Series Contents

Volume 1 Contents

BOOK 2

Medieval Europe and the World Beyond

PART ONE

The Shaping of the Middle Ages 175

8 A Flowering of Faith: Christianity and Buddhism 177

BOOK 3
The European Renaissance, the Reformation, and Global Encounter

PART ONE

The Age of the Renaissance 347

15 Adversity and Challenge: The Fourteenth-Century Transition 349

16 Classical Humanism in the Age of the Renaissance 369

Preface

"It's the most curious thing I ever saw in all my life!" exclaimed Lewis Carroll's Alice in Wonderland, as she watched the Cheshire Cat slowly disappear, leaving only the outline of a broad smile. "I've often seen a cat without a grin, but a grin without a cat!" A student who encounters an ancient Greek epic, a Yoruba mask, or a Mozart opera—lacking any context for these works—might be equally baffled. It may be helpful, therefore, to begin by explaining how the artifacts (the "grin") of the humanistic tradition relate to the larger and more elusive phenomenon (the "cat") of human culture.

The Humanistic Tradition and the Humanities

In its broadest sense, the term *humanistic tradition* refers to humankind's cultural legacy—the sum total of the significant ideas and achievements handed down from generation to generation. This tradition is the product of responses to conditions that have confronted all people throughout history. Since the beginnings of life on earth, human beings have tried to ensure their own survival by achieving harmony with nature. They have attempted to come to terms with the inevitable realities of disease and death. They have endeavored to establish ways of living collectively and communally. And they have persisted in the desire to understand themselves and their place in the universe. In response to these ever-present and universal challenges—*survival, communality,* and *self-knowledge*—human beings have created and transmitted the tools of science and technology, social and cultural institutions, religious and philosophic systems, and various forms of personal expression, the sum total of which we call *culture.*

Even the most ambitious survey cannot assess all manifestations of the humanistic tradition. This book therefore focuses on the creative legacy referred to collectively as *the humanities*: literature, philosophy, history (in its literary dimension), architecture, the visual arts (including photography and film), music, and dance. Selected examples from each of these disciplines constitute our *primary sources.* Primary sources (that is, works original to the age that produced them) provide first-hand evidence of human inventiveness and ingenuity. The primary sources in this text have been chosen on the basis of their authority, their beauty, and their enduring value. They are, simply stated, the great works of their time and, in some cases, of all time. Universal in their appeal, they have been transmitted from generation to generation.

Such works are, as well, the landmark examples of a specific time and place: they offer insight into the ideas and values of the society in which they were produced. *The Humanistic Tradition* joins "the grin" to "the cat" by examining them within their political, economic, and social contexts.

The humanities are the legacy of a given culture's values, ambitions, and beliefs. Poetry, painting, philosophy, and music are not, generally speaking, products of unstructured leisure or indulgent individuality; rather, they are tangible expressions of the human quest for the good (one might even say the "complete") life. Throughout history, these forms of expression have served the domains of the sacred, the ceremonial, and the communal. And even in the early days of the twenty-first century, as many time-honored traditions come under assault, the arts retain their power to awaken our imagination in the quest for survival, communality, and self-knowledge.

The Scope of the Humanistic Tradition

The humanistic tradition is not the exclusive achievement of any one geographic region, race, or class. For that reason, this text assumes a global and multicultural rather than exclusively Western perspective. At the same time, Western contributions are emphasized, first, because the audience for these books is predominantly Western, but also because in recent centuries the West has exercised a dominant influence on the course and character of global history. Since, the humanistic tradition belongs to all of humankind, the best way to understand the Western contribution to that tradition is to examine it in the arena of world culture.

As a survey, *The Humanistic Tradition* cannot provide an exhaustive analysis of our creative legacy. The critical reader will discover many gaps. Some aspects of culture that receive extended examination in traditional Western humanities surveys have been pared down to make room for the too often neglected contributions of Islam, Africa, and Asia. This book is necessarily selective—it omits many major figures and treats others only briefly. Primary sources are arranged, for the most part, chronologically, but they are presented as manifestations of the informing ideas of the age in which they were produced. The intent is to examine the evidence of the humanistic tradition thematically and topically, rather than to compile a series of mini-histories of the individual arts.

Studying the Humanistic Tradition

To study the creative record is to engage in a dialogue with the past, one that brings us face to face with the values of our ancestors, and, ultimately, with our own. This dialogue is (or should be) a source of personal revelation and delight; like Alice in Wonderland, our strange, new encounters will be enriched according to the degree of curiosity and patience we bring to them. Just as lasting friendships with special people are cultivated by extended familiarity, so our appreciation of a painting, a play, or a symphony depends on close attention and repeated contact. There are no shortcuts to the study of the humanistic tradition, but there are some techniques that may be helpful. It is useful, for instance, to approach each primary source from the triple perspective of its text, its context, and its subtext.

TEXT

The *text* of any primary source refers to its *medium* (that is, what it is made of), its *form* (its outward shape), and its *content* (the subject it describes).

LITERATURE Whether intended to be spoken or lead, literature depends on the medium of words—the American poet Robert Frost once defined literature as "performance in words." Literary form varies according to the manner in which words are arranged. So poetry, which shares with music and dance rhythmic organization, may be distinguished from prose, which normally lacks regular rhythmic pattern. The main purpose of prose is to convey information, to narrate, and to describe; poetry, by its freedom from conventional patterns of grammar, provides unique opportunities for the expression of intense emotions. Philosophy (the search for truth through reasoned analysis) and history (the record of the past) make use of prose to analyze and communicate ideas and information. In literature, as in most kinds of expression, content and form are usually interrelated. The subject matter or the form of a literary work determines its *genre*. For instance, a long narrative poem recounting the adventures of a hero constitutes an *epic*, while a formal, dignified speech in praise of a person or thing constitutes a *eulogy*.

THE VISUAL ARTS The *visual arts*—painting, sculpture, architecture, and photography—employ a wide variety of media, such as wood, clay, colored pigments, marble, granite, steel, and (more recently) plastic, neon, film, and computers. The form or outward shape of a work of art depends on the manner in which the artist manipulates the formal elements of color, line, texture, and space. Unlike words, these formal elements lack denotative meaning. The artist may manipulate form to describe and interpret the visible world (as in such genres as portraiture and landscape painting); to generate fantastic and imaginative kinds of imagery; or to create imagery that is non-representational—without identifiable subject matter. In general, however, the visual arts are spatial; that is, they operate and are apprehended in space.

MUSIC AND DANCE The medium of *music* is sound. Like literature, music is durational: it unfolds over the period of time in which it occurs. The formal elements of music are melody, rhythm, harmony, and tone color—elements that also characterize the oral life of literature. As with the visual arts, the formal elements of music are without symbolic content: literature, painting, and sculpture may imitate or describe nature, but music is almost always nonrepresentational—it rarely has meaning beyond the sound itself. For that reason, music is the most difficult of the arts to describe in words. It is also (in the view of some) the most affective of the arts. Dance, the artform that makes the human body itself a medium of expression, resembles music in that it is temporal and performance-oriented. Like music, dance exploits rhythm as a formal tool, but, like painting and sculpture, it unfolds in space as well as time.

In analyzing the text of a work of literature, art, or music, we ask how its formal elements contribute to its meaning and affective power. We examine the ways in which the artist manipulates medium and form to achieve a characteristic manner of execution and expression that we call *style*. And we try to determine the extent to which a style reflects the personal vision of the artist and the spirit of his or her time and place. Comparing the styles of various artworks from a single era, we may discover that they share certain defining features and characteristics. Similarities (both formal and stylistic) between, for instance, golden age Greek temples and Greek tragedies, between Chinese lyric poems and landscape paintings, and between postmodern fiction and pop sculpture, prompt us to seek the unifying moral and aesthetic values of the cultures in which they were produced.

CONTEXT

We use the word *context* to describe the historical and cultural environment. To determine the context, we ask: in what time and place did the artifact originate? How did it function within the society in which it was created? Was the purpose of the piece decorative, didactic, magical, propagandistic? Did it serve the religious or political needs of the community? Sometimes our answers to these questions are mere guesses. Nevertheless, understanding the function of an artifact often serves to clarify the nature of its form (and vice versa). For instance, much of the literature produced prior to the fifteenth century was spoken or sung rather than read; for that reason, such literature tends to feature repetition and rhyme, devices that facilitate memorization. We can assume that literary works embellished with frequent repetitions, such as the *Epic of Gilgamesh* and the Hebrew Bible, were products of an oral tradition. Determining the original function of an artwork also permits us to assess its significance in its own time and place: the paintings on the walls of Paleolithic caves, which are among the most compelling animal illustrations in the history of world art, are not "artworks" in the modern sense of the term but, rather, magical signs that accompanied hunting rituals, the performance of which was essential to the survival of the community. Understanding the relationship between text and context is one of the principal concerns of any inquiry into the humanistic tradition.

SUBTEXT

The *subtext* of the literary or artistic object refers to its secondary and implied meanings. The subtext embraces the emotional or intellectual messages embedded in, or implied by, a work of art. The epic poems of the ancient Greeks, for instance, which glorify prowess and physical courage in battle, suggest that such virtues are exclusively male. The state portraits of the seventeenth-century French ruler Louis XIV carry the subtext of unassailable and absolute power. In our own century, Andy Warhol's serial adaptations of soup cans and Coca-Cola bottles offer wry commentary on the supermarket mentality of postmodern American culture. Identifying the implicit message of an artwork helps us to determine the values and customs of the age in which it was produced and to assess those values against others.

Beyond *The Humanistic Tradition*

This book offers only small, enticing samples from an enormous cultural buffet. To dine more fully, students are encouraged to go beyond the sampling presented at this table; and for the most sumptuous feasting, nothing can substitute for first-hand experience. Students, therefore, should make every effort to supplement this book with visits to art museums and galleries, concert halls, theaters, and libraries. *The Humanistic Tradition* is designed for students who may or may not be able to read music, but who surely are able to cultivate an appreciation of music in performance. The music logos ♪ that appear in the margins of the text refer to the Music Listening Selections found on two accompanying compact discs, available from the publishers. Lists of suggestions for further reading are included at the end of each book, while a selected general bibliography of electronic humanities resources appears in the Online Learning Center at http://www.mhhe.com/fierotht5.

The Fifth Edition

In the fifth edition of *The Humanistic Tradition*, Study Questions follow each primary source readings; thse are desinged to provoke thought and discussion. Chapter 37 has been reorganized and expanded to explore a number of important global themes, such as ethnic identity and ecology. There is a reading selection from the Book of Psalms, a new modern translation of the *Quran*, and excerpts from the writings of Annie Dillard, E.O Wilson, Sandra Cisneros, Mahmoud Darwish, and Yehuda Amichai. Content has been expanded to a number of topics, including the life of Muhammad (Chapter 10), the Columbian Exchange (Chapter 18), artists' optical aids (Chapters 17 and 23), Islam since 1500 (Chapters 21, 35, 37), the training of female artists (Chapters 20 and 23, and the Middle Passage (Chapter 25). Among the new color illustrations for the fifth edition are Zoser's Pyramid, Nok sculpture, London's new Globe Theater, Bernini's *David*, Steen's *Drawing Lesson*, Hick's *Peaceable Kingdom*, Monet's Japanese Bridge, and Beardon's Empress of the Blues. This edition also updates the contemporary scene to include significant developments in architecture, photography, and film (Chapter 38). Two new Sony Music Listening CDs illustrate the muscial works discussed in the text, and new Music Listening Guides provide helpful analyses of these selections. Revised and expanded Timelines and Glossaries, along with Science and Technology boxes, locator maps, and pedagogical resources provide useful study aids (see the "Guided Tour" on page xii). Updated suggestions for additional reading appear at the end of each book, rather than by chapter.

A Note to Instructors

The key to successful classroom use of *The Humanistic Tradition* is *selectivity*. Although students may be assigned to read whole chapters that focus on a topic or theme, as well as complete works that supplement the abridged readings, the classroom should be the stage for a selective treatment of a single example or a set of examples. The organization of this textbook is designed to emphasize themes that cut across geographic boundaries—themes whose universal significance prompts students to evaluate and compare rather than simply memorize and repeat lists of names and places. To assist readers in achieving global cultural literacy, every effort has been made to resist isolating (or "ghettoizing") individual cultures and to avoid the inevitable biases we bring to our evaluation of relatively unfamiliar cultures.

Key Map Indicating Areas Shown as White Highlights on the Locator Maps

Acknowledgments

Writing *The Humanistic Tradition* has been an exercise in humility. Without the assistance of learned friends and colleagues, assembling a book of this breadth would have been an impossible task. James H. Dormon read all parts of the manuscript and made extensive and substantive editorial suggestions; as his colleague, best friend, and wife, I am most deeply indebted to him.

The following colleagues generously shared their knowledge and training in matters of content: in the sciences, Barbara J. Reeves (Virginia Tech); literature, Robert W. Butler, Darrell Bourque (University of Louisiana, Lafayette), and John Lowe (Louisiana State University); in the visual arts, Roy Barineau (Tallahassee Community College); music, Richard Harrison, Stephen Husarik (University of Arkansas), and Jack Jacobs; film, Joseph Warfield (New York University).

In the preparation of the fifth edition, I have also benefited from the suggestions and comments generously offered by Linda A. Austin (Glendale Community College), Edward Bonahue (Santa Fe Community College), Diane Boze (Northeastern State University), Peggy Brown (Collin County Community College), Michael Coste (Front Range Community College), Harry Coverston (University of Central Florida), Jaymes Dudding (Albuquerque Technical Vocational Institute), Scott Earle (Tacoma Community College), Joshua Fausty (New Jersey City University), Luis Samuel Gonzalez (Sinclair Community College), Jeanne McGlinn (University of North Carolina—Asheville), Khadijah O. Miller (Norfolk State University), Yvonne Milspaw (Harrisburg Area Community College), Thomas R. Moore (Maine Maritime Academy), Rachel M. Rumberger (Valencia Community College), Jerome P. Soneson (University of Northern Iowa), Sonia Sorrell (Pepperdine University), Nancy A. Taylor (California State University—Northridge), Mary Tripp (University of Central Florida), and Naomi Yavneh (University of South Florida).

The burden of preparing the fifth edition has been lightened by the assistance of Kristen N. Mellit (McGraw-Hill) and the editors at Laurence King Publishing. I am also indebted to Lyn Uhl, Lisa Pinto, and Elizabeth Sigal (McGraw-Hill) for their support and encouragement, and to Fiona Kinnear for discerning photographic research.

A Guided Tour of *The Humanistic Tradition*, FIFTH EDITION

Illustrated part-opening **TIMELINES** provide a chronological overview of major historical events, as well as key works of literature, art, and music featured in each part.

Science and Technology

2650 B.C.E. Pharaoh Khufu (or Cheops) orders construction of the Great Pyramid of Gizeh†

1500 B.C.E. Egyptians employ a simple form of the sundial

1450 B.C.E. the water clock is devised in Egypt

1400 B.C.E. glass in produced in Egypt and Mesopotamia

†All dates in this chapter are approximate

SCIENCE AND TECHNOLOGY BOXES offer a chronology of key scientific and technological developments.

READING 4.7   From Donne's *Meditation 17* (1623)

All mankind is of one author, and is one volume; when one man   1
dies, one chapter is not torn out of the book, but translated into
a better language; and every chapter must be so translated. God
employs several translators; some pieces are translated by age,
some by sickness, some by war, some by justice; but God's hand   5
is in every translation, and his hand shall bind up all our
scattered leaves again for that library where every book shall lie
open to one another. As therefore the bell that rings to a
sermon calls not upon the preacher only but upon the
congregation to come, so this bell calls us all. . . . No man is an   10
island entire of itself; every man is a piece of the continent, a
part of the main. If a clod be washed away by the sea, Europe is
the less, as well as if a promontory were, as well as if a manor
of thy friend's or of thine own were. Any man's death diminishes
me, because I am involved in mankind, and therefore never send   15
to know for whom the bell tolls; it tolls for thee.

 Q What three metaphors are invoked in *Meditation 17?*

PRIMARY SOURCE READINGS from a variety of genres provide a wealth of important and influential writings. New to the fifth edition, study questions designed to provoke thought and discussion follow each primary source reading.

GLOSSARY

asceticism strict self-denial and self-discipline

bodhisattva (Sanskrit, "one whose essence is enlightenment") a being who has postponed his or her own entry into *nirvana* in order to assist others in reaching that goal; worshiped as a deity in Mahayana Buddhism

Messiah Anointed One, or Savior; in Greek, *Christos*

rabbi a teacher and master trained in the Jewish law

sutra (Sanskrit, "thread") an instructional chapter or discourse in any of the sacred books of Buddhism

Terms marked in bold are defined in a **GLOSSARY** at the end of each chapter.

MUSICAL LOGOS in the margins refer to the Music Listening Selections found on accompanying compact disks, available separately from the publisher.

LOCATOR MAPS give readers their geographical bearings, alerting them to where events discussed in the section to follow took place.

EXPERIMENTAL FILM

Léger produced one of the earliest and most influential abstract films in the history of motion pictures. Developed in collaboration with the American journalist Dudley Murphy, *Ballet mécanique* (*Mechanical Ballet*, 1923–1924) puts into motion a series of abstract shapes and mundane objects (such as bottles and kitchen utensils), which, interspersed with human elements, convey a playful but dehumanized sense of everyday experience. The rhythms and juxtapositions of the images suggest—without any narrative—the notion of modern life as mechanized, routine, standardized, and impersonal. The repeated image of a laundry woman, for instance, alternating with that of a rotating machine part, plays on the associative qualities of visual motifs in ways that would influence film-makers for decades.

FILM ESSAYS explore various aspects of this important, relatively new medium.

Supplements for the Instructor and the Student

A number of useful supplements are available to instructors and students using *The Humanistic Tradition*. Please contact your sales representative to obtain these resources, or to ask for further details.

ONLINE LEARNING CENTER A complete set of web-based resources for *The Humanistic Tradition* can be found at www.mhhe.com/fierotht5.com. Materials for students include an audio pronunciation guide, self-tests, interactive maps, links to relevant images and complete primary source readings. Instructors will benefit from discussion and lecture suggestions, chapter summaries, music listening guides, and other resources. All resources from the Online Learning Center are also available in cartridges for WebCT and Blackboard course management systems.

INSTRUCTOR'S RESOURCE CD-ROM The Instructor's Resource CD-ROM (IRCD) is designed to assist instructors as they plan and prepare for classes. Chapter summaries emphasize key themes and topics that give focus to the primary source readings. Music listening guides provide instructors with ideas for integrating selections on the Music Listening CDs into their courses. Study questions for each chapter can be used for student discussion or written assignments. A list of suggested videos, DVDs, and recordings is also included. The CD-ROM also offers a Test Bank containing a comprehensive bank of multiple-choice questions for use in constructing student exams.

EZ TEST McGraw-Hill's EZ Test, also included on the IRCD, is a flexible and easy-to-use electronic testing program that allows instructors to create book-specific tests, drawing from a ready-made database and/or designing their own questions. Tests can be exported for use with course management systems such as WebCT, BlackBoard or PageOut. The program is available for use with Windows and Macintosh.

CORE CONCEPTS A groundbreaking *Core Concepts in the Humanities* DVD-ROM may be packaged free with every new copy of *The Humanistic Tradition* (ISBN 0073136433). The DVD-ROM augments students' understanding of the humanities through multimedia presentations on visual art, dance, theater, film, literature, and music. With over eighty interactive exercises, timelines, and extensive video clips, the DVD-ROM allows students to explore these disciplines in an exciting way. Study materials such as outlines,

summaries, and self-correcting quizzes are provided for every chapter of the text. Contact your McGraw-Hill representative at www.mhhe.com/rep for information about packaging this program with the textbook.

MUSIC LISTENING COMPACT DISCS Two audio compact discs have been designed exclusively for use with *The Humanistic Tradition*. CD One corresponds to the music listening selections discussed in Books 1-3 (Volume I), and CD Two contains the music in Books 4-6 (Volume II). Instructors may obtain copies of the recordings for classroom use, and the CDs are also available for individual purchase by students. They can be packaged with any or all of the six books or two-volume versions of the text. Consult your local sales representative for details.

SLIDE SETS A set of book-specific slides is available to qualified adopters of *The Humanistic Tradition*. These slides have been especially selected to include many of the key images in the books. Additional slides are available for purchase directly from Universal Color Slides. For further information, consult our web site at www.mhhe.com/fierotht5.com.

IMAGE VAULT Selected images from *The Humanistic Tradition*'s illustration program are available to adopting instructors in digital format in *The Image Vault*, McGraw-Hill's new web-based program. Instructors can incorporate images from *The Image Vault* in digital presentations that can be used in class offline, burned to CD-ROM, or embedded in course Web pages. See www.mhhe.com/theimagevault for more details.

Book 1
The First Civilizations and the Classical Legacy

Prehistory and the Birth of Civilization

*"But, after all, who knows and who can say
whence it all came, and how creation happened."*
Rig Veda

Whether or not one believes that the beginnings of life were divinely generated, it is clear that human beings belong to a long and complex process of evolutionary development. The story of human evolution is a record of the genetic and behavioral adaptation of human beings to their natural surroundings. It is the last chapter in a history that begins with the simplest forms of life that thrived in the primeval seas hundreds of millions of years ago and culminates in the astonishing achievements of modern human beings. Throughout their short history on this planet, human beings have faced the privations of the environment: of an often hostile geography and a threatening climate. Meeting such environmental challenges was the primary occupation of the earliest inhabitants.

Prehistory

The study of history before the appearance of written records, an enterprise that originated in France around 1860, is called **prehistory**. In the absence of written records, prehistorians depend on information about the past provided by the disciplines of geology, paleontology, anthropology, archeology, and ethnography. For instance, using instruments that measure the radioactive atoms remaining in the organic elements of the earth's strata, geologists have determined that our planet is approximately 4.5 billion years old. Paleontologists record the history of fossil remains and that of the earth's earliest living creatures. Anthropologists study human biology, society, and cultural practices, while archeologists uncover, analyze, and interpret the material remains of past societies. Finally, a special group of cultural anthropologists known as ethnographers study surviving preliterate societies. All of these specialists contribute to producing a detailed picture of humankind's earliest environment and the prehistoric past.

The earliest organic remains in the earth's strata are almost four billion years old. From one-celled organisms that inhabited the watery terrain of our planet, higher forms of life very gradually evolved. Some hundred million years ago, dinosaurs stalked the earth, eventually becoming extinct—possibly because they failed to adapt to climatic change. Eighty million years ago, mammals roamed the earth's surface. Although even the most approximate dates are much disputed, it is generally agreed that between ten and five million years ago ancestral humans first appeared on earth, probably in eastern and southern Africa. The exact genealogy of humankind is still a matter of intense debate. However, in the last fifty years, anthropologists have clarified some aspects of the relationship between human beings and earlier primates—the group of mammals that today includes monkeys, apes, and human beings. Fossil evidence reveals structural similarities between human beings and chimpanzees (and other apes). More recent research in molecular biology indicates that the DNA of chimpanzees is approximately 99% identical to human DNA, suggesting that humans are more closely related to chimpanzees than domestic cats are to lions.

Paleolithic ("Old Stone") Culture*
(ca. 7 million–10,000 B.C.E.**)

Early in the twentieth century, anthropologists discovered the first fossil remains of the near-human or proto-human creature known as **hominid**, who lived some five or more million years ago. Hominids lived in packs; they gathered seeds, berries, wild fruits, and vegetables, and possibly even hunted the beasts of the African savannas. Hominid footprints found in South Africa in the mid-1990s and fossil remains uncovered since 2002 in central Africa and near the Black Sea suggest that hominids may have walked upright as early as six million years ago. Two theories have

---

*The terms Paleolithic and Neolithic do not describe uniform time periods, but, rather, cultures that appeared at different times in different parts of the world.

**Dates are signified as B.C.E., "Before the Christian (or common) era," or C.E., "Christian (or common) era."

emerged to explain the evolution of the genus *Homo*, that is, modern humans and their closest now-extinct relatives. One, the "out of Africa" theory, holds that modern humans evolved only in Africa, from where they migrated elsewhere. A second, and more popular, "multi-regionalist" theory argues that many different populations of humans existed simultaneously; these mingled to produce modern human beings.

Whichever theory is correct, it is clear that some three million years ago, a South African variety of hominid known as *Australopithecus* was using sharp-edged pebbles for skinning animals and for chopping. Creating the first stone and bone tools and weapons, *Homo habilis* ("tool-making human") met the challenge of survival with problem-solving ingenuity. Anthropologists have long considered tool-making the distinguishing feature of modern humans. Tool-making represents the beginnings of **culture**, which, in its most basic sense, proceeds from the manipulation of nature; and the appearance of tools and weapons—humankind's earliest technology—constitutes the primary act of extending control over nature. Eventually, in parts of Africa and East Asia, hunter-gatherers known as *Homo erectus* ("upright human") made tools that were more varied and efficient than those used by earlier humans. These tools included hand-axes, cleavers, chisels, and a wide variety of choppers. The hand-axe became the standard tool for chopping, digging, cutting, and scraping. Fire, too, became an important part of the early culture of humankind, providing safety, warmth, and a means of cooking food. Although it is still not certain how long ago fire was first used, archeologists confirm that fire was a regular feature in the hearths of most *Homo erectus* dwellings.

Some 100,000 years ago, a group of human ancestors with anatomical features and brain size similar to our own appeared in the Neander Valley near Düsseldorf, Germany. The burial of human dead (their bodies dyed with red ocher) among Neanderthals and the practice of including tools, weapons, food, and flowers in Neanderthal graves are evidence of the self-conscious, symbol-making human known as *Homo sapiens*. Characterized by memory and foresight, these now-extinct cousins of modern-day humans were the first to demonstrate—by their ritual preparation and disposal of the deceased—a self-conscious concern with human mortality. That concern may have involved respect for, or fear of, the dead and the anticipation of life after death.

The development of the primate brain in both size and complexity was integral to the evolution of *Homo sapiens*: over millions of years, the average brain size of the human being grew to roughly three times the size of the gorilla's brain. Equally critical was the growth of more complex motor capacities. Gradually, verbal methods of communication complemented the nonverbal ones shared by animals and protohumans. Over time, our prehistoric ancestors came to use spoken language as a medium for transmitting information and patterns of culture. Communication by means of language distinguished *Homo sapiens* from other primates. Chimpanzees have

been known to bind two poles together in order to reach a bunch of bananas hanging from the top of a tree, but, short of immediate physical demonstration, they have developed no means of passing on this technique to subsequent generations of chimpanzees. *Homo sapiens*, on the other hand, have produced symbol systems that enable them to transmit their ideas and inventions. Thus, in the fullest sense, culture requires both the manipulation of nature and the formulation of a symbolic language for its transmission.

Paleolithic culture evolved during a period of climatic fluctuation called the Ice Age. Between roughly three million and 10,000 years ago, at least four large glacial advances covered the area north of the equator. As hunters and gatherers, Paleolithic people were forced either to migrate or adapt to changing climatic conditions. It is likely that more than fifteen species of humans co-existed with one another, and all but *Homo sapiens* became extinct. Ultimately, the ingenuity and imagination of *Homo sapiens* were responsible for the fact that they fared better than many other creatures.

Early modern humans devised an extensive technology of stone and bone tools and weapons that increased their comfort, safety, and almost certainly their confidence. A 7-foot stone-tipped spear enabled a hunter to attack an animal at a distance of six or more yards. Other devices increased the leverage of the arm and thus doubled that range. Spears and harpoons, and—toward the end of the Ice Age—bows and arrows, extended the efficacy and safety of Paleolithic people, just as axes and knives facilitated their food-preparing abilities.

During the last sixty years, archeologists have discovered thousands of paintings and carvings on the walls of caves and the surfaces of rocks at Paleolithic sites in Europe, Africa, Australia, and North America. Over one hundred limestone cave dwellings in southwestern France and still others discovered in 1996 in southeastern France contain images of animals (bears, bison, elk, lions, and zebras, among others), birds, fish, and other signs and symbols, all of which reveal a high degree of artistic and technical sophistication. Executed between 10,000 and 30,000 years ago, these wall-paintings provide a visual record of such long-extinct animals as the hairy mammoth and the woolly rhinoceros. Equally important, they document the

Science and Technology

2,500,000 B.C.E.	first stone tools are utilized in East Africa[†]
500,000 B.C.E.	in China, *Homo erectus* uses fire for domestic purposes
24,000 B.C.E.	fish hooks and lines are utilized in Europe
20,000 B.C.E.	bows and arrows are in use in North Africa and Spain; oil lamps, fueled by animal fat, come into use
13,000 B.C.E.	devices to hurl harpoons and spears are in use

[†]All dates in this introduction are approximate.

culture of a hunting people. Painted with **polychrome** mineral pigments and shaded with bitumen and burnt coal, realistically depicted bison, horses, reindeer, and a host of other creatures are shown standing, running, often wounded by spears and lances (Figure 0.1). What were the purpose and function of these vivid images? Located in the most inaccessible regions of the caves, and frequently drawn one over another, with no apparent regard for clarity of composition, they were probably *not* intended as decorations or even as records of the hunt. It seems more likely that, much like tools and weapons, cave art functioned as part of a hunting ritual. The following episode from Pygmy life in the African Congo, recorded by the twentieth-century German ethnographer Leo Frobenius, supports this hypothesis.

READING 1.1 The Story of Rock Picture Research

In 1905 we obtained further evidence from a Congo race, [1] hunting tribes, later famous as the "pygmies," which had been driven from the plateau to the refuge of the Congo [an area in South-central Africa bordering the Congo River]. We met in the jungle district between Kassai and Luebonn. Several of their members, three men and a woman, guided the expedition for almost a week and were soon on friendly terms with us. One afternoon, finding our larder rather depleted, I asked one of them to shoot me an antelope, surely an easy job for such an expert hunter. He and his fellows looked at me in [10] astonishment and then burst out with the answer that, yes, they'd do it gladly, but that it was naturally out of the question

for that day since no preparations had been made. After a long palaver they declared themselves ready to make these at sunrise. Then they went off as though searching for a good site and finally settled on a high place on a nearby hill.

As I was eager to learn what their preparations consisted of, I left camp before dawn and crept through the bush to the open place which they had sought out the night before. The pygmies appeared in the twilight, the woman with them. The [20] men crouched on the ground, plucked a small square free of weeds and smoothed it over with their hands. One of them then drew something in the cleared space with his forefinger, while his companions murmured some kind of formula or incantation. Then a waiting silence. The sun rose on the horizon. One of the men, an arrow on his bowstring, took his place beside the square. A few minutes later the rays of the sun fell on the drawing at his feet. In that same second the woman stretched out her arms to the sun, shouting words I did not understand, the man shot the arrow and the woman cried [30] out again. Then the three men bounded off through the bush while the woman stood for a few minutes and then went slowly towards our camp. As she disappeared I came forward and, looking down at the smoothed square of sand, saw the drawing of an antelope four hands long. From the antelope's neck protruded the pygmy's arrow.

I went back for my camera intending to photograph the drawing before the men returned. But the woman, when she saw what I was up to, made such a fuss that I desisted. We broke camp and continued our march. The drawing remained [40] unphotographed. That afternoon the hunters appeared with a fine "buschbock," an arrow in its throat. They delivered their booty and then went off to the hill we had left behind us, carrying a fistful of the antelope's hair and a gourd full of its

Figure 0.1 Hall of Bulls, left wall, Lascaux caves, Dordogne, France, ca. 15,000–10,000 B.C.E. Paint on limestone rock, length of individual bulls 13–16 ft.

Figure 0.2 Spotted horses and negative hand imprints, Pech-Merle caves, Lot, France, ca. 15,000–10,000 B.C.E. Length 11 ft. 2 in. Photo: Jean Vertut.

blood. Two days passed before they caught up with us again. Then, in the evening, as we were drinking a foamy palm wine, the oldest of the three men—I had turned to him because he seemed to have more confidence in me than the others—told me that he and his companions had returned to the scene of their preparations for the hunt in order to daub the picture **50** with the slain antelope's hair and blood, to withdraw the arrow and then to wipe the whole business away. The meaning of the formula was not clear, but I did gather that, had they not done as they did, the blood of the dead antelope would have destroyed them. The "wiping out," too, had to take place at sunrise.

 Q How does this reading illustrate the use of ritual to exercise control over nature?

This reading illuminates two concepts that are vital to an understanding of prehistoric art, and perhaps the art of the ancient world as well. First, the arts of the ancient world were not primarily decorative or intended as entertainment, as is the case with most modern art. Rather, drawing, painting, music, and dance held a sacred function, usually related to ritual or celebration. Among our ancient ancestors, "art" was a form of prayer, a vehicle by which humans petitioned superhuman forces. The Pygmy enactment of the hunt was a ritualized kind of *sympathetic magic*: a method by which one gains power over an object by manipulating its name or physical characteristics. Second, in the performance of such rituals, the arts were integrated: the success of the ritual depended upon the proper combination of words (chanted, sung, or spoken), visual images, and gestures (perhaps dance).

If the Pygmy episode is taken as a model, it is likely that prehistoric cave paintings belonged to rituals designed for a successful hunt.

Faith in the power to alter destiny by way of prayer and the manipulation of proper symbols has characterized religious ceremony throughout the history of humankind, but it was especially important to a culture in which control over nature was crucial to physical survival. A motif commonly found on cave walls is the image of the human hand, created in negative relief by blowing or splattering color around the actual hand of the hunter, shaman, or priest who interceded between the human realm and the spirit world (Figure 0.2). Since the hand was the hunter's most powerful ally in making and wielding a weapon, it is fitting that it appears enshrined in the sacred precinct amid the quarry of the hunt. The precise meaning of many of the markings on prehistoric cave walls continues to inspire speculation. In that some cave paintings depict beasts and sea-creatures that humans did not hunt, it may be that these images were cult-related. Some scholars hold that certain prehistoric markings were lunar calendars—notational devices used to predict the seasonal migration of animals. The cave, symbol of the cosmic underworld and the procreative womb, served as a ceremonial chamber, a shrine, and perhaps a council room. No matter how one interprets so-called "cave-art," it is surely an expression of our early ancestors' efforts to control their environment and thus ensure their survival.

Women played important roles in Paleolithic culture. The Pygmy ritual described by Frobenius suggests a clear division of labor in the performance of ritual: as the male shoots the arrow into the image of the antelope, his female companion issues special words and pious gestures. It is likely that similar kinds of shared responsibility characterized humankind's earliest societies. Women probably secured food by gathering fruits and berries; they acted also as healers and nurturers. Moreover, since the female (in her role as childbearer) assured the continuity of the tribe, she assumed a special importance: perceived as life-giver and identified with the mysterious powers of procreation, she was exalted as Mother Earth. Her importance in the prehistoric community is confirmed by the great numbers of female statuettes uncovered by archeologists throughout the world. A good many of these objects show the female nude with pendulous breasts, large buttocks, and a swollen abdomen, indicating pregnancy (Figure 0.3).

Figure 0.3 "Venus" of Willendorf, from Lower Austria, ca. 25,000–20,000 B.C.E. Limestone, height 4⅜ in. Museum of Natural History, Vienna.

Neolithic ("New Stone") Culture (ca. 8000–4000 B.C.E.)

Paleolithic people lived at the mercy of nature. However, during the transitional (or Mesolithic) phase that occurred shortly after 10,000 B.C.E., our ancient ancestors discovered that the seeds of wild grains and fruits might be planted to grow food, and wild animals might be domesticated. The rock art paintings discovered at Tassili in Africa's Sahara Desert—once fertile grasslands—tell the story of a transition from hunting to herding and the domestication of cattle and camels (Figure 0.4). Gradually, over a period of centuries, as hunters, gatherers, and herdsmen became farmers and food producers, a dynamic new culture emerged: the Neolithic. Food production freed people from a nomadic way of life. They gradually settled permanent farm communities, raising high-protein crops such as wheat and barley in Asia, rice in China, and maize in the Americas. They raised goats, pigs, cattle, and sheep that provided regular sources of food and valuable by-products such as wool and leather. The transition from the hunting-gathering phase of human subsistence to the agricultural-herding phase was a revolutionary development in human social organization, because it marked the shift from a nomadic to a sedentary way of life.

Neolithic sites excavated in Southwest Asia* (especially Israel, Jordan, Turkey, Iran, and Iraq), East Asia (China and Japan), and (as late as 1000 B.C.E.) in Meso-America, center on villages consisting of a number of mud- and limestone-faced huts—humankind's earliest architecture (Figure 0.5). At Jericho, in present-day Israel, massive defense walls surrounded the town, while tombs held the ornamented remains of local villagers. At Jarmo, in northern Iraq, a community of more than 150 people harvested wheat with stone sickles. Polished stone tools, some designed especially for farming, replaced the cruder tools of Paleolithic people. Ancient Japanese communities seem to have produced the world's oldest known pottery— handcoiled and fired clay vessels. But it is in Southwest Asia that some of the finest examples of painted pottery have come to light. Clay vessels, decorated with abstract motifs such as the long-necked birds that march around the rim of a beaker from Susa (Figure 0.6), held surplus foods for the lean months of winter, and woven rugs and textiles provided comfort against the wind, rain, and cold. Homemakers, artisans, and shepherds played significant roles in Neolithic society.

Agricultural life stimulated a new awareness of seasonal change and a profound respect for those life-giving powers, such as sun and rain, that were essential to the success of the harvest. The earth's fertility and the seasonal cycle were the principal concerns of the farming culture. A hand-modeled clay figurine from a Neolithic grave in Tlatilco in central Mexico (the region in which

---

*Also known as "the Near East" or "the Middle East." The geographic regions cited in this textbook are identified on the Key Map in the Preface.

Figure 0.4 Saharan rock painting, Tassili, Algeria, ca. 8000–4000 B.C.E. Copy of the original. AKG Images, London.

Figure 0.5 Isometric reconstruction of a Neolithic house at Hassuna (level 4). Originally mud and limestone. The Oriental Institute, The University of Chicago.

Figure 0.6 Beaker painted with goats, dogs, and long-necked birds, from Susa, southwest Iran, ca. 5000–4000 B.C.E. Baked clay, height 11¼ in. Louvre, Paris. Photo: © R.M.N.

Figure 0.7 Eternal duality of birth and death, figurine, Tlatilco, central Mexico, 1700–1300 B.C.E. Clay, height approx. 12 in. Regional Museum of Anthropology and History, Villahermosa, Tabasco. Richard Stirling/Photo © Ancient Art and Architecture Collection, Harrow.

the Olmec—Meso-America's earliest culture—flourished) illustrates the eternal duality of birth and death (Figure **0.7**): one half of the man-child appears plump and vigorous, but on the other the flesh is stripped away to reveal the skeletal remains of the body. The figure, like those of infants and dwarfs common in Olmec art, may be associated with rituals celebrating regeneration and the life cycle. Its startling conjunction of infancy and degeneration reflects a profound sensitivity to the course of birth and death that governs both the crops and the people who plant them.

The overwhelming evidence of female statuettes found in many Neolithic graves suggests that the cult of the Earth Mother may have become important in the transition from food-gathering to food production, when fertility and agricultural abundance were vital to the life of the community. Nevertheless, as with cave art, the exact meaning and function of the so-called "mother goddesses" remain a matter of speculation: they may have played a role in the performance of rites celebrating seasonal regeneration or they may have been associated with fertility cults that ensured successful childbirth. The symbolic association between the womb and "Mother Earth" played an important part in almost all ancient religions. In myth as well, female deities governed the earth, while male deities ruled the sky (see Reading 1.5). From culture to culture, the fertility goddess herself took many different forms. In contrast with the Paleolithic "Venus" of Willendorf (see Figure 0.3), for instance, whose sexual characteristics are boldly exaggerated, the marble statuettes produced in great number in the Cyclades, the Greek islands of the Aegean Sea, are as streamlined and highly stylized as some modern sculptures (Figure **0.8**). Though lacking the pronounced sexual characteristics of

Figure 0.8 Female figure, early Cycladic II, Late Spedos type, ca. 2600–2400 B.C.E. Marble, height 24¾ in. The Metropolitan Museum of Art, New York. Gift of Cristos B. Bastis, 1968. 68.148.

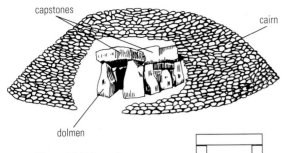

Figure 0.9 Dolmen site and post-and-lintel construction (right).

Figure 0.10 Burial site, Dolmen (upright stones supporting a horizontal slab), Crucuno, north of Carnac, France, Neolithic period. Ancient Art and Architecture Collection, Harrow.

the "Venus," the Cycladic figure probably played a similar role in rituals that sought the blessings of Mother Earth.

To farming peoples, the seasonal cycle—a primary fact of subsistence—was associated with death and regeneration. The dead, whose return to the earth put them in closer touch with the forces of nature, received careful burial. Almost all early cultures regarded the dead as messengers between the material world and the spirit world. Neolithic folk marked graves with **megaliths** (literally, "great stones"), upright stone slabs roofed by a capstone to form a stone tomb or **dolmen** (Figure 0.9). At some sites, the tomb was covered over with dirt and rubble to form a mound (Figure 0.10), symbolic of the sacred mountain (the abode of the gods) and the procreative womb (the source of regenerative life). The shape prevails in sacred architecture that ranges from the Meso-American temple (see Figure 2.8) to the Buddhist shrine (see chapter 9). The dolmen tomb made use of the simplest type of architectural construction: the **post-and-lintel** principle. At ceremonial centers and burial sites, megaliths might be placed upright in circles or multiple rows and capped by horizontal slabs. The most famous of these is the sanctuary at Stonehenge in southern England, where an elaborate group of stone circles, constructed in stages over a period of 2000 years, forms one of the most mysterious and impressive ritual spaces of the prehistoric world (Figure 0.11). To this wind-swept site, 20-foot megaliths, some weighing 25 tons each, were dragged from a quarry some twenty miles away, then shaped and assembled without metal tools to form a huge outer circle and an inner horseshoe of post-and-lintel stones (Figures 0.12, 0.13). A special **stele** that stands apart from the complex of stone circles marks the point—visible from the exact center of the inner circle—at which the sun rises at the midsummer solstice (the longest day of the year). It is probable that Stonehenge served as a celestial calendar predicting the movements of the sun and moon, clocking the seasonal

cycle, and thus providing information that would have been essential to an agricultural society.

Other Neolithic projects offer astounding testimony to ancient ingenuity. In the coastal deserts of Peru, enormous earthwork lines form geometric figures, spirals, and bird, animal, and insect designs, the meaning and function of which are yet to be deciphered. The giant hummingbird, whose wings span some 200 feet, is one of eighteen bird images pictured on the Peruvian plains (Figure 0.14). So complex are the designs of these earthworks that some modern writers have attributed their existence to the activity of beings from outer space—much as medieval people thought Stonehenge the work of Merlin, a legendary magician. Archeological analysis, however, severely challenges the credibility of such theories. Indeed, recent scholarship suggests that the Peruvian earthworks may have served as starmaps or astronomical calendars designed, like Stonehenge, to help ancient farmers determine dates for planting crops, for ritual celebrations, and thus for bringing human needs into harmony with the rhythms of nature.

Science and Technology

4500 B.C.E.	sailboats are used in Mesopotamia
4200 B.C.E.	the first known calendar (365 days) is devised in Egypt
4000 B.C.E.	copper ores are mined and smelted by Egyptians; bricks are fired in Mesopotamian kilns
3600 B.C.E.	bronze comes into use in Mesopotamia
3500 B.C.E.	the plow, wheeled cart, potter's wheel, tokens with pictographic impressions, fermentation processes for wine and beer are all introduced in Sumer

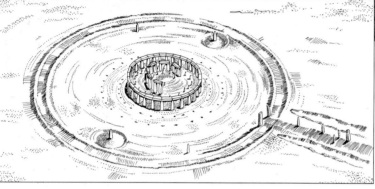

Figure 0.11 Stonehenge, Salisbury Plain, Wiltshire, England, ca. 3000–1800 B.C.E. Stone, diameter of circle 97 ft., tallest height 22 ft. Photo: Aerofilms, Hertfordshire.

Figure 0.12 (left) Stonehenge's construction. Of the roughly eighty 20-foot bluestones arranged in this horseshoe and circle formation, few survive. (below) Raising a sarsen stone into an upright setting. (bottom) Raising a lintel to the top of two sarsens.

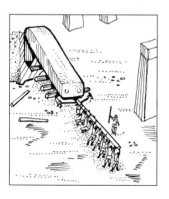
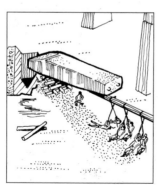
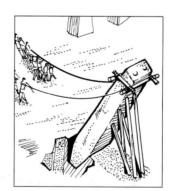

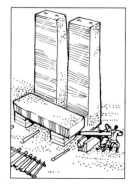
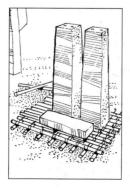

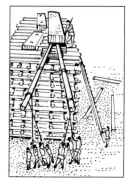

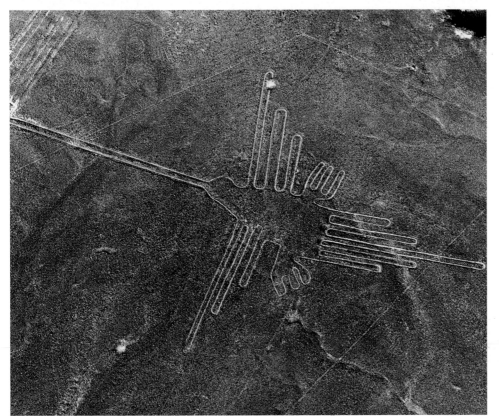

Figure 0.13 Stonehenge trilithons (lintel-topped pairs of stones at center), ca. 3000–1800 B.C.E. Tallest upright 22 ft. (including lintel). © English Heritage Photographic Library.

Figure 0.14 Giant hummingbird, Nasca culture, southwest Peru, ca. 200 B.C.E.–200 C.E. Wingspan 900 ft. The geoglyph was created by scraping away the weathered surface of the desert and removing stones. Photo: Parabola, New York.

The Birth of Civilization

Around 4000 B.C.E., a new chapter in the history of humankind began. Neolithic villages grew in population and size. They produced surplus amounts of food and goods that might be traded with neighboring villages. The demands of increased production and trade went hand in hand with changes in division and specialization of labor. Advances in technology, such as the invention of the wheel, the plow, and the solar calendar in the earliest known civilizations of Sumer and Egypt, enhanced economic efficiency. Wheeled carts transported people, food, and goods overland, and sailboats used the natural resource of wind for travel by water. Large-scale farming required artificial systems of irrigation, which, in turn, required cooperative effort and a high degree of communal organization. Neolithic villages grew in complexity to become the bustling cities of a new era. The birth of civilization (the word derives from the Latin *civitas*, or "city") marks the shift from rural/pastoral to urban/commercial life; or more specifically, the transition from simple village life to the more complex forms of social, economic, and political organization associated with urban existence.

The first civilization of the ancient world emerged in Mesopotamia, a fertile area that lay between the Tigris and Euphrates Rivers of the Southwest Asian land mass (Map 0.1). Mesopotamia formed the eastern arc of the Fertile Crescent, which stretched westward to the Nile delta. At the southeastern perimeter of the Fertile Crescent, about a dozen cities collectively constituted Sumer, the earliest civilization known to history. Shortly after the rise of Sumer, around 3500 B.C.E., Egyptian civilization emerged along the Nile River in Northeast Africa. In India, the earliest urban centers appeared in the valley of the Indus

River that runs through the northwest portion of the Indian subcontinent. Chinese civilization was born in the northern part of China's vast central plain, watered by the Yellow River. The appearance of these four river valley civilizations was not simultaneous. Fully a thousand years separates the birth of civilization in Sumer from the rise of cities in China.

By comparison with the self-sustaining Neolithic village, the early city reached outward. Specialization and the division of labor stimulated productivity and encouraged trade, which, in turn, enhanced the growth of the urban economy. Activities related to the production and distribution of goods could not be committed entirely to memory, but, rather, required a system of accounting and record keeping.

The Evolution of Writing

Writing, the principal means of record keeping, made it possible to transmit information by way of symbols. More a process than an invention, writing evolved from counting. As early as 7500 B.C.E., people used tokens—pieces of clay molded into shapes that represented specific commodities: a cone for a unit of grain, an egg shape for a unit of oil, and so on. These tokens were placed in hollow clay balls that accompanied shipments of goods. Upon arrival at their destination, the balls were broken open and the tokens—the "record" of the shipment—were counted. By the fourth millennium B.C.E., traders were stamping token shapes into wet clay, adding symbols to indicate the amounts of the actual goods. Around 3100 B.C.E., on clay tablets from Sumer, the **pictograph** (pictorial symbol) began to take the place of the token (Figure 0.15). In the following millennium, as scribes (using a stylus cut from a reed) found it difficult to execute the curves of pictographs

Map 0.1 Ancient River Valley Civilizations.

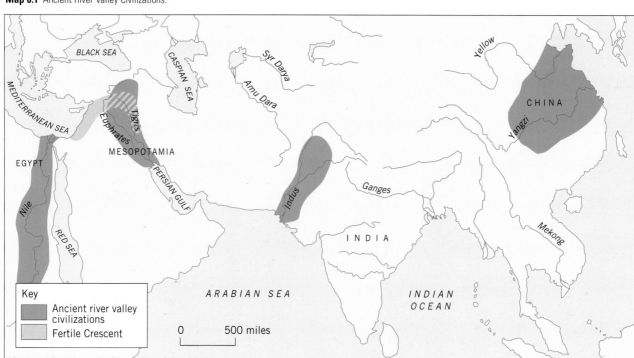

Key
- Ancient river valley civilizations
- Fertile Crescent

0   500 miles

on wet clay, these marks assumed a more angular and wedged shape. **Cuneiform** (from *cuneus*, the Latin word for "wedge"), a form of writing used throughout the Near East for well over 3000 years, ushered in the world's first information age (Figure 0.16). Thousands of clay tablets have survived. The earliest of them come from Sumer in Mesopotamia. Most bear notations concerning production and trade, while others are inventories and business accounts, historical records, myths, prayers, and genealogies of local rulers.

In Egypt, a set of "sacred signs" known as **hieroglyphs**, answered similar needs (see Figure 1.2). Ancient Egyptian writing remained a mystery to the world until 1822, when the Rosetta Stone (a black basalt slab discovered in 1799 in the Egyptian town of Rashid, or "Rosetta") was deciphered (Figure 0.17). The stone's inscription, written in two different types of Egyptian script and one Greek script, arranged in tiers, was understood only after a number of scholars, and ultimately Jean-François Champollion (1790–1832), matched the hieroglyphs for certain Egyptian rulers (such as Cleopatra) with their names in Greek. As Champollion showed, hieroglyphic writing combined **ideograms** (signs that represent ideas and things) and **phonograms** (signs that represent sounds).

The development of a written language is often isolated as the defining feature of a "civilized" society, but, in fact, some complex urban cultures (such as those of the Pueblo and Andean peoples in the ancient Americas) have existed without writing systems. Writing was only one of many inventions mothered by necessity on the threshold of the urban revolution. Technology itself would undergo dramatic development.

Figure 0.15 Reverse side of a pictographic tablet from Jamdat Nasr, near Kish, Iraq, ca. 3000 B.C.E., listing accounts involving animals and various commodities including bread and beer. Clay. Ashmolean Museum, Oxford.

Figure 0.16 The development of Sumerian writing from a pictographic script to cuneiform script to a phonetic system. Adapted from Samuel Noah Kramer, "The Sumerians," © 1957 by Scientific American, Inc. All rights reserved.

Earliest pictographs (3000 B.C.E.)	Denotation of pictographs	Pictographs in rotated position	Cuneiform signs ca. 1900 B.C.E.	Basic logographic values	
				Reading	Meaning
	Head and body of a man			lú	Man
	Head with mouth indicated			ka	Mouth
	Bowl of food			ninda	Food, bread
	Mouth + food			kú	To eat
	Stream of water			a	Water
	Mouth + water			nag	To drink
	Fish			kua	Fish
	Bird			mušen	Bird
	head of an ass			anše	Ass
	Ear of barley			še	Barley

Science and Technology

3100 B.C.E. cuneiform, the earliest known form of script, appears in Sumer; an early form of hieroglyphics appears in Egypt

3000 B.C.E. candles are manufactured in Egypt; cotton fabric is woven in India; Sumerian math evolves based on units of 60 (60 becomes basic unit for measuring time)

2600 B.C.E. Imhotep (Egyptian) produces the first known medical treatise

2600 B.C.E. a lost-wax method of bronze casting is used in East Mesopotamia

2500 B.C.E. the beginning of systematic standards in weights and measurement emerges in Sumer

Metallurgy

At about the same time that systems of writing emerged in Mesopotamia, metal began to replace stone and bone tools. Metallurgy, which was first practiced around Asia Minor during the period 4000 B.C.E., afforded humans a significant extension of control over nature by providing them with harder and more durable tools and weapons. At first, copper ore was extracted from surface deposits, but eventually metalsmiths devised sophisticated methods of mining and smelting ores. The result was bronze, an alloy of copper and tin that proved far superior to stone or bone in strength and durability. Since copper and tin were often located far apart, travel and trade were essential to Bronze Age cultures. (The 1995 discovery of Caucasian mummies in graves found in East Asia's Gobi desert argues for the existence of long distance trade and cross-cultural contact.) Metallurgy was a time-consuming process that required specialized training and the division of labor. Hence, bronze weapons were costly and available only to a small and well-to-do minority of the population. This minority formed a military elite who wielded power by virtue of superior arms. As the victory monument pictured in Figure **0.18** indicates, Sumerian warriors were outfitted with bronze shields, helmets, and lances.

Figure 0.17 Rosetta Stone, 196 B.C.E. Basalt, height 3 ft. 9 in. The same information is inscribed in hieroglyphic, a pictographic script (1); demotic script, a simplified form of hieroglyphic (2); and Greek (3). British Museum, London.

Figure 0.18 The King of Lagash leads his phalanx into battle. Detail of Eannatum's Stele of Victory, Tello, formerly Girsu, ca. 2450 B.C.E. Limestone, 5 ft. 10⅞ in. × 4 ft. 3⅜ in. Louvre, Paris. Photo: RMN.

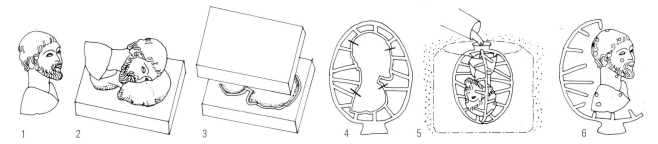

Figure 0.19 The lost-wax process of bronze casting developed in Mesopotamia, third millennium B.C.E. A positive model (1) is used to make a negative mold (2), which is then coated with wax. Cool fireclay is poured into the wax shell; the mold is then removed (3). Metal rods are added to hold the layers in place, as are wax vents for even flow of bronze (4). The whole structure is immersed in sand; the wax is burned out. Investment ready for molten bronze (5). Bronze head, ready for removal of gates and metal rods (6).

Figure 0.20 Chariot from Daimabad, Maharashtra, ca. 1500 B.C.E. Bronze, 8⅝ × 20½ × 6⅞ in. The Prince of Wales Museum of Western India, Bombay. Photo: Dirk Bakker.

The technology of bronze casting spread throughout the ancient world. Mesopotamians of the third millennium B.C.E. were among the first to use the **lost-wax** method of casting (Figure 0.19). Spreading eastward into the Indus valley, the lost-wax technique became popular for the manufacture of jewelry, musical instruments, horse fittings, and toys (Figure 0.20). The ancient Chinese cast the separate parts of bronze vessels in sectional clay molds, and then soldered the parts together. Master metallurgists, the Chinese transformed the techniques of bronze casting into one of the great artforms of the ancient world (see chapter 3).

People and Nature

Like their prehistoric ancestors, the inhabitants of the earliest civilizations lived in intimate association with nature. They looked upon the forces of nature—sun, wind, and rain—as vital and alive, indeed, as inhabited by living spirits—a belief known as **animism**. Just as they devised tools to manipulate the natural environment, so they devised strategies by which to understand and control that environment. *Myths*—that is, stories that explained the workings of nature—were part of the ritual fabric of everyday life. In legends and myths, the living spirits of

nature assumed human (and heroic) status: they might be vengeful or beneficent, ugly or beautiful, fickle or reliable. Ultimately, they became a family of superhumans—gods and goddesses who very much resembled humans in their physical features and personalities, but whose superior strength and intelligence far exceeded that of human beings. The gods were also immortal, which made them the envy of ordinary human beings. Ritual sacrifice, prayer, and the enactment of myths honoring one or more of the gods accompanied seasonal celebrations, rites of passage, and almost every other significant communal event. In the early history of civilization, goddesses seem to have outnumbered gods, and local deities reigned supreme within their own districts. By means of specially appointed priests and priestesses, who mediated between human and divine realms, ancient people forged contractual relationships with their gods: in return for divine benefits, they lived as they believed the gods would wish.

Myth and the Quest for Beginnings

Today, no less than thousands of years ago, humans feel the need to explain the origins of the universe and define their place in it. While modern speculation on the origins of life takes the form of scientific theory (advanced by physicists, geologists, paleontologists, and anthropologists), the ancient quest for beginnings assumed the guise of myth. Ritually celebrated and repeated generation after generation, myths became fixed in the popular memory. As in the Pygmy ritual (Reading 1.1), words, gestures, and images formed the powerful amalgam of sacred ceremony.

In modern parlance, the word "myth" has come to suggest misconception; but, more accurately, myth describes a particular kind of speculation that, although prescientific, bears historical significance. For while myth rationalizes the unknown in terms that may sound fantastic or quaint to modern ears, it constitutes the pattern of belief—the bedrock reality—of a given culture. Three further observations are noteworthy: first, the myths of ancient people are grounded in the evidence of the senses; thus, the imagery of myth is usually intensely visual. Second, the myths of a people are closely linked to that people's moral system, its rituals, and its religious beliefs, for what was taken as true was also held as sacred. Finally, the myths of humankind's earliest cultures show remarkable similarities, one of the most notable of which is the genesis of the first life forms from water.

In order to better understand these concepts, consider the following four creation myths. The first, a hymn from the *Rig Veda*—the oldest religious literature of India—locates our beginnings in a watery darkness. The second is but one example drawn from the huge fund of creation stories told by African tribal people and transmitted orally for centuries. It situates the origins of life in the slender grasses that grow in wet, marshy soil. The third, an account of creation from the *Popol Vuh* ("Sacred Book") of Central America's Maya Indians, links creation to the word, that is, to language itself. Finally, from the Native American Iroquois Federation, a Mohawk tale recounts how the Good Spirit fashioned humankind in its diversity.

READING 1.2 Creation Tales

"The Song of Creation" from the *Rig Veda*

Then even nothingness was not, nor existence. 1
    There was no air then, nor the heavens beyond it
    What covered it? Where was it? In whose keeping?
    Was there then cosmic water, in depths unfathomed?
Then there were neither death nor immortality, 5
    nor was there then the torch of night and day.
    The One breathed windlessly and self-sustaining.
    There was that One then, and there was no other.
At first there was only darkness wrapped in darkness.
    All this was only unillumined water. 10
    That One which came to be, enclosed in nothing,
    arose at last, born of the power of heat.
In the beginning desire descended on it—
    that was the primal seed, born of the mind.
    The sages who have searched their hearts with wisdom 15
    know that which is, is kin to that which is not.
And they have stretched their cord across the void,
    and know what was above, and what below.
    Seminal powers made fertile mighty forces.
    Below was strength, and over it was impulse. 20
But, after all, who knows, and who can say
    whence it all came, and how creation happened?
    The gods themselves are later than creation,
    so who knows truly whence it has arisen?
Whence all creation had its origin, 25
    he, whether he fashioned it or whether he did not,
    he, who surveys it all from highest heaven,
    he knows—or maybe even he does not know.

             (India)

An African Creation Tale

. . . It is said all men sprang from Unkulunkulu, who sprang 1
up first. The earth was in existence before Unkulunkulu. He
had his origin from the earth in a bed of reeds.

All things as well as Unkulunkulu sprang from a bed of reeds—everything, both animals and corn, everything came into being with Unkulunkulu.

He looked at the sun when it was finished (worked into form as a potter works clay) and said: "There is a torch which will give you light, that you may see." He looked down on the cattle and said: 10
"These are cattle. Be ye broken off, and see the cattle and let them be your food; eat their flesh and their milk." He looked on wild animals and said: "That is such an animal. That is an elephant. That is a buffalo." He looked on the fire and said: "Kindle it, and cook, and warm yourself; and eat meat when it has been dressed by the fire." He looked on all things and said: "So and so is the name of everything."

Unkulunkulu said: "Let there be marriage among men, that there may be those who can intermarry, that children may be born and men increase on earth." He said, "Let there be black 20 chiefs; and the chief be known by his people, and it be said, 'That is the chief: assemble all of you and go to your chief.'"

             (Amazulu)

From the *Popol Vuh*

This is the account of how all was in suspense, all calm, in 1 silence; all motionless, still, and the expanse of the sky was empty.

This is the first account, the first narrative. There was neither man, nor animal, birds, fishes, crabs, trees, stones, caves, ravines, grasses, nor forests; there was only the sky.

The surface of the earth had not appeared. There was only the calm sea and the great expanse of the sky.

There was nothing brought together, nothing which could make a noise, nor anything which might move, or tremble, or 10 could make noise in the sky.

There was nothing standing; only the calm water, the placid sea, alone and tranquil. Nothing existed.

There was only immobility and silence in the darkness in the night. Only the Creator, the Maker, Tepeu, Gucumatz, the Forefathers, were in the water surrounded with light. They were hidden under green and blue feathers, and were therefore called Gucumatz. By nature they were great sages and great thinkers. In this manner the sky existed and also the Heart of Heaven, which is the name of God and thus He is 20 called.

Then came the word. Tepeu and Gucumatz came together in the darkness, in the night, and Tepeu and Gucumatz talked together. They talked then, discussing and deliberating; they agreed, they united their words and their thoughts.

Then while they mediated, it became clear to them that when dawn would break, man must appear. Then they planned the creation, and the growth of the trees and the thickets and the birth of life and the creation of man. Thus it was arranged in the darkness and in the night by the Heart of Heaven who 30 is called Huracán.

Then Tepeu and Gucumatz came together; then they conferred about life and light, what they would do so that there would be light and dawn, who it would be who would provide food and sustenance.

Thus let it be done! Let the emptiness be filled! Let the water recede and make a void, let the earth appear and become solid; let it be done. Thus they spoke. Let there be light, let there be dawn in the sky and on the earth! There shall be neither glory nor grandeur in our creation and formation 40 until the human being is made, man is formed. So they spoke.

Then the earth was created by them. So it was, in truth, that they created the earth. Earth! . . . they said, and instantly it was made. . . .

(Maya)

A Native American Creation Tale, "How Man Was Created"

After Sat-kon-se-ri-io, the Good Spirit, had made the 1 animals, birds, and other creatures and had placed them to live and multiply upon the earth, he rested. As he gazed around at his various creations, it seemed to him that there was something lacking. For a long time the Good Spirit pondered over this thought. Finally he decided to make a creature that would resemble himself.

Going to the bank of a river he took a piece of clay, and out of it he fashioned a little clay man. After he had modeled it, he built a fire and, setting the little clay man in the fire, waited 10 for it to bake. The day was beautiful. The songs of the birds filled the air. The river sang a song and, as the Good Spirit listened to this song, he became very sleepy. He soon fell asleep beside the fire. When he finally awoke, he rushed to the fire and removed the clay man. He had slept too long. His little man was burnt black. According to the Mohawks, this little man was the first Negro. His skin was black. He had been overbaked.

The Good Spirit was not satisfied. Taking a fresh piece of clay, he fashioned another man and, placing him in the fire, 20 waited for him to bake, determined this time to stay awake

and watch his little man to see that he would not be overbaked. But the river sang its usual sleepy song. The Good Spirit, in spite of all he could do, fell asleep. But this time he slept only a little while. Awakening at last, he ran to the fire and removed his little man. Behold, it was half baked. This, say the Mohawks, was the first white man. He was half baked!

The Good Spirit was still unsatisfied. Searching along the riverbank he hunted until he found a bed of perfect red clay. 30 This time he took great care and modeled a very fine clay man. Taking the clay man to the fire, he allowed it to bake. Determined to stay awake, the Good Spirit stood beside the fire, after a while Sat-kon-se-ri-io removed the clay man. Behold, it was just right—a man the red color of the sunset sky. It was the first Mohawk Indian.

(Mohawk)

 Q What do all the creation myths in this reading have in common? How do they differ?

Civilization emerged not as a fleeting moment of change, but as a slow process of urban growth. By the operation of an increasingly refined abstract intelligence, and by means of ingenuity, imagination, and cooperation, the earliest human beings took the first steps in perpetuating their own survival and the security of their communities. Technology provided the tools for manipulating nature, while mythology and the arts lent meaning and purpose to nature's hidden mysteries. By such cultural achievements, the earliest human beings laid the foundations for the humanistic tradition.

GLOSSARY

animism the belief that the forces of nature are inhabited by spirits

culture the sum total of those things (including traditions, techniques, material goods, and symbol systems) that people have invented, developed, and transmitted

cuneiform ("wedge-shaped") one of humankind's earliest writing systems, consisting of wedge-shaped marks impressed into clay by means of a reed stylus

dolmen a stone tomb formed by two posts capped by a lintel

hieroglyph (Greek, "sacred sign") the pictographic script of ancient Egypt

hominid any of a family of bipedal primate mammals, including modern humans and their ancestors, the earliest of which is *Australopithecus*

ideogram a sign that represents an idea or a thing

lost wax (also French, *cire-perdu*) a method of metal-casting in which a figure is

modeled in wax, then enclosed in a clay mold that is fired; the wax melts, and molten metal is poured in to replace it; finally, the clay mold is removed and the solid metal form is polished (see Figure 0.18)

megalith a large, roughly shaped stone, often used in ancient architectural construction

phonogram a sign that represents a sound

pictograph a pictorial symbol used in humankind's earliest

systems of writing

polychrome having many or various colors

post-and-lintel the simplest form of architectural construction, consisting of vertical members (posts) and supporting horizontals (lintels); see Figure 0.9

prehistory the study of history before written records

stele an upright stone slab or pillar

The First Civilizations

The first chapters in the history of human life are often regarded as the most exciting. They present us with a gigantic puzzle that requires the piecing together of numerous fragments of information, most of which, like buried treasure, have been dug out of the earth. Reassembled, these fragments reveal the progress of humankind from its Bronze Age beginnings through the cultural history of ancient civilizations in Africa, Southwest Asia, India, and China. In the opening chapters of this book, history's four earliest civilizations are presented geographically and chronologically. It is not, however, the detailed histories of these individual civilizations that are our major concern. Rather, we pursue three principle *themes*: the formulation of belief systems that linked the secular and spiritual realms; the establishment of rulership within the earliest urban communities; and finally, the nature of the social order as revealed in law and other forms of cultural expression. These three themes address concerns that are universal; inevitably, they dominate the visual and literary works of humankind's earliest civilizations.

Common to all of the civilizations of the ancient world was the belief that the forces of nature are greater and more powerful than those of mere humans. The sun that nourishes a bountiful harvest, the winds that sweep away whole villages, the rains that cause rivers to flood the land —all of these natural forces affect daily life even in our own time. Among our early ancestors, however, those for whom survival was a day-to-day struggle, such forces, or the gods that represented them, assumed positions of primary importance. Belief systems and religious practices differed dramatically from one ancient civilization to another; but all systems and practices reflect the human effort to come to terms with the unknown: to understand the origins of life, the workings of nature, the meaning of death, and the destiny and purpose of humankind.

Throughout the ancient world, the survival of the community depended on strong leadership and communal cooperation. In Egypt, as in Mesopotamia, India, and China, rulership and the authority of law provided security and protection. The success of each civilization depended on a shared view of the earthly order as god-given or as immutably fixed in nature; as these civilizations matured, the bonds between the divine and secular realms gave shape to both social and moral life. In the arts—the astonishingly rich legacy of these four ancient civilizations—we discover a wealth of resources for an understanding of the dynamic interaction between the gods, the rulers, and the people who constituted the social order. In looking at the material evidence of the first civilizations, we come to understand not simply what happened in the ancient past, but how and why our forebears arrived at strategies and values that, in many instances, have shaped our own.

(opposite) Sphinx at Gizeh, Egypt, ca. 2540–2514 B.C.E. Limestone, length 240 ft., height 65 ft.

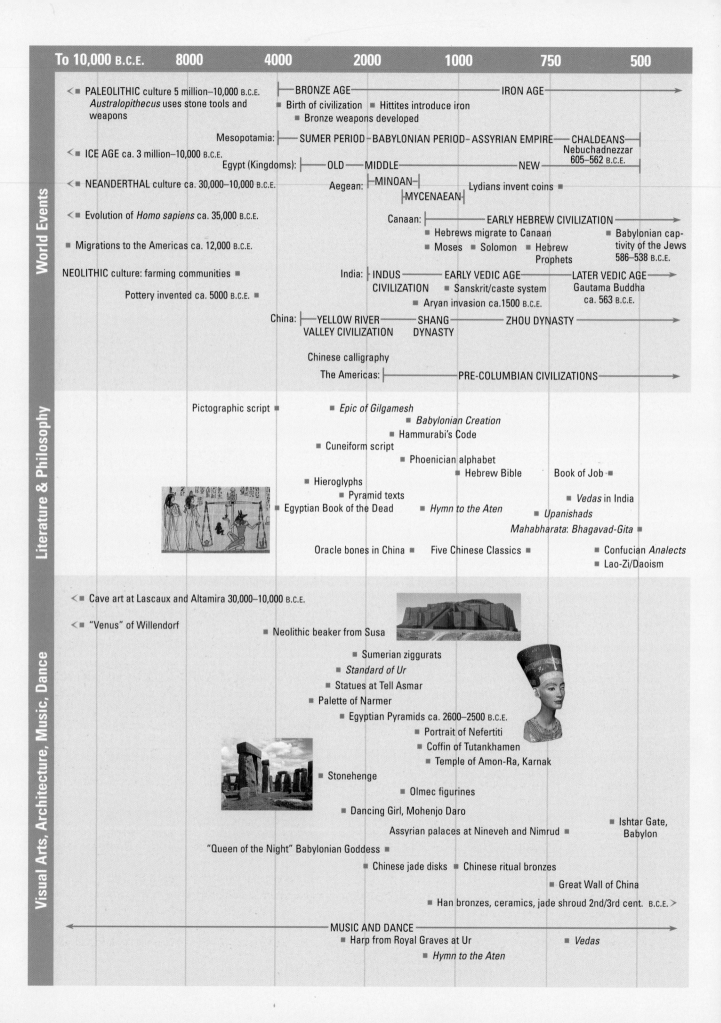

To 10,000 B.C.E.	8000	4000	2000	1000	750	500

World Events

◄ ■ PALEOLITHIC culture 5 million–10,000 B.C.E. *Australopithecus* uses stone tools and weapons

—BRONZE AGE—————————— IRON AGE——————
■ Birth of civilization ■ Hittites introduce iron
■ Bronze weapons developed

Mesopotamia: —SUMER PERIOD–BABYLONIAN PERIOD–ASSYRIAN EMPIRE— CHALDEANS
Nebuchadnezzar 605–562 B.C.E.

◄ ■ ICE AGE ca. 3 million–10,000 B.C.E.

Egypt (Kingdoms): —OLD—MIDDLE———————NEW———

◄ ■ NEANDERTHAL culture ca. 30,000–10,000 B.C.E.

Aegean: —MINOAN—
—MYCENAEAN—
Lydians invent coins ■

◄ ■ Evolution of *Homo sapiens* ca. 35,000 B.C.E.

Canaan: —————EARLY HEBREW CIVILIZATION————
■ Hebrews migrate to Canaan
■ Moses ■ Solomon ■ Hebrew Prophets
■ Babylonian captivity of the Jews 586–538 B.C.E.

■ Migrations to the Americas ca. 12,000 B.C.E.

NEOLITHIC culture: farming communities ■

India: —INDUS CIVILIZATION— EARLY VEDIC AGE
■ Sanskrit/caste system
■ Aryan invasion ca.1500 B.C.E.
LATER VEDIC AGE
Gautama Buddha ca. 563 B.C.E.

Pottery invented ca. 5000 B.C.E. ■

China: —YELLOW RIVER VALLEY CIVILIZATION— SHANG DYNASTY — ZHOU DYNASTY

Chinese calligraphy

The Americas: ———————PRE-COLUMBIAN CIVILIZATIONS————

Literature & Philosophy

Pictographic script ■

■ *Epic of Gilgamesh*
■ *Babylonian Creation*
■ Hammurabi's Code
■ Cuneiform script
■ Phoenician alphabet
■ Hebrew Bible
Book of Job ■
■ Hieroglyphs
■ Pyramid texts
Egyptian Book of the Dead
Hymn to the Aten
■ *Vedas* in India
■ *Upanishads*
Mahabharata: *Bhagavad-Gita* ■

Oracle bones in China ■ ■ Five Chinese Classics ■
■ Confucian *Analects*
■ Lao-Zi/Daoism

Visual Arts, Architecture, Music, Dance

◄ ■ Cave art at Lascaux and Altamira 30,000–10,000 B.C.E.

◄ ■ "Venus" of Willendorf

■ Neolithic beaker from Susa

■ Sumerian ziggurats
■ *Standard of Ur*
■ Statues at Tell Asmar
■ Palette of Narmer
■ Egyptian Pyramids ca. 2600–2500 B.C.E.
■ Portrait of Nefertiti
■ Coffin of Tutankhamen
■ Temple of Amon-Ra, Karnak

■ Stonehenge

■ Olmec figurines
■ Dancing Girl, Mohenjo Daro
Assyrian palaces at Nineveh and Nimrud ■
■ Ishtar Gate, Babylon

"Queen of the Night" Babylonian Goddess ■

■ Chinese jade disks ■ Chinese ritual bronzes
■ Great Wall of China
■ Han bronzes, ceramics, jade shroud 2nd/3rd cent. B.C.E. ►

————MUSIC AND DANCE————
■ Harp from Royal Graves at Ur
■ *Vedas*
■ *Hymn to the Aten*

CHAPTER 1

Egypt: Gods, Rulers, and the Social Order

*"The barges sail upstream and downstream too,
for every way is open at your rising."*
The Hymn to the Aten

Ancient Egyptian civilization emerged along the banks of the Nile River in northeast Africa. From the heart of Africa, the thin blue thread of the Nile flowed some 4000 miles to its fan-shaped delta at the Mediterranean Sea. Along this river, agricultural villages thrived, coming under the rule of a sole ruler around 3150 B.C.E. Surrounded by sea and desert, Egypt was relatively invulnerable to foreign invasion (Map **1.1**), a condition that lent stability to Egyptian history. Unlike Mesopotamia, home to many different civilizations, ancient Egypt enjoyed a fairly uniform religious, political, and cultural life that lasted for almost 3000 years. Its population shared a common language and a common world view. Although emerging slightly later than the first civilization in Mesopotamia, ancient Egypt thus provides a more accessible model for our understanding of the dynamics of the first civilizations.

The Gods of Ancient Egypt

Geography, climate, and the realities of the natural environment worked to shape the world views and religious beliefs of all ancient peoples. In the hot, arid climate of Northeast Africa, where ample sunlight made possible the cultivation of crops, the sun god held the place of honor. Variously called Amon, Re (Ra), or Aten, this god was considered greater than any other deity in the Egyptian pantheon. His cult dominated the **polytheistic** belief system of ancient Egypt for three millennia. Equally important to Egyptian life was the Nile, the world's longest river. Egypt, called by the Greek historian Herodotus "the gift of the Nile," depended on the annual overflow of the Nile, which left fertile layers of rich silt along its banks. The 365-day cycle of the river's inundation became the basis of the solar calendar and the primary source of Egypt's deep sense of order. In the regularity of the sun's daily cycle and the Nile's annual deluge, ancient Egyptians found security. From the natural elements—the sun, the Nile, and the largely flat topography of North Africa—they also constructed their **cosmology**, that is, their theory of the origin and structure of the universe. With graphic immediacy, they described the earth as a flat platter floating on the waters of the underworld. According to Egyptian myths, at the beginning of time, the Nile's primordial waters brought forth a mound of silt, out of which emerged the self-generating sun god; from that god, the rest of Egypt's gods were born.

Ancient Egyptians viewed the sun's daily ascent in the east as symbolic of the god's "rebirth"; his daily resurrection signified the victory of the forces of day, light, purity, goodness, and life over those of night, darkness, ignorance, evil, and death. In the cyclical regularity of nature evidenced by the daily rising and setting of the sun, the ancient Egyptians perceived both the inevitability of death and the promise of birth. "The Hymn to the Aten," a song of praise with numerous Egyptian antecedents, probably accompanied rituals of renewal honoring Egypt's pharaoh, the divinely appointed representative of the sun god. Depictions of such rituals on the walls of Egyptian temples and tombs show the pharaoh receiving from Amon the gift of immortality in the form of the *ankh*, the hieroglyphic symbol meaning "life" (Figure **1.1**). In both the visual arts and in poetry, the sun is exalted as the source of light and heat, but also as the proactive life force, the "creator of seed." The optimism and sense of security that pervades this hymn typifies ancient Egyptian culture.

READING 1.3 From "The Hymn to the Aten"

(ca. 1352–1336 B.C.E.)

You rise in perfection on the horizon of the sky	1
living Aten,[1] who started life.	
Whenever you are risen upon the eastern horizon	
you fill every land with your perfection.	
You are appealing, great, sparkling, high over every land;	5

---
[1] The sun disk.

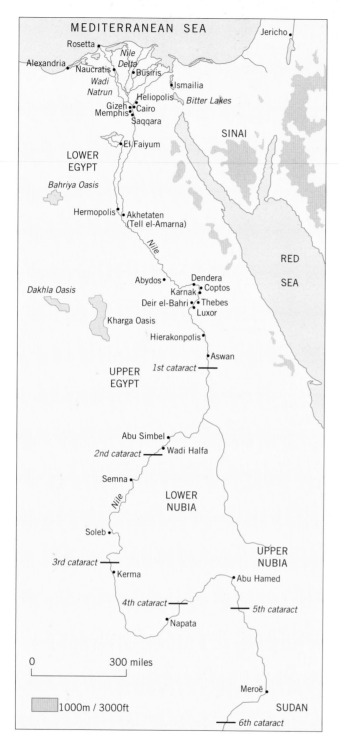

Map 1.1 Ancient Egypt.

and one eye does not see another.
  If all their possessions which are under their heads were
    stolen,   15
  they would not know it.
Every lion who comes out of his cave
  and all the serpents bite,
    for darkness is a blanket.
The land is silent now, because he who made them   20
  is at rest on his horizon

But when day breaks you are risen upon the horizon,
  and you shine as the Aten in the daytime.
When you dispel darkness and you give forth your rays
  the two lands[3] are in festival,   25
    alert and standing on their feet,
      now that you have raised them up.
Their bodies are clean,
  and their clothes have been put on;
    their arms are [lifted] in praise at your rising.   30
The entire land performs its work:
  all the cattle are content with their fodder,
    trees and plants grow,
      birds fly up to their nests,
        their wings [extended] in praise for your Ka.[4]   35
All the Kine[5] prance on their feet;
  everything which flies up and alights,
    they live when you
      have risen for them.
The barges sail upstream and downstream too,   40
  for every way is open at your rising.
The fishes in the river leap before your face
  when your rays are in the sea.

You who have placed seed in woman
  and have made sperm into man,   45
    who feeds the son in the womb of his mother,
      who quiets him with something to stop his crying;
        you are the nurse in the womb,
          giving breath to nourish all that has been begotten.

Q Which of Aten's powers are glorified in this hymn?

Q How did this god serve the ancient Egyptians?

your rays hold together the lands as far as everything
    you have made.
Since you are Re,[2] you reach as far as they do,
    and you curb them for your beloved son.
Although you are far away, your rays are upon the land;
    you are in their faces, yet your departure is not observed.   10
Whenever you set on the western horizon,
    the land is in darkness in the manner of death.
They sleep in a bedroom with heads under the covers,

Second only to the sun as the major natural force in Egyptian life was the Nile River. Ancient Egyptians identified the Nile with Osiris, ruler of the underworld and god of the dead. According to Egyptian myth, Osiris was slain

---

[2]Another name for the sun god, associated with his regenerative powers.

[3]The kingdoms of Upper and Lower Egypt, so designated because the Nile flows from the heart of Africa in the south to the Mediterranean Sea in the north. Upper Egypt extended south as far as the first cataract at Syene (Aswan); Lower Egypt comprised the Nile delta north of Memphis; see Map 1.1.

[4]The governing spirit or soul of a person or god.

[5]Cow.

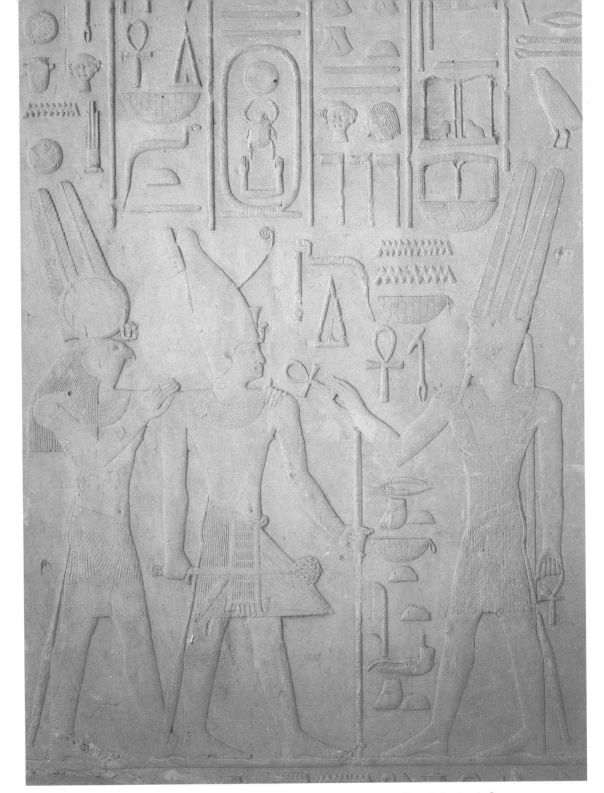

Figure 1.1 Amon receives Sesostris (Senusret) I, pillar relief, White Chapel, Karnak, ca. 1925 B.C.E. Photo: Andrea Jemolo, Rome.

by his evil brother, Set, who chopped his body into pieces and threw them into the Nile. But Osiris's loyal wife Isis, Queen of Heaven, gathered the fragments and restored Osiris to life. The union of Isis and the resurrected Osiris produced a son, Horus, who ultimately avenged his father by overthrowing Set and becoming ruler of Egypt. The Osiris myth vividly describes the idea of resurrection that was central to the ancient Egyptian belief system. Though the cult of the sun in his various aspects dominated the official religion of Egypt, local gods and goddesses—more

than 2000 of them—made up the Egyptian pantheon. These deities, most of whom held multiple powers, played protective roles in the daily lives of the ancient Egyptians. However, the following invocation to Isis, found inscribed on a sculpture of the goddess, suggests her central role among the female deities of Egypt:

> Praise to you, Isis, the Great One
> God's Mother, Lady of Heaven,
> Mistress and Queen of the Gods.

Principal Egyptian Gods

Name	Role	Depicted As
Amon	sun god, creator of heaven and earth	falcon, sun rays
Anubis	patron of embalmers, god of cemeteries	jackal
Aten	god of the solar disk	solar disk
Bes	helper of women in childbirth, protector against snakes	lion-faced dwarf
Hapi	god of the Nile	bull
Hathor	mother, wife, and daughter of Ra, sky goddess	cow
Horus	son of Isis and Osiris, sky god	falcon
Isis	wife of Osiris, mother of Horus, fertility goddess	female
Maat	goddess of truth and universal order	head-feather
Osiris	god of the underworld	mummified king
Ptah	creator of humans, patron of craftspeople	mummified man
Set	brother of Osiris, god of storms and violence	pig, ass, hippopotamus
Thoth	inventor of writing, patron of scribes	ibis

The Rulers of Ancient Egypt

Local rulers governed the Neolithic villages along the Nile until roughly 3150 B.C.E., when they were united under the authority of Egypt's first pharaoh, Narmer (also known as Menes). This important political event—the union of Upper and Lower Egypt—is commemorated on a two-foot-high slate object known as the Palette of Narmer (Figures **1.2** and **1.3**). The back of the slate palette shows the triumphant Narmer seizing a fallen enemy by the hair. Below his feet lie the bodies of the vanquished. To his left, a slave (represented smaller in size than Narmer) dutifully carries his master's sandals. At the upper right is the victorious falcon, symbol of the god Horus. Horus/Narmer holds by the leash the now-subdued lands of Lower Egypt, symbolized by a severed head and **papyrus**, the reed-like plants that grow along the Nile. On the front, the top register bears a victory procession flanked by rows of defeated soldiers, who stand with their decapitated heads between their legs. Narmer's conquest initiated Egypt's first **dynasty**. For some 2500 years to follow, ancient Egypt was ruled by a succession of dynasties, the history of which was divided into chronological periods by an Egyptian priest of the third century B.C.E.:

Early Dynastic period ca. 3100–2700 B.C.E. (Dynasties I–II)
Old Kingdom ca. 2700–2150 B.C.E. (Dynasties III–VI)
Middle Kingdom ca. 2050–1785 B.C.E. (Dynasties XI–XII)
New Kingdom ca. 1575–1085 B.C.E. (Dynasties XVIII–XX)

Civil dissent marked the intermediate period between the Old and Middle Kingdoms, while the era between the Middle and New Kingdoms (roughly 1785 to 1575) withstood the invasion of the Hyksos, warlike tribes who introduced the horse and chariot into Egypt. Following the expulsion of Hyksos, New Kingdom pharaohs (the word means "great house" in the sense of "first family") created Egypt's first empire, extending royal authority far into Syria, Palestine, and Nubia.

Throughout their long history, ancient Egyptians viewed the land as sacred. It was owned by the gods, ruled by the pharaohs, and farmed by the peasants with the assistance of slaves. The fruits of each harvest were shared according to the needs of the community. This divinely sanctioned way of life, known as *theocratic socialism*, provided Egypt with an abundance of food and a surplus that encouraged widespread trade. The land itself, however, passed from generation to generation not through the male but through the female line, that is, from the king's daughter to the man she married. For the pharaoh's son to come to the throne, he would have to marry his own sister or half-sister (hence the numerous brother–sister marriages in Egyptian dynastic history). This tradition, probably related to the practice of tracing parentage to the childbearer, lasted longer in Egypt than anywhere else in the ancient world. In the freestanding sculpture of the Old Kingdom pharaoh Mycerinus, the queen stands proudly at his side, one arm around his waist and the other gently touching his arm (Figure **1.4**). A sense of shared purpose is conveyed by their lifted chins and confident demeanor. While Egypt's rulers were traditionally male, women came to the throne three times. The most notable of all female pharaohs, Hatshepsut (ca. 1500–1447 B.C.E), governed Egypt for twenty-two years. She is often pictured in male attire, wearing the royal wig and false beard, and carrying the crook and the flail—traditional symbols of rulership.

Theocracy and the Cult of the Dead

From earliest times, political power was linked with spiritual power and superhuman might. The Egyptians held that divine power flowed from the gods to their royal agents. In this **theocracy** (rule by god or god's representative), reigning **monarchs** represented heaven's will on earth. While the pharaoh ruled in the name of the immortal and generative sun god, he was also identified with Horus, the avenging son of Osiris and Isis, symbolized by the falcon. So close was the association between rulers and

Science and Technology

2650 B.C.E.	Pharaoh Khufu (or Cheops) orders construction of the Great Pyramid of Gizeh†
1500 B.C.E.	Egyptians employ a simple form of the sundial
1450 B.C.E.	the water clock is devised in Egypt
1400 B.C.E.	glass in produced in Egypt and Mesopotamia

†All dates in this chapter are approximate

Figure 1.2 Palette of King Narmer (front and back), ca. 3100 B.C.E. Slate, height 25 in. Egyptian Museum, Cairo. © Hirmer Fotoarchiv.

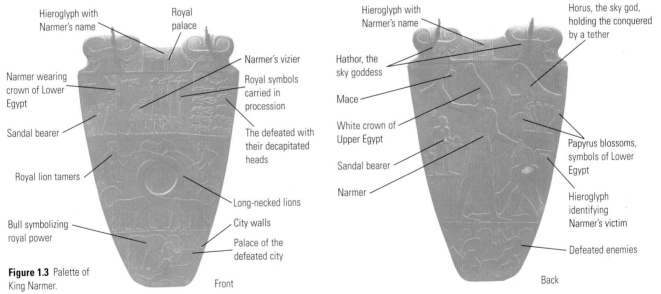

Figure 1.3 Palette of King Narmer.

Front labels:
- Hieroglyph with Narmer's name
- Royal palace
- Narmer wearing crown of Lower Egypt
- Narmer's vizier
- Royal symbols carried in procession
- Sandal bearer
- The defeated with their decapitated heads
- Royal lion tamers
- Long-necked lions
- Bull symbolizing royal power
- City walls
- Palace of the defeated city

Back labels:
- Hieroglyph with Narmer's name
- Horus, the sky god, holding the conquered by a tether
- Hathor, the sky goddess
- Mace
- White crown of Upper Egypt
- Sandal bearer
- Narmer
- Papyrus blossoms, symbols of Lower Egypt
- Hieroglyph identifying Narmer's victim
- Defeated enemies

gods that Egyptian hymns to the pharaoh address him in terms identical with those used in worshiping the gods. In the visual arts, rulers and gods alike were depicted with the attributes and physical features of powerful animals. Such is the case with the Great Sphinx, the recumbent creature that guards the entrance to the ceremonial complex at Gizeh (see Part I opener). This haunting figure, antiquity's largest and earliest surviving colossal statue, bears the portrait head of the Old Kingdom pharaoh Khafre and the body of a lion, king of the beasts. As such, it is a hybrid symbol of superhuman power and authority.

Ancient Egyptians venerated the pharaoh as the living representative of the sun god. They believed that on his death, the pharaoh would join with the sun to govern Egypt eternally. His body was prepared for burial by means of a special, ten-week embalming procedure that involved

Figure 1.4 Pair statue of Mycerinus and Queen Kha-merer-nebty II, Gizeh, Mycerinus, fourth dynasty, ca. 2599–1571 B.C.E. Slate schist, height 4 ft. 6½ in. (complete statue). Harvard University–Boston Museum of Fine Arts Expedition. Photograph © 2006 Museum of Fine Arts, Boston.

removing all of his internal organs (with the exception of his heart) and filling his body cavity with preservatives. His intestines, stomach, lungs, and liver were all embalmed separately—the brain was removed and discarded. The king's corpse was then wrapped in fine linen and placed in an elaborately ornamented coffin (Figure **1.5**), which was floated down the Nile on a royal barge to a burial site located at Gizeh and Saggara, near the southern tip of the Nile Delta (see Map 1.1). The earliest

Egyptian tombs—homes for the dead—were probably modeled on Egypt's domestic dwellings. These single-story mud-brick rectangular tombs, called **mastabas**, consisted of an offering chamber, a room that held a statue of the dead, and a shaft that descended to the burial chamber some 100 feet below the ground. Stacking five mastabas of decreasing size one on top of another, the third dynasty architect Imenhotep produced the impressive stepped pyramid for King Zoser, who ruled shortly before 2600 B.C.E. (Figure **1.6**). The pyramidal shape may have been inspired by the mythical mound of silt from which the primordial sun god was said to have risen. With the fourth-dynasty pharaohs of the Old Kingdom, the true geometric **pyramid** took shape.

Constructed between 2600 and 2500 B.C.E., the pyramids are technological wonders, as well as symbols of ancient Egypt's endurance through time (Figure **1.7**). A work force of some 50,000 men (divided into gangs of twenty-five) labored almost thirty years to raise the Great Pyramid of Khufu. According to recent DNA analysis of the workers found buried at Gizeh, the pyramid builders were Egyptians, not foreign slaves, as was previously assumed. This native work force quarried, transported, and assembled thousands of mammoth stone blocks, most weighing between 2 and 50 tons. These they lifted from tier to tier by means of levers—though some historians speculate they were slid into place on inclined ramps of

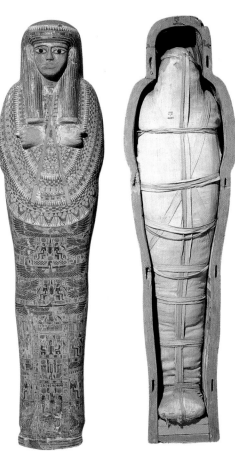

Figure 1.5 Egyptian mummy and coffin, ca. 1000 B.C.E. Reproduced by courtesy of the Trustees of the British Museum, London.

Figure 1.6 Stepped Pyramid of King Zoser, Saqqara, ca. 2630 B.C.E. © Paul M.R. Maeyart

Figure 1.7 Great Pyramids of Gizeh: from left to right, Menkure, ca. 2575 B.C.E., Khufu (Khefren), ca. 2650 B.C.E., Khafre, ca. 2600 B.C.E. Top height approx. 480 ft. Carolyn Clark/Spectrum Colour Library, London.

Figure 1.8 Pyramid construction. Some historians speculate that the vast stone building blocks were hauled into position using log sleds and inclined ramps made of packed sand.

Log sled

Mud and rubble ramp

connected to the exterior by tunnels (Figure 1.10), was prepared as a home for eternity—a tribute to communal faith in the eternal benevolence of the pharaoh. Its chambers were fitted with his most cherished possessions: priceless treasures of jewelry, weapons, and furniture, all of which he might require in the life to come. The chamber walls were painted in **fresco** and carved in **relief** with images recreating the pharaoh's life on earth (Figure **1.11**). Hieroglyphs formed an essential component of pictorial illustration, narrating the achievements of Egypt's rulers, listing the grave goods, and offering perpetual prayers for the deceased (see also Figures 1.1 and 1.2).

Figure **1.10** Burial chambers within a typical pyramid.

1 air shaft?
2 gallery to chambers
3 ascending corridor
4 descending corridor
5 weight-relieving chamber
6 burial chamber
7 abandoned
   burial chamber
8 escape route?
9 original burial chambers

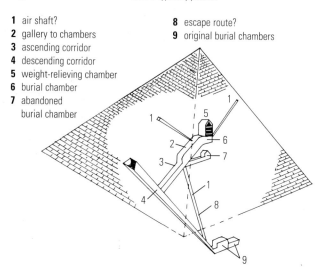

sand and rubble (Figure **1.8**). Finally, the laborers faced the surfaces of the great tombs with finely polished limestone. All of these feats were achieved with copper saws and chisels, and without pulleys or mortar. The Great Pyramid of Khufu, which stands as part of a large walled burial complex at Gizeh (Figure **1.9**), consists of more than two million stone blocks rising to a height of approximately 480 feet and covering a base area of thirteen acres. The royal burial vault, hidden within a series of chambers

Figure **1.9** Reconstruction of the Pyramids of Khufu and Khafre at Gizeh, ca. 2650–2600 B.C.E. (after Hoelscher). **1** Khafre, height approx. 470 ft. **2** Mortuary temple **3** Covered causeway **4** Valley temple **5** Great Sphinx **6** Khufu, height approx. 480 ft. **7** Pyramids of the royal family and mastabas of the nobles. From Horst de la Croix and Robert G. Tansey, *Art Through the Ages*, sixth edition, copyright © 1975 Harcourt Brace Jovanovich, Inc., reprinted by permission of the publisher.

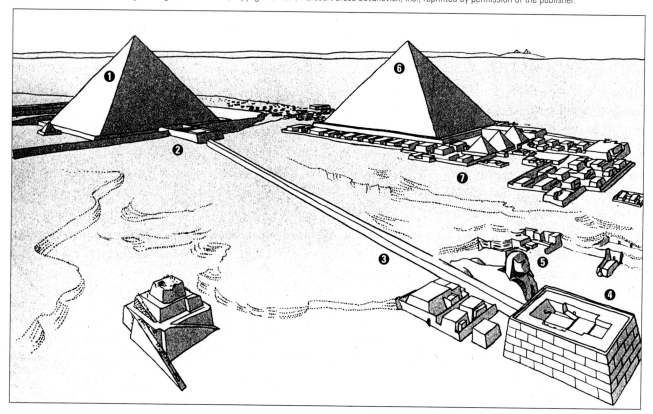

Figure 1.11 Scene of fowling, from the Tomb of Neb-amon at Thebes, Egypt, ca. 1400 B.C.E. Fragment of a fresco secco, height 32¼ in. Reproduced by courtesy of the Trustees of the British Museum, London.

Figure 1.12 A girl carrying meat in a box and a duck, produce of an estate of Meketre, ca. 2050 B.C.E. Height 3 ft. 8 in. The Metropolitan Museum, New York.

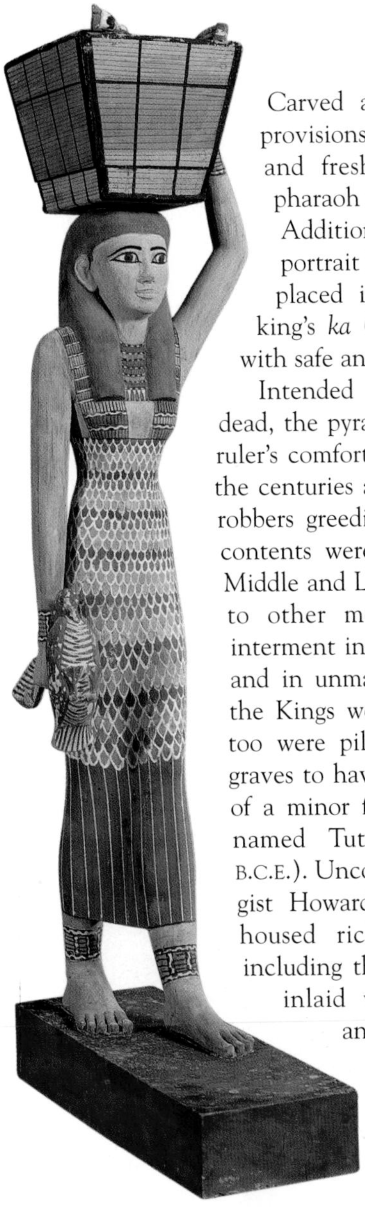

Carved and painted figures carrying provisions—loaves of bread, fowl, beer, and fresh linens—accompanied the pharaoh to the afterlife (Figure **1.12**). Additionally, death masks or "reserve" portrait heads of the pharaoh might be placed in the tomb to provide the king's *ka* (life force or divine essence) with safe and familiar dwelling places.

Intended primarily as homes for the dead, the pyramids were built to assure the ruler's comfort in the afterlife. However, in the centuries after their construction, grave robbers greedily despoiled them, and their contents were largely plundered and lost. Middle and Late Kingdom pharaohs turned to other methods of burial, including interment in the rock cliffs along the Nile and in unmarked graves in the Valley of the Kings west of Thebes. In time, these too were pillaged. One of the few royal graves to have escaped vandalism was that of a minor fourteenth-century B.C.E. ruler named Tutankhamen (ca. 1345–1325 B.C.E.). Uncovered by the British archeologist Howard Carter in 1922, the tomb housed riches of astonishing variety, including the pharaoh's solid gold coffin, inlaid with semiprecious carnelian and lapis lazuli (Figure **1.13**) and a lavish throne depicting Tutankhamen and his wife (Figure **1.14**). Standing below the shining disc of the sun god, the queen, in an ankle-length gown, tenderly straightens her consort's collar.

The promise of life after death seems to have dominated at all levels of Egyptian culture. The most elaborate homes for the dead were reserved for royalty and members of the aristocracy, but recent excavations of the lower cemetery at Gizeh reveal at least 700 graves of workmen and artisans. In the coffins of ancient Egypt's dead are found papyrus scrolls inscribed with prayers and incantations to guide the soul in the afterlife. *The Book of the Dead*, a collection of funerary prayers originating as far back as 4000 B.C.E., prepared each individual for final judgment. In the presence of the gods Osiris and Isis, the dead souls were expected to recite a lengthy confession attesting to their purity of heart, including:

I have not done iniquity.
I have not robbed with violence.
I have not done violence [to any man].
I have not committed theft.
I have not slain man or woman.
I have not made light the bushel.
I have not acted deceitfully.
I have not uttered falsehood.
I have not defiled the wife of a man.
I have not stirred up strife.
I have not cursed the god.
I have not behaved with insolence.
I have not increased my wealth, except with such things as are my own possessions.*

*Adapted from *The Egyptian Book of the Dead*, edited by E. Wallis Budge (Secaucus, New Jersey: University Books, Inc., 1977, pp. 576–577).

Figure 1.13 Egyptian cover of the coffin of Tutankhamen (portion), from the Valley of the Kings, ca. 1360 B.C.E. Gold with inlay of enamel, carnelian, lapis lazuli, and turquoise. Egyptian Museum, Cairo. Photo: Wim Swann, The Getty Center, Santa Monica.

Figure 1.14 Throne with Tutankhamen and Queen, detail of the back, late Marana period, New Kingdom, eighteenth dynasty, ca. 1360 B.C.E. Wood, plated with gold and silver, inlays of glass paste, approx 12 x 12 in. Egyptian Museum, Cairo. Photo: Andrea Jemolo, Rome.

A painted papyrus scroll from the *Book of the Dead* brings to life the last judgment itself: the enthroned Osiris, god of the underworld (far right) and his wife Isis (far left) oversee the ceremony in which the heart of the deceased Princess Entiu-ny is weighed against the figure of Truth (Figure **1.15**). Having made her testimony, the princess watches as the jackal-headed god of death, Anubis, prepares her heart for the ordeal. "Grant thou," reads the prayer to Osiris, "that I may have my being among the living, and that I may sail up and down the river among those who are in thy following." If the heart is not "found true by trial of the Great Balance," it will be devoured by the monster, Ament, thus meeting a second death. If pure, it might sail with the sun "up and down the river," or flourish in a realm where wheat grows high and the living souls of the dead enjoy feasting and singing. An image of this heavenly domain is depicted on the walls of the tomb of Sennudjem: the "fields of the blessed" are bordered by

Figure 1.15 Scene from a funerary papyrus, *Book of the Dead*. Height 11¾ in. The Metropolitan Museum of Art, New York, Rogers Fund. Princess Entiu-ny stands to the left of a set of scales on which Anubis, the jackal-headed god, weighs her heart against the figure of Truth, while Osiris, Lord of the Dead, judges from his throne. His wife, Isis, stands behind the princess.

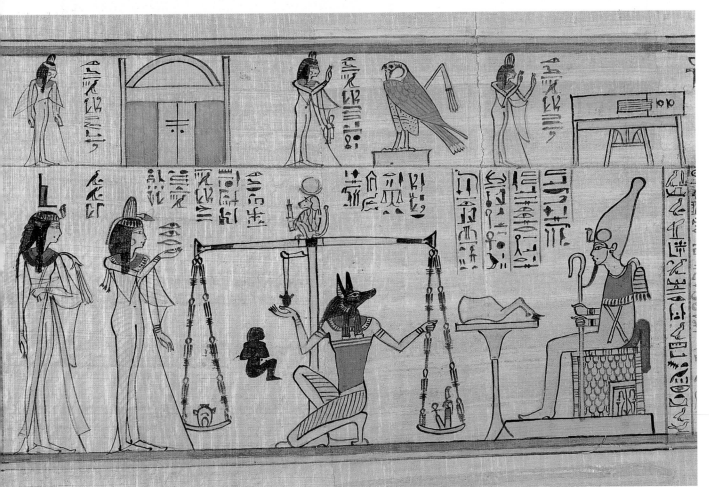

Figure 1.16 Illustration of Spell 110 from the *Book of the Dead* in the burial chamber of Sennudjem, ca. 1279 B.C.E. Photo: Axiom/James Austin.

beneficent gods (top) and flourishing fruit trees (bottom) (Figure **1.16**). Here death is a continuation of daily life in a realm that floats eternally on the primordial waters—indicated by the jagged blue lines that frame the registers.

Akhenaten's Reform

Throughout the dynastic history of Egypt, the central authority of the pharaoh was repeatedly contested by local temple priests, each of whom held religious and political sway in their own regions along the Nile. Perhaps in an effort to consolidate his authority against priestly encroachment, the New Kingdom pharaoh Amenhotep IV (ca. 1353–1336 B.C.E.) defied the tradition of polytheism by elevating Aten (God of the Sun Disk) to a position of supremacy over all other gods. "The Hymn to the Aten" (Reading 1.3), which is based on earlier Egyptian songs of praise, dates from the reign of Amenhotep IV. Changing his own name to Akhenaten ("Shining Spirit of Aten"), the pharaoh abandoned the political capital at Memphis and the religious center at Thebes to build a new palace midway between the two at a site called Akhetaten ("Place of the Sun Disk's Power") (see Map 2.1). In a small stone carving from Akhenaten's palace, the pharaoh is seen with his wife Nefertiti and one of their daughters making offerings to Aten (Figure **1.17**). The sun's rays end in human hands, some of which carry the *ankh*. The elongated figures and relaxed contours suggest a conscious departure from traditional (more formal) modes of representation. Akhenaten's chief wife, Queen Nefertiti, along with her mother-in-law, assisted in organizing the affairs of state. The mother of six daughters, Nefertiti is often pictured as Isis, the goddess from whom all Egyptian queens were said to have descended. Nefertiti's confident beauty inspired numerous sculpted likenesses, some of which are striking in their blend of realism and abstraction (Figure **1.18**). Akhenaten's monotheistic reform lasted only as long as his reign, and in the years following his death, Egypt's conservative priests and nobles returned to the polytheism of their forebears.

Nubia and Ancient Egypt

Throughout its history, ancient Egypt maintained commercial and cultural contact with other African civilizations—Libya in the north, Punt in the east, and Nubia in the south. The most significant of these, the civilization of Nubia was located between the first and sixth cataracts of

Figure 1.17 The royal family under the "Aten with Rays." New Kingdom, eighteenth dynasty, ca. 1345 B.C.E. Alabaster, height 3 ft. 4 in. Egyptian Museum, Cairo. Photo: Jürgen Liepe, Berlin.

the Nile (see Map 1.1). Nubia was the first literate urban society to appear in Africa south of the Sahara. Famous for its large quantities of gold, copper, iron, and cattle, it came under Egyptian rule as early as the Middle Kingdom. But during the ninth century B.C.E., the powerful state of Kush in Nubia came to rule all of southern Egypt. The history of Nubia, which dates from at least 2300 B.C.E., reflects the importation of Egyptian religion and culture, but its artifacts testify to a high level of native artistry and technical sophistication. This is especially visible in the area of metal-crafting, as reflected, for instance, in the bronze statue of the Kushan king Shabaqo (Figure **1.19**). In this small but forceful portrait, Nubia anticipated the birth of an African tradition in portraiture that flowered in the western Sudan as early as 500 B.C.E. and continued to flourish for at least a thousand years (see chapter 18).

Law in Ancient Egypt

In ancient Egypt, long-standing customs and unwritten rules preceded the codification and transcription of civil and criminal law. Indeed, Egyptian law consisted of the unwritten decrees of the pharaoh (passed down orally until they were transcribed during the New Kingdom). An inscription on an Old Kingdom tomb wall sums up this phenomenon as follows: "the law of the land is the mouth of the pharaoh." In Egypt, no written laws have been preserved from any period before the fourth century B.C.E. When one considers that toward the end of the thirteenth century B.C.E., the pharaoh Rameses II ruled approximately three million people, it is clear that the oral tradition—the verbal transmission of rules, conventions, and customs—played a vital part in establishing political continuity.

The Social Order

Like all ancient civilizations, Egypt could not have existed without a high level of cooperation among those whose individual tasks—governing, trading, farming, fighting—contributed to communal survival. Powerful families, tribes, and clans, usually those that had proved victorious in battle, established long-standing territorial claims. Such families often claimed descent from, or association with, the gods. Once royal authority was entrenched, it was almost impossible to unseat. The ruling dynasty, in conjunction with a priestly caste that supervised the religious activities of the community, formed an elite group of men and women who regulated the lives of the lower classes: merchants, farmers, herders,

Figure 1.19 King Shabaqo, from the area of the ancient Kush, ca. eighth century B.C.E. Solid cast bronze, height 6 in. National Museum, Athens, no. 632. Photo: courtesy National Museum.

artisans, soldiers, and servants. Nevertheless, the class structure in ancient Egypt seems to have been quite flexible. Ambitious individuals of any class were free to rise in status, usually by way of education. The westward migration of sub-Saharan (dark-skinned)* peoples and the thriving commercial activity between Egypt and Nubia produced a multiracial and multicultural population: at all levels, light- and dark-skinned people appear to have held similar social status.

For well over 2000 years, Egypt was administered by the pharaoh's vast bureaucracy, members of which collected taxes, regulated public works, and mobilized the army. In the social order, these individuals, along with large landowners and priests, constituted the upper classes. As in all ancient societies, power was not uniformly distributed but descended from the top rung of the hierarchy in diminishing degrees of influence. Those closest to the pharaoh participated most fully in his authority and prestige. Other individuals might advance their positions and improve their status through service to the pharaoh.

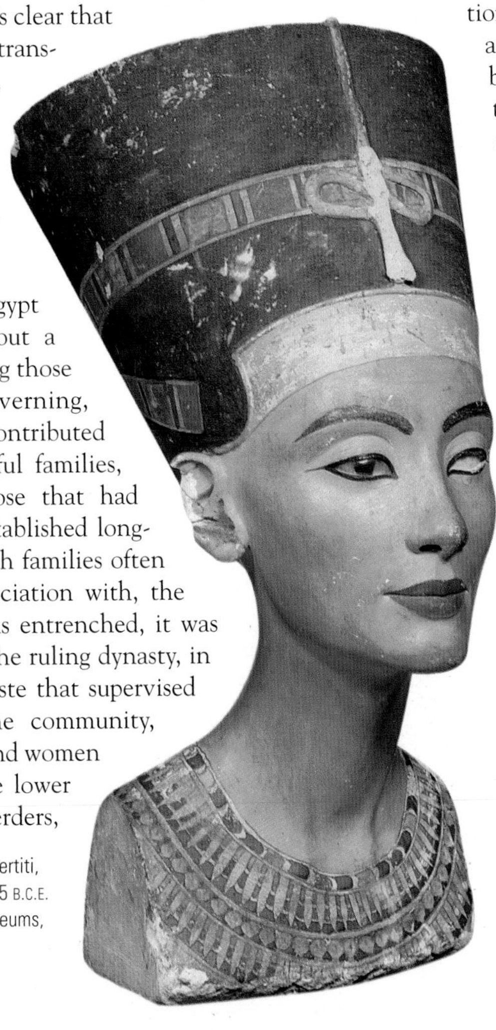

*Since skin pigmentation varies in accordance with the amount of melanin and keratin particles in the underskin (which regulates the permeation of sun rays), relative distance from the equator determined African skin colors, which differed from the very light brown of Mediterranean types to the very dark brown of black Nubian and sub-Saharan peoples.

Figure 1.18 Portrait of head of Queen Nefertiti, New Kingdom, eighteenth dynasty, ca. 1355 B.C.E. Painted limestone, height 20 in. State Museums, Berlin.

At the top of the bureaucratic pyramid stood the vizier. Essential to the administration and the security of the state, the vizier was in charge of appointing members of the royal bureaucracy and dispatching the local officials. He oversaw the mobilization of troops, the irrigation of canals, the taking of inventories, and, with the assistance of official scribes, he handled all litigation for the Egyptian state. Merchants, traders, builders, and scribes made up a prosperous middle class, who ranked in status just below the aristocracy. At the base of the social pyramid, the great masses of peasants constituted the agricultural backbone of ancient Egypt. Aided by slaves, peasant men and women worked side by side to farm the land. Even in the afterlife, husbands and wives shared the tasks of reaping and plowing (see Figure 1.16). Class status seems to have extended into the afterlife: in the cemeteries recently uncovered at Gizeh, artisans received separate and more elaborate burials than common laborers.

Slaves constituted a class of unfree men and women. In the ancient world, slaves were victims of military conquest. Enslaving one's enemy captives was a humane alternative to executing them. Some people became slaves as punishment for criminal acts, and still others as a result of falling into debt. Slaves might be sold or traded like any other form of property, but in Egypt and elsewhere in the ancient world, it appears that some slaves were able to acquire sufficient wealth to buy their own or their children's freedom.

Egyptian Women

Possibly because all property was inherited through the female line, Egyptian women seem to have enjoyed a large degree of economic independence, as well as civil rights and privileges. Women who could write and calculate might go into business. Women of the pharaoh's harem oversaw textile production, while others found positions as shop-keepers, midwives, musicians, and dancers (Figure 1.20). Nevertheless, men were wary of powerful women, as is indicated in a Middle Kingdom manual of good conduct, which offers the husband this advice concerning his wife: "Make her happy while you are alive, for she is land profitable to her lord. Neither judge her nor raise her to a position of power . . . her eye is a stormwind when she sees."

The Arts in Ancient Egypt

Literature

Ancient Egypt did not produce any literary masterpieces. Nevertheless, from tomb and temple walls, and from papyrus rolls, come prayers and songs, royal decrees and letters, prose tales, and texts that served to educate the young. One school text, which reflects the fragile relationship between oral and written traditions, reads, "Man decays, his corpse is dust,/All his kin have perished;/But a book makes him remembered,/Through the mouth of its reciter." The so-called "wisdom literature" of Egypt, which consists of words of advice and instruction, anticipates parts of the Hebrew Bible. From the New Kingdom, however, came a very personal type of poetry that would later be called **lyric** (literally, accompanied by the lyre or harp). In the following three poems, two in a male voice and one female, images drawn from nature are freely employed to color sentiments of love and desire. Lines 5 to 7 of the second poem illustrate the effective use of **simile**.

Figure 1.20 Procession of female musicians with instruments, including a harp, double pipes, and a lyre, Tomb of Djeserkarasneb, Thebes, ca. 1580–1314 BCE. Copy of the original. Egyptian Expedition of the Metropolitan Museum of Art, Rogers Fund, 1930. Photograph © 1985 The Metropolitan Museum of Art.

READING 1.4 Egyptian Poetry

Boy I will lie down within   1
      and feign to be ill, and then
my neighbors will come to see.
     My sister[1] will enter with them.
She'll put the physicians to shame,   5
    for she will understand
that I am sick for love.

— ◆ —

Boy My sister has come to me.   1
     My heart is filled with joy.
I open my arms wide
    that I may embrace her.
My heart is as happy in   5
    my breast as a red fish
swimming in its pond.
    O night, you are mine
forever, since my sister
    has come in love to me.   10

— ◆ —

Girl The Voice of the goose sounds forth   1
    as he's caught by the bait. Your love
ensnares me. I can't let it go.
    I shall take home my nets,
but what shall I tell my mother,   5
    to whom I return every day
laden with lovely birds?
    I set no traps today,
ensnared as I was by love.

 Q What natural images give color to these poems?

The Visual Arts

Egyptian art—at least that with which we are most familiar—comes almost exclusively from tombs and graves.
Such art was not intended as decoration; rather, it was
created to replicate the living world for the benefit of
the dead. In the Middle Kingdom "Tomb of the Sculptors,"
we see skilled craftsmen occupied with the production of
various artifacts (Figure **1.21**). Stylistically, Egyptian art
mirrors the deep sense of order and regularity that dominated ancient Egyptian life. Indeed, for 3000 years, Egypt
followed a set of conventions that dictated the manner
in which subjects should be depicted. In representations
of everyday life, figures are usually sized according to a
strict hierarchy, or graded order: upper-class individuals
are shown larger than lower-class ones, and males usually
outsize females and servants (see Figure 1.11). In monumental sculptures of royalty, however, the chief wife of

---

[1]Meaning "mistress" or "lady."

Figure 1.21 Craftsmen in a royal workshop, Tomb of the Sculptors, Thebes, eighteenth dynasty (ca. 1539–1292 B.C.E.). Copy of the original by Nina de Garis Davis. The British Museum, London.

the pharaoh is usually shown the same size as her husband
(see Figure 1.4).

Very early in Egyptian history, artists developed a
canon (or set of rules) by which to represent the human
form. The proportions of the human body were determined
according to a **module** (or standard of measurement) represented by the width of the clenched fist (Figure **1.22**).
More generally, Egyptian artists adhered to a set of guidelines by which they might "capture" the most characteristic and essential aspects of the subject matter: in depicting
the human figure the upper torso is shown from the front,
while the lower is shown from the side; the head is

Figure 1.22 The Egyptian canon of proportion.

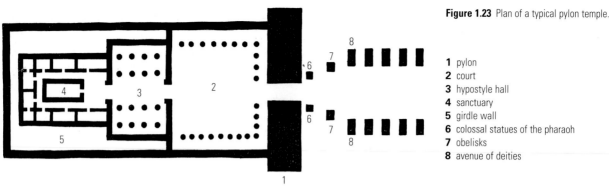

Figure 1.23 Plan of a typical pylon temple.

1 pylon
2 court
3 hypostyle hall
4 sanctuary
5 girdle wall
6 colossal statues of the pharaoh
7 obelisks
8 avenue of deities

depicted in profile, while the eye and eyebrow are frontal. This method of representation is *conceptual*—that is, based on ideas—rather than *perceptual*—that is, based on visual evidence. The conceptual approach represents a highly stylized record of reality.

The Egyptian artist's approach to space was also conceptual. Spatial depth is indicated by placing one figure above (rather than behind) the next, often in horizontal registers, or rows. Cast in this timeless matrix, Egyptian figures shared the symbolic resonance of the hieroglyphs by which they are framed (see Figure 1.1). Nowhere else in the ancient world do we see such an intimate and intelligible conjunction of images and words—a union designed to immortalize ideas rather than imitate reality. This is not to say that Egyptian artists ignored the world of the senses. Their love for realistic detail is evident, for example, in the hunting scene from the tomb of Nebamon at Thebes, where fish and fowl are depicted with such

Figure 1.24 Hypostyle Hall, Great Temple of Amon-Ra, Karnak, ca. 1220 B.C.E. Photo: Art Archive, London.

extraordinary accuracy that individual species of each can be identified (see Figure 1.11). It is in the union of the particular and the general that Egyptian art achieves its defining quality.

New Kingdom Temples

Temples were built by the Egyptians from earliest times, but most of those that have survived date from the New Kingdom. The basic plan of the temple mirrored the central features of the Egyptian cosmos: the **pylons** (two truncated pyramids that made up the gateway) symbolized the mountains that rimmed the edge of the world, while the progress from the open courtyard through the **hypostyle** hall into the dark inner sanctuary housing the cult statue represented the voyage from light to darkness (and back) symbolic of the sun's cyclical journey (Figure **1.23**). Oriented on an east–west axis, the temple received the sun's morning rays, which reached through the sequence of hallways into the sanctuary. The Great Temple of Amon-Ra at Karnak was the heart of a 5-acre religious complex that included a sacred lake, a sphinx-lined causeway, and numerous **obelisks** (commemorative stone pillars). The temple's hypostyle hall is adorned with painted reliefs that cover the walls and the surfaces of its 134 massive columns shaped like budding and flowering papyrus— these plants were identified with the marsh of creation (Figure **1.24**). Decorated with stars and other celestial images, the ceiling of the hall symbolized the heavens. Such sacred precincts were not intended for communal assembly—in fact, commoners were forbidden to enter. Rather, Egyptian temples were sanctuaries in which priests performed daily rituals of cosmic renewal on behalf of the pharaoh and the people. Temple rituals were celebrations of the solar cycle, associated not only with the birth of the sun god but with the regeneration of the ruler upon whom cosmic order depended.

Music in Ancient Egypt

Tomb paintings reveal much about ancient Egyptian culture. They are, for example, our main source of information about ancient Egyptian music and dance (see Figure 1.20). It is clear that song and poetry were interchangeable (hymns like those praising Aten were chanted, not spoken). Musical instruments, including harps, small stringed instruments, pipes, and sistrums (a type of rattle)—often found buried with the dead—accompanied song and dance. Greek sources indicate that Egyptian music was based in theory; nevertheless, we have no certain knowledge how that music actually sounded. Visual representations confirm, however, that music had a special place in religious rituals, in festive and funeral processions, and in many aspects of secular life (see Figure 1.20).

SUMMARY

Among ancient civilizations, nature and the natural environment influenced the formation of religious attitudes and beliefs. Egypt's relatively secure location, regular climate, and dependable Nile River encouraged a belief in a host of essentially benevolent nature deities, the most important of which were the gods of the sun and the Nile. The representative of the sun on earth, Egypt's theocratic monarch was accorded a burial befitting one who, after death, would work to ensure the well-being of his people. The belief in life after death, an expression of ancient Egypt's positive view of life, is evident in grave goods, tomb paintings, and hieroglyphic inscriptions, all of which manifest the artistic magnificence of ancient Egyptian civilization.

As elsewhere in the ancient world, the survival of the Egyptian community depended on cooperation among individuals with specialized responsibilities and tasks. It also depended on a shared view of the world as animated by the gods. Egypt's hierarchic social structure and its polytheistic belief system contributed to a deep sense of order. In the buoyant optimism of its poetry, the confident imagery of its tomb paintings, and the cosmic symbolism of its temple architecture, we detect a basic trust in forces that are greater and more powerful than those of perishable humankind.

GLOSSARY

canon a set of rules or standards used to establish proportions

cosmology the theory of the origins, evolution, and structure of the universe

dynasty a sequence of rulers from the same family

fresco (Italian, "fresh") a method of painting on walls or ceilings surfaced with fresh, moist, lime plaster

hypostyle a hall whose roof is supported by columns

lyric literally "accompanied by the lyre," hence, verse that is meant to be sung rather than spoken; usually characterized by individual and personal emotion

mastaba early rectangular Egyptian tomb with sloping sides and a flat roof.

module a unit of measurement used to determine proportion

monarch a single or sole ruler

obelisk a tall, four-sided pillar that tapers to a pyramidal apex

papyrus a reed-like plant from which the ancient Egyptians made paper

polytheism the belief in many gods

pylon a massive gateway in the form of a pair of truncated pyramids

pyramid a four-sided structure rising to a peak

relief a sculptural technique in which figures or forms are carved either to project from the background surface (raised relief) or cut away below the background level (sunk relief); the degree of relief is designated as high, low, or sunken

simile a figure of speech in which two unlike things are compared

theocracy rule by god or god's representative

CHAPTER 2

Mesopotamia: Gods, Rulers, and the Social Order

"From the days of old there is no permanence. The sleeping and the dead, how alike they are, they are like a painted death."
The Epic of Gilgamesh

Mesopotamia, literally "the land between the two rivers," describes the region in southwest Asia* that was the home of many civilizations over a period of 3000 years. The earliest of these civilizations appeared around 3500 B.C.E. at Sumer, where the Tigris and Euphrates Rivers empty into the Persian Gulf (Map **2.1**). Watered by these two rivers, the rich soil at the southeastern end of the Fertile Crescent made agricultural life possible and supported the growth of humankind's first cities—Uruk, Ur, Kish, Nippur, and Lagash. In contrast with the Nile River, which flooded its banks with comfortable regularity, the two rivers essential to food production in Mesopotamia overflowed unpredictably, often devastating whole villages and cities. Unlike Egypt, whose natural boundaries of desert and water worked to protect the civilization from foreign invasion, Mesopotamia's exposed and fertile plains invited the repeated attacks of tribal nomads, who descended from the mountainous regions north of the Fertile Crescent. And while Egypt's climate was regularly hot and dry, that of ancient Mesopotamia suffered fierce changes of weather, including drought, violent rainstorms, flood, wind, and hail. Mesopotamia's unpredictable rivers, vulnerable geographic situation, and erratic climate contributed to the mood of fear and insecurity that is reflected in all forms of Mesopotamian expression.

Mesopotamia was the stage on which many civilizations rose and fell. Some, like

Figure 2.1 The "Queen of the Night," Babylonian goddess, southern Iraq, 1800–1750 B.C.E. Painted terracotta plaque, height approx. 19½ in. The British Museum, London (ANE 2003-7-18.1).

*Also known by Westerners as the "Near East."

Map 2.1 Ancient Southwest Asia (Near and Middle East).

the Sumerian, formed small groups of city-states; others, like the Assyrian, founded great empires. And yet others, like the Hebrews, were tribal people who ultimately forged a political state. No one language or single, continuous form of government united these various Mesopotamian civilizations, yet they shared a common world view and—with the exception of the Hebrews—a polytheistic religious outlook.

The Gods of Mesopotamia

As in ancient Egypt, Mesopotamia's gods and goddesses were associated with nature and its forces (Figure **2.1**). However, like the environment of Mesopotamia, its gods and goddesses were fierce and capricious, its mythology filled with physical and spiritual woe, and its cosmology based in the themes of chaos and conflict. *The Babylonian Creation*, humankind's earliest cosmological myth, illustrates all of these conditions. *The Babylonian Creation* is a Sumerian poem recorded early in the second millennium B.C.E. Recited during the festival of the New Year, it celebrates the birth of the gods and the order of creation. It describes a universe that originated by means of spontaneous generation: at a moment when there was neither heaven nor earth, the sweet and bitter waters "mingled" to produce the first family of gods. As the story unfolds, chaos and discord prevail amid the reign of Tiamat, the Great Mother of the primeval waters, until Marduk, hero-god and offspring of Wisdom, takes matters in hand: he destroys the Great Mother and proceeds to establish a new order, bringing to an end the long and venerable tradition of matriarchy. Marduk founds the holy city of Babylon (literally, "home of the gods") and creates human beings, whose purpose it is to serve heaven's squabbling divinities.

Principal Mesopotamian Gods	
Name	**Role**
Adad	storm and rain god
Anu	father of the gods, god of heaven
Apsu	god of the primeval sweet waters
Dumuzi (Tammuz)	god of vegetation, fertility, and the underworld; husband of Ishtar
Ea	god of wisdom and patron of the arts
Enlil	god of earth, wind, and air
Ishtar (Innana)	goddess of love, fertility, and war; Queen of Heaven
Ninhursag	mother goddess, creator of vegetation; wife of Enlil
Nisaba	goddess of grain
Shamash	god of the sun; judge and law-giver; god of wisdom
Sin (Nanna)	goddess of the moon

READING 1.5   From *The Babylonian Creation*

When there was no heaven,   1
no earth, no height, no depth, no name,
    when Apsu[1] was alone,
the sweet water, the first begetter; and Tiamat[2]
    the bitter water, and that   5
return to the womb, her Mummu,[3]
    when there were no gods —

When sweet and bitter
mingled together, no reed was plaited, no rushes
    muddied the water,   10
the gods were nameless, natureless, futureless, then
    from Apsu and Tiamat
in the waters gods were created, in the waters
    silt precipitated,

Lahmu and Lahamu,[4]   15
were named; they were not yet old,
    not yet grown tall
when Anshar and Kishar[5] overtook them both,
    the lines of sky and earth
stretched where horizons meet to separate   20
    cloud from silt.

Days on days, years
on years passed till Anu,[6] the empty heaven,
    heir and supplanter,
first-born of his father, in his own nature   25
    begot of Nudimmud-Ea[7]
intellect, wisdom, wider than heaven's horizon,
    the strongest of all the kindred.

Discord broke out among the gods although they were
brothers, warring and jarring in the belly of Tiamat,   30
heaven shook, it reeled with the surge of the dance.
Apsu could not silence the clamour. Their behaviour was
bad, overbearing, and proud. . . .

[Ea kills Apsu; Marduk is born and Tiamat spawns serpents
and monsters to make war on the gods.]

When her labour of creation was ended, against her children   1
Tiamat began preparations of war. This was the evil she did
to requite Apsu, this was the evil news that came to Ea.

When he had learned how matters lay he was stunned, he
sat in black silence till rage had worked itself out; then he
remembered the gods before him. He went to Anshar, his
father's father, and told him how Tiamat plotted,

[1]The primeval sweet waters.
[2]The primeval bitter waters.
[3]One of the primordial beings of the universe.
[4]Male and female primordial beings.
[5]The horizon of the sky (male) and the horizon of the earth (female).
[6]God of the sky (the offspring of Anshar and Kishar).
[7]Another name for Ea, god of wisdom (the offspring of Anu).

'She loathes us, father, our mother Tiamat has raised up
that Company, she rages in turbulence and all have joined her,
all those gods whom you begot,   10

    'Together they jostle the ranks to march with Tiamat, day
and night furiously they plot, the growling roaring rout, ready
for battle, while the Old Hag, the first mother, mothers a new
brood. . . .'

[The gods make Marduk Supreme Commander of the wars;
he leads the attack on Tiamat.]

Then Marduk made a bow and strung it to be his own weapon,   1
he set the arrow against the bow-string, in his right hand he
grasped the mace and lifted it up, bow and quiver hung at his
side, lightnings played in front of him, he was altogether an
incandescence.

He netted a net, a snare for Tiamat; the winds from their
quarters held it, south wind, north, east wind, west, and no
part of Tiamat could escape. . . .

He turned back to where Tiamat lay bound, he straddled the
legs and smashed her skull (for the mace was merciless), he   10
severed the arteries and the blood streamed down the north
wind to the unknown ends of the world.

When the gods saw all this they laughed out loud, and they
sent him presents. They sent him their thankful tributes.

The lord rested; he gazed at the huge body, pondering how to
use it, what to create from the dead carcass. He split it apart
like a cockle-shell; with the upper half he constructed the arc
of sky, he pulled down the bar and set a watch on the waters,
so they should never escape. . . .

[Marduk makes Babylon "the home of the gods" and proceeds   20
to create Man.]

Now that Marduk has heard what it is the gods are saying, he
is moved with desire to create a work of consummate art. He
told Ea the deep thought in his heart.

        Blood to blood
        I join,
        blood to bone
        I form
        an original thing,
        its name is MAN,   30
        aboriginal man
        is mine in making.
        All his occupations
        are faithful service,
        the gods that fell
        have rest,
        I will subtly alter
        their operations,
        divided companies
        equally blest.   40

Ea answered with carefully chosen words, completing the
plan for the gods' comfort. He said to Marduk,
    "Let one of the kindred be taken; only one need die for the
new creation. Bring the gods together in the Great Assembly;
there let the guilty die, so the rest may live."

 Q How does this creation myth compare
with those in Reading 1.2?

The Search for Immortality

The theme of human vulnerability and the search for everlasting life are the central motifs in the *Epic of Gilgamesh*,
the world's first epic. An **epic**, that is, a long narrative
poem that recounts the deeds of a hero in quest of meaning
and identity, embodies the ideals and values of the culture
from which it comes. The *Epic of Gilgamesh* was recited
orally for centuries before it was recorded at Sumer in
the late third millennium B.C.E.
As literature, it precedes the
Hebrew Bible and all the other
major writings of antiquity. Its
hero is a semihistorical figure
who probably ruled the ancient
Sumerian city of Uruk around
2800 B.C.E. Described as two-
thirds god and one-third man,
Gilgamesh is blessed by the gods
with beauty and courage. But
when he spurns the affections of
the Queen of Heaven, Ishtar (a
fertility goddess not unlike the
Egyptian Isis), he is punished with
the loss of his dearest companion,
Enkidu. Despairing over Enkidu's
death, Gilgamesh undertakes a
long and hazardous quest in search
of everlasting life. He meets
Utnapishtim, a mortal whom the
gods have rewarded with eternal life
for having saved humankind from
a devastating flood. Utnapishtim
helps Gilgamesh locate the plant
that miraculously restores lost youth.
But ultimately, a serpent snatches
the plant, and Gilgamesh is left
with the haunting vision of death
as "a house of dust" and a place of
inescapable sadness. On the soundbox of a harp found in the royal
graves at Ur, Gilgamesh is depicted
standing between two human-headed
bulls, while some of the epic's fantastic

Figure 2.2 Gilgamesh between two human-headed bulls (top portion).
Soundbox of a harp, from Ur, Iraq, ca. 2600 B.C.E. Wood with inlaid gold, lapis
lazuli, and shell, height approx. 12 in. University Museum, University of
Pennsylvania, Philadelphia (Neg. #T4–109).

characters, such as the Man-Scorpion, appear in the registers below (Figure **2.2**). The meaning of these images is obscure; they may illustrate non-surviving portions of the epic, or they may refer to popular fables. The Great Harp itself (Figure **2.3**) may have been used to accompany the chanting of this epic.

Figure 2.3 Harp (reconstructed) from Ur, ca. 2600 B.C.E. Wood and inlays of gold, lapis lazuli, and shell, height 3 ft. 6 in. British Museum, London.

READING 1.6 From the *Epic of Gilgamesh*

O Gilgamesh, Lord of Kullab,[1] great is thy praise. This was   1
the man to whom all things were known; this was the king
who knew the countries of the world. He was wise, he saw
mysteries and knew secret things, he brought us a tale of the
days before the flood. He went on a long journey, was weary,
worn-out with labor, and returning engraved on a stone the
whole story.

When the Gods created Gilgamesh they gave him a perfect
body. Shamash the glorious sun endowed him with beauty,
Adad the god of the storm endowed him with courage, the   10
great gods made his beauty perfect, surpassing all others. Two
thirds they made him god and one third man.

In Uruk[2] he built walls, a great rampart, and the temple of
blessed Eanna for the god of the firmament Anu, and for Ishtar
the goddess of love.[3]

[Gilgamesh and his bosom companion, Enkidu, destroy
Humbaba, the guardian of the cedar forest, and perform other
heroic deeds. But Gilgamesh spurns the affections of Ishtar,
and in revenge, she takes Enkidu's life.]

Bitterly Gilgamesh wept for his friend Enkidu; he wandered
over the wilderness as a hunter, he roamed over the plains; in
his bitterness he cried, "How can I rest, how can I be at
peace? Despair is in my heart. What my brother is now, that
shall I be when I am dead. Because I am afraid of death I will   20
go as best I can to find Utnapishtim whom they call the
Faraway, for he has entered the assembly of the gods." So
Gilgamesh traveled over the wilderness, he wandered over the
grasslands, a long journey, in search of Utnapishtim, whom the
gods took after the deluge; and they set him to live in the land
of Dilmun,[4] in the garden of the sun; and to him alone of men
they gave everlasting life.

At night when he came to the mountain passes Gilgamesh
prayed: "In these mountain passes long ago I saw lions, I was
afraid and I lifted my eyes to the moon; I prayed and my   30
prayers went up to the gods, so now, O moon god Sin, protect
me." When he had prayed he lay down to sleep, until he was
woken from out of a dream. He saw the lions round him
glorying in life; then he took his axe in his hand, he drew his
sword from his belt, and struck and destroyed and scattered
them.

So at length Gilgamesh came to that great mountain whose
name is Mashu, the mountain which guards the rising and the
setting sun. Its twin peaks are as high as the wall of heaven
and its paps reach down to the underworld. At its gate the   40
Scorpions stand guard, half man and half dragon; their glory is
terrifying, their stare strikes death into men, their shimmering
halo sweeps the mountains that guard the rising sun. When

[1]Park of Uruk.
[2]A city located in Sumer. Gilgamesh was the fifth ruler in the dynasty of Uruk after the flood.
[3]Also associated with fertility and war.
[4]The Sumerian paradise, a mythical land resembling the Garden of Eden described in the Hebrew Bible.

Gilgamesh saw them he shielded his eyes for the length of a moment only; then he took courage and approached. When they saw him so undismayed the Man-Scorpion called to his mate, "This one who comes to us now is flesh of the gods." The mate of the Man-Scorpion answered, "Two thirds is god but one third is man."

Then he called to the man Gilgamesh, he called to the child **50** of the gods: "Why have you come so great a journey; for what have you traveled so far, crossing the dangerous waters; tell me the reason for your coming?" Gilgamesh answered, "For Enkidu; I loved him dearly, together we endured all kinds of hardships; on his account I have come, for the common lot of man has taken him. I have wept for him day and night, I would not give up his body for burial, I thought my friend would come back because of my weeping. Since he went, my life is nothing; that is why I have traveled here in search of Utnapishtim my father; for men say he has entered the **60** assembly of the gods, and has found everlasting life. I have a desire to question him concerning the living and the dead." The Man-Scorpion opened his mouth and said, speaking to Gilgamesh, "No man born of woman has done what you have asked, no mortal man has gone into the mountain; the length of it is twelve leagues[5] of darkness; in it there is no light, but the heart is oppressed with darkness. From the rising of the sun to the setting of the sun there is no light." Gilgamesh said, "Although I should go in sorrow and in pain, with sighing and with weeping, still I must go. Open the gate of the mountain." **70** And the Man-Scorpion said, "Go, Gilgamesh, I permit you to pass through the mountain of Mashu and through the high ranges; may your feet carry you safely home. The gate of the mountain is open."

When Gilgamesh heard this he did as the Man-Scorpion had said, he followed the sun's road to his rising, through the mountain. When he had gone one league the darkness became thick around him, for there was no light, he could see nothing ahead and nothing behind him. After two leagues the darkness was thick and there was no light, he could see **80** nothing ahead and nothing behind him. After three leagues the darkness was thick, and there was no light, he could see nothing ahead and nothing behind him. After four leagues the darkness was thick and there was no light, he could see nothing ahead and nothing behind him. At the end of five leagues the darkness was thick and there was no light, he could see nothing ahead and nothing behind him. At the end of six leagues the darkness was thick and there was no light, he could see nothing ahead and nothing behind him. When he had gone seven leagues the darkness was thick and there was **90** no light, he could see nothing ahead and nothing behind him. When he had gone eight leagues Gilgamesh gave a great cry, for the darkness was thick and he could see nothing ahead and nothing behind him. After nine leagues he felt the north wind on his face, but the darkness was thick and there was no light, he could see nothing ahead and nothing behind him. After ten leagues the end was near. After eleven leagues the dawn light appeared. At the end of twelve leagues the sun streamed out.

There was the garden of the gods; all round him stood **100**

bushes bearing gems. Seeing it he went down at once, for there was fruit of carnelian with the vine hanging from it, beautiful to look at; lapis lazuli leaves hung thick with fruit, sweet to see. For thorns and thistles there were hematite and rare stones, agate, and pearls from out of the sea. While Gilgamesh walked in the garden by the edge of the sea Shamash[6] saw him, and he saw that he was dressed in the skins of animals and ate their flesh. He was distressed, and he spoke and said, "No mortal man has gone this way before, nor will, as long as the winds drive over the sea." And to **110** Gilgamesh he said, "You will never find the life for which you are searching." Gilgamesh said to glorious Shamash, "Now that I have toiled and strayed so far over the wilderness, am I to sleep, and let the earth cover my head forever? Let my eyes see the sun until they are dazzled with looking. Although I am no better than a dead man, still let me see the light of the sun."

[Gilgamesh meets Siduri, the maker of wine, who advises him to give up his search and value more highly the good things of the earth. Gilgamesh prepares to cross the Ocean and, with the help of the ferryman Urshanabi, finally reaches Dilmun, the home of Utnapishtim.]

"Oh, father Utnapishtim, you who have entered the assembly of the gods, I wish to question you concerning the living and the dead, how shall I find the life for which I am **120** searching?"

Utnapishtim said, "There is no permanence. Do we build a house to stand for ever, do we seal a contract to hold for all time? Do brothers divide an inheritance to keep for ever, does the flood-time of rivers endure? It is only the nymph of the dragon-fly who sheds her larva and sees the sun in his glory. From the days of old there is no permanence. The sleeping and the dead, how alike they are, they are like a painted death. What is there between the master and the servant when both have fulfilled their doom? When the Annunaki, the judges, **130** come together, and Mammetun the mother of destinies, together they decree the fates of men. Life and death they allot but the day of death they do not disclose."

Then Gilgamesh said to Utnapishtim the Faraway, "I look at you now, Utnapishtim, and your appearance is no different from mine; there is nothing strange in your features. I thought I should find you like a hero prepared for battle, but you lie here taking your ease on your back. Tell me truly, how was it that you came to enter the company of the gods and to possess everlasting life?" Utnapishtim said to Gilgamesh, "I **140** will reveal to you a mystery, I will tell you a secret of the gods."

[Utnapishtim relates the story of the flood.]

In those days the world teemed, the people multiplied, the world bellowed like a wild bull, and the great god was aroused by the clamor. Enlil heard the clamor and he said to the gods in council, "The uproar of mankind is intolerable and sleep is no longer possible by reason of the babel." So the

---

[5]Approximately 36 miles.

[6]The Semitic sun god.

gods in their hearts were moved to let loose the deluge; but my lord Ea warned me in a dream. He whispered their words to my house of reeds.... "Tear down your house, I say, and **150** build a boat. These are the measurements of the barque as you shall build her: let her beam equal her length, let her deck be roofed like the vault that covers the abyss; then take up into the boat the seed of all living creatures...."

For six days and six nights the winds blew, torrent and tempest and flood overwhelmed the world, tempest and flood raged together like warring hosts. When the seventh day dawned the storm from the south subsided, the sea grew calm, the flood was stilled; I looked at the face of the world and there was silence, all mankind was turned to clay. The **160** surface of the sea stretched as flat as a roof-top; I opened a hatch and the light fell on my face. Then I bowed low, I sat down and I wept, the tears streamed down my face, for on every side was the waste of water.

[Utnapishtim leads Gilgamesh to Urshanabi the Ferryman.]

Then Gilgamesh and Urshanabi launched the boat on to the water and boarded it, and they made ready to sail away; but the wife of Utnapishtim the Faraway said to him, "Gilgamesh came here wearied out, he is worn out; what will you give him to carry him back to his own country?" So Utnapishtim spoke, and Gilgamesh took a pole and brought the boat in to the bank. **170** "Gilgamesh, you came here a man wearied out, you have worn yourself out; what shall I give you to carry you back to your own country? Gilgamesh, I shall reveal a secret thing, it is a mystery of the gods that I am telling you. There is a plant that grows under the water, it has a prickle like a thorn, like a rose; it will wound your hands, but if you succeed in taking it, then your hands will hold that which restores his lost youth to a man."

When Gilgamesh heard this he opened the sluices so that a sweet-water current might carry him out to the deepest channel; he tied heavy stones to his feet and they dragged him **180** down to the water-bed. There he saw the plant growing; although it pricked him he took it in his hands; then he cut the heavy stones from his feet, and the sea carried him and threw him on the shore. Gilgamesh said to Urshanabi the ferryman, "Come here, and see this marvelous plant. By its virtue a man may win back all his former strength. I will take it to Uruk of the strong walls; there I will give it to the old to eat. Its name shall be 'the Old Men are Young Again'; and at last I shall eat it myself and have back all my lost youth." So Gilgamesh **190** returned by the gate through which he had come, Gilgamesh and Urshanabi went together. They traveled their twenty leagues and then they broke their fast; after thirty leagues they stopped for the night.

Gilgamesh saw a well of cool water and he went down and bathed; but deep in the pool there was lying a serpent,[7] and the serpent sensed the sweetness of the flower. It rose out of the water and snatched it away, and immediately it sloughed its skin and returned to the well. Then Gilgamesh sat down and wept, the tears ran down his face, and he took the hand of Urshanabi; "O Urshanabi, was it for this that I toiled with **200** my hands, is it for this I have wrung out my heart's blood? For

myself I have gained nothing; not I, but the beast of the earth has joy of it now. Already the stream has carried it twenty leagues back to the channels where I found it. I found a sign and now I have lost it. Let us leave the boat on the bank and go."

 Q What makes Gilgamesh an epic hero? Are there any comparable figures in contemporary literature or life?

The *Epic of Gilgamesh* is important not only as the world's first epic poem, but also as the earliest known literary work that tries to come to terms with death, or nonbeing. It exemplifies the profound human need for an *immortality ideology**—a body of beliefs that anticipates the survival of some aspect of the self in a life hereafter. Typical of the mythic hero, Gilgamesh is driven to discover his human limits, to bring about change through human ingenuity, but his quest for personal immortality is frustrated and his goals remain unfulfilled. In the uncertainty of its conclusions, the *Epic of Gilgamesh* stands in stark contrast with Egyptian writings, which confidently celebrate the promise of life after death.

The Rulers of Mesopotamia

The area collectively known as Sumer was a loosely knit group of city-states, that is, urban centers that governed the neighboring countryside. Here, men and women produced humankind's earliest Bronze Age technology and refined the cuneiform script that became the first written language. They began the use of a base-60 number system that is the origin of the seconds and minutes still used today in telling time. In each of the city-states of Sumer, individual priest-kings ruled as agents of one or another of the gods. The priest-king led the army, regulated the supply and distribution of food, and provided political and religious leadership. From the temple at his palace, he conducted the services that were designed to win the favor of the gods.

Disunited and generally rivalrous, the city-states of Sumer were vulnerable to invasion from tribal warriors to the north. Around 2350 B.C.E. a gifted Akkadian warlord named Sargon I (Figure **2.4**) conquered the city-states of Sumer and united them under his command. Consolidating a variety of peoples and language groups under his administration, Sargon created the world's first **empire**. By 2000 B.C.E., however, Sargon's empire fell to the attacks of nomadic tribespeople from the north. The invaders—establishing the pattern that dominated all of Mesopotamian history—built on the accomplishments of the very states they conquered. So, theocratic monarchy, religious polytheism, a socialistic economy, and established traditions of trade and barter would prevail from

---

[7]More literally "earth lion" or "chameleon."

*The phrase is from Ernest Becker. *The Denial of Death*. New York: The Free Press, 1973.

civilization to civilization. The myths and legends, indeed the *Epic of Gilgamesh* itself, would be transmitted from century to century to be transcribed in ever more refined versions of cuneiform script.

Figure 2.4 Head of the Akkadian ruler Sargon I, from Nineveh, Iraq, ca. 2350 B.C.E. Bronze, height 12 in. Iraq Museum, Baghdad. © 1990, Photo Scala, Florence.

The Social Order

In the newly formed civilizations of the ancient world, community life demanded collective effort in matters of production and distribution, as well as in the irrigation of fields and the construction of roads, temples, palaces, and military defenses. As in Egypt, specialization of labor and the demands of urban life encouraged the development of social classes with different kinds of training, different responsibilities, and different types of authority. In the first civilizations, the magician-priest who prepared the wine in the ritual vessel, the soldier who protected the city, and the farmer who cultivated the field represented fairly distinct classes of people with unique duties and responsibilities to society as a whole. The social order and division of labor that prevailed in Mesopotamia around 2700 B.C.E. are depicted in the "Standard of Ur," a wooden panel found in the royal tombs excavated at the city of Ur (Figure **2.5** and **Frontispiece**). The double-sided panel, executed in shell, mother-of-pearl, and lapis lazuli, appears to commemorate a Sumerian victory. On one side, in the top and middle registers, the ruler and his soldiers are seen taking prisoners after a battle; the bottom register depicts part of the battle itself with horse-drawn chariots trampling the defeated. On the reverse side of the panel, the ruler and six high officials of the Sumerian community lift their goblets at a celebratory banquet where the entertainers include a harpist and his female companion (top register, far right). The two lower registers record the procession of bearers with cows, rams, fish, and tribute in the form of various bundles carried on the backs of foreigners, probably prisoners of war. Although the precise function of this object is unknown, the Standard of Ur provides a mirror of class divisions in Mesopotamia of the third millennium B.C.E.

Law and the Social Order in Babylon

Shortly after 2000 B.C.E., rulers of the city-state of Babylon unified the neighboring territories of Sumer to establish the first Babylonian empire. In an effort to unite these regions politically and provide them with effective leadership, Babylon's sixth ruler, Hammurabi, called for a systematic codification of existing legal practices. He sent out envoys to collect the local statutes and had them consolidated into a single body of law. Hammurabi's Code—a collection of 282 clauses engraved on an 7-foot-high stele—is our most valuable index to life in ancient Mesopotamia (Figure **2.6**). The Code is not the first example of recorded law among the Babylonian kings; it is, however, the most extensive and comprehensive set of laws to survive from ancient times. Although Hammurabi's Code addressed primarily secular matters, it bore the force of divine decree. This fact is indicated in the prologue to the Code, where Hammurabi claims descent from the gods. It is also manifested visually in the low-relief carving at the top of the stele: here, in a scene that calls to mind the story of the biblical Moses on Mount Sinai, Hammurabi is pictured receiving the law (symbolized by a staff) from the sun god Shamash. Wearing a conical crown topped with bull's

Figure 2.5 The Standard of Ur, ca. 2700 B.C.E. Double-sided panel inlaid with shell, lapis lazuli, and red limestone, approx. 8 x 19 in. Reproduced by courtesy of the Trustees of the British Museum, London.

horns, and discharging flames from his shoulders, the god sits enthroned atop a sacred mountain, symbolized by triangular markings beneath his feet.

Written law represented a landmark advance in the development of human rights in that it protected the individual from the capricious decisions of monarchs. Unwritten law was subject to the hazards of memory and the eccentricities of the powerful. Written law, on the other hand, permitted a more impersonal (if more objective and impartial) kind of justice than did oral law. It replaced the flexibility of the spoken word with the rigidity of the written word. It did not usually recognize exceptions and was not easily or quickly changed. Ultimately, recorded law shifted the burden of judgment from the individual ruler to the legal establishment. Although written law necessarily restricted individual freedom, it safeguarded the basic values of the community.

Hammurabi's Code covers a broad spectrum of moral, social, and commercial obligations. Its civil and criminal statutes specify penalties for murder, theft, incest, adultery, kidnapping, assault and battery, and many other crimes. More important for our understanding of ancient culture, it is a storehouse of information concerning the nature of class divisions, family relations, and human rights. The Code informs us, for instance, on matters of inheritance (clauses 162 and 168), professional obligations (clauses 218, 219, 229, and 232), and the individual's responsibilities to the community (clauses 109 and 152). It also documents the fact that under Babylonian law, individuals were not regarded as equals. Human worth was defined in terms of a person's wealth and status in society. Violence committed by one free person upon another was punished reciprocally (clause 196), but the same violence committed upon a lower-class individual drew considerably lighter punishment (clause 198), and penalties were reduced even further if the victim was a slave (clause 199). Similarly, a principle of "pay according to status" was applied in punishing thieves (clause 8): the upper-class thief was more heavily penalized or fined than the lower-class one. A thief who could not pay at all fell into slavery or was put to death. Slaves, whether captives of war or victims of debt, had no civil rights under law and enjoyed only the protection of the household to which they belonged.

In Babylonian society, women were considered intellectually and physically inferior to men and—much like slaves—were regarded as the personal property of the male head of the household. A woman went from her father's house to that of her husband, where she was expected to bear children (clause 138). Nevertheless, as indicated by the Code, women enjoyed commercial freedom (clause 109) and considerable legal protection (clause 134, 138, 209, and 210), their value as childbearers and housekeepers clearly acknowledged. Clause 142 is an astonishingly early example of no-fault divorce: since a husband's neglect of his spouse was not punishable, neither party to the marriage was legally "at fault."

Figure 2.6 Stele of Hammurabi, first Babylonian dynasty, ca. 1750 B.C.E. Basalt, entire stele approx. 7 ft. 4½ x 25½ in. Louvre, Paris. Photo: RMN.

READING 1.7 From Hammurabi's Code

(ca. 1750 B.C.E.)

. . . Hammurabi, the shepherd, named by Enlil am I, who increased plenty and abundance. The ancient seed of royalty, the powerful king, the sun of Babylon, who caused light to go forth over the lands of Sumer and Akkad . . . the favorite of Innana [Ishtar] am I. When Marduk sent me to rule the people and to bring help to the land, I established law and justice in the language of the land and promoted the welfare of the people.

Clause 8 If a man has stolen an ox, or sheep or an ass, or a pig or a goat, either from a god or a palace, he shall pay thirty-fold. If he is a plebeian,[1] he shall render ten-fold. If the thief has nothing to pay, he shall be slain.

14 If a man has stolen a man's son under age, he shall be slain.

109 If rebels meet in the house of a wine-seller and she does not seize them and take them to the palace, that wine-seller shall be slain.

129 If the wife of a man is found lying with another male, they shall be bound and thrown into the water; unless the husband lets his wife live, and the king lets his servant live.

134 If a man has been taken prisoner, and there is no food in his house, and his wife enters the house of another; then that woman bears no blame.

138 If a man divorces his spouse who has not borne him children, he shall give to her all the silver of the bride-price, and restore to her the dowry which she brought from the house of her father; and so he shall divorce her.

141 If a man's wife, dwelling in a man's house, has set her face to leave, has been guilty of dissipation, has wasted her house, and has neglected her husband; then she shall be prosecuted. If her husband says she is divorced, he shall let her go her way; he shall give her nothing for divorce. If her husband says she is not divorced, her husband may espouse another woman, and that woman shall remain a slave in the house of her husband.

142 If a woman hate her husband, and says "Thou shalt not possess me," the reason for her dislike shall be inquired into. If she is careful and has no fault, but her husband takes himself away and neglects her; then that woman is not to blame. She shall take her dowry and go back to her father's house.

---

[1]A member of the lower class, probably a peasant who worked the land for the ruling class.

Science and Technology

1800 B.C.E. multiplication tables are devised in Babylon

1750 B.C.E. mathematicians in Babylon develop quadratic equations, square roots, cube roots, and an approximate value of *pi*

1700 B.C.E. windmills are employed for irrigation in Babylon

All dates in this chapter are approximate

143 If she has not been careful, but runs out, wastes her house and neglects her husband; then that woman shall be thrown into the water.

152 If, after that woman has entered the man's house, they incur debt, both of them must satisfy the trader.

154 If a man has known his daughter, that man shall be banished from his city.

157 If a man after his father has lain in the breasts of his mother, both of them shall be burned.

162 If a man has married a wife, and she has borne children, and that woman has gone to her fate; then her father has no claim upon her dowry. The dowry is her children's.

168 If a man has set his face to disown his son, and has said to the judge, "I disown my son," then the judge shall look into his reasons. If the son has not borne a heavy crime which would justify his being disowned from filiation, then the father shall not disown his son from filiation.

195 If a son has struck his father, his hand shall be cut off.

196 If a man has destroyed the eye of a free man,[2] his own eye shall be destroyed.

198 If he has destroyed the eye of a plebeian, or broken the bone of a plebeian, he shall pay one mina[3] of silver.

199 If he has destroyed the eye of a man's slave, or broken the bone of a man's slave, he shall pay half his value.

209 If a man strike the daughter of a free man, and causes her foetus to fall; he shall pay ten shekels[4] of silver for her foetus.

210 If that woman die, his daughter shall be slain.

213 If he has struck the slave of a man, and made her foetus fall; he shall pay two shekels of silver.

214 If that slave die, he shall pay a third of a mina of silver.

218 If a doctor has treated a man with a metal knife for a severe wound, and has caused the man to die, or has opened a man's tumor with a metal knife, and destroyed the man's eye; his hands shall be cut off.

219 If a doctor has treated a slave of a plebeian with a metal knife for a severe wound, and caused him to die he shall render slave for slave.

229 If a builder has built a house for a man, and his work is not strong, and if the house he has built falls in and kills the householder, that builder shall be slain.

232 If goods have been destroyed, he shall replace all that has been destroyed; and because the house that he built was not made strong, and it has fallen in, he shall restore the fallen house out of his own personal property.

282 If a slave shall say to his master, "Thou are not my master," he shall be prosecuted as a slave, and his owner shall cut off his ear.

Q What does Hammurabi's Code tell us about women in ancient Babylon?

---

[2]Above the lower-class peasant, the free man who rented land owed only a percentage of the produce to the ruling class.

[3]A monetary unit equal to approximately one pound of silver.

[4]60 shekels = 1 mina.

The Arts in Mesopotamia

Although not as elaborate as the tombs of the Egyptians, the royal graves found at Ur and elsewhere in Mesopotamia have yielded artifacts of great beauty. Jewelry, weapons, household goods, and musical instruments testify to the wealth of Mesopotamia's princely rulers (see Figures 2.2 and 2.3). Rather than building elaborate homes for the dead, however, the inhabitants of Sumer and Babylon raised temple-towers that might bring them closer to heaven. The **ziggurat**—a massive terraced tower made of rubble and brick—symbolized the sacred mountain linking the realms of heaven and earth (Figure **2.7**). Ascended by a steep stairway, it provided a platform for sanctuaries dedicated to local deities and tended by priests and priestesses. Unlike the Egyptian pyramid, which functioned as a tomb, the ziggurat served as a shrine and temple. Hence, it formed the spiritual center of the city-state. Striking similarities exist between the ziggurats of Mesopotamia and the stepped platform pyramids of ancient Mexico (Figure **2.8**) and Peru, the earliest of which (found in the foothills of the Andes mountains) dates from 2627 B.C.E. Erected atop rubble mounds much like the Mesopotamian ziggurat, the temples of the Americas functioned as solar observatories, religious sanctuaries, and gravesites. Whether or not any historical link exists between these Mesopotamian and the structurally similar Native American monuments remains among the many mysteries of ancient history.

In the shrine rooms located some 250 feet atop the ziggurat, local priests stored clay tablets inscribed with cuneiform records of the city's economic activities, its religious customs, and its rites. The shrine room of the ziggurat at Tell Asmar in Sumer also housed a remarkable group of statues representing men and women of various sizes, with large, staring eyes and hands clasped across their chests (Figure **2.9**). Carved out of soft stone, some of these cult images may represent the gods, but it is more likely that they are votive (devotional) figures that represent the townspeople of Tell Asmar in the act of worshiping their local deities. The larger figures may be priests, and the smaller figures, laypersons. Rigid and attentive, they stand as if in perpetual prayer. Their enlarged eyes, inlaid with shell and black limestone convey the impression of dread and awe, visual testimony to the sense of human apprehension in the face of divine power. These images do not share the buoyant confidence of the Egyptians; rather, they convey the insecurities of a people whose vulnerability was an ever-present fact of life.

Figure 2.7 Ziggurat at Ur (partially reconstructed), third dynasty of Ur, Iraq, ca. 2150–2050 B.C.E. © Erwin Böhm, Mainz, Germany.

The Hebrews

Among the polytheistic Mesopotamians, in the city-state of Sumer, there originated a tribal people called by their neighbors "Hebrews." Most of what we know about the Hebrews comes from the Bible—the word derives from the Greek *biblia*, meaning "books." However, archeological investigation of the Near East offers additional information by which we can reconstruct the history of this unique people prior to the formation of their first political state around 1000 B.C.E. It is believed that shortly after 2000 B.C.E., under the leadership of Abraham of Ur, they migrated westward across the Fertile Crescent and settled in Canaan along the Mediterranean Sea (see Map 2.1). In Canaan, according to the Book of Genesis, Abraham received God's word that his descendants would return to that land and become a "great nation." God's promise to Abraham established the Hebrew claim to the land of Canaan (modern-day Israel). At the same time, a special bond between God and the Hebrews ("I will be your God; you will be my people," Genesis 17:7–8) marked the beginning of the Hebrew belief that they were God's Chosen (or Holy) People.

Some time after 1700 B.C.E., the Hebrews migrated into Egypt, but falling subject to pharaonic efforts to rid Egypt of the Hyksos, they were reduced to the status of state slaves. Around 1300 B.C.E., under a dynamic leader named Moses, they departed Egypt and headed back toward Canaan. This event became the basis for Exodus (literally, "going out"), the second book of the Hebrew Bible. Since Canaan was now occupied by local tribes with sizable military strength, the Hebrews settled briefly in an arid region near the Dead Sea. During a forty-year period—which archeologists place sometime between 1300 and 1150 B.C.E.—the Hebrews forged the fundamentals of their faith: **monotheism** (the belief in one and only one god); a set of ethical and spiritual obligations; and a **covenant** (or

Figure 2.8 Pyramid of the Sun, Teotihuacán, Mexico, 50–200 C.E. Photo: Photo Researchers, Inc/Carl Frank.

contract) that binds the Hebrew community to God in return for God's protection. The covenant rests in a set of ten laws (the Decalogue), which defines the proper relationship between God and the faithful, as well as between and among all members of the Hebrew community. The "Ten Commandments," like the testimonials of the Egyptian *Book of the Dead*, are framed in the negative. The consequence for the violation of each law is unspecified. There is no mention of reward or retribution in an afterlife; only the terrible warning that God will punish those who do not "keep the commandments" as well as their children "to the third and fourth generation" (Exodus 20.5).

Hebrew monotheism focused on devotion to a single Supreme Being, the god that came to be called Yahweh* (in Latin, Jehovah). The idea of a single creator-god appeared as well in Egypt around 1350 B.C.E., when the pharaoh Amenhotep IV (Akhenaten) made the sun god Aten the sole deity of Egypt (see chapter 1). Like other

---

*An acronym based on four Hebrew letters used to represent the Divine Name.

Figure 2.9 Statuettes from the Abu Temple, Tell Asmar, Iraq, ca. 2900–2600 B.C.E. Marble, tallest figure ca. 30 in. Iraq Museum, Baghdad, and Oriental Institute, University of Chicago.

ancient gods and goddesses, Aten was an arbitrary force associated with a specific natural phenomenon: the sun. The Hebrew deity, on the other hand, transcended nature and all natural phenomena. As Supreme Creator, the Hebrew god preceded the physical universe. Whereas in Babylonian myth the universe is spontaneously generated and initially chaotic, the Hebrew Creation describes a universe that is systematically planned and invested with a preconceived moral order; it is the miraculous feat of a single benevolent, all-knowing Being. In contrast to the Babylonian universe, where squabbling gods require human beings as their servants, the Hebrew universe is the gift given by God, its creator, to God's supreme creation: humankind. Hebrew monotheism stands apart from other ancient conceptions of divine power (including that of Akhenaten's Aten) in yet another essential dimension: its ethical charge. The veneration of Yahweh as the source of and guide for an ethical life was unique to the Hebrew faith. *Ethical monotheism*, the belief in a system of behavior and belief that derives from a sole, omnipotent God, dignified individual moral judgment. It became the most lasting of the Hebrew contributions to world culture.

The excerpts below belong to the Hebrew Bible, a collection of stories and songs passed down orally for hundreds of years. The first five books of the Bible, known as the **Torah** (literally "instruction"), were assembled from four main sources some time between the tenth and the seventh century B.C.E. Parts of Genesis, the first book of the Torah, belong to a common pool of traditions rooted in Mesopotamia, where the Hebrews originated; so the story of the Flood, for instance, appears in both Genesis and the *Epic of Gilgamesh* (as well as in other Mesopotamian texts). Two groups of laws are represented below: the first, whose penalties are unspecified, constitute the unconditional law of the Decalogue. The second, which belongs to a much larger body of Hebrew laws, resemble those of Hammurabi. Unlike the Ten Commandments, the latter, which deal primarily with social obligations, prescribe specific consequences for their violation. Some so closely parallel the laws of the First Babylonian Empire that scholars think both may look back to a common source. The Bible—like the *Epic of Gilgamesh*—conflates centuries of legend and fact, and its significance as great literature is unquestionable; but its value as a historical document has been hotly debated for well over a century. It is exalted by many as the revelation of divine authority, and it is regarded as sacred scripture by three world religions: Judaism, Christianity, and Islam. Even as it expounds a message of faith and moral instruction, it narrates the saga of a people who perceive history as divinely directed.

READING 1.8a From the Hebrew Bible (Genesis 1, 2)

The Creation

Chapter 1

[26]God said, "Let us make man in our own image, in the likeness of ourselves, and let them be masters of the fish of the sea, the birds of heaven, the cattle, all the wild animals and all the creatures that creep along the ground."

[27]God created man in the image of himself,
in the image of God he created him,
male and female he created them.

[28]God blessed them, saying to them, "Be fruitful, multiply, fill the earth and subdue it. Be masters of the fish of the sea, the birds of heaven and all the living creatures that move on earth." [29]God also said, "Look, to you I give all the seed-bearing plants everywhere on the surface of the earth, and all the trees with seed-bearing fruit; this will be your food. [30]And to all the wild animals, all the birds of heaven and all the living creatures that creep along the ground, I give all the foliage of the plants as their food." And so it was. [31]God saw all he had made, and indeed it was very good. Evening came and morning came: the sixth day.

Chapter 2

[1]Thus heaven and earth were completed with all their array. [2]On the seventh day God had completed the work he had been doing. He rested on the seventh day after all the work he had been doing. [3]God blessed the seventh day and made it holy, because on that day he rested after all his work of creating. [4]Such was the story of heaven and earth as they were created.

Paradise, and the test of free will

At the time when Yahweh God made earth and heaven [5]there was as yet no wild bush on the earth nor had any wild plant yet sprung up, for Yahweh God had not sent rain on the earth, nor was there any man to till the soil. [6]Instead, water flowed out of the ground and watered all the surface of the soil. [7]Yahweh God shaped man from the soil of the ground and blew the breath of life into his nostrils, and man became a living being. [8]Yahweh God planted a garden in Eden, which is in the east, and there he put the man he had fashioned. [9]From the soil, Yahweh God caused to grow every kind of tree, enticing to look at and good to eat, with the tree of life in the middle of the garden, and the tree of the knowledge of good and evil.

[10]A river flowed from Eden to water the garden, and from there it divided to make four streams. [11]The first is named the Pishon, and this winds all through the land of Havilah where there is gold. [12]The gold of this country is pure; bdellium* and cornelian** stone are found there. [13]The second river is named the Gihon, and this winds all through the land of Cush. [14]The third river is named the Tigris, and this flows to the east of Ashur. The fourth river is the Euphrates.

[15]Yahweh God took the man and settled him in the garden of Eden to cultivate and take care of it. [16]Then Yahweh God gave the man this command, "You are free to eat of all the trees in the garden. [17]But of the tree of the knowledge of good and evil you are not to eat; for, the day you eat of that, you are doomed to die."

[18]Yahweh God said, "It is not right that the man should be alone. I shall make him a helper." [19]So from the soil Yahweh God fashioned all the wild animals and all the birds of heaven. These he brought to the man to see what he would call them; each one was to bear the name the man would give it. [20]The man gave names to all the cattle, all the birds of heaven and all the wild animals. But no helper suitable for the man was found for him. [21]Then, Yahweh God made the man fall into a deep sleep. And, while he was asleep, he took one of his ribs and closed the flesh up again forthwith. [22]Yahweh God fashioned the rib he had taken from the man into a woman, and brought her to the man. [23]And the man said:

This one at last is bone of my bones
    and flesh of my flesh!
She is to be called Woman,
    because she was taken from Man.

[24]This is why a man leaves his father and mother and becomes attached to his wife, and they become one flesh. [25]Now, both of them were naked, the man and his wife, but they felt no shame before each other.

 Q How does this creation story differ from those in Readings 1.2 and 1.5?

READING 1.8b From the Hebrew Bible

(Exodus 20:1–20; 21:1–2, 18–27, 37; 23:1–9)

The Decalogue (Ten Commandments)

[1]Then God spoke all these words. He said, [2]"I am Yahweh your God who brought you out of Egypt, where you lived as slaves.

[3]"You shall have no other gods to rival me.

[4]"You shall not make yourself a carved image or any likeness of anything in heaven above or on earth beneath or in the waters under the earth.

[5]"You shall not bow down to them or serve them. For I, Yahweh your God, am a jealous God and I punish a parent's fault in the children, the grandchildren, and the great grandchildren among those who hate me; [6]but I act with faithful love towards thousands of those who love me and keep my commandments.

[7]"You shall not misuse the name of Yahweh your God, for Yahweh will not leave unpunished anyone who misuses his name.

[8]"Remember the Sabbath day and keep it holy. [9]For six days you shall labour and do all your work, [10]but the seventh day is a Sabbath for Yahweh your God. You shall do no work that day, neither you nor your son nor your daughter nor your

---

*Variously interpreted as a deep-red gem or a pearl.
**A semiprecious red stone (carnelian).

servants, men or women, nor your animals nor the alien living with you. ¹¹For in six days Yahweh made the heavens, earth and sea and all that these contain, but on the seventh day he rested; that is why Yahweh has blessed the Sabbath day and made it sacred.

¹²Honour your father and your mother so that you may live long in the land that Yahweh your God is giving you.

¹³"You shall not kill.

¹⁴"You shall not commit adultery.

¹⁵"You shall not steal.

¹⁶"You shall not give false evidence against your neighbour.

¹⁷"You shall not set your heart on your neighbour's house. You shall not set your heart on your neighbour's spouse, or servant, man or woman, or ox, or donkey, or any of your neighbour's possessions."

¹⁸Seeing the thunder pealing, the lightning flashing, the trumpet blasting and the mountain smoking, the people were all terrified and kept their distance. ¹⁹"Speak to us yourself," they said to Moses, "and we will obey; but do not let God speak to us, or we shall die." ²⁰Moses said to the people, "Do not be afraid; God has come to test you, so that your fear of him, being always in your mind, may keep you from sinning." ²¹So the people kept their distance while Moses approached the dark cloud where God was.

Laws Concerning Slaves

¹"These are the laws you must give them: ²When you buy a Hebrew slave, his service will last for six years. In the seventh year he will leave a free man without paying compensation."

Blows and Wounds

¹⁸"If people quarrel and one strikes the other a blow with stone or fist so that the injured party, though not dead, is confined to bed,¹⁹ but later recovers and can go about, even with a stick, the one who struck the blow will have no liability, other than to compensate the injured party for the enforced inactivity and to take care of the injured party until the cure is complete.

²⁰"If someone beats his slave, male or female, and the slave dies at his hands, he must pay the penalty. ²¹But should the slave survive for one or two days, he will pay no penalty because the slave is his by right of purchase.

²²"If people, when brawling, hurt a pregnant woman and she suffers a miscarriage but no further harm is done, the person responsible will pay compensation as fixed by the woman's master, paying as much as the judges decide. ²³If further harm is done, however, you will award life for life, ²⁴eye for eye, tooth for tooth, hand for hand, foot for foot, ²⁵burn for burn, wound for wound, stroke for stroke.

²⁶"If anyone strikes the eye of his slave, male or female, and destroys the use of it, he will give the slave his freedom to compensate for the eye. ²⁷If he knocks out the tooth of his slave, male or female, he will give the slave his freedom to compensate for the tooth."

Theft of Animals

³⁷"If anyone steals an ox or a sheep and slaughters or sells it, he will pay back five beasts from the herd for the ox, and four animals from the flock for the sheep."

Justice. Duties towards Enemies

¹"You will not spread false rumours. You will not lend support to the wicked by giving untrue evidence. ²You will not be led into wrong-doing by the majority nor, when giving evidence in a lawsuit, side with the majority to pervert the course of justice; ³nor will you show partiality to the poor in a lawsuit. ⁴"If you come on your enemy's ox or donkey straying, you will take it back to him. ⁵If you see the donkey of someone who hates you fallen under its load, do not stand back; you must go and help him with it. ⁶"You will not cheat the poor among you of their rights at law. ⁷Keep clear of fraud. Do not cause the death of the innocent or upright, and do not acquit the guilty. ⁸You will accept no bribes, for a bribe blinds the clear-sighted and is the ruin of the cause of the upright. ⁹"You will not oppress the alien; you know how an alien feels, for you yourselves were once aliens in Egypt. . . ."

Q Why are many of the Commandments framed in the negative?

Q How do these laws differ from those in Hammurabi's Code?

It is worth noting a major difference between the laws of the Hebrews and those of Babylon: among the Hebrews, punishment was not levied according to social class. This is not to say that class distinctions did not exist in Hebrew society, but rather that the law was meant to apply equally to all classes, with the exception of slaves. The humanitarian bias of the Hebrew laws is best reflected in God's frequent reminder to the Hebrews that since they themselves were once aliens and slaves, they must treat even the lowest members of the social order as worthy human beings. If Babylonian law prized economic prosperity and political stability, it was the unity of religious and moral life that lay at the heart of the Hebrew message.

The Hebrew State and the Social Order

By the beginning of the first millennium B.C.E., the Hebrews had reestablished themselves in Palestine—as ancient Canaan came to be called following its occupation by powerful tribes of Philistines ("People of the Sea") in the twelfth century B.C.E. Under the rule of the Hebrew kings, Saul (ca. 1040–1000 B.C.E.), David (ca. 1000–960 B.C.E.), and Solomon (ca. 960–920 B.C.E.), Canaan became a powerful state defended by armies equipped with iron war chariots. In the city of Jerusalem (see Map 2.1), King Solomon constructed a royal palace and a magnificent temple (no longer standing) to enshrine the Ark of the Covenant. The biblical injunction against carved images (Exodus 20.4) discouraged representation in three-dimensional form. (The implication of this rule went beyond any concern that the Hebrews might worship pagan idols; it reflected the view that human efforts to create lifelike images showed disrespect to Yahweh as Supreme Creator.) Instead, early **synagogues** (houses of worship) were embellished with symbols of the faith, such as the Ark that sheltered the Torah, the **menorah** (a seven-branched candelabrum) and a **shofar** (ram's horn used to call the faithful to prayer) (Figure **2.10**).

The social order of the Hebrews was shaped by biblical precepts. Between Hebrew kings and their people, there existed a covenant—protection in exchange for loyalty and obedience—similar to that which characterized the relationship between God and the Hebrews. This same patriarchal bond also prevailed between Jewish fathers and their families. Hebrew kings were considered the divinely appointed representatives of God; and Hebrew wives and children came under the direct control of the male head of the household and were listed among his possessions. In short, the covenant between God and the Hebrews, as expressed in the laws, established the model for both secular and familial authority.

In the course of his reign, Solomon divided the Hebrew state into two administrative divisions: a northern portion called Israel, and a southern portion called Judah (hence the name "Jews"). As commercial pursuits of the young Hebrew nation generated wealth and material comforts, the cults of the Canaanite fertility gods and goddesses seduced many Hebrews away from their rigorous moral obligations. By the eighth century B.C.E., a group of zealous teachers came forth to renew the ancient covenant: known as *prophets* (literally "those who speak for another"), Amos, Hosea, and Isaiah voiced urgent pleas for spiritual reform. They warned that violations of the covenant and the laws would result in divine punishment. A century after the fall of Israel to the Assyrians in 722 B.C.E., the prophet Jeremiah explained the event as an expression of divine chastisement. He warned the people of Judah to shun local religious cults and urged them to reaffirm the covenant or again feel God's wrath. The Hebrew concept of destiny as divinely governed is confirmed in Jeremiah's message: God rewards and punishes not in a life hereafter, but here on earth.

READING 1.8c From the Hebrew Bible

(Jeremiah 11: 1–14)

Jeremiah and the Observance of the Covenant

¹The word that came to Jeremiah from Yahweh, ²"Hear the terms of this covenant; tell them to the people of Judah and to the inhabitants of Jerusalem. ³Tell them, 'Yahweh, God of Israel, says this: Cursed be anyone who will not listen to the terms of this covenant ⁴which I ordained for your ancestors when I brought them out of Egypt, out of that iron-foundry. Listen to my voice, I told them, carry out all my orders, then you will be my people and I shall be your God, ⁵so that I may fulfil the oath I swore to your ancestors, that I may give them a country flowing with milk and honey, as is the case today.'" I replied, "So be it, Yahweh!" ⁶Then Yahweh said to me, "Proclaim all these terms in the towns of Judah and in the streets of Jerusalem, saying, 'Listen to the terms of this covenant and obey them. ⁷For when I brought your ancestors out of Egypt, I solemnly warned them, and have persistently warned them until today, saying: Listen to my voice. ⁸But they did not listen, did not pay attention; instead, each followed his own stubborn and wicked inclinations. And against them, in consequence, I put into action the words of this covenant which I had ordered them to obey and which they had not obeyed.'"

⁹Yahweh said to me, "Plainly there is conspiracy among the people of Judah and the citizens of Jerusalem. ¹⁰They have reverted to the sins of their ancestors who refused to listen to my words: they too are following other gods and serving them. The House of Israel and the House of Judah have broken my covenant which I made with their ancestors. ¹¹And so, Yahweh says this, 'I shall now bring a disaster on them which they cannot escape; they will call to me for help, but I shall not listen to them. ¹²The towns of Judah and the citizens of Jerusalem will then go and call

Figure 2.10 The Ark of the Covenant and sanctuary implements, Hammath near Tiberias, fourth century. Mosaic. Israel Antiquities Authority, Jerusalem. Photo: Zev Rodovan, Jerusalem.

for help to the gods to whom they burn incense, but these will be no help at all to them in their time of distress!

> [13]"For you have as many gods
> as you have towns, Judah!
> You have built as many altars to Shame,
> as many incense altars to Baal,
> as Jerusalem has streets!

[14]"You, for your part, must not intercede for this people, nor raise either plea or prayer on their behalf, for I will not listen when their distress forces them to call to me for help.'"

 Q For what failings does Jeremiah chastise the Hebrews?

The Babylonian Captivity and the Book of Job

In 586 B.C.E., Judah fell to Chaldean armies led by the mighty King Nebuchadnezzar (ca. 630–562 B.C.E.). Nebuchadnezzar burned Jerusalem, raided the Temple, and took the inhabitants of the city into captivity. In the newly restored city of Babylon, with its glazed brick portals (Figure **2.11**), its resplendent "hanging" gardens, its towering ziggurat—the prototype for the Tower of Babel described in Genesis—the Hebrews experienced almost fifty years of exile (586–538 B.C.E.). Their despair and doubt in the absolute goodness of God are voiced in the Book of Job, probably written in the years after the Babylonian Captivity. The finest example of wisdom literature in the Hebrew Bible, the Book of Job raises the question of unjustified suffering in a universe governed by a merciful god. The "blameless and upright" Job has obeyed the Commandments and has been a devoted servant of God throughout his life. Yet he is tested unmercifully by the loss of his possessions, his family, and his health. His wife begs him to renounce God, and his friends encourage him to acknowledge his sinfulness. But Job defiantly protests that he has given God no cause for anger. Job asks a universal question: "If there is no heaven (and thus no justice after death), how can a good man's suffering be justified?" or simply phrased, "Why do bad things happen to good people?"

READING 1.8d From the Hebrew Bible

(Job 1; 2; 3:1–5, 17–21; 13:28; 14; 38: 1–18; 42:1–6)

The Book of Job

Chapter 1

[1]There was once a man in the land of Uz called Job: a sound and honest man who feared God and shunned evil. [2]Seven sons and three daughters were born to him. [3]And he owned seven thousand sheep, three thousand camels, five hundred yoke of oxen and five hundred she-donkeys, and many servants besides. This man was the most prosperous of all the Sons of the East. [4]It was the custom of his sons to hold banquets in one another's houses in turn, and to invite their

Figure 2.11 A drawing of Babylon as it might have looked in the sixth century B.C.E. The Ishtar Gate stands at the center, with the palace of Nebuchadnezzar II and the Hanging Gardens behind and to its right. On the horizon and the east bank of the Euphrates looms the Marduk Ziggurat. Oriental Institute of the University of Chicago.

three sisters to eat and drink with them. [5]Once each series of banquets was over, Job would send for them to come and be purified, and at dawn on the following day he would make a burnt offering for each of them. "Perhaps," Job would say, "my sons have sinned and in their heart blasphemed." So that was what Job used to do each time.

[6]One day when the sons of God came to attend on Yahweh, among them came Satan.[*] [7]So Yahweh said to Satan, "Where have you been?" "Prowling about on earth," he answered, "roaming around there." [8]So Yahweh asked him, "Did you pay any attention to my servant Job? There is no one like him on the earth: a sound and honest man who fears God and shuns evil." [9]"Yes," Satan said, "but Job is not God-fearing for nothing, is he? [10]Have you not put a wall round him and his house and all his domain? You have blessed all he undertakes, and his flocks throng the countryside. [11]But stretch out your hand and lay a finger on his possessions: then, I warrant you, he will curse you to your face." [12]"Very well," Yahweh said to Satan, "all he has is in your power. But keep your hands off his person." So Satan left the presence of Yahweh.

[13]On the day when Job's sons and daughters were eating and drinking in their eldest brother's house, [14]a messenger came to Job. "Your oxen," he said, "were at the plough, with the donkeys grazing at their side, [15]when the Sabaeans swept down on them and carried them off, and put the servants to the sword: I alone have escaped to tell you." [16]He had not finished speaking when another messenger arrived. "The fire of God," he said, "has fallen from heaven and burnt the sheep and shepherds to ashes: I alone have escaped to tell you."

---

*Literally, "adversary."

[17]He had not finished speaking when another messenger arrived. "The Chaldeans," he said, "three bands of them, have raided the camels and made off with them, and put the servants to the sword: I alone have escaped to tell you." [18]He had not finished speaking when another messenger arrived. "Your sons and daughters," he said, "were eating and drinking at their eldest brother's house,[19] when suddenly from the desert a gale sprang up, and it battered all four corners of the house which fell in on the young people. They are dead: I alone have escaped to tell you."

[20]Then Job stood up, tore his robe and shaved his head. Then, falling to the ground, he prostrated himself [21] and said:

Naked I came from my mother's womb,
    naked I shall return again.
Yahweh gave, Yahweh has taken back.
Blessed be the name of Yahweh!

[22]In all this misfortune Job committed no sin, and he did not reproach God. . . .

Chapter 2

[1]Another day, the sons of God came to attend on Yahweh and Satan came with them too. [2]So Yahweh said to Satan, "Where have you been?" "Prowling about on earth," he answered, "roaming around there." [3]So Yahweh asked him, "Did you pay any attention to my servant Job? There is no one like him on the earth: a sound and honest man who fears God and shuns evil. He persists in his integrity still; you achieved nothing by provoking me to ruin him." [4]"Skin after skin!" Satan replied. "Someone will give away all he has to save his life. [5]But stretch out your hand and lay a finger on his bone and flesh; I warrant you, he will curse you to your face." [6]"Very well," Yahweh said to Satan, "he is in your power. But spare his life." [7]So Satan left the presence of Yahweh.

He struck Job down with malignant ulcers from the sole of his foot to the top of his head. [8]Job took a piece of pot to scrape himself, and went and sat among the ashes. [9]Then his wife said to him, "Why persist in this integrity of yours? Curse God and die." [10]"That is how a fool of a woman talks," Job replied. "If we take happiness from God's hand, must we not take sorrow too?" And in all this misfortune Job uttered no sinful word.

[11]The news of all the disasters that had fallen on Job came to the ears of three of his friends. Each of them set out from home—Eliphaz of Teman, Bildad of Shuah and Zophar of Naamath—and by common consent they decided to go and offer him sympathy and consolation. [12]Looking at him from a distance, they could not recognise him; they wept aloud and tore their robes and threw dust over their heads. [13]They sat there on the ground beside him for seven days and seven nights. To Job they spoke never a word, for they saw how much he was suffering.

Chapter 3: Job Curses the Day of his Birth

[1]In the end it was Job who broke his silence and cursed the day of his birth. [2]This is what he said:

[3]Perish the day on which I was born
    and the night that told of a boy conceived.
[4]May that day be darkness,

may God on high have no thought for it,
    may no light shine on it.
[5]May murk and shadow dark as death claim it for their own,
    clouds hang over it,
    eclipse swoop down on it.

. . . .

[17]What are human beings that you should take them so seriously,
    subjecting them to your scrutiny,
[18]that morning after morning you should examine them
    and at every instant test them?
[19]Will you never take your eyes off me
    long enough for me to swallow my spittle?
[20]Suppose I have sinned, what have I done to you,
    you tireless watcher of humanity?
Why do you choose me as your target?
    Why should I be a burden to you?
[21]Can you not tolerate my sin,
    not overlook my fault?
For soon I shall be lying in the dust,
    you will look for me and I shall be no more.

Chapter 14

[1]A human being, born of woman,
    [his] life is short but full of trouble.
[2]Like a flower, such a one blossoms and withers,
    fleeting as a shadow, transient.
[3]And this is the creature on whom you fix your gaze,
    and bring to judgement before you!
[4]But will anyone produce the pure from what is impure?
    No one can!
[5]Since his days are measured out,
    since his tale of months depends on you,
    since you assign him bounds he cannot pass,
[6]turn your eyes from him, leave him alone,
    like a hired labourer, to finish his day in peace.
[7]There is always hope for a tree:
    when felled, it can start its life again;
    its shoots continue to sprout.
[8]Its roots may have grown old in the earth,
    its stump rotting in the ground,
[9]but let it scent the water, and it buds,
    and puts out branches like a plant newly set.
[10]But a human being? He dies, and dead he remains,
    breathes his last, and then where is he?
[11]The waters of the sea will vanish,
    the rivers stop flowing and run dry:
[12]a human being, once laid to rest, will never rise again,
    the heavens will wear out before he wakes up,
    or before he is roused from his sleep.
[13]Will no one hide me in Sheol,
    and shelter me there till your anger is past,
    fixing a certain day for calling me to mind—
[14]can the dead come back to life?—
    day after day of my service, I should be waiting
    for my relief to come.
[15]Then you would call, and I should answer,
    you would want to see once more what you have made.
[16]Whereas now you count every step I take,

you would then stop spying on my sin;

¹⁷you would seal up my crime in a bag,
and put a cover over my fault.

¹⁸Alas! Just as, eventually, the mountain falls down,
the rock moves from its place,

¹⁹water wears away the stones,
the cloudburst erodes the soil;
so you destroy whatever hope a person has.

²⁰You crush him once for all, and he is gone;
first you disfigure him, then you dismiss him.

²¹His children may rise to honours—he does not know it;
they may come down in the world—he does not care.

²²He feels no pangs, except for his own body,
makes no lament, except for his own self.

Chapter 38: Job Must Bow to the Creator's Wisdom

¹Then from the heart of the tempest Yahweh gave Job his answer. He said:

²Who is this, obscuring my intentions
with his ignorant words?

³Brace yourself like a fighter;
I am going to ask the questions, and you are to inform me!

⁴Where were you when I laid the earth's foundations?
Tell me, since you are so well-informed!

⁵Who decided its dimensions, do you know?
Or who stretched the measuring line across it?

⁶What supports its pillars at their bases?
Who laid its cornerstone

⁷to the joyful concert of the morning stars
and the unanimous acclaim of the sons of God?

⁸Who pent up the sea behind closed doors
when it leapt tumultuous from the womb,

⁹when I wrapped it in a robe of mist
and made black clouds its swaddling bands;

¹⁰when I cut out the place I had decreed for it
and imposed gates and a bolt?

¹¹"Come so far," I said, "and no further;
here your proud waves must break!"

¹²Have you ever in your life given orders to the morning
or sent the dawn to its post,

¹³to grasp the earth by its edges
and shake the wicked out of it?

¹⁴She turns it as red as a clay seal,
she tints it as though it were a dress,

¹⁵stealing the light from evil-doers
and breaking the arm raised to strike.

¹⁶Have you been right down to the sources of the sea
and walked about at the bottom of the Abyss?

¹⁷Have you been shown the gates of Death,
have you seen the janitors of the Shadow dark as death?

¹⁸Have you an inkling of the extent of the earth?
Tell me all about it if you have!

Chapter 42: Job's Final Answer

¹This was the answer Job gave to Yahweh:

²I know that you are all-powerful:
what you conceive, you can perform.

³I was the man who misrepresented your intentions
with my ignorant words.
You have told me about great works that I cannot understand,
about marvels which are beyond me, of which I know
nothing.

⁴(Listen, please, and let me speak:
I am going to ask the questions, and you are to inform me.)

⁵Before, I knew you only by hearsay
but now, having seen you with my own eyes,

⁶I retract what I have said,
and repent in dust and ashes.

Q Why is the Book of Job called "wisdom literature"?

Q Why is this book essential to an understanding of the Hebrew covenant?

God's answer to Job is an eloquent vindication of unquestioned faith: God's power is immense and human beings cannot expect rational explanations of the divine will; indeed, they have no business demanding such. Proclaiming the magnitude of divine power and the fragility of humankind, the Book of Job confirms the pivotal role of faith (the belief and trust in God) that sustains the Hebrew covenant. The anxious sense of human vulnerability that pervades the Book of Job recalls the *Epic of Gilgamesh*. Job and Gilgamesh are tested by superhuman forces, and both come to realize that misfortune and suffering are typical of the human condition. Gilgamesh seeks but fails to secure personal immortality; Job solicits God's promise of heavenly reward but fails to secure assurance that once dead, he might return to life. Just as Utnapishtim tells Gilgamesh, "There is no permanence," so Job laments that man born of woman "Like a flower, such a one blossoms and withers, . . . He dies and dead he remains." Such pessimism was not uncommon in Mesopotamia, the region in which both the *Epic of Gilgamesh* and the Hebrew Bible originated. The notion of life after death (so prominent in Egyptian religious thought) is as elusive a concept in Hebraic literature as it is in Mesopotamian myth. Job anticipates a final departure to an underworld, an abode of the dead known among the Hebrews as *Sheol* or Shadowland. Yet, even without the promise of reward, Job remains stubbornly faithful to the covenant. His tragic vision involves the gradual but dignified acceptance of his place in a divinely governed universe.

The Book of Psalms

In 538 B.C.E., the Jewish remnant returned to Jerusalem to rebuild the temple of Solomon. The post-exile age—the period following the Babylonian Captivity—was marked by apocalyptic hopes and the renewal of the Covenant. This era also produced one of the best-loved books of the Hebrew Bible. The Book of Psalms (or "Psalter," from the Greek work *psalterion*, a stringed instrument) is a collection of 150 songs of praise, thanksgiving, confession, and supplication. Traditionally attributed to King David, whose name was associated with leadership in religious music, the Psalms were transmitted orally for more than half a century. In Hebrew culture, music was closely tied to prayer and worship. **Cantors** chanted biblical passages as part of the Hebrew **liturgy** (the rituals for public worship), and members of the congregation participated in the singing of psalms. Both prayers and psalms might be performed in the **responsory** style, in which the congregation answered the voice of the cantor, or in the **antiphonal** manner, in which the cantor and the congregation sang alternate verses. Sung in public worship, the psalms forge a link between the individual and the Hebrew community, as reflected in the line: "O magnify the Lord with me, and let us exalt his name together!" (Ps. 34:3). Psalm 8, reproduced below, is one of the most eloquent songs of praise in the Hebrew Bible.

READING 1.8e From the Hebrew Bible

(Psalms 8: 1–9)

The power of God's name
Yahweh our Lord,
how majestic is your name throughout the world!

Whoever keeps singing of your majesty higher than the heavens,
even through the mouths of children, or of babes in arms,
you make him a fortress, firm against your foes,
to subdue the enemy and the rebel.

I look up at your heavens, shaped by your fingers,
at the moon and the stars you set firm—
what are human beings that you spare a thought for them,
or the child of Adam that you care for him?

Yet you have made him little less than a god,
you have crowned him with glory and beauty,
made him lord of the works of your hands,
put all things under his feet,

sheep and cattle, all of them,
and even the wild beasts,
birds in the sky, fish in the sea,
when he makes his way across the ocean.

Yahweh our Lord,
how majestic your name throughout the world!

 Q How does this song of praise compare with "The Hymn to the Aten" (Reading 1.3)?

The Hebrew Bible played a major role in shaping the humanistic tradition in the West. It provided the religious and ethical foundations for Judaism, and, almost 2000 years after the death of Abraham, for Christianity and Islam.

The Hebrew Bible

The Torah	Genesis	Numbers
	Exodus	Deuteronomy
	Leviticus	
The Prophets	Joshua	Isaiah
	Judges	Jeremiah
	Samuel I & II	Ezekiel
	Kings I & II	Twelve Minor Prophets
The Writings	Psalms	Ecclesiastes
	Proverbs	Esther
	Job	Daniel
	Song of Songs	Ezra
	Ruth	Nehemiah
	Lamentations	Chronicles I & II

Biblical teachings, including the belief in a single, personal, caring god who intervenes on behalf of a faithful people, have become fundamental to Western thought. Bible stories—from Genesis to Job—have inspired some of humankind's greatest works of art, music, and literature. And Psalms, along with the later books of the Bible (see Box), have had a profound influence on the religious history of the West.

The Iron Age

During the course of the first millennium B.C.E., all of Mesopotamia felt the effects of a new technology: iron was introduced into Asia Minor by the Hittites, a nomadic tribe that entered the area before 2000 B.C.E. Cheaper to produce and more durable than bronze, iron represented new, superior technology. In addition to their iron weapons, the Hittites made active use of horse-drawn war chariots, which provided increased speed and mobility in battle. The combination of war chariots and iron weapons gave the Hittites clear military superiority over all of Mesopotamia.

As iron technology spread slowly throughout the Near East, it transformed the ancient world. Iron tools contributed to increased agricultural production, which in turn supported an increased population. In the wake of the Iron Age, numerous small states came to flower, bringing with them major cultural innovations. By 1500 B.C.E., for instance, the Phoenicians, an energetic, seafaring people located on the Mediterranean Sea (see Map 2.1), had developed an alphabet of twenty-two signs. These signs eventually replaced earlier forms of script and became the basis of all Western alphabets. In Asia Minor, the Lydians, successors to the Hittites, began the practice of minting coins.

Cheaper and stronger weapons also meant larger, more efficient armies: war was no longer the monopoly of the elite. Iron technology encouraged the rise of large and powerful empires. Equipped with iron weapons, the Assyrians (ca. 750–600 B.C.E.), Chaldeans (ca. 600–540 B.C.E.), and Persians (ca. 550–330 B.C.E.) followed one another in conquering vast portions of Mesopotamia. Each of these empires grew in size and authority by imposing military control over territories outside their own natural boundaries—a practice known as *imperialism*.

The Assyrian Empire

The first of the Iron Age empire-builders, the Assyrians earned a reputation as the most militant civilization of ancient Mesopotamia. Held together by a powerful army that systematically combined engineering and fighting techniques, the Assyrians turned their iron weapons against most of Mesopotamia. In 721 B.C.E., they conquered Israel and dispersed its population. By the middle of the seventh century B.C.E. they had swallowed up most of the land between the Persian Gulf and the Nile valley. Assyrian power is reflected in the imposing walled citadel of Khorsabad, located some 10 miles from Nineveh (see Map 2.1). Covering 25 acres, this walled complex featured a ziggurat and an elaborate palace with more than 200

Science and Technology

1800 B.C.E. Hittites introduce iron into Mesopotamia

850 B.C.E. first known arched bridge is constructed in Asia Minor

700 B.C.E. the Assyrians are the first to construct aqueducts

650 B.C.E. the Lydians introduce standard coinage

rooms: a maze of courtyards, harem quarters, treasuries, and state apartments (Figure 2.12). The palace walls were adorned with low-relief scenes of war and pillage and with cuneiform inscriptions celebrating Assyrian military victories. One seventh-century B.C.E. relief shows the imperial armies of King Ashurbanipal (668–627 B.C.E.) storming the battlements of an African city (Figure 2.13).

In the lower left, male captives (their chieftains still wearing the feathers of authority) are led away, followed in procession by women, children, and the spoils of war.

Flanking the scenes of military conquest on the palace walls at Nineveh and Nimrud are depictions of the royal lion hunt. Hunting and war, two closely related enterprises, were ideal vehicles by which to display the ruler's courage and physical might. In Assyrian reliefs, the lion, a traditional symbol of power throughout the ancient world (see page 16) is depicted as the adversary of the king. Ceremonial lion hunts symbolized the invincibility of the monarch, who, in earlier times, might have proved his prowess by combating wild animals in the field—in the manner of the legendary Gilgamesh (see Figure 2.2). One dramatic relief from Nimrud depicts a wounded lion fiercely pursuing the royal chariot as it speeds away, while another beast lies

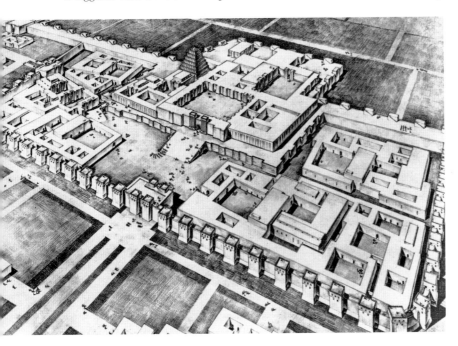

Figure 2.12 The citadel of Sargon II, Khorsabad, Iraq, ca. 720 B.C.E. Reconstruction drawing. Artist: Charles Altman. The Oriental Institute, University of Chicago.

Figure 2.13 Ashurbanipal besieging an Egyptian city, 667 B.C.E. Alabaster relief. Reproduced by courtesy of the Trustees of the British Museum, London.

Figure 2.14 King Ashurnasirpal II killing lions, from Palace of King Ashurnarsipal II, Nimrud, ca. 883–859 B.C.E. Alabaster relief, 3 ft. 3 in. x 8 ft. 4 in. Reproduced by courtesy of the Trustees of the British Museum, London.

dying before the wheels of the king's chariot (Figure 2.14). Spatial depth is indicated by superimposing the chariot wheels over the rear lion's legs. Yet the heads and legs of the horses are shown on a single plane, and clarity of design required that the second wounded lion, crouching in pain, fit precisely within the space between the front and rear legs of the prancing steeds. The balance between figures (positive shapes) and ground (negative or "empty"

Figure 2.15 Winged human-headed bull from Khorsabad, Iraq, ca. 720 B.C.E. Limestone, approx. height 13 ft. 10 in. Louvre, Paris.

space) results in a brilliant formal composition. The Assyrian reliefs—housed in large numbers at the British Museum in London—are superb examples of the artist's ability to infuse violent subject matter with narrative grandeur. If the lion hunt reliefs made implicit reference to the ruler's invincibility, colossal sculpture clearly manifested his superhuman status. Thirteen-foot-tall hybrid beasts guarded the gateways of Assyrian palaces (Figure 2.15), much in the way the sphinx guarded the royal tombs of Egypt. Bearing the facial features of the monarch, these colossi united the physical attributes of the bull (virility), the lion (physical strength), and the eagle (predatory agility). The winged, human-headed bulls from the citadel at Khorsabad were power-symbols designed to inspire awe and fear among those who passed beneath their impassive gaze. Clearly, the art of Assyria was visual propaganda, designed not only to celebrate Assyrian rulership, but to intimidate its enemies.

The Persian Empire

The Persian Empire, the last and the largest of the empires of Mesopotamia, was brought to its peak by Cyrus II (ca. 585–ca. 529 B.C.E.), called "the Great" for his conquests over territories ranging from the frontiers of India to the Mediterranean Sea. Persia's monarchs, aided by efficient administrators, oversaw a network of roads connecting the major cities of the Near East. Persian message-bearers traveled swiftly throughout the empire. Described by the Greek historian Herodotus as men unhindered "by snow, or rain, or heat, or by the darkness of night," they provided a model and a motto for the United States Postal Service.

The Persians devised a monotheistic religion based on the teachings of the prophet Zoroaster (ca. 628–ca. 551 B.C.E.). Denying the nature gods of earlier times, Zoroaster exalted the sole god Ahura-Mazda ("Wise Lord"), who demanded good thoughts, good works, and good deeds from his followers. Zoroaster taught that life was a battlefield on which the opposing forces of light and darkness contended for supremacy. Human beings took part in this cosmic struggle by way of their freedom to choose between good and evil, the consequences of which would determine their fate at the end of time. According to Zoroaster, a Last Judgment would consign the wicked to everlasting darkness, while the good would live eternally in an abode of luxury and light—the Persian *pairidaeza*, from which the English word "paradise" derives. Zoroastrianism came to influence the moral teachings of three great world religions: Judaism, Christianity, and Islam (see chapters 8 and 10).

At the Persian capital of Persepolis (in modern-day Iran), artists perpetuated the architectural and sculptural traditions of Assyria. The Persians also brought to perfection the art of metalworking that had flourished in Mesopotamia since the beginning of the Bronze Age. Utensils, vessels, and jewelry produced by Persian craftspeople, display some of the most intricate and sophisticated techniques of gold-working known to the history of that medium (Figure **2.16**). Many of these techniques would be practiced for centuries to come (see chapter 11).

SUMMARY

Mesopotamia's vulnerable geographic location contributed to the rise and fall of many different civilizations. Despite the differences in languages and ethnicity, the civilizations of this region, beginning with Sumer and ending with the Persian Empire, shared elements of a common culture. Unstable climate and the irregular overflow of the Tigris and Euphrates Rivers contributed to the formulation of a pantheon of fierce and capricious Mesopotamian deities and the evolution of a generally pessimistic world view. The world's first major literary work, the *Epic of Gilgamesh*, describes the futility of the human search for immortal life.

Neither the Sumerians nor the Hebrews inhabiting the region developed the deep sense of order that characterized ancient Egyptian culture; nor did any of the civilizations of the Near East (with the exception of Persia) produce a clearly defined picture of life after death comparable to that of the Egyptians. Among the Hebrews, the covenant with a single, personal, and transcendent god formed the basis for a religion that emphasized unswerving faith and high moral conduct. The Hebraic emphasis on ethical monotheism strongly influenced Western religious thought.

Mesopotamian rulers acted as agents of the gods. Within the civilizations of the Fertile Crescent, "divine-right monarchs" from Sargon to Cyrus the Great brought law and order to their societies. The close association between secular authority and spiritual power fostered the concept of law as a form of divine justice. From Mesopotamia came the world's first system of recorded law: under the Babylonian ruler Hammurabi, laws were recorded and codified. Unlike the Hebrews, whose laws applied equally to all classes, the Babylonians punished violators according to their status in society. Iron technology made possible the establishment of large armies and ushered in centuries of imperialism. Yet the empires of the Near East perpetuated cultural traditions that reached back to Sumer: civilization after civilization honored the gods with ziggurats, copied and recopied the *Epic of Gilgamesh*, and passed on the technology of metalworking. Yet it may be on Assyria's palace walls, inscribed with violent scenes of warfare, that the turbulent history of Mesopotamia is most vividly recorded. The arts of Mesopotamia reflect the lives of people for whom survival was a day-to-day struggle. These artworks proclaim the power of the ruler, the omnipotence of the gods, and the frailties of human beings as they try to understand the workings of nature, the meaning of death, and the destiny and purpose of humankind.

GLOSSARY

antiphonal a type of music in which two or more groups of voices or instruments alternate with one another

cantor the chief singer of the liturgy

covenant contract; the bond between the Hebrew people and their God

empire a state achieved militarily by the unification of territories under a single sovereign power

epic a long narrative poem that recounts the deeds of a legendary or historical hero in his quest for meaning or identity

liturgy the rituals for public worship

menorah a seven-branched candelabrum

monotheism the belief in one and only one god

responsory a type of music in which a single voice answers another voice or a chorus

shofar a trumpet made of a ram's horn, used to summon Jews to prayer

synagogue the Jewish house for worship and religious study

Torah (Hebrew, "instruction," "law," or "teaching") the first five books of the Hebrew Bible: Genesis, Exodus, Leviticus, Numbers, and Deuteronomy

ziggurat a terraced tower of rubble and brick that served ancient Mesopotamians as a temple-shrine

CHAPTER 3

India and China: Gods, Rulers, and the Social Order

"He knows peace who has forgotten desire.
He lives without craving:
Free from ego, free from pride."
The Bhagavad-Gita

India and China, two of the oldest continuous civilizations in world history, emerged somewhat later than the civilizations of Egypt and Mesopotamia. These ancient Asian cultures nevertheless contributed significantly to the humanistic tradition, producing literature, philosophy, art, and music that rank with that of the other great civilizations. But the Asian world view differs somewhat from that of the Western cultures we have examined. In India, for example, the fundamentals of spirituality were grounded in **pantheism**, the belief that all things in the universe are pervaded by an ineffable divine spirit. For the ancient Chinese, the natural order of the universe was central to all aspects of material and spiritual existence. In both of these cultures, all aspects of reality, whether human or divine, were thought to belong to the larger organic whole. This holistic outlook contributed to the evolution of rulership and the formation of the social order.

Ancient India

Indus Valley Civilization (ca. 2700–1500 B.C.E.)

India's earliest known civilization was located in the lower Indus valley, in an area called Sind—from which the words "India" and "Hindu" derive (Map **3.1**). At Mohenjo-daro (part of modern-day Pakistan) and other urban centers, a sophisticated Bronze Age culture flourished before 2500 B.C.E. India's first cities were planned communities: their streets, lined with fired-brick houses, were laid out in a grid pattern, and their covered sewage systems were unmatched in other parts of the civilized world. Bronze Age India also claimed a form of written language, although the 400 pictographic signs that constitute their earliest script are still undeciphered. There is little evidence of temple or tomb architecture, but a vigorous sculptural tradition existed in both bronze and stone. The lively female dancer pictured in Figure **3.1** is one of many objects (see also Figure 0.19)

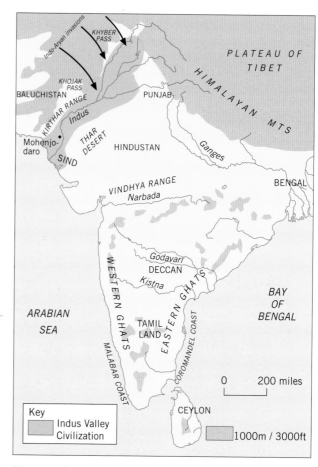

Map 3.1 Ancient India.

that reflect India's mastery of the lost-wax method of working bronze. In the medium of stone, the powerful portrait of a bearded man (possibly a priest or ruler) distinguished by an introspective expression, anticipates the meditative images of India's later religious art (Figure **3.2**).

The Vedic Era (ca. 1500–322 B.C.E.)

Some time after 1500 B.C.E., warring, seminomadic tribes known as Aryans ("lords" or "nobles") invaded the Indus valley. These light-skinned peoples enslaved or removed the dark-skinned populations of Sind and established a set of societal divisions that anticipated the **caste system**. While a hierarchical order marked the social systems of all ancient civilizations, India developed the most rigid kind of class stratification, which prevailed until modern times. By 1000 B.C.E., four principal castes existed: priests and scholars; rulers and warriors; artisans and merchants; and unskilled workers. Slowly, these castes began to subdivide according to occupation. At the very bottom of the social order—or, more accurately, outside it—lay those who held the most menial and degrading occupations. They became known as Untouchables.

It was the Aryans who introduced Sanskrit, which would become the classic language of India. The bards of India recounted stories of the bitter tribal wars between competing Aryan families. These stories were the basis for India's two great epics—the *Mahabharata* (*Great Deeds of the Bharata Clan*) and the *Ramayana* (*Song of Prince Rama*), transmitted orally for generations but not recorded until the eighth century B.C.E. The *Mahabharata*—the world's longest folk epic—recreates a ten-year-long struggle for control of the Ganges valley occurring around the year 1000 B.C.E. Along with the *Ramayana*, this epic assumed a role in the cultural history of India not unlike that of the *Iliad* and the *Odyssey* in Hellenic history. Indeed, the two epics have been treasured resources for much of the poetry, drama, and art produced throughout India's long history.

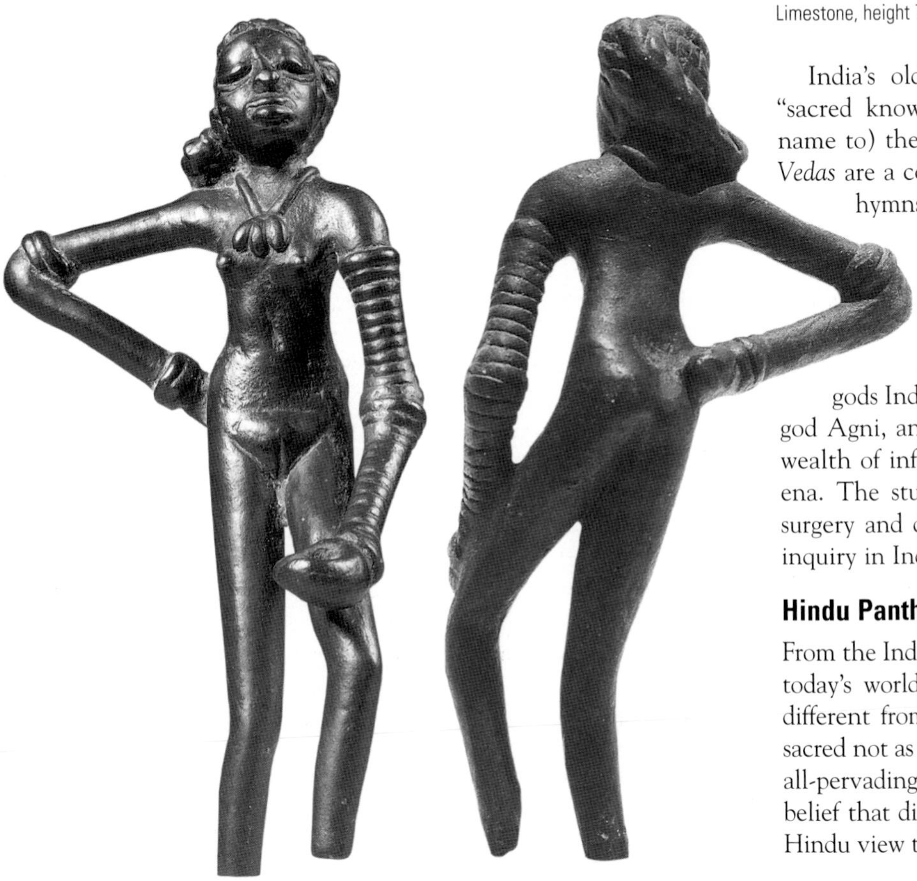

Figure 3.1 Dancing girl, from Mohenjo-daro, Indus valley, ca. 2300–1750 B.C.E. Bronze, height 4¼ in. National Museum, New Delhi.

Figure 3.2 Bearded man, from Mohenjo-daro, Indus valley, ca. 2000 B.C.E. Limestone, height 7 in. Karachi Museum. Photo: Robert Harding, London.

India's oldest devotional texts, the *Vedas* (literally, "sacred knowledge"), also originate in (and give their name to) the thousand-year period after 1500 B.C.E. The *Vedas* are a collection of prayers, sacrificial formulae, and hymns, one example of which appears in Reading 1.2 in the Introduction. Transmitted orally for centuries, the *Vedas* reflect a blending of the native folk traditions of the Indus valley and those of the invading Aryans. Among the chief Vedic deities were the sky gods Indra and Rudra (later known as Shiva), the fire god Agni, and the sun god Vishnu. The *Vedas* provide a wealth of information concerning astronomical phenomena. The study of the stars, along with the practice of surgery and dissection, mark the beginnings of scientific inquiry in India.

Hindu Pantheism

From the Indus valley civilization came the most ancient of today's world religions: Hinduism. Hinduism is markedly different from the religions of the West. It identifies the sacred not as a superhuman personality, but as an objective, all-pervading cosmic Spirit called **Brahman**. Pantheism, the belief that divinity is inherent in all things, is basic to the Hindu view that the universe itself is sacred. While neither polytheistic nor monotheistic in the traditional sense, Hinduism venerates all forms and manifestations of the all-pervasive Brahman. Hence, Hindus embrace all of the Vedic gods, a multitude of deities who are perceived as emanations of the divine. In the words of the *Rig Veda*, "Truth is one, but the wise call it by many names."

Hinduism is best understood by way of the religious texts known as the *Upanishads*, some 250 prose commentaries on the *Vedas*. Like the *Vedas* themselves, the *Upanishads* were orally transmitted and recorded in Sanskrit between the eighth and sixth centuries B.C.E. While the *Vedas* teach worship through prayer and sacrifice, the *Upanishads* teach enlightenment through meditation. They predicate the concept of the single, all-pervading cosmic force called Brahman. Unlike the nature deities of Egypt and Mesopotamia, Brahman is infinite, formless, and ultimately unknowable. Unlike the Hebrew Yahweh, Brahman assumes no personal and contractual relationship with humankind. Brahman is the Uncaused Cause and the Ultimate Reality. In every human being, there resides the individual manifestation of Brahman: the Self, or **Atman**, which, according to the *Upanishads*, is "soundless, formless, intangible, undying, tasteless, odorless, without beginning, without end, eternal, immutable, [and] beyond nature." Although housed in the material prison of the human body, the Self (Atman) seeks to be one with the Absolute Spirit (Brahman). The (re)union of Brahman and Atman—a condition known as **nirvana**—is the goal of every Hindu. This blissful reabsorption of the Self into Absolute Spirit must be preceded by one's gradual rejection of the material world, that is, the world of illusion and ignorance, and by the mastery of the techniques of meditation and through a system of spiritual exercises known as **yoga**. Yoga (literally "to yoke") seeks the joining of one's Atman to Brahman through control of the mind and body. A complex of physical positions and breathing exercises, which was not codified until the second century B.C.E., yoga (and its manifold schools) developed as one of the many Hindu ascetic disciplines aimed at achieving liberation of the Self and union with the Supreme Spirit.

Essentially a literature of humility, the *Upanishads* offer no guidelines for worship, no moral laws, and no religious dogma. They neither exalt divine power, nor do they interpret it. They do, however, instruct the individual Hindu on the subject of death and rebirth. The Hindu anticipates a succession of lives: that is, the successive return of the Atman in various physical forms. The physical form, whether animal or human and of whatever species or class, is determined by the level of spiritual purity that the Hindu has achieved by the time of his or her death. The Law of **Karma** holds that the collective spiritual energy gained from accumulated deeds determines one's physical state in the next life. Reincarnation, or the Wheel of Rebirth, is the fate of Hindus until they achieve nirvana. In this ultimate state, the enlightened Atman is both liberated and absorbed—a process that may be likened to the dissolution of a grain of salt in the vast waters of the ocean.

The *Bhagavad-Gita*

The fundamental teachings of Hinduism are lyrically expressed in one of India's most popular religious poems: the *Bhagavad-Gita (Song of God)*, which constitutes one episode from the *Mahabharata*. In this most famous part of the poem, a dialogue takes place between Arjuna, the warrior-hero, and Krishna, the incarnation of the god Vishnu and a divine manifestation of Brahman. Facing the prospect of shedding the blood of his own kinsmen in the battle to come, Arjuna seeks to reconcile his material obligations with his spiritual quest for selflessness. Krishna's answer to Arjuna—a classic statement of resignation—represents the essence of Hindu thought as distilled from the *Upanishads*. Although probably in existence earlier, the *Bhagavad-Gita* was not recorded until sometime between the fifth and second centuries B.C.E.

READING 1.9   From the *Bhagavad-Gita*

He [who] knows bliss in the Atman	1
And wants nothing else.	
Cravings torment the heart:	
He renounces cravings.	
I call him illumined.	5
Not shaken by adversity,	
Not hankering after happiness:	
Free from fear, free from anger,	
Free from the things of desire,	
I call him a seer, and illumined.	10
The bonds of his flesh are broken.	
He is lucky, and does not rejoice:	
He is unlucky, and does not weep.	
I call him illumined.	

. . . .

Thinking about sense-objects	15
Will attach you to sense-objects;	
Grow attached, and you become addicted;	
Thwart your addiction, it turns to anger;	
Be angry, and you confuse your mind;	
Confuse your mind, you forget the lesson of experience;	20
Forget experience, you lose discrimination;	
Lose discrimination, and you miss life's only purpose.	
When he has no lust, no hatred,	
A man walks safely among the things of lust and hatred.	
To obey the Atman	25
Is his peaceful joy:	
Sorrow melts	
Into that clear peace;	
His quiet mind	
Is soon established in peace.	30
The uncontrolled mind	
Does not guess that the Atman is present:	
How can it meditate?	
Without meditation, where is peace?	
Without peace, where is happiness?	35
The wind turns a ship	
From its course upon the waters:	

The wandering winds of the senses
Cast man's mind adrift
And turn his better judgment from its course. 40
When a man can still the senses
I call him illumined.
The recollected mind is awake
In the knowledge of the Atman
Which is dark night to the ignorant: 45
The ignorant are awake in their sense-life
Which they think is daylight:
To the seer it is darkness.
Water flows continually into the ocean
But the ocean is never disturbed: 50
Desire flows into the mind of the seer
But he is never disturbed.
The seer knows peace:
The man who stirs up his own lusts
Can never know peace. 55
He knows peace who has forgotten desire.
He lives without craving:
Free from ego, free from pride.
This is the state of enlightenment in Brahman:
A man who does not fall back from it 60
Into delusion.
Even at the moment of death
He is alive in that enlightenment:
Brahman and he are one. . . .

 Q What are the obstacles to the state of enlightenment, according to Krishna?

The Hindu view of the relationship between people and gods differs significantly from the religious views of ancient Egyptians and Mesopotamians. While the latter held human beings as separate from the gods, Hindus, guided by the *Upanishads* and the *Bhagavad-Gita*, asserted the oneness of matter and spirit. Where Western religions emphasized the imperishability of individual consciousness, Hinduism aspired to its sublimation, or rather, its reabsorption into the spiritual infinite. Although Hinduism still embraces the vast pantheon of Vedic gods and goddesses, it has remained relatively unaffected by the religious precepts of Western Judaism and Christianity. Unlike the latter, Hinduism has no institutional forms of worship and no doctrinal laws. On the other hand, since the nineteenth century, Hinduism's holistic view of nature has increasingly influenced Western thought and belief. And since the last decades of the twentieth century, Hindu techniques of deep meditation have made a notable impact on the disciplines of religion, philosophy, and medical science.

Figure 3.3 Ritual disk, Zhou dynasty, fifth to third century B.C.E. Jade, diameter 6½ in. Nelson Atkins Museum of Art, Kansas City, Missouri. 33–81.

Ancient China

 Ancient Chinese civilization emerged in the fertile valleys of two great waterways: the Yellow and the Yangzi* Rivers (Map 3.2). As early as 3500 B.C.E., the Neolithic villages of China were producing silk, a commodity that would bring wealth and fame to Chinese culture, but the hallmarks of civilization—urban centers, metallurgy, and writing—did not appear until the second millennium B.C.E. By 1750 B.C.E., the Chinese had developed a script that employed some 4500 characters (each character representing an individual word), some of which are still used today. Combining pictographic and phonetic elements, Chinese characters became the basis for writing throughout East Asia. It is likely that China's first dynasties flourished for some three centuries before the appearance of writing. But not until the rise of a warrior tribe known as the Shang is there evidence of a fully developed urban culture in Bronze Age China.

The Shang Dynasty (ca. 1520–1027 B.C.E.)

Shang rulers were hereditary kings who were regarded as intermediaries between the people and the spirit world. Limited in power by councils consisting of China's landholding nobility, they claimed their authority from the Lord on High (Shang-di). Hence, as in Egypt, they ruled by divine right. Royal authority was symbolized by the dragon, a hybrid beast that stood for strength, fertility, and life-giving water (Figure 3.3). Occupants of the "dragon

*All transcriptions of Chinese names appear in the system known as Hanyu Pinyin.

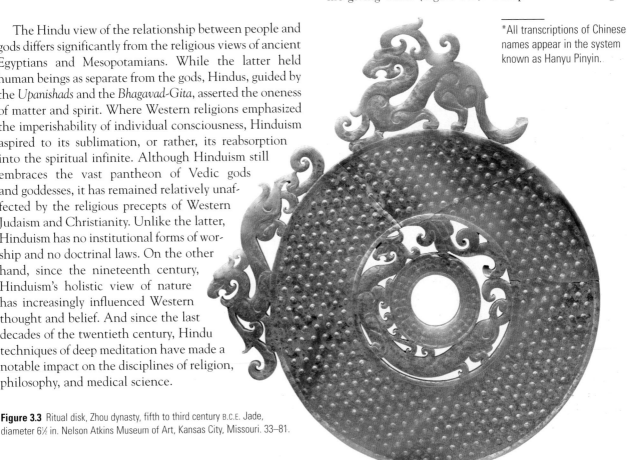

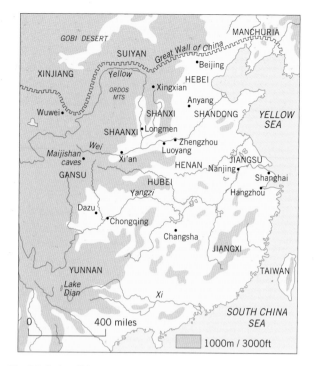

Map 3.2 Ancient China.

Figure 3.4 Ceremonial vessel with a cover, late Shang dynasty, China, ca. 1000 B.C.E. Bronze, height 20⅛ in. Freer Gallery of Art, Smithsonian Institution, Washington, D.C. Accession No. 30.26 AB.

throne," China's early kings defended their position by way of a powerful bureaucracy and huge armies of archer-warriors recruited from the provinces. The king's soldiers consisted of peasants, who, in peacetime, farmed the land with the assistance of slaves captured in war. The Chinese social order is clearly articulated in Shang royal tombs, where the king is surrounded by the men and women who served him. Royal graves also include several hundred headless bodies, probably those of the slaves who built the tombs. As in Egypt and Mesopotamia, China's royal tombs were filled with treasures—a vast array of ritual and grave goods that include silk fabrics, ceramic sculptures, jade artifacts, bronze vessels, and objects of personal adornment. (Unlike Egypt's tombs, China's were rarely plundered.) Bronze bells used in rituals and bronze vessels designed to hold food and drink for the deceased appear in great number (Figure 3.4). In their linear vitality, the surfaces of these ritual objects, adorned with a complex of dragons, birds, and maze-like motifs, express the ancient Chinese view of the cosmos as animated by natural spirits. In 1986, archeologists working in Sichuan province (an area beyond the rule of the Shang) uncovered graves that contained gold and silver objects, along with more than 200 bronze objects, including the earliest life-sized human figures in Chinese art (Figure 3.5). This and even more recent finds suggest that the early history of China is still largely hidden from us.

Beginning in Neolithic times and throughout ancient Chinese history, large numbers of jade objects—especially finely carved jade disks (see Figure 3.3)—were placed in royal graves. The meaning and function of these ubiquitous objects is a matter of some speculation. The Chinese used jade for tools, but also for carved insignias and talismans probably related to ceremonial ritual. As well as for its durability, jade was prized by the Chinese for its musical qualities, its subtle, translucent colors, and its alleged protective powers—it was thought to prevent fatigue and delay the decomposition of the body. Jade disks were usually placed at the center of the body in the tomb. In the tombs of later rulers, the deceased

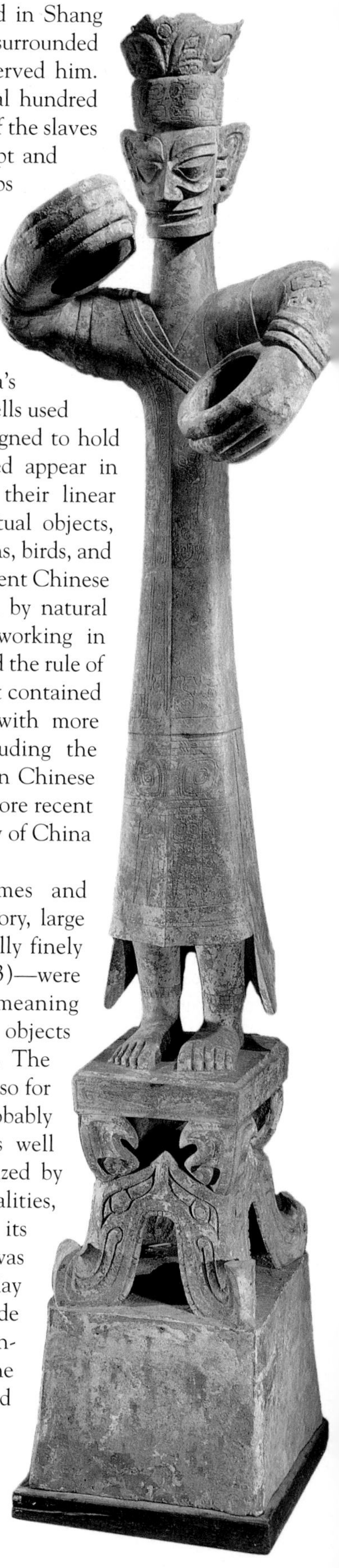

Figure 3.5 Standing figure, late Shang dynasty, ca. 1300–1100 B.C.E., from Pit 2 at Sanxingdui, Guanghan, Sichuan Province. Bronze, height 8 ft. 7 in.

Figure 3.6 Shroud, from the tomb of Liu Sheng at Lingshan, Mancheng, Hebei Province, Han dynasty, 206 B.C.E.–24 C.E. Jade and gold wire, length 6 ft. 2 in.

were encased with shrouds made up of thousands of carved jade plaques sewn with gold wire (Figure 3.6).

The Zhou Dynasty (1027–256 B.C.E.)

The sacred right to rule was known in China as the *Mandate of Heaven*. Although the notion of divine-right kingship began in the earliest centuries of China's dynasties, the concept of a divine mandate was not fixed until early in the Zhou era, when the rebel Zhou tribe justified their assault on the Shang by claiming that Shang kings had failed to rule virtuously; hence, Heaven had withdrawn its mandate. Charged with maintaining the will of heaven on earth, the king's political authority required obedience to pre-established moral law, which, in turn reflected the natural order.

According to the Chinese, the natural order—a holistic and primordial arrangement in nature—determined human intelligence and ability, as well as the individual's proper place in society. Within the natural hierarchy, those with greater intellectual abilities should govern, and those with lesser abilities should fulfill the physical needs of the state. Exactly how those with greater abilities were distinguished from those with lesser abilities is difficult to discern. Nevertheless, between the twelfth and eighth centuries B.C.E., when the Zhou kings controlled most of civilized China, the principle of the natural hierarchy already provided the basis for China's political and social hierarchy. Since the Zhou rulers delegated local authority to aristocrats of their choosing, it is probable that the assumptions of superiority and inferiority among people came after the fact of a division of labor among the members of society. Nevertheless, well before the second century B.C.E., the Chinese put into practice the world's first system whereby individuals were selected for government service on the basis of merit and education. Written examinations tested the competence and skill of those who sought government office. Such a system persisted for centuries and became the basis for an aristocracy of merit that has characterized Chinese culture well into modern times.

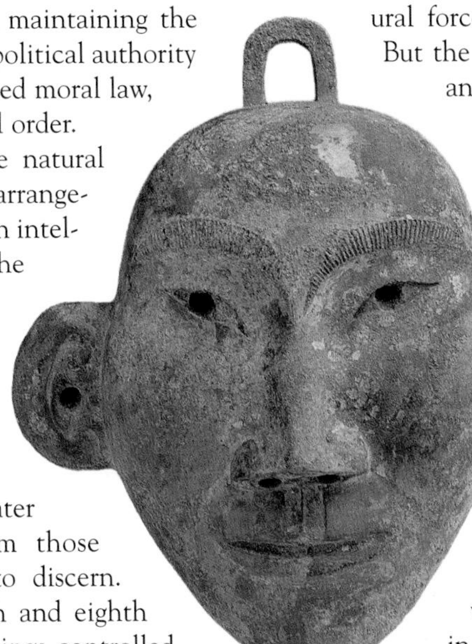

Spirits, Gods, and the Natural Order

The agricultural communities of ancient China venerated an assortment of local spirits associated with the natural forces, and with rivers, mountains, and crops. But the most powerful of the personalized spirits of ancient China were those of deceased ancestors, the members of an extended familial community (Figure 3.7). According to the Chinese, the spirits of deceased ancestors continued to exist in Heaven, where they assumed their role as mediators between Heaven and Earth. Since the ancestors exerted a direct influence upon human affairs, their eternal welfare was of deep concern to ancient Chinese families. They buried the dead in richly furnished tombs, regularly made sacrifices to them, and brought offerings of food and wine to their graves. One of the earliest odes in China's classic *Book of Songs* (*Shi jing*) celebrates the veneration of ancestors of both sexes:

Rich is the year with much millet and rice;
And we have tall granaries
With hundreds and thousands and millions of sheaves.
We make wind and sweet spirits
And offer them to our ancestors, male and female;
Thus to fulfill all the rites
And bring down blessings in full.*

Figure 3.7 Mask, Shang dynasty, ca. 1500–1600 B.C.E. Bronze, life-sized. Academia Sinica, Taipei.

*From William Theodore de Bry, and others, eds. *Sources of Chinese Tradition* (New York: Colombia University Press, 1960), 15.

The dead and the living shared a cosmos animated by nature and regulated by the natural order. In the regularity of the seasonal cycle, the growth of trees and plants, and the everyday workings of nature, the Chinese found harmony and order. The natural order might be symbolized by way of abstract symbols, such as the circle, but it was also worshiped in the form of nature spirits and celestial deities. The creative principle, for instance, was known interchangeably as the Lord on High (Shang-di) and, more abstractly, as Heaven (Tian). Although not an anthropomorphic deity of the kind found in ancient Egypt and Mesopotamia, Shang-di/Tian regulated the workings of the universe and impartially guided the destinies of all people. For the Chinese, the cosmic and human order was a single sacred system. This holistic viewpoint identified *qi* (pronounced "chee") as the substance of the universe and, thus, the vital energy that pervades the human body. An understanding of nature's order was deemed essential to the well-being of both the individual and the ancient Chinese community; hence, it became the job of a special group of priests to examine that order and to divine (or foretell) the future. Shang diviners inscribed questions—whether the harvest would be bountiful, whether to make war, and so on—on tortoise shells and animal bones. The bones were heated to produce cracks that the diviners might read and interpret. For modern-day scholars, the bones offer information about the ceremonies, wars, and administrative life of Shang rulers; they also reveal fascinating details about weather, disease, and many other routine topics. Inscriptions on oracle bones dating from between ca. 1500 and 1000 B.C.E. constitute some of the earliest examples of Chinese writing (Figure **3.8**).

The ancient Chinese perception of an inviolable natural order dominated all aspects of China's long his-tory. Unlike the civilizations of ancient Egypt and Mesopotamia, no great heroic epic survives from ancient China. China's oldest known text, *The Book of Changes (I jing)*, is a directory for interpreting the operations of the universe. *The Book of Changes*, which originated in the Shang era but was not recorded until the sixth century B.C.E., consists of cryptic symbols and commentaries on which diviners drew to predict the future. Order derived from the balance between the four seasons, the five elements (wood, fire, earth, metal, and water), and the five powers of creation (cold, heat, dryness, moisture, and wind). Cosmological diagrams featuring the square and the circle are inscribed on Chinese bronzes. And Chinese mythology described cosmic unity in terms of the marriage

Figure 3.8 Inscribed oracle bone, China, ca. 1500–1000 B.C.E. 7 x 4½ in. C. V. Starr. East Asian Library, Columbia University.

of Tian (the creative principle, or Heaven) and Kun (the receptive principle, or Earth). Signifying the order of nature most graphically, however, is the cosmological metaphor of the *yin/yang*. This principle, which ancient Chinese emperors called "the foundation of the entire universe," interprets all nature as the dynamic product of two interacting cosmic forces, or modes of energy, commonly configured as twin interpenetrating shapes enclosed within a circle (Figure **3.9**). The interaction of yang, the male principle (associated with lightness, hardness, brightness, warmth, and the sun) and yin, the female principle (associated with darkness, softness, moisture, coolness, the earth, and the moon) describes the creative energy of the universe and the natural order itself. For the Chinese, this order is inherent in the balance between the forces of hot and cold, day and night, heaven and earth, male and female, and so on. In the circle, a figure with no beginning or end, and the ring or disk, which unifies positive form and negative space, the complementary polarities of *yin/yang* are implicit. Perhaps, then, the jade disks found in such great numbers in Chinese graves served as cosmic talismans.

Figure 3.9 The yin and the yang as interpenetrating shapes in a circle.

Daoism

The most eloquent expression of the natural order as it relates to humankind is preserved in the ancient Chinese belief system known as Daoism. As much a philosophy as a religion, Daoism embraces a universal and natural principle—the Dao, or "Way." While the Dao is ineffable—indeed, it resists all intellectual analysis—it manifests itself in the harmony of things. It may be thought of as the unity underlying nature's multiplicity; and it is understood only by those who live in total simplicity and in harmony with nature. Daoists seek to cultivate tranquility, spontaneity, compassion, and spiritual insight. Like the Hindu, the Daoist practices meditation and breath control, along with dietary and other physical means of prolonging and enriching life.

Daoism existed in China as early as 1000 B.C.E., but its basic text, the *Dao de jing* (*The Way and Its Power*), did not appear until the sixth century B.C.E. This modest "scripture" of some 5000 words is associated with the name Lao Zi ("the Old One"), who may or may not have ever actually existed. The following poem, one of the eighty-one chapters of the *Dao de jing*, conveys the Daoist idea of nature's unity. It uses a series of simple images to illustrate the complementary and harmonious function of positive and negative elements in ordinary things, as in nature. Like all Daoist teaching, it relies on subtle wit and paradox as springboards to enlightenment.

READING 1.10 From the Dao de jing (ca. 550 B.C.E.)

Thirty spokes will converge	1
In the hub of a wheel;	
But the use of the cart	
Will depend on the part	
Of the hub that is void.	5
With a wall all around	
A clay bowl is molded;	
But the use of the bowl	
Will depend on the part	
Of the bowl that is void.	10
Cut out windows and doors	
In the house as you build;	
But the use of the house	
Will depend on the space	
In the walls that is void.	15
So advantage is had	
From whatever is there;	
But usefulness rises	
From whatever is not.	

 Q What images in this poem convey the idea of the Dao as a unity of opposites?

SUMMARY

India's first civilization, the Bronze Age culture at Mohenjo-daro, was overturned by the Aryans, who introduced the principal features of ancient Indian society: the caste system, epic poetry, India's earliest religious texts, and the religion known as Hinduism. Hinduism is a pantheistic faith that perceives all nature as an expression of the Absolute One or Brahman. Ancient Hindus viewed the life of the individual as one with, rather than subject to, an impersonal divine force. They sought the sublimation of the Self by means of meditation and a stilling of the senses. Achieving nirvana permitted the Hindu to escape the Wheel of Rebirth. To this day, Hinduism retains its holistic character and has remained relatively unaffected by Western religious precepts.

In ancient China, concepts of social and spiritual harmony were deeply rooted in the idea of an order governed by nature, rather than by individual and personal gods. The leaders of China's earliest dynasties ruled by the *Mandate of Heaven*, which enforced the order of heaven on earth. As in Egypt, China's kings were buried in elaborately furnished graves whose contents reflect a high level of artistic achievement. A holistic world view linked the realm of the dead with all living descendants. For the Chinese, the natural order was inseparable from the moral and social order; it governed China's doctrines of natural equality and justified its system of advancement based on merit. It also generated the school of thought known as Daoism, the way of nature. China's earliest dynasties established the foundations for a unified culture whose fundamental ideas and values endure well into our own time.

GLOSSARY

Atman the Hindu name for the Self; the personal part of Brahman

Brahman the Hindu name for the Absolute Spirit; an impersonal World Soul that pervades all things

caste system a rigid social stratification in India based on differences in wealth, rank, or occupation

karma (Sanskrit, "deed") the law that holds that one's deeds determine one's future life in the Wheel of Rebirth

nirvana (Sanskrit, "liberation" or "extinction") the blissful reabsorption of the Self into the Absolute Spirit (Brahman): release from the endless cycle of rebirth (see also Buddhism, chapters 8, 9)

pantheism the belief that a divine spirit pervades all things in the universe

qi (Chinese, "substance" or "breath") the material substance or vital force of the universe

yoga (Sanskrit, "to yoke or join") a system of spiritual exercises aimed at joining the Self and the One through control of mind and body

PART 2

The Classical Legacy

Between 500 B.C.E. and 500 C.E., the civilizations of ancient Greece and Rome came to flower in the Mediterranean world. Their influence on the humanistic tradition was both profound and long-lasting, far exceeding that of any culture preceding them. To the civilizations of Greece and Rome the West owes the refinement of almost all of the basic forms of literary expression (including drama, the epistle, lyric poetry, satire, and historical narrative), the fundamentals of philosophic and scientific inquiry, the development of civil and judicial law, and the formulation of aesthetic norms in art and music that have persisted for well over a thousand years.

Greek civilization emerged at the western end of the Asian landmass, north and west of the ancient civilizations of Egypt and Mesopotamia. Between 1200 and 750 B.C.E., the first Greek city-states appeared on the islands and peninsulas in the Aegean Sea, the coast of Asia Minor, at the southern tip of Italy, and in Sicily. This ancient civilization called itself "Hellas" and its people "Hellenes" (the name "Greece" derives from the Latin *Graecus*). During and just after the Golden Age, the Hellenic city-states produced some of the most engaging works of art, literature, and philosophy in the history of culture. Hellenic culture would not die with the fall of Greece in 338 B.C.E.; rather, by way of the imperial ambitions of Alexander the Great, it would permeate all of Asia, generating a Greek-like, or Hellenistic, era. And well into the period of Roman dominance in the Mediterranean, the legacy of Greece would continue to influence the history of culture.

While Greek culture was savoring its Golden Age, Rome was establishing itself as the leading city-state of the Italian peninsula. Rome's history is usually divided into two phases: the Republic (509–31 B.C.E.) and the Empire (31 B.C.E.–476 C.E.). The Romans created the largest and most powerful empire in the ancient world. Their achievements in engineering, architecture, literature, and law would be imitated in the West long after the collapse of Rome itself. Moreover, Roman civilization would transmit westward the legacy of classical Greek culture as well as the fundamentals of a young religious faith called Christianity.

Because the civilizations of Greece and Rome have provided authoritative models in the arts and ideas of the West, they are called "classical," and the age in which they flourished is known as the Classical Age. The word "classical," however, is used in several ways. Most generally, the words "classic" and "classical" mean first-rate, enduring, the best of its kind. So, classic cars refer to vintage automobiles, and classic films are those that attract generation after generation of viewers. In this usage, "classic" implies lasting quality. The term "classical" is also used to designate the characteristic phase of a culture or civilization, especially if that phase has had an enduring influence on subsequent cultures. Finally, the word "classical" is used stylistically: it describes the mode of expression characterized by the principles of clarity, harmony, balance, simplicity (or moderation), and refinement, which came to its peak in Golden Age Greece, the fifth century B.C.E.

Between 500 B.C.E. and 500 C.E., yet another great classical culture came to flower. Emerging as a rich and populous empire, China developed a body of learning and a legacy in the arts that would endure for thousands of years. The era of the Han (ca. 200 B.C.E. to 200 C.E.) is regarded as China's Classical Age. As the legacy of the Greco-Roman culture shaped the destiny of the West, so that of China prevailed to mold the culture of East Asia.

(opposite) Myron, *Discobolus (Discus Thrower)*, reconstructed Roman marble copy of a bronze Greek original of ca. 450 B.C.E. Height 5 ft. 1 in. Museo Nazionale delle Terme, Rome. Photo: © Vincenzo Pirozzi, Rome fotopirozzi@inwind.it.

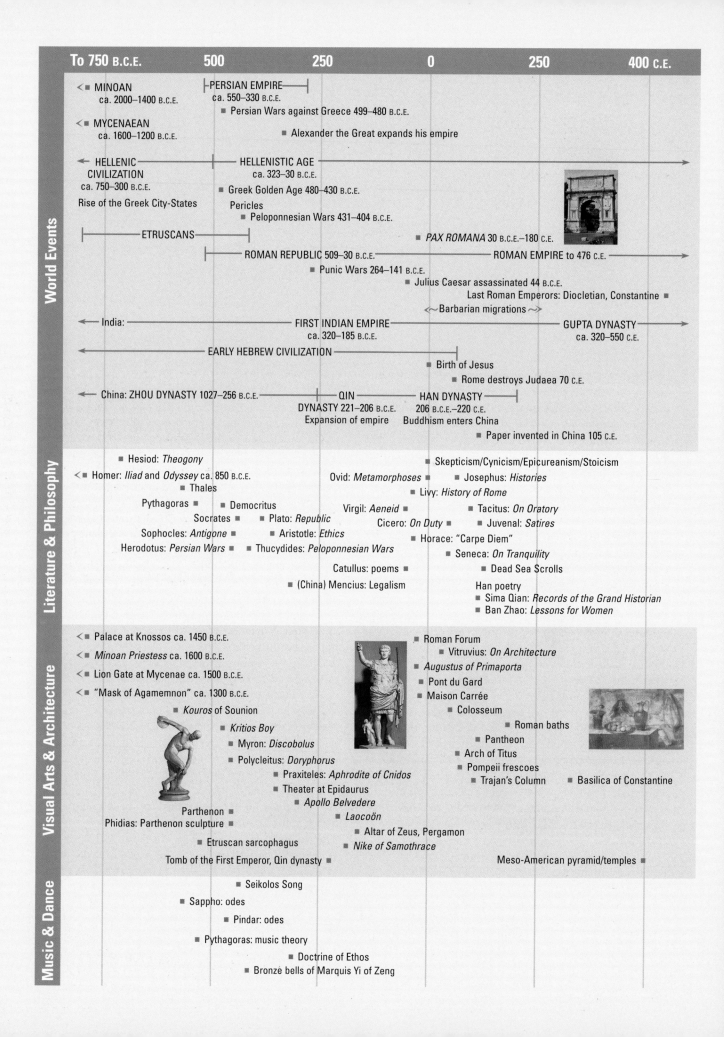

To 750 B.C.E.   500   250   0   250   400 C.E.

World Events

◄ ■ MINOAN ca. 2000–1400 B.C.E.

├ PERSIAN EMPIRE ┤ ca. 550–330 B.C.E.

■ Persian Wars against Greece 499–480 B.C.E.

◄ ■ MYCENAEAN ca. 1600–1200 B.C.E.

■ Alexander the Great expands his empire

◄— HELLENIC CIVILIZATION ca. 750–300 B.C.E.

Rise of the Greek City-States

HELLENISTIC AGE ca. 323–30 B.C.E. —►

■ Greek Golden Age 480–430 B.C.E.

Pericles

■ Peloponnesian Wars 431–404 B.C.E.

├— ETRUSCANS —┤

■ *PAX ROMANA* 30 B.C.E.–180 C.E.

├— ROMAN REPUBLIC 509–30 B.C.E. —┤   ROMAN EMPIRE to 476 C.E. —►

■ Punic Wars 264–141 B.C.E.

■ Julius Caesar assassinated 44 B.C.E.

■ Last Roman Emperors: Diocletian, Constantine ■

◄— Barbarian migrations —►

◄— India: ——— FIRST INDIAN EMPIRE ca. 320–185 B.C.E. ——— GUPTA DYNASTY ca. 320–550 C.E. —►

◄— EARLY HEBREW CIVILIZATION ———

■ Birth of Jesus

■ Rome destroys Judaea 70 C.E.

◄— China: ZHOU DYNASTY 1027–256 B.C.E. —

QIN DYNASTY 221–206 B.C.E.
Expansion of empire

HAN DYNASTY 206 B.C.E.–220 C.E.
Buddhism enters China

■ Paper invented in China 105 C.E.

Literature & Philosophy

■ Hesiod: *Theogony*

■ Skepticism/Cynicism/Epicureanism/Stoicism

◄ ■ Homer: *Iliad* and *Odyssey* ca. 850 B.C.E.

Ovid: *Metamorphoses* ■   ■ Josephus: *Histories*

■ Thales

■ Livy: *History of Rome*

Pythagoras ■   ■ Democritus

Virgil: *Aeneid* ■   ■ Tacitus: *On Oratory*

Socrates ■   ■ Plato: *Republic*

Cicero: *On Duty* ■   ■ Juvenal: *Satires*

Sophocles: *Antigone* ■   ■ Aristotle: *Ethics*

■ Horace: "Carpe Diem"

Herodotus: *Persian Wars* ■   ■ Thucydides: *Peloponnesian Wars*

■ Seneca: *On Tranquility*

Catullus: poems ■   ■ Dead Sea Scrolls

■ (China) Mencius: Legalism

Han poetry
■ Sima Qian: *Records of the Grand Historian*
■ Ban Zhao: *Lessons for Women*

Visual Arts & Architecture

◄ ■ Palace at Knossos ca. 1450 B.C.E.

■ Roman Forum

◄ ■ *Minoan Priestess* ca. 1600 B.C.E.

■ Vitruvius: *On Architecture*

◄ ■ Lion Gate at Mycenae ca. 1500 B.C.E.

■ *Augustus of Primaporta*

◄ ■ "Mask of Agamemnon" ca. 1300 B.C.E.

■ Pont du Gard

■ *Kouros* of Sounion

■ Maison Carrée

■ *Kritios Boy*

■ Colosseum

■ Myron: *Discobolus*

■ Roman baths

■ Polycleitus: *Doryphorus*

■ Pantheon

■ Praxiteles: *Aphrodite of Cnidos*

■ Arch of Titus

■ Theater at Epidaurus

■ Pompeii frescoes

■ *Apollo Belvedere*

■ Trajan's Column   ■ Basilica of Constantine

Parthenon ■
Phidias: Parthenon sculpture ■

■ *Laocoön*

■ Altar of Zeus, Pergamon

■ Etruscan sarcophagus

■ *Nike of Samothrace*

Tomb of the First Emperor, Qin dynasty ■

Meso-American pyramid/temples ■

Music & Dance

■ Seikolos Song

■ Sappho: odes

■ Pindar: odes

■ Pythagoras: music theory

■ Doctrine of Ethos

■ Bronze bells of Marquis Yi of Zeng

CHAPTER 4

Greece: Humanism and the Speculative Leap

"I say that Athens is the school of Hellas, and that the individual Athenian in his own person seems to have the power of adapting himself to the most varied forms of action with the utmost versatility and grace."
Thucydides

The nineteenth-century British poet Percy Bysshe Shelley once proclaimed, "We are all Greeks." He meant by this that modern humankind—profoundly influenced by Hellenic notions of reason, beauty, and the good life—bears the stamp of ancient Greece. Few civilizations have been so deeply concerned with the quality of human life as that of the ancient Greeks. And few have been so committed to the role of the individual intellect in shaping the destiny of the community. Because their art, their literature, and their religious beliefs celebrate human interests and concerns, the Greeks have been called the humanists of the ancient world. The worldliness and robust optimism that marks Hellenic culture is apparent even in the formative stages of Greek civilization.

Bronze Age Civilizations of the Aegean (ca. 3000–1200 B.C.E.)

The Bronze Age culture of Mycenae was not known to the world until the late nineteenth century, when an amateur German archeologist named Heinrich Schliemann uncovered the first artifacts of ancient Troy (Map **4.1**). Schliemann's excavations brought to light the civilization of an adventuresome tribal people, the Mycenaeans, who had established themselves on the Greek mainland around 1600 B.C.E. Subsequent discoveries by other archeologists disclosed an even earlier pre-Greek civilization located on the island of Crete in the Aegean Sea. Named Minoan

Map 4.1 Ancient Greece.

Figure 4.1 Palace of Minos, Knossos, Crete, ca. 1500 B.C.E. Photo: Gloria K. Fiero.

after the legendary King Minos, this maritime civilization flourished between 2000 and 1400 B.C.E., when it seems to have been absorbed or destroyed by the Mycenaeans.

Minoan Civilization (ca. 2000–1400 B.C.E.)

Centered in the Palace of Minos at Knossos on the island of Crete (Figure **4.1**), Minoan culture was prosperous and seafaring. The absence of protective walls around

the palace complex suggests that the Minoans enjoyed a sense of security. The three-story palace at Knossos was a labyrinthine masonry structure with dozens of rooms and corridors built around a central courtyard. The interior walls of the palace bear magnificent frescoes illustrating natural and marine motifs (Figure **4.2**), ceremonial processions, and other aspects of Cretan life. The most famous of the palace frescoes, the so-called "bull-leaping" fresco,

Figure 4.2 The Queen's Quarters, Palace of Minos, Knossos, Crete, ca. 1450 B.C.E. Ancient Art and Architecture Collection, Middlesex.

Figure 4.3 Bull-leaping fresco from the Palace of Minos, Knossos, Crete, ca. 1500 B.C.E. Height 32 in. Archeological Museum, Heraklion, Crete. Scala, Florence.

Figure 4.4 Priestess with snakes, Minoan, ca. 1600 B.C.E. Faience, height 13½ in. Archeological Museum, Heraklion, Crete. Photo: © Craig & Marie Mauzy, Athens.

shows two women and a man, the latter vigorously somersaulting over the back of a bull (Figure **4.3**). Probably associated with the cult of the bull—ancient symbol of virility (see Figures 1.3 and 2.15)—the ritual game prefigures the modern bullfight, the "rules" of which were codified in Roman times by Julius Caesar. Since 1979, when modern archeologists uncovered the evidence of human sacrifice in Minoan Crete, historians have speculated on the meaning of ancient bull-vaulting (a sport still practiced in Portugal), and its possible relationship to rituals of blood sacrifice. Nevertheless, the significance of the representation lies in the authority it bestows upon the players: human beings are pictured here not as pawns in a divine game, but, rather, as challengers in a contest of wit and physical agility. Other Minoan artifacts suggest the persistence of ancient fertility cults honoring gods traditionally associated with procreation: the small statue of a bare-breasted female brandishing snakes may represent a popular fertility goddess; or it may depict a priestess performing specific cult rites, such as those accompanying ancient Greek dances that featured live snakes (Figure **4.4**). Minoan writing (known as "Linear A") has not yet been deciphered, but a later version of the script ("Linear B") found on mainland Greece appears to be an early form of Greek. Modern archeologists were not the first to prize Minoan culture; the Greeks immortalized the Minoans in myth and legend. The most famous of these legends describes a Minotaur—a monstrous half-man, half-bull hybrid born of the union of Minos' queen and a sacred white bull. According to the story, the clever Athenian hero Theseus, aided by the king's daughter Ariadne, threaded his way through the Minotaur's labyrinthine lair to kill the monster, thus freeing Athens from its ancient bondage to the Minoans. Around 1700 B.C.E., some three centuries before mainland Greece absorbed Crete, an earthquake brought devastation to Minoan civilization.

Mycenaean Civilization (ca. 1600–1200 B.C.E.)

By 1600 B.C.E., the Mycenaeans had established themselves in the Aegean. By contrast with the Minoans, the Mycenaeans were a militant and aggressive people: their warships challenged other traders for control of the eastern Mediterranean. On mainland Greece at Tiryns and Mycenae (see Map 4.1), the Mycenaeans constructed heavily fortified citadels and walls so massive that later generations thought they had been built by a mythical race of giants known as the Cyclops. These "cyclopean" walls were guarded by symbols of royal power: in the triangular arch above the entrance gate to the citadel, two 9-foot-high stone lions flank a column that rests on a stone altar (Figure **4.5**). Master stonemasons, the Mycenaeans buried their rulers in beehive-shaped tombs. The royal graves, uncovered by Schliemann in 1876, are filled with weapons and jewelry fit for an Egyptian pharaoh. These items, and in particular the gold death mask that once covered the face of the deceased, Schliemann identified as belonging to Agamemnon (Figure **4.6**), the legendary king who led the ancient Greeks against the city of Troy. This tale is immortalized in the first of the Greek epic poems, the *Iliad*. Although later archeologists have proved Schliemann wrong—the tombs are earlier than he thought—the legends and the myths of the Greek world would flower in Mycenaean soil.

Around 1200 B.C.E., the Mycenaeans attacked Troy ("Ilion" in Greek), a commercial stronghold on the northwest coast of Asia Minor. The ten-year-long war between Mycenae and Troy would provide the historical context for the two great epic poems of the ancient Greeks: the *Iliad* and the *Odyssey*.

The Heroic Age (ca. 1200–750 B.C.E.)

Soon after 1200 B.C.E., more powerful, iron-bearing tribes of Dorians, a Greek-speaking people from the north, destroyed Mycenaean civilization. During the long period of darkness that followed, storytellers kept alive the history of early Greece, the adventures of the Mycenaeans, and the tales of the Trojan War, passing them orally from generation to generation. It was not until at least the ninth century B.C.E that these stories were transcribed; and it was yet another three hundred years before they reached their present form. The *Iliad* and the *Odyssey* became the "national" poems of ancient Greece, uniting Greek-speaking people by giving literary authority to their common heritage. Although much of what is known about the early history of the Greeks comes from these epic poems, little is known about the blind poet

Figure 4.5 Lion Gate, Citadel at Mycenae, ca. 1500–1300 B.C.E. Limestone, height of relief 9 ft. 6 in. Photo: © Craig & Marie Mauzy, Athens.

Figure 4.6 Funerary mask, possibly of Agamemnon, ca. 1500 B.C.E. Gold, height 12 in. National Archeological Museum, Athens. Photo: © Craig & Marie Mauzy, Athens.

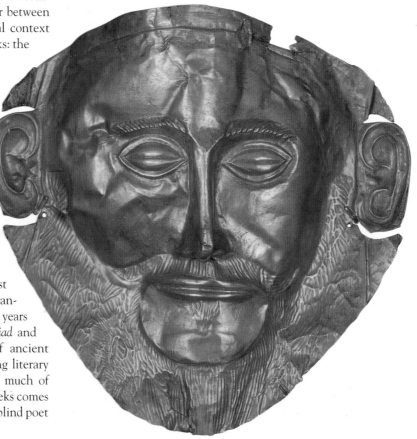

Homer, to whom they are traditionally attributed. Scholars are not sure when or where he lived, or, indeed, if he existed at all. It is unlikely that he composed the poems, though legend has it that he actually memorized the whole of each poem. The only fact of which we can be fairly certain is that Homer represents the culmination of a long and vigorous tradition in which oral recitation—possibly to instrumental accompaniment—was a popular kind of entertainment.

The *Iliad* takes place in the last days of the Trojan War. It is the story of the Achaean (ancient Greek) hero Achilles (or Achilleus), who, moved to anger by an affront to his honor, refuses to join the battle against Troy alongside his Achaean comrades. However, when his dearest friend Patroclus is killed by Hector (leader of the Trojan forces), Achilles finally and vengefully goes to war. The *Odyssey*, the second of the two epics, recounts the long, adventure-packed sea journey undertaken by Odysseus, a resourceful hero of the Trojan War, in his effort to return to his home and family in Ithaca. Like the *Epic of Gilgamesh*, the *Iliad* and the *Odyssey* belong to the oral tradition of a heroic age, but whereas the *Epic of Gilgamesh* takes as its theme the pursuit of everlasting life, the Greek epics give voice to the quest for individual honor and glory.

The *Iliad* is a robust tale of war, but its true subject is the personality of Achilles as he attempts to reconcile selfhood and communal responsibility. Achilles is the offspring of Peleus, King of Thessaly, and the sea nymph Thetis, who had dipped her infant son in the river Styx, thus making him invulnerable except for the heel by which she held him. Like Gilgamesh, Achilles is part-god and part-man, but the Greek superhero is a more psychologically complex character than Gilgamesh; the emotions he exhibits—anger, love, rage, and grief—are wholly human. The plot of the *Iliad* turns on Achilles' decision to take action that will bring glory to his tribe and to himself. The importance of heroic action in proving virtue, or excellence (the Greek word *arete* connotes both), is central to the *Iliad* and to the male-dominated culture of the Heroic Age. To the ancient Greeks, moral value lay in proper action, even if the consequence of that action meant death (Figure **4.7**). Indeed, death in battle was a sure path to honor.

The language of the *Iliad*, no less than its theme, is charged with heroic vigor. It makes use of vivid similes (anger "blinds like smoke"), graphic **epithets** ("the bronze-armed Achaeans"), and lengthy **catalogs** of particulars. Both in its almost 16,000 lines of majestic poetry and for its heroic personalities, the *Iliad* has inspired generations of Western writers, including Virgil and Milton (to be discussed in later chapters). The following excerpts from the *Iliad*, rendered in a 1990 translation by Robert Fagles, illustrate the qualities that have made the work a classic.

Figure 4.7 Attr. The "Botkin Class" painter, *Contest of Two Warriors*, ca. 540-530 B.C.E. Attic black-figured amphora, terracotta, 11½ × 9½ in. Museum of Fine Arts, Boston, Henry Lillie Pierce Fund. Photograph © 2006 Museum of Fine Arts, Boston.

READING 1.11 From the *Iliad* (ca. 850 B.C.E.)

(Book 18, ll. 1–42, 82–150; Book 19, ll. 423–477; Book 24, ll. 471–707)

So the men fought on like a mass of whirling fire   1
as swift Antilochus raced the message toward Achilles.
Sheltered under his curving, beaked ships he found him,
foreboding, deep down, all that had come to pass.
Agonizing now he probed his own great heart: 5
"Why, why? Our long-haired Achaeans[1] routed again,
driven in terror off the plain to crowd the ships, but why?
Dear gods, don't bring to pass the grief that haunts my
      heart—
the prophecy that mother revealed to me one time . . .
she said the best of the Myrmidons[2]—while I lived—   10
would fall at Trojan hands and leave the light of day.
And now he's dead, I know it: Menoetius' gallant son,[3]
my headstrong friend! And I told Patroclus clearly,
'Once you have beaten off the lethal fire, quick,
come back to the ships—you must not battle Hector!'"   15

---

[1]The Mycenaeans, who inhabited the kingdom near Thessaly, and, more broadly, the Greek army that besieged Troy.
[2]The name by which the subject warriors of Peleus and Achilles are known in Homer. It derives from the Greek word for ants, the creatures out of which Zeus was said to have created the inhabitants of the island of Aegina, ruled by Peleus.
[3]Patroclus, Achilles' favorite companion and friend.

As such fears went churning through his mind
the warlord Nestor's son drew near him now,
streaming warm tears, to give the dreaded message:
"Ah son of royal Peleus, what you must hear from me!
What painful news—would to god it had never happened!   20
Patroclus has fallen. They're fighting over his corpse.
He's stripped, naked—Hector with that flashing helmet,
Hector has your arms!"
                                        So the captain reported.
A black cloud of grief came shrouding over Achilles.
Both hands clawing the ground for soot and filth,   25
he poured it over his head, fouled his handsome face
and black ashes settled onto his fresh clean war-shirt.
Overpowered in all his power, he sprawled in the dust.
Achilles lay there, fallen . . .
tearing his hair, defiling it with his own hands.   30
And the women he and Patroclus carried off as captives
caught the grief in their hearts and keened and wailed,
out of the tents they ran to ring the great Achilles,
all of them beat their breasts with clenched fists,
sank to the ground, each woman's knees gave way.   35
Antilochus kneeling near, weeping uncontrollably,
clutched Achilles' hands as he wept his proud heart out—
for fear he would slash his throat with an iron blade.
Achilles suddenly loosed a terrible, wrenching cry
and his noble mother heard him, seated near her father,   40
the Old Man of the Sea[4] in the salt green depths,
and she cried out in turn.

              ·   ·   ·   ·   ·   ·   ·   ·   ·

As he groaned from the depths his mother rose before him
and sobbing a sharp cry, cradled her son's head in her hands
and her words were all compassion, winging pity: "My child—   45
why in tears? What sorrow has touched your heart?
Tell me, please. Don't harbor it deep inside you.
Zeus has accomplished everything you wanted,
just as you raised your hands and prayed that day.
All the sons of Achaea are pinned against the ships   50
and all for want of you—they suffer shattering losses."

     And groaning deeply the matchless runner answered,
"O dear mother, true! All those burning desires
Olympian Zeus has brought to pass for me—
but what joy to me now? My dear comrade's dead—   55
Patroclus—the man I loved beyond all other comrades,
loved as my own life—I've lost him—Hector's killed him,
stripped the gigantic armor off his back, a marvel to behold—
my burnished gear! Radiant gifts the gods presented Peleus
that day they drove you into a mortal's marriage bed . . .   60
I wish you'd lingered deep with the deathless sea-nymphs,
lived at ease, and Peleus carried home a mortal bride.
But now, as it is, sorrows, unending sorrows must surge
within your heart as well—for your own son's death.
Never again will you embrace him striding home.   65
My spirits rebel—I've lost the will to live,
to take my stand in the world of men—unless,
before all else, Hector's battered down by my spear

and gasps away his life, the blood-price for Patroclus,
Menoetius' gallant son he's killed and stripped!"   70

     But Thetis answered, warning through her tears,
"You're doomed to a short life, my son, from all you say!
For hard on the heels of Hector's death your death
must come at once—"
                    "Then let me die at once"—
Achilles burst out, despairing—"since it was not my fate   75
to save my dearest comrade from his death! Look,
a world away from his fatherland he's perished,
lacking me, my fighting strength, to defend him.
But now, since I shall not return to my fatherland . . .
nor did I bring one ray of hope to my Patroclus,   80
nor to the rest of all my steadfast comrades,
countless ranks struck down by mighty Hector—
No, no, here I sit by the ships . . .
a useless, dead weight on the good green earth—
I, no man my equal among the bronze-armed Achaeans,   85
not in battle, only in wars of words that others win.
If only strife could die from the lives of gods and men
and anger that drives the sanest man to flare in outrage—
bitter gall, sweeter than dripping streams of honey,
that swarms in people's chests and blinds like smoke—   90
just like the anger Agamemnon[5] king of men
has roused within me now . . .
                    Enough.
Let bygones be bygones. Done is done.
Despite my anguish I will beat it down,
the fury mounting inside me, down by force.   95
But now I'll go and meet that murderer head-on,
that Hector who destroyed the dearest life I know.
For my own death, I'll meet it freely—whenever Zeus
and the other deathless gods would like to bring it on!
Not even Heracles fled his death, for all his power,   100
favorite son as he was to father Zeus the King.
Fate crushed him, and Hera's savage anger.
And I too, if the same fate waits for me . . .
I'll lie in peace, once I've gone down to death.
But now, for the moment, let me seize great glory!—   105
and drive some woman of Troy or deep-breasted Dardan
to claw with both hands at her tender cheeks and wipe away
her burning tears as the sobs come choking from her throat—
they'll learn that I refrained from war a good long time!
Don't try to hold me back from the fighting, mother,   110
love me as you do. You can't persuade me now."

              ·   ·   ·   ·   ·   ·   ·   ·   ·

[Hephaestus (Hephaistos), god of fire and of metalworking,
has forged a special set of arms for Achilles. In the following
lines from Book 19, Achilles prepares to lead the Achaeans
into battle.]

Thick-and-fast as the snow comes swirling down from Zeus,
frozen sharp when the North Wind born in heaven blasts it
              on—
so massed, so dense the glistening burnished helmets shone,

---

[4]A sea god, the "Old Man" of the sea and father of some fifty to one
hundred daughters, including Thetis, mother of Achilles.

---

[5]King of Mycenae, who led the Greek forces in the Trojan War.

streaming out of the ships, and shields with jutting bosses,   115
breastplates welded front and back and the long ashen spears.
The glory of armor lit the skies and the whole earth laughed,
rippling under the glitter of bronze, thunder resounding
under trampling feet of armies. And in their midst
the brilliant Achilles began to arm for battle . . .   120
A sound of grinding came from the fighter's teeth,
his eyes blazed forth in searing points of fire,
unbearable grief came surging through his heart
and now, bursting with rage against the men of Troy,
he donned Hephaestus' gifts—magnificent armor   125
the god of fire forged with all his labor.
First he wrapped his legs with well-made greaves,
fastened behind his heels with silver ankle-clasps,
next he strapped the breastplate round his chest
then over his shoulder Achilles slung his sword,   130
the fine bronze blade with its silver-studded hilt,
then hoisted the massive shield flashing far and wide
like a full round moon—and gleaming bright as the light
that reaches sailors out at sea, the flare of a watchfire
burning strong in a lonely sheepfold up some mountain slope   135
when the gale-winds hurl the crew that fights against them
far over the fish-swarming sea, far from loved ones—
so the gleam from Achilles' well-wrought blazoned shield
shot up and hit the skies. Then lifting his rugged helmet
he set it down on his brows, and the horsehair crest   140
shone like a star and the waving golden plumes shook
that Hephaestus drove in bristling thick along its ridge.
And brilliant Achilles tested himself in all his gear,
Achilles spun on his heels to see if it fit tightly,
see if his shining limbs ran free within it, yes,   145
and it felt like buoyant wings lifting the great captain.
And then, last, Achilles drew his father's spear
from its socket-stand—weighted, heavy, tough.
No other Achaean fighter could heft that shaft,
only Achilles had the skill to wield it well;   150
Pelian ash it was, a gift to his father Peleus
presented by Chiron[6] once, hewn on Pelion's crest
to be the death of heroes.
                    Now the war-team—
Alcimus and Automedon worked to yoke them quickly.
They clinched the supple breast-straps round their chests   155
and driving the bridle irons home between their jaws,
pulled the reins back taut to the bolted chariot.
Seizing a glinting whip, his fist on the handgrip,
Automedon leapt aboard behind the team and behind him
Achilles struck his stance, helmed for battle now,   160
glittering in his armor like the sun astride the skies,
his ringing, daunting voice commanding his father's horses:
"Roan Beauty and Charger, illustrious foals of Lightfoot!
Try hard, do better this time—bring your charioteer
back home alive to his waiting Argive comrades   165
once we're through with fighting. Don't leave Achilles
there on the battlefield as you left Patroclus—dead!"

                    . . . .

---

[6]A centaur (half-man, half-horse), one of the creatures driven from
Mount Pelion by the Lapiths (see Figure 5.22).

[After Achilles defeats Hector, Priam, Hector's father and king
of Troy, comes to the Achaean camp. In the following lines
from Book 24, Priam begs for the return of his son's body.]

. . . the old king went straight up to the lodge
where Achilles dear to Zeus would always sit.
Priam found the warrior there inside . . .   170
many captains sitting some way off, but two,
veteran Automedon and the fine fighter Alcimus
were busy serving him. He had just finished dinner,
eating, drinking, and the table still stood near.
The majestic king of Troy slipped past the rest   175
and kneeling down beside Achilles, clasped his knees
and kissed his hands, those terrible, man-killing hands
that had slaughtered Priam's many sons in battle.
Awesome—as when the grip of madness seizes one
who murders a man in his own fatherland and flees   180
abroad to foreign shores, to a wealthy, noble host,
and a sense of marvel runs through all who see him—
so Achilles marveled, beholding majestic Priam.
His men marveled too, trading startled glances.
But Priam prayed his heart out to Achilles: 185
"Remember your own father, great godlike Achilles—
as old as I am, past the threshold of deadly old age!
No doubt the countrymen round about him plague him now,
with no one there to defend him, beat away disaster.
No one—but at least he hears you're still alive   190
and his old heart rejoices, hopes rising, day by day,
to see his beloved son come sailing home from Troy.
But I—dear god, my life so cursed by fate . . .
I fathered hero sons in the wide realm of Troy
and now not a single one is left, I tell you.   195
Fifty sons I had when the sons of Achaea came,
nineteen born to me from a single mother's womb
and the rest by other women in the palace. Many,
most of them violent Ares cut the knees from under.
But one, one was left me, to guard my walls, my people—   200
the one you killed the other day, defending his fatherland,
my Hector! It's all for him I've come to the ships now,
to win him back from you—I bring a priceless ransom.
Revere the gods, Achilles! Pity me in my own right,
remember your own father! I deserve more pity . . .   205
I have endured what no one on earth has ever done before—
I put to my lips the hands of the man who killed my son."

    Those words stirred within Achilles a deep desire
to grieve for his own father. Taking the old man's hand
he gently moved him back. And overpowered by memory   210
both men gave way to grief. Priam wept freely
for man-killing Hector, throbbing, crouching
before Achilles' feet as Achilles wept himself,
now for his father, now for Patroclus once again,
and their sobbing rose and fell throughout the house.   215
Then, when brilliant Achilles had his fill of tears
and the longing for it had left his mind and body,
he rose from his seat, raised the old man by the hand
and filled with pity now for his gray head and gray beard,
he spoke out winging words, flying straight to the heart: 220
"Poor man, how much you've borne—pain to break the spirit!

What daring brought you down to the ships, all alone,
to face the glance of the man who killed your sons,
so many fine brave boys? You have a heart of iron.
Come, please, sit down on this chair here...   225
Let us put our griefs to rest in our own hearts,
rake them up no more, raw as we are with mourning.
What good's to be won from tears that chill the spirit?
So the immortals spun our lives that we, we wretched men
live on to bear such torments—the gods live free of sorrows. 230
There are two great jars that stand on the floor of Zeus's halls
and hold his gifts, our miseries one, the other blessings.
When Zeus who loves the lightning mixes gifts for a man,
now he meets with misfortune, now good times in turn.
When Zeus dispenses gifts from the jar of sorrows only,   235
he makes a man an outcast—brutal, ravenous hunger
drives him down the face of the shining earth,
stalking far and wide, cursed by gods and men.
So with my father, Peleus. What glittering gifts
the gods rained down from the day that he was born!   240
He excelled all men in wealth and pride of place,
he lorded the Myrmidons, and mortal that he was,
they gave the man an immortal goddess for a wife.
Yes, but even on him the Father piled hardships,
no powerful race of princes born in his royal halls,   245
only a single son he fathered, doomed at birth,
cut off in the spring of life—
and I, I give the man no care as he grows old
since here I sit in Troy, far from my fatherland,
a grief to you, a grief to all your children.   250
And you too, old man, we hear you prospered once:
as far as Lesbos, Macar's kingdom, bounds to seaward,
Phrygia east and upland, the Hellespont vast and north—
that entire realm, they say, you lorded over once,
you excelled all men, old king, in sons and wealth.   255
But then the gods of heaven brought this agony on you—
ceaseless battles round your walls, your armies slaughtered.
You must bear up now. Enough of endless tears,
the pain that breaks the spirit.
Grief for your son will do no good at all.   260
You will never bring him back to life—
sooner you must suffer something worse."

    But the old and noble Priam protested strongly:
"Don't make me sit on a chair, Achilles, Prince,
not while Hector lies uncared-for in your camp!   265
Give him back to me, now, no more delay—
I must see my son with my own eyes.
Accept the ransom I bring you, a king's ransom!
Enjoy it, all of it—return to your own native land,
safe and sound . . . since now you've spared my life."   270
    A dark glance—and the headstrong runner answered,
"No more, old man, don't tempt my wrath, not now!
My own mind's made up to give you back your son.
A messenger brought me word from Zeus—my mother,
Thetis who bore me, the Old Man of the Sea's daughter.   275
And what's more, I can see through you, Priam—
no hiding the fact from me: one of the gods
has led you down to Achaea's fast ships.
No man alive, not even a rugged young fighter,

would dare to venture into our camp. Never—   280
how could he slip past the sentries unchallenged?
Or shoot back the bolt of my gates with so much ease?
So don't anger me now. Don't stir my raging heart still more.
Or under my own roof I may not spare your life, old man—
suppliant that you are—may break the laws of Zeus!"   285

    The old man was terrified. He obeyed the order.
But Achilles bounded out of doors like a lion—
not alone but flanked by his two aides-in-arms,
veteran Automedon and Alcimus, steady comrades,
Achilles' favorites next to the dead Patroclus.   290
They loosed from harness the horses and the mules,
they led the herald in, the old king's crier,
and sat him down on a bench. From the polished wagon
they lifted the priceless ransom brought for Hector's corpse
but they left behind two capes and a finely-woven shirt   295
to shroud the body well when Priam bore him home.
Then Achilles called the serving-women out:
"Bathe and anoint the body—
bear it aside first. Priam must not see his son."
He feared that, overwhelmed by the sight of Hector,   300
wild with grief, Priam might let his anger flare
and Achilles might fly into fresh rage himself,
cut the old man down and break the laws of Zeus.
So when the maids had bathed and anointed the body
sleek with olive oil and wrapped it round and round   305
in a braided battle-shirt and handsome battle-cape,
then Achilles lifted Hector up in his own arms
and laid him down on a bier, and comrades helped him
raise the bier and body onto the sturdy wagon . . .
Then with a groan he called his dear friend by name: 310
"Feel no anger at me, Patroclus, if you learn—
even there in the House of Death—I let his father
have Prince Hector back. He gave me worthy ransom
and you shall have your share from me, as always,
your fitting, lordly share."
                So he vowed   315
and brilliant Achilles strode back to his shelter,
sat down on the well-carved chair that he had left,
at the far wall of the room, leaned toward Priam
and firmly spoke the words the king had come to hear:
"Your son is now set free, old man, as you requested.   320
Hector lies in state. With the first light of day
you will see for yourself as you convey him home.
Now, at last, let us turn our thoughts to supper."

 Q How would you describe the personality of Achilles?

Q How do Achilles and Gilgamesh compare as epic heroes?

The Greek Gods

The ancient Greeks envisioned their gods as a family of immortals who intervened in the lives of human beings. Originating in the cultures of Crete and Mycenae, the Greek pantheon exalted Zeus, the powerful sky god, and his wife, Hera, as the ruling deities. Among the lesser gods were Poseidon, god of the sea; Apollo, god of light, medicine, and music; Dionysus, god of wine and vegetation; Athena, goddess of wisdom and war; and Aphrodite, goddess of love, beauty, and procreation. Around these and other deities there emerged an elaborate mythology.

Many Greek myths look back to the common pool of legends and tales that traveled throughout the Mediterranean and the Near East. In the *Theogony* (*The Birth of the Gods*), a poem recounting the history and genealogy of the gods, Homer's contemporary Hesiod (fl. 700 B.C.E.) describes the origins of the universe in a manner reminiscent of *The Babylonian Creation*:

> First of all, the Void came into being, next broad-bosomed Earth, the solid and eternal home of all, and Eros [Desire], the most beautiful of the immortal gods, who in every man and every god softens the sinews and overpowers the prudent purpose of the mind. Out of Void came Darkness and black Night, and out of Night came Light and Day, her children conceived after union in love with Darkness. Earth first produced starry Sky, equal in size with herself . . .*

The Greeks also had their own version of the Isis/Osiris myth. When Hades, god of the underworld, abducts the beautiful Persephone, her mother, Demeter, rescues her; tricked by Hades, however, this goddess of vegetation is forced to return annually to the underworld, leaving the earth above barren and desolate. Cults based in myths of death and rebirth offered their devotees the hope of personal regeneration.

The Greeks traced their origins to events related to the fury of Zeus: angered by human evil, Zeus decided to destroy humankind by sending a flood. Deucalion, the Greek Noah, built a boat for himself and his wife and obeyed an oracle that commanded them to throw the "bones" of Mother Earth overboard. From these stones sprang up human beings, the first of whom was Hellen, the legendary ancestor of the Greeks, or "Hellenes."

Although immortal, the Greek gods were much like the human beings who worshiped them: they were amorous, adulterous, capricious, and quarrelsome. They lived not in some remote heaven, but (conveniently enough) atop a mountain in northern Greece—that is, among the Greeks themselves. From their home on Mount Olympus, the gods might take sides in human combat (as they regularly do in the *Iliad*), seduce mortal women, and meddle in the lives of those they felt were worthy of their attention. The Greek gods were not always benevolent or just. Unlike the Hebrew God, they set forth no clear principles of moral conduct and no guidelines for religious worship. Priests and priestesses tended the temples and shrines and oversaw rituals, including human and animal sacrifices performed to win the favor of the gods. Popular

*Hesiod, *Theogony*, translated by Norman O. Brown (New York: Bobbs-Merrill, 1953), 56.

The Principal Greek Gods

Greek Name	Roman Name	Signifies
Aphrodite	Venus	Love, beauty, procreation
Apollo	Phoebus	Solar light, medicine, music
Ares	Mars	War, strife
Artemis	Diana	Hunting, wildlife, the moon
Athena	Minerva	War, wisdom
Demeter	Ceres	Agriculture, grain
Dionysus	Bacchus	Wine, vegetation
Eros	Amor/Cupid	Erotic love, desire
Hades	Pluto	Underworld
Helios	Phoebus	Sun
Hephaestus	Vulcan	Fire, metallurgy
Hera	Juno	Queen of the gods
Heracles	Hercules	Strength, courage
Hermes	Mercury	Male messenger of the gods
Hestia	Vesta	Hearth, domestic life
Nike		Victory
Persephone	Proserpina	Underworld
Poseidon	Neptune	Sea
Selene	Diana	Moon
Zeus	Jupiter	King of the gods, sky

Greek religion produced no sacred scripture and no doctrines—circumstances that may have contributed to the freedom of intellectual inquiry for which the Greeks became famous. Equally famous, at least in ancient times, was the oracle at Delphi, the shrine of Apollo and the site that marked for the Greeks the center of the universe and the "navel" of the earth. Here the priestess of Apollo sat on a tripod over a fissure in the rock, and, in a state of ecstasy (which recent archeologists attribute to hallucinogenic fumes from narcotic gases in two geologic faults below) uttered inscrutable replies to the questions of suppliants from near and far. The oracle at Delphi remained the supreme source of prophecy and mystical wisdom until the temple-shrine was destroyed in late Roman times.

The Greek City-State and the Persian Wars (ca. 750–480 B.C.E.)

Toward the end of the Homeric Age, the Greeks formed small rural colonies that gradually grew into urban communities, mainly through maritime trade. Geographic conditions—a rocky terrain interrupted by mountains, valleys, and narrow rivers—made overland travel and trade difficult. At the same time, Greek geography (see Map 4.1) encouraged the evolution of the independent city-state (in Greek, *polis*). Ancient Greece consisted of a constellation of some 200 city-states, a few as large as 400 square miles and others as tiny as 2 square miles. Many of these (Athens, for instance) were small enough that a person might walk around their walls in only a few hours. Although all of the Greek city-states shared the same language, traditions, and religion, each *polis* governed itself, issued its own coinage, and provided its own military defenses. The autonomy of the Greek city-states—so unlike the monolithic Egyptian state—fostered fierce competition and commercial rivalry. However, like the squabbling members of a family who are suddenly menaced by aggressive neighbors, the Greek city-states, confronted by the rising power of Persia, united in self-defense.

By the sixth century B.C.E., the Persian Empire had conquered most of the territories between the western frontier of India and Asia Minor. Advancing westward, Persia annexed Ionia, the Greek region on the coast of Asia Minor (see Map 4.1), a move that clearly threatened mainland Greece. Thus, when in 499 B.C.E. the Ionian cities revolted against Persian rule, their Greek neighbors came to their aid. In retaliation, the Persians sent military expeditions to punish the rebel cities of the Greek mainland. In 490 B.C.E., on the plain of Marathon, 25 miles from Athens, a Greek force of 11,000 men met a Persian army with twice its numbers and defeated them, losing only 192 men. Persian casualties exceeded 6,000. The Greek warrior who brought news of the victory at Marathon to Athens died upon completing the 26-mile run. (Hence the word "marathon" has come to designate a long-distance endurance contest.) But the Greeks soon realized that without a strong navy even the combined land forces of all the city-states could not hope to oust the Persians. They thus proceeded to build a fleet of warships, which, in 480 B.C.E., ultimately defeated the Persian armada at Salamis, one of the final battles of the Persian Wars.

Herodotus

The story of the Persian Wars intrigued the world's first known historian, Herodotus (ca. 485–425 B.C.E), the "father of history." Writing not as an eyewitness to the wars, but a half-century later, Herodotus nevertheless brought keen critical judgment to sources that included hearsay as well as record. His sprawling narrative is filled with fascinating anecdotes and colorful digressions, including a "travelogue" of his visits to Egypt and Asia—accounts that remain among our most detailed sources of information about ancient African and West Asian life. He is our earliest source of information on Scythian royal burials and on the use of hemp as a hallucinogen. The chapters on Africa, filled with numerous comparisons between Greek and Egyptian social practices and religious beliefs, show Herodotus as an early investigator of what would today be called "comparative culture." By presenting various (and often contradictory) pieces of evidence and weighing them before arriving at a conclusion, Herodotus laid the basis for the historical method. His procedures and his writings established a boundary between myth and history. *The Persian Wars*, which followed the Homeric poems by some 300 years, remains significant as the Western world's first major work in prose.

Athens and the Greek Golden Age (ca. 480–430 B.C.E.)

Although all of the city-states had contributed to expelling the Persians, it was Athens that claimed the crown of victory. Indeed, in the wake of the Persian Wars, Athens assumed political dominion among the city-states, as well as commercial supremacy in the Aegean Sea. The defeat of Persia inspired a mood of confidence and a spirit of vigorous chauvinism. This spirit ushered in an age of drama, philosophy, music, art, and architecture. In fact, the period between 480 and 430 B.C.E., known as the Greek Golden Age, was one of the most creative in the history of the world. In Athens, it was as if the heroic idealism of the *Iliad* had bloomed into civic patriotism.

Athens, the most cosmopolitan of the city-states, was unique among the Greek communities, for the democratic government that came to prevail there was the exception rather than the rule in ancient Greece. In its early history, Athens—like most of the other Greek city-states—was an **oligarchy**, that is, a government controlled by an elite minority. But a series of enlightened rulers who governed Athens between roughly 600 and 500 B.C.E. introduced reforms that placed increasing authority in the hands of its citizens. The Athenian statesman, poet, and legislator Solon (ca. 638–558 B.C.E) fixed the democratic course of Athenian history by abolishing the custom of debt slavery and encouraging members of the lower classes to serve in public office. By broadening the civic responsibilities of Athenians, Solon educated citizens of all classes in the activities of government. By 550 B.C.E., the Popular Assembly of Citizens (made up of all citizens) was operating alongside the Council of Five Hundred (made up of aristocrats who handled routine state business) and the Board of Ten Generals (an annually elected executive body). When, at last, in the year 508 B.C.E., the Popular Assembly acquired the right to make laws, Athens became the first direct democracy in world history.

The word "**democracy**" derives from Greek words describing a government in which the people (*demos*) hold power (*kratos*). In the democracy of ancient Athens, Athenian citizens exercised political power directly, thus—unlike the United States, where power rests in the hands of representatives of the people—the citizens of Athens themselves held the authority to make the laws and approve state policy. Athenian democracy was, however, highly exclusive. Its citizenry included only landowning males over the age of eighteen. Of an estimated population of 250,000, this probably constituted some 40,000 people. Women, children, resident aliens, and slaves did not qualify as citizens. Athenian women could not inherit or own property and had few legal rights. (Slaves, as in earlier civilizations, arrived at their unfree condition as a result of warfare or debt, not race or skin color.) Clearly, in the mind of the Athenian, Hellenes were superior to non-Greeks (or outsiders, whom the Greeks called *barbaros*, from which comes the English word "barbarians"), Athenians were superior to non-Athenians, Athenian males were superior to Athenian females, and all classes of free men and women were superior to slaves.

Fundamental to Athenian democracy was a commitment to the legal equality of its participants: one citizen's vote weighed as heavily as the next. Equally important to Athenian (as to any) democracy was the hypothesis that individuals who had the right to vote would do so, and, moreover, were willing to take responsible action in the interest of the common good. (Such ideals are still highly valued in many parts of the modern world.) The small size of Athens probably contributed to the success of its unique form of government. Although probably no more than 5000 Athenians attended the Assembly that met four times a month to make laws in the open-air marketplace (the Agora) located at the foot of the Acropolis, these men were the proponents of a brave new enterprise in governing.

Golden Age Athens stands in vivid contrast to those ancient civilizations whose rulers—the incarnate representatives of the gods—held absolute power while its citizens held none. Athens also stands in contrast to its rival, Sparta, the largest *polis* on the Peloponnesus (see Map 4.1). In Sparta, an oligarchy of five officials, elected annually, held tight reins on a society whose male citizens (from the age of seven on) were trained as soldiers. All physical labor fell to a class of unfree workers called *helots*, the captives of Sparta's frequent local wars. Spartan soldiers were renowned for their bravery; their women, expected to live up to the ideals of a warrior culture, enjoyed a measure of freedom that was unknown in Athens. Yet, the history of Sparta would be one in which a strict social order left little room for creativity, in government or in the arts.

Pericles' Glorification of Athens

The leading proponent of Athenian democracy was the statesman Pericles (ca. 495–429 B.C.E.) (Figure **4.8**), who dominated the Board of Ten Generals for more than thirty years until his death. An aristocrat by birth, Pericles was a democrat at heart. In the interest of broadening the democratic system, he initiated some of Athens' most sweeping domestic reforms, such as payment for holding public office and a system of public audit in which the finances of outgoing magistrates were subject to critical scrutiny. In Pericles' time many public offices were filled by lottery—a procedure that invited all citizens to seek governmental office, and one so egalitarian as to be unthinkable today. Pericles' foreign policy was even more ambitious than his domestic policies. In the wake of the Persian Wars, he encouraged the Greek city-states to form a defensive alliance against future invaders. At the outset, the league's collective funds were kept in a treasury on the sacred island of Delos (hence the name "Delian League"). But, in a bold display of chauvinism, Pericles moved the fund to Athens and expropriated its monies to rebuild the Athenian temples that had been burned by the Persians.

Pericles' high-handed actions, along with his imperialistic efforts to dominate the commercial policies of league members, led to antagonism and armed dispute between Athens and a federation of rival city-states led by Sparta. The ensuing Peloponnesian Wars (431–404 B.C.E.), which culminated in the defeat of Athens, brought an end to the Greek Golden Age. Our knowledge of the Peloponnesian Wars is based mainly on the account written by the great historian Thucydides (ca. 460–400 B.C.E.), himself a general in the combat. Thucydides went beyond merely recording the events of the war to provide insights into its causes and a first-hand assessment of its political and moral consequences. Thucydides' terse, graphic descriptions and his detached analyses of events distinguish his style from that of Herodotus.

The following speech by Pericles, excerpted from Thucydides' *History of the Peloponnesian Wars*, was presented on the occasion of a mass funeral held outside the walls of Athens to honor those who had died in the first battles of the war. Nowhere are the concepts of humanism and individualism more closely linked to civic patriotism than in this speech. Pericles reviews the "principles of action" by which Athens rose to power. He describes Athens as "the school of Hellas," that is, as the ultimate model for other Greek communities in matters of political, social, and cultural significance. The greatness of Athens, according to Pericles, lies not merely in its military might and in the superiority of its political institutions, but in the quality of its citizens, their nobility of spirit, and their love of beauty and wisdom. Pericles' views, which were shared by most Athenians as primary articles of faith, reflect the spirit of civic pride that characterized Hellenic culture at its peak.

Figure 4.8 Bust inscribed with the name of Pericles, from Tivoli. Roman copy after a bronze original of 450–425 B.C.E. Marble, height 23 in. Reproduced by courtesy of the Trustees of the British Museum, London.

READING 1.12 From Thucydides' *Peloponnesian Wars* (ca. 410 B.C.E.)

Pericles' Funeral Speech

"I will speak first of our ancestors, for it is right and 1
becoming that now, when we are lamenting the dead, a
tribute should be paid to their memory. There has never been a
time when they did not inhabit this land, which by their valor
they have handed down from generation to generation, and
we have received from them a free state. But if they were
worthy of praise, still more were our fathers, who added to
their inheritance, and after many a struggle transmitted to us
their sons this great empire. And we ourselves assembled
here today, who are still most of us in the vigor of life, have 10
chiefly done the work of improvement, and have richly
endowed our city with all things, so that she is sufficient for
herself both in peace and war. Of the military exploits by
which our various possessions were acquired, or of the energy
with which we or our fathers drove back the tide of war,
Hellenic or barbarian, I will not speak; for the tale would be
long and is familiar to you. But before I praise the dead, I
should like to point out by what principles of action we rose to
power, and under what institutions and through what manner
of life our empire became great. For I conceive that such 20
thoughts are not unsuited to the occasion, and that this
numerous assembly of citizens and strangers may profitably
listen to them.

"Our form of government does not enter into rivalry with
the institutions of others. We do not copy our neighbors, but are
an example to them. It is true that we are called a democracy,
for the administration is in the hands of the many and not of
the few. But while the law secures equal justice to all alike in
their private disputes, the claim of excellence is also
recognized; and when a citizen is in any way distinguished, 30
he is preferred to the public service, not as a matter of
privilege, but as the reward of merit. Neither is poverty a bar,
but a man may benefit his country whatever be the obscurity
of his condition. There is no exclusiveness in our public life,
and in our private intercourse we are not suspicious of one
another, nor angry with our neighbor if he does what he likes;
we do not put on sour looks at him which, though harmless,
are not pleasant. While we are thus unconstrained in our
private intercourse, a spirit of reverence pervades our public
acts; we are prevented from doing wrong by respect for 40
authority and for the laws, having an especial regard to those
which are ordained for the protection of the injured as well as
to those unwritten laws which bring upon the transgressor of
them the reprobation of the general sentiment.

"And we have not forgotten to provide for our weary spirits
many relaxations from toil; we have regular games[1] and
sacrifices throughout the year; at home the style of our life is
refined; and the delight which we daily feel in all these things
helps to banish melancholy. Because of the greatness of our
city the fruits of the whole earth flow in upon us; so that we 50
enjoy the goods of other countries as freely as of our own.

"Then, again, our military training is in many respects superior
to that of our adversaries. Our city is thrown open to the
world, and we never expel a foreigner or prevent him from
seeing or learning anything of which the secret if revealed to
an enemy might profit him. We rely not upon management or
trickery, but upon our own hearts and hands. And in the matter
of education, whereas they from early youth are always
undergoing laborious exercises which are to make them brave,
we live at ease, and yet are equally ready to face the perils 60
which they face. And here is the proof. The Lacedaemonians[2]
come into Attica not by themselves, but with their whole
confederacy following; we go alone into a neighbor's country;
and although our opponents are fighting for their homes and
we on a foreign soil, we have seldom any difficulty in
overcoming them. Our enemies have never yet felt our united
strength; the care of a navy divides our attention, and on land
we are obliged to send our own citizens everywhere. But they,
if they meet and defeat a part of our army, are as proud as if
they had routed us all, and when defeated they pretend to 70
have been vanquished by us all.

"If then we prefer to meet danger with a light heart but
without laborious training, and with a courage which is gained
by habit and not enforced by law, are we not greatly the
gainers? Since we do not anticipate the pain, although, when
the hour comes, we can be as brave as those who never allow
themselves to rest; and thus too our city is equally admirable
in peace and in war.

"For we are lovers of the beautiful, yet with economy, and
we cultivate the mind without loss of manliness. Wealth we 80
employ, not for talk and ostentation, but when there is a real
use for it. To avow poverty with us is no disgrace; the true
disgrace is in doing nothing to avoid it. An Athenian citizen
does not neglect the state because he takes care of his own
household; and even those of us who are engaged in business
have a very fair idea of politics. We alone regard a man who
takes no interest in public affairs, not as a harmless, but as a
useless character; and if few of us are originators, we are all
sound judges of a policy. The great impediment to action is, in
our opinion, not discussion, but the want of that knowledge 90
which is gained by discussion preparatory to action. For we
have a peculiar power of thinking before we act and of acting
too, whereas other men are courageous from ignorance but
hesitate upon reflection. And they are surely to be esteemed
the bravest spirits who, having the clearest sense both of the
pains and pleasures of life, do not on that account shrink from
danger. In doing good, again, we are unlike others; we make
our friends by conferring, not by receiving favors. . . . We alone
do good to our neighbors not upon a calculation of interest,
but in the confidence of freedom and in a frank and fearless 100
spirit.

"To sum up: I say that Athens is the school of Hellas, and
that the individual Athenian in his own person seems to have
the power of adapting himself to the most varied forms of
action with the utmost versatility and grace. This is no passing
and idle word, but truth and fact; and the assertion is verified
by the position to which these qualities have raised the state.
For in the hour of trial Athens alone among her

---

[1]Athletic games were part of many Greek festivals, the most famous of
which was the Panhellenic festival (see below).

[2]Citizens of the city-state of Sparta, ideologically opposed to Athens.

contemporaries is superior to the report of her. No enemy who comes against her is indignant at the reverses which he sustains at the hands of such a city; no subject complains that his masters are unworthy of him. And we shall assuredly not be without witnesses; there are mighty monuments of our power which will make us the wonder of this and of succeeding ages; we shall not need the praises of Homer or of any other panegyrist whose poetry may please for the moment, although his representation of the facts will not bear the light of day. For we have compelled every land and every sea to open a path for our valor, and have everywhere planted eternal memorials of our friendship and of our enmity. Such is the city for whose sake these men nobly fought and died; they could not bear the thought that she might be taken from them; and every one of us who survive should gladly toil on her behalf. **120**

"I have dwelt upon the greatness of Athens because I want to show you that we are contending for a higher prize than those who enjoy none of these privileges, and to establish by manifest proof the merit of these men whom I am now commemorating. Their loftiest praise has been already spoken. For in magnifying the city I have magnified them, and men like them whose virtues made her glorious." **130**

Q In what way does Pericles find Athens unique?
Q What does he mean by saying "Athens is the school of Hellas"?

The Olympic Games

Pericles makes proud reference to the "regular games" that provide Athenians with "relaxations from toil." But, in fact, the most famous of the "games" were athletic contests in which all the city-states of Greece participated. These games were the chief feature of the Panhellenic ("all-Greek") Festival, instituted in 776 B.C.E. in honor of the Greek gods. Located in Olympia, one of the great religious centers of Greece, the festival took place at midsummer every four years, even during wartime: a sacred truce guaranteed safe conduct to all visitors. So significant were the games that they became the basis for the reckoning of time. While Egypt and Mesopotamia calculated time according to the rule of dynasties and kings, the ancient Greeks marked time in "Olympiads," four-year periods beginning with the first games in 776 B.C.E. The central event of the games was a 200-yard sprint (Figure **4.9**) called the *stadion* (hence our word "stadium"). But there were also many other contests: a footrace of one and a half miles, the discus-throw, the long-jump, wrestling, boxing, and other games that probably looked back to Minoan tradition (see Figure 4.3). Greek athletes competed in the nude—from the Greek word *gymnos* ("naked") we get "gymnasium." Winners received **amphoras** filled with olive oil, garlands consisting of wild olive or laurel leaves, and the enthusiastic acclaim of Greek painters and poets (see Reading 1.20), but no financial reward.

Although women were not permitted to compete in the Olympics, they could hold games of their own. Prowess rather than cunning was valued in all games: in wrestling, hair-pulling and finger-bending were permitted, but biting and finger-breaking were forbidden. A match terminated when either wrestler gave up, lost consciousness, or fell dead. True "sport" was that which gave athletes an opportunity to rival the divinity of the gods. Nevertheless, the Olympics were a national event that, typically, promoted both individual excellence and communal pride.

Greek Drama

While the Olympic Games were held only once in four years, theatrical performances in the city of Athens occurred twice annually. Like the games, Greek drama was a form of play that addressed the dynamic relationship between the individual, the community, and the gods. The ancient Greeks were the first masters in the art of drama,

Figure 4.9 Attr. The Euphiletos painter, detail from Greek black-figured Panathenaic prize amphora showing foot race, from Vulci, ca. 530 B.C.E. Terracotta, height 24½ in. The Metropolitan Museum of Art, New York. Rogers Fund, 1914 (14.130.12).

Figure 4.10 Polycleitus the Younger, Theater at Epidaurus, Greece, ca. 350 B.C.E. This view shows the great size (13,000 capacity) typical of Greek theaters. Nevertheless, actors and chorus could be heard even from the top row.

the literary genre that tells a story through the imitation of action. Recitation and chant, music, dance, and mime animated the enactment of myths that celebrated rites of passage or marked seasonal change. As evidenced by the Pygmy hunting ceremony discussed in the Introduction (Reading 1.1), dramatic action served to bring about favorable results in hunting, farming, and in ensuring the survival of the community.

Greek drama grew out of a complex of rituals associated with the worship of Dionysus, god of wine, vegetation, and seasonal regeneration. In early Homeric times, religious rites performed in honor of Dionysus featured a dialogue between two choruses or between a leader (originally perhaps the shaman or priest) and a chorus (the worshipers or ritual participants). With the advent of the poet Thespis (fl. 534 B.C.E.), actor and chorus (the performers) seem to have become separate from those who witnessed the action (the audience). At the same time, dramatic action assumed two principal forms: *tragedy* and *comedy*. Although the origins of each are still the subject of speculation among scholars, tragedy probably evolved from fertility rituals surrounding the death and decay of the crops, while comedy seems to have developed out of village revels celebrating seasonal rebirth. It is possible, as well, that such performances had something to do with the healing cults of ancient Greece: the great Theater at Epidaurus (Figure 4.10) was dedicated to Aesclepius, the god of medicine. Like the more ancient theater of Dionysus in Athens, it stood adjacent to a chief sanctuary for the worship of the god of healing.

The two annual festivals dedicated to Dionysus were the occasion for the performances of tragedies and comedies, and on each occasion (lasting several days) the author of the best play in its category received a prize. By the fifth century B.C.E. Greece had become a mecca for theater, and while hundreds of plays were performed during the century in which Athenian theater flourished, only forty-four have survived.* They are the products of but four playwrights: Aeschylus (ca. 525–456 B.C.E.), Sophocles (496–406 B.C.E.), Euripides (480–406 B.C.E.), and Aristophanes (ca. 450–ca. 388 B.C.E.). Their plays were staged in the open-air theaters built into the hillsides at sacred sites throughout Greece. These acoustically superb structures, which seated between 13,000 and 27,000 people, featured a *proscenium* (the ancient "stage"), an *orchestra* (the circular "dancing space" in front of the stage), a *skene* (an area that functioned as a stage set or dressing room), and an *altar* dedicated to the god Dionysus (Figure 4.11). Music, dance, and song were essential to dramatic performance; scenery and props were few; and actors (all of whom were male) wore elaborate costumes, along with masks that served to amplify their voices.

The tragedies of Aeschylus, Sophocles, and Euripides deal with human conflicts as revealed in Greek history, myth, and legend. Since such stories would have been generally familiar to the average Greek who attended the Dionysian theater, the way in which the playwright intrigued the theatergoer would depend upon his treatment of the story or the manner in which the story was enacted. The tragic drama concentrated on issues involving a specific moment of friction between the individual and fate, the gods, or the community. The events of the play unfolded by way of dialogue spoken by individual characters but also through the commentary of the chorus. Aeschylus, the author of the oldest surviving Western tragedy, introduced a second actor and gave the chorus

_____
*All of the Greek plays in English translation may be found at the website: http://classics.mit.edu.

a principal role in the drama. He brought deep religious feeling to his tragedies, the most famous of which is the series of three plays, or trilogy, known as the *Oresteia* (Orestes plays). These plays deal with the history of the family of Agamemnon, who led the Greeks to Troy, and whose murder at the hands of his wife upon his return from Troy is avenged by their son, Orestes.

While Aeschylus advanced the story of the play by way of sonorous language, Sophocles, the second of the great tragedians, developed his plots through the actions of the characters. He modified the ceremonial formality of earlier Greek tragedies by individualizing the characters and introducing moments of great psychological intimacy. Euripides, the last of the great tragedians, brought even greater realism to his characters; his striking psychological portraits explore the human soul in its experience of grief.

Tragedy, which gave formal expression to the most awful kinds of human experience—disaster and death—invited the spectator to participate vicariously in the dramatic action, thus undergoing a kind of emotional liberation. Comedy, on the other hand, drew its ability to provoke laughter from incongruity and the unexpected. Probably originating in association with fertility rites, comedy involved satires and parodies of sexual union and erotic play of the kind found to this day in seasonal festivals and carnivals such as Mardi Gras. Obscene jokes, grotesque masks, fantastic costumes, and provocative dance and song were common to ancient comedy, as they are in various forms of modern slapstick and burlesque. In the history of ancient Greek drama, the only comic plays to survive are those of Aristophanes. His inventive wit, sharply directed against Athenian politics and current affairs, is best revealed in the comedy *Lysistrata*, the oldest of his eleven surviving works. In *Lysistrata*, written in the wake of the bitter military conflict between Athens and Sparta, the playwright has the leading character—the wife of an Athenian soldier—launch a "strike" that will deprive all husbands of sexual satisfaction until they agree to refrain from war. As timely today as it was in ancient Athens, *Lysistrata* is a hilarious attack on the idealized, heroic image of armed combat.

Figure 4.11 Plan of the theater at Epidaurus. **1** gangway **2** aisles **3** tiered seating for audience **4** ramp **5** *orchestra* **6** *skene* **7** *proscenium*

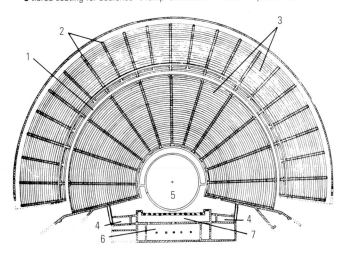

The Individual and the Community

The Case of Antigone

The drama that is most relevant to the theme of this chapter is Sophocles' *Antigone*, the third of a group of plays that includes *Oedipus the King* and *Oedipus at Colonus*. The story of *Antigone* proceeds from the last phase of the history of Thebes, a history with which most Athenians would have been familiar, since it recalled the ancient ascendancy of Athens over Thebes: following the death of Oedipus, King of Thebes, his sons Polynices and Eteocles kill each other in a dispute over the throne, thus leaving the crown to Creon, the brother-in-law of Oedipus and the only surviving male member of the ill-fated royal family. Upon becoming king, Creon forbids the burial of Polynices, contending that Eteocles had been the rightful ruler of Thebes. Driven by familial duty and the wish to fulfill the divine laws requiring burial of the dead, Oedipus' daughter Antigone violates Creon's decree and buries her brother Polynices. These circumstances provoke further violence and tragic death.

Antigone is a play that deals with many issues: it explores the conflict between the rights of the individual and the laws of the state; between dedication to family and loyalty to community; between personal and political obligations; between female willpower and male authority; and, finally, between human and divine law. It reflects Sophocles' effort to reconcile human passions, the will of the gods, and the sovereignty of the *polis*. Heroic idealism is a major motif in *Antigone*. It drives the action of the play, which weighs the grandeur of human beings against their frailties.

READING 1.13 From Sophocles' *Antigone*

(ca. 440 B.C.E.)

Characters

Antigone and Ismene, daughters of Oedipus
Creon, king of Thebes, brother of Jocasta
Haemon, son of Creon
Teiresias, a blind prophet
A Sentry
A Messenger
Eurydice, wife of Creon
Chorus of Theban elders
Attendants of the king and queen
Soldiers
A Boy who leads Teiresias

Scene

An open space before the house of Creon. The house is at the back, with gates opening from it. On the right, the city is to be supposed; to the left and in the distance, the Theban plain and the hills rising beyond it. Antigone and Ismene come from the middle door of three in the King's house.

Antigone: Ismene, O my dear, my little sister, of all the griefs bequeathed us by our father Oedipus, is there any that Zeus will share with us while we live? There is no sorrow and no shame we have not known. And now what is this new edict they tell about, that our Captain has published all through Thebes? Do you know? Have you heard? Or is it kept from you that our friends are threatened with the punishment due to foes?

Ismene: I have heard no news, Antigone, glad or sad, about our friends, since we two sisters lost two brothers at a single blow; and since the Argive army fled last night, I do not know whether my fortune is better or worse.

Antigone: I know, I know it well. That is why I sent for you to come outside the gates, to speak to you alone.

Ismene: What is it? I can see that you are troubled.

Antigone: Should I not be?—when Creon gives honors to one of our brothers, but condemns the other to shame? Eteocles, they say, he has laid in the earth with due observance of right and custom, that all may be well with him among the shades below. But the poor corpse of Polynices— it has been published to the city that none shall bury him, none shall mourn him; but he shall be left unwept and unsepulchred, and the birds are welcome to feast upon him!

Such, they say, are the orders the good Creon has given for you and me—yes, for me! He is coming now to make his wishes clear; and it is no light matter, for whoever disobeys him is condemned to death by stoning before all the people. Now you know!—and now you will show whether you are nobly bred, or the unworthy daughter of a noble line.

Ismene: Sister, sister!—if we are caught in this web, what could I do to loose or tighten the knot?

Antigone: Decide if you will share the work and the danger.

Ismene: What are you planning?—what are you thinking of?

Antigone: Will you help this hand to lift the dead?

Ismene: Oh, you would bury him!—when it is forbidden to anyone in Thebes?

Antigone: He is still my brother, if he is not yours. No one shall say I failed in my duty to him.

Ismene: But how can you dare, when Creon has forbidden it?

Antigone: He has no right to keep me from my own.

Ismene: Alas, sister, remember how our father perished hated and scorned, when he had struck out his eyes in horror of the sins his own persistency had brought to light. Remember how she who was both his mother and his wife hung herself with a twisted cord. And only yesterday our two brothers came to their terrible end, each by the other's hand. Now only we two are left, and we are all alone. Think how we shall perish, more miserably than all the rest, if in defiance of the law we brave the King's decree and the King's power. No, no, we must remember we were born women, not meant to strive with men. We are in the grip of those stronger than ourselves, and must obey them in this and in things still more cruel. Therefore I will ask forgiveness of the gods and spirits who dwell below, for they will see that I yield to force, and I will hearken to our rulers. It is foolish to be too zealous even in a good cause.

Antigone: I will not urge you. No, if you wished to join me now I would not let you. Do as you think best. As for me, I will bury him; and if I die for that, I am content. I shall rest like a loved one with him whom I have loved, innocent in my guilt. For I owe a longer allegiance to the dead than to the living; I must dwell with them forever. You, if you wish, may dishonor the laws which the gods have established.

Ismene: I would not dishonor them, but to defy the State— I am not strong enough for that!

Antigone: Well, make your excuses—I am going now to heap the earth above the brother whom I love.

Ismene: Oh, I fear something terrible will happen to you!

Antigone: Fear not for me; but look to your own fate.

Ismene: At least, then, tell no one what you intend, but hide it closely—and so too will I.

Antigone: No, but cry it aloud! I will condemn you more if you are silent than if you proclaim my deed to all.

Ismene: You have so hot a heart for deeds that make the blood run cold!

Antigone: My deeds will please those they are meant to please.

Ismene: Ah yes, if you can do what you plan—but you cannot.

Antigone: When my strength fails, I shall confess my failure.

Ismene: The impossible should not be tried at all.

Antigone: If you say such things I will hate you, and the dead will haunt you!—But leave me, and the folly that is mine alone, to suffer what I must; for I shall not suffer anything so dreadful as an ignoble death.

Ismene: Go then, if you must, though your errand is mad; and be sure of this, my love goes with you!

(Antigone goes toward the plain. Ismene retires into the King's house. The Chorus, being the elders of Thebes, comes into the place before the house.)

Chorus: Over the waters, see!—over the stream of Dirke, the golden eye of the dawn opens on the seven gates; Terror crouched in the night, how welcome to Thebes is the morning, when the warriors of the white shields flee from the spears of the sun.

From Argos mailed they came, swords drawn for Polynices; like eagles that scream in the air these plumed ones fell on our land. They ravened around our towers, and burst the doors of our dwellings; their spears sniffed at our blood—but they fled without quenching that thirst.

They heaped the eager pine-boughs, flaming, against our bastions, calling upon Hephaestos; but he the fire-god failed them. The clash of battle was loud, the clamor beloved of the war-god; but a thing they found too hard was to conquer the dragon's brood.

And a thing abhorred by Zeus is the boastful tongue of the haughty: one proud chief, armored in gold, with triumph in his throat,

The stormy wave of the foe flung to the crest of our rampart—the god, with a crooked bolt, smites him crashing to earth.

At the seven gates of the city, seven of the host's grim captains yielded to Zeus who turns the tide of battle, their arms of bronze;
And woe to those two sons of the same father and mother, they crossed their angry spears, and brought each other low.

But now since Victory, most desired of all men, to 120
Thebes of the many chariots has come scattering joy,
Let us forget the wars, and dance before the temples; and Bacchus be our leader, loved by the land of Thebes!

But see, the King of this land comes yonder—Creon, son of Menoekeus, our new ruler by virtue of the new turn the gods have given things. What counsel is he pondering, that he has called by special summons this gathering of the elders?

Creon: Sirs, our State has been like a ship tossed by 130 stormy waves; but thanks to the gods, it sails once more upon a steady keel. You I have summoned here apart from all the people because I remember that of old you had great reverence for the royal power of Laius; and I know how you upheld Oedipus when he ruled this land, and, when he died, you loyally supported his two sons. Those sons have fallen, both in one moment, each smitten by the other, each stained with a brother's blood; now I possess the throne and all its powers, since I am nearest kindred of the dead.

No man's worthiness to rule can be known until his mind 140 and soul have been tested by the duties of government and lawgiving. For my part, I have always held that any man who is the supreme guardian of the State, and who fails in his duty through fear, remaining silent when evil is done, is base and contemptible; nor have I any regard for him who puts friendship above the common welfare. Zeus, who sees all things, be my witness that I will not be silent when danger threatens the people; nor will I ever call my country's foe my friend. For our country is the ship that bears us all, and he only is our friend who helps us sail a prosperous course. 150

Such are the rules by which I will guard this city's greatness; and in keeping with them is the edict I have published touching the sons of Oedipus. For Eteocles, who fell like a true soldier defending his native land, there shall be such funeral as we give the noblest dead. But as to his brother Polynices—he who came out of exile and sought to destroy with fire the city of his fathers and the shrines of his fathers' gods—he who thirsted for the blood of his kin, and would have led into slavery all who escaped death—as to this man, it has been proclaimed that none shall honor him, none shall 160 lament over him, but he shall lie unburied, a corpse mangled by birds and dogs, a gruesome thing to see. Such is my way with traitors.

Chorus: Such is your way, Creon, son of Menoekeus, with the false and with the faithful; and you have power, I know, to give such orders as you please, both for the dead and for all of us who live.

Creon: Then look to it that my mandate is observed.
Chorus: Call on some younger man for this hard task.
Creon: No, watchers of the corpse have been appointed. 170
Chorus: What is this duty, then, you lay on us?
Creon: To side with no one breaking this command.
Chorus: No man is foolish enough to go courting death.
Creon: That indeed shall be the penalty; but men have been lured even to death by the hope of gain.

(A Guard, coming from the direction of the plain, approaches Creon.)

Guard: Sire, I will not say that I am out of breath from hurrying, nor that I have come here on the run; for in fact my thoughts made me pause more than once, and even turn in my path, to go back. My mind was telling me two different things. "Fool," it said to me, "why do you go where you are sure to 180 be condemned?" And then on the other hand, "Wretch, tarrying again? If Creon hears of this from another, you'll smart for it." Torn between these fears, I came on slowly and unwillingly, making a short road long. But at last I got up courage to come to you, and though there is little to my story, I will tell it; for I have got a good grip on one thought—that I can suffer nothing but what is my fate.

Creon: Well, and what is it that makes you so upset?
Guard: First let me tell you that I did not do the deed and I did not see it done, so it would not be just to make me suffer 190 for it.

Creon: You have a good care for your own skin, and armor yourself well against blame. I take it that you have news to tell?

Guard: Yes, that I have, but bad news is nothing to be in a hurry about.

Creon: Tell it, man, will you?—tell it and be off.
Guard: Well, this is it. The corpse—someone has done it funeral honors—sprinkled dust upon it, and other pious rites.
Creon: What—what do you say? What man has dared 200 this deed?

Guard: That I cannot tell you. There was no sign of a pick being used, no earth torn up the way it is by a mattock. The ground was hard and dry, there was no track of wheels. Whoever did it left no trace; when the first day-watchman showed it to us, we were struck dumb. You couldn't see the dead man at all; not that he was in any grave, but dry dust was strewn that thick all over him. It was the hand of someone warding off a curse did that. There was no sign that any dog or wild beast had been at the body. 210

Then there were loud words, and hard words, among us of the guard, everyone accusing someone else, 'til we nearly came to blows, and it's a wonder we didn't. Everyone was accused and no one was convicted, and each man stuck to it that he knew nothing about it. We were ready to take red-hot iron in our hands—to walk through fire—to swear by the gods that we did not do the deed and were not in the secret of whoever did it.

At last, when all our disputing got us nowhere, one of the men spoke up in a way that made us look down at the ground 220 in silence and fear; for we could not see how to gainsay him, nor how to escape trouble if we heeded him. What he said was, that this must be reported to you, it was no use hiding it. There was no doubt of it, he was right; so we cast lots, and it was my bad luck to win the prize. Here I am, then, as unwelcome as unwilling, I know; for no man likes the bearer of bad news.

Chorus: O King, my thoughts have been whispering, could this deed perhaps have been the work of gods?

Creon: Silence, before your words fill me with anger, and 230 you prove yourself as foolish as you are old! You say what is not to be borne, that the gods would concern themselves with this corpse. What!—did they cover his nakedness to reward the reverence he paid them, coming to burn their pillared shrines and sacred treasures, to harry their land, to put scorn upon their laws? Do you think it is the way of the gods to honor the wicked? No! From the first there were some in this city who muttered against me, chafing at this edict, wagging their heads in secret; they would not bow to the yoke, not they, like men contented with my rule. 240

I know well enough, it is such malcontents who have bribed and beguiled these guards to do this deed or let it be done. Nothing so evil as money ever arose among men. It lays cities low, drives peoples from their homes, warps honest souls 'til they give themselves to works of shame; it teaches men to practice villainies and grow familiar with impious deeds.

But the men who did this thing for hire, sooner or later they shall pay the price. Now, as Zeus still has my reverence, know this—I tell you on my oath: Unless you find the very man whose hand strewed dust upon that body, and bring him here 250 before mine eyes, death alone shall not be enough for you, but you shall first be hung up alive until you reveal the truth about this outrage; that henceforth you may have a better idea about how to get money, and learn that it is not wise to grasp at it from any source. I will teach you that ill-gotten gains bring more men to ruin than to prosperity.

Guard: May I speak? Or shall I turn and go?

Creon: Can you not see that your voice offends me?

Guard: Are your ears troubled, or your soul?

Creon: And why should you try to fix the seat of my pain? 260

Guard: The doer of the deed inflames your mind, but I, only your ears.

Creon: Bah, you are a babbler born!

Guard: I may be that, but I never did this deed.

Creon: You did, for silver; but you shall pay with your life.

Guard: It is bad when a judge misjudges.

Creon: Prate about "judgment" all you like; but unless you show me the culprit in this crime, you will admit before long that guilty wages were better never earned.

(Creon goes into his house.)

Guard: Well, may the guilty man be found, that's all I ask. 270 But whether he's found or not—fate will decide that—you will not see me here again. I have escaped better than I ever hoped or thought—I owe the gods much thanks.

(The Guard departs, going toward the plain.)

Chorus: Wonders are many in the world, and the wonder of all is man.
With his bit in the teeth of the storm and his faith in a fragile prow,

Far he sails, where the waves leap white-fanged, wroth [wrathful] at his plan.
And he has his will of the earth by the strength of his hand on the plough.

The birds, the clan of the light heart, he snares with his woven cord,
And the beasts with wary eyes, and the stealthy fish in the sea;
That shaggy freedom-lover, the horse, obeys his word, 280
And the sullen bull must serve him, for cunning of wit is he.

Against all ills providing, he tempers the dark and the light,
The creeping siege of the frost and the arrows of sleet and rain,
The grievous wounds of the daytime and the fever that steals in the night;
Only against Death man arms himself in vain.

With speech and wind-swift thought he builds the State to his mood,
Prospering while he honors the gods and the laws of the land.
Yet in his rashness often he scorns the ways that are good—
May such as walk with evil be far from my hearth and hand!

(The Guard reappears leading Antigone.)

Chorus: But what is this?—what portent from the gods is 290 this? I am bewildered, for surely this maiden is Antigone; I know her well. O luckless daughter of a luckless father, child of Oedipus, what does this mean? Why have they made you prisoner? Surely they did not take you in the folly of breaking the King's laws?

Guard: Here she is, the doer of the deed! We caught this girl burying him. But where is Creon?

Chorus: Look, he is coming from the house now.

(Creon comes from the house.)

Creon: What is it? What has happened that makes my coming timely? 300

Guard: Sire, a man should never say positively "I will do this" or "I won't do that," for things happen to change the mind. I vowed I would not soon come here again, after the way you scared me, lashing me with your threats. But there's nothing so pleasant as a happy turn when we've given up hope, so I have broken my sworn oath to hurry back here with this girl, who was taken showing grace to the dead. This time there was no casting of lots; no, this is my good luck, no one else's. And now, Sire, take her yourself, question her, examine her, all you please; but I have a right to free and final 310 quittance of this trouble.

Creon: Stay!—this prisoner—how and where did you take her?

Guard: She was burying the man; that's all there is to tell you.

Creon: Do you mean what you say? Are you telling the truth?

Guard: I saw her burying the corpse that you had forbidden to bury. Is that plain and clear?

Creon: What did you see? Did you take her in the act? 320

Guard: It happened this way. When we came to the place where he lay, worrying over your threats, we swept away all the dirt, leaving the rotting corpse bare. Then we sat us down on the brow of the hill to windward, so that the smell from him would not strike us. We kept wide awake frightening each other with what you would do to us if we didn't carry out your command. So it went until the sun was bright in the top of the sky, and the heat began to burn. Then suddenly a whirlwind came roaring down, making the sky all black, hiding the plain under clouds of choking dust and leaves torn from 330 the trees. We closed our eyes and bore this plague from the gods.

And when, after a long while, the storm had passed, we saw this girl, and she crying aloud with the sharp cry of a bird in its grief; the way a bird will cry when it sees the nest bare and the nestlings gone, it was that way she lifted up her voice when she saw the corpse uncovered; and she called down dreadful curses on those that did it. Then straightway she scooped up dust in her hands, and she had a shapely ewer of bronze, and she held that high while she honored the dead 340 with three drink-offerings.

We rushed forward at this and closed on our quarry, who was not at all frightened at us. Then we charged her with the past and present offences, and she denied nothing—I was both happy and sorry for that. It is good to escape danger one's self, but hard to bring trouble to one's friends. However, nothing counts with me so much as my own safety.

Creon: You, then—you whose face is bent to the earth—do you confess or do you deny the deed?

Antigone: I did it; I make no denial. 350

Creon (*to Guard*); You may go your way, wherever you will, free and clear of a grave charge. (*To Antigone*); Now tell me—not in many words, but briefly—did you know of the edict that forbade what you did?

Antigone: I knew it. How could I help knowing?—it was public.

Creon: And you had the boldness to transgress that law?

Antigone: Yes, for it was not Zeus made such a law; such is not the Justice of the gods. Nor did I think that your decrees had so much force, that a mortal could override the unwritten 360 and unchanging statutes of heaven. For their authority is not of today nor yesterday, but from all time, and no man knows when they were first put forth.

Not through dread or any human power could I answer to the gods for breaking these. That I must die I knew without your edict. But if I am to die before my time, I count that a gain; for who, living as I do in the midst of many woes, would not call death a friend?

It saddens me little, therefore, to come to my end. If I had let my mother's son lie in death an unburied corpse, that 370 would have saddened me, but for myself I do not grieve. And if my acts are foolish in your eyes, it may be that a foolish judge condemns my folly.

Chorus: The maiden shows herself the passionate daughter of a passionate father, she does not know how to bend the neck.

Creon: Let me remind you that those who are too stiff and stubborn are most often humbled; it is the iron baked too hard in the furnace you will oftenest see snapped and splintered. But I have seen horses that show temper brought to order by 380 a little curb. Too much pride is out of place in one who lives subject to another. This girl was already versed in insolence when she transgressed the law that had been published; and now, behold, a second insult—to boast about it, to exult in her misdeed!

But I am no man, she is the man, if she can carry this off unpunished. No! She is my sister's child, but if she were nearer to me in blood than any who worships Zeus at the altar of my house, she should not escape a dreadful doom—nor her sister either, for indeed I charge her too with plotting this 390 burial.

And summon that sister—for I saw her just now within, raving and out of her wits. That is the way minds plotting evil in the dark give away their secret and convict themselves even before they are found out. But the most intolerable thing is that one who has been caught in wickedness should glory in the crime.

Antigone: Would you do more than slay me?

Creon: No more than that—no, and nothing less.

Antigone: Then why do you delay? Your speeches give me 400 no pleasure, and never will; and my words, I suppose, buzz hatefully in your ear. I am ready; for there is no better way I could prepare for death than by giving burial to my brother. Everyone would say so if their lips were not sealed by fear. But a king has many advantages, he can do and say what he pleases.

Creon: You slander the race of Cadmus,[1] not one of them shares your view of this deed.

Antigone: They see it as I do, but their tails are between their legs. 410

Creon: They are loyal to their king; are you not ashamed to be otherwise?

Antigone: No; there is nothing shameful in piety to a brother.

Creon: Was it not a brother also who died in the good cause?

Antigone: Born of the same mother and sired by the same father.

Creon: Why then do you dishonor him by honoring that other? 420

Antigone: The dead will not look upon it that way.

Creon: Yes, if you honor the wicked equally with the virtuous.

Antigone: It was his brother, not his slave, that died.

Creon: One perished ravaging his fatherland, the other defending it.

Antigone: Nevertheless, Hades desires these rites.

Creon: Surely the good are not pleased to be made equal with the evil!

Antigone: Who knows how the gods see good and evil? 430

---

[1]The ancestor of the noble families of Thebes.

Creon: A foe is never a friend—even in death.

Antigone: It is not my nature to join in hating, but in loving.

Creon: Your place, then, is with the dead. If you must love, love them. While I live, no woman shall overbear me.

(Ismene is led from the King's house by two attendants.)

Chorus: See, Ismene come through the gate shedding such tears as loving sisters weep. It seems as if a cloud gathers about her brow and breaks in rain upon her cheek.

Creon: And you, who lurked like a viper in my house, sucking the blood of my honor, while I knew not that I was nursing two reptiles ready to strike at my throne—come, tell me now, will you confess your part in this guilty burial, or will you swear you knew nothing of it? 440

Ismene: I am guilty if she is, and share the blame.

Antigone: No, no! Justice will not permit this. You did not consent to the deed, nor would I let you have part in it.

Ismene: But now that danger threatens you, I am not ashamed to come to your side.

Antigone: Who did the deed, the gods and the dead know; a friend in words is not the friend I love.

Ismene: Sister, do not reject me, but let me die with you, and duly honor the dead. 450

Antigone: Do not court death, nor claim a deed to which you did not put your hand. My death will suffice.

Ismene: How could life be dear to me without you?

Antigone: Ask Creon, you think highly of his word.

Ismene: Why taunt me so, when it does you no good?

Antigone: Ah, if I mock you, it is with pain I do it.

Ismene: Oh tell me, how can I serve you, even now?

Antigone: Save yourself; I do not grudge your escape.

Ismene: Oh, my grief! Can I not share your fate? 460

Antigone: You chose to live, and I to die.

Ismene: At least I begged you not to make that choice.

Antigone: This world approved your caution, but the gods my courage.

Ismene: But now I approve, and so I am guilty too.

Antigone: Ah little sister, be of good cheer, and live. My life has long been given to death, that I might serve the dead.

Creon: Behold, one of these girls turns to folly now, as the other one has ever since she was born.

Ismene: Yes, Sire, such reason as nature gives us may break under misfortune, and go astray. 470

Creon: Yours did, when you chose to share evil deeds with the evil.

Ismene: But I cannot live without her.

Creon: You mistake; she lives no more.

Ismene: Surely you will not slay your own son's betrothed?

Creon: He can plough other fields.

Ismene: But he cannot find such love again.

Creon: I will not have an evil wife for my son.

Antigone: Ah, Haemon, my beloved! Dishonored by your father! 480

Creon: Enough! I'll hear no more of you and your marriage!

Chorus: Will you indeed rob your son of his bride?

Creon: Death will do that for me.

Chorus: It seems determined then, that she shall die.

Creon: Determined, yes—for me and for you. No more delay—servants, take them within. Let them know that they

are women, not meant to roam abroad. For even the boldest seek to fly when they see Death stretching his hand their way.

(Attendants lead Antigone and Ismene into the house.)

Chorus: Blest are they whose days have not tasted of sorrow: 490
For if a house has dared the anger of heaven,
Evil strikes at it down the generations,
Wave after wave, like seas that batter a headland.

I see how fate has harried the seed of Labdakos;
Son cannot fly the curse that was laid on the sire,
The doom incurred by the dead must fall on the living:
When gods pursue, no race can find deliverance.

And even these, the last of the children of Oedipus—
Because of the frenzy that rose in a passionate heart,
Because of a handful of blood-stained dust that was sprinkled— 500
The last of the roots is cut, and the light extinguished.

O Zeus, how vain is the mortal will that opposes
The Will Immortal that neither sleeps nor ages,
The Imperturbable Power that on Olympus
Dwells in unclouded glory, the All-Beholding!
Wise was he who said that ancient saying:
Whom the gods bewilder, at last takes evil for virtue;
And let no man lament if his lot is humble—
No great things come to mortals without a curse.

But look, Sire: Haemon, the last of your sons, approaches. I 510
wonder if he comes grieving over the doom of his promised bride, Antigone, and bitter that his marriage-hopes are baffled?

(Haemon comes before his father.)

Creon: We shall know soon, better than seers could tell us. My son, you have heard the irrevocable doom decreed for your betrothed. Do you come to rage against your father, or do you remember the duty of filial love, no matter what I do.

Haemon: Father, I am yours; and knowing you are wise, I follow the paths you trace for me. No marriage could be more to me than your good guidance. 520

Creon: Yes, my son, this should be your heart's first law, in all things to obey your father's will. Men pray for dutiful children growing up about them in their homes, that such may pay their father's foe with evil, and honor as their father does, his friend. But if a man begets undutiful children, what shall we say that he has sown, only sorrow for himself and triumph for his enemies? Do not then, my son, thinking of pleasures, put aside reason for a woman's sake. If you brought an evil woman to your bed and home, you would find that such embraces soon grow hateful; and nothing can wound so 530 deeply as to find a loved one false. No, but with loathing, and as if she were your enemy, let this girl go to find a husband in the house of Hades. For she alone in all the city defied and disobeyed me; I have taken her in the act, and I will not be a liar to my people—I will slay her.

Let her appeal all she pleases to the claims of kindred

blood. If I am to rear my own kin to evil deeds, certainly I must expect evil among the people. Only a man who rules his own household justly can do justice in the State. If anyone transgresses, and does violence to the laws, or thinks to dictate to the ruler, I will not tolerate it. No!—whoever the city shall appoint to rule, that man must be obeyed, in little things and great things, in just things and unjust; for the man who is a good subject is the one who would be a good ruler, and it is he who in time of war will stand his ground where he is placed, loyal to his comrades and without fear, though the spears fall around him like rain in a storm. 540

But disobedience is the worst of evils. It desolates households; it ruins cities; it throws the ranks of allies into confusion and rout. On the other hand, note those whose lives are prosperous: they owe it, you will generally find, to obedience. Therefore we must uphold the cause of order; and certainly we must not let a woman defy us. It would be better to fall from power by a man's hand, than to be called weaker than a woman. 550

Chorus: Unless the years have stolen our wits, all that you say seems wise.

Haemon: Father, the gods implant reason in men, the highest of all things that we call our own. I have no skill to prove, and I would not wish to show, that you speak unwisely; and yet another man, too, might have some useful thought. I count it a duty to keep my ears alert for what men say about you, noting especially when they find fault. The people dare not say to your face what would displease you; but I can hear the things murmured in the dark, and the whole city weeps for this maiden. "No woman ever," they say, "so little merited a cruel fate. None was ever doomed to a shameful death for deeds so noble as hers; who, when her brother lay dead from bloody wounds, would not leave him unburied for the birds and dogs to mangle. Does not so pious an act deserve golden praise?" 560 570

Such is the way the people speak in secret. To me, father, nothing is so precious as your welfare. What is there father or son can so rejoice in as the other's fair repute? I pray you therefore do not wear one mood too stubbornly, as if no one else could possibly be right. For the man who thinks he is the only wise man always proves hollow when we sound him. No, though a man be wise, it is no shame for him to learn many things, and to yield at the right time. When the streams rage and overflow in Winter, you know how those trees that yield come safely through the flood; but the stubborn are torn up and perish, root and branch. Consider too, the sailor who keeps his sheet always taut, and never slackens it; presently his boat overturns and his keel floats uppermost. So, though you are angry, permit reason to move you. If I, young as I am, may offer a thought, I would say it were best if men were by nature always wise; but that being seldom so, it is prudent to listen to those who offer honest counsel. 580

Chorus: Sire, it is fitting that you should weigh his words, if he speaks in season; and you, Haemon, should mark your father's words; for on both parts there has been wise speech. 590

Creon: What! Shall men of our age be schooled by youths like this?

Haemon: In nothing that does not go with reason; but as to my youth, you should weigh my merits, not my years.

Creon: Is it your merit that you honor the lawless?

Haemon: I could wish no one to respect evil-doers.

Creon: This girl—is she not tainted with that plague?

Haemon: Our Theban folk deny it, with one voice.

Creon: Shall Thebes, then, tell me how to rule? 600

Haemon: Now who speaks like a boy?

Creon: Tell me—am I to rule by my own judgment or the views of others?

Haemon: That is no city which belongs to one man.

Creon: Is not the city held to be the ruler's?

Haemon: That kind of monarchy would do well in a desert.

Creon: Ho, this boy, it seems, is the woman's champion!

Haemon: Yes, if you are a woman, for my concern is for you.

Creon: Shameless, to bandy arguments with your father! 610

Haemon: Only because I see you flouting justice.

Creon: Is it wrong for me to respect my royal position?

Haemon: It is a poor way to respect it, trampling on the laws of the gods.

Creon: This is depravity, putting a woman foremost!

Haemon: At least you will not find me so depraved that I fear to plead for justice.

Creon: Every word you speak is a plea for that girl.

Haemon: And for you, and for me, and for the gods below.

Creon: Marry her you shall not, this side the grave. 620

Haemon: She must die then, and in dying destroy others?

Creon: Ha, you go so far as open threats?

Haemon: I speak no threats, but grieve for your fatal stubbornness.

Creon: You shall rue your unwise teaching of wisdom.

Haemon: If you were not my father, I would call you unwise.

Creon: Slave of a woman, do not think you can cajole me.

Haemon: Then no one but yourself may speak, you will hear no reason? 630

Creon: Enough of this—now, by Olympus, you shall smart for baiting me this way! Bring her here, that hateful rebel, that she may die forthwith before his eyes—yes, at her bridegroom's side!

Haemon: No, no, never think it, I shall not witness her death; but my face your eyes shall never see again. Give your passion its way before those who can endure you!

(Haemon rushes away.)

Chorus: He has gone, O King, in angry haste; a youthful mind, when stung, is impetuous.

Creon: Let him do what he will, let him dream himself more than a common man, but he shall not save those girls from their doom. 640

Chorus: Are you indeed determined to slay them both?

Creon: Not the one whose hands are clean of the crime— you do well to remind me of that.

Chorus: But how will you put the other one to death?

Creon: I will take her where the path is loneliest, and hide her, living, in a rocky vault, with only so much food as the pious laws require, that the city may avoid reproach. There she can pray to Hades, whose gods alone she worships; perhaps they will bargain with death for her escape. And if 650 they do not, she will learn, too late, that it is lost labor to revere the dead.

[Antigone engages in an impassioned lament over her destiny. Creon will not relent, and the guards lead Antigone to the tomb.]

Teiresias: Princes of Thebes, it is a hard journey for me to come here, for the blind must walk by another's steps and see with another's eyes; yet I have come.

Creon: And what, Teiresias, are your tidings?

Teiresias: I shall tell you; and listen well to the seer.

Creon: I have never slighted your counsel.

Teiresias: It is that way you have steered the city well. 660

Creon: I know, and bear witness, to the worth of your words.

Teiresias: Then mark them now: for I tell you, you stand on fate's thin edge.

Creon: What do you mean? I shudder at your message.

Teiresias: You will know, when you hear the signs my art has disclosed. For lately, as I took my place in my ancient seat of augury, where all the birds of the air gather about me, I heard strange things. They were screaming with feverish rage, their usual clear notes were a frightful jargon; and I knew 670 they were rending each other murderously with their talons: the whir of their wings told an angry tale.

Straightway, these things filling me with fear, I kindled fire upon an altar, with due ceremony, and laid a sacrifice among the faggots; but Hephaestus would not consume my offering with flame. A moisture oozing out from the bones and flesh trickled upon the embers, making them smoke and sputter. Then the gall burst and scattered on the air, and the steaming thighs lay bared of the fat that had wrapped them.

Such was the failure of the rites by which I vainly asked a 680 sign, as this boy reported them; for his eyes serve me, as I serve others. And I tell you, it is your deeds that have brought a sickness on the State. For the altars of our city and the altars of our hearths have been polluted, one and all, by birds and dogs who have fed on that outraged corpse that was the son of Oedipus. It is for this reason the gods refuse prayer and sacrifice at our hands, and will not consume the meat-offering with flame; nor does any bird give a clear sign by its shrill cry, for they have tasted the fatness of a slain man's blood.

Think then on these things, my son. All men are liable to 690 err; but he shows wisdom and earns blessings who heals the ills his errors caused, being not too stubborn; too stiff a will is folly. Yield to the dead, I counsel you, and do not stab the fallen; what prowess is it to slay the slain anew? I have sought your welfare, it is for your good I speak; and it should be a pleasant thing to hear a good counselor when he counsels for your own gain.

Creon: Old man, you all shoot your shafts at me, like archers at a butt—you must practice your prophecies on me! Indeed, the tribe of augurs has long trafficked in me and 700 made me their merchandise! Go, seek your price, drive your trade, if you will, in the precious ore of Sardis and the gold of India; but you shall not buy that corpse a grave! No, though the eagles of Zeus should bear their carrion dainties to their Master's throne—no, not even for dread of that will I permit this burial!—for I know that no mortal can pollute the gods.

So, hoary prophet, the wisest come to a shameful fall when they clothe shameful counsels in fair words to earn a bribe.

Teiresias: Alas! Does no man know, does none consider . . .

Creon: What pompous precept now? 710

Teiresias: . . . that honest counsel is the most priceless gift?

Creon: Yes, and folly the most worthless.

Teiresias: True, and you are infected with that disease.

Creon: This wise man's taunts I shall not answer in kind.

Teiresias: Yet you slander me, saying I augur falsely.

Creon: Well, the tribe of seers always liked money.

Teiresias: And the race of tyrants was ever proud and covetous.

Creon: Do you know you are speaking to your king? 720

Teiresias: I know it: you saved the city when you followed my advice.

Creon: You have your gifts, but you love evil deeds.

Teiresias: Ah, you will sting me to utter the dread secret I have kept hidden in my soul.

Creon: Out with it!—but if you hope to earn a fee by shaking my purpose, you babble in vain.

Teiresias: Indeed I think I shall earn no reward from you.

Creon: Be sure you shall not trade on my resolve.

Teiresias: Know then—aye, know it well!—you will not 730 live through many days, seeing the sun's swift chariot coursing heaven, 'til one whose blood comes from your own heart shall be a corpse, matching two other corpses; because you have given to the shadows one who belongs to the sun, you have lodged a living soul in the grave; yet in this world you detain one who belongs to the world below, a corpse unburied, unhonored, and unblest. These things outrage the gods; therefore those dread Airiness, who serve the fury of the gods, lie now in wait for you, preparing a vengeance equal to your guilt. 740

And mark well if I speak these things as a hireling. A time not long delayed will waken the wailing of men and women in your house. But after these cries I hear a more dreadful tumult. For wrath and hatred will stir to arms against you every city whose mangled sons had the burial-rite from dogs and wild beasts, or from birds that will bear the taint of this crime even to the startled hearths of the unburied dead.

Such arrows I do indeed aim at your heart, since you provoke me—they will find their mark, and you shall not escape the sting.—Boy, lead me home, that he may spend 750 his rage on younger men, or learn to curb his bitter tongue and temper his violent mind.

(Teiresias is led away.)

Chorus: The seer has gone, O King, predicting terrible things. And since the days when my white hair was dark, I know that he has never spoken false auguries for our city.

Creon: I know that too, I know it well, and I am troubled in soul. It is hard to yield; but if by stubbornness I bring my pride to ruin—that too would be hard.

Chorus: Son of Menoekeus, it is time to heed good counsel. 760

Creon: What shall I do, then? Speak, and I will obey.

Chorus: Go free the living maiden from her grave, and make a grave for the unburied dead.

Creon: Is this indeed your counsel? Do you bid me yield?

Chorus: Yes, and without delay; for the swift judgments of the gods cut short the folly of men.

Creon: It is hard to do—to retreat from a firm stand— but I yield, I will obey you. We must not wage a vain war with Fate.

Chorus: Go then, let your own hand do these things; do not leave them to others.   770

Creon: Even as I am I will go: come, servants, all of you, bring tools to raise one grave and open another. Since our judgment has taken this turn, I who buried the girl will free her myself.—My heart misgive me, it is best to keep the established laws, even to life's end.

(Creon and his servants go toward the plain.)

[The Chorus sings a hymn in praise of Dionysus.]

(A Messenger appears, from the direction of the plain.)

Messenger: Neighbors of the house of Cadmus, dwellers within Amphion's[2] walls, there is no state of mortal life that I would praise or pity, for none is beyond swift change. Fortune raises men up and fortune casts them down from day to day, and no man can foretell the fate of things established. For   780 Creon was blest in all that I count happiness; he had honor as our savior; power as our king; pride as the father of princely children. Now all is ended. For when a man is stripped of happiness, I count him not with the living—he is but a breathing corpse. Let a man have riches heaped in his house, and live in royal splendor; yet I would not give the shadow of a breath for all, if they bring no gladness.

Chorus: What fearful news have you about our princes?

Messenger: Death; and the living are guilty of the dead.

Chorus: Who is the slayer—who is slain?   790

Messenger: Haemon has perished, and it was no stranger shed his blood.

Chorus: His father's hand, or his own?

Messenger: His own, maddened by his father's crime.

Chorus: O prophet, how true your word has proved!

Messenger: This is the way things are: consider then, how to act.

Chorus: Look!—the unhappy Eurydice, Creon's consort, comes from the house; is it by chance, or has she heard these tidings of her son?   800

(Eurydice comes from the house.)

Eurydice: I heard your words, citizens, as I was going to the shrine of Pallas with my prayers. As I loosed the bolts of the gate, the message of woe to my household smote my ear. I sank back, stricken with horror, into the arms of my handmaids, and my senses left me. Yet say again these tidings. I shall hear them as one who is no stranger to grief.

Messenger: Dear lady, I will tell you what I saw, I will hide nothing of the truth. I would gladly tell you a happier tale, but it would soon be found out false. Truth is the only way.—I guided your lord the King to the furthest part of the plain,   810 where the body of Polynices, torn by dogs, still lay unpitied. There we prayed to the goddess of the roads, and to Pluto,[3] in mercy to restrain their wrath. We washed the dead with holy rites, and all that was left of the mortal man we burned with fresh-plucked branches; and over the ashes at last we raised a mound of his native earth.

That done, we turned our steps toward those fearsome caves where in a cold nuptial chamber, with couch of stone, that maiden had been given as a bride of Death. But from afar off, one of us heard a voice wailing aloud, and turned to   820 tell our master Creon.

And as the King drew nearer, the sharp anguish of broken cries came to his ears. Then he groaned and said like one in pain, "Can my sudden fear be true? Am I on the saddest road I ever went? That voice is my son's! Hurry, my servants, to the tomb, and through the gap where the stones have been torn out, look into the cell— tell me if it is Haemon's voice I hear, or if my wits are tortured by the gods."

At these words from our stricken master, we went to make that search; and in the dim furthest part of the tomb we saw   830 Antigone hanging by the neck, her scarf of fine linen twisted into a cruel noose. And there too we saw Haemon—his arms about her waist, while he cried out upon the loss of his bride, and his father's deed, and his ill-starred love.

But now the King approached, and saw him, and cried out with horror, and went in and called with piteous voice, "Unhappy boy, what a deed have you done, breaking into this tomb! What purpose have you? Has grief stolen your reason? Come forth, my son! I pray you—I implore!" The boy answered no word, but glared at him with fierce eyes, spat in   840 his face, and drew his cross-hilted sword. His father turned and fled, and the blow missed its mark. Then that maddened boy, torn between grief and rage and penitence, straightway leaned upon his sword, and drove it half its length into his side; and in the little moment before death, he clasped the maiden in his arms, and her pale cheek was red where his blood gushed forth.

Corpse enfolding corpse they lie; he has won his bride, poor lad, not here but in the halls of Death; to all of us he has left a terrible witness that man's worst error is to reject good   850 counsel.

(Eurydice goes into the house.)

Chorus: What does this mean? The lady turns and goes without a word.

Messenger: I too am startled; but I think it means she is too proud to cry out before the people. Within the house, with her handmaids about her, the tears will flow. Life has taught her prudence.

Chorus: It may be; yet I fear. To me such silence seems more ominous than many lamentations.

Messenger: Then I will go into the house, and learn if   860 some tragic purpose has formed in her tortured heart. Yes, you speak wisely; too much silence may hide terrible meanings.

(The Messenger enters the house. As he goes, Creon comes into the open place before the house with attendants carrying the shrouded body of Haemon on a bier.)

---

[2]Son of Zeus and Antiope; with his twin brother Zethus, he built the walls of Thebes.

[3]Another name for Hades, the Greek god of the netherworld, the shadowy realm where the souls of the dead were thought to rest.

Chorus: See, the King himself draws near, with the sad proof of his folly; this tells a tale of no violence by strangers, but—if I may say it—of his own misdeeds.

Creon: Woe for the sins of a darkened soul, the sins of a stubborn pride that played with death! Behold me, the father who has slain, behold the son who has perished! I am punished for the blindness of my counsels. Alas my son, cut down in youth untimely, woe is me!—your spirit fled—not yours the fault and folly, but my own! 870

Chorus: Too late, too late your eyes are opened!

Creon: I have learned that bitter lesson. But it was some god, I think, darkened my mind and turned me into ways of cruelty. Now my days are overthrown and my joys trampled. Alas, man's labors come but to foolish ends!

(The Messenger comes from the house.)

Messenger: Sire, one sees your hands are not empty, but there is more laid up in store for you. Woeful is the burden you bear, and you must look on further woes within your house. 880

Creon: Why, how can there be more?

Messenger: Your queen is dead, the mother of that lad—unhappy lady! This is Fate's latest blow.

Creon: Death, Death, how many deaths will stay your hunger? For me is there no mercy? O messenger of evil, bearer of bitter tidings, what is this you tell me? I was already dead, but you smite me anew. What do you say?—what is this news you bring of slaughter heaped on slaughter?

(The doors of the King's house are opened, and the corpse of Eurydice is disclosed.)

Chorus: Behold with your own eyes!

Creon: Oh, horror!—woe upon woe! Can any further 890 dreadful thing await me? I have but now raised my son in these arms—and here again I see a corpse before me. Alas, unhappy mother—alas, alas my child!

Messenger: At the altar of your house, self-stabbed with a keen knife, she suffered her darkening eyes to close, while she lamented that other son, Megareus, who died so nobly but a while ago, and then this boy whose corpse is here beside you. But with her last breath and with a bitter cry she invoked evil upon you, the slayer of your sons.

Creon: Will no one strike me to the heart with the two- 900 edged sword?—miserable that I am, and plunged in misery!

Messenger: Yes, both this son's death and that other son's were charged to you by her whose corpse you see.

Creon: But how did she do this violence upon herself?

Messenger: Her own hand struck her to the heart, when she had heard how this boy died.

Creon: I cannot escape the guilt of these things, it rests on no other of mortal kind. I, only I, am the slayer, wretched that I am—I own the truth. Lead me away, my servants, lead me quickly hence, for my life is but death. 910

Chorus: You speak well, if any speech is good amid so much evil. When all is trouble, the briefest way is best.

Creon: Oh let it come now, the fate most merciful for me, my last day—that will be the best fate of all. Oh let it come

swiftly, that I may not look upon tomorrow's light!

Chorus: That is hidden in the future. Present tasks claim our care. The ordering of the future does not rest with mortals.

Creon: Yet all my desire is summed up in that prayer.

Chorus: Pray no more: no man evades his destiny.

Creon: Lead me away, I pray you; a rash, foolish man, who 920 has slain you, O my son, unwittingly, and you too my wife—unhappy that I am! Where can I find comfort, where can I turn my gaze?—for where I have turned my hand, all has gone wrong; and this last blow breaks me and bows my head.

(Creon is led into his house as the Chorus speaks.)

Chorus: If any man would be happy, and not broken by Fate, Wisdom is the thing he should seek, for happiness hides there. Let him revere the gods and keep their words inviolate, for proud men who speak great words come in the end to despair. And learn wisdom in sorrow, when it is too late.

Q Who is the tragic figure in this play: Antigone or Creon?

Q How does the play illustrate "heroic idealism" and the conflict between personal and communal obligations?

The tragic action in *Antigone* springs from the irreconcilability of Antigone's personal idealism and Creon's hard-headed political realism. Creon means well by the state; he is committed to the exercise of justice under the law. As a king newly come to power, he perceives his duty in terms of his authority: "whoever the city shall appoint to rule," says Creon, "that man must be obeyed, in little things and in great things, in just things and unjust; for the man who is a good subject is the one who would be a good ruler . . ." But Creon ignores the ancient imperatives of divine law and familial duty. His blind devotion to the state and his unwillingness to compromise trap him into making a decision whose consequences are disastrous.

In the Greek tragedy, the weakness or "tragic flaw" of the **protagonist** (the leading character) brings that character into conflict with fate or with the **antagonist** (one who opposes the protagonist), and ultimately to his or her fall. Creon's excessive pride (in Greek, *hubris*) results in the loss of those who are dearest to him. But Antigone is also a victim of self-righteous inflexibility. In an age that confined women to the domestic household and expected them to conform to male opinion, Antigone was unique. In ancient Greece, a girl in her early teens might marry a man considerably older than she. Along with the other female members of the household, she oversaw the daily chores associated with child-rearing, food preparation, and the production of clothing—spinning, weaving, and sewing. She could not inherit or own property and could not choose to divorce her husband (though he could divorce her); hence she was subordinate to her husband, as she had been to her father. While there were exceptions to this pattern (usually among the courtesans of male aristocrats), it seems clear that by challenging male authority, Antigone threatened the status quo: "*She* is the man," Creon angrily objects, "if she can carry this off unpunished." Antigone's sister, Ismene, argues, "We must remember we were born women, not meant to strive with men." But Antigone persists: her heroism derives from her unswerving dedication to the ideals of divine justice and to the duty of the individual to honor family, even if it challenges the laws of the state.

Sophocles perceived the difficulties involved in reconciling public good and private conscience, and in achieving harmony between the individual and the community. In *Antigone*, he offers a moving plea for sound judgment and rational action, a plea that rings with the unbounded optimism of the choral chant: "Wonders are many in the world, and the wonder of all is man. . . . With speech and wind-swift thought he builds the State to his mood / Prospering while he honors the gods and the laws of the land" (lines 284, 296–297).

Aristotle on Tragedy

In modern parlance, the word "tragedy" is often used to describe a terrible act of fate that befalls an unwitting individual. With regard to drama, however, the word (and the form it describes) has a very different meaning. As a literary genre, tragedy deals not so much with catastrophic events as with *how* these events work to affect individuals in shaping their character and in determining their fate. The protagonist becomes a tragic hero not because of what befalls him, but rather as a result of the manner in which he confronts his destiny. In the *Poetics*, the world's first treatise on literary criticism, the Greek philosopher Aristotle (384–322 B.C.E.) describes tragedy as an imitation of an action involving incidents that arouse pity and fear. Tragic action, he argues, should involve an error in judgment made by an individual who is "better than the ordinary man" but with whom the audience may sympathize.

The *Poetics* further clarifies the importance of "proper construction": the play must have a balanced arrangement of parts, and the action of the story should be limited to the events of a single day. The plot should consist of a single action made up of several closely connected incidents (without irrelevant additions). If we apply Aristotle's aesthetic principles of tragedy to Sophocles' *Antigone*, we arrive at an understanding of the so-called "unities" of action and time that characterize classic Greek tragedy. (Seventeenth-century playwrights added "unity of place" to neoclassical drama.) In *Antigone*, the action rests on a single incident: the rash decision of Creon. The events of the play occur within a single place and are acted out within a time span comparable to their occurrence in real life. Every episode in the play is relevant to the central action. Proportion and order apply to the writing of drama, suggests Aristotle, even as they must apply to the conduct and the fate of the tragic hero.

READING 1.14 From Aristotle's *Poetics* (ca. 340 B.C.E.)

. . . let us now consider the proper construction of the Fable or Plot, as that is at once the first and the most important thing in Tragedy. We have laid it down that a tragedy is an imitation of an action that is complete in itself, as a whole of some magnitude; for a whole may be of no magnitude to speak of. Now a whole is that which has beginning, middle, and end. A beginning is that which is not itself necessarily after anything else, and which has naturally something else after it; an end is that which is naturally after something itself, either as its necessary or usual consequent, and with nothing **10** else after it; and a middle, that which is by nature after one thing and has also another after it. A well-constructed Plot, therefore, cannot either begin or end at any point one likes; beginning and end in it must be of the forms just described. Again: to be beautiful, a living creature, and every whole made up of parts, must not only present a certain order in its arrangement of parts, but also be of certain definite magnitude. Beauty is a matter of size and order, and therefore impossible either (1) in a very minute creature, since our perception becomes indistinct as it approaches instantaneity; **20** or (2) in a creature of vast size—one, say, 1000 miles long—as in that case, instead of the object being seen all at once, the unity and wholeness of it is lost to the beholder. Just in the same way, then, as a beautiful whole made up of parts, or a beautiful living creature, must be of some size, but a size to be taken in by the eye, so a story or Plot must be of some length, but of a length to be taken in by the eye, so a story or Plot must be of some length, but of a length to be taken in by the memory. . . . The truth is that, just as in the other imitative arts one imitation is always of one thing, so in poetry the **30** story, as an imitation of action, must represent one action, a complete whole, with its several incidents so closely connected that the transposal or withdrawal of any one of them will disjoin and dislocate the whole. For that which makes no perceptible difference by its presence or absence is no real part of the whole. . . . The perfect Plot, accordingly, must have a single, and not (as some tell us) a double issue; the change in the hero's fortunes must be not from misery to happiness, but on the contrary from happiness to misery; and the cause of it must lie not in any depravity, but in some **40** great error on his part; . . . As Tragedy is an imitation of personages better than the ordinary man, we in our way should follow the example of good portrait-painters, who reproduce the distinctive features of a man, and at the same time, without losing the likeness, make him handsomer than he is. . . .

Q Why does Aristotle require the length of a play to be equivalent to the course of its plot in real life?

Q How does a "great error" figure in the plot of a tragedy?

Greek Philosophy:
The Speculative Leap

In the ancient world, where most people saw themselves at the mercy of forces they could not comprehend, shamans and priestesses explored the unknown by means of sympathetic magic, myth, and ritual. During the sixth century B.C.E., a small group of Greek thinkers offered an intellectual alternative that combined careful observation, systematic analysis, and the exercise of pure reason. These individuals, whom we call philosophers (literally, "lovers of wisdom"), laid the foundations for Western scientific and philosophic inquiry. Instead of making nature the object of worship, they made it the object of study. To those who interpreted disasters such as earthquakes and lightning as expressions of divine anger, they submitted that such events might have natural, not supernatural, causes. Challenging all prevailing myths, the Greek philosophers made the speculative leap from supernatural to natural explanations of the unknown.

The Greeks were not the first to argue that the universe was governed by a natural order. The ancient Chinese, for instance, described the cosmos in terms of complimentary and interacting polarities, the *yin* and the *yang* (see chapter 3). In India, Hindu culture had stressed the oneness of all things in the universe. But while Asians might hypothesize on the wholeness of nature, the Greeks subjected it to rigorous analysis, a process that required the separation of the whole into its component parts. The ancient Greeks defended rationalism and objectivity as alternatives to intuition, holism, and supernaturalism. Their claims to intellectual detachment and objectivity—the fundamentals of the scientific method—put them at odds with East Asian claims to intuitively grasped truths. They also stand in clear contrast to the Hebrew call for unswerving faith. Indeed, the Greek glorification of reason provides a sharp contrast to the Hebrew exaltation of faith, as exemplified, for instance, in the Book of Job. These two modes of experience—reason (rooted in the Greco-Roman tradition) and faith (rooted in the Judeo-Christian tradition)—have competed for primacy in shaping Western culture from earliest times to the present.

Naturalist Philosophy: The Pre-Socratics

The earliest of the Greek philosopher-scientists lived just prior to the time of Socrates in the city of Miletus on the Ionian coast of Asia Minor (see Map 4.1). Although their senses reported a world of constant change, they reasoned that there must be a single, unifying substance that formed the basic "stuff" of nature. They asked, "What is everything made of?" "How do things come into existence?" and "What permanent substance lies behind the world of appearance?" Thales (ca. 625–ca. 547 B.C.E.), history's first philosopher, held that water was the fundamental substance and source from which all things proceeded. Water's potential for change (from solid to liquid to gas) and its pervasiveness on earth convinced him that water formed the primary matter of the universe. While Thales argued that water formed the basic stuff of nature, his followers challenged this view: "Air," said one, "fire," countered another, and still others identified the basic substance as a mixture of the primordial elements. The concept that a single, unifying substance underlay reality drew opposition from some of the pre-Socratics. The universe, argued Heraclitus of Ephesus (ca. 540–ca. 480 B.C.E.), has no permanence, but, rather, is in constant process or flux. Heraclitus defended the idea that change itself was the basis of reality. "You cannot step twice into the same river," he wrote, "for fresh waters are ever flowing in upon you." Yet, Heraclitus believed that an underlying Form or Guiding Force (in Greek, *logos*) permeated nature, an idea that resembles Hindu pantheism and anticipates the Christian concept (found in the Gospel of John) of a Great Intelligence governing the beginning of time. For Heraclitus the Force was impersonal, universal, and eternal.

Around 500 B.C.E., Leucippus of Miletus theorized that physical reality consisted of minute, invisible particles that moved ceaselessly in the void. These he called *atoms*, the Greek word meaning "indivisible." Democritus (ca. 460–370 B.C.E.), a follower of Leucippus and the best known of the naturalist philosophers, developed the atomic theory of matter. For Democritus, the mind consisted of the same indivisible physical substances as everything else in nature. According to this materialist view, atoms moved constantly and eternally according to chance in infinite time and space. The atomic theory survived into Roman times, and although forgotten for two thousand years thereafter, it was validated by physicists of the early twentieth century.

Yet another pre-Socratic thinker, named Pythagoras (ca. 580–ca. 500 B.C.E.), advanced an idea that departed from both the material and nonmaterial views of the universe. Pythagoras believed that proportion, discovered through number, was the true basis of reality. According to Pythagoras, all universal relationships may be expressed through numbers, the truths of which are eternal and unchanging. The formula in plane geometry that equates the square of the hypotenuse in right angle triangles to the sum of the square of the other two sides—a theorem traditionally associated with Pythagoras—is an example of such an unchanging and eternal truth, as is the simplest of mathematical equations: $2 + 2 = 4$. Pythagoras was the founding father of pure mathematics. He was also the first to demonstrate the relationship between musical harmonics and numbers. His view that number gives order and harmony to the universe is basic to the principles of balance and proportion that dominate classical art and music (see chapter 5).

In contrast with the Egyptians and the Mesopotamians, who deified the sun, the rivers, and other natural elements, the pre-Socratics stripped nature of all supernatural associations. They made accurate predictions of solar and lunar eclipses, plotted astronomical charts, and hypothesized on the processes of regeneration in plants and animals. Yet, in the areas of geometry, astronomy, and mathematics, it is likely that they inherited a large body of practical and theoretical data from the pyramid

Science and Technology

600 B.C.E. Thales of Miletus produces an accurate theory of the solar eclipse; he also advances the study of deductive geometry[†]

540 B.C.E. Anaximander claims that life evolved from beginnings in the sea and that man evolved from a more primitive species

530 B.C.E. Pythagoras argues for a spherical earth around which five planets revolve; he also develops the "Pythagorean Theorem"

500 B.C.E. Leucippus theorizes that all matter is composed of "atoms"

480 B.C.E. Anaxagoras postulates that the sun is a large, glowing rock; he explains solar eclipses

[†]All dates in this chapter are approximate

builders and calendar keepers of Egypt, and from the astrologists and palace engineers of Babylon, who knew how to solve linear and quadratic equations. It is also likely that the philosophic and religious theories originating in China and India influenced the speculative systems of Heraclitus, Pythagoras, and other pre-Socratics. Ideas, along with goods like silk, ivory, and cotton, moved back and forth along the overland trade routes that linked East Asia to the Mediterranean. For example, the Pythagorean proscription against eating animal flesh and certain plants suggests Greek familiarity with the Hindu belief in reincarnation and the transmigration of souls (see chapter 1). And the Chinese association between illness and an imbalance of vital body energy seems to have made its way westward into the purview of Hippocrates. Hippocrates (ca. 460–377 B.C.E.), the most famous of the Greek physicians and so-called "father of medicine," investigated the influence of diet and environment on general health and advanced the idea that an imbalance among bodily "humors"—blood, phlegm, black bile, and yellow bile—was the cause of disease. He insisted on the necessary relationship of cause and effect in matters of physical illness, and he raised questions concerning the influence of the mind on the body. He may also be deemed the "father of medical ethics": to this day, graduating physicians are encouraged to practice medicine according to the precepts of the Hippocratic Oath (probably not written by Hippocrates himself), which binds them to heal the sick and abstain from unprofessional medical practices.

The separation of the natural from the supernatural was as essential to the birth of medical science as it was to speculative philosophy. And although no agreement as to the nature of reality was ever reached among the pre-Socratics, these intellectuals laid the groundwork and the methodology for the rational investigation of the universe. Their efforts represent the beginnings of Western science and philosophy as formal disciplines.

Humanist Philosophy

The Sophists

The naturalist philosophers were concerned with describing physical reality in terms of the unity that lay behind the chaos of human perceptions. The philosophers who followed them pursued a different course: they turned their attention from the world of nature to the world of the mind, from physical matters to moral concerns, and from the gathering of information to the cultivation of wisdom. Significantly, these thinkers fathered the field of inquiry known as metaphysics (literally, "beyond physics"), that branch of philosophy concerned with abstract thought. They asked not simply "*What* do we know (about nature)?" but "*How* do we know what we know?" The transition from the examination of matter to the exploration of mind established the humanistic direction of Greek philosophy for at least two centuries (Figure **4.12**).

The first humanist philosophers were a group of traveling scholar-teachers called Sophists. Masters of formal debate, the Sophists were concerned with defining the limits of human knowledge. The Thracian Sophist Protagoras (ca. 485–410 B.C.E.) believed that knowledge could not exceed human opinion, a position summed up in his memorable dictum: "Man is the measure of all things." His contemporary Gorgias (ca. 483–ca. 376 B.C.E.) tried to prove that reality is incomprehensible and that even if one could comprehend it, one could not describe the real to others. Such skepticism was common to the Sophists, who argued that truth and justice were relative: what might be considered just and true for one individual or situation might not be just and true for another.

Socrates and the Quest for Virtue

Athens' foremost philosopher, Socrates (ca. 470–399 B.C.E.), vigorously opposed the views of the Sophists. Insisting on the

Figure 4.12 Interior of a red-figured *kylix* (a Greek drinking cup), Douris, ca. 480 B.C.E. Terracotta, height 4⅜ in, diameter 11¾ in. The Metropolitan Museum of Art, New York. Rogers Fund, 1952 (52.11.4).

Science and Technology

470 B.C.E. Greek physicians practice dissection in the study of human anatomy

430 B.C.E. Democritus argues that atoms move freely in space and are eternal

400 B.C.E. Hippocrates' treatises on medicine include a study of epidemics, a description of phobias, and an examination of the effects of the environment on health

330 B.C.E. Agnodike, a female physician, successfully challenges the law that prohibits women from practicing medicine in Athens

absolute nature of truth and justice, he described the ethical life as belonging to a larger set of universal truths and an unchanging moral order. For Socrates, virtue was not discovered by means of clever but misleading argumentation—a kind of reasoning that would come to be called (after the Sophists) *sophistry*, nor was it relative to individual circumstances. Rather, virtue was a condition of the *psyche**, the seat of both the moral and intellectual faculties of the individual. Hence, understanding the true meaning of virtue was preliminary to acting virtuously: to know good is to do good.

The question of right conduct was central to Socrates' life and teachings. A stonemason by profession, Socrates preferred to roam the streets of Athens and engage his fellow citizens in conversation and debate (Figure **4.13**). Insisting that the unexamined life was not worth living, he challenged his peers on matters of public and private virtue, constantly posing the question, "What is the greatest good?" In this pursuit, Socrates employed a rigorous question-and-answer technique known as the **dialectical method**. Unlike the Sophists, he refused to charge fees for teaching: he argued that wealth did not produce excellence; rather, wealth derived *from* excellence. Socrates described himself as a large horsefly, alighting upon and pestering the well-bred but rather sluggish horse—that is, Athens. So Socrates "alighted" on the citizens of Athens, arousing, persuading, and reproaching them and—most important—demanding that they give rational justification for their actions.

Socrates established philosophy as a lived experience, rather than a set of doctrines. His style of cross-examination, the question-and-answer method, proceeded from his first principle of inquiry, "Know thyself," while the progress of his analysis moved from specific examples to general principles, and from particular to universal truths, a type of reasoning known as *inductive*. The inductive method demands a process of abstraction: a shift of focus from the individual thing (the city) to all things (cities) and from the individual action (just or unjust) to the idea of justice. Central to Socratic inquiry was discourse. The notion that talk itself humanizes the individual is typically Greek and even more typically Socratic. Indeed, the art of conversation—the dialectical exchange of ideas—united the citizens of the *polis* (Figure 4.13).

As gadfly, Socrates won as many enemies as he won friends. The great masses of Greek citizens found comfort in the traditional Greek gods and goddesses. They had little use for Socrates' religious skepticism and stringent methods of self-examination. Outspoken in his commitment to free inquiry, Socrates fell into disfavor with the reactionary regime that governed Athens after its defeat in the Peloponnesian Wars. Although he had fought bravely in the wars, he vigorously opposed the new regime and the moral chaos of post-war Athens. In the year 399 B.C.E., when he was over seventy years old, he was brought to trial for subversive behavior, impiety, and atheism. The Athenian jury found him guilty by a narrow margin of votes and sentenced him to death by drinking hemlock, a poisonous herb.

In his lifetime, Socrates wrote no books or letters: what we know of him comes mainly from his students' writings. The dialogue called *Crito* (written by Plato) narrates the last events of Socrates' life: Crito, Socrates' friend and pupil, urges him to escape from prison, but the old philosopher refuses. He explains that to run away would be to subvert the laws by which he has lived. His escape would represent an implicit criticism of the democratic system and the city-state that he had defended throughout his life. For Socrates, the loyalty of the citizen to the *polis*, like that of the child to its parents, is a primary obligation. To violate the will of the community to which he belongs would constitute dishonor. Like Antigone, Socrates prefers death to dishonor. In the excerpt from *Crito*, Socrates explains why right action is crucial to the destiny of both the individual and the community. These words reaffirm the Hellenic view that immortality is achieved through human deeds, which outlast human lives.

Figure 4.13 Portrait bust of Socrates, supposedly created by Lysippos. Roman marble copy of an original bronze, ca. 350 B.C.E. © Hirmer Fotoarchiv.

---

*"*Psyche*" is often translated as "soul" or "mind," as distinguished from "body" or "matter."

Crito: . . . O my good Socrates, I beg you for the last time   1
to listen to me and save yourself. For to me your death will be
more than a single disaster: not only shall I lose a friend the
like of whom I shall never find again, but many persons who
do not know you and me well will think that I might have
saved you if I had been willing to spend money, but that I
neglected to do so. And what reputation could be more
disgraceful than the reputation of caring more for money than
for one's friends? The public will never believe that we were
anxious to save you, but that you yourself refused to escape.   10

Socrates: But, my dear Crito, why should we care so much
about public opinion? Reasonable men, of whose opinion it is
worth our while to think, will believe that we acted as we
really did.

Crito: But you see, Socrates, that it is necessary to care
about public opinion, too. This very thing that has happened to
you proves that the multitude can do a man not the least, but
almost the greatest harm, if he is falsely accused to them.

Socrates: I wish that the multitude were able to do a man
the greatest harm, Crito, for then they would be able to do   20
him the greatest good, too. That would have been fine. But, as
it is, they can do neither. They cannot make a man either wise
or foolish: they act wholly at random . . . . Consider it in this
way. Suppose the laws and the commonwealth were to come
and appear to me as I was preparing to run away (if that is the
right phrase to describe my escape) and were to ask, "Tell us,
Socrates, what have you in your mind to do? What do you
mean by trying to escape but to destroy us, the laws, and the
whole state, so far as you are able? Do you think that a state
can exist and not be overthrown, in which the decisions of   30
law are of no force, and are disregarded and undermined by
private individuals?" How shall we answer questions like that,
Crito? Much might be said, especially by an orator, in defense
of the law which makes judicial decisions supreme. Shall I
reply, "But the state has injured me by judging my case
unjustly." Shall we say that?

Crito: Certainly we will, Socrates.

Socrates: And suppose the laws were to reply, "Was that
our agreement? Or was it that you would abide by whatever
judgments the state should pronounce?" And if we were   40
surprised by their words, perhaps they would say, "Socrates,
don't be surprised by our words, but answer us; you yourself
are accustomed to ask questions and to answer them. What
complaint have you against us and the state, that you are
trying to destroy us? Are we not, first of all, your parents?
Through us your father took your mother and brought you into
the world. Tell us, have you any fault to find with those of us
that are the laws of marriage?" "I have none," I should reply.
"Or have you any fault to find with those of us that regulate
the raising of the child and the education which you, like   50
others, received? Did we not do well in telling your father to
educate you in music and athletics?" "You did," I should say.
"Well, then, since you were brought into the world and raised
and educated by us, how, in the first place, can you deny that
you are our child and our slave, as your fathers were before
you? And if this be so, do you think that your rights are on a

level with ours? Do you think that you have a right to retaliate
if we should try to do anything to you? You had not the same
rights that your father had, or that your master would have
had if you had been a slave. You had no right to retaliate if   60
they ill-treated you, or to answer them if they scolded you, or
to strike them back if they struck you, or to repay them evil
with evil in any way. And do you think that you may retaliate
in the case of your country and its laws? If we try to destroy
you, because we think it just, will you in return do all that you
can to destroy us, the laws, and your country, and say that in
so doing you are acting justly—you, the man who really thinks
so much of excellence? Or are you too wise to see that your
country is worthier, more to be revered, more sacred, and held
in higher honor both by the gods and by all men of   70
understanding, than your father and your mother and all your
ancestors; and that you ought to reverence it, and to submit to
it, and to approach it more humbly when it is angry with you
than you would approach your father; and either to do
whatever it tells you to do or to persuade it to excuse you; and
to obey in silence if it orders you to endure flogging or
imprisonment, or if it sends you to battle to be wounded or
die? That is just. You must not give way, nor retreat, nor
desert your station. In war, and in the court of justice, and
everywhere, you must do whatever your state and your   80
country tell you to do, or you must persuade them that their
commands are unjust. But it is impious to use violence against
your father or your mother; and much more impious to use
violence against your country." What answer shall we make,
Crito? Shall we say that the laws speak the truth, or not?

Crito: I think that they do.

Socrates: "Then consider, Socrates," perhaps they would
say, "if we are right in saying that by attempting to escape
you are attempting an injustice. We brought you into the
world, we raised you, we educated you, we gave you and   90
every other citizen a share of all the good things we could. Yet
we proclaim that if any man of the Athenians is dissatisfied
with us, he may take his goods and go away wherever he
pleases; we give that privilege to every man who chooses to
avail himself of it, so soon as he has reached manhood, and
sees us, the laws, and the administration of our state. No one
of us stands in his way or forbids him to take his goods and go
wherever he likes, whether it be to an Athenian colony, or to
any foreign country, if he is dissatisfied with us and with the
state. But we say that every man of you who remains here,   100
seeing how we administer justice, and how we govern the
state in other matters, has agreed, by the very fact of
remaining here, to do whatsoever we tell him. And, we say, he
who disobeys us acts unjustly on three counts: he disobeys us
who are his parents, and he disobeys us who reared him, and
he disobeys us after he has agreed to obey us, without
persuading us that we are wrong. Yet we did not tell him
sternly to do whatever we told him. We offered him an
alternative; we gave him his choice either to obey us or to
convince us that we were wrong; but he does neither. "These   110
are the charges, Socrates, to which we say that you will
expose yourself if you do what you intend; and you are more
exposed to these charges than other Athenians." And if I were
to ask, "Why?" they might retort with justice that I have bound
myself by the agreement with them more than other

Athenians. They would say, "Socrates, we have very strong evidence that you were satisfied with us and with the state. You would not have been content to stay at home in it more than other Athenians unless you had been satisfied with it more than they. You never went away from Athens to the festivals, nor elsewhere except on military service; you never made other journeys like other men; you had no desire to see other states or other laws; you were contented with us and our state; so strongly did you prefer us, and agree to be governed by us. And what is more, you had children in this city, you found it so satisfactory. Besides, if you had wished, you might at your trial have offered to go into exile. At that time you could have done with the state's consent what you are trying now to do without it. But then you gloried in being willing to die. You said that you preferred death to exile. And now you do not honor those words: you do not respect us, the laws, for you are trying to destroy us; and you are acting just as a miserable slave would act, trying to run away, and breaking the contracts and agreement which you made to live as our citizen. First, therefore, answer this question. Are we right, or are we wrong, in saying that you have agreed not in mere words, but in your actions, to live under our government?" What are we to say, Crito? Must we not admit that it is true?

Crito: We must, Socrates. . . . 140

Q What reasons does Socrates give for refusing to escape from prison?

Q How does this reading illustrate the relationship between the individual and the community?

Plato and the Theory of Forms

Socrates' teachings were an inspiration to his pupil Plato (ca. 428–ca. 347 B.C.E.). Born in Athens during the Peloponnesian Wars, Plato reaped the benefits of Golden Age culture along with the insecurities of the post-war era. In 387 B.C.E, more than a decade after the death of his master, he founded the world's first school of philosophy, the Academy. Plato wrote some two dozen treatises, most of which were cast in the dialogue or dialectical format that Socrates had made famous. Some of the dialogues may be precise transcriptions of actual conversations, whereas others are clearly fictional, but the major philosophical arguments in almost all of Plato's treatises are put into the mouth of Socrates. Since Socrates himself wrote nothing, it is almost impossible to distinguish between the ideas of Plato and those of Socrates.

Plato's most famous treatise, the *Republic*, asks two central questions: "What is the meaning of justice?" and "What is the nature of a just society?" In trying to answer these questions, Plato introduces a theory of knowledge that is both visionary and dogmatic. It asserts the existence of a two-level reality, one consisting of constantly changing particulars available to our senses, the other consisting of unchanging eternal truths understood by way of the intellect. According to Plato, the higher reality of

eternal truths, which he calls Forms, is distinct from the imperfect and transient objects of sensory experience, which are mere copies of Forms. Plato's Theory of Forms proposes that all sensory objects are imitations of the Forms, which, like the simplest mathematical equations, are imperishable and forever true. For example, the circle and its three-dimensional counterpart, the sphere, exist independent of any *particular* circle and sphere. They have always existed and will always exist. But the beach ball I toss in the air, an imperfect copy of the sphere, is transitory. Indeed, if all of the particular beach balls in the world were destroyed, the Universal Form—Sphere—would still exist. Similarly, suggests Plato, Justice, Love, and Beauty (along with other Forms) stand as unchanging and eternal models for the many individual and particular instances of each in the sensory world.

According to Plato, Forms descend from an ultimate Form, the Form of the Good. Plato never located or defined the Ultimate Good, except by analogy with the sun. Like the sun, the Form of the Good illuminates all that is intelligible and makes possible the mind's perception of Forms as objects of thought. The Ultimate Good, knowledge of which is the goal of dialectical inquiry, is the most difficult to reach.

In the *Republic*, Plato uses a literary device known as **allegory** to illustrate the dilemma facing the *psyche* in its ascent to knowledge of the imperishable and unchanging Forms. By way of allegory—the device by which the literal meaning of the text implies a figurative or "hidden" meaning—Plato describes a group of ordinary mortals chained within an underground chamber (the *psyche* imprisoned within the human body). Their woeful position permits them to see only the shadows on the walls of the cave (the imperfect and perishable imitations of the Forms that occupy the world of the senses), which the prisoners, in their ignorance, believe to be real (Figure **4.14**). Only when one of the prisoners (the philosopher-hero) ascends to the domain of light (true knowledge, or knowledge of the Forms) does it become clear that what the cave-dwellers perceive as truth is nothing more than shadows of Reality. This intriguing parable is presented as a dialogue between Socrates and Plato's older brother, Glaucon.

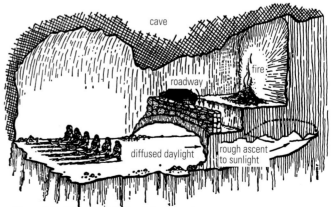

Figure 4.14 "Allegory of the Cave" from *The Great Dialogues of Plato*, translated by W.H.D. Rouse, translation copyright © 1956, renewed 1984 by J.C.G. Rouse. Used by permission of Dutton Signet, a division of Penguin Books USA Inc.

READING 1.16 The "Allegory of the Cave" from Plato's *Republic* (ca. 375 B.C.E.)

Next, said [Socrates], here is a parable to illustrate the **1**
degrees in which our nature may be enlightened or
unenlightened. Imagine the condition of men living in a sort of
cavernous chamber underground, with an entrance open to the
light and a long passage all down the cave. Here they have
been from childhood, chained by the leg and also by the neck,
so that they cannot move and can see only what is in front of
them, because the chains will not let them turn their heads. At
some distance higher up is the light of a fire burning behind
them; and between the prisoners and the fire is a track[1] with **10**
a parapet built along it, like the screen at a puppet-show,
which hides the performers while they show their puppets
over the top.

I see, said he.

Now behind this parapet imagine persons carrying along
various artificial objects, including figures of men and animals
in wood or stone or other materials, which project above the
parapet. Naturally, some of these persons will be talking,
others silent.[2]

It is a strange picture, he said, and a strange sort of **20**
prisoners.

Like ourselves, I replied; for in the first place prisoners so
confined would have seen nothing of themselves or of one
another, except the shadows thrown by the fire-light on the
wall of the Cave facing them, would they?

Not if all their lives they had been prevented from moving
their heads.

And they would have seen as little of the objects carried
past.

Of course. **30**

Now, if they could talk to one another, would they not
suppose that their words referred only to those passing
shadows which they saw?

Necessarily.

And suppose their prison had an echo from the wall facing
them? When one of the people crossing behind them spoke,
they could only suppose that the sound came from the shadow
passing before their eyes.

No doubt.

In every way, then, such prisoners would recognize as **40**
reality nothing but the shadows of those artificial objects.

Inevitably.

Now consider what would happen if their release from the
chains and the healing of their unwisdom should come about

---

[1]The track crosses the passage into the cave at right angles and is
above the parapet built along it.
[2]A modern Plato would compare his Cave to an underground cinema,
where the audience watch the play of shadows thrown by the film
passing before a light at their backs. The film itself is only an image of
"real" things and events in the world outside the cinema. For the film
Plato has to substitute the clumsier apparatus of a procession of
artificial objects carried on their heads by persons who are merely part
of the machinery, providing for the movement of the objects and the
sound whose echo the prisoners hear. The parapet prevents these
persons' shadows from being cast on the wall of the Cave.

in this way. Suppose one of them were set free and forced
suddenly to stand up, turn his head, and walk with eyes lifted
to the light; all these movements would be painful, and he
would be too dazzled to make out the objects whose shadows
he had been used to see. What do you think he would say, if
someone told him that what he had formerly seen was **50**
meaningless illusion, but now, being somewhat nearer to
reality and turned towards more real objects, he was getting a
truer view? Suppose further that he were shown the various
objects being carried by and were made to say, in reply to
questions, what each of them was. Would he not be perplexed
and believe the objects now shown him to be not so real as
what he formerly saw?

Yes, not nearly so real.

And if he were forced to look at the fire-light itself, would
not his eyes ache, so that he would try to escape and turn **60**
back to the things which he could see distinctly, convinced
that they really were clearer than these other objects now
being shown to him?

Yes.

And suppose someone were to drag him away forcibly up
the steep and rugged ascent and not let him go until he had
hauled him out into the sunlight, would he not suffer pain and
vexation at such treatment, and, when he had come out into
the light, find his eyes so full of its radiance that he could not
see a single one of the things that he was now told were **70**
real?

Certainly he would not see them all at once.

He would need, then, to grow accustomed before he could
see things in that upper world. At first it would be easiest to
make out shadows, and then the images of men and things
reflected in water, and later on the things themselves. After
that, it would be easier to watch the heavenly bodies and the
sky itself by night, looking at the light of the moon and stars
rather than the Sun and the Sun's light in the day-time.

Yes, surely. **80**

Last of all, he would be able to look at the Sun and
contemplate its nature, not as it appears when reflected in
water or any alien medium, but as it is in itself in its own
domain.

No doubt.

And now he would begin to draw the conclusion that it is
the Sun that produces the seasons and the course of the year
and controls everything in the visible world, and moreover is in
a way the cause of all that he and his companions used to
see. **90**

Clearly he would come at last to that conclusion.

Then if he called to mind his fellow prisoners and what
passed for wisdom in his former dwelling-place, he would
surely think himself happy in the change and be sorry for
them. They may have had a practice of honoring and
commending one another, with prizes for the man who had the
keenest eye for the passing shadows and the best memory for
the order in which they followed or accompanied one another,
so that he could make a good guess as to which was going to
come next. Would our released prisoner be likely to covet **100**
those prizes or to envy the men exalted to honor and power in
the Cave? Would he not feel like Homer's Achilles, that he
would far sooner "be on earth as a hired servant in the house

of a landless man"[3] or endure anything rather than go back to his old beliefs and live in the old way?

Yes, he would prefer any fate to such a life.

Now imagine what would happen if he went down again to take his former seat in the Cave. Coming suddenly out of the sunlight, his eyes would be filled with darkness. He might be required once more to deliver his opinion on those shadows, 110 in competition with the prisoners who had never been released, while his eyesight was still dim and unsteady; and it might take some time to become used to the darkness. They would laugh at him and say that he had gone up only to come back with his sight ruined; it was worth no one's while even to attempt the ascent. If they could lay hands on the man who was trying to set them free and lead them up, they would kill him.[4]

Yes, they would.

Every feature in this parable, my dear Glaucon, is meant to 120 fit our earlier analysis. The prison dwelling corresponds to the region revealed to us through the sense of sight, and the fire-light within it to the power of the Sun. The ascent to see the things in the upper world you may take as standing for the upward journey of the soul into the region of the intelligible; then you will be in possession of what I surmise, since that is what you wish to be told. Heaven knows whether it is true; but this, at any rate, is how it appears to me. In the world of knowledge, the last thing to be perceived and only with great difficulty is the essential Form of Goodness. Once it is 130 perceived, the conclusion must follow that, for all things, this is the cause of whatever is right and good; in the visible world it gives birth to light and to the lord of light, while it is itself sovereign in the intelligible world and the parent of intelligence and truth. Without having had a vision of this Form no one can act with wisdom, either in his own life or in matters of state.

So far as I can understand, I share your belief.

Then you may also agree that it is no wonder if those who have reached this height are reluctant to manage the affairs 140 of men. Their souls long to spend all their time in that upper world—naturally enough, if here once more our parable holds true. Nor, again, is it at all strange that one who comes from the contemplation of divine things to the miseries of human life should appear awkward and ridiculous when, with eyes still dazed and not yet accustomed to the darkness, he is compelled, in a law-court or elsewhere, to dispute about the shadows of justice or the images that cast those shadows, and to wrangle over the notions of what is right in the minds of men who have never beheld Justice itself. 150

It is not at all strange.

No; a sensible man will remember that the eyes may be confused in two ways—by a change from light to darkness or from darkness to light; and he will recognize that the same thing happens to the soul. When he sees it troubled and unable to discern anything clearly, instead of laughing thoughtlessly, he will ask whether, coming from a brighter existence, its unaccustomed vision is obscured by the darkness, in which case he will think its condition enviable and its life a happy one; or whether, emerging from the 160 depths of ignorance, it is dazzled by excess of light. If so, he will rather feel sorry for it; or, if he were inclined to laugh, that would be less ridiculous than to laugh at the soul which has come down from the light.

That is a fair statement.

If this is true, then, we must conclude that education is not what it is said to be by some, who profess to put knowledge into a soul which does not possess it, as if they could put sight into blind eyes. On the contrary, our own account signifies that the soul of every man does possess the power 170 of learning the truth and the organ to see it with; and that, just as one might have to turn the whole body round in order that the eye should see light instead of darkness, so the entire soul must be turned away from this changing world, until its eye can bear to contemplate reality and that supreme splendor which we have called the Good. Hence there may well be an art whose aim would be to effect this very thing, the conversion of the soul, in the readiest way; not to put the power of sight into the soul's eye, which already has it, but to ensure that, instead of looking in the wrong direction, it is 180 turned the way it ought to be.

Yes, it may well be so.

It looks, then, as though wisdom were different from those ordinary virtues, as they are called, which are not far removed from bodily qualities, in that they can be produced by habituation and exercise in a soul which has not possessed them from the first. Wisdom, it seems, is certainly the virtue of some diviner faculty, which never loses its power, though its use for good or harm depends on the direction towards which it is turned. You must have noticed in dishonest men 190 with a reputation for sagacity the shrewd glance of a narrow intelligence piercing the objects to which it is directed. There is nothing wrong with their power of vision, but it has been forced into the service of evil, so that the keener its sight, the more harm it works.

Quite true.

And yet if the growth of a nature like this had been pruned from earliest childhood, cleared of those clinging overgrowths which come of gluttony and all luxurious pleasure and, like leaden weights charged with affinity to this mortal world, 200 hang upon the soul, bending its vision downwards; if, freed from these, the soul were turned round towards true reality, then this same power in these very men would see the truth as keenly as the objects it is turned to now.

Yes, very likely.

Is it not also likely, or indeed certain after what has been said, that a state can never be properly governed either by the uneducated who know nothing of truth or by men who are allowed to spend all their days in the pursuit of culture? The ignorant have no single mark before their eyes at which they 210 must aim in all the conduct of their own lives and of affairs of state; and the others will not engage in action if they can help it, dreaming that, while still alive, they have been translated to the Island of the Blest.

Quite true.

It is for us, then, as founders of a commonwealth, to bring

---

[3]This verse, spoken by the ghost of Achilles, suggests that the Cave is comparable with Hades, the Greek underworld.
[4]An allusion to the fate of Socrates.

compulsion to bear on the noblest natures. They must be made to climb the ascent to the vision of Goodness, which we called the highest object of knowledge; and, when they have looked upon it long enough, they must not be allowed, as **220** they now are, to remain on the heights, refusing to come down again to the prisoners or to take any part in their labors and rewards, however much or little these may be worth.

Shall we not be doing them an injustice, if we force on them a worse life than they might have?

You have forgotten again, my friend, that the law is not concerned to make any one class specially happy, but to ensure the welfare of the commonwealth as a whole. By persuasion or constraint it will unite the citizens in harmony, making them share whatever benefits each class can **230** contribute to the common good; and its purpose in forming men of that spirit was not that each should be left to go his own way, but that they should be instrumental in binding the community into one.

True, I had forgotten.

You will see, then, Glaucon, that there will be no real injustice in compelling our philosophers to watch over and care for the other citizens. We can fairly tell them that their compeers in other states may quite reasonably refuse to collaborate: there they have sprung up, like a self-sown **240** plant, in despite of their country's institutions; no one has fostered their growth, and they cannot be expected to show gratitude for a care they have never received. "But," we shall say, "it is not so with you. We have brought you into existence for your country's sake as well as for your own, to be like leaders and king-bees in a hive; you have been better and more thoroughly educated than those others and hence you are more capable of playing your part both as men of thought and as men of action. You must go down, then, each in his turn, to live with the rest and let your eyes grow accustomed **250** to the darkness. You will then see a thousand times better than those who live there always; you will recognize every image for what it is and know what it represents, because you have seen justice, beauty, and goodness in their reality; and so you and we shall find life in our commonwealth no mere dream, as it is in most existing states, where men live fighting one another about shadows and quarreling for power, as if that were a great prize; whereas in truth government can be at its best and free from dissension only where the destined rulers are least desirous of holding office." **260**

Quite true.

Then will our pupils refuse to listen and to take their turns at sharing in the work of the community, though they may live together for most of their time in a purer air?

No; it is a fair demand, and they are fair-minded men. No doubt, unlike any ruler of the present day, they will think of holding power as an unavoidable necessity.

Yes, my friend; for the truth is that you can have a well-governed society only if you can discover for your future rulers a better way of life than being in office; then only will power **270** be in the hands of men who are rich, not in gold, but in the wealth that brings happiness, a good and wise life. All goes wrong when, starved for lack of anything good in their own lives, men turn to public affairs hoping to snatch from thence the happiness they hunger for. They set about fighting for

power, and this internecine conflict ruins them and their country. The life of true philosophy is the only one that looks down upon offices of state; and access to power must be confined to men who are not in love with it; otherwise rivals will start fighting. So whom else can you compel to **280** undertake the guardianship of the commonwealth, if not those who, besides understanding best the principles of government, enjoy a nobler life than the politician's and look for rewards of a different kind?

There is indeed no other choice. . . .

Q What does each allegorical figure (the Cave, the Sun, and so on) represent?

Q How does this education of the *psyche* contribute (according to Socrates) to the life of a "well-governed society"?

The "Allegory of the Cave" illustrates some key theories in the teachings of Plato. The first of these is **idealism**, the theory that holds that reality lies in the realm of unchanging Forms, rather than in sensory objects. Platonic idealism implies a dualistic (spirit-and-matter or mind-and-body) model of the universe: the *psyche* (mind) belongs to the world of the eternal Forms, while the *soma* (body) belongs to the sensory or material world. Imprisoned in the body, the mind forgets its once-perfect knowledge of the Forms. It is, nevertheless, capable of recovering its prenatal intelligence. The business of philosophy is to educate the *psyche*, to draw it out of its material prison so that it can regain perfect awareness.

Plato's concept of an unchanging force behind the flux of our perceptions looks back to the theories of Heraclitus, while his description of the Forms resembles Pythagorean assertions of the unchanging reality of number. It is not without significance that Plato's Theory of Forms has been hailed in modern physics: the celebrated twentieth-century German physicist Werner Heisenberg argued that the smallest units of matter are not physical objects in the ordinary sense; rather, he asserted, they are "forms," or ideas that can be expressed unambiguously only in mathematical language. In constructing the Theory of Forms, Plato may also have been influenced by Asian religious thought. The spiritual "spark" with which humans are born, according to Plato, and which must be kindled and cultivated, resembles the Hindu Atman (see chapter 3). And Plato's distinction between the realm of the senses and the ultimate, all-embracing Form recalls the Hindu belief that the illusory world of matter stands apart from Ultimate Being or Brahman. In contrast with Hinduism, however, Plato's teachings do not advocate enlightenment as escape from the material world. Rather, Plato perceives the mind's ascent to knowledge as a prerequisite of individual well-being and the attainment of the good life here on earth. Such enlightenment is essential to achieving a just state and a healthy society. Unlike the Hindu philosophers, whose mystical ascent to enlightenment is accomplished through withdrawal from the world, meditation, and self-denial, Plato defends a practical system of education by which individuals might arrive at knowledge of the Good. That educational system is expounded in the *Republic*.

Plato's utopian community permits no private property and little family life, but exalts education as fundamental to society. While everyone (male and female) would be educated equally, the ability of each would determine that person's place within society. Thus the duties of all citizens—laborers, soldiers, or governors—would be consistent with their mental and physical abilities. Plato has little use for democracy of the kind practiced in Athens. Governing, according to Plato, should fall to those who are the most intellectually able. That is, those who have most fully recovered a knowledge of the Forms are obliged to act as "king-bees" in the communal hive. (Plato might have been surprised to discover that the ruling bee in a beehive is female.) The life of contemplation carries with it heavy responsibilities, for in the hands of the philosopher-kings lies "the welfare of the commonwealth as a whole." Plato's views on the ideal state were remarkably compatible with the ancient Chinese belief that a natural hierarchy determined who was intellectually fit to govern (see chapter 3).

Aristotle and the Life of Reason

Among Plato's students at the Academy was a young Macedonian named Aristotle, whose contributions to philosophy ultimately rivaled those of his teacher. After a period of travel in the eastern Mediterranean and a brief career as tutor to the young prince of Macedonia (the future Alexander the Great), Aristotle returned to Athens and founded a school known as the Lyceum. Aristotle's habit of walking up and down as he lectured gave him the nickname the "peripatetic philosopher." His teachings, which exist only in the form of lecture notes compiled by his students, cover a wider and more practical range of subjects than those of Plato. Aristotle did not accept the Theory of Forms. Insisting that mind and matter could not exist independently of each other, he rejected Plato's notion of an eternal *psyche*. Nevertheless, he theorized that a portion of the soul identified with reason (and with the impersonal force he called the Unmoved Mover) might be immortal.

Aristotle's interests spanned many fields, including those of biology, physics, politics, poetry, drama, logic, and ethics. The son of a physician, Aristotle was inspired by his education to gather specimens of plant and animal life and classify them according to their physical similarities and differences. Over five hundred different animals, some of which Aristotle himself dissected, are mentioned in his zoological treatises. Though he did little in the way of modern scientific experimentation, Aristotle's practice of basing conclusions on very careful observation advanced the **empirical method**—a method of inquiry dependent on direct experience. Indeed, whereas Plato was the traditional rationalist, Aristotle pursued the path of the empiricist. He brought to his analysis of political life, literature, and human conduct the same principles he employed

in classifying plants and animals: objectivity, clarity, and consistency. Before writing the *Politics*, he examined the constitutions of more than 150 Greek city-states. And in the *Poetics* he defined the various genres of literary expression (see chapter 5). In the fields of biology, astronomy, and physics, Aristotle's conclusions (including many that were incorrect) remained unchallenged for centuries. For instance, Aristotle theorized that in sexual union, the male was the "generator" and the female the "receptacle," while procreation involved the imposition of life-giving form (the male) on chaotic matter (the female). In short, Aristotle's views on female biology and sexuality led centuries of scholars to regard woman as an imperfect and incomplete version of man.

Aristotle's application of scientific principles to the reasoning process was the basis for the science of logic. Aristotelian logic requires the division of an argument into individual terms, followed—in Socratic fashion—by an examination of the meaning of those terms. Aristotle formulated the **syllogism**, a deductive scheme that presents two premises from which a conclusion may be drawn. As a procedure for reasoned thought without reference to specific content, the syllogism is a system of notation that is similar to mathematics.

Aristotle's Ethics

Not the least of Aristotle's contributions was that which he made to **ethics**, that branch of philosophy that sets forth the principles of human conduct. Proceeding from an examination of human values, Aristotle hypothesizes that happiness or "the good life" (the Greek word *eudaimonia* means both) is the only human value that might be considered a final goal or end (*telos*) in itself, rather than a means to any other end. Is not happiness the one goal to which all human beings aspire? If so, then how does one achieve it? The answer, says Aristotle, lies in fulfilling one's unique function. The function of any thing is that by which it is defined: the function of the eye is to see; the function of the racehorse is to run fast; the function of a knife is to cut, and so on. How well a thing performs is synonymous with its excellence or virtue (in Greek, the word *arete* denotes both): the excellence of the eye, then, lies in seeing well; the excellence of a racehorse lies in how fast it runs; the excellence of a knife depends on how well it cuts, and so on. The unique function of the human being, observes Aristotle, is the ability to reason; hence, the excellence of any human creature lies in the exercise of reason.

In the *Ethics*, edited by Aristotle's son Nicomachus, Aristotle examines the Theory of the Good Life and the Nature of Happiness. He explains that action in accordance with reason is necessary for the acquisition of excellence, or virtue. Ideal conduct, suggests Aristotle, lies in the Golden Mean—the middle ground between any two extremes of behavior. Between cowardice and recklessness,

> **THE SYLLOGISM**
>
> All men are mortal.
> a:b
> Socrates is a man.
> c:a
> Therefore, Socrates
> is mortal.
> ∴ c = b

for instance, one should seek the middle ground: courage. Between boastfulness and timidity, one should cultivate modesty. The Doctrine of the Mean rationalized the classical search for moderation and balance. In contrast with the divinely ordained moral texts of other ancient cultures, Aristotle's teachings required individuals to reason their way to ethical conduct.

READING 1.17 From Aristotle's Nicomachean Ethics (ca. 340 B.C.E.)

The Supreme Good

If it is true that in the sphere of action there is an end which we wish for its own sake, and for the sake of which we wish for everything else, and that we do not desire all things for the sake of something else (for, if that is so, the process will go on *ad infinitum*, and our desire will be idle and futile) it is clear that this will be the good or the supreme good. Does it not follow then that the knowledge of this supreme good is of great importance for the conduct of life, and that, if we know it, we shall be like archers who have a mark at which to aim, we shall have a better chance of attaining what we want? But, if this is the case, we must endeavor to comprehend, at **10** least in outline, its nature, and the science or faculty to which it belongs. . . .

It seems not unreasonable that people should derive their conception of the good or of happiness from men's lives. Thus ordinary or vulgar people conceive it to be pleasure, and accordingly approve a life of enjoyment. For there are practically three prominent lives, the sensual, the political, and, thirdly, the speculative. Now the mass of men present an absolutely slavish appearance, as choosing the life of brute beasts, but they meet with consideration because so many **20** persons in authority share the tastes of Sardanapalus.[1] Cultivated and practical people, on the other hand, identify happiness with honor, as honor is the general end of political life. But this appears too superficial for our present purpose; for honor seems to depend more upon the people who pay it than upon the person to whom it is paid, and we have an intuitive feeling that the good is something which is proper to a man himself and cannot easily be taken away from him. It seems too that the reason why men seek honor is that they may be confident of their own goodness. Accordingly they **30** seek it at the hands of the wise and of those who know them well, and they seek it on the ground of virtue; hence it is clear that in their judgment at any rate virtue is superior to honor. . . .

We speak of that which is sought after for its own sake as more final than that which is sought after as a means to something else; we speak of that which is never desired as a means to something else as more final than the things which are desired both in themselves and as means to something else; and we speak of a thing as absolutely final, if it is always desired in itself and never as a means to something **40** else.

It seems that happiness preeminently answers to this description, as we always desire happiness for its own sake

and never as a means to something else, whereas we desire honor, pleasure, intellect, and every virtue, partly for their own sakes (for we should desire them independently of what might result from them) but partly also as being means to happiness, because we suppose they will prove the instruments of happiness. Happiness, on the other hand, nobody desires for the sake of these things, nor indeed as a means to anything **50** else at all. . . .

Perhaps, however, it seems a truth which is generally admitted, that happiness is the supreme good; what is wanted is to define its nature a little more clearly. The best way of arriving at such a definition will probably be to ascertain the function of Man. For, as with a flute- player, a statuary, or any artisan, or in fact anybody who has a definite function and action, his goodness, or excellence seems to lie in his function, so it would seem to be with Man, if indeed he has a definite function. Can it be said then that, while a carpenter **60** and a cobbler have definite functions and actions, Man, unlike them, is naturally functionless? The reasonable view is that, as the eye, the hand, the foot, and similarly each . . . part of the body has a definite function, so Man may be regarded as having a definite function apart from all these. What then, can this function be? It is not life; for life is apparently something which man shares with the plants; and it is something peculiar to him that we are looking for. We must exclude therefore the life of nutrition and increase. There is next what may be called the life of sensation. But this too, is **70** apparently shared by Man with horses, cattle, and all other animals. There remains what I may call the practical life of the rational part of *Man's being*. But the rational part is twofold; it is rational partly in the sense of being obedient to reason, and partly in the sense of possessing reason and intelligence. The practical life too may be conceived of in two ways, viz., *either as a moral state, or as a moral activity*; but we must understand by it the life of activity, as this seems to be the truer form of the conception.

The function of Man then is an activity of soul in accordance **80** with reason, or not independently of reason. . . .

The Golden Mean

Our present study is not, like other studies, purely speculative in its intention; for the object of our inquiry is not to know the nature of virtue but to become ourselves virtuous, as that is the sole benefit which it conveys. It is necessary therefore to consider the right way of performing actions, for it is actions as we have said that determine the character of the resulting moral states. . . .

The first point to be observed then is that in such matters as we are considering[,] deficiency and excess are equally **90** fatal. It is so, as we observe, in regard to health and strength; for we must judge of what we cannot see by the evidence of what we do see. Excess or deficiency of gymnastic exercise is fatal to strength. Similarly an excess or deficiency of meat and drink is fatal to health, whereas a suitable amount produces, augments and sustains it. It is the same then with temperance, courage, and the other virtues. A person who avoids and is afraid of everything and faces nothing becomes a coward; a person who is not afraid of anything but is ready to face everything becomes foolhardy. **100**

---

[1]The legendary king of Assyria, known for his sensuality.

Similarly he who enjoys every pleasure and never abstains from any pleasure is licentious; he who eschews all pleasures like a boor is an insensible sort of person. For temperance and courage are destroyed by excess and deficiency but preserved by the mean [middle] state. . . .

The nature of virtue has been now generically described. But it is not enough to state merely that virtue is a moral state, we must also describe the character of that moral state.

It must be laid down then that every virtue or excellence has the effect of producing a good condition of that of which it 110 is a virtue or excellence, and of enabling it to perform its function well. Thus the excellence of the eye makes the eye good and its function good, as it is by the excellence of the eye that we see well. Similarly, the excellence of the horse makes a horse excellent and good at racing, at carrying its rider and at facing the enemy. If then this is universally true, the virtue or excellence of man will be such a moral state as makes a man good and able to perform his proper function well. We have already explained how this will be the case, but another way of making it clear will be to study the nature 120 or character of this virtue.

Now in everything, whether it be continuous or discrete, it is possible to take a greater, a smaller, or an equal amount, and this either absolutely or in relation to ourselves, the equal being a mean between excess and deficiency. By the mean in respect of the thing itself, or the absolute mean, I understand that which is equally distinct from both extremes; and this is one and the same thing for everybody. By the mean considered relatively to ourselves I understand that which is neither too much nor too little; but this is not one thing, nor is it the same 130 for everybody. Thus if 10 be too much and 2 too little we take 6 as a mean in respect of the thing itself; for 6 is as much greater than 2 as it is less than 10, and this is a mean in arithmetical proportion. But the mean considered relatively to ourselves must not be ascertained in this way. It does not follow that if 10 pounds of *meat* be too much and 2 be too little for a man to eat, a trainer will order him 6 pounds, as this may itself be too much or too little for the person who is to take it; it will be too little [for instance] for Milo,[2] but too much for a beginner in gymnastics. It will be the same with 140

running and wrestling; *the right amount will vary with the individual*. This being so, everybody who understands his business avoids alike excess and deficiency; he seeks and chooses the mean, not the absolute mean, but the mean considered relatively to ourselves.

Every science then performs its function well, if it regards the mean and refers the works which it produces to the mean. This is the reason why it is usually said of successful works that it is impossible to take anything from them or to add anything to them, which implies that excess or deficiency is 150 fatal to excellence but that the mean state ensures it. Good artists too, as we say, have an eye to the mean in their works. But virtue, like Nature herself, is more accurate and better than any art; virtue therefore will aim at the mean;—I speak of moral virtue, as it is moral virtue which is concerned with emotions and actions, and it is these which admit of excess and deficiency and the mean. Thus it is possible to go too far, or not to go far enough, in respect of fear, courage, desire, anger, pity, and pleasure and pain generally, and the excess and the deficiency are alike wrong; but to experience these 160 emotions at the right times and on the right occasions and towards the right persons and for the right causes and in the right manner is the mean or the supreme good, which is characteristic of virtue. Similarly there may be excess, deficiency, or the mean, in regard to actions. But virtue is concerned with emotions and actions, and here excess is an error and deficiency a fault, whereas the mean is successful and laudable, and success and merit are both characteristics of virtue.

Virtue then is a state of deliberate moral purpose consisting 170 in a mean that is relative to ourselves, the mean being determined by reason, or as a prudent man would determine it. . . .

Q What, according to Aristotle, is the supreme good?

Q How does one arrive at the Golden Mean?

Science and Technology

390 B.C.E. Plato coins the term "elements" to describe four primary substances: earth, air, fire, and water (earlier introduced by Empedocles)

350 B.C.E. Aristotle posits a spherical earth based on observations of a lunar eclipse

340 B.C.E. Eudemus of Rhodes writes the *History of Mathematics*

330 B.C.E. Aristotle's *Historia Animalium* classifies animals and records details of animal life; other of his writings advance the study of medicine, biology, and physics

---

[2]A famous athlete from the Greek city-state of Crotona in southern Italy. As a teenager, he began lifting a calf each day, until, as both his strength and the calf grew, he could lift a full-grown bullock.

Aristotle and the State

While the Golden Mean gave every individual a method for determining right action, Aristotle was uncertain that citizens would put it to efficient use in governing themselves. Like Plato, he questioned the viability of the democratic state. Political privilege, argued Aristotle, was the logical consequence of the fact that some human beings were naturally superior to others: from the hour of their birth some were marked out for subjection and others for rule. Aristotle also insisted that governments must function in the interest of the state, not in the interest of any single individual or group. He criticized democracy because, at least in theory, it put power in the hands of great masses of poor people who might rule in their own interests. He also pointed out that Athenian demagogues were capable of persuading the Assembly to pass less-than-worthy laws. In his *Politics*, the first treatise on political theory produced in the West, Aristotle concluded that the best type of government was a constitutional one ruled by the middle class. Aristotle defined the human being as a *polis*-person (the term from which we derive the word "political"). Humans are, in other words, political creatures, who can reach their full potential only within the political framework of the state. Only beasts and gods, he noted, have no need for the state—he gracefully excluded women from such considerations. Aristotle resolved the relationship between the individual and the state as follows:

> [The] state is by nature clearly prior to the family and to the individual, since the whole is of necessity prior to the part. . . . The proof that the state is a creation of nature and prior to the individual is that the individual, when isolated, is not self-sufficing; and therefore he is like a part in relation to the whole. But he who is unable to live in society, or who has no need because he is sufficient for himself, must be either a beast or a god: he is no part of a state. A social instinct is implanted in all men by nature, and yet he who first founded the state was the greatest of benefactors.
>
> For man, when perfected, is the best of animals, but, when separated from law and justice, he is the worst of all; since armed injustice is the more dangerous, and he is equipped at birth with arms, meant to be used by intelligence and virtue, he is the most unholy and the most savage of animals, and the most full of lust and gluttony. But justice is the bond of men in states, for the administration of justice, which is the determination of what is just, is the principle of order in political society.

SUMMARY

The Aegean civilizations of Crete and Mycenae laid the foundations for much of Greek life and legend. Based in these pre-Greek cultures, the Homeric epics describe an aggressive and warlike people who balance vigorous individualism against a deep devotion to the tribal community. The heroes of the *Iliad*, unlike those of other ancient civilizations, do not place themselves at the mercy of the gods; rather, they determine their own destinies.

This spirit of individualism also shaped the values of the emerging Greek city-states. It contributed to the creation of Athenian democracy—the world's first and only direct democracy—and to the Golden Age in cultural productivity that followed the Persian Wars. In Pericles' Funeral Speech the heroic ideal assumes a civic context. In Sophocles' *Antigone* individual choice challenges the inflexible demands of the state. These works illustrate the humanistic thrust of Greek culture. In them, we encounter the Hellenic claim that freedom was no gift of heaven, but rather, a human enterprise involving the active engagement of the individual in the life of the community. The literary achievements of the ancient Greeks in epic poetry, historical narrative, and drama are memorable for the majesty of their language and the profundity of their insights into the human condition. They convey the enduring belief that the good life is within the grasp of mortals.

The ancient Greeks made the speculative leap from belief to reason and from supernatural to natural explanations of the universe. The naturalist philosophers tried to determine the material basis of the universe: Democritus advanced the atomic theory of matter, and Pythagoras held that proportion based on number constituted the underlying cosmic order. The Sophists and the humanist philosophers Socrates, Plato, and Aristotle moved "beyond physics" to probe the limits of human knowledge and the nature of moral action. The Sophists argued that knowledge and virtue were relative, while their critic Socrates pursued absolute standards for moral conduct. Induction and the dialectical method served Socrates in his quest for virtue. Plato's Theory of Forms laid the basis for philosophical idealism and for the separation of mind and matter. In the *Republic*, Plato explained how virtue might be cultivated for the mutual benefit of the individual and the community. The more practical Aristotle investigated a wide variety of subjects ranging from logic and zoology to the art of poetry and the science of statecraft. In his *Ethics*, Aristotle asserted that the good life was identical with the life of reason, a life guided by the Golden Mean. The writings of Plato and Aristotle are the fountainhead of Western philosophic thought. They explore methods of critical thinking that lie at the heart of Western rationalism. As such, they have made an immeasurable contribution to the humanistic tradition.

GLOSSARY

allegory a literary device in which objects, persons, or actions are equated with secondary, figurative meanings that underlie their literal meaning

amphora a two-handled vessel used for oil or wine (see Figures 4.7 and 5.4)

antagonist the character that directly opposes the protagonist in drama or fiction

catalog a list of people, things, or attributes, characteristic of biblical and Homeric literature

democracy a government in which supreme power is vested in the people

dialectical method a question-and-answer style of inquiry made famous by Socrates

empirical method a method of inquiry dependent on direct experience or observation

epithet a characterizing word or phrase; in Homeric verse, a compound adjective used to identify a person or thing

ethics that branch of philosophy that sets forth the principles of human conduct

hubris excessive pride; arrogance

idealism (Platonic) the theory that holds that things in the material world are manifestations of an independent realm of unchanging, immaterial ideas of forms (see also Kantian idealism, chapter 25)

oligarchy a government in which power lies in the hands of an elite minority

protagonist the leading character in a play or story

syllogism a deductive scheme of formal argument, consisting of two premises from which a conclusion may be drawn

CHAPTER 5

The Classical Style

*"Men are day-bound. What is a man? What is he not? Man is a shadow's dream.
But when divine advantage comes, men gain a radiance and a richer life."*
Pindar

The words "classic" or "classical" are commonly used to mean "first-rate" and "enduring"; but they also describe the unique style that dominated the arts during the Greek Golden Age, that is, the period that followed the Persian Wars. The classical style embraced principles of clarity, harmony, and proportioned order in the visual arts, as well as in literature and music. At its height (ca. 480–400 B.C.E.) the so-called High Classical style provided a standard of beauty and excellence that was imitated for centuries, but most immediately by the civilizations that came to prominence after the collapse of Hellenic power. During the fourth century B.C.E., Alexander the Great carried Greek language and culture into North Africa and Central Asia, thus "Hellenizing" a vast part of the civilized world. Thereafter, the Romans absorbed Greek culture and, by imitation and adaptation, ensured the survival of classicism. In music and literature, as in the visual arts, the Greeks provided models that the Romans ultimately transmitted to the West.* Most of the freestanding sculptures of the Greek masters survive only in Roman replicas, and what remains is a fraction of what once existed. The balance fell to the ravages of time and barbarian peoples, who pulverized marble statues to make mortar and melted down bronze pieces to mint coins and cast cannons.

Despite these losses, the classical conception of beauty has had a profound influence on Western cultural expression. Its mark is most visible in the numerous neoclassical ("new classical") revivals that have flourished over the centuries, beginning with the Renaissance in Italy (see chapters 16–17). Some analysis of the defining features of the classical style is essential to an appreciation (and an understanding) of how and why that style became the touchstone by which creative expression was to be judged for centuries.

---

*The Roman contribution to the classical style is discussed in chapter 6.

Key Features of the Classical Style

Order and Proportion

The quest for harmonious order was the driving force behind the evolution of the classical style, even as it was the impetus for the rise of Greek philosophy. In chapter 4, we saw that the naturalist philosophers made every effort to identify the fundamental order underlying the chaos of human perception. Pythagoras, for example, tried to show that the order of the universe could be understood by observing proportion (both geometric and numerical) in nature: he produced a taut string that, when plucked, sounded a specific pitch; by pinching that string in the middle and plucking either half he generated a sound exactly consonant with (and one **octave** higher than) the first pitch. Pythagoras claimed that relationships between musical sounds obeyed a natural symmetry that might be expressed numerically and geometrically. If music was governed by proportion, was not the universe as a whole subject to similar laws? And, if indeed nature itself obeyed laws of harmony and proportion, then should not artists work to imitate them?

Among Greek artists and architects, such ideas generated the search for a canon, or set of rules for determining physical proportion. To arrive at a canon, the artist fixed on a module, or standard of measurement, that governed the relationships between all parts of the work of art and the whole. The size of the module was not absolute, but varied according to the subject matter. In the human body, for instance, the distance from the chin to the top of the forehead, representing one-tenth of the whole body height, constituted a module by which body measurements might be calculated. Unlike the Egyptian canon (see Figure 1.22), the Greek canon was flexible: it did not employ a grid on which the human form was mapped, with fixed positions for parts of the body. Nevertheless, the Greek canon made active use of that principle of proportion known as *symmetry*, that is, correspondence of

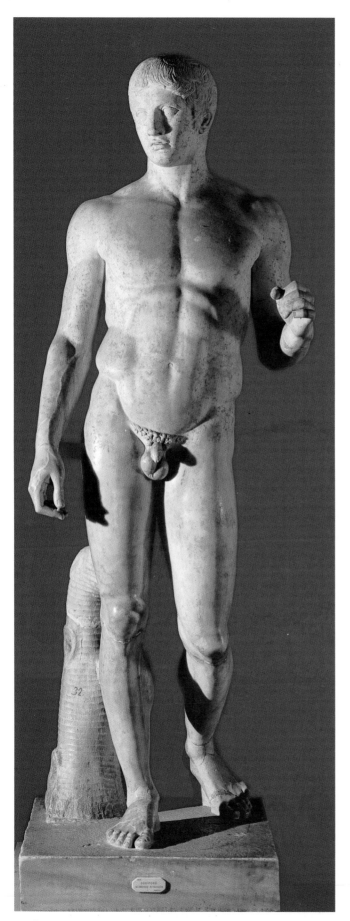

Figure 5.1 Polycleitus, *Doryphorus (Spear-Bearer)*, Roman copy after a bronze Greek original of ca. 450–440 B.C.E. Marble, height 6 ft. 11½ in. National Museum, Naples. Photo: Fotografica Foglia, Naples.

opposite parts in size, shape, or position, as is evident in the human body.

Although little survives in the way of Greek literary evidence, Roman sources preserve information that helps us to understand the canon that, after three centuries of experimentation, artists of the Greek Golden Age put into practice. Among these sources, the best is the *Ten Books on Architecture* written by the Roman architect and engineer, Vitruvius Pollio (?–26 B.C.E.). Vitruvius recorded many of the aesthetic principles and structural techniques used by the ancient Greeks. In defining the classical canon, Vitruvius advised that the construction of a building and the relationship between its parts must imitate the proportions of the human body. Without proportion, that is, the correspondence between the various parts of the whole, there can be no design, argued Vitruvius. And without design, there can be no art. The eminent Golden Age Greek sculptor Polycleitus, himself the author of a manual on proportion (no longer in existence), is believed to have employed the canon Vitruvius describes (Figure **5.1**). But it was the Vitruvian model itself that, thanks to the efforts of the Renaissance artist/scientist Leonardo da Vinci (see chapter 17), became a symbol for the centrality of the ideally proportioned human being in an ideally proportioned universe (Figure **5.2**).

Figure 5.2 Leonardo da Vinci, *Proportional Study of a Man in the Manner of Vitruvius*, ca. 1487. Pen and ink, 13½ × 9⅜ in. Galleria dell'Accademia, Venice.

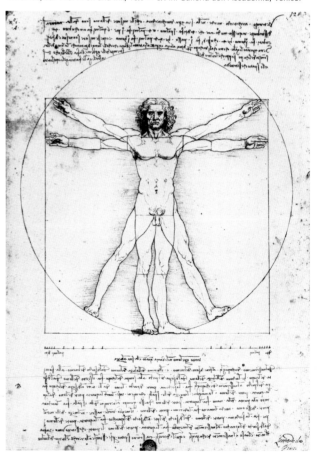

READING 1.18 From Vitruvius' Principles of Symmetry (ca. 46–30 B.C.E.)

On Symmetry: In Temples and in the Human Body

1 The Design of a temple depends on symmetry, the principles of which must be most carefully observed by the architect. They are due to proportion. . . . Proportion is a correspondence among the measures of the members of an entire work, and of the whole to a certain part selected as standard. From this result the principles of symmetry. Without symmetry and proportion there can be no principles in the design of any temple; that is, if there is no precise relation between its members, as in the case of those of a well shaped man. **10**

2 For the human body is so designed by nature that the face, from the chin to the top of the forehead and lowest roots of the hair, is a tenth part of the whole height; the open hand from the wrist to the tip of the middle finger is just the same; the head from the chin to the crown is an eighth, and with the neck and shoulder from the top of the breast to the lowest roots of the hair is a sixth; from the middle of the breast to the summit of the crown is a fourth. If we take the height of the face itself, the distance from the bottom of the chin to the under side of the nostrils is one third of it; the nose from the underside of the **20** nostrils to a line between the eyebrows is the same; from there to the lowest roots of the hair is also a third, comprising the forehead. The length of the foot is one sixth of the height of the body; of the forearm, one fourth; and the breadth of the breast is also one fourth. The other members, too, have their own symmetrical proportions, and it was by employing them that famous painters and sculptors of antiquity attained to great and endless renown.

3 Similarly, in the members of a temple there ought to be the greatest harmony in the symmetrical relations of the different **30** parts to the general magnitude of the whole. Then again, in the human body the central point is naturally the navel. For if a man be placed flat on his back, with hands and feet extended, and a pair of compasses centered at his navel, the fingers and toes of his two hands and feet will touch the circumference of a circle described therefrom. And just as the human body yields a circular outline, so too a square figure may be found from it [see Figure 5.2]. For if we measure the distance from the soles of the feet to the top of the head, and then apply that measure to the outstretched arms, the breadth will be found to be the same as **40** the height, as in the case of plane surfaces which are perfectly square.

4 Therefore, since nature has designed the human body so that its members are duly proportioned to the frame as a whole, it appears that the ancients had good reason for their rule, that in perfect buildings the different members must be in exact symmetrical relations to the whole general scheme. Hence, while transmitting to us the proper arrangements for buildings of all kinds, they are particularly careful to do so in the case of temples of the gods, buildings in which merits and **50** faults usually last forever. . . .

Q Should the proportions of the human body govern architectural design, as Vitruvius suggests?

Humanism, Realism, and Idealism

While proportion and order are two guiding principles of the classical style, other features informed Greek classicism from earliest times. One of these is *humanism*. Greek art is said to be humanistic not only because it observes fundamental laws derived from the human physique, but because it focuses so consistently on the actions of human beings. Greek art is fundamentally *realistic*, that is, faithful to nature; but it refines nature in a process of *idealization*, that is, the effort to achieve a perfection that surpasses nature. Humanism, realism, and idealism are hallmarks of Greek art.

Because almost all evidence of Greek wall-painting has disappeared, decorated vases are our main source of information about Greek painting. During the first three hundred years of Greek art—the *Geometric period* (ca. 1200–700 B.C.E)—artists painted their ceramic wares with angular figures and complex geometric patterns arranged to enhance the shape of the vessel. Scenes from a warrior's funeral dominate the upper register of a **krater** (a vessel used for mixing wine and water); the funeral procession, with horse-drawn chariots, occupies the lower register (Figure **5.3**). By the *Archaic period* (ca. 700–480 B.C.E.), scenes from mythology, literature, and everyday life, came to dominate the central zone of the vase (Figure **5.4**; see

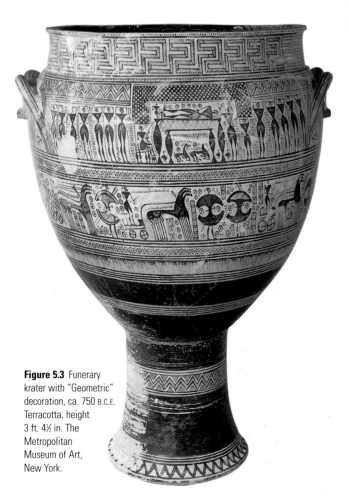

Figure 5.3 Funerary krater with "Geometric" decoration, ca. 750 B.C.E. Terracotta, height 3 ft. 4½ in. The Metropolitan Museum of Art, New York.

Figure 5.4 Exekias, black-figured amphora with Achilles and Ajax playing dice, ca. 530 B.C.E. Height 24 in. Vatican Museums, Rome.

(Figure **5.5**). They refined their efforts to position figures and objects to complement the shape of the vessel (see also Figures 4.12 and 5.4). However, with the newly developed red-figured style, artists might delineate physical details on the buff-colored surface, thereby making the human form appear more lifelike. Although still flattened and aligned side by side, figures are posed naturally. *Realism*, that is, fidelity to nature, has overtaken the decorative aspect of the Geometric and Archaic styles. At the same time, artists of the Classical period moved toward aesthetic *idealism*. Socrates is noted for having described the idealizing process: he advised the painter Parrhasius that he must reach beyond the flawed world of appearances by selecting and combining the most beautiful details of many different models. To achieve ideal form, the artist must simplify the subject matter, free it of incidental detail, and impose the accepted canon of proportion. Accordingly, the art object will surpass the imperfect and transient objects of sensory experience. Like Plato's Ideal Forms, the artist's imitations of reality are lifelike in appearance, but they aim to improve upon or perfect sensory reality. Among the Greeks, as among the Egyptians, conception played a large part in the art-making process; with the Greeks, however, the created object was no longer a static sacred sign, but a dynamic, rationalized replica of the physical world.

The Evolution of the Classical Style

Greek Sculpture: The Archaic Period (ca. 700–480 B.C.E.)

Nowhere is the Greek affection for the natural beauty of the human body so evident as in Hellenic sculpture, where the male nude form assumed major importance as a subject. Freestanding Greek sculptures fulfilled the same purpose as Egyptian and Mesopotamian votive statues: they paid perpetual homage to the gods. They also served as cult statues, funerary monuments, and memorials designed to honor the victors of the athletic games. Since athletes both trained and competed in the nude, representation of the unclothed body was completely appropriate. Ultimately, however, the centrality of the nude in Greek art reflects the Hellenic regard for the human body as nature's perfect creation. (The fig leaves that cover the genitals of some Greek sculptures are additions dating from the Christian era.)

As in painting, so in sculpture, the quest for realism was offset by the will to idealize form. Achieving the

Figure 5.5 Epictetus, cup (detail), ca. 510 B.C.E. Terracotta, diameter 13 in. Reproduced by courtesy of the Trustees of the British Museum, London.

also Figures 4.7 and 4.9). Water jars, wine jugs, storage vessels, drinking cups, and bowls all record the keen enjoyment of everyday activities among the Greeks: working, dancing, feasting, fighting, and gaming. In these compositions, little if any physical setting is provided for the action. Indeed, in their decorative simplicity, the flat, black figures often resemble the abstract shapes that ornament the rim, handle, and foot of the vessel (see Figure 5.4). The principles of clarity and order so apparent in the Geometric style (see Figure 5.3) remain dominant in the decoration of later black-figured vases, where a startling clarity of design is produced by the interplay of dark and light areas of figure and ground.

During the *Classical period* (480–323 B.C.E.), artists replaced the black-figured style with one in which the human body was left the color of the clay and the ground was painted black

delicate balance between real and ideal was a slow process, one that had its beginnings early in Greek history. During the Archaic phase of Greek sculpture, freestanding representations of the male youth (***kouros***) still resembled the blocklike statuary of ancient Egypt (see Figure 1.4). A *kouros* from Attica is rigidly posed, with arms close to its sides and its body weight distributed equally on both feet (Figure **5.6**). Like most Archaic statues, the figure retains the rigid verticality of tree trunks from which the earliest Greek sculptures were carved.

Produced some fifty years after the Attica *kouros*, the *Calf-Bearer* is more gently and more realistically modeled—note especially the abdominal muscles and the sensitively carved bull calf (Figure **5.7**). The hollow eyes of the shepherd once held inlays of semiprecious stones (mother-of-pearl, gray agate, and lapis lazuli) that would have given the face a strikingly realistic appearance. Such lifelike effects were enhanced by the brightly colored

Figure 5.7 *Calf-Bearer*, ca. 575–550 B.C.E. Marble, height 5 ft. 6 in. Acropolis Museum, Athens. © Hirmer Fotoarchiv.

paint (now almost gone) that enlivened the lips, hair, and other parts of the figure. A quarter of a century later, the robust likeness of a warrior named Kroisos (found marking his grave) shows close anatomical attention to knee and calf muscles. Like his archaic predecessors, he strides aggressively forward, but his forearms now turn in toward his body, and his chest, arms, and legs swell with powerful energy (Figure **5.8**). He also bears a blissful smile that, in contrast with the awestruck countenances of Mesopotamian votive statues (see Figure 2.9), reflects the buoyant optimism of the early Greeks.

Greek Sculpture: The Classical Period (480–323 B.C.E.)

By the early fifth century B.C.E., a major transformation occurred in Hellenic art. With the *Kritios Boy* (Figure 5.9), the Greek sculptor had arrived at the natural positioning of the human body that would characterize the classical style: the sensuous torso turns on the axis of the spine, and the weight of the body shifts from equal distribution on both legs to greater weight on the left leg—a kind of

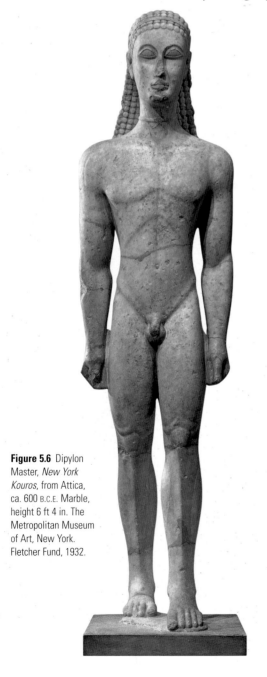

Figure 5.6 Dipylon Master, *New York Kouros*, from Attica, ca. 600 B.C.E. Marble, height 6 ft. 4 in. The Metropolitan Museum of Art, New York. Fletcher Fund, 1932.

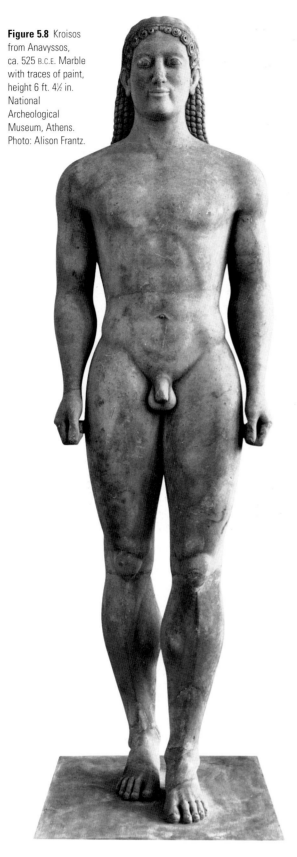

Figure 5.8 Kroisos from Anavyssos, ca. 525 B.C.E. Marble with traces of paint, height 6 ft. 4½ in. National Archeological Museum, Athens. Photo: Alison Frantz.

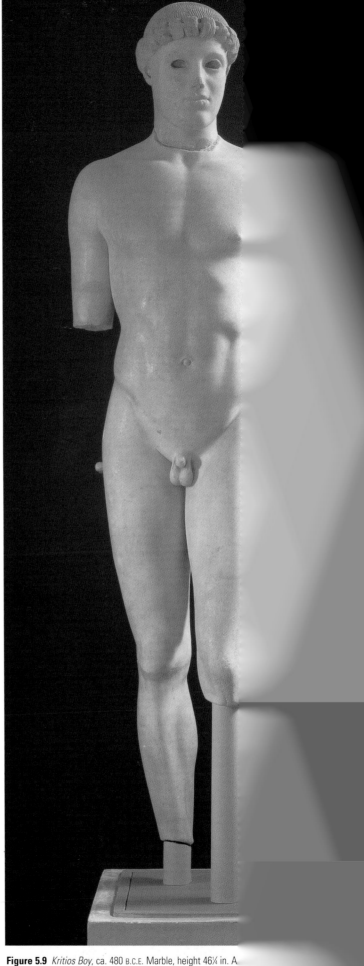

Figure 5.9 *Kritios Boy*, ca. 480 B.C.E. Marble, height 46¼ in. A Athens. Photo: © Craig & Marie Mauzy, Athens.

balanced opposition that is at once natural and graceful. (This counterpositioning would be called **contrapposto** by Italian Renaissance artists.) The muscles of the *Kritios Boy* are no longer geometrically schematized, but protrude subtly at anatomical junctures. And the figure is no longer smiling, but instead solemn and contemplative. The new poised stance, along with a complete mastery of human

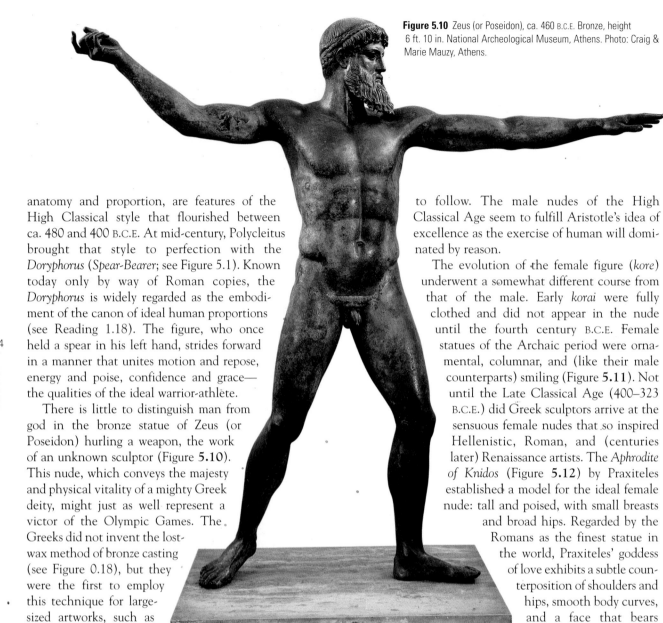

anatomy and proportion, are features of the High Classical style that flourished between ca. 480 and 400 B.C.E. At mid-century, Polycleitus brought that style to perfection with the *Doryphorus* (*Spear-Bearer*; see Figure 5.1). Known today only by way of Roman copies, the *Doryphorus* is widely regarded as the embodiment of the canon of ideal human proportions (see Reading 1.18). The figure, who once held a spear in his left hand, strides forward in a manner that unites motion and repose, energy and poise, confidence and grace—the qualities of the ideal warrior-athlete.

There is little to distinguish man from god in the bronze statue of Zeus (or Poseidon) hurling a weapon, the work of an unknown sculptor (Figure **5.10**). This nude, which conveys the majesty and physical vitality of a mighty Greek deity, might just as well represent a victor of the Olympic Games. The Greeks did not invent the lost-wax method of bronze casting (see Figure 0.18), but they were the first to employ this technique for large-sized artworks, such as the monumental Zeus (or Poseidon) itself. This sophisticated technique allowed artists to depict more vigorous physical action and to include greater detail than was possible in the more restrictive medium of marble. Dynamically posed—the artist has deliberately exaggerated the length of the arms—the god fixes the decisive moment just before the action, when every muscle in the body is tensed, ready to achieve the mark. The sculptor has also idealized the physique in the direction of geometric clarity. Hence the muscles of the stomach are indicated as symmetrical trapezoids, and the strands of his hair and beard assume a distinctive pattern of parallel wavy lines.

Greek and Roman sculptors often made marble copies of popular bronze-cast figures. The *Discobolus* (*Discus Thrower*), originally executed in bronze by Myron around 450 B.C.E, but surviving only in various Roman marble copies, is one such example (see page 66). Like the statue in Figure 5.10, it captures the moment before the action, the ideal moment when intellect guides the physical effort

to follow. The male nudes of the High Classical Age seem to fulfill Aristotle's idea of excellence as the exercise of human will dominated by reason.

The evolution of the female figure (*kore*) underwent a somewhat different course from that of the male. Early *korai* were fully clothed and did not appear in the nude until the fourth century B.C.E. Female statues of the Archaic period were ornamental, columnar, and (like their male counterparts) smiling (Figure **5.11**). Not until the Late Classical Age (400–323 B.C.E.) did Greek sculptors arrive at the sensuous female nudes that so inspired Hellenistic, Roman, and (centuries later) Renaissance artists. The *Aphrodite of Knidos* (Figure **5.12**) by Praxiteles established a model for the ideal female nude: tall and poised, with small breasts and broad hips. Regarded by the Romans as the finest statue in the world, Praxiteles' goddess of love exhibits a subtle counterposition of shoulders and hips, smooth body curves, and a face that bears a dreamy, melting gaze. She is distinguished by the famous Praxitelean technique of carving that coaxed a translucent shimmer from the fine white marble. This classical icon is a Roman copy of a Greek original, and the bar bracing the hip suggests that the original may have been executed in bronze. Some sixty versions of this celebrated nude exist.

A careful study of Greek statuary from the Archaic through the Late Classical Age reflects increasing refinements in realism and idealism: all imperfections (wrinkles, warts, blemishes) have been purged in favor of a radiant flawlessness. The classical nude is neither very old nor very young, neither very thin nor very fat. He or she is eternally youthful, healthy, serene, and dignified, and liberated from all accidents of nature. This synthesis of humanism, realism, and idealism in the representation of the freestanding nude was one of the great achievements of Greek art. Indeed, the Hellenic conception of the nude defined the standard of beauty in Western art for centuries.

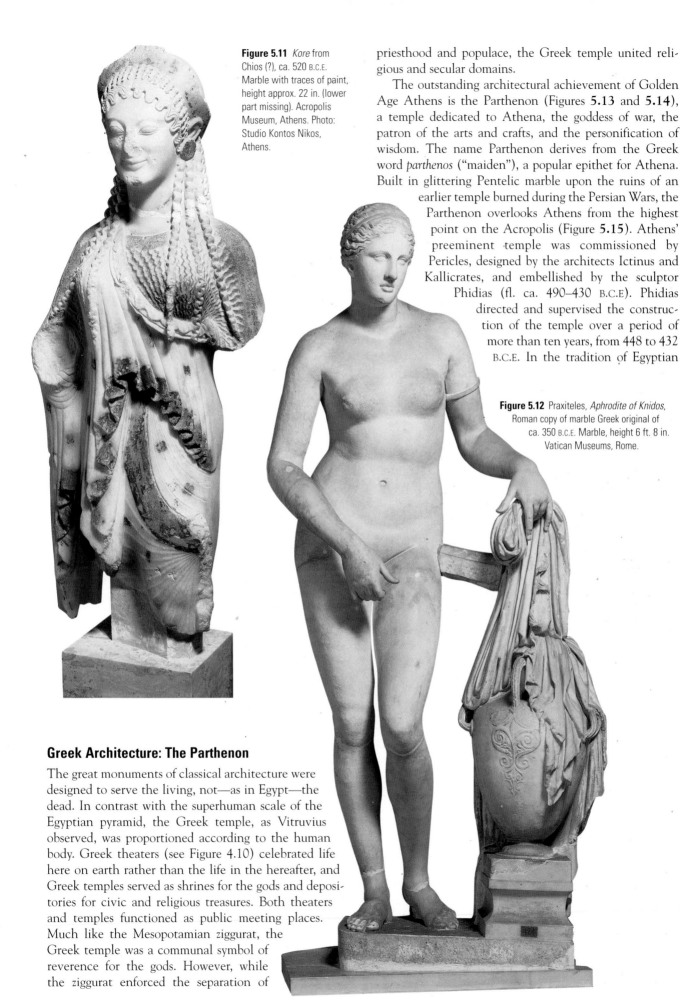

Figure 5.11 *Kore* from Chios (?), ca. 520 B.C.E. Marble with traces of paint, height approx. 22 in. (lower part missing). Acropolis Museum, Athens. Photo: Studio Kontos Nikos, Athens.

priesthood and populace, the Greek temple united religious and secular domains.

The outstanding architectural achievement of Golden Age Athens is the Parthenon (Figures **5.13** and **5.14**), a temple dedicated to Athena, the goddess of war, the patron of the arts and crafts, and the personification of wisdom. The name Parthenon derives from the Greek word *parthenos* ("maiden"), a popular epithet for Athena. Built in glittering Pentelic marble upon the ruins of an earlier temple burned during the Persian Wars, the Parthenon overlooks Athens from the highest point on the Acropolis (Figure **5.15**). Athens' preeminent temple was commissioned by Pericles, designed by the architects Ictinus and Kallicrates, and embellished by the sculptor Phidias (fl. ca. 490–430 B.C.E). Phidias directed and supervised the construction of the temple over a period of more than ten years, from 448 to 432 B.C.E. In the tradition of Egyptian

Figure 5.12 Praxiteles, *Aphrodite of Knidos*, Roman copy of marble Greek original of ca. 350 B.C.E. Marble, height 6 ft. 8 in. Vatican Museums, Rome.

Greek Architecture: The Parthenon

The great monuments of classical architecture were designed to serve the living, not—as in Egypt—the dead. In contrast with the superhuman scale of the Egyptian pyramid, the Greek temple, as Vitruvius observed, was proportioned according to the human body. Greek theaters (see Figure 4.10) celebrated life here on earth rather than the life in the hereafter, and Greek temples served as shrines for the gods and depositories for civic and religious treasures. Both theaters and temples functioned as public meeting places. Much like the Mesopotamian ziggurat, the Greek temple was a communal symbol of reverence for the gods. However, while the ziggurat enforced the separation of

Figure 5.13 Ictinus and Kallicrates, West end of the Parthenon, Athens, 448–432 B.C.E. Pentelic marble, height of columns 34 ft. Photo: Sonia Halliday, Weston Turville.

builders, Greek architects used no mortar. Rather, they employed bronze clamps and dowels to fasten the individually cut marble segments.

The Parthenon represents the apex of a long history of post-and-lintel temple building among the Greeks. That history, like the history of Greek painting and sculpture, entailed a search for harmonious proportion, which came to fruition in the Parthenon. The plan of the temple, a rectangle delimited on all four sides by a colonnaded walkway, reflects the typically classical reverence for clarity and symmetry (see Figure 5.14). Freestanding columns (each 34 feet tall) make up the exterior, while two further rows of columns on the east and west ends of the temple provide inner **porticos** (see Figure 5.18). The interior of the Parthenon is divided into two rooms, a central hall (or *cella*), which held the colossal cult statue of Athena, and a smaller room

used as a treasury. It was here that the much-disputed Delian League funds were stored. Entirely elevated on a raised platform, the Parthenon invited the individual to move around it, as if it were a piece of monumental sculpture. Indeed, scholars have suggested that the Parthenon was both a shrine to Athena and a victory monument.

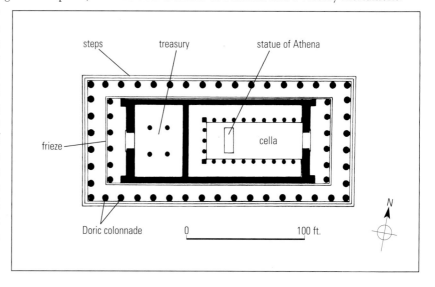

Figure 5.14 Plan of the Parthenon, Athens.

Figure 5.15 Model of the classical Acropolis at Athens. American School of Classical Studies at Athens: Agora Excavations.

1 Erechtheion
2 picture gallery
3 Propylaia (entrance gate)
4 Sacred Way
5 Temple of Athena Nike
6 Chalkotheke (armory)
7 Parthenon (Temple of Athena Parthenos)

The Parthenon makes use of the Doric **order**, one of three programs of architectural design developed by the ancient Greeks (Figure **5.16**). Each of the orders—Doric, Ionic, and (in Hellenistic times) Corinthian—prescribes a fundamental set of structural and decorative parts that stand in fixed relation to each other. Each order differs in details and in the relative proportions of the parts. The Doric order, which originated on the Greek mainland, is simple and severe. In the Parthenon it reached its most refined expression. The Ionic order, originating in Asia Minor and the Aegean Islands, is more delicate and ornamental. Its slender columns terminate in capitals with paired volutes or scrolls. The Ionic order is employed in some of the small temples on the Acropolis (Figure **5.17**). The Corinthian, the most ornate of the orders, is characterized by capitals consisting of acanthus leaves. It is often

Figure 5.16 The Greek orders: (a) Doric; (b) Ionic; and (c) Corinthian.

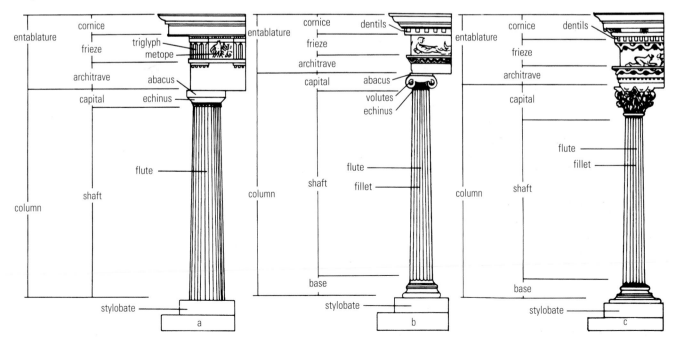

found on victory monuments, in **tholos** (circular) sanctuaries and shrines, as well as in various Hellenistic and Roman structures (see Figures 6.10 and 6.13).

If an ideal system governed the parts of the Greek building, a similar set of laws determined its proportions. The precise canon of proportion adopted by Phidias for the construction of the Parthenon is still, however, the subject of debate. Most architectural historians agree that a module was used, but whether the module was geometric or numerical, and whether it followed a specific ratio—such as the famous "Golden Section"—has not been resolved. The system of proportions known as the "Golden Section" or "Golden Ratio" is expressed numerically by the ratio of 1.618:1, or approximately 8:5. This ratio, which governs the proportions of the ground plan of the Parthenon and the Vitruvian canon, represents an aesthetic ideal found in nature and in the human anatomy. The question of the Parthenon's construction is further complicated by the fact that there are virtually no straight lines in the entire building. Its Doric columns, for instance, swell out near the center to counter the optical effect of thinning that occurs when the normal eye views an uninterrupted set of parallel lines. All columns tilt slightly inward. Corner columns are thicker than the others to compensate for the attenuating effect produced by the bright light of the sky against which the columns are viewed, and also to ensure their ability to bear the weight of the terminal segments of the superstructure. The top step of the platform on which the columns rest is not parallel to the ground, but rises four and a quarter inches at the center, allowing for rainwater to run off the convex surface even as it corrects the optical impression of sagging along the extended length of the platform. Consistently, the architects of the Parthenon corrected negative optical illusions produced by strict conformity to geometric regularity. Avoiding rigid systems of proportion, they took as their primary consideration the aesthetic and functional integrity of the building. Today the Parthenon stands as a noble ruin, the victim of an accidental gunpowder explosion in the seventeenth century, followed by centuries of vandalism, air pollution, and unrelenting tourist traffic.

The Sculpture of the Parthenon

Between 448 and 432 B.C.E. Phidias and the members of his workshop executed the sculptures that would appear in three main locations on the Parthenon: in the **pediments**

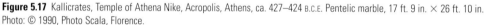

Figure 5.17 Kallicrates, Temple of Athena Nike, Acropolis, Athens, ca. 427–424 B.C.E. Pentelic marble, 17 ft. 9 in. × 26 ft. 10 in. Photo: © 1990, Photo Scala, Florence.

Figure 5.18 Sculptural and architectural detail of the Parthenon. **Frieze**, a decorative band along the top of a wall; **metopes**, segmented spaces on a frieze; **pediment**, a gable.

metope

pedimental sculpture

Ionic frieze

of the roof **gables**, on the **metopes** or square panels between the beam ends under the roof, and in the area along the outer wall of the *cella* (Figure **5.18**). Brightly painted, as were some of the decorative portions of the building, the Parthenon sculptures relieved the stark angularity of the post-and-lintel structure. In subject matter, the temple sculptures paid homage to the patron deity of Athens: the east pediment narrates the birth of Athena with gods and goddesses in attendance (Figures **5.19** and **5.20**). The west pediment shows the contest between Poseidon and Athena for domination of Athens. The ninety-two metopes that occupy the **frieze** (see Figure 5.18) illustrate the legendary combat between the Greeks (the bearers of civilization) and Giants, Amazons, and Centaurs (the forces of barbarism). Figure **5.21**, for instance, shows one of the Lapiths (an ancient Greek tribe) defeating a centaur (a fabulous hybrid of horse and man) after a group of drunken centaurs tried to abduct the Lapiths' women. Carved in high relief, each metope is a masterful depiction of two contestants, one human and the other bestial. Appropriate to a temple honoring the Goddess of Wisdom, the sculptural program of the Parthenon celebrates the victory of intellect over unbridled passion, hence barbarism.

Completing Phidias' program of architectural decoration for the Parthenon is the continuous frieze that winds

Figure 5.19 Drawing of a reconstruction of the east pediment of the Parthenon, central section. Acropolis Museum, Athens.

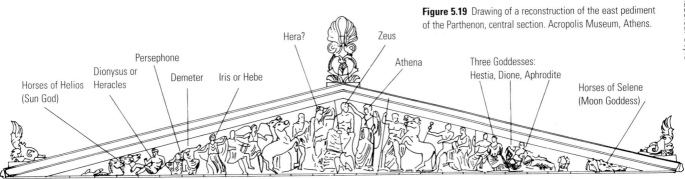

Hera?   Zeus

Persephone

Dionysus or Heracles

Demeter   Iris or Hebe

Athena

Three Goddesses: Hestia, Dione, Aphrodite

Horses of Helios (Sun God)

Horses of Selene (Moon Goddess)

Figure 5.20 Three Goddesses: Hestia, Dione, Aphrodite, from east pediment of the Parthenon, Athens, ca. 437–432 B.C.E. Marble, over life-sized. Reproduced by courtesy of the Trustees of the British Museum, London.

Figure 5.21 Lapith overcoming a centaur, south metope 27, Parthenon, Athens, 447–438 B.C.E. Marble, height 4 ft. 5 in. Reproduced by courtesy of the Trustees of the British Museum, London.

Figure 5.22 Group of young horsemen, from the north frieze of the Parthenon, Athens, 447–438 B.C.E. Marble, height 3 ft. 7 in. Reproduced by courtesy of the Trustees of the British Museum, London.

Figure 5.24 Gold pendant disk with the head of Athena (one of a pair), from Kul Oba, ca. 400–350 B.C.E. Height 3 19/20 in., diameter of disk 1½ in. Photo: Hermitage KO 5. NOVOSTI, London.

around the outer wall of the *cella* where that wall meets the roofline. The 524-foot-long sculptured band is thought to depict the Panathenaic Festival, a celebration held every four years in honor of the goddess Athena. Hundreds of figures—a cavalcade of horsemen (Figure **5.22**), water bearers, musicians, and votaries—are shown filing in calm procession toward an assembled group of gods and goddesses (Figure **5.23**). The figures move with graceful rhythms, in tempos that could well be translated into music. Once brightly painted and ornamented with metal details, these noble images must have appeared impressively lifelike. To increase this effect and satisfy a viewpoint from below, Phidias graded the relief, cutting the marble more deeply at the top than at the bottom. Housed today in the British Museum in London, where it is hung at approximately eye level, the Parthenon frieze loses much of its illusionistic subtlety. Nevertheless, this masterpiece of the Greek Golden Age reveals the harmonious reconciliation of humanism, realism, and idealism that is the hallmark of the classical style.

The Gold of Greece

The famous statue of Athena that stood in the *cella* of the Parthenon disappeared many centuries ago. However, images of the goddess abound in Hellenic art. One of the most spectacular appears in the form of a gold pendant disk that shows the head of Athena wearing a helmet bearing a sphinx, deer and griffin heads, and an elaborate triple crest (Figure **5.24**). From Athena's shoulders snakes spring forth, and by her head stands an owl (the symbol of wisdom)—both motifs recalling the powers of the Minoan priestess (see Figure **4.4**). Rosettes of gold filigree and enamel-colored buds ornament the complex of looped chains that hang from the disk.

The Greeks gained international acclaim for their gold-working techniques, many of which had been inherited

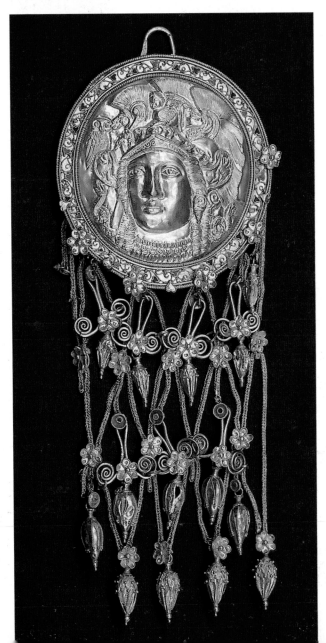

from Persia and from the nomadic Scythians of northern Asia. Gold-rich mining areas of northern Greece provided craftspeople with materials for the manufacture of jewelry. Particularly popular were pendants, earrings, and headpieces in the form of miniature sculptures, some of which (like the pendant of Athena) reproduced familiar images of the gods. Much like today, gold jewelry was a mark of wealth that also bore sentimental and religious value. In Greece and especially in the cities of Asia Minor, men as well as women adorned themselves with stylish earrings and bracelets.

The Classical Style in Poetry

In classical Greece, as in other parts of the ancient world, distinctions between various forms of artistic expression were neither clear-cut nor definitive. A combination of the arts prevailed in most forms of religious ritual and in public and private entertainment. In *Antigone*, for instance, Sophocles used choric pantomime and dance to complement dramatic poetry. And in processions and festivals, music, poetry, and dance all served a common purpose. The intimate relationship between music and poetry is revealed in the fact that many of the words we use to describe lyric forms, such as "**ode**" and "**hymn**," are also musical terms. The word lyric, meaning "accompanied by the lyre," describes verse that was meant to be sung, not read silently. Lyric poetry was designed to give voice to deep emotions.

Hellenic culture produced an impressive group of lyric poets, the greatest of whom was Sappho (ca. 610–ca. 580 B.C.E.). Her personal life remains a mystery. Born into an aristocratic family, she seems to have married and mothered a daughter. She settled on the island of Lesbos, where she led a group of young women dedicated to the cult of Aphrodite. At Lesbos, Sappho trained women in the production of love poetry and music. She herself produced some nine books of poetry, of which only fragments remain. Her highly self-conscious poems, many of which come to us only as fragments, are filled with passion and tenderness. They offer only a glimpse of a body of poetry that inspired Sappho's contemporaries to regard her as "the female Homer."

Ancient and modern poets alike admired Sappho for her powerful economy of expression and her inventive combinations of sense and sound—features that are extremely difficult to convey in translation. The first of the five poems reproduced below gives lyric voice to Sappho's homoerotic attachment to the women of the Lesbian cult. That bisexual and homosexual relationships were common among the ancient Greeks is given ample evidence in Hellenic literature and art. The scene on the elegant drinking cup by Douris (see Figure 4.12), for instance, is generally interpreted as depicting an older man propositioning a younger one. The last of the selections, a terse and pensive poem, reflects the intense spirit of this-worldliness and the generally negative view of death that typified Sappho's verse and ancient Greek expression in general.

READING 1.19 Sappho's Poems (ca. 590 B.C.E.)

He is more than a hero   1
He is a god in my eyes
the man who is allowed
to sit beside you—he

who listens intimately   5
to the sweet murmur of
your voice, the enticing

laughter that makes my own
heart beat fast. If I meet
you suddenly, I can't   10

speak—my tongue is broken;
a thin flame runs under
my skin; seeing nothing,

hearing only my own ears
drumming, I drip with sweat;   15
trembling shakes my body

and I turn paler than
dry grass. At such times
death isn't far from me

———◆———

With his venom   1
Irresistible
and bittersweet
that loosener
of limbs, Love   5
reptile-like
strikes me down

———◆———

I took my lyre and said: 1
Come now, my heavenly
tortoise shell; become
a speaking instrument

———◆———

Although they are   1
Only breath, words
which I command
are immortal

———◆———

We know this much   1
Death is an evil;
we have the gods'
word for it; they too
would die if death   5
were a good thing

Q What themes are treated in these five poems?

Q How do the poems illustrate "economy of expression"?

Science and Technology

500 B.C.E.	steel is first produced in India; the corpus of Indian geometry is summarized in the Sulvasutras ("Rules of the Cord")
400 B.C.E.	Hellenistic Greeks invent the catapult for use as an artillery weapon
300 B.C.E.	Euclid completes his *Elements*, a compilation of mathematics that includes geometry and number theory
300 B.C.E.	a school of medicine is established in Alexandria
290 B.C.E.	Theophrastus, a student of Plato, writes the detailed *History of Plants*

While lyric poetry often conveyed deeply personal feelings, certain types of lyrics, namely odes, served as public eulogies or songs of praise. Odes honoring Greek athletes bear strong similarities to songs of divine praise, such as the Egyptian "Hymn to the Aten" (see chapter 1), the Hebrew Psalms, and Greek invocations. But the sentiments conveyed in the odes of the noted Greek poet Pindar (ca. 522–438 B.C.E.) are firmly planted in the secular world. They celebrate the achievements of the athletes who competed at the games held at the great sanctuaries of Olympia, Delphi, Nemea, and elsewhere (see Figure 4.9). Perpetuating the heroic idealism of the *Iliad*, Pindar's odes make the claim that prowess, not chance, leads to victory, which in turn renders the victor immortal. The first lines of his *Nemean Ode VI* honoring Alcimidas of Aegina (winner in the boys' division of wrestling) assert that gods and men share a common origin. The closest human beings can come to achieving godlike immortality, however, lies in the exercise of "greatness of mind/Or of body." The ode thus narrows the gap between hero-athletes and their divine prototypes. In his *Pythian Ode VIII* (dedicated to yet another victorious wrestler), Pindar develops a more modest balance of opposites: he sets the glories of youth against the adversities of aging and mortality itself. Although mortal limitations separate human beings from the ageless and undying gods, "manly action" secures the "richer life."

READING 1.20 From Pindar's Odes (ca. 420 B.C.E.)

From *Nemean Ode VI*

Single is the race, single	1
Of men and of gods;	
From a single mother we both draw breath.	
But a difference of power in everything	
Keeps us apart;	5
For the one is as nothing, but the brazen sky	
Stays a fixed habitation for ever.	
Yet we can in greatness of mind	
Or of body be like the Immortals,	
Though we know not to what goal	10
By day or in the nights	
Fate has written that we shall run.	

From *Pythian Ode VIII*

In the Pythian games	1
you pinned four wrestlers	
unrelentingly, and sent	
them home in losers' gloom;	
no pleasant laughter cheered them as they reached	5
their mothers' sides; shunning ridicule,	
they took to alleys, licking losers' wounds.	
And he, who in his youth	
secures a fine advantage	
gathers hope and flies	10
on wings of manly action,	
disdaining cost. Men's happiness is early-	
ripened fruit that falls to earth	
from shakings of adversity.	
Men are day-bound. What is a man? What is	15
he *not*? Man is a shadow's dream. But when divine	
advantage comes, men gain a radiance and a richer life.	

Q How does Pindar answer his own question (line 15), "What is a man?"

Q How does his answer compare to other responses to this question in Readings 1.6, 1.8e, and 1.13, lines 274–89?

The Classical Style in Music and Dance

The English word *music* derives from *muse*, the Greek word describing any of the nine mythological daughters of Zeus and the Goddess of Memory. According to Greek mythology, the muses presided over the arts and the sciences. Pythagoras observed that music was governed by mathematical ratios and therefore constituted both a science and an art. As was true of the other arts, music played a major role in Greek life. However, we know almost as little about how Greek music sounded as we do in the cases of Egyptian or Sumerian music. The ancient Greeks did not invent a system of notation with which to record instrumental or vocal sounds. Apart from written and visual descriptions of musical performances, there exist only a few fourth-century-B.C.E. treatises on music theory and some primitively notated musical works. The only complete piece of ancient Greek music that has survived is an ancient song found chiseled on a first-century-B.C.E. gravestone. It reads: "So long as you live, be radiant, and do not grieve at all. Life's span is short and time exacts the final reckoning." Both vocal and instrumental music were commonplace, and contests between musicians, like those between playwrights, were a regular part of public life. Vase paintings reveal that the principal musical instruments of ancient Greece were the **lyre**, the **kithara**—both belonging to the harp family and differing only in shape, size, and number of strings

♪ See Music Listening Selections at end of chapter.

(Figure **5.25**)—and the **aulos**, a flute or reed pipe (see Figure 5.5). Along with percussion devices often used to accompany dancing, these string and wind instruments were probably inherited from Egypt.

The Greeks devised a system of **modes**, or types of **scales** characterized by fixed patterns of pitch and tempo within the octave. (The sound of the ancient Greek Dorian mode is approximated by playing the eight white keys of the piano beginning with the white key two notes above middle C.) Modified variously in Christian times, the modes were preserved in Gregorian chant and Byzantine church hymnology (see chapter 9). Although the modes themselves may have been inspired by the music of ancient India, the diatonic scale (familiar to Westerners as the series of notes C, D, E, F, G, A, B, C) originated in Greece. Greek music lacked harmony as we know it. It was thus **monophonic**, that is, confined to a single unaccompanied line of melody. The strong association between poetry and music suggests that the human voice had a significant influence in both melody and rhythm.

From earliest times, music was believed to hold magical powers and therefore exercise great spiritual influence. Greek and Roman mythology describes gods and heroes who used music to heal or destroy. Following Pythagoras, who equated musical ratios with the unchanging cosmic order, many believed that music might put one "in tune with" the universe. The planets, which Pythagoras described as a series of spheres moving at varying speeds in concentric orbits around the earth, were said to produce a special harmony, the so-called *music of the spheres*. The Greeks believed, moreover, that music had a moral influence. This argument, often referred to as the "Doctrine of Ethos," held that some modes strengthened the will, whereas others undermined it and thus damaged the development of moral character. In the *Republic*, Plato encouraged the use of the Dorian mode, which settled the temper and inspired courage, but he condemned the Lydian mode, which aroused sensuality. Because of music's potential for affecting character and mood, both Plato and Aristotle recommended that the types of music used in the education of young children be regulated by law. As with other forms of classical expression, music was deemed essential to the advancement of the individual and the well-being of the community.

Dance was prized for its moral value, as well as for its ability to give pleasure and induce good health (see Figure 5.5). For Plato the uneducated man was a "danceless" man. Both Plato and Aristotle advised that children be instructed at an early age in music and dancing. However, both men distinguished noble dances from ignoble ones—Dionysian and comic dances, for instance. These they considered unfit for Athenian citizens and therefore inappropriate to the educational curriculum. Nevertheless, the dancing *maenad*, a cult follower of Dionysus, was a favorite image of revelry and intoxication in ancient Greece (Figure **5.26**).

The Diffusion of the Classical Style: The Hellenistic Age (323–30 B.C.E.)

The fourth century B.C.E. was a turbulent era marked by rivalry and warfare among the Greek city-states. Ironically, however, the failure of the Greek city-states to live in peace would lead to the spread of Hellenic culture throughout the civilized world. Manipulating the shifting confederacies and internecine strife to his advantage, Philip of Macedonia eventually defeated the Greeks in 338 B.C.E. When he was assassinated two years later, his twenty-year-old son Alexander (356–323 B.C.E.) assumed the Macedonian throne (Figure **5.27**). A student of Aristotle, Alexander brought to his role as ruler the same kind of far-reaching ambition and imagination that his teacher had exercised in the intellectual realm. Alexander was a military genius: within twelve years, he created an empire that stretched from Greece to the borders of modern India (Map **5.1**). To all parts of his empire, but especially to the cities he founded—many of which he named after himself—Alexander carried Greek language and culture. Greek art and literature made a major impact on civilizations as far east as India, where it influenced Buddhist art and Sanskrit literature (see chapter 9).

Alexander carved out his empire with the help of an army of 35,000 Greeks and Macedonians equipped with

Figure 5.25 The Berlin painter, red-figured amphora, ca. 490 B.C.E. Terracotta, height of vase 16⅜ in. The Metropolitan Museum of Art, New York. Fletcher Fund, 1956.

weapons that were superior to any in the ancient world. Siege machines such as catapults and battering rams were used to destroy the walls of the best-defended cities of Asia Minor, Egypt, Syria, and Persia. Finally, in northwest India, facing the prospect of confronting the formidable army of the King of Ganges and his force of five thousand elephants, Alexander's troops refused to go any further. Shortly thereafter, the thirty-two-year-old general died (probably of malaria), and his empire split into three segments: Egypt was governed by the Ptolemy dynasty; Persia came under the leadership of the Seleucid rulers; and

Figure 5.26 A *maenad* leaning on a thyrsos, Roman copy of Greek original, ca. 420–410 B.C.E. Marble relief. The Metropolitan Museum of Art, New York. Fletcher Fund, 1935.

Figure 5.27 Head of Alexander, from Pergamon, Hellenistic portrait, ca. 200 B.C.E. Marble, height 16 in. Archeological Museum, Istanbul.

Macedonia-Greece was governed by the family of Antigonus the One-Eyed (see Map 5.1, inset).

The era that followed, called Hellenistic ("Greek-like"), lasted from 323 to 30 B.C.E. The defining features of the Hellenistic Age were cosmopolitanism, urbanism, and the blending of Greek, African, and Asian cultures. Trade routes linked Arabia, east Africa, and central Asia, bringing great wealth to the cities of Alexandria, Antioch, Pergamon, and Rhodes. Alexandria, which replaced Athens as a cultural center, boasted a population of more than one million people and a library of half a million books (the collection was destroyed by fire when Julius Caesar besieged the city in 47 B.C.E.). The Great Library, part of the cultural complex known as the Temple of the Muses (or "Museum"), was an ancient "think tank" that housed both scholars and books. At the rival library of Pergamon (with some 200,000 books), scribes prepared sheepskin to produce "pergamene paper," that is, parchment, the medium that would be used for centuries of manuscript production prior to the widespread dissemination of paper.

The Hellenistic Age made important advances in geography, astronomy, and mathematics. Euclid, who lived in Alexandria during the late fourth century B.C.E., produced a textbook of existing geometric learning that systematized the theorems of plane and solid geometry. Archimedes of Syracuse, who flourished a century later, calculated the value of *pi* (the ratio of the circumference of a circle to its diameter). An engineer as well as a mathematician, he invented the compound pulley, a windlass for moving heavy weights, and many other mechanical devices. "Give me a place to stand," he is said to have

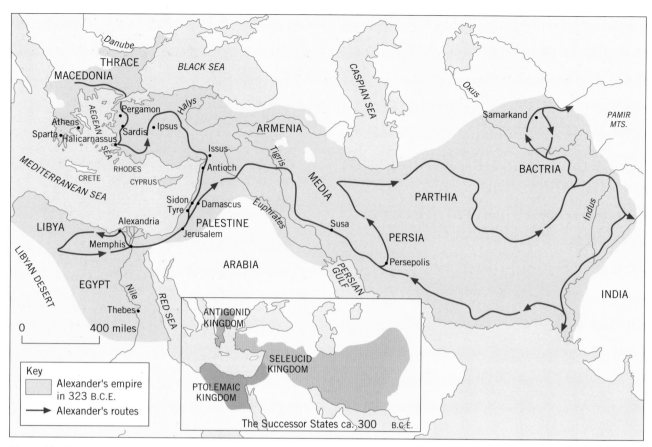

Map 5.1 The Hellenistic World.

boasted, "and I shall move the earth." Legend describes Archimedes as the typical absent-minded scientist, who often forgot to eat; upon realizing that the water he displaced in his bathtub explained the law of specific gravity, he is said to have jumped out of the bathtub and run naked through the streets of Syracuse, shouting *"Eureka"* ("I have found it!").

Hellenistic Schools of Thought

The Hellenistic world was considerably different from the world of the Greek city-states. In the latter, citizens identified with their community, which was itself the state; but in Alexander's vast empire, communal loyalties were unsteady and—especially in sprawling urban centers—impersonal. The intellectuals of the Hellenistic Age did not formulate rational methods of investigation in the style of Plato and Aristotle; rather they espoused philosophic schools of thought that guided everyday existence: Skepticism, Cynicism, Epicureanism, and Stoicism. The Skeptics—much like the Sophists of Socrates' time—denied the possibility of knowing anything with certainty: they argued for the suspension of all intellectual judgment. The Cynics held that spiritual satisfaction was only possible if one renounced societal values, conventions, and material wealth. The Epicureans, followers of the Greek thinker Epicurus (341–270 B.C.E.), taught that happiness depended on avoiding all forms of physical excess; they valued plain living and the perfect union of body and mind. Epicurus held that the gods played no part in human life, and that death was nothing more than the rearrangement

of atoms of which the body and all of nature consisted. Finally, the Stoics found tranquility of mind in a doctrine of detachment that allowed them to accept even the worst of life's circumstances. The aim of the Stoic was to bring the individual will into complete harmony with the will of nature, which they believed was governed by an impersonal intelligence. Stoicism, which became increasingly influential among Roman intellectuals (see chapter 6), also advanced the notion of universal equality. All four of these schools of thought placed the personal needs and emotions of the individual over and above the good of the community at large; in this, they constituted a practical and radical departure from the Hellenic quest for universal truth.

Hellenistic Art

The shift from city-state to empire that accompanied the advent of the Hellenistic era was reflected in larger, more monumental forms of architecture and in the construction of utilitarian structures, such as lighthouses, theaters, and libraries. Circular sanctuaries and colossal Corinthian temples with triumphant decorative friezes were particularly popular in the fourth century B.C.E. and thereafter. At Pergamon (see Map 5.1) stood the largest sculptural complex in the ancient world: the Altar of Zeus (see Figure **5.28**). Erected around 180 B.C.E. to celebrate the victory of the minor kingdom of Pergamon over the invading tribal Gauls achieved some fifty years earlier, the altar stands atop a 20-foot-high platform enclosed by an Ionic colonnade. A massive stairway reaches upward to the

Science and Technology

280 B.C.E. the lighthouse at Pharos, north of Alexandria, is the tallest tower in existence

260 B.C.E. Archimedes establishes the law of specific gravity, invents the compound pulley, studies the mechanical properties of the lever, and lays the foundations for calculus

240 B.C.E. Aristarchus of Samos proposes that the earth and all the planets rotate on their axes and revolve around the sun (the heliocentric theory)

230 B.C.E. Eratosthenes of Cyrene calculates the circumference of the earth with near accuracy

220 B.C.E. Herophilus of Alexandria discovers the human nervous system; he proposes that the arteries carry blood (not air, as previously believed) from the heart

150 B.C.E. Hipparchus of Nicea invents trigonometry; he catalogs 805 fixed stars

shrine. Around the base of the platform runs a 300-foot-long sculptured frieze depicting the mythological battle between the Olympic gods and the race of giants known as Titans. The subject matter, symbolizing the victory of intellect over barbarism, recalls the metopes of the Parthenon, but both the altar and the frieze are far more theatrical in style than anything created in the Hellenic *polis*. The drama of the structure itself, which more resembles a stage than a temple, is made emphatic in the frieze: here, high-relief figures writhe in rhythmic patterns, engaging each other in fierce combat. The goddess

Athena, some 7 feet tall, grasps by the hair a serpent-tailed male, the son of the earth mother who rises from the ground on the lower right (see Figure 5.29). The deeply cut figures create strong light and dark contrasts; indeed, some seem to break free of their architectural frame. In the Altar of Zeus, classical restraint has given way to violent passion.

In free-standing Hellenistic sculpture, the new emphasis on private emotion and discrete personality gave rise to portraits that were more lifelike and less idealized than those of the Hellenic era. A marble portrait of the ruler Alexander (Figure 5.27) manifests the new effort to capture fleeting mood and momentary expression. Hellenistic art is also notable for its sensuous female nude sculptures: the fondness for erotic expression is especially evident in works carved in the tradition of Praxiteles (see Figure 5.12). Perhaps the most notable example of the new sensuousness, however, is the male nude statue known as the *Apollo Belvedere* (Figure **5.30**). This Roman copy of a Hellenistic statue was destined to exercise a major influence in Western art from the moment it was recovered in Rome in 1503. A comparison of the *Apollo* with its Hellenic counterpart, the *Spear-Bearer* (see Figure 5.1), reveals the subtle move of Hellenistic sculpture away from the High Classical to a more animated, feminized, and self-conscious style. Hellenistic artists departed from classical idealism by broadening the range of subjects to include young children and old, even deformed, people. Hellenistic sculptors continue to demonstrate a high degree of technical virtuosity, but their carving techniques are used increasingly to emphasize dynamic contrasts of light and dark and the subtleties of semitransparent robes. These features, in addition to a bold display of vigorous movement, are evident in the larger-than-life **Nike** (the

Figure 5.28 The Altar of Zeus (reconstructed), Pergamon, ca. 175 B.C.E. Marble. Pergamonmuseum, Berlin.

Figure 5.29 Athena battling with Acyoneus, from the frieze of the Altar of Zeus, Pergamon, ca. 180 B.C.E. Marble, Height 7 ft. 6 in. Pergamonmuseum, Berlin.

Figure 5.30 *Apollo Belvedere.* Roman marble copy of a Greek original, late fourth century B.C.E. Height 7ft 4in. Vatican Museum, Rome.

Figure 5.31 Pythocritos of Rhodes, *Nike of Samothrace*, ca. 190 B.C.E. Marble, height 8 ft. Louvre, Paris. Photo: R.M.N, Paris.

Figure 5.32 Agesander, Polydorus, and Athenodorus of Rhodes, *Laocoön and His Sons*, second to first century B.C.E. or a Roman copy of first century C.E. Marble, height 7 ft. 10½ in. Vatican Museums. Photo: Araldo de Luca.

The work that best sums up the Hellenistic aesthetic is the remarkable *Laocoön and His Sons* (Figure **5.32**). This monumental marble sculpture recreates the dramatic moment when Laocoön, priest of Apollo, and his two sons are attacked by sea serpents. Legend had it that the gods had sent these creatures as punishment for Laocoön's effort to warn the Trojans against the Greek ruse—a wooden horse filled with armed soldiers—that would bring an end to the Trojan War. The tortuous pose, strained muscles, and anguished face of the doomed priest create a sense of turbulence and agitation that contrasts sharply with the mild tranquility and dignified restraint of Hellenic art. Indeed, the *Laocoön* is a memorable symbol of an age in which classical idealism had already become part of history.

Greek personification of Victory) erected at Rhodes to celebrate a naval triumph over Syria (Figure **5.31**). The deeply cut drapery of the *Nike of Samothrace* clings sensuously to her body as the winged figure strides into the wind, like some gigantic ship's prow.

SUMMARY

No style in the history of the arts has been more influential than that which emerged during the Greek Golden Age. The classical style reflects the Hellenic devotion to rational laws of proportion, order, clarity, and balance. It is also characterized by humanism, a this-worldly belief in the dignity and inherent worth of human beings, by realism, or fidelity to nature, and by idealism, that is, the commitment to an underlying standard of perfection. The human body and human experience are central to all the arts of classical Greece. In the paintings found on Greek vases, as in the evolution of the freestanding nude figure, Hellenic artists achieved a sublime balance between realistic representation and idealized form.

The monument that best mirrors the classical style is the Parthenon, the Greek temple built atop the Acropolis to honor Athens' patron goddess of wisdom and war. In its application of the Doric order, the integration of technical refinements, and the intelligent application of architectural decoration, the Parthenon stands as one of the most noble buildings in the history of architecture.

The Hellenic synthesis of humanism and idealism, harnessed to an impassioned quest for order and proportion, also characterized literature and music. The lyric poetry of Sappho and Pindar makes the human being the measure of earthly experience. In Greek music, where the clarity of the single line of melody prevails, modal patterns of pitch and tempo were held to influence the moral condition of the listener.

During the fourth century B.C.E. Alexander the Great spread Greek language and culture throughout a vast, though short-lived, empire that extended from Macedonia to India. During the Hellenistic Age, metaphysics gave way to science and practical philosophy, and the classical style moved further toward realism and melodramatic expressiveness. Nevertheless, the Hellenistic (and thereafter, the Roman) era perpetuated the fundamental features of classicism. Indeed, for centuries to come, Western artists—like newly liberated prisoners from Plato's mythical cave—would try to throw off the chains that bound them to the imperfect world of the senses in pursuit of the classical ideal.

MUSIC LISTENING SELECTION

CD One Selection 1   Anonymous, "Seikolos Song." Greek, ca. 50 C.E.

GLOSSARY

aulos a wind instrument used in ancient Greece; it had a double reed (held inside the mouth) and a number of finger holes and was always played in pairs, that is, with the performer holding one in each hand; a leather band was often tied around the head to support the cheeks, thus enabling the player to blow harder (see Figure 6.5)

contrapposto (Italian, "counterpoised") a position assumed by the human body in which one part is turned in opposition to another part

frieze in architecture, a sculptured or ornamented band

gable the triangular section of a wall at the end of a pitched roof

hymn a lyric poem offering divine praise or glorification

kithara a large version of the lyre (having seven to eleven strings) and the principal instrument of ancient Greek music

kouros (Greek, "youth"; pl. *kouroi*) a youthful male figure, usually depicted nude in ancient Greek sculpture; the female counterpart is the *kore* (Greek, "maiden"; pl. *korai*)

krater a vessel used for mixing wine and water

lyre any one of a group of plucked stringed instruments; in ancient Greece usually made of tortoise shell or horn and therefore light in weight

metope the square panel between the beam ends under the roof of a structure (see Figure 5.19)

mode a type of musical scale characterized by a fixed pattern of pitch and tempo within the octave; because the Greeks associated each of the modes with a different emotional state, it is likely that the mode involved something more than a particular musical scale, perhaps a set of rhythms and melodic turns associated with each scale pattern

monophony (Greek, "one voice") a musical texture consisting of a single, unaccompanied line of melody

Nike the Greek goddess of victory

octave the series of eight tones forming any major or minor scale

ode a lyric poem expressing exalted emotion in honor of a person or special occasion

order in classical architecture, the parts of a building that stand in fixed and constant relation to each other; the three classical orders are the Doric, the Ionic, and the Corinthian (see Figure 5.17)

pediment the triangular space forming the gable of a two-pitched roof in classical architecture; any similar triangular form found over a portico, door, or window

portico a porch with a roof supported by columns

scale (Latin, *scala*, "ladder") a series of tones arranged in ascending or descending consecutive order; the *diatonic* scale, characteristic of Western music, consists of the eight tones (or series of notes C, D, E, F, G, A, B, C) of the twelve-tone octave; the *chromatic* scale consists of all twelve tones (represented by the twelve piano keys, seven white and five black) of the octave, each a semitone apart

tholos a circular structure, generally in classical Greek style and probably derived from early tombs

CHAPTER 6

Rome: The Rise to Empire

". . . remember, Roman,
To rule the people under law, to establish
The way of peace, to battle down the haughty,
To spare the meek. Our fine arts, these forever."
Virgil

"In the second century of the Christian Era, the empire of Rome comprehended the fairest part of the earth, and the most civilized portion of mankind. The frontiers of that extensive monarchy were guarded by ancient renown and disciplined valor. The gentle, but powerful, influence of laws and manners had gradually cemented the union of the provinces." So wrote the eighteenth-century historian Edward Gibbon, who voiced universal and abiding respect for the longest-lasting and most complex empire in Western history. The rise and fall of the Roman Empire is too long a story to be told in these pages. Rather, this chapter explores Rome's imperial presence in Classical Antiquity and its enduring contribution to the humanistic tradition.

The Roman Rise to Empire

Rome's Early History

Rome's origins are to be found among tribes of Iron Age folk called Latins, who invaded the Italian peninsula just after the beginning of the first millennium B.C.E. By the mid-eighth century B.C.E., these people had founded the city of Rome in the lower valley of the Tiber River, a spot strategically located for control of the Italian peninsula and for convenient access to the Mediterranean Sea (Map 6.1). While central Italy became the domain of the Latins, the rest of the peninsula received a continuous infusion of eastern Mediterranean people—Etruscans, Greeks, and Phoenicians—who brought with them cultures richer and more complex than that of the Latins. The Etruscans, whose origins are unknown (and whose language remains undeciphered), established themselves in northwest Italy. A sophisticated, Hellenized people with commercial contacts throughout the Mediterranean, they were experts in the arts of metallurgy, town building, and city planning. The Greeks, who colonized the tip of the Italian peninsula and Sicily, were masters of philosophy and the arts. The Phoenicians, who settled on the northern coast of Africa, brought westward their alphabet and their commercial

and maritime skills. From all of these people, but especially from the first two groups, the Latins borrowed elements that would enhance their own history. From the Etruscans, the Romans absorbed the fundamentals of urban planning, chariot racing, the toga, bronze and gold crafting, and the most ingenious structural principle of Mesopotamian architecture—the arch. The Etruscans provided their dead with tombs designed to resemble the lavish dwelling places of the deceased. On the lids of the **sarcophagi** (stone coffins) that held their remains, Etruscan artists carved portraits of the dead, depicting husbands and wives relaxing and socializing on their dining couch, as if still enjoying a family banquet (Figure **6.1**).

From the Greeks, the Romans borrowed a pantheon of gods and goddesses, linguistic and literary principles, and the aesthetics of the classical style. As the Latins absorbed Etruscan and Greek culture, so they drew these and other peoples into what would become the most powerful world-state in ancient history.

The Roman Republic (509–133 B.C.E.)

For three centuries, Etruscan kings ruled the Latin population, but in 509 B.C.E. the Latins overthrew the Etruscans. Over the next two hundred years, monarchy slowly gave way to a government "of the people" (***res publica***). The agricultural population of ancient Rome consisted of a powerful class of large landowners, the *patricians,* and a more populous class of farmers and small landowners called *plebeians.* The plebeians constituted the membership of a Popular Assembly. Although this body conferred civil and military authority (the **imperium**) upon two elected magistrates (called *consuls*), its lower-class members had little voice in government. The wealthy patricians—life members of the Roman Senate—controlled the lawmaking process. But step by step, the plebeians gained increasing political influence. Using as leverage their service as soldiers in the Roman army and their power to veto laws initiated by the Senate, the plebeians—through their leaders, the *tribunes*—made themselves heard.

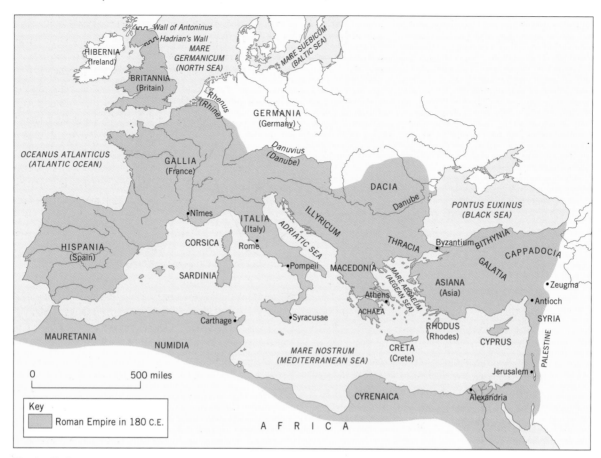

Map 6.1 The Roman Empire in 180 C.E.

Eventually, they won the freedom to intermarry with the patricians, the right to hold executive office, and, finally, in 287 B.C.E., the privilege of making laws. The stern and independent population of Roman farmers had arrived at a *res publica* by peaceful means. But no sooner had Rome become a Republic than it adopted an expansionist course that would erode these democratic achievements.

Obedience to the Roman state and service in its powerful army were essential to the life of the early Republic. Both contributed to the rise of Roman imperialism, which proceeded by means of long wars of conquest similar to those that had marked the history of earlier empires. After expelling the last of the Etruscan kings, Rome extended its power over all parts of the Italian peninsula. By the middle of the third century B.C.E., having united all of Italy by force or negotiation, Rome stood poised to rule the Mediterranean. A longstanding distrust of the Phoenicians, and rivalry with the city of Carthage, Phoenicia's commercial stronghold in northeastern Africa, led Rome into the Punic (Latin for "Phoenician") Wars—a 150-year-period of intermittent violence that ended with the destruction of Carthage in 146 B.C.E. With the defeat of Carthage, Rome assumed naval and commercial leadership in

the western Mediterranean, the sea they would come to call *mare nostrum* ("our sea"). But the ambitions of army generals and the impetus of a century of warfare fueled the fire of Roman imperialism. Rome seized every opportunity for conquest, and by the end of the first century B.C.E.,

Figure 6.1 Sarcophagus from Cerveteri, ca. 520 B.C.E. Painted terracotta, length 6 ft. 7 in. Museo Nazionale di Villa Giulia, Rome

the Empire included most of North Africa, the Iberian peninsula, Greece, Egypt, much of Southwest Asia, and the territories constituting present-day Europe as far as the Rhine River (see Map 6.1).

Despite the difficulties presented by the task of governing such far-flung territories, the Romans proved to be efficient administrators. They demanded from their foreign provinces taxes, soldiers to serve in the Roman army, tribute, and slaves. Roman governors, appointed by the Senate from among the higher ranks of the military, ruled within the conquered provinces. Usually, local customs and even local governments were permitted to continue unmodified, for the Romans considered tolerance of provincial customs politically practical. The Romans introduced the Latin language and Roman law in the provinces. They built paved roads, freshwater aqueducts, bridges, and eventually granted the people of their conquered territories Roman citizenship.

Rome's highly disciplined army was the backbone of the Empire. During the Republic, the army consisted of citizens who served two-year terms, but by the first century C.E., the military had become a profession to which all free men might devote twenty-five years (or more) of their lives. Since serving for this length of time allowed a non-Roman to gain Roman citizenship for himself and his children, military service acted as a means of Romanizing foreigners. The Roman army was the object of fear and admiration among those familiar with Rome's rise to power. Josephus (ca. 37–100 C.E.), a Jewish historian who witnessed the Roman destruction of Jerusalem in 70 C.E., described the superiority of the Roman military machine, which he estimated to include more than three hundred thousand armed men. According to Josephus, Roman soldiers performed as though they "had been born with weapons in their hands." The efficiency of the army, reported Josephus, was the consequence of superior organization and discipline. The following description of a Roman military camp reflects the admiration and awe with which non-Romans viewed Roman might. It also describes the nature of that "perfect discipline" and dedication to duty that characterized the Roman ethos and Roman culture in general.

READING 1.21 Josephus' *Description of the Roman Army* (ca. 70 C.E.)

. . . one cannot but admire the forethought shown in this particular by the Romans, in making their servant class useful to them not only for the ministrations of ordinary life but also for war. If one goes on to study the organization of their army as a whole, it will be seen that this vast empire of theirs has come to them as the prize of valor, and not as a gift of fortune. [5]

For their nation does not wait for the outbreak of war to give men their first lesson on arms; they do not sit with folded hands in peace time only to put them in motion in the hour of need. On the contrary, as though they had been born with [10] weapons in hand, they never have a truce from training, never wait for emergencies to arise. Moreover, their peace maneuvers are no less strenuous than veritable warfare; each soldier daily throws all his energy into his drill, as though he were in action. Hence that perfect ease with which they sustain the shock of battle: no confusion breaks their customary formation, no panic paralyzes, no fatigue exhausts them; and as their opponents cannot match these qualities, victory is the invariable and certain consequence. Indeed, it would not be wrong to describe their maneuvers as bloodless [20] combats and combats as sanguinary maneuvers.

The Romans never lay themselves open to a surprise attack; for, whatever hostile territory they may invade, they engage in no battle until they have fortified their camp. This camp is not erected at random or unevenly; they do not all work at once or in disorderly parties; if the ground is uneven, it is first leveled; a site for the camp is then measured out in the form of a square. For this purpose the army is accompanied by a multitude of workmen and of tools for building.

The interior of the camp is divided into rows of tents. The [30] exterior circuit presents the appearance of a wall and is furnished with towers at regular intervals; and on the spaces between the towers are placed "quick-firers," catapults, "stone-throwers," and every variety of artillery engines, all ready for use. In this surrounding wall are set four gates, one on each side, spacious enough for beasts of burden to enter without difficulty and wide enough for sallies of troops in emergencies. The camp is intersected by streets symmetrically laid out; in the middle are the tents of the officers, and precisely in the center the headquarters of the commander-in- [40] chief, resembling a small temple. Thus, as it were, an improvised city springs up, with its market-place, its artisan quarter, its seats of judgment, where captains and colonels adjudicate upon any differences which may arise. . . .

Once entrenched, the soldiers take up their quarters in their tents by companies, quietly and in good order. All their fatigue duties are performed with the same discipline, the same regard for security; the procuring of wood, food-supplies, and water, as required—each party has its allotted task. . . . The same precision is maintained on the battle-field: the troops [50] wheel smartly round in the requisite direction, and, whether advancing to the attack or retreating, all move as a unit at the word of command.

When the camp is to be broken up, the trumpet sounds a first call; at that none remain idle: instantly, at this signal, they strike the tents and make all ready for departure. The trumpets sound a second call to prepare for the march: at once they pile their baggage on the mules and other beasts of burden and stand ready to start, like runners breasting the cord on the race-course. They then set fire to the encampment, both [60] because they can easily construct another [on the spot], and to prevent the enemy from ever making use of it. . . .

Then they advance, all marching in silence and in good order, each man keeping his place in the ranks, as if in face of the enemy. . . . By their military exercises the Romans instil into their soldiers fortitude not only of body but also of soul; fear, too, plays its part in their training. For they have laws which punish with death not merely desertion of the ranks, but even a slight neglect of duty; and their generals are held in even greater awe than the laws. For the high honors with [70] which they reward the brave prevent the offenders whom they punish from regarding themselves as treated cruelly.

This perfect discipline makes the army an ornament of peace-time and in war welds the whole into a single body; so compact are their ranks, so alert their movements in wheeling to right or left, so quick their ears for orders, their eyes for signals, their hands to act upon them. Prompt as they consequently ever are in action, none are slower than they in succumbing to suffering, and never have they been known in any predicament to be beaten by numbers, by ruse, by **80** difficulties of ground, or even by fortune; for they have more assurance of victory than of fortune. Where counsel thus precedes active operations, where the leaders' plan of campaign is followed up by so efficient an army, no wonder that the Empire has extended its boundaries on the east to the Euphrates, on the west to the ocean,[1] on the south to the most fertile tracts of Libya, on the north to the Ister[2] and the Rhine. One might say without exaggeration that, great as are their possessions, the people that won them are greater still. . . .

 Q What, according to Josephus, are the admirable features of the Roman army?

The Collapse of the Republic (133–30 B.C.E.)

By the beginning of the first millennium C.E., Rome had become the watchdog of the ancient world. Roman imperialism, however, worked to effect changes within the Republic itself. By its authority to handle all military matters, the Senate became increasingly powerful, as did a new class of men, wealthy Roman entrepreneurs (known as *equestrians*), who filled the jobs of provincial administration. The army, by its domination of Rome's overseas provinces, also became more powerful. Precious metals, booty, and slaves from foreign conquests brought enormous wealth to army generals and influential patricians; corruption became widespread. Captives of war were shipped back to Rome and auctioned off to the highest bidders, usually patrician landowners, whose farms soon became large-scale plantations (*latifundia*) worked by slaves. The increased agricultural productivity of the *latifundia* gave economic advantage to large landowners who easily undersold the lesser landowners and drove them out of business. Increasingly, the small farmers were forced to sell their farms to neighboring patricians in return for the right to remain on the land. Or, they simply moved to the city to join, by the end of the first century B.C.E., a

growing unemployed population. The disappearance of the small farmer signaled the decline of the Republic.

As Rome's rich citizens grew richer and its poor citizens poorer, the patricians fiercely resisted efforts to redistribute wealth more equally. But reform measures failed and political rivalries increased. Ultimately, Rome fell victim to the ambitions of army generals, who, having conquered in the name of Rome, now turned to conquering Rome itself. The first century B.C.E. was an age of military dictators, whose competing claims to power fueled a spate of civil wars. As bloody confrontations replaced reasoned compromises, the Republic crumbled.

In 46 B.C.E., an extraordinary army commander named Gaius Julius Caesar (Figure **6.2**) triumphantly entered the city of Rome and established a dictatorship. Caesar, who had spent nine years conquering Gaul (present-day France and Belgium), was as shrewd in politics as he was brilliant in war. These campaigns are described in his prose *Commentaries on the Gallic War*. His brief but successful campaigns in Syria, Asia Minor, and Egypt— where his union with the Egyptian Queen Cleopatra (69–30 B.C.E.) produced a son—inspired his famous boast: *veni, vidi, vici* ("I came, I saw, I conquered"). A superb organizer, Caesar took strong measures to restabilize Rome: he codified the laws, regulated taxation, reduced debts, sent large numbers of the unemployed proletariat to overseas colonies, and inaugurated public works projects. He also granted citizenship to non-Italians and reformed the Western calendar to comprise 365 days and twelve months (one of which—July—he named after himself). Threatened by Caesar's populist reforms and his contempt for republican institutions, a group of his senatorial opponents, led by Marcus Junius Brutus, assassinated him in 44 B.C.E. Despite Caesar's inglorious death, the name *Caesar* would be used as an honorific title by all his imperial successors well into the second century C.E., as well as by many modern-day dictators.

The Roman Empire (30 B.C.E.–180 C.E.)

Following the assassination of Julius Caesar, a struggle for power ensued between Caesar's first lieutenant, Mark Anthony (ca. 80–30 B.C.E.) and his grandnephew (and adopted son) Octavian (63 B.C.E.–14 C.E.). The contest between the two was resolved at Actium in 31 B.C.E., when Octavian's

[1]The Atlantic.
[2]The Roman name for the Danube River.

Figure 6.2 Bust of Julius Caesar, first century B.C.E. Green schist, height 16⅛ in. Photo: The State Museum, Berlin.

navy routed the combined forces of Mark Anthony and Queen Cleopatra. The alliance between Anthony and Cleopatra, like that between Cleopatra and Julius Caesar, advanced the political ambitions of Egypt's most seductive queen, who sought not only to unite the eastern and western portions of Rome's great empire, but to govern a vast Roman world state. That destiny, however, would fall to Octavian. In 43 B.C.E., Octavian usurped the consulship and gained the approval of the Senate to rule for life. Although he called himself "first citizen" (*princeps*), his title of Emperor betrayed the reality that he was first and foremost Rome's army general (*imperator*). The Senate, however, bestowed on him the title *Augustus* ("the Revered One"). Augustus shared legislative power with the Senate, but retained the right to veto legislation. Thus, to all intents and purposes, the Republic was defunct. The destiny of Rome lay once again in the hands of a military dictator. It is in this guise that Augustus appears in Roman sculpture (Figure **6.3**). In this freestanding, larger-than-life statue from Primaporta, Octavian raises his arm in a gesture of leadership and imperial authority. He wears a breastplate celebrating his victory over the Parthians in 20 B.C.E. At his feet appear Cupid and a dolphin, reminders of his alleged divine descent from Venus—the mother of Aeneas, Rome's legendary founder. Octavian's stance and physical proportions are modeled on the *Doryphorus* by Polycleitus (see Figure 5.1). His handsome face and tall, muscular physique serve to complete the heroic image. In reality, however, the emperor was only 5 feet 4 inches tall—the average height of the Roman male.

Augustus' reign ushered in an era of peace and stability, a *Pax Romana*: from 30 B.C.E. to 180 C.E. the Roman peace prevailed throughout the Empire, and Rome enjoyed active commercial contact with all parts of the civilized world, including India and China. Augustus tried to arrest the tide of moral decay that had swept into Rome: in an effort to restore family values and the begetting of legitimate children, he passed laws (which ultimately failed in their purpose) to curb adultery and to prevent bachelors from receiving inheritances. The *Pax Romana* was also a time of artistic and literary productivity. An enthusiastic patron of the arts, Augustus commissioned literature,

Figure 6.3 Augustus of Primaporta, early first century C.E., after a bronze of ca. 20 B.C.E. Marble, height 6 ft. 8 in. Vatican Museums, Rome. Photo: © 1990, Photo Scala, Florence.

Principal Roman Emperors

The Julio-Claudian Dynasty

27 B.C.E.–14 C.E.	Augustus
14–37	Tiberius
37–41	Gaius Caligula
41–54	Claudius
54–68	Nero

The Flavian Dynasty

68–79	Vespasian
79–81	Titus
81–96	Domitian

The "Good Emperors"

96–98	Nerva
97–117	Trajan
117–138	Hadrian
138–161	Antoninus Pius
161–180	Marcus Aurelius

Beginning of Decline

180–192	Commodus

The Severan Dynasty

193–211	Septimius Severus
211–217	Caracalla
222–235	Alexander Severus
235–284	Anarchy
284–305	Diocletian
306–337	Constantine I

sculpture, and architecture. He boasted that he had come to power when Rome was a city of brick and would leave it a city of marble. In most cases, this meant a veneer of marble that was, by standard Roman building practices, laid over the brick surface. In a city blighted by crime, noise, poor hygiene, and a frequent scarcity of food and water, Augustus initiated many new public works (including three new aqueducts and some 500 fountains) and such civic services as a police force and a fire department. The reign of Octavian also witnessed the birth of a new religion, Christianity, which, in later centuries, would spread throughout the Empire (see chapters 8 and 9).

Augustus put an end to the civil wars of the preceding century, but he revived neither the political nor the social equilibrium of the early Republic. Following his death, Rome continued to be ruled by military officials. Since there was no machinery for succession to the imperial throne, Rome's rulers held office until they either died or were assassinated. Of the twenty-six emperors who governed Rome during the fifty-year period between 335 and 385 C.E., only one died a natural death. Government by and for the people had been the hallmark of Rome's early history, but the enterprise of imperialism ultimately overtook these lofty republican ideals.

Roman Law

Against this backdrop of conquest and dominion, it is no surprise that Rome's contributions to the humanistic tradition were practical rather than theoretical. The sheer size of the Roman Empire inspired engineering programs, such as bridge and road building, that united all regions under Roman rule. Law—a less tangible means of unification—was equally important in this regard. The development of a system of law was one of Rome's most original and influential achievements.

Roman law (the Latin *jus* means both "law" and "justice") evolved out of the practical need to rule a worldstate, rather than—as in ancient Greece—as the product of a dialectic between the citizen and the *polis*. Inspired by the laws of Solon, the Romans published their first civil code, the Twelve Tables of Law, in 450 B.C.E. They placed these laws on view in the Forum, the public meeting area for the civic, religious, and commercial activities of Rome. The Twelve Tables of Law provided Rome's basic legal code for almost a thousand years. To this body of law were added the acts of the Assembly and the Senate, and public decrees of the emperors. For some five hundred years, *praetors* (magistrates who administered justice) and *jurisconsults* (experts in the law) interpreted the laws, bringing commonsense resolutions to private disputes. Their interpretations constituted a body of "case law." In giving consideration to individual needs, these magistrates cultivated the concept of equity, which puts the spirit of the law above the letter of the law. The decisions of Roman jurists became precedents that established comprehensive guidelines for future judgments. Thus, Roman law was not fixed, but was an evolving body of opinions on the nature and dispensation of justice.

Early in Roman history, the law of the land (*jus civile*) applied only to Roman citizens, but as Roman citizenship was extended to the provinces, so too was the law. Law that embraced a wider range of peoples and customs, the law of the people (*jus gentium*), assumed an international quality that acknowledged compromises between conflicting customs and traditions. The law of the people was, in effect, a law based on universal principles, that is, the law of nature (*jus naturale*). The full body of Roman law came

Science and Technology

312 B.C.E.	Consul Appius Claudius orders construction of the "Appian Way," the first in a strategic network of Roman roads
101 B.C.E.	the Romans use water power for milling grain
46 B.C.E.	Caesar inaugurates the "Julian Calendar" on which the modern calendar is based
77 C.E.	Pliny the Elder completes a 37-volume encyclopedia called *Natural History*, which summarized information about astronomy, geography, and zoology
79 C.E.	Pliny the Younger writes a detailed account of the eruption of Mount Vesuvius

to incorporate the decisions of the jurists, the acts passed by Roman legislative assemblies, and the edicts of Roman emperors. In the sixth century C.E., two hundred years after the division of the Empire into eastern and western portions and a hundred years after the collapse of Rome, the Byzantine (East Roman) Emperor Justinian would codify this huge body of law, thereafter known as the *Corpus Juris Civilis*. The Roman system of law influenced the development of codified law in all European countries with the exception of England.

The Roman Contribution to Literature

Roman Philosophic Thought

Roman contributions to law were numerous, but such was not the case with philosophy. More a practical than a speculative people, the Romans produced no systems of philosophic thought comparable to those of Plato and Aristotle. Yet they respected and preserved the writings of Hellenic and Hellenistic thinkers. Educated Romans admired Aristotle and absorbed the works of the Epicureans and the Stoics. The Latin poet Lucretius (ca. 95–ca. 55 B.C.E.) popularized the materialist theories of Democritus and Leucippus, which describe the world in purely physical terms and deny the existence of the gods and other supernatural beings. Since all of reality, including the human soul, consists of atoms, he argues in his only work, *On the Nature of Things*, there is no reason to fear death: "We shall not feel because we shall not be."

In the vast, impersonal world of the Empire, many Romans cultivated the attitude of rational detachment popular among the Stoics (see chapter 5). Like their third-century-B.C.E. forebears, Roman Stoics believed that an impersonal force (Providence or Divine Reason) governed the world, and that happiness lay in one's ability to accept the will of the universe. Stoics rejected any emotional attachments that might enslave them. The ideal spiritual condition and the one most conducive to contentment, according to the Stoic point of view, depended on self-control and the subjugation of the emotions to reason.

The commonsense tenets of Stoicism encouraged the Roman sense of duty. At the same time, the Stoic belief in the equality of all people had a humanizing effect on Roman jurisprudence and anticipated the all-embracing outlook of early Christian thought (see chapter 8). Stoicism was especially popular among such intellectuals as the noted playwright and essayist Lucius Annaeus Seneca (ca. 4 B.C.E.–65 C.E.) and the Emperor Marcus Aurelius (121–180 C.E.), both of whom wrote stimulating treatises on the subject. Seneca's *On Tranquility of Mind*, an excerpt from which follows, argues that one may achieve peace of mind by avoiding burdensome responsibilities, gloomy companions, and excessive wealth. Stoicism offered a reasoned retreat from psychic pain and moral despair, as well as a practical set of solutions to the daily strife between the self and society.

READING 1.22 From Seneca's *On Tranquility of Mind* (ca. 40 C.E.)

... our question, then, is how the mind can maintain a consistent and advantageous course, be kind to itself and take pleasure in its attributes, never interrupt this satisfaction but abide in its serenity, without excitement or depression. This amounts to tranquility. We shall inquire how it may be attained. ... 1

A correct estimate of self is prerequisite, for we are generally inclined to overrate our capacities. One man is tripped by confidence in his eloquence, another makes greater demands upon his estate than it can stand, another burdens a 10 frail body with an exhausting office. Some are too bashful for politics, which requires aggressiveness; some are too headstrong for court; some do not control their temper and break into unguarded language at the slightest provocation; some cannot restrain their wit or resist making risky jokes. For all such people retirement is better than a career; an assertive and intolerant temperament should avoid incitements to outspokenness that will prove harmful.

Next we must appraise the career and compare our strength with the task we shall attempt. The worker must be stronger 20 than his project; loads larger than the bearer must necessarily crush him. Certain careers, moreover, are not so demanding in themselves as they are prolific in begetting a mass of other activities. Enterprises which give rise to new and multifarious activities should be avoided; you must not commit yourself to a task from which there is no free egress. Put your hand to one you can finish or at least hope to finish; leave alone those that expand as you work at them and do not stop where you intend they should.

In our choice of men we should be particularly careful to 30 see whether they are worth spending part of our life on and whether they will appreciate our loss of time; some people think we are in their debt if we do them a service. Athenadorus said he would not even go to dine with a man who would not feel indebted for his coming. Much less would he dine with people, as I suppose you understand, who discharge indebtedness for services rendered by giving a dinner and count the courses as favors, as if their lavishness was a mark of honor to others. Take away witnesses and spectators and they will take no pleasure in secret 40 gormandizing.

But nothing can equal the pleasures of faithful and congenial friendship. How good it is to have willing hearts as safe repositories for your every secret, whose privity you fear less than your own, whose conversation allays your anxiety, whose counsel promotes your plans, whose cheerfulness dissipates your gloom, whose very appearance gives you joy! But we must choose friends who are, so far as possible, free from passions. Vices are contagious; they light upon whoever is nearest and infect by contact. During a plague we must be 50 careful not to sit near people caught in the throes and burning with fever, because we would be courting danger and drawing poison in with our breath; just so in choosing friends we must pay attention to character and take those least tainted. To mingle the healthy with the sick is the beginning of disease.

But I would not prescribe that you become attached to or attract no one who is not a sage. Where would you find him? We have been searching for him for centuries. Call the least bad man the best. You could not have a more opulent choice, if you were looking for good men, than among the Platos and **60** Xenophons[1] and the famous Socratic brood, or if you had at your disposal the age of Cato,[2] which produced many characters worthy to be his contemporaries (just as it produced many unprecedentedly bad, who engineered monstrous crimes. Both kinds were necessary to make Cato's quality understood: he needed bad men against whom he could make his strength effective and good men to appreciate his effectiveness). But now there is a great dearth of good men, and your choice cannot be fastidious. But gloomy people who deplore everything and find reason to complain you must **70** take pains to avoid. With all his loyalty and good will, a grumbling and touchy companion militates against tranquility.

We pass now to property, the greatest source of affliction to humanity. If you balance all our other troubles—deaths, diseases, fears, longings, subjection to labor and pain—with the miseries in which our money involves us, the latter will far outweigh the former. Reflect, then, how much less a grief it is not to have money than to lose it, and then you will realize that poverty has less to torment us with in the degree that it has less to lose. If you suppose that rich men take their losses **80** with greater equanimity you are mistaken; a wound hurts a big man as much as it does a little. Bion[3] put it smartly: a bald man is as bothered when his hair is plucked as a man with a full head. The same applies to rich and poor, you may be sure; in either case the money is glued on and cannot be torn away without a twinge, so that both suffer alike. It is less distressing, as I have said, and easier not to acquire money than to lose it, and you will therefore notice that people upon whom Fortune never has smiled are more cheerful than those she has deserted. . . . **90**

All life is bondage. Man must therefore habituate himself to his condition, complain of it as little as possible, and grasp whatever good lies within his reach. No situation is so harsh that a dispassionate mind cannot find some consolation in it. If a man lays even a very small area out skillfully it will provide ample space for many uses, and even a foothold can be made livable by deft arrangement. Apply good sense to your problems; the hard can be softened, the narrow widened, and the heavy made lighter by the skillful bearer. . . .

 Q How, according to Seneca, does one achieve "tranquility of mind"?
Q What, in his view, is humanity's greatest source of affliction?

---

[1] A Greek historian and biographer who lived ca. 428–354 B.C.E.
[2] Marcus Porcius Cato (234–149 B.C.E.), known as "the Censor," a Roman champion of austerity and simplicity.
[3] A Greek poet who lived around 100 B.C.E.

Latin Prose Literature

Roman literature reveals a masterful use of Latin prose for the purposes of entertainment, instruction, and record keeping. Ever applying their resources to practical ends, the Romans found prose the ideal vehicle for compiling and transmitting information. Rome gave the West its first geographies and encyclopedias, as well as some of its finest biographies, histories, and manuals of instruction. In the writing of history, in particular, the Romans demonstrated their talent for the collection and analysis of factual evidence. Although Roman historians tended to glorify Rome and its leadership, their attention to detail often surpassed that of the Greek historians. One of Rome's greatest historians, Titus Livius ("Livy," ca. 59 B.C.E.–17 C.E.), wrote a history of Rome from the eighth century B.C.E. to his own day. Although only a small portion of Livy's original 142 books survive, this monumental work—commissioned by Octavian himself—constitutes our most reliable account of political and social life in the days of the Roman Republic.

The Romans were masters, as well, in **oratory**, that is, the art of public speaking, and in the writing of **epistles** (letters). In both of these genres, the statesman Marcus Tullius Cicero (106–43 B.C.E.) excelled. A contemporary of Julius Caesar, Cicero produced more than 900 letters—sometimes writing three a day to the same person—and more than one hundred speeches and essays. Clarity and eloquence are the hallmarks of Cicero's prose style, which Renaissance humanists hailed as the model for literary excellence (see chapter 16). While Cicero was familiar with the theoretical works of Aristotle and the Stoics, his letters reflect a profound concern for the political realities of his own day. In his lifetime, Cicero served Rome as consul, statesman, and orator; his carefully reasoned speeches helped to shape public opinion. While he praised Julius Caesar's literary style, he openly opposed his patron's dictatorship. (Caesar congenially confessed to Cicero, "It is nobler to enlarge the boundaries of human intelligence than those of the Roman Empire.") As we see in the following excerpt from his essay *On Duty*, Cicero considered public service the noblest of human activities—one that demanded the exercise of personal courage equal to that required in military combat.

READING 1.23 From Cicero's *On Duty* (44 B.C.E.)

. . . that moral goodness which we look for in a lofty, high- **1** minded spirit is secured, of course, by moral, not by physical, strength. And yet the body must be trained and so disciplined that it can obey the dictates of judgment and reason in attending to business and in enduring toil. But that moral goodness which is our theme depends wholly upon the thought and attention given to it by the mind. And, in this way, the men who in a civil capacity direct the affairs of the nation render no less important service than they who conduct its wars: by their statesmanship oftentimes wars are either **10** averted or terminated; sometimes also they are declared.

Upon Marcus Cato's[1] counsel, for example, the Third Punic War was undertaken, and in its conduct his influence was dominant, even after he was dead. And so diplomacy in the friendly settlement of controversies is more desirable than courage in settling them on the battlefield; but we must be careful not to take that course merely for the sake of avoiding war rather than for the sake of public expediency. War, however, should be undertaken in such a way as to make it evident that it has no other object than to secure peace. 20

But it takes a brave and resolute spirit not to be disconcerted in times of difficulty or ruffled and thrown off one's feet, as the saying is, but to keep one's presence of mind and one's self-possession and not to swerve from the path of reason.

Now all this requires great personal courage; but it calls also for great intellectual ability by reflection to anticipate the future, to discover some time in advance what may happen whether for good or for ill, and what must be done in any possible event, and never to be reduced to having to say 30 "I had not thought of that."

These are the activities that mark a spirit strong, high, and self-reliant in its prudence and wisdom. But to mix rashly in the fray and to fight hand to hand with the enemy is but a barbarous and brutish kind of business. Yet when the stress of circumstances demands it, we must gird on the sword and prefer death to slavery and disgrace.

As to destroying and plundering cities, let me say that great care should be taken that nothing be done in reckless cruelty or wantonness. And it is a great man's duty in troublous times 40 to single out the guilty for punishment, to spare the many, and in every turn of fortune to hold to a true and honorable course. For whereas there are many, as I have said before, who place the achievements of war above those of peace, so one may find many to whom adventurous, hot-headed counsels seem more brilliant and more impressive than calm and well-considered measures.

We must, of course, never be guilty of seeming cowardly and craven in our avoidance of danger; but we must also beware of exposing ourselves to danger needlessly. Nothing 50 can be more foolhardy than that. Accordingly, in encountering danger we should do as doctors do in their practice: in light cases of illness they give mild treatment; in cases of dangerous sickness they are compelled to apply hazardous and even desperate remedies. It is, therefore, only a madman who, in a calm, would pray for a storm; a wise man's way is, when the storm does come, to withstand it with all the means at his command, and especially when the advantages to be expected in case of a successful issue are greater than the hazards of the struggle. 60

The dangers attending great affairs of state fall sometimes upon those who undertake them, sometimes upon the state. In carrying out such enterprises, some run the risk of losing their lives, others their reputation and the good-will of their fellow-citizens. It is our duty, then, to be more ready to endanger our own than the public welfare and to hazard honor and glory more readily than other advantages. . . .

Q According to Cicero, under what circumstances is war justified?

Q What are the main duties of a statesman?

As Cicero indicates, Roman education emphasized civic duty. It aimed at training the young for active roles in civic life. For careers in law and political administration, the art of public speaking was essential. Indeed, in the provinces, where people of many languages mingled, oratory was the ultimate form of political influence. Since the art of public speaking was the distinctive mark of the educated Roman, the practical skills of grammar and rhetoric held an important place in Roman education. One of the greatest spokesmen for the significance of oratory in public affairs was the Roman historian and politician, P. Cornelius Tacitus (ca. 56–120 C.E.). Tacitus' *Dialogue on Oratory* describes the role of public speaking in ancient Roman life. It bemoans the passing of a time when "eloquence led not only to great rewards, but was also a sheer necessity."

READING 1.24 From Tacitus' *Dialogue on Oratory* (ca. 100–105 C.E.)

. . . great oratory is like a flame: it needs fuel to feed it, 1 movement to fan it, and it brightens as it burns.

At Rome too the eloquence of our forefathers owed its development to [special] conditions. For although the orators of today have also succeeded in obtaining all the influence that it would be proper to allow them under settled, peaceable, and prosperous political conditions, yet their predecessors in those days of unrest and unrestraint thought they could accomplish more when, in the general ferment and without the strong hand of a single ruler, a speaker's political 10 wisdom was measured by his power of carrying conviction to the unstable populace. This was the source of the constant succession of measures put forward by champions of the people's rights, of the harangues of state officials who almost spent the night on the hustings,[1] of the impeachments of powerful criminals and hereditary feuds between whole families, of schisms among the aristocracy and never-ending struggles between the senate and the commons.[2] All this tore the commonwealth in pieces, but it provided a sphere for the oratory of those days and heaped on it what one saw were 20 vast rewards. The more influence a man could wield by his powers of speech, the more readily did he attain to high office, the further did he, when in office, outstrip his colleagues in the race for precedence, the more did he gain favor with the great, authority with the senate, and name and fame with the common people. These were the men who had whole nations of foreigners under their protection, several at a time; the men to whom state officials presented their humble duty on the eve of their departure to take up the government

---

of a province, and to whom they paid their respects on their return; the men who, without any effort on their own part, seemed to have praetorships and consulates at their beck and call; the men who even when out of office were in power, seeing that by their advice and authority they could bend both the senate and the people to their will. With them, moreover, it was a conviction that without eloquence it was impossible for anyone either to attain to a position of distinction and prominence in the community, or to maintain it; and no wonder they cherished this conviction, when they were called on to appear in public even when they would rather not, when it was not enough to move a brief resolution in the senate, unless one made good one's opinion in an able speech, when persons who had in some way or other incurred odium, or else were definitely charged with some offence, had to put in an appearance in person, when, moreover, evidence in criminal trials had to be given not indirectly or by affidavit, but personally and by word of mouth. So it was that eloquence not only led to great rewards, but was also a sheer necessity; and just as it was considered great and glorious to have the reputation of being a good speaker, so, on the other hand, it was accounted discreditable to be inarticulate and incapable of utterance. . . .

 Q What role, according to Tacitus, did oratory play in Roman life? Is this true of oratory today?

Roman Epic Poetry

While the Romans excelled in didactic prose, they also produced some of the world's finest verse. Under the patronage of Octavian, Rome enjoyed a Golden Age of Latin literature whose most notable representative was Virgil (Publius Vergilius Maro, 70–19 B.C.E.). Rome's foremost poet-publicist, Virgil wrote the semilegendary epic that immortalized Rome's destiny as world ruler. The *Aeneid* was not the product of an oral tradition, as were the Homeric epics; rather, it was a literary epic, undertaken as a work that might rival the epics of Homer. The hero of Virgil's poem is Rome's mythical founder, the Trojan-born Aeneas. As the typical epic hero, Aeneas undertakes a long journey and undergoes a series of adventures that test his prowess. The first six books of the *Aeneid* recount the hero's journey from Troy to Italy and his love affair with the beautiful Carthaginian princess, Dido. The second six books describe the Trojan conquest of Latium and the establishment of the Roman state. No summary of the *Aeneid* can represent adequately the monumental impact of a work that was to become the foundation for education in the Latin language. Yet, the following two excerpts capture the spirit of Virgil's vision. In the first, Aeneas, pressed to fulfill his divine mission, prepares to take leave of the passionate Dido. Here, his Stoic sense of duty overcomes his desire for personal fulfillment. The second passage, selected from the lengthy monologue spoken by the ghost of Aeneas' father, Anchises, eloquently sums up the meaning and purpose of Rome's historic mission.

READING 1.25 From Virgil's *Aeneid* (Books Four and Six) (ca. 20 B.C.E.)

[Mercury, the divine herald, urges Aeneas to leave Carthage and proceed to Italy.]

Mercury wastes no time:—"What are you doing,   1
Forgetful of your kingdom and your fortunes,
Building for Carthage? Woman-crazy fellow,
The ruler of the Gods, the great compeller
Of heaven and earth, has sent me from Olympus   5
With no more word than this: what are you doing,
With what ambition wasting time in Libya?
If your own fame and fortune count as nothing,
Think of Ascanius[1] at least, whose kingdom
In Italy, whose Roman land, are waiting   10
As promise justly due." He spoke, and vanished
Into thin air. Apalled, amazed, Aeneas
Is stricken dumb; his hair stands up in terror,
His voice sticks in his throat. He is more than eager
To flee that pleasant land, awed by the warning   15
Of the divine command. But how to do it?
How get around that passionate queen?[2] What opening
Try first? His mind runs out in all directions,
Shifting and veering. Finally, he has it,
Or thinks he has: he calls his comrades to him,   20
The leaders, bids them quietly prepare
The fleet for voyage, meanwhile saying nothing
About the new activity; since Dido
Is unaware, has no idea that passion
As strong as theirs is on the verge of breaking,   25
He will see what he can do, find the right moment
To let her know, all in good time. Rejoicing,
The captains move to carry out the orders.

    Who can deceive a woman in love? The queen
Anticipates each move, is fearful even   30
While everything is safe, foresees this cunning,
And the same trouble-making goddess, Rumor,
Tells her the fleet is being armed, made ready
For voyaging. She rages through the city
Like a woman mad, or drunk, the way the Maenads[3]   35
Go howling through the night-time on Cithaeron[4]
When Bacchus' cymbals summon with their clashing.
She waits no explanation from Aeneas;
She is the first to speak: "And so, betrayer,
You hoped to hide your wickedness, go sneaking   40
Out of my land without a word? Our love
Means nothing to you, our exchange of vows,
And even the death of Dido could not hold you.
The season is dead of winter, and you labor
Over the fleet; the northern gales are nothing—   45
You must be cruel, must you not? Why, even,
If ancient Troy remained, and you were seeking

---

[1] Aeneas' son.
[2] Dido, Queen of Carthage.
[3] "Mad women," the votaries of Bacchus (Dionysus).
[4] A mountain range between Attica and Boetia.

Not unknown homes and lands, but Troy again,
Would you be venturing Troyward in this weather?
I am the one you flee from: true? I beg you   50
By my own tears, and your right hand—(I have nothing
Else left my wretchedness)—by the beginnings
Of marriage, wedlock, what we had, if ever
I served you well, if anything of mine
Was ever sweet to you, I beg you, pity   55
A falling house; if there is room for pleading
As late as this, I plead, put off that purpose.
You are the reason I am hated; Libyans,
Numidians, Tyrians, hate me; and my honor
Is lost, and the fame I had, that almost brought me   60
High as the stars, is gone. To whom, O guest—
I must not call you husband any longer—
To whom do you leave me? I am a dying woman;
Why do I linger on? Until Pygmalion,
My brother, brings destruction to this city?   65
Until the prince Iarbas leads me captive?
At least if there had been some hope of children
Before your flight, a little Aeneas playing
Around my courts, to bring you back, in feature
At least, I would seem less taken and deserted."   70
    There was nothing he could say. Jove bade him keep
Affection from his eyes, and grief in his heart
With never a sign. At last, he managed something:—
"Never, O Queen, will I deny you merit
Whatever you have strength to claim; I will not   75
Regret remembering Dido, while I have
Breath in my body, or consciousness of spirit.
I have a point or two to make. I did not,
Believe me, hope to hide my flight by cunning;
I did not, ever, claim to be a husband,   80
Made no such vows. If I had fate's permission
To live my life my way, to settle my troubles
At my own will, I would be watching over
The city of Troy, and caring for my people,
Those whom the Greeks had spared, and Priam's palace   85
Would still be standing; for the vanquished people
I would have built the town again. But now
It is Italy I must seek, great Italy,
Apollo orders, and his oracles
Call me to Italy. There is my love,   90
There is my country. If the towers of Carthage,
The Libyan citadels, can please a woman
Who came from Tyre,[5] why must you grudge the Trojans
Ausonian land?[6] It is proper for us also
To seek a foreign kingdom. I am warned   95
Of this in dreams: when the earth is veiled in shadow
And the fiery stars are burning, I see my father,
Anchises, or his ghost, and I am frightened;
I am troubled for the wrong I do my son,
Cheating him out of his kingdom in the west,   100
And lands that fate assigns him. And a herald,

Jove's[7] messenger—I call them both to witness—
Has brought me, through the rush of air, his orders;
I saw the god myself, in the full daylight,
Enter these walls, I heard the words he brought me.   105
Cease to inflame us both with your complainings;
I follow Italy not because I want to."

[In the Underworld described in Book 6, Aeneas
encounters the soul of his father, Anchises, who foretells
the destiny of Rome.]

"Others, no doubt, will better mould the bronze
To the semblance of soft breathing, draw from marble,
The living countenance; and others please   110
With greater eloquence, or learn to measure
Better than we, the pathways of the heavens,
The risings of the stars: remember, Roman,
To rule the people under law, to establish
The way of peace, to battle down the haughty,   115
To spare the meek. Our fine arts, these forever."

Q Why does Aeneas abandon Dido?
Q How do Aeneas and Achilles (Reading
1.11) compare as epic heroes?

Roman Lyric Poetry and Satire

While Virgil is best known for the *Aeneid*, he also wrote
pastoral poems, or **eclogues**, that glorify the natural landscape and its rustic inhabitants. Virgil's *Eclogues* found
inspiration in the pastoral sketches of Theocritus, a third-
century-B.C.E. Sicilian poet. Many classicists besides Virgil
looked to Hellenic prototypes. The poetry of Catullus
(ca. 84–54 B.C.E.), for instance, reflects familiarity with the
art of Sappho, whose lyrics he admired. The greatest of the
Latin lyric poets, Catullus came to Rome from Verona. A
young man of some wealth and charm, he wrote primarily
on the subjects that consumed his short but intense life:
friendship, love, and sex. His passionate affair with Clodia,
the adulterous wife of a Roman consul, inspired some of his
finest poems, three of which appear below. These trace the
trajectory from the poet's first fevered amorous passions to
his despair and bitterness at the collapse of the affair. The
fourth poem betrays the raw invective and caustic wit that
Catullus brought to many of his verses, including those
with themes of jealousy and possession related to his bisexual liaisons. Candid and deeply personal, these poems
strike us with the immediacy of a modern, secular voice.

READING 1.26 The Poems of Catullus (ca. 60 B.C.E.)

Come, Lesbia,[1] let us live and love,   1
nor give a damn what sour old men say.
The sun that sets may rise again
but when our light has sunk into the earth,
it is gone forever.   5

---
[5]A maritime city of ancient Phoenicia, ruled by Dido's father.
[6]From *Ausones*, the ancient name for the inhabitants of middle and
southern Italy.
[7]Jupiter, the sky god.

---
[1]The name Catullus gave to Clodia, a reference to Sappho of Lesbos.

Give me a thousand kisses,
then a hundred, another thousand,
another hundred
    and in one breath
still kiss another thousand,   10
another hundred.
    O then with lips and bodies joined
many deep thousands;
    confuse
their number,   15
    so that poor fools and cuckolds (envious
even now) shall never
learn our wealth and curse us
with their
evil eyes.   20

——————◆——————

He is changed to a god he who looks on her,   1
godlike he shines when he's seated beside her,
immortal joy to gaze and hear the fall of
    her sweet laughter.

All of my senses are lost and confounded;   5
Lesbia rises before me and trembling
I sink into earth and swift dissolution
    seizes my body.

Limbs are pierced with fire and the heavy tongue fails,
ears resound with noise of distant storms shaking   10
this earth, eyes gaze on stars that fall forever
    into deep midnight.

This languid madness destroys you Catullus,
long day and night shall be desolate, broken,
as long ago ancient kings and rich cities   15
    fell into ruin.

——————◆——————

Lesbia, forever spitting fire at me, is never silent, And now   1
if Lesbia fails to love me, I shall die. Why
do I know in truth her passion burns for me? Because I am
    like her,
because I curse her endlessly. And still, O hear me gods,   5
I love her.

——————◆——————

Furius, Aurelius, I'll work your own perversions   1
upon you and your persons, since you say my poems
prove that I'm effeminate, deep in homosexual
    vice.
A genuine poet must be chaste, industrious,
though his verse may give us   5
rich, voluptuous passion to please the
taste of those who read him and not only
delicate boys, but bearded men whose limbs are
stiff and out of practice. And you because my verses
contain many (thousands of) kisses, look at me   10
as though I were a girl. Come at me, and I'll be ready
to defile you and seduce you.

 Q How do the poems of Catullus compare
with those of Sappho?

The poetry of Catullus notwithstanding, passion and personal feeling were not typical of Latin literature, which inclined more usually toward instruction and satire. One of Rome's most notable poets, Publius Ovidius Naso, or Ovid (43 B.C.E.–17 C.E.), earned centuries of fame for his narrative poem, the *Metamorphoses*; this vast collection of stories about Greek and Roman gods develops the theme of supernatural transformation. Ovid himself pursued a career of poetry and love. Married three times, he seems to have been a master in the art of seduction. His witty guide on the subject, *The Art of Love*, brought him into disfavor with Augustus, who (finding the work morally threatening) sent Ovid into exile. Though written with tongue in cheek, *The Art of Love* swelled an already large canon of misogynistic, or antifemale, classical literature. In this humorous "handbook," Ovid offers vivid glimpses into everyday life in Rome, but he clearly holds that the greatest human crimes issue from women's lust, which, according to the poet, is "keener, fiercer, and more wanton" than men's.

Roman poets were at their most typical when they were moralizing. Octavian's poet laureate, Quintus Haeredes Flaccus, better known as Horace (65–8 B.C.E.), took a critical view of life. Though lacking the grandeur of Virgil and the virtuosity of Ovid, Horace composed verse that pointed up the contradictions between practical realities and philosophic ideals. Having lived through the devastating civil wars of the first century B.C.E., Horace brought a commonsense insight to the subject of war, as we see in the first of the following poems. The second poem exemplifies the Roman taste for **satire**, a literary genre that uses humor to denounce human vice and folly. Satire—Rome's unique contribution to world literature—is a kind of moralizing in which human imperfection is not simply criticized, but rather mocked through biting wit and comic exaggeration. *To Be Quite Frank* is a caustic description of a middle-aged lady with teenage pretensions, a characterization as unvarnished and true-to-life as most Roman portraits. Finally, in the third poem below, Horace discloses his Stoic disbelief in human perfection: he advises us to "Seize the day" (*carpe diem*) and "Learn to accept whatever is to be."

READING 1.27 The Poems of Horace (ca. 30–15 B.C.E.)

Civil War

Why do ye rush, oh wicked folk,   1
    To a fresh war?
Again the cries, the sword, the smoke—
    What for?

Has not sufficient precious blood   5
    Been fiercely shed?
Must ye spill more until ye flood
    The dead?

Not even armed in rivalry
    Your hate's employed;   10

But 'gainst yourselves until ye be
    Destroyed!

Even when beasts slay beasts, they kill
    Some other kind.
Can it be madness makes ye still   15
    So blind?

Make answer! Is your conscience numb?
    Each ashy face
Admits, with silent lips, the dumb
    Disgrace.   20

Murder of brothers! Of all crime,
    Vilest and worst!
Pause—lest ye be, through all of time,
    Accursed.

To Be Quite Frank

Your conduct, naughty Chloris, is   1
    Not just exactly Horace's
Ideal of a lady
    At the shady
Time of life;   5
You mustn't throw your soul away
On foolishness, like Pholoë—
    Her days are folly-laden—
    She's a maiden,
        You're a wife.   10

Your daughter, with propriety,
May look for male society,
    Do one thing and another
    In which mother
        Shouldn't mix;   15
But revels Bacchanalian
Are—or should be—quite alien
    To you a married person,
    Something worse'n
        Forty-six!   20

Yes, Chloris, you cut up too much,
You love the dance and cup too much,
    Your years are quickly flitting—
    To your knitting
        Right about!   25
Forget the incidental things
That keep you from parental things—
    The World, the Flesh, the Devil,
    On the level,
        Cut 'em out!   30

Carpe Diem

Pry not in forbidden lore,   1
    Ask no more, Leuconoë,
How many years—to you?—to me?—
The gods will send us

Before they end us;   5
Nor, questing, fix your hopes
On Babylonian horoscopes.
Learn to accept whatever is to be:
Whether Jove grant us many winters,
Or make of this the last, which splinters   10
Now on opposing cliffs the Tuscan sea.

Be wise; decant your wine; condense
Large aims to fit life's cramped circumference.
We talk, time flies—you've said it!
Make hay today,   15
Tomorrow rates no credit.

 Q How does each of these poems reflect Horace's "critical view of life"?

While Horace's satirical lyrics are, for the most part, genial, those of Rome's most famous satirist, Juvenal (Decimus Junius Juvenalis, ca. 60–130 C.E.), are among the most devastating ever written. Juvenal came to Rome from the provinces. His subsequent career as a magistrate and his experience of poverty and financial failure contributed to his negative perception of Roman society, which he describes in his sixteen bitter *Satires* as swollen with greed and corruption. Juvenal's attack on the city of Rome paints a picture of a noisy, dirty, and crowded urban community inhabited by selfish, violent, and self-indulgent people.

READING 1.28a From Juvenal's "Against the City of Rome" (ca. 110–127 C.E.)

"Rome, good-bye! Let the rest stay in the town if they
    want to,   1
Fellows like A, B, and C, who make black white at their
    pleasure,
Finding it easy to grab contracts for rivers and harbors,
Putting up temples, or cleaning out sewers, or hauling
    off corpses,
Or, if it comes to that, auctioning slaves in the market.   5
Once they used to be hornblowers, working the carneys;
Every wide place in the road knew their puffed-out
    cheeks and their squealing.
Now they give shows of their own. Thumbs up! Thumbs
    down![1] And the killers
Spare or slay, and then go back to concessions for
    private privies.
Nothing they won't take on. Why not?—since the
    kindness of Fortune   10
(Fortune is out for laughs) has exalted them out of the
    gutter.

    . . . .

[1]To turn the thumb down was the signal to kill a wounded gladiator; to turn it up signaled that he should be spared.

"If you're poor, you're a joke, on each and every occasion.
What a laugh, if your cloak is dirty or torn, if your toga
Seems a little bit soiled, if your shoe has a crack in the
    leather,
Or if more than one patch attests to more than one
    mending!   15
Poverty's greatest curse, much worse than the fact of it,
    is that
It makes men objects of mirth, ridiculed, humbled,
    embarrassed.
'Out of the front-row seats!' they cry when you're out of
    money,
Yield your place to the sons of some pimp, the spawn of
    some cathouse,
Some slick auctioneer's brat, or the louts some trainer
    has fathered   20
Or the well-groomed boys whose sire is a gladiator.

   . . . .

"Here in town the sick die from insomnia mostly.
Undigested food, on a stomach burning with ulcers,
Brings on listlessness, but who can sleep in a flophouse?
Who but the rich can afford sleep and a garden
    apartment?   25
That's the source of infection. The wheels creak by on
    the narrow
Streets of the wards, the drivers squabble and brawl
    when they're stopped,
More than enough to frustrate the drowsiest son of a sea
    cow.
When his business calls, the crowd makes way, as the
    rich man,
Carried high in his car, rides over them, reading or
    writing,   30
Even taking a snooze, perhaps, for the motion's composing.
Still, he gets where he wants before we do; for all of our
    hurry
Traffic gets in our way, in front, around and behind us.
Somebody gives me a shove with an elbow, or two-by-
    four scantling.[2]
One clunks my head with a beam, another cracks down
    with a beer keg.   35
Mud is thick on my shins, I am trampled by somebody's
    big feet.
Now what?—a soldier grinds his hobnails into my toes."

Q What urban ills does Juvenal describe
in this poem? Are they exclusive to
ancient Rome?

If Juvenal found much to criticize among his peers, he was
equally hostile toward foreigners and women. His sixth
Satire, "Against Women," is one of the most bitter antifemale diatribes in the history of Western literature. Here,
the poet laments the disappearance of the chaste Latin

woman whose virtues, he submits, have been corrupted by
luxury. Though Juvenal's bias against womankind strikes a
personal note, it is likely that he was reflecting the public
outcry against the licentiousness that was widespread in
his own day. Increasingly during the second century, men
openly enjoyed concubines, mistresses, and prostitutes.
Infidelity among married women was on the rise, and
divorce was common, as were second and third marriages
for both sexes.

The women of imperial Rome did not have many more
civil rights than did their Golden Age Athenian sisters.
They could neither vote nor hold public office. However,
they did not occupy separate household quarters from
males, they could own property, and they were free to
manage their own legal affairs. Roman girls were educated
along with boys, and most middle-class women could read
and write. Some female aristocrats were active in public
life, and the consorts of Rome's rulers often shaped matters
of succession and politics by way of their influence on
their husbands and sons. Roman records confirm that in
addition to the traditional occupations of women in food
and textile production and in prostitution, they also held
positions as musicians, painters, priestesses, midwives, and
gladiators.

READING 1.28b From Juvenal's "Against Women" (ca. 110–127 C.E.)

Where, you ask, do they come from, such monsters as
    these? In the old days   1
Latin women were chaste by dint of their lowly fortunes.
Toil and short hours for sleep kept cottages free from
    contagion,
Hands were hard from working the wood, and husbands
    were watching,
Standing to arms at the Colline Gate, and the shadow of
    Hannibal's looming.[1]   5
Now we suffer the evils of long peace. Luxury hatches
Terrors worse than the wars, avenging a world beaten
    down.
Every crime is here, and every lust, as they have been
Since the day, long since, when Roman poverty perished.
Over our seven hills,[2] from that day on, they came
    pouring.   10
The rabble and rout of the East, Sybaris, Rhodes, Miletus,
Yes, and Tarentum[3] too, garlanded, drunken, shameless.
Dirty money it was that first imported among us
Foreign vice and our times broke down with
    overindulgence.
Riches are flabby, soft. And what does Venus care for   15
When she is drunk? She can't tell one end of a thing
    from another,

_____
[1]In 213 B.C.E. the Carthaginian general, Hannibal, Rome's most
formidable enemy, was camped only a few miles outside Rome, poised
to attack (see Livy, xxvi:10).
[2]The hills surrounding the city of Rome.
[3]Greek cities associated with luxury and vice.

_____
[2]A piece of lumber.

Gulping big oysters down at midnight, making the
    unguents
Foam in the unmixed wine, and drinking out of a
    conchhorn
While the walls spin round, and the table starts in
    dancing,
And the glow of the lamps is blurred by double their
    number.   **20**

. . . .

There's nothing a woman won't do, nothing she thinks is
    disgraceful
With the green gems at her neck, or pearls distending
    her ear lobes.
Nothing is worse to endure than your Mrs. Richbitch,
    whose visage
Is padded and plastered with dough, in the most
    ridiculous manner.
Furthermore, she reeks of unguents, so God help her
    husband   **25**
With his wretched face stunk up with these, smeared by
    her lipstick.
To her lovers she comes with her skin washed clean. But
    at home
Why does she need to look pretty? Nard[4] is assumed for
    the lover,
For the lover she buys all the Arabian perfumes.
It takes her some time to strip down to her face,
    removing the layers   **30**
One by one, till at last she is recognizable, almost,
Then she uses a lotion, she-asses' milk; she'd need
    herds
Of these creatures to keep her supplied on her
    northernmost journeys.
But when she's given herself the treatment in full, from
    the ground base
Through the last layer of mud pack, from the first wash
    to a poultice,   **35**
What lies under all this—a human face, or an ulcer?

 Q What complaints does Juvenal launch
against the women of imperial Rome?
Q What does he mean by saying Rome
suffers "the evils of long peace"?

Roman Drama

Roman tragedies were roughly modeled on those of
Greece. They were moral and didactic in intent, and their
themes were drawn from Greek and Roman history.
Theatrical performances in Rome did not share, however,
the religious solemnity of those in Greece. Rather, they
were a form of entertainment offered along with the public games that marked the major civic festivals known
as *ludi*. Unlike the rituals and athletic contests of the
Greeks, *ludi* featured displays of armed combat and other

---
[4]Spikenard, a fragrant ointment.

violent amusements. The nature of these public spectacles
may explain why many of the tragedies written to compete with them were bloody and ghoulish in character.
The lurid plays of the Stoic writer Seneca drew crowds
in Roman times and were to inspire—some 1500 years
later—such playwrights as William Shakespeare.

The Romans seem to have preferred comedies to
tragedies, for most surviving Roman plays are in the comic
genre. Comic writers employed simple plots and broad
(often obscene) humor. The plays of Plautus (ca. 250–
184 B.C.E.) and Terence (ca. 185–159 B.C.E.) are filled with
stock characters, such as the good-hearted prostitute, the
shrewish wife, and the clever servant. The characters
engage in farcical schemes and broad slapstick action of
the kind common to today's television situation comedies.
In the comic theater of the Romans, as in Roman culture
in general, everyday life took precedence over fantasy, and
the real, if imperfect, world was the natural setting for
down-to-earth human beings.

The Arts of the Roman Empire

Roman Architecture

Rome's architecture reflected the practical needs of a
sprawling empire whose urban centers suffered from the
congestion, noise, and filth described by Juvenal. To link
the provinces that ranged from the Atlantic Ocean to
the Euphrates River, Roman engineers built fifty thousand
miles of paved roads, many of which are still in use today.
The need to house, govern, and entertain large numbers of
citizens inspired the construction of tenements, meeting
halls, baths, and amphitheaters. Eight- and nine-story
tenements provided thousands with cheap (if often
rat-infested) housing. Roman bridges and tunnels defied
natural barriers, while some eighteen aqueducts brought
fresh water to Rome's major cities. The aqueducts, some of
which delivered well over forty million gallons of water
per day to a single site, were the public works that the
Romans considered their most significant technological
achievement.

Science and Technology

45 C.E. the Romans invent the technique of
glassblowing

90 C.E. a system of aqueducts provide water for the city of
Rome

122 C.E. in Roman Britain, the emperor Hadrian begins
construction of a wall to protect against invasion from
the North

140 C.E. the Alexandrian astronomer Ptolemy produces the
Almagest, which posits a geocentric (earth-centered)
universe (and becomes the basis for Western
astronomy for centuries)

160 C.E. Claudius Galen writes over 100 medical treatises
(despite errors, they became the basis for Western
medical practice for centuries)

Superb engineers, the Romans employed the structural advantages of the arch (the knowledge of which they inherited from the Etruscans) to enclose greater volumes of uninterrupted space than any previously known. The arch constituted a clear technical advance over the post-and-lintel construction used by the Greeks in buildings like the Parthenon (see Figure 5.14). The Romans adapted this structural principle inventively: they placed arches back to back to form a barrel **vault**, at right angles to each other to form a cross or groined vault, and around a central point to form a dome (Figure **6.4**). Roman building techniques reveal a combination of practicality and innovation: the Romans were the first to use concrete (an aggregate of sand, lime, brick-and-stone rubble, and water), a medium that made possible cheap large-scale construction. They laid their foundations with concrete, raised structures with brick, rubble, and stone, and finished exterior surfaces with veneers of marble, tile, bronze, or plaster.

Roman architecture and engineering were considered one and the same discipline. Vitruvius' *Ten Books on Architecture* (see chapter 5), the oldest and most influential work of its kind, includes instructions for hydraulic systems, city planning, and mechanical devices. For the Roman architect, the function of a building determined its formal design. The design of villas, theaters, and temples received the same close attention as that given to hospitals, fortresses, and—as Josephus reveals—military camps. One of Rome's most spectacular large-scale engineering projects is the 900-foot-long Pont du Gard, part of a 25-mile-long aqueduct that brought fresh water to

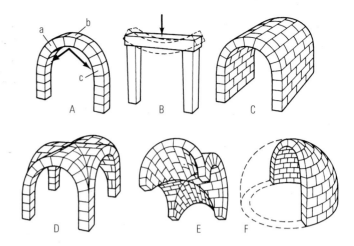

Figure 6.4 Arch principle and arch construction. (A) Arch consisting of voussoirs, wedge-shaped blocks (a,b,c,); (B) Post-and-lintel; (C) Barrel or tunnel vault; (D and E) Groined vault; (F) Dome.

the city of Nîmes in southern France (Figure **6.5**). Built of 6-ton stones and assembled without mortar, the structure reflects the practical function of arches at three levels, the bottom row supporting a bridge and the second row undergirding the top channel through which water ran by gravity to its destination.

The sheer magnitude of such Roman amphitheaters as the Circus Maximus, which seated 200,000 spectators (Figure **6.6**, foreground) and the Colosseum, which covered six acres and accommodated 50,000 (Figure **6.7**), is a reminder that during the first century C.E., Rome's population exceeded one million people. Many of them were the

Figure 6.5 Pont du Gard, near Nîmes, France, ca. 20–10 B.C.E. Stone, height 180 ft., length ca. 900 ft. Photo: Paul M.R. Maeyaert, Belgium.

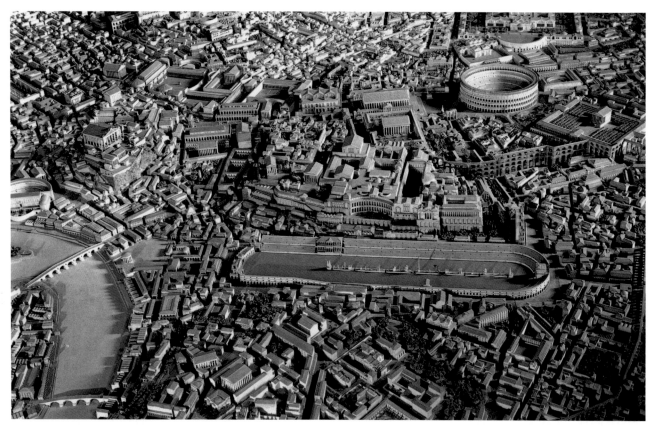

Figure 6.6 Reconstruction of fourth-century C.E. Rome by I. Gismondi. Museum of Roman Civilization, Rome.

impoverished recipients of relief in the form of wheat and free entertainment, hence the phrase "bread and circuses." The Roman amphitheaters testify to the popular taste for entertainments that included chariot races, mock sea battles, gladiatorial contests, and a variety of brutal blood sports. At the Colosseum, three levels of seating rose above the arena floor. Beneath the floor was a complex of rooms and tunnels from which athletes, gladiators, and wild animals emerged to entertain the cheering crowd. To provide shade from the sun, an awning at the roof level could be extended by means of a system of pulleys. On each level of the exterior, arches were framed by a series of decorative, or engaged, columns displaying the three Greek orders: Doric (at ground level), Ionic, and Corinthian (Figure **6.8**). The ingenious combination of arch and post-and-lintel structural elements in the design

Figure 6.7 Colosseum, Rome (aerial view), 70–82 C.E. Photo: Alinari, Florence.

Figure 6.8 Outer wall of the Colosseum, Rome, 70–82 C.E. Photo: A. F. Kersting, London.

Figure 6.9 The Pantheon, Rome, ca. 118–125 C.E. Photo: R. Liebermann.

Figure 6.10 Plan and section of the Pantheon (after Sir Banister Fletcher). From Horst de la Croix and Richard Tansey, *Art Through the Ages*, sixth edition, © 1975 by Harcourt Brace Jovanovich, Inc., reprinted by permission of the publisher.

of the Colosseum would be widely imitated for centuries, and especially during the Italian Renaissance. More generally, the longstanding influence of this Roman amphitheater is apparent in the design of the modern sports arena.

Roman architectural genius may be best illustrated by the Pantheon, a temple whose structural majesty depends on the combination of Roman technical ingenuity and dramatic spatial design. Dedicated to the seven planetary deities, the Pantheon was built in the early second century C.E. Its monumental exterior—once covered with a veneer of white marble and bronze—features a portico with eight Corinthian columns originally elevated by a flight of stairs that now lie buried beneath the city street (Figure **6.9**). One of the few buildings from classical antiquity to have remained almost intact, the Pantheon boasts a 19-foot-thick rotunda that is capped by a solid dome consisting of

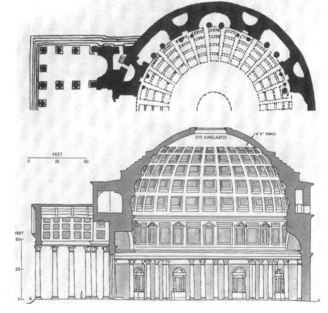

5000 tons of concrete (Figure **6.10**). The interior of the dome, once painted blue and gold to resemble the vault of heaven, is pierced by a 30-foot-wide *oculus*, or "eye," that admits light and air (Figure **6.11**). The proportions of the Pantheon observe the classical principles of symmetry and harmony as described by Vitruvius (see Reading 1.18): the height from the floor to the apex of the dome (143 feet) equals the diameter of the rotunda. The Pantheon has inspired more works of architecture than any other monument in Greco-Roman history. It awed and delighted such eminent late eighteenth-century neoclassicists as Thomas Jefferson, who used it as the model for many architectural designs, including that of the Rotunda of the University of Virginia (Figure **6.12**).

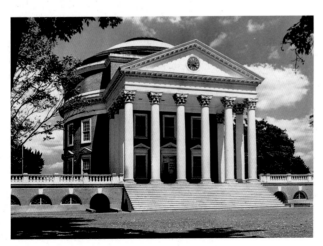

Figure 6.12 Thomas Jefferson, The Rotunda, University of Virginia, Charlottesville, Virginia, 1822–1826. Photo: Ralph Thompson. Albert and Shirley Small Special Collections Library, University of Virginia.

Figure 6.11 Giovanni Paolo Panini, *The Interior of the Pantheon*, ca. 1734–1735. Oil on canvas, 4 ft. 2½ in. × 3 ft. 3 in. National Gallery of Art, Washington, D.C. Samuel H. Kress Collection.

Figure 6.13 (above) Maison Carrée, Nîmes, France, ca. 19 B.C.E. Photo: Paul M. R. Maeyaert, Belgium.

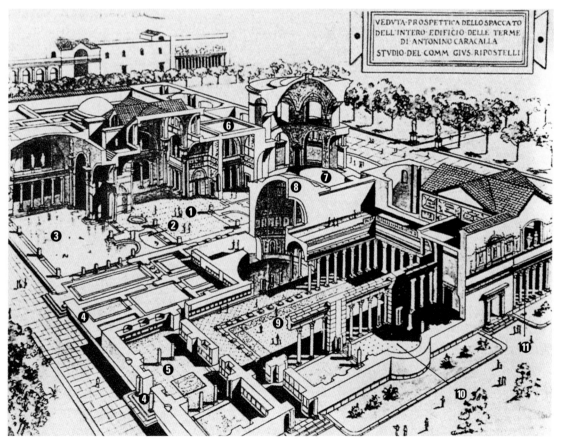

Figure 6.14
Restoration of the Baths of Caracalla in Rome, 211–217 C.E.

1 Great Hall
2 Oval pools (cool baths)
3 Swimming pool
4 Entrance
5 Vestibule
6 Heated rooms
7 Hot baths
8 Steam baths
9 Colonnaded court
10 Lecture halls
11 Lounges

Engraving. The Bettmann Archive.

Figure 6.15 Great Bath, Roman bath complex, Bath, England, 54 C.E. Part of the finest group of Roman remains in England, this sumptuous pool is still fed by natural hot springs. Photo: Spectrum Picture Library, London.

The Pantheon is distinctly Roman in spirit; however, other Roman buildings imitated Greek models. The temple in Nîmes, France, for instance, known as the Maison Carrée, stands like a miniature Greek shrine atop a high podium (Figure **6.13**). A stairway and a colonnaded portico accentuate the single entranceway and give the building a frontal "focus" usually lacking in Greek temples. The Corinthian order (see Figure 5.16) appears in the portico, and engaged columns adorn the exterior wall. The epitome of classical refinement, the Maison Carrée inspired numerous European and American copies. Indeed, the Virginia State Capitol, designed by Thomas Jefferson, offers clear evidence of the use of classical models to convey the dignity, stability, and authority that neoclassicists associated with the world of Greece and Rome.

If temples such as the Pantheon and the Maison Carrée answered the spiritual needs of the Romans, the baths, such as those named for the Emperor Caracalla, satisfied some of their temporal requirements (Figure **6.14**). Elaborate structures fed by natural hot springs (Figure **6.15**), the baths provided a welcome refuge from the noise and grime of the city streets. In addition to rooms in which pools of water were heated to varying degrees, such spas often included steam rooms, exercise rooms, art galleries, shops, cafés, reading rooms, and chambers for physical intimacy. Though most baths had separate women's quarters, many permitted mixed bathing. The popularity of the baths is reflected in the fact that by the third century C.E., there were more than 900 of them in the city of Rome.

Roman baths centered on a **basilica**, a rectangular colonnaded hall commonly used for public assemblies. The basilica was the ideal structure for courts of law, meeting halls, and marketplaces. The huge meeting hall known as the Basilica of Maxentius consisted of a 300-foot-long central nave, four side aisles, and a semicircular recess called an **apse** (Figure **6.16**). The Roman basilica might be roofed by wooden beams or—as in the case of the Basilica of Maxentius (Figure **6.17**)—by gigantic stone vaults. Completed by the Emperor Constantine in the

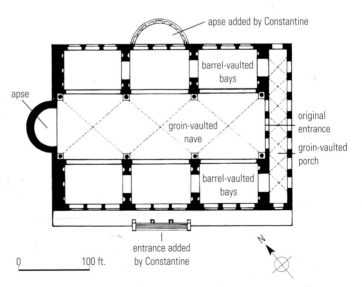

Figure 6.16 Plan of the Basilica of Maxentius and Constantine.

Figure 6.17 Basilica of Maxentius, Rome, begun 306–310 C.E., completed by Constantine after 313 C.E. Photo: © 1990, Photo Scala, Florence – courtesy of the Ministero Beni e Att. Culturali.

fourth century C.E., these enormous vaults rested on brick-faced concrete walls some twenty feet thick. In floor plan and construction features, the Roman basilica became the model for the early Christian Church in the West.

Roman Sculpture

Like its imperialistic predecessors, Rome advertised its military achievements in monumental public works of art. These consisted mainly of triumphal arches and victory columns, which, like the obelisks of Egyptian pharaohs, commemorated the conquests of strong rulers. The 100-foot-tall marble column erected in 113 C.E. by Emperor Trajan to celebrate his victory over the Dacians includes 2500 figures—a huge picture scroll carved in brilliant low relief (Figures **6.18** and **6.19**). Here, a documentary vitality is achieved by the piling up of figures in illusionistic space, and by a plethora of realistic details describing Roman military fortifications and weaponry. Triumphal arches were landmarks of Roman imperial victory. More rightly classed with sculpture than with architecture (since, unlike architecture, the Roman arch did not enclose interior space), these monumental structures functioned as visual propaganda and monumental gateways that celebrated Rome's military conquests. First used by Augustus, some thirty-four triumphal arches in Rome (and many more throughout the Empire) bear witness to the power and the geographic reach of the Roman state. The arch of Titus, which stands at the upper end of the Roman Forum, commemorates the final days of the Jewish Wars (66–70 C.E.) fought by the emperors Vespasian and Titus (Figure **6.20**). The marble-faced concrete vault of the arch is elevated between two massive piers that bear engaged Corinthian columns and an **attic** or superstructure carrying a commemorative inscription. Narrative relief panels on the interior sides of the vault depict a typical Roman triumphal procession: it celebrates the destruction of Jerusalem and the pillage of the Temple of Solomon (Figure **6.21**). Crowned with laurel wreaths of victory, Roman soldiers march through a city gate carrying the menorah and other spoils of victory. Subtly carved in

Figure 6.18 Trajan's Victory Column, Rome, C.E. 113. Marble, height (with base) 125 ft. Photo: © 1990, Photo Scala, Florence – courtesy of the Ministero Beni e Att. Culturali

Figure 6.19 Detail from Trajan's Victory Column, Rome, 113 C.E. Marble. Photo: © 1990, Photo Scala, Florence – courtesy of the Ministero Beni e Att. Culturali.

various depths from low to high relief, the scene evokes the illusion of deep space. Even in its damaged state, *The Spoils of Jerusalem* remains a vivid record of conquest and triumph. It is the product of an age that depended on realistic narrative relief—as we today depend on photography and film—to document (and immortalize) key historical events.

While triumphal arches served as visual propaganda for Rome's military exploits, monumental sculpture glorified Roman rulers. The statue of Augustus from Primaporta (see Figure 6.3), is one of the best examples of Roman heroic portraiture. It exemplifies the classical synthesis of realistic detail (most evident in the treatment of the breastplate and toga) and the idealized form (obviously in the handsome face and canonic proportions) that dominated official Roman art, including that found on Rome's mass-produced coins.

During the second century C.E., the tradition of heroic portraiture assumed an even more magisterial stamp in the image of the ruler on horseback: the **equestrian** statue (Figure **6.22**). The equestrian portrait of the Roman Emperor Marcus Aurelius depicts the general addressing his troops with the traditional gesture of imperial authority. The body of a conquered warrior once lay under the raised right hoof of the spirited charger, whose veins and muscles seem to burst from beneath his bronze skin.

Figure 6.20 Arch of Titus, Rome, ca. 81 C.E. Marble, height approx. 50 ft., width approx. 40 ft. Photo: © 1990, Photo Scala, Florence – courtesy of the Ministero Beni e Att. Culturali.

While public portrayal of the ruler usually demanded a degree of flattering idealization, images intended for private use invited realistic detail. The Roman taste for realism is perhaps best illustrated in three-dimensional portraits of Roman men and women, often members of the ruling class or wealthy patricians. In contrast to the idealized portraits of Golden Age Greece (see Figure 4.8), many Roman likenesses reflect obsessive fidelity to nature. So true to life seem some Roman portrait heads that scholars suspect they may have been executed from wax death masks. Roman portrait sculpture tends to reflect the personality and character of the sitter, a fact perhaps related to the ancient custom of honoring the "genius" or in-dwelling spirit of the dead ancestor. The lifelike portrait bust of Julius Caesar, carved in green schist with inset crystal eyes, captures the spirit of resolute determination (see Figure 6.2). It is the record of a particular person at a particular time in his life; as such it conveys a degree of psychological realism absent from most classical Greek portraits. In that portrait sculpture served much as our photographs do today—as physical reminders of favorite relatives and friends—the emphasis on realism is understandable. The balding patrician who carries two portrait busts of his ancestors (Figure **6.23**) reminds us that the Roman family placed extraordinary emphasis on its lineage and honored the father of the family (*paterfamilias*) no less devotedly than did the ancient Chinese. Such intimate sculptured likenesses of the deceased would have been displayed and venerated at special altars and shrines within the Roman home. Finally, the portrait of the square-jawed aristocratic woman, whose wig or hairdo

Figure 6.21 Spoils from the Temple in Jerusalem. Relief from the Arch of Titus, Rome, ca. 81 C.E. Marble, height approx. 7 ft. Alinari, Florence.

Figure 6.22 Equestrian statue of Marcus Aurelius, ca. 173 C.E. Bronze, height 16 ft. 8 in. Piazza del Campidoglio, Rome. Photo: Photo: © 1990, Photo Scala, Florence.

Figure 6.23 Roman aristocrat holding portrait busts of his ancestors, late first century B.C.E. Marble, height 5 ft. 5 in. Capitoline Museum, Rome. Photo: Alinari, Florence.

surely required the fastidious application of the curling iron, discloses the proud confidence of a Roman matron (Figure 6.24). Whether cast in bronze, or carved in marble, slate, or terracotta, these psychologically penetrating studies are often as unflattering as they are honest. In their lack of idealization and their affection for literal detail, they are representative of Roman sculpture as a record of commonplace reality.

Roman Painting

A similar taste for realism appears in the frescoes with which the Romans decorated their meeting halls, baths, and country villas. Possibly inspired by Greek murals, of which only a few examples survive, Roman artists painted scenes drawn from literature, mythology, and everyday life. Among the finest examples of Roman frescoes are those found in and around Pompeii and Herculaneum, two southern Italian cities that attracted a population of wealthy Romans. But even in the outer reaches of the empire, such as at Zeugma in modern Turkey (uncovered as recently as 1992), the Roman taste for visual representation is evident in magnificently decorated palatial villas, a legacy soon to be submerged in the waters of an urgently needed hydroelectric dam. Pompeii and Herculaneum remain the showcases of Roman suburban life: both cities were engulfed and destroyed by a mountain of ash from the volcanic eruption of Mount Vesuvius of 79 C.E., but the

Figure 6.24 Flavian woman, ca. 89 C.E. Marble, life-sized. Capitoline Museum, Rome.

Figure 6.25 Atrium, House of the Silver Wedding, Pompeii, Italy, first century C.E. Alinari/Art Resource, New York.

lava from the disaster preserved many of the area's suburban homes. These residential villas, constructed around an **atrium** (a large central hall open to the sky), are valuable sources of information concerning the lifestyles of upper-class Romans (Figure **6.25**).

At a villa in Boscoreale, about a mile north of Pompeii, floor surfaces display fine, ornamental motifs and scenes illustrated in **mosaic**, a technique by which small pieces of stone or glass are embedded into wet cement surfaces. The walls of many rooms are painted with frescoes designed to give viewers the impression that they are looking out upon gardens and distant buildings (Figure **6.26**). Such illusionism is a kind of visual artifice known by the French phrase ***trompe l'oeil*** ("fool the eye"). Designed to deceive the eye, they reveal the artist's competence in mastering *empirical perspective*, the technique of achieving a sense of three-dimensional space on a two-dimensional surface. Other devices, such as light and shade, are also employed to seduce the eye into believing it perceives

real objects in deep space: in the extraordinary *Still Life With Eggs and Thrushes*, for instance, one of a series of frescoes celebrating food and found in a villa at Pompeii, light seems to bounce off the metal pitcher, whose shiny surface contrasts with the densely textured towel and the ceramic plate holding ten lifelike eggs (Figure **6.27**). Roman artists integrated illusionistic devices in ways that would not be seen again in Western art for a thousand years (see chapter 23).

The invention of still life as an independent genre (or type) of art confirmed the Roman fondness for the tangible things of the material world. Similarly, their affection for nature led them to pioneer the genre of landscape painting. First-century-B.C.E. frescoes illustrating the adventures of the Greek hero Odysseus feature spacious landscapes filled with rocky plains, feathery trees, animals, and people (Figure **6.28**). Bathed in light and shade, the naturalistically modeled figures cast shadows to indicate their physical presence in atmospheric space. Evident in

Figure 6.26 Bedroom from the Villa of P. Fannius Synistor, Boscoreale, Italy, first century B.C.E. Mosaic floor, couch, and footstool come from other Roman villas of later date. Fresco on lime plaster, 8 ft. 8½ in. × 19 ft. 1⅛ in. × 10 ft. 11½ in. The Metropolitan Museum of Art, New York, Rogers Fund, 1903 (03.14.13). Photo: Schecter Lee.

these Roman landscapes is a deep affection for the countryside and for the pleasures of nature. Arcadia, the mountainous region in the central Peloponnesus inhabited by the peaceloving shepherds and nymphs of ancient Greek legend, provided the model for the classical landscape, which celebrated (as did Greek and Latin **pastoral** poetry) a life of innocence and simplicity. The glorification of bucolic freedom—the "Arcadian Myth"—reflected the Roman disenchantment with city life. The theme was to reappear frequently in the arts of the West, especially during periods of rising urbanization.

Roman Music

While Roman civilization left abundant visual and literary resources, the absence of surviving examples in music make it almost impossible to evaluate the Roman contribution in this domain. Passages from the writings of Roman historians suggest that Roman music theory was adopted from the Greeks, as were most Roman instruments. In drama, musical interludes replaced the Greek choral odes—a change that suggests the growing distance between drama and its ancient ritual function. Music was, however, essential to most forms of public entertainment and also played an important role in military life; for the latter, the Romans developed brass instruments, such as trumpets and horns, and drums for military processions.

SUMMARY

A genius for practical organization marked all aspects of Roman history. From its Latin beginnings, Rome showed an extraordinary talent for adopting and adapting the

best of other cultures: Etruscan and Greek. Although the Roman Republic engaged all citizens in government, power rested largely with the wealthy and influential patrician class. As Rome built an empire and assumed mastery of the civilized world, the Republic fell increasingly into the hands of military dictators, the greatest of whom was Julius Caesar. Caesar's heir, the emperor Octavian, ushered in the *Pax Romana*, a time of peace and high cultural productivity.

The Romans produced no original philosophy but cultivated Hellenistic schools of thought such as Stoicism. Roman literature manifests a practical bias for factual information. The Romans gave the world its first encyclopedias, as well as memorable biographies, essays, speeches, histories, and letters. The high moral tone and lucid prose of Cicero and Tacitus characterize Roman writing at its best. In poetry, Virgil paid homage to the Roman state in the *Aeneid*, Catullus sang of love and loss, while Horace and Juvenal offered a critical view of Roman life in satiric verse, the genre that constitutes Rome's most original contribution to literature.

Rome's most enduring accomplishments lay in the practical areas of law, language, and political life. However, Rome's architectural and engineering projects, which engaged the inventive use of the arch and the techniques of concrete and brick construction, exercised an equally important influence on subsequent civilizations in the West. To the classical style in architecture, the Romans contributed domed and stone-vaulted types of construction that enclosed vast areas of space. Rome borrowed Hellenic models in all of the arts, but the Roman taste for realism dominated narrative relief sculpture,

Figure 6.27 *Still Life with Eggs and Thrushes,* from the House (or Villa) of Julia Felix, Pompeii, before 79 C.E. Fresco, 35 in. × 48 in. Photo: Fotografic Foglia, Naples.

portrait busts, and fresco painting. These genres disclose a love for literal truth that contrasts sharply with the Hellenic effort to generalize and idealize form.

For almost a thousand years, the Romans held together a geographically and ethnically diverse realm, providing a large population with such a high quality of life as to move future generations to envy and praise. The Roman contribution is imprinted on the language, laws, and architecture of the West. By its preservation and transmission of the classical legacy, Rome's influence on the humanistic tradition was felt long after Roman glory and might had faded.

Figure 6.28 *Ulysses in the Land of the Lestrygonians*, part of the *Odyssey Landscapes*, second-style ("architectural") wall-painting from a house in Rome, late first century B.C.E. Height approx. 5 ft. Vatican Library, Rome.

GLOSSARY

apse a vaulted semicircular recess at one or both ends of a basilica

atrium the inner courtyard of a Roman house, usually colonnaded and open to the sky

attic the superstructure or low upper story above the main order of a façade

basilica a large, colonnaded hall commonly used for public assemblies, law courts, baths, and marketplaces

eclogue a pastoral poem, usually involving shepherds in an idyllic rural setting

epistle a formal letter

equestrian mounted on horseback

imperium (Latin, "command," "empire") the civil and military authority exercised by the rulers of ancient Rome (and the root of the English words "imperialism" and "empire"); symbolized in ancient Rome by an eagle-headed scepter and the *fasces*, an ax bound in a bundle of rods

mosaic a medium by which small pieces of glass or stone are embedded in wet cement

on wall and floor surfaces; any picture or pattern made in this manner

oratory the art of public speaking

pastoral pertaining to the country, to shepherds, and the simple rural life; also, any work of art presenting an idealized picture of country life

res publica (Latin, "of the people") a government in which power resides in citizens entitled to vote and is exercised by representatives responsible to them and to a body of law

sarcophagus (plural, **sarcophagi**) a stone coffin

satire a literary genre that ridicules or pokes fun at human vices and follies

trompe l'oeil (French, "fool the eye") a form of illusionistic painting that tries to convince the viewer that the image is real and not painted

vault a roof or ceiling constructed on the arch principle (see Figure 6.5)

CHAPTER 7

China: The Rise to Empire

"He who learns but does not think is lost.
He who thinks but does not learn is in great danger."
Confucius

In the thousand-year period (ca. 500 B.C.E. to 500 C.E.) in which Greco-Roman civilization flourished in the West, China and India brought forth cultures that were both definitive and enduring, hence "classical." China and India* each generated a body of learning and an artistic heritage that served for centuries as models for the rest of East Asia. Their legacies, like those of Greece and Rome, also reached beyond the East. In this chapter, Classical China receives our attention. The culture of classical China, as well as China's rise to empire, offer intriguing parallels with the histories of ancient Greece and Rome, and in particular the latter. These two great empires—Han China and Imperial Rome—located at either end of the Eurasian landmass, brought political stability and cultural unity to vast stretches of territory. Both were profoundly secular in their approach to the world and to the conduct of human beings. Both inherited age-old forms and practices in religion, law, literature, and the arts; these they self-consciously preserved and transmitted to future generations. The classical legacies of China and Rome would come to shape the respective histories of East and West.

Confucius and the Classics

After 771 B.C.E., as warring rebels competed for political power, the Zhou dynasty, which had ruled since 1027 B.C.E., slowly disintegrated. But in the waning years of the Zhou, trade and urban life continued to flourish, and China developed some of her most significant and lasting material and philosophic traditions. Chopsticks, cast iron, square-holed coins, and finely lacquered objects were all developed during the sixth century B.C.E. At the same time, and parallel with (but totally independent of) the rise of philosophic thought in Greece, China experienced a burst of intellectual creativity: China's classical texts date from this period, and with them came the formulation

of some of China's oldest moral and religious precepts. As we saw in chapter 3, the ancient Chinese regarded the natural order as the basis for spiritual life, political stability (witness the *Mandate of Heaven*), and the social order. To know one's place within the order and to act accordingly were essential to the well-being of both the individual and the community. The Chinese describe this ethical imperative with the word *li*, which translates variously as "propriety," "ritual," and "arrangement." The original meaning of the word *li* is found in the act of ritual sacrifice, that is, the proper performance of traditional Chinese rites. But by the middle of the Zhou era, *li* had come to refer to the pattern or principles governing appropriate behavior, or action in conformity with the rules of decorum and propriety. Formative in the evolution of this concept were the teachings of the philosopher Kong-fuzi (551–479 B.C.E.), better known as Confucius, a Latinization of his Chinese name. Confucius was China's most notable thinker. According to tradition, he was also the compiler and editor of the "Five Chinese Classics." A self-educated man, who served as a local administrator, Confucius pursued the career of a teacher and social reformer. Like his Greek contemporary, Socrates, he

---

*India's classical history—the birth of Buddhism and the revival of Hindu culture—are surveyed in chapters 8, 9, and 14.

The Five Chinese Classics*

1 The Book of Changes (I jing)—a text for divination

2 The Book of History (Shu jing)—government records: speeches, reports, and announcements by rulers and ministers of ancient China

3 The Book of Songs (Shi jing)—an anthology of some 300 poems: folk songs, ceremonial and secular poems

4 The Book of Rites (Li ji)—a collection of texts centering on rules of conduct for everyday life

5 The Spring and Autumn Annals (Lushi chunqiu)—commentaries that chronicle events up to the fifth century B.C.E.

*A sixth classic, on music, is no longer in existence

himself wrote nothing. He earned renown through the force of his teachings, which his disciples transcribed after his death. This collection of writings came to be known as the *Analects*. As eclectic in their origins and dating as the Hebrew Bible, the *Analects* embody the words of Confucius on matters as diverse as music, marriage, and death. But they center on questions of conduct: the proper behavior of the individual in the society at large. They articulate the ancient Chinese conviction that human beings must heed a moral order that is fixed in nature, not in divine pronouncement (see chapter 3). Confucius confidently maintained that human character, not birth, determined the worth and status of the individual. He had little to say about gods and spirits; nor did he pursue ultimate truth (in the manner of the Greek philosophers). Rather, he taught the importance of tradition, filial piety (respect for one's elders), and the exercise of *li*. In doing so, he formulated the first expression of the so-called "Golden Rule": "What you do not wish for yourself, do not do to others."

The teachings of Confucius preserved social and political ideas as old as the Shang and Zhou dynasties. In that Confucius lived during the turbulent years just prior to the collapse of the Zhou and the era of the Warring States (403–221 B.C.E.), he may have sought to insure the survival of traditional values and ideals. Basic to these was the notion that the ruler was the "parent" of the people. The cultivation of character and the successful regulation of the family preceded the ruler's ability to govern. The good influence and high moral status of the ruler—a figure much like Plato's philosopher-king—was of greater political value than physical force or the threat of punishment. If a ruler was not himself virtuous, he could not expect to inspire virtue among his subjects. For Confucius, as for Plato, moral and political life were one. Moral harmony was the root of political harmony, and moral rectitude made government all but unnecessary. Such precepts were basic to humanist thought in China for well over 2000 years.

READING 1.29 From the *Analects* of Confucius

2.1 The Master said: "He who rules by virtue is like the polestar, which remains unmoving in its mansion while all the other stars revolve respectfully around it."

2.2 The Master said: "The three hundred *Poems* are summed up in one single phrase: 'Think no evil.' "

2.3 The Master said: "Lead them by political maneuvers, restrain them with punishments: the people will become cunning and shameless. Lead them by virtue, restrain them with ritual: they will develop a sense of shame and a sense of participation."

2.13 Zigong asked about the true gentleman. The Master said: "He preaches only what he practices."

2.14 The Master said: "The gentleman considers the whole rather than the parts. The small man considers the parts rather than the whole."

2.15 The Master said: "To study without thinking is futile. To think without studying is dangerous."

2.17 The Master said: "Zilu, I am going to teach you what knowledge is. To take what you know for what you know, and what you do not know for what you do not know, that is knowledge indeed."

2.20 Lord Ji Kang asked: "What should I do in order to make the people respectful, loyal, and zealous?" The Master said: "Approach them with dignity and they will be respectful. Be yourself a good son and a kind father, and they will be loyal. Raise the good and train the incompetent, and they will be zealous."

2.24 The Master said: "To worship gods that are not yours, that is toadyism. Not to act when justice commands, that is cowardice."

4.7 The Master said: "Your faults define you. From your very faults one can know your quality."

4.11 The Master said: "A gentleman seeks virtue; a small man seeks land. A gentleman seeks justice; a small man seeks favors."

4.14 The Master said: "Do not worry if you are without a position; worry lest you do not deserve a position. Do not worry if you are not famous; worry lest you do not deserve to be famous."

4.16 The Master said: "A gentleman considers what is just; a small man considers what is expedient."

4.17 The Master said: "When you see a worthy man, seek to emulate him. When you see an unworthy man, examine yourself."

4.19 The Master said: "While your parents are alive, do not travel afar. If you have to travel, you must leave an address."

4.21 The Master said: "Always keep in mind the age of your parents. Let this thought be both your joy and your worry."

4.24 The Master said: "A gentleman should be slow to speak and prompt to act."

12.16 The Master said: "A gentleman brings out the good that is in people, he does not bring out the bad. A vulgar man does the opposite."

12.21 Fan Chi was taking a walk with Confucius under the Rain Dance Terrace. He said: "May I ask how one can accumulate moral power, neutralize hostility, and recognize emotional incoherence?" The Master said: "Excellent question! Always put the effort before the reward: is this not the way to accumulate moral power? To attack evil in itself and not the evil that is in people: is this not the way to neutralize hostility? To endanger oneself and one's kin in a sudden fit of anger: is this not an instance of incoherence?"

15.6 Zizhang asked about conduct. The Master said: "Speak with loyalty and good faith, act with dedication and deference, and even among the barbarians your conduct will be irreproachable. If you speak without loyalty and good faith, if you act without dedication or deference, your conduct will be unacceptable, even in your own village. Wherever you stand, you should have this precept always in front of your eyes; have it carved upon the yoke of your chariot, and only then will you be able to move ahead." Zizhang wrote it on his sash.

15.8 The Master said: "When dealing with a man who is capable of understanding your teaching, if you do not teach him, you waste the man. When dealing with a man who is incapable of understanding your teaching, if you do teach him, you waste your teaching. A wise teacher wastes no man and wastes no teaching."

15.9 The Master said: "A righteous man, a man attached to humanity, does not seek life at the expense of his humanity; there are instances where he will give his life in order to fulfill his humanity."

15.12 The Master said: "A man with no concern for the future is bound to worry about the present."

15.13 The Master said: "The fact remains that I have never seen a man who loved virtue as much as sex."

15.15 The Master said: "Demand much from yourself, little from others, and you will prevent discontent."

15.18 The Master said: "A gentleman takes justice as his basis, enacts it in conformity with the ritual, expounds it with modesty, and through good faith, brings it to fruition. This is how a gentleman proceeds."

15.19 The Master said: "A gentleman resents his incompetence; he does not resent his obscurity."

15.20 The Master said: "A gentleman worries lest he might disappear from this world without having made a name for himself."

15.21 The Master said: "A gentleman makes demands on himself; a vulgar man makes demands on others."

15.24 Zigong asked: "Is there any single word that could guide one's entire life?" The Master said: "Should it not be *reciprocity*? What you do not wish for yourself, do not do to others."

Q What aspects of moral conduct occupy Confucius in the *Analects*?

Q What do the *Analects* reveal about ancient Chinese values?

Confucianism and Legalism

The two centuries following the death of Confucius marked an era of turbulence and social upheaval inflicted by the armies of China's warring states. But during that time (and perhaps because of its instability) there emerged competing schools of thought on questions concerning human nature and, by extension, the ideal form of government. Such speculation took place among the class of China's scholars, who, much like the Hellenic Aristotle, took a practical approach to the investigation of morality. Mencius (372–289 B.C.E.), China's most significant voice after Confucius, expanded Confucian concepts of government as a civilizing force and the ruler as the moral model. Mencius held that human beings are born good; they fall into evil only by neglect or abuse. In defining human nature, Mencius insisted:

> The tendency of human nature to do good is like that of water to flow downward. There is no man who does not tend to do good; there is not water that does not flow downward. Now you may strike water and make it splash over your forehead, or you may even force it up the hills. But is this in the nature of water? It is of course due to the force of circumstances. Similarly, man may be brought to do evil, and that is because the same is done to his nature.*

Based on this view of humankind, Mencius envisioned the state as an agent for cultivating the goodness of the individual.

An opposing body of thought challenged this point of view. In contrast to the Confucians, who generally perceived humankind as good, those who came to be called Legalists described the nature of humankind as inherently evil. From this negative premise, the Legalists concluded that the best state was one in which rulers held absolute authority to uphold (strict) laws and dole out punishment to violators. The leading Legalist, Han Fei Zi (?–233 B.C.E.), argued that the rationality of an adult was no more reliable than that of an infant. The innate selfishness of humankind justified strong central authority and harsh punishment. "Now take a young fellow who is a bad character," he writes:

> His parents may get angry at him, but he never makes any change. The villagers may reprove him, but he is not moved. His teachers and elders may admonish him, but he never reforms. The love of his parents, the efforts of the villagers, and the wisdom of his teachers and elders . . . are applied to him, and yet not even a hair on his chin is altered. It is only after the district magistrate sends out his soldiers and in the name of the law searches for wicked individuals that the young man becomes afraid and changes his ways and alters his deeds. So while the love of parents is not sufficient to discipline the children, the severe penalties of the district magistrate are. This is because men become naturally spoiled by love, but are submissive to authority.**

The Legalism of Han Fei would become the fundamental philosophy of China's first empire.

Sources of Chinese Tradition, compiled by Wm. Theodore de Bary and others (New York: Columbia University Press, 1960), 103.
**Sources of Chinese Tradition*, compiled by Wm. Theodore de Bary and others (New York: Columbia University Press, 1960), 146–147.

The Chinese Rise to Empire

The Qin Dynasty (221–206 B.C.E.)

Even as the great Roman *imperium* came to dominate the Western world, a comparable empire arose on the eastern end of the vast Asian landmass. The first great period of unity in China came about under the Qin (pronounced "chin"), the dynasty from which the English word "China" is derived. By the 5th century B.C.E., the different autonomous states into which the Zhou realm had dissolved were in open warfare, vying with one another for supremacy. In 221 B.C.E. King Zheng (ca. 259–210 B.C.E.) of the state of Qin finally succeeded in conquering all the other rival states, unifying their domains under his rule. He declared himself "First Emperor" (Shi Huang Di), and—like the first Roman emperor, Augustus—immediately set about eliminating the possibility of further conflict. Like the Shang and Zhou kings, the Qin emperors held absolute responsibility for maintaining order and harmony. However, the First Emperor took the additional step of replacing the old system of governing based upon a land-based aristocracy with a new imperial government centered on his capital Xianyang (near present day Xi'an) and organized into a network of provinces and districts governed by non-hereditary officials. By way of these governors, the Qin enforced the laws, collected taxes, and drafted men to defend the newly annexed regions of their former rival states.

This large, salaried bureaucracy worked to centralize political power by various administrative devices. These included a census of China's population (the first of its kind in world history), the standardization of the written Chinese language, the creation of uniform coinage, as well as a system of weights and measures, and the division of China into provinces that exists more or less intact to this day. In a practical move worthy of the Romans, the First Emperor standardized the width of all axles manufactured for Chinese wagons, so that the wagons would fit the existing ruts in Chinese roads (thus speeding travel and trade). Royal promotion of the silk industry attracted long-distance merchants and brought increasing wealth to China, whom the Romans called the Seres ("Silk People"). While imperial policies fostered the private ownership of land by peasant farmers, the new system permitted the governors to tax those farmers, which they did mercilessly. Peasant protest was a constant threat to imperial power, but the most serious challenge to Qin safety came from the repeated invasions by the nomadic Central Asian tribes along China's northern borders. To discourage invasion, the Qin commissioned the construction (and in some stretches the reconstruction) of the 1500-mile-long Great Wall of China (Figure 7.1). This spectacular

Figure 7.1 The Great Wall, near Beijing, China, begun 214 B.C.E. Length approx. 1500 miles, height and width approx. 25 ft. This photo shows watchtowers placed strategically along the wall. Photo: Spectrum, London.

Figure 7.2 Terracotta army of soldiers, horses, and chariots, tomb of the First Emperor of the Qin dynasty, 221–206 B.C.E. Spectrum Picture Library, London.

engineering feat may be compared with the wall built by the Roman Emperor Hadrian: Hadrian's Wall, only 73 miles long, would be raised in the early second century C.E. in an effort to deter barbarian attacks on Roman Britain's northernmost border. Like Hadrian's Wall, the Great Wall of China could not stop an army on foot; rather, it discouraged mounted men, wagons, and the like from making raids across the borders.

The building of the Great Wall required the labor of some 700,000 people. An equal number of workers is said to have labored for eleven years on the Emperor's tomb. The entrance to that tomb, part of a twenty-one-square-mile burial site near the Qin capital, provides an immortal record of the Qin military machine. It contains almost 8000 life-sized **terracotta** soldiers, most of which are armed with actual swords, spears, and crossbows (Figure 7.2). Standing at strict attention, the huge army of footsoldiers and cavalry guards the tomb itself, which has not yet been opened. These figures may have served to replace the living sacrifices that went into the graves of the Shang kings (see chapter 3). The bodies of the ceramic warriors seem to have been mass-produced from molds, but the faces, no two of which are exactly alike, were individually carved and painted (Figure 7.3). In their lifelike intensity, these images resemble Roman portrait busts (see Figure 6.2). Yet the portraits of Rome were created for the appreciation

Science and Technology

350 B.C.E.   Shin Shen completes a catalog of some 800 stars

300 B.C.E.   cast iron is produced in China

250 B.C.E.   the crossbow is invented in China

214 B.C.E.   the First Emperor orders construction to begin on the Great Wall (which will not take its final form until the seventeenth century)

of the living, while those of Qin China were intended for the dead. Nevertheless, the subterranean legions of the First Emperor glorify an armed force that the Romans might have envied.

Legalist theory provided justification for the stringency of the law under the Qin, as well as for the civil and political oppressiveness of imperial authority. The Legalist First Emperor so feared public opposition and the free exercise of thought that he required all privately owned copies of the Confucian classics burned and all who opposed his government beheaded, along with their families. On the other hand, they were loyal students of the *The Art of War* (*Bing Fa*) of Sun Zi, the world's first treatise on military

strategy. This military classic, dating from the era of the Warring States, emphasized the tactical, as well as the strategic and psychological aspects of combat.

The Han Dynasty (206 B.C.E.–220 C.E.)

The Qin dynasty survived only fifteen years, but the succeeding Han empire would last more than four centuries. Just as the Roman Empire marked the culmination of classical civilization in the West, so the Han dynasty represented the high point and the classical phase of Chinese civilization. The intellectual and cultural achievements of the Han also made an indelible mark on the history of neighboring Korea, Vietnam, and Japan, whose cultures adopted Chinese methods of writing and the Confucian precepts of filial piety and propriety. The Chinese have long regarded the era of the Han as their classical age, and to this day refer to themselves as the "children of the Han." Han intellectual achievements ranged from the literary and artistic to the domains of **cartography**, medicine, mathematics, and astronomy. The invention of paper, block printing, the seismograph, the crossbow, the horse collar, and the wheelbarrow are but a few of the technological advances of the late Han era.

Han rulers tripled the size of the empire they inherited from the Qin. At its height, the Han empire was roughly equivalent to that of Rome in power and prestige, but

Figure 7.3 Two terracotta soldiers, tomb of the First Emperor of the Qin dynasty, 221–206 B.C.E. Height 6 ft. 3½ in. and 4 ft. Photo: Dagli Orti, Paris.

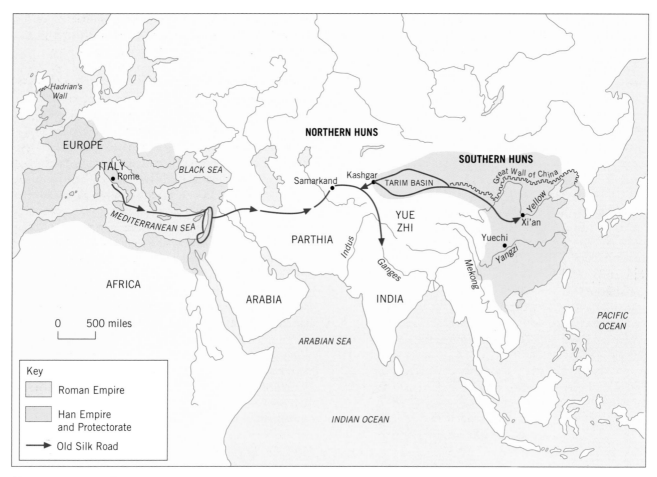

Map 7.1 Han and Roman Empires.

larger in actual population—a total of 57 million people, according to the census of 2 C.E. (Map **7.1**). Improvements in farming and advances in technology insured economic prosperity, which in turn stimulated vigorous long-distance trade. In exchange for Western linen, wool, glass, and metalware, the Chinese exported silk, ivory, gems, and spices. Trade proceeded by way of Asian intermediaries, who led camel caravans across the vast "Silk Road" that stretched from Asia Minor to the Pacific Ocean. In accordance with Confucian thought, China traditionally scorned its merchants (who were perceived as profiting from the labor of others) and regarded its farmers as honorable. Nevertheless, while Chinese merchants flourished, Chinese peasants failed to reap the benefits of Han prosperity. Conscripted for repeated wars, they fought the nomadic tribes along the bitter cold northern frontier. They also served in the armies that conquered western Korea and northern

Vietnam. Heavy taxes levied on Chinese farmers to support the Han machinery of state forced many to sell their lands. Wealthy landowners purchased these lands, on which (in a manner reminiscent of the late Roman republic) bankrupt farmers became tenants or unfree peasants. By the early third century, violent peasant revolts accompanied by "barbarian" incursions, led to the overthrow of the Han dynasty. Like the Roman empire, the great Han empire fell victim to internal and external pressures it could not withstand.

The Literary Contributions of Imperial China

Just as the Romans borrowed the best of the cultural achievements that preceded them, so Han rulers preserved the enduring works of their forebears. These they passed on to future generations as a body of classical learning and thought. Where the Qin rulers had preferred Legalist thought, the Han emperors restored Confucianism to its place at the heart of China's intellectual traditions, and with it came the restoration of Confucian texts and the Confucian scholar/official.

Chinese Prose Literature

As with the Greeks and the Romans, the Chinese placed high value on record keeping. Hence, the writing of

Science and Technology

150 B.C.E. iron wheels are designed for shaping jade and reeling silk

110 B.C.E. the Chinese devise the collar harness (for horses)

100 B.C.E. the Chinese invent the crank (for turning wheels)

1 B.C.E. cast iron is used in Chinese suspension bridges

history was one of China's greatest achievements. According to tradition, Chinese court historians kept chronicles of events as far back as one thousand years before the Han Era. Unfortunately, many of these chronicles were lost in the wars and notorious "book-burnings" of the Qin era. Beginning with the second century B.C.E., however, palace historians kept a continuous record of rulership. Ancient China's greatest historian Sima Qian (145–90 B.C.E.), the rival of both Thucydides and Livy, produced the monumental *Shi Ji* (*Records of the Grand Historian*), a narrative account of Chinese history from earliest times through the lifetime of the author. Sima Qian, himself the son of a palace historian–astronomer, served at the court of the Emperor Wudi, the vigorous ruler who brought Han China to the peak of its power. After Sima's death, China's first woman historian Ban Zhao (45–114 C.E.) continued his court chronicle. Ban also won fame for her handbook, *Lessons for Women*, which outlined the obligations and duties of the wife to her husband.

The following excerpt from Sima Qian's chapter on "Wealth and Commerce" offers a detailed description of the Han economy, as well as its social and moral life. Whereas economic activity follows the natural order, morals, observes the author, "come as the effects of wealth." In Sima's view, wealth and virtue are interdependent. A flourishing economy will encourage the people to be virtuous, while poverty leads inevitably to moral decay. Stylistically, Sima Qian's *Records* display the economy and vigor of expression that characterizes the finest Han prose.

READING 1.30 From Sima Qian's *Records of the Grand Historian* (ca. 100 B.C.E.)

I do not know about prehistoric times before Shennong,[1] but 1
since [Emperor Yu and the Xia dynasty, after the] twenty-
second century B.C.E. during the period discussed by the
historical records, human nature has always struggled for
good food, dress, amusements, and physical comfort, and has
always tended to be proud of wealth and ostentation. No
matter how the philosophers may teach otherwise, the people
cannot be changed. Therefore, the best of men leave it alone,
and next in order come those who try to guide it, then those
who moralize about it, and then those who try to make 10
adjustments to it, and lastly come those who get into the
scramble themselves. Briefly, Shanxi produces timber, grains,
linen, ox hair, and jades. Shandong produces fish, salt, lacquer,
silks, and musical instruments. Jiangnan [south of the Yangzi]
produces cedar, *zi* [a hard wood for making wood blocks],
ginger, cinnamon, gold and tin ores, cinnabar, rhinoceros horn,
tortoise shell, pearls, and hides. Longmen produces stone for
tablets. The north produces horses, cattle, sheep, furs, and
horns. As for copper and iron, they are often found in
mountains everywhere, spread out like pawns on a 20
chessboard. These are what the people of China like and what

provide the necessities for their living and for ceremonies for
the dead. The farmers produce them, the wholesalers bring
them from the country, the artisans work on them, and the
merchants trade on them. All this takes place without the
intervention of government or of the philosophers. Everybody
exerts his best and uses his labor to get what he wants.
Therefore prices seek their level, cheap goods going to where
they are expensive and higher prices are brought down. People
follow their respective professions and do it on their own 30
initiative. It is like flowing water which seeks the lower level
day and night without stop. All things are produced by the
people themselves without being asked and transported to
where they are wanted. Is it not true that these operations
happen naturally in accord with their own principles? *The
Book of Zhou*[2] says, "Without the farmers, food will not be
produced; without the artisans, industry will not develop;
without the merchants, the valuable goods will disappear; and
without the wholesalers, there will be no capital and the
natural resources of lakes and mountains will not be opened 40
up." Our food and our dress come from these four classes, and
wealth and poverty vary with the size of these sources. On a
larger scale, it benefits a country, and on a smaller scale, it
enriches a family. These are the inescapable laws of wealth
and poverty. The clever ones have enough and to spare, while
the stupid ones have not enough. . . .

Therefore, first the granaries must be full before the people
can talk of culture. The people must have sufficient food and
good dress before they can talk of honor. The good customs
and social amenities come from wealth and disappear when 50
the country is poor. Even as fish thrive in a deep lake and the
beasts gravitate toward a deep jungle, so the morals of
mankind come as effects of wealth. The rich acquire power
and influence, while the poor are unhappy and have no place
to turn to. This is even truer of the barbarians. Therefore it is
said: "A wealthy man's son does not die in the market place,"
and it is not an empty saying. It is said:

The world hustles
    Where money beckons.
The world jostles 60
    Where profit thickens.

Even kings and dukes and the wealthy gentry worry about
poverty. Why wonder that the common people and the slaves
do the same? . . .

[Here follows a long section on the economic products and
conditions and the people's character and way of living of the
different regions.]

Therefore you see the distinguished scholars who argue at
courts and temples about policies and talk about honesty and
self-sacrifice, and the mountain recluses who achieve a great 70
reputation. Where do they go? They seek after the rich. The
honest officials acquire wealth as time goes on, and the
honest merchants become wealthier and wealthier. For wealth
is something which man seeks instinctively without being

---

[1]A legendary cultural hero, inventor of agriculture and commerce, ca. 2737 B.C.E.

[2]The book of documents devoted to the Zhou dynasty (1111–221 B.C.E.)

taught. You see soldiers rush in front of battle and perform great exploits in a hail of arrows and rocks and against great dangers, because there is a great reward. You see young men steal and rob and commit violence and dig up tombs for treasures, and even risk the punishments by law, throwing all considerations of their own safety to the winds—all because of money. The courtesans of Zhao and Zheng dress up and play music and wear long sleeves and pointed dancing shoes. They flirt and wink, and do not mind being called to a great distance, irrespective of the age of the men—all are attracted by the rich. The sons of the rich dress up in caps and carry swords and go about with a fleet of carriages just to show off their wealth. The hunters and the fishermen go out at night, in snow and frost, roam in the wooded valleys haunted by wild beasts, because they want to catch game. Others gamble, have cock fights, and match dogs in order to win. Physicians and magicians practice their arts in expectation of compensation for their services. Bureaucrats play hide-and-seek with the law and even commit forgery and falsify seals at the risk of penal sentences because they have received bribes. And so all farmers, artisans, and merchants and cattle raisers try to reach the same goal. Everybody knows this, and one hardly ever hears of one who works and declines pay for it. . . .

80

90

Q What is Sima Qian's attitude toward wealth?

Q Based on this reading, how might one describe second-century B.C.E Chinese society?

Sima Qian's narrative describes the men and women of the Han era as practical and this-worldly, in fact, as remarkably similar to Romans. This sensibility, which unites a typically Chinese holism with sober realism, is also visible in the large body of Confucianist essays from the Han period. Of these, only one brief example may be cited, for its similarity to the rationalism of Seneca, Lucretius, and other Roman thinkers is striking. A *Discussion of Death* by Wang Chong (17–100 C.E.), offers a skeptical view of the supernaturalism that attracted the vast majority of Chinese people. Wang writes,

> Before a man is born he has no consciousness, so when he dies and returns to this original unconscious state how could he still have consciousness? The reason a man is intelligent and understanding is that he possesses the forces of the five virtues [humanity, righteousness, decorum, wisdom, and faith]. The reason he possesses these is that he has within him the five organs [heart, liver, stomach, lungs, and kidneys]. If these five organs are unimpaired, a man has understanding, but if they are diseased, then he becomes vague and confused and behaves like a fool or an idiot. When a man dies, the five organs rot away and the five virtues no longer have any place to reside. Both the seat and the faculty of understanding are destroyed. The body must await

the vital force [*qi*] before it is complete, and the vital force must await the body before it can have consciousness. Nowhere is there a fire that burns all by itself. How then could there be a spirit with consciousness existing without a body?*

Chinese Poetry

The writing of poetry has a long and rich history in China. While China's earliest poems drew on an ancient oral tradition (see chapter 3), the poems of the Han era originated as written works—a circumstance that may have been encouraged by the Chinese invention of paper. Chinese poetry is striking in its simplicity and its refinement. Humanism and common sense are fundamental to Han poetic expression, and Han verse seems to have played an indispensable part in everyday life. As with Greek and Roman lyrics, Chinese poetry took the form of hymns and ritual songs accompanied by the lute or other stringed instruments. Poems served as entertainments for various occasions, such as banquets, and as expressions of affection that were often exchanged as gifts. In contrast with the Greco-Roman world, however, the Chinese produced neither epics nor heroic poems. Their poetry does not so much glorify individual prowess or valorous achievement as it meditates on human experience. Han poetry, much of which takes the form of the "prose-poem," is personal and intimate rather than moralizing and eulogistic. Even in cases where the poem is the medium for social or political complaint, it is more a mirror of the poet's mood than a vehicle of instruction. Notable too (especially in contrast with Roman poetry) is the large number of female poets among the Chinese. The four poems that appear below (translated by Burton Watson) are drawn from the vast collection of Han poetry. They have been selected not only for their lyric beauty, but as expressions of some of the deepest concerns of Han poets, such as the practice of bestowing women upon neighboring tribes as "conciliatory" gifts and the conscription of laborers for public works projects. The perceptive reader should discover a number of interesting parallels, as well as contrasts, between these poems and those of the Greeks, Sappho and Pindar, and the Romans, Virgil, Horace, and Juvenal.

---

*Translated by Burton Watson in *Anthology of Chinese Literature*, edited by Cyril Birch (New York: Grove Press, Inc., 1965), pp. 89–90.

READING 1.31 A Selection of Han Poems

Song of Sorrow

My family has married me   1
  in this far corner of the world,
sent me to a strange land,
  to the king of the Wu-sun.
A yurt[1] is my chamber,   5
  felt is my walls,
flesh my only food,[2]
  kumiss[3] to drink.
My thoughts are all of my homeland,
  my heart aches within.   10
Oh to be the yellow crane
  winging home again!

Liu Xijun, ca. 107 B.C.E.

Song: I Watered My Horse at the Long Wall Caves

I watered my horse at the Long Wall caves,   1
water so cold it hurt his bones;
I went and spoke to the Long Wall boss:
"We're soldiers from Tai-yuan—will you keep us here
  forever?"
"Public works go according to schedule—   5
swing your hammer, pitch your voice in with the rest!"
A man'd be better off to die in battle
than eat his heart out building the Long Wall!
The Long Wall—how it winds and winds,
winds and winds three thousand li;[4]   10
here on the border, so many strong boys;
in the houses back home, so many widows and wives.
I sent a letter to my wife:
"Better remarry than wait any longer—
serve your new mother-in-law with care   15
and sometimes remember the husband you once had."
In answer her letter came to the border:
"What nonsense do you write me now?
Now when you're in the thick of danger,
how could I rest by another man's side?"   20
(HE) If you bear a son, don't bring him up!
  But a daughter—feed her good dried meat.
  Only *you* can't see, here by the Long Wall,
  the bones of the dead men heaped about!
(SHE) I bound up my hair and went to serve you;   25
  constant constant was the care of my heart.
  Too well I know your borderland troubles;
  and I—can I go on like this much longer?

Chen Lin (d. 217 C.E.)

Two Selections from "Nineteen Old Poems of the Han"

I turn the carriage, yoke and set off,   1
far, far, over the never-ending roads.
In the four directions, broad plain on plain;
east wind shakes the hundred grasses.
Among all I meet, nothing of the past;   5
what can save us from sudden old age?
Fullness and decay, each has its season;
success—I hate it, so late in coming!
Man is not made of metal or stone;
how can he hope to live for long?   10
Swiftly he follows in the wake of change.
A shining name—let that be the prize!

Anonymous, late second century C.E.

Man's years fall short of a hundred;   1
a thousand years of worry crowd his heart.
If the day is short and you hate the long night,
why not take the torch and go wandering?
Seek out happiness in season;   5
who can wait for the coming year?
Fools who cling too fondly to gold
earn no more than posterity's jeers.
Prince Qiao,[2] that immortal man—
small hope we have of matching him!   10

Anonymous, late second century C.E.

Q What human sentiments are expressed
  in each of these poems?

Q How do these poems compare with
  those of Sappho, Catullus, and Horace
  (Readings 1.19, 1.26, and 1.27)?

The Visual Arts and Music in Han China

Because the Chinese built primarily in the impermanent medium of wood, nothing remains of the palaces and temple structures erected during the Han era, and therefore no monumental architecture survives from China's classical period comparable to that of Rome. Yet some idea of Chinese architecture is provided by the polychromed, glazed earthenware models of the traditional multiroofed buildings—houses and watchtowers—that are found in Chinese tombs (Figure 7.4). Such engineering projects as the Great Wall testify to the high level of Qin and Han building skills. China's royal tombs were replicas of the imperial palace, which was laid out according to a cosmological model: the central building was symmetrical and bisected by a north–south axis. Its foundation was square, symbolizing the earth (*kun*), and its roof was round, symbolizing heaven (*tian*). In its geometric regularity, such designs share the Greco-Roman search for harmony and

---

[1]A circular tent of felt and skins on a framework of poles, the common habitation of the nomads of Mongolia.
[2]Meat was a staple of the Mongol diet.
[3]The fermented milk of a horse, mule, or donkey.
[4]A *li* equals approximately one-third of a mile.

---

[2]According to Chinese legend, a prince who became an immortal spirit.

Figure 7.4 Tomb model of a house, Eastern Han dynasty, first century C.E. Earthenware with unfired pigments, 52 × 33½ × 27 in. The Nelson-Atkins Museum of Art, Kansas City, Missouri. Purchase: Nelson Trust 33–521.

Science and Technology

140 C.E.   early Chinese compass devised with magnetic silver that always points north–south

190 C.E.   Chinese mathematicians use powers of 10 to express numbers

200 C.E.   the double yoke harness is invented in China

220 C.E.   Chinese make ink from lamp black for early block printing

270 C.E.   Chinese alchemists create gunpowder

302 C.E.   the stirrup is depicted for the first time in Chinese art

balanced proportion. However, classical design among the Chinese was less an effort to idealize nature than it was a means of representing the natural order.

During the Han era, the visual arts flourished. Like their forebears, the Han excelled in bronze casting: bronze chariots, horses (Figure **7.5**), weapons, mirrors, and jewelry are found in royal burial tombs. Han craftspeople also produced exquisite works in jade and gold, lacquered wood, and silk. But it is in the medium of terracotta—glazed for durability—that the Han left a record of daily life almost as detailed as that found in ancient Egyptian

tombs. Scenes of threshing, baking, juggling, music-making, game-playing, and other everyday activities appear routinely in three-dimensional polychromed ceramic models recovered from Han funerary chambers (Figure **7.6**). Han art does not consistently demonstrate the high degree of realism that is apparent in Greek and Roman representation. Yet the central place given to figural subject matter in art (as in literature) suggests a similar this-worldly bias. The carved, low reliefs on one Han stone tomb entrance depict an interesting combination of secular and spiritual subjects (Figure **7.7**). The top register of the lintel depicts a lively procession of chariots and horses; beneath are scenes of hunting, while on either side human guardians and winged spirits protect the chamber from evil. On the doors themselves appear fabulous creatures—elegant phoenixes and raging unicorns.

The technical and aesthetic achievement of the Han in the visual arts seems to have been matched in music. As early as the Shang era, bronze bells were buried in royal tombs (see Chapter 3), and the tradition of burying sets of bells continued for centuries. A set of sixty-five bells, seven large zithers, two panpipes, three transverse flutes, three drums, and other musical instruments accompanied the fifth-century B.C.E. Marquis Yi of Zeng to his grave (Figure **7.8**). The instruments (along with the bodies of eight young women and a dog) occupied a subterranean room that replicated the great hall of a palace. Each bell can produce two notes (depending on where the bell is struck) and the name of each note is inscribed in gold on the bell. A set of bells was thus able

Figure 7.5 Prancing horse, Eastern Han dynasty, second century C.E. Bronze. Cultural Relics Publishing House, Beijing

Figure 7.6 Musicians, Chinese, early sixth century C.E. Mold-pressed clay with traces of unfired pigments, each: height 11 in. Nelson-Atkins Museum of Art, Kansas City, Missouri. 32-186/1-7

to range over several octaves, each containing up to ten notes. Whether the bells were used in ceremonial, ritual, or secular events is unclear, but other evidence of other sorts, such as the small ceramic orchestra pictured in Figure 7.6 and the bronze buckle with dancers holding cymbals (Figure **7.9**) suggests the Han enjoyed a variety of musical entertainments.

SUMMARY

In a period approximately parallel to the Greco-Roman era, the civilization of China produced many of the definitive and enduring features of its 3,000-year-old culture. During the fifth century B.C.E., Confucius, China's leading thinker, articulated the fundamental rules of proper conduct. Under this influence, the Five Classics came to provide the basis for Chinese education and culture. Confucian thought confirmed ancient Chinese notions of proper behavior and proper rule, which held that the ruler, by his virtuous conduct, exercised the will of heaven on earth.

Two centuries after the death of Confucius, the short-lived and militant Qin dynasty created China's first unified empire. Qin emperors embraced the harsh principles of Legalism, rather than the humanistic teachings of

Figure 7.7 Reliefs of tomb entrance, Eastern Han dynasty, 25–220 C.E.

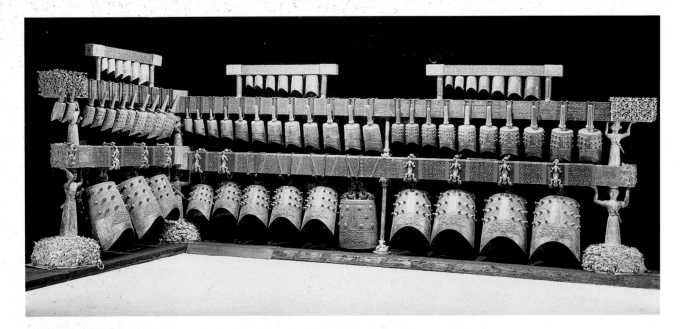

Figure 7.8 Bells from the tomb of the Marquis Yi of Zeng, Hubei province, fifth century B.C.E. Bronze, height of largest nearly 5 ft. Cultural Relics Publishing House, Beijing.

Figure 7.9 Buckle ornament with dancers, Western Han dynasty, 206–8 C.E. Gilt bronze, 4¾ × 7¼ in. Yunnan Provincial Museum, Kunming, China.

Confucius. Like the Romans, the Chinese expanded the empire by way of an aggressive military machine, a detailed record of which survives in the tombs of its emperors. Successors to the Qin, the Han rulers played a vital part in establishing classical Chinese culture. In the 400 years of Han rule, Chinese culture flourished: an educated bureaucracy revived the teachings of Confucius, while a healthy economy encouraged long-distance trade between East and West. As in the Greco-Roman world, the Han produced a body of literature and art that displays a this-worldly affection for nature and a passion for the good life. Han historians and poets assessed the secular world with critical insight and candor. The Han talent for technological invention challenged and even surpassed

that of Rome. Nevertheless, it was Han humanism that would come to hold the pivotal place in the classical legacy of East Asia.

GLOSSARY

cartography the art of making maps or charts

li (Chinese, "propriety", "ritual," or "arrangement") originally, the proper performance of ritual, but eventually also the natural

and moral order, thus, appropriate behavior in all aspects of life

terracotta (Italian, "baked earth") a clay medium that may be glazed or painted; also called "earthenware"

Book 2
Medieval Europe and the World Beyond

PART 1

The Shaping of the Middle Ages

Scholars once described the thousand-year period between the fall of Rome and the age of the European Renaissance as a "dark" age whose cultural achievements fell far short of those of ancient Greece and Rome. Our present understanding of the Middle Ages suggests otherwise. As the following chapters indicate, this was one of the most creative periods in the history of Western culture. During the Early Middle Ages—that is, the first seven centuries of the first millennium of the common era—a transition from classical to Christian culture took place in the West. Elsewhere in the world, the same period witnessed the vitalizing effects of two world religions: Buddhism and Islam. So powerful were these religious faiths—Christianity, Buddhism, and Islam—that by the year 1000, the Eastern hemisphere could be described as being divided among them (Map **8.1**). In fact, the Early Middle Ages was a time in which religious communities took hold: people began to identify with a religion, rather than with a region or state.

From the perspective of world history, the transition to the Middle Ages encompassed several significant developments: the decline of classical civilization and the rise of the Christian West, centered in the territories that would come to be called "Europe"; the diffusion of Germanic tribal peoples into the lands of the West Roman Empire; the golden age of Byzantine (or East Roman) civilization, which would outlive the West Roman Empire by a thousand years; the expansion of the teachings of the Buddha from India to China and East Asia; and, finally, the birth and expansion of Islam in Southwest Asia and beyond.

Christianity flowered in the fertile soil of three cultures: Greco-Roman, Hebraic, and West Asian—the area called by Westerners "the Near East." Centering on the teachings of the Hebrew prophet Jesus of Nazareth, the fledgling faith spread westward. In the West, the transition from classical to Christian culture was marked by new modes of expression: literary narrative and realistic forms of representation came to be replaced by religious allegory and symbolism. In the East, yet another significant world religion was on the rise. Buddhism, rooted in the Hinduism of ancient India, spread into China and Japan, its religious vocabulary at once absorbing the older traditions of East Asia and projecting a new, more personalized spiritual message.

Before the end of the seventh century, the youngest of the world religions, Islam, had spread from its birthplace in Arabia into the larger world. Islam, the religious faith practiced today by more than a billion people, would play a major role in the shaping of the Middle Ages, not only in terms of the cultural contributions of its artists and scholars but also as the commercial and cultural intermediary between East and West.

(opposite) Detail of *Empress Theodora and Retinue*, ca. 547. Mosaic. San Vitale, Ravenna. © Cameraphoto Arte, Venice..

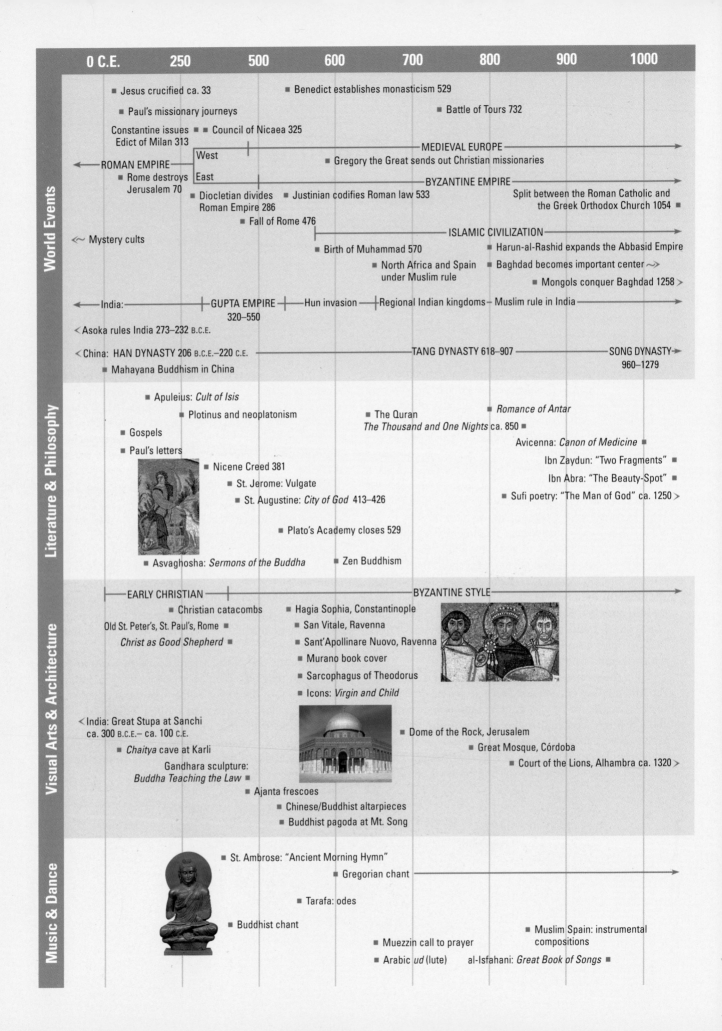

World Events

| 0 C.E. | 250 | 500 | 600 | 700 | 800 | 900 | 1000 |

- Jesus crucified ca. 33
- Paul's missionary journeys
- Benedict establishes monasticism 529
- Battle of Tours 732
- Constantine issues Edict of Milan 313
- Council of Nicaea 325

MEDIEVAL EUROPE

West
- Gregory the Great sends out Christian missionaries

← ROMAN EMPIRE
- Rome destroys Jerusalem 70

East

BYZANTINE EMPIRE

- Diocletian divides Roman Empire 286
- Justinian codifies Roman law 533
- Split between the Roman Catholic and the Greek Orthodox Church 1054
- Fall of Rome 476

~ Mystery cults

ISLAMIC CIVILIZATION

- Birth of Muhammad 570
- Harun-al-Rashid expands the Abbasid Empire
- North Africa and Spain under Muslim rule
- Baghdad becomes important center ~
- Mongols conquer Baghdad 1258 >

← India:
GUPTA EMPIRE 320–550
Hun invasion
Regional Indian kingdoms
Muslim rule in India

< Asoka rules India 273–232 B.C.E.

< China: HAN DYNASTY 206 B.C.E.–220 C.E.
TANG DYNASTY 618–907
SONG DYNASTY> 960–1279

- Mahayana Buddhism in China

Literature & Philosophy

- Apuleius: *Cult of Isis*
- Plotinus and neoplatonism
- The Quran
- *Romance of Antar*
- *The Thousand and One Nights* ca. 850
- Gospels
- Paul's letters
- Avicenna: *Canon of Medicine*
- Ibn Zaydun: "Two Fragments"
- Ibn Abra: "The Beauty-Spot"
- Nicene Creed 381
- St. Jerome: Vulgate
- St. Augustine: *City of God* 413–426
- Sufi poetry: "The Man of God" ca. 1250 >
- Plato's Academy closes 529
- Asvaghosha: *Sermons of the Buddha*
- Zen Buddhism

Visual Arts & Architecture

EARLY CHRISTIAN

BYZANTINE STYLE

- Christian catacombs
- Old St. Peter's, St. Paul's, Rome
- *Christ as Good Shepherd*
- Hagia Sophia, Constantinople
- San Vitale, Ravenna
- Sant'Apollinare Nuovo, Ravenna
- Murano book cover
- Sarcophagus of Theodorus
- Icons: *Virgin and Child*

< India: Great Stupa at Sanchi ca. 300 B.C.E.– ca. 100 C.E.
- *Chaitya* cave at Karli
- Gandhara sculpture: *Buddha Teaching the Law*
- Dome of the Rock, Jerusalem
- Great Mosque, Córdoba
- Court of the Lions, Alhambra ca. 1320 >
- Ajanta frescoes
- Chinese/Buddhist altarpieces
- Buddhist pagoda at Mt. Song

Music & Dance

- St. Ambrose: "Ancient Morning Hymn"
- Gregorian chant
- Tarafa: odes
- Buddhist chant
- Muslim Spain: instrumental compositions
- Muezzin call to prayer
- Arabic *ud* (lute)
- al-Isfahani: *Great Book of Songs*

CHAPTER 8

A Flowering of Faith: Christianity and Buddhism

*"Do not imagine that I have come to abolish the Law or the
Prophets. I have come not to abolish but to complete them."*
Gospel of Matthew

Shortly after the reign of the Roman Emperor Octavian, in the province of Judea (the Roman name for Palestine), an obscure Jewish preacher named Joshua (in Greek, *Jesus*) brought forth a message that became the basis for a new world religion: Christianity. Christianity came to provide an alternative to the secular, rational values associated with classical culture in the West. The pursuit of reason and earthly wisdom gave way to the promise of messianic deliverance and eternal life.

As Christianity began to win converts within the Roman Empire, a somewhat older set of religious teachings

was spreading in the East. The message of Siddhartha Gautama, the fifth-century-B.C.E.* founder of Buddhism, swept through Asia. By the third century B.C.E., Buddhism had become India's state religion, and by the fifth century C.E., it was the principal religious faith of China. The similarities and differences between Buddhism and Christianity

---

*B.C.E. designates dates "Before the Christian (or common) era," while dates from the "Christian (or common) era" are either designated by C.E. where necessary to distinguish them from B.C.E. dates or are left undesignated.

Map 8.1 Distribution of Major Religious Faiths, ca. 1000 C.E.

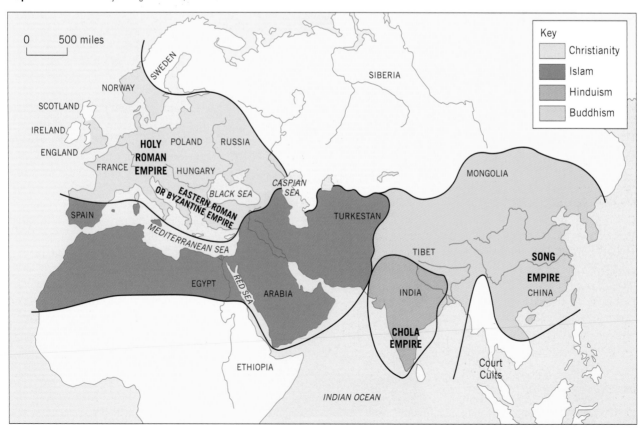

offer valuable insights into the spiritual communities of the East and West. While no in-depth analysis of either religion can be offered here, a brief look at the formative stages of these two world faiths provides some understanding of their significance within the humanistic tradition.

The Background to Christianity

Both as a religious faith and as a historical phenomenon, Christianity emerged out of three distinctly different cultural traditions: Greco-Roman, Near Eastern (West Asian), and Hebraic. All three of these cultures have been examined in the first seven chapters of this book; however, by focusing on the religious life of each at the turn of the first millennium—just prior to the birth of Jesus—we are better able to understand the factors that contributed to the evolution and the rise of the religion that would become the largest of the world's faiths.

The Greco-Roman Background

Roman religion, like Roman culture itself, was a blend of native and borrowed traditions. Ancient pagan religious rituals marked seasonal change and celebrated seedtime and harvest. Augury, the interpretation of omens (a practice borrowed from the Etruscans), was important to Roman religious life as a means of predicting future events. As with the Greeks, Rome's favorite deities were looked upon as protectors of the household, the marketplace, and the state: Vesta, for instance, guarded the hearth fire, and Mars, god of war, ministered to soldiers. The Romans welcomed the gods of non-Roman peoples and honored them along with the greater and lesser Roman gods. They embraced the Greek gods, who had assumed Latin names (see Table, chapter 4). Tolerance for non-Roman cults and creeds contributed to the lack of religious uniformity in the Empire, as well as to wide speculation concerning the possibility of life after death. Roman poets pictured a shadowy underworld in which the souls of the dead survived (similar to the Greek Hades and the Hebrew Sheol), but Roman religion promised neither retribution in the afterlife nor the reward of eternal life.

Rome hosted a wide variety of religious beliefs and practices, along with a number of quasi-religious Hellenistic philosophies (see chapter 6).

Figure 8.1 *Isis and Horus Enthroned,* Middle Egyptian, fourth century C.E. Limestone, height 35 in. Staatliche Museen, Berlin.

Of these, Stoicism and neoplatonism were the most influential. Stoicism's ethical view of life and its emphasis on equality among human beings offered an idealized alternative to a social order marked by wide gaps between rich and poor, and between citizens and slaves. Neoplatonism was a school of philosophy developed in Alexandria that took as its inspiration some of the principal ideas in the writings of Plato and his followers. It anticipated a mystical union between the individual soul and "the One" or Ultimate Being—comparable with Plato's Form of Goodness. According to Plotinus, a third-century Egyptian-born neoplatonist, union with the One could be achieved only by the soul's ascent through a series of levels or degrees of spiritual purification. Neoplatonism's view of the soul as eternal and divine, and its perception of the universe as layered in ascending degrees of perfection, would have a shaping influence on early Christian thought.

Following the decline of the Roman Republic and in the wake of repeated diplomatic contacts with the royal courts of Persia and Egypt (especially that of Cleopatra), Rome absorbed a number of uniquely Eastern traditions. Roman emperors came to be regarded as theocratic monarchs and assumed titles such as *dominus* ("lord") and *deus* ("god"). By the second century, Rome enjoyed a full-blown imperial cult that honored the living emperor as semidivine and deified him after his death. At the same time, widespread social, political, and economic unrest fed a rising distrust of reason and a growing impulse toward mysticism.

The Near Eastern Background

In Greece, Egypt, and throughout Southwest Asia, there had long flourished numerous religious cults whose appeal was less intellectual than that of neoplatonism and far more personal than that of the prevailing Greco-Roman religious philosophies. The promise of personal immortality was the central feature of the so-called "mystery cults" because their initiation rituals were secret (in Greek, *mysterios*). The cults of Isis in Egypt, Cybele in Phrygia, Dionysus in Greece, and Mithra in Persia, to name but four, had a heritage dating back to Neolithic times. As we have seen in earlier chapters, ancient agricultural societies celebrated seasonal change by means of symbolic performances of the birth, death, and rebirth of gods and goddesses associated with the regeneration of crops. The mystery cults perpetuated these practices. Their initiates participated in symbolic acts of spiritual death and rebirth, including ritual baptism and a communal meal at which they might consume the flesh or blood of the deity.

The cult of Isis originated in the Egyptian myth of the descent of the

Figure 8.2 Mithraic relief, early third century C.E. Bronze. Metropolitan Museum of Art. Gift of Mr. and Mrs. Klaus G. Perls, 1997. 145.3.

goddess Isis into the underworld to find and resurrect her mate Osiris (see chapter 1). Followers identified Isis as Earth Mother and Queen of Heaven and looked to her to ensure their own salvation (Figure **8.1**). Initiation into the cult included formal processions, a ritual meal, purification of the body, and a ten-day period of fasting that culminated in the ecstatic vision of the goddess herself. During the second century, in a Latin novel entitled *The Golden Ass,* or *Metamorphoses,* the Roman writer Lucius Apuleius described the initiation rites of the cult of Isis. At the close of the solemn rites, according to Apuleius, the initiate fell prostrate before the image of the Queen of Heaven and recited the prayer that is reproduced in part in the passage that follows. The ecstatic tone of this prayer—a startling departure from the measured, rational cast of most Greco-Roman literature—reflects the mood of religious longing that characterized the late classical era.

READING 2.1   From Apuleius' *Initiation into the Cult of Isis* (ca. 155)

"O holy and eternal savior of mankind, you who ever   1
bountifully nurture mortals, you apply the sweet affection of a
mother to the misfortunes of the wretched. Neither a day nor
a night nor even a tiny moment passes empty of your
blessings: you protect men on sea and land, and you drive
away the storm-winds of life and stretch forth your rescuing
hand, with which you unwind the threads of the Fates even
when they are inextricably twisted, you calm the storms of
Fortune, and you repress harmful motions of the stars. The
spirits above revere you, the spirits below pay you homage.   10
You rotate the earth, light the sun, rule the universe, and tread
Tartarus[1] beneath your heel. The stars obey you, the seasons
return at your will, deities rejoice in you, and the elements are
your slaves. At your nod breezes breathe, clouds give
nourishment, seeds sprout, and seedlings grow. Your majesty
awes the birds traveling the sky, the beasts wandering upon
the mountains, the snakes lurking in the ground, and the
monsters that swim in the deep. But my talent is too feeble to
speak your praises and my inheritance too meager to bring you
sacrifices. The fullness of my voice is inadequate to express   20

what I feel about your majesty; a thousand mouths and as
many tongues would not be enough, nor even an endless flow
of inexhaustible speech. I shall therefore take care to do the
only thing that a devout but poor man can: I shall store your
divine countenance and sacred godhead in the secret places of
my heart, forever guarding it and picturing it to myself. . . ."

Q What are the powers of Isis that are praised in this reading?

Q How does this compare to "The Hymn to the Aten" (Reading 1.3)?

While the worship of Isis, Dionysus, and Cybele was peculiar to the Mediterranean, Mithraism, the most popular of the mystery cults, originated in Persia. Mithraism looked back to one of the oldest religious philosophies of the ancient world, Zoroastrianism (see chapter 2). Over the centuries, the ancient hero-god Mithra, who had appeared as judge in the Zoroastrian Judgment ceremony, came to play a major part in this Persian belief system. Associated with the forces of Light and the Good, Mithra's slaughter of the Sacred Bull, one of many heroic "labors," was thought to render the earth fertile (Figure 8.2). By their personal attachment to Mithra, his devotees looked forward to spiritual well-being and everlasting life.

---

[1]In Greek mythology, a part of the underworld where the wicked are punished.

Mithraism featured strict initiation rites, periods of fasting, ritual baptism, and a communal meal of bread and wine. Mithra's followers celebrated his birth on December 25—that is, just after the sun's "rebirth" at the winter solstice. While Mithraism excluded the participation of women, it quickly became the favorite religion of Roman soldiers, who identified with Mithra's physical prowess and heroic self-discipline.

From Persia, Mithraism spread throughout Europe and North Africa, where archeologists have discovered the remains of numerous Mithraic chapels. Indeed, for the first two centuries of the common era, Mithraism was the chief rival of Christianity. The similarities between Mithraism and Christianity—a man-god hero, ritual baptism, a communal meal, and the promise of deliverance from evil—suggest that some of the basic features of Christianity already existed in the religious history of the Roman world prior to the time of Jesus. It is no surprise that many educated Romans considered Christianity to be an imitation of Mithraism.

Although the mystery cults often involved costly and demanding rituals, they were successful in attracting devotees. The Romans readily accommodated the exotic gods and goddesses of these cults as long as their worship did not challenge the authority of the Roman imperial cult or threaten the security of the Roman state.

The Jewish Background

Judaism, the oldest living religion in the Western world, differed from the other religions and religious cults of this period in its strongly ethical bias, its commitment to monotheism, and its exclusivity—that is, its emphasis on a special relationship (or covenant) between God and the Chosen People, the Jews themselves. As discussed in chapter 2, the early history of the Hebrews followed a dramatic narrative of wandering, settlement, and conquest at the hands of foreign powers. Following the sixty years of exile known as the Babylonian Captivity (586–539 B.C.E.), the Hebrews returned to Jerusalem, rebuilt the Temple of Solomon, and renewed their faith in the Torah. Under the influence of the scholar and teacher, Ezra (fl. 428 B.C.E.), the books of the Bible became ever more central in shaping the Hebrew identity. With the eastward expansion of Alexander the Great, the Jews were "hellenized," and by the second century B.C.E., a Greek translation of Hebrew Scriptures appeared. Called the *Septuagint* ("Seventy"), as it was reputed to have been translated by seventy or seventy-two scholars in a period of seventy-two days, this edition is the first known translation of a sacred book into another language.

The homeland of the Jews became the Roman province of Judea in 63 B.C.E., when the Roman general Pompey (106–48 B.C.E.) captured Jerusalem and the neighboring territories. Imperial taxes and loyalty to Rome were among the traditional demands of the conquerors, but Judaism, a monotheistic faith, forbade the worship of Rome's rulers and Rome's gods. Hence the Roman presence in Jerusalem caused mutual animosity and perpetual discord, conditions that would culminate in the Roman assault on the city and the destruction of the Second Temple in 70 C.E.* (see Figure 6.21). In 135, the Romans renamed Judea

---

*Hereafter, unless otherwise designated, all dates refer to the Christian (or common) era.

Figure 8.3 *The Good Shepherd*, ca. 425–450 C.E. Mosaic. Mausoleum of Galla Placidia, Ravenna, Italy. Giraudon/Bridgeman Art Library, London.

"Provincial Syria Palaestina," after the Philistines ("Sea People") who had settled there in the twelfth century B.C.E. Not until 1948, when the independent state of Israel came into being, did Judaism have a primary location in the world. During the first century B.C.E., however, unrest in Judea was complicated by disunity of opinion and biblical interpretation. Even as a special group of **rabbis** (Jewish teachers) met in 90 C.E. to draw up the authoritative list of thirty-six books that would constitute the canonic Hebrew Bible,** there was no agreement concerning the meaning of many Scriptural references. What, for instance, was the destiny of the Jew in the hereafter? What was the nature and the mission of the figure called by the Hebrew prophets the **Messiah** (the "Anointed One")? The Sadducees, a learned sect of Jewish aristocrats who advocated cultural and religious solidarity among the Jews, envisioned the Messiah as a temporal leader who would consolidate Jewish ideals and lead the Jews to political freedom. Defending a strict interpretation of the Torah, they denied that the soul survived the death of the body. The Pharisees, the more influential group of Jewish teachers and the principal interpreters of Hebrew law, believed in the advent of a messianic redeemer who, like a shepherd looking after his flock, would lead the righteous to salvation (Figure **8.3**). In their view, (one that recognized oral tradition along with Scripture), the human soul was imperishable and the wicked would suffer eternal punishment.

In addition to the Sadducees and the Pharisees, there existed in Judea a minor religious sect called the Essenes, whose members lived in monastic communities near the Dead Sea. The Essenes renounced worldly goods and practiced **asceticism**—strict self-denial and self-discipline. The Essenes believed in the immortality of the soul and its ultimate release and liberation from the body. They anticipated the coming of a teacher of truth who would appear at the end of time. The Dead Sea Scrolls—found in the 1840s in caves near Essene ruins at Qumran—include some of the oldest extant fragments of the Hebrew Bible along with scriptures that forecast a final apocalyptic age. In Judea, where all of these groups along with scores of self-proclaimed miracle workers and preachers competed for an audience, the climate of intense religious expectation was altogether receptive to the appearance of a charismatic leader.

The Message of Jesus

That charismatic leader proved to be a young Jewish rabbi from the city of Nazareth. Since Jesus of Nazareth (d. 33) is not mentioned in non-Christian literature until almost the end of the first century, the historical Jesus is an elusive figure. Our most important sources of information concerning Jesus are the Christian Gospels (literally,

"good news"). The oldest, dating from at least forty years after Jesus' death, provides the earliest biographical evidence of the life of Jesus. Yet, since the authors of the Gospels—the evangelists Matthew, Mark, Luke, and John—gave most of their attention to the last months of Jesus' life, these biblical books are not biographies in the true sense of the word. Perhaps because Jesus' followers anticipated his imminent return, they made no effort to keep a careful historical record of their master's life.

Recorded in Greek, the Gospels describe the life and miracles of an eloquent and inspiring teacher. Like all great teachers, Jesus was concerned with ethical matters. His message, cast in simple and direct language and in parables that carried moral lessons, was essentially pacifistic and antimaterialistic. He warned of the perils of riches and the temptations of the temporal world. Jesus' insistence upon the evils of material wealth represented a radically new direction in ancient culture. Despite such exceptions as the Essenes, the neoplatonists, and the Stoics, the classical world was fundamentally materialistic and secular. Jesus preached the renunciation of material goods ("do not lay up for yourselves treasures on earth") not merely as a means of freeing the soul from temporal enslavement, but as a preparation for eternal life.

With a reformer's zeal, Jesus criticized the Judaism of his day, especially its emphasis on strict observance of ritual. He embraced the spirit (rather than the letter) of Hebrew law and proclaimed the primacy of faith over ritual. Asked which of the laws were primary, Jesus cited love of God and love of one's neighbor (Matthew 22:34–40). He pictured God as stern but merciful, loving and protective, rather than chastising (recall Job's Yahweh; see chapter 2) or remote and inaccessible (as with the deities of the mystery cults). Finally, and most importantly, Jesus preached the cultivation of compassion, righteousness, and trust in God, the rewards for which would be reaped in the "kingdom of heaven." For all its simplicity and directness, however, the message of Jesus prescribed an almost impossibly altruistic ideal—an ideal of unconditional love linked to an equally lofty imperative: "You must . . . be perfect, just as your heavenly Father is perfect" (Matthew 5:48). The Sermon on the Mount, as recorded by the apostle Matthew, is probably the most representative of Jesus' sermons. Here Jesus sets forth the basic injunctions of an uncompromising ethic to which moral intention is more important than outward behavior: love your neighbor; accept persecution with humility; pass no judgment on others; and treat others as you would have them treat you.

READING 2.2 From the Gospel of Matthew (ca. 80–90)

Sermon on the Mount

Chapter 5: The Beatitudes

¹Seeing the crowds, he went onto the mountain. And when he was seated his disciples came to him. ²Then he began to speak. This is what he taught them:

**Following ancient Hebrew tradition, these were grouped into three divisions: the Law (the first five books of instruction, called the *Torah*), the Prophets, and the Writings—that is, wisdom literature (see chapter 2).

³How blessed are the poor in spirit:
the kingdom of Heaven is theirs.

⁴Blessed are *the gentle*:
they shall have the earth as inheritance.

⁵Blessed are those who mourn:
they shall be comforted.

⁶Blessed are those who hunger and thirst for uprightness:
they shall have their fill.

⁷Blessed are the merciful:
they shall have mercy shown them.

⁸Blessed are the pure in heart:
they shall see God.

⁹Blessed are the peacemakers:
they shall be recognised as children of God.

¹⁰Blessed are those who are persecuted in the cause of uprightness:
the kingdom of Heaven is theirs.

¹¹"Blessed are you when people abuse you and persecute you and speak all kinds of calumny against you falsely on my account. ¹²Rejoice and be glad, for your reward will be great in heaven; this is how they persecuted the prophets before you.

Salt for the earth and light for the world

¹³"You are salt for the earth. But if salt loses its taste, what can make it salty again? It is good for nothing, and can only be thrown out to be trampled under people's feet.

¹⁴"You are light for the world. A city built on a hill-top cannot be hidden. ¹⁵No one lights a lamp to put it under a tub; they put it on the lamp-stand where it shines for everyone in the house. ¹⁶In the same way your light must shine in people's sight, so that, seeing your good works, they may give praise to your Father in heaven.

The fulfilment of the Law

¹⁷"Do not imagine that I have come to abolish the Law or the Prophets. I have come not to abolish but to complete them. ¹⁸In truth I tell you, till heaven and earth disappear, not one dot, not one little stroke, is to disappear from the Law until all its purpose is achieved. ¹⁹Therefore, anyone who infringes even one of the least of these commandments and teaches others to do the same will be considered the least in the kingdom of Heaven; but the person who keeps them and teaches them will be considered great in the kingdom of Heaven.

The new standard higher than the old

²⁰"For I tell you, if your uprightness does not surpass that of the scribes and Pharisees, you will never get into the kingdom of Heaven.

²¹"You have heard how it was said to our ancestors, *You shall not kill*; and if anyone does kill he must answer for it before the court. ²²But I say this to you, anyone who is angry with a brother will answer for it before the court; anyone who calls a brother 'Fool' will answer for it before the Sanhedrin; and anyone who calls him 'Traitor' will answer for it in hell fire. ²³So then, if you are bringing your offering to the altar and there remember that your brother has something against you, ²⁴leave your offering there before the altar, go and be

reconciled with your brother first, and then come back and present your offering. ²⁵Come to terms with your opponent in good time while you are still on the way to the court with him, or he may hand you over to the judge and the judge to the officer, and you will be thrown into prison. ²⁶In truth I tell you, you will not get out till you have paid the last penny.

²⁷"You have heard how it was said, *You shall not commit adultery*. ²⁸But I say this to you, if a man looks at a woman lustfully, he has already committed adultery with her in his heart. ²⁹If your right eye should be your downfall, tear it out and throw it away; for it will do you less harm to lose one part of yourself than to have your whole body thrown into hell. ³⁰And if your right hand should be your downfall, cut it off and throw it away; for it will do you less harm to lose one part of yourself than to have your whole body go to hell.

³¹"It has also been said, *Anyone who divorces his wife must give her a writ of dismissal*. ³²But I say this to you, everyone who divorces his wife, except for the case of an illicit marriage, makes her an adulteress; and anyone who marries a divorced woman commits adultery.

³³"Again, you have heard how it was said to our ancestors, *You must not break your oath, but must fulfil your oaths to the Lord*. ³⁴But I say this to you, do not swear at all, either by *heaven*, since that is *God's throne*; ³⁵or by *earth*, since that is *his footstool*; or by Jerusalem, since that is *the city of the great King*. ³⁶Do not swear by your own head either, since you cannot turn a single hair white or black. ³⁷All you need say is 'Yes' if you mean yes, 'No' if you mean no; anything more than this comes from the Evil One.

³⁸"You have heard how it was said: *Eye for eye and tooth for tooth*. ³⁹But I say this to you: offer no resistance to the wicked. On the contrary, if anyone hits you on the right cheek, offer him the other as well; ⁴⁰if someone wishes to go to law with you to get your tunic, let him have your cloak as well. ⁴¹And if anyone requires you to go one mile, go two miles with

The New Testament

Gospels		
	Matthew	Luke
	Mark	John
Acts of the Apostles		
Letters of Paul		
	Romans	I Thessalonians
	I Corinthians	II Thessalonians
	II Corinthians	I Timothy
	Galatians	II Timothy
	Ephesians	Titus
	Philippians	Philemon
	Colossians	Hebrews
Letters of		
	James	II John
	I Peter	III John
	II Peter	Jude
	I John	
The Book of Revelations		
	(The Apocalypse)	

him. [42]Give to anyone who asks you, and if anyone wants to borrow, do not turn away.

[43]"You have heard how it was said, *You will love your neighbor* and hate your enemy. [44]But I say this to you, love your enemies and pray for those who persecute you; [45]so that you may be children of your Father in heaven, for he causes his sun to rise on the bad as well as the good, and sends down rain to fall on the upright and the wicked alike. [46]For if you love those who love you, what reward will you get? Do not even the tax collectors do as much? [47]And if you save your greetings for your brothers, are you doing anything exceptional? [48]Do not even the gentiles do as much? You must therefore be perfect, just as your heavenly Father is perfect."

Chapter 6: Almsgiving in secret

[1]"Be careful not to parade your uprightness in public to attract attention; otherwise you will lose all reward from your Father in heaven. [2]So when you give alms, do not have it trumpeted before you; this is what the hypocrites do in the synagogues and in the streets to win human admiration. In truth I tell you, they have had their reward. [3]But when you give alms, your left hand must not know what your right is doing; [4]your almsgiving must be secret, and your Father who sees all that is done in secret will reward you.

Prayer in secret

[5]"And when you pray, do not imitate the hypocrites; they love to say their prayers standing up in the synagogues and at the street corners for people to see them. In truth I tell you, they have had their reward. [6]But when you pray, *go to your private room*, shut yourself in, and so pray to your Father who is in that secret place, and your Father who sees all that is done in secret will reward you.

How to pray. The Lord's Prayer

[7]"In your prayers do not babble as the gentiles do, for they think that by using many words they will make themselves heard. [8]Do not be like them; your Father knows what you need before you ask him. [9]So you should pray like this:

Our Father in heaven,
may your name be held holy,
[10]your kingdom come,
your will be done,
on earth as in heaven.
[11]Give us today our daily bread.
[12]And forgive us our debts,
as we have forgiven those who are in debt to us.
[13]And do not put us to the test,
but save us from the Evil One.

[14]"Yes, if you forgive others their failings, your heavenly Father will forgive you yours; [15]but if you do not forgive others, your Father will not forgive your failings either.

Fasting in secret

[16]"When you are fasting, do not put on a gloomy look as the hypocrites do: they go about looking unsightly to let people know they are fasting. In truth I tell you, they have had their reward. [17]But when you fast, put scent on your head and wash your face, [18]so that no one will know you are fasting except your Father who sees all that is done in secret; and your Father who sees all that is done in secret will reward you.

True treasures

[19]"Do not store up treasures for yourselves on earth, where moth and woodworm destroy them and thieves can break in and steal. [20]But store up treasures for yourselves in heaven, where neither moth nor woodworm destroys them and thieves cannot break in and steal. [21]For wherever your treasure is, there will your heart be too."

Chapter 7: Do not judge

[1]"Do not judge, and you will not be judged; [2]because the judgements you give are the judgements you will get, and the standard you use will be the standard used for you. [3]Why do you observe the splinter in your brother's eye and never notice the great log in your own? [4]And how dare you say to your brother, 'Let me take that splinter out of your eye,' when, look, there is a great log in your own? [5]Hypocrite! Take the log out of your own eye first, and then you will see clearly enough to take the splinter out of your brother's eye.

Do not profane sacred things

[6]"Do not give dogs what is holy; and do not throw your pearls in front of pigs, or they may trample them and then turn on you and tear you to pieces.

Effective prayer

[7]"Ask, and it will be given to you; search, and you will find; knock, and the door will be opened to you. [8]Everyone who asks receives; everyone who searches finds; everyone who knocks will have the door opened. [9]Is there anyone among you who would hand his son a stone when he asked for bread? [10]Or would hand him a snake when he asked for a fish? [11]If you, then, evil as you are, know how to give your children what is good, how much more will your Father in heaven give good things to those who ask him!

The golden rule

[12]"So always treat others as you would like them to treat you; that is the Law and the Prophets.

The two ways

[13]"Enter by the narrow gate, since the road that leads to destruction is wide and spacious, and many take it; [14]but it is a narrow gate and a hard road that leads to life, and only a few find it."

Q What moral injunctions form the core of this sermon, as recounted by Matthew?

Q Which might be the most difficult to fulfill?

The Teachings of Paul

Jesus' urgent and prophetic words, along with the stories of his miraculous acts, spread like wildfire throughout Judea; but his message won few converts from among the Jewish population. Both the Pharisees and the Sadducees opposed Jesus and accused him of violating Jewish law. While the learned community of Judea rejected Jesus as the biblical Messiah, the Romans condemned him as a subversive and a threat to imperial stability. By the authority of the Roman governor, Pontius Pilate, Jesus was put to death by crucifixion (Figure **8.4**), the punishment that the Romans dispensed to thieves and traitors.

Despite the missionary activities of the apostles, the disciples of Jesus, only a small percentage of the population of the Roman Empire—scholarly estimates range from ten to fifteen percent—became Christians in the first hundred years after Jesus' death. And those who did convert came mainly from communities where Jewish tradition was not strong. However, through the efforts of the best-known of the apostles, Paul (d. 65), the message of Jesus gained widespread appeal. A Jewish tentmaker from Tarsus in Asia Minor, Paul had been schooled in both Greek and Hebrew. Following a mystical experience in which Jesus is said to have revealed himself to Paul, he became a passionate convert to the teachings of the preacher from Nazareth. Paul is generally believed to have written ten to fourteen of the twenty-seven books of the Christian Scriptures called by Christians the "New Testament," to distinguish it from the Hebrew Bible, which they referred to as the "Old Testament." Paul's most important contributions lie in his having universalized and systematically explained Jesus' message. While Jesus preached only to the Jews, Paul spread the message of Jesus in the non-Jewish communities of Greece, Asia Minor, and Rome, thus earning the title "Apostle to the Gentiles." Preaching among non-Jews, Paul stressed that the words of Jesus were directed not exclusively to Jews, but to non-Jews ("gentiles") as well. Identifying Jesus as the *Christos* (Greek for "Messiah"), Paul explained the meaning of Jesus's life on earth and the purpose of his death. He described Jesus as a living sacrifice who died for the sins of humankind, and specifically, for the sin that had entered the world through Adam and Eve's defiance of God in the Garden of Eden. For Paul, the death of Jesus was the act of atonement that "acquitted" humankind from the condemnation merited by original sin. Where Adam's sin had condemned humankind, Jesus—the New Adam—would redeem humankind. Finally, and perhaps most important, Paul emphasized that faith itself guaranteed eternal salvation among the followers of Christ.

These concepts, which indelibly separated Christianity from both its parent faith, Judaism, and from the classical belief in the innate goodness and freedom of human nature, are set forth in Paul's Epistle to the Church in Rome, parts of which follow. Written ten years before his death, the epistle imparts a message of faith laden with a view of humankind as condemned by "the law of sin and death." Paul anticipates, however, that those who are "baptized in Christ" will "live a new life." The view of Jesus as a sacrifice for human sin accommodated ancient religious practices in which guilt for communal (or individual) transgressions was ritually displaced onto a living sacrifice. It also embraced basic aspects of the mystery cults, such as the promise of eternal life as reward for devotion to a savior deity. However, Paul's focus on moral renewal and redemption from sin would set Christianity apart from the mystery religions. So important was Paul's contribution to the foundations of the new faith that he has been called "the co-founder of Christianity."

Figure 8.4 *Crucifixion*, west doors of Santa Sabina, Rome, ca. 430 C.E. Wood, 11 × 15¾ in. © 1990, Photo Scala, Florence - courtesy of the Ministero Beni e Att. Culturali.

READING 2.3 From Paul's Epistle to the Church in Rome (ca. 57)

Chapter 1: Thanksgiving and prayer

[8]First I give thanks to my God through Jesus Christ for all of you because your faith is talked of all over the world. [9]God, whom I serve with my spirit in preaching the gospel of his Son, is my witness that I continually mention you in my prayers, [10]asking always that by some means I may at long last be enabled to visit you, if it is God's will. [11]For I am longing to see you so that I can convey to you some spiritual gift that will be a lasting strength, [12]or rather that we may be strengthened together through our mutual faith, yours and mine. [13]I want you to be quite certain too, brothers, that I have often planned to visit you—though up to the present I have always been prevented—in the hope that I might work as fruitfully among you as I have among the gentiles elsewhere. [14]I have an obligation to Greeks as well as barbarians, to the educated as well as the ignorant, [15]and hence the eagerness on my part to preach the gospel to you in Rome too.

Chapter 2: The Jews are not exempt from the retribution of God

[1]So no matter who you are, if you pass judgement you have no excuse. It is yourself that you condemn when you judge others, since you behave in the same way as those you are condemning. [2]We are well aware that people who behave like that are justly condemned by God. [3]But you—when you judge those who behave like this while you are doing the same yourself—do you think you will escape God's condemnation? [4]Or are you not disregarding his abundant goodness, tolerance and patience, failing to realise that this generosity of God is meant to bring you to repentance? [5]Your stubborn refusal to repent is only storing up retribution for yourself on that Day of retribution when God's just verdicts will be made known. [6]*He will repay everyone as their deeds deserve.* [7]For those who aimed for glory and honour and immortality by persevering in doing good, there will be eternal life; [8]but for those who out of jealousy have taken for their guide not truth but injustice, there will be the fury of retribution. [9]Trouble and distress will come to every human being who does evil—Jews first, but Greeks as well; [10]glory and honour and peace will come to everyone who does good—Jews first, but Greeks as well. [11]*There is no favouritism with God.*

Chapter 5: Faith guarantees salvation

[1]So then, now that we have been justified by faith, we are at peace with God through our Lord Jesus Christ; [2]it is through him, by faith, that we have been admitted into God's favour in which we are living, and look forward exultantly to God's glory. [3]Not only that; let us exult, too, in our hardships, understanding that hardship develops perseverance, [4]and perseverance develops a tested character, something that gives us hope, [5]and a hope which will not let us down, because the love of God has been poured into our hearts by the Holy Spirit which has been given to us. [6]When we were still helpless, at the appointed time, Christ died for the godless. [7]You could hardly find anyone ready to die even for someone upright; though it is just possible that, for a really good person, someone might undertake to die. [8]So it is proof of God's own love for us, that Christ died for us while we were still sinners. [9]How much more can we be sure, therefore, that, now that we have been justified by his death, we shall be saved through him from the retribution of God. [10]For if, while we were enemies, we were reconciled to God through the death of his Son, how much more can we be sure that, being now reconciled, we shall be saved by his life. [11]What is more, we are filled with exultant trust in God, through our Lord Jesus Christ, through whom we have already gained our reconciliation.

Adam and Jesus Christ

[12]Well then; it was through one man that sin *came into the world*, and through sin death, and thus death has spread through the whole human race because everyone has sinned. [13]Sin already existed in the world before there was any law, even though sin is not reckoned when there is no law. [14]Nonetheless death reigned over all from Adam to Moses, even over those whose sin was not the breaking of a commandment, as Adam's was. He prefigured the One who was to come. . . . [15]There is no comparison between the free gift and the offense. If death came to many through the offense of one man, how much greater an effect the grace of God has had, coming to so many and so plentifully as the free gift through the one man Jesus Christ! [16]Again, there is no comparison between the gift and the offense of one man. One single offense brought condemnation, but now, after many offenses, have come the free gift and so acquittal! [17]It was by one man's offense that death came to reign over all, but how much greater the reign in life of those who receive the fullness of grace and the gift of saving justice, through the one man, Jesus Christ. [18]One man's offense brought condemnation on all humanity; and one man's good act has brought justification and life to all humanity. [19]Just as by one man's disobedience many were made sinners, so by one man's obedience are many to be made upright. [20]When law came on the scene, it was to multiply the offenses. But however much sin increased, grace was always greater; [21]so that as sin's reign brought death, so grace was to rule through saving justice that leads to eternal life through Jesus Christ our Lord.

Chapter 6: Baptism

[1]What should we say then? Should we remain in sin so that grace may be given the more fully? [2]Out of the question! We have died to sin; how could we go on living in it? [3]You cannot have forgotten that all of us, when we were baptised into Christ Jesus, were baptised into his death. [4]So by our baptism into his death we were buried with him, so that as Christ was raised from the dead by the Father's glorious power, we too should begin living a new life. [5]If we have been joined to him by dying a death like his, so we shall be by a resurrection like his; [6]realising that our former self was crucified with him, so that the self which belonged to sin should be destroyed and we should be freed from the slavery of sin. [7]Someone who has died, of course, no longer has to answer for sin.

[8]But we believe that, if we died with Christ, then we shall live with him too. [9]We know that Christ has been raised from the dead and will never die again. Death has no power over

him any more. ¹⁰For by dying, he is dead to sin once and for all, and now the life that he lives is life with God. ¹¹In the same way, you must see yourselves as being dead to sin but alive for God in Christ Jesus.

Chapter 8: The life of the spirit

¹Thus, condemnation will never come to those who are in Christ Jesus, ²because the law of the Spirit which gives life in Christ Jesus has set you free from the law of sin and death. ³What the Law could not do because of the weakness of human nature, God did, sending his own Son in the same human nature as any sinner to be a sacrifice for sin, and condemning sin in that human nature. ⁴This was so that the Law's requirements might be fully satisfied in us as we direct our lives not by our natural inclinations but by the Spirit. ⁵Those who are living by their natural inclinations have their minds on the things human nature desires; those who live in the Spirit have their minds on spiritual things. ⁶And human nature has nothing to look forward to but death, while the Spirit looks forward to life and peace, ⁷because the outlook of disordered human nature is opposed to God, since it does not submit to God's Law, and indeed it cannot, ⁸and those who live by their natural inclinations can never be pleasing to God. . . .

Q How does Paul explain the death of Jesus?

Q What is his position on sin and salvation?

The Spread of Christianity

A variety of historical factors contributed to the slow but growing receptivity to Christianity within the Roman Empire. The decline of the Roman Republic had left in its wake large gaps between the rich and the poor. Octavian's efforts to restore the old Roman values of duty and civic pride had failed to offset increasing impersonalism and bureaucratic corruption. Furthermore, as early as the second century B.C.E., Germanic tribes had been migrating into the West and assaulting Rome's borders (see chapter 11). Repeatedly, these nomadic people put Rome on the defensive and added to the prevailing sense of insecurity. Amid widespread oppression and grinding poverty, Christianity promised redemption from sins, personal immortality, and a life to come from which material adversities were absent. The message of Jesus was easy to understand, free of cumbersome regulations (characteristic of Judaism) and costly rituals (characteristic of the mystery cults), and, in contrast to Mithraism, it was accessible to all—male and female, rich and poor, free and enslaved. The unique feature of the new faith, however, was its historical credibility, that is, the fact that Jesus—unlike the elusive gods of the mystery cults or the remote Yahweh—had actually lived among men and women and had practiced the morality he preached.

Nevertheless, at the outset the new religion failed to win official approval. While both Roman religion and the mystery cults were receptive to many gods, Christianity—like Judaism—professed monotheism. Christians not only refused to worship the emperor as divine but also denied the existence of the Roman gods. Even more threatening to the state was the Christian refusal to serve in the Roman army. While the Romans dealt with the Jews by destroying Jerusalem, how might they annihilate a people whose kingdom was in heaven? During the first century, Christian converts were simply expelled from the city of Rome, but during the late third century—a time of famine, plague, and war—Christians who refused to make sacrifices to the Roman gods of state suffered horrific forms of persecution: they were tortured, burned, beheaded, or thrown to wild beasts in the public amphitheaters. Christian martyrs astonished Roman audiences by going to their deaths joyously proclaiming their anticipation of a better life in the hereafter.

Not until 313 C.E., when the emperor Constantine issued the Edict of Milan, did the public persecution of Christians come to an end. The Edict, which proclaimed religious toleration in the West, not only liberated Christians from physical and political oppression, but encouraged the development of Christianity as a legitimate faith. Christian leaders were free to establish a uniform doctrine of belief, an administrative hierarchy, the guidelines for worship, and a symbolic vocabulary for religious expression (see chapter 9). By the end of the fourth century, the minor religious sect called Christianity had become the official religion of the Roman Empire.

The Message of the Buddha

The reasons why similar world-historical developments occur at approximately the same time within two remotely related cultures is a mystery that historians have never solved. One of the most interesting such parallels is that between the spread of Buddhism in the East and the emergence of Christianity in the West, both of which occurred during the first century of the Christian era. Siddhartha Gautama, known as the Buddha ("Enlightened One"), lived in India some three to five centuries before Jesus—scholars still disagree as to whether his life spanned the years 560–480 or 440–360 B.C.E. Born into a princely Hindu family, Siddhartha was well-educated and protected from the experience of pain and suffering. At the age of nineteen, he married his cousin and fathered a son. As he matured, however, he began to realize that the lives of most people were far from pleasant. His discovery of the three "truths" of existence—sickness, old age, and death—led the twenty-nine-year-old Siddhartha to renounce his wealth, abandon his wife and child, and begin the quest for inner illumination. With shaven head, yellow robe, and begging bowl, he followed the way of the Hindu ascetic. After six years, however, he concluded that the life of self-denial was futile. Turning inward, Siddhartha sat beneath a bo (fig) tree (Figure **8.5**) and began the work of meditation

Figure 8.5 *Seated Buddha*, from the Gandharan region of northwest Pakistan, ca. 200 C.E. Gray schist, 4 ft. 3 in. × 31 in. The Cleveland Museum of Art. Leonard Hanna, Jr. Bequest. CMA 61.418.

that would bring him to enlightenment—the omniscient consciousness of reality. Meditation would lead Siddhartha to the full perception that the cause of human sufferings was desire, that is, attachment to material things and ignorance and, hence, illusion. For the next forty years—he died at the age of eighty—Siddhartha preached a message of humility and compassion, the pursuit of which might lead his followers to *nirvana*, the ultimate release from illusion and from the Wheel of Rebirth.

With his earliest sermons, the Buddha set in motion the Wheel of the Law (*dharma*). His message was simple. The path to enlightenment (*nirvana*) begins with the Four Noble Truths:

1. pain is universal
2. desire causes pain
3. ceasing to desire relieves pain
4. right conduct leads to release from pain.

Right conduct takes the form of the Middle Way, or Eightfold Path: right views, right intention, right speech, right action, right livelihood, right effort, right mindfulness, and right concentration. The practice of the Eightfold Path leads to insight and knowledge, and, ultimately, to *nirvana*. The Buddhist's goal is not, as with Christianity, the promise of personal immortality, but rather escape from the endless cycle of birth, death, and rebirth. For the Buddhist, "salvation" lies in the extinction of the Self.

Like Jesus, the Buddha was an eloquent teacher whose concerns were profoundly ethical. Just as Jesus criticized Judaism's heavy emphasis on ritual, so Siddhartha attacked the existing forms of Hindu worship, including animal sacrifice and the authority of the Vedas. He encouraged the annihilation of worldly desires and the renunciation of material wealth, in full accordance with Hinduism. But in contrast to the caste-oriented Hinduism of his time, the Buddha held that enlightenment could be achieved by all people, regardless of caste. Opposing the existing forms of religious worship, and renouncing reliance on the popular gods of the Vedas (see chapter 3), the Buddha urged his followers to work out their own salvation. Clearly, Jesus and Siddhartha were reformers of older world faiths: Judaism and Hinduism. Soon after his enlightenment, Siddhartha assembled a group of disciples, five of whom founded the first Buddhist monastic order. As with Jesus, Siddhartha's life came to be surrounded by

miraculous tales, which, along with his sermons, were preserved and recorded by his followers. For instance, legend has it that Siddhartha was born miraculously from the right side of his mother, Queen Maya, and at that very moment the tree she touched in the royal garden burst into bloom.

The Buddha himself wrote nothing, but his disciples memorized his teachings and set them down during the first century B.C.E. in three main books, the *Pitakas* or "Baskets of the Law." These works, written in Pali and Sanskrit, were divided into instructional chapters known as **sutras** (Sanskrit for "thread"). The most famous of the Buddha's sermons is one that he preached to his disciples at the Deer Park in Benares (modern Varanasi in Northeast India). The Sermon at Benares, part of which is reproduced here, urges the abandonment of behavioral extremes and the pursuit of the Eightfold Path of right conduct. In its emphasis on faith over good works and on the renunciation of worldly pleasures, it has much in common with Jesus' Sermon on the Mount. Comparable also to Jesus' teachings (see Matthew 5:11, for instance) is the Buddha's regard for loving kindness that "commends the return of good for evil"—a concept central to the Sermon on Abuse.

READING 2.4a From the Buddha's Sermon at Benares (recorded ca. 100 B.C.E.)

"There are two extremes, O bhikkhus,[1] which the man who has given up the world ought not to follow—the habitual practice, on the one hand, of self-indulgence which is unworthy, vain and fit only for the worldly-minded—and the habitual practice, on the other hand, of self-mortification, which is painful, useless and unprofitable.   1

"Neither abstinence from fish or flesh, nor going naked, nor shaving the head, nor wearing matted hair, nor dressing in a rough garment, nor covering oneself with dirt, nor sacrificing to Agni,[2] will cleanse a man who is not free from delusions.   10

"Reading the Vedas, making offerings to priests, or sacrifices to the gods, self-mortification by heat or cold, and many such penances performed for the sake of immortality, these do not cleanse the man who is not free from delusions.

"Anger, drunkenness, obstinacy, bigotry, deception, envy, self-praise, disparaging others, superciliousness and evil intentions constitute uncleanness; not verily the eating of flesh.

[1] Disciples.
[2] The Vedic god of fire, associated with sun and lightning.

"A middle path, O bhikkhus, avoiding the two extremes, had been discovered by the Tathāgata[3]—a path which opens the eyes, and bestows understanding, which leads to peace of mind, to the higher wisdom, to full enlightenment, to Nirvāna! 20

"What is that middle path, O bhikkhus, avoiding these two extremes, discovered by the Tathāgata—that path which opens the eyes, and bestows understanding, which leads to peace of mind, to the higher wisdom, to full enlightenment, to Nirvāna?

"Let me teach you, O bhikkhus, the middle path, which keeps aloof from both extremes. By suffering, the emaciated devotee produces confusion and sickly thoughts in his mind. 30 Mortification is not conducive even to worldly knowledge; how much less to a triumph over the senses!

"He who fills his lamp with water will not dispel the darkness, and he who tries to light a fire with rotten wood will fail. And how can any one be free from self by leading a wretched life, if he does not succeed in quenching the fires of lust, if he still hankers after either worldly or heavenly pleasures. But he in whom self has become extinct is free from lust; he will desire neither worldly nor heavenly pleasures, and the satisfaction of his natural wants will not 40 defile him. However, let him be moderate, let him eat and drink according to the needs of the body.

"Sensuality is enervating; the self-indulgent man is a slave to his passions, and pleasure-seeking is degrading and vulgar.

"But to satisfy the necessities of life is not evil. To keep the body in good health is a duty, for otherwise we shall not be able to trim the lamp of wisdom, and keep our mind strong and clear. Water surrounds the lotus-flower, but does not wet its petals.

"This is the middle path, O bhikkhus, that keeps aloof from 50 both extremes."

And the Blessed One spoke kindly to his disciples, pitying them for their errors, and pointing out the uselessness of their endeavors, and the ice of ill-will that chilled their hearts melted away under the gentle warmth of the Master's persuasion.

Now the Blessed One set the wheel of the most excellent law[4] rolling, and he began to preach to the five bhikkhus, opening to them the gate of immortality, and showing them the bliss of Nirvāna. 60

The Buddha said:

"The spokes of the wheel are the rules of pure conduct: justice is the uniformity of their length; wisdom is the tire; modesty and thoughtfulness are the hub in which the immovable axle of truth is fixed.

"He who recognizes the existence of suffering, its cause, its remedy, and its cessation has fathomed the four noble truths. He will walk in the right path.

"Right views will be the torch to light his way. Right aspirations will be his guide. Right speech will be his 70 dwelling-place on the road. His gait will be straight, for it is right behavior. His refreshments will be the right way of earning his livelihood. Right efforts will be his steps: right

thoughts his breath; and right contemplation will give him the peace that follows in his footprints.

"Now, this, O bhikkhus, is the noble truth concerning suffering:

"Birth is attended with pain, decay is painful, disease is painful, death is painful. Union with the unpleasant is painful, painful is separation from the pleasant; and any craving that is 80 unsatisfied, that too is painful. In brief, bodily conditions which spring from attachment are painful.

"This, then, O bhikkhus, is the noble truth concerning suffering.

"Now this, O bhikkhus, is the noble truth concerning the origin of suffering:

"Verily, it is that craving which causes the renewal of existence, accompanied by sensual delight, seeking satisfaction now here, now there, the craving for the gratification of the passions, the craving for a future life, and 90 the craving for happiness in this life.

"This, then, O bhikkhus, is the noble truth concerning the origin of suffering.

"Now this, O bhikkhus, is the noble truth concerning the destruction of suffering:

"Verily, it is the destruction, in which no passion remains, of this very thirst; it is the laying aside of, the being free from, the dwelling no longer upon this thirst.

"This, then, O bhikkhus, is the noble truth concerning the destruction of suffering. 100

"Now this, O bhikkhus, is the noble truth concerning the way which leads to the destruction of sorrow. Verily! it is this noble eightfold path; that is to say:

"Right views; right aspirations; right speech; right behavior; right livelihood; right effort; right thoughts; and right contemplation.

"This, then, O bhikkhus, is the noble truth concerning the destruction of sorrow.

"By the practice of loving kindness I have attained liberation of heart, and thus I am assured that I shall never return in 110 renewed births. I have even now attained Nirvāna."

And when the Blessed One had thus set the royal chariot wheel of truth rolling onward, a rapture thrilled through the universes. . . .

 Q How does the Buddhist Middle Path compare with Aristotle's Doctrine of the Mean (Reading 1.17)?
Q How might a Stoic (Reading 1.22) respond to the Buddha's sermon?

READING 2.4b From the Buddha's Sermon on Abuse (recorded ca. 100 B.C.E.)

And the Blessed One observed the ways of society and 1 noticed how much misery came from malignity and foolish offenses done only to gratify vanity and self-seeking pride.

And the Buddha said: "If a man foolishly does me wrong, I will return to him the protection of my ungrudging love; the

---

[3]"The successor to his predecessors in office," another name for the Buddha.
[4]The Wheel of the Law.

more evil comes from him, the more good shall go from me; the fragrance of goodness always comes to me, and the harmful air of evil goes to him."

A foolish man learning that the Buddha observed the principle of great love which commends the return of good for evil, came and abused him. The Buddha was silent, pitying his folly. [10]

When the man had finished his abuse, the Buddha asked him, saying: "Son, if a man declined to accept a present made to him, to whom would it belong?" And he answered: "In that case it would belong to the man who offered it."

"My son," said the Buddha, "thou has railed at me, but I decline to accept thy abuse, and request thee to keep it thyself. Will it not be a source of misery to thee? As the echo belongs to the sound, and the shadow to the substance, so [20] misery will overtake the evil-doer without fail."

The abuser made no reply, and the Buddha continued:

"A wicked man who reproaches a virtuous one is like one who looks up and spits at heaven; the spittle soils not the heaven, but comes back and defiles his own person.

"The slanderer is like one who flings dust at another when the wind is contrary; the dust does but return on him who threw it. The virtuous man cannot be hurt and the misery that the other would inflict comes back on himself."

The abuser went away ashamed, but he came again and took [30] refuge in the Buddha, the Dharma,[1] and the Sangha[2]. . . .

Q As reflected in their sermons, how do the teachings of Jesus (Reading 2.2) and the Buddha compare ?

The Spread of Buddhism

During the third century B.C.E., the emperor Asoka (273–232 B.C.E.) made Buddhism the state religion of India. Asoka's active role in spreading Buddhism foreshadowed Constantine's labors on behalf of Christianity; but Asoka went even further: he sent Buddhist missionaries as far west as Greece and southeast into Ceylon (present-day Sri Lanka). In spite of Asoka's efforts to give the world a unified faith, the Buddha's teachings generated varying interpretations and numerous factions. By the first century C.E., there were as many as five hundred major and minor Buddhist sects in India alone. In general, however, two principal divisions of Buddhism emerged: Hinayana ("Lesser Vehicle") Buddhism and Mahayana ("Greater Vehicle") Buddhism. Hinayana Buddhism emphasized the personal pursuit of *nirvana*, and its followers consider that in doing so they remain close to the teachings of the Buddha and his emphasis on self-destiny. Mahayana Buddhism, on the other hand, elevated the Buddha to the level of a divine being. It taught that the Buddha was the path to salvation, that he had come to earth in the form of

a man to guide humankind. Mahayana Buddhists regarded Siddhartha Gautama as but one of the Buddha's earthly incarnations, of which there had been many in the past and would be many in the future. The gods of other religions, including those of Hindusim, were held to be incarnations of the Buddha, who had appeared in various bodily forms in his previous lives. Mahayana Buddhism developed the concept of many different Buddhist divinities who inhabit the heavens, but also manifested themselves in earthly form in order to help believers attain enlightenment. These "Buddhas-to-be" or ***bodhisattvas*** (Figure **8.6**) are beings who have reached enlightenment, but who—out of compassion—have held back from entering *nirvana* until every last soul has been brought to enlightenment. *Bodhisattvas* are the heroes of Buddhism; and much like the Christian saints, they became objects of many popular Buddhist cults. Images of *bodhisattvas* are distinguished from those of the Buddha by their rich drapery and jewelry, which indicate their worldly associations. The most famous *bodhisattva* is Avalokiteshvara (known in Chinese as Guanyin and in Japanese as Kannon). Although *bodhisattvas*, like the Buddha, are beings beyond sexual gender, they are generally depicted as male. However, in East Asia Avalokiteshvara came to be regarded as a goddess of

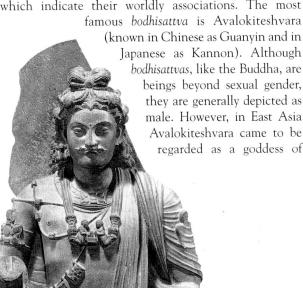

Figure 8.6 *Standing Bodhisattva*, from the Gandharan region of northwest Pakistan, late second century C.E. Gray schist, height approx. 3 ft. Courtesy Museum of Fine Arts, Boston. Helen and Alice Colburn Fund. Photograph © 2006 Museum of Fine Arts, Boston.

---
[1] The law of Righteousness; the Wheel of the Law.
[2] An assemblage of those who vow to pursue the Buddhist life.

mercy, hence depicted as a woman (see Fig. 14.13) and worshiped much in the way that Roman Catholics and Orthodox Christians honor the Virgin Mary.

Despite Asoka's efforts, Buddhism never gained widespread popularity in India. The strength of the established Hindu tradition in India (like that of Judaism in Judea) and the resistance of the Brahmin caste to Buddhist egalitarianism ultimately hindered the success of the new faith. By the middle of the first millennium, Hinduism was at least as prevalent as Buddhism in India, and by the year 1000, Buddhism was the religion of a minority. Buddhist communities nevertheless continued to flourish in India until the Islamic invasion of northern India in the twelfth and thirteenth centuries (see chapter 14); while Hindu establishments soon revived, Buddhism became all but extinct. Buddhism did, however, continue to thrive in lands far from its place of birth. In China, Mahayana Buddhism gained an overwhelming following and influence. From China, the new religion spread also to Korea, Japan, and Vietnam, where its impact was similarly great. Buddhism's tolerance for other religions enhanced its popularity and universal appeal. Mahayana Buddhism brought a message of hope and salvation to millions of people in East Asia. Hinayana Buddhism dominated as the faith in Ceylon (Sri Lanka), and spread from there to Burma (Myanmar), Thailand, and Cambodia.

Buddhism entered China during the first century C.E. and rose to prominence during the last, turbulent decades of the Han era (see chapter 7). At that time, Buddhist texts were translated into Chinese; over the following centuries, Buddhism was popularized in China by the writings of the Indian poet Asvaghosha (ca. 80–ca. 150). Asvaghosha's Sanskrit descriptions of the life of the Buddha, which became available in the year 420, was the literary medium for Mahayana Buddhism. Here, as in many other parts of Asia, the Buddha was regarded not simply as a teacher or reformer, but as a divine being. Daoism and Buddhism made an early and largely amicable contact in China, where their religious traditions would contribute to the formation of a syncretic popular faith. Buddhist "paradise sects," closely resembling the mystery cults of Southwest Asia promised their adherents rebirth in an idyllic, heavenly realm presided over by a heavenly Buddha. The most popular of these came to be the "Pure Land of the West" of Amitabha Buddha. Still another Buddhist sect, known in China as Chan ("meditation") and in Japan as Zen, rose to prominence in the later centuries of the first millennium. Chan emphasized the role of meditation and visionary insight in reaching *nirvana*. Strongly influenced by Daoist thought, this sect held that enlightenment could not be attained by rational means but, rather, through intense concentration that led to a spontaneous awakening of the mind. Among the tools of Zen masters were such mind-sharpening riddles as: "You know the sound of two hands clapping; what, then, is the sound of one hand clapping?" The Zen monk's attention to such queries forced him to move beyond reason. Legend has it that heavily caffeinated tea was introduced from India to China and Japan as an aid to prolonging

meditation. In contrast with Christianity, Buddhism (in all its variant forms) extolled the practice of meditation, the act by which the mind is emptied of thoughts, individual identity is obliterated, and total harmony with nature is achieved.

SUMMARY

The world into which Jesus was born was ripe for religious revitalization. Roman religion focused on nature deities and civic gods who provided little in the way of personal spiritual comfort. The mystery cults promised rebirth and resurrection to devotees of fertility gods and goddesses. The province of Judea, beset by religious and political factionalism, sought apocalyptic deliverance from the Roman yoke. The message preached by Jesus demanded an abiding faith in God, compassion for one's fellow human beings, and the renunciation of material wealth. In an age when people were required to serve the state, Jesus asked that they serve God. The apostle Paul universalized Jesus' message by preaching among non-Jews. He explained Jesus' death as atonement for sin and anticipated eternal life for the followers of the *Christos*.

The religion that had begun with the teachings of Siddhartha Gautama in India swept through East Asia in the very centuries that Christianity emerged in the West. Although rooted in different traditions, the two world faiths had much in common, especially in the message of compassion, humility, and right conduct preached by their founders. They also differed considerably—for instance, Buddhism did not share the Pauline concepts of sin and redemption. Ultimately, Christianity and Buddhism would only have limited impact in the lands in which their founders were born, but both religions gained popularity in empires that flourished at the same time: Christianity in the Roman world-state, and Buddhism under the late Han dynasty in China. With Pauline Christianity, as with Mahayana Buddhism, the belief in a savior god, the promise of salvation for all human beings, and the practice of uncompromising moral goodness provided spiritual alternatives to the prevailing materialism of imperial Rome and Han China. On the soil of these great but declining empires were cast the seeds of two world-historical religions that are still followed by millions of people today.

GLOSSARY

asceticism   strict self-denial and self-discipline

bodhisattva   (Sanskrit, "one whose essence is enlightenment") a being who has postponed his or her own entry into *nirvana* in order to assist others in reaching that goal; worshiped as a deity in Mahayana Buddhism

Messiah   Anointed One, or Savior; in Greek, *Christos*

rabbi   a teacher and master trained in the Jewish law

sutra   (Sanskrit, "thread") an instructional chapter or discourse in any of the sacred books of Buddhism

CHAPTER 9

The Language of Faith: Symbolism and the Arts

"The earthly city loves its own strength as revealed in its men of power, the heavenly city says to its God: 'I will love thee, O Lord, my strength.'"
Augustine of Hippo

Christianity began its rise to world significance amidst an empire beset by increasing domestic difficulties and the assaults of barbarian nomads (see chapter 11). The last great Roman emperors, Diocletian (245–316) and Constantine (ca. 274–337), made valiant efforts to restructure the Empire and reverse military and economic decline. In order to govern Rome's sprawling territories more efficiently, Diocletian divided the Empire into western and eastern halves and appointed a co-emperor to share the burden of administration and defense. After Diocletian retired, Constantine levied new taxes and made unsuccessful efforts to revive a money economy. By means of the Edict of Milan (313), which proclaimed toleration of all religions (including the fledgling Christianity), Constantine tried to heal Rome's internal divisions. Failing to breathe new life into the waning Empire, however, in 330 he moved the seat of power from the beleaguered city of Rome to the Eastern capital of the Empire, Byzantium, which he renamed Constantinople.

While the Roman Empire languished in the West, the East Roman or Byzantine Empire—the economic heart of the Roman world—prospered. Located at the crossroads of Europe and Asia, Constantinople was the hub of a vital trade network and the heir to the cultural traditions of Greece, Rome, and Asia. Byzantine emperors formed a firm alliance with Church leaders and worked to create an empire that flourished until the mid-fifteenth century. The Slavic regions of Eastern Europe (including Russia) converted to Orthodox Christianity during the ninth and tenth centuries, thus extending the religious influence of the city that Constantine had designated the "New Rome."

As Christians in Rome and Byzantium worked to formulate an effective language of faith, Buddhists in India, China, and Southeast Asia were developing their own vocabulary of religious expression. Buddhism inspired a glorious outpouring of art, architecture, and music that—like Early Christian art in the West—nourished the spiritual needs of millions of people throughout the East.

The Christian Identity

Between the fourth and sixth centuries, Christianity grew from a small, dynamic sect into a full-fledged religion; and its ministerial agent, the Roman Catholic Church, came to replace the Roman Empire as the dominant authority in the West. The history of these developments sheds light on the formation of the Christian identity.

In the first centuries after the death of Jesus, there was little unity of belief and practice among those who called themselves Christians. But after the legalization of the faith in 313, the followers of Jesus moved toward resolving questions of Church hierarchy, **dogma** (prescribed doctrine), and **liturgy** (the rituals for public worship). From Rome, Church leaders in the West took the Latin language, the Roman legal system (which would become the basis for Church or **canon law**), and Roman methods of architectural construction. The Church retained the Empire's administrative divisions, appointing archbishops to oversee the provinces, bishops in the dioceses, and priests in the parishes. As Rome had been the hub of the Western Empire, so it became the administrative center of the new faith. When Church leaders in Constantinople and Antioch contested the administrative primacy of Rome, the bishop of Rome, Leo the Great (ca. 400–461), advanced the "Petrine Doctrine," claiming that Roman pontiffs inherited their position as the successors to Peter, the First Apostle and the principal evangelist of Rome. As Roman emperors had held supreme authority over the state, so Roman Catholic popes—the temporal representatives of Christ—would govern Western Christendom. The new spiritual order in the West was thus patterned after imperial Rome.

A functional administrative hierarchy was essential to the success of the new faith; so too was the formulation of a uniform doctrine of belief. As Christianity spread, the story of Jesus and the meaning of his message provoked various kinds of inquiry. Was Jesus human or divine? What was the status of Jesus in relation to God? Such fundamental questions drew conflicting answers. To resolve them, Church officials would convene to hammer out a systematic explanation of the life, death, and resurrection of Jesus. The first **ecumenical** (worldwide) council of churchmen was called by the emperor Constantine. It met at Nicaea (present-day Iznik) in 325. At the Council of Nicaea, a consensus of opinion among Church representatives laid the basis for Christian dogma. It was resolved—to the objection of some dissenting Eastern churchmen—that Jesus was of one substance (or essence) with God the Father. The council issued a statement of Christian belief known as the Nicene Creed. A version of the Nicene Creed issued in 381 and still used by Eastern Orthodox Christians is reproduced below. It pledges commitment to a variety of miraculous phenomena, including virgin birth, the resurrection of the dead, and a mystical Trinity comprising Jesus, God the Father, and the Holy Spirit. The principal formula of Christian belief, it stands as the turning point between classical rationalism and Christian mysticism. Challenging reason and the evidence of the senses, it embraces faith and the intuition of truths that transcend ordinary understanding. As such, it anticipates the shift from a homocentric classical worldview to the God-centered medieval worldview.

READING 2.5 The Nicene Creed (381)

We believe in one God the Father All-Sovereign, maker of   1
heaven and earth, and of all things visible and invisible;
    And in one Lord Jesus Christ, the only-begotten Son of God,
Begotten of the Father before all the ages, Light of Light, true
God of true God, begotten not made, of one substance with
the Father, through whom all things were made; who for us
men and for our salvation came down from the heavens, and
was made flesh of the Holy Spirit and the Virgin Mary, and
became man, and was crucified for us under Pontius Pilate,
and suffered and was buried, and rose again on the third day   10
according to the Scriptures, and ascended into the heavens,
and sitteth on the right hand of the Father, and cometh again
with glory to judge living and dead, of whose kingdom there
shall be no end:
    And in the Holy Spirit, the Lord and the Life-giver, that
proceedeth from the Father, who with Father and Son is
worshipped together and glorified together, who spake
through the prophets:
    In one holy Catholic and Apostolic Church:
    We acknowledge one baptism unto remission of sins. We   20
look for a resurrection of the dead, and the life of the age to
come.

Q What is a "creed"?
Q How does the Nicene Creed illustrate the "leap of faith" that is basic to all religious belief?

Christian Monasticism

Even before the coming of Christ, communal asceticism (self-denial) was a way of life among those who sought an an environment for study and prayer and an alternative to the decadence of urban life. Such was the case with the Essenes in the West and the Buddhist monks of Asia. The earliest Christian monastics (the word comes from the Greek *monas*, meaning "alone") pursued sanctity in the deserts of Egypt. Fasting, poverty, and celibacy were the essential features of the ascetic lifestyle instituted by the Greek bishop Saint Basil (ca. 329–379) and still followed by monastics of the Eastern Church.

In the West, the impulse to retreat from the turmoil of secular life became more intense as the last remnants of classical civilization disappeared. In 529, the same year that Plato's Academy closed its doors in Athens, the first Western monastic community was founded at Monte Cassino in Southern Italy. Named after its founder, Benedict of Nursia (ca. 480–547), the Benedictine rule (in Latin, *regula*) required that its members take vows of poverty (the renunciation of all material possessions), chastity (abstention from sexual activity), and obedience to the governing **abbot**, or father of the monastic community. Benedictine monks followed a routine of work that freed them from dependence on the secular world, balanced by religious study and prayer: the daily recitation of the Divine Office, a cycle of prayers that marked eight devotional intervals in the twenty-four-hour period. This program of *ora et labora* ("prayer and work") gave structure and meaning to the daily routine, and provided a balanced standard best expressed by the Benedictine motto, *mens sana in corpore sano* ("a sound mind in a sound body").

Monastics and church fathers alike generally regarded women as the daughters of Eve, inherently sinful and dangerous as objects of sexual temptation. The Church prohibited women from holding positions of Church authority and from receiving ordination as **secular clergy** (priests). However, women were not excluded from joining the ranks of the religious. In Egypt, some 20,000 women—twice the number of men—lived in monastic communities as nuns. In the West, aristocratic women often turned their homes into Benedictine nunneries, where they provided religious education for women of all classes. Saint Benedict's sister, Scholastica (d. 543), became abbess of a monastery near Monte Cassino. A refuge for female intellectuals, the convent offered women an alternative to marriage.

From the fifth century on, members of the **regular clergy** (those who follow the rule of a monastic order) played an increasingly important role in Western intellectual history. As Greek and Roman sources of education dried up and fewer men and women learned to read and write, the task of preserving the history and literature of the past fell to the last bastions of literacy: the monasteries. Benedictine monks and nuns hand-copied and illustrated Christian as well as classical manuscripts, and stored them in their libraries. Over the centuries, Benedictine monasteries provided local education, managed hospices, sponsored sacred music and art, and produced a continuous stream of missionaries, scholars, mystics, and Church reformers. One little-known sixth-century abbot, Dionysius Exiguus (Denis the Little, fl. 525), was responsible for establishing the calendar that is most widely used in the world to this day. In an effort to fix the Church timetable for the annual celebration of Easter, Dionysius reckoned the birth of Jesus at 754 years after the founding of Rome. Although he was inaccurate by at least three years, he applied his chronology to establish the year one as *Anno domini nostri Jesu Christi* ("the Year of Our Lord Jesus Christ"). This method of dating became the standard practice in the West after the English abbot and scholar known as the Venerable Bede (673–735) employed the Christian calendar in writing his monumental history of England.

The Latin Church Fathers

In the formation of Christian dogma and liturgy in the West, the most important figures were four Latin scholars who lived between the fourth and sixth centuries: Jerome, Ambrose, Gregory, and Augustine. Saint Jerome (ca. 347–420), a Christian educated in Rome, translated into Latin both the Hebrew Bible and the Greek books of the "New Testament." This mammoth task resulted in the Vulgate, the Latin edition of Scripture that became the official Bible of the Roman Catholic Church. Although Jerome considered pagan culture a distraction from the spiritual life, he admired the writers of classical antiquity and did not hesitate to plunder the spoils of classicism—and Hebraism—to build the edifice of a new faith.

Like Jerome, Ambrose (339–397) drew on Hebrew, Greek, and Southwest Asian traditions in formulating Christian doctrine and liturgy. A Roman aristocrat who became bishop of Milan, Ambrose wrote some of the earliest Christian hymns for congregational use. Influenced by eastern Mediterranean chants and Hebrew psalms, Ambrose's hymns are characterized by a lyrical simplicity that made them models of religious expression. In the hymn that follows, divine light is the unifying theme. The reference to God as the "Light of light" distinctly recalls the cult of Mithras, as well as Plato's analogy between the Good and the Sun. Culminating in a burst of praise for the triune God, the hymn conveys a mood of buoyant optimism.

READING 2.6 Saint Ambrose's "Ancient Morning Hymn" (ca. 380)

O Splendor of God's glory bright,   1
O Thou who bringest light from light,
O Light of light, light's living spring,
O Day, all days illumining!

O Thou true Sun, on us Thy glance   5
Let fall in royal radiance;
The Spirit's sanctifying beam
Upon our earthly senses stream.

The Father, too, our prayers implore,
Father of glory evermore,   10
The Father of all grace and might,
To banish sin from our delight.

To guide whate'er we nobly do,
With love all envy to subdue,
To make ill-fortune turn to fair,   15
And give us grace our wrongs to bear.

Rejoicing may this day go hence;
Like virgin dawn our innocence,
Like fiery noon our faith appear,
Nor know the gloom of twilight drear.   20

Morn in her rosy car is borne:
Let him come forth, our perfect morn,
The Word in God the Father one,
The Father perfect in the Son.

All laud to God the Father be;   25
All praise, eternal Son, to Thee;
All glory, as is ever meet,
To God the holy Paraclete.[1]

Q How does this song of praise compare to "The Hymn to the Aten" (Reading 1.3) and to Psalm 8 (Reading 1.8e)?

The contribution of the Roman aristocrat Gregory the Great (ca. 540–604) was vital to the development of early Church government. Elected to the papacy in 590, Gregory established the administrative machinery by which all subsequent popes would govern the Church of Rome. A born organizer, Gregory sent missionaries to convert England to Christianity; he extended the temporal authority of the Roman Church throughout Western Europe; and with equal efficiency he organized the liturgical music of the early Church.

The most profound and influential of all the Latin church fathers was Augustine of Hippo (354–430). A native of Roman Africa and an intellectual who came under the spell of both Paul and Plotinan neoplatonism, Augustine converted to Christianity at the age of thirty-three. His treatises on the nature of the soul, free will, and the meaning of evil made him the greatest philosopher of Christian antiquity. Before his conversion to Christianity, Augustine had enjoyed a sensual and turbulent youth, marked by womanizing, gambling, and fathering an illegitimate child. Augustine's lifelong conflict between his love of worldly pleasures, dominated by what he called his "lower self," and his love of God, exercised by the "higher part of our nature," is the focus of his fascinating and self-scrutinizing autobiography known as the *Confessions*. Here, Augustine makes a fundamental distinction between physical and spiritual satisfaction, arguing that "no bodily pleasure, however great it might be . . . [is] worthy

---

[1] Holy Spirit.

of comparison, or even of mention, beside the happiness of the life of the saints." The dualistic model of the human being as the locus of warring elements—the "unclean body" and the "purified soul"—drew heavily on the neo-platonist duality of Matter and Spirit and the Pauline promise that the sin of Adam might be cleansed by the sacrifice of Jesus.

In the extract below from his *Confessions*, Augustine identifies the three temptations that endanger his soul: the lust of the flesh, the lust of the eyes, and the ambition of the world. Nowhere is Augustine's motto, "Faith seeking understanding," so intimately reflected as in the self-examining prose of the *Confessions*.

READING 2.7 From Saint Augustine's *Confessions* (ca. 400)

Certainly you command me to restrain myself from the *lust of* 1
the flesh, the lust of the eyes, and the ambition of the world.
You commanded me to abstain from sleeping with a mistress,
and with regard to marriage you advised me to take a better
course than the one that was permitted me. And since you
gave me the power, it was done, even before I became a
dispenser of your Sacrament. But there still live in that
memory of mine, of which I have spoken so much, images of
the things which my habit has fixed there. These images come
into my thoughts, and, though when I am awake they are   10
strengthless, in sleep they not only cause pleasure but go so
far as to obtain assent and something very like reality. These
images, though real, have such an effect on my soul, in my
flesh, that false visions in my sleep obtain from me what true
visions cannot when I am awake. Surely, Lord my God, I am
myself when I am asleep? And yet there is a very great
difference between myself and myself in that moment of time
when I pass from being awake to being asleep or come back
again from sleep to wakefulness. Where then is my reason
which, when I am awake, resists such suggestions and   20
remains unshaken if the realities themselves were presented
to it? Do reason's eyes close with the eyes of the body? Does
reason go to sleep when the bodily senses sleep? If so, how
does it happen that even in our sleep we do often resist and,
remembering our purpose and most chastely abiding by it, give
no assent to enticements of this kind? Nevertheless, there is a
great difference, because, when it happens otherwise, we
return on waking to a peace of conscience and, by the very
remoteness of our state now and then, discover that it was
not we who did something which was, to our regret, somehow 30
or other done in us.

Almighty God, surely your hand is powerful enough to cure
all the sickness in my soul and, with a more abundant
measure of your grace, to quench even the lustful impulses of
my sleep. Lord, you will increase your gifts in me more and
more, so that my soul, disentangled from the birdlime of
concupiscence,[1] may follow me to you; so that it may not be in
revolt against itself and may not, even in dreams, succumb to
or even give the slightest assent to those degrading

---

[1]Strong desire, especially sexual desire.

corruptions which by means of sensual images actually disturb 40
and pollute the flesh. . . .

I must now mention another form of temptation which is in
many ways more dangerous. Apart from the concupiscence of
the flesh which is present in the delight we take in all the
pleasures of the senses (and the slaves of it perish as they put
themselves far from you), there is also present in the soul, by
means of these same bodily senses, a kind of empty longing
and curiosity which aims not at taking pleasure in the flesh
but at acquiring experience through the flesh, and this empty
curiosity is dignified by the names of learning and science.   50
Since this is in the appetite for knowing, and since the eyes
are the chief of our senses for acquiring knowledge, it is
called in the divine language the lust of the eyes. For "to see"
is used properly of the eyes; but we also use this word of the
other senses when we are employing them for the purpose of
gaining knowledge. We do not say: "Hear how it flashes" or
"Smell how bright it is" or "Taste how it shines" or "Feel how
it gleams"; in all these cases we use the verb "to see." But
we not only say: "See how it shines," a thing which can only
be perceived by the eyes; we also say "See how it sounds,"   60
"See how it smells," "See how it tastes," "See how hard it
is." Therefore, the general experience of the senses is, as was
said before, called "the lust of the eyes," because seeing,
which belongs properly to the eyes, is used by analogy of the
other senses too when they are attempting to discover any
kind of knowledge.

In this it is easy to see how pleasure and curiosity have
different objects in their use of the senses. Pleasure goes
after what is beautiful to us, sweet to hear, to smell, to taste,
to touch; but curiosity, for the sake of experiment, may go   70
after the exact opposites of these, not in order to suffer
discomfort, but simply because of the lust to find out and to
know. What pleasure can there be in looking at a mangled
corpse, which must excite our horror? Yet if there is one near,
people flock to see it, so as to grow sad and pale at the sight.
They are actually frightened of seeing it in their sleep, as
though anyone had forced them to see it when they were
awake or as if they had been induced to look at it because it
had the reputation of being a beautiful thing to see. The same
is true of the other senses. There is no need to go to the   80
length of producing examples. Because of this disease of
curiosity monsters and anything out of the ordinary are put on
show in our theaters. From the same motive men proceed to
investigate the workings of nature which is beyond our ken—
things which it does no good to know and which men only
want to know for the sake of knowing. So too, and with this
same end of perverted science, people make enquiries by
means of magic. Even in religion we find the same thing: God
is tempted when signs and portents are demanded and are not
desired for any salutary purpose, but simply for the experience 90
of seeing them. . . .

We are tempted, Lord, by these temptations every day;
without intermission we are tempted. The tongue of man is
the furnace in which we are tried every day. Here too you
command us to be continent. Give what you command, and
command what you will. You know how on this matter my
heart groans to you and my eyes stream tears. For I cannot
easily discover how far I have become cleaner from this

disease, and I much fear my hidden sins which are visible to your eyes, though not to mine. For in other kinds of temptation **100** I have at least some means of finding out about myself; but in this kind it is almost impossible. With regard to the pleasures of the flesh and the unnecessary curiosity for knowledge I can see how far I have advanced in the ability to control my mind simply by observing myself when I am without these things, either from choice or when they are not available. For I can then ask myself how much or how little I mind not having them. So too with regard to riches, which are desired for the satisfaction of one or two or all of those three concupiscences; if one is not able to be quite sure in one's own mind whether **110** or not one despises them when one has them, it is possible to get rid of them so as to put oneself to the test. But how can we arrange things so as to be without praise and make the same experiment with regard to it? Are we to live a bad life, to live in such a wicked and abandoned way that everyone who knows us will detest us? Nothing could be madder than such a suggestion as that. On the contrary, if praise both goes with and ought to go with a good life and good works, we should no more part with it than with the good life itself. Yet unless a thing is not there I cannot tell whether it is difficult **120** or easy for me to be without it. . . .

Q Which temptation does Augustine seem to find the most difficult of resist?

Q How might he respond to Buddhism's Four Noble Truths?

A living witness to the decline of the Roman Empire, Augustine defended his faith against recurrent pagan charges that Christianity was responsible for Rome's downfall. In his multivolume work the *City of God*, he distinguishes between the earthly city of humankind and the heavenly city that is the eternal dwelling place of the Christian soul. Augustine's earthly abode, a place where "wise men live according to man," represents the classical world prior to the coming of Jesus. By contrast, the heavenly city—the spiritual realm where human beings live according to divine precepts—is the destiny of those who embrace the "New Dispensation" of Christ.

Augustine's influence in shaping Christian dogma cannot be overestimated. His rationalization of evil as the perversion of the good created by God, and his defense of "just war"—that is, war as reprisal for the abuse of morality—testify to the analytic subtlety of his mind. His description of history as divinely ordered and directed toward a predestined end became fundamental to the Christian philosophy of history. Finally, his dualistic model of reality—matter and spirit, body and soul, earth and heaven, Satan and God, state and Church—governed Western thought for centuries to come. The conception of the visible world (matter) as an imperfect reflection of the divine order (spirit) determined the allegorical character of Christian culture. According to this model, matter was the matrix in which God's message was hidden. In Scripture, as well as in every natural and created thing,

God's invisible order might be discovered. For Augustine, the Hebrew Bible was a symbolic prefiguration of Christian truths, and history itself was a cloaked message of divine revelation.

The extract from the *City of God* illustrates Augustine's dual perception of reality and suggests its importance to the tradition of Christian allegory. Augustine's description of Noah's ark as symbolic of the City of God, the Church, and the body of Christ exemplifies the way in which a single image might assume various meanings within the language of Christian faith.

READING 2.8 From Saint Augustine's *City of God Against the Pagans* (413–426)

On the character of the two cities, the earthly and the heavenly.

The two cities then were created by two kinds of love: the **1** earthly city by a love of self carried even to the point of contempt for God, the heavenly city by a love of God carried even to the point of contempt for self. Consequently, the earthly city glories in itself while the other glories in the Lord.[1] For the former seeks glory from men, but the latter finds its greatest glory in God, the witness of our conscience. The earthly city lifts up its head in its own glory; the heavenly city says to its God: "My glory and the lifter of my head."[2] In the one, the lust for dominion has dominion over its princes as **10** well as over the nations that it subdues; in the other, both those put in charge and those placed under them serve one another in love, the former by their counsel, the latter by their obedience. The earthly city loves its own strength as revealed in its men of power; the heavenly city says to its God: "I will love thee, O Lord, my strength."[3]

Thus in the earthly city its wise men who live according to man have pursued the goods either of the body or of their own mind or of both together; or if any of them were able to know God, "they did not honor him as God or give thanks to him, but **20** they became futile in their thinking and their senseless minds were darkened; claiming to be wise," that is, exalting themselves in their own wisdom under the dominion of pride, "they became fools, and exchanged the glory of the immortal God for images resembling mortal man or birds or beasts or reptiles," for in the adoration of idols of this sort they were either leaders or followers of the populace, "and worshiped and served the creature rather than the creator, who is blessed forever."[4] In the heavenly city, on the other hand, man's only wisdom is the religion that guides him rightly to worship the **30** true God and awaits as its reward in the fellowship of saints, not only human but also angelic, this goal, "that God may be all in all."[5] . . .

That the ark which Noah was ordered to make symbolizes Christ and the church in every detail.

---
[1]Cf. 2 Corinthians 10:17.
[2]Psalms 3:3.
[3]Psalms 18:1.
[4]Romans 1:21–23, 25.
[5]1 Corinthians 15:28.

Figure 9.1 Sarcophagus of Archbishop Theodorus, sixth century. Marble. Sant'Apollinare in Classe, Ravenna, Italy. Alinari, Florence.

Now God, as we know, enjoined the building of an ark upon Noah, a man who was righteous and according to the true testimony of Scripture, perfect in his generation,[6] that is, perfect, not as the citizens of the City of God are to become in that immortal state where they will be made equal with the **40** angels of God, but as they can be during their sojourn here on earth. In this ark he was to be rescued from the devastation of the flood with his family, that is, his wife, sons and daughters-in-law, as well as with the animals that came to him in the ark at God's direction. We doubtless have here a symbolic representation of the City of God sojourning as an alien in this world, that is, of the church which wins salvation by virtue of the wood on which the mediator between God and men, the man Christ Jesus,[7] was suspended.

The very measurements of the ark's length, height and **50** breadth symbolize the human body, in the reality of which it was prophesied that Christ would come to mankind, as, in fact, he did come. For the length of the human body from top to toe is six times its breadth from one side to the other and ten times its thickness measured on a side from back to belly. Thus if you measure a man lying on his back or face down, his length from head to foot is six times his breadth from right to left or from left to right and ten times his elevation from the ground. This is why the ark was made three hundred cubits in length, fifty in breadth and thirty in height. And as for the door that it received **60** on its side, that surely is the wound that was made when the side of the crucified one was pierced by the spear.[8] This is the way by which those who come to him enter, because from this opening flowed the sacraments with which believers are initiated. Moreover, the order that it should be made of squared beams contains an allusion to the foursquare stability of saints' lives, for in whatever direction you turn a squared object, it will stand firm. In similar fashion, everything else mentioned in the construction of this ark symbolizes some aspect of the church....

Q How is allegory used in this reading?
Q Why was allegory such an important tool in shaping the "New Dispensation"?

[6]Cf. Genesis 6:9.
[7]1 Timothy 2:5.
[8]Cf. John 19:34.

Symbolism and Early Christian Art

Christian signs and symbols linked the visible to the invisible world. They worked by analogy, in much the same way that allegory operated in Augustine's *The City of God*. Since in Christian art the symbolic significance of a representation is often more important that its literal meaning, the identification and interpretation of the subject matter (a discipline known as **iconography**) is especially important. Before Christianity was legalized in 313, visual symbols served the practical function of identifying new converts to the faith among themselves. Followers of Jesus adopted the sign of the fish because the Greek word for fish (*ichthys*) is an acrostic combination of the first letters of the Greek words "Jesus Christ, Son of God, Savior." They also used the first and last letters of the Greek alphabet, *alpha* and *omega*, to designate Christ's presence at the beginning and the end of time. Roman converts to Christianity saw in the Latin word for peace, *pax*, a symbolic reference to Christ, since the last and first letters could also be read as *chi* and *rho*, the first two letters in the Greek word *Christos*. Indeed, *pax* was emblazoned on the banner under which the emperor Constantine was said to have defeated his enemies. Such symbols soon found their way into Early Christian art.

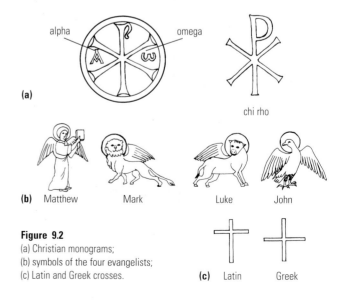

Figure 9.2
(a) Christian monograms;
(b) symbols of the four evangelists;
(c) Latin and Greek crosses.

On a sixth-century sarcophagus (stone coffin) of the archbishop Theodorus of Ravenna (Figure **9.1**), the *chi* and *rho* and the *alpha* and *omega* have been made into an insignia that resembles both a crucifix (symbolizing Christ as Savior) and a pastoral cross (symbolizing Christ as Shepherd, Figure **9.2**). Three laurel wreaths, Roman imperial symbols of triumph, encircle the medallions on the coffin lid. On either side of the central medallion are grapevines designating the wine that represents the blood of Christ. The tiny birds that stand beneath the vines—derived from Greek funerary art—refer to the human soul. Also included in the iconographic program are two popular Southwest Asian symbols of immortality: the peacock or phoenix, a legendary bird that was thought to be reborn from its own ashes, and the rosette, an ancient symbol of Isis in her regenerative role. Taken as a whole, the archbishop's coffin is the vehicle of a sacred language signifying Christ's triumph and the Christian promise of resurrection and salvation.

In Early Christian art, music, and literature, almost every number and combination of numbers was thought to bear allegorical meaning. The number 3, for example, signified the Trinity; 4 signified the evangelists; 5 symbolized the wounds of Jesus; 12 stood for the apostles, and so on. The evangelists were usually represented by four winged creatures: the man for Matthew, the lion for Mark, the ox for Luke, and the eagle for John (see Figure 9.2 and the upper portion of Figure 9.11). Prefigured in the Book of Revelation (4:1–8), each of the four creatures came to be

Figure 9.4 *Christ as Good Shepherd*, mid-fourth century. Fresco. Catacombs of Saints Pietro and Marcellino, Rome. Pontificia-Commissione per l'Archeologia Cristiana, Rome.

associated with a particular Gospel. The lion, for example, was appropriate to Mark because in his Gospel he emphasized the royal dignity of Christ; the heaven-soaring eagle suited John, who produced the most lofty and mystical of the Gospels. The halo, a zone of light used in Roman art to signify divinity or holiness, became a favorite symbolic device in the visual representation of Jesus, the evangelists, and others whom the Church canonized as holy persons capable of interceding for sinners.

Some of the earliest evidence of Christian art comes from the **catacombs**, subterranean burial chambers outside the city of Rome. These vast networks of underground galleries and rooms include gravesites whose walls are covered with frescoes illustrating scenes from the Old and New Testaments. One figure is shown in the ***orans*** position—with arms upraised in an attitude of prayer—an ancient gesture (see Figure 2.1) used in the performance of ritual (Figure **9.3**). Like the story of Noah's ark, "decoded" by Augustine to reveal its hidden significance, Early Christian imagery was multilayered and pregnant with symbolic meaning. For example, the popular figure of Jesus as Good Shepherd, an adaptation of the calf- or lamb-bearing youth of Greco-Roman art (see chapter 5), symbolizes Jesus' role as savior-protector (shepherd) and sacrificial victim (lamb). Featured in catacomb frescoes (Figure **9.4**) and in freestanding sculpture (see Figure 9.5),

Figure 9.3 *Orans* (praying figure), ca. 300. Fresco. Catacombs of Saint Priscilla, Rome. © 1990, Photo Scala, Florence.

the Good Shepherd evokes the early Christian theme of deliverance. But while the message of the catacomb frescoes is one of salvation and deliverance, the style of these paintings resembles that of secular Roman art (see chapter 6): figures are small but substantial and deftly shaded to suggest three-dimensionality. Setting and specific indications of spatial depth are omitted, however, so that human forms appear to float in ethereal space.

In the centuries following the legalization of Christianity, stories about the life of Jesus came to form two main narrative cycles: The Youth of Christ and The Passion of Christ. Not until the fifth century, however, when the manner of Jesus' death began to lose its ignoble associations, was Jesus depicted on the Cross. One of the earliest of such scenes is that carved in low relief on the wooden west doors of Santa Sabina in Rome (see Figure 8.4). Christ assumes the *orans* in a rigid and static frontal position that also signifies a crucified body. The tripartite composition of the relief includes the smaller (because less important) figures of the thieves who flanked Jesus at the

crucifixion. Despite its narrative content, the image is far from being a representation of the crucifixion of Jesus. Rather, it is a symbolic statement of Christian redemption.

Early Christians had little use for the Roman approach to art as a window on the world. Roman realism, with its scrupulous attention to time, place, and personalities, was ill-suited to convey the timeless message of a universal faith and the miraculous events surrounding the life of a savior god. Moreover, Christian artists inherited the Jewish prohibition against "graven images." As a result, very little freestanding sculpture was produced between the second and eleventh centuries; that which was produced, such as the fourth-century *Good Shepherd* (Figure 9.5), retains only the rudimentary features—such as the *contrapposto* stance—of high classical statuary. On the other hand, hand-illuminated manuscripts and **diptychs** (two-leaved hinged tablets or panels) designed for private devotional use were produced in great numbers. A sixth-century ivory book cover from Murano, Italy (Figure 9.6), is typical of the Early Christian artist's

Iconography of the Life of Jesus

THE YOUTH OF CHRIST (principal events)

1	**The Annunciation**	The Archangel Gabriel announces to the Virgin Mary that God has chosen her to bear his son
2	**The Visitation**	The pregnant Mary visits her cousin Elizabeth, who is pregnant with the future John the Baptist
3	**The Nativity**	Jesus is born to Mary in Bethlehem
4	**The Annunciation to the Shepherds**	An angel announces the birth of Jesus to humble shepherds, who hasten to Bethlehem
5	**The Adoration of the Magi**	Three wise men from the East follow a star to Bethlehem where they present the Christ child with precious gifts (gold, frankincense, and myrrh)
6	**The Presentation in the Temple**	Mary and Joseph present Jesus to the high priest at the Temple in Jerusalem
7	**The Massacre of the Innocents and the Flight to Egypt**	King Herod murders all the newborn of Bethlehem; the Holy Family (Mary, Joseph, and Jesus) flee to Egypt
8	**The Baptism**	John the Baptist, a preacher in the wilderness of Judea, baptizes Jesus in the Jordan River
9	**The Temptation**	Jesus fasts for forty days and nights in the wilderness; he rejects the worldly wealth offered to him by the Devil
10	**The Calling of the Apostles**	Near the Sea of Galilee, Jesus calls the brothers Simon (Peter) and Andrew into his service
11	**The Raising of Lazarus**	Jesus restores to life Lazarus, the brother of Mary and Martha
12	**The Transfiguration**	On Mount Tabor in Galilee, among his disciples Peter, James, and John the Evangelist, the radiantly transfigured Jesus is hailed by God as his beloved Son

THE PASSION OF CHRIST (principal events)

1	**The Entry into Jerusalem**	Jesus, riding on a donkey, enters Jerusalem amidst his disciples and receptive crowds
2	**The Last Supper**	At the Passover *seder*, Jesus reveals to his disciples his impending death and instructs them to consume the bread (his body) and the wine (his blood) in remembrance of him
3	**The Agony in the Garden**	At the Garden of Gethsemane on the Mount of Olives, while the disciples Peter, James, and John sleep, Jesus reconciles his soul to death
4	**The Betrayal**	Judas Iscariot, who has been bribed to point Jesus out to his enemies, identifies him by kissing him as he leaves the Garden of Gethsemane
5	**Jesus Before Pilate**	Jesus comes before the Roman governor of Judea and is charged with treason; when the crowd demands Jesus be put to death, Pilate washes his hands to signify his innocence of the deed
6	**The Flagellation**	Jesus is scourged by his captors, the Roman soldiers
7	**The Mocking of Jesus**	Pilate's soldiers dress Jesus in royal robes and a crown of thorns
8	**The Road to Calvary**	Jesus carries the Cross to Golgotha (Calvary), where he is to be executed affixed to a cross raised to stand
9	**The Crucifixion**	At Golgotha, the body of Jesus is between two crucified thieves
10	**The Descent from the Cross and the Lamentation**	Grief-stricken followers remove the body of Jesus from the Cross; the Virgin, Mary Magdalene, and others grieve over the body
11	**The Entombment**	Mary and the followers of Jesus place his body in a nearby tomb
12	**The Resurrection**	Three days after his death, Jesus rises from the tomb

preoccupation with didactic content and surface adornment. Scenes of Jesus' miracles are wedged together in airless compartments surrounding the central image of the enthroned Jesus with Peter and Paul (Figure **9.7**). A royal canopy flanked by **Latin crosses** (see Figure **9.2**) crowns the holy space. In the top register, two angels

Figure 9.6 (above) Book cover, from Murano, Italy, sixth century. Ivory. © 1990, Photo Scala, Florence - courtesy of the Ministero Beni e Att. Culturali.

Triumphal wreath

Angels

Christ healing the blind

Saint Peter

Christ exorcising demons

Jonah under the gourd tree

Greek Cross

The Raising of Lazarus

Saint Paul

Christ Enthroned

Christ healing at the Pool of Bethesda

The Three Hebrews in the Fiery Furnace

Jonah thrown overboard

Figure 9.5 (above) *The Good Shepherd*, ca. 300. Marble, height 3 ft. Vatican Museums, Rome. (The legs are restored.)

Figure 9.7 Book cover from Murano, Italy.

modeled on classical **putti** (winged angelic beings) carry a **Greek cross** encircled by a triumphal wreath, while below, scenes from the life of Jonah ("reborn" from the belly of the whale) make reference to redemption and resurrection in Christ. Despite its classical borrowings, the piece abandons Greco-Roman realism in favor of symbolic abstraction.

Early Christian Architecture

The legalization of Christianity made possible the construction of monumental houses for public religious worship. In the West, the Early Christian church building was modeled on the Roman basilica (see Figure 6.16). As with the sacred temples of Antiquity, the Christian church consisted of a hierarchy of spaces that ushered the devotee

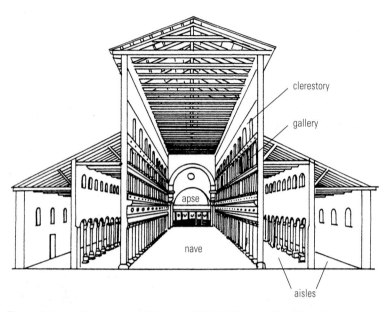

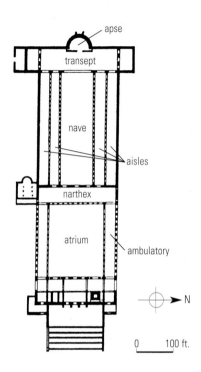

Figure 9.8 (above) Cross section and floor plan of Old Saint Peter's Basilica, Rome, fourth century. Interior of basilica approx. 208 × 355 ft., height of nave 105 ft.

Figure 9.9 (below) Interior of Saint Paul's Outside the Walls, Rome, begun 386. Etching by Giambattista Piranesi, 1749. Reproduced by courtesy of the Trustees of the British Museum.

from the chaos of the everyday world to the serenity of the sacred chamber, and ultimately, to the ritual of deliverance. One entered Rome's earliest Christian basilicas, Saint Peter's and Saint Paul's, through the unroofed atrium that was surrounded on three sides by a covered walkway or **ambulatory**, and on the fourth side (directly in front of the church entrance) by a vestibule, or **narthex**. This outer zone provided a transition between temporal and spiritual realms. Having crossed the vestibule and entered through the west portal, one proceeded down the long, colonnaded central hall or **nave**, flanked on either side by two aisles; the upper wall of the nave consisted of the **gallery** and the **clerestory** (Figure 9.8). The gallery was often decorated with mosaics or frescoes illuminated by light that entered the basilica through the clerestory windows (Figures **9.9, 9.10**).

Toward the east end of the church, lying across the axis of the nave, was a rectangular area called the **transept**. The north and south arms of the transept, which might be extended to form a Latin cross, provided entrances additional to the main doorway at the west end of the church. Crossing the transept, one continued toward the triumphal arch that framed the **apse**, the semicircular space beyond the transept. In the apse, at an altar that

Figure 9.10 Interior of the nave of Saint Paul's Outside the Walls, Rome (after reconstruction), begun 386. © Canali Photobank, Capriolo (BS) Italy.

Figure 9.11 *Christ Teaching the Apostles in the Heavenly Jerusalem*, ca. 401–417. Mosaic. Apse of Santa Pudenziana, Rome. © 1990, Photo Scala, Florence.

stood on a raised platform, one received the sacrament of Holy Communion. As in ancient Egypt, which prized the eastern horizon as the site of the sun's daily "rebirth," so in Christian ritual the most important of the sacraments was celebrated in the East. The Christian pilgrimage from secular to sacred space thus symbolized the soul's progress from sin to salvation.

Early Christian churches served as places of worship, but they also entombed the bones of Christian martyrs, usually beneath the altar. Hence, church buildings were massive shrines, as well as settings for the performance of the liturgy. Their spacious interiors—Old Saint Peter's basilica was approximately 355 feet long and 208 feet wide—accommodated thousands of Christian pilgrims. However, the wood-trussed roofs of these churches made them especially vulnerable to fire. None of the great Early Christian structures has survived, but the heavily restored basilica of Saint Paul Outside the Walls offers some idea of the magnificence of the early church interior.

The Latin cross plan (see Figure 9.2) became the model for medieval churches in the West. The church exterior, which clearly reflected the functional divisions of the interior, was usually left plain and unadorned, while the interior was lavishly decorated with mosaics consisting of tiny pieces of colored glass or marble set in wet cement. The technique had been invented by the Romans, who used it largely to decorate the floors of public or private buildings (see Figure 6.26). In Early Christian art, it became the ideal means of conveying the transcendental character of the Christian message. The medium encouraged the

invention of flat, simplified shapes arranged in radiant color patterns. Glass backed with gold leaf added splendor to the total effect. As daylight or candlelight flickered across walls embellished with mosaic, surface designs were transformed into sparkling and ethereal apparitions.

In the fifth-century mosaic of *Christ Teaching the Apostles* from the apse of Santa Pudenziana in Rome (Figure **9.11**), the heavenly city unfolds below the hovering image of a magnificent jeweled cross flanked by winged symbols of the four evangelists. The bearded Jesus, here conceived as a Roman emperor, rules the world from atop "the throne set in heaven" as described in Revelation 4. Two female figures, personifications of the Old and New Testaments, offer wreaths of victory to Peter and Paul. Looking like an assembly of Roman senators, the apostles receive the Law, symbolized by the open book, and the **benediction** (blessing) of Jesus.

Byzantine Art and Architecture

In the churches of Byzantium, the mosaic technique reached its artistic peak. Byzantine church architects favored the Greek cross plan by which all four arms of the structure were of equal length (see Figure 9.2). At the crossing point rose a large and imposing dome. Occasionally, as with the most notable example of Byzantine architecture, Hagia Sophia ("Holy Wisdom"), the longitudinal axis of the Latin cross plan was combined with the Greek cross plan (Figure **9.12**). The crowning architectural glory and principal church of Constantinople, Hagia Sophia (Figures **9.13**, **9.14**) was commissioned in

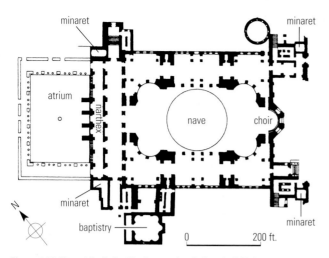

Figure 9.12 Plan of Hagia Sophia, Constantinople (Istanbul), Turkey.

532 by the East Roman emperor Justinian (481–565). Its massive dome—112 feet in diameter—rises 184 feet above the pavement (40 feet higher than the Pantheon; see chapter 6). Triangular **pendentives** make the transition between the square base of the building and the super-structure (Figure **9.15**). Light filtering through the forty closely set windows at the base of the dome creates the impression that the dome is floating miraculously above the substance of the building. That light, whose symbolic value was as important to Byzantine liturgy as it was to Saint Ambrose's "Ancient Morning Hymn," illuminated the resplendent mosaics and colored marble surfaces that once filled the interior of the church. After the fall of Constantinople to the Turks in 1453, the Muslims trans-formed Hagia Sophia into a mosque and whitewashed its mosaics (in accordance with the Islamic prohibition against images). Modern Turkish officials, however, have made the building a museum and restored some of the original mosaics.

Hagia Sophia marks the Golden Age of Byzantine art and architecture that took place under the leadership of the emperor Justinian. Assuming the throne in 527,

Justinian envisioned Constantinople as the "New Rome." Of his most monumental architectural commission, Hagia Sophia, he is said to have boasted that he had surpassed King Solomon. Encouraged by his clever and ambitious consort Theodora, he sought to reunify the eastern and western portions of the old Roman Empire (Map **9.1**). Though he did not achieve this goal, he nevertheless restored the prestige of ancient Rome by commissioning one of the monumental projects of his time: the revision and codification of Roman law. The monumental *Corpus juris civilis* (the *Collected Civil Law*) consisted of four parts: the *Code*, a compilation of Roman laws; the *Digest*, summaries of the opinions of jurists; the *Institutes*, a legal textbook; and the *Novels*, a collection of laws issued after 533. This testament to the primacy of law over imperial authority would have an enormous influence on legal and political history in the West, especially after the eleventh century, when it became the basis for the legal systems in most of the European states. Justinian's influence was equally important to the Byzantine economy. By directing his ambassadors to smuggle silkworm eggs out of China, Justinian initiated the silk industry that came to compete with Eastern markets. The city that served as Justinian's western imperial outpost was Ravenna, located in north-west Italy (see Map 9.1). Here Justinian commissioned the construction of one of the small gems of Byzantine archi-tecture: the church of San Vitale (Figure **9.16**). The drab exterior of this domed octagonal structure hardly prepares one for the radiant interior, the walls of which are embell-ished with polychrome marble, carved alabaster columns, and some of the most magnificent mosaics in the history of world art (Figure **9.17**). The mosaics on either side of the altar show Justinian and his consort Theodora, each carry-ing offerings to Christ (Figures **9.18**, **9.19**). The iconog-raphy of the Justinian representation illustrates the bond between Church and state that characterized Byzantine history: Justinian is flanked by twelve companions, an allu-sion to Christ and the apostles. On his right are his soldiers, the defenders of Christ (note the *chi* and *rho*

Figure 9.13 Anthemius of Tralles and Isidorus of Miletus, Hagia Sophia, from the southwest, Constantinople, Turkey, 532–537. Dome height 184 ft.; diameter 112 ft. The body of the original church is now surrounded by later additions, including the minarets built after 1453 under the Ottoman Turks. Sonia Halliday Photographs.

Figure 9.14 (opposite) Hagia Sophia, Constantinople. © AKG Images/Erich Lessing

Figure 9.15 (right) Schematic drawing of the dome of Hagia Sophia, showing pendentives.

Figure 9.16 (below) San Vitale, Ravenna, Italy, ca. 526–547. Art Archive, London.

Figure 9.17 (far right) San Vitale, Ravenna. © 1990, Photo Scala, Florence.

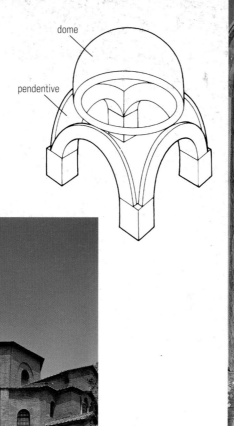

dome
pendentive

Map 9.1 The Byzantine World Under Justinian, 565.

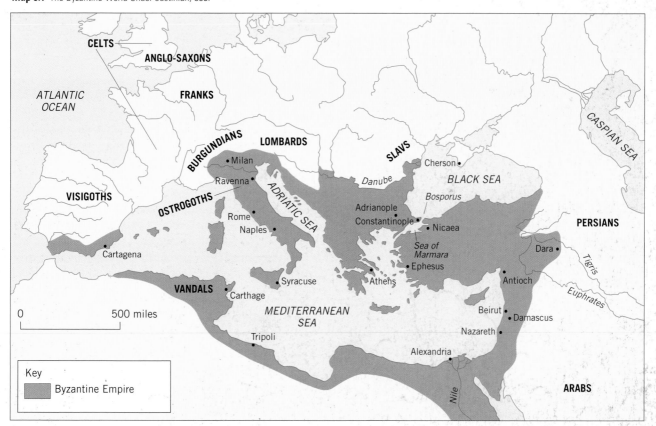

CELTS

ANGLO-SAXONS

ATLANTIC OCEAN

FRANKS

BURGUNDIANS   LOMBARDS

SLAVS

Cherson •

BLACK SEA

CASPIAN SEA

VISIGOTHS

• Milan

Ravenna •

ADRIATIC SEA

Danube

Bosporus

Adrianople •

OSTROGOTHS

Rome •

Constantinople •   • Nicaea

PERSIANS

Naples •

Sea of Marmara

Dara •

Tigris

• Cartagena

ADRIATIC SEA

• Ephesus

Antioch •

Euphrates

VANDALS   •

Syracuse •

Athens •

Beirut •

• Damascus

Carthage •

MEDITERRANEAN SEA

Nazareth •

0   500 miles

Tripoli •

Alexandria •

Nile

Key

☐ Byzantine Empire

ARABS

Figure 9.18 *Emperor Justinian and His Courtiers*, ca. 547. Mosaic. San Vitale, Ravenna. © Cameraphoto Arte, Venice.

emblazoned on the shield), while on his left are representatives of the clergy, who bear the instruments of the liturgy: the crucifix, the book, and the incense vessel. Crowned by a solar disc or halo—a device often used in Persian and late Roman art to indicate divine status—Justinian assumes the sacred authority of Christ on earth, thus uniting temporal and spiritual power in the person of the emperor. At the same time, Justinian and his empress reenact the ancient rite of royal donation, a theme underscored by the illustration of the Three Magi on the hem of Theodora's robe (see Figure 9.19).

The style of the mosaic conveys the solemn formality of the event: Justinian and his courtiers stand grave and motionless, as if frozen in ceremonial attention. They are slender, elongated, and rigidly positioned—like the notes of a musical score—against a gold background that works to eliminate spatial depth. Minimally shaded, these "paper cut-out" figures with small, flapperlike feet seem to float on the surface of the picture plane, rather than stand anchored in real space. A comparison of this composition with, for instance, any Roman paintings or sculptural reliefs (see chapter 6) underlines the vast differences between the aesthetic aims and purposes of classical and Christian art. Whereas the Romans engaged a realistic narrative style

to glorify temporal power, the Christians cultivated an abstract language of line and color to celebrate otherworldly glory.

The sixth-century mosaic of *Jesus Calling the First Apostles, Peter and Andrew* (Figure **9.20**) found in Sant'Apollinare Nuovo in Ravenna—a Christian basilica ornamented by Roman and Byzantine artisans—provides yet another example of the surrender of narrative detail to symbolic abstraction. In the composition, setting is minimal: a gold background shuts out space and provides a supernatural screen against which ritualized action takes place. The figures, stiff and immovable, seem to lack substance. There is almost no sense of muscle and bone beneath the togas of Christ and the apostles. The enlarged eyes and solemn gestures (reminiscent of Mesopotamian votive sculpture; see chapter 2) impart a powerful sense of otherworldly vision and omniscience.

The Byzantine Icon

Although religious imagery was essential to the growing influence of Christianity, a fundamental disagreement concerning the role of **icons** (images) in divine worship led to conflict between the Roman Catholic and Eastern Orthodox Churches. Most Roman Catholics held that

Figure 9.19 *Empress Theodora and Retinue*, ca. 547. Mosaic. San Vitale, Ravenna. © Cameraphoto Arte, Venice.

Figure 9.20 *Jesus Calling the First Apostles, Peter and Andrew*, early sixth century. Mosaic. Detail of upper register of north wall, Sant'Apollinare Nuovo, Ravenna. © 1990 Photo Scala, Florence - courtesy of the Ministero Beni e Att. Culturali.

visual representations of God the Father, Jesus, the Virgin, and the saints worked to inspire religious reverence. On the other hand, iconoclasts (those who favored the destruction of icons) held that such images were no better than pagan idols, which were worshiped in and of themselves. During the eighth century, Byzantine iconoclasm resulted in the wholesale destruction of images, while the Iconoclastic Controversy, which remained unresolved until the middle of the ninth century, generated a schism between the Eastern and Western Churches. Nevertheless, for over a thousand years, Byzantine monastics produced solemn portraits of Jesus, Mary, and the saints. The faithful regarded these devotional images as sacred; indeed, some icons were thought to have supernatural and miraculous powers. The idea of the icon as epiphany or "appearance" was linked to the belief that the image (usually that of Mary) was the tangible confirmation of the Blessed Virgin's miraculous appearance. The anonymity of icon painters and the formulaic quality of the image from generation to generation reflects the unique nature of the icon as an archetypal image—one that cannot be altered by the human imagination. Executed in glowing colors and gold paint on small, portable panels, Byzantine icons usually featured the Virgin and Child (alone or surrounded by saints) seated frontally in a formal, stylized manner (Figure **9.21**; compare Figure 9.19). While such representations look back to portrayals of Isis and other East Mediterranean mother cult deities (see Figure 8.1), they also prefigure medieval representations of the Virgin as the seat or throne of wisdom (see Figures 13.28, 13.32).

Following the conversion of Russia to Orthodox Christianity in the tenth century, artists brought new splendor to the art of the icon, often embellishing the painted panel with gold leaf and semiprecious jewels, or enhancing the garments of the saint with thin sheets of hammered gold or silver. To this day, the icon assumes a special importance in the Eastern Orthodox Church and home, where it may be greeted with a kiss, a bow, and the sign of the cross.

Figure 9.21 *Virgin and Child with Saints and Angels,* second half of sixth century. Icon: encaustic on wood, 27 × 18⅞ in. Monastery of Saint Catherine, Mount Sinai, Egypt.

Early Christian Music

Early Christians distrusted the sensuous and emotional powers of music, especially instrumental music. Saint Augustine noted the "dangerous pleasure" of music and confessed that on those occasions when he was more "moved by the singing than by what was sung" he felt that he had "sinned criminally." For such reasons, the early Church was careful to exclude all forms of individual expression from liturgical music. Ancient Hebrew religious ritual, especially the practice of chanting daily prayers and singing psalms (see chapter 2), directly influenced Church music. Hymns of praise such as those produced by Saint Ambrose were sung by the Christian congregation led by a **cantor**. But the most important music of Christian antiquity, and that which became central to the liturgy of the Church, was the music of the Mass.

The most sacred rite of the Christian liturgy, the Mass celebrated the sacrifice of Christ's body and blood as enacted at the Last Supper. The service culminated in the sacrament of Holy Communion (or Eucharist), by which Christians ritually shared the body and blood of their Redeemer. In the West, the service called High Mass featured a series of Latin chants known as either plainsong, plainchant, or Gregorian chant—the last because Gregory the Great codified and made uniform the many types of religious chant that existed in early Christian times. The invariable or "ordinary" parts of the Mass—that is, those used throughout the year—included "Kyrie eleison" ("Lord have mercy"), "Gloria" ("Glory to God"), "Credo" (the affirmation of the Nicene Creed), "Sanctus" ("Holy, Holy, Holy"), "Benedictus" ("Blessed is He that cometh in the name of the Lord"), and "Agnus Dei" ("Lamb of God"). Eventually, the "Sanctus" and the "Benedictus" appeared as one chant, making a total of five parts to the ordinary of the Mass.

One of the oldest bodies of liturgical song still in everyday use, Gregorian chant stands among the great treasures of Western music. Like all Hebrew and Early Christian hymnody, it is monophonic, that is, it consists of a single line of melody. Sung *a cappella* (without instrumental accompaniment), the plainsong of the early Christian era was performed by the clergy and by choirs of monks rather than by members of the congregation. Both the Ambrosian hymns and plainsong could be performed in a responsorial style, with the chorus answering the voice of the cantor, or antiphonally, with parts of the choir or congregation singing alternating verses. In general, the rhythm of the words dictated the rhythm of the music. Plainsong might be **syllabic** (one note to one syllable), or it might involve **melismatic** embellishments (with many notes to one syllable). Since no method for notating music existed before the ninth century, choristers depended on memory and on **neumes**—marks entered above the words of the text to indicate the rise and fall of the voice.

The duration and exact pitch of each note, however, had to be committed to memory.

Lacking fixed meter or climax, the free rhythms of Gregorian chant echoed through Early Christian churches, whose cavernous interiors enshrined sound and produced effects that were otherworldly and hypnotic. These qualities, conveyed only to a limited degree by modern recordings, are best appreciated when Gregorian chant is performed in large, acoustically resonant basilicas such as the remodeled Saint Peter's in Rome.

The Buddhist Identity

Buddhism, as it spread through India and China, followed a very different path from that of Christianity. Under the leadership of Asoka (see chapter 8), councils of Buddhist monks tried to organize the Master's teachings into a uniform, official canon; but they did not succeed in creating a single, monolithic interpretation of the Buddha's teachings—one adhered to by the entire Buddhist community, or even a majority thereof. Despite the unifying influence of the Buddha's sermons as collected in the *Pitakas*, Buddhism established no church hierarchy or uniform liturgy—a standardized ritual for public worship—comparable to that of the Roman and Orthodox communities of Christianity. The Buddhist identity was embellished, however, by a large body of folklore and legend, along with stories of the Master's previous lives, known as *jatakas* ("birth-stories"). The heart of Buddhist scripture, however, is a body of discourses informed by the Master's sermons. Devoted to uncovering "the truth of life," these teachings deal with such subjects as the nature of the Self, the cultivation of infinite consciousness, and the development of proper breathing. The essential element of the Buddhist "creed" calls for adherence to the Law of Righteousness (*dharma*) and the Eightfold Path. In its purist (Hinayana) form, it urges Buddhists to work out their own salvation. In its later (Mahayana) development, it seeks divine help in the quest for enlightenment. Within every Buddhist sect, however, can be found the monastic community—a place for religious retreat and spiritual practice similar to that of the early Benedictine community. The ancient Buddhist monastic complex centered on a hall used for teaching and meditation. An adjacent shrine or pagoda might hold relics or ashes of the Buddha.

While the majority of Buddhists belong to the laity, the Buddhist monk became the model of religious life. To this day, religious "services" consist only of the chanting of Buddhist texts (mainly the Buddha's sermons), the recitation of hymns and **mantras** (sacred word and sound formulas), meditation, and confession. And despite the deification of the Buddha among Mahayana Buddhists and the popular adulation of *bodhisattvas* who might aid humans to achieve *nirvana*, Buddhism never abandoned its profoundly contemplative character.

♪ See Music Listening Selections at end of chapter.

Buddhist Art and Architecture in India

Buddhist texts relate that upon his death, the body of the Buddha was cremated and his ashes divided and enshrined in eight burial mounds or *stupas*. When the emperor Asoka made Buddhism the state religion of India in the third century B.C.E., he further divided the ashes, distributing them among some 60,000 shrines. These came to house the relics of the Buddha (and his disciples) and mark the places at which he had taught. The most typical of Buddhist structures, the *stupa* is a beehivelike mound of earth encased by brick or stone. Derived from the prehistoric burial mound, it symbolizes at once the World Mountain, the Dome of Heaven, and the hallowed Womb of the Universe. A hemisphere set atop a square base, the *stupa* is also the three-dimensional realization of the cosmic *mandala*—a diagrammatic map of the universe used as a visual aid to meditation. Separating the shrine from the secular world are stone balustrades. Four gates mark the cardinal points of the compass; the walls and gates are carved with symbols of the Buddha and his teachings. As Buddhist pilgrims pass through the east gate and circle the *stupa* clockwise, they make the sacred journey that awakens the mind to the rhythms of the universe. The spiritual journey of the early Christian pilgrim is linear (from narthex to apse), marking the movement from sin to salvation, while the Buddhist journey is circular, symbolizing the cycle of regeneration and the quest for *nirvana*.

Begun in the third century B.C.E., the Great Stupa at Sanchi in Central India was one of Asoka's foremost

achievements (Figure **9.22**). Elevated on a 20-foot drum and surrounded by a circular stone railing, the shrine is 105 feet in diameter and rises to a height of 50 feet. It is surmounted by a series of *chatras*, umbrellalike shapes that signify the sacred bo tree under which the Buddha reached *nirvana*. The *chatras* also symbolize the levels of human consciousness through which the soul ascends in seeking enlightenment. Occasionally, *stupas* were enclosed in massive, rock-cut caves or placed at the end of arcaded halls adjacent to monastic dwellings (Figures **9.23**, **9.24**). Known as *chaitya* halls, these sacred spaces are not used for congregational worship, as with Early Christian churches; rather, they are sanctuaries for individual contemplation. Nevertheless, the *chaitya* hall bears a striking resemblance to the Early Christian basilica. Like the basilica, a long colonnaded hall leads the devotee from the veranda at the entrance to the semicircular apse in which the *stupa* is situated. The ceilings of both the Early Christian church and the *chaitya* hall were made of wood, but the latter was usually barrel vaulted, its curved rafters carrying the eye downward toward an ornate frieze or rows of elephants—ancient symbols of royal authority and spiritual strength associated with the Buddha.

Buddhism's prohibition of idolatry influenced art in the first centuries after the Master's death, during which time artists avoided portraying the Buddha in human form. Like the early Christians, who devised a body of sacred signs to represent the Christos (see Figure 9.2), Buddhists adopted symbols for the Buddha, such as the fig tree under which

Figure 9.22 West gateway, the Great Stupa, Sanchi, central India, Shunga and early Andhra periods, third century B.C.E.–early first century C.E. Shrine height 50 ft.; diameter 105 ft. © 1990, Photo Scala, Florence.

Figure 9.23 Interior of carved *chaitya* cave, Karli, India, ca. 50. Government of India, Archeological Survey of India.

he meditated, his footprints, elephants, and, most important, the wheel (signifying both the sun and the Wheel of the Law). These devices, along with sensuous images of nature deities retained from Vedic tradition, make up the densely ornamented surface of the 34-foot-high ***toranas*** (stone gateways) that mark the entrances to the Great Stupa at Sanchi (Figure **9.25**). Notably different from the Augustinian antagonism of flesh and spirit, and Christianity's general abhorrence of carnal pleasure, Buddhism (like Hinduism) regarded sexuality and spirituality as variant forms of a single, fundamental cosmic force. Hence, Buddhist art—in contrast with Christian art—did not condemn the representation of the nude

body. Indeed, Sanchi's voluptuous fertility goddesses, whose globular breasts and tubelike limbs swell with life, celebrate female sexuality as sensuously as any classically carved Venus (Figure **9.26**).

Mahayana Buddhism, however, glorified the Buddha as a savior, and thus, by the second century C.E., the image of the Buddha himself became important in popular worship. Contacts between Northwest India (Gandhara) and the West influenced the emergence of a distinctly human Buddha icon inspired by Hellenistic and Roman representations of the god Apollo. Gandharan artists created classically draped and idealized freestanding figures of the Buddha and the *bodhisattvas* (see Figures 8.5, 8.6). They

Figure 9.24 Elevation and ground plan of *chaitya* cave, Karli, ca. 50.

1 Stupa
2 Column
3 Aisle
4 Main Hall (Nave)
5 Entrance
6 Ambulatory
7 Apse
8 Veranda

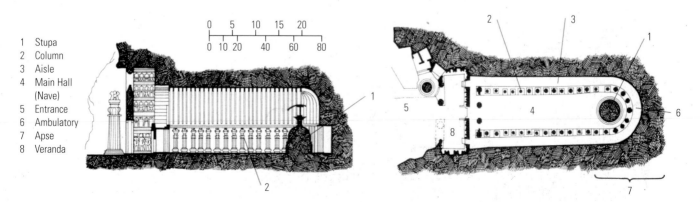

also carved elaborate stone reliefs depicting the life of the Buddha. One well-preserved frieze shows scenes from this narrative: the birth of the Buddha—shown miraculously emerging from the hip of his mother Queen Maya; the demonic assault on the Buddha as he achieves enlightenment beneath the Bodhi tree, his right hand touching the earth in the **mudra** (symbolic gesture) that calls the earth to witness his enlightenment (Figures **9.27**, **9.28**); the Buddha preaching the *Sermon at Benares*; and the death of the Buddha. In its union of realistic narrative and stylized symbolism, the frieze has much in common with Early Christian devotional images (see Figure 9.6).

Between the fourth and sixth centuries, under the sway of the Gupta Empire, India experienced a golden age in the arts as well as in the sciences. Gupta rulers commissioned Sanskrit prose and poetry that ranged from adventure stories and plays to sacred and philosophical works. Gupta mathematicians were the first to use a special sign for the numeric zero and Hindu physicians made significant advances in medicine. (As we shall see in chapter 10, the Arabs transmitted many of these innovations to the West.) In the hands of Gupta sculptors, the image of the Buddha assumed its classic form: a figure seated cross-legged in the position of yoga meditation (Figure **9.29**). The Buddha's oval head, framed by an elaborately ornamented halo, features a mounded protuberance (symbolizing spiritual wisdom), elongated earlobes (a reference to Siddhartha's princely origins), and a third "eye"—a symbol of spiritual vision—between the eyebrows (see Figure 8.5).

Figure 9.25 (above) East *torana* (gate), Great Stupa, Sanchi, India, early Andhra period, mid-first century B.C.E. Sandstone, height of gate 34 ft. Photo: A. F. Kersting, London.

Figure 9.26 (right) *Yakshi* (female fertility spirit) bracket figure, east *torana*, Great Stupa, Sanchi, India. Sandstone, height approx. 5 ft. Photo: Douglas Dickins, London.

Figure 9.27 *Enlightenment*, detail of frieze showing four scenes from the life of Buddha: *Birth*, *Enlightenment*, *First Preaching*, and *Nirvana*, from the Gandharan region of northwest Pakistan, Kushan dynasty, late second–early third century. Dark gray-blue slate, height 26⅜ in., width 114⅛ in., thickness 31⅜ in. Courtesy of the Freer Gallery of Art, Smithsonian Institution, Washington, D.C. 49.9.

His masklike face, with downcast eyes and gentle smile, denotes the still state of inner repose. His hands form a *mudra* that indicates the Wheel of the Law, the subject of the Buddha's first sermon (see Figure 9.28). Wheels, symbolizing the Wheel of the Law, are additionally engraved on the palms of his hands and the soles of his feet. The lotus, a favorite Buddhist symbol of enlightenment (and an ancient symbol of procreativity), appears on the seat of the throne and in the decorative motifs on the halo. Finally, in the relief on the base of the throne is the narrative

Figure 9.28 (below) *Mudras.*

abhaya mudra
reassurance and
protection

*bhumisparsha
mudra*
calling the earth
to witness

vitarka mudra
intellectual debate

dharmachakra mudra
teaching

dhyana mudra
meditation

Figure 9.29 *Teaching Buddha*, from Sarnath, India, Gupta period, fifth century. Sandstone, height 5 ft. 2 in. Archeological Museum, Sarnath.

depiction of the Buddha preaching: six disciples flank the Wheel of the Law, while two rampant deer signify the site of the sermon, the Deer Park in Benares (see Reading 2.4a). More stylized than their Gandharan predecessors, Gupta figures are typically full-bodied and smoothly modeled with details reduced to decorative linear patterns.

The Gupta period also produced some of the earliest surviving examples of Indian painting. Hundreds of frescoes found on the walls of some thirty rock-cut sanctuaries at Ajanta in Central India show scenes from the lives and incarnations of the Buddha (as told in Mahayana literature), as well as stories from Indian history and legend. In the Ajanta frescoes, musicians, dancers, and lightly clad *bodhisattvas* (Figure **9.30**) rival the sensual elegance of the carved goddesses at Sanchi. The Ajanta frescoes are among the best-preserved and most magnificent of Indian paintings. They rank with the frescoes of the catacombs and the mosaic cycles of Early Christian and Byzantine churches, though in their naturalistic treatment of form and in their mythic subject matter (which includes depictions of erotic love), they have no equivalent in the medieval West. They underline the fact that, in Buddhist thought, the divine and the human, the spirit and the body, are considered complementary rather than antagonistic.

Figure 9.30 Palace scene, Cave 17, Ajanta, India, Gupta period, fifth century. Wall painting.

Buddhist Art and Architecture in China

Between the first and third centuries, Buddhist missionaries introduced many of the basic conventions of Indian art and architecture into China. The Chinese adopted the *stupa* as a temple-shrine and place of private worship, transforming its moundlike base and umbrellalike structure into a **pagoda**, or multitiered tower with many roofs. These temple-towers are characterized by sweeping curves and upturned corners similar to those used in ancient watchtowers and multistoried houses (see chapter 7). At the same time, they recreate the image of the spreading pine tree, a beneficent sign in Chinese culture. Favoring timber as the principal building medium, Chinese architects devised complex vaulting systems for the construction of pagodas, of which no early examples have survived.

The earliest Buddhist building in China whose date is known is the twelve-sided brick pagoda on Mount Song in Henan, which served as a shrine for the nearby Buddhist monastery (Figure **9.31**). Constructed in the early sixth century, this pagoda has a hollow interior that may once have held a large statue of the Buddha. Pagodas, whether built in brick or painted wood, became popular throughout Southeast Asia and provided a model for all religious shrines—Daoist and Confucian—as well as for Hindu temples in medieval India.

In addition, the Chinese produced rock-cut sanctuaries modeled on India's monastic shrines. These contain colossal images of the Buddha and his *bodhisattvas*. Once sheltered by a sandstone cave front that collapsed centuries ago, the gigantic Buddha and standing *bodhisattva* at Yungang Cave 20 reveal sharply cut, masklike faces and calligraphic folds of clinging draperies (Figure **9.32**). The Chinese preference for abstract patterns and flowing, rhythmic lines also dominates the relief carvings in the limestone rock walls of late fifth- and sixth-century Buddhist caves (Figure **9.33**). Once painted with bright colors, the reliefs showing the emperor Xuanwu and his consort bearing ritual gifts to the shrine of the Buddha may be compared with the almost contemporaneous mosaics of Justinian and Theodora in San Vitale, Ravenna (see Figures 9.18, 9.19). Both the Ravenna mosaics and the Longmen reliefs are permanent memorials of rulers in the act of religious devotion. Lacking the ceremonial formality of its Byzantine counterpart, the image of *The Empress as Donor with Attendants* achieves an ornamental elegance that is as typical of Chinese relief sculpture as it is of Chinese calligraphy and painting.

By the sixth century, the Maitreya Buddha—the Buddha of the Future—had become the favorite devotional image of Mahayana Buddhism, and his cult promised rebirth in his paradise. This Buddha and his paradise would in later centuries be supplanted by Amitabha Buddha and his western paradise in popular Buddhist devotions (see chapter 14). In an elegant bronze altarpiece (Figure **9.34**), the Maitreya Buddha raises his right hand in the gesture of reassurance. Standing above a group of

Figure 9.31 Pagoda of the Song Yue Temple, Mount Song, Henan, China, 523. © the Huntington Archive, Columbus, Ohio

bodhisattvas and monks, he is framed by a perforated, flame-shaped halo from which winged angelic creatures sprout. An ornamental and calligraphic vitality infuses the design. Comparison of this devotional object with one from the Christian West—such as the ivory book cover from Murano (see Figure 9.6)—reveals certain formal similarities: in both the sacred personages (Jesus and the Buddha) are pictured centrally and physically larger than the accompanying figures, thus indicating their greater importance. Both depend on special symbols, such as the halo and the throne, to indicate divine status; and both employ stylization and abstraction to produce an iconic image. These devices, employed by artists East and West, worked to evoke spiritual truths that transcended the realm of ordinary reality.

Buddhist Music in India and China

In its origins and development, the music of India was inseparable from India's religious history. For thousands of years, Hindu priests chanted Vedic hymns (see chapter 3). Like the ancient Greeks, Hindus identified sound and rhythm with the cosmic principle and considered music a powerful curative. Moreover, to the Hindu, music represented the marriage of physical breath and spiritual being, a union of the personal life force (*Atman*) and the Absolute Spirit (*Brahman*).

Figure 9.32 (above) *Large Seated Buddha with Standing Bodhisattva*, Cave 20, Yungang, Shanxi, China, Northern Wei dynasty, ca. 460–470. Stone, height 44 ft. Werner Forman Archive, London.

Figure 9.33 (right) *The Empress as Donor with Attendants*, from the Binyang cave chapel, Longmen, Henan, China, Northern Wei dynasty, ca. 522. Fine gray limestone with traces of color, 6 ft. 4 in. × 9 ft. 1 in. The Nelson-Atkins Museum of Art, Kansas City, Missouri. Purchase: Nelson Trust.

chant proceeded, the pace of recitation increased, causing an overlapping of voices and instruments that produced a hypnotic web of sound.

Sliding, nasal tones characterized the performance of Chinese music. Such tones were achieved by both the voice and by the instruments peculiar to Chinese culture. China's earliest and most important instrument was the **zither**, a five- or seven-stringed instrument that is generally plucked with a plectrum and the fingertips (see Figure 14.11). Associated with ancient religious and ceremonial music, the zither was quickly adopted by Buddhist monks. The vibrato or hum produced by plucking the strings of the zither is audible long after the instrument is touched, a phenomenon that Buddhists found comparable to the pervasive resonance of chant (and to the human breath seeking union with the One).

SUMMARY

Between the fourth and sixth centuries, Christianity and Buddhism became world religions, each with its own set of religious symbols and its own identity. The Roman Empire was the vehicle by which Christianity rose to prominence in the West. It provided the early Christian Church with unique forms of administrative and cultural expression. A governing Church hierarchy and periodic Church councils worked to transform Christianity from a minor sect to an institutionalized religion. Christian monasticism, established in the West by Saint Benedict, played a large part in preserving and spreading the Christian message. Four Latin church fathers—Augustine, Jerome, Ambrose, and Gregory—helped to formulate a uniform Christian doctrine and a distinctive liturgy. The writings of Augustine of Hippo, the most important of the Latin church fathers, were crucial to the development of the allegorical tradition.

The Christian promise of personal salvation encouraged intuition and faith as primary modes of experience. In the visual arts, Christianity inspired a turning away from objective representation and the world of the senses. The language of symbolism and allegory came to convey the Christian message of deliverance.

Parallel with the rise of Roman Catholicism in the West, the Eastern Orthodox Church flourished in the East. The fifth and sixth centuries were a time of great church construction. Saint Peter's in Rome and Hagia Sophia in Constantinople typify the respective Western and Eastern church styles. During the reign of the Byzantine emperor Justinian, in Constantinople and Ravenna, some of the finest mosaics in the history of art were produced. In these mosaics, as in other examples of Early Christian art, formal abstraction replaced realism, and symbolism replaced literal representation. Christian churches provided splendid settings for the performance of the liturgy. The principal parts of the Mass, the ceremony celebrating the sacrament of Holy Communion, were recited in fluid, monophonic Gregorian chant.

Figure 9.34 Altar with Maitreya Buddha, Northern Wei dynasty, 524. Gilt bronze, height 30¼ in. The Metropolitan Museum of Art, New York. 38.158.1a–n.

Scholars did not begin to survey Buddhist music until the early twentieth century. It seems clear, however, that Buddhist religious practices were based in India's ancient musical traditions, specifically those that involved the intoning of sacred Hindu texts. The recitation of *mantras* and the chanting of Sanskrit prayers were central acts of meditation among Buddhist monks throughout Asia, and the performance of such texts assumed a trancelike quality similar to that of Western plainsong. Buddhist chant was monophonic and lacked a fixed beat; but, unlike Western Church music, it was usually accompanied by percussion instruments (such as drums, bells, cymbals, and gongs) that imparted a rich rhythmic texture. Complex drumming techniques were among the most notable of Indian musical contributions.

As in India, Buddhist chant in China and Japan was performed in the monasteries. It featured the intoning of statements and responses interrupted by the sounding of percussion instruments such as bells or drums. As the

♪ See Music Listening Selections at end of chapter.

Buddhist art and architecture flourished in India three centuries before the time of Jesus, but Buddhism spread into China and Southeast Asia only from the beginning of the first millennium C.E. Unlike Christianity, Buddhism provided no sacramental ceremonies comparable to the Mass and no clerical hierarchy to mediate between human beings and God. Essentially a religion of self-destiny, Buddhism did not devise a liturgy for congregational worship. Buddhism shared with Christianity a strong monastic component and a reverence for the relics of its founder. But while Early Christian churches were resplendent precincts for public ritual, Buddhist religious shrines and temples were primarily sites for devotional meditation. Music was not developed to serve any sacramental ceremony comparable with the Mass; nevertheless religious chant was essential to monastic Buddhism throughout Asia.

MUSIC LISTENING SELECTIONS

CD One Selection 2   Gregorian chant, "Alleluya, vidimus stellam," codified 590–604.

CD One Selection 3   Buddhist chant, Morning prayers (based on the Lotus Scripture) at Nomanji, Japan, excerpt.

GLOSSARY

abbot (Latin, "father") the superior of an abbey or monastery for men; the female equivalent in a convent of nuns is called an "abbess"

a cappella choral singing without instrumental accompaniment

ambulatory a covered walkway, outdoors or indoors (see Figures 9.8, 13.4)

apse the semicircular recess at the east end of a Roman basilica or a Christian church (see Figure 9.8)

benediction the invocation of a blessing; in art, indicated by the raised right hand with fore and middle fingers extended

canon law the ecclesiastical law that governs the Christian Church

cantor the official in Judaism who sings or chants the liturgy; the official in medieval Christianity in charge of music at a cathedral, later a choir leader and soloist for the responsorial singing

catacomb a subterranean complex consisting of burial chambers and galleries with recesses for tombs

chaitya a sacred space, often applied to arcaded assembly halls that enclose a *stupa*

chatra an umbrellalike shape that signifies the sacred tree

under which the Buddha reached *nirvana*

clerestory (also "clerstory") the upper part of the nave, whose walls contain openings for light (see Figure 9.8)

diptych a two-leaved hinged tablet; a two-paneled altarpiece

dogma a prescribed body of doctrines concerning faith or morals, formally stated and authoritatively proclaimed by the Church

ecumenical worldwide in extent; representing the whole body of churches

gallery the area between the clerestory and the nave arcade, usually adorned with mosaics in Early Christian churches (see Figure 9.8)

Greek cross a cross in which all four arms are of equal length

icon (Greek, "likeness") the image of a saint or other religious figure

iconography the study, identification, and interpretation of subject matter in art; also the visual imagery that conveys specific concepts and ideas

Latin cross a cross in which the vertical member is longer than the horizontal member it intersects

liturgy the prescribed rituals or body of rites for public worship

mandala a diagrammatic map of the universe used as a visual aid to meditation and as a ground plan for Hindu and Buddhist temple shrines

mantra a sacred formula of invocation or incantation common to Hinduism and Buddhism

melismatic with many notes of music to one syllable

mudra (Sanskrit, "sign") a symbolic gesture commonly used in Buddhist art

narthex a porch or vestibule at the main entrance of a church (see Figure 9.8)

nave the central aisle of a church between the altar and the apse, usually demarcated from the side aisles by columns or piers (see Figure 9.8)

neume a mark or symbol indicating the direction of the voice in the early notation of Gregorian chant

orans a gesture involving the raising of the arms in an attitude of prayer

pagoda an East Asian shrine in the shape of a tower, usually with roofs curving upward at the division of each of several stories

pendentive a concave piece of masonry that makes the transition between the angle of

two walls and the base of the dome above (see Figure 9.15)

putto (Italian, "child," plural *putti*) a nude, male child, usually winged; related to the classical Cupid (see chapter 6) and to Greco-Roman images of the angelic *psyche* or soul

regular clergy (Latin, *regula*, meaning "rule") those who have taken vows to obey the rules of a monastic order; as opposed to secular clergy (see below)

secular clergy (Latin, *seculum*, meaning "in the world") those ordained to serve the Christian Church in the world

stupa a hemispherical mound that serves as a Buddhist shrine

syllabic with one note of music per syllable

torana a gateway that marks one of the four cardinal points in the stone fence surrounding a *stupa*

transept the part of a basilican-plan church that runs perpendicular to the nave (see Figure 9.8)

zither a five- or seven-stringed instrument that is usually plucked with a plectrum and the fingertips; the favorite instrument of ancient China

CHAPTER 10

The Islamic World: Religion and Culture

"Whoever goes aright, for his own soul does he go aright; and whoever goes astray, to its detriment only does he go astray . . ."
The Quran

Islam, the world's youngest major religion, was born among the tribal peoples of the Arabian peninsula. The faith of the followers of Muhammad (ca. 570–632), it became the unifying force in the rise of the first global civilization since the fall of Rome. Islamic civilization was the geographic bridge between Europe and East Asia, as well as the historical link between the classical and early modern eras. But beyond its role as intermediary between the cultures of the East and the medieval West, Islam generated a rich cultural heritage of its own.

Between the eighth and fourteenth centuries, Islam brought spiritual unity and cultural cohesiveness to people

of a wide variety of languages and customs. Indeed, by the mid-eighth century an international Islamic community stretched from Spain (Al-Andalus) across North Africa and into India (Map 10.1). Just as Christianity absorbed the cultural legacy of the Mediterranean in its reach across the Roman world, so, in its rise, Islam drew on the cultures of Arabia, Southwest Asia, and Persia. Islam's control of the Mediterranean snuffed out the waning Western sea trade and ushered in a period of incubation in Christian Europe. At the same time, Muslim expansion played a key role in defining the geographic borders of Western Europe. During the Middle Ages, Muslim communities in

Map 10.1 The Expansion of Islam, 622–ca. 750.

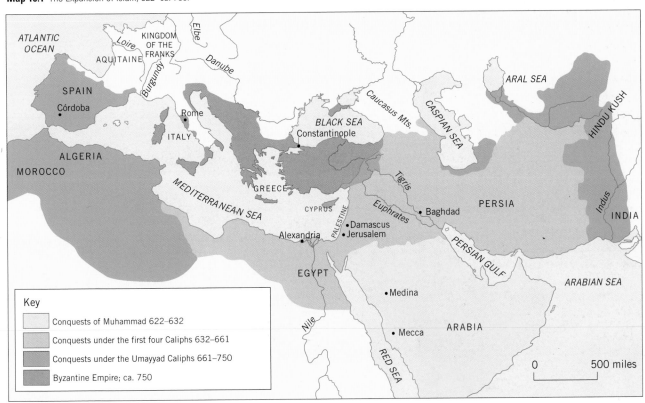

Key

- Conquests of Muhammad 622–632
- Conquests under the first four Caliphs 632–661
- Conquests under the Umayyad Caliphs 661–750
- Byzantine Empire; ca. 750

Spain, North Africa, and the Near East cultivated rich traditions in the arts and sciences. Muslim scholars in the cities of Baghdad (in present-day Iraq) and Córdoba (in Andalusia, or southern Spain) copied Greek manuscripts, creating a rich preserve of classical literature; and Islamic intermediaries carried into the West many of the greatest innovations of Asian culture. These achievements had far-reaching effects on global culture, on the subsequent rise of the European West and, more broadly, on the global humanistic tradition.

The religion of Islam is practiced today by some one billion people, more than two-thirds of whom live outside of Southwest Asia. In the United States, home to over six million Muslims, Islam is the fastest growing religion. These facts suggest that, despite a decline in Islamic culture after 1350, Islam remains one of the most powerful forces in world history.

The Religion of Islam

Muhammad and Islam

Centuries before the time of Christ, nomadic Arabs known as Bedouins lived in the desert peninsula of Arabia east of Egypt. At the mercy of this arid land, they traded along the caravan routes of Southwest Asia. Bedouin Arabs were an animistic, tribal people who worshiped some three hundred different nature deities. Idols of these gods, along with the sacred Black Stone (probably an ancient meteorite), were housed in the *Kaaba*, a sanctuary located in the city of Mecca (in modern Saudi Arabia). Until the sixth century

C.E., the Arabs remained polytheistic and disunited, but the birth of the prophet Muhammad in 570 in Mecca changed these circumstances dramatically.

Orphaned at the age of six, Muhammad received little formal education. He traveled with his uncle as a camel driver on caravan journeys that brought him into contact with communities of Jews, Christians, and pagans. At the age of twenty-five he married Khadijah, a wealthy widow fifteen years his senior, and assisted in running her flourishing caravan trade. Periods of retreat and solitary meditation in the desert, however, led to a transformation in Muhammad's life: according to Muslim teachings, the Angel Gabriel commanded Muhammad to proclaim his role as the prophet of the one and only Allah (the Arabic word for "God"). Now forty-one years old, Muhammad declared himself the final messenger in a history of religious revelation that had begun with Abraham and continued through Moses and Jesus.

At the outset, Muhammad's message attracted few followers. Since his attack on idolatry threatened Mecca's prominence as a prosperous pilgrimage site, the polytheistic Meccan elite actively resisted the new faith. Tribal loyalties among Meccans ran deep, and armed conflict was common. In 622, after twelve years of indecisive warfare with the Meccan opposition, the Prophet abandoned his native city. Along with some seventy Muslim families, he emigrated to Medina—a journey known as the *hijra* ("migration"). Eight more years marked by sporadic warfare were to elapse before the population of Medina was converted. When Muhammad returned to Mecca with a following of ten thousand men, the city opened its gates to him. Muhammad conquered Mecca and destroyed the idols in the *Kaaba*, with the exception of the Black Stone.

Figure 10.1 The *Kaaba*, Mecca, Saudi Arabia. Photo: Mohamed Amin/Robert Harding Picture Library, London.

Thereafter, Muhammad assumed spiritual and political authority—establishing a theocracy that bound religious and secular realms in a manner not unlike that of the early Hebrew kings. By the time Muhammad died in 632, the entire Arabian peninsula was united in its commitment to Islam. Since the history of Muhammad's successful missionary activity began with the *hijra* of 622, that date marks the first years of the Muslim calendar.

Submission to God

Muhammad preached the revealed word of Allah to his followers, who called themselves "Muslims" ("those who submit"). Identical with the god of the Jews and the Christians, Allah fulfilled the long Judeo-Christian biblical tradition of deliverance, making Muhammad "the last of the Prophets." The religion that would be called "Islam" ("submission to God's will") thus completed God's revelation. Addressed to all people, the message of Islam holds simply: "There is no god but Allah, and Muhammad is the Messenger of God." This declaration of faith is the first of the so-called "Five Pillars" of Muslim religious practice.

The Five Pillars
1 confession of faith
2 recitation of prayers five times daily
3 charitable contributions to the welfare of the Islamic community
4 fasting from dawn to sunset during the sacred month of Ramadan (during which Muhammad received his calling)
5 the *hajj* (pilgrimage) to the holy city of Mecca (and to the *Kaaba*)

The origins of the sacred shrine known as the *Kaaba* are variously explained. According to Muslim tradition, it was built by Abraham and his son Ishmael as a physical reminder of the links between Islam and Judaism. It is also identified as the spot where, at God's command, the biblical Abraham prepared to sacrifice his son Isaac.

Nevertheless, pilgrims who throng to Mecca, Muhammad's birthplace, consider the *hajj* an essential spiritual journey. At least once in their life, the devout Muslim makes the ritual procession that circles the *Kaaba* (Figure **10.1**) seven times (compare Buddhist ritual as described in chapter 9).

The Quran

Muhammad himself wrote nothing, but his disciples memorized his teachings and recorded them some ten years after his death. Written in Arabic, the Quran (literally, "recitation") is the Holy Book of Islam (Figure **10.2**). The Muslim guide to spiritual and secular life, the Quran consists of 114 chapters (*suras*) that reveal the nature of God and the inevitability of judgment and resurrection. The Quran is the supreme authority and fundamental source of the Muslim creed, rituals, ethics, and laws. It provides guidelines for worship and specific moral and social injunctions for everyday conduct. It condemns drinking wine, eating pork, and all forms of gambling. Islam limits **polygyny** (marriage to several women at the same time) to no more than four wives, provided that a man can support and protect all of them. Although the Quran defends the equality of men and women before God (see Sura 4.3–7), it describes men as being "a degree higher than women" (in that they are the providers) and endorses the pre-Islamic tradition requiring women to veil their bodies from public view (Sura 24:31; see Figure 10.3). Moreover, a husband has unrestricted rights of divorce and can end a marriage by renouncing his wife publicly. Nevertheless, Muhammad's teachings actually raised the status of women by condemning female infanticide, according women property rights, and ensuring their financial support in an age when such protections were not commonly guaranteed.

The Quran calls upon Muslims to undertake **jihad**, aggressive religious struggle. Often translated narrowly as "holy war," the word signifies all aspects of the Muslim drive toward spiritual and religious perfection, including the militant defense and spread of Islam. In Muslim thought and practice, there are multiple interpretations of this term;

Figure 10.2 Kufic calligraphy from the Quran, from Persia, ninth–tenth centuries. Ink and gold leaf on vellum, 8½ × 21 in. The Nelson-Atkins Museum of Art, Kansas City, Missouri. Purchase: Nelson Trust.

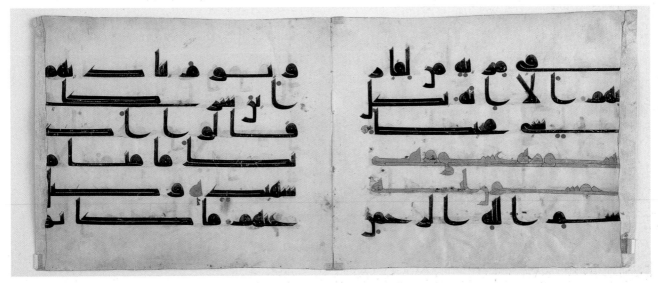

however, its dual aspect may be understood in Muhammad's distinction between "the lesser *jihad*" (war) and the "greater *jihad*" (individual self-control), the struggle to contain personal anger, lust, and other forms of indulgence.

Muslims consider the Quran the eternal and absolute word of God, and centuries of Muslim leaders have governed according to its precepts. It is sacred verse, intended to be chanted or recited, not read silently. Committed to memory by devout Muslims, the Quran is considered untranslatable, not only because its contents are deemed holy, but because it is impossible to capture in other languages the musical nuances of the original Arabic. Since the main textbook of the Muslim world is written in Arabic, many non-Arab-speaking Muslims have felt it necessary to learn that language. The foundation for all the Islamic sciences, including law and astronomy, the Quran is also the primary text for the study of the Arabic language.

READING 2.9 From the Quran[1]

Chapter 5 The Feast
In the name of God, the Lord of Mercy, the Giver of Mercy

. . . .

6. You who believe, when you are about to pray, wash your faces and your hands up to the elbows, wipe your heads, wash your feet up to the ankles and, if required, wash your whole body. If any of you is sick or on a journey, or has just relieved himself, or had intimate contact with a woman, and can find no water, then take some clean sand and wipe your face and hands with it. God does not wish to place any burden on you: He only wishes to cleanse you and perfect His blessing on you, so that you may be thankful.

7. So remember God's blessing on you and the pledge with which you were bound when you said, "We hear and we obey." Be mindful of God: God has full knowledge of the secrets of the heart.

8. You who believe, be steadfast in your devotion to God and bear witness impartially: do not let hatred of others lead you away from justice, but adhere to justice, for that is closer to awareness of God. Be mindful of God: God is well aware of all that you do.

9. God has promised forgiveness and a rich reward to those who have faith and do good works;

10. those who reject faith and deny Our revelations will inhabit the blazing Fire.

11. You who believe, remember God's blessing on you when a certain people were about to raise their hands against you and He restrained them. Be mindful of God: let the believers put their trust in Him.

. . . .

19. People of the Book[2], Our Messenger comes to you now, after a break in the sequence of messengers, to make things clear for you in case you should say, "No one has come to give us good news or to warn us." So someone has come to you to give you good news and warn you: God has the power to do all things.

. . . .

65. If only the People of the Book would believe and be mindful of God, We would take away their sins and bring them into the Gardens of Delight.

66. If they had upheld the Torah and the Gospel and what was sent down to them from their Lord, they would have been given abundance from above and from below: some of them are on the right course, but many of them do evil.

67. Messenger, proclaim everything that has been sent down to you from the Lord—if you do not, then you will not have communicated His message—and God will protect you from people. God does not guide those who defy Him.

68. Say, "People of the Book, you have no true basis [for your religion] unless you uphold the Torah, the Gospel, and that which has been sent down to you from your Lord," but what has been sent down to you [Prophet] from your Lord is sure to increase many of them in their insolence and defiance: do not worry about those who defy [God].

69. The [Muslim] believers, the Jews, the Sabians[3], and the Christians—those who believe in God and the Last Day and do good deeds—will have nothing to fear or to regret.

70. We took a pledge from the Children of Israel, and sent messengers to them. Whenever a messenger brought them anything they did not like, they accused some of lying and put others to death;

71. they thought no harm could come to them and so became blind and deaf [to God]. God turned to them in mercy but many of them again became blind and deaf: God is fully aware of their actions.

72. Those who say, "God is the Messiah, son of Mary," although the Messiah himself said, "Children of Israel, worship God, my Lord and your Lord," have defied [what he said]: if anyone associates others with God, God will forbid him from the Garden, and Hell will be his home. No one will help such evildoers.

73. Those people who say that God is the third of three[4] are defying [the truth]: there is only One God. If they persist in what they are saying, a painful punishment will afflict those of them who defy [the truth].

74. Why do they not turn to God and ask His forgiveness, when God is most forgiving, most merciful?

75. The Messiah, son of Mary, was only a messenger; other messengers had come and gone before him; his mother was a virtuous woman; both ate food [like other mortals]. See how clear We make these signs for them; see how deluded they are.

76. Say, "How can you worship something other than God, that has no power to do you harm or good? God alone is the All Hearing and All Knowing."

77. Say, "People of the Book, do not overstep the bounds of truth in your religion and do not follow the whims of those who went astray before you—they led many others astray themselves, and continue to stray from the right path."

. . . .

---

[1]Muhammad's followers arranged the 114 chapters of the Quran in order of length, from longest to shortest. The shorter chapters are, however, earlier in date.
[2]Jews and Christians

---

[3]Semitic merchants from the Saba, a kingdom in southern Arabia.
[4]The Trinity

Chapter 17 The Israelites

In the name of God, the Lord of Mercy, the giver of Mercy.

. . . .

9. This Quran does indeed show the straightest way. It gives the faithful who do right the good news that they will have a great reward and

10. warns that We have prepared an agonizing punishment for those who do not believe in the world to come.

11. Yet man prays for harm, just as he prays for good: man is ever hasty.

12. We made the night and the day as two signs, then darkened the night and made the day for seeing, for you to seek your Lord's bounty and to know how to count the years and calculate. We have explained everything in detail.

13. We have bound each human being's destiny to his neck. On the Day of Resurrection, We shall bring out a record for each of them, which you will find spread wide open,

14. "Read your record. Today your own soul is enough to calculate your account."

15. Whoever accepts guidance does so for his own good; whoever strays does so at his own peril. No soul will bear another's burden, nor do We punish until We have sent a messenger.

16. When We decide to destroy a town, We command those corrupted by wealth [to reform], but they [persist in their] disobedience; Our sentence is passed, and We destroy them utterly.

17. How many generations We have destroyed since Noah! Your Lord knows and observes the sins of His servants well enough.

18. If anyone desires [only] the fleeting life, We speed up whatever We will in it, for whoever We wish; then We have prepared Hell for him in which to burn, disgraced and rejected.

19. But if anyone desires the life to come and strives after it as he should, as a true believer, his striving will be thanked.

20. To both the latter and the former, We give some of your Lord's bounty. [Prophet], your Lord's bounty is not restricted—

21. see how We have given some more than others—but the Hereafter holds greater ranks and greater favors.

22. Set up no other god beside God, or you will end up disgraced and forsaken.

23. Your Lord has commanded that you should worship none but Him, and that you be kind to your parents. If either or both of them reach old age with you, say no word that shows impatience with them, and do not be harsh with them, but speak to them respectfully

24. and, out of mercy, lower your wing in humility toward them and say, "Lord, have mercy on them, just as they cared for me when I was little."

25. Your Lord knows best what is in your heart. If you are good, He is most forgiving to those who return to Him.

26. Give relatives their due, and the needy, and travelers—do not squander your wealth wastefully:

27. those who squander are the brothers of Satan, and Satan is most ungrateful to his Lord—

28. but if, while seeking some bounty that you expect from your Lord, you turn them down, then at least speak some word of comfort to them.

29. Do not be tight-fisted, nor so open-handed that you end up blamed and overwhelmed with regret.

30. Your Lord gives abundantly to whoever He will, and sparingly to whoever He will: He knows and observes His servants thoroughly.

31. Do not kill your children for fear of poverty—We shall provide for them and for you—killing them is a great sin.

32. And do not go anywhere near adultery: it is an outrage, and an evil path.

33. Do not take life—which God has made sacred—except by right. If anyone is killed wrongfully, We have given authority to the defender of his rights, but he should not be excessive in taking life, for he is already aided [by God].

34. Do not go near the orphan's property, except with the best intentions, until he reaches the age of maturity. Honor your pledges: you will be questioned about your pledges.

35. Give full measure when you measure, and weigh with accurate scales: that is better and fairer in the end.

36. Do not follow blindly what you do not know to be true: ears, eyes, and heart, you will be questioned about all these.

37. Do not strut arrogantly about the earth: you cannot break it open, nor match the mountains in height.

38. The evil of all these is hateful to your Lord.

. . . .

Chapter 47 Muhammad

In the name of God, the Lord of Mercy, the Giver of Mercy

1. God will bring to nothing the deeds of those who disbelieve and bar others from the way of God,

2. but He will overlook the bad deeds of those who have faith, do good deeds, and believe in what has been sent down to Muhammad—the truth from their Lord—and He will put them into a good state.

3. This is because the disbelievers follow falsehood, while the believers follow the truth from their Lord. In this way God shows people their true type.

4. When you meet the disbelievers in battle, strike them in the neck, and once they are defeated, bind any captives firmly—later you can release them by grace or by ransom—until the toils of war have ended. That [is the way]. God could have defeated them Himself if He had willed, but His purpose is to test some of you by means of others. He will not let the deeds of those who are killed for His cause come to nothing;

5. He will guide them and put them into a good state;

6. He will admit them into the Garden He has already made known to them.

7. You who believe! If you help God, He will help you and make you stand firm.

8. As for the disbelievers, how wretched will be their state! God has brought their deeds to nothing.

9. It is because they hate what God has sent down that He has caused their deeds to go to waste.

10. Have they not traveled the earth and seen how those before them met their end? God destroyed them utterly: a similar fate awaits the disbelievers.

11. That is because God protects the believers while the disbelievers have no one to protect them:

12. God will admit those who believe and do good deeds to

Gardens graced with flowing streams; the disbelievers may take their fill of pleasure in this world, and eat as cattle do, but the Fire will be their home.

13. We have destroyed many a town stronger than your own [Prophet]—the town which [chose to] expel you—and they had no one to help them.

. . . .

Chapter 76 Man

In the name of God, the Lord of Mercy, the Giver of Mercy

1. Was there not a period of time when man was nothing to speak of?[5]
2. We created man from a drop of mingled fluid to put him to the test; We gave him hearing and sight;
3. We guided him to the right path, whether he was grateful or not.
4. We have prepared chains, iron collars, and blazing Fire for the disbelievers, but
5. the righteous will have a drink mixed with *kafur*,[6]
6. a spring for God's servants, which flows abundantly at their wish.
7. They fulfill their vows; they fear a day of widespread woes;
8. they give food to the poor, the orphan, and the captive, though they love it themselves,
9. saying, "We feed you for the sake of God alone: We seek neither recompense nor thanks from you.
10. We fear the Day of our Lord—a woefully grim Day."
11. So God will save them from the woes of that Day, give them radiance and gladness,
12. and reward them, for their steadfastness, with a Garden and silken robes.
13. They will sit on couches, feeling neither scorching heat nor biting cold,
14. with shady [branches] spread above them and clusters of fruit hanging close at hand.
15. They will be served with silver plates
16. and gleaming silver goblets according to their fancy,
17. and they will be given a drink infused with ginger
18. from a spring called Salsabil.[7]
19. Everlasting youths will attend them—if you could see them, you would think they were scattered pearls,
20. and if you were to look around, you would see a vast, blissful kingdom—
21. and they will wear garments of green silk and brocade. They will be adorned with silver bracelets. Their Lord will give them a pure drink.
22. [It will be said], "This is your reward. Your endeavors are appreciated."
23. We Ourself have sent down this Quran to you [Prophet] in gradual revelation.

24. Await your Lord's Judgment with patience; do not yield to any of these sinners and disbelievers;
25. remember the name of your Lord at dawn and in the evening;
26. bow down before Him, and glorify Him at length by night.
27. These people love the fleeting life. They put aside [all thoughts of] a Heavy Day.
28. Yet We created them; We strengthened their constitution; if We please, We can replace such people completely.
29. This is a reminder. Let whoever wishes, take the way to his Lord.
30. But you will only wish to do so if God wills—God is all knowing, all wise—
31. He admits whoever He will into His Mercy and has prepared a painful punishment for the disbelievers.

Q How does the Quran describe the "People of the Book?"
Q How does the Muslim view of reward and punishment compare with that of other world faiths?

The Spread of Islam

To righteous Muslims of the hot and arid Arab desert, the Quran promised a paradisiacal garden filled with flowing rivers, shade-providing fruit trees, and handsome youths serving cool liquids in silver goblets. But paired with the sensuous pleasures of the Muslim Heaven were the terrifying punishments of Hell—as hot and dusty as the desert itself—the destination of the wicked and of **infidels** (nonbelievers). For those who accepted Allah, Islam provided a system of social justice and the guidelines for obedient worship. It offered, as well, a universal ethic that emphasized equality among all members of the Islamic community.

Islam's success in becoming a world faith is a remarkable historical phenomenon, one that is explained in part by the fact that, at the outset, religious, political, and military goals were allied. However, other factors were crucial to the success of Islam. The new faith offered rules of conduct that were easy to understand and to follow—a timely alternative, perhaps, to the complexities of Jewish ritual and Christian theology. In contrast with Christianity and Judaism, Islam remained free of dogma and liturgy and unencumbered by a priestly hierarchy. Orthodox Muslims venerated no intercessors and regarded the Trinity and the Christian cult of saints as polytheistic. The core Islamic texts, the Quran and the *Hadith* (a compilation of Muhammad's sayings and deeds compiled after his death), provide the all-embracing code of ethical conduct known as the **sharia** ("the path to follow"). Spiritual supervision lies (to this day) in the hands of prayer leaders (**imams**) and scholars trained in Muslim law (**mullahs**), whose duty it is to interpret the *sharia*.

Islam unified the tribal population of Arabia in a common religious and ethnic bond that propelled Muslims out of their desert confines into East Asia, Africa, and the West. The young religion assumed a sense of historical

CHAPTER 10 The Islamic World: Religion and Culture

---

[5]Literally, "Has there not come over man a period of time when he was not mentioned?" This refers to the time before a person is born, the point being that he was nothing, then God created him, just as He will bring him to life again for Judgment.
[6]A fragrant herb.
[7]Literally, "Seek the Way"; the word also means "sweet" and "rapid-flowing."

Figure 10.3 *The Slave Market at Zabīd, Yemen*, from the *Maqāmāt of al-Harīrī*, 1237. Bibliothèque Nationale, Paris. MS Arabe 5847, fol. 105.

mission much like that which drove the ancient Romans or the early Christians. In fact, the militant expansion of Islam—like the militant expansion of the Christian West (discussed in chapter 11)—was the evangelical counterpart of *jihad*. Militant Muslims would have agreed with Augustine that a "just cause" made warfare acceptable in the eyes of God (see chapter 9). Indeed, Christian soldiers anticipated heavenly rewards if they died fighting for Christ, while Muslims looked forward to Paradise if they died in the service of Allah.

Generally speaking, early Muslim expansion succeeded not so much by the militant coercion of foreign populations as it did by the economic opportunities Muslims offered conquered people. Unlike Christianity and Buddhism, Islam neither renounced nor condemned material wealth. Jews and Christians ("People of the Book") living in Muslim lands were taxed but not persecuted. Converts to Islam were exempt from paying a poll-tax levied on all non-Muslim subjects. Into the towns that would soon become cultural oases, Muslims brought expertise in navigation, trade, and commercial exchange. They fostered favorable associations between Arab merchants and members of the ruling elite (in Africa, for instance) and rewarded converts with access to positions of power and authority. While many subject people embraced Islam out of genuine spiritual conviction, others found clear commercial and social advantages in conversion to the faith of Muhammad.

Muhammad never designated a successor; hence, after his death, bitter controversies arose concerning Muslim leadership. Rival claims to authority produced major divisions within the faith and armed conflicts that still

exist today; the Sunni (from *sunna*, "the tradition of the Prophet") consider themselves the orthodox of Islam. Representing approximately ninety percent of the modern Muslim world population, they hold that religious rulers should be chosen by the faithful. By contrast, the Shiites (living primarily in modern Iran and Iraq today) claim descent through Muhammad's cousin and son-in-law Ali and believe that only his direct descendants should rule. Following Muhammad's death, the **caliphs**, theocratic successors to Muhammad, were appointed by his followers. The first four caliphs, who ruled until 661, assumed political and religious authority, and their success in carrying Islam outside of Arabia (see Map 10.1) resulted in the establishment of a Muslim empire. Damascus fell to Islam in 634, Persia in 636, Jerusalem in 638, and Egypt in 640. Within another seventy years, all of North Africa and Spain also lay under Muslim rule. The Muslim advance upon the West encountered only two significant obstacles: the first was Constantinople, where Byzantine forces equipped with "Greek fire" (an incendiary compound catapulted from ships) deterred repeated Arab attacks. The second was in southwest France near Tours, where, in 732, Frankish soldiers led by Charles Martel (the grandfather of Charlemagne) turned back the Muslims, barring the progress of Islam into Europe. Nevertheless, in less than a century, Islam had won more converts than Christianity had gained in its first three hundred years.

Islam's success in Africa was remarkable. As early as the seventh century, on the edges of the Sahara Desert and in North Africa, Muslim traders came to dominate commerce in salt, gold, and slaves (Figure 10.3). They soon commanded the trans-Saharan network that linked West

Africa to Cairo and continued through Asia via the Silk Road to China (see chapters 7, 14). Islam quickly became Africa's fastest growing religion, mingling with various aspects of local belief systems as it attracted a following primarily among the ruling elite of the continent's burgeoning kingdoms: in West Africa, Ghana, Mali, and Songhai (see chapter 18). The kings of Mali incorporated Islamic rituals into native African ceremonies; adopted the Arabic language for administrative purposes; hired Muslim scribes and jurists; and underwrote the construction of mosques and universities, the greatest of which was located at Timbuktu. In East Africa, as elsewhere, Swahili rulers who converted to Islam did not actively impose the religion on their subjects, so that only the larger African towns and centers of trade became oases of Islamic culture.

Between 661 and 750, Damascus (in modern Syria) served as the political center of the Muslim world. However, as Islam spread eastward under the leadership of a new Muslim dynasty—the Abbassids—the capital shifted to Baghdad (in modern Iraq). In Baghdad, a multiethnic city of more than 300,000 people, a golden age would come to flower. Between the eighth and tenth centuries, the city became an international trade center and expansive commercial activity enriched the growing urban population. Arab merchants imported leopards and rubies from India; silk, paper, and porcelain from China; horses and camels from Arabia; and topaz and cotton cloth from Egypt. The court of the caliph Harun al-Rashid (r. 786–809) attracted musicians, dancers, writers, and poets. Harun's sons opened a House of Wisdom (*Dar al-Hikmet*) in which scholars prepared Arabic translations of Greek, Persian, Syriac, and Sanskrit manuscripts. In the ninth century, no city in the world could match the breadth of educational instruction or boast a library as large as that of Baghdad. Al-Yaqubi, a late ninth-century traveler, called Baghdad "the navel of the earth" and "the greatest city, which has no peer in the east or the west of the world in extent, size, prosperity, abundance of water, or health of climate. . . ." He continued:

To [Baghdad] they come from all countries, far and near, and people from every side have preferred Baghdad to their own homelands. There is no country, the peoples of which have not their own quarter and their own trading and financial arrangements. In it there is gathered that which does not exist in any other city in the world. On its flanks flow two great rivers, the Tigris and the Euphrates, and thus goods and foodstuffs come to it by land and water with the greatest ease, so that every kind of merchandise is completely available, from east and west, from Muslim and non-Muslim lands. Goods are brought from India, Sind [modern Pakistan], China, Tibet, the lands of the Turks, . . . the Ethiopians, and others to such an extent that [products] are more plentiful in Baghdad than in the countries from which they come. They can be procured so readily and so certainly that it is as if all the good things of

the world are sent there, all the treasures of the earth assembled there, and all the blessings of creation perfected there. . . . The people excel in knowledge, understanding, letters, manners, insight, discernment, skill in commerce and crafts, cleverness in every argument, proficiency in every calling, and mastery of every craft. There is none more learned than their scholars, better informed than their traditionists, more cogent than their theologians, more perspicuous than their grammarians, more accurate than their [calligraphers], more skillful than their physicians, more melodious than their singers, more delicate than their craftsmen, more literate than their scribes, more lucid than their logicians, more devoted than their worshipers, more pious than their ascetics, more juridical than their [magistrates], more eloquent than their preachers, more poetic than their poets, and more reckless than their rakes.*

Although this description may reflect the sentiments of an overly enthusiastic tourist, it is accurate to say that, between the eighth and tenth centuries, the cosmopolitan cities of the Muslim world boasted levels of wealth and culture that far exceeded those of Western Christendom. Even after invading Turkish nomads gained control of Baghdad during the eleventh century, the city retained cultural primacy within the civilized world—although Córdoba, with a library of some 400,000 volumes, came to rival Baghdad as a cultural and educational center. The destruction of Baghdad in 1258 at the hands of the Mongols ushered in centuries of slow cultural decline. However, Mongols and Turks, themselves converts to Islam, carried Islamic culture into India and China. In Egypt, an independent Islamic government ruled until the sixteenth century. The Tunisian historian Ibn Khaldun, visiting fourteenth-century Egypt, called Cairo "the mother of the world, the great center of Islam and the

*Bernard Lewis, ed. and trans., *Islam from the Prophet Muhammad to the Capture of Constantinople*. New York: Oxford University Press, 1987, 69–71.

mainspring of the sciences and the crafts." Until the mid-fourteenth century, Muslims continued to dominate a system of world trade that stretched from Western Europe to China. Thereafter, the glories of medieval Muslim culture began to wane, to be revived only in the lavish court of the sixteenth-century Ottoman Turks and by the Moguls of seventeenth-century India (see chapter 21). The same cannot be said of the religion of Islam: over the centuries of Islamic expansion, millions of people found Islam responsive to their immediate spiritual needs, and in most of the Asiatic and African regions conquered prior to the late seventh century (see Map 10.1), it is still the dominant faith. To date, Islam has experienced less change and remains closer to its original form than any other world religion.

Islamic Culture

From its beginnings, Islam held the status of a state-sponsored religion; however, the unique feature of Islamic civilization is its diversity, the product of its assimilation of the many different cultures and peoples it encountered. The principal languages of the Islamic world, for instance, are Arabic, Persian, and Turkish, but dozens of other languages, including Berber, Swahili, Kurdish, Tamil, Malay, and Javanese, are spoken by Muslims. Moreover, as Islam expanded, it absorbed many different styles from the arts of non-Arab cultures. "Islamic," then, is a term used to describe the culture of geographically diverse regions—Arab and non-Arab—dominated by Islam.

Scholarship in the Islamic World

Following Muhammad's dictum to "seek knowledge," Islam was enthusiastically receptive to the intellectual achievements of other cultures and aggressive in its will to understand the workings of the natural world. At a time when few Westerners could read or write Latin and even fewer could decipher Greek, Arab scholars preserved hundreds of ancient Greek manuscripts—the works of Plato, Aristotle, Archimedes, Hippocrates, Galen, Ptolemy, and others—copying and editing them in Arabic translations. An important factor in this burst of literary creativity was the availability of paper, which originated in China as early as the second century and came into use in Baghdad during the ninth century. In the copying of classical manuscripts, in the codification of religious teachings (that had heretofore been passed orally), and in the production of new types of literature, such as scientific treatises, cookbooks, poems and tales (see Readings 2.10–12), paper provided a major advance over parchment and papyrus, expensive materials from whose surfaces ink could easily be erased. Between the ninth and twelfth century, Muslims absorbed and preserved much of the medical, botanical, and astrological lore of the Hellenized Mediterranean. This fund of scientific and technological knowledge, along with Arabic translations of Aristotle's works in logic and natural philosophy, and Muslim commentaries on Aristotle, filtered into the urban centers of Europe. There, in the twelfth century, they stimulated a rebirth of learning and contributed to the rise of Western universities (see chapter 12). Muslim philosophers compared the theories of Aristotle and the neoplatonists with the precepts of Islam, seeking a unity of truth that would become the object of inquiry among Italian Renaissance humanists. Crucial to the advancement of learning was the Muslim transmission of Hindu numbers, which replaced cumbersome Roman numerals with so-called "Arabic numbers" such as those used to paginate this book. Muslims also provided the West with such technological wonders as block printing (after the eighth century) and gunpowder (after the thirteenth century), both of which originated in China. Muslims thus borrowed and diffused the knowledge of Greek, Chinese, and Indian culture as energetically as they circulated commercial goods.

But the scholars of the Islamic world were not merely copyists; they made original contributions in mathematics, medicine, optics, chemistry, geography, philosophy, and astronomy. In the field of medicine, Islamic physicians wrote treatises on smallpox, measles, and diseases transmitted by animals (such as rabies), on the cauterization of wounds, and on the preparation of medicinal drugs (Figure 10.4). The single most important medieval health handbook, the *Tacuinum Sanitatis*, originated among Arab physicians

Figure 10.4 *Preparing Medicine from Honey*, from an Arabic manuscript of *Materia Medica* by Dioscorides, thirteenth century. Colors and gilt on paper, 12⅜ × 9 in. The Metropolitan Museum of Art, New York. Cora Timken Burnett Collection of Persian Miniatures and Other Persian Art Objects. Bequest of Cora Timken Burnett, 1956. 57.51.21.

Figure 10.5 Abd al-Karim al-Misri, Astrolabe, from Cairo, 1235–1236. Brass, height 15½ in. British Museum, London.

Science and Technology

1005	a comprehensive science library is founded in Cairo
1030	Ibn al-Haytham (Alhazen) publishes the first major work on optics since Hellenistic times
1035	publication of Ibn Sina's *Canon of Medicine*, an Arab compilation of Greek and Arab medical principles
1075	Arab astronomers posit the elliptical orbits of the planets
ca. 1150	al-Idrisi prepares a geographical survey of the world with maps for climatic sections

who examined the effects of various foods, drinks, and clothing on human well-being. Translated into Latin in the eleventh century, this manuscript came into widespread popular use throughout the West. The vast *Canon of Medicine* compiled by the Persian physician and philosopher Ibn Sina (Avicenna, 980–1037) was a systematic repository of medical knowledge in use well into the sixteenth century. Muslim chemists invented the process of distillation and produced a volatile liquid (and forbidden intoxicant) called *alkuhl* (alcohol). At a time when most Europeans knew little of the earth's physical size or shape, geographers in Baghdad estimated with some accuracy the earth's circumference, as well as its shape and curvature. Muslim astronomers made advances in spherical geometry and trigonometry that aided religious observance, which required an accurate lunar calendar and the means of determining the direction of Mecca from any given location. By refining the astrolabe, an ancient instrument for measuring the altitude of heavenly bodies above the horizon (Figure **10.5**), Muslims were able to determine the time of day, hence estimate the correct hours for worship.

Islamic Poetry

In the Islamic literary tradition—a tradition dominated by two highly lyrical languages, Arabic and Persian—poetry played an infinitely more important role than prose. As within the cultures of ancient Greece, Africa, and China, poetry and music were intimately related, and local bards or wandering minstrels were the "keepers" of a popular oral verse tradition. The Bedouin minstrels of pre-Islamic culture celebrated in song themes of romantic love, tribal warfare, and nomadic life. Bedouin songs, like the Arabic language itself, are rich in rhyme, and a single rhyme often dominates an entire poem. No English translation can capture the musical qualities of Arabic verse, and only some translations succeed in preserving its colorful descriptive imagery. Such is the case with the sixth-century ode by Tarafa in Reading 2.10, which uses vivid

similes to convey a memorable portrait of the camel that has captured his heart.

Following the rise of Islam, no literature was prized more highly than the Arabic lyrics that constituted the Quran. However, the pre-Islamic affection for secular verse persisted: the dominant themes in Islamic poetry included laments over injustice, elegies for the departed, and celebrations of the physical delights of nature. Romantic love—both heterosexual and homosexual, and often strongly erotic—was a favorite subject, especially among those who came under the influence of Persian literature. The eighth-century "Romance of Antar," a eulogy in honor of a beautiful and bewitching female, attributed to al-Asmai, reflects the sensual power of the finest Islamic lyrics. The poet's "ailment" of unrequited love, or "love-sickness," was a popular conceit in Arabic verse and one that became central to the code of courtly love in the medieval West. With their frank examination of physical desire and their reverence for female beauty, the poems of al-Asmai (740–828), Ibn Zaydun (1003–1071), and Ibn Abra—the latter two representative of Moorish* Islam—influenced the various genres of literature in Western Europe. This includes *troubadour* poetry, the medieval romance (see chapter 11), and the sonnets and songs of the Renaissance poet Petrarch (see chapter 16).

READING 2.10 Secular Islamic Poems (ca. 800–1300)

From Tarafa's "Praise for His Camel"

. . . .

Yet I have means to fly from grief, when such pursues me, on a lean high beast, which paces swiftly by day and by night,	1
A camel sure of foot, firm and thin as the planks of a bier, whom I guide surely over the trodden ways, ways etched in earth as texture is in cloth;	5
A she-camel, rival of the best, swift as an ostrich. When she trots her hind feet fall in the marks of her forefeet on the beaten road.	

---

*The term "Moor" describes a Northwest African Muslim of mixed Arab and Berber descent. The Moors invaded and occupied Spain in the eighth century and maintained a strong presence there until they were expelled from Granada, their last stronghold, in 1492.

With her white feathery tail she lashes backward and　10
　　forward. Sometimes the lash falls on her rider,
　　sometimes on her own dried udder, where no milk is,
　　flaccid as an old bottle of leather.
Firm and polished are her haunches as two worn jambs of
　　a castle gate.　15
The bones of her spine are supple and well-attached, and
　　her neck rises solidly.

When she raises her long neck it is like the rudder of a
　　boat going up the Tigris.
She carries her strong thighs well apart, as a carrier of　20
　　water holds apart his buckets.
Red is the hair under her chin. Strong she is of back, long
　　of stride; easily she moves her forelegs.

The marks of the girths on her sides are as the marks of
　　water-courses over smooth rock.　25
Sometimes the marks unite and sometimes are distinct,
　　like the gores in fine linen, well-cut and stitched.
Her long skull is like an anvil, and where the bones unite
　　their edges are sharp as the teeth of a file.
Her cheek is smooth as paper of Syria, and her upper lip　30
　　like leather of Yemen, exactly and smoothly cut.
The two polished mirrors of her eyes gleam in the caverns
　　of their sockets as water gleams in rocky pools.

Her ears are sharp to hear the low voices of the night, and
　　not inattentive to the loud call,　35
Pricked ears, that show her breeding, like those of a lone
　　wild bull in the groves of Haumel.
Her upper lip is divided and her nose pierced. When she
　　stretches them along the ground her pace increases.
I touch her with my whip and she quickens her step, even　40
　　though it be the time when the mirage shimmers on
　　the burning sands.
She walks with graceful gait, as the dancing girl walks,
　　showing her master the skirts of her trailing garment.

From Al-Asmai's "Romance of Antar"

　　　　. . . . .

The lovely virgin has struck my heart with the arrow of a　1
　　glance, for which there is no cure.
Sometimes she wishes for a feast in the sand-hills, like a
　　fawn whose eyes are full of magic.
My disease preys on me; it is in my entrails: I conceal it;　5
　　but its very concealment discloses it.
She moves: I should say it was the branch of the tamarisk[1]
　　that waves its branches to the southern breeze.
She approaches: I should say her face was truly the sun
　　when its luster dazzles the beholders.　10
She walks away: I should say her face was truly the sun
　　when its luster dazzles the beholders.
She gazes: I should say it was the full moon of the night
　　when Orion[2] girds it with stars.
She smiles: and the pearls of her teeth sparkle, in which　15

there is the cure for the sickness of lovers.
She prostrates herself in reverence towards her God;
　　and the greatest of men bow down to her beauties.
O Abla! when I most despair, love for thee and all its
　　weaknesses are my only hope!　20

Ibn Zaydun's "Two Fragments"

I

The world is strange
For lack of you;
Times change their common hue—
The day is black, but very night
With you was shining white.

II

Two secrets in the heart of night
We were until the light
Of busybody day
Gave both of us away.

Ibn Abra's "The Beauty-Spot"

A mole on Ahmad's cheek
Draws all men's eyes to seek
The love they swear reposes
In a garden there.
That breathing bed of roses
In a Nubian's care.

Q　What are the principal themes in these
　　poems?
Q　What similes and metaphors make
　　these poems distinctive?

Sufi Poetry

One of the richest sources of literary inspiration in Islamic history was the movement known as Sufism. As early as the eighth century, some followers of Muhammad began to pursue a meditative, world-renouncing religious life that resembled the spiritual ideals of Christian and Buddhist ascetics and neoplatonic mystics. The Sufi, so-called for the coarse wool (*suf*) garments they wore, were committed to purification of the soul and mystical union with God through meditation, fasting, and prayer. As the movement grew, Sufism placed increasing emphasis on visionary experience and the practice of intensifying physical sensation through music, poetry, and dance. Religious rituals involving whirling dances (associated with Persian sufis, known as "dervishes") functioned to transport the pious to a state of ecstasy (Figure 10.6). The union of the senses and the spirit sought by the members of this ascetic brotherhood is also evident in Sufi poetry.

Sufi poetry, as represented in the works of the great Persian mystic and poet Jalal al-Din Rumi (ca. 1207–1273), draws on the intuitive, nonrational dimensions of the religious experience. In the first of the following three poems, a number of seeming contradictions work to characterize the unique nature of the spiritual master. The

---

[1]A small tree or shrub from the Mediterranean region.
[2]A constellation of bright stars represented by the figure of a hunter with belt and sword.

Figure 10.6 *Dancing Dervishes*, from a manuscript of the *Diwan* (*Book of Poems*) of Hafiz, Herat School, Persia, ca. 1490. Colors and gilt on paper, 11¾ x 7⅜ in. The Metropolitan Museum of Art, New York. Rogers Fund.

body of Sufi instructions outlined in the second poem might be equally appropriate to the Buddhist or the Christian mystic. In the third piece, "The One True Light," from *Love is a Stranger*, Rumi rehearses an ancient parable that illuminates the unity of God: seeing beyond the dim gropings of the ordinary intellect, the mystic perceives that religions are many, but God is One.

READING 2.11 Rumi's Poems (ca. 1250)

The Man of God   *Spiritual Master*

The man of God is drunken while sober.	1
The man of God is full without meat.	
The man of God is perplexed and bewildered.	

The man of God neither sleeps nor eats.	
The man of God is a king clothed in rags.	5
The man of God is a treasure in the streets.	
The man of God is neither of sky nor land.	
The man of God is neither of earth nor sea.	
The man of God is an ocean without end.	
The man of God drops pearls at your feet.	10
The man of God has a hundred moons at night.	
The man of God has a hundred suns' light.	
The man of God's knowledge is complete.	
The man of God doesn't read with his sight.	
The man of God is beyond form and disbelief.	15
The man of God sees good and bad alike.	
The man of God is far beyond non-being.	
The man of God is seen riding high.	

The man of God is hidden, Shamsuddin.
The man of God you must seek and find. 20

Empty the Glass of Your Desire

Join yourself to friends 1
and know the joy of the soul.
Enter the neighborhood of ruin
with those who drink to the dregs.

Empty the glass of your desire 5
so that you won't be disgraced.
Stop looking for something out there
and begin seeing within.

Open your arms if you want an embrace.
Break the earthen idols and release the radiance. 10
Why get involved with a hag like this world?
You know what it will cost.

And three pitiful meals a day
is all that weapons and violence can earn.
At night when the Beloved comes 15
will you be nodding on opium?

If you close your mouth to food,
you can know a sweeter taste.
Our Host is no tyrant. We gather in a circle.
Sit down with us beyond the wheel of time. 20

Here is the deal: give one life
and receive a hundred.
Stop growling like dogs,
and know the shepherd's care.

You keep complaining about others 25
and all they owe you?
Well, forget about them;
just be in His presence.

When the earth is this wide,
why are you asleep in a prison? 30
Think of nothing but the source of thought.
Feed the soul; let the body fast.

Avoid knotted ideas;
untie yourself in a higher world.
Limit your talk 35
for the sake of timeless communion.

Abandon life and the world,
and find the life of the world.

The One True Light

The lamps are different, but the Light is the same: it
comes from Beyond. 1
If thou keep looking at the lamp, thou art lost: for thence
arises the appearance of number and plurality.
Fix thy gaze upon the Light, and thou art delivered from
the dualism inherent in the finite body.
O thou who art the kernel of Existence, the disagreement
between Moslem, Zoroastrian and Jew depends on the
standpoint.

Some Hindus brought an elephant, which they exhibited
in a dark shed. 5
As seeing it with the eye was impossible, every one felt it
with the palm of his hand.
The hand of one fell on its trunk: he said, "This animal
is like a water-pipe."
Another touched its ear: to him the creature seemed like
a fan.
Another handled its leg and described the elephant as
having the shape of a pillar.
Another stroked its back. "Truly," said he, "this elephant
resembles a throne." 10
Had each of them held a lighted candle, there would
have been no contradiction in their words.

Q What aspects of these poems reflect
religious mysticism?
Q Do they also put forth practical
insights or advice?

Islamic Prose Literature

Islam prized poetry over prose, but both forms drew on enduring oral tradition and on the verbal treasures of many regions. Unique to Arabic literature was rhyming prose, which brought a musical quality to everyday speech. One of the most popular forms of prose literary entertainment was a collection of eighth-century animal fables, which instructed as they amused. Another, which narrated the adventures of a rogue or vagabond characters, anticipated by five centuries the picaresque novel in the West (see chapter 24).

The rich diversity of Islamic culture is nowhere better revealed, however, than in the collection of prose tales known as *The Thousand and One Nights*. This literary classic, gradually assembled between the eighth and tenth centuries, brought together in the Arabic tongue various tales from Persian, Arabic, and Indian sources. The framework for the whole derives from an Indian fairy tale: Shahrasad (in English, Scheherazade) marries a king who fears female infidelity so greatly that he kills each new wife on the morning after the wedding night. In order to forestall her own death, Scheherazade entertains the king by telling stories, each of which she carefully brings to a climax just before dawn, so that, in order to learn the ending, the king must allow her to live. Scheherazade—or, more exactly, her storytelling—has a humanizing effect upon the king, who, after a thousand nights, comes to prize his clever wife. *The Thousand and One Nights*, which exists in many versions, actually contains only some 250 tales, many of which have become favorites with readers throughout the world: the adventures of Ali Baba, Aladdin, Sinbad, and other post-medieval stories are filled with fantasy, exotic characters, and spicy romance. The manner in which each tale loops into the next, linking story to story and parts of each story to each other, resembles the regulating principles of design in Islamic art, which include repetition, infinite extension, and the looping together of motifs to form a meandering, overall pattern (Figures **10.7** and **10.8**).

The story of Prince Behram and the Princess Al-Datma, reproduced below, addresses some of the major themes in Islamic literary culture: the power of female beauty, survival through cunning, and the "battle" of the sexes. While the story provides insight into Islamic notions of etiquette, it confirms the subordinate role of women in this, as in Western, society (see Reading 2.15). Nevertheless, ingenuity (exercised by both of the major characters in their efforts to achieve what they most desire) plays a saving role in both the tale told by Scheherazade and in the destiny of the storyteller herself, whose beauty, wit, and verbal powers prove to be a civilizing force.

READING 2.12 From *The Thousand and One Nights* (ca. 850)

"Prince Behram and the Princess Al-Datma"

There was once a king's daughter called Al-Datma who, in her **1** time, had no equal in beauty and grace. In addition to her lovely looks, she was brilliant and feisty and took great pleasure in ravishing the wits of the male sex. In fact, she used to boast, "There is nobody who can match me in anything." And the fact is that she was most accomplished in horsemanship and martial exercises, and all those things a cavalier should know.

Given her qualities, numerous princes sought her hand in marriage, but she rejected them all. Instead, she proclaimed, **10** "No man shall marry me unless he defeats me with his lance and sword in fair battle. He who succeeds I will gladly wed. But if I overcome him, I will take his horse, clothes, and arms and brand his head with the following words: 'This is the freedom of Al-Datma.'"

Now the sons of kings flocked to her from every quarter far and near, but she prevailed and put them to shame, stripping them of their arms and branding them with fire. Soon, a son of the king of Persia named Behram ibn Taji heard about her and journeyed from afar to her father's court. He brought men and **20** horses with him and a great deal of wealth and royal treasures. When he drew near the city, he sent her father a rich present, and the king came out to meet him and bestowed great honors on him. Then the king's son sent a message to him through his vizier and requested his daughter's hand in marriage. However, the king answered, "With regard to my daughter Al-Datma, I have no power over her, for she has sworn by her soul to marry no one but him who defeats her in the listed field."

"I journeyed here from my father's court with no other **30** purpose but this," the prince declared. "I came here to woo her and to form an alliance with you."

"Then you shall meet her tomorrow," said the king.

So the next day he sent for his daughter, who got ready for battle by donning her armor of war. Since the people of the kingdom had heard about the coming joust, they flocked from all sides to the field. Soon the princess rode into the lists, armed head to toe with her visor down, and the Persian king's son came out to meet her, equipped in the fairest of fashions.

Figure 10.7 Wooden doors carved with a geometric and floral design, twelfth century. Ethnological Museum, Konya. Photo: D. Talbot Rice.

Then they charged at each other and fought a long time, **40** wheeling and sparring, advancing and retreating, and the princess realized that he had more courage and skill than she had ever encountered before. Indeed, she began to fear that he might put her to shame before the bystanders and defeat her. Consequently, she decided to trick him, and raising her visor, she showed her face, which appeared more radiant than the full moon, and when he saw it, he was bewildered by her beauty. His strength failed, and his spirit faltered. When she perceived this moment of weakness, she attacked and knocked him from his saddle. Consequently, he became like a **50** sparrow in the clutches of an eagle. Amazed and confused, he did not know what was happening to him when she took his steed, clothes, and armor. Then, after branding him with fire, she let him go his way.

When he recovered from his stupor, he spent several days without food, drink, or sleep. Indeed, love had gripped his heart. Finally, he decided to send a letter to his father via a

Figure 10.8 Niche (*mihrab*) showing Islamic calligraphy, from Iran. The Metropolitan Museum of Art, New York. 39.20.

messenger, informing him that he could not return home until he had won the princess or died for want of her. When his sire received the letter, he was extremely distressed about his son **60** and wanted to rescue him by sending troops and soldiers. However, his ministers dissuaded him from this action and advised him to be patient. So he prayed to Almighty Allah for guidance.

In the meantime, the prince thought of different ways to attain his goal, and soon he decided to disguise himself as a decrepit old man. So he put a white beard over his own black one and went to the garden where the princess used to walk most of the days. Here he sought out the gardener and said to him, "I'm a stranger from a country far away, and from my **70** youth onward I've been a gardener, and nobody is more skilled than I am in the grafting of trees and cultivating fruit, flowers, and vines."

When the gardener heard this, he was extremely pleased and led him into the garden, where he let him do his work. So the prince began to tend the garden and improved the Persian waterwheels and the irrigation channels. One day, as he was occupied with some work, he saw some slaves enter the garden leading mules and carrying carpets and vessels, and he asked them what they were doing there. **80**

"The princess wants to spend an enjoyable afternoon here," they answered.

When he heard these words, he rushed to his lodging and fetched some jewels and ornaments he had brought with him from home. After returning to the garden, he sat down and spread some of the valuable items before him while shaking and pretending to be a very old man.

And Scheherazade noticed that dawn was approaching and stopped telling her story. When the next night arrived, however, she received the king's permission to continue her tale and said, **90**

In fact, the prince made it seem as if he were extremely decrepit and senile. After an hour or so a company of damsels and eunuchs entered the garden with the princess, who looked just like the radiant moon among the stars. They ran about the garden, plucking fruits and enjoying themselves, until they caught sight of the prince disguised as an old man sitting under one of the trees. The man's hands and feet were trembling from old age, and he had spread a great many precious jewels and regal ornaments before him. Of course, they were astounded by this and asked him what he was **100** doing there with the jewels.

"I want to use these trinkets," he said, "to buy me a wife from among the lot of you."

They all laughed at him and said, "If one of us marries you, what will you do with her?"

"I'll give her one kiss," he replied, "and then divorce her."

"If that's the case," said the princess, "I'll give this damsel to you for your wife."

So he rose, leaned on his staff, staggered toward the damsel, and gave her a kiss. Right after that he gave her the **110** jewels and ornaments, whereupon she rejoiced and they all went on their way laughing at him.

The next day they came again to the garden, and they found him seated in the same place with more jewels and ornaments than before spread before him.

"Oh sheikh," they asked him, "what are you going to do with all this jewelry?"

"I want to wed one of you again," he answered, "just as I did yesterday."

So the princess said, "I'll marry you to this damsel." **120**

And the prince went up to her, kissed her, and gave her the jewels, and they all went their way.

After seeing how generous the old man was to her slave girls, the princess said to herself, "I have more right to these fine things than my slaves, and there's surely no danger involved in this game." So when morning arrived, she went down by herself into the garden dressed as one of her own damsels, and she appeared all alone before the prince and said to him, "Old man, the king's daughter has sent me to you so that you can marry me." **130**

When he looked at her, he knew who she was. So he answered, "With all my heart and love," and he gave her the finest and costliest of jewels and ornaments. Then he rose to kiss her, and since she was not on her guard and thought she had nothing to fear, he grabbed hold of her with his strong hands and threw her down on the ground, where he deprived her of her maidenhead. Then he pulled the beard from his face and said, "Do you recognize me?"

"Who are you?"

"I am Behram, the King of Persia's son," he replied. "I've **140** changed myself and have become a stranger to my people, all for your sake. And I have lavished my treasures for your love."

She rose from him in silence and did not say a word to him. Indeed, she was dazed by what had happened and felt that it was best to be silent, especially since she did not want to be shamed. All the while she was thinking to herself, "If I kill myself, it will be senseless, and if I have him put to death, there's nothing that I'd really gain. The best thing for me to do is to elope with him to his own country."

So, after leaving him in the garden, she gathered together **150** her money and treasures and sent him a message informing him what she intended to do and telling him to get ready to depart with his possessions and whatever else he needed. Then they set a rendezvous for their departure.

At the appointed time they mounted racehorses and set out under cover of darkness, and by the next morning they had traveled a great distance. They kept traveling at a fast pace until they drew near his father's capital in Persia, and when his father heard about his son's coming, he rode out to meet him with his troops and was full of joy. **160**

After a few days went by, the king of Persia sent a splendid present to the princess's father along with a letter to the effect that his daughter was with him and requested her wedding outfit. Al-Datma's father greeted the messenger with a happy heart (for he thought he had lost his daughter and had been grieving for her). In response to the king's letter, he summoned the kazi[1] and the witnesses and drew up a marriage contract between his daughter and the prince of Persia. In addition, he bestowed robes of honor on the envoys from the king of Persia and sent his daughter her marriage **170** equipage. After the official wedding took place, Prince Behram lived with her until death came and sundered their union.

---

[1] Chief justice.

No sooner had Scheherazade concluded her tale than she said, "And yet, oh king, this tale is no more wondrous than the tale of the three apples."

Q Does this tale have a "moral"? If so, what does it teach?

Islamic Art and Architecture

Five times a day, at the call of **muezzins** (criers) usually located atop **minarets** (tall, slender towers; see Figure 9.13), Muslims are summoned to interrupt their activities to kneel and pray facing Mecca. Such prayer is required whether believers are in the heart of the desert or in their homes. The official Muslim place of worship, however, is the **mosque**: a large, columned hall whose square or rectangular shape derives from the simple urban house made of sun-dried bricks. The design of the mosque is not, as with the Early Christian church, determined by the needs of religious liturgy. Rather, the mosque is first and foremost a place of prayer. Every mosque is oriented toward Mecca, and that direction is marked by a niche (**mihrab**) located in the wall (Figure 10.8). Occasionally, the niche holds a lamp that symbolizes Allah as the light of the heavens and the earth (Sura 24.35). To the right of the *mihrab* is a small, elevated platform (**minbar**) at which the Quran may be read.

The Great Mosque in Córdoba, Spain, begun in 784 and enlarged over a period of three hundred years, is one of the noblest examples of early Islamic architecture. Its interior consists of more than five hundred double-tiered columns that originally supported a wooden roof (Figure 10.9). The floor plan of the Great Mosque (now a Catholic cathedral), with its seemingly infinite rows of columns, represents a sharp contrast with the design of the Early Christian basilica, which moves the worshiper in a linear fashion from portal to altar. At Córdoba, horseshoe-shaped arches consisting of contrasting wedges of white marble and red sandstone crown a forest of ornamental pillars (Figure 10.10). Such arches seem to "flower" like palm fronts from their column "stems." In some parts of the structure, multilobed arches are set in "piggyback" fashion, creating further ornamental rhythms. The dome of the *mihrab*, constructed on eight intersecting arches and lavishly decorated with mosaics, is clear evidence of Muslim proficiency in mathematics, engineering, and artistic virtuosity (Figure 10.11).

Islam was self-consciously resistant to image-making. Like the Jews, Muslims condemned the worship of pagan idols and considered making likenesses of living creatures an act of pride that "competed" with the Creator God. Hence, in Islamic religious art, there is almost no three-dimensional sculpture, and, with the exception of occasional scenes of the Muslim Paradise, no pictorial representations of the kind found in Christian art. Islamic art also differs from Christian art in its self-conscious avoidance of symbols. But such self-imposed limitations did not prevent Muslims from creating one of the richest

NO Symbols

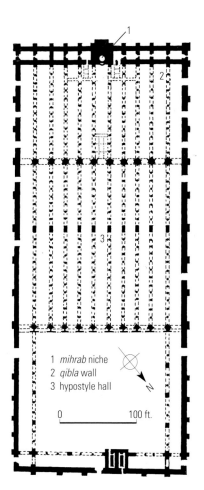

Figure 10.9 Plan of the Great Mosque, Córdoba. The additions of 832–848 and 961 are shown, but not the final enlargement of 987.

1 *mihrab* niche
2 *qibla* wall
3 hypostyle hall

0   100 ft.

bodies of visual ornamentation in the history of world art. Three types of motifs dominate the Islamic decorative repertory: *geometric*, *floral*, and *calligraphic*. Geometric designs, drawn largely from a classical repertory, were developed in complex and variegated patterns. Abstract, interlocking shapes often enclose floral motifs that feature the **arabesque**, a type of ornamentation based on plant and flower forms inspired by Byzantine and Persian art (Figure 10.7). Calligraphy, that is "beautiful writing," completes the vocabulary of ornamentation. In Islamic art, where the written word takes precedence over the human form, calligraphy assumes a sacramental character. Most calligraphic inscriptions were drawn from the Quran. In carved, painted, and enameled surfaces, the Word of Allah, written in elegant **Kufic**, the earliest form of Arabic script (originating in the Iraqi town of Kufa) plays an essential part in both embellishment and revelation. Whether calligraphic, floral, or geometric, Islamic motifs are repeated in seemingly infinite, rhythmic extension, bound only by the borders of the frame. "Meander and frame"—an expression of the universal theme of variety and unity in nature—is a fundamental principle of the Islamic decorative tradition and (as noted earlier) of Islamic aesthetics. The aesthetic of infinite extension sees Truth as intuitive and all-pervasive in time and space, rather than (as in Western Christian thought) as apocalyptic and self-fulfilling.

Complex surface designs executed in mosaics and polychrome patterned glazed tiles regularly transformed the exteriors of mosques and palaces into shimmering veils of

Figure 10.10 Columns in the Moorish part of the Great Mosque, Córdoba, 784–987. White marble and red sandstone. Photo: A. F. Kersting, London.

Figure 10.11 Dome of the *mihrab*, Great Mosque, Córdoba, Spain, originally built 784–787; additions 832–848, 961, and 987. Raffaello Bencini Fotografo Firenze.

light and color. Indeed, the bold use of color in monumental buildings is one of the unique features of Islamic architecture over the centuries. At the Dome of the Rock (Figure **10.12**), the earliest surviving Islamic sanctuary, Quranic inscriptions in gold mosaic cubes on a blue ground wind around the spectacular octagon. Constructed on a 35-acre plateau in east Jerusalem, the sanctuary (also known as the Mosque of Omar) is capped by a **gilded** dome. While much of the exterior has been refaced with glazed pottery tiles, the interior still shelters the original dazzling mosaics. Both in its harmonious proportions and its lavishly ornamented surfaces, the structure is a landmark of the Muslim faith. It is believed to crown the site of the creation of Adam and mark the spot from which Muhammad ascended to Heaven. It is also said to be the site of the biblical Temple of Solomon. Hence, the Dome of the Rock is a sacred monument whose historical significance—like that of Jerusalem itself—is shared, but also bitterly contested, by Jews, Muslims, and Christians.

The lavish combination of geometric, floral, and calligraphic designs distinguishes Islamic frescoes, carpets, ivories, manuscripts, textiles, and ceramics but, occasionally, calligraphy alone provides ornamentation. Along the rim of a tenth-century earthenware bowl, for instance, elegant Kufic script imparts Muhammad's injunction: "Planning before work protects one from regret; prosperity and peace" (Figure **10.13**). Here, as on the pages of an

Figure 10.12 Dome of the Rock, Jerusalem, Israel, ca. 687–691. Photo: Spectrum Picture Library, London.

early **illuminated manuscript** of the Quran (see Figure 10.2), fluid calligraphic strokes (with red and yellow dots to indicate vowels) provide the sole "decoration." While figural subjects are avoided in religious art, they abound in secular manuscripts, and especially in those produced after 1200. Travel tales (see Figure 10.3), fables, romances, chronicles, and medical treatises (see Figure 10.4) are freely illustrated with human and animal activities. In one miniature from an illustrated manuscript of Sufi poetry, dervishes (some of whom have succumbed to vertigo), musicians, and witnesses congregate in a tapestrylike landscape filled with flowers and blooming trees (see Figure 10.6).

Islamic art and architecture often feature the garden and garden motifs as symbolic of the Muslim Paradise, (which is mentioned in the Quran no fewer than 130 times). Like the biblical Garden of

Eden and the Babylonian Dilmun (see Reading 1.6), the paradisal garden is a place of spiritual and physical refreshment. Watered by cool rivers and filled with luscious fruit trees, the Garden of the Afterlife takes its earthly form in Islamic architecture. Luxuriant palaces throughout the Muslim world—real-life settings for the fictional Scheherazade—as well as royal tombs like the Taj Mahal (see chapter 21) normally feature gardens and park pavilions with fountains and water pools. At the oldest well-preserved Islamic palace in the world, the Alhambra in Granada, Spain, rectangular courtyards are cooled by clear, reflecting pools of water and bubbling, central fountains from which flow (in the

Figure 10.13 Islamic bowl with inscription. Glazed earthenware, height 7 in., diameter 18 in. The Metropolitan Museum of Art, New York. Rogers Fund, 1965.

Figure 10.14 Court of the Lions, the Alhambra, Granada, Spain, fourteenth century.

Two additional characteristics of Arab music (to this day) are its use of microtones (the intervals that lie between the semitones of the Western twelve-note system) and its preference for improvisation (the performer's original, spur-of-the-moment variations on the melody or rhythm of a given piece). Both of these features, which also occur in modern jazz, work to give Arab music its unique sound. The melodic line of the Arab song weaves and wanders, looping and repeating themes in a kind of aural arabesque; the voice slides and intones in subtle and hypnotic stretches. In its linear ornamentation and in its repetitive rhythmic phrasing, Arab music has much in common with literary and visual forms of Islamic expression. This vocal pattern, resembling Hebrew, Christian, or Buddhist chant, is not unlike the sound of the *muezzin* calling Muslims to prayer. Instrumental music took second place to the voice everywhere in the Islamic world, except in Persia, where a strong pre-Islamic instrumental tradition flourished. Lyres, flutes, and drums—all light, portable instruments—were used to accompany the songs of Bedouin camel drivers, while bells and tambourines might provide percussion for dancing. At the end of the sixth century, the Arabs developed the lute (in Arabic, *ud*, meaning "wood"), a half-pear-shaped wooden string instrument that was used to accompany vocal performance (Figures **10.15**, **10.16**). The forerunner of the guitar, the lute has a right-angled neck and is played with a small quill. Some time after the eighth century, Muslim musicians in Spain began to compose larger orchestral pieces divided into five or more distinct movements, to be performed by string and wind

cardinal directions) the four "paradisal rivers" (Figure **10.14**). This fourteenth-century palace—the stronghold of Muslim culture in the West until 1492—makes use of polychrome **stucco** reliefs, glazed tiles, lacy arabesque designs, and lush gardens simulating Heaven on earth.

Music in the Islamic World

For the devout Muslim, there was no religious music other than the sound of the chanted Quran and the *muezzin's* call to prayer. Muslims regarded music as a forbidden pleasure and condemned its "killing charm" (as *The Thousand and One Nights* describes it). Nevertheless, the therapeutic uses of music were recognized by Arab physicians and its sensual powers were celebrated by Sufi mystics. During Islam's golden age, secular music flourished in the courts of Córdoba and Baghdad, and, even earlier, Arab song mingled with the music of Persia, Syria, Egypt, and Byzantium.

The music of the Islamic world originated in the songs of the desert nomads—songs featuring the solo voice and unmeasured rhythms. (The meter of one type of caravan song, however, is said to resemble the rhythm of the camel's lurching stride.) As in ancient Greece, India, and China, the music of Arabia consisted of a single melodic line, either unaccompanied or with occasional instrumental accompaniment. It was, as well, modal (each mode bearing association with a specific quality of emotion).

See Music Listening Selections at end of chapter.

Figure 10.15 (above) Lute with nine strings. Spanish miniature from the *Cantigas de Santa Maria*, 1221–1289. El Escorial de Santa Maria, MS E-Eb-1-2, f.162.

Figure 10.16 (below) Drawing of a lute.

instruments, percussion, and voices. It is possible that the Western tradition of orchestral music, along with the development of such instruments as oboes, trumpets, viols, and kettledrums, originated among Arab musicians during the centuries of Muslim rule in Spain. Indeed, the renowned ninth-century musician Ziryab (known for his dark complexion as "the Blackbird") traveled from Baghdad through North Africa to Córdoba to become the founder of the first conservatory of music and patriarch of Arabo-Andalusian musical art. Music composition and theory reached a peak between the ninth and eleventh centuries, when noted Islamic scholars wrote almost two hundred treatises on musical performance and theory. They classified the aesthetic, ethical, and medicinal functions of the modes, recommending specific types of music to relieve specific illnesses. One Arab writer, al-Isfahani (897–967), compiled the _Great Book of Songs_, a twenty-one-volume encyclopedia that remains the most important source of information about Arab music and poetry from its beginnings to the tenth century. The wide range of love songs, many with motifs of complaint and yearning, would have a distinct influence on both the secular and the religious music of the Western Middle Ages and the Renaissance.

SUMMARY

In seventh-century Arabia, Islam emerged as the third of the global monotheistic religions. As the teachings of Muhammad, the Prophet of Allah, came to be recorded in the Quran, Muslims throughout Arabia followed the religious, social, and ethical mandates of a vibrant new faith. Islam rapidly expanded beyond the Arabian homeland to establish the most culturally productive civilization since

Roman times. Dominating the Mediterranean and much of Southwest Asia, Muslim traders and travelers formed a global community whose internal cohesiveness was based on a set of common moral and religious values.

Between the eighth and thirteenth centuries, the great centers of Muslim urban life—Baghdad in Iraq, Córdoba in Spain, and Cairo in Egypt—outshone the cities of Western Europe in learning and the arts. Muslims made unique contributions in the realms of poetry and prose, as well as in architecture, the visual arts, and music. The high degree of technical craftsmanship in these forms of expression is matched by a sophisticated taste for complex abstract design. Compositions marked by lyrical repetition and infinite extension are as evident in _The Thousand and One Nights_ as in the Great Mosque at Córdoba. Muslim scholars translated into Arabic the valuable corpus of Greek writings, which they transmitted to the West along with the technological and scientific inventions of Asian civilizations. But the scholars of the Islamic world also produced original work in the fields of mathematics, optics, philosophy, geography, and medicine, much of which had profound effects on the course of European culture. As the geographic intermediaries between Asia and Europe, the Muslims created the first truly global culture—a culture united by a single system of belief, but embracing a wide variety of regions, languages, and customs. To this day, Islam, with over one billion adherents, has preserved with little change the teachings of its founder. And, in our own time, Muslim countries and their populations have reassumed positions of worldwide consequence.

MUSIC LISTENING SELECTIONS

CD One Selection 4 Islamic Call to Prayer.
CD One Selection 5 Anonymous, Twisya no. 3 of the Nouba.

♪ See Music Listening Selections at end of chapter.

GLOSSARY

arabesque a type of ornament featuring plant and flower forms

caliph (Arabic, "deputy") the official successor to Muhammad and theocratic ruler of an Islamic state

gilded (or **gilt**) gold-surfaced; covered with a thin layer of gold, gold paint, or gold foil

hajj pilgrimage to Mecca, the fifth Pillar of the Faith in Islam

hijra (Arabic, "migration" or "flight") Muhammad's journey from Mecca to Medina in the year 622

illuminated manuscript a handwritten and ornamented book, parts of which (the script, illustrations, or decorative devices) may be embellished with gold or silver paint or with gold foil, hence "illuminated"

imam a Muslim prayer leader

infidel a nonbeliever

jihad (Arabic, "struggle" [to follow God's will]) the struggle to lead a virtuous life and to further the universal mission of Islam through teaching, preaching, and, when necessary, warfare

Kaaba (Arabic, "cube") a religious sanctuary in Mecca; a square shrine containing the sacred Black Stone thought to have been delivered to Abraham by the Angel Gabriel

Kufic the earliest form of Arabic script; it originated in the Iraqi town of Kufa

mihrab a special niche in the wall of a mosque that indicates the direction of Mecca

minaret a tall, slender tower usually attached to a mosque and surrounded by a balcony from which the _muezzin_ summons Muslims to prayer

minbar a stepped pulpit in a mosque

mosque the Muslim house of worship

muezzin a "crier" who calls the hours of Muslim prayer five times a day

mullah a Muslim trained in Islamic law and doctrine

polygyny the marriage of one man to several women at the same time

sharia the body of Muslim law based on the Quran and the Hadith

stucco fine plaster or cement used to coat or decorate walls

PART 2

The Medieval West

The popular picture of the Middle Ages is colored by knights in shining armor, hooded monks, walled castles, and bloody crusades. There is, indeed, much about the medieval world that provides food for fantasy; but, in reality, the era had a powerful impact on the evolution of Western values, beliefs, and practices. The geographic contours of modern European states and the basic political, religious, and linguistic traditions of Western Europe (to which Americans are deeply indebted) took shape during the Middle Ages. The prototypes of nation-states, cities, and universities emerged at this time, and the Roman Catholic Church reached its peak as a powerful political and spiritual institution. The feudal epic, the courtly romance, and the morality play appeared, along with the vernacular languages used in the West today. Medieval artists and artisans produced works of art and architecture that still dazzle modern beholders.

Three distinctly different cultures combined to produce the Middle Ages: Greco-Roman, Judeo-Christian, and Germanic. As these three strands mingled and blended, a new culture, whose mainstay was Christianity, came to dominate Western Europe. The Greco-Roman and the Judeo-Christian strands have been examined in previous chapters. Our examination, therefore, begins with an appraisal of Germanic culture and the ways in which the tribal invasions of the West affected the identity of the late Roman world. The empire of Charlemagne provides an excellent example of cultural synthesis: Germanic, Classical, and Christian. Though interrupted by Viking invasions, Carolingian culture laid the basis for medieval patterns of life. The feudal and manorial traditions of the Early Middle Ages (ca. 500–1000) established patterns of class and social status that came to shape the economic and political history of the West. In the masterworks of this period—the Song of Roland, the Bayeux Tapestry, Gregorian chant, and the gloriously illuminated pages of Christian liturgical manuscripts—we see reflected some of the principal features of early medieval culture: the spirit of rugged warfare, the obligations of feudal loyalty, and the rising tide of Christian piety. Between 700 and 1300, the approximate time frame for chapters 11 to 13, the population of medieval Europe rose from 27 million to 73 million people. The High Middle Ages (ca. 1000–1300) saw the onset of the Crusades, the revival of trade, the emergence of towns, and the rise of universities. Medieval Europe's centuries of incubation had given way to a new era, marked by urban growth and global outreach.

Throughout the Middle Ages the Catholic Church assumed a major role in shaping the belief system of medieval Christians. Catholic mystics and preachers articulated the promise of life after death in vivid terms that inspired such great literary works as Everyman and Dante's Divine Comedy. The great monastic centers, the Romanesque and Gothic churches, the lavishly adorned liturgical objects and manuscripts, and the rise of polyphonic religious music all give evidence of the spiritual yearnings of an age of faith. In the synthesis of all of these forms of expression—architecture, sculpture, painting, stained glass, metalwork, music, poetry, and drama—the Middle Ages provided a unique chapter in the history of the humanistic tradition.

(opposite) *The Ascension*, from the Sacramentary of Archbishop Drogo of Metz, ca. 842. Bibliothèque Nationale, Paris, MS Lat. 9428, f.71v.

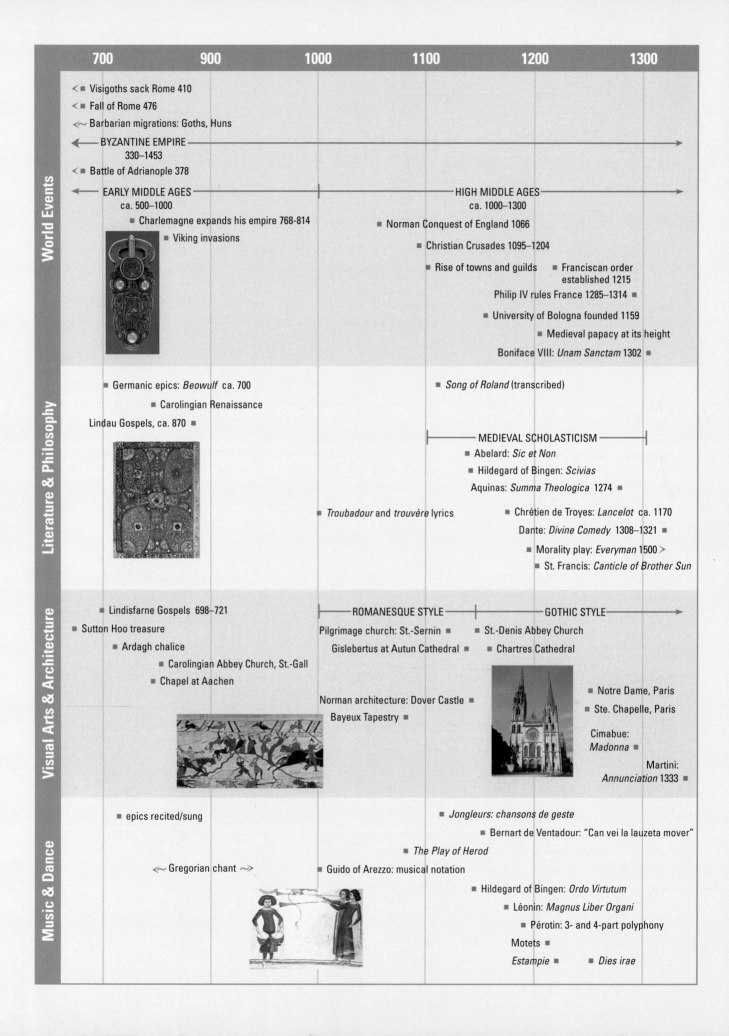

	700	900	1000	1100	1200	1300

World Events

< ■ Visigoths sack Rome 410
< ■ Fall of Rome 476
⌇ Barbarian migrations: Goths, Huns
← BYZANTINE EMPIRE → 330–1453
< ■ Battle of Adrianople 378

← EARLY MIDDLE AGES → ca. 500–1000
← HIGH MIDDLE AGES → ca. 1000–1300

■ Charlemagne expands his empire 768-814
■ Viking invasions

■ Norman Conquest of England 1066
■ Christian Crusades 1095–1204
■ Rise of towns and guilds   ■ Franciscan order established 1215
Philip IV rules France 1285–1314 ■
■ University of Bologna founded 1159
■ Medieval papacy at its height
Boniface VIII: *Unam Sanctam* 1302 ■

Literature & Philosophy

■ Germanic epics: *Beowulf* ca. 700
■ *Song of Roland* (transcribed)
■ Carolingian Renaissance
Lindau Gospels, ca. 870 ■

— MEDIEVAL SCHOLASTICISM —
■ Abelard: *Sic et Non*
■ Hildegard of Bingen: *Scivias*
Aquinas: *Summa Theologica* 1274 ■

■ *Troubadour* and *trouvère* lyrics   ■ Chrétien de Troyes: *Lancelot* ca. 1170
Dante: *Divine Comedy* 1308–1321 ■
■ Morality play: *Everyman* 1500 >
■ St. Francis: *Canticle of Brother Sun*

Visual Arts & Architecture

■ Lindisfarne Gospels 698–721
■ Sutton Hoo treasure
■ Ardagh chalice
■ Carolingian Abbey Church, St.-Gall
■ Chapel at Aachen

— ROMANESQUE STYLE —   — GOTHIC STYLE →
Pilgrimage church: St.-Sernin ■   ■ St.-Denis Abbey Church
Gislebertus at Autun Cathedral ■   ■ Chartres Cathedral

Norman architecture: Dover Castle ■
Bayeux Tapestry ■

■ Notre Dame, Paris
■ Ste. Chapelle, Paris

Cimabue: *Madonna* ■

Martini: *Annunciation* 1333 ■

Music & Dance

■ epics recited/sung

■ *Jongleurs: chansons de geste*
■ Bernart de Ventadour: "Can vei la lauzeta mover"
■ *The Play of Herod*

⌇ Gregorian chant ⌇   ■ Guido of Arezzo: musical notation

■ Hildegard of Bingen: *Ordo Virtutum*
■ Léonin: *Magnus Liber Organi*
■ Pérotin: 3- and 4-part polyphony
Motets ■
Estampie ■   ■ *Dies irae*

CHAPTER 11

Patterns of Medieval Life

*"When they mount chargers, take up their swords and shields,
Not death itself could drive them from the field.
They are good men; their words are fierce and proud."*
Song of Roland

In the five centuries following the fall of Rome in 476—a period often called the Dark Ages—Western Europe struggled for order and stability. During this formative era, more aptly termed the Early Middle Ages (ca. 500–1000), three traditions—classical, Christian, and Germanic—came together to produce the vigorous new culture of the medieval West. The Germanic tribes that moved upon the West in the first centuries of the Christian era (Map 11.1) contributed to the decline and decentralization of Roman civilization. Ultimately, however, Germanic tribal people and practices blended with those of classical Rome and Western Christianity to forge the basic economic, social, and cultural patterns of medieval life. The system of feudalism came to dominate early medieval society, while in the centuries immediately following the Crusades the revival of trade stimulated the rise of cities and the development of an urban culture.

Map 11.1 The Early Christian World and the Barbarian Invasions, ca. 500.

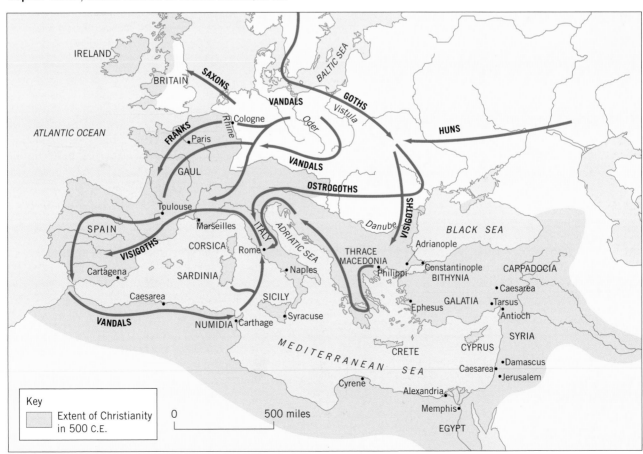

The Germanic Tribes

The Germanic peoples were a tribal folk who followed a migratory existence. Dependent on their flocks and herds, they lived in pre-urban village communities throughout Asia and frequently raided and plundered nearby lands for material gain, yet they settled no territorial state. As early as the first century B.C.E., a loose confederacy of Germanic tribes began to threaten Roman territories, but it was not until the fourth century C.E. that these tribes, driven westward by the fierce Central Asian nomads known as Huns, pressed into the Roman Empire. Lacking the hallmarks of civilization—urban settlements, monumental architecture, and the art of writing—the Germanic tribes struck the Romans as inferiors, as outsiders, hence, as "barbarians." Ethnically distinct from the Huns, the Germanic folk, including East Goths (Ostrogoths), West Goths (Visigoths), Franks, Vandals, Burgundians, Angles, and Saxons, belonged to one and the same language family, dialects of which differed from tribe to tribe. The Ostrogoths occupied the steppe region between the Black and Baltic seas, while the Visigoths settled in territories closer to the Danube River (see Map 11.1). As the tribes pressed westward, an uneasy alliance was forged: the Romans allowed the barbarians to settle on the borders of the Empire, but in exchange the Germanic warriors were obliged to protect Rome against other invaders. Antagonism between Rome and the West Goths led to a military showdown. At the Battle of Adrianople (130 miles northwest of Constantinople, near modern Edirne in Turkey) in 378, the Visigoths defeated the "invincible" Roman army, killing the East Roman Emperor Valens and dispersing his army. Almost immediately thereafter, the Visigoths swept across the Roman border, raiding the cities of the declining West, including Rome itself in 410.

The Battle of Adrianople opened the door to a sequence of barbarian invasions. During the fifth century, the Empire fell prey to the assaults of many Germanic tribes, including the Vandals, whose willful, malicious destruction of Rome in 455 produced the English word "vandalize." In 476, a Germanic commander named Odoacer deposed the reigning Roman emperor in the West, an event that is traditionally taken to mark the official end of the Roman Empire. Although the Germanic tribes leveled the final assaults on an already declining empire, they did not utterly destroy Rome's vast resources, nor did they ignore the culture of the late Roman world. The Ostrogoths embraced Christianity and sponsored literary and architectural enterprises modeled on those of Rome and Byzantium, while the Franks and the Burgundians chose to commit their legal traditions to writing, styling their codes of law on Roman models.

Germanic culture differed dramatically from that of Rome: in the agrarian and essentially self-sufficient communities of these nomadic peoples, fighting was a way of life and a highly respected skill. Armed with javelins and shields, Germanic warriors fought fiercely on foot and on horseback. Superb horsemen, the Germanic cavalry would come to borrow from the Mongols spurs and foot stirrups—devices (originating in China) that firmly secured the rider in his saddle and improved his driving force. In addition to introducing to the West superior methods of fighting on horseback, the Germanic tribes imposed their own longstanding traditions on medieval Europe. Every Germanic chieftain retained a band of warriors that followed him into battle, and every warrior anticipated sharing with his chieftain the spoils of victory. At the end of the first century, the Roman historian Tacitus (see chapter 6) wrote an account of the habits and customs of the Germanic peoples. He observes:

> All [men] are bound, to defend their leader . . . and to make even their own actions subservient to his renown. If he dies in the field, he who survives him survives to live in infamy. . . . This is the bond of union, the most sacred obligation. The chief fights for victory; the followers for their chief. . . . The chief must show his liberality, and the follower expects it. He demands, at one time this warlike horse, at another, that victorious lance drenched with the blood of the enemy.*

The bond of **fealty**, or loyalty, between the Germanic warrior and his chieftain and the practice of rewarding the warrior would become fundamental to the medieval practice of feudalism.

Germanic Law

Germanic law was not legislated by the state, as in Roman tradition, but was, rather, a collection of customs passed orally from generation to generation. The Germanic dependence on custom would have a lasting influence on the development of law, and especially **common law**, in parts of the West. Among the Germanic peoples, tribal chiefs were responsible for governing, but general assemblies met to make important decisions: fully armed, clan warriors demonstrated their assent to propositions "in a military manner," according to Tacitus—by brandishing their javelins. Since warlike behavior was commonplace, tribal law was severe, uncompromising, and directed toward publicly shaming the guilty. Tacitus records that punishment for an adulterous wife was "instant, and inflicted by the husband. He cuts off the hair of his guilty wife, and having assembled her relations, expels her naked from his house, pursuing her with stripes through the village. To public loss of honor no favor is shown. She may

---

Science and Technology

568	Germanic tribes introduce stirrups (from China) into Europe
600	a heavy iron plow is used in Northern Europe
770	iron horseshoes are used widely in Western Europe

---

*_Tacitus: Historical Works_, translated by Arthur Murphey. London: J. M. Dent, 1907, 320–321.

possess beauty, youth and riches; but a husband she can never obtain."

As in most ancient societies—Hammurabi's Babylon, for instance—penalties for crimes varied according to the social standing of the guilty party. Among the Germanic tribes, however, a person's guilt or innocence might be determined by an ordeal involving fire or water; such trials reflected the faith Germanic peoples placed in the will of nature deities. Some of the names of these gods came to designate days of the week; for example, the English word "Wednesday" derives from "Woden's day" and "Thursday" from "Thor's day."

Germanic Literature

Germanic traditions, including those of personal valor and heroism associated with a warring culture, are reflected in the epic poems of the Early Middle Ages. The three most famous of these, *Beowulf*, *The Song of the Nibelungen*, and the *Song of Roland*, were transmitted orally for hundreds of years before they were written down some time between the tenth and thirteenth centuries. *Beowulf*, which originated among the Anglo-Saxons around 700, was recorded in Old English—the Germanic language spoken in the British Isles between the fifth and eleventh centuries. *The Song of the Nibelungen*, a product of the Burgundian tribes, was recorded in Old German; and the Frankish *Song of Roland*, in Old French. Celebrating the deeds of warrior-heroes, these three epic poems have much in common with the *Iliad*, the *Mahabharata*, and other orally transmitted adventure poems.

The 3,000-line epic known as *Beowulf* is the first monumental literary composition in a European vernacular language. The tale of a daring Scandinavian prince, *Beowulf* brings to life the heroic world of the Germanic people with whom it originated. In unrhymed Old English verse embellished with numerous two-term metaphors known as **kennings** ("whale-path" for "sea," "ring-giver" for "king"), the poem recounts three major adventures: Beowulf's encounter with the monster Grendel, his destruction of Grendel's hideous and vengeful mother, and (some five decades later) his effort to destroy the fire-breathing dragon which threatens his people. These adventures—the stuff of legend, folk tale, and fantasy—immortalize the mythic origins of the Anglo-Saxons. Composed in the newly Christianized England of the eighth century, the poem was not written down for another two centuries. Only a full reading of *Beowulf* offers an appreciation of its significance as a work of art. However, the passage that follows—from a modern translation by Burton Raffel—offers an idea of the poem's vigorous style and narrative. The excerpt (lines 2510–2601 of the work), which describes Beowulf's assault on the fire-dragon, opens with a "battle-vow" that broadcasts the boastful courage of the epic hero. Those who wish to know the outcome of this gory contest must read further in the poem.

READING 2.13 From *Beowulf*

And Beowulf uttered his final boast: 1
  "I've never known fear; as a youth I fought
In endless battles. I am old, now,
But I will fight again, seek fame still,
If the dragon hiding in his tower dares 5
To face me."
  Then he said farewell to his followers,
Each in his turn, for the last time:
  "I'd use no sword, no weapon, if this beast
Could be killed without it, crushed to death
Like Grendel, gripped in my hands and torn 10
Limb from limb. But his breath will be burning
Hot, poison will pour from his tongue.
I feel no shame, with shield and sword
And armor, against this monster: when he comes to me
I mean to stand, not run from his shooting 15
Flames, stand till fate decides
Which of us wins. My heart is firm,
My hands calm: I need no hot
Words. Wait for me close by, my friends.
We shall see, soon, who will survive 20
This bloody battle, stand when the fighting
Is done. No one else could do
What I mean to, here, no man but me
Could hope to defeat this monster. No one
Could try. And this dragon's treasure, his gold 25
And everything hidden in that tower, will be mine
Or war will sweep me to a bitter death!"
  Then Beowulf rose, still brave, still strong,
And with his shield at his side, and a mail shirt on his breast,
Strode calmly, confidently, toward the tower, under 30
The rocky cliffs: no coward could have walked there!
And then he who'd endured dozens of desperate
Battles, who'd stood boldly while swords and shields
Clashed, the best of kings, saw
Huge stone arches and felt the heat 35
Of the dragon's breath, flooding down
Through the hidden entrance, too hot for anyone
To stand, a streaming current of fire
And smoke that blocked all passage. And the Geats'[1]
Lord and leader, angry, lowered 40
His sword and roared out a battle cry,
A call so loud and clear that it reached through
The hoary rock, hung in the dragon's
Ear. The beast rose, angry,
Knowing a man had come—and then nothing 45
But war could have followed. Its breath came first,
A steaming cloud pouring from the stone,
Then the earth itself shook. Beowulf
Swung his shield into place, held it
In front of him, facing the entrance. The dragon 50
Coiled and uncoiled, its heart urging it
Into battle. Beowulf's ancient sword
Was waiting, unsheathed, his sharp and gleaming

[1] The Scandinavian tribe led by Beowulf.

Blade. The beast came closer; both of them
Were ready, each set on slaughter. The Geats'   **55**
Great prince stood firm, unmoving, prepared
Behind his high shield, waiting in his shining
Armor. The monster came quickly toward him,
Pouring out fire and smoke, hurrying
To its fate. Flames beat at the iron   **60**
Shield, and for a time it held, protected
Beowulf as he'd planned; then it began to melt,
And for the first time in his life that famous prince
Fought with fate against him, with glory
Denied him. He knew it, but he raised his sword   **65**
And struck at the dragon's scaly hide.
The ancient blade broke, bit into
The monster's skin, drew blood, but cracked
And failed him before it went deep enough, helped him
Less than he needed. The dragon leaped   **70**
With pain, thrashed and beat at him, spouting
Murderous flames, spreading them everywhere.
And the Geats' ring-giver did not boast of glorious
Victories in other wars: his weapon
Had failed him, deserted him, now when he needed it   **75**
Most, that excellent sword. Edgetho's
Famous son stared at death,
Unwilling to leave this world, to exchange it
For a dwelling in some distant place—a journey
Into darkness that all men must make, as death   **80**
Ends their few brief hours on earth.

    Quickly, the dragon came at him, encouraged
As Beowulf fell back; its breath flared,
And he suffered, wrapped around in swirling
Flames—a king, before, but now   **85**
A beaten warrior. None of his comrades
Came to him, helped him, his brave and noble
Followers; they ran for their lives, fled
Deep in a wood. And only one of them
Remained, stood there, miserable, remembering,   **90**
As a good man must, what kinship should mean. . . .

Q How does the poet bring color and excitement to Beowulf's assault on the fire-dragon?

Figure 11.1 Sutton Hoo purse cover, East Anglia, England, ca. 630. Gold with garnets and *cloisonné* enamel, 8 in. long. British Museum, London.

Germanic Art

The artistic production of nomadic peoples consists largely of easily transported objects such as carpets, jewelry, and weapons. Germanic folk often buried the most lavish of these items with their chieftains in boats that were cast out to sea (as described in *Beowulf*). In 1939, archeologists at Sutton Hoo in eastern England excavated a seventh-century Anglo-Saxon grave that contained weapons, coins, utensils, jewelry, and a small lyre. These treasures were packed, along with the corpse of their chieftain, into an 89-foot-long ship that served as a tomb.

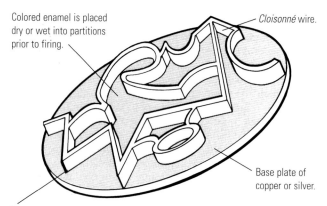

Colored enamel is placed dry or wet into partitions prior to firing.

Cloisonné wire.

Base plate of copper or silver.

Base plate is enameled and permanently holds the partitions in place. They may also be soldered to the base metal before the first firing.

Figure 11.2 *Cloisonné* enameling process. From Richard Phipps and Richard Wink, *Introduction to the Gallery*. Copyright © 1987 Wm. C. Brown Publishers, Dubuque, Iowa. All rights reserved. Reprinted by permission.

Among the remarkable metalwork items found at Sutton Hoo were gold buckles, shoulder clasps, and the lid of a purse designed to hang from the chieftain's waist-belt (Figure **11.1**). These objects are adorned with semiprecious stones and **cloisonné**—enamelwork produced by pouring molten colored glass between thin gold partitions (Figure **11.2**). The purse lid is ornamented with a series of motifs: interlaced fighting animals, two frontal male figures between pairs of rampant beasts (compare Figure 2.2), and two curved-beaked predators attacking wild birds. These motifs explore the interface between man and beast in what was primarily a hunting society. A 5-pound gold belt buckle is richly ornamented with a dense pattern of interlaced snakes incised with a black sulfurous substance called **niello** (Figure **11.3**). The high quality of so-called "barbarian" art, as evidenced at Sutton Hoo and elsewhere, shows that technical sophistication and artistic originality were by no means the monopoly of "civilized" societies. It also demonstrates the continuous diffusion and exchange of styles across Asia and into Europe. The **zoomorphic** (animal-shaped) motifs found on the artifacts at Sutton Hoo, along with many of the metalwork techniques used in their fabrication, are evidence of contact between the Germanic tribes and the nomadic populations of Central Asia, who perpetuated the decorative traditions of ancient Persian, Scythian, and Chinese craftspeople.

As the Germanic tribes poured into Europe, their art and their culture commingled with that of the people with whom they came into contact. A classic example is the fusion of Celtic and Anglo-Saxon styles. The Celts were a non-Germanic, Iron Age folk that had migrated throughout Europe between the fifth and third centuries B.C.E., settling in the British Isles before the time of Christ. A great flowering of Celtic art and literature occurred in Ireland and England following the conversion of the Celts to Christianity in the fifth century C.E. The instrument of this conversion was the fabled Saint Patrick (ca. 385–461), the British monk who is said to have baptized more than 120,000 people and founded three hundred churches in Ireland. In the centuries thereafter, Anglo-Irish monasteries produced a number of extraordinary illuminated manuscripts, whose decorative style is closely related to the dynamic linear ornamentation of the Sutton Hoo artifacts.

The seventh-century Lindisfarne Gospels is the oldest surviving translation of the Gospels into the English language. The visual masterpiece of an otherwise bleak period in the West, it comes from a monastery located on an island off the east coast of England. In the pages of this remarkable book, naturalistic representation of the kind associated with classical culture has disappeared entirely.

The precisely drawn Lindisfarne "carpet page"—so called for its resemblance to Asian prayer rugs—is dominated by a magnificent **cruciform** (cross-shaped) design (Figure **11.4**), but the entire spatial field writhes with knotted, ribbonlike shapes resembling those on the Sutton Hoo belt buckle (see Figure 11.3). Looking every bit like a metalwork surface or a woven rug, the carpet page combines the illusion of compositional order with a sense of labyrinthine movement. Analysis of the design shows, however, that one's initial impression of perfect symmetry is mistaken, for the composition involves a complex system of mirror images and subtly varied shapes, lines, and colors. The influence of Germanic design in Christian manuscript illumination is a dramatic example of cultural syncretism (the combination of different practices and principles), but it also raises another matter—the similarity between Germanic and Islamic art styles. As did Islamic artists, the Germanic tribes distilled the decorative traditions of Persia, Egypt, and the Mediterranean into a style marked by complex, rhythmically meandering surface designs. Whether the sophisticated abstract vocabularies of these two bodies of art—Germanic and Islamic—are symbolic of the wandering lifestyles of these originally nomadic peoples (as some scholars have suggested), or

Figure 11.3 Buckle, from Sutton Hoo, first half of seventh century. Gold and niello, length 5¼ in., weight 5 lb. Reproduced by courtesy of the Trustees of the British Museum, London.

Figure 11.4 Bishop Eadfrith (?), "Carpet Page," from the Lindisfarne Gospels, ca. 698–721. Vellum, 13½ × 9¾ in. British Library, London.

Figure 11.5 Ardagh Chalice, from Ireland, early eighth century. Silver, gilt bronze, gold wire, glass, and enamel. National Museum of Ireland, Dublin.

whether closeness to nature generated a set of unique but similar design principles, may be left to speculation.

The Germanic style influenced not only the illumination of Christian manuscripts, but also the decoration of Christian liturgical objects, such as the **paten** (Eucharistic plate) and the **chalice** (Eucharistic cup). Used in the celebration of the Mass, these objects usually commanded the finest and most costly materials; and, like the manuscripts that accompanied the sacred rites, they received inordinate care in execution. The Ardagh Chalice, made of silver, gilded bronze, gold wire, glass, and enamel, displays the technical virtuosity of early eighth-century metalworkers in Ireland (Figure 11.5). On the surface of the vessel, a band of interlace designs is offset by raised roundels worked in enamel and gold thread. Clearly, in the liturgical objects and illuminated manuscripts of the Early Middle Ages, the abstract, ornamental Germanic style provided Christian art with an aesthetic alternative to classical modes of representation.

Charlemagne and the Carolingian Renaissance

From the time he came to the throne in 768 until his death in 814, the Frankish chieftain Charles the Great (in French, "Charlemagne") pursued the dream of restoring the Roman Empire under Christian leadership. A great warrior and an able administrator, the fair-haired heir to the Frankish kingdom conquered vast areas of land (Map 11.2). His holy wars—the Christian equivalent of the Muslim *jihad*—resulted in the forcible conversion of the Saxons east of the Rhine River, the Lombards of northern Italy, and the Slavic peoples along the Danube.

Map 11.2 The Empire of Charlemagne, 814.

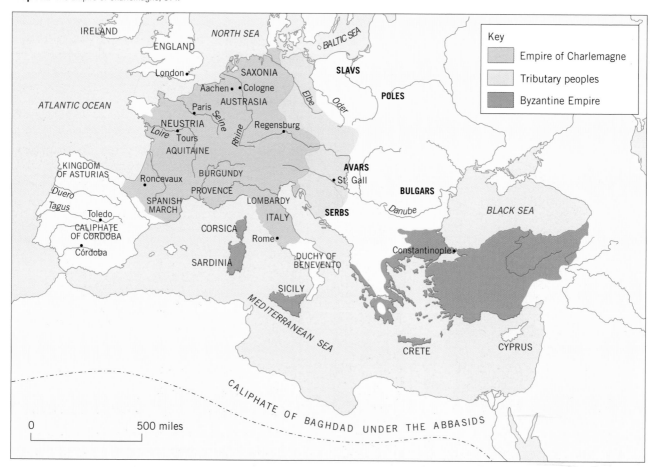

Charlemagne's campaigns also pushed the Muslims back beyond the Pyrenees into Spain.

In the year 800, Pope Leo III crowned Charlemagne "Emperor of the Romans," thus establishing a firm relationship between Church and state. But, equally significantly, Charlemagne's role in creating a Roman Christian or "Holy" Roman Empire cast him as the prototype of Christian kingship. For the more than thirty years during which he waged wars in the name of Christ, Charlemagne sought to control conquered lands by placing them in the hands of local administrators—on whom he bestowed the titles "count" and "duke"—and by periodically sending out royal envoys to carry his edicts abroad. He revived trade with the East, stabilized the currency of the realm, and even pursued diplomatic ties with Baghdad, whose caliph, Harun al-Rashid, graced Charlemagne's court with the gift of an elephant.

Charlemagne's imperial mission was animated by a passionate interest in education and the arts. Having visited San Vitale in Ravenna (see Figures 9.16, 9.17), he had its architectural plan and decorative program imitated in the Palatine Chapel at Aachen (Figure 11.6). The topmost tier, crowned by a mosaic dome, represented Heaven and the bottom tier the earth, where priest and congregation met for worship; enthroned in the gallery between, which was connected by a passageway to the royal palace, Charlemagne assumed his symbolic role as mediator between God and ordinary mortals. Alert to the legacy of his forebears, he revived the bronze-casting techniques of Roman sculptors, though on a small scale (Figure 11.7). Despite the fact that he himself could barely read and write—his sword hand was, according to his biographers, so callused that he had great difficulty forming letters—he sponsored a revival of learning and literacy. To oversee this educational program, Charlemagne invited to his court missionaries and scholars from all over Europe. He established schools at Aachen (Aix-la-Chapelle), in town centers

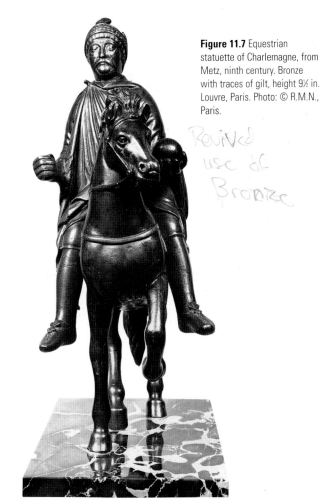

Figure 11.7 Equestrian statuette of Charlemagne, from Metz, ninth century. Bronze with traces of gilt, height 9½ in. Louvre, Paris. Photo: © R.M.N., Paris.

throughout the Empire, and in Benedictine monasteries such as that at Saint-Gall in Switzerland, where monks and nuns copied religious manuscripts, along with texts on medicine, drama, and other secular subjects. The scale of this **renaissance** or "rebirth" of learning is evident in that eighty percent of the oldest surviving classical Latin manuscripts exist in Carolingian copies.

Carolingian copyists rejected Roman script, which lacked punctuation and spaces between words, in favor of a neat, uniform writing style known as the minuscule (Figure 11.8), the ancestor of modern typography. The decorative programs of many Carolingian manuscripts reflect the

Figure 11.6 Odo of Metz, Palatine Chapel of Charlemagne, Aachen, Germany, 792–805 Roebild, Frankfurt.

Figure 11.8 Comparison of Merovingian (pre-Carolingian) book script and Caroline (Carolingian) minuscule.

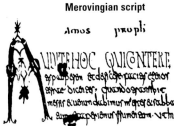

Figure 11.9 *The Ascension*, from the Sacramentary of Archbishop Drogo of Metz, ca. 842. Bibliothèque Nationale, Paris, MS Lat. 9428, f.71v.

Figure 11.10 Back cover of the Lindau Gospels, ca. 870. Silver gilt with *cloisonné* enamel and precious stones, 13⅜ × 10⅜ in. © The J. Pierpont Morgan Library, New York. Art Resource, NY.

union of late Roman realism and Germanic abstraction. The former is revealed in the pictorial narrative that fills (or "historiates") the capital letter in Figure **11.9**, while the latter is seen in the ribbonlike pattern of the initial itself. But the Carolingian Renaissance was not limited to the copying of manuscripts. Among the most magnificent artifacts of the period were liturgical and devotional objects, often made of ivory or precious metals. Dating from the decades after Charlemagne's death, the book cover for the Lindau Gospels testifies to the superior technical abilities of Carolingian metalsmiths (Figure **11.10**). The surface of the back cover, worked in silver gilt, inlaid with *cloisonné* enamel, and encrusted with precious gems, consists of an ornate Greek cross that dominates a field of writhing, interlaced creatures similar to those found in Anglo-Saxon metalwork (see Figure 11.3) and Anglo-Irish manuscripts (see Figure 11.4). At the corners of the inner rectangle of the book cover are four tiny scenes showing the evangelists at their writing desks. These realistically conceived representations contrast sharply with the more stylized figural images that appear in the arms of the cross. The integration of Germanic, Roman, and Byzantine stylistic traditions evident in the cover of the Lindau Gospels typifies the Carolingian Renaissance, the glories of which would not be matched for at least three centuries.

Feudal Society

When Charlemagne died in the year 814, the short-lived unity he had brought to Western Europe died with him. Although he had turned the Frankish kingdom into an empire, he failed to establish any legal and administrative machinery comparable with that of imperial Rome. There was no standing army, no system of taxation, and no single code of law to unify the widely diverse population. Inevitably, following his death, the fragile stability of the Carolingian Empire was shattered by Scandinavian seafarers known as Vikings. Charlemagne's sons and grandsons could not repel the raids of these fierce invaders, who ravaged the northern coasts of the Empire; at the same time, neither were his heirs able to arrest the repeated forays of the Muslims along the Mediterranean coast. Lacking effective leadership, the Carolingian Empire disintegrated. In the mid-ninth century, Charlemagne's three grandsons divided the Empire among themselves, separating French- from German-speaking territories. Increasingly, however, administration and protection fell to members of the local ruling aristocracy—heirs of the counts and dukes whom Charlemagne had appointed to administer portions of the realm, or simply those who had taken land by force. The fragmentation of the Empire and the insecurity generated by the Viking invasions caused people at all social levels to attach themselves to members of a military nobility who were capable of providing protection. These circumstances enhanced the growth of a unique system of political and military organization known as **feudalism**.

Derived from Roman and Germanic traditions of rewarding warriors with the spoils of war, feudalism involved the exchange of land for military service. In return for the grant of land, known as a **fief** or *feudum* (the Germanic word for "property"), a **vassal** owed his **lord** a certain number of fighting days (usually forty) per year. The contract between lord and vassal also involved a number of other obligations, including the lord's provision of a court of justice, the vassal's contribution of ransom if his lord were captured, and the reciprocation of hospitality between the two. In an age of instability, feudalism provided a rudimentary form of local government while answering the need for security against armed attack.

Those engaged in the feudal contract constituted roughly the upper ten percent of European society. The feudal nobility, which bore the twin responsibilities of military defense and political leadership, was a closed class of men and women whose superior status was inherited at birth. A male member of the nobility was first and foremost a mounted man-at-arms—a *chevalier* (from the French *cheval*, for "horse") or knight (from the Germanic *Knecht*, a youthful servant or soldier). The medieval knight was a cavalry warrior equipped with stirrups, protected by **chain mail** (flexible armor made of interlinked metal rings), and armed with such weapons as broadsword and shield.

The knight's conduct and manners in all aspects of life were guided by a strict code of behavior called **chivalry**. Chivalry demanded that the knight be courageous in battle, loyal to his lord and fellow warriors, and reverent toward women. Feudal life was marked by ceremonies and symbols almost as extensive as those of the Christian Church. For instance, a vassal received his fief by an elaborate procedure known as **investiture**, in which oaths of fealty were formally exchanged (Figure **11.11**). In warfare, adversaries usually fixed the time and place of combat in advance. Medieval warfare was both a profession and a pastime, as knights entertained themselves with **jousts** (personal combat between men on horseback) or war games that imitated the trials of combat (Figure **11.12**).

Women helped to shape the chivalric society of the Middle Ages. In many parts of Europe they inherited land, which they usually defended by means of hired soldiers. A woman controlled her fief until she married, and

Figure 11.11 MATTHEW PARIS, *Vassal Paying Homage to his Lord*, from the Westminster Psalter, ca. 1250. Reproduced by permission of the British Library, London.

regained it upon becoming a widow. Men and women took great pride in their aristocratic lineage and advertised the family name by means of heraldic devices emblazoned on tunics, pennants, and shields (see Figure 11.11).

The Literature of the Feudal Nobility

The ideals of the fighting nobility in a feudal age are best captured in the oldest and greatest French epic poem, the *Song of Roland*. It is based on an event that took place in 778—the ambush of Charlemagne's rear guard, led by Charlemagne's nephew Roland, as they returned from an expedition against the Muslims in Spain. This four-thousand-line *chanson de geste* ("song of heroic deeds") was transmitted orally for three centuries and not written down until the early 1100s. Generation after generation of *jongleurs* (professional entertainers) wandered from court to court, chanting the story (and possibly embellishing it with episodes of folklore) to the accompaniment of a lyre. Although the music for the poem has not survived, it is likely that it consisted of a single and highly improvised line of melody. The tune was probably syllabic (setting one note to each syllable) and—like folk song—dependent on simple repetition.

Figure 11.12 French plaque from a casket, fourteenth century. Ivory, 3⅛ × ⅝ in. The Metropolitan Museum of Art, New York. Gift of J. Pierpont Morgan, 1917.

As with other works in the oral tradition (the *Epic of Gilgamesh* and the *Iliad*, for instance), the *Song of Roland* is grandiose in its dimensions and profound in its lyric power. Its rugged Old French verse describes a culture that prized the performance of heroic deeds that brought honor to the warrior, his lord, and his religion. The strong bond of loyalty between vassal and chieftain that characterized the Germanic way of life resonates in Roland's declaration of unswerving devotion to his temporal overlord, Charlemagne.

The *Song of Roland* brings to life such aspects of early medieval culture as the practice of naming one's battle gear and weapons (often considered sacred), the dependence on cavalry, the glorification of blood-and-thunder heroism, and the strong sense of comradeship among men-at-arms. Women play almost no part in the epic. The feudal contract did not exclude members of the clergy; hence Archbishop Turpin fights with lance and spear, despite the fact that Church law forbade members of the clergy to shed another man's blood. (Some members of the clergy got around this law by arming themselves with a **mace**—a spike-headed club that could knock one's armored opponent off his horse or do damage short of bloodshed.) Roland's willingness to die for his religious beliefs, fired by the Archbishop's promise of admission into Paradise for those who fall fighting the infidels (in this case, the Muslims), suggests that the militant fervor of Muslims was matched by that of early medieval Christians. Indeed, the *Song of Roland* captures the powerful antagonism between Christians and Muslims that dominated all of medieval history and culminated in the Christian Crusades described later in this chapter.

The descriptive language of the *Song of Roland* is stark, unembellished, and vivid: "He feels his brain gush out," reports the poet in verse 168. Such directness and simplicity lend immediacy to the action. Characters are stereotypical ("Roland's a hero, and Oliver is wise," verse 87), and groups of people are characterized with epic expansiveness: *all* Christians are good and *all* Muslims are bad. The figure of Roland epitomizes the ideals of physical courage, religious devotion, and personal loyalty. Yet, in his refusal to call for assistance from Charlemagne and his troops, who have already retreated across the Pyrenees, he exhibits a foolhardiness—perhaps a "tragic flaw"—that leads him and his warriors to their deaths.

READING 2.14 From the *Song of Roland*

81

Count Oliver has climbed up on a hill;	1
From there he sees the Spanish lands below,	
And Saracens[1] assembled in great force.	
Their helmets gleam with gold and precious stones,	

Their shields are shining, their hauberks[2] burnished gold, 5
Their long sharp spears with battle flags unfurled.
He tries to see how many men there are:
Even battalions are more than he can count.
And in his heart Oliver is dismayed;
Quick as he can, he comes down from the height, 10
And tells the Franks what they will have to fight.

82

Oliver says, "Here come the Saracens—
A greater number no man has ever seen!
The first host carries a hundred thousand shields,
Their helms are laced, their hauberks shining white, 15
From straight wood handles rise ranks of burnished spears.
You'll have a battle like none on earth before!
Frenchmen, my lords, now God give you the strength
To stand your ground, and keep us from defeat."
They say, "God's curse on those who quit the field! 20
We're yours till death—not one of us will yield."   AOI[3]

83

Oliver says, "The pagan might is great—
It seems to me, our Franks are very few!
Roland, my friend, it's time to sound your horn;
King Charles[4] will hear, and bring his army back." 25
Roland replies, "You must think I've gone mad!
In all sweet France I'd forfeit my good name!
No! I will strike great blows with Durendal,[5]
Crimson the blade up to the hilt of gold.
To those foul pagans I promise bitter woe— 30
They all are doomed to die at Roncevaux!"[6]   AOI

84

"Roland, my friend, let the Oliphant[7] sound!
King Charles will hear it, his host will all turn back,
His valiant barons will help us in this fight."
Roland replies, "Almighty God forbid 35
That I bring shame upon my family,
And cause sweet France to fall into disgrace!
I'll strike that horde with my good Durendal;
My sword is ready, girded here at my side,
And soon you'll see its keen blade dripping blood. 40
The Saracens will curse the evil day
They challenged us, for we will make them pay."   AOI

85

"Roland, my friend I pray you, sound your horn!
King Charlemagne, crossing the mountain pass,

---

[1] Another name for Muslims.

[2] Long coats of chain mail.
[3] The letters AOI have no known meaning but probably signify a musical appendage or refrain that occurred at the end of each stanza.
[4] Charlemagne.
[5] Roland's sword.
[6] "The gate of Spain," a narrow pass in the Pyrenees where the battle takes place.
[7] A horn made from an elephant's tusk.

Won't fail, I swear it, to bring back all his Franks." 45
"May God forbid!" Count Roland answers then.
"No man on earth shall have the right to say
That I for pagans sounded the Oliphant!
I will not bring my family to shame.
I'll fight this battle; my Durendal shall strike 50
A thousand blows and seven hundred more;
You'll see bright blood flow from the blade's keen steel.
We have good men; their prowess will prevail,
And not one Spaniard shall live to tell the tale."

86

Oliver says, "Never would you be blamed; 55
I've seen the pagans, the Saracens of Spain.
They fill the valleys, cover the mountain peaks;
On every hill, and every wide-spread plain,
Vast hosts assemble from that alien race;
Our company numbers but very few." 60
Roland replies, "The better, then, we'll fight!
If it please God and His angelic host,
I won't betray the glory of sweet France!
Better to die than learn to live with shame—
Charles loves us more as our keen swords win fame." 65

87

Roland's a hero, and Oliver is wise;
Both are so brave men marvel at their deeds.
When they mount chargers, take up their swords and shields,
Not death itself could drive them from the field.
They are good men; their words are fierce and proud. 70
With wrathful speed the pagans ride to war.
Oliver says, "Roland, you see them now.
They're very close, the king too far away.
You were too proud to sound the Oliphant:
If Charles were with us, we would not come to grief. 75
Look up above us, close to the Gate of Spain:
There stands the guards—who would not pity them!
To fight this battle means not to fight again."
Roland replies, "Don't speak so foolishly!
Cursed be the heart that cowers in the breast! 80
We'll hold our ground; if they will meet us here,
Our foes will find us ready with sword and spear." AOI

88

When Roland sees the fight will soon begin,
Lions and leopards are not so fierce as he.
Calling the Franks, he says to Oliver: 85
"Noble companion, my friend, don't talk that way!
The Emperor Charles, who left us in command
Of twenty thousand he chose to guard the pass,
Made very sure no coward's in their ranks.
In his lord's service a man must suffer pain, 90
Bitterest cold and burning heat endure;
He must be willing to lose his flesh and blood.
Strike with your lance, and I'll wield Durendal—
The king himself presented it to me—
And if I die, whoever takes my sword 95
Can say its master has nobly served his lord."

89

Archbishop Turpin comes forward then to speak.
He spurs his horse and gallops up a hill,
Summons the Franks, and preaches in these words:
"My noble lords, Charlemagne left us here, 100
And may our deaths do honor to the king!
Now you must help defend our holy Faith!
Before your eyes you see the Saracens.
Confess your sins, ask God to pardon you;
I'll grant you absolution to save your souls. 105
Your deaths would be a holy martyrdom,
And you'll have places in highest Paradise."
The French dismount; they kneel upon the ground.
Then the archbishop, blessing them in God's name,
Told them, for penance, to strike when battle came. 110

. . . .

91

At Roncevaux Count Roland passes by,
Riding his charger, swift-running Veillantif.[8]
He's armed for battle, splendid in shining mail.
As he parades, he brandishes his lance.
Turning the point straight up against the sky, 115
And from the spearhead a banner flies, pure white,
With long gold fringes that beat against his hands.
Fair to behold, he laughs, serene and gay.
Now close behind him comes Oliver, his friend,
With all the Frenchmen cheering their mighty lord. 120
Fiercely his eyes confront the Saracens;
Humbly and gently he gazes at the Franks,
Speaking to them with gallant courtesy:
"Barons, my lords, softly now, keep the pace!
Here come the pagans looking for martyrdom. 125
We'll have such plunder before the day is out,
As no French king has ever won before!"
And at this moment the armies join in war. AOI

. . . .

161

The pagans flee, furious and enraged,
Trying their best to get away in Spain. 130
Count Roland lacks the means to chase them now,
For he has lost his war-horse Veillantif;
Against his will he has to go on foot.
He went to give Archbishop Turpin help,
Unlaced his helmet, removed it from his head, 135
And then took off the hauberk of light mail;
The under-tunic he cut into long strips
With which he stanched the largest of his wounds.
Then lifting Turpin, carried him in his arms
To soft green grass, and gently laid him down. 140
In a low voice Roland made this request:
"My noble lord, I pray you, give me leave,
For our companions, the men we held so dear,
Must not be left abandoned now in death.
I want to go and seek out every one, 145

---

[8]Roland's horse.

Carry them here, and place them at your feet."
Said the archbishop, "I grant it willingly.
The field belongs, thank God, to you and me."

162

Alone, Count Roland walks through the battlefield,
Searching the valleys, searching the mountain heights. 150
He found the bodies of Ivon and Ivoire,
And then he found the Gascon Engelier.
Gerin he found, and Gerier his friend,
He found Aton and then Count Bérengier,
Proud Anseïs he found, and then Samson, 155
Gérard the Old, the Count of Roussillon.
He took these barons, and carried every one
Back to the place where the archbishop was,
And then he put them in ranks at Turpin's knees.
Seeing them, Turpin cannot restrain his tears; 160
Raising his hand, he blesses all the dead.
And then he says, "You've come to grief, my lords!
Now in His glory, may God receive your souls,
Among bright flowers set you in Paradise!
It's my turn now; death keeps me in such pain, 165
Never again will I see Charlemagne."

163

Roland goes back to search the field once more,
And his companion he finds there, Oliver.
Lifting him in his arms he holds him close,
Brings him to Turpin as quickly as he can, 170
Beside the others places him on a shield;
Turpin absolves him, signing him with the cross,
And then they yield to pity and to grief.
Count Roland says, "Brother in arms, fair friend,
You were the son of Renier, the duke 175
Who held the land where Runers valley lies.
For breaking lances, for shattering thick shields,
Bringing the proud to terror and defeat,
For giving counsel, defending what is right,
In all the world there is no better knight." 180

164

When Roland sees that all his peers are dead,
And Oliver whom he so dearly loved,
He feels such sorrow that he begins to weep;
Drained of all color, his face turns ashen pale,
His grief is more than any man could bear, 185
He falls down, fainting whether he will or no.
Says the archbishop, "Baron, you've come to woe."

. . . .

168

Now Roland knows that death is very near.
His ears give way, he feels his brain gush out.
He prays that God will summon all his peers; 190
Then, for himself, he prays to Gabriel.
Taking the horn, to keep it from all shame,
With Durendal clasped in his other hand,

He goes on, farther than a good cross-bow shot,
West into Spain, crossing a fallow field. 195
Up on a hilltop, under two lofty trees.
Four marble blocks are standing on the grass.
But when he comes there, Count Roland faints once more,
He falls down backward; now he is at death's door.

. . . .

174

Count Roland feels the very grip of death 200
Which from his head is reaching for his heart.
He hurries then to go beneath a pine;
In the green grass he lies down on his face,
Placing beneath him the sword and Oliphant;
He turns his head to look toward pagan Spain. 205
He does these things in order to be sure
King Charles will say, and with him all the Franks,
The noble count conquered until he died.
He makes confession, for all his sins laments.
Offers his glove to God in penitence. AOI 210

 Q What aspects of European feudalism are brought to life in the *Song of Roland*?

The Norman Conquest and the Arts

As early as the eighth century the seafarers known as Vikings (but also as Norsemen, Northmen, and later, Normans) had moved beyond the bounds of their Scandinavian homelands. They constructed long wooden ships equipped with sailing gear that allowed them to tack into the wind. Expert shipbuilders, sailors, and navigators, they soon came to control the North Atlantic. The western Vikings were the first to colonize Iceland, and they set up a colony in Greenland before the year 1000. The eastern Vikings sailed across the North Sea to establish trading centers at Kiev and Novgorod. Known among Arab traders of this area as "*rus,*" they gave their name to Russia. They traded animal hides, amber, and other valued items, including captive Eastern Europeans—Slavs—from which the English word "slave" derives.

The Vikings began their raids on England with an attack on the Lindisfarne monastery in 793, and by the end of the ninth century, they had settled throughout northern Europe. Within one hundred years, these aggressive Normans made Normandy one of the strongest fiefs in France. In 1066, under the leadership of William of Normandy, some 5,000 men crossed the English Channel; at the Battle of Hastings, William defeated the Anglo-Saxon Duke Harold and seized the throne of England. The Norman Conquest had enormous consequences for the histories of England and France, for it marked the transfer of power in England from Anglo-Saxon rulers to Norman noblemen who were already vassals of the king of France. The Normans brought feudalism to England. To raise money, William ordered a detailed census of all property in the realm—the *Domesday Book*—which laid the basis for the collection of taxes. King William controlled all aspects of government with the aid of the *Curia Regis*—the royal court and council consisting of his feudal barons. Under the Norman kings, England would become one of Europe's leading medieval states.

The Normans led the way in the construction of stone castles and churches. Atop hills and at such vulnerable sites as Dover on the southeast coast of England, Norman kings erected austere castle-fortresses (Figure **11.13**). The castle featured a **keep** (square tower) containing a dungeon, a main hall, and a chapel, and incorporated a central open space with workshops and storehouses (Figure **11.14**). The enclosing stone walls were usually surmounted by turrets with **crenellations** that provided archers with protection in defensive combat. A **moat** (a trench usually filled with water) often surrounded the castle walls to deter enemy invasion. The brilliance of the Normans' achievements in architecture, apparent in their fortresses and in some of the earliest Romanesque churches (see chapter 13), lies in the use of stone to replace earlier timber fortifications and in the clarity with which the form of the building reflects its function.

One of the most famous Norman artifacts is the Bayeux Tapestry, an unusual visual record of the conquest of England by William of Normandy. This eleventh-century embroidered wallhanging, named for the city in northwestern France where it was made and where it is still displayed today, documents the history and folklore of the Normans with the same energetic spirit that animates the *Song of Roland*. Sewn into the linen cloth, which is some 20 inches deep and 231 feet long, are lively pictorial representations of the incidents leading up to and including the Battle of Hastings (Figure **11.15**). Above and alongside the images are Latin captions that serve to identify characters, places, and events. The text in the scene in Figure 11.15 reads, "Here the English and French have

Figure 11.13 Dover Castle, Kent, England, twelfth century. Photo: Skyscan Balloon Photography

At first, Norman castles in England had two parts: a flattened area called a bailey and a large mound called a motte. Buildings were of wood.

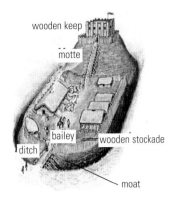

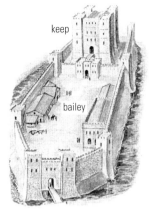

Later castles were built of stone. There was no motte, for the heavy keep had to stand on flat, firm earth that would not collapse.

Figure 11.14 Development of the Norman Castle, from Patrick Rook, *The Normans*. Macdonald Education Ltd., 1977.

fallen together in battle." In the margin below the spectacle appear fallen soldiers, weapons, and a bodiless head. The seventy-nine scenes progress in the manner of a parchment scroll or a cartoon comic strip (although they also call to mind the style of ancient Assyrian narrative reliefs, pictured in chapter 2). Rendered in only eight colors of wool yarn, the ambitious narrative includes 626 figures, 190 horses, and over 500 other animals. Since embroidery was almost exclusively a female occupation, it is likely that the Bayeux Tapestry was the work of women—although women are depicted only four times in the entire piece.

The *Song of Roland* and the Bayeux Tapestry have much in common: both are epic in theme and robust in style. Both consist of sweeping narratives whose episodes are irregular rather than uniform in length. Like the stereotypical (and almost exclusively male) characters in the *chanson*, the figures of the Tapestry are delineated by means of expressive gestures and simplified physical features; the Normans, for instance, are distinguished by the shaved backs of their heads. Weapons and armor in both epic and embroidery are described with loving detail. Indeed, in the Bayeux Tapestry, scenes of combat provide a veritable encyclopedia of medieval battle gear: kite-shaped shields, conical iron helmets, hauberks, short bows, double-edged swords, battle axes, and lances. Both the *Song of Roland* and the Bayeux Tapestry offer a vivid record of feudal life in all its heroic splendor.

The Lives of Medieval Serfs

Although the feudal class monopolized land and power within medieval society, this elite group represented only a tiny percentage of the total population. The majority of people—more than ninety percent—were unfree peasants or **serfs** who, along with freemen, farmed the soil. Medieval serfs lived quite differently from their landlords. Bound to large farms or manors they, like the farmers of the old Roman *latifundia* (see chapter 6), provided food in exchange for military protection furnished by the nobility.

Figure 11.15 *The Battle Rages,* detail from the Bayeux Tapestry, late eleventh century. Wool embroidery on linen, depth approx. 20 in., entire length 231 ft. Town of Bayeux, France. Photo: By special permission of the City of Bayeux.

They owned no property. They were forbidden to leave the land, though, on the positive side, they could not be evicted. Their bondage to the soil assured them the protection of feudal lords who, in an age lacking effective central authority, were the sole sources of political authority.

During the Middle Ages, the reciprocal obligations of serfs and lords and the serf's continuing tenure on the land became firmly fixed. At least until the eleventh century, the interdependence between the two classes was generally beneficial to both; serfs needed protection, and feudal lords, whose position as gentlemen-warriors excluded them from menial toil, needed food. For upper and lower classes alike, the individual's place in medieval society was inherited and bound by tradition.

A medieval fief usually included one or more manors. The average manor community comprised fifteen to twenty families, while a large manor of 5,000 acres might contain some fifty families. The lord usually appointed the local priest, provided a court of justice, and governed the manor from a fortified residence or castle. Between the eighth and tenth centuries, such residences were simple wooden structures but, by the twelfth century, elaborate stone manor houses with crenellated walls and towers became commonplace. On long winter nights, the lord's castle might be the scene of reveling and entertainment by *jongleurs* singing epic tales like the *Song of Roland* (see Reading 2.14).

The typical medieval manor consisted of farmlands, woodland, and pasture, and included a common mill, winepress, and oven (Figure **11.16**). Serfs cultivated the major crops of oats and rye on strips of arable land. In addition to the food they produced from fields reserved for the lord, they owed the lord a percentage—usually a third—of their own agricultural yield. They also performed services in the form of labor. In the medieval world, manor was isolated from manor, and a subsistence economy similar to that of the Neolithic village prevailed. The annual round of peasant labor, beset by a continuing war with the elements, was harsh and demanding. Nevertheless, during the Early Middle Ages, serfs made considerable progress in farm technology and agricultural practices. They developed the heavy-wheeled plow and the tandem harness, utilized wind and water mills, recovered land by dredging swamps and clearing forests, and offset soil

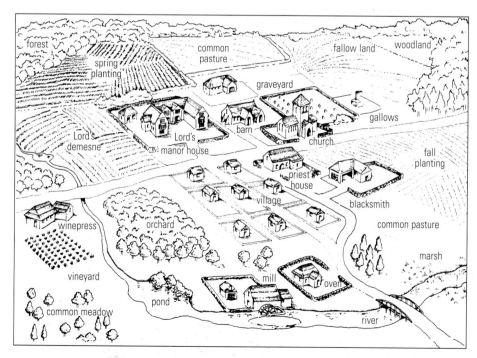

Figure 11.16 The Medieval Manor.

Figure 11.17 Carpenters' Guild Signature window, detail, early thirteenth century. Stained glass. Chartres Cathedral, France. Photo: Sonia Halliday, Weston Turville, U.K.

Figure 11.18 *Women and Men Reaping*, from the Luttrell Psalter, ca. 1340. Reproduced by permission of the British Library, London, Add. MS 42130, f.172.

exhaustion by devising systems of crop rotation. The "three-field system," for example, left one-third of the land fallow to allow it to recover its fertility. Such innovations eventually contributed to the production of a food surplus, which in turn stimulated the revival of trade.

Medieval serfs were subject to perennial toil and constant privations, including those of famine and disease. Most could neither read nor write. Unfortunately, art and literature leave us little insight into the lives and values of the lower classes of medieval society. Occasionally, however, in the sculptures of laboring peasants found on medieval cathedrals, in stained glass windows (Figure 11.17), and in medieval manuscripts, we find visual representations of lower-class life. As illustrations from the Luttrell Psalter indicate, peasant women worked alongside men in raising crops: sowing, reaping, gleaning, threshing, and assisting even in the most backbreaking of farming tasks (Figure 11.18). Medieval women were associated with the professions that involved food preparation (milking, raising vegetables, brewing, and baking) and the making of cloth (sheep-shearing,

Science and Technology

800	rigging (gear that controls ships' sails to take advantage of the wind) is invented by the Vikings
900	horse collars come into use in Europe
1050	crossbows are first used in France
ca. 1150	the first windmills appear in Europe

carting, spinning, and weaving). The distaff, the pole on which fibers were wound prior to spinning, came to be a symbol of women's work and (universally) of womankind. But lower-class women also shared their husbands' domestic tasks and day to day responsibilities that few noblewomen shared with their upper-class partners.

The Christian Crusades

During the eleventh century, numerous circumstances contributed to a change in the character of medieval life. The Normans effectively pushed the Muslims out of the Mediterranean Sea and, as the Normans and other marauders began to settle down, Europeans enjoyed a greater degree of security. At the same time, rising agricultural productivity and surplus encouraged trade and travel. The Crusades of the eleventh to thirteenth centuries were directly related to these changes. They were both a cause of economic revitalization and a symptom of the increased freedom and new mobility of Western Europeans during the High Middle Ages (ca. 1000–1300).

The Crusades began in an effort to rescue Jerusalem from Muslim Turks who were threatening the Byzantine Empire and denying Christian pilgrims access to the Holy Land. At the request of the Byzantine emperor, the Roman Catholic Church launched a series of military expeditions designed to regain territories dominated by the Turks. The First Crusade, called by Pope Urban II in 1095, began in the spirit of a holy war but, unlike the Muslim *jihad*, the intention was to recover land, not to convert pagans. Thousands of people—both laymen and clergy—"took up the Cross" and marched overland through Europe to the Byzantine East (Map **11.3**).

It soon became apparent, however, that the material benefits of the Crusades outweighed the spiritual ones, especially since the campaigns provided economic and military opportunities for the younger sons of the nobility. While the eldest son of an upper-class family inherited his father's fief under the principle of **primogeniture**, his younger brothers were left to seek their own fortunes. The Crusades stirred the ambitions of these disenfranchised young men. Equally ambitious were the Italian city-states. Eager to expand their commercial activities, they encouraged the Crusaders to become middlemen in trade between Italy and the East. In the course of the Fourth Crusade, Venetian profit seekers persuaded the Crusaders to sack Constantinople and capture trade ports in the Aegean. Moral inhibitions failed to restrain the vampires of greed and, in 1204, the Fourth Crusade deteriorated into a contest for personal profit. A disastrous postscript to

the Fourth Crusade was the Children's Crusade of 1212, in which thousands of children, aged between ten and fourteen, set out to recapture Jerusalem. Almost all died or were taken into slavery before reaching the Holy Land.

Aside from such economic advantages as those enjoyed by individual Crusaders and the Italian city-states, the gains made by the Crusades were slight. In the first of the four major expeditions, the Crusaders did retake some important cities, including Jerusalem. But by 1291, all recaptured lands were lost again to the Muslims. Indeed, in over two hundred years of fighting and seven major Crusades, the Crusaders did not secure any territory permanently, nor did they stop the westward advance of the Turks. Constantinople finally fell in 1453 to a later wave of Muslim Turks.

Despite their failure as religious ventures, the Crusades had enormous consequences for the West: the revival of trade between East and West enhanced European commercial life, encouraging the rise of towns and bringing great wealth to the Italian cities of Venice, Genoa, and Pisa. Then, too, in the absence or at the death of crusading noblemen, feudal lords (including emperors and kings) seized every opportunity to establish greater authority over the lands within their domains, thus consolidating and centralizing political power in the embryonic nation-states of England and France. Finally, renewed contact with Byzantium promoted an atmosphere of commercial and cultural receptivity that had not existed since Roman times. Luxury goods, such as saffron, citrus, silks, and damasks, entered Western Europe, as did sacred relics associated with the lives of Jesus, Mary, and the Christian saints. And, to the delight of the literate, Arabic translations of Greek manuscripts poured into France, along with all genres of Islamic literature (see chapter 10).

The Medieval Romance and the Code of Courtly Love

The Crusades inspired the writing of chronicles that were an admixture of historical fact, Christian lore, and stirring fiction. As such histories had broad appeal in an age of increasing upper-class literacy, they came to be written in the everyday language of the layperson—the vernacular—rather than in Latin. The Crusades also contributed to the birth of the **medieval romance**, a fictitious tale of love and adventure that became the most popular form of literary entertainment in the West between the years 1200 and 1500. Medieval romances first appeared in twelfth-century France in the form of rhymed verse, but later ones were written in prose. While romances were probably recited before a small, courtly audience rather than read individually, the development of the form coincided with the rise of a European "textual culture," that is, a culture dependent on written language rather than on oral tradition. In this textual culture, vernacular languages gained importance for intimate kinds of literature, while Latin remained the official language of Church and state.

The "spice" of the typical medieval romance was an illicit relationship or forbidden liaison between a man and woman of the upper class. During the Middle Ages, marriage among members of the nobility was usually an

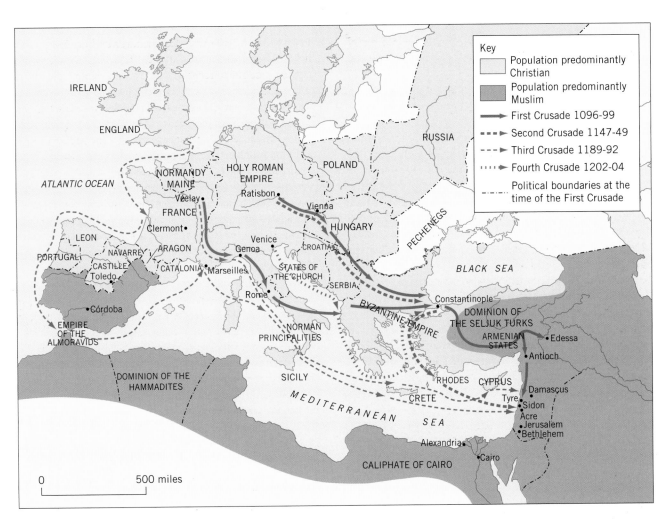

Map 11.3 The Major Crusades, 1096–1204.

alliance formed in the interest of securing land. Indeed, noble families might arrange marriages for offspring who were still in the cradle. In such circumstances, romantic love was more likely to flourish outside marriage. An adulterous affair between Lancelot, a knight of King Arthur's court, and Guinevere, the king's wife, is central to the popular twelfth-century verse romance *Lancelot*. Written in vernacular French by Chrétien de Troyes (d. ca. 1183), *Lancelot* belongs to a cycle of stories associated with a semilegendary sixth-century Welsh chieftain named Arthur. Chrétien's poem (a portion of which appears in prose translation in the following pages) stands at the beginning of a long tradition of Arthurian romance literature. Filled with bloody combat, supernatural events, and romantic alliances, medieval romances introduced a new and complex picture of human conduct and courtship associated with the so-called "code of courtly love."

Science and Technology

ca. 1150 magnetic compasses appear in Europe

1233 the first coal mines are opened in Newcastle, England

1240 European shipbuilders adopt the use of the rudder from the Arabs

1249 Muslims use gunpowder against Christian Crusaders

Courtly love, as the name suggests, was a phenomenon cultivated in the courts of the medieval nobility. Characterized by the longing of a nobleman for a (usually unattainable) woman, the courtly love tradition, with its "rules" of wooing and winning a lady, laid the basis for concepts of romantic love in Western literature and life. Popularized in twelfth-century manuals of conduct for European aristocrats, the code held that love (whether requited or not) had a purifying and ennobling influence on the lover. To love was to suffer; witness, in the excerpt below, Queen Guinevere's distress upon hearing the false report of Lancelot's death. Courtly love was also associated with a variety of distressing physical symptoms, such as an inability to eat or sleep. The tenets of courtly love required that a knight prove his love for his lady by performing daring and often impossible deeds; he must even be willing to die for her. In these features, the medieval romance is far removed from the rugged, bellicose spirit of earlier literary works like the *Song of Roland*. Indeed, *Lancelot* dramatizes the feminization of the chivalric ideal. The *Song of Roland* pictures early medieval culture in terms of heroic idealism and personal loyalty between men. The Arthurian romance, however, redefined these qualities in the direction of sentiment and sensuality. Lancelot fights not for his country, nor even for his lord, but to win the affections of his mistress. His prowess is not exercised, as with Roland, on a field of battle, but as individual combat undertaken in the courtyard of his host. While Roland is motivated by the ideal of glory in battle, Lancelot is driven by his love for Guinevere.

The courtly love tradition contributed to shaping modern Western concepts of gender and courtship. It also worked to define the romantic perception of women as objects, particularly objects of reward for the performance of brave deeds. For although courtly love elevated the woman (and her prototype, the Virgin Mary) as worthy of adoration, it defined her exclusively in terms of the interests of men. Nevertheless, the medieval romance, which flattered and exalted the aristocratic lady as an object of desire, was directed toward a primarily female audience. A product of the aristocratic (and male) imagination, the lady of the medieval romance had no counterpart in the lower classes of society, where women worked side by side with men in the fields (see Figure 11.18) and in a variety of trades. Despite its artificiality, however, the theme of courtly love and the romance itself had a significant influence on Western literary tradition. In that tradition, even into modern times, writers have tended to treat love more as a mode of spiritual purification or as an emotional affliction than as a condition of true affection and sympathy between the sexes.

READING 2.15 From Chrétien de Troyes' *Lancelot* (ca. 1170)

[Gawain and Lancelot, knights of King Arthur's court, set out in quest of Queen Guinevere. In the forest, they meet a damsel, who tells them of the Queen's whereabouts.]

Then the damsel relates to them the following story: "In truth, **1** my lords, Meleagant, a tall and powerful knight, son of the King of Gorre, has taken her off into the kingdom whence no foreigner returns, but where he must perforce remain in servitude and banishment." Then they ask her: "Damsel, where is this country? Where can we find the way thither?" She replies: "That you shall quickly learn; but you may be sure that you will meet with many obstacles and difficult passages, for it is not easy to enter there except with the permission of the king, whose name is Bademagu; however, it is possible to **10** enter by two very perilous paths and by two very difficult passage-ways. One is called 'the water-bridge,' because the bridge is under water, and there is the same amount of water beneath it as above it, so that the bridge is exactly in the middle; and it is only a foot and a half in width and in thickness. This choice is certainly to be avoided, and yet it is the less dangerous of the two.... The other bridge is still more impracticable and much more perilous, never having been crossed by man. It is just like a sharp sword, and therefore all the people call it 'the sword-bridge.' Now I have **20** told you all the truth I know...."

[They reach the sword-bridge.]

At the end of this very difficult bridge they dismount from their steeds and gaze at the wicked-looking stream, which is as swift and raging, as black and turgid, as fierce and terrible as if it were the devil's stream; and it is so dangerous and bottomless that anything falling into it would be as completely lost as if it fell into the salt sea. And the bridge, which spans it, is different from any other bridge; for there never was such a one as this. If any one asks of me the truth, there never was such a bad bridge, nor one whose flooring was so bad. The **30** bridge across the cold stream consisted of a polished, gleaming sword; but the sword was stout and stiff, and was as long as two lances. At each end there was a tree-trunk in which the sword was firmly fixed. No one need fear to fall because of its breaking or bending, for its excellence was such that it could support a great weight.... [Lancelot] prepares, as best he may, to cross the stream, and he does a very marvelous thing in removing the armor from his feet and hands. He will be in a sorry state when he reaches the other side [Figure **11.19**]. He is going to support himself with his **40** bare hands and feet upon the sword, which was sharper than a scythe, for he had not kept on his feet either sole or upper[1] or hose. But he felt no fear of wounds upon his hands or feet; he preferred to maim himself rather than to fall from the bridge and be plunged in the water from which he could never escape. In accordance with this determination, he passes over with great pain and agony, being wounded in the hands, knees, and feet. But even this suffering is sweet to him: for Love, who conducts and leads him on, assuages and relieves the pain. Creeping on his hands, feet, and knees, he proceeds **50** until he reaches the other side....

[Lancelot confronts the Queen's captors: King Bademagu's son, Meleagant, refuses to make peace with Lancelot and promptly challenges him to battle.]

... Very early, before prime[2] had yet been sounded, both of the knights fully armed were led to the place, mounted upon two horses equally protected. Meleagant was very graceful, alert, and shapely; the hauberk with its fine meshes, the helmet, and the shield hanging from his neck—all these became him well.... Then the combatants without delay make all the people stand aside; then they clash the shields with their elbows, and thrust their arms into the straps, and spur at each other so violently that each sends his lance two **60** arms' length through his opponent's shield, causing the lance to split and splinter like a flying spark. And the horses meet head on, clashing breast to breast, and the shields and helmets crash with such a noise that it seems like a mighty thunder-clap; not a breast-strap, girth, rein or surcingle[3] remains unbroken, and the saddle-bows, though strong, are broken to pieces. The combatants felt no shame in falling to earth, in view of their mishaps, but they quickly spring to their feet, and without waste of threatening words rush at each other more fiercely than two wild boars, and deal great blows **70** with their swords of steel like men whose hate is violent. Repeatedly they trim the helmets and shining hauberks so fiercely that after the sword the blood spurts out. They

---

[1]Parts of the shoe or boot.
[2]The second of the Canonical Hours, around 6 A.M. The devout recited special devotional prayers at each of the Canonical Hours: lauds, prime, terce, sext, none, vespers, and compline.
[3]A band passing around a horse's body to bind the saddle.

Figure 11.19 *Lancelot Crossing the Swordbridge and Guinevere in the Tower*, from the *Romance of Lancelot*, ca. 1300. 13½ × 10 in.
© The J. Pierpont Morgan Library, New York, 1990, MS 806 f. 166. Art Resource, NY.

furnished an excellent battle, indeed, as they stunned and wounded each other with their heavy, wicked blows. Many fierce, hard, long bouts they sustained with equal honor, so that the onlookers could discern no advantage on either side. But it was inevitable that he who had crossed the bridge should be much weakened by his wounded hands. The people who sided with him were much dismayed, for they notice that 80 his strokes are growing weaker, and they fear he will get the worst of it; it seemed to them that he was weakening, while Meleagant was triumphing, and they began to murmur all around. But up at the window of the tower there was a wise maiden who thought within herself that the knight had not undertaken the battle either on her account or for the sake of the common herd who had gathered about the list, but that his only incentive had been the Queen; and she thought that, if he knew that she was at the window seeing and watching him, his strength and courage would increase. . . . Then she came 90 to the Queen and said: "Lady, for God's sake and your own as well as ours, I beseech you to tell me, if you know, the name of yonder knight, to the end that it may be of some help to him." "Damsel," the Queen replies, "you have asked me a question in which I see no hate or evil, but rather good intent; the name of the knight, I know, is Lancelot of the Lake." "God, how happy and glad at heart I am!" the damsel says. Then she leans forward and calls to him by name so loudly that all the people hear: "Lancelot, turn about and see who is here taking note of thee!" 100

When Lancelot heard his name, he was not slow to turn around: he turns and sees seated up there at the window of the tower her whom he desired most in the world to see. From the moment he caught sight of her, he did not turn or take his eyes and face from her, defending himself with backhand blows. . . . Lancelot's strength and courage grow, partly because he has love's aid, and partly because he never hated any one so much as him with whom he is engaged. Love and mortal hate, so fierce that never before was such hate seen, make him so fiery and bold that Meleagant ceases to treat it 110 as a jest and begins to stand in awe of him, for he had never met or known so doughty a knight, nor had any knight ever wounded or injured him as this one does. . . .

[Lancelot spares Meleagant but thereafter is taken prisoner. Rumor reaches the Queen that Lancelot is dead.]

The news of this spread until it reached the Queen, who was sitting at meat. She almost killed herself on hearing the false report about Lancelot, but she supposes it to be true, and therefore she is in such dismay that she almost loses the power to speak; but, because of those present, she forces herself to say: "In truth, I am sorry for his death, and it is no wonder that I grieve, for he came into this country for my 120 sake, and therefore I should mourn for him." Then she says to herself, so that the others should not hear, that no one need ask her to drink or eat, if it is true that he is dead, in whose life she found her own. Then grieving she rises from the table, and makes her lament, but so that no one hears or notices her. She is so beside herself that she repeatedly grasps her throat with the desire to kill herself; but first she confesses to herself, and repents with self-reproach, blaming and censuring herself, for the wrong she had done him, who, as she knew, had always been hers, and would still be hers, if he were 130 alive. . . . "Alas how much better I should feel, and how much comfort I should take, if only once before he died I had held him in my arms! What? Yes, certainly, quite unclad, in order the better to enjoy him. If he is dead, I am very wicked not to destroy myself. Why? Can it harm my lover for me to live on after he is dead, if I take no pleasure in anything but in the woe I bear for him? In giving myself up to grief after his death, the very woes I court would be sweet to me, if he were only still alive. It is wrong for a woman to wish to die rather than to suffer for her lover's sake. It is certainly sweet for me to 140 mourn him long. I would rather be beaten alive than die and be at rest."

[Once freed, Lancelot makes his way to the castle and Guinevere agrees to meet with him secretly.]

Lancelot . . . was so impatient for the night to come that his restlessness made the day seem longer than a hundred ordinary days or than an entire year. If night had only come, he would gladly have gone to the trysting place. Dark and somber night at last won its struggle with the day, and wrapped it up in its covering, and laid it away beneath its cloak. When he saw the light of day obscured, he pretended to be tired and worn, and said that, in view of his protracted vigils, he needed 150 rest. You, who have ever done the same, may well understand and guess that he pretends to be tired and goes to bed in order to deceive the people of the house; but he cared nothing about his bed, nor would he have sought rest there for anything, for he could not have done so and would not have dared, and furthermore he would not have cared to possess the courage or the power to do so. Soon he softly rose, and was pleased to find that no moon or star was shining, and that in the house there was no candle, lamp or lantern burning. Thus he went out and looked about, but there was no one on 160 the watch for him, for all thought that he would sleep in his bed all night. Without escort or company he quickly went out into the garden, meeting no one on the way, and he was so fortunate as to find that a part of the garden-wall had recently fallen down. Through this break he passes quickly and proceeds to the window, where he stands, taking good care not to cough or sneeze, until the Queen arrives clad in a very white chemise. She wore no cloak or coat, but had thrown over her a short cape of scarlet cloth and shrew-mouse fur. As soon as Lancelot saw the Queen leaning on the window-sill 170 behind the great iron bars, he honored her with a gentle salute. She promptly returned his greeting, for he was desirous of her, and she of him. Their talk and conversation are not of vulgar, tiresome affairs. They draw close to one another, until each holds the other's hand. But they are so distressed at not being able to come together more completely, that they curse the iron bars. Then Lancelot asserts that, with the Queen's consent, he will come inside to be with her, and that the bars cannot keep him out. And the Queen replies: "Do you not see how the bars are stiff to bend 180 and hard to break? You could never so twist, pull or drag at them as to dislodge one of them." "Lady," says he, "have no fear of that. It would take more than these bars to keep me out. . . ."

Then the Queen retires, and he prepares to loosen the window. Seizing the bars, he pulls and wrenches them until he makes them bend and drags them from their places. But the iron was so sharp that the end of his little finger was cut to the nerve, and the first joint of the next finger was torn; but he who is intent upon something else paid no heed to any of his 190 wounds or to the blood which trickled down. Though the window is not low, Lancelot gets through it quickly and easily . . . then he comes to the bed of the Queen, whom he adores and before whom he kneels, holding her more dear than the relic of any saint. And the Queen extends her arms to him and, embracing him, presses him tightly against her bosom, drawing him into the bed beside her and showing him every possible satisfaction: her love and her heart go out to him. It is love that prompts her to treat him so; and if she feels great love for him, he feels a hundred thousand times as much for 200 her. For there is no love at all in other hearts compared with what there is in his; in his heart love was so completely embodied that it was niggardly toward all other hearts. Now Lancelot possesses all he wants, when the Queen voluntarily seeks his company and love, and when he holds her in his arms, and she holds him in hers. Their sport is so agreeable and sweet, as they kiss and fondle each other, that in truth such a marvellous joy comes over them as was never heard or known. But their joy will not be revealed by me, for in a story it has no place. Yet, the most choice and delightful 210 satisfaction was precisely that of which our story must not speak. That night Lancelot's joy and pleasure was very great. But, to his sorrow, day comes when he must leave his mistress' side. It cost him such pain to leave her that he suffered a real martyr's agony. His heart now stays where the Queen remains; he has not the power to lead it away, for it finds such pleasure in the Queen that it has no desire to leave her: so his body goes, and his heart remains; . . .

Q How do Roland (Reading 2.14) and Lancelot compare as medieval heroes?

Q What "brave deeds" does each undertake to achieve his goal?

Lancelot's worship of Guinevere (cc. 205–206) and his repeated references to her "saintliness" illustrate the confusion of sensual and spiritual passions that characterized the culture of the High Middle Ages. The fact that Lancelot uses the terminology of religious worship to flatter an unfaithful wife suggests the paradoxical nature of the so-called "religion of love" associated with courtly romance. However one explains this phenomenon, *Lancelot* remains representative of the climate of shifting values and the degeneration of feudal ideals, especially those of honor and loyalty among gentleman-warriors.

The Poetry of the *Troubadours*

During the Early Middle Ages, few men and women could read or write. But by the eleventh century, literacy was spreading beyond the cathedral schools and monasteries. The popularity of such forms of vernacular literature as lyric poetry, the chronicle, and the romance gives evidence of increasing lay literacy among upper-class men and women. To entertain the French nobility, *trouvères* (in the north) and *troubadours* (in the south) composed and performed poems devoted to courtly love, chivalry, religion, and politics. The most famous collection of such lyric poems, the *Carmina Burana*, came from twelfth-century France. In German-speaking courts, *Minnesingers* provided a similar kind of entertainment, while *Meistersingers*, masters of the guilds of poets and musicians, flourished somewhat later in German towns.

Unlike the minstrels of old, *troubadours* were usually men and women of noble birth. Their poems, like the *chansons* of the Early Middle Ages, were monophonic and syllabic, but they were more expressive in content and more delicate in style, betraying their indebtedness to Arab poetic forms. Often, *troubadours* (or the professional musicians who recited their poems) accompanied themselves on a lyre or a lute (see Figure 10.15). Many of the 2,600 extant *troubadour* poems exalt the passionate affection of a gentleman for a lady, or, as in those written

Figure 11.20 *Konrad von Altstetten Smitten by Spring and His Beloved*, from the Manesse Codex, Zürich, ca. 1300. Manuscript illumination, 14 x 9⅞ in. University Library, Heidelberg, Germany, Codex pal. germ. 848, f.249v. Rheinisches Köln Bildarchiv, Cologne, Germany.

by the twenty identifiable *trobairitzes* (female *troubadours*), the reverse (Figure **11.20**).

Influenced by Islamic verse such as that found in chapter 10, *troubadour* poems generally manifest a positive, even joyous, response to physical nature and the world of the senses. An eleventh-century poem by William IX, Duke of Aquitaine and one of the first *troubadours*, compares the anticipation of sexual fulfillment with the coming of spring. It opens with these high-spirited words:

> In the sweetness of the new season
> when woods burst forth and birds
> sing, each in its own voice
> to the lyrics of a new song,
> *then* should one seize
> the pleasures one most desires.

In a more melancholic vein, the mid-twelfth-century poet Bernart de Ventadour explored the popular theme of unrequited love in the poem "When I behold the lark." Occasionally, *troubadour* verse gives evidence of hostility between upper and lower social classes. Such is the case with the second of the poems printed here, in which the *troubadour* Peire Cardenal levels a fierce attack on social inequity and upper-class greed. The third voice represented below is that of a woman: the countess of Dia (often called "Beatriz") was a twelfth-century *trobairitz*; her surviving four songs are filled with personal laments for lost love ("I've been in great anguish") and impassioned enticements of physical pleasure.

READING 2.16 *Troubadour* Poems (ca. 1050–1200)

Bernart de Ventadour's "When I behold the lark"

When I behold the lark arise 1
with wings of gold for heaven's height,
to drop at last from flooded skies,
lost in its fullness of delight,
such sweetness spreads upon the day 5
I envy those who share the glee.
My heart's so filled with love's dismay
I wait its breaking suddenly.

I thought in love's ways I was wise,
yet little do I know aright. 10
I praised a woman as love's prize

🎜 See Music Listening Selection at end of chapter.

and she gives nothing to requite.
My heart, my life she took in theft,
she took the world away from me,
and now my plundered self is left 15
only desire and misery.

Her rule I'm forced to recognize
since all my broken joys took flight.
I looked within her lifted eyes,
that mirror sweet with treacherous might: 20
O mirror, here I weep and dream
of depths once glimpsed and now denied.
I'm lost in you as in the stream
comely Narcissus looked and died.

Now trust in indignation dies 25
and womanhood I henceforth slight.
I find that all her worths are lies.
I thought her something made of light.
And no one comes to plead for me
with her who darkens all my days. 30

Woman I doubt and now I see
that she like all the rest betrays.

Aye, pity women all despise.
Come face the truth and do not fight.
The smallest kindness she denies,   35
yet who but she should soothe my plight?
So gentle and so fair is she,
it's hard for others to believe.
She, who could save, in cruelty
watches her wasting lover grieve.   40

My love has failed and powerless lies;
devotion bears for me no right.
She laughs to hear my deepest sighs—
then silently I'll leave her sight.
I cast my love of her away.   45
She struck and I accept the blow.
She will not speak and I must stray
in exile. Where, I do not know.

Tristan, I've made an end, I say.
I'm going—where, I do not know.   50
My song is dying, and away
all love and joy I cast, and go.

Peire Cardenal's "Lonely the rich need never be"

Lonely the rich need never be,   1
they have such constant company.
For Wickedness in front we see,
behind, all round, and far and wide.
The giant called Cupidity   5
is always hulking at their side.
Injustice waves the flag, and he
is led along by Pride . . .

If a poor man has snitched a bit of rag,
he goes with downcast head and frightened eye.   10
But when the rich thief fills his greedy bag,
he marches on with head still held as high.
The poor man's hanged, he stole a rotten bridle.
The man who hanged him stole the horse. O fie.
To hang poor thieves the rich thieves still aren't idle. 15
That kind of justice arrow-swift will fly . . .

The rich are charitable? Yes,
as Cain who slew his brother Abel.
They're thieves, no wolves as merciless.
They're liars, like a whoreshop-babel.   20
O stick their ribs, O stick their souls!
No truth comes bubbling from the holes,
but lies. Their greedy hearts, abhorrent,
are rabid as a mountain-torrent . . .

With loving-kindness how they quicken,   25
what hoards of charity they spread.
If all the stones were loaves of bread,
if all the streams with wine should thicken,
the hills turn bacon or boiled chicken,
they'd give no extra crumb. That's flat,   30
    Some people are like that.

The Countess of Dia's "I've been in great anguish"

I've been in great anguish   1
over a noble knight I once had,
and I want everyone to know, for all time,
that I loved him—too much!
Now I see I'm betrayed   5
because I didn't yield my love to him.

For that I've suffered greatly,
both in my bed and when I'm fully clad.

How I'd yearn to have my knight
in my naked arms for one night!   10
He would feel a frenzy of delight
only to have me for his pillow.
I'm more in love with him
than Blancheflor ever was with Floris.[1]
To him I'd give my heart, my love,   15
my mind, my eyes, my life.

Beautiful, gracious, sweet friend,
when shall I hold you in my power?
If I could lie with you for one night,
and give you a kiss of love,   20
you can be sure I would desire greatly
to grant you a husband's place,
as long as you promised
to do everything I wished!

Q On what specific topics and themes are these songs focused?

Q What do these themes reveal about the culture that produced the *troubadours*?

The Rise of Medieval Towns

Observing the plight of the poor at the hands of the rich, Peire Cardenal condemns a universal condition; but his poem discloses a new social consciousness associated with economic change. During the High Middle Ages, a class of people "midway" between serfs and landlords—the middle class—was emerging. Many factors, including increased agricultural production and the reopening of trade routes, encouraged the rise of the middle class. During the eleventh century, merchants (often younger sons of noble families) engaged in commercial enterprises that promoted the growth of local markets. Usually located near highways or rivers, outside the walls of a fortified castle (*bourg* in French, *burg* in German, *borough* in English), the trade market became an essential part of manorial life. The permanent market (or *faubourg*) provided the basis for the medieval town—an urban center that attracted farmers and artisans who might buy freedom from their lord or simply run away from the manor. "City air makes a man free" was the cry of those who had discovered the urban alternative to manorial life.

In the newly established towns, the middle class pursued profit from commercial exchange. Merchants and

---

[1] The lovers in a popular medieval romance.

Figure 11.21 The walled city of Carcassonne, France, twelfth–thirteenth centuries. Topham Picturepoint/Roger Viollet, Paris

ernments and regulate their own economic activities. Such commercial centers as Milan, Florence, and Venice became completely self-governing city-states similar to those of ancient Greece and Rome. The self-governing Flemish cities of Bruges and Antwerp exported fine linen and wool to England and to towns along the Baltic Sea. The spirit of urban growth was manifested in the construction of defensive stone walls that protected the citizens, as at Carcassonne in southwestern France (Figure **11.21**), and in the building of cathedrals and guildhalls that flanked the open marketplace. Although by the twelfth century town dwellers constituted less than fifteen percent of the total European population, the middle class continued to expand and ultimately it came to dominate Western society.

craftspeople in like occupations formed **guilds** for the mutual protection of buyers and sellers. The guilds regulated prices, fixed wages, established standards of quality in the production of goods, and provided training for newcomers in each profession. During the eleventh and twelfth centuries, urban dwellers purchased charters of self-government from lords in whose fiefs their towns were situated. Such charters allowed townspeople (*bourgeois* in French; *Burghers* in German) to establish municipal gov-

Middle-class values differed considerably from those of the feudal nobility. Whereas warfare and chivalry preoccupied the nobility, financial prosperity and profit were the principal concerns of the middle class. In European cities, there evolved a lively vernacular literature expressive of middle-class concerns. It included humorous narrative tales (*fabliaux*) and poems (*dits*) describing urban occupations, domestic conflict, and street and tavern life (Figure **11.22**). These popular genres, which feature such stereotypes as the miserly husband and the lecherous monk, slyly reflect many of the social tensions and sexual prejudices of the day. A favorite theme of medieval *fabliaux* and *dits* was the antifemale diatribe, a denunciation of women as bitter as Juvenal's (see chapter 6), and one that was rooted in a long tradition of misogyny (the hatred of women). While medieval romances generally cast the female in a positive light, *fabliaux* and *dits* often described women as sinful and seductive. The hostile attitude toward womankind, intensified perhaps by women's increasing participation in some of the commercial activities traditionally dominated by men, is readily apparent in both urban legislation and in the popular literature of the late thirteenth century. The following verse, based on a widely circulated proverb, voices a popular male complaint:

Figure 11.22 *Young Lady Shopping for Belts and Purses*, from the Manesse Codex, Zürich, ca. 1315–1333. Universitätsbibliothek, Heidelberg, Germany, MS Pal. germ. 848, f.64. Rheinisches Köln Bildarchiv, Cologne, Germany.

He who takes a wife trades peace for strife,
Long weariness, despair, oppress his life,
A heavy load, a barrel full of chatter,
Uncorkable, her gossip makes a clatter,
Now, ever since I took a wife,
Calamity has marred my life.*

SUMMARY

The progress of the medieval West reflects the commingling of three cultural ingredients: classical, Christian, and

---

*"The Vices of Women," in *Three Medieval Views of Women*, translated by Gloria K. Fiero et al. New Haven: Yale University Press, 1989, 129, 131.

Germanic. The westward migrations of the Germanic tribes threatened the stability of the already waning Roman civilization. Nevertheless, these tribes introduced customs and values that came to shape the character of the European Middle Ages. In the first five hundred years of the first millennium, Germanic languages, laws, and forms of artistic expression fused with those of the late Roman and newly Christianized world to fix the patterns of early medieval life. The epic *Beowulf* and the art of Sutton Hoo are landmarks of Germanic cultural achievement. By the eighth century, the Empire of the Frankish ruler Charlemagne had become the cultural oasis of the West. Under Charlemagne's influence, much of Europe converted to Christianity, while members of his court worked to encourage education and the arts.

In the turbulent century following the fragmentation of the Carolingian Empire, feudalism—the exchange of land for military service—gave noblemen the power to rule locally while providing protection from outside attack. The artistic monuments of the Early Middle Ages—the *Song of Roland*, the Norman castle, and the Bayeux Tapestry—all describe a heroic age that glorified feudal combat, male prowess, and the conquest of land. Manorialism, the economic basis for medieval society, offered the lower classes physical protection in exchange for food production, but it left in its wake little tangible evidence of the lives and values of the majority of the population.

The Christian Crusades—the definitive medieval expression of Christian–Muslim hostility—altered patterns of economic and cultural life, even as they reflected the new mobility of Europe's High Middle Ages. In the literature of the medieval court, sentiment and sensuousness replaced heroic idealism and chivalric chastity. Romantic love, a medieval invention, dominated both the vernacular romance and *troubadour* poetry. The Crusades also encouraged the rise of towns and trade dominated by a new middle class, whose ambitions were distinctly materialistic and profit-oriented. The values of merchants and craftspeople differed from those of the feudal nobility, for whom land provided the basis of wealth and chivalry dictated manners and morals. Vernacular tales and poems often satirized inequality between classes and antagonism between sexes. Changing patterns of secular life between the years 750 and 1300 reflect the shift from a feudal society to an urban one distinguished by increasingly complex social interactions between male and female, lord and vassal, farmer and merchant.

MUSIC LISTENING SELECTION

CD One Selection 6 Bernart de Ventadour, "Can vei la lauzeta mover" ("When I behold the lark"), ca. 1150, excerpt.

GLOSSARY

chain mail a flexible medieval armor made of interlinked metal rings

chalice a goblet; in Christian liturgy, the Eucharistic cup

chanson de geste (French, "song of heroic deeds") an epic poem of the Early Middle Ages

chivalry a code of behavior practiced by upper-class men and women of medieval society

cloisonné (French, *cloison*, meaning "fence") an enameling technique produced by pouring molten colored glass between thin metal strips secured to a metal surface; any object ornamented in this manner (see Figure 11.2)

common law the body of unwritten law developed primarily from judicial decisions based on custom and precedent; the basis of the English legal system and that of all states in the United States with the exception of Louisiana

crenellations tooth-shaped battlements surmounting a wall and used for defensive combat

cruciform cross-shaped

fealty loyalty; the fidelity of the warrior to his chieftain

feudalism the system of political organization prevailing in Europe between the ninth and fifteenth centuries and having as its basis the exchange of land for military defense

fief in feudal society, land or property given to a warrior in return for military service

guild an association of merchants or craftspeople organized according to occupation

investiture the procedure by which a feudal lord granted a vassal control over a fief

jongleur a professional entertainer who wandered from court to court in medieval Europe

joust a form of personal combat, usually with lances on horseback, between men-at-arms

keep a square tower, the strongest and most secure part of the medieval castle (see Figure 11.14)

kenning a two-term metaphor used in Old English verse

lord any member of the feudal nobility who invested a vassal with a fief

mace a heavy, spike-headed club used as a weapon in medieval combat

medieval romance a tale of adventure that deals with knights, kings, and ladies acting under the impulse of love, religious faith, or the desire for adventure

moat a wide trench, usually filled with water, surrounding a fortified place such as a castle (see Figure 11.14)

niello a black sulfurous substance used as a decorative inlay for incised metal surfaces; the art or process of decorating metal in this manner

paten a shallow dish; in Christian liturgy, the Eucharistic plate

primogeniture the principle by which a fief was passed from father to eldest son

renaissance (French, "rebirth") a revival of the learning of former and especially classical culture

serf an unfree peasant

vassal any member of the feudal nobility who vowed to serve a lord in exchange for control of a fief

zoomorphic animal-shaped; having the form of an animal

CHAPTER 12

Christianity and the Medieval Mind

"All earthly things is but vanity:
Beauty, Strength, and Discretion do man forsake,
Foolish friends and kinsmen, that fair spake,
All fleeth save Good Deeds . . ."
Everyman

For a thousand years after the fall of Rome (ca. 500–1500), the Catholic Church was the primary source of spiritual authority and religious leadership in the European West. Longstanding disagreements over doctrinal, political, and liturgical matters resulted, in 1054, in a permanent breach between the Roman Catholic Church in the West and the Greek Orthodox Church in the East. Both churches, however, shared the view that the terrestrial world mirrored a divine order that was sustained through the ministry of God's representatives on earth. Church doctrine and liturgy gave coherence and meaning to everyday life. More important, the Church offered the sole means by which the medieval Christian might achieve life everlasting.

The Christian Way of Life and Death

The promise of personal immortality was central to Christianity and to the medieval worldview. With the exception of the purest forms of Hinduism and Buddhism, which anticipate the extinction of the Self, most world religions have met the fear of death with an ideology (a body of doctrine supported by myth and symbols) that promises the survival of some aspect of the Self in a life hereafter. The nature of that hereafter usually depends on the moral status of the believer—that is, his or her conduct on earth.

Christianity addressed the question of personal salvation more effectively than any other world religion. Indeed, the Christian immortality ideology provided a system by which medieval Christians achieved final victory over death. Through the **sacraments**, a set of sacred acts that impart **grace** (the free and unearned favor of God), medieval Christians were assured of the soul's redemption from sin and, ultimately, of eternal life in the world to come. The seven sacraments—the number fixed by the Fourth Lateran Council of 1215—touched every significant phase of human life: at birth, baptism purified the recipient of Original Sin; confirmation admitted the

baptized to full church privileges; ordination invested those entering the clergy with priestly authority; matrimony blessed the union of man and woman; penance acknowledged repentance of sins and offered absolution; Eucharist—the central and most important of the sacraments—joined human beings to God by means of the body and blood of Jesus; and finally, just prior to death, extreme unction provided final absolution from sins.

By way of the sacraments, the Church participated in virtually every major aspect of the individual's life, enforcing a set of values that determined the collective spirituality of Christendom. Since only church officials could administer the sacraments, the clergy held a "monopoly" on personal salvation. Medieval Christians thus looked to representatives of the Mother Church as shepherds guiding the members of their flock on their long and hazardous journey from cradle to grave. Their conduct on earth determined whether their souls went to Heaven, Hell, or Purgatory (the place of purification from sins). But only by way of the clergy might they receive the gifts of grace that made salvation possible.

By the twelfth century, the Christian concepts of sin and divine justice had become ever more complex: church councils defined Purgatory as an intermediate realm occupied by the soul after death (and before the Last Judgment). In Purgatory punishment was imposed for the unexpiated but repented sins committed in mortal life. While ordinary Christians might suffer punishment in Purgatory, they might also benefit from prayers and good works offered on their behalf. The role of the priesthood in providing such forms of remission from sin would give the medieval Church unassailable power and authority.

The Literature of Mysticism

Most of the religious literature of the Middle Ages was didactic—that is, it served to teach and instruct. Visionary literature, however, functioned in two other ways. It reflected an individual's intuitive and direct knowledge of God (thus constituting a form of autobiography); and it conjured vivid images of the supernatural (thus providing a vocabulary by which the unknowable might actually be known). The leading mystic of the twelfth century, Hildegard of Bingen (1098–1179) was an extraordinary individual. Entering a Benedictine convent at the age of eight, she went on to become its abbess. A scholar of both Latin and her native Germany, she wrote three visionary tracts, treatises on natural science, medicine and the treatment of disease, an allegorical dialogue between the vices and the virtues, and a cycle of seventy-seven songs arranged for devotional performance (see Chapter 13). While some regard Hildegard as the *first* of the female visionaries, she actually follows a long line of mystics and seers whose history begins in antiquity (most famously represented by the Delphic priestesses and the Roman sibyls). One of the first great Christian mystics, however, Hildegard produced original works on such topics as the nature of the universe, the meaning of Scripture, and the destiny of the Christian soul. The Church confirmed the divine source of her visions and, along with most of her contemporaries, acknowledged her prophetic powers. In the following selection from *Scivias*, short for *Scito vias domini (Know the Ways of the Lord)*, her encounter with the "voice from heaven" is followed by two of her most compelling visions. The miniature accompanying one of these visions (Figure **12.1**)—like all of those that illustrate her manuscripts—was supervised by Hildegard herself.

READING 2.17 From Hildegard of Bingen's *Know the Ways of the Lord*

(ca. 1146)

1. A Solemn Declaration Concerning the True Vision Flowing from God: *Scivias.* Protestificatio

Lo! In the forty-third year of my temporal course, when I clung   **1**
to a celestial vision with great fear and tremulous effort, I saw
a great splendor. In it came a voice from heaven, saying:

"O frail mortal, both ash of ashes, and rottenness of
rottenness, speak and write down what you see and hear. But
because you are fearful of speaking, simple at expounding,
and unlearned in writing—speak and write, not according to
the speech of man or according to the intelligence of human
invention, or following the aim of human composition, but
according to what you see and hear from the heavens above in   **10**
the wonders of God! Offer explanations of them, just as one
who hears and understands the words of an instructor
willingly makes them public, revealing and teaching them
according to the sense of the instructor's discourse. You,
therefore, O mortal, speak also the things you see and hear.
Write them, not according to yourself or to some other person,
but according to the will of the Knower, Seer, and Ordainer of
all things in the secrets of their mysteries."

And again I heard the voice from heaven saying to me:
"Speak these wonders and write the things taught in this   **20**
manner—and speak!"

It happened in the year 1141 of the Incarnation of the Son
of God, Jesus Christ, when I was forty-two years and seven

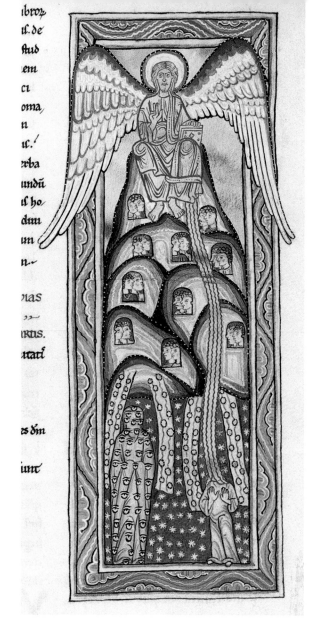

Figure 12.1 Hildegard of Bingen, *Scivias*, ca. 1146. Rheinisches Bildarchiv, MS 13 321, Wiesbaden Codex B, folio 1.

months old, that a fiery light of the greatest radiance coming
from the open heavens flooded through my entire brain. It
kindled my whole breast like a flame that does not scorch but
warms in the same way the sun warms anything on which it
sheds its rays.

Suddenly I understood the meaning of books, that is, the
Psalms and the Gospels; and I knew other catholic books of   **30**
the Old as well as the New Testaments—not the significance
of the words of the text, or the division of the syllables, nor
did I consider an examination of the cases and tenses.

Indeed, from the age of girlhood, from the time that I was
fifteen until the present, I had perceived in myself, just as until
this moment, a power of mysterious, secret, and marvelous
visions of a miraculous sort. However, I revealed these things
to no one, except to a few religious persons who were living
under the same vows as I was. But meanwhile, until this time
when God in his grace has willed these things to be revealed,   **40**
I have repressed them in quiet silence.

But I have not perceived these visions in dreams, or asleep,
or in a delirium, or with my bodily eyes, or with my external

mortal ears, or in secreted places, but I received them awake and looking attentively about me with an unclouded mind, in open places, according to God's will. However this may be, it is difficult for carnal man to fathom. . . .

2. The Iron-Colored Mountain and the Radiant One: *Scivias*. Book I, Vision 1

I saw what seemed to be a huge mountain having the color of iron. On its height was sitting One of such great radiance that it stunned my vision. On both sides of him extended a gentle 50
shadow like a wing of marvelous width and length. And in front of him at the foot of the same mountain stood a figure full of eyes everywhere. Because of those eyes, I was not able to distinguish any human form.

In front of this figure there was another figure, whose age was that of a boy, and he was clothed in a pale tunic and white shoes. I was not able to look at his face, because above his head so much radiance descended from the One sitting on the mountain. From the One sitting on the mountain a great many living sparks cascaded, which flew around those figures 60
with great sweetness. In this same mountain, moreover, there seemed to be a number of little windows, in which men's heads appeared, some pale and some white.

And see! The One sitting on the mountain shouted in an extremely loud, strong voice, saying: "O frail mortal, you who are of the dust of the earth's dust, and ash of ash, cry out and speak of the way into incorruptible salvation! Do this in order that those people may be taught who see the innermost meaning of Scripture, but who do not wish to tell it or preach it because they are lukewarm and dull in preserving God's 70
justice. Unlock for them the mystical barriers. For they, being timid, are hiding themselves in a remote and barren field. You, therefore, pour yourself forth in a fountain of abundance! Flow with mystical learning, so that those who want you to be scorned because of the guilt of Eve may be inundated by the flood of your refreshment!

"For you do not receive this keenness of insight from man, but from that supernal and awesome judge on high. There amidst brilliant light, this radiance will brightly shine forth among the luminous ones. Arise, therefore, and shout and 80
speak! These things are revealed to you through the strongest power of divine aid. For he who potently and benignly rules his creatures imbues with the radiance of heavenly enlightenment all those who fear him and serve him with sweet love in a spirit of humility. And he leads those who persevere in the path of justice to the joys of everlasting vision!"

3. The Fall of Lucifer, the Formation of Hell, and the Fall of Adam and Eve: *Scivias*. Book I, Vision 2

Then I saw what seemed to be a great number of living torches, full of brilliance. Catching a fiery gleam, they received a most radiant splendor from it. And see! A lake appeared here, of great length and depth, with a mouth like a well, 90
breathing forth a stinking fiery smoke. From the mouth of the lake a loathsome fog also arose until it touched a thing like a blood vessel that had a deceptive appearance.

And in a certain region of brightness, the fog blew through the blood vessel to a pure white cloud, which had emerged

from the beautiful form of a man, and the cloud contained within itself many, many stars. Then the loathsome fog blew and drove the cloud and the man's form out of the region of brightness.

Once this had happened, the most luminous splendor 100
encircled that region. The elements of the world, which previously had held firmly together in great tranquility, now, turning into great turmoil, displayed fearful terrors. . . .

Now "that lake of great length and depth" which appeared to you is Hell. In its length are contained vices, and in its deep abyss is damnation, as you see. Also, "it has a mouth like a well, breathing forth a stinking, fiery smoke" means that drowning souls are swallowed in its voracious greed. For although the lake shows them sweetness and delights, it leads them, through perverse deceit, to a perdition of 110
torments. There the heat of the fire breathes forth with an outpouring of the most loathsome smoke, and with a boiling, death-dealing stench. For these abominable torments were prepared for the Devil and his followers, who turned away from the highest good, which they wanted neither to know nor to understand. For this reason they were cast down from every good thing, not because they did not know them but because they were contemptuous of them in their lofty pride. . . .

Q What role does revelation play in Hildegard's visions?

Q Which of her visionary images do you find most vivid?

Sermon Literature

While the writings of Hildegard of Bingen addressed individual, literate Christians, medieval sermons, delivered orally from the pulpit of the church, were directed to the largely illiterate Christian community. Both visionary tracts and sermon literature, however, described grace and salvation in vivid terms. The classic medieval sermon, *On the Misery of the Human Condition*, was written by one of Christendom's most influential popes, Innocent III (d. 1216). This sermon is a compelling description of the natural sinfulness of humankind and a scathing condemnation of the "vile and filthy [human] condition." Such motifs, like those found in Hildegard's visions, proceeded from prevailing views of the human condition: weighed down by the burden of the flesh, the body is subject to corruption, disease, and carnal desire. As the temple of the soul, the body will be resurrected on Judgment Day, but not before it suffers the trials of mortality. Warning of the "nearness of death," Innocent's sermon functioned as a **memento mori**, a device by which listeners in a predominantly oral culture might "remember death" and thus prepare themselves for its inevitable arrival. Innocent's portrayal of the decay of the human body reflects the medieval disdain for the world of matter, a major theme in most medieval didactic literature. During the Late Middle Ages, especially after the onslaught of the bubonic plague (see chapter 15), the motif of the body as "food for worms"—one of Innocent's most vivid images—

Figure 12.2 Detail of *transi* (effigy of the dead) of François de la Sarra, ca. 1390. La Sarraz, Switzerland. Photo: De Jongh, Lausanne. © Musée de l'Elysée, Lausanne, Switzerland.

became particularly popular in gruesomely forthright tomb sculptures (Figure **12.2**).

Innocent's vivid account of the Christian Hell transforms the concept of corruption into an image of eternal punishment for unabsolved sinners—a favorite subject matter for medieval artists (Figure **12.3**). The contrast that Innocent draws between physical death and spiritual life has its visual counterpart in the representations of the Last Judgment depicted in medieval manuscripts and on Romanesque and Gothic church portals (see Figure 13.9).

READING 2.18 From Pope Innocent III's *On the Misery of the Human Condition* (ca. 1200)

Of the Miserable Entrance upon the Human Condition

... Man was formed of dust, slime, and ashes: what is even more vile, of the filthiest seed. He was conceived from the itch of the flesh, in the heat of passion and the stench of lust, and worse yet, with the stain of sin. He was born to toil, dread, and trouble; and more wretched still, was born only to die. He commits depraved acts by which he offends God, his neighbor, and himself; shameful acts by which he defiles his name, his person, and his conscience; and vain acts by which he ignores all things important, useful, and necessary. He will become fuel for those fires which are forever hot and burn forever **10** bright; food for the worm which forever nibbles and digests; a mass of rottenness which will forever stink and reek. . . .

On the Nearness of Death

A man's last day is always the first in importance, but his first day is never considered his last. Yet it is fitting to live always on this principle, that one should act as if in the moment of death. For it is written: "Remember that death is not slow."[1] Time passes, death draws near. In the eyes of the dying man a thousand years are as yesterday, which is past. The future is forever being born, the present forever dying and what is past is utterly dead. We are forever dying while we are alive; we **20** only cease to die when we cease to live. Therefore it is better to die to life than to live waiting for death, for mortal life is but a living death. . . .

On the Putrefaction of the Dead Body

. . . Man is conceived of blood made rotten by the heat of lust; and in the end worms, like mourners, stand about his corpse. In life he produced lice and tapeworms; in death he will produce worms and flies. In life he produced dung and vomit; in death he produces rottenness and stench. In life he fattened one man; in death he fattens a multitude of worms. What then is more foul than a human corpse? What is more horrible than **30** a dead man? He whose embrace was pure delight in life will be a gruesome sight in death.

Of what advantage, then, are riches, food, and honors? For riches will not free us from death, neither food protect us from the worm nor honors from the stench. That man who but now sat in glory upon a throne is now looked down on in the grave; the dandy who once glittered in his palace lies now naked and

———
[1] Ecclesiastes 14:12.

Figure 12.3 *The Mouth of Hell,* from the Psalter of Henry of Blois, Bishop of Winchester, twelfth century. Reproduced by permission of the British Library, London, MS Cotton Nero, C.IV, f.39.

vile in his tomb; and he who supped once on delicacies in his hall is now in his sepulcher food for worms. . . .

That Nothing Can Help the Damned

. . . O strict judgment!—not only of actions, but "of every idle **40** word that men shall speak, they shall render an account";[2] payment with the usurer's interest will be exacted to the last penny. "Who hath showed you to flee from the wrath to come?"[3]

"The Son of Man shall send his angels and they shall gather out of his kingdom all scandals, and them that work iniquity, and they will bind them as bundles to be burnt, and shall cast them into the furnace of fire. There shall be weeping and gnashing of teeth,"[4] there shall be groaning and wailing, shrieking and flailing of arms and screaming, screeching, and **50** shouting; there shall be fear and trembling, toil and trouble, holocaust and dreadful stench, and everywhere darkness and anguish; there shall be asperity, cruelty, calamity, poverty, distress, and utter wretchedness; they will feel an oblivion of loneliness and namelessness; there shall be twistings and piercings, bitterness, terror, hunger and thirst, cold and hot, brimstone and fire burning, forever and ever world without end. . . .

Q How does Innocent describe the nature and the destiny of humankind?

Q How does this sermon compare with the Sermon on the Mount (Reading 2.2)?

The Medieval Morality Play

While medieval churches rang with sermons like those preached by Innocent III, town squares (often immediately adjacent to a cathedral) became open-air theaters for the dramatization of Christian history and legend. To these urban spaces, townspeople flocked to see dramatic performances that might last from sunrise to sunset. The **mystery play** dramatized biblical history from the fall of Lucifer to the Last Judgment, while the **miracle play** enacted stories from the Life of Christ, the Virgin, or the saints. The **morality play**, the third type of medieval drama, dealt with the struggle between good and evil and the destiny of the soul in the hereafter. The first medieval morality play, Hildegard of Bingen's *Ordo virtutum* (*Play of the Virtues*) was a twelfth-century allegorical dialogue between vice and virtue. All of these types of plays were performed by members of the local guilds, and mystery plays were usually produced on **pageants** (roofed wagon-stages) that were rolled into the town square. Medieval plays were a popular form of entertainment, as well as a source of religious and moral instruction.

Medieval drama, like Greek drama, had its roots in religious performance. The Catholic Mass, the principal rite of Christian worship, admitted all of the trappings of theater: colorful costumes, symbolic props, solemn processions, dramatic gestures, and ceremonial music. It is likely that the gradual dramatization of Church liturgy (see chapter 13) influenced the genesis of mystery and miracle plays. The morality play, however, had clear precedents in allegorical poetry and sermon literature. Allegory—a literary device we have encountered in Plato's *Republic* (Reading 1.16) and in Augustine's *City of God* (Reading 2.8)—uses symbolic figures to capture the essence of a person, thing, or idea. The characters in the morality play are personifications of abstract qualities and universal conditions. In the play *Everyman*, for instance, the main character represents *all* Christian souls, Fellowship stands for friends, Goods for worldly possessions, and so forth.

Although *Everyman* has survived only in fifteenth-century Dutch and English editions, plays similar to it originated considerably earlier. The most popular of all medieval morality plays, *Everyman* symbolically recreates the pilgrimage of the Christian soul to its ultimate destiny. The play opens with the Messenger, who expounds on the transitory nature of human life. The subsequent conversation between Death and God, somewhat reminiscent of that between Satan and God in the Book of Job (see chapter 2), shows God to be an angry, petulant figure who finds human beings "drowned in sin." If left to their own devices, he opines, "they will become much worse than beasts." As the action unfolds, Everyman realizes that Death has come for him. Frightened and unprepared, he soon discovers that his best friends, his kin, his worldly possessions—indeed, all that he so treasured in life—will not accompany him to the grave. Knowledge, Wits, Beauty, and Discretion may point the way to redemption, but they cannot save him. His only ally is Good Deeds, which, with the assistance of the Catholic priesthood, will help him win salvation. Everyman is essentially a moral allegory that dramatizes the pilgrimage of the Christian soul from earthly existence to Last Judgment. Like Innocent's sermon, it teaches that life is transient, that worldly pleasures are ultimately valueless, and that sin can be mitigated solely by salvation earned through grace as dispensed by the Church.

READING 2.19 From *Everyman* (ca. 1500)

Characters

Messenger	Cousin	Strength
God (Adonai)	Goods	Discretion
Death	Good-Deeds	Five-Wits
Everyman	Knowledge	Angel
Fellowship	Confession	Doctor
Kindred	Beauty	

HERE BEGINNETH A TREATISE HOW THE HIGH FATHER OF HEAVEN SENDETH DEATH TO SUMMON EVERY CREATURE TO COME AND GIVE ACCOUNT OF THEIR LIVES IN THIS WORLD AND IS IN MANNER OF A MORAL PLAY.

---

[2]Matthew 12:36.
[3]Luke 3:7.
[4]Matthew 13:41–42.

Messenger: I pray you all give your audience, 1
And hear this matter with reverence,
By figure a moral play—
The Summoning of Everyman called it is,
That of our lives and ending shows
How transitory we be all day.[1]
This matter is wondrous precious,
But the intent of it is more gracious,
And sweet to bear away.
The story saith—Man, in the beginning, 10
Look well, and take good heed to the ending,
Be you never so gay!
Ye think sin in the beginning full sweet,
Which in the end causeth thy soul to weep,
When the body lieth in clay.
Here shall you see how *Fellowship* and *Jollity*,
Both *Strength, Pleasure,* and *Beauty,*
Will fade from thee as flower in May.
For ye shall hear, how our heaven king
Calleth *Everyman* to a general reckoning: 20
Give audience, and hear what he doth say.

    God: I perceive here in my majesty,
How that all creatures be to me unkind,[2]
Living without dread in worldly prosperity:
Of ghostly[3] sight the people be so blind,
Drowned in sin, they know me not for their God:
In worldly riches is all their mind,
They fear not my right wiseness, the sharp rod:
My law that I shewed, when I for them died,
They forget clean, and shedding of my blood red: 30
I hanged between two, it cannot be denied:
To get them life I suffered to be dead:
I healed their feet, with thorns hurt was my head:
I could do no more than I did truly,
And now I see the people do clean forsake me,
They use the seven deadly sins damnable;
As pride, covetise, wrath, and lechery,
Now in the world be made commendable;
And thus they leave of angels the heavenly company;
Everyman liveth so after his own pleasure, 40
And yet of their life they be nothing sure:
I see the more that I them forbear
The worse they be from year to year;
All that liveth appaireth[4] fast,
Therefore I will in all the haste
Having a reckoning of Everyman's person
For and[5] I leave the people thus alone
In their life and wicked tempests,
Verily they will become much worse than beasts;
For now one would by envy another up eat; 50
Charity they all do clean forget.
I hoped well that Everyman
In my glory should make his mansion,

And thereto I had them all elect;
But now I see, like traitors deject,
They thank me not for the pleasure that I to them meant
Nor yet for their being that I them have lent;
I proffered the people great multitude of mercy,
And few there be that asketh it heartily;
They be so combered with worldly riches, 60
That needs of them I must do justice,
On Everyman living without fear.
Where art thou, Death, thou mighty messenger?

    Death: Almighty God, I am here at your will,
Your commandment to fulfil.

    God: Go thou to Everyman,
And show him in my name
A pilgrimage he must on him take,
Which he in no wise may escape:
And that he bring with him a sure reckoning 70
Without delay or any tarrying.

    Death: Lord, I will in the world go run over all,
And cruelly outsearch both great and small;
Every man will I beset that liveth beastly
Out of God's laws, and dreadeth not folly:
He that loveth riches I will strike with my dart,
His sight to blind, and from heaven to depart,
Except that alms be his good friend,
In hell for to dwell, world without end.
Lo, yonder I see Everyman walking; 80
Full little he thinketh on my coming;
His mind is on fleshly lusts and his treasure,
And great pain it shall cause him to endure
Before the Lord Heaven King.
Everyman, stand still; whither art thou going
Thus gaily? Hast my Maker forgot?

    Everyman: Why askst thou?
Wouldest thou wete?[6]

    Death: Yea, sir, I will show you;
In great haste I am sent to thee 90
From God out of his majesty.

    Everyman: What, sent to me?

    Death: Yea, certainly.
Though thou have forget him here,
He thinketh on thee in the heavenly sphere,
As, or we depart, thou shalt know.

    Everyman: What desireth God of me?

    Death: That shall I show thee;
A reckoning he will needs have
Without any longer respite. 100

    Everyman: To give a reckoning longer leisure I crave;
This blind matter troubleth my wit.

    Death: On thee thou must take a long journey:
Therefore thy book of count with thee thou bring:
For turn again thou can not by no way.
And look thou be sure of thy reckoning:
For before God thou shalt answer, and show
Thy many bad deeds and good but a few;
How thou hast spent thy life, and in what wise,
Before the chief lord of paradise. 110

---

[1]Always.
[2]Ungrateful.
[3]Spiritual.
[4]Decays.
[5]If.

---

[6]Know.

Have ado that we were in that way,
For, wete thou well, thou shalt make none attournay.[7]

    Everyman: Full unready I am such reckoning to give.
I know thee not: what messenger art thou?

    Death: I am Death, that no man dreadeth.
For every man I rest[8] and no man spareth;
For it is God's commandment
That all to me should be obedient.

    Everyman: O Death, thou comest when I had thee least
      in mind,
In thy power it lieth me to save,   120
Yet of my good[s] will I give thee, if ye will be kind,
Yea, a thousand pound shalt thou have,
And defer this matter till another day.

    Death: Everyman, it may not be by no way;
I set not by gold, silver, nor riches,
Ne by pope, emperor, king, duke, ne princes,
For and I would receive gifts great,
All the world I might get;
But my custom is clean contrary.
I give thee no respite: come hence, and not tarry. 130

    Everyman: Alas, shall I have no longer respite?
I may say Death giveth no warning:
To think on thee, it maketh my heart sick,
For all unready is my book of reckoning.
But twelve year and I might have abiding,
My counting book I would make so clear,
That my reckoning I should not need to fear.
Wherefore, Death, I pray thee, for God's mercy.
Spare me till I be provided of remedy.

    Death: Thee availeth not to cry, weep, and pray: 140
But haste thee lightly that you were gone the journey.
And prove thy friends if thou can.
For, wete thou well, the tide abideth no man,
And in the world each living creature
For Adam's sin must die of nature.

    Everyman: Death, if I should this pilgrimage take,
And my reckoning surely make,
Show me, for saint charity,
Should I not come again shortly?

    Death: No, Everyman; and thou be once there, 150
Thou mayst never more come here,
Trust me verily.

    Everyman: O gracious God, in the high seat celestial,
Have mercy on me in this most need;
Shall I have no company from this vale terrestrial
Of mine acquaintance that way me to lead?

    Death: Yea, if any be so hardy,
That would go with thee and bear thee company.
Hie thee that you were gone[9] to God's magnificence,
Thy reckoning to give before his presence. 160
What, weenest[10] thou thy life is given thee,
And thy worldly goods also?

    Everyman: I had wend[11] so, verily.

    Death: Nay, nay; it was but lent thee;
For as soon as thou art go,
another awhile shall have it, and then go therefrom
Even as thou has done.
Everyman, thou art mad; thou hast thy wits five,
And here on earth will not amend thy life,
For suddenly I do come.   170

    Everyman: O wretched caitiff, whither shall I flee,
That I might scape this endless sorrow!
Now, gentle Death, spare me till to-morrow,
That I may amend me
With good advisement.

    Death: Nay, thereto I will not consent,
Nor no man will I respite,
But to the heart suddenly I shall smite
Without any advisement.
And now out of thy sight I will me nie; 180
See thou make thee ready shortly,
For thou mayst say this is the day
That no man living may scape away.

    Everyman: Alas, I may well weep with sighs deep,
Now have I no manner of company
To help me in my journey, and me to keep;
And also my writing is full unready.
How shall I do now for to excuse me?
I would to God I had never be gete![12]
To my soul a full great profit it had be; 190
For now I fear pains huge and great.
The time passeth; Lord, help that all wrought;
For though I mourn it availeth nought.
The day passeth, and is almost a-go;
I wot not well what for to do.
To whom were I best my complaint to make?
What, and I to Fellowship thereof spake,
And showed him of this sudden chance?
For in him is all mine affiance;[13]
We have in the world so many a day 200
Be on good friends in sport and play.
I see him yonder, certainly;
I trust that he will bear me company;
Therefore to him will I speak to ease my sorrow.
Well met, good Fellowship, and good morrow!

    Fellowship: Everyman, good morrow by this day.
Sir, why lookest thou so piteously?
If any thing be amiss, I pray thee, me say,
That I may help to remedy.

    Everyman: Yea, good Fellowship, yea. 210
I am in great jeopardy.

    Fellowship: My true friend, show to me your mind;
I will not forsake thee, unto my life's end,
In the way of good company.

    Everyman: That was well spoken, and lovingly.

    Fellowship: Sir, I must needs know your heaviness;
I have pity to see you in any distress;
If any have ye wronged he shall revenged be,
Though I on the ground be slain for thee—

---

[7]Mediator.
[8]Arrest.
[9]Hurry and go.
[10]Do you suppose.
[11]Supposed.

[12]Been born.
[13]Trust.

Thou that I know before that I should die.   220
    Everyman: Verily, Fellowship, gramercy.[14]
    Fellowship: Tush! by thy thanks I set not a straw;
Show me your grief, and say no more.
    Everyman: If I my heart should to you break,
And then you to turn your mind from me,
And would not me comfort, when you hear me speak,
Then should I ten times sorrier be.
    Fellowship: Sir, I say as I will do in deed.
    Everyman: Then be you a good friend at need:
I have found you true here before.   230
    Fellowship: And so ye shall evermore;
For, in faith, and thou go to Hell,
I will not forsake thee by the way!
    Everyman: Ye speak like a good friend: I believe you well;
I shall deserve[15] it, and I may.
    Fellowship: I speak of no deserving, by this day.
For he that will say and nothing do
Is not worthy with good company to go;
Therefore show me the grief of your mind,
As to your friend most loving and kind.   240
    Everyman: I shall show you how it is;
Commanded I am to go a journey,
A long way, hard and dangerous,
And give a strait count without delay
Before the high judge Adonai.[16]
Wherefore I pray you, bear me company,
As ye have promised, in this journey.
    Fellowship: That is matter indeed! Promise is duty,
But, and I should take such a voyage on me,
I know it well, it should be to my pain: 250
Also it make me afeard, certain.
But let us take counsel here as well as we can,
For your words would fear[17] a strong man.
    Everyman: Why, ye said, if I had need,
Ye would me never forsake, quick nor dead,
Though it were to Hell truly.
    Fellowship: So I said, certainly,
But such pleasures be set aside, thee sooth to say:
And also, if we took such a journey,
When should we come again?   260
    Everyman: Nay, never again till the day of doom.
    Fellowship: In faith, then will not I come there!
Who hath you these tidings brought?
    Everyman: Indeed, Death was with me here.
    Fellowship: Now, by God that all hath bought,
If Death were the messenger,
For no man that is living today
I will not go that loath journey—
Not for the father that begat me!
    Everyman: Ye promised other wise, pardie.[18]   270
    Fellowship: I wot well I say so truly
And yet if thou wilt eat, and drink, and make good cheer,

Or haunt to women, the lusty company,
I would not forsake you, while the day is clear,
Trust me verily!
    Everyman: Yea, thereto ye would be ready;
To go to mirth, solace, and play
Your mind will sooner apply
Than to bear me company in my long journey.
    Fellowship: Now, in good faith, I will not that way.   280
But and thou wilt murder, or any man kill,
In that I will help thee with a good will!
    Everyman: O that is a simple advice indeed!
Gentle fellow: help me in my necessity;
We have loved long, and now I need,
And now, gentle Fellowship, remember me.
    Fellowship: Whether ye have loved me or no,
By Saint John, I will not with thee go.
    Everyman: Yet I pray thee, take the labour, and do so
      much for me
To bring me forward, for saint charity,   290
And comfort me till I come without the town.
    Fellowship: Nay, and thou would give me a new gown,
I will not a foot with thee go;
But and you had tarried I would not have left thee so.
And as now, God speed thee in thy journey,
For from thee I will depart as fast as I may.
    Everyman: Whither away, Fellowship? Will you forsake me?
    Fellowship: Yea, by my fay,[19] to God I betake thee.
    Everyman: Farewell, good Fellowship; for this my heart
      is sore;
Adieu for ever, I shall see thee no more.   300
    Fellowship: In faith, Everyman, farewell not at the end; For you
I will remember that parting is mourning.
    Everyman: Alack! shall we thus depart indeed?
Our Lady, help, without any more comfort,
Lo, Fellowship forsaketh me in my most need:
For help in this world whither shall I resort?
Fellowship herebefore with me would merry make;
And now little sorrow for me doth he take.
It is said, in prosperity men friends may find,
Which in adversity be full unkind.   310
Now whither for succour shall I flee,
[since] Fellowship hath forsaken me?
To my kinsmen I will truly,
Praying them to help me in my necessity:
I believe that they will do so,
For kind will creep where it may not go,
Where be ye now, my friends and kinsmen?
    Kindred: Here be we now at your commandment.
Cousin, I pray you show us your intent
In any wise, and not spare.   320
    Cousin: Yea, Everyman, and to us declare
If ye be disposed to go any whither,
For wete you well, we will live and die together.
    Kindred: In wealth and woe we will with you hold,
For over his kin a man may be bold.
    Everyman: Gramercy, my friends and kinsmen kind.
Now shall I show you the grief of my mind:

---

[14]Many thanks.
[15]Repay.
[16]God.
[17]Terrify.
[18]By God.

---

[19]Faith.

I was commanded by a messenger,
That is an high king's chief officer;
He bade me go a pilgrimage to my pain,   330
And I know well I shall never come again;
Also I must give a reckoning straight,
For I have a great enemy, that hath me in wait,
Which intendeth me for to hinder.

    Kindred: What account is that which ye must render?
That would I know.

    Everyman: Of all my works I must show
How I have lived and my days spent;
Also of ill deeds, that I have used
In my time, sith[20] life was me lent;   340
And of all virtues that I have refused.
Therefore I pray you go thither with me,
To help to make mine account, for saint charity.

    Cousin: What, to go thither? Is that the matter?
Nay, Everyman, I had liefer[21] fast bread and water
All this five year and more.

    Everyman: Alas, that ever I was bore![22]
For now shall I never be merry
If that you forsake me.

    Kindred: Ah, sir, what, ye be a merry man!   350
Take good heart to you, and make no moan.
But one thing I warn you, by Saint Anne,
As for me, ye shall go alone.

    Everyman: My Cousin, will you not with me go?

    Cousin: No, by our Lady; I have the cramp in my toe.
Trust not to me, for, so God me speed,
I will deceive you in your most need.

    Kindred: It availeth not us to tice.[23]
Ye shall have my maid with all my heart;
She loveth to go to feasts, there to be nice,   360
And to dance, and abroad to start:
I will give her leave to help you in that journey,
If that you and she may agree.

    Everyman: Now show me the very effect of your mind. Will you
go with me, or abide behind?

    Kindred: Abide behind? Yea, that I will and I may! Therefore
farewell until another day.

    Everyman: How should I be merry or glad?
For fair promises to me make,
But when I have most need, they me forsake.   370
I am deceived; that maketh me sad.

    Cousin: Cousin Everyman, farewell now,
For verily I will not go with you;
Also of mine own an unready reckoning
I have to account: therefore I make tarrying.
Now, God keep thee, for now I go.

    Everyman: Ah, Jesus, is all come hereto?
Lo, fair words maketh fools feign;
They promise and nothing will do certain.
My kinsmen promised me faithfully   380
For to abide with me steadfastly,

And now fast away do they flee:
Even so Fellowship promised me.
What friend were best me of to provide?
I lose my time here longer to abide.
Yet in my mind a thing there is:—
All my life I have loved riches;
If that my goods now help me might,
He would make my heart full light.
I will speak to him in this distress.—   390
Where art thou, my Goods and riches?

    Goods: Who calleth me? Everyman? What haste thou
       hast!
I lie here in corners, trussed and piled so high,
And in chests I am locked so fast,
Also sacked in bags, thou mayst see with thine eye,
I cannot stir; in packs low I lie,
What would ye have, lightly me say.[24]

    Everyman: Come hither, Good, in all the haste thou
       may,
For of counsel I must desire thee.

    Goods: Sir, and ye in the world have trouble or adversity. 400
That can I help you to remedy shortly.

    Everyman: It is another disease that grieveth me;
In this world it is not, I tell thee so.
I am sent for another way to go,
To give a straight account general
Before the highest Jupiter of all;
And all my life I have had joy and pleasure in thee.
Therefore I pray thee go with me,
For, peradventure, thou mayst before God Almighty
My reckoning help to clean and purify;   410
For it is said ever among,
That money maketh all right that is wrong.

    Goods: Nay, Everyman, I sing another song.
I follow no man in such voyages;
For and I went with thee
Thou shouldst fare much the worse for me;
For because on me thou did set thy mind,
Thy reckoning I have made blotted and blind
That thine account thou cannot make truly;
And that has thou for the love of me.   420

    Everyman: That would grieve me full sore,
When I should come to that fearful answer.
Up, let us go thither together.

    Goods: Nay, no so, I am too brittle, I may not endure:
I will follow no man one foot, be ye sure.

    Everyman: Alas, I have thee loved, and had great
pleasure
All my life-days on good and treasure.

    Goods: That is to thy damnation without lesing,[25]
For my love is contrary to the love everlasting
But if thou had me loved moderately during,   430
As, to the poor give part of me,
Then shouldst thou not in this dolour[26] be,
Nor in this great sorrow and care.

---

[20]Since.
[21]Rather.
[22]Born.
[23]It is useless to try to entice us.

---

[24]Quickly tell me.
[25]Loosing, releasing.
[26]Distress.

Everyman: Lo, now was I deceived or I was ware,
And all I may wyte[27] my spending of time.

    Goods: What, weenest thou that I am thine?

    Everyman: I had wend so.

    Goods: Nay, Everyman, I say no;
As for a while I was lent thee,
A season thou hast had me in prosperity   440
My condition is man's soul to kill;
If I save one, a thousand I do spill;[28]
Weenest thou that I will follow thee?
Nay, from this world, not verily.

    Everyman: I had wend otherwise.

    Goods: Therefore to thy soul Good is a thief;
For when thou art dead, this is my guise
Another to deceive in the same wise
As I have done thee, and all to his soul's reprief.[29]

    Everyman: O false Good, cursed thou be!   450
Thou traitor to God, that has deceived me,
And caught me in thy snare.

    Goods: Marry,[30] thou brought thyself in care,
Whereof I am glad,
I must needs laugh, I cannot be sad.

    Everyman: Ah, Goods, thou has had long my heartly love; I gave thee that which should be the Lord's above.
But wilt thou not go with me in deed?
I pray thee truth to say.

    Goods: No, so God me speed,   460
Therefore farewell, and have good day.

    Everyman: O, to whom shall I make moan
For to go with me in that heavy journey?
First Fellowship said he would with me gone;
His words were very pleasant and gay,
But afterward he left me alone.
Then spake I to my kinsmen all in despair,
And also they gave me words fair,
They lacked no fair speaking,
But all forsake me in the ending.   470
Then went I to my Goods that I loved best,
In hope to have comfort, but there had I least:
For my Goods sharply did me tell
That he bringeth many into hell.
Then of myself I was ashamed;
And so I am worthy to be blamed;
Thus may I well myself hate,
Of whom shall I now counsel take?
I think that I shall never speed
Till that I go to my Good-Deeds,   480
But alas, she is so weak,
That she can neither go nor speak,
Yet will I venture on her now.—
My Good-Deeds, where be you?

    Good-Deeds: Here I lie cold on the ground,
Thy sins hath me sore bound,
That I cannot stir.

    Everyman: O, Good-Deeds, I stand in fear;
I must you pray of counsel,
For help now should come right well.   490

    Good-Deeds: Everyman, I have understanding
That ye be summoned account to make
Before Messias, of Jerusalem King;
And you by me[31] that journey what[32] you will I take.

    Everyman: Therefore I come to you, my moan to make; I pray you, that ye will go with me.

    Good-Deeds: I would full fain,[33] but I cannot stand verily.

    Everyman: Why, is there anything on you fall?

    Good-Deeds: Yea, sir, I may think you of all;
If ye had perfectly cheered me,   500
Your book of account now full ready had be.
Look, the books of your works and deeds eke;[34]
Oh, see how they lie under the feet,
To your soul's heaviness.

    Everyman: Our Lord Jesus, help me!
For one letter here I can not see.

    Good-Deeds: There is a blind reckoning in time of distress!

    Everyman: Good-Deeds, I pray you, help me in this need,
Or else I am for ever damned indeed;
Therefore help me to make reckoning   510
Before the redeemer of all thing,
That king is, and was, and ever shall.

    Good-Deeds: Everyman, I am sorry of your fall,
And fain would I help you, and I were able.

    Everyman: Good-Deeds, your counsel I pray you give me.

    Good-Deeds: That shall I do verily;
Though that on my feet I may not go,
I have a sister, that shall with you also,
Called Knowledge, which shall with you abide,
To help you to make that dreadful reckoning.   520

[Knowledge guides Everyman to Confession, Discretion, Strength, Beauty, and Five-Wits, who direct him to receive the sacrament of extreme unction.]

Knowledge: Everyman, hearken what I say;
Go to priesthood, I you advise,
And receive of him in any wise
The holy sacrament and ointment together;
Then shortly see ye turn again hither;
We will all abide you here.

    Five-Wits: Yea, Everyman, hie[35] you that ye ready were, There is no emperor, king, duke, ne baron,
That of God hath commission,
As hath the least priest in the world being;   530
For of the blessed sacraments pure and benign,
He beareth the keys and thereof hath the cure
For man's redemption, it is ever sure;
Which God for our soul's medicine
Gave us out of his heart with great pine;[36]

---

[27]Blame.

[28]Ruin.

[29]Shame.

[30]The Virgin Mary! (An interjection of surprise or agreement.)

[31]If you do as I advise.

[32]With.

[33]Very willingly.

[34]Also.

[35]Hasten.

[36]Suffering.

Here in this transitory life, for thee and me
The blessed sacraments seven there be.
Baptism, confirmation, with priesthood good,
And the sacrament of God's precious flesh and blood,
Marriage, the holy extreme unction, and penance; 540
These seven be good to have in remembrance,
Gracious sacraments of high divinity.

    Everyman: Fain would I receive that holy body
And meekly to my ghostly father I will go.

    Five-Wits: Everyman, that is the best that ye can do:
God will you to salvation bring,
For priesthood exceedeth all other thing;
To us Holy Scripture they do teach,
And converteth man from sin heaven to reach;
God hath to them more power given, 550
Than to any angel that is in heaven;
With five words he may consecrate
God's body in flesh and blood to make,
And handleth his maker between his hands;
The priest bindeth and unbindeth all bands,
Both in earth and in heaven;
Thou ministers all the sacraments seven;
Though we kissed thy feet thou were worthy;
Thou art surgeon that cureth sin deadly:
No remedy we find under God 560
But all only priesthood.
Everyman, God gave priest that dignity,
And setteth them in his stead among us to be;
Thus be they above angels in degree.

    Knowledge: If priests be good it is so surely;
But when Jesus hanged on the cross with great smart
There he gave, out of his blessed heart,
The same sacrament in great torment:
He sold them not to us, that Lord Omnipotent.
Therefore Saint Peter the apostle doth say 570
That Jesu's curse hath all they
Which God their Savior do buy or sell,
Or they for any money do take or tell.
Sinful priests giveth the sinners example bad;
Their children sitteth by other men's fires, I have heard;
And some haunteth women's company,
With unclean life, as lusts of lechery:
These be with sin made blind.

    Five-Wits: I trust to God no such may we find;
Therefore let us priesthood honour, 580
And follow their doctrine for our souls' succour;
We be their sheep, and they shepherds be
By whom we all be kept in surety.
Peace, for yonder I see Everyman come,
Which hath made true satisfaction.

    Good-Deeds: Methinketh it is he indeed.

    Everyman: Now Jesu be our alder speed.[37]
I have received the sacrament for my redemption,
And then mine extreme unction:
Blessed be all they that counselled me to take it! 590
And now, friends, let us go without longer respite;
I thank God that ye have tarried so long.

---
[37]Speed in help of all.

Now set each of you on this rood[38] your hand,
And shortly follow me:
I go before, there I would be; God be our guide.

[All but Good-Deeds then abandon Everyman.]

Everyman: Methinketh, alas, that I must be gone
To make my reckoning and my debts pay,
For I see my time is nigh spent away.
Take example, all ye that this do hear or see,
How they that I loved best do forsake me, 600
Except my Good-Deeds that bideth truly.

    Good-Deeds: All earthly things is but vanity:
Beauty, Strength, and Discretion, do man forsake,
Foolish friends and kinsmen, that fair spake,
All fleeth save Good-Deeds, and that am I.

    Everyman: Have mercy on me, God most mighty;
And stand by me, thou Mother and Maid, holy Mary.

    Good-Deeds: Fear not, I will speak for thee.

    Everyman: Here I cry God mercy.

    Good-Deeds: Short our end, and minish[39] our pain; 610
Let us go and never come again.

    Everyman: Into thy hands, Lord, my soul I commend; Receive it,
Lord, that it be not lost;
As thou me boughtest, so me defend,
And save me from the fiend's boast,
That I may appear with that blessed host
That shall be saved at the day of doom.
In mannus tuas—of might's most
For ever—*commendo spiritum meum.*[40]

    Knowledge: Now hath he suffered that we all shall 620
        endure:
The Good-Deeds shall make all sure.
Now hath he made ending;
Methinketh that I hear angels sing
And make great joy and melody,
Where Everyman's soul received shall be.

    Angel: Come, excellent elect spouse to Jesu:[41]
Hereabove thou shalt go
Because of thy singular virtue:
Now the soul is taken the body fro;
Thy reckoning is crystal-clear. 630
Now shalt thou into the heavenly sphere,
Unto the which all ye shall come
That liveth well before the day of doom.

    Doctor: This moral men may have in mind;
Ye hearers, take it of worth, old and young,
And forsake pride, for he deceiveth you in the end,
And remember Beauty, Five-Wits, Strength, and
        Discretion,
They all at the last do Everyman forsake,
Save his Good-Deeds, there doth he take.
But beware, and they be small 640
Before God, he hath not help at all.
None excuse may be there for Everyman:

---
[38]Cross.
[39]Diminish.
[40]Into your hands I commend my spirit.
[41]Bride of Christ, a term symbolizing the soul's union with God.

Alas, how shall he do then?
For after death amends may no man make,
For then mercy and pity do him forsake.
If his reckoning be not clear when he do come,
God will say—*ite maledicti in ignem aeternum.*[42]
And he that hath his account whole and sound,
High in heaven he shall be crowned;
Unto which place God brings us all thither   **650**
That we may live body and soul together.
Thereto help the Trinity,
Amen, say ye, for saint Charity
THUS ENDETH THIS MORAL PLAY OF EVERYMAN.

 Q What key aspects of the medieval mind are represented in this play?

Dante's *Divine Comedy*

The medieval view of life on earth as a vale of tears was balanced by a triumphant belief in the divine promise of deliverance and eternal bliss. By far the most profound and imaginative statement of these ideas is the epic poem known as the *Commedia Divina* or *Divine Comedy*. Begun ca. 1308 by the Florentine poet Dante Alighieri (1265–1321), the *Commedia* records, on the literal level, an adventure-packed journey through the realm of the dead (Figure **12.4**). On a symbolic level, the poem describes the spiritual pilgrimage of the Christian soul from sin (Hell), through purification (Purgatory), and ultimately, to salvation (Paradise) (Figure **12.5**). The *Divine Comedy* is the quintessential expression of the medieval mind in that it gives dramatic form to the fundamental precepts of the Christian way of life and death. The structure of the

---

[42]Be damned to the eternal fire.

Figure 12.4 DOMENICO DI MICHELINO, *Dante and His Poem*, 1465. Fresco, 10 ft. 6 in. × 9 ft. 7 in. Florence Cathedral, Italy. Dante, with an open copy of the *Commedia*, points to Hell with his right hand. The mount of Purgatory with its seven terraces is behind him. Florence's cathedral (with its newly finished dome) represents Paradise on the poet's left. Alinari, Florence.

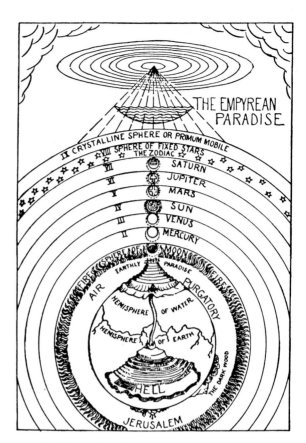

Figure 12.5 Plan of Dante's Universe.

poem reflects the medieval view of nature as the mirror of God's plan, while the content of the poem provides an invaluable picture of the ethical, political, and theological concerns of Dante's own time.

Every aspect of Dante's *Commedia* carries symbolic meaning. For instance, Dante is accompanied through Hell by the Roman poet Virgil, who stands for human reason. Dante deeply admired Virgil's great epic, the *Aeneid*, and was familiar with the hero's journey to the underworld included in the sixth book of the poem. As Dante's guide, Virgil may travel only as far as the top of Mount Purgatory, for while human reason serves as the pilgrim's initial guide to salvation, it cannot penetrate the divine mysteries of the Christian faith. In Paradise, Dante is escorted by Beatrice, the symbol of Divine Wisdom, modeled on a Florentine woman who had, throughout the poet's life, been the object of his physical desire and spiritual devotion. Dante structured the *Commedia* according to a strict moral hierarchy. The three parts of the poem correspond to the Aristotelian divisions of the human psyche: reason, will, and love. They also represent the potential moral conditions of the Christian soul: perversity, repentance, and grace.

Sacred numerology—especially the number 3, symbolic of the Trinity—permeates the design of the *Commedia*. The poem is divided into

three canticles (books); and each canticle has thirty-three **cantos**, to which Dante added one introductory canto to total a sublime one hundred (the number symbolizing pleni-tude and perfection). Each canto consists of stanzas composed in *terza rima*—interlocking lines that rhyme a/b/a, b/c/b, c/d/c. There are three guides to escort Dante, three divisions of Hell and Purgatory, three main rivers in Hell. Three squared (9) are the regions of sinners in Hell, the circles of penitents in Purgatory, and the spheres of Heaven.

The elaborate numerology of the *Commedia* is matched by multileveled symbolism that draws into synthesis theological, scientific, and historical information based in ancient and medieval sources. Given this wealth of symbolism, it is remarkable that the language of the poem is so sharply realistic. For, while the characters in the *Commedia*, like those in *Everyman*, serve an allegorical function, they are, at the same time, convincing flesh-and-blood creatures. The inhabitants of Dante's universe are real people, some drawn from history and legend, others from his own era—citizens of the bustling urban centers of Italy through which Dante had wandered for nineteen years after his exile from his native Florence for political offenses. By framing the poem on both a literal level and an allegorical one, Dante reinforces the medieval (and essentially Augustinian) view of the bond between the City of Man and the City of God. At the same time, he animates a favorite theme of medieval sermons: the

warning that actions in this life bring inevitable consequences in the next.

Well versed in both classical and Christian literature, Dante had written Latin treatises on political theory and on the origins and development of language. But for the poem that constituted his epic masterpiece, he rejected the Latin of churchmen and scholars and wrote in his native Italian, the language of everyday speech. Dante called his poem a comedy because the piece begins with affliction (Hell) and ends with joy (Heaven). Later admirers added the adjective "divine" to the title, not simply to describe its religious character, but also to praise its sublime lyrics and its artful composition.

The most lively of the canticles, and the one that best manifests Dante's talent for creating realistic images with words, is the "Inferno," the first book of the *Commedia*. With grim moral logic, the sinners are each assigned to one of the nine rings in Hell (Figure **12.6**), where they are punished according to the nature of their sins: the violent are immersed for eternity in boiling blood and the gluttons wallow like pigs in their own excrement. By the law of symbolic retribution, the sinners are punished not *for* but *by* their sins. Those condemned for sins of passion—the least grave of sins—inhabit the conical rings at the top of Hell, while those who have committed sins of the will lie farther down. Those guilty of sins of the intellect are imprisoned still lower, deep within the pit ruled by Satan (Figure **12.7**). Thus, Dante's Hell proclaims a moral hierarchy and a divinely graded system in which the damned suffer their proper destiny.

In the last canto of the "Inferno," Dante describes the ninth circle of Hell, the very bottom of the infernal pit. Lodged in ice up to his chest, a three-faced Satan beats his six batlike wings to create a chilling wind—the setting provides sharp contrast with the flaming regions of Upper Hell. Surrounding Satan, whom Dante calls "the Emperor of the Universe of Pain," those guilty of treachery—the most foul of all sins, according to Dante—are imprisoned in the ice, "like straws in glass." Satan, weeping tears "mixed with bloody froth and pus," chews with "rake-like teeth" on the bodies of the three most infamous traitors of Christian and classical history respectively: Judas, Brutus, and Cassius. The dark and brooding despair that pervades the "Inferno" reflects the medieval view of Hell as the condition of the soul farthest from the light of God. Nevertheless, the last canto of the "Inferno" ends with Dante and Virgil climbing from the frozen pit "into the shining world," a motif of ascent that pervades the second and third canticles.

Satan's domain stands in grim contrast to the blissful and brilliant experience of God enjoyed by those in Paradise. Light, the least material of natural elements, is a prime image in Dante's evocation of Heaven, and light imagery—as central to the *Commedia* as it is to Saint Ambrose's hymn (see Reading 2.6)—pervades Dante's vision of God's mystery and majesty. The last eight stanzas of Canto 33 of "Paradiso" (reproduced below) are the culminating phase of that vision. In the perfect shape of the circle, as in a cathedral rose window, Dante sees the image

Figure 12.6 Plan of Dante's "Inferno."

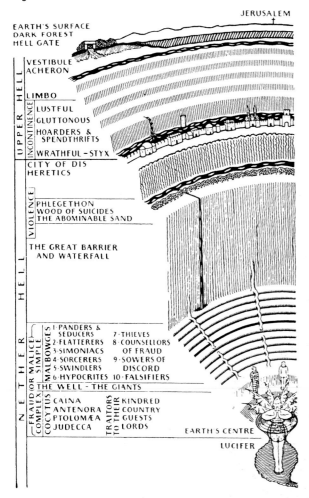

Figure 12.7 *Satan Eating and Excreting the Souls of the Damned in Hell.* Louvre, Paris. Photo: Roger Viollet, Paris.

of humankind absorbed into the substance of God. And as that wheel of love turns, the poet discovers the redemptive radiance of God.

It is impossible to recreate the grandeur of the *Commedia* by means of a single canto, especially since, translated into English, a great deal of the richness of the original Tuscan dialect is lost. Nevertheless, some of the majesty of Dante's poem may be conveyed by the excerpts reproduced here.

READING 2.20 From Dante's *Divine Comedy* (ca. 1308–1321)

The Dark Wood of Error ("Inferno," Canto 1)

Midway in our life's journey, I went astray
   from the straight road and woke to find myself
   alone in a dark wood. How shall I say   **3**

what wood that was! I never saw so drear,
   so rank, so arduous a wilderness!
   Its very memory gives a shape to fear.   **6**

Death could scarce be more bitter than that place!
   But since it came to good, I will recount
   all that I found revealed there by God's grace.   **9**

How I came to it I cannot rightly say,
   so drugged and loose with sleep had I become
   when I first wandered there from the True Way.   **12**

But at the far end of the valley of evil
   whose maze had sapped my very heart with fear!
   I found myself before a little hill   **15**

and lifted up my eyes. Its shoulders glowed
   already with the sweet rays of that planet
   whose virtue leads men straight on every road,   **18**

and the shining strengthened me against the fright
   whose agony had wracked the lake of my heart
   through all the terrors of that piteous night.   **21**

Just as a swimmer, who with his last breath
   flounders ashore from perilous seas, might turn
   to memorize the wide water of his death—   **24**

so did I turn, my soul still fugitive
   from death's surviving image, to stare down
   that pass that none had ever left alive.   **27**

And there I lay to rest from my heart's race
   till calm and breath returned to me. Then rose
   and pushed up that dead slope at such a pace   **30**

each footfall rose above the last. And lo!
   almost at the beginning of the rise
   I faced a spotted Leopard, all tremor and flow   **33**

and gaudy pelt. And it would not pass, but stood
   so blocking my every turn that time and again
   I was on the verge of turning back to the wood.   **36**

This fell at the first widening of the dawn
   as the sun was climbing Aries with those stars
   that rode with him to light the new creation.   **39**

Thus the holy hour and the sweet season
   of commemoration did much to arm my fear
   of that bright murderous beast with their good omen.   **42**

Yet not so much but what I shook with dread
  at sight of a great Lion that broke upon me
  raging with hunger, its enormous head   **45**

held high as if to strike a mortal terror
  into the very air. And down his track,
  a She-Wolf drove upon me, a starved horror   **48**

ravening and wasted beyond all belief.
  She seemed a rack for avarice, gaunt and craving.
  Oh many the souls she has brought to endless grief!   **51**

She brought such heaviness upon my spirit
  at sight of her savagery and desperation,
  I died from every hope of that high summit.   **54**

And like a miser—eager in acquisition
  but desperate in self-reproach when Fortune's wheel
  turns to the hour of his loss—all tears and attrition   **57**

I wavered back; and still the beast pursued,
  forcing herself against me bit by bit
  till I slid back into the sunless wood.   **60**

And as I fell to my soul's ruin, a presence
  gathered before me on the discolored air,
  the figure of one who seemed hoarse from long silence. **63**

At sight of him in that friendless waste I cried:
  "Have pity on me, whatever thing you are,
  whether shade or living man." And it replied: **66**

"Not man, though man I once was, and my blood
  was Lombard, both my parents Mantuan.
  I was born, though late, *sub Julio*, and bred   **69**

in Rome under Augustus in the noon
  of the false and lying gods. I was a poet
  and sang of old Anchises' noble son   **72**

who came to Rome after the burning of Troy.
  But you—why do *you* return to these distresses
  instead of climbing that shining Mount of Joy   **75**

which is the seat and first cause of man's bliss?"
  "And are you then that Virgil and that fountain
  of purest speech?" My voice grew tremulous: **78**

"Glory and light of poets! now may that zeal
  and love's apprenticeship that I poured out
  on your heroic verses serve me well!   **81**

For you are my true master and first author,
  the sole maker from whom I drew the breath
  of that sweet style whose measures have brought me honor. **84**

See there, immortal sage, the beast I flee.
  For my soul's salvation, I beg you, guard me from her,
  for she has struck a mortal tremor through me."   **87**

And he replied, seeing my soul in tears:
  "He must go by another way who would escape
  this wilderness, for that mad beast that fleers*   **90**

---
*sneers

before you there, suffers no man to pass.
  She tracks down all, kills all, and knows no glut,
  but, feeding, she grows hungrier than she was.   **93**

She mates with any beast, and will mate with more
  before the Greyhound comes to hunt her down.
  He will not feed on lands nor loot, but honor   **96**

and love and wisdom will make straight his way.
  He will rise between Feltro and Feltro, and in him
  shall be the resurrection and new day   **99**

of that sad Italy for which Nisus died,
  and Turnus, and Euryalus, and the maid Camilla.
  He shall hunt her through every nation of sick pride   **102**

till she is driven back forever to Hell
  whence Envy first released her on the world.
  Therefore, for your own good, I think it well   **105**

you follow me and I will be your guide
  and lead you forth through an eternal place.
  There you shall see the ancient spirits tried   **108**

in endless pain, and hear their lamentation
  as each bemoans the second death of souls.
  Next you shall see upon a burning mountain   **111**

souls in fire and yet content in fire,
  knowing that whensoever it may be
  they yet will mount into the blessed choir.   **114**

To which, if it is still your wish to climb,
  a worthier spirit shall be sent to guide you.
  With her shall I leave you, for the King of Time,   **117**

who reigns on high, forbids me to come there
  since, living, I rebelled against his law.
  He rules the waters and the land and air   **120**

and there holds court, his city and his throne.
  Oh blessed are they he chooses!" And I to him:
  "Poet, by that God to you unknown,   **123**

lead me this way. Beyond this present ill
  and worse to dread, lead me to Peter's gate
  and be my guide through the sad halls of Hell."   **126**

And he then: "Follow." And he moved ahead
in silence, and I followed where he led.

Notes to "Inferno" (Canto 1)

line 1 *midway in our life's journey*: The biblical life span is three-score years and ten. The action opens in Dante's thirty-fifth year, i.e., 1300.

line 17 *that planet*: The sun. Ptolemaic astronomers considered it a planet. It is also symbolic of God as He who lights man's way.

line 31 *each footfall rose above the last*: The literal rendering would be: "So that the fixed foot was ever the lower." "Fixed" has often been translated "right" and an ingenious reasoning can support that reading, but a simpler explanation offers itself and seems more competent: Dante is saying that he climbed with such zeal and haste that every footfall carried him above the last despite the steepness of the climb. At a slow pace, on the other hand, the rear foot might be brought up only as far as the forward foot. This device of selecting a minute but exactly centered detail to convey the whole of a larger action is one of the central characteristics of Dante's style.

lines 33, 44, 48 *Leopard, Lion, She-Wolf*: These three beasts are undoubtedly taken from Jeremiah 5.6. Many additional and incidental interpretations have been advanced for them, but the central interpretation must remain as noted. They foreshadow the three divisions of Hell (incontinence, violence, and fraud) that Virgil explains at length in Canto 11, 16–111. I am not at all sure but what the She-Wolf is better interpreted as Fraud and the Leopard as Incontinence. Good arguments can be offered either way.

lines 38–39 *Aries . . . that rode with him to light the new creation*: The medieval tradition had it that the sun was in Aries at the time of the Creation. The significance of the astronomical and religious conjunction is an important part of Dante's intended allegory. It is just before dawn of Good Friday 1300 when he awakens in the Dark Wood. Thus his new life begins under Aries, the sign of creation, at dawn (rebirth), and in the Easter season (resurrection). Moreover the moon is full and the sun is in the equinox, conditions that did not fall together on any Friday of 1300. Dante is obviously constructing poetically the perfect Easter as a symbol of his new awakening.

line 69 *sub Julio*: In the reign of Julius Caesar.

lines 95–98 *the Greyhound . . .Feltro and Feltro*: Almost certainly refers to Can Grande della Scala (1290–1329), a great Italian leader born in Verona, which lies between the towns of Feltre and Montefeltro.

lines 100–101 *Nisus, Turnus, Euryalus, Camilla*: All were killed in the war between the Trojans and the Latians when, according to legend, Aeneas led the survivors of Troy into Italy. Nisus and Euryalus (*Aeneid* IX) were Trojan comrades-in-arms who died together. Camilla (*Aeneid* XI) was the daughter of the Latian king and one of the warrior women. She was killed in a horse charge against the Trojans after displaying great gallantry. Turnus (*Aeneid* XII) was killed by Aeneas in a duel.

line 110 *the second death*: Damnation. "This is the second death, even the lake of fire." (Revelation 20.14)

lines 118–119 *forbids me to come there since, living, etc.*: Salvation is only through Christ in Dante's theology. Virgil lived and died before the establishment of Christ's teachings in Rome, and therefore cannot enter Heaven.

line 125 *Peter's gate*: The gate of Purgatory. (See "Purgatorio" 9, 76 ff.) The gate is guarded by an angel with a gleaming sword. The angel is Peter's vicar (Peter, the first pope, symbolized all popes; i.e., Christ's vicar on earth) and is entrusted with the two great keys.

Some commentators argue that this is the gate of Paradise, but Dante mentions no gate beyond this one in his ascent to Heaven. It should be remembered, too, that those who pass the gate of Purgatory have effectively entered Heaven.

The three great gates that figure in the entire journey are: the gate of Hell (Canto 3, 1–11), the gate of Dis (Canto 8, 79–113, and Canto 9, 86–87), and the gate of Purgatory, as above.

The Ninth Circle of Hell ("Inferno," Canto 34)

"On march the banners of the King of Hell,"
   my Master said. "Toward us. Look straight ahead:
   can you make him out at the core of the frozen shell?"   **3**

Like a whirling windmill seen afar at twilight,
   or when a mist has risen from the ground—
   just such an engine rose upon my sight   **6**

stirring up such a wild and bitter wind
   I cowered for shelter at my Master's back
   there being no other windbreak I could find.   **9**

I stood now where the souls of the last class
   (with fear my verses tell it) were covered wholly:
   they shone below the ice like straws in glass.   **12**

Some lie stretched out; others are fixed in place
   upright, some on their heads, some on their
   soles; another, like a bow, bends foot to face.   **15**

When we had gone so far across the ice
   that it pleased my Guide to show me the foul creature
   which once had worn the grace of Paradise,   **18**

he made me stop, and, stepping aside, he said:
   "Now see the face of Dis! This is the place
   where you must arm your soul against all dread."   **21**

Do not ask, Reader, how my blood ran cold
   and my voice choked up with fear. I cannot write it:
   this is a terror that cannot be told.   **24**

I did not die, and yet I lost life's breath:
   imagine for yourself what I became,
   deprived at once of both my life and death.   **27**

The Emperor of the Universe of Pain
   jutted his upper chest above the ice;
   and I am closer in size to the great mountain   **30**

the Titans make around the central pit,
   than they to his arms. Now starting from this part,
   imagine the whole that corresponds to it.   **33**

If he was once as beautiful as now
   he is hideous, and still turned on his Maker,
   well may he be the source of every woe!   **36**

With what a sense of awe I saw his head
   towering above me! for it had three faces:
   one was in front, and it was fiery red,   **39**

the other two, as weirdly wonderful,
   merged with it from the middle of each shoulder
   to the point where all converged at the top of the skull;   **42**

the right was something between white and bile;
   the left was about the color that one finds
   on those who live along the banks of the Nile.   **45**

Under each head two wings rose terribly,
   their span proportioned to so gross a bird:
   I never saw such sails upon the sea.   **48**

They were not feathers—their texture and their form
   were like a bat's wings—and he beat them so
   that three winds blew from him in one great storm: **51**

it is these winds that freeze all Cocytus. [The final pit of Hell.]
   He wept from his six eyes, and down three chins
   the tears ran mixed with bloody froth and pus.   **54**

In every mouth he worked a broken sinner
   between his rake-like teeth. Thus he kept three
   in eternal pain at his eternal dinner.   **57**

For the one in front the biting seemed to play
   no part at all compared to the ripping: at times
   the whole skin of his back was flayed away.   **60**

"That soul that suffers most," explained the Guide,
  "is Judas Iscariot, he who kicks his legs
  on the fiery chin and has his head inside.   63

Of the other two, who have their heads thrust forward
  the one who dangles down from the black face
  is Brutus: note how he writhes without a word.   66

And there, with the huge and sinewy arms, is the soul
  of Cassius. But the night is coming on
  and we must go, for we have seen the whole."   69

Then, as he bade, I clasped his neck, and he,
  watching for a moment when the wings
  were opened wide, reached over dexterously   72

and seized the shaggy coat of the king demon;
  then grappling matted hair and frozen crusts
  from one tuft to another, clambered down.   75

When we had reached the joint where the great thigh
  merges into the swelling of the haunch,
  my Guide and Master, straining terribly,   78

turned his head to where his feet had been
  and began to grip the hair as if he were climbing;
  so that I thought we moved toward Hell again.   81

"Hold fast!" my Guide said, and his breath came shrill
  with labor and exhaustion. "There is no way
  but by such stairs to rise above such evil."   84

At last he climbed out through an opening
  in the central rock, and he seated me on the rim;
  then joined me with a nimble backward spring.   87

I looked up, thinking to see Lucifer
  as I had left him, and I saw instead
  his legs projecting high into the air.   90

Now let all those whose dull minds are still vexed
  by failure to understand what point it was
  I had passed through, judge if I was perplexed.   93

"Get up. Up on your feet," my Master said.
  "The sun already mounts to middle tierce,
  and a long road and hard climbing lie ahead."   96

It was no hall of state we had found there,
  but a natural animal pit hollowed from rock
  with a broken floor and a close and sunless air.   99

"Before I tear myself from the Abyss,"
  I said when I had risen, "O my Master,
  explain to me my error in all this: 102

where is the ice? and Lucifer—how has he
  been turned from top to bottom: and how can the sun
  have gone from night to day so suddenly?"   105

And he to me: "You imagine you are still
  on the other side of the center where I grasped
  the shaggy flank of the Great Worm of Evil   108

which bores through the world—you *were* while I climbed down,
  but when I turned myself about, you passed
  the point to which all gravities are drawn.   111

You are under the other hemisphere where you stand;
  the sky above us is the half opposed
  to that which canopies the great dry land.   114

Under the mid-point of that other sky
  the Man who was born sinless and who lived
  beyond all blemish, came to suffer and die.   117

You have your feet upon a little sphere
  which forms the other face of the Judecca. [Named
    for Judas Iscariot.]
  There it is evening when it is morning here.   120

And this gross Fiend and Image of all Evil
  who made a stairway for us with his hide
  is pinched and prisoned in the ice-pack still.   123

On this side he plunged down from heaven's height,
  and the land that spread here once hid in the sea
  and fled North to our hemisphere for fright;   126

and it may be that moved by that same fear,
  the one peak that still rises on this side
  fled upward leaving this great cavern here."   129

Down there, beginning at the further bound
  of Beelzebub's dim tomb, there is a space
  not known by sight, but only by the sound   132

of a little stream descending through the hollow
  it has eroded from the massive stone
  in its endlessly entwining lazy flow.   135

My Guide and I crossed over and began
  to mount that little known and lightless road
  to ascend into the shining world again.   138

He first, I second, without thought of rest
  we climbed the dark until we reached the point
  where a round opening brought in sight the blest   141

and beauteous shining of the Heavenly cars.
And we walked out once more beneath the Stars.

Notes to "Inferno" (Canto 34)

line 1 *On march the banners of the King*: The hymn ("Vexilla regis prodeunt") was written in the sixth century by Venantius Fortunatus, Bishop of Poitiers. The original celebrates the Holy Cross, and is part of the service for Good Friday to be sung at the moment of uncovering the cross.

line 17 *the foul creature*: Satan.

line 38 *three faces*: Numerous interpretations of these three faces exist. What is essential to all explanations is that they be seen as perversions of the qualities of the Trinity.

line 54 *bloody froth and pus*: The gore of the sinners he chews which is mixed with his slaver.

line 62 *Judas*: His punishment is patterned closely on that of the Simoniacs whom Dante describes in Canto 19.

line 67 *huge and sinewy arms*: The Cassius who betrayed Caesar was more generally described in terms of Shakespeare's "lean and hungry look." Another Cassius is described by Cicero (*Catiline* III) as huge and sinewy. Dante probably confused the two.

line 68 *the night is coming on*: It is now Saturday evening.

line 82 *his breath came shrill*: Cf. Canto 23, 85, where the fact that Dante breathes indicates to the Hypocrites that he is alive. Virgil's breathing is certainly a contradiction.

line 95 *middle tierce*: In the canonical day tierce is the period from about six to nine a.m. Middle tierce, therefore, is seven-thirty. In going through the center point, they have gone from night to day. They have moved ahead twelve hours.

line 128 *the one peak*: The Mount of Purgatory.

line 129 *this great cavern*: The natural animal pit of line 98. It is also "Beelzebub's dim tomb," line 131.

line 133 *a little stream*: Lethe. In classical mythology, the river of forgetfulness, from which souls drank before being born. In Dante's symbolism it flows down from Purgatory, where it has washed away the memory of sin from the souls who are undergoing purification. That memory it delivers to Hell, which draws all sin to itself.

line 143 *Stars*: As part of his total symbolism Dante ends each of the three divisions of the *Commedia* with this word. Every conclusion of the upward soul is toward the stars, God's shining symbols of hope and virtue. It is just before dawn of Easter Sunday that the Poets emerge—a further symbolism.

From The Vision of God ("Paradiso," Canto 33)

O Light Eternal fixed in Itself alone,
  by Itself alone understood, which from Itself
  loves and glows, self-knowing and self-known;   126

that second aureole which shone forth in Thee,
  conceived as a reflection of the first—
  or which appeared so to my scrutiny—   129

seemed in Itself of Its own coloration
  to be painted with man's image. I fixed my eyes
  on that alone in rapturous contemplation.   132

Like a geometer wholly dedicated
  to squaring the circle, but who cannot find,
  think as he may, the principle indicated—   135

so did I study the supernal face.
  I yearned to know just how our image merges
  into that circle, and how it there finds place;   138

but mine were not the wings for such a flight.
  Yet, as I wished, the truth I wished for came
  cleaving my mind in a great flash of light.   141

Here my powers rest from their high fantasy,
  but already I could feel my being turned—
  instinct and intellect balanced equally   144

as in a wheel whose motion nothing jars—
  by the Love that moves the Sun and the other stars.

Notes to "Paradiso" (Canto 33)

lines 130–144 *seemed in Itself of Its own coloration . . . instinct and intellect balanced equally*: The central metaphor of the entire Comedy is the image of God and the final triumphant in Godding of the elected soul returning to its Maker. On the mystery of that image, the metaphoric symphony of the *Comedy* comes to rest.

In the second aspect of Triple-unity, in the circle reflected from the first, Dante thinks he sees the image of mankind woven into the very substance

and coloration of God. He turns the entire attention of his soul to that mystery, as a geometer might seek to shut out every other thought and dedicate himself to squaring the circle. In *Il Convivio II*, 14, Dante asserted that the circle could not be squared, but that impossibility had not yet been firmly demonstrated in Dante's time and mathematicians still worked at the problem. Note, however, that Dante assumes the impossibility of squaring the circle as a weak mortal example of mortal impossibility. How much more impossible, he implies, to resolve the mystery of God, study as man will.

The mystery remains beyond Dante's mortal power. Yet, there in Heaven, in a moment of grace, God revealed the truth to him in a flash of light—revealed it, that is, to the God-enlarged power of Dante's emparadised soul. On Dante's return to the mortal life, the details of that revelation vanished from his mind but the force of the revelation survives in its power on Dante's feelings.

So ends the vision of the *Comedy* and yet the vision endures, for ever since that revelation, Dante tells us, he feels his soul turning ever as one with the perfect motion of God's love.

Q Why is Dante's *Commedia* considered a medieval epic?
Q Whom does Dante find in the ninth circle of Hell? Why are they there?

The Medieval Church

During the High Middle Ages, the Catholic Church exercised great power and authority not only as a religious force, but also as a political institution. The papacy took strong measures to ensure the independence of the Church from secular interference, especially that of the emerging European states. In 1022, for instance, the Church formed the College of Cardinals as the sole body responsible for the election of popes. Medieval pontiffs functioned much like secular monarchs, governing a huge and complex bureaucracy that incorporated financial, judicial, and disciplinary branches. The Curia, the papal council and highest Church court, headed a vast network of ecclesiastical courts, while the Camera (the papal treasury) handled financial matters. The medieval Church was enormously wealthy. Over the centuries, Christians had donated and bequeathed to Christendom so many thousands of acres of land that, by the end of the twelfth century, the Catholic Church was the largest single landholder in Western Europe.

Among lay Christians of every rank the Church commanded religious obedience. It enforced religious conformity by means of such spiritual penalties as **excommunication** (exclusion from the sacraments) and **interdict**, the excommunication of an entire city or state—used to dissuade secular rulers from opposing papal policy. In spite of these spiritual weapons, **heresy** (denial of the revealed truths of the Christian faith) spread rapidly within the increasingly cosmopolitan centers of twelfth-century Europe. Such anticlerical groups as the Waldensians (followers of the French thirteenth-century reformer Peter Waldo) denounced the growing worldliness of the Church. Waldo proposed that lay Christians administer the sacraments and that the Bible—sole source of religious authority—should be translated into the vernacular.

Condemning such views as threats to civil and religious order, the Church launched antiheretical crusades that were almost as violent as those advanced against the Muslims. Further, in 1233, the pope established the Inquisition, a special court designed to stamp out heresy. The Inquisition brought to trial individuals whom local townspeople denounced as heretics. Deprived of legal counsel, the accused were usually tried in secret. Inquisitors might use physical torture to obtain confession, for the Church considered injury to the body preferable to the eternal damnation of the soul. If the Inquisition failed to restore accused heretics to the faith, it might impose such penalties as exile or excommunication, or it might turn over the defendants to the state to be hanged or burned at the stake—the latter being the preferred punishment for female heretics. With the same energy that the Church persecuted heretics, it acted as a civilizing agent. It preserved order by enforcing periods in which warfare was prohibited. It assumed moral and financial responsibility for the poor, the sick, and the homeless; and it provided for the organization of hospitals, refuges, orphanages, and other charitable institutions.

The power and prestige of the Church were enhanced by the outstanding talents of some popes as diplomats, canon lawyers, and administrators. Under the leadership of the lawyer/pope Innocent III, the papacy emerged as the most powerful political institution in Western Europe. Pope Innocent enlarged the body of canon law and refined the bureaucratic machinery of the Church. He used his authority to influence secular rulers and frequently intervened in the political, financial, and personal affairs of heads of state. Innocent confirmed church restrictions prohibiting nuns from hearing confession, preaching, and singing the Gospel—measures that limited the freedoms and privileges of the holy women. At the Fourth Lateran Council (1215), he endorsed the establishment of the Franciscans, a monastic order that would revive the humane candor and devotional simplicity of the Sermon on the Mount.

The Franciscans took their name from their founder, Giovanni Bernardone (1181–1226), whose father had nicknamed him "Francesco." The son of a wealthy Italian cloth merchant, Francis renounced a life of luxury and dedicated himself to preaching and serving the poor. In imitation of the apostles, he practiced absolute poverty and begged for his food and lodging as he traveled from town to town. Unlike Saint Benedict (see chapter 9) and other cloistered followers of Christ, Francis chose to evangelize among the citizens of the rapidly rising Italian city-states. His mendicant (begging) lifestyle made him an icon of humility; and his attention to the poor and the sickly revived the compassionate ideals of early Christianity and of Jesus himself. Some of the legends written after the death of Francis reported that the body of the saint bore the stigmata, the marks of crucifixion. Others described Francis as a missionary to all of God's creations, hence, the popular depiction of the saint sermonizing to the beasts

Figure 12.8 GIOTTO, *Sermon to the Birds*, ca. 1290. Fresco. Upper Church of San Francesco, Assisi, Italy. Photo: Dagli Orti, Paris.

and the birds (Figure **12.8**). In the song of praise written by Francis two years before his death, his reverence for nature is displayed with a forthright simplicity that resembles both the hymns of Ambrose (Reading 2.6) and the ritual prayers chanted by Native Americans in praise of nature (see Reading 3.18).

READING 2.21 Saint Francis' *The Canticle of Brother Sun* (1224)

Most High, all-powerful, good Lord,   1
Yours are the praises, the glory, the honor, and all blessing.
To You alone, Most High, do they belong,
and no man is worthy to mention Your name.
Praised be You, my Lord, with all your creatures,
especially Sir Brother Sun,
Who is the day and through whom You give us light.
And he is beautiful and radiant with great splendor;
and bears a likeness of You, Most High One.
Praised be You, my Lord, through Sister Moon and the stars,   10
in heaven You formed them clear and precious and beautiful.
Praised be You, my Lord, through Brother Wind,
and through the air, cloudy and serene, and every kind of weather
through which You give sustenance to Your creatures.
Praised be You, my Lord, through Sister Water,
which is very useful and humble and precious and chaste.
Praised be You, my Lord, through Brother Fire,
through whom You light the night
and he is beautiful and playful and robust and strong.
Praised be You, my Lord, through our Sister Mother Earth,   20
who sustains and governs us,

and who produces varied fruits with colored flowers and herbs.
Praised be You, my Lord, through those who give pardon for Your love
and bear infirmity and tribulation.
Blessed are those who endure in peace
for by You, Most High, they shall be crowned.
Praised be You, my Lord, through our Sister Bodily Death,
from whom no living man can escape.
Woe to those who die in mortal sin.
Blessed are those whom death will find in Your most holy will,   30
for the second death shall do them no harm.
Praise and bless my Lord and give Him thanks
and serve Him with great humility.

 Q What is the relationship between God and nature in this song of praise?

The Franciscans were not the sole exemplars of the wave of humanitarianism that swept through the Christian West during the thirteenth century: in 1216 the followers of the well-educated Spanish priest Saint Dominic (ca. 1170–1221) founded a second mendicant order devoted to teaching and preaching. Deeply committed to the study of theology, the Dominicans educated many renowned scholars, including Thomas Aquinas, discussed later in this chapter. The Franciscan and Dominican friars ("brothers") and their female counterparts, the Poor Clares and the Dominican nuns, earned longlasting respect and acclaim for educating the young, fighting heresy, and ministering to the sick and needy.

The Conflict Between Church and State

As secular rulers grew in power among the burgeoning nation-states of medieval Europe, the early medieval alliance between Church and state deteriorated. The attempts of kings and emperors to win the allegiance of their subjects—especially those in the newly formed towns—and to enlarge their financial resources often interfered with papal ambitions and Church decree. When, for example, King Philip IV ("the Fair") of France (1268–1314) attempted to tax the clergy as citizens of the French realm, Pope Boniface VIII (ca. 1234–1303) protested, threatening to excommunicate and depose the king. In the dispute that followed, Pope Boniface issued the edict *Unam sanctam* ("One [and] Holy [Church]"), the boldest assertion of spiritual authority ever published. The edict rested upon the centuries-old papal claim that the Church held primacy over the state, since, while the Church governed the souls of all Christians, the state governed only their bodies. Although in the ensuing struggle between popes and kings, the latter emerged victorious, *Unam sanctam* remained the classic justification for Church supremacy in both temporal and spiritual realms.

The Medieval University

Of the many medieval contributions to modern Western society—including trial by jury and the Catholic Church itself—one of the most significant was the university.

Education in medieval Europe was almost exclusively a religious enterprise, and monastic schools had monopolized learning for many centuries. By the twelfth century, however, spurred by the resurgence of economic activity, the rise of towns, and the influx of heretofore unavailable classical texts, education shifted from monastic and parish settings to cathedral schools located in the new urban centers of Western Europe. Growing out of these schools, groups of students and teachers formed guilds for higher learning; the Latin word *universitas* describes a guild of learners and teachers.

In medieval Europe, as in our own day, universities were arenas for intellectual inquiry and debate. At Bologna, Paris, Oxford, and Cambridge, to name but four among some eighty universities founded during the Middle Ages, the best minds of Europe grappled with the compelling ideas of their day, often testing those ideas against the teachings of the Church. The universities offered a basic Liberal Arts curriculum divided into two parts: the *trivium*, consisting of grammar, logic, and rhetoric; and the *quadrivium*, which included arithmetic, geometry, astronomy, and music. Programs in professional disciplines, such as medicine, theology, and law, were also available. Textbooks—that is, handwritten manuscripts—were expensive and difficult to obtain, therefore teaching took the form of oral instruction, and students took copious notes based on class lectures (Figure **12.9**). Exams for the bachelor of arts (B.A.) degree, usually taken upon completion of a three- to five-year course of study, were oral. Beyond the B.A. degree, one might pursue additional study leading to mastery of a specialized field. The master of arts (M.A.) degree qualified the student to teach theology or practice law or medicine. Still another four years of study were usually required for the doctoral candidate, whose efforts culminated in his defense of a thesis before a board of learned masters. (Tradition required the successful candidate to honor his examiners with a banquet.)

Among the first universities was that founded at Bologna in northern Italy in 1159. Bologna was a center for the study of law. Its curriculum was run by students who hired professors to teach courses in law and other fields. University students brought pressure on townsfolk to maintain reasonable prices for food and lodging. They controlled the salaries and teaching schedules of their professors, requiring a teacher to obtain permission from his students for even a single day's absence and docking his pay if he was tardy. In contrast to the student-run university at Bologna, the university in Paris was a guild of teachers organized primarily for instruction in theology. This institution, which grew out of the cathedral school of Notre Dame, became independent of Church control by way of a royal charter issued in the year 1200. Its respected degree in theology drew an international student body that made Paris the intellectual melting pot of the medieval West.

Until the thirteenth century, upper-class men and women received basically the same kinds of formal education. But with the rise of the university women were excluded from receiving a higher education, much as they

Figure 12.9 *University Lecture by Henry of Germany*, from a medieval German edition of Aristotle's *Ethics*, second half of fourteenth century. Manuscript illumination, parchment, 7 × 8¾ in. State Museum, Berlin. Preussischer Kulturbesitz, Kupferstichkabinett. Photo: Bildarchiv Preussischer Kulturbesitz, Berlin.

were forbidden from entering the priesthood. Ranging between the ages of seventeen and forty, students often held minor orders in the Church. The intellectual enterprise of the most famous of the theologically trained schoolmen (or *scholastics*, as they came to be called), inspired an important movement in medieval intellectual life known as Scholasticism.

Medieval Scholasticism

Before the twelfth century, intellectuals (as well as ordinary men and women) considered Scripture and the writings of the church fathers the major repositories of knowledge. Faith in these established sources superseded rational inquiry and preempted the empirical examination of the physical world. Indeed, most intellectuals upheld the Augustinian credo that faith preceded reason. They maintained that since both faith and reason derived from God, the two could never stand in contradiction. When, in the late twelfth century, Arab transcriptions

of the writings of Aristotle and Arab commentaries on his works filtered into the West from Muslim Spain and Southwest Asia, a new intellectual challenge confronted churchmen and scholars. How were they to reconcile Aristotle's rational and dispassionate views of physical reality with the supernatural truths of the Christian faith? The Church's initial reaction was to ban Aristotle's works (with the exception of the *Logic*, which had long been available in the West), but by the early thirteenth century, all of the writings of the venerated Greek philosopher were in the hands of medieval scholars. For the next hundred years, the scholastics engaged in an effort to reconcile the two primary modes of knowledge: faith and reason, the first as defended by theology, the second as exalted in Greek philosophy.

Even before the full body of Aristotle's works was available, a brilliant logician and popular teacher at the University of Paris, Peter Abelard (1079–ca. 1144), had inaugurated a rationalist approach to Church dogma—one that emphasized the freedom to doubt and to question authority. In his treatise *Sic et Non* (*Yes and No*), written several years before the high tide of Aristotelian influence, Abelard puts into practice one of the principal devices of the scholastic method—that of balancing opposing points of view. *Sic et Non* presents 150 conflicting opinions on important religious matters from such sources as the Old Testament, the Greek philosophers, the Latin church fathers, and the decrees of the Church. Abelard's methodical compilation of Hebrew, classical, and Christian thought is an expression of the scholastic inclination to collect and reconcile vast amounts of information. This impulse toward synthesis also inspired the many *compendia* (collections), *specula* ("mirrors" of knowledge), and *summa* (comprehensive treatises) that were written during the twelfth and thirteenth centuries.

The greatest of the scholastics and the most influential teacher of his time was the Dominican theologian Thomas Aquinas (1225–1274). Aquinas lectured and wrote on a wide variety of theological and biblical subjects, but his major contribution was the *Summa Theologica*, a vast compendium of virtually all of the major theological issues of the High Middle Ages. In this unfinished work, which exceeds Abelard's *Sic et Non* in both size and conception, Aquinas poses 631 questions on topics ranging from the

Science and Technology

1120	the English introduce the use of latitude and longitude measured in degrees and minutes
1120s	Arabic works on mathematics, optics, and astronomy are introduced into Europe
1249	Roger Bacon (English) uses glass lenses to correct faulty eyesight
1250s	Albertus Magnus (German) produces a biological classification of plants based on Aristotle
1250s	returning Crusaders introduce Arabic numbering and the decimal system to Europe

nature of God to the ethics of money lending. The comprehensiveness of Aquinas' program is suggested by the following list of queries drawn arbitrarily from the *Summa*:

Whether God exists
Whether God is the highest good
Whether God is infinite
Whether God wills evil
Whether there is a trinity in God
Whether it belongs to God alone to create
Whether good can be the cause of evil
Whether angels assume bodies
Whether woman should have been made in the first production of things
Whether woman should have been made from man
Whether the soul is composed of matter and form
Whether man has free choice
Whether paradise is a corporeal place
Whether there is eternal law
Whether man can merit eternal life without grace
Whether it is lawful to sell a thing for more than it is worth

In dealing with each question, Aquinas follows Abelard's method of marshaling opinions that seem to oppose or contradict each other. But where Abelard merely mediates, Aquinas offers carefully reasoned answers; he brings to bear all the intellectual ammunition of his time in an effort to prove that the truths of reason (those proceeding from the senses and from the exercise of logic) are compatible with the truths of revelation (those that have been divinely revealed). Aquinas begins by posing an initial question—for instance, "Whether woman should have been made in the first production of things"; then he offers objections or negations of the proposition, followed by positive responses drawn from a variety of authoritative sources—mainly Scripture and the works of the early church fathers (see chapter 9). The exposition of these "seeming opposites" is followed by Aquinas' own opinion, a synthesis that invariably reconciles the contradictions. Finally, Aquinas provides "reply objections" answering the original objections one by one. So, for example, Objection 3, which argues that woman should not have been created because she constituted an "occasion for sin" is countered by Reply Objection 3, which asserts God's power to "direct any evil (even that of womankind) to a good end."

In the following excerpt, Aquinas deals with the question of whether and to what purpose God created women, whom most medieval churchmen regarded as the "daughters of Eve" and hence the source of humankind's depravity. Following Aristotle, Aquinas concludes that, though inferior to man in "the discernment of reason," woman was created as man's helpmate in reproducing the species. Significantly, however, Aquinas denies Aristotle's claim that woman is a defective male and, elsewhere in the *Summa*, he holds that women should retain property rights and their own earnings. Even this brief examination of the *Summa Theologica* reveals its majestic intellectual sweep, its hierarchic rigor, and its power of synthesis—three of the principal characteristics of medieval cultural expression.

READING 2.22 From Aquinas' *Summa Theologica* (1274)

Whether Woman Should Have Been Made in the First Production of Things?
We proceed thus to the First Article:

Objection 1. It would seem that woman should not have been made in the first production of things. For the Philosopher[1] says that the *female is a misbegotten male*. But nothing misbegotten or defective should have been in the first production of things. Therefore woman should not have been made at that first production.

Objection 2. Further, subjection and limitation were a result of sin, for to the woman was it said after sin (*Gen.* iii. 16): *Thou shalt be under the man's power*, and Gregory[2] says that, *Where there is no sin, there is no inequality*. But woman is naturally of less strength and dignity than man, *for the agent is always more honorable than the patient*, as Augustine says. Therefore woman should not have been made in the first production of things before sin.

Objection 3. Further, occasions of sin should be cut off. But God foresaw that woman would be an occasion of sin to man. Therefore He should not have made woman.

On the contrary, It is written (*Gen.* ii. 18): *It is not good for man to be alone; let us make him a helper like to himself.*

I answer that, It was necessary for woman to be made, as the Scripture says, as a *helper* to man; not, indeed, as a helpmate in other works, as some say, since man can be more efficiently helped by another man in other works: but as a helper in the work of generation. . . . Among perfect animals, the active power of generation belongs to the male sex, and the passive power to the female. And as among animals there is a vital operation nobler than generation, to which their life is principally directed, so it happens that the male sex is not found in continual union with the female in perfect animals, but only at the time of coition; so that we may consider that by coition the male and female are one, as in plants they are always united, even though in some cases one of them preponderates, and in some the other. But man is further ordered to a still nobler work of life, and that is intellectual operation. Therefore there was greater reason for the distinction of these two powers in man; so that the female should be produced separately from the male, and yet that they should be carnally united for generation. Therefore directly after the formation of woman, it was said: *And they shall be two in one flesh* (*Gen.* ii. 24).

Reply Objection 1. As regards the individual nature, woman is defective and misbegotten, for the active power in the male seed tends to the production of a perfect likeness according to the masculine sex; while the production of woman comes from defect in the active power, or from some material indisposition, or even from some external influence, such as that of a south wind, which is moist, as the Philosopher observes. On the other hand, as regards universal human nature, woman is not misbegotten, but is included in nature's intention as directed to

---

[1]Aristotle.
[2]Gregory the Great (see chapter 9).

the work of generation. Now the universal intention of nature depends on God, Who is the universal Author of nature. Therefore, in producing nature, God formed not only the male but also the female.

Reply Objection 2. Subjection is twofold. One is servile, by virtue of which a superior makes use of a subject for his own benefit; and this kind of subjection began after sin. There is another kind of subjection, which is called economic or civil, whereby the superior makes use of his subjects for their own benefit and good; and this kind of subjection existed even before sin. For the good of order would have been wanting in the human family if some were not governed by others wiser than themselves. So by such a kind of subjection woman is naturally subject to man, because in man the discernment of reason predominates. Nor is inequality among men excluded by the state of innocence, as we shall prove.

Reply Objection 3. If God had deprived the world of all those things which proved an occasion of sin, the universe would have been imperfect. Nor was it fitting for the common good to be destroyed in order that individual evil might be avoided; especially as God is so powerful that He can direct any evil to a good end....

 Q What does this reading reveal about the potential conflict between reason and authority?

The scholastics aimed at producing a synthesis of Christian and classical learning, but the motivation for and the substance of their efforts were still largely religious. Despite their attention to Aristotle's writings and their respect for his methods of inquiry, medieval scholastics created no system of knowledge that completely dispensed with supernatural assumptions. Nevertheless, the scholastics were the humanists of the medieval world; they held that the human being, the noblest and most rational of God's creatures, was the link between the created universe and divine intelligence. They believed that human reason was the handmaiden of faith, and that reason—though incapable of transcending revelation—was essential to the understanding of God's divine plan.

SUMMARY

The Catholic Church was the dominant political, religious, and cultural force of the European Middle Ages. As spiritual caretaker, the Church guided medieval men and women through the rites of passage that marked the soul's pilgrimage to salvation. The Christian immortality ideology taught that life on earth was transient and that, depending on their conduct on earth, Christian souls would reap reward or punishment in an eternal hereafter. These concepts colored all aspects of medieval expression.

The visionary tracts of Hildegard of Bingen brought Scripture to life in dazzling allegorical prose. Medieval sermons and morality plays warned Christians of the perpetual struggle between good and evil and reminded them of the need to prepare for death. As the *Everyman* illustrates, the medieval mind interpreted reality in symbolic and hierarchic terms: the visible world was a mere reflection of invisible truths, which, in God's universal scheme, followed a predesigned and unchanging order. The late medieval work that best reflects these ideas is Dante's *Commedia*, a sublime moral vision of the Christian universe.

The Church was the mainstay of medieval life. Wealthy and powerful, it governed vast lands, a complex bureaucracy, and a large body of secular and regular clergymen. By means of excommunication, interdict, and the Inquisition, the Church challenged a rising tide of heresy. And despite the challenge of increasingly powerful secular rulers among the European states, the Church maintained a position of political dominance in the West until the sixteenth century. With the rise of universities in twelfth-century Bologna, Paris, and elsewhere, intellectual life flourished. The leading teachers at the University of Paris, Abelard and Aquinas, were proponents of Scholasticism, a movement aimed at reconciling faith and reason. Fueled by the newly available writings of Aristotle, students and scholars alike applied the principles of logic to the study of theology. Among scholastics, as among less learned Christians, matters concerning the eternal destiny of the soul and the fulfillment of God's design were central to daily life and creative expression.

GLOSSARY

canto one of the main divisions of a long poem

excommunication ecclesiastical censure that excludes the individual from receiving the sacraments

grace the free, unearned favor of God

heresy the denial of the revealed truths or orthodox doctrine by a baptized member of the Church; an opinion or doctrine contrary to Church dogma

interdict the excommunication of an entire city, district, or state

memento mori (Latin, "remember death") a warning of the closeness of death and the need to prepare for one's own death

miracle play a type of medieval play that dramatized the lives of, and especially the miracles performed by, Christ, the Virgin Mary, or the saints

morality play a type of medieval play that dramatized moral themes, such as the conflict between good and evil

mystery play a type of medieval play originating in Church liturgy and dramatizing biblical history from the fall of Satan to the Last Judgment

pageant a roofed wagon-stage on which medieval plays and spectacles were performed

sacrament a sacred act or pledge; in medieval Christianity, a visible sign (instituted by Jesus Christ) of God's grace

CHAPTER 13

The Medieval Synthesis in the Arts

"That which is united in splendor, radiates in splendor
And the magnificent work inundated with the new light shines."
Abbot Suger

If the Catholic Church was the major source of moral and spiritual instruction in the West, it was also the wellspring of artistic productivity and the patron of some of the most glorious works of art ever created. The great monastic complexes and majestic cathedrals, the spirited sculptures and radiant stained glass windows, the richly illuminated manuscripts, and the polyphonic Masses and motets—all reflect the irrepressible religious vitality of an age of faith. Although each of these genres is distinct from every other, they all functioned in close relationship to form a grand synthesis—a union of separate elements to form an all-embracing whole. In the arts, as in Aquinas' *Summa* or Dante's *Commedia*, the enterprise of synthesis harmonized many diverse components, which nevertheless retained their individual identities. Church architecture, sculpture, stained glass, and painted altarpieces, for instance, along with the liturgy and the music of the Mass, formed the synthesis or "whole" of Christian worship. The medieval synthesis drew inspiration from the idea of God as Master Architect (Figure **13.1**). If the macrocosm, the greater universe, was ordered by God so that no part of it could stand independent of the whole, then the microcosm, the lesser universe of the Christian on earth, must mirror that orderly design. The arts operated collectively to point the way to salvation, but they also worked to unite the temporal and divine realms.

The Carolingian Abbey Church

During the Carolingian Renaissance of the ninth century (see chapter 11), Charlemagne authorized the construction of numerous Benedictine monasteries, or abbeys. Central to each abbey was a church that served as a place of worship and as a shrine that housed sacred relics. Though built on a smaller scale than that of Early Christian churches, most abbey churches were simple basilicas with square towers added at the west entrance and at the crossing of the nave and transept.

In the construction of the abbey church, as in the arrangement of the monastic complex as a whole, Carolingian architects pursued a strict geometry governed by classical principles of symmetry and order. The plan for an ideal monastery (Figure **13.2**) found in a manuscript in

Figure 13.1 *God as Architect of the Universe*, from the Bible Moralisée, thirteenth century. Österreichische Nationalbibliothek, Vienna. MS Cod. 2554, f.1.

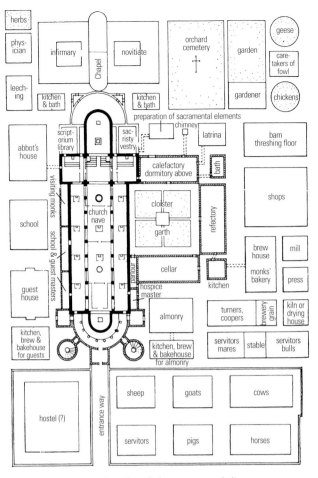

Figure 13.2 Plan for an ideal Benedictine monastery, ninth century. 13½ × 10¼ in. Monastery Library of Saint-Gall, Switzerland.

the library of the monastery of Saint-Gall, Switzerland, reflects these concerns: each part of the complex, from **refectory** (dining hall) to cemetery, is fixed on the gridlike plan according to its practical function. Monks gained access to the church, for example, by means of both the adjacent dormitory and the cloister. At the abbey church of Saint-Gall, where a second transept provided longitudinal symmetry, the monks added chapels along the aisles and transepts to house relics of saints and martyrs whose bones had been exhumed from the Roman catacombs.

The Romanesque Pilgrimage Church

After the year 1000, devout Christians, who had expected the return of Jesus at the end of the millennium, reconciled themselves to the advent of a new age. The Benedictine abbey of Cluny in southeastern France launched a movement for monastic revitalization that witnessed—within a period of 150 years—the construction of more than

one thousand monasteries and abbey churches throughout Western Europe. The new churches, most of which were modeled on Cluny itself, enshrined relics brought back from the Holy Land by the Crusaders or collected locally. Such relics—the remains of saints and martyrs, a piece of the cross on which Jesus was crucified, and the like—became objects of holy veneration. They were housed in ornamented containers, or **reliquaries**, some in the shape of the body part they held. The reliquary statue pictured in Figure **13.3** held the cranium of the child martyr and favorite local saint of Conques. On feast days, the image, sheathed in thin sheets of gold and semiprecious stones, was carried through the streets in sacred procession. The monastic churches that housed the holy relics of saints and martyrs attracted thousands of Christian pilgrims. Some traveled to the shrine to seek pardon for sins or pay homage to a particular saint. Suppliants afflicted with blindness, leprosy, and other illnesses often slept near the saint's tomb in hope of a healing vision or a miraculous cure.

There were four major pilgrimage routes that linked the cities of France with the favorite shrine of Christian pilgrims: the cathedral of Santiago de Compostela in northwestern Spain (Map **13.1**). Santiago—that is, Saint James Major (brother of Saint John the Evangelist)—was said to have brought Christianity to Spain. Martyred upon his return to Judea, his body was miraculously recovered in the early ninth century and buried at Compostela, where repeated miracles made his shrine a major pilgrimage center. Along the roads that carried pilgrims from Paris across to the Pyrenees, old churches were rebuilt and new churches erected, prompting one eleventh-century chronicler to observe, "The whole world seems to have shaken off her slumber, cast off her old rags, and clothed herself in a white mantle of new churches."

Like the Crusades, the pilgrimage was an expression of increased mobility and economic revitalization (see chapter 11). Since pilgrims, like modern tourists, constituted a major source of revenue for European towns and churches, parishes competed for them by enlarging church interiors and by increasing

Figure 13.3 Reliquary statue of Sainte Foy, Conques, France, late tenth–eleventh century. Gold and gemstones over a wooden core, height 33½ in. © Paul M. R. Maeyaert, Belgium.

Map 13.1 Romanesque and Gothic Sites in Western Europe.

the number of reliquary chapels. The practical requirement for additional space in which to house these relics safely and make them accessible to Christian pilgrims determined the plan of the pilgrimage church. To provide additional space for shrines, architects enlarged the eastern end of the church to include a number of radiating chapels. They also extended the side aisles around the transept and behind the apse to form an ambulatory (walkway). The ambulatory allowed lay visitors to move freely into the chapels without disturbing the monks at the main altar (Figure **13.4**). In the Early Christian church, as in the Carolingian abbey, the width of the nave was limited by the size and availability of roofing timber, and the wooden superstructure itself was highly susceptible to fire. The use of cut stone as the primary vaulting medium provided a solution to both of these problems. Indeed, the

medieval architect's return to stone barrel and groin vaults of the kinds first used by the Romans (see chapter 6) inaugurated the *Romanesque style.*

Romanesque architects employed round arches and a uniform system of stone vaults in the upper zones of the nave and side aisles. While the floor plan of the typical Romanesque church followed the Latin cross design of Early Christian and Carolingian churches, the new system of stone vaulting allowed medieval architects to build on a grander scale than ever before. In the construction of these new, all-stone structures, the Normans led the way. The technical superiority of Norman stonemasons, apparent in their castles (see Figure 11.14), is reflected in the abbey churches at Caen and Jumièges in northwestern France. At the abbey of Jumièges, consecrated in 1067 in the presence of William the Conqueror, little remains

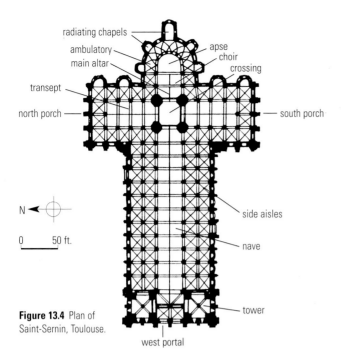

Figure 13.4 Plan of Saint-Sernin, Toulouse.

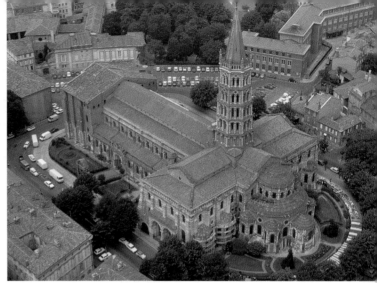

Figure 13.6 Saint-Sernin, Toulouse, France, ca. 1080–1120 (tower enlarged in the thirteenth century). Photo: Yan, Toulouse.

other than the **westwork** (west façade), with its 141-foot-high twin towers (Figure **13.5**). This austere entrance portal, with its **tripartite** (three-part) division and three round arches, captures the geometric simplicity and rugged severity typical of the Romanesque style in France and England. It also anticipates some of the central features of medieval church architecture: massive towers pointed heavenward and made the church visible from great distances; stone portals separated the secular from the divine realm (see chapter 9) and dramatized the entrance door as the gateway to paradise.

Figure 13.5 West façade of the Abbey of Jumièges, on the lower Seine near Rouen, France, 1037–1067. Height of towers 141 ft. Photo: Serge Chirol, Paris.

The church of Saint-Sernin at Toulouse, on the southernmost pilgrimage route to Compostela, is one of the largest of the French pilgrimage churches (Figure **13.6**). Constructed of magnificent pink granite, Saint-Sernin's spacious nave is covered by a barrel vault divided by ornamental transverse arches (Figure **13.7**). Thick stone walls and heavy piers carry the weight of the vault and provide

Figure 13.7 Nave and choir of Saint-Sernin, Toulouse. Pink granite, length of nave 377 ft. 4 in. Photo: Serge Chirol, Paris.

lateral (sideways) support (see Figure 13.19). Since window openings might have weakened the walls that buttressed the barrel vault, the architects of Saint-Sernin eliminated the clerestory. Beneath the vaults over the double side-aisles, a gallery that served weary pilgrims as a place of overnight refuge provided additional lateral buttressing.

The formal design of Saint-Sernin follows rational and harmonious principles: the square represented by the crossing of the nave and transept is the module for the organization of the building and its parts (see Figure 13.4). Each nave **bay** (vaulted compartment) equals one-half the module, while each side-aisle bay equals one-fourth of the module. Clarity of design is also visible in the ways in which the exterior reflects the geometry of the interior: at the east end of the church, for instance, five reliquary chapels protrude uniformly from the ambulatory, while at the crossing of the nave and transept, a tower (enlarged in the thirteenth century) rises as both a belfry and a beacon to approaching pilgrims (see Figure 13.5). Massive and stately in its exterior, dignified and somber in its interior, Saint-Sernin conveys the effect of a monumental spiritual fortress.

Romanesque architects experimented with a wide assortment of regional variation in stone vaulting techniques. At the pilgrimage church of Sainte Madeleine (Mary Magdalene) at Vézelay in France—the site from which the Second Crusade was launched—the nave was covered with groin vaults separated by pronounced transverse arches. The concentration of weight along the arches, along with lighter masonry, allowed the architect to enlarge the width of the nave to 90 feet and to include a clerestory that admitted light into the dark interior (Figure **13.8**). The alternating light and dark stone **voussoirs**

Figure 13.8 Nave of Sainte Madeleine, Vézelay, France, ca. 1104–1132. Width 90 ft. © Paul M. R. Maeyaert, Belgium.

Figure 13.9 (below) **GISLEBERTUS**, *Last Judgment*, ca. 1130–1135. West tympanum, Autun Cathedral, France. © Paul M. R. Maeyaert.

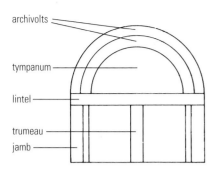

archivolts

tympanum

lintel

trumeau

jamb

Figure 13.10 Diagram of a portal.

Labors of the month

Signs of the zodiac

Heaven

Saint Peter

Angel with trumpet

Souls of the dead rising

Christ in judgment

Hell

The Angel Michael

Angel with trumpet

Figure 13.11 West tympanum, Autun Cathedral, France.

(wedges) in the arches of this dramatic interior indicate the influence of Muslim architecture (see Figure 10.10) on the development of the Romanesque church.

Romanesque Sculpture

Pilgrimage churches of the eleventh and twelfth centuries heralded the revival of monumental stone sculpture—a medium that, for the most part, had been abandoned since Roman antiquity. Scenes from the Old and New Testaments—carved in high relief and brightly painted— usually appeared on the entrance portals of the church, as well as in the capitals of columns throughout the basilica and its cloister. The entrance portal, normally located at the west end of the church, marked the dividing point between the earthly city and the City of God. Passage through the portal marked the beginning of the symbolic journey from sin (darkness/west) to salvation (light/east).

As they passed beneath the elaborately carved west portal of the church of Saint Lazarus at Autun in France, medieval Christians were powerfully reminded of the inevitability of sin, death, and judgment. The forbidding image of Christ as Judge greeted them from the center of the **tympanum** (the semicircular space within the arch of the portal) just above their heads (Figures **13.9, 13.10, 13.11**). Framed by an almond-shaped halo, Jesus displays his wounds and points to the realms of the afterlife: Heaven (on his right) and Hell (on his left). Surrounding the awesome Christ, flamelike saints and angels and grimacing devils await the souls of the resurrected. Saint Michael weighs a soul in order to determine its eternal destiny, a motif that recalls late Egyptian art (see Figure 1.15), while a wraithlike devil tries to tip the scales in his own favor (Figure **13.12**). In the **lintel** (the horizontal band below the tympanum), the resurrected are pictured

Figure 13.12 GISLEBERTUS, detail of *Last Judgment*, ca. 1130–1135. Autun Cathedral, France. © RMN/Bulloz, Paris.

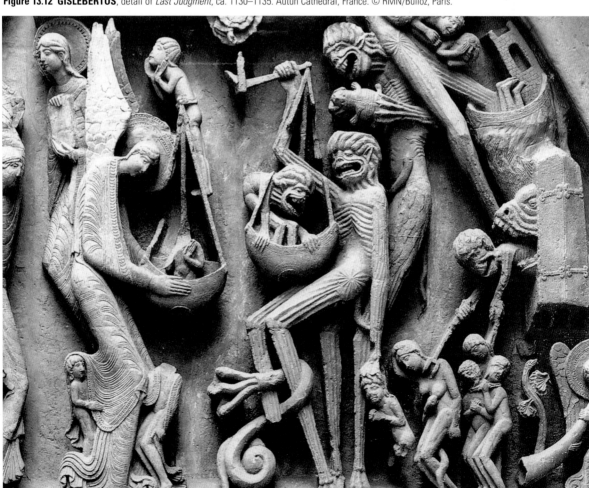

as a *memento mori*, reminding Christians of the inevitability of death and judgment. Indeed, beneath his signature, the artist Gislebertus added the warning, "Let this terror frighten those bound by earthly sin."

The tympanum at Autun preserves the tradition of abstract stylization typical of early medieval manuscripts (see Figure 11.10). With graphic subtlety, Gislebertus carved his figures to fit the shapes of the stone segments that comprise the portal. These lively, elongated figures bend and twist, as if animated by the restless energy that suffused the age. Similarly, at the abbey church of Saint Pierre at Moissac in France, the Hebrew prophet Jeremiah stretches like taffy to conform to the shape of the **trumeau** (the post that supports the superstructure) of the west portal (Figure **13.13**). The Moissac sculptor unites form and content symbolically: the post supports the superstructure just as the Old Testament prophets were said to "support" the New Testament revelation of Last Judgment.

Among the most compelling examples of Romanesque sculpture are those that adorn the capitals of columns in churches and cloisters. These so-called **historiated capitals** feature narrative scenes depicting the life of Christ. One of the largest extant groups of historiated capitals comes from the west porch of the pilgrimage church of Saint Benoît-sur-Loire in France, which housed the relics of Saint Benedict. In *The Flight to Egypt*, a moon-faced Mary sits awkwardly upon a toylike donkey led by a bearded Joseph (Figure **13.14**). The six-pointed star above Mary's right shoulder and the naively shortened figures—altered to fit into the shape of the capital—give the scene a whimsical quality. Romanesque artisans plumbed their

rising from their graves. Just beneath the mouth of Hell, a pair of disembodied claws clutch at the damned, who cower in anticipation of eternal punishment. And in the **archivolts** that frame the tympanum are roundels with signs of the zodiac and depictions of the labors of the months, symbols of the calendar year and the passage of time between the First and Second Coming of Christ. Like a medieval morality play, the tympanum at Autun served

Figure 13.14 *The Flight to Egypt*, late eleventh century. Capital, Saint Benoît-sur-Loire, France. Photo: James Austin, Cambridge, U.K.

imaginations to generate the legions of fantastic beasts and hybrid demons that embellish church portals and capitals. The popularity of such imagery moved some medieval churchmen to debate whether the visual arts inspired or distracted the faithful from contemplation and prayer. Nevertheless, the fusion of dogma and fantasy that characterizes so much Romanesque sculpture must have made a tremendous impact on the great percentage of people who could neither read nor write.

The Gothic Cathedral

Romanesque architects drew on Greco-Roman principles and building techniques. Gothic architects, on the other hand, represented a clear break with the classical past. Whereas classical temples seemed to hug the earth, Gothic cathedrals soared heavenward; whereas classical structures enforced a static relationship between building parts, Gothic structures engaged a dynamic system of thrusts and counterthrusts; and whereas classical architects rationalized form, Gothic architects infused form with symbolism. Seventeenth-century neoclassicists coined the term "Gothic" to condemn a style they judged to be a "rude and barbarous" alternative to the classical style. But modern critics have recognized the *Gothic style* as a sophisticated and majestic expression of the age of faith.

The Gothic style was born in northern France and spread quickly throughout medieval Europe. In France alone, 80 Gothic cathedrals and nearly 500 cathedral-class churches were constructed between 1170 and 1270. Like all Christian churches, the Gothic cathedral was a sanctuary for the celebration of the mass. But, reflecting a shift of intellectual life from the monastery to the town, the Gothic cathedral was also the administrative seat (*cathedra*) of a bishop, the site of ecclesiastical authority, and an educational center—a fount of theological doctrine and divine precept. The Gothic cathedral honored one or more saints, including and especially the Virgin Mary—the principal intercessor between God and the Christian believer. Indeed, most of the prominent churches of the Middle Ages were dedicated to Notre Dame ("Our Lady"). On a symbolic level, the church was both the Heavenly Jerusalem (the City of God) and a model of the Virgin as Womb of Christ and Queen of Heaven. In the cathedral, the various types of religious expression converged: sculpture appeared in its portals, capitals, and choir screens; stained glass diffused divine light through its windows; painted altarpieces embellished its chapels; religious drama was enacted both within its walls and outside its doors; liturgical music filled its choirs.

Finally, the Gothic cathedral, often large enough to hold the entire population of a town, was the municipal center. If the Romanesque church constituted a rural retreat for monastics and pilgrims, the Gothic cathedral served as the focal point for an urban community. Physically dominating the town, its spires soaring above the houses and shops below (Figure **13.15**), the cathedral attracted civic events, public festivals, and even local business. The actual construction of a Gothic cathedral was a town effort, supported by the funds and labors of local citizens and guild members, including stonemasons (Figure **13.16**), carpenters, metalworkers, and glaziers.

Figure 13.15 Chartres Cathedral, France, begun 1194. Sonia Halliday Photographs.

The definitive features of the Gothic style were first assembled in a monastic church just outside the gates of Paris: the abbey church of Saint-Denis—the church that held the relics of the patron saint of France and, for centuries, the burial place of French royalty. Between 1122 and 1144, Abbot Suger (1085–1151), a personal friend and adviser of the French kings Louis VI and VII, enlarged and remodeled the old Carolingian structure. Suger's designs for the east end of the church called for a combination of three architectural innovations that had been employed only occasionally or experimentally: the pointed arch, the rib vault, and stained glass windows. The result was a spacious choir and ambulatory, free of heavy stone supports and flooded with light (Figure **13.17**).

While Gothic cathedrals followed Saint-Denis in adopting a new look, their floor plan—the Latin cross—remained basically the same as that of the Romanesque church; only the transept might be moved further west to create a larger choir area (Figure **13.18**). The ingenious combination of rib vault and pointed arch, however, had a major impact on the size and elevation of Gothic structures. Stone ribs replaced the heavy stone masonry of Romanesque vaults, and pointed arches raised these vaults to new heights. Whereas the rounded vaults of the Romanesque church demanded extensive lateral buttressing, the steeply pointed arches of the Gothic period, which directed weight downward, required only the combination of slender vertical piers and thin lateral ("flying") buttresses (Figures **13.19**, **13.20**). In place of masonry, broad areas of glass filled the interstices of this "cage" of stone. The nave wall consisted of an arcade of pier bundles that swept from floor to ceiling, an ornamental **triforium**

Figure 13.17 Choir and ambulatory of the Abbey Church of Saint-Denis, France, 1140–1144. © Paul M. R. Maeyaert, Belgium.

gallery (the arcaded passage between the nave arcade and the clerestory), and a large clerestory consisting of **rose** (from the French *roue*, "wheel") and **lancet** (vertically pointed) windows (see Figure 13.20). Above the clerestory hung elegant canopies of **quadripartite** (four-part; Figure **13.21**) or **sexpartite** (six-part) rib vaults. Lighter and more airy than Romanesque churches, Gothic interiors

Figure 13.16 *Thirteenth-Century Masons*, French miniature from an Old Testament building scene, ca. 1240. 15⅓ × 11⅞ in. © The J. Pierpont Morgan Library, New York, 1991, MS 638 f.3. Art Resource, NY. Stones, shaped by the two men (bottom right), are lifted by a hoisting engine powered by the treadwheel on the left. Another man is carrying mortar up the ladder on his back.

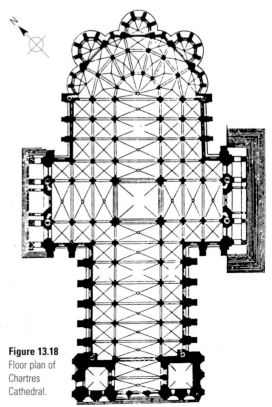

Figure 13.18
Floor plan of Chartres Cathedral.

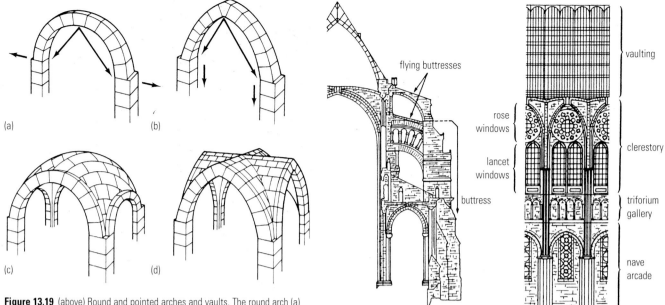

Figure 13.19 (above) Round and pointed arches and vaults. The round arch (a) spreads the load laterally, while the pointed arch (b) thrusts its load more directly toward the ground. The pointed arch can rise to any height while the height of the semicircular arch is governed by the space it spans. Round arches create a dome-shaped vault (c). The Gothic rib-vault (d) permits a lighter and more flexible building system with larger wall-openings that may accommodate windows.

Figure 13.20 Diagram of vaulting and section of nave wall, Chartres Cathedral.

Figure 13.21 Nave facing east, Chartres Cathedral. Nave completed in 1220. Height of nave 122 ft. © Paul M. R. Maeyaert, Belgium.

seem to expand and unfold in vertical space. The pointed arch, the rib vault, and stained glass windows, along with the flying buttress (first used at the cathedral of Notre Dame in Paris around 1170), became the fundamental ingredients of the Gothic style.

Medieval towns competed with one another in the grandeur of their cathedrals: at Chartres, a town located 50 miles southwest of Paris (see Map 13.1), the nave of the cathedral rose to a height of 122 feet (Figure **13.22**; see also Figures 13.15, 13.21); architects at Amiens (see Figure 13.25) took the space from the floor to the apex of the vault to a breathtaking 144 feet. At Beauvais, the 157-foot

Science and Technology

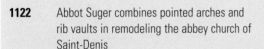

1122	Abbot Suger combines pointed arches and rib vaults in remodeling the abbey church of Saint-Denis
ca. 1175	flying buttresses are first used in the cathedral of Notre Dame in Paris
ca. 1225	Villard de Honnecourt (French) begins a sketchbook of architectural plans, elevations, and engineering devices
1291	Venetian glassmakers produce the first clear (as opposed to colored) glass

Figure 13.22 West façade of Chartres Cathedral, lower parts 1134–1150, mainly after 1194. John Elk III, Oakland, California.

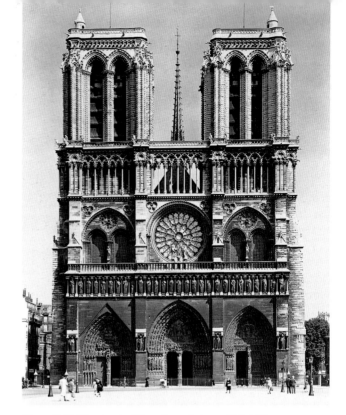

Figure 13.23 West façade of Notre Dame, Paris, ca. 1200–1250. Photo: © Museum of Notre Dame de Paris.

vault of the choir (the equivalent of a fourteen-story high-rise) collapsed twelve years after its completion and had to be reconstructed over a period of forty years. These major enterprises in engineering design and craftsmanship often took decades to build, and many were never finished. In contrast to the Romanesque church, with its well-defined cubic volumes and its simple geometric harmonies, the Gothic cathedral was an intricate web of stone, a dynamic network of open and closed spaces that evoked a sense of unbounded extension. Despite its visual complexity, however, the Gothic interior obeyed a set of proportional principles aimed at achieving harmonious design: at Chartres, for instance, the height of the clerestory and the height of the nave arcade are each exactly three times the height of the triforium (see Figure 13.21). At the cathedral of Notre Dame in Paris, these interior sections are mirrored in the three-story elevation of the façade: the height of the nave arcade corresponds to that of the west portals; the triforium arcade is echoed in the rows of saints standing above those portals; and the clerestory is marked by a majestic rose window (Figure **13.23**).

Gothic architects embellished the structural extremities of the cathedral with stone **crockets** (stylized leaves) and **finials** (crowning ornamental details). At the upper portions of the building, **gargoyles**—waterspouts in the form of grotesque figures or hybrid beasts—were believed to ward off evil (Figure **13.24**). During the thirteenth century and thereafter, cathedrals

Figure 13.24 Grotesques and a gargoyle waterspout on a tower terrace of Notre Dame, Paris, as restored in the nineteenth century. © 1996 Photo Scala, Florence.

increased in structural and ornamental complexity (Figure 13.25). Flying buttresses became ornate stone wings terminating in minichapels that housed individual statues of saints and martyrs. Crockets and finials sprouted in greater numbers from gables and spires (compare the façades of

Figure 13.25 West façade of Notre Dame of Amiens, France, ca. 1220–1288. Height of nave 144 ft. Scala/Art Resource, New York.

Chartres and Amiens; see Figures 13.22 and 13.25), and sculptural details became more numerous. But, like an Aquinan proposition, the final design represents the reconciliation of all individual parts into a majestic and harmonious synthesis.

The Cult of the Virgin

From the earliest years of its establishment as a religion, Christianity exalted the Virgin Mary as an object of veneration. Long revered as "the second Eve," Mary was honored as the woman who redeemed humankind from damnation and death, the twin consequences of the first Eve's disobedience. The image of Mary as a paragon of virtue and chastity constituted an ideal feminine type not unlike that held by Isis in the ancient world. The great cathedrals, most of which were dedicated to the Virgin, portrayed her as Mother of God, Bride of Christ, and Queen of Heaven. Enthroned alongside Jesus—often no smaller in size—she appears as co-equal in authority (see Figure 13.29). During the twelfth century, as emphasis came to be placed on the humanity of Jesus, Mary was depicted as the suffering Mother and compassionate intercessor, her praises recounted in literature and song. As legends of her miracles proliferated, the Cult of the Virgin inspired worship at shrines in her honor (Figure 13.26) and special prayers of supplication. Increasingly, images

Figure 13.26 *Yolande de Soissons Kneeling before a Statue of the Virgin and Child*, from Psalter and Book of Hours, northern France, ca. 1290. The Pierpont Morgan Library NY. Art Resource, NY.

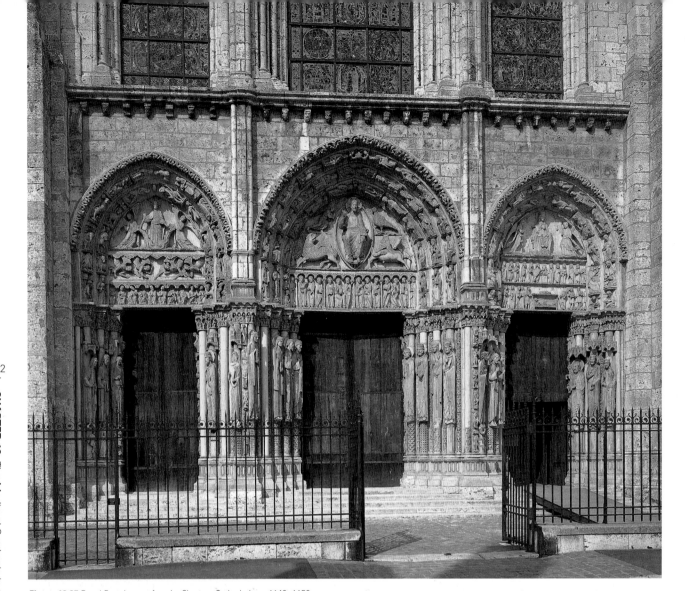

Figure 13.27 Royal Portal, west façade, Chartres Cathedral, ca. 1140–1150.

of Mary and depictions of her life came to adorn church portals, stained glass windows, altarpieces, and illuminated manuscripts.

Gothic Sculpture

The sculpture of the Gothic cathedral was an exhaustive compendium of Old and New Testament history, classical and Christian precepts, and secular legend and lore. Like the stained glass of the Gothic cathedral, the sculptural program—that is, the totality of its carved representations—conveyed Christian doctrine and liturgy in terms that were meaningful to both scholars and laity. Learned churchmen might glean from these images a profound symbolic message, while less educated Christians might see in them a history of their faith and a mirror of daily experience. Designed to be "read" by the laity, the Gothic façade was both a "bible in stone" and an encyclopedia of the religious and secular life of an age of faith.

In the sculpture of the cathedral, as in the stained glass window scenes, the Virgin Mary holds a prominent place. This is especially so at Chartres cathedral, which, from earliest times, had housed the tunic that the Virgin Mary

was said to have worn at the birth of Jesus. When, in 1194, the tunic survived the devastating fire that destroyed most of the old cathedral, it was taken as a miracle indicating the Virgin's desire to see her shrine gloriously rebuilt. Contributions for its reconstruction poured in from all of Christendom. Chartres' west portal, which survived the fire, is called the Royal Portal for its jamb figures of the kings and queens of the Old Testament (Figure **13.27**). Its central tympanum features Christ in Majesty; but on the right tympanum, the Mother of God is honored as Queen of the Liberal Arts (Figure **13.28**). She appears as the Seat of Wisdom (compare *La Belle Verrière*, Figure 13.32). Crowning scenes from the youth of Christ, she is framed by archivolts that include allegorical representations of grammar, rhetoric, arithmetic, and the other four Liberal Arts (Figure **13.29**). Each of the disciplines is accompanied by the appropriate historical authority. For instance, the inner archivolt on the lower right shows Music, who holds a **psaltery** (a stringed instrument; see also Figure 13.41) and strikes a set of bells. She stands just above Pythagoras (celebrated for having discovered the numerical relation between the length of strings and musical notes), shown hunched over his lap desk.

Figure 13.28 *Scenes from the Life of the Virgin Mary*, between 1145 and 1170. Right tympanum of the royal portal, west façade, Chartres Cathedral. Photo: © James Austin, London.

Figure 13.29 *Scenes from the Life of the Virgin Mary.*

Angels

Mary as the seat of wisdom

Presentation of Jesus in the Temple

Gemini (zodiac)

Annunciation

Visitation

Pisces (zodiac)

Angels

Music (Liberal Arts)

Annunciation to the Shepherds

Pythagoras

Nativity

Figure 13.30 *Virgin and Child* (above) and *Temptation of Adam and Eve* (below), thirteenth century. Central trumeau of the west portal, Notre Dame, Paris. © RMN/Bulloz.

On cathedral façades, the Virgin Mary appears frequently as Mother of God and Queen of Heaven. The central trumeau of the west portal at Notre Dame in Paris shows the regal Mary carrying the Christ child (Figure 13.30). Beneath her feet is an image of the fallen Eve, standing alongside Adam in the Garden of Eden. The conjunction of Mary and Eve alluded to the popular medieval idea that Mary was the "new Eve," who brought salvation as a remedy for the sentence of death resulting from the disobedience of the "old Eve."

The thousands of individually carved figures on the façades of the cathedrals at Chartres, Paris, Amiens, and elsewhere required the labor of many sculptors working over long periods of time. Often, the variety of styles on a single façade reflects the efforts of different workshops and different eras. The present cathedral at Chartres, at least the fifth on that site, was the product of numerous building campaigns: its north and south portals were added in the early thirteenth century, and its north tower was adorned with an ornate spire following a fire in 1507. The Royal Portal retains the linear severity of the Romanesque style (see Figure 13.27). In the central tympanum sits a rigidly posed Christ in Majesty flanked by symbols of the four evangelists and framed by the Elders of the Apocalypse in the outer archivolts. In the lintel below, the apostles are ordered into formal groups of threes. Yet, if one compares this late twelfth-century portal with that at Autun, carved only a few decades earlier (see Figure 13.9), it is apparent that medieval sculpture was moving in the direction of heightened realism.

During the thirteenth century, figural representation became gradually more detailed and lifelike. The figures on Chartres' north portal (1200–1220)—a veritable throng of angels, prophets, kings, and patriarchs—assume natural poses, their robes shifting with the positions of their bodies and their gestures varied and subtle. Rather than conform stiffly to the architectural framework, they seem to detach themselves from the stone, a fact quickly grasped when one observes the live pigeons darting in and out of the spaces behind and between the stone representations of the Virgin Mary and Jesus seated on the central tympanum (see Figure 13.31). The trend toward greater realism in Gothic sculpture accompanied the proliferation of religious imagery and architectural details—indeed, at Amiens, the entire west façade seems to dissolve into a lacy skein of stone (see Figure 13.25).

Stained Glass

Stained glass was to the Gothic cathedral what mosaics were to the Early Christian church: a source of religious edification, a medium of divine light, and a delight to the eye. Produced on the site of the cathedral by a process of mixing metal oxides into molten glass, colored sheets of glass were cut into fragments to fit preconceived designs. They were then fixed within lead bands, bound by a grid of iron bars, and set into stone **mullions** (vertical frames). Imprisoned in this lacelike armature, the glass vibrated with color, sparkling in response to the changing natural

Figure 13.31 *Coronation of the Virgin*, ca. 1225. Central tympanum of the north portal, Chartres Cathedral. © Hirmer Fotoarchiv, Munich.

light and casting rainbows of color that seemed to dissolve the stone walls. The faithful of Christendom regarded the cathedral windows as precious objects—glass tapestries that clothed the House of God with radiant light. They especially treasured the windows at Chartres, with their rich blues, which, in contrast to other colors, required a cobalt oxide that came from regions far beyond France. Legend had it that Abbot Suger, the first church man to exploit the aesthetic potential of stained glass, produced blue glass by grinding up sapphires—a story that, although untrue, reflects the popular equation of precious gems with sacred glass.

Suger exalted stained glass as a medium that filtered divine truth. To the medieval mind, light was a symbol of Jesus, who had proclaimed to his apostles, "I am the light of the world" (John 8:12). Drawing on this mystical bond between Jesus and light, Suger identified the *lux nova* ("new light") of the Gothic church as the symbolic equivalent of God and the windows as mediators of God's love. But for Suger, light—especially as it passed through the stained glass windows of the church—also signified the sublime knowledge that accompanied the progressive purification of the ascending human spirit (compare Canto 33 of Dante's "Paradiso," Reading 2.20). Suger's mystical interpretation of light, inspired by his reading of neoplatonic treatises (see chapter 8), sustained his belief that contemplation of the "many-colored gems" of church

glass could transport the Christian from "the slime of this earth" to "the purity of heaven." On the wall of the ambulatory at Saint-Denis, Abbot Suger had these words inscribed: "That which is united in splendor, radiates in splendor/And the magnificent work inundated with the new light shines."

The light symbolism that Suger embraced was as distinctive to medieval sermons and treatises as it was to the everyday liturgy of the church. It permeates the writings of Hildegard of Bingen (see Reading 2.17), who referred to God as "the Living Light," and it is the principal theme in Saint Ambrose's sixth-century song of praise, the "Ancient Morning Hymn" (see Reading 2.6).

The Windows at Chartres

The late twelfth and early thirteenth centuries were, without doubt, the golden age of stained glass. At Chartres, the 175 surviving glass panels with representations of more than four thousand figures comprise a cosmic narrative of humankind's religious and secular history. Chartres' windows, which were removed for safekeeping during World War II and thereafter returned to their original positions, follow a carefully organized theological program designed, as Abbot Suger explained, "to show simple folk . . . what they ought to believe." In one of Chartres' oldest windows, whose vibrant combination of red and blue glass inspired the title *Notre Dame de la Belle Verrière* ("Our Lady of the

Beautiful Glass"), the Virgin appears in her dual role as Mother of God and Queen of Heaven (Figure **13.32**). Holding the Christ child on her lap and immediately adjacent to her womb, she also symbolizes the Seat of Wisdom. In the lancet windows below the rose of the south transept wall (Figure 13.33), Mary and the Christ child are flanked by four Old Testament prophets who carry on their shoulders the four evangelists, a symbolic rendering of the Christian belief that the Old Dispensation upheld the New (compare Figure 13.13). Often, the colors chosen for parts of the design carry symbolic value. For instance, in scenes of the Passion from the west-central lancet window, the cross carried by Jesus is green—the color of vegetation—to symbolize rebirth and regeneration.

Many of Chartres' windows were donated by members of the nobility, who are frequently shown kneeling in prayer below the images of the saints (see Figure 13.33)—the activities of bakers, butchers, stonemasons, and other

Figure 13.32 *Notre Dame de la Belle Verrière* ("Our Lady of the Beautiful Glass"), twelfth century. Stained glass. Chartres Cathedral. Photo: Sonia Halliday, Weston Turville, U.K.

Figure 13.33 (opposite) South rose and lancets, thirteenth century. Chartres Cathedral. Photo: © Sonia Halliday, Western Turville, UK.

Figure 13.34 Sainte Chapelle, Paris, from the southwest, 1245–1248. Photo: A. F. Kersting, London.

workers often appear among the windows commemorating the patron saints of each guild (see Figure 11.17).

Sainte Chapelle: Medieval "Jewelbox"

The art of stained glass reached its highest point in Sainte Chapelle, the small palace chapel commissioned for the Ile de France by King Louis IX ("Saint Louis") (Figure 13.34). Executed between 1245 and 1248, the chapel was designed to hold the Crown of Thorns, a prized relic that Christian Crusaders claimed to have recovered along with other symbols of Christ's Passion. The lower level of the chapel is richly painted with frescoes that imitate the canopy of Heaven, while the upper level consists almost entirely of 49-foot-high lancet windows dominated by ruby red and purplish blue glass (Figure 13.35). More than a thousand individual stories are depicted within the stained glass windows that make up two-thirds of the upper chapel walls. In its vast iconographic program and its dazzling, ethereal effect, this medieval "jewelbox" is the crowning example of French Gothic art.

Medieval Painting

Medieval painting shared the graphic character of Romanesque sculpture. Responsive to the combined influence of Germanic, Islamic, and Byzantine art, medieval artists developed a taste for decorative abstraction through line. In fresco, manuscript illumination, and panel painting, line worked to flatten form, eliminate space, and enhance the iconic nature of the image. Line also helped to emphasize gesture, an important symbolic device. In an age dominated by sermons, liturgical chant, and other oral genres, a single, symbolic gesture was truly "worth a thousand words."

Graceful draftsmanship characterizes the illustrations in the thirteenth-century Psalter of Saint Swithin (Figure 13.36). Like the figures at Moissac and Autun, those depicted in the *Capture and Flagellation of Christ* are tall, thin, and lively, their gestures and facial expressions exaggerated to emphasize the contrasting states of arrogance and humility. The artist who painted the *Crucifixion and Deposition of Christ* for the Psalter of Blanche of Castile (the mother of Saint Louis) imitates the geometric compositions and strong, simple colors of stained glass windows (Figure 13.37). To the right and left of Jesus are depicted the Church (representing the New Dispensation)

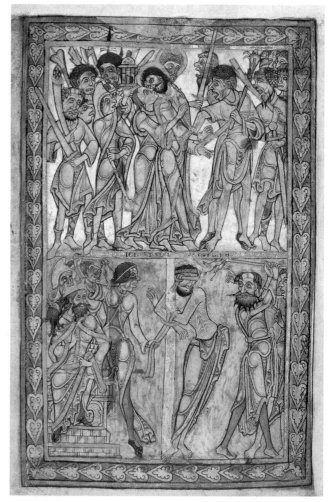

Figure 13.36 *Capture and Flagellation of Christ,* from the Psalter of Saint Swithin, ca. 1250. Reproduced by permission of the British Library, London.

Figure 13.35 Upper chapel of Sainte Chapelle, Paris. Height of lancet windows 49 ft. Sonia Halliday Photographs.

and the Synagogue (representing the Old Dispensation). Book illuminators often used pattern books filled with stock representations of standard historical and religious subjects, a practice that encouraged stylistic conservatism. Nevertheless, in the execution of thousands of miniatures and marginal illustrations for secular and religious manuscripts, the imagination of medieval artists seems

unbounded. The preparation of medieval manuscripts was a time-consuming and expensive enterprise, usually shared by many different workers. The production of a bible might require the slaughter of some two hundred sheep or calves, whose hides were then scraped, bleached, and carefully processed before becoming the folded sheets of parchment (or, if derived from calves, vellum) that made up the book

Figure 13.37 *Crucifixion and Deposition of Christ with the Church and the Synogogue*, from the Psalter of Blanche of Castile, ca. 1235. Bibliothèque de l'Arsenal, Paris. MS 1186, f.24.

Such hierarchic grading, which was typical of medieval art, also characterized Egyptian and Byzantine compositional design.

Cimabue's lavishly gilded devotional image has a schematic elegance: line elicits the sharp, metallic folds of the Virgin's dark blue mantle, the crisp wings of the angels, the chiseled features of the Christ child, and the decorative

Figure 13.38 CIMABUE, *Madonna Enthroned*, ca. 1280–1290. Tempera on wood, 12 ft. 7½ in. × 7 ft. 4 in. Uffizi Gallery, Florence. © Studio Fotografico Quattrone, Florence.

itself. Gold was used lavishly to "illuminate" the images, while rich colors, such as the blue used in Figure 13.37, might come from places as far away as Afghanistan, hence the name "ultramarine" ("beyond the sea") to designate that color.

Some of the finest examples of medieval painting appear in the form of altarpieces installed on or behind chapel altars dedicated to the Virgin or one of the saints. The typical Gothic altarpiece consisted of a wooden panel or group of panels coated with **gesso** (a chalky white plaster), on which figures were painted in **tempera** (a powdered pigment that produces dry, flat surface colors), and embellished with gold leaf that reflected the light of altar candles. The object of devotional prayer, the altarpiece usually displayed scenes from the Life of Jesus, the Virgin Mary, or a favorite saint or martyr. A late thirteenth-century altarpiece by the Florentine painter Cimabue (1240–1302) shows the Virgin and Child elevated on a monumental seat that is both a throne and a tower (Figure **13.38**). Angels throng around the throne, while, beneath the Virgin's feet, four Hebrew prophets display scrolls predicting the coming of Jesus. To symbolize their lesser importance, angels and prophets are pictured considerably smaller than the enthroned Mary.

surface of the throne. The figure of the Virgin combines the hypnotic grandeur of Byzantine icons (by which many Italian artists were influenced) and the weightless, hieratic clarity of Gislebertus' Christ in Majesty at Autun (see Figure 13.9). Although Cimabue's Virgin is more humanized than either of these, she is every bit as regal an object of veneration.

Medieval artists often imitated the ornamental vocabulary of Gothic architecture and the bright colors of stained glass windows. The Sienese painter Simone Martini (1284–1344) made brilliant use of Gothic architectural motifs in his *Annunciation* altarpiece of 1333 (Figure **13.39**).

The frame of the altarpiece consists of elegant Gothic spires and heavily gilded **ogee** arches (pointed arches with S-shaped curves near the apex) sprouting finials and crockets. Set on a gold leaf ground, the petulant Virgin, the Angel Annunciate, and the vase of lilies (symbolizing Mary's purity) seem suspended in time and space. Martini's composition depends on a refined play of lines: the graceful curves of the Angel Gabriel's wings are echoed in his fluttering vestments, in the contours of the Virgin's body as she shrinks from the angel's greeting, and in the folds of her mantle, the pigment for which was ground from semiprecious lapis lazuli.

Figure 13.39 SIMONE MARTINI, *Annunciation*, 1333. (Saints in side panels by **LIPPO MEMMI**.) Tempera on wood, 8 ft. 8 in. × 10 ft. Uffizi Gallery, Florence. © 2002, Photo Scala, Florence - courtesy of the Ministero Beni e Att. Culturali.

Medieval Music

Early Medieval Music and Liturgical Drama

The major musical developments of the Early Middle Ages, like those in architecture, came out of the monasteries. In Charlemagne's time, monastic reforms in Church liturgy and in sacred music accompanied the renaissance in the visual arts. Early Church music took the form of unaccompanied monophonic chant (see chapter 9), a solemn sound that inspired one medieval monk to write in the margin of his songbook, "The tedious plainsong grates my tender ears." Perhaps to remedy such complaints, the monks at Saint-Gall enlarged the range of expression of the classical Gregorian chant by adding **antiphons**, or verses sung as responses to the religious text. Carolingian monks also embellished plainsong with the **trope**, an addition of music or words to the established liturgical chant. Thus, "Lord, have mercy upon us" became "Lord, omnipotent Father, God, Creator of all, have mercy upon us." A special kind of trope, called a **sequence**, added words to the long, melismatic passages—such as the alleluias and amens—that occurred at the end of each part of the Mass (Figure **13.40**).

By the tenth century, singers began to divide among themselves the parts of the liturgy for Christmas and Easter, now embellished by tropes and sequences. As more and more dramatic incidents were added to the texts for these Masses, full-fledged music-drama emerged. Eventually, liturgical plays broke away from the liturgy and were performed in the intervals between the parts of the

Mass. Such was the case with the twlefth-century *Play of Daniel*, whose dramatic "action" brought to life episodes from the Book of Daniel (in the Hebrew Bible) that Christians took to prophesize the birth of the Messiah—a story appropriate to the Christmas season. By the twelfth century, spoken dialogue and possibly musical instruments were introduced. At the monastery of the German abbess, Hildegard of Bingen, Benedictine nuns may have performed her *Ordo virtutum* (see chapter 12). In this music-drama, the earliest known morality play in Western history, the Virtues contest with the Devil for the Soul of the Christian. The Devil's lines are spoken, not sung, consistent with Hildegard's belief that satanic evil was excluded from knowing music's harmony and order. Hildegard's most important musical compositions, however, were liturgical. Her monophonic hymns and antiphons in honor of the saints, performed as part of the Divine Office, are exercises in musical meditation. Some offer praise for womankind and for the virgin saints, while others such as the chant *O Successores* celebrate the holy confessors—Christ's "successors," who hear confession and give absolution.

Medieval Musical Notation

Musical notation was invented in the monasteries. As with Romanesque architecture, so with medieval musical theory and practice, Benedictine monks at Cluny and elsewhere were especially influential. During the eleventh

_____

♪ See Music Listening Selections at end of chapter.

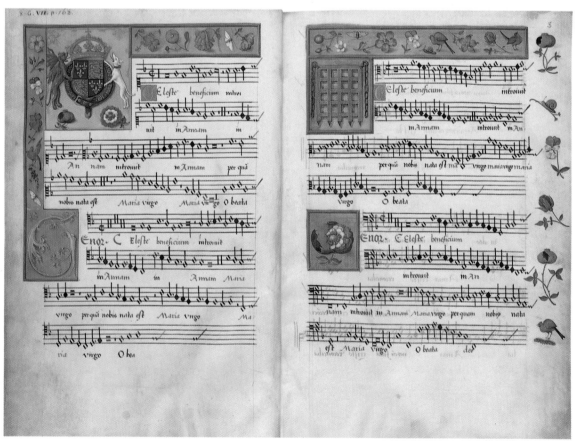

Figure 13.40 Mainz Troper (Sequences and Tropes), Mainz, Germany, ca. 970. British Library. MS 19768, ff.10v-11.

century, they devised the first efficient Western system of musical notation, thus facilitating the performance and transmission of liturgical music. They arranged the tones of the commonly used scale in progression from A through G and developed a formal system of notating pitch. The Italian Benedictine Guido of Arezzo (ca. 990–ca. 1050) introduced a staff of colored lines (yellow for C, red for F, etc.) on which he registered neumes—notational signs traditionally written above the words to indicate tonal ascent or descent (see chapter 9). Guido's system established a precise means of indicating shifts in pitch. Instead of relying on memory alone, singers could consult songbooks inscribed with both words and music. Such advances encouraged the kinds of compositional complexity represented by medieval polyphony.

Medieval Polyphony

Although our knowledge of early medieval music is sparse, there is reason to believe that, even before the year 1000, choristers were experimenting with multiple lines of music as an alternative to the monophonic style of Gregorian chant. **Polyphony** (music consisting of two or more lines of melody) was a Western invention; it did not make its appearance in Asia until modern times. The earliest polyphonic compositions consisted of Gregorian melodies sung in two parts simultaneously, with both voices moving note-for-note in parallel motion (parallel **organum**), or with a second voice moving in contrary motion (free organum), perhaps also adding many notes to the individual syllables of the text (melismatic organum). Consistent with rules of harmony derived from antiquity, and with the different ranges of the voice, the second musical part was usually pitched a fourth or a fifth above or below the first, creating a pure, hollow sound.

Throughout the High Middle Ages, northern France—and the city of Paris in particular—was the center of polyphonic composition. From the same area that produced the Gothic cathedral came a new musical style that featured several lines of melody arranged in counterpoised rhythms. The foremost Parisian composer was Pérotin (ca. 1160–1240). A member of the Notre Dame School, Pérotin enhanced the splendor of the Christian Mass by writing three- and four-part polyphonic compositions based on Gregorian chant. Pérotin's music usually consisted of a principal voice or "tenor" (from the Latin *tenere*, meaning "to hold") that sang the chant or "fixed song" (Latin, *cantus firmus*) and one or more voices that moved in shorter phrases and usually faster tempos. The combination of two or three related but independent voices, a musical technique called **counterpoint**, enlivened late twelfth- and thirteenth-century music. Indeed, the process of vertical superimposition of voice on voice enhanced sonority and augmented the melodic complexity of medieval music much in the way that the counterbalanced parts of the Gothic structure enriched its visual texture.

As medieval polyphony encouraged the addition of voices and voice parts, the choir areas of Gothic cathedrals were enlarged to accommodate more singers. Performed within the acoustically resonant bodies of such cathedrals as Notre Dame in Paris, the polyphonic Mass produced an aural effect as resplendent as the multicolored glass that shimmered throughout the interior. Like the cathedral itself, the polyphonic Mass was a masterful synthesis of carefully arranged parts—a synthesis achieved in *time* rather than in *space*.

The "Dies Irae"

One of the best examples of the medieval synthesis, particularly as it served the Christian immortality ideology, is the "Dies irae" ("Day of Wrath"). The fifty-seven-line hymn, which originated among the Franciscans during the thirteenth century, was added to the Roman Catholic **requiem** (the Mass for the Dead) and quickly became a standard part of the Christian funeral service. Invoking a powerful vision of the end of time, the "Dies irae" is the musical counterpart of the apocalyptic sermons and Last Judgment portals (see Figure 13.9) that issued solemn warnings of final doom. The hymn opens with the words:

> Day of Wrath! O day of mourning!
> See fulfilled the prophets' warning,
> Heaven and earth in ashes burning!

But, as with most examples of apocalyptic art, including Dante's *Commedia*, the hymn holds out hope for absolution and deliverance:

> With Thy favored sheep, oh, place me!
> Nor among the goats abase me,
> But to Thy right hand upraise me.
>
> While the Wicked are confounded,
> Doomed to flames of woe unbounded,
> Call me, with Thy saints surrounded.

Like so many other forms of medieval expression, the "Dies irae" brings into vivid contrast the destinies of sinners and saints. In later centuries, it inspired the powerful requiem settings of Mozart, Berlioz, and Verdi, and its music became a familiar symbol of death and damnation.

The Motet

The thirteenth century also witnessed the invention of a new religious musical genre, the **motet**—a short, polyphonic choral composition based on a sacred text. Performed both inside and outside the church, it was the most popular kind of medieval religious song. Like the trope, the motet (from the French *mot*, meaning "word") developed from the practice of adding words to the melismatic parts of a melody. Medieval motets usually juxtaposed two or more uncomplicated themes, each with its own lyrics and metrical pattern, in a manner that was lilting and lively. Motets designed to be sung outside the church often borrowed secular tunes with vernacular words. A three-part motet might combine a love song in

♩ See Music Listening Selections at end of chapter.

♩ See Music Listening Selections at end of chapter.

the vernacular, a well-known hymn of praise to the Virgin, and a Latin liturgical text in the *cantus firmus*. Thirteenth-century motets were thus polytextual as well as polyphonic and polyrhythmic. A stock of melodies (like the stock of images in medieval pattern books) was available to musicians for use in secular and sacred songs, and the same one might serve both types of song. Subtle forms of symbolism occurred in many medieval motets, as for instance where a popular song celebrating spring might be used to refer to the Resurrection of Jesus, the awakening of romantic love, or both.

Instrumental Music

Musical instruments first appeared in religious music not for the purpose of accompanying songs, as with *troubadour* poems and folk epics, but to substitute for the human voice in polyphonic compositions. Medieval music depended on **timbre** (tone color) rather than volume for its effect, and most medieval instruments produced sounds that were gentle and thin by comparison with their modern (not to mention electronically amplified) counterparts. Medieval string instruments included the harp, the psaltery, and the lute (all three are plucked), and bowed fiddles such as the vielle and the rebec (Figure **13.41**). Wind instruments included portable pipe organs, recorders, and bagpipes. Percussion was produced by chimes, cymbals, bells, tambourines, and drums. Instrumental music performed without voices accompanied medieval dancing. Percussion instruments established the basic rhythms for a wide variety of high-spirited dances, including the estampie, a popular round dance consisting of short, repeated phrases.

SUMMARY

Medieval churches and cathedrals were the monumental expressions of an age of faith. In Carolingian times, the abbey church became the focal point of monastic life as well as the repository of sacred relics that drew pilgrims from neighboring areas. After the year 1000, Romanesque pilgrimage churches were constructed in great numbers throughout Western Europe. They feature all-stone masonry with round arches and thick barrel and groin vaults. Their stone portals and capitals displayed Christian themes of redemption and salvation.

While the Romanesque church was essentially a rural phenomenon, the Gothic cathedral was the focus and glory of the medieval town. First developed in the region of Paris, the cathedral was an ingenious synthesis of three structural elements—rib vaults, pointed arches, and flying buttresses—the combination of which permitted the extensive use of stained glass. Raised to breathtaking heights, the

See Music Listening Selections at end of chapter.

Figure 13.41 *Music and Her Attendants*, from **BOETHIUS**, *De Arithmetica*, fourteenth century. © 1990, Photo Scala, Florence - courtesy of the Ministero Beni e Att. Culturali. Holding a portable pipe organ, the elegant lady who symbolizes the civilized art of courtly music is surrounded by an ensemble of female court musicians. In the circle at the top, King David plays a psaltery, the instrument named after the Psalms (Psaltery) of David. Clockwise from right: lute, clappers, trumpets, nakers (kettledrums), bagpipe, shawm, tambourine, rebec (viol).

Gothic cathedral was, in the words recited at the Mass for the consecration of a Catholic church, "the Court of God and the Gate of Heaven." The sculptural façade, a "bible in stone," presented a panorama of Old and New Testament history, medieval lore, and everyday life. Medieval sculpture and painting styles were generally abstract, symbolic, and characterized by expressive linearity, the use of bright colors, and a decorative treatment of form. Gradually, Gothic art moved in the direction of greater realism and descriptive detail.

As in the visual arts, the music of the Middle Ages was closely related to religious ritual. In Carolingian times, tropes and sequences came to embellish Christian chant, a process that led to the birth of liturgical drama. In the eleventh century, Benedictine monks devised a system of musical notation that facilitated performance and made possible the accurate transmission of music from generation to generation. At about the same time, polyphony, a uniquely Western kind of expression that featured multiple, independent lines of melody, brought a new richness to medieval music. Polyphonic religious compositions known as motets often integrated vernacular texts and secular melodies.

Like the Gothic cathedral, the polyphonic motet may be said to illustrate the medieval practice of juxtaposing and reconciling opposing elements. Collectively, all of the arts worked to form a coherent whole—a synthesis that projected the medieval view of nature as the expression of a preordained, divine order.

MUSIC LISTENING SELECTIONS

CD One Selection 7 Medieval liturgical drama, *The Play of Daniel*, "Incipit: Ad honorem, Astra tementi."

CD One Selection 8 Hildegard of Bingen, *O Successores* (Your Successors), ca. 1150.

CD One Selection 9 Two examples of early medieval polyphony: parallel organum, "Rex caeli, Domine," excerpt; melismatic organum, "Alleluia, Justus ut palma," ca. 900–1150; excerpts.

CD One Selection 10 Pérotin, three-part organum, "Alleluya" (Nativitas), twelfth century.

CD One Selection 11 Anonymous, Motet, "En non Diu! Quant voi; Eius in Oriente," thirteenth century, excerpt.

CD One Selection 12 French dance, "Estampie," thirteenth century.

GLOSSARY

antiphon a verse sung in response to the text

archivolt a molded or decorated band around an arch or forming an archlike frame for an opening

bay a regularly repeated spatial unit of a building; in medieval architecture, a vaulted compartment

counterpoint a musical technique that involves two or more independent melodies; the term is often used interchangeably with "polyphony"

crocket a stylized leaf used as a terminal ornament

finial an ornament, usually pointed and foliated, that tops a spire or pinnacle

gargoyle a waterspout usually carved in the form of a grotesque figure

gesso a chalky white plaster used to prepare the surface of a panel for painting

historiated capital the uppermost member of a column, ornamented with figural scenes

lancet a narrow window topped with a pointed arch

lintel a horizontal beam or stone that spans an opening (see Figure 13.10)

motet a short, polyphonic religious composition based on a sacred text

mullion the slender, vertical pier dividing the parts of a window, door, or screen

ogee a pointed arch with an S-shaped curve on each side

organum the general name for the oldest form of polyphony: In *parallel organum*, the two voices move exactly parallel to one another; in *free organum* the second voice moves in contrary motion; *melismatic organum* involves the use of multiple notes for the individual syllables of the text

polyphony (Greek, "many voices") a musical texture consisting of two or more lines of melody that are of equal importance

psaltery a stringed instrument consisting of a flat soundboard and strings that are plucked

quadripartite consisting of or divided into four parts

refectory the dining hall of a monastery

reliquary a container for a sacred relic or relics

requiem a Mass for the Dead; a solemn chant to honor the dead

rose (from the French *roue*, "wheel") a large circular window with stained glass and stone tracery

sequence a special kind of trope consisting of words added to the melismatic passages of Gregorian chant

sexpartite consisting of or divided into six parts

tempera a powdered pigment that produces dry, flat colors

timbre tone color; the distinctive tone or quality of sound made by a voice or a musical instrument

triforium in a medieval church, the shallow arcaded passageway above the nave and below the clerestory (see Figure 13.20)

tripartite consisting of or divided into three parts

trope an addition of words, music, or both to Gregorian chant

trumeau the pillar that supports the superstructure of a portal (see Figure 13.10)

tympanum the semicircular space enclosed by the lintel over a doorway and the arch above it (see Figure 13.10)

voussoir (French, "wedge") a wedge-shaped block or unit in an arch or vault

westwork (from the German, *Westwerk*) the elaborate west end of a Carolingian or Romanesque church

PART 3

The World Beyond the West

Western students often overlook the fact that Europe—home of the culture that is most familiar to them—occupies only a tiny area at the far western end of the vast continental landmass of Asia. At the eastern end of that landmass lie two geographic and cultural giants, India and China, and the small but mighty Japan (see Maps 14.1 and 14.2). During the European Middle Ages, East and West had little contact with each other, apart from periodic exchanges of goods and technology facilitated by Muslim intermediaries. Although neither India nor China nor Japan had a direct impact on the West, their indirect influence was considerable, especially in the areas of science and technology.

Between 500 and 1300 C.E., India produced some of the finest Sanskrit literature ever written. Hindu temple architecture and sculpture reached new levels of imagination and complexity, and Indian music flourished. In China, during roughly the same period, the Tang and Song dynasties fostered a golden age in poetry and painting. The Chinese surpassed the rest of the world in technological

invention and led global production in fine pottery and textiles. Even at the peak of productivity in medieval Europe, and especially between the years 1250 and 1350, China's technical sophistication, naval power, and cultural fertility exceeded that of any country in the West.

Japan represents the third of the notable Pacific cultures. Medieval Japan originated the world's oldest prose fiction, as well as a unique form of theatrical performance known as Nō drama. In both secular and Buddhist art, the Japanese cultivated a style governed by elegance and artless simplicity. Deeply infused with the values of Buddhism, Hinduism, Daoism, and the precepts of Confucius, the artistic record of India, China, and Japan reflects a holistic view of nature that has worked broadly to universalize the human experience. A brief examination of these achievements puts our study of the humanistic tradition in global perspective and provides a basis for the appreciation of three of Asia's most highly venerated cultures.

(opposite) Attributed to Li Cheng, *A Solitary Temple Amid Clearing Peaks* (detail), Northern Song dynasty, ca. 950. Ink and slight color on silk hanging scroll, 3 ft. 8 in. × 22 in. The Nelson-Atkins Museum of Art, Kansas City, Missouri. Purchase: Nelson Trust. 47–71.

	800	1000	1100	1200	1300	1400

World Events

India: Era of Regional States →

■ India: Turkish Muslims capture Delhi 1192

■ Delhi sultanate

← China: TANG DYNASTY 618–907 — SONG DYNASTY 960–1279 — MING DYNASTY →
1368–1644

■ *Diamond Sutra* earliest printed book 868

■ Movable type invented
1041

■ Introduction of paper currency

■ Mongol rule 1260–1368

■ Marco Polo reaches China ca. 1275

Japan: HEIAN ERA 794–1185 — KAMAKURA SHOGUNATE 1185–1333 — ASHIKAGA ERA →
1336–1573

◄ ■ Buddhism enters Japan 580s

■ Rise of the *samurai*

Literature & Philosophy

← India: Sanskrit poetry →

■ Vidyakara: *Treasury of Well-Turned Verse* 1050

← Chinese poetry →

◄ ■ Li Bo ca. 730

■ Chinese theater

◄ ■ Du Fu ca. 730

Luo Guanzhong: *Three Kingdoms* ■

■ Bo Zhuyi

■ World's earliest printed book: *Diamond Sutra* 868

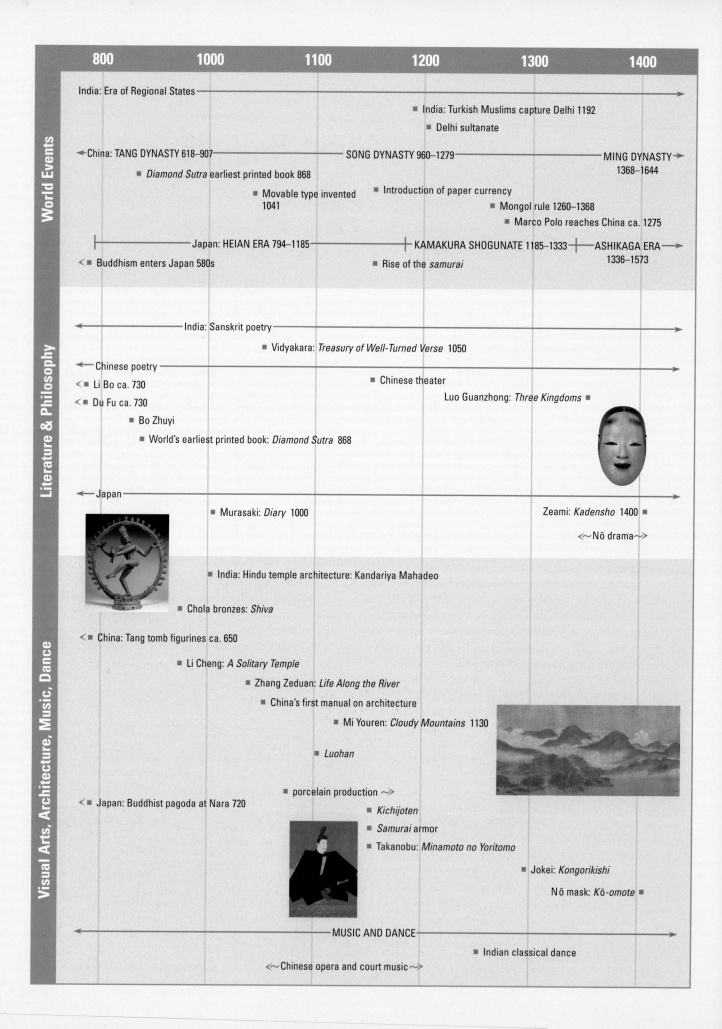

← Japan →

■ Murasaki: *Diary* 1000

Zeami: *Kadensho* 1400 ■

←~ Nō drama ~→

Visual Arts, Architecture, Music, Dance

■ India: Hindu temple architecture: Kandariya Mahadeo

■ Chola bronzes: *Shiva*

◄ ■ China: Tang tomb figurines ca. 650

■ Li Cheng: *A Solitary Temple*

■ Zhang Zeduan: *Life Along the River*

■ China's first manual on architecture

■ Mi Youren: *Cloudy Mountains* 1130

■ *Luohan*

■ porcelain production ~→

◄ ■ Japan: Buddhist pagoda at Nara 720

■ *Kichijoten*

■ *Samurai* armor

■ Takanobu: *Minamoto no Yoritomo*

■ Jokei: *Kongorikishi*

Nō mask: *Kō-omote* ■

← MUSIC AND DANCE →

■ Indian classical dance

←~ Chinese opera and court music ~→

CHAPTER 14

Asian Civilizations: The Artistic Record

"Heaven is my father and earth is my mother, and even such a small creature as I finds an intimate place in their midst."
Zhang Zai

The Medieval Period in India

Although the term "medieval" does not apply to the history of India in the Western sense of an interlude between classical and early modern times, scholars have used that term to designate the era between the end of the Gupta dynasty (ca. 500) and the Mongol invasion of India in the fourteenth century—a thousand-year period that roughly approximates the Western Middle Ages. The dissolution of the Gupta Empire at the hands of Central Asian Huns, an event that paralleled the fall of Rome in the West and the collapse of the Han Empire in China, destroyed the remains of South Asia's greatest culture. Following this event, amidst widespread political turmoil and anarchy, India reverted to a conglomeration of fragmented, rival local kingdoms dominated by a warrior caste (not unlike the feudal aristocracy of medieval Europe). Ruling hereditary chiefs or *rajputs* ("sons of kings") followed a code of chivalry that set them apart from the lower classes. The caste system (see chapter 3), which had been practiced in India for many centuries, worked to enforce the distance between rulers and the ruled. And as groups were subdivided according to occupation and social status, caste distinctions became more rigid and increasingly fragmented. Extended families of the same caste were ruled by the eldest male, who might take a number of wives. Children were betrothed early in life and women's duties—to tend the household and raise children (preferably sons)—were carefully prescribed. In a society where males were masters, a favorite Hindu proverb ran, "A woman is never fit for independence." The devotion of the upper-caste Hindu woman to her husband was dramatically expressed in *sati*, a custom by which the wife threw herself on her mate's funeral pyre.

Early in the eighth century, Arab Muslims entered India and began to convert members of the native population to Islam. Muslim authority took hold in northern India, and Muslims rose to power as members of the ruling caste. During the tenth century, the invasions of Turkish Muslims brought further chaos to India, resulting in the

capture of Delhi (Map **14.1**) in 1192 and the destruction of the Buddhist University of Nalanda in the following year. Muslim armies destroyed vast numbers of Hindu and Buddhist religious statues, which they regarded as idols, and Islam ultimately supplanted Hinduism and Buddhism in the Indus valley (modern Pakistan) and in Bengal (modern Bangladesh). Elsewhere, however, the native

Map 14.1 India in the Eleventh Century.

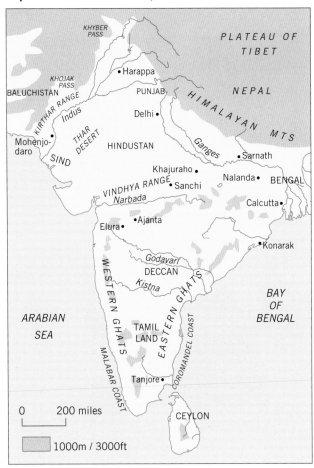

traditions of India and Hinduism itself prevailed. Indeed, most of India—especially the extreme south, which held out against the Muslims until the fourteenth century—remained profoundly devoted to the Hindu faith. Today, approximately eighty-five percent of India's population is Hindu. Buddhism, on the other hand, would virtually disappear from India by the thirteenth century.

Hinduism in Medieval India

In the medieval period, the philosophic aspects of Hinduism (as defined in the principal religious writings, the *Upanishads* and the *Bhagavad-Gita*; see chapter 3) were overshadowed by growing devotion to the gods and goddesses of Hindu mythology. These personal deities, rooted in India's most ancient texts—the *Vedas*—are personifications of the powerful, life-giving forces of nature. Although the worship of these gods suggests that Hindus are

Figure 14.1 *Standing Vishnu*, from southern India, Chola period, tenth century. Bronze, with greenish-blue patination, height 33¾ in. The Metropolitan Museum of Art, New York. Purchase 1962. Gift of Mr. and Mrs. John D. Rockefeller.

Figure 14.2 *Shiva Nataraja, Lord of the Dance*, from southern India, Chola period, eleventh century. Copper, height 3 ft. 7⅞ in. © The Cleveland Museum of Art, 2002. Purchase from the J.H. Wade Fund, 1930.331.

polytheistic, it is more accurate to say that Hinduism, fundamentally pantheistic, perceives all of nature—divine, human, and animal—as one. At the very core of Indian civilization, Hinduism confirms the oneness of nature. It teaches that all individual aspects of being belong to the same divine substance: the impersonal, all-pervading Absolute Spirit known as Brahman. Hindus view regional deities and the gods of ancient India as **avatars** (Sanskrit, "incarnations") of Brahman, much in the way that Christians regard Jesus as the incarnate form of God. Indeed, since Hindus believe that the avatars of Brahman may assume different names and forms (even those of animals), they freely honor the Buddha and Jesus as human guises of the Absolute Spirit. Like Buddhism, Hinduism is characterized by a multitude of sects headed by a variety of teachers, or gurus. There is, therefore, no monolithic single organization comparable to either the Roman or Orthodox Christian churches in Hinduism's history. Devotional practices are not united by a single, orthodox liturgy. Hinduism encourages its devotees to seek union with Brahman in their own fashion, or in the fashion taught by their guru, placing a fundamental faith in the concept that there are infinite ways of expressing the truth of Brahman—whether through the meditative pursuits of the wandering hermit or in paying reverence to the many gods and spirits within the Hindu pantheon. The plural character of Hinduism, which it shares with Buddhism, contrasts sharply with Judaism, Christianity, and Islam, all of which hold divinity as a singular concept. The many gods of the Hindus—like the facets of a diamond—exist only as individual aspects (or manifestations) of Brahman.

Images of deities, however, play a major role in Hinduism, as it is believed that the god is present in its representation. Hindus regard visual contact with an image of the deity as a form of direct contact with the divine; this they call *darshan* (literally, "seeing and being seen by the god"). The very act of beholding the image is thus an act of worship and an expression of intense personal devotion by which divine blessings are received.

Out of the host of deities that characterized Hindu worship in medieval India, three principal gods came to dominate the Hindu pantheon: Brahma, Vishnu, and Shiva. Hindus associate this "trinity" with the three main expressions of Brahmanic power: creation, preservation, and destruction. They honor Brahma—his name is the masculine form of Brahman—as the creator of the world. They prize Vishnu (identified with the sun in ancient Vedic hymns) as the preserver god. Hindu mythology recounts Vishnu's appearance on earth in nine different incarnations, including that of Krishna, the hero-god of the *Mahabharata* (see chapter 3). Icons of Vishnu often resemble those of the Buddha, who is accepted by Hindus as an avatar of Vishnu. The conically crowned Vishnu pictured in Figure **14.1** holds in his upper right hand a flaming solar disc; his upper left hand displays a conch shell, a reminder of his association with the primeval ocean, but also a symbol of the ancient war trumpet used by Vishnu to terrorize his enemies. With his lower right hand, he makes the *mudra* of protection (see Figure 9.28), while his lower left hand points to the earth and the sacred lotus, symbol of the cosmic womb. Such ritual icons, cast in bronze by the lost-wax method (see Figure 0.18), are among the finest freestanding figural sculptures executed since golden-age Greece. Produced in large numbers in tenth-century Tamil Nadu in South India, bronze effigies of the god were often bedecked with flowers and carried in public processions. (Note the rings at the four corners of the base of the *Standing Vishnu*, which once held poles for transporting the statue.) As a ninth-century Tamil poet explained, "The god comes within everyone's reach."

The third god of the trinity, Shiva, is the Hindu lord of regeneration. A god of destruction and creation, of disease and death, and of sexuality and rebirth, Shiva embodies the dynamic rhythms of the universe. While often shown in a dual male and female aspect, Shiva is most commonly portrayed as Lord of the Dance, an image that evokes the Hindu notion of time. Unlike the Western view of time, which is linear and progressive, the Hindu perception of time is cyclical; it moves like an ever-turning cosmic wheel. The four-armed figure of Shiva as Lord of the Dance is one of medieval India's most famous Hindu icons (Figure **14.2**)—so popular, in fact, that Tamil sculptors cast multiple versions of the image. Framed in a celestial ring of fire or circle of life, Shiva enacts the dance of cosmic creation and destruction, the living cycle of birth and death. His serpentine body bends at the neck, waist, and knees in accordance with specific and prescribed dance movements (Figure **14.3**). Every part of the statue has symbolic meaning: Shiva's earrings are mismatched to represent the male/female duality. One right hand holds a small drum, the symbol of creation; a second right hand (the arm wreathed by a snake, ancient

Figure 14.3 Temple sculptures showing classical dance postures, inspired by the *Karanas*, from the Devi temple, Chidambaram, India, thirteenth century. © Government of India, Department of Archeology.

symbol of regeneration) forms the *mudra* meaning protection; one left hand holds a flame, the symbol of destruction; the second left hand points toward Shiva's feet, the left "released" from worldliness, the right one crushing a demon-dwarf that symbolizes egotism and ignorance. Utterly peaceful in countenance, Shiva embodies the five activities of the godhead: creation, protection, destruction, release from destiny, and enlightenment. By these activities, the god dances the universe in and out of existence.

Indian Religious Literature

Medieval Indian literature drew heavily on the mythology and legends of early Hinduism as found in the Vedic hymns and in India's two great epics, the *Mahabharata* and the *Ramayana* (see chapter 3). This body of classic Indian literature was recorded in Sanskrit, the language of India's educated classes. Serving much the same purpose that Latin served in the medieval West, Sanskrit functioned for centuries as a cohesive force amidst India's diverse groups of regional vernacular dialects.

Among the most popular forms of Hindu literature in the medieval period were the *Puranas* (Sanskrit, "old stories"), a collection of eighteen religious books that preserved the myths and legends of the Hindu gods. Transmitted orally for centuries, they were not written down until well after 500 C.E. Many of the tales in the *Puranas* illustrate the special powers of Vishnu and Shiva or their avatars. In the *Vishnu Purana*, for instance, Krishna (the eighth and most venerated incarnation of Vishnu), is pictured as the "cosmic lover" who courts his devotees with sensual abandon, seducing them to become one with the divinity. In contrast to medieval Christianity's somber condemnation of the sensual life, Hinduism regards the physical union of male and female as symbolic of the eternal mingling of flesh and spirit, a sublime metaphor for the fusion of the Self (Atman) and the Absolute Spirit (Brahman) that culminates in *nirvana*. The *Upanishads* make clear the analogy:

> In the embrace of his beloved a man forgets the
> whole world—everything both within and without.
> In the same manner, he who embraces the Self
> knows neither within nor without.

The Hindu view of human sexuality as a metaphor for spiritual knowledge recalls the rituals of pre-Christian fertility cults, which exalted the life-affirming and regenerative aspects of erotic love. In the following passage from the *Vishnu Purana*, Krishna's cajoling and sensuous courtship, culminating in the circle of the dance, symbolizes the god's love for the human soul and the soul's unswerving attraction to the One.

READING 2.23 From the *Vishnu Purana*

(recorded after 500)

... [Krishna], observing the clear sky, bright with the autumnal   **1**
moon, and the air perfumed with the fragrance of the wild
water-lily, in whose buds the clustering bees were murmuring

their songs, felt inclined to join with the milkmaids [Gopis] in
sport. . . .

Then Madhava [Krishna], coming amongst them, conciliated some with soft speeches, some with gentle looks; and some he took by the hand: and the illustrious deity sported with them in the stations of the dance. As each of the milkmaids, however, attempted to keep in one place, close to the side of **10** Krishna, the circle of the dance could not be constructed; and he, therefore, took each by the hand, and when their eyelids were shut by the effects of such touch, the circle was formed. Then proceeded the dance, to the music of their clashing bracelets, and songs that celebrated, in suitable strain, the charms of the autumnal season. Krishna sang of the moon of autumn—a mine of gentle radiance; but the nymphs repeated the praises of Krishna alone. At times, one of them, wearied by the revolving dance, threw her arms, ornamented with tinkling bracelets, round the neck of the destroyer of Madhu **20** [Krishna]; another, skilled in the art of singing his praises, embraced him. The drops of perspiration from the arms of Hari [Krishna] were like fertilizing rain, which produced a crop of down upon the temples of the milkmaids. Krishna sang the strain that was appropriate to the dance. The milkmaids repeatedly exclaimed "Bravo, Krishna!" to his song. When leading, they followed him; when returning they encountered him; and whether he went forwards or backwards, they ever attended on his steps. Whilst frolicking thus, they considered every instant without him a myriad of years; and prohibited (in **30** vain) by husbands, fathers, brothers, they went forth at night to sport with Krishna, the object of their affection.

Thus, the illimitable being, the benevolent remover of all imperfections, assumed the character of a youth among the females of the herdsmen of [the district of] Vraja; pervading their natures and that of their lords by his own essence, all-diffusive like the wind. For even as the elements of ether, fire, earth, water, and air are comprehended in all creatures, so also is he everywhere present, and in all . . .

 Q How do "seduction" and "the dance" function as metaphors of Hindu spirituality?

Indian Poetry

If the religious literature of India is sensuous in nature, so too is the secular literature, much of which is devoted to physical pleasure. Sanskrit lyric poetry is the most erotic of all world literatures. Unlike the poetry of other ancient cultures, that of India was meant to be spoken, not sung. On the other hand, Sanskrit poetry shares with most ancient Greek and Latin verse a lack of rhyme. It also exploits such literary devices as **alliteration** (the repetition of initial sounds in successive words, as in "panting and pale") and **assonance** (similarity between vowel sounds, as in "lake" and "fate").

In Sanskrit verse, implication and innuendo are more important than direct statement or assertion. The multiplicity of synonyms in Sanskrit permits a wide range of meanings, puns, and verbal play. And although this wealth of synonyms and near-synonyms contributes to the richness of Indian poetry, it makes English translation quite difficult. For example, there are some fifty expressions in Sanskrit for "lotus"; in English there is but one. Sanskrit poets employ a large number of stock similes: the lady's face is like the moon, her eyes resemble lotuses, and so on. Sanskrit poems are rarely intimate or personal; rather, they describe general and universal conditions. But classical rules of style dictate that every poem must exhibit a single characteristic sentiment, such as anger, courage, wonder, or passion. Grief, however—the emotion humans seek to avoid—may not dominate any poem or play.

A great flowering of Indian literature occurred between the fourth and tenth centuries, but it was not until the eleventh century and thereafter that the renowned anthologies of Sanskrit poetry appeared. One of the most honored of these collections, an anthology of 1,739 verses dating from between 700 and 1050, was compiled by the late eleventh-century Buddhist monk Vidyakara. It is entitled *The Treasury of Well-Turned Verse*. As with most Indian anthologies, poems on the subject of love outnumber those in any other category, and many of the love lyrics feature details of physical passion. As suggested by the selection that follows, Indian poetry is more frank and erotic than ancient or medieval European love poetry and less concerned with the romantic aspects of courtship than most Islamic verse.

READING 2.24 From *The Treasury of Well-Turned Verse* (ca. 1050)

"When we have loved, my love"

When we have loved, my love,
Panting and pale from love,
Then from your cheeks my love,
Scent of the sweat I love:
And when our bodies love
Now to relax in love
After the stress of love,
Ever still more I love
Our mingled breath of love.

"When he desired to see her breast"

When he desired to see her breast
She clasped him tight in an embrace;
And when he wished to kiss her lip
She used cosmetics on her face.
She held his hand quite firmly pressed
Between her thighs in desperate grip;
   Nor yielded to his caress,
   Yet kept alive his wantonness.

"If my absent bride were but a pond"

If my absent bride were but a pond,
her eyes the water lilies and her face the lotus,
her brows the rippling waves, her arms the lotus stems;

then might I dive into the water of her loveliness
and cool of limb escape the mortal pain
exacted by the flaming fire of love.

Q How do these poems compare with similar expressions of love in Egypt (Reading 1.4), Greece (Reading 1.19), and Rome (Reading 1.26)?

Indian Architecture

The medieval period generated some of the finest works of Hindu art and architecture in India's long history. Buddhist imagery influenced the style of medieval Hindu art, and Buddhist rock-cut temples and shrines provided models for Hindu architects. Between the sixth and fourteenth centuries, Hindus built thousands of temple-shrines to honor Vishnu and Shiva. These structures varied in shape from region to region, but generally they took the shape of a mound (often square or rectangular) topped with lofty towers or spires. Such structures were built of stone or brick with iron dowels frequently substituting for mortar. As with the early Buddhist *stupa* (see Figure 9.22), the Hindu temple symbolized the sacred mountain. Some temples were even painted white to resemble the snowy peaks of the Himalayas. The Buddhist *stupa* was invariably a solid mound; however, the Hindu temple, more akin to the *chaitya* hall (see Figures 9.23, 9.24), enclosed a series of interior spaces leading to a shrine—the dwelling place of the god on earth. Devotees entered the temple by way of an ornate porch or series of porches, each porch having its own roof and spire. Beyond these areas stood a large hall designed for sacred dancing, and, finally, the dim, womblike sanctuary that enshrined the cult image of the god. The Hindu temple did not serve as a place for congregational worship (as did the medieval church); rather, its basic function was as a place of private, individual devotion, a place in which the devotee might contemplate or make offerings to the god. A temple could also be the focus of pilgrimage and at particular times of the year, it would also be the focus of religious festivals specific to the god (or gods) to which it was dedicated. The design of the Hindu temple is based on the cosmic mandala and governed by divine numerology. The sacred space at the center is the primordial Brahman; the surrounding squares correspond to gods, whose roles in this context are as guardians of the Absolute Spirit. Although the Hindu temple and the Gothic cathedral were very different in terms of design and building function, both signified the

Science and Technology

499	Indian mathematicians complete a compilation of known mathematical and astronomical principles
ca. 600	the decimal system is in use in India
876	the symbol for "zero" is first used in India

profoundly human impulse to forge a link between Heaven and earth and between matter and spirit.

The Kandariya Mahadeo temple in Khajuraho is but one of twenty-five remaining Hindu temple-shrines that rise like cosmic mountains out of the dusty plains of central north India (see Map 14.1). Dedicated in the early eleventh century to the god Shiva, the temple rests on a high masonry terrace and is entered through an elevated porch (Figures **14.4, 14.5**). Like most Indian temples, Kandariya Mahadeo consists of a series of extensively ornamented horizontal cornices that ascend in narrowing diameter to their lotus-shaped peaks. At each tier of the beehivelike tower is a row of high-relief sculptures: human beings and animals drawn from India's great epics appear at the lower levels, while divine nymphs and celestial deities adorn the upper sections. The ornamental ensemble comprises a total of some six hundred figures (Figure **14.6**).

Like the Gothic cathedral, the Hindu temple was a kind of "bible" in stone. Yet no two artistic enterprises could have been further apart: whereas the medieval Church discouraged the depiction of nudity as suggestive of sexual pleasure and sinfulness, Hinduism exalted the representation of the human body as symbolic of abundance, prosperity, and regeneration. The sinuous nudes that animate the surface of the Kandariya Mahadeo temple assume languid, erotic poses. Deeply carved, and endowed with supple limbs and swelling breasts and buttocks, their bodies signify the divine attributes of life breath and

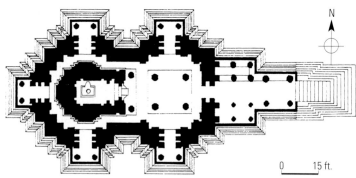

Figure 14.5 Plan of Kandariya Mahadeo temple, Khajuraho.

"fullness." The loving couples (known as **mithunas**)—men and women locked in passionate embrace (Figure **14.7**)—call to mind the imagery of the dance in the *Vishnu Purana.* They symbolize regenerative bliss and the ultimate union of human and divine love.

Figure 14.6 Celestial deities, Kandariya Mahadeo temple, Khajuraho, ca. 1000. Stone. Photo: © Richard Lucas/The Image Works, Inc.

Figure 14.4 Kandariya Mahadeo temple, Khajuraho, India, ca. 1000. Stone, height approx. 102 ft. A. F. Kersting, London.

Figure 14.7 *Mithuna* couple, from Orissa, India, twelfth–thirteenth centuries. Stone, height 6 ft. The Metropolitan Museum of Art, New York. Florence Waterbury Fund, 1970.

Indian Music and Dance

As noted in chapter 9, the music of India is inseparable from religious practice. Moreover, a single musical tradition—one that goes back some three thousand years—dominates both secular and religious music. In ancient times, India developed a system of music characterized by specific melodic sequences (**ragas**) and rhythms (**talas**). The centuries have produced thousands of *ragas*, sixty of which remain in standard use; nine are considered primary. Each *raga* consists of a series of seven basic tones arranged in a specific order. The performer may improvise on a chosen *raga* in any manner and at any length. As with the Greek modes (see chapter 5), each of the basic Indian *ragas* is associated with a different emotion, mood, or time of day. A famous Indian anecdote tells how a sixteenth-century court musician, entertaining at midday, once sang a night *raga* so beautiful that darkness instantly fell where he stood. Governing the rhythmic pattern of an Indian musical composition is the *tala*, which, in union with the *raga*, shapes the mood of the piece. Indian music divides the octave into twenty-two principal tones and many more microtones, all of which are treated equally. There is, therefore, no tonal center and no harmony in traditional Indian music. Rather, the character of a musical composition depends on the choice of the *raga* and on its exposition. A typical *raga* opens with a slow portion that establishes a particular mood, moves into a second portion that explores rhythmic variations, and closes with rapid, complex, and often syncopated improvisations that culminate in a frenzied finale.

India developed a broad range of stringed instruments that were either bowed or plucked. The most popular of these was the **sitar**, a long-necked stringed instrument with a gourd resonator, which came into use during the thirteenth century (Figure **14.8**). Related to the cithara, an instrument used in ancient Greece (see chapter 5), the sitar provided a distinctive rhythmic "drone," while its strings were plucked for melody. Accompanied by flutes, drums, bells, and horns, sitar players were fond of improvising patterns of notes in quick succession against a resonating bass sound.

The Sanskrit word for music (*sangeeta*) means both "sound" and "rhythm," suggesting that the music of India, like that of ancient Greece, was inseparable from the art of the dance. Indian dance, like the *raga* that accompanied it, set a mood or told a story by way of rigidly observed steps and hand gestures (*mudra*). India trained professional dancers to achieve difficult leg and foot positions (see Figure 14.3), some of which may be seen on the façades of Indian temples (see Figure 14.6). Each of some thirty traditional dances requires a combination of complex body positions, of which there are more than one hundred. The close relationship among the arts of medieval India provides something of a parallel with the achievement of the medieval synthesis in the West. On the other hand, the sensual character of the arts of India distinguishes them sharply from the arts of Christian Europe.

See Music Listening Selections at end of chapter.

Figure 14.8 Ravi Shankar
playing the sitar (right);
others with tabla (hand
drums) and tamboura
(plucked string instrument).
Photo:
© Silverstone/Magnum
Photos, Inc.

The Medieval Period in China

Nowhere else in the world has a single cultural tradition dominated so consistently over so long a period as in China. When European merchants visited China in the thirteenth century, the Chinese had already enjoyed 1,700 years of civilization. China's agrarian landmass, rich in vast mineral, vegetable, and animal resources, readily supported a large and self-sufficient population, the majority of which constituted a massive land-bound peasantry. Despite internal shifts of power and repeated attacks from its northern nomadic neighbors, China experienced a single form of government—imperial monarchy—and a large degree of political order until the invasion of the Mongols in the thirteenth century. But even after the establishment of Mongol rule under Kubilai Khan (1215–1294), the governmental bureaucracy on which China had long depended remained intact, and Chinese culture continued to flourish. The wealth and splendor of early fourteenth-century China inspired the awe and admiration of Western visitors, such as the famous Venetian merchant-adventurer Marco Polo (1254–1324). Indeed, in the two centuries prior to Europe's rise to economic dominion (but especially between 1250 and 1350), China was "the most extensive, populous, and technologically advanced region of the medieval world."*

China in the Tang Era

Tang China (618–907) was a unified, centralized state that had no equal in Asia or the West. In contrast with India, class distinctions in China were flexible and allowed a fair degree of social mobility: thanks to the imperial meritocratic system, even commoners could rise to become members of the ruling elite. Nevertheless, as in all Asian and European civilizations of premodern times, the great masses of Chinese peasants had no voice in political matters.

*Janet L. Abu-Lughod, *Before European Hegemony: The World System A.D. 1250–1350*. New York: Oxford University Press, 1989, 316.

Despite the success of Buddhism in China, Confucianism remained China's foremost moral philosophy. Confucian teachings encouraged social harmony and respect for the ruling monarch, whom the Chinese called the "Son of Heaven." The Confucian equation of virtue and authority, which linked the destiny of the community with the ruler's obedience to moral law, and Confucian respect for the universal order (expressed in the creative interaction of *yin* and *yang*) were humanizing forces in Chinese culture. Confucianism was generally tolerant of all religious creeds, though it disapproved of the Buddhist commitment to celibacy, which contravened the Confucian esteem for family. Nevertheless, the vast wealth and political influence accumulated by the Chinese Buddhist community, in addition to the loss of large numbers of talented men to the cloister, encouraged some emperors to restrict the number of Buddhist monasteries and to limit the ordination of new monks and nuns. This culminated in the brief but catastrophic ban of the religion within the empire in the year 845, which saw the confiscation of Buddhist temple and monastic property, and the enforced return of monks and nuns to the population at large. Although short in duration, the effect of this ban had longlasting effects on Chinese Buddhism. While future emperors would be devoted Buddhists, their political counsel would almost always remain Confucian.

Science and Technology

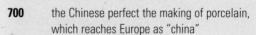

700	the Chinese perfect the making of porcelain, which reaches Europe as "china"
725	the Chinese build a water clock with a regulating device anticipating mechanical clocks
748	the first printed newspaper appears in Beijing
868	the *Diamond Sutra*, the first known printed book, is produced in China

Nevertheless, the monkish image of the Buddhist *luohan* ("worthy one"), humbly attired and transfixed in a state of deep meditation (Figure **14.9**), became a popular model of self-control and selflessness—an ideal type not unlike that of the Christian saint. Like the Christian promise of reward in an afterlife, an important feature in China's Mahayana Buddhism was the believer's aspiration to be reborn into a Buddhist paradise. Similarly, medieval Daoism aspired to reach the isle of the immortals. In contrast, Confucian culture held firmly to a secular ethic that emphasized proper conduct (*li*) and the sanctity of human life on earth. These Confucian tenets—renewed in the neo-Confucian movement of the eleventh century—challenged neither the popular worship of a large number of Chinese nature deities nor ancient rites that honored the souls of the dead. Confucian ideals of order, harmony, and filial duty were also easily reconciled with holistic Daoism. Tolerant of all religions, the Chinese never engaged in religious wars or massive crusades of the kind that disrupted both Christian and Islamic civilizations.

Under the rule of the Tang emperors, China experienced a flowering of culture that was unmatched anywhere in the world. Often called the greatest dynasty in Chinese history, the Tang brought unity and wealth to a vast Chinese empire (Map **14.2**). Tang emperors perpetuated the economic policies of their immediate predecessors, but they employed their vast powers to achieve a remarkable series of reforms. They completed the Grand Canal connecting the lower valley of the Yellow River to the eastern banks of the Yangzi, a project that facilitated shipping and promoted internal cohesion and wealth. They initiated a full census of the

population (some four centuries before a similar survey was undertaken in Norman England), which was repeated every three years. They also humanized the penal code and tried to guarantee farmlands to the peasants. They stimulated agricultural production, encouraged the flourishing silk trade, launched a tax reform that based assessments on units of land rather than agricultural output, and they commuted payments from goods to coins.

The Tang Empire dwarfed the Carolingian Empire in the West not only in terms of its geographic size and population but also with respect to its intellectual and educational accomplishments. Tang bureaucrats, steeped in Confucian traditions and rigorously trained in the literary classics, were members of an intellectual elite that rose to service on the basis of merit. Beginning in the seventh century (but rooted in a long tradition of leadership based on education and ability), every government official was subject to a rigorous civil service examination. A young man gained a political position by passing three levels of examinations (district, provincial, and national) that tested his familiarity with the Chinese classics as well as his grasp of contemporary political issues. For lower-ranking positions, candidates took exams in law, mathematics, and calligraphy. As in the Islamic world and the Christian West, higher education in China required close familiarity with the basic religious and philosophical texts. But because Chinese characters changed very little over the centuries, students could read 1,500-year-old texts as easily as they could read contemporary ones. Chinese classics were thus accessible to Chinese scholars in a way that the Greco-Roman classics were not accessible to Western scholars. Training for the

Figure 14.9 *Luohan*, China, tenth to thirteenth centuries. Pottery with three-color glaze, height 3 ft. 10½ in. The Nelson-Atkins Museum of Art, Kansas City, Missouri. Purchase: Nelson Trust.

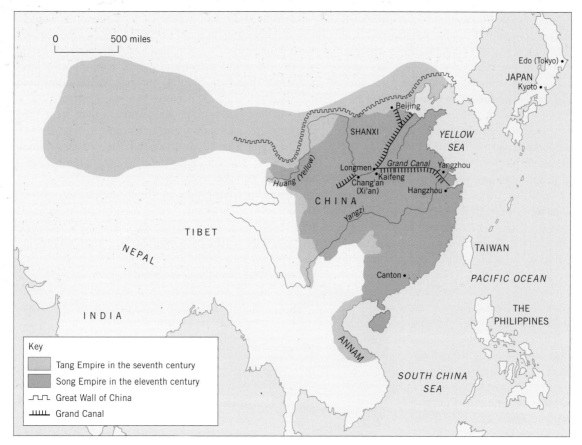

Map 14.2 East Asia.

Figure 14.10 Attributed to the Song emperor **HUIZONG** (reigned 1101–1125), but probably by court academician, after a lost painting by Zhang Xuan (fl. 713–741), *Women Combing Silk*, detail of *Court Ladies Preparing Newly Woven Silk*, Northern Song dynasty, early twelfth century. Ink, color, and gold on silk handscroll, height 14½ in., length4 ft. 9¾ in. Courtesy Museum of Fine Arts, Boston. Special Chinese and Japanese Fund. Photograph © 2006 Museum of Fine Arts, Boston.

Figure 14.11 Attributed to **GU HONGZHONG**, detail of *Night Revels of Han Xizai*, ca. twelfth-century copy of a tenth-century composition. Ink and color on silk handscroll, 11¼ in. × 11 ft. 1 in. The Palace Museum, Beijing.

arduous civil service examinations required a great degree of memorization and a thorough knowledge of the Chinese literary tradition, but originality was also important: candidates had to prove accomplishment in the writing of prose and poetry, as well as in the analysis of administrative policy. Strict standards applied to grading, and candidates who failed the exams (only one to ten percent passed the first level) could take them over and over, even into their middle and old age.

During the seventh century, the imperial college in the capital city of Chang'an (present-day Xi'an) prepared some three thousand men for the civil service examinations. (As in the West, women were excluded from education in colleges and universities.) Such scholar officials constituted China's highest social class. And while the vast population of Chinese peasants lived in relative ignorance and poverty, the aristocratic bureaucracy of the Tang generally enjoyed lives of wealth and position. Nowhere else in the world (except perhaps ninth-century Baghdad) was such prestige attached to scholarship and intellectual achievement. Despite instances in which family connections influenced political position, the imperial examination system remained the main route to official status in China into the twentieth century.

A less enlightened Chinese practice survived into the modern period: the binding of women's feet. From earliest times, Chinese women participated in agricultural activities as well as in the manufacture of silk (Figure **14.10**); many were trained in dance and musical performance (Figure **14.11**). In the early 900s, however, as women seem to have assumed a more ornamental role in Chinese society, footbinding became common among the upper classes. To indicate that their female offspring were exempt from common labor, prosperous urban families bound the feet of their infant daughters—a practice that broke the arch and dwarfed the foot to half its normal growth. Footbinding, a cruel means of signifying social status, persisted into the early twentieth century.

China in the Song Era

After a brief period of political turmoil resulting from the collapse of the Tang dynasty and attacks of nomadic tribes, the Song dynasty (960–1279) reestablished a unified Chinese empire. Although its territory was much reduced compared to that of the Tang Empire, and it had powerful and land-hungry neighbors to the north and west, the Song nevertheless is a period of great advancement both in terms of culture and technology. The three centuries of Song rule corresponded roughly to the golden age of Muslim learning, the waning of the Abbasid Empire and the era of Norman domination in Europe (see chapters 10, 11). The Song Era was a period of population growth, agricultural productivity, and vigorous commercial trade centering on the exportation of tea, silk, and ceramics. China's new economic prosperity caused a population shift from the countryside to the city, where social mobility was on the rise. The imperial capitals of Kaifeng and Hangzhou (see Map 14.2), with populations of over one million people, boasted a variety of restaurants, teahouses, temples, gardens, and shops, including bookstores and pet shops (Figure **14.12**). Chinese cities were larger and more populous than those in the West and city dwellers enjoyed conditions of safety that are enviable even today—in Hangzhou, the streets were patrolled at night, and bridges and canals were guarded and fitted with balustrades to prevent drunken revelers from falling into the water.

Given the constant threat posed by their northern neighbors, a ready army was a necessity in the Song period. Mercenaries, however, characterize the military of the Song state. Where medieval Islam and the feudal West prized heroism and the art of war, the Chinese despised military life. A Chinese proverb claimed that just as good steel should not be made into common nails, good men should not become soldiers. Chinese poets frequently lamented the disruption of family life as soldiers left home to defend remote regions of the Empire. In combat, the Chinese generally preferred starving out their enemies to

Figure 14.12 ZHANG ZEDUAN, detail from *Life Along the River on the Eve of the Qing Ming Festival*, late eleventh to early twelfth century. Handscroll, ink on silk. Collection of the Palace Museum, Beijing.

confronting them in battle. The peaceful nature of the Chinese impressed its first Western visitors: arriving in China a half century after the end of the Song Era, Marco Polo observed with some astonishment that no one carried arms. Indeed, from the twelfth to the early twentieth century, China espoused the Confucian idea that everything partakes of a single Nature—a notion of cosmic harmony best expressed in the writings of the Neo-Confucian philosopher Zhang Zai (1020–1077):

> Heaven is my father and earth is my mother, and even such a small creature as I finds an intimate place in their midst. Therefore that which extends throughout the universe I regard as my body and that which directs the universe I consider as my nature. All people are my brothers and sisters, and all things are my companions.*

Confucian, Dao, and Buddhist practices continued to flourish during the Song era. It was at this time within Chinese Buddhist sects (especially the more popular ones) that the image and person of the *bodhisattva* of compassion, Guanyin, became feminized (Figure **14.13**). This beloved icon, like that of the Virgin Mother in medieval Christendom, embodied the loving, forgiving aspect of devotional faith. Brightly painted and gilded, the wood-carved Guanyin wears sumptuous robes, an ornate headdress, and a profusion of jewels.

_____
*William H. McNeill and J. W. Sedlar, eds. *China, India, and Japan: The Middle Period*. New York: Oxford University Press, 1971, 78.

Figure 14.13 *Guanyin*, tenth to early twelfth century. Wood with painted decoration, height 7 ft 11 in. The Nelson-Atkins Museum of Art, Kansas City, Missouri. Purchase: Nelson Trust. Photo: Jamison Miller.

Technology in the Tang and Song Eras

Chinese civilization is exceptional in the extraordinary number of its technological inventions, many of which came into use elsewhere in the world only long after their utilization in China. A case in point is printing, which

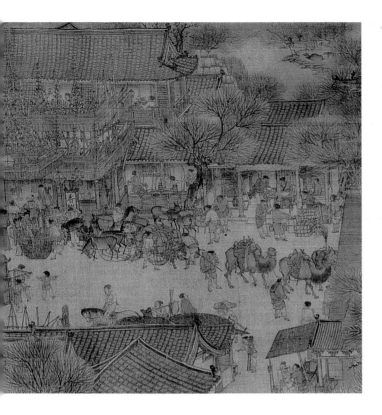

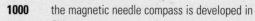

Science and Technology

1000   the magnetic needle compass is developed in China

1009   the Chinese first use coal as fuel

ca. 1040 three varieties of gunpowder are described by Zeng Kongliang

1041   movable type is utilized in China

Chinese technology often involved the intelligent application of natural principles to produce labor-saving devices. Examples include the water mill (devised to grind tea leaves and to provide power to run machinery), the wheelbarrow (used in China from at least the third century but not found in Europe until more than ten centuries later), and the stern-post rudder and magnetic compass (Song inventions that facilitated maritime trade). The latter two devices had revolutionary consequences for Western Europeans, who used them to inaugurate an age of exploration and discovery (see chapter 18). Gunpowder, invented by the Chinese as early as the seventh century and used in firework displays, was employed (in the form of fire-arrow incendiary devices) for military purposes in the mid-tenth century, but arrived in the West only in the fourteenth century. Other contrivances, such as the abacus and the hydromechanical clock, and such processes as iron-casting (used for armaments, for suspension bridges, and for the construction of some Tang and Song pagodas) were unknown in the West for centuries or were invented independently of Chinese prototypes. Not until the eighteenth century, for instance, did Western Europeans master the technique of steel-casting, which had been in use in China since the sixth century C.E.; and the seismograph (invented in China around 100 B.C.E.) remained unknown to Europe until modern times.

Some of China's most important technological contributions, such as the foot stirrup (in use well before the fifth century) and gunpowder, improved China's ability to withstand the attacks of Huns, Turks, and other tribal peoples who repeatedly attacked China's northern frontiers.

originated in ninth-century China but was not perfected in the West until the fifteenth century. The earliest printed document, the *Diamond Sutra*, dated 868, is a Buddhist text produced from large woodcut blocks (Figure **14.14**). In the mid-eleventh century, the Chinese invented movable type and, by the end of the century, the entire body of Buddhist and Confucian classics, including the commentaries, were available in printed editions. One such classic (a required text for civil service candidates) was *The Book of Songs*, a venerable collection of over three hundred poems dating from the first millennium B.C.E. By the twelfth century, the Chinese were also printing paper money—a practice that inevitably gave rise to the "profession" of counterfeiting. Although in China movable type did not inspire a revolution in the communication of ideas (as it would in Renaissance Europe), it encouraged literacy, fostered scholarship, and facilitated the preservation of the Chinese classics.

Figure 14.14 The *Diamond Sutra*, the world's earliest printed book, dated 868. 6 ft. × 30 in. Reproduced by courtesy of the British Library, London. Department of Oriental Manuscripts and Books.

In the West, however, these devices had revolutionary results: the former ushered in the military aspect of medieval feudalism; and the latter ultimately undermined siege warfare and inaugurated modern forms of combat. While thirteenth-century China was far ahead of the medieval West in science and technology, its wealth in manpower—a population of some hundred million people—may have made a technology of industrial power unnecessary.

In addition to their ingenuity in engineering and metallurgy, the Chinese advanced the practice of medicine. From the eleventh century on, they used vaccination to prevent diseases, thus establishing the science of immunology. Their understanding of human anatomy and their assumption that illness derives from an imbalance of *qi* (life energy) gave rise to acupuncture—the practice of applying needles to specific parts of the body to regulate and restore proper energy flow. Chinese medical encyclopedias dating from the twelfth century were far in advance of any produced in the medieval West. In both India and China, the belief in the unity of mind and body generated healing practices (such as meditation and yoga) that have met enthusiastic reception in the West only in recent decades.

Chinese Literature

Chinese literature owes little to other cultures. It reflects at every turn a high regard for native traditions and for the concepts of universal harmony expressed in Confucian and Daoist thought. Philosophic in nature, it is, however, markedly free of religious sentiment. Even between the fifth and ninth centuries, when Buddhism was at its height in China, Chinese literature was largely secular, hence quite different from most of the writings of medieval Europe and the rest of Asia.

The literature of the Tang and Song eras embraced a wide variety of genres including treatises on history, geography, religion, economics, and architecture; monographs on botany and zoology; essays on administrative and governmental affairs; drama, fiction, and lyric poetry. Experts in the art of compiling information, the Chinese produced a vast assortment of encyclopedias, manuals of divination and ritual, ethical discourses, and anthologies based on the teachings of Confucius and others. Like the medieval scholastics in the West, Chinese scholars esteemed their classical past, but, unlike the Europeans, they acknowledged no conflict between (and therefore no need to reconcile) faith and reason.

During the twelfth and thirteenth centuries, in Song urban centers, storytelling flourished, and popular theater arose in the form of dramatic performance. Popular genres included comedy, historical plays, and tales of everyday life—many of which featured love stories. As dramatists began to adapt literary plots to music, **opera** (musical drama) became the fashionable entertainment among ordinary townspeople and at the imperial court. The first Chinese **novels**—products of a long tradition of oral narrative—also appeared during the twelfth century, their themes focusing on the adventures of contemporary heroes.

The novel, however, was not original to China. Rather, it was a product of the aristocratic and feudal culture of medieval Japan (discussed later in this chapter). In China, early fiction writing reached a high point with the monumental historical novel entitled *Three Kingdoms* (attributed to the fourteenth-century playwright Luo Guanzhong). This one-thousand-page work, filled with hundreds of characters and lengthy, epic descriptions of martial prowess, brings alive the turbulent era (220–280) that followed the breakup of the Han dynasty.

Chinese Music and Poetry

To the Chinese, music functioned to imitate and sustain the harmony of nature. Both Daoists and Confucians regarded music as an expression of cosmic order, and Daoists even made distinctions between *yin* and *yang* notes. Like most of the music of the ancient world, that of China was monophonic, but it assumed a unique timbre produced by nasal tones that were often high in pitch and subtle in inflection. The sliding nasal tones that typify Chinese music resemble those of the zither. Frequently used for Buddhist chant (see chapter 9), the zither was the favorite Chinese instrument, and musical notation to guide the performer was devised as early as the second century B.C.E. The Chinese employed the zither, along with the short-necked lute and various flutes, bells, and chimes in instrumental ensembles (see Figure 14.11).

The most popular Chinese musical genre was the solo song, performed with or without instrumental accompaniment. A close kinship between Chinese music and speech was enforced by the unique nature of the Chinese language. Consisting of some fifty thousand characters, spoken Chinese demands subtle intonations: the pitch or tonal level at which any word is pronounced gives it its meaning. A single word, depending on how it is uttered, may have more than a hundred meanings. In this sense, all communication in the Chinese language is musical—a phenomenon that has particular importance for Chinese poetry. Chinese poetry is a kind of vocal music: a line of spoken poetry is—like music—essentially a series of tones that rise and fall in various rhythms. Moreover, since Chinese is a monosyllabic language with few word endings, rhyme is common to speech. All Chinese verse is rhymed, often in long runs that are almost impossible to imitate in English. And, finally, it is characterized by

♪ See Music Listening Selections at end of chapter.

extraordinary kinds of condensation and innuendo that most English translations cannot capture.

During the Tang Era, China produced some of the most beautiful poetry in world literature. The poems of the eighth and ninth centuries—an era referred to as the Golden Age of Chinese poetry—resemble diary entries that record the intimate experience of everyday life. Unlike the poetry of India, Chinese lyrics are rarely sensuous or erotic and only infrequently attentive to either physical affection or romantic love. Restrained and sophisticated, the poetry of the Tang period was written by scholar-poets (the so-called *literati*) who considered verse making, along with calligraphy and painting, the mark of educational and intellectual refinement. From earliest times, nature and natural imagery played a large part in Chinese verse. Tang poets continued this long tradition: their poems are filled with the meditative spirit of Daoism and a sense of oneness with nature.

Two of the greatest poets of the Tang period, Li Bo (ca. 700–762) and Du Fu (712–770), belonged to the group of cultivated individuals who made up China's cultural elite. Although Li Bo was not a scholar-official, as was his friend Du Fu, he was familiar with the Chinese classics. Both Li Bo and Du Fu were members of the Eight Immortals of the Wine Cup, an informal association of poets who celebrated the kinship of ink and drink and the value of inebriation to poetic inspiration. Du Fu, often regarded as China's greatest poet, wrote some 1,400 poems, many of which are autobiographical reflections that impart genuine emotion and humor. In contrast with these poets, the ninth-century poet Bo Zhuyi, who headed the Tang Bureau of War, brought to his poetry a note of cynicism and worldliness that is particularly typical of the late Tang period and that of the succeeding Song. Like most of the poets of his time, he was a statesman, a calligrapher, an aesthetician, and a moralist. He thus epitomized the ideal well-rounded individual long before that concept became important among Renaissance Europeans.

READING 2.25 Poems of the Tang and Song Eras (750–900)

Li Bo's "Watching the Mount Lushan Waterfall"

Incense-Burner Peak shimmers in the sun,	1
Purple mist slowly rising.	
A flying stream, seen from below,	
Hangs like clouds down the crag.	
The waterfall pours itself	5
Three thousand feet straight down,	
Roaring like the Milky Way	
Tumbling from high heaven.	

Li Bo's "Zhuang Zhou and the Butterfly"

Zhuang Zhou[1] in dream became a butterfly,	1

[1]A fourth-century follower of Lao Zi (see chapter 3), whose writings describe how, in a dream, he became a butterfly.

And the butterfly became Zhuang Zhou at waking.	
Which was the real—the butterfly or the man?	
Who can tell the end of the endless changes of things?	
The water that flows into the depth of the distant sea	5
Returns anon to the shallows of a transparent stream.	
The man, raising melons outside the green gate of the city,	
Was once the Prince of the East Hill,[2]	
So must rank and riches vanish.	
You know it, still you toil and toil,—What for?	10

Du Fu's "Spring Rain"

Oh lovely spring rain!	1
You come at the right time, in the right season.	
Riding the night winds you creep in,	
Quietly wetting the world.	
Roads are dark, clouds are darker.	5
Only a light on a boat, gleaming.	
And in the morning the city is drunk with red flowers,	
Cluster after cluster, moist, glistening.	

Du Fu's "Farewell Once More"
(To my friend Yan at Feng Ji Station)

Here we part.	1
You go off in the distance,	
And once more the forested mountains	
Are empty, unfriendly.	
What holiday will see us	5
Drunk together again?	
Last night we walked	
Arm in arm in the moonlight,	
Singing sentimental ballads	
Along the banks of the river.	10
Your honor outlasts three emperors.	
I go back to my lonely house by the river,	
Mute, friendless, feeding the crumbling years.	

Bo Zhuyi's "On His Baldness"

At dawn I sighed to see my hairs fall;	1
At dusk I sighed to see my hairs fall.	
For I dreaded the time when the last lock should go . . .	
They are all gone and I do not mind at all!	
I have done with that cumbrous washing and getting dry;	5
My tiresome comb forever is laid aside.	
Best of all, when the weather is hot and wet,	
To have no topknot weighing down on one's head!	
I put aside my dusty conical cap;	
And loose my collar fringe,	10
In a silver jar I have stored a cold stream;	
On my bald pate I trickle a ladle-full.	
Like one baptized with the Water of Buddha's Law,	
I sit and receive this cool, cleansing joy.	
Now I know why the priest who seeks repose	15
Frees his heart by first shaving his head.	

[2]The Marquis of Dongling, a third-century-B.C.E. official, lost his exalted position at court after the fall of the Qin dynasty, and retired to grow melons outside of the city of Chang'an.

Bo Zhuyi's "Madly Singing in the Mountains"

There is no one among men that has not a special failing: **1**
And my failing consists in writing verses.
I have broken away from the thousand ties of life:
But this infirmity still remains behind.
Each time that I look at a fine landscape: **5**
Each time that I meet a loved friend,
I raise my voice and recite a stanza of poetry
And am glad as though a god had crossed my path.
Ever since the day I was banished to Xunyang
Half my time I have lived among the hills.   **10**
And often, when I have finished a new poem,
Alone I climb the road to the Eastern Rock.
I lean my body on the banks of white stone:
I pull down with my hands a green cassia[1] branch.
My mad singing startles the valleys and hills: **15**
The apes and birds all come to peep.
Fearing to become a laughing-stock to the world,
I choose a place that is unfrequented by men.

Q What themes dominate these six poems?

Q How do these poems differ from those of medieval India (Reading 2.24)?

Chinese Landscape Painting

During the Tang Era, figural subjects dominated Chinese art (see Figure 14.10), but by the tenth century, landscape painting became the favorite genre. The Chinese, and especially the literati of Song China, referred to landscape paintings as wordless poems and poems as formless paintings; such metaphors reflect the intimate relationship between painting and poetry in Chinese art. In subjects dealing with the natural landscape, both Chinese paintings and Chinese poems seek to evoke a mood rather than provide a literal, objective description of reality. Chinese landscapes work to convey a spirit of harmony between heaven and earth. This cosmic approach to nature, fundamental to Confucianism, Daoism, and Buddhism, asks the beholder to contemplate, rather than simply to view the painted image. The contemplative landscape may require the beholder to integrate multiple viewpoints, and to shift between foreground, middleground, and background in ways that resemble the mental shifts employed in reading lines of poetry.

Chinese paintings generally assume one of three basic formats: the handscroll, the hanging scroll, or the album leaf (often used as a fan). Between one and forty feet long, the handscroll is viewed continuously from right to left (Figure 14.15). Like a poem, the visual "action" unfolds in time—an object of lingering contemplation and delight. The hanging scroll, on the other hand, is vertical in format and is meant to be read from the bottom up—from earth to heaven, so to speak (see Figure 14.16). The album leaf usually belongs to a book that combines poems and paintings in a sequence. Both leaves and scrolls are made of silk or paper and ornamented with ink or thin washes of paint applied in monochrome or in muted colors. An interesting Chinese practice is the addition of the seals or signatures of collectors who have owned the work of art. These appear along with occasional marginal comments or brief poems inspired by the visual image. The poem may also serve as an extension of the content of the work of art. The Chinese painting, then, is a repository of the personal expressions of both artist and art lover.

By comparison with medieval and Renaissance art in the West, much of which is religious in subject matter, Chinese painting draws heavily on the everyday activities of men, women, and children. Whereas Western artists exalt the heroic deeds and historical achievements of individuals, Chinese artists rarely glorify human accomplishments. Indeed, in Chinese paintings, the landscape often dwarfs the figures so that human occupations seem mundane and incidental within the vast sweep of nature.

A Solitary Temple Amid Clearing Peaks, attributed to Li Cheng (active 940–967), is meditative in mood and subtle in composition (Figure **14.16**). There is no single viewpoint from which to observe the mountains, trees, waters, and human habitations. Rather, we perceive the whole from what one eleventh-century Chinese art critic called the "angle of totality." We look down upon some elements, such as the rooftops, and up to others, such as the mountains. The lofty mountains and gentle waterfall seem protective of the infinitely smaller images of temples, houses, and people. Misty areas provide transition between foreground, middleground, and background, but each plane—even the background—is delineated with identical precision. The visual voyage through discontinuous space engages our recognition of the subtle relationships between all parts of the painting, putting us in touch with the physical and spiritual energies of nature. Mountains, Chinese symbols of immortality, were regarded as living organisms that emanated the life force (*qi*) in the form of cloud vapor. As with Chinese poetry, in which a few well-chosen words may convey a distinct mood,

---

[1]A tree whose bark is used as a source of cinnamon.

Figure 14.15 MI YOUREN, *Cloudy Mountains*, 1130. Ink, white lead, and slight touches of color on silk handscroll, 13 ft. 6 in. × 6 ft. 3 in. The Cleveland Museum of Art. Purchase from the J. H. Wade Fund.

Figure 14.16 Attributed to **LI CHENG**, *A Solitary Temple Amid Clearing Peaks*, Northern Song dynasty, ca. 950. Ink and slight color on silk hanging scroll, 3 ft. 8 in. × 22 in. The Nelson-Atkins Museum of Art, Kansas City, Missouri. Purchase: Nelson Trust. 47–71.

Chinese painting displays a remarkable economy of line and color—that is, a memorable image is achieved by means of a limited number of brushstrokes and tones. Li Cheng fulfilled the primary aim of the Chinese landscape painter (as defined by Song critics): to capture the whole universe within a few inches of space.

More intimate in detail but equally subtle in its organization of positive and negative space, *Apricot Blossoms* by Ma Yuan reflects the Song taste for decorative works featuring floral motifs (Figure **14.17**). Refined nature studies like this one, executed in ink and color on silk, dwell on a single element in nature (the "broken branch") rather than the expansive landscape. The couplet at the right (added by the Empress Yang (1162–1232) extends the "message" of the image as fragile, elegant, fleeting:

> Meeting the wind, they offer their artful charm;
> Moist with dew, they boast their pink beauty.*

The earliest treatises on Chinese painting appeared in the Song era. They describe the artist's practice of integrating complementary pictorial elements: dark and light shapes, bold and muted strokes, dense and sparse textures, large and small forms, and positive and negative shapes, each pair interacting in imitation of the *yin/yang* principle that underlies cosmic wholeness. Specific brushstrokes, each bearing an individual name, are prescribed for depicting different natural phenomena: pine needles, rocks, mountains, and so forth. A form of calligraphy, the artist's brushstrokes are the "bones" of the Chinese painting. Economy, gestural expressiveness, and spontaneity are hallmarks of the finest Chinese paintings, as they are of the best Chinese poems. In premodern China, tradition rather than originality governed creativity: artists freely copied the works of the masters and honored their forebears by "quoting" from their poems or paintings.

*Maxwell Hearn, *Splendors of Imperial China: Treasures from the National Palace Museum, Taipei.* New York: The Metropolitan Museum of Art, 1996, 33.

Figure 14.17 MA YUAN, *Apricot Blossoms*, Song dynasty. Fan mounted as an album leaf, ink and color on silk, 10 × 10¾ in. National Palace Museum, Taipei.

Chinese Crafts

From earliest times, the Chinese excelled in the production of ceramic wares. They manufactured fine terracotta and earthenware objects for everyday use and for burial in the tombs of the dead (see chapter 7). During the Tang era, Chinese craftspeople produced thousands of realistic clay images: a terracotta court dancer wears an elegant dress with long sleeves designed to sway with her body movements (Figure 14.18), while other female figures are shown playing polo and performing on musical instruments—evidence of the wide range of activities enjoyed by aristocratic women. Representations of horsemen and horses—the treasured animals of China—appear in great numbers in Tang graves (as they had in the tombs of earlier dynasties, see Figure 7.5). Such figures were usually cast from molds, assembled in sections, and glazed with green, yellow, and brown (Figure **14.19).**

In addition to earthenware pottery, Tang and Song craftspeople perfected various types of stoneware, the finest of which was **porcelain**—a hard, translucent ceramic ware fired at extremely high heat. Glazed with delicate colors, and impervious to water, porcelain vessels display a level of sophistication that is not merely technical; their elegant shapes, based on natural forms, such as lotus blossoms and buds, are marvels of calculated simplicity in form and design (Figure **14.20**). Describing the magnificent porcelain vessels of the Tang era, a ninth-century merchant observed that one could see the sparkle of water through Chinese bowls that were "as fine as glass." International trade featuring porcelain did not begin, however, until the Song era. Exported along with silk, lacquerware, and carved ivory, porcelain became one of the most sought-after of Chinese luxury goods—indeed, it was so popular that Westerners still refer to dishes and plates as "china." Classic porcelains reflect the refinement of age-old traditions: their shapes often drew inspiration from those conceived by early bronze

workers of the Shang era (see chapter 3), while the cool blues and yellowish greens of the finest Chinese porcelains recall the color and texture of Chinese jades. Still other types, such as the cobalt blue and white porcelains that influenced Islamic art, originated in the thirteenth century. In subtlety of design, Chinese ceramics compare favorably with the most sublime Chinese landscape paintings.

The somber restraint of Chinese pottery stands in sharp contrast to the ornate richness of Chinese metalwork, inlaid wood, carved lacquers, and textiles. Weavers of the Song era produced exquisite silks embroidered to imitate flower-and-bird-paintings. The luxury silks and embroideries of the Chinese were valued so highly that they were often buried, along with fine ceramics and gold and silver objects, in the graves of wealthy Asians.

Figure 14.18 *Standing Court Lady*, Tang dynasty, mid-seventh century. Pottery with painted decoration, height 15¼ in. The Metropolitan Museum of Art, New York, anonymous gift, in memory Louise G. Dillingham, 1978 (1978.345). Photo: Lynton Gardiner, © 1989 The Metropolitan Museum of Art.

Figure 14.20 Ru ware, bowl in the shape of a lotus, Northern Sung dynasty, twelfth century. Porcelain, height 4 in. National Palace Museum, Taiwan.

Figure 14.19 (below) *Horse and Rider*, Tang dynasty, early eighth century. Pottery with three-color glaze and painted decoration, height 15 in. The Metropolitan Museum of Art, New York. Rogers Fund, 1954. 54.169.

So famous was Chinese silk that the 8,000-mile overland trade route connecting West and East (from Constantinople on the Atlantic to Chang'an on the Pacific) was dubbed "the Silk Road." Between roughly 500 B.C.E. and 1450 C.E., this route (and the nomadic peoples who traversed it) facilitated the exchange of goods and ideas between China, the great cities of Central Asia, and the West as far as Venice.

Chinese Architecture

Chinese architects embraced a system of design that reflected the ancient Daoist quest for harmony with nature. Structures were emphatically horizontal—built to hug the earth—and both whole towns and individual buildings were laid out according to a cosmic axis that ran from north to south. Celestial symbolism governed Chinese palace design: for instance, four doors represented the four seasons, eight windows signified the eight winds, and twelve halls stood for the number of months in the year. House doors faced the "good" southerly direction of the summer sun, and rear walls were closed to the cold North, homeland of barbarian hordes that had threatened China throughout its history. Chinese residences were normally self-enclosed and looked inward to courtyards or gardens.

During the Tang and Song eras, the multiroofed pagoda, a shrine sheltering the relics of the Buddha or the *bodhisattvas*, remained the locus of Buddhist worship (see chapter 9). From earliest times, pagodas were constructed of wood, a building material that was plentiful in China and one that was highly valued for its natural beauty. Chinese architectural ingenuity lay in the invention of a unique timber frame that—in place of walls—bore the entire weight of the roof while making the structure earthquake-resistant (Figure **14.21**). Perfected during the Tang era, the Chinese system of vaulting consisted of an intricate series of wooden cantilevers (horizontal brackets extending beyond the vertical supports) that provided support for centrally pitched, shingled, or glazed-tile roofs. By the tenth century, the aesthetics of wood construction were firmly established and, during the following century, scholars enshrined these principles in China's first manual on architecture. Because wooden buildings were highly vulnerable to fire—almost all examples of early Chinese shrines had been destroyed by the end of the first millennium—Chinese architects began to build in brick and in cast iron. Regardless of medium, however, Chinese pagodas, pavilions, and domestic structures, with their projecting upturned eaves, became models of elegant design. As indicated by the many magnificent pagodas found throughout Japan and Southeast Asia, China was influential in disseminating an architectural style that, in its dependence on the wooden cantilever and its harmonious relationship with the natural site, remains stylistically distinctive.

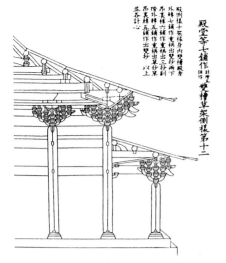

Figure 14.21
Seven-tiered bracket for a Chinese palace hall, from the Song dynasty architectural manual, *Yingzao fashin* (1925 edition). Woodcut.

The Medieval Period in Japan

Buddhism entered Japan from China by way of Korea in the early sixth century, bringing in its wake a restructuring of the government on Chinese imperial models and the embracing by Japan's elite of all things Chinese. The Chinese system of writing, record keeping, and governing, as well as the fundamentals of Chinese art and architecture, had a profound influence upon the Japanese. By the eighth century, Japan absorbed both Buddhism and Chinese culture. For roughly four centuries (794–1185), Japan enjoyed a cultural golden age centered on the imperial capital of Heian (modern Kyoto), from which came Japan's first wholly original literature and a set of aesthetic norms that left a permanent mark on Japanese culture.

It was Japan that introduced to world literature the prose form known as the novel. *The Tale of Genji* (ca. 1004), a Japanese classic, tells the story of the "shining prince" of the Heian court. Because the novel exposes the inner life of Genji and other characters, it has been called the world's first psychological novel. However, it also paints a detailed picture of Japanese life within a small segment of the population: the aristocracy. The men and women of this class prized elegant clothes (women usually wore five to twelve layers of silk robes), refined manners, and poetic versatility: inability to compose the appropriate on-the-spot poem was considered a serious social deficiency. The Heian aristocracy regarded as essential education in the (Chinese) Confucian classics, and the cultivation of dance, music, and fine calligraphy—in all, a set of values that prefigured the Renaissance ideal of the well-rounded courtier by some five hundred years. The author of *The Tale of Genji*, Murasaki Shikibu (978–1016), was one of a group of outstanding female writers and members of Heian court society. Upper-class women like Murasaki were unique in East Asian literary history: their fame in writing polished intimate prose was so great that one tenth-century male diarist pretended his work had been penned by a woman. The achievement of medieval Japanese women is all the more remarkable in that (like their Chinese counterparts) they were excluded from the world of scholarly education and, hence, from training in written Chinese. Nevertheless, using a system of phonetic symbols derived from Chinese characters, these women produced the outstanding monuments of medieval Japanese prose.

The Tale of Genji—in English translation some six volumes long—cannot be represented adequately here. But it is possible to gain insight into both the talents of Murasaki Shikibu and the character of the Heian court by means of a brief look at Murasaki's *Diary*, which she wrote between the years 1008 and 1010. Her keen eye for visual detail, for instance, is revealed in her vivid descriptions of court attire:

> . . . the older women wore plain jackets in yellow-green or dark red, each with five damask cuffs. The brightness of the wave pattern printed on their trains caught the eye, and their waistlines too were heavily embroidered. They had white robes lined with dark red in either three or five layers but of plain silk. The younger women wore jackets with five cuffs of various colors, white on the outside with dark red on yellow-green, white with just one green lining, and pale red shading to dark red with one white layer interposed; they were all arranged most intelligently.*

Beyond its importance as a historical record, Lady Murasaki's *Diary* is significant as an exercise in self-analysis. Not an autobiography, it is, rather, a series of reminiscences, anecdotes, and experiences. Nevertheless, it documents the author's quest to understand her role as a writer and her place in the highly artificial Heian court. As such, the *Diary* displays a dimension of self-consciousness that has long been considered an exclusively Western phenomenon.

READING 2.26 From Murasaki's *Diary* (ca.1000)

. . . The wife of the Governor of Tanba is known to everyone in the service of Her Majesty and His Excellency as Masahira Emon. She may not be a genius but she has great poise and does not feel that she has to compose a poem on everything she sees merely because she is a poet. From what I have seen, her work is most accomplished, even her occasional verse. People who think so much of themselves that, at the drop of a hat, they compose lame verses that only just hang together or produce the most pretentious compositions imaginable are quite odious and rather pathetic. 10

Sei Shōnagon,[1] for instance, was dreadfully conceited. She thought herself so clever, and littered her writings with Chinese characters, but if you examined them closely, they left a great deal to be desired. Those who think of themselves as being superior to everyone else in this way will inevitably suffer and come to a bad end, and people who have become so precious that they go out of their way to be sensitive in the most unpromising situations, trying to capture every moment of interest, however slight, are bound to look ridiculous and superficial. How can the future turn out well for them? 20

*Murasaki Shikibu, *Her Diary and Poetic Memoirs*, translated by Richard Bowring. Princeton, N. J.: Princeton University Press, 1982, 79.
[1]Female writer (ca. 968–1025) famous for her *Pillow Book*, a long collection of notes, stories, and descriptions of everyday life among members of the Heian upper class.

I criticize other women like this, but here is one who has managed to survive this far without having achieved anything of note and has nothing to rely on in the future that might afford her the slightest consolation. Yet, perhaps because I still retain the conviction that I am not the kind of person to abandon herself completely to despair, on autumn evenings, when nostalgia is at its most poignant, I go out and sit on the veranda to gaze in reverie. "Is this the moon that used to praise my beauty?" I say to myself, as I conjure up memories of the past. Then, realizing that I am making precisely that mistake which must be avoided, I become uneasy and move inside a little, while still, of course, continuing to fret and worry.

I remember how in the cool of the evening I used to play the koto[2] to myself, rather badly; I was always worried lest someone were to hear me and realize that I was just "adding to the sadness of it all." How silly of me, and yet how sad! So now my two kotos, one of thirteen strings and the other of six, stand in a miserable little closet blackened with soot, ready tuned but idle. Through neglect—I forgot, for example, to ask that the bridges be removed on rainy days—they have accumulated the dust and lean there now against a cupboard, their necks jammed between that and a pillar, with a biwa standing on either side.

There is also a pair of large cupboards crammed full to bursting point. One is full of old poems and tales that have become the home for countless silverfish that scatter in such an unpleasant manner that no one cares to look at them any more; the other is full of Chinese books which have lain unattended ever since he who carefully collected them passed away. Whenever my loneliness threatens to overwhelm me, I take out one or two of them to look at. But my women gather together behind my back. "It's because she goes on like that that she is so miserable. What kind of lady is it who reads Chinese books?" they whisper. "In the past it was not even the done thing to read sutras!"[3] "Yes," I feel like replying, "but I've never seen anyone who lived longer just because they obeyed a prohibition!" But that would be inconsiderate of me, for what they say is not unreasonable.

Everyone reacts differently. Some are cheerful, open-hearted, and forthcoming; others are born pessimists, amused by nothing, the kind who search through old letters, carry out penances, intone sutras without end, and clack their beads, all of which I find most unseemly. So aware am I of my women's prying eyes that I hesitate to do even those things a woman in my position should allow herself to do. How much more so at court, where I do have many things I wish to say but always think better of it. There would be no point, I tell myself, in explaining to people who would never understand, and as it would only be causing trouble with women who think of nothing but themselves and are always carping, I just keep my thoughts to myself. It is very rare that one finds people of true understanding; for the most part they judge everything by their own standards and ignore everyone else's opinion.

So I seem to be misunderstood, and they think that I am shy. There have been times when I have been forced to sit in their company, and on such occasions I have tried to avoid their petty criticisms, not because I am particularly shy but because I consider it all so distasteful; as a result, I am now known as somewhat of a dullard.

"Well, we never expected this!" they all say. "No one liked her. They all said she was pretentious, awkward, difficult to approach, prickly, too fond of her tales, haughty, prone to versifying, disdainful, cantankerous, and scornful. But when you meet her, she is strangely meek, a completely different person altogether!"

How embarrassing! Do they really look upon me as such a dull thing, I wonder? But I am what I am and so act accordingly. Her Majesty too has often remarked that she had thought I was not the kind of person with whom she could ever relax, but that now I have become closer to her than any of the others. I am so perversely standoffish; if only I can avoid putting off those for whom I have genuine respect.

The key to everything is to be pleasant, gentle, properly relaxed, and self-possessed; this is what makes for charm and composure in a woman. No matter how amorous or capricious one may be, as long as you are well-meaning at heart and refrain from anything that might cause embarrassment to others, you will be forgiven.

On the other hand, women who think too highly of themselves and act in a pretentious and overbearing manner become the object of attention, even when they take great care over their least move, and, once this happens, people are bound to find fault with whatever they say or do, going so far as to criticize how they sit down or how they take their leave. Those, of course, who tend to contradict themselves when they talk and disparage their companions are watched and listened to all the more. As long as one is free from such faults, people will be prepared to give you the benefit of the doubt and show you good will, no matter how superficial it might be.

Those who go out of their way to hurt others, as well as those who do stupid things by mistake, deserve, I think, to be ridiculed. Some people are so good-natured they can still care for someone even though that person hates them, but most people are just not capable of such magnanimity. Does the compassionate Buddha himself ever teach that taking the name of the three treasures in vain is merely a trivial offense? How much more so in this sullied world of ours should he who is hard on others be hardly done by. And yet one can clearly tell the differences in people's natures in the way that some glare at you openly with malicious intent and spread the most dreadful rumors, hoping to enhance themselves thereby, whereas others hide their feelings and appear on the surface to be quite friendly. . . .

[2] A Japanese musical instrument of the zither family.
[3] Buddhist discourses (see chapter 8).

Q. What does this reading reveal about the court culture of medieval Japan, and about the role of women in that culture?

Buddhism in Japan

As Buddhism spread throughout Japan, it inspired the construction of hundreds of shrines and temples, the oldest of which are found just outside Japan's early capital city of Nara. The site of the oldest wooden buildings in the world, this eighth-century temple complex at Yakushiji with its graceful five-storied pagoda (Figure 14.22) preserves the timber style that originated in China. The Buddhism that arrived in sixth-century Japan was of the Mahayana variety (see chapter 8). As it did with Daoism in China, Mahayana Buddhism coexisted with Japan's native Shinto religion, which venerated the divinity of the emperor as well as the host of local and nature spirits of the countryside. Indeed, the two faiths, Buddhism and Shintoism, formed a vigorous amalgam that accommodated many local beliefs and practices. As in China, the aspiration of the Buddhist faithful to be reborn in a Buddhist paradise also proved very popular in Japan. The Pure Land sect, venerated the Buddha known as

Figure 14.22 (below) East pagoda of Yakushiji, Nara, Japan, ca. 720. Robert Harding World Images, London.

Figure 14.23 (above) *Kichijoten*, Late Heian period, late twelfth century. Painted wood, height 35½ in. Joruriji, Kyoto, Japan.

Amitabha (or, in Japanese, Amida), who presides over the western paradise (the "pure land"). According to his followers, simply uttering the name of Amitabha many times a day was an aid to salvation and a means of assuring that he would deliver their dying souls to Paradise. True to its practice across Asia, Mahayana Buddhist sects in Japan assimilated the divine beings of India and China as well as those of Japan and honored them in painting and sculpture often based on Korean or Indian prototypes. Kichijoten, for instance, a female Buddhist deity of Indian derivation, is represented in a richly polychromed wooden statue of the Late Heian period (Figure 14.23). The popular goddess of abundance and good fortune, she is shown dressed in the elegant robes and jewelry of a Heian aristocrat.

The Age of the *Samurai*: The Kamakura Shogunate (1185–1333)

Toward the mid-twelfth century, Heian authority gave way to a powerful group of local clans that competed for political and military preeminence. Two in particular—the Taira and the Minamoto—engaged in outright war. The strength of any clan depended on the *samurai* (literally, "those who serve"), skilled warriors who held land in return for military service to aristocratic lords—a system of local protection not unlike that of feudalism in the West. Outfitted with warhorses and elaborate armor made of iron plated with lacquer to protect against the rain (Figure **14.24**), and trained in the arts of archery and swordsmanship, the *samurai* were a class of warrior aristocrats. They upheld chivalric values similar to those of the European knight (see chapter 11) and embraced a code of conduct called *bushido* ("the way of the warrior"), which required selflessness in battle, fierce loyalty to one's superior, and a disdain for death. The code demanded ritual suicide, usually by disembowelment, for any *samurai* warrior who fell into dishonor. Not surprisingly, the sword was the distinctive symbol of this warrior class.

When the civil wars came to an end in 1192, the generals of the Minamoto clan became the rulers of Japan. They established the seat of their government at Kamakura, near modern Tokyo. Minamoto no Yoritomo (1147–1199) adopted the title of *shogun* ("general-in-chief") and set up a form of military dictatorship that ruled in the emperor's name. Yoritomo is pictured on a silk scroll in magnificent ceremonial dress, the stiff formality of which provides a startling contrast with the personalized features of the head and face (Figure **14.25**). The blend of naturalism and abstraction in this painting is typical of Japanese portraiture at its best. During the thirteenth century, Japanese sculptors—master woodcarvers—moved toward a more intense pictorial realism. The artist Jokei executed a series of painted wood temple guardians that reveal the Japanese fascination with the human figure in violent action (Figure **14.26**). These superhuman sentinels, with their taut muscles and their grimacing faces, direct their wrath toward those who would oppose the Buddhist law. By means of exaggeration and

Figure 14.25 Attributed to **FUJIWARA TAKANOBU**, *Minamoto no Yoritomo*, Kamakura period, second half of twelfth century. Ink and color on silk hanging scroll, height 4 ft. 6¾ in. Jingoji, Kyoto, Japan.

Figure 14.26 JOKEI, *Kongorikishi*, Kamakura period, ca. 1288. Painted wood, height 5 ft. 4 in. Kofukuji, Nara, Japan.

forthright detail, Jokei achieved a balletic union of martial-arts grace and *samurai* fierceness. The Kamakura shogunate remained the source of Japanese government only until 1333, but the values of the *samurai* prevailed well into modern times.

Nō Drama

Nō drama, the oldest form of Japanese theater, evolved from performances in dance, song, and mime popular in the Heian era and possibly even earlier. Like Greek drama, the Nō play treats serious themes drawn from a legacy of history and literature. Just as Sophocles recounted the history of Thebes, so Nō playwrights recalled the civil wars of the *samurai* and episodes from *The Tale of Genji*. Nō drama, however, was little concerned with character development or the realistic reenactment of actual events.

Rather, by means of a rigidly formalized selection of text, gestures, dance, and music (usually performed on flute and drum), the play explored a given story to expose its underlying meaning.

Nō plays—still flourishing in modern-day Japan—are performed on a square wooden stage that opens to the audience on three sides and is connected by a raised passageway to an offstage dressing room. Though roofed, the stage holds almost no scenery and that which does appear serves a symbolic function. As in ancient Greek drama, all roles are played by men. A chorus that sits at the side of the stage expresses the thoughts of the actors. Elegant costumes and masks, often magnificently carved and painted (Figure **14.27**), may be used to represent individual characters. This mask of a young woman reveals the classic Heian preference for the white-powdered face, plucked eyebrows, and blackened teeth—marks of high fashion among medieval Japanese females. A single program of Nō drama (which lasts some six hours) consists of a group of plays, with a selection from each of the play-types, such as god-plays, warrior-plays, and women-plays. Comic interludes are provided between them to lighten the serious mood.

The formalities of Nō drama were not set down until the early fifteenth century, when the playwright and actor Zeami Motokiyo (1363–1443) wrote an instructional manual for Nō actors. Zeami's manual, the *Kadensho*, prescribes demanding training exercises for the aspiring actor; it also analyzes the philosophic and aesthetic purposes of Nō theater. In the excerpt that follows, certain hallmarks of Japanese culture emerge, including a high regard for beauty of effect, an emphasis on refinement of form, and a melancholic sensitivity to the pathos of human life.

READING 2.27 From Zeami's *Kadensho* (ca. 1400)

Yūgen is considered to be the mark of supreme attainment in all of the arts and accomplishments. In the art of the Nō in particular the manifestation of *yūgen* is of the first importance. In general, a display of *yūgen* in the Nō is apparent to the eye, and it is the one thing which audiences most admire, but actors who possess *yūgen* are few and far between. This is because they do not in fact know the true meaning of *yūgen*. There are thus none who reach that stage.   **1**

    In what sort of place, then, is the stage of *yūgen* actually to be found? Let us begin by examining the various classes of   **10** people on the basis of the appearance that they make in society. May we not say of the courtiers, whose behavior is distinguished and whose appearance far surpasses that of other men, that theirs is the stage of *yūgen*? From this we may see that the essence of *yūgen* lies in a true state of beauty and gentleness. Tranquility and elegance make for *yūgen* in personal appearance. In the same way, the *yūgen* of discourse lies in a grace of language and a complete mastery of the speech of the nobility and gentry, so that even the most casual utterance will be graceful. With respect to a musical   **20** performance, it may be said to possess *yūgen* when the melody flows beautifully and sounds smooth and sensitive. In the dance there will be *yūgen* when the discipline has been thoroughly mastered and the audience is delighted by the beauty of the performer's movements and by his serene appearance. In acting, there will be *yūgen* when the performance of the Three Roles is beautiful. If the characterization calls for a display of anger or for the representation of a devil, the actions may be somewhat forceful, but as long as the actor never loses sight of the beauty of the effect and bears in mind always the correct balance between his mental and physical actions and between the movements of his body and feet, his appearance will be so beautiful that it may be called "the *yūgen* of a devil."

All these aspects of *yūgen* must be kept in mind and made a part of the actor's body, so that whatever part he may be playing *yūgen* will never be absent. . . . It is through the use of intelligence that the above principles are thoroughly grasped; that poetry is learned so as to impart *yūgen* to his discourse; that the most elegant costuming is studied so as to impart *yūgen* to his bearing: though the characterization varies according to the different parts, the actor should realize that the ability to appear beautiful is the seed of *yūgen*. It is all too apt to happen that an actor, believing that once he has mastered the characterization of the various parts he has attained the highest stage of excellence, forgets his appearances and therefore is unable to enter the realm of *yūgen*. Unless an actor enters the realm of *yūgen* he will not attain the highest achievements. If he fails to attain the highest achievements, he will not become a celebrated master. That is why there are so few masters. The actor must consider *yūgen* as the most important aspect of his art and study to perfect his understanding of it.

The "highest achievement" of which I have spoken refers to beauty of form and manners. The most careful attention must therefore be given to the appearance presented. Accordingly, when we thoroughly examine the principles of *yūgen* we see that when the form is beautiful, whether in dancing, singing, or in any type of characterization, it may properly be called the "highest achievement." When the form is poor, the performance will be inferior. The actor should realize that *yūgen* is attained when all of the different forms of visual or aural expression are beautiful. It is when the actor himself has worked out these principles and made himself their master that he may be said to have entered the realm of *yūgen*. If he fails to work out these principles for himself, he will not master them, and however much he may aspire to attain *yūgen*, he will never in all his life do so.

. . . .

Sometimes spectators of the Nō say, "The moments of 'no-action' are the most enjoyable." This is an art which the actor keeps secret. Dancing and singing, movements and the different types of miming are all acts performed by the body. Moments of "no-action" occur in between. When we examine why such moments without actions are enjoyable, we find that it is due to the underlying spiritual strength of the actor which unremittingly holds the attention. He does not relax the tension when the dancing or singing come to an end or at intervals between the dialogue and the different types of miming, but maintains an unwavering inner strength. This feeling of inner strength will faintly reveal itself and bring enjoyment. However, it is undesirable for the actor to permit this inner strength to become obvious to the audience. If it is obvious, it becomes an act, and is no longer "no-action." The actions before and after an interval of "no-action" must be linked by entering the state of mindlessness in which one conceals even from oneself one's intent. This, then, is the faculty of moving audiences, by linking all the artistic powers with one mind.

> Life and death, past and present—
> Marionettes on a toy stage.
> When the strings are broken,
> Behold the broken pieces.

This is a metaphor describing human life as it transmigrates between life and death. Marionettes on a stage appear to move in various ways, but in fact it is not they who really move—they are manipulated by strings. When these strings are broken, the marionettes fall and are dashed to pieces. In the art of the Nō too, the different sorts of miming are artificial things. What holds the parts together is the mind. This mind must not be disclosed to the audience. If it is seen, it is just as if a marionette's strings were visible. The mind must be made the strings which hold together all the powers of the arts. If this is done the actor's talent will endure. This resolution must not be confined to the times when the actor is appearing on the stage. Day or night, wherever he may be, whatever he may be doing, he should not forget this resolution, but should make it his constant guide, uniting all

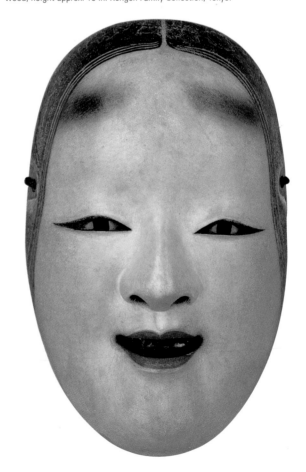

Figure 14.27 *Ko-omote* Nō mask, Ashikaga period, fifteenth century. Painted wood, height approx. 10 in. Kongoh Family Collection, Tokyo.

his powers. If he unremittingly works at this his talent will steadily grow. This article is the most secret of the secret teachings.... **110**

 Q What is *yūgen*? What role does it play in Japanese theater and culture?

SUMMARY

Between roughly 500 and 1300, India, China, and Japan produced arts and ideas that, although markedly different from those of the European West, contributed richly to the corpus of the humanistic tradition. Asian art of this period reveals a profound respect for the interdependence of natural and divine forces, of body and mind, and of matter and spirit. The sacred literature of Hinduism, as well as the rich fund of Sanskrit secular poetry, manifests a distinctly sensual approach to nature. In literature, architecture, and sculpture, the Hindu gods are identified with the creative, cyclical, and regenerative forces of the Absolute Spirit. The Hindu notion that nature and humankind belong to one and the same unifying, organic order differs sharply from the medieval Christian view that humankind is distinct and separate from both lower (animal) and higher (divine) forms of reality. In Indian visual art, as in Indian music and dance, the holistic view is expressed as a celebration of cyclical and natural universal rhythms.

The arts of China blossomed under the centralized leadership of the Tang and Song dynasties. Chinese religious philosophy—a synthesis of Buddhist, Confucian, and Daoist precepts—emphasized natural harmony and the unity of all living things. These concepts found sublime expression in Chinese poetry and landscape painting—

two of China's greatest contributions to world culture. The Chinese produced an elite class of scholar-officials and scholar-poets known as literati. China manufactured high-quality luxury goods and exported these to the rest of the world. Until at least the fourteenth century, China's technological and commercial achievements (such as the invention of printing, the magnetic compass, gunpowder, and the manufacture of magnificent porcelains and silks) far outstripped those of the West.

Japan's artistic record bears the stamp of Chinese culture. In the Heian period, however, a literary form unique to medieval Japan—the psychological novel—made its way into world literature. The samurai culture that began with the Kamakura shogunate and a rich heritage of Mahayana Buddhism played distinctive roles in the arts: the former commissioned magnificent weapons, armor, and palace portraiture, while the latter supported a flourishing industry in religious architecture and sculpture. The medieval Japanese preference for refined form and beauty of effect is illustrated in the visual arts, in literature, and perhaps most distinctively in Nō theater, the classic drama of Japan.

As modern forms of communication have worked to bring all parts of the world closer together, the Asian contributions to the humanistic tradition have gained greater recognition, better understanding, and deeper appreciation among Westerners.

MUSIC LISTENING SELECTIONS

CD One Selection 13 Indian music, *Thumri*, played on the sitar by Ravi Shankar.

CD One Selection 14 Chinese music: Cantonese music drama for male solo, zither, and other instruments, "Ngoh wai heng kong" ("I'm Mad About You").

GLOSSARY

alliteration a literary device involving the repetition of initial sounds in successive or closely associated words or syllables

assonance a literary device involving a similarity in sound between vowels followed by different consonants

avatar (Sanskrit, "incarnation") the incarnation of a Hindu deity

luohan (Chinese, "worthy one") a term for enlightened being, portrayed as a sage or mystic

mithuna the Hindu representation of a male and a female locked in passionate embrace

novel an extended fictional prose narrative

opera a drama set to music and making use of vocal pieces with orchestral accompaniment

porcelain a hard, translucent ceramic ware made from clay fired at high heat

raga a mode or melodic form in Hindu music; a specific combination of notes associated

with a particular mood or atmosphere

sitar a long-necked stringed instrument popular in Indian music

tala a set rhythmic formula in Hindu music

PART 1

The Age of the Renaissance

The three hundred years between 1300 and 1600 brought Western Europe out of the Middle Ages and onto the threshold of modernity. In economic life, manorialism succumbed to entrepreneurial capitalism. In political life, the medieval order gave way to centralized forms of government and the advent of national states. Ascendant individualism, secularism, and rationalism challenged devotional sentiment and religious fervor. The printing press made liberal education available to an increasingly literate population, while the science of navigation and advancing technology encouraged European expansion and cross-cultural contacts. By 1600, Europe would assume a dominant presence in parts of the world whose geography had only recently been mapped with any accuracy.

The Renaissance, or "rebirth" of classicism, was the cultural hinge between medieval and modern times. Originating in fourteenth-century Italy, and spreading northward during the fifteenth and sixteenth centuries, this dynamic movement shaped some of the West's most fundamental political, economic, and cultural values—values associated with the rise of nation-states, the formation of the middle class, and the advancement of classically based education and classically inspired art.

The fourteenth century was a period of transition marked by the struggle for survival against the devastating bubonic plague, the trials of a long and debilitating war between England and France, and the dramatic decline of the Roman Catholic Church. These events radically altered all aspects of Western European life and cultural expression. In the arts of this era there are distinct signs of a revived self-consciousness, increasing fidelity to nature, and a growing preoccupation with gender and class. But it was in Italy that the definitive aspect of the Renaissance—classical humanism—unfolded. Classical humanism—the movement to recover, study, and disseminate ancient Greek and Latin texts—stimulated a sense of individualism, a boundless vitality, and an optimistic view of the human potential for fulfillment on earth. The writings of Petrarch, Alberti, Pico, Castiglione, and Machiavelli are evidence of the Renaissance effort to apply classical precepts to matters of education, diplomacy, politics, and social life.

Renaissance artists looked to classical Greece and Rome as sources of aesthetic authority, but competed with their classical predecessors in the search for more scientific methods of describing the visual world. To portraiture and landscape painting, they brought keen objectivity; to monumental sculpture a sense of heroic individualism, and to architecture a new unity of design. The development of vernacular song forms, the rise of instrumental music, and the beginnings of choreography all mark the growing secularism of an age of rebirth.

(opposite) **AMBROGIO LORENZETTI**, *Effects of Good Government in the City and the Country*, from *The Allegory of Good Government*, 1338–1339, Sala della Pace, Palazzo Pubblico, Siena. © Quattrone, Florence.

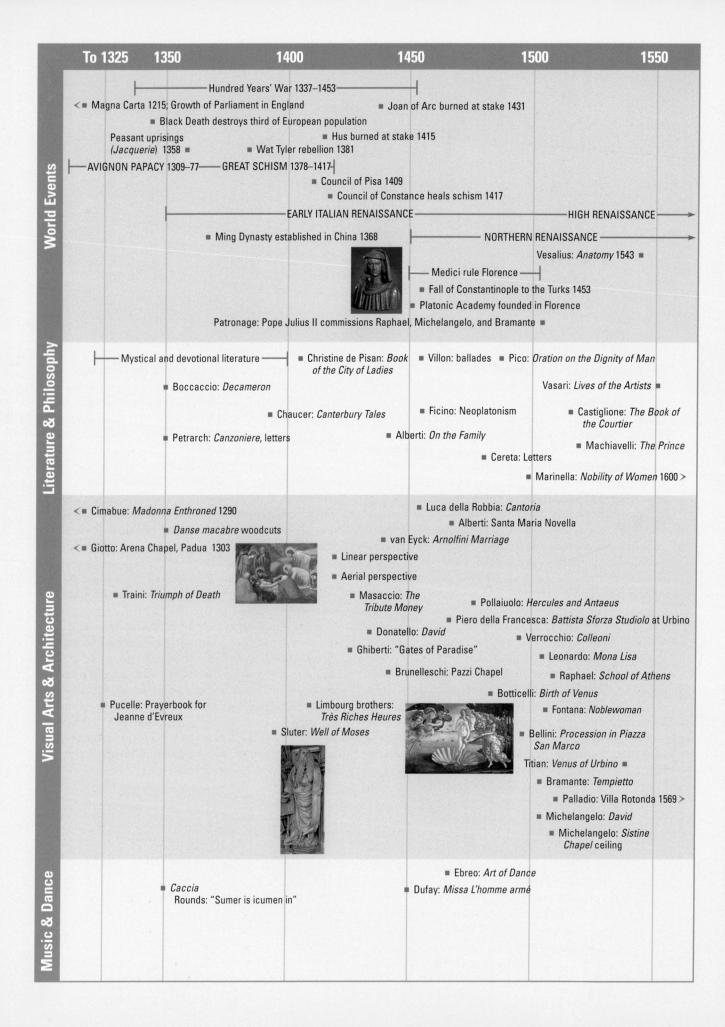

	To 1325	1350	1400	1450	1500	1550

World Events

Hundred Years' War 1337–1453

◄ ■ Magna Carta 1215; Growth of Parliament in England   ■ Joan of Arc burned at stake 1431

■ Black Death destroys third of European population

Peasant uprisings   ■ Hus burned at stake 1415
(Jacquerie) 1358 ■   ■ Wat Tyler rebellion 1381

├─ AVIGNON PAPACY 1309–77 ──── GREAT SCHISM 1378–1417 ─┤

■ Council of Pisa 1409

■ Council of Constance heals schism 1417

├──────── EARLY ITALIAN RENAISSANCE ────────   ──── HIGH RENAISSANCE ──→

■ Ming Dynasty established in China 1368   ├──── NORTHERN RENAISSANCE ────→

Vesalius: *Anatomy* 1543 ■

├── Medici rule Florence ──┤

■ Fall of Constantinople to the Turks 1453

■ Platonic Academy founded in Florence

Patronage: Pope Julius II commissions Raphael, Michelangelo, and Bramante ■

Literature & Philosophy

├── Mystical and devotional literature ──┤   ■ Christine de Pisan: *Book   ■ Villon: ballades   ■ Pico: *Oration on the Dignity of Man*
of the City of Ladies*

■ Boccaccio: *Decameron*   Vasari: *Lives of the Artists* ■

■ Chaucer: *Canterbury Tales*   ■ Ficino: Neoplatonism   ■ Castiglione: *The Book of
the Courtier*

■ Petrarch: *Canzoniere*, letters   ■ Alberti: *On the Family*   ■ Machiavelli: *The Prince*

■ Cereta: Letters

■ Marinella: *Nobility of Women* 1600 ►

Visual Arts & Architecture

◄ ■ Cimabue: *Madonna Enthroned* 1290   ■ Luca della Robbia: *Cantoria*

■ *Danse macabre* woodcuts   ■ Alberti: Santa Maria Novella

◄ ■ Giotto: Arena Chapel, Padua 1303   ■ van Eyck: *Arnolfini Marriage*

■ Linear perspective

■ Traini: *Triumph of Death*   ■ Aerial perspective

■ Masaccio: *The   ■ Pollaiuolo: *Hercules and Antaeus*
Tribute Money*

■ Piero della Francesca: *Battista Sforza Studiolo* at Urbino

■ Donatello: *David*   ■ Verrocchio: *Colleoni*

■ Ghiberti: "Gates of Paradise"   ■ Leonardo: *Mona Lisa*

■ Brunelleschi: Pazzi Chapel   ■ Raphael: *School of Athens*

■ Botticelli: *Birth of Venus*

■ Pucelle: Prayerbook for   ■ Limbourg brothers: ■ Fontana: *Noblewoman*
Jeanne d'Evreux   *Très Riches Heures*

■ Sluter: *Well of Moses*   ■ Bellini: *Procession in Piazza
San Marco*

Titian: *Venus of Urbino* ■

■ Bramante: *Tempietto*

■ Palladio: Villa Rotonda 1569 ►

■ Michelangelo: *David*

■ Michelangelo: *Sistine
Chapel* ceiling

Music & Dance

■ Ebreo: *Art of Dance*

■ *Caccia*   ■ Dufay: *Missa L'homme armé*
Rounds: "Sumer is icumen in"

CHAPTER 15

Adversity and Challenge: The Fourteenth-Century Transition

"So many bodies were brought to the churches every day that the consecrated ground did not suffice to hold them . . ."
Boccaccio

Traditions normally undergo modification only over long periods of time. However, natural disasters, epidemic disease, and protracted warfare generally accelerate cultural change. The fourteenth century provides a case in point, for during that dramatic time all of these catalytic phenomena occurred in Western Europe, causing widespread havoc and wrenching medieval customs and practices out of their steady, dependable rhythms. As a result, the period between roughly 1300 and 1400 became a time of transition between medieval and early modern history. During this age, many medieval traditions were revised or discarded and new cultural patterns contributed to the formation of a modern world system dominated by the rise of the West.

The Black Death

The most devastating natural catastrophe of the early modern era was the bubonic plague, which struck Europe in 1347 and destroyed one third to one half of its population within less than a century. Originating in Asia and spread by the Mongol tribes that dominated that vast area, the disease devastated China and the Middle East, interrupting long-distance trade and cross-cultural encounters that had flourished for two centuries. The plague was carried into Europe by flea-bearing black rats infesting the commercial vessels that brought goods to Mediterranean ports. Within two years of its arrival it ravaged much of the Western world. In its early stages, it was transmitted by the bite of either the infected flea or the host rat; in its more severe stages, it was passed on by those infected with the disease. The symptoms of the malady were terrifying: buboes (or abscesses) that began in the lymph glands of the groin or armpits of the afflicted slowly filled with pus, turning the body a deathly black, hence the popular label "the Black Death." Once the boils and accompanying fever

appeared, death usually followed within two to three days. Traditional treatments, such as the bleeding of victims and fumigation with vapors of vinegar, proved useless. No connection was perceived between the ubiquitous rats and the plague itself, and in the absence of a clinical understanding of bacterial infection, the medical profession of the day was helpless. (Indeed, the bacillus of the bubonic plague was not isolated until 1894.)

The plague hit hardest in the towns, where the concentration of population and the lack of sanitation made the disease all the more difficult to contain. Four waves of bubonic plague spread throughout Europe between 1347 and 1375, infecting some European cities several times and nearly wiping out their entire populations (Figure **15.1**). The virulence of the plague and the mood of mounting despair horrified the Florentine writer Giovanni Boccaccio (1313–1375). In his preface to the *Decameron*, a collection of tales told by ten young people who abandoned plague-ridden Florence for the safety of a country estate, Boccaccio described the physical conditions of the pestilence, as well as its psychological consequences. He recorded with somber precision how widespread death had forced Florentine citizens to abandon the traditional forms of grieving and the rituals associated with death and burial. The stirring vernacular prose captured the mood of dread that prevailed in Florence, as people fled their cities, homes, and even their families.

READING 3.1 From Boccaccio's Introduction to the *Decameron* (1351)

In the year of Our Lord 1348 the deadly plague broke out in the great city of Florence, most beautiful of Italian cities. Whether through the operation of the heavenly bodies or because of our own iniquities which the just wrath of God sought to correct, the plague had arisen in the East some years before, causing the death of countless human beings. It spread without stop from one

1

place to another, until, unfortunately, it swept over the West. Neither knowledge nor human foresight availed against it, though the city was cleansed of much filth by chosen officers in charge and sick persons were forbidden to enter it, while advice was broadcast for the preservation of health. Nor did humble supplications serve. Not once but many times they were ordained in the form of processions and other ways for the propitiation of God by the faithful, but, in spite of everything, toward the spring of the year the plague began to show its ravages in a way short of miraculous.

It did not manifest itself as in the East, where if a man bled at the nose he had certain warning of inevitable death. At the onset of the disease both men and women were afflicted by a sort of swelling in the groin or under the armpits which sometimes attained the size of a common apple or egg. Some of these swellings were larger and some smaller, and all were commonly called boils. From these two starting points the boils began in a little while to spread and appear generally all over the body. Afterwards, the manifestation of the disease changed into black or livid spots on the arms, thighs and the whole person. In many these blotches were large and far apart, in others small and closely clustered. Like the boils, which had been and continued to be a certain indication of coming death, these blotches had the same meaning for everyone on whom they appeared.

Neither the advice of physicians nor the virtue of any medicine seemed to help or avail in the cure of these diseases. Indeed, whether the nature of the malady did not suffer it, or whether the ignorance of the physicians could not determine the source and therefore could take no preventive measures against it, the fact was that not only did few recover, but on the contrary almost everyone died within three days of the appearance of the signs—some sooner, some later, and the majority without fever or other ill. Moreover, besides the qualified medical men, a vast number of quacks, both men and women, who had never studied medicine, joined the ranks and practiced cures. The virulence of the plague was all the greater in that it was communicated by the sick to the well by contact, not unlike fire when dry or fatty things are brought near it. But the evil was still worse. Not only did conversation and familiarity with the diseased spread the malady and even cause death, but the mere touch of the clothes or any other object the sick had touched or used, seemed to spread the pestilence. . . .

Because of such happenings and many others of a like sort, various fears and superstitions arose among the survivors, almost all of which tended toward one end—to flee from the sick and whatever had belonged to them. In this way each man thought to be safeguarding his own health. Some among them were of the opinion that by living temperately and guarding against excess of all kinds, they could do much toward avoiding the danger; and forming a band they lived away from the rest of the world. Gathering in those houses where no one had been ill and living was more comfortable, they shut themselves in. They ate moderately of the best that could be had and

drank excellent wines, avoiding all luxuriousness. With music and whatever other delights they could have, they lived together in this fashion, allowing no one to speak to them and avoiding news either of death or sickness from the outer world.

Others, arriving at a contrary conclusion, held that plenty of drinking and enjoyment, singing and free living and the gratification of the appetite in every possible way, letting the devil take the hindmost, was the best preventative of such a malady; and as far as they could, they suited the action to the word. Day and night they went from one tavern to another drinking and carousing unrestrainedly. At the least inkling of something that suited them, they ran wild in other people's houses, and there was no one to prevent them, for everyone had abandoned all responsibility for his belongings as well as for himself, considering his days numbered. Consequently most of the houses had become common property and strangers would make use of them at will whenever they came upon them even as the rightful owners might have done. Following this uncharitable way of thinking, they did their best to run away from the infected.

Meanwhile, in the midst of the affliction and misery that had befallen the city, even the reverend authority of divine and human law had almost crumbled and fallen into decay, for its ministers and executors, like other men, had either died or sickened, or had been left so entirely without assistants that they were unable to attend to their duties. As a result everyone had leave to do as he saw fit.

[Others, in an effort to escape the plague, abandoned the city, their houses, their possessions, and their relatives.] The calamity had instilled such horror into the hearts of men and women that brother abandoned brother, uncles, sisters and wives left their dear ones to perish, and, what is more serious and almost incredible, parents avoided visiting or nursing their very children, as though these were not their own flesh. . . . So great was the multitude of those who died in the city night and day, what with lack of proper care and the virulence of the plague, that it was terrible to hear of, and worse still to see. Out of sheer necessity, therefore, quite different customs arose among the survivors from the original laws of the townspeople.

It used to be common, as it is still, for women, friends and neighbors of a dead man, to gather in his house and mourn there with his people, while his men friends and many other citizens collected with his nearest of kin outside the door. Then came the clergy, according to the standing of the departed, and with funereal pomp of tapers and singing he was carried on the shoulders of his peers to the church he had elected before death. Now, as the plague gained in violence, these customs were either modified or laid aside altogether, and new ones were instituted in their place, so that, far from dying among a crowd of women mourners, many passed away without the benefit of a single witness. Indeed, few were those who received the piteous wails and bitter tears of friends and relatives, for often, instead of mourning, laughter, jest and carousal accompanied the dead—usages which even

Figure 15.1 *The Black Death*, miniature from a rhymed Latin chronicle of the events of 1349–1352 by Egidius, abbot of Saint Martin's, Tournai, France, ca. 1355. Manuscript illumination. Bibliothèque Royale, Brussels. MS13076–77, f.24v.

naturally compassionate women had learned to perfection for their health's sake. It was a rare occurrence for a corpse to be followed to church by more than ten or twelve mourners—not the usual respectable citizens, but a class of vulgar grave-diggers who called themselves "sextons" and did these services for a price. They crept under the bier and shouldered it, and then with hasty steps rushed it, not to the church the deceased had designated before death, but oftener than not to the nearest one. . . . 130

More wretched still were the circumstances of the common people and, for a great part, of the middle class, for, confined to their homes either by hope of safety or by poverty, and restricted to their own sections, they fell sick daily by thousands. There, devoid of help or care, they died almost without redemption. A great many breathed their last in the public streets, day and night; a large number perished in their homes, and it was only by the stench of their decaying bodies that they proclaimed their death to their neighbors. Everywhere the city was teeming with corpses. A general course was now adopted by the people, more out of fear of contagion than of any charity they felt toward the dead. Alone, or with the assistance of whatever bearers they could muster, they would drag the corpses out of their homes and pile them in front of the doors, where often, of a morning, countless bodies might be seen. Biers were sent for. When none was to be had, the dead were laid upon ordinary boards, two or three at once. It was not infrequent to see a single bier carrying husband and wife, two or three brothers, father and son, and others besides. . . . 140

150

So many bodies were brought to the churches every day that the consecrated ground did not suffice to hold them, particularly according to the ancient custom of giving each corpse its individual place. Huge trenches were dug in the crowded churchyards and the new dead were piled in them, layer upon layer, like merchandise in the hold of a ship. A little earth covered the corpses of each row, and the procedure continued until the trench was filled to the top. 160

Q What aspects of Boccaccio's Introduction to the *Decameron* reflect a shift to realism in prose literature?

Q Are there any modern analogies to the pandemic that Boccaccio describes?

The Effects of the Black Death

Those who survived the plague tried to fathom its meaning and purpose. Some viewed it as the manifestation of God's displeasure with the growing worldliness of contemporary society, while others saw it as a divine warning to all Christians, but especially to the clergy, whose profligacy and moral laxity were commonly acknowledged facts. Those who perceived the plague as God's scourge urged a return to religious orthodoxy, and some devised fanatic kinds of atonement. Groups of flagellants, for instance, wandered the countryside lashing their bodies with whips in frenzies of self-mortification. At the other extreme, there were many who resolved to "eat, drink, and be merry" in what might be the last hours of their lives; while still others, in a spirit of doubt and inquiry, questioned the very existence of a god who could work such evils on humankind.

The abandonment of the church-directed rituals of funeral and burial described by Boccaccio threatened tradition and shook the confidence of medieval Christians. Inevitably, the old medieval regard for death as a welcome release from earthly existence began to give way to a gnawing sense of anxiety and a new self-consciousness. Some of these changes are mirrored in the abundance of death-related pictorial images, including purgatorial visions and gruesome depictions of death and burial, that appeared during the century of the Black Death. Of all the plague-related themes depicted in the arts, the most popular was the "Dance of Death," or *danse macabre*. Set forth in both poetry and the visual arts, the Dance of Death portrayed death as a grinning skeleton or cadaver shepherding a parade of his victims to the grave (Figure **15.2**). The procession (which might have originated in conjunction with popular dances) included men, women, and children from all walks of life and social classes: peasants and kings, schoolmasters and merchants, priests and nuns—all succumb to Death's ravishment. The Dance of Death objectified the new regard for death as "the Great Equalizer," that is, as an impartial phenomenon threatening every individual, regardless of status or wealth. This vulnerability of humankind is a prevailing motif in fourteenth- and fifteenth-century verse. Note, for example, these lines written by François Villon (1431–ca. 1463), the greatest French poet of his time.

> I know this well, that rich and poor
> Fools, sages, laymen, friars in cowl,
> Large-hearted lords and each mean boor,[1]
> Little and great and fair and foul,
> Ladies in lace, who smile or scowl,
> From whatever stock they stem,
> Hatted or hooded, prone to prowl,
> Death seizes every one of them.

Figure 15.2 HANS HOLBEIN THE YOUNGER, *Dance of Death*, ca. 1490. Woodcut. Library of Congress, Washington, D.C. Lessing J. Rosenwald Collection.

[1]Peasant; a rude and illiterate person.

The theme of the Dance of Death captured the imagination of fourteenth-century artists and appeared in almost every medium of expression, including woodcut and engraving, for two centuries thereafter. In the medieval morality play *Everyman* (see chapter 12), Death is a powerful antagonist. But in visual representations, he assumes subtle guises—ruler, predator, and seducer—and is a sly and cajoling figure who mocks the worldly pursuits of his unsuspecting victims.

If the psychological impact of the Black Death was traumatic, its economic effects were equally devastating. Widespread death among the poor caused a shortage of labor, which in turn created a greater demand for workers. The bargaining power of those who survived the plague was thus improved. In many parts of Europe, workers pressed to raise their status and income. Peasants took advantage of opportunities to become tenant farmers on lands leased by lords in need of laborers. Others fled their rural manors for cities where jobs were readily available. This exodus from the countryside spurred urban growth and contributed to the slow disintegration of manorialism.

All of Europe, however, was disadvantaged by the climatic disasters that caused frequent crop failure and famine, and by the continuing demands of financially threatened feudal overlords. Violent working-class revolts—the first examples of labor rebellion in Western history—broke out in France and England in the mid-fourteenth century. In 1358, French peasants (known as *jacques*) staged an angry protest (the *Jacquerie*) that took the lives of hundreds of noblemen before it was suppressed by the French king. In England, the desperation of the poor was manifested in the Peasants' Revolt of 1381, led by Wat Tyler and described in the *Chronicles* of the French historian Jean Froissart (1338–1410). Despite their ultimate failure, these revolts left their imprint on the social history of the West. They frightened landowners everywhere and lent an instability to class relationships that hastened the demise of the old feudal order.

Europe in Transition

The Rise of Constitutional Monarchy

While the peasant rebellions achieved no immediate reforms, the lower classes had taken a major step toward demanding equality with the rest of society. England's laborers were not the first, however, to have contested the absolute authority of the English monarch. As early as the year 1215, the barons of the realm had forced King John of England (1167–1216) to sign the landmark document called the Magna Carta (Latin, meaning "great charter"), which forbade the king to levy additional feudal taxes without the consent of his royal council. The Magna Carta, which was also interpreted as guaranteeing such other freedoms as trial by jury, asserted the primacy of law over the will of the ruler—a principle that paved the way for the development of constitutional monarchy.

Only fifty years after the signing of the Magna Carta, the English nobility, demanding equal authority in ruling

Figure 15.3 *The End of the Siege of Ribodane: English Soldiers Take a French Town*, late fifteenth century. Manuscript illumination. Note longbow and light cannon. By permission of the British Library, London. MS Roy.14.E.IV, f.281v.

England, imprisoned King Henry III (1207–1272) and invited middle-class representatives to participate in the actions of the Great Council (Parliament), thus initiating the first example of representative government among the burgeoning nation-states of the West. During the fourteenth century, as Parliament met frequently to raise taxes for England's wars with France, it bargained for greater power, including the right to initiate legislation. Peasants and laborers still exercised no real political influence, but by the end of the century the English had laid the groundwork for a constitutional monarchy that would bridge the gap between medieval feudalism and modern democracy.

The Hundred Years' War

In France, the ills of plague, famine, and civil disturbance were compounded by a war with England that lasted more than one hundred years (1337–1453) and that was fought entirely on French soil. Larger and more protracted than any previous medieval conflict, the Hundred Years' War was the result of a longstanding English claim to continental lands: from the time of the Norman Conquest, the

kings of England had held land in France, a situation that caused chronic resentment among the French. But the immediate cause of the war was the English claim to the French throne, occasioned by the death of Charles IV (1294–1328), the last of the male heirs in a long line of French kings that had begun with Hugh Capet in 987.

The war that began in 1337 was marked by intermittent battles, in many of which the French outnumbered the English by three or four to one. Nevertheless, the English won most of the early battles of the war, owing to their use of three new "secret" weapons: the foot soldier, the longbow, and gunpowder—the invisible enemy that would ultimately eliminate the personal element in military combat. Along with the traditional cavalry, the English army depended heavily on foot soldiers armed with longbows (Figure **15.3**). The thin, steel-tipped arrows of the 6-foot longbow could be fired more quickly and at a longer range than those of the traditional crossbow. Because the thin arrows of the longbow easily pierced the finest French chain mail, plate mail soon came to replace chain mail. However, within the next few centuries, even plate mail

Science and Technology

1300s	mechanical clocks appear in Europe
1346	gunpowder and longbows are utilized by the English army at the Battle of Crécy
1370	the steel crossbow is adopted as a weapon of war

became obsolete, since it proved useless against artillery that employed gunpowder.

Introduced into Europe by the Muslims, who acquired it from the Chinese, gunpowder was first used in Western combat during the Hundred Years' War. In the first battle of the war, however, the incendiary substance proved too potent for the poorly cast English cannons, which issued little more than terrifying noise. Still, gunpowder, which could lay waste a city, constituted an extraordinary advance in military technology, one that ultimately outmoded hand-to-hand combat and rendered obsolete the medieval code of chivalry. Froissart's account of the Hundred Years' War—which reads like a Crusade chronicle—glorifies the performance of chivalric deeds, even though many of the methods of combat Froissart describes clearly anticipate a new era. For instance, because the English were greatly outnumbered by the French, they resorted to ambush, thus violating medieval rules of war. It can be said, then, that the Hundred Years' War inaugurated the impersonal style of combat that has come to dominate modern warfare.

Throughout the Hundred Years' War the English repeatedly devastated the French armies; nevertheless, the financial and physical burdens of garrisoning French lands ultimately proved too great for the English. Facing a revitalized army under the charismatic leadership of Joan of Arc, England finally withdrew from France in 1450. Of peasant background, the seventeen-year-old Joan begged the French king to allow her to obey the voices of the Christian saints who had directed her to expel the English (Figure **15.4**). Donning armor and riding a white horse, she led the French into battle. Her success forced the English to withdraw from Orléans, but initiated her martyrdom. Betrayed by her supporters in 1431, she was condemned as a heretic and burned at the stake.

The Hundred Years' War dealt a major blow to feudalism. By the mid-fifteenth century, the French nobility was badly depleted, and those knights who survived the war found themselves "outdated." In France, feudal allegiances were soon superseded by systems of national conscription, and in the decades following the English withdrawal, both countries were ready to move in separate directions, politically and culturally.

The Decline of the Church

The growth of the European nation-states contributed to the weakening of the Christian commonwealth, especially where Church and state competed for influence and authority. The two events that proved most damaging to the prestige of the Catholic Church were the Avignon

Papacy (1309–1377) and the Great Schism (1378–1417). The term "Avignon Papacy" describes the relocation of the papacy from Rome to the city of Avignon in Southern France (see Map 16.1) in response to political pressure from the French king Philip IV ("the Fair"). Attempting to compete in prestige and political influence with the secular rulers of Europe, the Avignon popes established a luxurious and powerful court, using stringent (and occasionally corrupt) means to accomplish their purpose. The increasing need for Church revenue led some of the Avignon popes to sell Church office (a practice known as **simony**), to levy additional taxes upon clergymen, to elect members of their own families to ecclesiastical office, and to step up the sale of **indulgences** (pardons from temporal penalties for sins committed by lay Christians). From the twelfth century on, the Church had sold these certificates of grace—drawn from the "surplus" of good works left by the saints—to lay Christians who bought them as a means of speeding their own progress to Heaven or to benefit their relatives and friends in Purgatory. While the seven popes who ruled from Avignon were able administrators, their unsavory efforts at financial and political aggrandizement damaged the reputation of the Church.

The return of the papacy to Rome in 1377 was followed by one of the most devastating events in Church history: a rift between French and Italian factions of the College of Cardinals led to the election of two popes, one who ruled from Avignon, the other from Rome. This schism produced two conflicting claims to universal sovereignty and violent controversy within the Church. As each pope excommunicated the other, lay people questioned whether any Christian soul might enter Heaven. The Great Schism proved even more detrimental to Church prestige than the Avignon Papacy, for while the latter had prompted strong anticlerical feelings—even shock—in Christians who regarded Rome as the traditional home of the papacy, the Schism violated the very sanctity of the Holy Office. The ecumenical council at Pisa in 1409 tried to remedy matters by deposing both popes and electing another (the "Pisan pope"), but, when the popes at Rome and Avignon refused to step down, the Church was rent by *three* claims to the throne of Christ, a disgraceful situation that lasted for almost a decade.

Anticlericalism and the Rise of Devotional Piety

In 1417, the Council of Constance healed the Schism, authorizing Pope Martin V to rule from Rome, but ecclesiastical discord continued. Fifteenth-century popes refused to acknowledge limits to papal power, thus hampering the efforts of church councils to exercise authority over the papacy. The Avignon Papacy and the Great Schism drew criticism from uneducated Christians and intellectuals alike. Two of the most vocal Church critics were the Oxford scholar John Wycliffe (ca. 1330–1384) and the Czech preacher Jan Hus (ca. 1373–1415). Wycliffe and Hus attacked papal power and wealth. They called for the abolition of pilgrimages and relic worship, insisting that Christian belief and practice must rest solidly in

Figure 15.4 Joan of Arc, from **ANTOINE DUFOUR'S** *Lives of Famous Women*, 1504. French manuscript. Musée Dobrée, Nantes, France. MS 17, f. 176. Photo: Bridgeman Art Library.

the Scriptures, which they sought to translate into the vernacular. The Church vigorously condemned Wycliffe and his bands of followers, who were called Lollards. Hus stood trial for heresy and was burned at the stake in 1415. Disenchanted with the institutional Church, lay Christians increasingly turned to private forms of devotional piety and to mysticism—the effort to know God directly and intuitively.

Popular mysticism challenged the authority of the institutional Church and threatened its corporate hold over Catholicism. Throughout the Middle Ages, mystics— many of whom came from the cloister—had voiced their passionate commitment to Christ. The twelfth-century mystic Hildegard of Bingen (see chapter 12), whose visionary interpretations of Scripture were intensely personal, received the approval of the institutional Church.

By the thirteenth century, however, as churchmen sought to centralize authority in the hands of male ecclesiastics, visionary literature was looked upon with some suspicion. The Church condemned the lyrical descriptions of divine love penned by the thirteenth-century mystic Marguerite of Porete, for instance, and Marguerite herself was burned at the stake in 1310. Nonetheless, during the fourteenth century a flood of mystical and devotional literature engulfed Europe. The writings of the great fourteenth-century German mystics Johannes Eckhart (ca. 1260–1327) and Heinrich Suso, of the English Julian of Norwich (1342–ca. 1416), and of the Swedish Saint Bridget (ca. 1303–1373) describe—in language that is at once intimate and ecstatic—the heightened personal experience of God. Such writings—the expression of pious individualism—mark an important shift from the scholastic reliance on religious authority to modern assertions of faith based on inner conviction.

Literature in Transition

The Social Realism of Boccaccio

Fourteenth-century Europeans manifested an unprecedented preoccupation with differences in class, gender, and personality. Both in literature and in art, there emerged a new fidelity to nature and to personal experience in the everyday world. This close, objective attention to human society and social interaction may be described as "social realism." The new realism is evident in the many woodcuts of the Dance of Death (see Figure 15.2), where class differences are clearly drawn, and in the one hundred lively vernacular tales that make up Boccaccio's *Decameron* (part of the preface to which appeared earlier in this chapter). The framework for the *Decameron* is provided by the plague itself: eager to escape the contagion, seven young women and three young men retreat to a villa in the suburbs of Florence, where, to pass the time, each tells a story on each of ten days. The stories, designed as distractions from the horrors of the pandemic, are, in effect, amusing secular entertainments. They provide insight, however, into the social concerns and values of both the fictional narrators and Boccaccio's reading public.

Boccaccio borrowed many stories in the *Decameron* from popular fables, *fabliaux* (humorous narrative tales), and contemporary incidents. His characters resemble neither the allegorical figures of *Everyman* nor the courtly stereotypes of *Lancelot*. Rather, they are realistically conceived, high-spirited individuals who prize cleverness, good humor, and the world of the flesh over the classic medieval virtues of chivalry, piety, and humility. A case in point is the "Tale of Filippa," a delightful story that recounts how a woman from the Italian town of Prato shrewdly escapes legal punishment for committing adultery. The heroine, Madame Filippa, candidly confesses that she has a lover; however, she bitterly protests the city ordinance that serves a double standard of justice: one law for men, another for women. Filippa's proposal that women should not waste the passions unclaimed by their husbands but, rather, be allowed to enjoy the

"surplus" with others—a view that might enlist the support of modern-day feminists—rings with good-humored defiance. Boccaccio's Filippa strikes a sharp note of contrast with the clinging heroines of the medieval romance. While Guinevere, for instance, wallows in longing for Lancelot (see Reading 2.15), Filippa boldly defends her right to sexual independence. Like many a male protagonist, she fearlessly challenges and exploits fortune to serve her own designs.

The *Decameron* must have had special appeal for men and women who saw themselves as the heroes and heroines of precarious and rapidly changing times. Toward the end of his life, Boccaccio repented writing what he himself called his "immoral tales;" nevertheless, his stories, as the following example illustrates, remain a lasting tribute to the varieties of human affection and desire.

READING 3.2 From Boccaccio's "Tale of Filippa" from the *Decameron*

(1351)

Once upon a time, in the town of Prato, there used to be a law in force—as pernicious, indeed, as it was cruel, to the effect that any woman caught by her husband in the act of adultery with a lover, was to be burned alive, like any vulgar harlot who sold herself for money.

While this statute prevailed, a beautiful lady called Filippa, a devout worshiper of Cupid, was surprised in her bedroom one night by her husband, Rinaldo de' Pugliesi, in the arms of Lazzarino de' Guazzagliotri, a high-born Adonis of a youth of that city, whom she loved as the apple of her eye. 10

Burning with rage at the discovery, Rinaldo could scarcely forbear running upon them, and slaying them on the spot. Were it not for the misgivings he had for his own safety, if he gave vent to his wrath, he would have followed his impulse. However, he controlled his evil intent, but could not abandon his desire to demand of the town's statute, what it was unlawful for him to bring about—in other words, the death of his wife.

As he had no lack of evidence to prove Filippa's guilt, 20 he brought charges against her, early in the morning, at daybreak, and without further deliberation, had her summoned before the court.

Now Filippa was a high-spirited woman, as all women are who truly love, and though many of her friends and relatives advised her against going, she resolved to appear before the magistrate, preferring a courageous death, by confessing the truth, to a shameful life of exile, by a cowardly flight that would have proved her unworthy of the lover in whose arms she had lain that night. 30

Accordingly, she presented herself before the provost, with a large following of men and women who urged her to deny the charges. She asked him firmly and without moving a muscle what he desired of her. The provost, seeing her so beautiful, courteous and so brave—as her words demonstrated—felt a certain pity stirring in his heart at the thought that she might confess a crime for which he would be obliged to sentence her to death to save his honor. But then, seeing he could not avoid cross-questioning her on the charge proffered against her, he said:

"Madam, here as you see, is Rinaldo, your husband, who is suing you on the grounds of finding you in the act of adultery with another man, and who therefore demands that I sentence you to death for it, as the law, which is in force, requires. I cannot pass sentence if you do not confess your guilt with your own lips. Be careful of your answers, then, and tell me if what your husband charges you with is true."

Filippa, not at all daunted, replied in a very agreeable voice: "Your honor, it is true that Rinaldo is my husband, and that last night he found me in the arms of Lazzarino, where I had lain many another time, out of the great and true love I bear him. Far be it from me ever to deny it.

"As you are doubtless aware, laws should be equal for all, and should be made with the consent of those whom they affect. Such is not the case with this particular statute, which is stringent only with us poor women, who, after all, have it in our power to give pleasure to many more people than men ever could. Moreover, when this law was drawn up, not a single woman gave her consent or was so much as invited to give it. For all these reasons, it surely deserves to be considered reprehensible. If you insist upon enforcing it, not at the risk of my body, but of your immortal soul, you are at liberty to do so; but before you proceed to pass judgment, I beg you to grant me a small request. Simply ask my husband whether I have ever failed to yield myself to him entirely, whenever he chose, and as often as he pleased."

Without waiting for the magistrate to question him, Rinaldo immediately answered that there was no doubt Filippa had always granted him the joy of her body, at each and every request of his.

"That being the case, your honor," she went on, directly, "I'd like to ask him, since he has always had all he wanted of me and to his heart's content, what was I to do with all that was left over? Indeed, what am I to do with it? Throw it to the dogs? Isn't it far better to let it give enjoyment to some gentleman who loves me more than his life, than to let it go to waste or ruin?"

As it happened, the whole town had turned out to attend the sensational trial that involved a lady of such beauty and fame, and when the people heard her roguish question, they burst into a roar of laughter, shouting to a man that she was right and had spoken well.

That day, before court was adjourned, that harsh statute was modified at the magistrate's suggestion to hold only for such women as made cuckolds of their husbands for love of money.

As for Rinaldo, he went away crest-fallen at his mad venture, while Filippa returned home victorious, feeling in her joy that she had, in a sense, been delivered from the flames.

 Q How does Boccaccio's tale illustrate new attitudes toward women in Italian society?

The Feminism of Christine de Pisan

Just decades after Boccaccio took the woman's view in the "Tale of Filippa," the world's first feminist writer, Christine de Pisan (1364–1428?), emerged in France. The daughter of an Italian physician, Christine wedded a French nobleman when she was fifteen—medieval women usually married in their mid to late teens. Ten years later, when her husband died, Christine was left to support three children, a task she met by becoming the first female professional writer (Figure 15.5). Christine attacked the long antifemale tradition that had demeaned women and denied them the right to a university education. Her feminism is all the more significant because it occurred in a time in which men were making systematic efforts to restrict female inheritance of land and female membership in the guilds. In an early poem, the "Epistle to the God of Love" (1399), she protested the persistent antifemale bias of churchmen and scholars with these words:

> Some say that many women are deceitful,
> Wily, false, of little worth;
> Others that too many are liars,
> Fickle, flighty, and inconstant;
> Still others accuse them of great vices,
> Blaming them much, excusing them nothing,
> Thus do clerics, night and day,

Figure 15.5 *Christine de Pisan at Her Writing Desk*, frontispiece to Christine's *Livre de la Mutacion de Fortune*, early fifteenth century. Bibliothèque Royale, Brussels. MS9508, f.2r.

First in French verse, then in Latin,
Based on who knows what books
That tell more lies than drunkards do.

Christine was keenly aware of the fact that Western literary tradition did not offer a representative picture of women's importance to society. Eager to correct this inequity, she became a spokesperson for female achievements and talents. In her *Book of the City of Ladies*, Christine attacks male misogyny and exalts the accomplishments of famous women throughout the ages. Patterned as an allegorical debate, *The City of Ladies* pictures Christine herself "interviewing" three goddesses—Lady Reason, Lady Rectitude, and Lady Justice—as she seeks moral guidance on matters such as whether women can and should be educated in the same manner as men (I.27) and why men claim it is not good for women to be educated at all (II.36). Excerpts from these two portions of Christine's landmark feminist work follow.

READING 3.3　From Christine de Pisan's *Book of the City of Ladies* (1405)

Book I. 27 Christine Asks Reason Whether God Has Ever Wished to Ennoble the Mind of Woman With the Loftiness of the Sciences; and Reason's Answer.

. . . please enlighten me again, whether it has ever pleased this God, who has bestowed so many favors on women, to honor the feminine sex with the privilege of the virtue of high understanding and great learning, and whether women ever have a clever enough mind for this. I wish very much to know this because men maintain that the mind of women can learn only a little."

She answered, "My daughter, since I told you before, you know quite well that the opposite of their opinion is true, and to show you this even more clearly, I will give you proof through examples. I tell you again—and don't doubt the contrary—if it were customary to send daughters to school like sons, and if they were then taught the natural sciences, they would learn as thoroughly and understand the subtleties of all the arts and sciences as well as sons. And by chance there happen to be such women, for, as I touched on before, just as women have more delicate bodies than men, weaker and less able to perform many tasks, so do they have minds that are freer and sharper whenever they apply themselves."

"My lady, what are you saying? With all due respect, could you dwell longer on this point, please. Certainly men would never admit this answer is true, unless it is explained more plainly, for they believe that one normally sees that men know more than women do."

She answered, "Do you know why women know less?"

"Not unless you tell me, my lady."

"Without the slightest doubt, it is because they are not involved in many different things, but stay at home, where it is enough for them to run the household, and there is nothing which so instructs a reasonable creature as the exercise and experience of many different things."

"My lady, since they have minds skilled in conceptualizing and learning, just like men, why don't women learn more?"

She replied, "Because, my daughter, the public does not require them to get involved in the affairs which men are commissioned to execute, just as I told you before. It is enough for women to perform the usual duties to which they are ordained. As for judging from experience, since one sees that women usually know less than men, that therefore their capacity for understanding is less, look at men who farm the flatlands or who live in the mountains. You will find that in many countries they seem completely savage because they are so simple-minded. All the same, there is no doubt that Nature provided them with the qualities of body and mind found in the wisest and most learned men. All of this stems from a failure to learn, though, just as I told you, among men and women, some possess better minds than others. . . .

Book II. 36 Against Those Men Who Claim It Is Not Good for Women to Be Educated.

Following these remarks, I, Christine, spoke, "My lady, I realize that women have accomplished many good things and that even if evil women have done evil, it seems to me, nevertheless, that the benefits accrued and still accruing because of good women—particularly the wise and literary ones and those educated in the natural science whom I mentioned above—outweigh the evil. Therefore, I am amazed by the opinion of some men who claim that they do not want their daughters, wives, or kinswomen to be educated because their mores[1] would be ruined as a result."

She responded, "Here you can clearly see that not all opinions of men are based on reason and that these men are wrong. For it must not be presumed that mores necessarily grow worse from knowing the moral sciences, which teach the virtues, indeed, there is not the slightest doubt that moral education amends and ennobles them. How could anyone think or believe that whoever follows good teaching or doctrine is the worse for it? Such an opinion cannot be expressed or maintained. I do not mean that it would be good for a man or a woman to study the art of divination or those fields of learning which are forbidden—for the holy Church did not remove them from common use without good reason—but it should not be believed that women are the worse for knowing what is good.

"Quintus Hortensius,[2] a great rhetorician and consummately skilled orator in Rome, did not share this opinion. He had a daughter, named Hortensia, whom he greatly loved for the subtlety of her wit. He had her learn letters and study the science of rhetoric, which she mastered so thoroughly that she resembled her father Hortensius not only in wit and lively memory but also in her excellent delivery and order of speech—in fact, he surpassed her in nothing. As for the subject discussed

---

[1] Customs.
[2] Quintus Hortensius (114–50 B.C.E.).

above, concerning the good which comes about through women, the benefits realized by this woman and her learning were, among others, exceptionally remarkable. That is, during the time when Rome was governed by three men, this Hortensia began to support the cause of women and to undertake what no man dared to undertake. There was a question whether certain taxes should be levied on women and on their jewelry during a needy period in Rome. This woman's eloquence was so compelling that she was listened to, no less readily than her father would have been, and she won her case.

"Similarly, to speak of more recent times, without searching for examples in ancient history, Giovanni Andrea, a solemn law professor in Bologna not quite sixty years ago, was not of the opinion that it was bad for women to be educated. He had a fair and good daughter, named Novella, who was educated in the law to such an advanced degree that when he was occupied by some task and not at leisure to present his lectures to his students, he would send Novella, his daughter, in his place to lecture to the students from his chair. And to prevent her beauty from distracting the concentration of her audience, she had a little curtain drawn in front of her. In this manner she could on occasion supplement and lighten her father's occupation. He loved her so much that, to commemorate her name, he wrote a book of remarkable lectures on the law which he entitled *Novella super Decretalium*, after his daughter's name.

"Thus, not all men (and especially the wisest) share the opinion that it is bad for women to be educated. But it is very true that many foolish men have claimed this because it displeased them that women knew more than they did. Your father, who was a great scientist and philosopher, did not believe that women were worth less by knowing science; rather, as you know, he took great pleasure from seeing your inclination to learning. The feminine opinion of your mother, however, who wished to keep you busy with spinning and silly girlishness, following the common custom of women, was the major obstacle to your being more involved in the sciences. But just as the proverb already mentioned above says, 'No one can take away what Nature has given,' your mother could not hinder in you the feeling for the sciences which you, through natural inclination, had nevertheless gathered together in little droplets. I am sure that, on account of these things, you do not think you are worth less but rather that you consider it a great treasure for yourself; and you doubtless have reason to."

And I, Christine, replied to all of this, "Indeed, my lady, what you say is as true as the Lord's Prayer."

Q With what arguments does Lady Reason defend the intelligence of women?

Q What role does education play in matters of gender equality?

The Social Realism of Chaucer

Geoffrey Chaucer (1340–1400) was a contemporary of Boccaccio and Christine de Pisan and one of the greatest masters of fourteenth-century vernacular literature. A middle-class civil servant and diplomat, soldier in the Hundred Years' War, and a citizen of the bustling city of London, Chaucer left an indelible image of his time in a group of stories known as the *Canterbury Tales*. Modeled broadly on Boccaccio's *Decameron*, this versified human comedy was framed by Chaucer in the setting of a pilgrimage whose participants tell stories to entertain each other while traveling to the shrine of Saint Thomas à Becket in Canterbury. Chaucer's twenty-nine pilgrims, who include a miller, a monk, a plowman, a knight, a priest, a scholar, and a prioress, provide a literary cross-section of late medieval society. Although they are type characters, they are also individual personalities. (The Pardoner, for instance, is portrayed as effeminate, while the Wife of Bath is lusty.) Chaucer characterizes each pilgrim by description, by their lively and humorous conversations, and by the twenty stories they tell, which range from moral tales and beast fables to *fabliaux* of the most risqué and bawdy sort.

Like his medieval predecessors, Chaucer tended to moralize, reserving special scorn for clerical abuse and human hypocrisy. But unlike his forebears, whose view of human nature often produced stereotypes, Chaucer brought his characters to life by means of memorable details. His talent in this direction is best realized through a brief comparison. In a twelfth-century verse narrative called *Equitan*, written by Marie de France, a notable poet in the Norman court of England, we find the following description of the heroine:

> Very desirable was the lady; passing tender of body and sweet of vesture, coiffed and fretted with gold. Her eyes were blue, her face warmly colored, with a fragrant mouth, and a dainty nose. Certainly she had no peer in all the realm.

Compare Chaucer's descriptions of the Wife of Bath and the Miller (from the "Prologue"). Then, in direct comparison with the lines from *Equitan*, consider Chaucer's evocation of Alison (the Miller's wife) in "The Miller's Tale" which, though too long to reproduce here, is recommended to all who might enjoy a spicy yarn.

READING 3.4 From Chaucer's "Prologue" and "The Miller's Tale" in the *Canterbury Tales* (ca. 1390)

Here begins the Book of the Tales of Canterbury: When April with its gentle showers has pierced the March drought to the root and bathed every plant in the moisture which will hasten the flowering; when Zephyrus with his sweet breath has stirred the new shoots in every wood and field, and the young sun has run its half-course in the Ram, and small birds sing melodiously, so touched in their hearts by Nature that they sleep all night with open eyes—then folks long to go on pilgrimages, and palmers to visit foreign shores and distant shrines, known in various lands; and especially from every shire's end of England they travel to Canterbury, to seek the holy blessed martyr who helped them when they were sick.

One day in that season when I stopped at the Tabard in Southwark, ready to go on my pilgrimage to Canterbury with a truly devout heart, it happened that a group of twenty-nine people came into that inn in the evening. They were people of various ranks who had come together by chance, and they were all pilgrims who planned to ride to Canterbury. The rooms and stables were large enough for each of us to be well lodged, and, shortly after the sun had gone down, I had talked with each of these pilgrims and had soon made myself one of their group. We made our plans to get up early in order to start our trip, which I am going to tell you about. But, nevertheless, while I have time and space, before I go farther in this account, it seems reasonable to tell you all about each of the pilgrims, as they appeared to me; who they were, and of what rank, and also what sort of clothes they wore.

. . . .

There was a good Wife from near Bath, but she was somewhat deaf, which was a shame. She had such skill in clothmaking that she surpassed the weavers of Ypres and Ghent. In all her parish there was no woman who could go before her to the offertory; and if someone did, the Wife of Bath was certainly so angry that she lost all charitable feeling. Her kerchiefs were of fine texture; those she wore upon her head on Sunday weighed, I swear, ten pounds. Her fine scarlet hose were carefully tied, and her shoes were uncracked and new. Her face was bold and fair and red. All of her life she had been an estimable woman: she had had five husbands, not to mention other company in her youth—but of that we need not speak now. And three times she had been to Jerusalem; she had crossed many a foreign river; she had been to Rome, to Bologna, to St. James' shrine in Galicia, and to Cologne. About journeying through the country she knew a great deal. To tell the truth she was gap-toothed. She sat her gentle horse easily, and wore a fine headdress with a hat as broad as a buckler or a shield, a riding skirt about her large hips, and a pair of sharp spurs on her heels. She knew how to laugh and joke in company, and all the remedies of love, for her skill was great in that old game.

. . . .

The Miller was a very husky fellow, tremendous in bone and in brawn which he used well to get the best of all comers; in wrestling he always won the prize. He was stocky, broad, and thickset. There was no door which he could not pull off its hinges or break by ramming it with his head. His beard was as red as any sow or fox, and as broad as a spade. At the right on top of his nose he had a wart, from which there grew a tuft of hairs red as the bristles of a sow's ears, and his nostrils were wide and black. A sword and a shield hung at his side. His mouth was as huge as a large furnace, and he was a jokester and a ribald clown, most of whose jests were of sin and scurrility. He knew quite well how to steal grain and charge thrice over, but yet he really remained reasonably honest. The coat he wore was white and the hood blue. He could play the bagpipe well and led us out of town to its music.

. . . .

The young wife was pretty, with a body as neat and graceful as a weasel. She wore a checked silk belt, and around her loins a flounced apron as white as fresh milk. Her smock was white also, embroidered in front and in back, inside and outside and around the collar, with coal-black silk. The strings of her white hood were of the same material as her collar; her hair was bound with a wide ribbon of silk set high on her head. And, truly, she had a wanton eye. Her eyebrows were plucked thin and were arched and black as any sloe.[1] She was even more delightful to look at than a young, early-ripe pear tree, and she was softer than lamb's wool. A leather purse, with a silk tassel and metal ornaments, hung from her belt. In all the world there is no man so wise that, though he looked far and near, he could imagine so gay a darling or such a wench. Her coloring was brighter than that of a coin newly forged in the Tower, and her singing was as loud and lively as a swallow's sitting on a barn. In addition, she could skip about and play like any kid or calf following its mother. Her mouth was as sweet as honey or mead, or a pile of apples laid up in hay or heather. She was as skittish as a young colt, and tall and straight as a mast or wand. On her low collar she wore a brooch as broad as the boss on a shield. Her shoes were laced high on her legs. She was a primrose, a trillium,[2] fit to grace the bed of any lord or to marry any good yeoman.

 Q Which of Chaucer's descriptive devices are most effective in evoking character and personality?

Chaucer uses sprightly similes ("graceful as a weasel," "as sweet as honey") and vivid details ("a checked silk belt," "high laced" shoes) to bring alive the personality and physical presence of the Miller's wife. (He also hints at the contradiction between her chaste exterior and her sensual nature, a major feature in the development of the story in which she figures.) By comparison, Marie de France's portrait is a pallid and stereotypical adaptation of the standard medieval female image: the courtly lady, the Virgin Mary, and the female saint. Chaucer's humanizing techniques bring zesty realism to both his pilgrim-narrators and the characters featured in their tales. Writing in the everyday language of his time (Middle English, as distinguished from the more Germanic Old English that preceded it), Chaucer shaped the development of English literature, much as Dante, a century earlier, had influenced the course of Italian poetry.

---

[1] A small, dark berry.
[2] A lily.

Art and Music in Transition

Giotto's New Realism

A half century before Boccaccio and Chaucer began to write, the Florentine artist Giotto (1266–1337) anticipated the shift to realism that accompanied the transition from medieval to modern times. A comparison of Cimabue's *Madonna Enthroned*, completed around 1290 (see Figure 13.38), with Giotto's rendering of the same subject executed in 1310 (Figure **15.6**), provides visual evidence of that shift. Cimabue's Virgin looks back to the flat, decorative, and idealized style of Byzantine icons, while Giotto's Madonna—robust, lifelike, and set in deep space—anticipates the pictorialism and humanism of Italian Renaissance painting (see chapter 17). As with Cimabue, Giotto shows an oversized Virgin on a Gothic throne that is set against a gold background. But Giotto renounces the graceful Gothic line that etherealizes Cimabue's

Figure 15.6 GIOTTO, *Madonna Enthroned*, ca. 1310. Tempera on panel, 10 ft. 8 in. × 6 ft. 8 in. Uffizi Gallery, Florence. © 1991 Photo Scala, Florence - courtesy of the Ministero Beni e Att. Culturali.

Figure 15.7 GIOTTO, Arena Chapel (Cappella Scrovegni), Padua, interior looking toward the choir. Height 42 ft., width 27 ft. 10 in., length 96 ft. © Quattrone, Florence.

Figure 15.8 GIOTTO, *Lamentation*, 1305–1306. Fresco, 7 ft. 7 in. × 7 ft. 9 in. Arena Chapel, Padua.

Madonna. Instead, by means of **chiaroscuro** (the technique of modeling form by gradations of light and shade), Giotto gives the figure an imposing three-dimensional presence (note the forward projection of her knees, which provide physical support for the baby Jesus). Instead of placing the angels above one another around the throne, Giotto arranges them in positions that define their presence in three-dimensional space. In contrast with Cimabue's stylized and idealized Madonna, Giotto has created a natural and lifelike image.

Giotto brought this same naturalism to his frescoes. In 1303, the wealthy banker and money-lender Enrico Scrovegni commissioned Giotto to paint a series of frescoes for the family chapel in Padua. On the walls of the Arena Chapel, Giotto illustrated familiar episodes from the narrative cycle that recounts the lives of the Virgin and Christ (Figure **15.7**). While wholly traditional in subject matter (see chapter 9), the enterprise constituted an innovative approach to representation: Giotto transformed the tiny barrel-vaulted chapel into a theater in which individual events, as viewed from the center of the chapel and lit from the west, appear to take place in real space. This illusionistic approach to representation is also evident in the individual scenes in the cycle. For the *Lamentation* over Jesus (Figure **15.8**), Giotto gave weight and volume to figures whose nobility and dignity call to mind classical sculpture (see chapter 5). Giotto placed these figures in a shallow but carefully defined theatrical space delimited by craggy rocks and a single, barren tree. He enhanced dramatic expression by subtly varying the gestures of lament among the ten principal witnesses and by introducing emphatically grief-stricken responses among the ten angels that flutter above the scene. Like the characters in Boccaccio's *Decameron* and Chaucer's *Canterbury Tales*, Giotto's figures are convincingly human: while they are not individualized to the point of portraiture, neither are they stereotypes. Giotto's style advanced

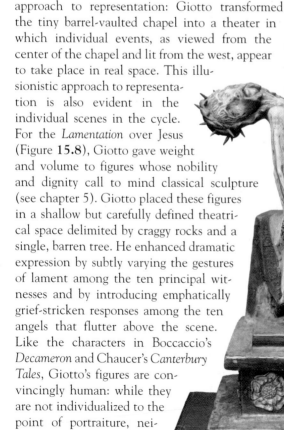

the trend toward realism already evident in late Gothic sculpture (see chapter 13). At the same time, it gave substance to the spirit of lay piety and individualism that marked the fourteenth century.

Devotional Realism and Portraiture

In religious art, realism enhanced the devotional mood of the age. Traditional scenes of the lives of Christ and the Virgin became at once more pictorial and detailed, a reflection of the new concern with Christ's human nature and his suffering. Images of the Crucifixion and the *Pietà* (the Virgin holding the dead Jesus), which had been a popular object of veneration since the tenth century, were now depicted with a new expressive intensity. One anonymous German artist of the mid-fourteenth century rendered the *Pietà* (the word means both "pity" and "piety") as a traumatic moment between a despairing Mother and her Son, whose broken torso and elongated arms are as rigid as the wood from which they were carved (Figure **15.9**). The sculpture captures the torment of Christ's martyrdom with a fierce energy more frequently found in African wood sculpture (see Figures 18.8, 18.11) than in traditional European art.

Figure 15.9 Anonymous, *The Röttgen Pietà*, c. 1370. Rheinisches Landesmuseum, Bonn.

Figure 15.10 CLAUS SLUTER, figure of Moses on the *Well of Moses*, 1395–1406. Painted stone, height approx. 6 ft. Carthusian Monastery of Champmol, Dijon, France. Photo: Erich Lessing/Art Resource. NY.

However, time has robbed the piece of the brightly colored paint and metal accessories (the scholarly Jeremiah bore a pair of copper spectacles) that once gave it a startlingly lifelike presence. Carrying scrolls engraved with their messianic texts, the life-sized prophets are swathed in deeply cut, voluminous draperies. Facial features are individualized so as to render each prophet with a distinctive personality. As in Giotto's *Lamentation*, mourning angels (at the corners of the pedestal above the heads of the prophets) cover their faces or wring their hands in gestures of anguish and despair. So intensely theatrical is the realism of the Champmol ensemble that scholars suspect Sluter might have been inspired by contemporary mystery plays, where Old Testament characters regularly took the stage between the acts to "prophesy" New Testament events.

Devotional realism is equally apparent in illuminated manuscripts, and especially in the popular prayerbook known as the Book of Hours. This guide to private prayer featured traditional recitations for the canonical hours—the sets of prayers recited daily at three-hour intervals: matins, lauds, prime, terce, sext, none, vespers, and compline—as well as prayers to the Virgin and the saints. As manuals for personal piety and alternatives to daily Church ritual, Books of Hours were in great demand, especially among prosperous Christians.

In the miniatures of these prayer books, scenes from sacred history are filled with realistic and homely details drawn from everyday life. Even miraculous events are made more believable as they are presented in lifelike settings and given new dramatic fervor. Such is the case with the animated **grisaille** (gray-toned) miniatures found in a prayer book executed around 1325 for Jeanne d'Evreux, Queen of France, by the French court painter Jean Pucelle (Figure **15.11**). The Betrayal of Christ, in contrast with thirteenth-century versions (see chapter 13), features accurately proportioned figures modeled in subtle *chiaroscuro*. In the Annunciation illustrated above, Pucelle employed receding diagonal

The most notable personality in the domain of fourteenth-century monumental sculpture was the Dutch artist Claus Sluter (ca. 1350–1406). Sluter's *Well of Moses*, executed between 1395 and 1406 for the Carthusian monastery at Champmol just outside of Dijon, France, was originally part of a 25-foot-tall stone fountain designed to celebrate the sacraments of Eucharist and Baptism. The Crucifixion group that made up the superstructure is lost, but the pedestal of the fountain with its six Old Testament prophets—Moses, David, Jeremiah, Zachariah, Daniel, and Isaiah—survives in its entirety (Figure **15.10**).

Figure 15.11 JEAN PUCELLE, *Betrayal* and *Annunciation* from the *Book of Hours of Jeanne d'Evreux, Queen of France*, 1325–1328. Miniature on vellum, each folio 3½ × 2⅜ in. The Metropolitan Museum of Art, New York. The Cloisters Collection, 1954 (54.1.2. ff.15v and 16r).

lines to create the illusion of a "doll's house" that holds an oversized Madonna.

Pucelle's experiments in empirical perspective and his dramatic renderings of traditional subjects were carried further by the three brothers Jean, Pol, and Herman Limbourg, who flourished between 1385 and 1415. Their generous patron Jean, Duke of Berry and brother of the King of France, commissioned from them a remarkable series of Books of Hours illustrated with religious and secular subjects. For the calendar pages of the *Très Riches Heures* (*Very Precious Hours*), the Limbourgs painted scenes illustrating the mundane activities and labors peculiar to each month of the year. In the scene for the month of February—the first snowscape in Western art—three peasants warm themselves by the fire, while others hurry to complete their chores (Figure **15.12**). The Limbourgs show a new fascination with natural details: dovecote and beehives covered with new-fallen snow, sheep that huddle together in a thatched pen, smoke curling from a chimney, and even the genitalia of two of the laborers who warm themselves by the fire.

Devotional realism also overtook the popular subject of the Madonna and Child: the new image of the Virgin as a humble matron tenderly nurturing the Infant Jesus (Figure 15.13) replaced earlier, more hieratic representations of Mary as Queen of Heaven (see Figures 13.31 and 13.38). In paintings of the Virgin as humble matron and as "Nursing Madonna," the Infant is shown as a lively baby, not as the miniature adult of previous renderings. Fourteenth-century artists frequently introduced narrative details from mystery plays or from the writings of mystics like Saint Bridget of Sweden. Indeed, the interchange of imagery between devotional literature, medieval drama, and the visual arts was commonplace.

In light of the growing interest in the human personality—so clearly revealed in the literature of Boccaccio and Chaucer—it is no surprise that fourteenth-century artists produced the first portrait paintings since classical antiquity. Many such portraits appear in manuscripts. In panel painting, the anonymous portrait of John the Good, King of France (Figure 15.14), documents the new consciousness of the particular as opposed to the generalized image of humankind.

The *Ars Nova* in Music

Imagination and diversity characterized fourteenth-century music, which composers of that era self-consciously labeled the **ars nova** ("new art"). The music of the *ars*

Figure 15.12 JEAN, POL, AND HERMAN LIMBOURG, *February,* plate 3 from the *Très Riches Heures* (*Very Precious Hours*) *du Duc de Berry,* ca. 1413–1416. Illumination, 8¾ × 5⁵⁄₁₆ in. Musée Condé, Chantilly, France. Giraudon/Bridgeman Art Library, London.

of Our Lady). Departing from the medieval tradition of treating the Mass as five separate compositions (based on Gregorian chant), he unified the parts into a single musical composition. He is the first known composer to have provided this type of unified setting for the textually fixed portions of the Mass. Machaut's effort at coherence of design is clear evidence that composers had begun to rank musical effect as equal to liturgical function. He also added to the Mass a sixth movement, the "Ite missa est." Machaut's new treatment of the Catholic liturgy set a precedent for such composers as the sixteenth-century Palestrina and the baroque master Johann Sebastian Bach (see chapter 22).

Machaut's sacred compositions represent only a small part of his total musical output. Indeed, his secular music parallels the rise of vernacular art in his time. Typical of this trend are his 142 polyphonic **ballades** (secular songs), which look back to the music of the *trouvères*. They introduce new warmth and lyricism, as well as vivid poetic imagery—features that parallel the humanizing currents in

Figure 15.13 AMBROGIO LORENZETTI, *Madonna del Latte* (*Nursing Madonna*), ca. 1340. Fresco. San Francesco, Siena, Italy. © 1990, Photo Scala, Florence.

nova featured increased rhythmic complexity and aural expressiveness, achieved in part by **isorhythm** (literally, "same rhythm"): the close repetition of identical rhythmic patterns in different portions of a composition. Isorhythm, which gave unprecedented unity to a musical composition, reflected a new interest in the manipulation of pitches and rhythms.

In France, the leading proponent of the *ars nova* was the French poet, priest, and composer Guillaume de Machaut (1300–1377). In his day, Machaut was more widely known and acclaimed than Chaucer and Boccaccio. Like the Limbourg brothers, Machaut held commissions from the French aristocracy, including the Duke of Berry. Machaut penned hundreds of poems, including a verse drama interspersed with songs, but his most important musical achievement was his *Messe de Notre Dame* (Mass

Figure 15.14 *King John the Good*, ca. 1356–1359(?). Canvas on panel, 21⅞ × 13⅜ in. Louvre, Paris. © Photo Josse, Paris.

♪ See Music Listening Selections at end of chapter.

fourteenth-century art and literature. "One who does not compose according to feelings," wrote Machaut, "falsifies his work and his song."

Although fourteenth-century polyphony involved both voices and instruments, manuscripts of the period did not usually specify whether a given part of a piece was instrumental or vocal. Custom probably dictated the performance style, not only for vocal and instrumental ensembles, but for dance as well. Outside France, polyphonic music flourished. The blind Italian composer Francesco Landini (ca. 1325–1397) produced graceful instrumental compositions and eloquent two- and three-part songs. Landini's 150 works constitute more than one third of the surviving music of the fourteenth century—evidence of his enormous popularity. Italian composers anticipated Renaissance style (see chapter 17) with florid polyphonic compositions that featured a close relationship between musical parts. The *caccia* (Italian for "chase"), for instance, which dealt with such everyday subjects as hunting, was set to lively music in which one voice part "chased" another. Another popular fourteenth-century polyphonic composition, the **round**, featured successive voices that repeated a single melody (as in "Row, Row, Row Your Boat"). The English round "Sumer is icumen in" is an example of fourteenth-century polyphony at its freshest and most buoyant.

SUMMARY

The fourteenth century witnessed the transition from medieval to early modern culture in the West. During this era, violence uprooted tradition, corruption bred cynicism, and widespread death generated insecurity and fear. The two great catalysts of the age—the Black Death and the Hundred Years' War—brought about a collapse of the medieval order, along with distinct political, military, and economic unrest. By the end of the century, the population of Western Europe had declined by approximately sixty percent. At the same time, as a result of the Avignon Papacy and the Great Schism, the Church of

Rome lost, in great measure, its aura of sanctity. Demands for Church reform echoed throughout the fourteenth century (though actual reform would not occur for nearly two more centuries).

Rising secularism paralleled the decline of the Church. In the wake of the Black Death and during the Great Schism, Boccaccio and Chaucer penned vernacular tales to entertain urban audiences. Rejecting literary stereotypes, allegorical intent, and religious purpose, these writers brought to life the personalities of self-motivated men and women. In France, Chaucer's contemporary Christine de Pisan ushered in the birth of feminism in Western literature.

The new realism of fourteenth-century literature was also evident in the visual arts, both in the rise of portraiture and in a more humanized and personal approach to traditional religious subjects such as that seen in the art of Giotto. In manuscript illumination and in devotional sculpture, as in panel and fresco painting, true-to-life narrative detail and emotional expressiveness came to replace Gothic abstraction and stylization. The term *ars nova*, coined by composers of that time to describe the trend toward novel rhythmic and harmonic patterns in music, is, therefore, equally appropriate for all of the arts of the fourteenth century.

If medieval people thought and acted communally, as members of a manor, a guild, or the Holy Church, fourteenth-century Westerners began to see themselves in terms of class, gender, and personality—categories that are essentially secular and modern. An era of turmoil and yet of remarkable artistic productivity, the fourteenth century challenged the feudal and corporate traditions of medieval life in the West, introducing new kinds of warfare, new forms of political organization, and a general retreat from the all-embracing spirituality of medieval Christendom.

MUSIC LISTENING SELECTIONS

CD One Selection 15   Machaut, *Messe de Notre Dame* (*Mass of Our Lady*), "Ite missa est, Deo gratias" 1364.

CD One Selection 16   Anonymous, English round, "Sumer is icumen in," fourteenth century.

♪ See Music Listening Selections at end of chapter.

GLOSSARY

ars nova (Latin, "new art") a term used for the music of fourteenth-century Europe to distinguish it from that of the old art (*ars antiqua*); it featured new rhythms, new harmonies, and more complicated methods of musical notation

ballade a secular song that tells a story in simple verse, usually repeating the same music for each stanza

caccia (Italian, "chase") a lively fourteenth-century Italian musical form that deals with everyday subjects, such as hunting and fishing

chiaroscuro (Italian, "light–dark") in drawing and painting, the technique of modeling form in gradations of light and shade to produce the illusion of three-dimensionality

grisaille (French, "gray-toned") the use of exclusively gray tones in painting or drawing

indulgence a Church pardon from the temporal penalties for sins; the remission of purgatorial punishment

isorhythm the close repetition of identical rhythmic patterns in different sections of a musical composition

round a type of polyphonic composition that features successive voices repeating exactly the same melody and text

simony the buying or selling of Church office or preferment (see Simon Magus, Acts of the Apostles 8:9–24)

CHAPTER 16

Classical Humanism in the Age of the Renaissance

". . . man is, with complete justice, considered and called a great miracle and a being worthy of all admiration."
Pico della Mirandola

Humanism, in its most general sense, describes an attitude centered on human interests and values. The term *classical humanism*, however, refers to the revival of Greco-Roman culture—a phenomenon that gave the Renaissance (the word literally means "rebirth") its distinctly secular stamp. Classical culture did not disappear altogether with the fall of Rome in 476 C.E. It was preserved by countless Christian and Muslim scholars, revived by Charlemagne in the early Middle Ages, and championed by such medieval intellectuals as Aquinas (who took Aristotle as his master) and Dante (who chose Virgil as his guide). But the classical revival of the fourteenth to sixteenth centuries—the age of the Renaissance—generated new and more all-embracing attitudes toward Greco-Roman antiquity than any that had preceded it.

Renaissance humanists advocated the recovery and uncensored study of the entire body of Greek and Latin manuscripts and the self-conscious imitation of classical art and architecture. They regarded classical authority not exclusively as a means of clarifying Christian truths, but as the basis for a new appraisal of the role of the individual in the world order. Thus, although Renaissance humanists still prized the Liberal Arts as the basis for intellectual advancement, they approached the classics from a different point of view than that of their scholastic predecessors. Whereas the scholastics had studied the Greco-Roman legacy as the foundation for Christian dogma and faith, Renaissance humanists discovered in the Greek and Latin classics a rational guide to the fulfillment of the human potential. Moreover, the Renaissance revival of humanism differed from earlier revivals because it attracted the interest of a broad base of the population and not a mere handful of theologians, as was the case, for instance, in Carolingian or later medieval times.

The humanists of the Renaissance were the cultural archeologists of their age. They uncovered new evidence of the splendor of Greco-Roman antiquity and consumed the fruits of their Western heritage. Unattached to any single school or university, this new breed of humanists pursued what the ancient Romans had called *studia humanitatis*, a program of study that embraced grammar, rhetoric, history, poetry, and moral philosophy. These branches of learning fostered training in the moral and aesthetic areas of human knowledge—the very areas of experience with which this textbook is concerned. While such an educational curriculum was assuredly not antireligious—indeed, most Renaissance humanists were devout Catholics—its focus was secular rather than religious. For these humanists, life on earth was not a vale of tears but, rather, an extended occasion during which human beings might cultivate their unique talents and abilities. Classical humanists saw no conflict between humanism and religious belief. They viewed their intellectual mission as both pleasing to God and advantageous to society in general. Humanism, then, grounded in a reevaluation of classical literature and art, represented a shift in emphasis rather than an entirely new pursuit; it involved a turning away from exclusively otherworldly preoccupations to a robust, this-worldly point of view.

Italy: Birthplace of the Renaissance

The Renaissance designates that period in European history between roughly 1300 and 1600, during which time the revival of classical humanism spread from its birthplace in Florence, Italy, throughout Western Europe. Italy was the homeland of Roman antiquity, the splendid ruins of which stood as reminders of the greatness of classical civilization. The least feudalized part of the medieval world and Europe's foremost commercial and financial center, Italy had traded with Southwest Asian cities even in the darkest days of the Dark Ages. It had also maintained cultural contacts with Byzantium, the heir to Greek culture. The cities of Italy, especially Venice and Genoa (Map **16.1**), had profited financially from the Crusades (see chapter 11) and—despite the ravages of the plague—continued to enjoy a high level of commercial prosperity. In fourteenth-century Florence, shopkeepers devised a

Map 16.1 Renaissance Europe, ca. 1500.

practical system (based on Arab models) of tracking deb-its and credits: double-entry book-keeping helped mer-chants to maintain systematic records of transactions in what was the soundest currency in the West, the Florentine gold florin. Fifteenth-century handbooks on arithmetic, foreign currency, and even good penmanship encouraged the commercial activities of traders and bankers.

The pursuit of money and leisure, rather than a pre-occupation with feudal and chivalric obligations, marked the lifestyle of merchants and artisans who lived in the bustling city-states of Italy. In a panoramic cityscape commissioned for the Palazzo Pubblico (Town Hall) of Siena, Ambrogio Lorenzetti (whom we met in chapter 15) celebrated the positive effects of good government on urban life (Figure **16.1**), while a matching fresco illus-trated the evil effects of bad government. Throughout Italy, the Avignon Papacy and the Great Schism had pro-duced a climate of anticlericalism and intellectual skepti-cism. Middle-class men and women challenged canonical sources of authority that frowned upon profit-making and

the accumulation of wealth. In this materialistic and often only superficially religious society, the old medieval values no longer made sense, while those of pre-Christian antiq-uity seemed more compatible with the secular interests and ambitions of the rising merchant class. The ancient Greeks and Romans were indeed ideal historical models for the enterprising citizens of the Italian city-states.

Politically, Renaissance Italy had much in common with ancient Greece. Independent and disunited, the city-states of Italy, like those of ancient Greece, were fiercely competitive. As in golden-age Greece, commercial rivalry among the Italian city-states led to frequent civil wars. In Italy, however, such wars were not always fought by citizens (who, as merchants, were generally ill prepared for combat), but by **condottieri** (professional soldiers) whose loyalties, along with their services, were bought for a price. The papacy, a potential source of political leader-ship, made little effort to unify the rival Italian communes. Rather, as temporal governors of the Papal States (the lands located in central Italy), Renaissance popes joined

Figure 16.1 AMBROGIO LORENZETTI, *Effects of Good Government in the City and the Country*, from *The Allegory of Good Government*, 1338–1339. Sala della Pace, Palazzo Pubblico, Siena, Italy. © Quattrone, Florence.

Figure 16.2 ANDREA DEL VERROCCHIO, *Lorenzo de' Medici*, ca. 1478. Terracotta, 25⅞ × 23¼ × 12⅞ in. © 2000 Board of Trustees, National Gallery of Art, Washington, D.C. Samuel H. Kress Collection.

in the game of power politics, often allying with one group of city-states against another.

Italian Renaissance cities were ruled either by members of the petty nobility, by mercenary generals, or—as in the case of Florence and Venice—by wealthy middle-class families. In Florence, a city of approximately 50,000, some one hundred families dominated political life. The most notable of these was the Medici, a wealthy banking family that rose to power during the fourteenth century and gradually assumed the reins of state. Partly because the commercial ingenuity of the Medici enhanced the material status of the Florentine citizens, and partly because strong, uninterrupted leadership guaranteed local economic stability, the Medici ruled Florence for four generations. The Medici merchant-princes, especially Cosimo (1389–1464) and Lorenzo "the Magnificent" (1449–1492) (Figure **16.2**), supported scholarship and patronized the arts. Affluence coupled with intellectual discernment and refined taste inspired the Medici to commission works from such artists as Brunelleschi, Botticelli, Verrocchio, and Michelangelo, who produced some of the West's most brilliant art. For almost two centuries, scholars, poets, painters, and civic leaders shared common interests, acknowledging one another as leaders of a vigorous cultural revival.

Petrarch: "Father of Humanism"

The most famous of the early Florentine humanists was the poet and scholar Francesco Petrarch (1304–1374). Often called the "father of humanism," Petrarch devoted his life to the recovery, copying, and editing of Latin manuscripts. In quest of these ancient sources of wisdom, he traveled all over Europe, hand-copying manuscripts he could not beg or buy from monastic libraries, borrowing others from friends, and gradually amassing a private library of more than two hundred volumes. Petrarch was a tireless popularizer of classical studies. Reviving the epistolary (letter-writing) tradition that had practically disappeared since Roman times, he wrote hundreds of letters describing his admiration for antiquity and his enthusiasm for the classics, especially the writings of the Roman statesman Cicero (see chapter 6). In his letters, Petrarch eulogized and imitated Cicero's polished prose style, which stood in refined contrast to the corrupt Latin of his own time.

The intensity of Petrarch's passion for antiquity and his eagerness to rescue it from neglect come across powerfully in a letter addressed to his friend Lapo da Castiglionchio. Here, he laments the scarcity and incompetence of copyists, bemoans the fact that books that are difficult to understand have "sunk into utter neglect," and defends his ambition to preserve them, despite the inordinate amount of time it takes to copy them. (Such fervor, shared by his successors, surely motivated the invention of print technology within one hundred years of his death.) In the letter to Lapo, part of which is reproduced below, Petrarch vows to sacrifice the precious hours of his old age to the pleasures of copying Cicero (whom he calls fondly by his middle name, Tullius).

READING 3.5 From Petrarch's Letter to Lapo da Castiglionchio (ca. 1351)

Your Cicero has been in my possession four years and 1
more. There is a good reason, though, for so long a delay;
namely, the great scarcity of copyists who understand
such work. It is a state of affairs that has resulted in an
incredible loss to scholarship. Books that by their nature
are a little hard to understand are no longer multiplied,
and have ceased to be generally intelligible, and so have
sunk into utter neglect, and in the end have perished.
This age of ours consequently has let fall, bit by bit, some
of the richest and sweetest fruits that the tree of 10
knowledge has yielded; has thrown away the results of the
vigils and labors of the most illustrious men of genius,
things of more value, I am almost tempted to say, than
anything else in the whole world. . . .

But I must return to your Cicero. I could not do without
it, and the incompetence of the copyists would not let me
possess it. What was left for me but to rely upon my own
resources, and press these weary fingers and this worn
and ragged pen into service? The plan that I followed was
this. I want you to know it, in case you should ever have 20
to grapple with a similar task. Not a single word did I read
except as I wrote. But how is that, I hear someone say;

did you write without knowing what it was that you were
writing? Ah! but from the very first it was enough for me to
know that it was a work of Tullius, and an extremely rare
one too. And then as soon as I was fairly started I found
at every step so much sweetness and charm, and felt so
strong a desire to advance, that the only difficulty which I
experienced in reading and writing at the same time came
from the fact that my pen could not cover the ground so 30
rapidly as I wanted it to, whereas my expectation had
been rather that it would outstrip my eyes, and that my
ardor for writing would be chilled by the slowness of my
reading. So the pen held back the eye, and the eye drove
on the pen, and I covered page after page, delighting in
my task, and committing many and many a passage to
memory as I wrote. For just in proportion as the writing is
slower than the reading does the passage make a deep
impression and cling to the mind.

And yet I must confess that I did finally reach a point 40
in my copying where I was overcome by weariness; not
mental, for how unlikely that would be where Cicero was
concerned, but the sort of fatigue that springs from
excessive manual labor. I began to feel doubtful about this
plan that I was following, and to regret having undertaken
a task for which I had not been trained; when suddenly I
came across a place where Cicero tells how he himself
copied the orations of—someone or other; just who it was I
do not know, but certainly no Tullius, for there is but one
such man, one such voice, one such mind. These are his 50
words: "You say that you have been in the habit of reading
the orations of Cassius[1] in your idle moments. But I," he
jestingly adds, with his customary disregard of his
adversary's feelings, "have made a practice of *copying*
them, so that I might *have* no idle moments." As I read this
passage I grew hot with shame, like a modest young soldier
who hears the voice of his beloved leader rebuking him. I
said to myself, "So Cicero copied orations that another
wrote, and you are not ready to copy his? What ardor! What
scholarly devotion! what reverence for a man of godlike 60
genius!" These thoughts were a spur to me, and I pushed
on, with all my doubts dispelled. If ever from my darkness
there shall come a single ray that can enhance the splendor
of the reputation which his heavenly eloquence has won
for him, it will proceed in no slight measure from the fact
that I was so captivated by his ineffable sweetness that I
did a thing in itself most irksome with such delight and
eagerness that I scarcely knew I was doing it at all.

So then at last your Cicero has the happiness of
returning to you, bearing you my thanks. And yet he also 70
stays, very willingly, with me; a dear friend, to whom I give
the credit of being almost the only man of letters for whose
sake I would go to the length of spending my time, when
the difficulties of life are pressing on me so sharply and
inexorably and the cares pertaining to my literary labors
make the longest life seem far too short, in transcribing
compositions not my own. I may have done such things in
former days, when I thought myself rich in time, and had

---

[1] More probably Lucius Licenius Crassus (140–91 B.C.E.), one of the great Roman orators and a principal figure in Cicero's treatise *On Oratory*.

not learned how stealthily it slips away: but I now know that this is of all our riches the most uncertain and fleeting; the years are closing in upon me now, and there is no longer any room for deviation from the beaten path. I am forced to practice strict economy; I only hope that I have not begun too late. But Cicero! he assuredly is worthy of a part of even the little that I have left. Farewell. 80

Q In what ways does Petrarch's letter exemplify the aims and passions of the Renaissance humanist?

Nothing in the letter to Lapo suggests that Petrarch was a devout Christian; yet, in fact, Petrarch's affection for Cicero was matched only by his devotion to Saint Augustine and his writings. Indeed, in their introspective tone and their expression of intimate feelings and desires, Petrarch's letters reveal the profound influence of Augustine's *Confessions*, a work that Petrarch deeply admired. Torn between Christian piety and his passion for classical antiquity, Petrarch experienced recurrent psychic conflict. In his writings there is a gnawing and unresolved dissonance between the dual imperatives of his heritage: the Judeo-Christian will to believe and the classical will to reason. Such self-torment—evident in Petrarch's poems, over 300 examples of which make up the *Canzoniere* (*Songbook*)—implies that Petrarch remained, in part, a medieval man. Yet it did not prevent him from pursuing worldly fame. At Rome in 1341, he proudly received the laurel crown for outstanding literary achievement (Figure **16.3**). The tradition, which looks back to the ancient Greek practice of honoring victors in the athletic games with wreaths made from the foliage of the laurel tree, survives in our modern honorary title "poet *laureate*."

The object of Petrarch's affection and the inspiration for the *Canzoniere* was a married Florentine woman named Laura de Sade. Petrarch dedicated hundreds of love lyrics to Laura, many of which were written after she died of bubonic plague in 1348. While Petrarch used Latin, the language of learning, for his letters and essays, he wrote his poems and songs in vernacular Italian. His favorite poetic form was the **sonnet**, a fourteen-line lyric poem. The sonnet form originated among the poets of Sicily, but it was Petrarch who brought it to perfection. Influenced by the "sweet style" of his Italian forebears and, more generally, by *troubadour* songs and Islamic lyric verse, Petrarch's sonnets are a record of his struggle between the flesh and the spirit. In their self-reflective and even self-indulgent tone, they are strikingly modern, especially where they explore Petrarch's love for Laura—and for love itself. In the first of the two sonnets below, Petrarch explores the conflicting emotional states evoked by his unfulfilled desire. These are phrased intriguingly in contrasting sets: peace/war, burn/freeze, tears/laughter, and so on. In the second sonnet, Petrarch employs vivid imagery—"a field without flowers," "[a] ring without gem"—to picture the void left by Laura's death.

Figure 16.3 *Petrarch in his study*, late fifteenth century. Manuscript illumination. Darmstadt, Hessische Landesbibliothek. MS 101, f. iv.

READING 3.6 From Petrarch's *Canzoniere*

(ca. 1350)

Sonnet 132

I find no peace and I am not at war; 1
I fear and hope, and I burn and I freeze;
I rise up to the sky, lie on earth's floor;
And I grasp nothing and I hug the trees.

She has jailed me, and nor opens nor shuts, 5
Nor keeps me for her own, nor tears the noose,
Love does not slay and does not set me loose,
He wants me nor alive nor out of ruts.

I see and have no eyes; no tongue, and cry;
I wish to perish and call help to fly; 10
And I abhor myself and love another.

I feed on grief, in tears and laugh I smother;
Death and life are the objects of my hate:
Lady, because of you, such is my state.

Sonnet 338

Death, you have left the world without its sun, 1
Gloomy and cold, Love blind and without arms,
Loveliness bare, and sick all beauty's charms,
Myself distressed and by this load undone,

Courtesy banished, honesty pretext: 5
I alone mourn, though not alone I should;
For you uprooted a clear shoot of good.
Torn the first valour, which will be the next?

They ought to weep, the earth, the sea, the air,
The human lineage that without her is   10
Like a field without flowers, ring without gem.

They did not know her while she was with them;
I did, who am left here and weep for this,
And the sky did, that with my grief grows fair.

Q What are the main features of the
Petrarchan sonnet?

In his own time, Petrarch was acclaimed as the finest prac-
titioner of the sonnet form. His sonnets were translated by
Chaucer and set to music by Landini (see chapter 15).
During the sixteenth century, Michelangelo Buonarroti in
Italy and the English poets Thomas Wyatt, Edmund
Spenser, and William Shakespeare (see chapter 19) wrote
sonnets modeled on those of Petrarch. Petrarch's influence
as a classical humanist was equally significant: he established the standards for the study of the Latin classics,
and, by insisting on the union of ethics and eloquence, he

pioneered the modern ideal of the educated individual.
Although Petrarch never learned to read Greek, he
encouraged his contemporaries and friends (including
Boccaccio) to master the language of the first philosophers. Petrarch's passion for classical learning initiated
something of a cult, which at its worst became an infatua-
tion with everything antique, but which at its best called
forth a diligent examination of the classical heritage.

Italian Renaissance Humanism

The effort to recover, copy, and produce accurate editions
of classical writings dominated the early history of the
Renaissance in Italy. By the middle of the fifteenth century,
almost all of the major Greek and Latin manuscripts
of antiquity were available to scholars. Throughout
Italy, the small study retreat, or *studiolo*, filled with manuscripts, musical instruments, and the artifacts of scientific
inquiry, came to be considered essential to the advancement
of intellectual life. Wealthy patrons like Federico da
Montefeltro, Duke of Urbino and his wife Battista Sforza
(Figures **16.4** and **16.5**) encouraged humanistic education, commissioning private studies for their villas and for
the ducal palace itself (Figure **16.6**). Among the humanists of Italy, classical writings kindled new attitudes
concerning the importance of active participation in civic
life. Aristotle's view of human beings as "political animals"

Figure 16.4 and **16.5 PIERO DELLA FRANCESCA**, *Battista Sforza, Duchess of Urbino* and *Federico da Montefeltro, Duke of Urbino*, after 1475. Oil and tempera on panel, each 18½ x 13 in. Galleria degli Uffizi, Florence. © 1992, Photo Scala, Florence - courtesy of the Ministero Beni e Att. Culturali.

Figure 16.6 The *studiolo* of Federico da Montefeltro in the Palazzo Ducale, Urbino, Italy, 1476. Scala, Florence.

(see chapter 4) and Cicero's glorification of duty to the state (see chapter 6) encouraged humanists to perceive that the exercise of civic responsibility was the hallmark of the cultivated individual. Such civic humanists as Leonardo Bruni and Coluccio Salutati, who served Florence as chancellors and historians during the Renaissance, defended the precept that one's highest good was activity in the public interest.

Alberti and Renaissance *Virtù*

A formative figure of the Early Renaissance was the multitalented Florentine humanist Leon Battista Alberti (1404–1474) (Figure **16.7**). A mathematician, architect, engineer, musician, and playwright, Alberti's most original literary contribution (and that for which he was best known in his own time) was his treatise *On the Family*. Published in 1443, *On the Family* is the first sociological inquiry into the structure, function, and responsibilities of the family. It is also a moralizing treatise that defends the importance of a classical education and hard work as prerequisites for worldly success. In Alberti's view, skill, talent, fortitude, ingenuity, and the ability to determine one's destiny—qualities summed up in the single Italian word *virtù*—are essential to human enterprise. *Virtù*, Alberti observes, is not inherited; rather, it must be cultivated. Not to be confused with the English word "virtue," *virtù* describes the self-confident vitality of the self-made Renaissance individual.

In *On the Family*, Alberti warns that idleness is the enemy of human achievement, while the performance of "manly tasks" and the pursuit of "fine studies" are sure means to worldly fame and material fortune. Pointing to the success of his own family, he defends the acquisition of wealth as the reward of free-spirited *virtù*. The buoyant optimism so characteristic of the age of the Renaissance is epitomized in Alberti's statement that "man can do anything he wants." Alberti himself—architect, mathematician, and scholar—was living proof of that viewpoint.

Figure 16.7 LEON BATTISTA ALBERTI, *Self-Portrait*, ca. 1435. Bronze, 7²⁹⁄₃₂ × 5¹¹⁄₃₂ in. © 2000 Board of Trustees, National Gallery of Art, Washington, D.C. Samuel H. Kress Collection.

READING 3.7 From Alberti's *On the Family*

(1443)

Let Fathers . . . see to it that their sons pursue the   1
study of letters assiduously and let them teach them to
understand and write correctly. Let them not think they
have taught them if they do not see that their sons have
learned to read and write perfectly, for in this it is almost
the same to know badly as not to know at all. Then let
the children learn arithmetic and gain a sufficient
knowledge of geometry, for these are enjoyable sciences
suitable to young minds and of great use to all regardless
of age or social status. Then let them turn once more to   10
the poets, orators, and philosophers. Above all, one must
try to have good teachers from whom the children may
learn excellent customs as well as letters. I should want
my sons to become accustomed to good authors. I
should want them to learn grammar from Priscian and
Servius and to become familiar, not with collections of
sayings and extracts, but with the works of Cicero, Livy,
and Sallust above all, so that they might learn the
perfection and splendid eloquence of the elegant Latin
tongue from the very beginning. They say that the same   20
thing happens to the mind as to a bottle: if at first one
puts bad wine in it, its taste will never disappear. One
must, therefore, avoid all crude and inelegant writers and
study those who are polished and elegant, keeping their
works at hand, reading them continuously, reciting them
often, and memorizing them. . . .

   Think for a moment: can you find a man—or even
imagine one—who fears infamy, though he may have no
strong desire for glory, and yet does not hate idleness
and sloth? Who can ever think it possible to achieve   30
honors and dignity without the loving study of excellent
arts, without assiduous work, without striving in difficult
manly tasks? If one wishes to gain praise and fame, he
must abhor idleness and laziness and oppose them as
deadly foes. There is nothing that gives rise to dishonor
and infamy as much as idleness. Idleness has always
been the breeding-place of vice. . . .

   Therefore, idleness which is the cause of so many evils
must be hated by all good men. Even if idleness were not
a deadly enemy of good customs and the cause of every   40
vice, as everyone knows it is, what man, though inept,
could wish to spend his life without using his mind, his
limbs, his every faculty? Does an idle man differ from a
tree trunk, a statue, or a putrid corpse? As for me, one
who does not care for honor or fear shame and does not
act with prudence and intelligence does not live well.
But one who lies buried in idleness and sloth and
completely neglects good deeds and fine studies is
altogether dead. One who does not give himself body and
soul to the quest for praise and virtue is to be deemed   50
unworthy of life. . . .

   [Man] comes into this world in order to enjoy all
things, be virtuous, and make himself happy. For he who
may be called happy will be useful to other men, and he
who is now useful to others cannot but please God. He
who uses things improperly harms other men and incurs
God's displeasure, and he who displeases God is a fool if
he thinks he is happy. We may, therefore, state that man
is created by Nature to use, and reap the benefits of, all
things, and that he is born to be happy. . . .   60

   I believe it will not be excessively difficult for a
man to acquire the highest honors and glory, if he
perseveres in his studies as much as is necessary,
toiling, sweating, and striving to surpass all others by far.
It is said that man can do anything he wants. If you will
strive with all your strength and skill, as I have said, I
have no doubt you will reach the highest degree of
perfection and fame in any profession. . . .

   To those of noble and liberal spirit, no occupations
seem less brilliant than those whose purpose is to make   70
money. If you think a moment and try to remember
which are the occupations for making money, you will
see that they consist of buying and selling, lending and
collecting. I believe that these occupations whose
purpose is gain may seem vile and worthless to you, for
you are of noble and lofty spirit. In fact, selling is a
mercenary trade; you serve the buyer's needs, pay
yourself for your work, and make a profit by charging
others more than you yourself have paid. You are not
selling goods, therefore, but your labors; you are   80

reimbursed for the cost of your goods, and for your labor
you receive a profit. Lending would be a laudable
generosity if you did not seek interest, but then it would
not be a profitable business. Some say that these
occupations, which we shall call pecuniary, always entail
dishonesty and numerous lies and often entail dishonest
agreements and fraudulent contracts. They say,
therefore, that those of liberal spirit must completely
avoid them as dishonest and mercenary. But I believe
that those who judge all pecuniary occupations in this   90
manner are wrong. Granted that acquiring wealth is not a
glorious enterprise to be likened to the most noble
professions. We must not, however, scorn a man who is
not naturally endowed for noble deeds if he turns to
these other occupations in which he knows he is not
inept and which, everyone admits, are of great use to the
family and to the state. Riches are useful for gaining
friends and praise, for with them we can help those in
need. With wealth we can gain fame and prestige if we
use it munificently for great and noble projects.   100

 Q What is Alberti's opinion of the business of money-making? What, according to him, is the value of wealth?

After the fall of Constantinople to the Ottoman Turks in 1453, Greek manuscripts and Byzantine scholars poured into Italy, contributing to the efflorescence of what the humanist philosopher Marsilio Ficino (1433–1499) called "a golden age." Encouraged by the availability of Greek resources and supported by his patron Cosimo de' Medici, Ficino translated the entire corpus of Plato's writings from Greek into Latin, making them available to Western scholars for the first time since antiquity. Ficino's translations and the founding of the Platonic Academy in Florence (financed by Cosimo) launched a reappraisal of Plato and the neoplatonists that had major consequences in the domains of art and literature. Plato's writings—especially the *Symposium*, in which love is exalted as a divine force—advanced the idea, popularized by Ficino, that "platonic" (or spiritual) love attracted the soul to God. Platonic love became a major theme among Renaissance poets and painters, who held that spiritual love was inspired by physical beauty.

While Ficino was engaged in popularizing Plato, one of his most learned contemporaries, Giovanni Pico della Mirandola (1463–1494), undertook the translation of various ancient literary works in Hebrew, Arabic, Latin, and Greek. Humanist, poet, and theologian, Pico sought not only to bring to light the entire history of human thought, but to prove that all intellectual expression shared the same divine purpose and design. This effort to discover a "unity of truth" in all philosophic thought—similar to but more comprehensive than the medieval quest for synthesis and so dramatically different from our own modern pluralistic outlook—dominated the arts and ideas of the High Renaissance (see chapter 17).

Pico's program to recover the past and his reverence for the power of human knowledge continued a tradition that looked back to Petrarch; at the same time, his monumental efforts typified the activist spirit of Renaissance *individualism*—the affirmation of the unique, self-fashioning potential of the human being. In Rome, at the age of twenty-four, Pico boldly challenged the Church to debate some 900 theological propositions that challenged the institutional Church in a variety of theological and philosophical matters. The young scholar did not get the opportunity to debate his theses; indeed, he was persecuted for heresy and forced to flee Italy. As an introduction to the disputation, Pico had prepared the Latin introduction that has come to be called the *Oration on the Dignity of Man*. In this "manifesto of humanism," Pico drew on a wide range of literary sources to build an argument for free will and the perfectibility of the individual. Describing the individual's position as only "a little lower than the angels," he stressed man's capacity to determine his own destiny on the hierarchical "chain of being" that linked the divine and brute realms. Although Pico's *Oration* was not circulated until after his death, its assertion of free will and its acclamation of the unlimited potential of the individual came to symbolize the collective ideals of the Renaissance humanists. The Renaissance view that the self-made individual occupies the center of a rational universe is nowhere better described than in the following excerpt.

READING 3.8 From Pico's *Oration on the Dignity of Man* (1486)

Most esteemed Fathers,[1] I have read in the ancient writings   1
of the Arabians that Abdala the Saracen[2] on being asked
what, on this stage, so to say, of the world, seemed to him
most evocative of wonder, replied that there was nothing to
be seen more marvelous than man. And that celebrated
exclamation of Hermes Trismegistus,[3] "What a great miracle
is man, Asclepius"[4] confirms this opinion.

And still, as I reflected upon the basis assigned for these
estimations, I was not fully persuaded by the diverse
reasons advanced by a variety of persons for the   10
preeminence of human nature; for example: that man is the
intermediary between creatures, that he is the familiar
of the gods above him as he is lord of the beings beneath
him; that, by the acuteness of his senses, the inquiry of his
reason and the light of his intelligence, he is the interpreter
of nature, set midway between the timeless unchanging and
the flux of time; the living union (as the Persians say), the
very marriage hymn of the world, and, by David's testimony[5]

[1]The assembly of clergymen to whom the oration was to be addressed.
[2]The Arabic philosopher and translator Abd-Allah Ibn al Muqaffa
(718–775).
[3]The Greek name (Hermes Thrice-Great) for the Greek god Thoth, the
presumed author of a body of occult philosophy that mingled
neoplatonism, alchemy, and mystical interpretations of the Scriptures.
[4]The Greek god of healing and medicine.
[5]In Psalms 8.6.

but little lower than the angels. These reasons are all, without question, of great weight; nevertheless, they do not touch the principal reasons, those, that is to say, which justify man's unique right to such unbounded admiration. Why, I asked, should we not admire the angels themselves and the beatific choirs more?

At long last, however, I feel that I have come to some understanding of why man is the most fortunate of living things and, consequently, deserving of all admiration; of what may be the condition in the hierarchy of beings assigned to him, which draws upon him the envy, not of the brutes alone, but of the astral beings and of the very intelligences which dwell beyond the confines of the world. A thing surpassing belief and smiting the soul with wonder. Still, how could it be otherwise? For it is on this ground that man is, with complete justice, considered and called a great miracle and a being worthy of all admiration.

Hear then, oh Fathers, precisely what this condition of man is; and in the name of your humanity, grant me your benign audition as I pursue this theme.

God the Father, the Mightiest Architect, had already raised, according to the precepts of His hidden wisdom, this world we see, the cosmic dwelling of divinity, a temple most august. He had already adorned the supercelestial region with Intelligences, infused the heavenly globes with the life of immortal souls and set the fermenting dung-heap of the inferior world teeming with every form of animal life. But when this work was done, the Divine Artificer still longed for some creature which might comprehend the meaning of so vast an achievement, which might be moved with love at its beauty and smitten with awe at its grandeur. When, consequently, all else had been completed, . . . in the very last place, He bethought Himself of bringing forth man. Truth was, however, that there remained no archetype according to which He might fashion a new offspring, nor in His treasure-houses the wherewithal to endow a new son with a fitting inheritance, nor any place, among the seats of the universe, where this new creature might dispose himself to contemplate the world. All space was already filled; all things had been distributed in the highest, the middle and the lowest orders. Still, it was not in the nature of the power of the Father to fail in this last creative élan; nor was it in the nature of that supreme Wisdom to hesitate through lack of counsel in so crucial a matter; nor, finally, in the nature of His beneficent love to compel the creature destined to praise the divine generosity in all other things to find it wanting in himself.

At last, the Supreme Maker decreed that this creature, to whom He could give nothing wholly his own, should have a share in the particular endowment of every other creature. Taking man, therefore, this creature of indeterminate image, He set him in the middle of the world and thus spoke to him:

"We have given you, Oh Adam, no visage proper to yourself, nor any endowment properly your own, in order that whatever place, whatever form, whatever gifts you may, with premeditation, select, these same you may have and possess through your own judgment and decision. The nature of all other creatures is defined and restricted within laws which

We have laid down; you, by contrast, impeded by no such restrictions, may, by your own free will, to whose custody We have assigned you, trace for yourself the lineaments of your own nature. I have placed you at the very center of the world, so that from that vantage point you may with greater ease glance round about you on all that the world contains. We have made you a creature neither of heaven nor of earth, neither mortal nor immortal, in order that you may, as the free and proud shaper of your own being, fashion yourself in the form you may prefer. It will be in your power to descend to the lower, brutish forms of life; [or] you will be able, through your own decision, to rise again to the superior orders whose life is divine."

Oh unsurpassed generosity of God the Father, Oh wondrous and unsurpassable felicity of man, to whom it is granted to have what he chooses, to be what he wills to be! The brutes, from the moment of their birth, bring with them, as Lucilius[6] says, "from their mother's womb" all that they will ever possess. The highest spiritual beings were, from the very moment of creation, or soon thereafter, fixed in the mode of being which would be theirs through measureless eternities. But upon man, at the moment of his creation, God bestowed seeds pregnant with all possibilities, the germs of every form of life. Whichever of these a man shall cultivate, the same will mature and bear fruit in him. If vegetative, he will become a plant; if sensual, he will become brutish; if rational, he will reveal himself a heavenly being; if intellectual, he will be an angel and the son of God. And if, dissatisfied with the lot of all creatures, he should recollect himself into the center of his own unity, he will there, become one spirit with God, in the solitary darkness of the Father, Who is set above all things, himself transcend all creatures.

Who then will not look with awe upon this our chameleon, or who, at least, will look with greater admiration on any other being? This creature, man, whom Asclepius the Athenian, by reason of this very mutability, this nature capable of transforming itself, quite rightly said was symbolized in the mysteries by the figure of Proteus. This is the source of those metamorphoses, or transformations, so celebrated among the Hebrews and among the Pythagoreans;[7] . . . . while the Pythagoreans transform men guilty of crimes into brutes or even, if we are to believe Empedocles,[8] into plants; and Mohamet,[9] imitating them, was known frequently to say that the man who deserts the divine law becomes a brute. And he was right; for it is not the bark that makes the tree, but its insensitive and unresponsive nature; nor the hide which makes the beast of burden, but its brute and sensual soul; nor the orbicular form which makes the heavens, but their harmonious order. Finally, it is not freedom from a body, but its spiritual intelligence, which makes the angel. If you see a man dedicated to his stomach, crawling on the ground, you see a plant and not a man; or if you see a man bedazzled by the empty forms of the imagination, as

---

[6]A Roman writer of satires (180–102 B.C.E.).
[7]Followers of the Greek philosopher and mathematician Pythagoras (fl. 530 B.C.E.); see chapter 5.
[8]A Greek philosopher and poet (495–435 B.C.E.).
[9]The prophet Muhammad (570–632); see chapter 10.

by the wiles of Calypso,[10] and through their alluring solicitations made a slave to his own senses, you see a brute and not a man. If, however, you see a philosopher, judging and distinguishing all things according to the rule of reason, him shall you hold in veneration, for he is a creature of heaven and not of earth; if, finally, a pure contemplator, unmindful of the body, wholly withdrawn into the inner chambers of the mind, here indeed is neither a creature of earth nor a heavenly creature, but some higher divinity, clothed with human flesh.

Q In what ways, according to Pico, is man "a great miracle" (line 6)?

Q Why does he call man "our chameleon" (line 110)?

Castiglione: The Well-Rounded Person

By far the most provocative analysis of Renaissance individualism is that found in *The Book of the Courtier*, a treatise written between 1513 and 1518 by the Italian diplomat and man of letters Baldassare Castiglione (1478–1529) (Figure **16.8**). Castiglione's *Courtier* was inspired by a series of conversations that had taken place among a group of sixteenth-century aristocrats at the court of Urbino, a mecca for humanist studies located in central Italy. The subject of these conversations, which Castiglione probably recorded from memory, concerns the qualifications of the ideal Renaissance man and woman. Debating this subject at length, the members of the court arrive at a consensus that affords the image of *l'uomo universale*: the well-rounded person. Castiglione reports that the ideal man should master all the skills of the medieval warrior and display the physical proficiency of a champion athlete. But, additionally, he must possess the refinements of a humanistic education. He must know Latin and Greek (as well as his own native language), be familiar with the classics, speak and write well, and be able to compose verse, draw, and play a musical instrument. Moreover, all that the Renaissance gentleman does, he should do with an air of nonchalance and grace, a quality summed up in the Italian word *sprezzatura*. This unique combination of breeding and education would produce a cultured individual to serve a very special end: the perfection of the state. For, as Book Four of *The Courtier* explains, the primary duty of the well-rounded person is to influence the ruler to govern wisely.

Although, according to Castiglione, the goal of the ideal gentleman was to cultivate his full potential as a human being, such was not the case with the Renaissance gentlewoman. The Renaissance woman should have a knowledge of letters, music, and art—that is, like the gentleman, she should be privileged with a humanistic education—but in no way should she violate that "soft and delicate tenderness that is her defining quality." Castiglione's peers agreed that "in her ways, manners, words, gestures, and bearing, a woman ought to be very unlike a man." Just as the success of the courtier depends on his ability to influence those who rule, the success of the lady rests with her skills in entertaining the male members of the court.

Castiglione's handbook of Renaissance etiquette was based on the views of a narrow, aristocratic segment of society. But despite its selective viewpoint, it was immensely popular: in 1527, the Aldine Press in Venice printed *The Courtier* in an edition of more than 1000 copies. It was translated into five languages and went through fifty-seven editions before the year 1600. Historically, *The Book of the Courtier* is an index to cultural changes that were taking place between medieval and early modern times. It departs from exclusively feudal and Christian educational ideals and formulates a program for the cultivation of both mind *and* body that has become fundamental to modern Western education. Representative also of the shift from medieval to modern values is Castiglione's preoccupation with manners rather than morals; that is, with *how* individuals act and how their actions may impress their peers, rather than with the intrinsic moral value of those actions.

Figure 16.8 RAPHAEL, *Portrait of Baldassare Castiglione*, ca. 1515. Oil on canvas, approx. 30¼ × 26½ in. Louvre, Paris. © R.M.N.

---

[10]In Greek mythology, a sea nymph who lured Odysseus to remain with her for seven years.

[Count Ludovico de Canossa says:] "I am of opinion that the principal and true profession of the Courtier ought to be that of arms; which I would have him follow actively above all else, and be known among others as bold and strong, and loyal to whomsoever he serves. And he will win a reputation for these good qualities by exercising them at all times and in all places, since one may never fail in this without severest censure. And just as among women, their fair fame once sullied never recovers its first lustre, so the reputation of a gentleman who bears arms, if once it be in the least tarnished with cowardice or other disgrace, remains forever infamous before the world and full of ignominy.[1] Therefore the more our Courtier excels in this art, the more he will be worthy of praise. . . .

"Then coming to the bodily frame, I say it is enough if this be neither extremely short nor tall, for both of these conditions excite a certain contemptuous surprise, and men of either sort are gazed upon in much the same way that we gaze on monsters. Yet if we must offend in one of the two extremes, it is preferable to fall a little short of the just measure of height than to exceed it, for besides often being dull of intellect, men thus huge of body are also unfit for every exercise of agility, which thing I should much wish in the Courtier. And so I would have him well built and shapely of limb, and would have him show strength and lightness and suppleness, and know all bodily exercises that befit a man of war; whereof I think the first should be to handle every sort of weapon well on foot and on horse, to understand the advantages of each, and especially to be familiar with those weapons that are ordinarily used among gentlemen; for besides the use of them in war, where such subtlety in contrivance is perhaps not needful, there frequently arise differences between one gentleman and another, which afterwards result in duels often fought with such weapons as happen at the moment to be within reach; thus knowledge of this kind is a very safe thing. Nor am I one of those who say that skill is forgotten in the hour of need; for he whose skill forsakes him at such a time, indeed gives token that he has already lost heart and head through fear.

"Moreover I deem it very important to know how to wrestle, for it is a great help in the use of all kinds of weapons on foot. Then, both for his own sake and for that of his friends, he must understand the quarrels and differences that may arise, and must be quick to seize an advantage, always showing courage and prudence in all things. Nor should he be too ready to fight except when honor demands it. . . .

"There are also many other exercises, which although not immediately dependent upon arms, yet are closely connected therewith, and greatly foster manly sturdiness; and one of the chief among these seems to me to be the chase [hunting], because it bears a certain likeness to war: and truly it is an amusement for great lords and befitting a man at court, and furthermore it is seen to have been much cultivated among the ancients. It is fitting also to know how to swim, to leap, to run, to throw stones, for besides the use that may be made of this in war, a man often has occasion to show what he can do in such matters; whence good esteem is to be won, especially with the multitude, who must be taken into account withal. Another admirable exercise, and one very befitting a man at court, is the game of tennis, in which are well shown the disposition of the body, the quickness and suppleness of every member, and all those qualities that are seen in nearly every other exercise. Nor less highly do I esteem vaulting on horse, which although it be fatiguing and difficult, makes a man very light and dexterous more than any other thing; and besides its utility, if this lightness is accompanied by grace, it is to my thinking a finer show than any of the others.

"Our Courtier having once become more than fairly expert in these exercises, I think he should leave the others on one side: such as turning somersaults, rope-walking, and the like, which savor of the mountebank and little befit a gentleman.

"But since one cannot devote himself to such fatiguing exercises continually, and since repetition becomes very tiresome and abates the admiration felt for what is rare, we must always diversify our life with various occupations. For this reason I would have our Courtier sometimes descend to quieter and more tranquil exercises, and in order to escape envy and to entertain himself agreeably with everyone, let him do whatever others do, yet never departing from praiseworthy deeds, and governing himself with that good judgment which will keep him from all folly; but let him laugh, jest, banter, frolic and dance, yet in such fashion that he shall always appear genial and discreet, and that everything he may do or say shall be stamped with grace."

[Cesare Gonzaga says:] "But having before now often considered whence this grace springs, laying aside those men who have it by nature, I find one universal rule concerning it, which seems to me worth more in this matter than any other in all things human that are done or said: and that is to avoid affectation to the uttermost and as it were a very sharp and dangerous rock; and, to use possibly a new word, to practice in everything a certain nonchalance that shall conceal design and show that what is done and said is done without effort and almost without thought[2]. . . ."

[Count Ludovico says:] "I think that what is chiefly important and necessary for the Courtier, in order to speak and write well, is knowledge; for he who is ignorant and has nothing in his mind that merits being heard, can neither say it nor write it.

"Next he must arrange in good order what he has to say or write; then express it well in words, which (if I do

___
[1] Shame, dishonor.

[2] That is, with nonchalance (in Italian, *sprezzatura*).

not err) ought to be precise, choice, rich and rightly formed, but above all, in use even among the masses; because such words as these make the grandeur and pomp of speech, if the speaker has good sense and carefulness, and knows how to choose the words most expressive of his meaning, and to exalt them, to mould position and order that they shall at a glance show and make known their dignity and splendor, like pictures placed in good and proper light.

"And this I say as well of writing as of speaking: in which however some things are required that are not needful in writing—such as a good voice, not too thin and soft like a woman's, nor yet so stern and rough as to smack of the rustic's—but sonorous, clear, sweet and well sounding, with distinct enunciation, and with proper bearing and gestures; which I think consist in certain movements of the whole body, not affected or violent, but tempered by a calm face and with a play of the eyes that shall give an effect of grace, accord with the words, and as far as possible express also, together with the gestures, the speaker's intent and feeling.

"But all these things would be vain and of small moment, if the thoughts expressed by the words were not beautiful, ingenious, acute, elegant and grave—according to the need.

"I would have him more than passably accomplished in letters, at least in those studies that are called the humanities, and conversant not only with the Latin language but with the Greek, for the sake of the many different things that have been admirably written therein. Let him be well versed in the poets, and not less in the orators and historians, and also proficient in writing verse and prose, especially in this vulgar[3] tongue of ours; for besides the enjoyment he will find in it, he will by this means never lack agreeable entertainment with ladies, who are usually fond of such things. And if other occupations or want of study prevent his reaching such perfection as to render his writings worthy of great praise, let him be careful to suppress them so that others may not laugh at him. . . .

"My lords, you must know that I am not content with the Courtier unless he be also a musician and unless, besides understanding and being able to read notes, he can play upon divers[4] instruments. For if we consider rightly, there is to be found no rest from toil or medicine for the troubled spirit more becoming and praiseworthy in time of leisure, than this; and especially in courts, where besides the relief from tedium that music affords us all, many things are done to please the ladies, whose tender and gentle spirit is easily penetrated by harmony and filled with sweetness. Thus it is no marvel that in both ancient and modern times they have always been inclined to favor musicians, and have found refreshing spiritual food in music. . . .

"I wish to discuss another matter, which I deem of great importance and therefore think our Courtier ought by no means to omit: and this is to know how to draw and to have acquaintance with the very art of painting.

"And do not marvel that I desire this art, which to-day may seem to savor of the artisan and little to befit a gentleman; for I remember having read that the ancients, especially throughout Greece, had their boys of gentle birth study painting in school as an honorable and necessary thing, and it was admitted to the first rank of liberal arts; while by public edict they forbade that it be taught to slaves. Among the Romans too, it was held in highest honor. . . ."

[The discussion turns to defining the court lady. Giuliano de' Medici addresses the company of ladies and gentlemen:] ". . . although my lord Gaspar has said that the same rules which are set the Courtier serve also for the Lady, I am of another mind; for while some qualities are common to both and as necessary to man as to woman, there are nevertheless some others that befit woman more than man, and some are befitting man to which she ought to be wholly a stranger. The same I say of bodily exercises; but above all, methinks that in her ways, manners, words, gestures and bearing a woman ought to be very unlike a man; for just as it befits him to show a certain stout and sturdy manliness, so it is becoming in a woman to have a soft and dainty tenderness with an air of womanly sweetness in her every movement. . . .

"Now, if this precept be added to the rules that these gentlemen have taught the Courtier, I certainly think she ought to be able to profit by many of them, and to adorn herself with admirable accomplishments, as my lord Gaspar says. For I believe that many faculties of the mind are as necessary to woman as to man; likewise gentle birth, to avoid affectation, to be naturally graceful in all her doings, to be mannerly, clever, prudent, not arrogant, not envious, not slanderous, not vain, not quarrelsome, not silly, to know how to win and keep the favor of her mistress and of all others, to practice well and gracefully the exercises that befit women. I am quite of the opinion, too, that beauty is more necessary to her than to the Courtier, for in truth that woman lacks much who lacks beauty. . . .

[The Court Lady:] "must have not only the good sense to discern the quality of him with whom she is speaking, but knowledge of many things, in order to entertain him graciously; and in her talk she should know how to choose those things that are adapted to the quality of him with whom she is speaking, and should be cautious lest occasionally, without intending it, she utter words that may offend him. Let her guard against wearying him by praising herself indiscreetly or by being too prolix. Let her not go about mingling serious matters with her playful or humorous discourse, or jests and jokes with her serious discourse. Let her not stupidly pretend to know that which she does not know, but modestly seek to do herself credit in that which she does know—in all things avoiding affectation, as has been said. In this way she will be adorned with good manners, and will perform with perfect grace the bodily exercises proper to women;

120

130

140

150

160

170

180

190

200

210

220

her discourse will be rich and full of prudence, virtue and pleasantness; and thus she will be not only loved but revered by everyone, and perhaps worthy to be placed side by side with this great Courtier as well in qualities of the mind as in those of the body. . . .   230

"Since I may fashion this Lady as I wish, not only am I unwilling to have her practice such vigorous and rugged manly exercises, but I would have her practice even those that are becoming to women, circumspectly and with that gentle daintiness which we have said befits her; and thus in dancing I would not see her use too active and violent movements, nor in singing or playing those abrupt and oft-repeated diminutions[5] which show more skill than sweetness; likewise the musical instruments that she uses ought, in my opinion, to be   240 appropriate to this intent. Imagine how unlovely it would be to see a woman play drums, fifes or trumpets, or other like instruments; and this because their harshness hides and destroys that mild gentleness which so much adorns every act a woman does. Therefore when she starts to dance or make music of any kind, she ought to bring herself to it by letting herself be urged a little, and with a touch of shyness which shall show that noble shame which is the opposite of effrontery. . . .

"And to repeat in a few words part of what has been   250 already said, I wish this Lady to have knowledge of letters, music, painting, and to know how to dance and make merry; accompanying the other precepts that have been taught the Courtier with discreet modesty and with the giving of a good impression of herself. And thus, in her talk, her laughter, her play, her jesting, in short, in everything, she will be very graceful, and will entertain appropriately, and with witticisms and pleasantries befitting her, everyone who shall come before her. . . ."

Q What are the primary characteristics of Castiglione's courtier? What are those of his court lady?

Q How do Castiglione's views of the well-rounded individual compare with your own?

Renaissance Women

As *The Book of the Courtier* suggests, the Renaissance provided greater opportunities for education among upper-class women than were available to their medieval counterparts. The Renaissance woman might have access to a family library and, if it pleased her parents, to a humanistic education. The Bolognese painter Lavinia Fontana (1552–1614), a product of family tutelage in painting and the arts, continued her career well after her marriage to a fellow artist, who gave up his own career and helped to rear their eleven children. Noted for her skillful portraits, Fontana received numerous commissions for works that

commemorated the luxurious weddings of the nobility. Her *Portrait of a Noblewoman* depicts a lavishly dressed young bride (whose identity is unknown) adorned with gold earrings, headdress, belt and pectoral chains, all of which are encrusted with pearls and rubies (Figure **16.9**). A bodice of shimmering satin ribbons and a red velvet dress enhance the image of wealth, loyalty (symbolized by the dog), and gentility—virtues that (along with her dowry) the young woman would likely bring to the marriage. Once married, Renaissance women's roles and rights were carefully limited by men, most of whom considered women their social and intellectual inferiors. Even such enlightened humanists as Alberti perpetuated old prejudices that found women "almost universally timid by nature, soft, and slow." Indeed, according to Alberti, nature had decreed "that men should bring things home and women care for them." Although Renaissance women were held in high esteem as housekeepers and mothers, they were not generally regarded as respectable models for male children, who, Alberti explained, should be "steered away from womanly customs and ways." Married (usually between the ages of thirteen and sixteen) to men considerably older than themselves, women often inherited large fortunes and lucrative businesses; and, as they came into such positions, they enjoyed a new sense of independence that often discouraged them from remarrying.

Renaissance women's occupations remained limited to service tasks, such as midwifery and innkeeping, but there is ample evidence that by the sixteenth century they reaped the advantages of an increasingly commercialized economy in which they might compete successfully with men. If, for centuries, women had dominated the areas of textiles, food preparation, and healthcare, many also rose to prominence in positions of political power. Elizabeth, Queen of England, and Caterina Sforza of Milan are but two of the more spectacular examples of women whose strong will and political ingenuity shaped history. The seeds of feminism planted by Christine de Pisan (see chapter 15) flowered among increasing numbers of women writers and patrons. Battista Sforza, niece of Francesco Sforza, the powerful ruler of Milan, shared the efforts of her husband Duke Federico da Montefeltro in making Urbino a cultural and intellectual center. The Duchess of Urbino (see Figure 16.4) was admired for her knowledge of Greek and Latin and for her role as patron of the arts. Women humanists, a small but visible group often bred among wealthy aristocrats, often had to choose between marriage, the convent, and the pursuit of a Liberal Arts education. Italy produced some notable female humanists, including the poet Vittoria Colonna (1490–1547), whom her admirer, Michelangelo, compared to "a block of marble whose talent was hidden deep within."

Humanist study of Greek and Latin and (in particular) intellectual inquiry into the moral philosophy of Plato, Aristotle, and Cicero, attracted a small group of women, mostly from Northern Italy. To her patrons and friends throughout Europe, the Venetian humanist Cassandra Fedele (1465–1558) penned elegant Latin letters in the tradition of Petrarch (see Reading 3.5). Female humanists,

---

[5]Rapid ornamentation or variation of a line of music, here implying excessive virtuosity.

Figure 16.9 LAVINIA FONTANA, *Portrait of a Noblewoman*, ca. 1580. Oil on canvas, 3 ft. 9¼ in. × 35¼ in. The National Museum of Women in the Arts, Washington, DC. Gift of Wallace and Wilhelmina Holladay.

however, had to contend with the criticisms of their male peers. In their writings they repeatedly defend their own efforts by citing the achievements of famous women who preceded them—a theme that earlier appeared in the writings of Boccaccio and Christine de Pisan (see Reading 3.3). Such was the case with Laura Cereta (1468–1499), the daughter of a Brescian aristocrat, who married at the age of fifteen and continued her studies even after the death of her husband (some eighteen months later). In her letters, she denounces the frivolous attention to outward forms of luxury among the women of her time and describes the difficulties encountered by intelligent women. The letter known as the *Defense of Liberal Instruction of Women* (1488) is Cereta's bitter counterattack against a critic who had praised her as a prodigy, implicitly condemning her female humanist contemporaries. "With just cause," objects Cereta, "I am moved to demonstrate how great a reputation for learning and virtue women have won by their inborn excellence." To the conventional list of famous women—Babylonian sibyls, Biblical heroines, ancient goddesses, and notable Greek and Roman writers and orators—Cereta adds the female humanists of her own time. Finally, she tries to explain why outstanding women are so few in number:

> The explanation is clear: women have been able by nature to be exceptional, but have chosen lesser goals. For some women are concerned with parting their hair correctly, adorning themselves with lovely dresses, or decorating their fingers with pearls and other gems. Others delight in mouthing carefully composed phrases, indulging in dancing, or managing spoiled puppies. Still others wish to gaze at lavish banquet tables, to rest in sleep, or, standing at mirrors, to smear their lovely faces. But those in whom a deeper integrity yearns for virtue, restrain from the start their youthful souls, reflect on higher things, harden the body with sobriety and trials, and curb their tongues, open their ears, compose their thoughts in wakeful hours, their minds in contemplation, to letters bonded to righteousness. For knowledge is not given as a gift, but [is gained] with diligence. The free mind, not shirking effort, always soars zealously toward the good, and the desire to know grows ever more wide and deep. It is because of no special holiness, therefore, that we [women] are rewarded by God the Giver with the gift of exceptional talent. Nature has generously lavished its gifts upon all people, opening to all the doors of choice through which reason sends envoys to the will, from which they learn and convey its desires. The will must choose to exercise the gift of reason.
>
> [But] where we [women] should be forceful we are [too often] devious; where we should be confident we are insecure.*

*In Margaret L. King and Albert Rabil, eds., *Her Immaculate Hand: Selected Works By and About the Women Humanists of Quattrocento Italy* (Binghampton, N.Y.: Pegasus, 1992), p. 83.

The most extraordinary of sixteenth-century female humanists, the Venetian writer Lucretia Marinella (1571–1653), was neither devious nor insecure. The daughter and the wife of physicians, Marinella published a great many works, including religious verse, madrigals, a pastoral drama, a life of the Virgin, and an epic poem that celebrated the role of Venice in the Fourth Crusade (see chapter 11). However, the work that marks Marinella's dual importance as humanist and feminist was her treatise *The Nobility and Excellence of Women and the Defects and Vices of Men*. This formal polemic (the first of its kind written by a woman) was a direct response to a contemporary diatribe on the defects of women—an attack that rehearsed the traditional misogynistic litany that found woman vain, jealous, lustful, fickle, idle, and inherently flawed. The first part of Marinella's treatise observes the standard model for dispute and debate (employed by Christine de Pisan, Laura Cereta, and others) in which womankind is defended by a series of examples of illustrious women drawn from history. More remarkable—indeed, unique to its time—is Marinella's attack on what she perceived as the defects and vices of men. Using the very techniques that prevailed in humanist polemics, Marinella presents each defect—brutality, obstinacy, ingratitude, discourtesy, inconstancy, vanity—and proceeds to illustrate each by the evidence of illustrious men from classical and biblical antiquity. Moreover, and in a manner worthy of modern feminists, she attempts to analyze the psychological basis for misogyny, contending that certain flaws—specifically anger, envy, and self-love—drive even the wisest and most learned men to attack women. The excerpts below suggest that while humanism was an enterprise dominated by men, it provided women with the tools by which they might advance their intellectual status and voice their own complaints.

READING 3.10 From Marinella's *The Nobility and Excellence of Women and the Defects of Men* (1600)

A reply to the flippant and vain reasoning adopted by men in their own favor

It seems to me that I have clearly shown that women are far nobler and more excellent than men. Now it remains for me to reply to the false objections of our slanderers. These are of two sorts, some founded on specious reasonings and others solely on authorities and their opinions. Commencing with the latter, I maintain that I am not obliged to reply to them at all. If I should affirm that the element of air does not exist, I would not be obliged to reply to the authority of Aristotle or of other writers who say that it does.

I do not, however, wish to wrong famous men in denying their conclusions, since certain obstinate people would regard this as being unjust. I say, therefore, that various reasons drove certain wise and learned men to reprove and vituperate women. They included anger, self-love, envy, and insufficient intelligence. It can be stated therefore that when Aristotle or some other man reproved women, the reason for it was either anger, envy, or too much self-love.

It is clear to everyone that anger is the origin of indecent accusations against women. When a man wishes to fulfill his unbridled desires and is unable to because of the temperance and continence of a woman, he immediately becomes angry and disdainful and in his rage says every bad thing he can think of, as if the woman were something evil and hateful. The same can be said of the envious man, who when he sees someone worthy of praise can only look at them with a distorted view. And thus when a man sees that a woman is superior to him, both in virtue and in beauty, and that she is justly honored and loved even by him, he tortures himself and is consumed with envy. Not being able to give vent to his emotions in any other way, he resorts with sharp and biting tongue to false and specious vituperation and reproof. The same occurs as a result of the too great love that men bear for themselves, which causes them to believe that they are more outstanding in wit and intelligence and by nature superior to women—an exaggerated arrogance and over-inflated and haughty pride. But if with a subtle intelligence they should consider their own imperfections, oh how humble and low they would become! Perhaps one day, God willing, they will perceive it.

All these reasons therefore induced the good Aristotle to blame women—the principal among them, I believe, being the envy he bore them. For three years, as Diogenes Laertius[1] relates, he had been in love with a lady concubine of Hermias[2] who, knowing of his great and mad love for her, gave her to him as his wife. He, arrogant with joy, made sacrifices in honor of his new lady and goddess—as it was the custom in those times to make to Ceres of Eleusis[3]—and also to Hermias who had given her to him. Pondering then on all those worthy and memorable matters, he became envious of his wife and jealous of her state, since, not being worshiped like a god by anyone, he could not equal it. Thus he turned to reviling women even though he knew they were worthy of every praise.

It can also be added that, like a man of small intelligence (pardon me you Aristotelians who are reading this . . .) he attributed the reasons for his long error to Hermias's lady, and not to his own unwise intellect, and proceeded to utter shameful and dishonorable words in order to cover up the error he had committed and to lower the female sex, which was an unreasonable thing to do.

To these two motives can also be added self-love, since he judged himself to be a miracle of nature and grew so excessively conceited that he reputed every other person in the world to be unworthy of his love. Therefore, whenever he remembered the time when he had been subservient to women and was secretly ashamed of it, he sought to cover up his failing by speaking badly of them.

The fact that it was disdain against certain women that induced him to injure the female sex is something that must of necessity be believed. He had been a lover, and as I have shown above, an unbridled lover. These were the reasons that induced poor Aristotle to say that women were more dishonest and given to gossiping than men, and more envious and slanderous. He did not see that in calling them slanderous, he too was joining the ranks of the slanderers.

In *History of Animals*, book IX, and in other places, he says that women are composed of matter, imperfect, weak, deficient and poor-spirited—things we have discussed. It could also be thoughtlessness that caused him to deceive himself about the nature and essence of women. Perhaps a mature consideration of their nobility and excellence would have proved too great a burden for his shoulders. As we know, there are many people who believe that the earth moves and the sky remains still,[4] others that there are infinite worlds,[5] still others that there is only one, and some that the fly is nobler than the heavens. Each and every person defends his or her opinion obstinately and with infinite arguments, and these are the replies that we give to those who vituperate the female sex.

There have also been some men who, on discovering a woman who was not very good, have bitingly and slanderously stated that all women are bad and wicked. They have made the grave error of basing a universal criticism on one particular case. It is true, however, that, having realized their error, they have then astutely praised good women. One reply is sufficient for the moral philosophers and poets who, when they criticize women are merely criticizing the worst ones. . . .

Of men who are ornate, polished, painted, and bleached

For men born to politics and civil life it is becoming, to a certain extent, to be elegant and polished. Everyone knows this, and it has been verified by Della Casa, Guazzo, Sabba, and *The Book of the Courtier*.[6] If, according to these authors' reasoning, this is right for men, we must believe that it is even more right for women, since beauty shines brighter among the rich and elegantly dressed than among the poor and rude. Tasso[7] demonstrates this in *Torrismondo*, by means of the Queen's speech to Rosmonda:

Why do you not adorn your pleasing limbs and with pleasing clothes augment that beauty which heaven has given you courteously and generously? Unadorned beauty in humble guise is like a rough, badly polished gem, which in a humble setting shines dully.

Since beauty is woman's special gift from the Supreme Hand, should she not seek to guard it with all diligence?

---

[1]The third century C.E. author of *Lives and Opinions of Eminent Philosophers*.
[2]The ruler of Atarneus whom Aristotle was said to have tutored.
[3]A nature deity whose cult was celebrated annually in Greece.
[4]A reference to the heliocentric theory defended by Copernicus in his treatise *On the Revolution of the Heavenly Spheres* published in 1543 (see chapter 23).
[5]A reference to the claim made by Giordorno Bruno (1548–1600) that the universe was infinite and might contain many solar systems. Bruno was burned at the stake in Rome the year that Marinella's treatise was published.
[6]A reference to four famous sixteenth-century handbooks on manners.
[7]The Italian poet Torquato Tasso (1495–1544), whose tragedy *Torrismondo* was published in 1586.

And when she is endowed with but a small amount of that excellent quality, should she not seek to embellish it by every means possible, provided it is not ignoble? I certainly believe that it is so. When man has some special gift such as physical strength, which enables him to perform as a gladiator or swagger around, as is the common usage, does he not seek to conserve it? If he were born courageous, would he not seek to augment his natural courage with the art of defense? But if he were born with little courage would he not practice the martial arts and cover himself with plate and mail and constantly seek out duels and fights in order to demonstrate his courage rather than reveal his true timidity and cowardice? 120

I have used this example because of the impossibility of finding a man who does not swagger and play the daredevil. If there is such a one people call him effeminate, which is why we always see men dressed up like soldiers with weapons at their belts, bearded and menacing, and walking in a way that they think will frighten everyone. Often they wear gloves of mail and contrive for their weapons to clink under their clothing so people realize they are armed and ready for combat and feel intimidated by them. 130

What are all these things but artifice and tinsel? Under these trappings of courage and valor hide the cowardly souls of rabbits or hunted hares, and it is the same with all their other artifices. Since men behave in this way, why should not those women who are born less beautiful than the rest hide their less fortunate attributes and seek to augment the little beauty they possess through artifice, provided it is not offensive? 140

Why should it be a sin if a woman born with considerable beauty washes her delicate face with lemon juice and the water of beanflowers and privets[8] in order to remove her freckles and keep her skin soft and clean? Or if with columbine, white bread, lemon juice, and pearls she creates some other potion to keep her face clean and soft? I believe it to be merely a small one. If roses do not flame within the lily pallor of her face, could she not, with some art, create a similar effect? Certainly she could, without fear of being reproved, because those who possess beauty must conserve it and those who lack it must make themselves as perfect as possible, removing every obstacle that obscures its splendor and grace. And if writers and poets, both ancient and modern, say that her golden hair enhances her beauty, why should she not color it blonde and make ringlets and curls in it so as to embellish it still further?.... 150 160

But what should we say of men who are not born beautiful and who yet make great efforts to appear handsome and appealing, not only by putting on clothes made of silk and cloth of gold as many do, spending all their money on an item of clothing, but by wearing intricately worked neckbands? What should we say of the medallions they wear in their caps, the gold buttons, the pearls, the pennants and plumes and the great number of liveries[9] that bring ruin on their houses? They go around with their hair waved, greased, and 170

perfumed so that many of them smell like walking perfumeries. How many are there who go to the barbers every four days in order to appear close-shaven, rosy-cheeked, and like young men even when they are old? How many dye their beards when the dread arrival of old age causes them to turn white? How many use lead combs to tint their white hairs? How many pluck out their white hairs in order to make it appear that they are in the flower of youth? I pass over the earrings that Frenchmen and other foreigners wear and the necklaces, of Gallic invention, which we read of in Livy. 180

How many spend three or four hours each day combing their hair and washing themselves with those balls of soap sold by mountebanks in the *piazza*[10]? Let us not even mention the time they spend perfuming themselves and putting on their shoes and blaspheming against the saints because their shoes are small and their feet are big, and they want their big feet to get into their small shoes. How ridiculous!

Q What, according to Marinella, motivates men to slander women?

Q How does Marinella defy traditional male attacks on female vanity?

Machiavelli and Power Politics

The modern notion of progress as an active process of improving the lot of the individual was born during the Renaissance. Repeatedly, Renaissance humanists asserted that society's leaders must exercise *virtù* in order to master Fate (often personified in Western art and literature as a female) and fashion their destinies in their own interests. Balanced against the ideals of human perfectibility championed by Castiglione and Pico were the realities of human greed, ignorance, and cruelty. Such technological innovations as gunpowder made warfare increasingly impersonal and devastating, while the rise of strong national rulers occasioned the worst kinds of aggression and brute force. Even the keepers of the spiritual kingdom on earth—the leaders of the Church of Rome—had become notorious for their self-indulgence and greed, as some Renaissance popes actually took mistresses, led armed attacks upon neighboring states, and lived at shocking levels of luxury.

The most acute critic of these conditions was the Florentine diplomat and statesman Niccolò Machiavelli (1469–1527). A keen political observer and a student of Roman history, Machiavelli lamented Italy's disunity in the face of continuous rivalry among the city-states. He anticipated that outside powers might try to take advantage of Italy's internal weaknesses. The threat of foreign invasion became a reality in 1494, when French armies marched into Italy, thus initiating a series of wars that left Italy divided and impoverished. Exiled from Florence upon the collapse of the republican government he had served from 1498 to 1512 and eager to win favor with the Medici now

[8]Flowering shrub.
[9]Servants.

[10]A broad, open public space.

that they had returned to power, Machiavelli penned *The Prince*, a political treatise that called for the unification of Italy under a powerful and courageous leader. This notorious little book laid out the guidelines for how an aspiring ruler might gain and maintain political power.

In *The Prince*, Machiavelli argued that the need for a strong state justified strong rule. He pictured the secular prince as one who was schooled in war and in the lessons of history. The ruler must trust no one, least of all mercenary soldiers. He must imitate the lion in his fierceness, but he must also act like a fox to outsmart his enemies. Finally, in the interest of the state, he must be ruthless, and, if necessary, he must sacrifice moral virtue. In the final analysis, the end—that is, the preservation of a strong state—will justify any means of maintaining power, however cunning or violent. As indicated in the following excerpts, Machiavelli formulated the idea of the state as an entity that remains exempt from the bonds of conventional morality.

READING 3.11 From Machiavelli's *The Prince* (1513)

XII How Many Different Kinds of Soldiers There Are, and of Mercenaries

. . . a Prince must lay solid foundations since otherwise he will inevitably be destroyed. Now the main foundations of all States, whether new, old, or mixed, are good laws and good arms. But since you cannot have the former without the latter, and where you have the latter, are likely to have the former, I shall here omit all discussion on the subject of laws, and speak only of arms.

I say then that the arms wherewith a Prince defends his State are either his own subjects, or they are mercenaries, or they are auxiliaries, or they are partly one and partly another. Mercenaries and auxiliaries are at once useless and dangerous, and he who holds his State by means of mercenary troops can never be solidly or securely seated. For such troops are disunited, ambitious, insubordinate, treacherous, insolent among friends, cowardly before foes, and without fear of God or faith with man. Whenever they are attacked defeat follows; so that in peace you are plundered by them, in war by your enemies. And this because they have no tie or motive to keep them in the field beyond their paltry pay, in return for which it would be too much to expect them to give their lives. They are ready enough, therefore, to be your soldiers while you are at peace, but when war is declared they make off and disappear. I ought to have little difficulty in getting this believed, for the present ruin of Italy is due to no other cause than her having for many years trusted to mercenaries, who though heretofore they may have helped the fortunes of some one man, and made a show of strength when matched with one another, have always revealed themselves in their true colors as soon as foreign enemies appeared. . . .

XIV Of the Duty of a Prince in Respect of Military Affairs

A Prince, therefore, should have no care or thought but for war, and for the regulations and training it requires, and should apply himself exclusively to this as his peculiar province; for war is the sole art looked for in one who rules and is of such efficacy that it not merely maintains those who are born Princes, but often enables men to rise to that eminence from a private station; while, on other hand, we often see that when Princes devote themselves rather to pleasure than to arms, they lose their dominions. And as neglect of this art is the prime cause of such calamities, so to be proficient in it is the surest way to acquire power. . . .

XV Of the Qualities in Respect of which Princes are Praised or Blamed

It now remains for us to consider what ought to be the conduct and bearing of a Prince in relation to his subjects and friends. And since I know that many have written on this subject, I fear it may be thought presumptuous in me to write of it also; the more so, because in my treatment of it I depart widely from the views that others have taken.

But since it is my object to write what shall be useful to whosoever understands it, it seems to me better to follow the real truth of things than an imaginary view of them. For many Republics and Princedoms have been imagined that were never seen or known. It is essential, therefore, for a Prince who would maintain his position, to have learned how to be other than good, and to use or not to use his goodness as necessity requires.

Laying aside, therefore, all fanciful notions concerning a Prince, and considering those only that are true, I say that all men when they are spoken of, and Princes more than others from their being set so high, are noted for certain of those qualities which attach either praise or blame. Thus one is accounted liberal, another miserly . . . ; one is generous, another greedy; one cruel, another tender-hearted; one is faithless, another true to his word; one effeminate and cowardly, another high-spirited and courageous; one is courteous, another haughty; one lewd, another chaste; one upright, another crafty; one firm, another facile; one grave, another frivolous; one devout, another unbelieving; and the like. Every one, I know, will admit that it would be most laudable for a Prince to be endowed with all of the above qualities that are reckoned good; but since it is impossible for him to possess or constantly practice them all, the conditions of human nature not allowing it, he must be discreet enough to know how to avoid the reproach of those vices that would deprive him of his government, and, if possible, be on his guard also against those which might not deprive him of it; though if he cannot wholly restrain himself, he may with less scruple indulge in the latter. But he need never hesitate to incur the reproach of those vices without which his authority can hardly be preserved; for if he well consider the whole matter, he will find that there may be

Line numbers: 1, 10, 20, 30, 40, 50, 60, 70, 80

a line of conduct having the appearance of virtue, to follow which would be his ruin, and that there may be another course having the appearance of vice, by following which his safety and well-being are secured.

XVII Whether It is Better to Be Loved Than Feared

[We now consider] the question whether it is better to be loved rather than feared, or feared rather than loved. It might perhaps be answered that we should wish to be both; but since love and fear can hardly exist together, if we must choose between them, it is far safer to be feared than loved. For of men it may generally be affirmed that they are thankless, fickle, false, studious to avoid danger, greedy of gain, devoted to you while you are able to confer benefits upon them, and ready, as I said before, while danger is distant, to shed their blood, and sacrifice their property, their lives, and their children for you; but in the hour of need they turn against you. The Prince, therefore, who without otherwise securing himself builds wholly on their professions is undone. For the friendships which we buy with a price, and do not gain by greatness and nobility of character, though they be fairly earned are not made good, but fail us when we have occasion to use them.

Moreover, men are less careful how they offend him who makes himself loved than him who makes himself feared. For love is held by the tie of obligation, which, because men are a sorry breed, is broken on every whisper of private interest; but fear is bound by the apprehension of punishment which never relaxes its grasp.

Nevertheless a Prince should inspire fear in such a fashion that if he do not win love he may escape hate. For a man may very well be feared and yet not hated, and this will be the case so long as he does not meddle with the property or with the women of his citizens and subjects. And if constrained to put any to death, he should do so only when there is manifest cause or reasonable justification. But, above all, he must abstain from the property of others. For men will sooner forget the death of their father than the loss of their property. . . .

XVIII How Princes Should Keep Faith

Every one understands how praiseworthy it is in a Prince to keep faith, and to live uprightly and not craftily. Nevertheless, we see from what has taken place in our own days that Princes who have set little store by their world, but have known how to overreach men by their cunning, have accomplished great things, and in the end got the better of those who trusted to honest dealing.

Be it known, then, that there are two ways of contending, one in accordance with the laws, the other by force; the first of which is proper to men, the second to beasts. But since the first method is often ineffectual, it becomes necessary to resort to the second. A Prince should, therefore, understand how to use well both the man and the beast . . . of beasts [the Prince should

90

100

110

120

130

choose as his models] both the lion and the fox; for the lion cannot guard himself from traps, nor the fox from wolves. He must therefore be a fox to discern traps, and a lion to drive off wolves.

To rely wholly on the lion is unwise; and for this reason a prudent Prince neither can nor ought to keep his word when to keep it is hurtful to him and the causes which led him to pledge it are removed. If all men were good, this would not be good advice, but since they are dishonest and do not keep faith with you, you, in return, need not keep faith with them; and no Prince was ever at a loss for plausible reasons to cloak a breach of faith. Of this numberless recent instances could be given, and it might be shown how many solemn treaties and engagements have been rendered inoperative and idle through want of faith in Princes, and that he who has best known to play the fox has had the best success.

It is necessary, indeed, to put a good disguise on this nature, and to be skillful in simulating and dissembling. But men are so simple, and governed so absolutely by their present needs, that he who wishes to deceive will never fail in finding willing dupes. . . .

And you are to understand that a Prince, and most of all a new Prince, cannot observe all those rules of conduct in respect whereof men are accounted good, being often forced, in order to preserve his Princedom, to act in opposition to good faith, charity, humanity, and religion. He must therefore keep his mind to shift as the winds and tides of Fortune turn, and, as I have already said, he ought not to quit good courses if he can help it, but should know how to follow evil courses if he must. . . . Moreover, in the actions of all men, and most of all Princes, where there is no tribunal to which we can appeal, we look to results. Therefore if a Prince succeeds in establishing and maintaining his authority, the means will always be judged honorable and be approved by every one. For the vulgar are always taken by appearances and by results, and the world is made up of the vulgar, the few only finding room when the many have no longer ground to stand on. . . .

140

150

160

170

Q What are the primary qualities of the Machiavellian ruler?

Q Why is Machiavelli often called "the first political realist"?

The advice Machiavelli gives in his handbook of power politics is based on an essentially negative view of humankind: if, by nature, human beings are "thankless," "fickle," "false," "greedy," "dishonest," and "simple" (as Machiavelli describes them), how better to govern them than by ruthless unlimited power that might keep this "sorry breed" in check? Machiavelli's treatise suggests, furthermore, that personal morality, guided by the principles of justice and benevolence, differs from the morality of the collective entity, the state. It implies, further, that the state, an impersonal phenomenon, may be declared amoral, that is, exempt from any moral judgment. In either case, Machiavelli's separation of the value-principles of governance from the principles of personal morality—of which there are all too many examples in modern political history—stunned the European community. The rules of power advertised in *The Prince* appeared to Renaissance thinkers not as idealized notions, but, rather, as expedient solutions based on a realistic analysis of contemporary political conditions. Indeed, Machiavelli's political theories rested on an analysis of human nature not as it should be, but as it was. Widely circulated, *The Prince* was hailed not simply as a cynical examination of political expediency, but as an exposé of real-life politics—so much so that the word "Machiavellian" soon became synonymous with the idea of political duplicity.

Throughout *The Prince*, Machiavelli cites examples of power drawn from Roman history and contemporary politics. In defense of the successful use of power, for instance, one of Machiavelli's favorite models was Cesare Borgia (the illegitimate son of the Renaissance Pope Alexander VI), who, along with other thoroughly corrupt and decadent members of his family, exercised a ruthless military campaign to establish a papal empire in central Italy. In such figures, Machiavelli located the heroic aspects of *virtù*: imagination, resilience, ingenuity, and canny intelligence. Machiavelli provided ample evidence to justify his denunciation of the secular ruler as the divinely appointed model of moral rectitude—a medieval conception staunchly defended by Castiglione. Machiavelli's profound grasp of past and present history, which he summed up as his "knowledge of the actions of man," made him both a critic of human behavior and modern Europe's first political scientist.

SUMMARY

Classical humanism, the movement to recover, edit, and study ancient Greek and Latin manuscripts, took shape in fourteenth-century Italy, where it marked the beginnings of the Renaissance. This revival of Greco-Roman culture was to spread throughout Western Europe over the following three hundred years. Petrarch, the father of humanism, provided the model for Renaissance scholarship and education. He glorified Ciceronian Latin, encouraged textual criticism, and wrote introspective and passionate sonnets that were revered and imitated for centuries to come.

The city of Florence was the unrivaled center of classical humanism for the first 150 years of the Renaissance. A thriving commercial and financial center dominated by a prosperous middle class, Florence found political and cultural leadership in such wealthy and sophisticated families as the Medici. Classical humanism helped to cultivate a sense of civic pride, a new respect for oral and written eloquence, and a set of personal values that sustained the ambitions of the rising merchant class.

Fifteenth-century humanists carried on Petrarch's quest to recover the classical past. Ficino translated the entire body of Plato's writings, while Pico's investigations in Hebrew and Arabic led him to believe that the world's great minds shared a single, universal truth. Pico's *Oration on the Dignity of Man* proclaimed the centrality of humankind and defended the unlimited freedom of the individual within the universal scheme.

Renaissance humanists cultivated the idea of the good life. Following Alberti's maxim, "A man can do anything he wants," they applied the moral precepts of the classical past to such contemporary pursuits as diplomacy, politics, and the arts. While Petrarch and his peers were concerned primarily with the recovery of classical manuscripts and the production of critical editions, Alberti, Castiglione, and Machiavelli eagerly infused scholarship with action. Allying their scrutiny of the past with an empirical study of the present, they championed a heroic ideal of the individual that surpassed all classical models. For Alberti, material wealth and authority proceeded from the exercise of *virtù*; for Castiglione, the superior breed of human being was *l'uomo universale*, the well-rounded and well-educated individual; for Machiavelli, only a ruthless master of power politics could ensure the survival of the state. Alberti, Castiglione, and Machiavelli are representative of those thinkers who asserted the infinite capacity for self-knowledge and exalted the role of the individual in the secular world. Their views shaped the modern character of the humanistic tradition in the European West.

GLOSSARY

condottiere (plural *condottieri*) a professional soldier; a mercenary who typically served the Renaissance city-state

sonnet a fourteen-line lyric poem with a fixed scheme of rhyming

CHAPTER 17

Renaissance Artists: Disciples of Nature, Masters of Invention

"The eye, which is called the window of the soul, is the chief means whereby the understanding may most fully and abundantly appreciate the infinite works of nature."
Leonardo

The Renaissance produced a flowering in the visual arts rarely matched in the annals of world culture. Artists embraced the natural world with an enthusiasm that was equalled only by their ambition to master the lessons of classical antiquity. The result was a unique and sophisticated body of art that set the standards for most of the painting, sculpture, and architecture produced in the West until the late nineteenth century.

During the Early Renaissance, the period from roughly 1400 to 1490, Florentine artists worked side by side with literary humanists to revive the classical heritage. These artist–scientists combined their interest in Greco-Roman art with an impassioned desire to understand the natural world and imitate its visual appearance. As disciples of nature, they studied its operations and functions; as masters of invention, they devised techniques by which to represent the visible world more realistically. In the years of the High Renaissance—approximately 1490 to 1530—the spirit of individualism reached heroic proportions, as artists such as Leonardo da Vinci, Raphael, and Michelangelo integrated the new techniques of naturalistic representation with the much respected principles of classical art.

While the subject matter of Renaissance art was still largely religious, the style was more lifelike than ever. Indeed, in contrast with the generally abstract and symbolic art of the Middle Ages, Renaissance art was concrete and realistic. Most medieval art served liturgical or devotional ends; increasingly, however, wealthy patrons commissioned paintings and sculptures to embellish their homes and palaces or to commemorate secular and civic achievements. Portrait painting, a genre that glorified the individual, became popular during the Renaissance, along with other genres that described the physical and social aspects of urban life. These artistic developments reflect the needs of a culture driven by material prosperity, civic pride, and personal pleasure.

Renaissance Art and Patronage

In the commercial cities of Italy and the Netherlands, painting, sculpture, and architecture were the tangible expressions of increased affluence. In addition to the traditional medieval source of patronage—the Catholic Church—merchant princes and petty despots vied with growing numbers of middle-class patrons and urban centered guilds whose lavish commissions brought prestige to their businesses and families. Those who supported the arts did so at least in part with an eye on leaving their mark upon society or immortalizing themselves for posterity. Thus art became evidence of material well-being as well as a visible extension of the ego in an age of individualism.

Active patronage enhanced the social and financial status of Renaissance artists. Such artists were first and foremost craftspeople, apprenticed to studios in which they might achieve mastery over a wide variety of techniques, including the grinding of paints, the making of brushes, and the skillful copying of images. While trained to observe firmly established artistic convention, the more innovative amongst them moved to create a new visual language. Indeed, for the first time in Western history, artists came to wield influence as humanists, scientists, and poets: a new phenomenon of the artist as hero and genius was born. The image of the artist as hero was promoted by the self-publicizing efforts of these artists, as well as by the adulation of their peers. The Italian painter, architect, and critic Giorgio Vasari (1511–1574) immortalized hundreds of Renaissance artists in his monumental biography *The Lives of the Most Excellent Painters, Architects, and Sculptors*, published in 1550. Vasari drew to legendary proportions the achievements of notable Renaissance figures, many of whom he knew personally. Consider, for instance, this terse characterization of Leonardo da Vinci (an artist whose work is featured in this chapter):

. . . He might have been a scientist if he had not been so versatile. But the instability of his character caused him to take up and abandon many things. In arithmetic, for example, he made such rapid progress during the short time he studied it that he often confounded his teacher by his questions. He also began the study of music and resolved to learn to play the lute, and as he was by nature of exalted imagination, and full of the most graceful vivacity, he sang and accompanied himself most divinely, improvising at once both verses and music. He studied not one branch of art only, but all. Admirably intelligent, and an excellent geometrician besides, Leonardo not only worked in sculpture . . . but, as an architect, designed ground plans and entire buildings; and, as an engineer, was the one who first suggested making a canal from Florence to Pisa by altering the river Arno. Leonardo also designed mills and water-driven machines. But, as he had resolved to make painting his profession, he spent most of his time drawing from life. . . .

The Early Renaissance

The Revival of the Classical Nude

Like the classical humanists, artists of the Renaissance were the self-conscious beneficiaries of ancient Greek and Roman culture. One of the most creative forces in Florentine sculpture, Donato Bardi, known as Donatello (1386–1466), traveled to Rome to study antique statuary. The works he observed there inspired his extraordinary likeness of the biblical hero David (Figure **17.1**). Completed in 1432, Donatello's bronze was the first freestanding, life-sized nude sculpture since antiquity. While not an imitation of any single Greek or Roman statue, the piece reveals an indebtedness to classical models in its correct anatomical proportions and gentle **contrapposto** stance (compare the *Kritios Boy* and *Doryphorus* in chapter 5). However, the sensuousness of the youthful figure—especially apparent in the surface modeling—surpasses that of any antique statue. Indeed, in this tribute to male beauty, Donatello rejected the medieval view of the human body as the wellspring of sin and anticipated the modern Western exaltation of the body as the seat of pleasure.

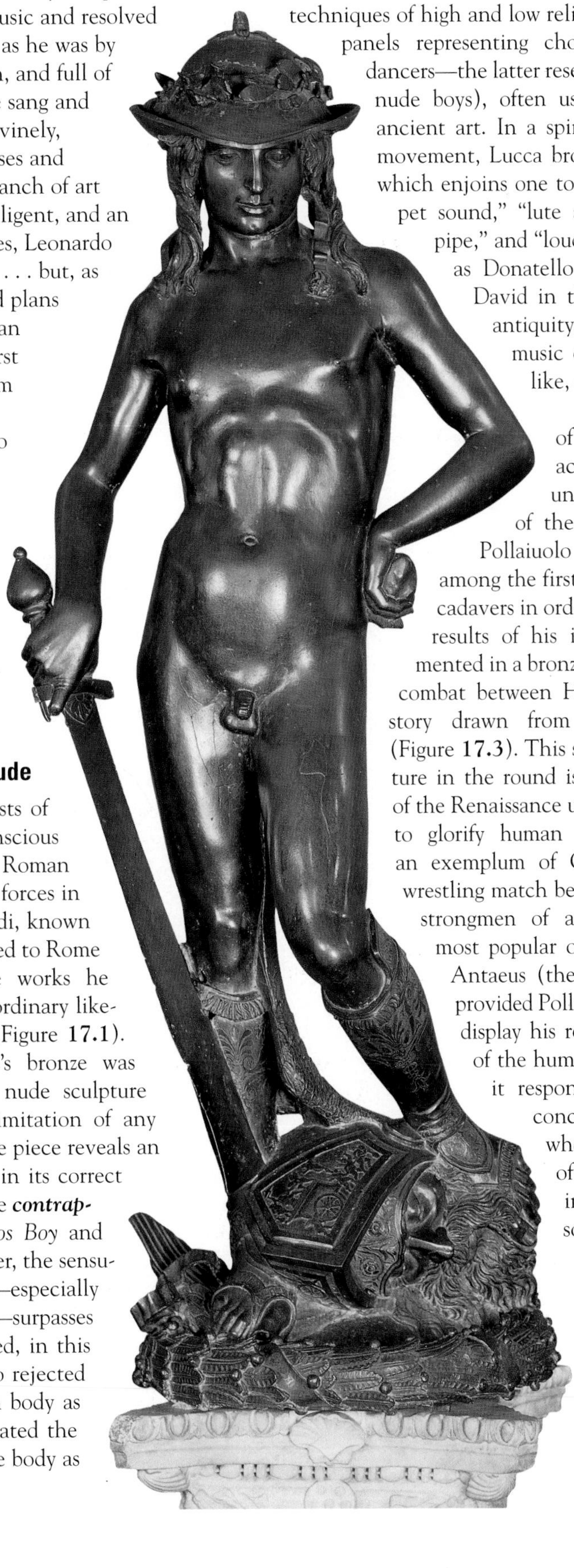

Donatello's colleague Lucca della Robbia (1400–1482) would become famous for his enameled terracotta religious figures; but in his first documented commission—the *Cantoria* (Singing Gallery) for the Cathedral of Florence—he exhibited his talents as a sculptor of marble and as a student of antiquity (Figure **17.2**). Greco-Roman techniques of high and low relief are revived in the ten panels representing choristers, musicians, and dancers—the latter resembling the *putti* (plump, nude boys), often used to depict Cupid in ancient art. In a spirited display of physical movement, Lucca brought to life Psalm 150, which enjoins one to praise God with "trumpet sound," "lute and harp," "strings and pipe," and "loud clashing cymbals." Just as Donatello conceived the biblical David in the language of classical antiquity, so Lucca invested the music of Scripture with a lifelike, classicized vigor.

The Renaissance revival of the classical nude was accompanied by a quest to understand the mechanics of the human body. Antonio Pollaiuolo (ca. 1431–1498) was among the first artists to dissect human cadavers in order to study anatomy. The results of his investigations are documented in a bronze sculpture depicting the combat between Hercules and Antaeus, a story drawn from Greco-Roman legend (Figure **17.3**). This small but powerful sculpture in the round is one of many examples of the Renaissance use of classical mythology to glorify human action, rather than as an exemplum of Christian morality. The wrestling match between the two legendary strongmen of antiquity, Hercules (the most popular of all Greek heroes) and Antaeus (the son of Mother Earth), provided Pollaiuolo with the chance to display his remarkable understanding of the human phyique, especially as it responds to stress. Pollaiuolo concentrates on the moment when Hercules lifts Antaeus off the ground, thus divesting him of his maternal source of strength and crushing him in a "body

Figure 17.1 DONATELLO, *David*, completed 1432. Bronze, height 5 ft. 2 in. Museo Nazionale del Bargello, Florence. © Studio Fotografico Quattrone, Florence.

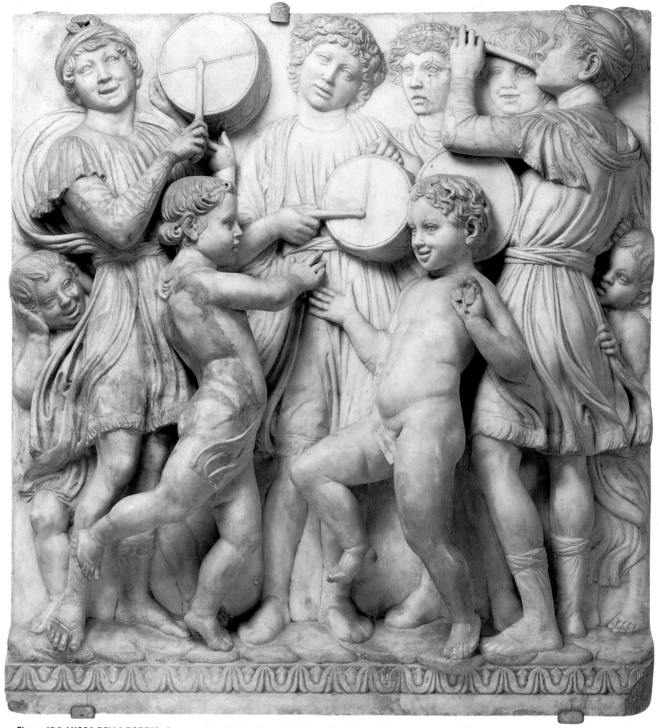

Figure 17.2 LUCCA DELLA ROBBIA, *Drummers* (detail of the *Cantoria*). Marble, 3 ft. 6⅛ in. × 3 ft. 4¹⁹⁄₂₀ in. Museo dell'Opera del Duomo, Florence.
© 1990, Photo Scala, Florence.

lock." The human capacity for tension and energy is nowhere better captured than in the straining muscles and tendons of the two athletes in combat.

The classically inspired nude fascinated Renaissance painters as well as sculptors. In the *Birth of Venus* (Figure **17.4**) by Sandro Botticelli (1445–1510), the central image is an idealized portrayal of womankind based on an antique model, possibly a statue in the Medici collection (Figure **17.5**). Born of sea foam (according to the Greek poet Hesiod), Venus floats on a pearlescent scallop shell to the shore of the island of Cythera. To her right are

two wind gods locked in sensuous embrace, while to her left is the welcoming figure of Pomona, the ancient Roman goddess of fruit trees and fecundity. Many elements in the painting—water, wind, flowers, trees—suggest procreation and fertility, powers associated with Venus as goddess of earthly love. But Botticelli, inspired by a contemporary neoplatonic poem honoring Aphrodite/ Venus as goddess of divine love, renders Venus also as an object of ethereal beauty and spiritual love. He pictorializes ideas set forth at the Platonic Academy of Florence (see chapter 16), particularly the neoplatonic notion that

objects of physical beauty move the soul to desire union with God, divine fount of beauty and truth. Botticelli's wistful goddess assumes the double role accorded her by the neoplatonists: goddess of earthly love and goddess of divine (or Platonic) love.

Botticelli executed the *Birth of Venus* in tempera on a large canvas. He rendered the figures with a minimum of shading, so that they seem weightless, suspended in space. An undulating line animates the wind-blown hair, the embroidered robes, and the delicate flowers that lie on the tapestrylike surface of the canvas. Gold accents and pastel colors (including the delicious lime of the water) further remove this idyllic vision from association with the mundane world.

Figure 17.4 SANDRO BOTTICELLI, *Birth of Venus*, after 1482. Tempera on canvas, 5 ft. 9 in. × 9 ft. ½ in. Uffizi Gallery, Florence. © 1991, Photo Scala, Florence - courtesy of the Ministero Beni e Att. Culturali.

Figure 17.5 *Medici Venus*, first century C.E. Marble, height 5 ft. ¼ in. Uffizi Gallery, Florence. Alinari, Florence.

Figure 17.6 Florence Cathedral. A.F. Kersting, © 1990, Photo Scala, Florence.

Early Renaissance Architecture

The art of the Early Renaissance was never a mere imitation of antique models (as was often the case with Roman copies of Greek sculpture), but rather an original effort to reinterpret Greco-Roman themes and principles. The same is true of Renaissance architecture. The revival of classical architecture was inaugurated by the architect, sculptor, and theorist Filippo Brunelleschi (1377–1446). In 1420, Brunelleschi won a civic competition for the design of the dome of Florence Cathedral (Figure **17.6**). His ingeniously conceived dome—the largest since that of the Pantheon in Rome—consisted of two octagonal shells. Each incorporated eight curved panels joined by massive ribs that soar upward from the octagonal **drum**—the section immediately beneath the dome—to converge at an elegant **lantern** through which light enters the interior. In the space between the two shells, Brunelleschi designed an interlocking system of ribs that operate like hidden flying buttresses (Figure **17.7**). To raise the dome, he devised new methods of hoisting stone and new masonry techniques, all of which won him acclaim in Florence. Indeed, Brunelleschi's colleague Alberti hailed the completed dome as "a feat of engineering . . . unknown and unimaginable among the ancients."

Brunelleschi was among the first architects of the Renaissance to defend classical principles of symmetry

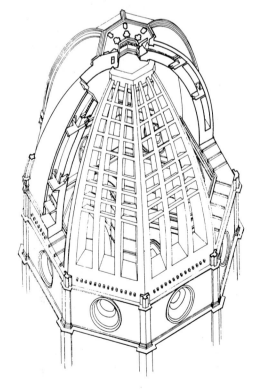

Figure 17.7 Axonometric section of the dome of Florence cathedral. Cross-section at base 11 ft. × 7 ft.

and proportion in architectural design. In the graceful little chapel he produced for the Pazzi family of Florence (Figure **17.8**), he placed a dome over the central square of the inner hall and buttressed the square with two short barrel vaults. Since the exterior of this self-contained structure was later modified by the addition of a portico, it is in the interior that Brunelleschi's break with the medieval past is fully realized (Figure **17.9**). Here, the repetition of geometric shapes enforces a new kind of visual clarity wherein all parts of the structure are readily accessible to the eye and to the mind. Gray stone moldings and gray Corinthian **pilasters**—shallow, flattened, rectangular columns that adhere to the wall surface—emphasize the "seams" between the individual segments of the stark white interior, producing a sense of order and harmony that is unsurpassed in Early Renaissance architecture. Whereas the medieval cathedral coaxes one's gaze heavenward, the Pazzi Chapel fixes the beholder decisively on earth.

Brunelleschi's enthusiasm for an architecture of harmonious proportions was shared by his younger colleague, the multitalented Florentine humanist Leon Battista Alberti (see chapter 16). Alberti's

Figure 17.8 FILIPPO BRUNELLESCHI, Pazzi Chapel, cloister of Santa Croce, Florence, ca. 1441–1460. © 1990, Photo Scala, Florence.

Figure 17.9 FILIPPO BRUNELLESCHI, Pazzi Chapel, Santa Croce, Florence, ca. 1441–1460. © Studio Fotografico Quattrone, Florence.

scientific treatises on painting, sculpture, and architecture reveal his admiration for Roman architecture and his familiarity with the writings of the Roman engineer Vitruvius (see Reading 1.18). In his *Ten Books on Architecture* (modeled after Vitruvius' *De architectura*), Alberti argued that architectural design should proceed from the square and the circle, the two most perfect geometric shapes. This proposition was the guiding precept for all of Alberti's buildings (a total of only six); it would become the definitive principle of High Renaissance composition (see Figures 17.25, 17.32, 17.33).

In the townhouse Alberti designed for the wealthy Rucellai family of Florence (Figure **17.10**)—a structure for which there were no direct antique precedents—each story is ornamented with a different classical order (see chapter

5). Rows of crisply defined arcaded windows appear on the upper stories, while square windows placed well above the street (for safety and privacy) accent the lowest level. From the Roman Colosseum (see chapter 6), Alberti borrowed the device of alternating arches and engaged columns, flattening the latter into pilasters. Here the principles of clarity and proportion prevail. For the west front of Santa Maria Novella in Florence (Figure **17.11**), Alberti produced an eloquent pattern of geometric shapes ordered by a perfect square: the height of the dominantly gray and green marble façade (from the ground to the tip of the pediment) exactly equals its width. All parts are related by harmonic proportions based on numerical ratios; for instance, the upper portion is one fourth the size of the square into which the entire face of the church would fit.

Figure 17.10 LEON BATTISTA ALBERTI (designer) and **BERNARDO ROSSELLINO** (architect), Palazzo Rucellai, Florence, 1446–1451. © 1990, Photo Scala, Florence.

Figure 17.11 LEON BATTISTA ALBERTI, Santa Maria Novella, Florence, completed 1470. Green and gray marble. © Studio Fotografico Quattrone, Florence.

Huge scrolls—imitated by generations of Western architects to come—link the upper and lower divisions of the façade. At Santa Maria Novella, as in the churches he designed at Rimini and Mantua, Alberti imposed the defining features of classical architecture upon a Latin cross basilica, thus uniting Greco-Roman and Christian traditions.

Both Alberti and Brunelleschi espoused the Hellenic theory that the human form mirrored the order inherent in the universe. The human microcosm (or "lesser world")

was the natural expression of the divine macrocosm (or "greater world"). Accordingly, the study of nature and the understanding and exercise of its underlying harmonies put one in touch with the macrocosm. Rational architecture, reflecting natural laws, would help to cultivate rational individuals. Just as the gentler modes in music elicited refined behavior (the Doctrine of Ethos; see chapter 5), so harmoniously proportioned buildings might produce ideal citizens.

Figure 17.12 JAN VAN EYCK, *Marriage of Giovanni Arnolfini and His Bride*, 1434. Tempera and oil on panel, 32¼ × 23½ in. National Gallery, London.

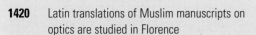

Science and Technology

1420	Latin translations of Muslim manuscripts on optics are studied in Florence
1421	Brunelleschi receives the world's first patent of monopoly for an invention (related to shipping marble)
1436	Alberti proposes the use of mathematics for obtaining graphic perspective
1545	Geronimo Cardano (Italian) publishes a new algebra text, commencing the age of modern mathematics

The Renaissance Portrait

The revival of portraiture during the Renaissance was an expression of two impulses: the desire to immortalize oneself by way of one's physical appearance and the wish to publicize one's greatness in the traditional manner of Greek and Roman antiquity. Like biography and autobiography—two literary genres that were revived during the Renaissance—portraiture and self-portraiture were hallmarks of a new self-consciousness. The bronze self-portrait of Alberti, a medal bearing the artist's personal emblem of a winged eye (see Figure 16.7), looks back to the small fourteenth-century portrait profile of King John of France (see Figure 15.14). But the former is more deliberate in its effort to recreate an accurate likeness and, at the same time, more clearly imitative of Roman coins and medals.

In the Netherlandish cities of northern Europe, affluence among members of a rising urban elite stimulated the demand for portraits. The full-length double portrait by the Netherlandish artist Jan van Eyck (1370/90–1441) was the first painting in Western art to portray a secular couple in a domestic interior (Figure **17.12**). Long thought to be a document recording the marriage of the Italian merchant Giovanni Nicolas Arnolfini to Jeanne Cenami, the so-called "Arnolfini Marriage" has been the object of debate among scholars who question both its purpose and the true identity of the sitters (though it is generally agreed that the male figure belongs to the Arnolfini family of merchants who represented the Medici bank in Bruges). Clearly the couple are in the process of making some type of vow: witness the joined hands and the raised right hand of the richly dressed man. Above the convex mirror on the wall behind the couple is the inscription *"Johannes de Eyck fuit hic"* ("Jan van Eyck was here"), information reiterated by the reflection in the mirror of the artist and a second observer. Many other objects in this domestic setting suggest a sacred union: the burning candle (traditionally carried to the marriage ceremony by the bride) symbolizes the divine presence of Christ; the dog represents fidelity; the ripening fruit that lies near and on the window sill alludes to the union of the first Couple in the Garden of Eden; and the carved image of Saint Margaret (on the chairback near the bed), patron of women in childbirth, signifies aspirations for a fruitful alliance. We may never know for certain whom these figures represent. However, the enduring vitality of the

painting lies not with the identity of the sitters, but with Jan's consummate mastery of minute, realistic details—from the ruffles on the female's headcovering to the whiskers of the monkey-faced dog. The immediacy of the material world is enhanced by the technique of oil painting, which Jan brought to perfection. By applying thin, translucent glazes of pigments bound with linseed oil, he achieved the impression of dense, atmospheric space and simulated the naturalistic effect of light reflecting off the surfaces of objects. Jan's uncanny fidelity to nature, especially evident in his portraits, has provoked the question of whether he (and other Renaissance masters) made use of optical aids, such as mirrors and lenses, or a combination of the two, to capture detailed likenesses of his subjects.* Whether or not such aids were employed by artist–scientists, it is indisputable that Jan brought to his paintings a degree of optical veracity that had never before been achieved.

To the Renaissance passion for realistic representation, Jan introduced the phenomenon of the psychological portrait—the portrait that probed the temperament, character, or unique personality of the subject. In his brilliant self-image (Figure **17.13**), whose level gaze and compressed lips suggest the personality of a shrewd realist, facial features are finely (almost photographically)

Figure 17.13 JAN VAN EYCK, *Man in a Turban* (*Self-Portrait?*), 1433. Tempera and oil on panel, 13⅜ × 10¼ in. National Gallery, London.

---

* See David Hockney, *Secret Knowledge: Rediscovering the Lost Techniques of the Old Masters*. New York: Viking, 2001.

detailed. Complex folds of crimson fabric make up the turban that crowns his head. Jan deliberately abandoned the profile portrait (see Figure 15.14) in favor of a three-quarter view that gave the figure a more aggressive spatial presence.

While Early Renaissance artists usually represented their sitters in domestic interiors, High Renaissance masters preferred to situate them in *plein-air* (outdoor) settings, as if to suggest human consonance with nature. Leonardo da Vinci's *Mona Lisa* (Figure 17.14), the world's best-known portrait, brings figure and landscape into exquisite harmony: the pyramidal shape of the sitter (probably the wife of the Florentine banker Francesco del Giocondo) is echoed in the rugged mountains; the folds of her tunic are repeated in the curves of distant roads and rivers. Soft golden tones highlight the figure, which, like the landscape, is modeled in soft, smoky (in Italian, *sfumato*) gradations of light and shade. The setting, a rocky and ethereal wilderness, is as elusive as the sitter, whose eyes and mouth are delicately blurred to produce a facial expression that is almost impossible to decipher—a smile both melancholic and mocking. While the shaved eyebrows and plucked hairline are hallmarks of fifteenth-century female fashion, the figure resists classification by age and (in the opinion of some) by gender. Praised by Renaissance copyists for its "lifelikeness," the *Mona Lisa*

Figure 17.14 LEONARDO DA VINCI, *Mona Lisa*, ca. 1503–1505. Oil on panel, 30¼ × 21 in. Louvre, Paris. Photo: © Studio Fotografico Quattrone, Florence.

Figure 17.15 (left and above) **ANDREA DEL VERROCCHIO** (completed by Alessandro Leopardi), equestrian statue of Bartolommeo Colleoni, ca. 1481–1496. Bronze, height approx. 13 ft. Campo Santi Giovanni e Paolo, Venice.
(left image) Angelo Hornak, London.

has remained an object of fascination and mystery for generations of beholders. ·

Renaissance portraits often took the form of life-sized sculptures in the round, some of which were brightly painted to achieve naturalistic effects. Such is also the case with the polychrome terracotta likeness of Lorenzo de' Medici (see Figure 16.2), executed by the Florentine sculptor Andrea del Verrocchio (1435–1488), which reveals a spirited naturalism reminiscent of Roman portraiture (see chapter 6). Verrocchio (a nickname meaning "true eye") was the Medici court sculptor and the close companion of Lorenzo, whose luxurious lifestyle and opulent tastes won him the title "Il Magnifico" ("the Magnificent"). Verrocchio immortalized the physical appearance of the Florentine ruler, who was also a humanist, poet, and musician. At the same time, he captured the willful vitality of the man whose *virtù* made him a legend in his time.

Renaissance sculptors revived still another antique genre: the equestrian statue. Verrocchio's monumental

bronze statue of the *condottiere* Bartolommeo Colleoni (Figure **17.15**), commissioned to commemorate the mercenary soldier's military victories on behalf of the city of Venice, recalls the Roman statue of Marcus Aurelius on horseback (see Figure 6.22) as well as the considerably smaller equestrian statue of Charlemagne (see Figure 11.7). However, compared with these works, Verrocchio's masterpiece displays an unprecedented degree of scientific naturalism and a close attention to anatomical detail—note the bulging muscles of Colleoni's mount. Verrocchio moreover makes his towering mercenary twist dramatically in his saddle and scowl fiercely. Such expressions of *terribilità*, or awe-inspiring power, typify the aggressive spirit that fueled the Renaissance.

Early Renaissance Artist–Scientists

If Renaissance artists took formal and literary inspiration from classical antiquity, they were equally motivated by a desire to analyze and record the natural world. The empirical study of the physical world—the reliance on direct observation—was the first step in their effort to capture in art the "look" of nature. Medieval artists had little reason to simulate the world of the senses, a world they regarded as the imperfect reflection of the divine order. For Renaissance artist–scientists, however, the visible, physical world could be mastered only if it were understood. To this end, they engaged in a program of examination, experimentation, and record keeping. They drew from live studio models, studied human and animal anatomy, and analyzed the effects of natural light on objects in space. Art became a form of rational inquiry or, as in the case of Leonardo, of scientific analysis.

For Renaissance artists, the painting constituted a window on nature: the **picture plane**, that is, the two-dimensional surface of the panel or canvas, was conceived as a transparent glass or window through which one might perceive the three-dimensional world. Various techniques aided artists in the task of recreating the illusion of reality. The technique of oil painting, refined by Jan van Eyck, was among the first of these. The application of thin oil glazes, which also became popular in Italy, produced a sense of atmospheric space rarely achieved in fresco (see Figure 15.7) or tempera (see Figure 17.4). But the more revolutionary "breakthrough" in Renaissance painting was the invention of **linear perspective**, an ingenious tool for the translation of three-dimensional space onto a two-dimensional surface. Around 1420, encouraged by research in optics stemming from humanist investigations into Arab science, Brunelleschi formulated the first laws of linear perspective. These laws describe the manner by which all parallel lines in a given visual field appear to converge at a single vanishing point on the horizon (an illusion familiar to anyone who, from the rear of a train, has watched railroad tracks "merge" in the distance). Brunelleschi projected the picture plane as a cross-section through which diagonal lines (orthogonals) connected the eye of the beholder with objects along those lines and hence with the vanishing point (Figure **17.16**; see also

Figures 17.22, 17.41). The new perspective system, stated mathematically and geometrically by Alberti in 1435 and advanced thereafter by Leonardo and Dürer (see chapter 19), enabled artists to represent objects "in depth" at various distances from the viewer and in correct proportion to one another. Linear perspective satisfied the Renaissance craving for an exact and accurate description of the physical world. It also imposed a fixed relationship—both in time and space—between the image and the eye of the beholder, making the latter the exclusive point of reference

Figure 17.16 One-point perspective.

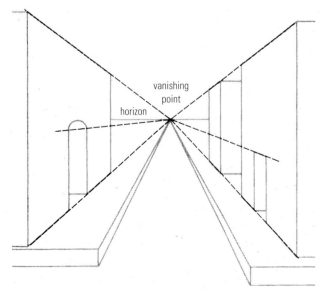

Figure 17.17 MASACCIO, *Trinity with the Virgin, Saint John the Evangelist, and Donors*, ca. 1426–1427. Fresco (now detached from wall), 21 ft. 10⅝ in. × 10 ft. 4¾ in. Santa Maria Novella, Florence. Photo: © Studio Fotografico Quattrone, Florence.

within the spatial field and thus, metaphorically, placing the individual at the center of the macrocosm.

The first artist to master Brunelleschi's new spatial device was the Florentine painter Tommaso Guidi, called Masaccio, or "Slovenly Tom" (1401–1428). Before his untimely death (possibly by poison) at age twenty-seven, Masaccio demonstrated his remarkable artistic talents in frescoes he painted for the churches of Florence. Masaccio's *Trinity with the Virgin, Saint John the Evangelist, and Donors* (Figure **17.17**), in Santa Maria Novella, reflects the artist's mastery over the new perspective system: the lines of the painted barrel vault above the *Trinity* recede and converge at a vanishing point located at the foot of the Cross, thus corresponding precisely with the eye-level of viewers standing below the scene in the church itself (Figure **17.18**). Masaccio further enhanced the illusion of real space by placing the figures of the kneeling patrons "outside of" the classical architectural forms that frame the sacred space.

The cycle of frescoes Masaccio executed for the Brancacci Chapel in Santa Maria del Carmine in Florence (Figure **17.19**) represents an even more elaborate synthesis of illusionistic techniques. In *The Tribute Money*, a scene based on the Gospel story in which Jesus honors the

Figure 17.18 (above) **MASACCIO**, *Trinity with the Virgin, Saint John the Evangelist, and Donors*, showing perspective lines.

Figure 17.19 (right) Brancacci Chapel (after restoration), Santa Maria del Carmine, Florence. Photo: © Studio Fotografico Quattrone, Florence.

Figure 17.20 MASACCIO, *The Tribute Money*, ca. 1425. Fresco (after restoration), 8 ft. 4 in. × 19 ft. 8 in. Brancacci Chapel, Santa Maria del Carmine, Florence. Photo: © Studio Fotografico Quattrone, Florence.

demands of the Roman state by paying a tax or "tribute," the artist depicted Christ instructing the Apostle Peter to gather money from the mouth of a fish, an event seen at the left; at the right, Peter is shown delivering the coins to the Roman tax collector (Figure 17.20). Masaccio's application of linear perspective—the orthogonals of the building on the right meet at a vanishing point just behind the head of Jesus—provides spatial unity to the three separate episodes. Tonal unity is provided by means of **aerial perspective**—the subtle blurring of details and diminution of color intensity in objects perceived at a distance. Refining the innovative techniques explored by Giotto at the Arena Chapel in Padua (see Figures 15.7, 15.8), Masaccio also made use of light and shade (*chiaroscuro*) to model his figures as though they actually stood in the light of the chapel window located to the right of the fresco.

Eager to represent nature as precisely as possible, Masaccio worked from live models as well as from the available antique sources. From classical statuary he borrowed the graceful stance of the Roman tax collector, who is shown twice in the fresco—viewed from front and back. Antique sculpture also probably inspired the Roman togas and the head of John the Evangelist (on Jesus' right). In the Brancacci Chapel frescoes, Masaccio anticipated the three principal features of Early Renaissance painting: the adaptation of classical prototypes, the empirical study of nature, and the application of the new techniques of spatial illusionism.

Masaccio was not alone in the rush to explore the new illusionism: artists throughout Italy refined the technique of perspective **intarsia**, the inlay of various kinds of wood to achieve new levels of pictorial illusion. They found numerous opportunities to devise *trompe l'oeil* ("fool-the-eye") illusions such as those that delighted visitors to the *studiolo* of Federico da Montefeltro (see Figure 16.6). In the domain of sculpture, the Early Renaissance master of pictorial illusionism was the Florentine goldsmith Lorenzo Ghiberti (1378–1455). His bronze panels for the east doors of the Baptistry of Florence make use of linear perspective to stage dramatic narratives filled with graceful figures and fine details (Figure 17.21). The doors bring to life ten milestones of the Hebrew bible, from the Creation of Adam and Eve to the Reign of Solomon. Overwhelmed by the majesty of these doors, the great sculptor of the next generation, Michelangelo, exclaimed that they were worthy of being the Gates of Paradise. The bottom panel on the right, which depicts the biblical meeting of Solomon and Sheba (Figure 17.22), illustrates the centrally focused use of one-point perspective that profoundly influenced High Renaissance art (see Figure 17.29).

Leonardo da Vinci as Artist–Scientist

Among all the artist–scientists of the Renaissance, Leonardo da Vinci (1452–1519) best deserves that title. A diligent investigator of natural phenomena, Leonardo examined the anatomical and organic functions of plants, animals, and human beings. He also studied the properties of wind and water and invented several hundred ingenious mechanical devices, including an armored tank, a diving bell, and a flying machine, most of which never left the

Figure 17.21 (opposite) **LORENZO GHIBERTI**, "Gates of Paradise," 1425–1442. The east portal of the Florentine baptistry contains Lorenzo Ghiberti's immense (18 ft. 6 in. tall) gilt-bronze doors, brilliantly depicting in low relief ten episodes from the Old Testament. Canali Photobank, Capriolo, Italy.

Figure 17.22 LORENZO GHIBERTI, *Meeting of Solomon and Sheba* (single panel of the "Gates of Paradise," Figure 17.21). Gilt-bronze relief, 31¼ × 31¼ in. Museo dell'Opera del Duomo, Florence. © Quattrone, Florence.

notebook stage. Between 1489 and 1518, Leonardo produced thousands of drawings accompanied by notes (Figure **17.23**) written in mirror-image script (devised perhaps to discourage imitators and plagiarists). This annotated record of the artist–scientist's passion to master nature includes anatomical drawings whose accuracy remained unsurpassed until 1543, when the Flemish physician Andreas Vesalius published the first medical illustrations of the human anatomy. Some of Leonardo's studies explore ideas (for example, the standardization of machine parts) that were far in advance of their time. Although Leonardo's notebooks—unpublished until 1898—had little influence upon European science, they remain a symbol of the Renaissance imagination and a timeless source of inspiration: the comic book hero Batman, according to its twentieth-century creator Bob Kane, was born when Kane first viewed Leonardo's sketches related to the mechanics of flight (Figure **17.24**).

Following Alberti, Leonardo maintained that proportional principles govern both nature and art. Indeed, Leonardo's belief in a universal order led him to seek a basic correspondence between human proportions and ideal geometric shapes, as Vitruvius and his followers had advised. Leonardo's so-called "Vitruvian Man" (Figure **17.25**), whose strict geometry haunts the compositions of High Renaissance painters and architects, is the metaphor for the Renaissance view of the microcosm as a mirror of the macrocosm. Yet, more than any other artist of his time, Leonardo exalted the importance of empirical experience for discovering the general rules of nature. Critical of abstract speculation bereft of sensory confirmation, he held that the human eye was the most dependable instrument for obtaining true knowledge of nature. When Leonardo wrote, "That painting is the most to be praised which agrees most exactly with the thing imitated," he was articulating the Renaissance view of art as the imitation of nature. Although Leonardo never established a strict methodology for the formulation of scientific laws, his insistence on direct experience and experimentation made him the harbinger of the Scientific Revolution that would sweep through Western Europe during the next two centuries. In the following excerpts from his notebooks, Leonardo defends the superiority of sensory experience over "book learning" and argues that painting surpasses poetry as a form of human expression.

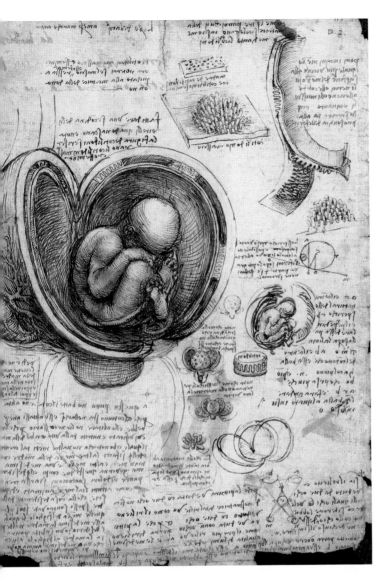

Figure 17.23 (left) **LEONARDO DA VINCI**, *Embryo in the Womb*, ca. 1510. Pen and brown ink, 11¾ × 8½ in. The Royal Collection, Royal Library, Windsor Castle. © 2005 Her Majesty Queen Elizabeth II.

READING 3.12 From Leonardo da Vinci's *Notes* (ca. 1510)

I am fully aware that the fact of my not being a man of   1
letters may cause certain arrogant persons to think that
they may with reason censure me, alleging that I am a man
ignorant of book-learning. Foolish folk! Do they not know
that I might retort by saying, as did Marius to the Roman
Patricians, "They who themselves go about adorned in the
labor of others will not permit me my own." They will say
that because of my lack of book-learning, I cannot properly
express what I desire to treat of. Do they not know that
my subjects require for their exposition experience rather   10
than the words of others? And since experience has been
the mistress of whoever has written well, I take her as my
mistress, and to her in all points make my appeal.

I wish to work miracles. . . . And you who say that it is
better to look at an anatomical demonstration than to see
these drawings, you would be right, if it were possible to
observe all the details shown in these drawings in a single
figure, in which, with all your ability, you will not see nor
acquire a knowledge of more than some few veins, while,
in order to obtain an exact and complete knowledge of   20
these, I have dissected more than ten human bodies,
destroying all the various members, and removing even

Figure 17.24 **LEONARDO DA VINCI**, *Wing Construction for a Flying Machine*, ca. 1500. Pen and brown ink. Biblioteca Ambrosiana, Milan. Codex Atlanticus, f.309v–a.

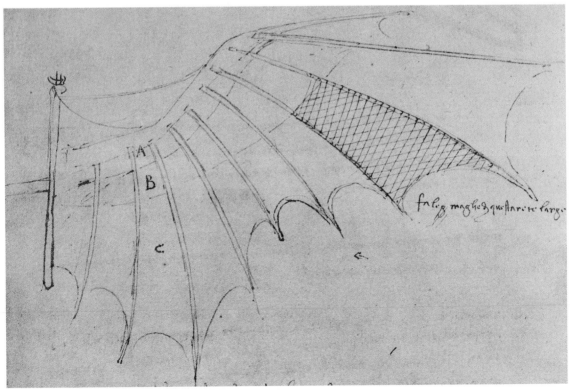

Figure 17.25 LEONARDO DA VINCI, *Proportional Study of a Man in the Manner of Vitruvius*, ca. 1487. Pen and ink, 13½ × 9⅝ in. Galleria dell'Accademia, Venice.

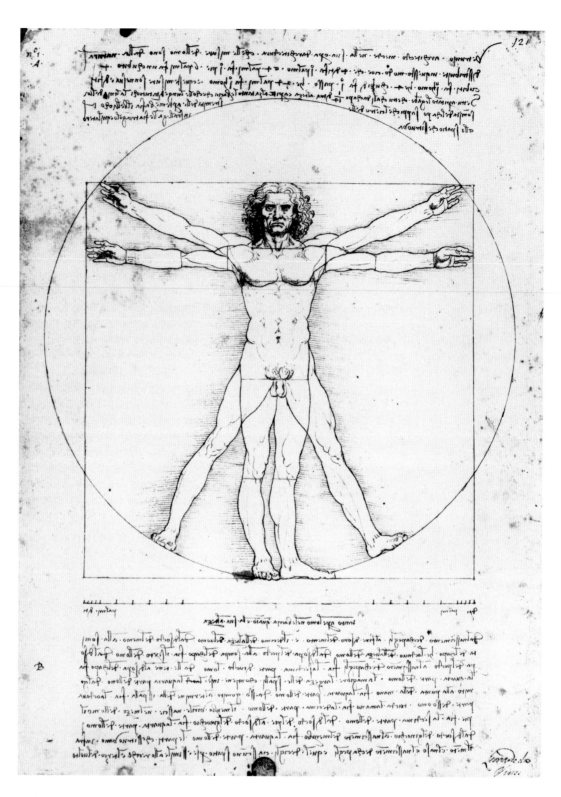

the very smallest particles of the flesh which surrounded these veins without causing any effusion of blood other than the imperceptible bleeding of the capillary veins. And, as one single body did not suffice for so long a time, it was necessary to proceed by stages with so many bodies as would render my knowledge complete; and this I repeated twice over in order to discover the differences. . . .

The eye, which is called the window of the soul, is the chief means whereby the understanding may most fully and abundantly appreciate the infinite works of nature; and the ear is the second inasmuch as it acquires its **30**

importance from the fact that it hears the things which the eye has seen. If you historians, or poets, or mathematicians had never seen things with your eyes you would be ill able to describe them in your writings. And if you, O poet, represent a story by depicting it with your pen, the painter with his brush will so render it as to be more easily satisfying and less tedious to understand. If you call painting "dumb poetry," then the painter may say of the poet that his art is "blind painting." Consider then which is the more grievous affliction, to be blind or be dumb! Although the poet has as wide a choice of subjects **40** as the painter, his creations fail to afford as much satisfaction to mankind as do paintings, for while poetry attempts with words to represent forms, actions, and scenes, the painter employs the exact images of the forms in order to reproduce these forms. Consider, then, which is more fundamental to man, the name of man or **50** his image? The name changes with change of country; the form is unchanged except by death.

And if the poet serves the understanding by way of the ear, the painter does so by the eye which is the nobler sense. I will only cite as an instance of this how if a good painter represents the fury of a battle and a poet also describes one, and the two descriptions are shown together to the public, you will soon see which will draw most of the spectators, and where there will be most discussion, to which most praise will be given and which **60** will satisfy the more. There is no doubt that the painting which is by far the more useful and beautiful will give the greater pleasure. Inscribe in any place the name of God and set opposite to it his image, you will see which will be held in greater reverence!. . .

If you despise painting, which is the sole imitator of all the visible works of nature, it is certain that you will be despising a subtle invention which with philosophical and ingenious speculation takes as its theme all the various kinds of forms, airs, and scenes, plants, animals, grasses **70** and flowers, which are surrounded by light and shade. And this truly is a science and the true-born daughter of nature, since painting is the offspring of nature. But in order to speak more correctly we may call it the grandchild of nature; for all visible things derive their existence from nature, and from these same things is born painting. So therefore we may justly speak of it as the grandchild of nature and as related to God himself.

Q How does this reading illustrate Leonardo's role as an artist–scientist?

Q In what ways is painting, according to Leonardo, superior to poetry?

The High Renaissance

Leonardo

By the end of the fifteenth century, Renaissance artists had mastered all of the fundamental techniques of visual illusionism, including linear and aerial perspective and the use of light and shade. They now began to employ these techniques in ever more heroic and monumental ways. To the techniques of scientific illusionism they wedded the classical principles of clarity, symmetry, and order, arriving at a unity of design that would typify High Renaissance art. The two artists whose paintings best represent the achievements of the High Renaissance are Leonardo da Vinci and Raphael.

In his few (and largely unfinished) religious narratives, Leonardo da Vinci fused narrative and symbolic content to achieve an ordered, grand design. The classic example is his *Last Supper*, executed in the late 1490s to adorn the wall of the refectory (the monastery dining room) of Santa Maria delle Grazie in Milan (Figure **17.26**). The *Last Supper* is one of the great religious paintings of all time. Leonardo intended that the sacred event *appear* to take place within the monastic dining room: the receding lines of the ceiling beams and side niches in the fresco create a sense of spatial depth and link the scene illusionistically with the interior walls of the refectory. Leonardo fixed the vanishing point at the center of the composition directly behind the head of Jesus so that the orthogonals of the composition (see Figure 17.16) radiate out from the head of the figure whose message would illuminate the world. Topped by a pediment, the open doorway (one of three, symbolic of the Trinity) acts as a halo, reinforcing the centrality of Christ and his mission as "light of the world." The formal elements of the composition thereby underscore the symbolic aspects of the religious narrative. To this masterful rationalization of space, Leonardo added high drama: he divided the apostles into four groups of three who interact in response to the Master's declaration that one of them would betray him (Matthew 26:21). The somber mood, enhanced by Christ's meditative look and submissive gesture indicating the bread and wine as symbols of the Eucharist, is heightened by the reactions of the apostles—astonishment, anger, disbelief—appropriate to their biblical personalities. (The angry Peter, for instance—fifth from the left—wields the knife he later uses to cut off the ear of Christ's assailant, Malchus.)

Slow in his working methods, Leonardo rejected the traditional (fast-drying) fresco technique of applying paint to the wet-plastered wall. Instead, he experimented with a mixture of oil, tempera, and varnish that proved to be non-durable. The use and abuse of the refectory over the centuries—especially after it was hit by an Allied bomb in 1943—further precipitated the deterioration of the painting. Between the eighteenth and twentieth centuries, the fresco underwent many retouchings, repaintings, and cleanings, the most recent of which was a twenty-two-year Italian-led rehabilitation enterprise (completed in 1999) that made use of various technologies, but left many of the figures with no facial features (Figure **17.27**). Bitter controversy has followed on the heels of this (and other) restorations of landmark artworks. While some scholars praise the recent restoration of the *Last Supper*, others claim that the cleaning has done additional damage and has distorted Leonardo's colors beyond repair. Most agree, however, that what is left of the masterpiece is not much more than a ghost of the original.

Science and Technology

1494	Leonardo devises plans to harness the waters of the Arno River
1508	Leonardo records the results of cadaver dissections and analyzes the movements of birds in flight in unpublished manuscripts
1513	Leonardo undertakes scientific studies of botany, geology, and hydraulic power

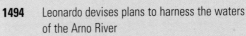

The following excerpt from Vasari's biography of Leonardo offers a glimpse into the circumstances surrounding the creation of the *Last Supper*.

READING 3.13 From Vasari's *Lives of the Most Excellent Painters, Architects, and Sculptors* (1550)

Biography of Leonardo da Vinci

The master gave so much beauty and majesty to the heads of the Apostles that he was constrained to leave the Christ unfinished, convinced as he was that he could not render the divinity of the Redeemer. Even so, this work has always been held in the highest estimation by the Milanese and by foreigners as well. Leonardo rendered to perfection the doubts and anxieties of the Apostles, their desire to know by whom their Master is to be betrayed. All their faces show their love, terror, anger, grief, or bewilderment, unable as they are to fathom the meaning of the Lord. The spectator is also struck by the determination, hatred, and treachery of Judas [fourth figure from the left]. The whole is executed with the most minute exactitude. The texture of the tablecloth seems actually made of linen.

The story goes that the prior was in a great hurry to see the picture done. He could not understand why Leonardo should sometimes remain before his work half a day together, absorbed in thought. He would have him work away, as he compelled the laborers to do who were digging in his garden, and never put the pencil down. Not content with seeking to hurry Leonardo, the prior even complained to the duke, and tormented him so much that, at length, he sent for Leonardo and courteously entreated him to finish the work. Leonardo, knowing the duke to be an intelligent man, explained himself as he had never bothered to do to the prior. He made it clear that men of genius are sometimes producing most when they seem least to labor, for their minds are then occupied in the shaping of those conceptions to which they afterward give form. He told the duke that two heads were yet to be done: that of the Savior, the likeness of which he could not hope to find on earth and had not yet been able to create in his imagination in perfection of celestial grace: and the other, of Judas. He said he wanted to find features fit to render the appearance of a man so depraved as to betray his benefactor, his Lord, and the Creator of the world. He said he would still search but as a last resort he could always use the head of the troublesome and impertinent prior. This made the duke laugh with all his heart. The prior was utterly confounded and went away to speed the digging in his garden. Leonardo was left in peace.

Figure 17.26 LEONARDO DA VINCI, *Last Supper*, ca. 1485–1498 Fresco: oil, tempera, and varnish on plaster, 15 ft. 1⅛ in × 28 ft. 10½ in. Refectory, Santa Maria delle Grazie, Milan. AKG Images, London. This shows the fresco before restoration.

Q What aspects of Leonardo's *Last Supper* does Vasari admire? What does this suggest about Renaissance standards in the visual arts?

Raphael

The second of the great High Renaissance artists was Urbino-born Raphael (Raffaello Sanzio; 1483–1520). Less devoted to scientific speculation than Leonardo, Raphael was first and foremost a master painter. His fashionable portraits were famous for their accuracy and incisiveness. A case in point is the portrait of Raphael's lifelong friend Baldassare Castiglione (see Figure 16.8), which captures the self-confidence and thoughtful intelligence of this celebrated Renaissance personality.

Raphael's compositions are notable for their clarity, harmony, and unity of design. In *The Alba Madonna* (Figure 17.28), one of Raphael's many renderings of the Madonna and Child, he sets the Virgin in a landscape framed by the picturesque hills of central Italy. Using clear, bright colors and precise draftsmanship, Raphael organized the composition according to simple geometric shapes: the triangle (formed by the Virgin, Christ child, and the infant John the Baptist), the circle (the painting's basic shape and the head of the Virgin), and the trapezoid (one length of which is formed by the Virgin's outstretched leg). Despite the dignity of the composition and the nobility of the figures, the scene might be construed as a record of an ordinary woman with two children in a landscape, for Raphael has avoided obvious religious symbolism, such as the traditional halo. In Raphael's world, all is sweetness and light. Raphael idealized his figures, especially his female saints, and often gave them sentimental facial expressions and theatrical poses—features that were taken to extremes by the artist's many imitators.

In 1510 Pope Julius II, the greatest of Renaissance Church patrons, commissioned Raphael to execute a series of frescoes for the Vatican Stanza della Segnatura—the Pope's personal library and the room in which official church papers were signed. The paintings were to represent the four domains of human learning: theology, philosophy, law, and the arts. To illustrate philosophy, Raphael painted *The School of Athens*. In this landmark fresco, the artist immortalized with unsurpassed dignity the company of the great philosophers and scientists of ancient history. At the center of the composition appear, as if in scholarly debate, the two giants of classical philosophy: Plato, who points heavenward to indicate his view of reality as fixed in universal Forms, and Aristotle, who points to the earth to indicate that universal truth depends on the study of nature. Framed by a series of receding arches, the two

Figure 17.27 LEONARDO DA VINCI, *Last Supper*, ca. 1485–1498. © Quattrone, Florence. This shows the painting in Figure 17.26 after the restoration completed in 1999.

Figure 17.28 RAPHAEL, *The Alba Madonna*, ca. 1510. Oil on wood transferred to canvas, diameter 37¼ in. © 2000 Board of Trustees, National Gallery of Art, Washington, D.C. Andrew W. Mellon Collection.

philosophers stand against the bright sky, beneath the lofty vaults of a Roman basilica that resembles the newly remodeled Saint Peter's Cathedral (Figure **17.29**). Between their heads lies the invisible vanishing point at which all the principal lines of sight converge. On either side of the great hall appear historical figures (Figure **17.30**) belonging to each of the two philosophic "camps": the Platonists (left) and the Aristotelians (right).

The School of Athens is a portrait gallery of Renaissance artists whose likenesses Raphael borrowed to depict his classical heroes. The stately, bearded Plato is an idealized portrait of Leonardo, who was visiting Rome while Raphael was at work in the Vatican. The balding Euclid, seen bending over his slate in the lower right corner of the composition, resembles Raphael's good friend, the architect Bramante. In the far right corner, Raphael himself (wearing a dark hat) appears discreetly among the Aristotelians. And in final revisions of the fresco, Raphael added to the left foreground the likeness of Michelangelo in the guise of the brooding and solitary Greek philosopher Heraclitus. *The School of Athens* is the ultimate tribute to the rebirth of classical humanism in the age of the Renaissance, for here, in a unified, imaginary space, the artists of Raphael's day are presented as the incarnations of the intellectual titans of antiquity.

In the restrained nobility of the near life-sized figures and the measured symmetry of the composition, Raphael's *School of Athens* marked the culmination of a style that had begun with Giotto and Masaccio; here, Raphael gave concrete vision to a world purged of accident and emotion. Monumental in conception and size and flawless in execution, *The School of Athens* advanced a set of formal principles that came to epitomize the *Grand Manner*: spatial clarity, decorum (that is, propriety and good taste), balance, unity of design, and grace (the last especially evident in the subtle symmetries of line and color). These principles remained touchstones for Western academic art until the late nineteenth century.

Architecture of the High Renaissance: Bramante and Palladio

During the High Renaissance, the center of artistic activity shifted from Florence to Rome as the popes undertook a campaign to restore the ancient city of Rome to its original grandeur as the capital of Christendom. When Pope Julius II commissioned Donato Bramante (1444–1514) to rebuild Saint Peter's Cathedral, the architect designed a monumentally proportioned, centrally planned church to be capped by an immense dome. Bramante's plan was much modified in the 120 years it took to complete the

Figure 17.29 RAPHAEL, *The School of Athens*, 1509–1511. Fresco, 26 ft. × 18 ft. Stanza della Segnatura, Vatican, Rome. © 1990, Photo Scala, Florence.

Figure 17.30 Plan of *The School of Athens*.

1 Apollo
2 Alcibiades or Alexander
3 Socrates
4 Plato (Leonardo)
5 Aristotle
6 Minerva
7 Sodoma
8 Raphael
9 Ptolemy
10 Zoroaster (Pietro Bembo?)
11 Euclid (Bramante)
12 Diogenes
13 Heraclitus (Michelangelo)
14 Parmenides, Xenocrates, or Aristossenus
15 Francesco Maria della Rovere
16 Telauges
17 Pythagoras
18 Averhöes
19 Epicurus
20 Federigo Gonzaga
21 Zeno

new Saint Peter's. But his ideal of a building organized so that all structural elements were evenly disposed around a central point took shape on a smaller scale in his Tempietto, the "little temple" that marked the site of Saint Peter's martyrdom in Rome (Figure **17.31**). Modeled on the classical *tholos* (see chapter 5), Bramante's circular stone chapel is ringed by a simple Doric colonnade and topped by a dome elevated upon a niched drum. Although the interior affords little light and space, the exterior gives the appearance of an elegant marble reliquary, a perfect structure from which nothing can be added or subtracted without damage to the whole.

The Renaissance passion for harmonious design had an equally powerful influence on the history of domestic architecture, a circumstance for which the Italian architect Andrea Palladio (1518–1580) was especially responsible. In his *Four Books on Architecture*, published in Venice in 1570, Palladio defended symmetry and centrality as the controlling elements of architectural design. He put his ideals into practice in a number of magnificent country houses he built for patrons in northern Italy. The Villa

Rotonda near Vicenza—a centrally planned, thirty-two-room country house—is a perfectly symmetrical structure featuring a central room (or rotunda) covered by a dome (Figure **17.32**). All four façades of the villa are identical, featuring a projecting Ionic portico approached by a flight of steps (Figure **17.33**). In its geometric clarity, its cool elegance, and its dominance over its landscape setting, the Villa Rotonda represents the Renaissance distillation of classical principles as applied to secular architecture. With this building, Palladio established the definitive ideal in domestic housing for the wealthy and provided a model of solemn dignity that would inspire generations of neoclassical architects in England and America (see chapter 26).

Michelangelo and Heroic Idealism

The works of the High Renaissance master Michelangelo Buonarroti (1475–1564) are some of the most heroic in Renaissance art. An architect, poet, painter, and engineer, Michelangelo regarded himself first and foremost as a sculptor. At the age of twenty-one, he launched his career with a commission for a marble *Pietà* that would serve as a tomb monument in Old Saint Peter's Cathedral in Rome (Figure **17.34**). Boasting that he would produce the most beautiful marble sculpture in Rome, Michelangelo carved the image of the young Virgin holding the lifeless body of Jesus (as was traditional to this subject), but, at the same time, caught in a moment of sorrowful meditation. The figure of Mary, disproportionately large in comparison with that of Jesus, creates a protective pyramidal shape that not only supports, but enfolds the Son. All elements of the composition—the position of the left arm of Jesus, the angles formed by his knees, and the folds of Mary's drapery—work toward a gentle unity of design that contrasts sharply with earlier versions of the subject (see Figure 15.9). Indeed, Michelangelo's *Pietà* transformed the late medieval devotional image into a monumental statement on the meaning of Christian sacrifice.

Michelangelo went on to establish his reputation in Florence at the age of twenty-seven, when he undertook to carve a freestanding larger-than-life statue of the biblical David from a gigantic block of Carrara marble that no other sculptor had dared to tackle (Figure **17.35**). When Michelangelo completed the statue in 1504, the rulers of Florence placed it at the entrance to the city hall as a symbol of Florentine vigilance. Compared to Donatello's lean and introspective youth (see Figure 17.1), Michelangelo's

Figure 17.31 DONATO BRAMANTE, Tempietto, San Pietro in Montorio, Rome, 1502. Height 46 ft., external diameter 29 ft. Photo: © Vincenzo Pirozzi, Rome.

Figure 17.32 ANDREA PALLADIO (Andrea di Pietro Gondola), Villa Rotonda, Vicenza, Italy, completed 1569. Photo: Bridgeman Art Library, London.

David is a defiant presence—the offspring of a race of giants. While indebted to classical tradition, Michelangelo deliberately violated classical proportions by making the head and hands of his figure too large for his trunk. The body of the fearless adolescent, with its swelling veins and taut muscles, is tense and brooding, powerful rather than graceful. Indeed, in this image, Michelangelo drew to heroic proportions the Renaissance ideals of *terribilità* and *virtù*.

Although Michelangelo considered himself primarily a sculptor, he spent four years fulfilling a papal commission to paint the 5,760-square-foot ceiling of the Vatican's Sistine Chapel (Figure **17.36**). The scope and monumentality of this enterprise reflect both the ambitions of Pope Julius II and the heroic aspirations of Michelangelo himself. Working from scaffolds poised some 70 feet above the floor, Michelangelo painted a vast scenario illustrating the Creation and Fall of Humankind as recorded in

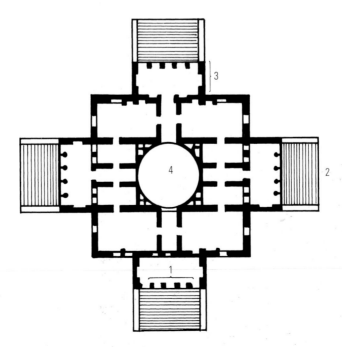

Figure 17.33
Plan of the Villa Rotonda, Vicenza, Italy.
1 Columns
2 Steps
3 Portico
4 Central domed space

Genesis (1:1 through 9:27; Figure **17.37**). In the nine principal scenes, as well as in the hundreds of accompanying prophets and sibyls, he used high-keyed, clear, bright colors (restored by recent cleaning). He overthrew many traditional constraints, minimizing setting and symbolic details and maximizing the grandeur of figures that—like those he carved in stone—seem superhuman in size and spirit. A significant archeological event influenced Michelangelo's treatment of the figure after 1506: in that year, diggers working in Rome uncovered the Laocoön (see Figure 5.32), the celebrated Hellenistic sculpture that had been known to Western scholars only by way of the Roman writer, Pliny. The sculpture—with its bold contortions and its powerfully rendered anatomy—had as great an impact on Michelangelo and the course of High Renaissance art as Cicero's prose had exercised on Petrarch and early Renaissance literature. Indeed, the twisted torsos, taut muscles, and stretched physiques of the Sistine Chapel figures reflect the influence of the Laocoön

and other recovered classical antiquities. In the *Creation of Adam* (Figure **17.38**), God and Man—equal in size and muscular grace—confront each other like partners in the divine plan. Adam reaches longingly toward God, seeking the moment of fulfillment, when God will charge his languid body with celestial energy. If the image depicts Creation, it is also a metaphor for the Renaissance belief in the potential divinity of humankind—the visual analogue of Pico's *Oration on the Dignity of Man* (see chapter 16). Creation and creativity are themes that dominate Michelangelo's sonnets. In some of the sonnets, he likens the creative act to the workings of neoplatonic love, which move to purge the base (or lower) elements of the human being. In others, he suggests that the task of the sculptor is to "liberate" the "idea" that is embedded within the marble block. Hailed as a major poet even in his own time, Michelangelo reflected upon all aspects of the creative life; reflecting on the Sistine Chapel ceiling, he describes his hardships with comic eloquence:

Figure 17.34 MICHELANGELO, *Pietà*, 1497–1500. Marble, 15 ft 8½ in. St. Peter's, Rome. © 1990, Photo Scala, Florence.

In this hard toil I've such a goiter grown,
Like cats that water drink in Lombardy,
(Or wheresoever else the place may be)
That chin and belly meet perforce in one.
My beard doth point to heaven, my scalp its place
Upon my shoulder finds; my chest, you'll say,
A harpy's is, my paint-brush all the day
Doth drop a rich mosaic on my face.
My loins have entered my paunch within,
My nether end my balance doth supply,
My feet unseen move to and fro in vain.
In front to utmost length is stretched my skin
And wrinkled up in folds behind, while I
Am bent as bowmen bend a bow in [Spain].*

In 1546, Michelangelo accepted the papal commission to complete the dome and east end of the new Saint Peter's Cathedral in Rome—a project that followed numerous earlier efforts to make the basilica a centrally planned, domed church (Figure **17.39**). For Saint Peter's, Michelangelo designed an elliptically shaped dome on a huge drum ornamented with double columns of the "colossal order" (Figure **17.40**). He lived to build the drum, but it was not until 1590 that the dome was completed. Rising some 450 feet from the floor of the nave to the top of its tall lantern, Michelangelo's dome was heroic in size and dramatic in contour. But its enormous double shell of brick and stone proved impractical: cracks in the substructure appeared less than ten years after completion, and the superstructure had to be bolstered repeatedly over the centuries, most recently by means of chains. Nevertheless, the great dome inspired numerous copies, such as that of Saint Paul's Cathedral in London (see Figure 22.2) and the United States Capitol in Washington, D.C.

Michelangelo shared the neoplatonic belief that the soul, imprisoned in the body, yearned to return to its sacred origins. In his last works of art, as in his impassioned sonnets, he explored the conflict between flesh and spirit that had burdened many humanists, including Petrarch. The restless, brooding figures of Michelangelo's late paintings and sculptures writhe and twist, like spirits trying to free themselves of physical matter. Ever the master of invention, the aging Michelangelo moved the gravity and solemnity of High Renaissance art in the direction of mannered theatricality (see Figure 20.3).

Figure 17.35 MICHELANGELO, *David*, 1501–1504. Marble, height 13 ft. 5 in. Galleria dell' Accademia, Florence. Photo: © Studio Fotografico Quattrone, Florence.

Figure 17.36 (following pages) **MICHELANGELO**, Sistine Chapel ceiling (after cleaning), Vatican, Rome, 1508–1512. Fresco, 45 ft. × 128 ft. Vatican Museums.

*Robert J. Clements. *The Poetry of Michelangelo*. N.Y: New York University Press, 1966. pp. 91–92.

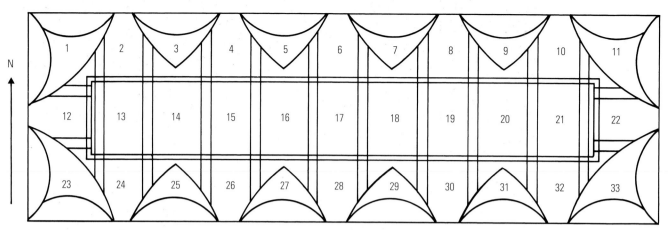

Figure 17.37 Sistine Chapel ceiling, plan of scenes (after Hibbard).

1 Death of Haman
2 Jeremiah
3 Salmon
4 Persian Sibyl
5 Roboam
6 Ezekiel
7 Ozias
8 Eritrean Sibyl
9 Zorobabel

10 Joel
11 David and Goliath
12 Jonah
13 Separation of Light from
   Darkness
14 Creation of Sun, Moon, Planets
15 Separation of Land from Water
16 Creation of Adam
17 Creation of Eve

18 Temptation and Expulsion
19 Sacrifice of Noah
20 The Flood
21 Drunkenness of Noah
22 Zechariah
23 Moses and the Serpent of Brass
24 Libyan Sibyl
25 Jesse
26 Daniel

27 Asa
28 Cumaean Sibyl
29 Ezekias
30 Isaiah
31 Josiah
32 Delphic Sibyl
33 Judith and Holofernes

Figure 17.38 (below) **MICHELANGELO**, *Creation of Adam*, detail of Figure 17.36. Fresco. Vatican Museums, Rome.

Figure 17.40
MICHELANGELO, dome
of Saint Peter's, Vatican,
Rome, ca. 1546–1564
(view from the south).
Dome completed by
Giacomo della Porta,
1590. Photo: © James
Morris, London.

Figure 17.39 (below)
MICHELANGELO, plan
for the new Saint Peter's,
Vatican, Rome,
ca. 1537–1550.

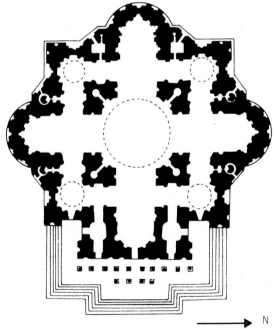

→ N

The High Renaissance in Venice

The most notable artworks of the High Renaissance did not come from Florence, which suffered severe political upheavals at the end of the fifteenth century, but from the cities of Rome, Milan, and Venice. Venice, the Jewel of the Adriatic and a thriving center of trade, was a cluster of islands whose main streets consisted of canals lined with richly ornamented palaces. The pleasure-loving Venetians, governed by a merchant aristocracy, regularly imported costly tapestries, jewels, and other luxury goods from all parts of Asia. During the sixteenth century, Venice outshone all of the other city-states of Italy in its ornate architecture and its taste for pageantry, both of which are recreated in the *Procession of the Reliquary of the Cross in Piazza San Marco* (Figure **17.41**) by one of Venice's leading artists, Gentile Bellini (1429?–1507). In this panoramic canvas, which employs the new system of one-point perspective to dramatize the union of civic and religious ritual, the Cathedral of Saint Mark resembles a monumental version of the ornate reliquary shrine carried in the foreground. A symbol of Venetian opulence and one of the city's most prized architectural treasures, San Marco reflects the cross-cultural heritage of Byzantine, Islamic, and Western Christian decorative styles. The multidomed cathedral was begun during the eleventh century and ornamented over many centuries with dazzling mosaics that adorn both the interior and the exterior. As befitting this city of jeweled altarpieces, radiant mosaics, and sparkling lagoons, Renaissance Venice produced an art of color and light. While Florentine artists depended primarily on *line* as fundamental to design and the articulation of form, the Venetians delighted in the subjective use of *color*. In preference to fresco-painting and tempera applied on wood panels, Venetian painters favored the oil medium, by which they might build up fine color glazes on rough canvas surfaces.

The two greatest Venetian colorists were Giorgio Barbarelli, known as Giorgione (ca. 1477–1511), and Tiziano Vecelli, called Titian (ca. 1488–1576). Little is known of Giorgione's life, but his influence on his younger colleague was significant. The *Pastoral Concert* (Figure **17.42**), a work that some scholars hold to be an early Titian, was probably begun by Giorgione and completed by Titian. This intriguing canvas shows two magnificently dressed Venetian courtiers—one playing a lute—in the presence of two female nudes. One woman holds a recorder,

Figure 17.41 GENTILE BELLINI, *Procession of the Reliquary of the Cross in Piazza San Marco*, 1496. Oil on canvas, 12 ft. ½ in. × 24 ft. 5¼ in. Galleria dell'Accademia, Venice. © Cameraphoto Arte, Venice.

while the other pours water into a well. The precise subject of the painting is unclear, but its sensuousness—more a product of mood than of narrative content—is enhanced by textural contrasts: the satin costume of the lute player versus the golden flesh tones of bare skin, the dense foliage of the middle ground versus the thin atmosphere on the distant horizon, and so forth. In its evocation of untroubled country life, *Pastoral Concert* may be considered the visual equivalent of pastoral verse, a genre that became popular among Renaissance humanists. But the painting

also introduces a new subject that would become quite fashionable in Western art: the nude in a landscape setting. During the sixteenth century, the female nude—often bearing the name of a classical goddess—became a favorite subject of patrons seeking sensuous or erotic art for private enjoyment. The most famous of such commissions, the so-called *Venus of Urbino* (Figure **17.43**), was painted for Guidobaldo della Rovera, the Duke of Urbino, during the last stage of Titian's artistic career. Here, a curvaceous nude reclines on a bed in the curtained alcove

Figure 17.42 TITIAN (begun by Giorgione), *Pastoral Concert*, ca. 1505. Oil on canvas, 3 ft. 7¼ in. × 4 ft. 6¼ in. Louvre, Paris. Photo: © R.M.N., Paris.

of a typical upper-class Venetian palace. The tiny roses in her hand, the myrtle plant (a symbol of Venus, goddess of love and fertility) on the window sill, the faithful dog at her feet, and the servants who rummage in the nearby wedding chest all suggest impending marriage, while her seductive pose and arresting gaze are manifestly sexual. Titian enhanced the sensuality of the image by means of exquisitely painted surfaces: the delicate nuances of creamy skin modeled with glowing pinks, the reddish blond locks of hair, the deep burgundies of tapestries and cushions, and the cooler bluish whites of the sheets—all bathed in a pervasive golden light. Titian, who worked almost exclusively in oils, applied paint loosely, building up forms with layers of color so that contours seem to melt into each other, a technique best described as "painterly." He preferred broken and subtle tones of color to the flat, bright hues favored by such artists as Raphael. Titian's painterly style became the definitive expression of the coloristic manner in High Renaissance painting and a model for such artists as Rubens in the seventeenth century and Delacroix in the nineteenth.

The Music of the Renaissance

Like Renaissance art, Renaissance music was increasingly secular in subject matter and function. However, the perception of the Renaissance as a time when secular music overtook ecclesiastical music may be due to the fact that after 1450 more secular music was committed to paper. The printing press, perfected in Germany in the mid-fifteenth century, encouraged the preservation and dissemination of all kinds of musical composition. With the establishment

of presses in Venice in the late fifteenth century, printed books of lute music and part-books for individual instruments appeared in great numbers. (Most music was based on preexisting melodies, and manuscripts normally lacked tempo markings and other indications as to how a piece was to be performed.) Publishers also sold handbooks that offered instructions on how to play musical instruments. It is no surprise, then, that during the Renaissance, music was composed by both professional and amateur musicians. Indeed, Castiglione observed that making music was the function of all well-rounded individuals. Music was an essential ingredient at intimate gatherings, court celebrations, and public festivals (Figure **17.44**). And virtuosity in performance, a hallmark of Renaissance music, was common among both amateurs and professionals. Such Renaissance princes as Lorenzo de' Medici took pleasure in writing songs for the carnivals that traditionally preceded the Lenten season. On pageant wagons designed for holiday spectacles in Florence and other cities, masked singers, dancers, and mimes enacted mythological, religious, and contemporary tales in musical performance.

While the literary and visual evidence of classical antiquity was readily available to the humanists of the Renaissance, few musical examples had survived, and none could be accurately deciphered. For that reason, medieval tradition maintained a stronger influence in the development of music than it did in art and literature. (Not until the late sixteenth century did composers draw on Greek drama as the inspiration for a new genre: opera—discussed in chapter 20.) Moreover, perhaps because performing music was believed to be within everyone's reach, musicians were not held in such high esteem

Figure 17.43 TITIAN, *Venus of Urbino*, 1538–1539. Oil on canvas, 3 ft. 11 in. × 5 ft. 5 in. Uffizi Gallery, Florence.
© 1996, Photo Scala, Florence - courtesy of the Ministero Beni e Att. Culturali.

Figure 17.44 LORENZO COSTA, *The Concert*, ca. 1485–95. Oil on poplar, 3 ft. 1½ in. × 29¾ in. National Gallery, London.

as painters, sculptors, or architects of the Renaissance. Most theorists, including Leonardo da Vinci (himself a musician of some renown), considered poetry—and by extension, music—inferior to painting. Nevertheless, just as Renaissance artists pursued a more "natural-looking" art, Renaissance composers sought a more "natural-sounding" music. By the early fifteenth century, the trend toward consonant sounds encouraged the use of **intervals** of thirds in place of the traditional medieval (and ancient) intervals of fourths and fifths.

Early Renaissance Music: Dufay

While in the visual arts Italy took the lead, in music, French and Franco-Flemish composers outshone their Italian counterparts. During the fifteenth and much of the sixteenth centuries, composers from Burgundy and

Flanders dominated the courts of Europe, including those of Italy. The leading Franco-Flemish composer of the fifteenth century, Guillaume Dufay (1400–1474), spent more than thirteen years of his career in Italy, during which time he set to music the verses of Petrarch and Lorenzo de' Medici (unfortunately, the latter compositions have been lost). In Dufay's more than two hundred surviving vocal and instrumental compositions, including motets, masses, and *chansons* (secular songs), he made extensive use of late medieval polyphonic techniques. At the same time, he introduced a close melodic and rhythmic kinship between all parts of a musical composition.

Just as religious subject matter inspired much of the art of Renaissance painters and sculptors, so religious music—and especially compositions for the Mass—held a prominent place in Dufay's output. However, sacred and secular themes are often indistinguishable in Dufay's works, and both are suffused by warmth of feeling. For his Mass settings, Dufay followed the common practice of using melodies borrowed from popular folk tunes. In the *Missa L'homme armé*, for instance, he employed the best known of all fifteenth-century French folksongs, "The Armed Man," as the *cantus firmus* for all sections of the piece.

High Renaissance Music: Josquin

If Dufay was the leading composer of the Early Renaissance, the outstanding figure in High Renaissance music was Josquin des Prez (ca. 1440–1521). Josquin followed the example of his predecessors by serving at the courts of France and Italy, including that of the papacy. A master of masses, motets, and secular songs, he earned international recognition as "the prince of music." Like Dufay, Josquin unified each polyphonic mass around a single musical theme, but, more in the grand style of the painter Raphael, Josquin contrived complex designs in which melody and harmony were distributed symmetrically and with "geometric" clarity. He might give focus to a single musical phrase in the way that Raphael might center the Virgin and Child within a composition. And, in an effort to increase compositional balance, he might group voices into pairs, with the higher voices repeating certain phrases of the lower ones. The expressive grace of Josquin's music followed from the attention he gave to the relationship between words and music. He tailored musical lines so that they followed the natural flow of the words, a device inspired perhaps by his appreciation of the classical kinship of song and text. Josquin was among the first to practice **word painting**, the manipulation of music to convey the literal meaning of the text—as, for example, where the text describes a bird's ascent, the music might rise in pitch. Word painting characterized both the religious and secular music of the Renaissance.

In music, as in the visual arts, composers of the Renaissance valued unity of design. Josquin achieved a homogeneous musical texture by the use of **imitation**, a technique whereby a melodic fragment introduced in the first voice is repeated closely (though usually at a different pitch) in the second, third, and fourth voices, so that one overlaps the next. Simple rhythmic lines and the ingenious use of imitation contributed to the smooth and sonorous style of such motets as "Tulerunt Dominum meum." A master of the integration of multiple voice lines—one of his motets has as many as twenty-four parts—Josquin wrote motets that featured a continuous flow of interwoven melodies and a graceful design comparable to that of Raphael's High Renaissance compositions.

The Madrigal

During the sixteenth century, the secular counterpart of the motet and the most popular type of vernacular song was the **madrigal**, a composition for three to six unaccompanied voices. Usually polyphonic in texture, the madrigal often incorporated a large degree of vocal freedom, including the playful use of imitation and word painting. An intimate kind of musical composition, the madrigal might develop a romantic theme from a sonnet by Petrarch or give expression to a trifling and whimsical complaint. The Flemish composer Roland de Lassus (Orlando di Lasso; 1532–1594), who graced princely courts throughout Renaissance Europe, produced almost two hundred madrigals among his more than two thousand compositions. In 1550, at age eighteen, Lassus wrote one of the most delightful madrigals of the Renaissance: "Matona, mia cara" ("My lady, my beloved"). The piece, which describes a suitor's effort to seduce his ladyfriend, ends each stanza with a frivolous group of nonsense syllables.

> My lady, my beloved,
> Such pleasure would I choose
> To sing beneath your window
> Of love you'll never lose.
>
> > *Dong, dong, dong, derry, derry,*
> > *Dong, dong, dong, dong.*
>
> I beg you, only hear me,
> This song of sweetest news,
> My love for you is boundless
> Like lovebirds I enthuse.
>
> > *Dong, dong, dong, derry, derry,*
> > *Dong, dong, dong, dong.*
>
> For I would go a-hunting
> And falcons I would use
> To bring you spoils a-plenty
> Plump woodfowl as your dues.
>
> > *Dong, dong, dong, derry, derry,*
> > *Dong, dong, dong, dong.*
>
> But though my words should fail me,
> Lest fear my cause should lose,
> E'en Petrarch could not help me
> Nor Helicon's fair Muse.
>
> > *Dong, dong, dong, derry, derry,*
> > *Dong, dong, dong, dong.*

♪ See Music Listening Selections at end of chapter.

♪ See Music Listening Selections at end of chapter.

But only say you'll love me
And if you'll not refuse
I'll boldly sing of my love
Night long until the dews.

Dong, dong, dong, derry, derry,
*Dong, dong, dong, dong.**

Madrigals flourished primarily in the courts of Italy and England. At the fashionable court of Queen Elizabeth I of England, the madrigal became the rage. Usually based on Italian models, the English madrigal was generally lighter in mood than its Italian counterpart and often technically simple enough to be performed by amateurs. Two of the most popular Elizabethan composers, John Dowland (1563–1626) and Thomas Morley (1557–1602), composed English-language solo songs and madrigals that are still enjoyed today.

Instrumental Music of the Renaissance

Although most Renaissance music was composed to be sung, the sixteenth century made considerable advances in the development of instrumental music. Music for solo instruments was popular, with the lute still the favorite. In London, its popularity as a solo instrument and to accompany madrigals (see Figure 17.44) warranted the importation of almost 14,000 lute strings in the one-year period between 1567 and 1568. A wide variety of other instruments, such as shawms, cromornes, cornets, trumpets, trombones, stringed instruments, and drums, were used for accompaniment and in small instrumental ensembles (Figure 17.45). Renaissance composers wrote music for portable **organs** (popular in private homes and princely courts) and for two other types of keyboard instruments: the **clavichord** and the **harpsichord** (also called the *spinet*, the *clavecin*, and the *virginal*—the last possibly after the "Virgin Queen," Elizabeth I of England, who was an accomplished musician). Harpsichord sounds are made by quills that pluck a set of strings, while clavichord notes are produced by metal tangents that strike the strings. Such instruments create bright, sharp sounds, somewhat more robust in the harpsichord. Since Renaissance instruments produce a less dynamic and smaller range of sound than do modern instruments, they demand greater attention to nuances of *timbre*—the "color" or quality of musical sound.

During the late Middle Ages, instruments occasionally took the place of one or more voice parts. It was not until the Renaissance, however, that music for instruments alone regularly appeared. Instrumental compositions developed out of dance tunes with strong rhythms and distinctive melodic lines. Indeed, the earliest model for the instrumental suite was a group of dances arranged according to contrasting rhythms. Instrumental music was characterized by the same kind of complex invention that marked the vocal compositions of Josquin, and the skillful performance of difficult instrumental passages brought acclaim to both performer and composer.

Renaissance Dance

In the Renaissance, dance played an important role in all forms of entertainment: town pageants, courtly rituals, festal displays sponsored by trade and merchant guilds, and in almost all nonecclesiastical celebrations. Folk dancing, of the kind illustrated by the Flemish painter Pieter Brueghel (see Figure 19.14), was a collective experience that fostered a powerful sense of community. In contrast with folk dances, court dances stressed individual grace and poise. Renaissance dancing masters distinguished folk dance from courtly dance, a move that eventually resulted in the development of dance as a form of theatrical entertainment.

The Renaissance witnessed the first efforts to establish dance as an independent discipline. Guglielmo Ebreo (1439–1482), dancing master at the court of Urbino, –wrote one of the first treatises on the art of dancing. He emphasized the importance of grace, the memorization of fixed steps, and the coordination of music and motion. Guglielmo also choreographed a number of lively dances

Figure 17.45 HANS BURGKMAIR, *The Music Room*, from *Der Weiss Kunig*, late sixteenth century. Woodcut. The J. Pierpont Morgan Library, New York. © 1990. Art Resource, NY.

*Translation by Susan Peach, copyright © Calmann & King 1998.

♪ See Music Listening Selections at end of chapter.

or *balli*—the Italian word from which the French *ballet* derives. Three favorite forms of Italian court dance were the *basse* (a slow, solemn ceremonial dance), the *saltarello* (a vigorous, three-beat dance featuring graceful leaps), and the *piva* (a dance in rapid tempo with double steps). In Guglielmo's day, such dances were still performed by members of the court, rather than by professional dancers.

SUMMARY

Renaissance artists were disciples of nature in that they brought a scientific curiosity to the study of the natural world and diligently probed its operations. Donatello, Pollaiuolo, Masaccio, and Brunelleschi studied the mechanics of the human body, the effects of light on material substances, and the physical appearance of objects in three-dimensional space. At the same time, Renaissance artists were masters of invention: they perfected the technique of oil painting, formulated laws of perspective, and applied the principles of classical art to the representation of Christian and contemporary subjects. Patronized by a wealthy European middle class, they revived such this-worldly genres as portraiture and gave new attention to the nude body as an object of beauty.

The art of the High Renaissance marks the culmination of a hundred-year effort to wed the techniques of naturalistic representation to classical ideals of proportion and order. Leonardo, the quintessential artist–scientist, tried to reconcile empirical experience with abstract principles of design. The compositions of Raphael, with their monumental grace and unity of design, became standards by which Western paintings would be judged for centuries.

The multitalented Michelangelo brought a heroic idealism to the treatment of traditional Christian and classical themes. In Venice, Titian's painterly handling of the female nude represented a new and more sensuous naturalism. In architecture, the centrally planned buildings of Bramante and Palladio fulfilled the quest of such Early Renaissance architects as Brunelleschi and Alberti for an architecture of harmony, balance, and clarity.

The Renaissance produced an equally splendid flowering in music, especially among Franco-Flemish composers. Secular compositions began to outnumber religious ones. The techniques of imitation and word painting infused both religious and secular music with homogeneity and increased expressiveness. Printed sheet music helped to popularize the madrigal and other secular, vernacular song forms. Instrumental music and dance emerged as independent genres. Like their classical predecessors, Renaissance artists exalted technical skill, ingenuity, and imagination. Their optimism, combined with intellectual curiosity and increasing worldliness, fueled the early modern era in the West.

MUSIC LISTENING SELECTIONS

CD One Selection 17 Guillaume Dufay, *Missa L'homme armé (The Armed Man Mass)*, "Kyrie I," ca. 1450.

CD One Selection 18 Roland de Lassus (Orlando di Lasso), Madrigal, "Matona, mia cara" ("My lady, my beloved"), 1550.

CD One Selection 19 Thomas Morley, Madrigal, "My bonnie lass she smileth," 1595.

CD One Selection 20 Josquin des Prez, Motet, "Tulerunt Dominum meum," ca. 1520.

GLOSSARY

aerial perspective the means of representing distance that relies on the imitation of the ways atmosphere affects the eye—outlines are blurred, details lost, contrasts of light and shade diminished, hues bluer, and colors less vivid; also called "atmospheric perspective"

clavichord (French, *clavier*, meaning "keyboard") a stringed keyboard instrument widely used between the sixteenth and eighteenth centuries; when the player presses down on a key, a brass tangent or blade rises and strikes a string

contrapposto (Italian, "counterpoised") a position assumed by the human body

in which one part is turned in opposition to another part

drum the cylindrical section immediately beneath the dome of a building

harpsichord a stringed keyboard instrument widely used between the sixteenth and eighteenth centuries; when the player presses down on a key, a quill, called a plectrum, plucks the string

imitation a technique whereby a melodic fragment introduced in the first voice of a composition is repeated closely (though usually at a different pitch) in the second, third, and fourth voices, so that one voice overlaps the next; the repetition may be exactly

the same as the original, or it may differ somewhat

intarsia a type of marquetry (see chapter 21) involving the technique of wood inlay

interval the distance between the pitches of two musical tones

lantern a small, windowed tower on top of a roof or dome that allows light to enter the interior of a building

linear perspective (or **optical perspective**) a method of creating the semblance of three-dimensional space on a two-dimensional surface; it derives from two optical illusions: (1) parallel lines appear to converge as they recede toward a vanishing point on a horizon level with the viewer's eye, and

(2) objects appear to shrink and move closer together as they recede from view

madrigal a vernacular song, usually composed for three to six unaccompanied voices

organ a keyboard instrument in which keyboards and pedals are used to force air into a series of pipes, causing them to sound

picture plane the two-dimensional surface of a panel or canvas

pilaster a shallow, flattened, rectangular column or pier attached to a wall surface

word painting the manipulation of music to convey a specific object, thought, or mood—that is, the content of the text

PART 2

A Brave New World

"O brave new world, That has such people in it," exclaims Miranda, a character in Shakespeare's *The Tempest*, as she considers the "many goodly creatures" of the playwright's fictional island. With similar astonishment but perhaps a little less optimism, mid-sixteenth-century Europeans contemplated their brave new world—one that witnessed the fragmentation of Christendom, the onset of devastating religious wars, and the discovery of strange cultures in remote parts of the world.

By the sixteenth century, the old medieval order was crumbling. Classical humanism and the influence of Renaissance artist–scientists were spreading throughout Northern Europe. Ambition and commerce drove Westerners to undertake a program of expansion by which they came to encounter the peoples of Africa, Asia, and the Americas. Spanish campaigns of geographic exploration resulted in the colonization of the Americas. Overseas ventures led to a more accurate appreciation of world geography and the proliferation of commercial traffic. Muslim travelers and Christian explorers participated in cross-cultural exchanges that were to bring massive economic, political, and cultural transformation to all parts of the modern world.

The brave new world of the sixteenth century saw the rise of a global economy and vast opportunities for material wealth. Europe's population rose from 69 million in 1500 to 188 million in 1600. As European nation-states tried to strengthen sovereignty and international influence, rivalry among Western nations intensified. The "superpowers"—Spain, under the Habsburg ruler Philip II (1527–1598) and England under Elizabeth I (1533–1603)—contended for advantages in Atlantic shipping and trade. In order to resist the encroachment of the stronger nation-states, weaker states formed balance-of-power alliances that often invited war.

While political turmoil threatened the medieval order, sixteenth-century science challenged age-old traditions. In 1530, the Polish astronomer Nicolas Copernicus (1473–1543) completed a treatise that opposed the earth-centered view of the universe. Contrary to the position supported by Scripture and the Church, *De revolutionibus* (*On the Revolution of the Heavenly Spheres*) contended that the planets moved around the sun. Scientific theory, geographic exploration, and commercial expansion all worked to move the West toward modernity; but the event that most effectively destroyed the old medieval order was the Protestant Reformation. In the wake of Protestantism, the unity of European Christendom disappeared forever. And, as religious factionalism compounded the political rivalries among the nation-states, the future of Western civilization seemed grim indeed.

During the 300-year "seam" between old and new, Westerners reassessed their relationship with the classical and medieval past, created the first global trade empires, and virtually determined the futures of Africa and the Americas. Such devices as firearms, eyeglasses, the printing press, and the clock—all products of this period—gave Europeans considerable mastery over nature. But the very people who invented these technological wonders also pursued cruel wars of religion, widespread trade in chattel slavery, and ruthless campaigns of witch burnings—activities that seem to give the lie to any optimistic theory of human progress. Nevertheless, the sixteenth century set the humanistic tradition on an irreversibly modern course.

(opposite) **HIERONYMUS BOSCH**, *Hell*, ca. 1510–1515. Oil on wood, 7 ft. 2⅜ in. × 3 ft. 2¼ in. © Museo del Prado, Madrid

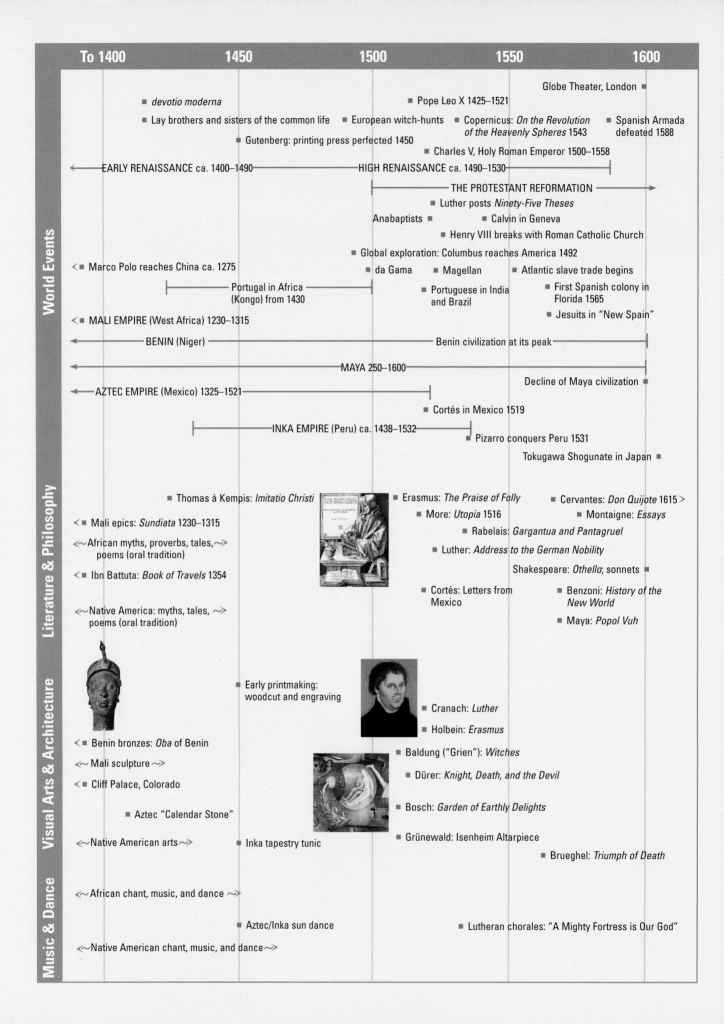

	To 1400	1450	1500	1550	1600

World Events

- Globe Theater, London ■
- ■ *devotio moderna*
- Pope Leo X 1425–1521
- ■ Lay brothers and sisters of the common life
- ■ European witch-hunts
- ■ Copernicus: *On the Revolution of the Heavenly Spheres* 1543
- ■ Spanish Armada defeated 1588
- ■ Gutenberg: printing press perfected 1450
- ■ Charles V, Holy Roman Emperor 1500–1558
- ←————EARLY RENAISSANCE ca. 1400–1490————————HIGH RENAISSANCE ca. 1490–1530——→
- ————————THE PROTESTANT REFORMATION————————→
- ■ Luther posts *Ninety-Five Theses*
- Anabaptists ■   ■ Calvin in Geneva
- ■ Henry VIII breaks with Roman Catholic Church
- ■ Global exploration: Columbus reaches America 1492
- ◄■ Marco Polo reaches China ca. 1275
- ■ da Gama   ■ Magellan   ■ Atlantic slave trade begins
- ■ Portuguese in India and Brazil
- ■ First Spanish colony in Florida 1565
- ————Portugal in Africa (Kongo) from 1430————
- ◄■ MALI EMPIRE (West Africa) 1230–1315
- ■ Jesuits in "New Spain"
- ←————BENIN (Niger)————————Benin civilization at its peak————→
- ←————————MAYA 250–1600————————→
- Decline of Maya civilization ■
- ←——AZTEC EMPIRE (Mexico) 1325–1521——→
- ■ Cortés in Mexico 1519
- ——INKA EMPIRE (Peru) ca. 1438–1532——
- ■ Pizarro conquers Peru 1531
- Tokugawa Shogunate in Japan ■

Literature & Philosophy

- ■ Thomas à Kempis: *Imitatio Christi*
- ■ Erasmus: *The Praise of Folly*
- ■ Cervantes: *Don Quijote* 1615 ►
- ■ More: *Utopia* 1516
- ■ Montaigne: *Essays*
- ◄■ Mali epics: *Sundiata* 1230–1315
- ■ Rabelais: *Gargantua and Pantagruel*
- ◄~African myths, proverbs, tales,~► poems (oral tradition)
- ■ Luther: *Address to the German Nobility*
- ◄■ Ibn Battuta: *Book of Travels* 1354
- Shakespeare: *Othello*; sonnets ■
- ■ Cortés: Letters from Mexico
- ■ Benzoni: *History of the New World*
- ◄~Native America: myths, tales,~► poems (oral tradition)
- ■ Maya: *Popol Vuh*

Visual Arts & Architecture

- ■ Early printmaking: woodcut and engraving
- ■ Cranach: *Luther*
- ■ Holbein: *Erasmus*
- ◄■ Benin bronzes: *Oba* of Benin
- ■ Baldung ("Grien"): *Witches*
- ◄~ Mali sculpture ~►
- ■ Dürer: *Knight, Death, and the Devil*
- ◄■ Cliff Palace, Colorado
- ■ Aztec "Calendar Stone"
- ■ Bosch: *Garden of Earthly Delights*
- ◄~Native American arts~►
- ■ Inka tapestry tunic
- ■ Grünewald: Isenheim Altarpiece
- ■ Brueghel: *Triumph of Death*

Music & Dance

- ◄~African chant, music, and dance~►
- ■ Aztec/Inka sun dance
- ■ Lutheran chorales: "A Mighty Fortress is Our God"
- ◄~Native American chant, music, and dance~►

Africa, the Americas, and Cross-Cultural Encounter

". . . the world is old, but the future springs from the past."
Sundiata: An Epic of Old Mali

Global Travel and Trade

The period between 1400 and 1600 was the greatest age of trans-Eurasian travel since the days of the Roman Empire. However, even earlier, and especially after 1000 C.E., long-range trade, religious pilgrimage, missionary activity, and just plain curiosity had stimulated cross-cultural contact between East and West. Arab merchants dominated North African trade routes. Converts to Islam—especially Turks and Mongols—carried the Muslim faith across Asia into India and Anatolia. Mongol tribes traversed the vast overland Asian Silk Route, which stretched from Constantinople to the Pacific Ocean. Enterprising families, like that of the Venetian merchant Marco Polo (ca. 1254–1324), established cultural and commercial links with the court of the Mongol emperor of China, Kubilai Khan. Boasting that "brotherhood among peoples" had reached a new height during his rule (1260–1294), Kublai encouraged long-distance travel and cross-cultural dialogue. The same roads that brought thirteenth-century Franciscan and Dominican monks into China sped the exchange of goods and religious beliefs between Muslims and Hindus, Confucians and Buddhists. Even after Mongol rule came to an end in China, policies of outreach prevailed: during the brief period from 1405 to 1433, 300 Chinese ships—the largest wooden vessels ever constructed—and 28,000 men sailed the Indian Ocean to the coasts of India and Africa as China moved to expand its political and commercial influence.

Although the great plague that swept through Asia and Europe interrupted long-established patterns of East–West exchange, the appearance of fourteenth-century hand-books, such as that written by the Florentine merchant Francesco Pegolotti, suggests that global travel did not completely disappear (Pegolotti journeyed as far as China). Nor did regional travel cease: Chaucer's pilgrims traveled to local Christian shrines, while Buddhists visited their sanctuaries throughout East Asia, and Muslims often made even longer journeys to participate in the ritual of the *hajj*, that is, the pilgrimage to Mecca.

By the mid-fifteenth century, new factors fueled the enterprise of cross-cultural encounter. In 1453 the formidable armies of the Ottoman Empire captured Constantinople, renaming it Istanbul and bringing a thousand years of Byzantine civilization to an end. At the height of Ottoman power, as the Turkish presence in Southwest Asia threatened the safety of European overland caravans to the East, Western rulers explored two main offensive strategies: warfare against the Turks and the search for all-water routes to the East. The first strategy yielded some success when the allied forces of Venice, Spain, and the papacy defeated the Ottoman navy in Western Greece at the Battle of Lepanto in 1571. Although this event briefly reduced the Ottoman presence in the Mediterranean— the Turks quickly rebuilt their navy—it did not answer the need for faster and more efficient trade routes to the East. Greed for gold, slaves, and spices—the major commodities of Africa and Asia—also encouraged the emerging European nations to compete with Arab and Turkish traders for control of foreign markets.

Science and Technology

1405   China launches the first of seven overseas expeditions with over three hundred of the largest wooden ships ever built

1418   Prince Henry of Portugal opens a school of navigation

1420   the Portuguese develop the three-masted caravel for ocean travel

1448   Andreas Walsperger (Flemish) uses the coordinates of longitude, latitude, and climatic divisions in his *mappa mundi* (world map)

1522   the circumnavigation of the globe (begun by Magellan) is completed

The technology of navigation was crucial to the success of these ventures. With the early fifteenth-century Latin translation of Ptolemy's *Geography*, mapmakers began to order geographic space with the coordinates of latitude and longitude. The Portuguese, encouraged by Prince Henry the Navigator (1394–1460), came to produce maps and charts that exceeded the accuracy of those drafted by classical and Muslim cartographers. Renaissance Europeans improved such older Arab navigational devices as the compass and the astrolabe (an instrument that measures the angle between the horizon and heavenly bodies and thus fixes latitude; see chapter 10).

Portugal and Spain adopted the Arab lateen sail and built two- and three-masted caravels with multiple sails—ships that were faster, safer, and more practical for rough ocean travel than the oar-driven galleys that sailed the Mediterranean Sea (Figure **18.1**). The new caravels were outfitted with brass cannons and sufficient firepower to fend off severe enemy attack. By 1498, Vasco da Gama (1460–1524) had navigated around Southern Africa to establish Portuguese trading posts in India. Christopher Columbus (1451–1506), an Italian in the employ of Spain, sailed west in search of an all-water route to China. His discovery of the Americas—the existence of which no Europeans had ever suspected—was to change the course of world history. While the Spanish sought to reach China by sailing across the Atlantic Ocean, the Portuguese set off eastward around Africa and across the Indian Ocean (Map **18.1**). These enterprises initiated an era of exploration and cross-cultural encounter the consequences of which would transform the destinies of Africa and the Americas. Indeed, the era of expansion would mark the beginning of a modern world-system dominated by the West.

The African Cultural Heritage

Africa, long known to Europeans as the "Dark Continent," was unaffected by the civilizations of both Asia and the West for thousands of years. Even after the Muslim conquest of North Africa in the seventh century, many parts of Africa remained independent of foreign influence and Africans continued to preserve local traditions and culture.

Diversity has characterized all aspects of African history, for Africa is a continent of widely varying geographic regions and more than eight hundred different native languages. The political organization of African territories over the centuries has ranged from small village communities to large states and empires.

Map 18.1 World Exploration, 1271–1295; 1486–1611.

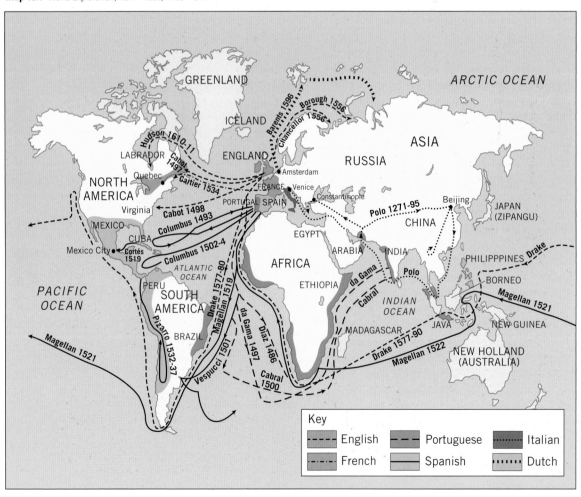

Figure 18.1 ALEJO FERNANDEZ, *Our Lady of the Navigators*, 1535. Alcazar, Seville. Photo: Institut Amatller D'Art Hispanic, Barcelona.

Despite their geographic, linguistic, and political differences, however, Africans share some distinct cultural characteristics, especially a kinship system that emphasizes the importance and well-being of the group as essential to that of the individual. Historically, the African kinship system was based on the extended family, a group of people who were both related to each other and dependent on each other for survival. The tribe consisted of a federation of extended families or clans ruled by chiefs or elders—either hereditary or elected—who held semidivine status. All those who belonged to the same family, clan, or tribe—the living, the dead, and the yet unborn—made up a single cohesive community irrevocably linked in time and space. While this form of social organization was not unique to Africa—indeed, it has characterized most agricultural societies in world history—it played an especially important role in shaping the character of African society and culture.

While tribal structure was traditionally the primary feature of African culture, **animism**—the belief that spirits inhabit all things in nature—was equally characteristic. Africans perceived the natural world as animated by supernatural spirits (including those of the dead). Most Africans honored a Supreme Creator, but they also recognized a great many lesser deities and spirits. For Africans, the spirits of ancestors, as well as those of natural objects, carried great potency. Since the spirits of the dead and the spirits of natural forces (rain, wind, forests, and so on) were thought to influence the living and to act as guides and protectors, honoring them was essential to tribal security. Hence, ritual played a major part in assuring the well-being of the community, and the keepers of ritual—shamans, diviners, and priests—held prominent positions in African society. For centuries, most of Africa consisted of farming villages united by kinship ties and ruled by chieftains. At a first millennium B.C.E. farming site called Nok, located along the Niger River (Map 18.2), artisans produced remarkable terracotta figures of animals and human beings (Figure 18.2). These sculptures, hand-modeled rather than produced with molds, are the earliest

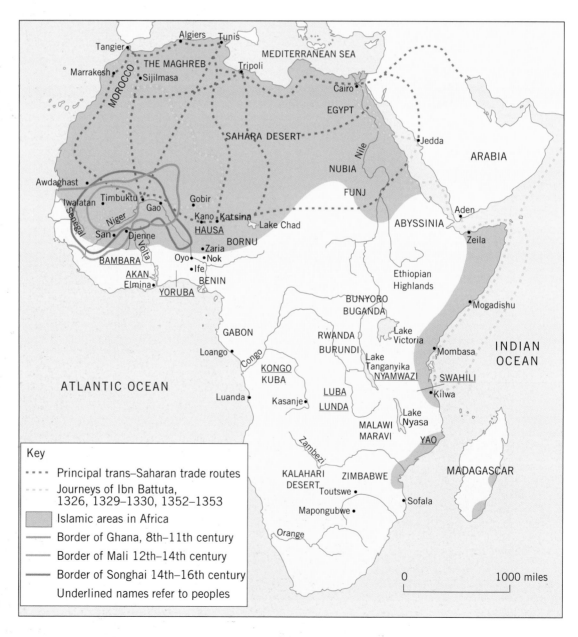

Map 18.2 Africa, 1000–1500.

known artworks of sub-Saharan Africa. The Nok heads, probably once joined to life-sized bodies, display strongly individualized personalities; they may have represented tribal ancestors or revered chieftains.

West African Kingdoms

By the ninth century (encouraged by the demands of Muslim merchants and a lucrative trans-Saharan trade) the first of a number of African states emerged in the *Sudan* (the word means "Land of the Blacks"): the region that stretches across Africa south of the Sahara Desert (see Map 18.2). The very name of the first Sudanic state, Ghana, which means "war chief," suggests how centralization came about: a single powerful chieftain took control of the surrounding villages. Ghana's rulers, who were presumed to have divine ancestors, regulated the exportation of gold to the north and the importation of salt from the desert fringes. These two products—gold and salt—along with iron, slaves, and ivory, were the principal African commodities. After Ghana fell to the Muslims in the eleventh century, the native kings, along with much of the local culture, came under Arabic influence. The history of Ghana and other ancient African kingdoms is recorded primarily in Arabic sources describing the courts of kings, but little is known of African life in areas removed from the centers of power. Scholars estimate that in the hands of the Muslims, the trans-Saharan market in slaves—war captives, for the most part—increased from roughly three hundred thousand in the ninth century to over a million in the twelfth century.

Figure 18.2 Head, Nok culture, ca. 500 B.C.E.–200 C.E. Terracotta, height 14 ⅜ in. National Museum, Lagos, Nigeria. Photo: Held Collection/Bridgeman Art Library, London

Figure 18.3 Prostrate Muslims in front of a mosque in the town of San, Mali, 1971. Photographic Archives, National Museum of African Art, Smithsonian Institution, Washington, D.C. (neg. no. VII–11, 37). Photo: Eliot Elisofon. The worshipers pray facing Mecca, birthplace of Muhammad and the holiest city of Islam.

During the thirteenth century, West Africans speaking the Mande language brought much of the Sudan under their dominion to form the Mali Empire. This dramatic development is associated with the powerful warrior-king Sundiata, who ruled Mali from around 1230 to 1255. The wealth and influence of the Mali Empire, which reached its zenith in the early fourteenth century, derived from its control of northern trade routes. On one of these routes lay the prosperous city of Timbuktu (see Map 18.2), the greatest of early African trading centers and the site of a flourishing Islamic university. In Mali, as in many of the African states, the rulers were converts to Islam; they employed Muslim scribes and jurists and used Arabic as the language of administration. The hallmarks of Islamic culture—its great mosques (Figure 18.3) and libraries and the Arabic language itself—did not penetrate deeply into the vast interior of Africa, however, where native African traditions dominated everyday life.

Prior to the fourteenth century, neither Arabs nor Europeans traveled to the parts of Africa south of the great savanna, a thickly vegetated area of tropical rainforest. Here, at the mouth of the Niger, in the area of present-day Nigeria, emerged the culture known as Benin, which absorbed the traditions of the cultures that had preceded it. By the twelfth century, Benin dominated most of the West African territories north of the Niger delta. The Benin *obas* (rulers) established an impressive royal tradition, building large, walled cities and engaging in trade with other African states. Like most African rulers, the *obas* of Benin regarded themselves as descendants of the gods. Craftspeople specially trained in the technique of lost-wax bronze and copper casting—a process probably begun in Mesopotamia—immortalized the *oba* and their queens in magnificent portraits that capture their dignity and authority. The queen mother pictured in Figure 18.4 bears on her forehead the marks of **scarification** (the process of incising the flesh) that designated her membership or status within a group and functioned as a form of body art. (A contrasting scarification pattern of thin parallel lines appears on the idealized face of the *oba* in Figure 18.5.) She wears a conical, netted headdress patterned on a distinctive royal hairstyle and embellished with coral beads. This compelling image stood on the royal altar for some 300 years after Benin culture reached its peak in the sixteenth century.

African Literature

Black Africa transmitted native folk traditions orally rather than in writing. As a result, the literary contributions of Africans remained unrecorded for hundreds of years—in some cases until the nineteenth century and thereafter. During the tenth century, Arab scholars in Africa began to transcribe popular native tales and stories into Arabic. Over time, several of the traditional African languages have developed written forms and produced a literature of note. Even to this day, however, a highly prized oral tradition dominates African literature.

Ancient Africa's oral tradition was the province of **griots**, a special class of professional poet–historians who preserved the legends of the past by chanting or singing them from memory. Like the *jongleurs* of the early Middle Ages, *griots* transmitted the history of the people by way of stories that had been handed down from generation to generation. The most notable of these narratives is *Sundiata*, an epic describing the formative phase of Mali history. *Sundiata* originated around 1240, in the time of Mali's great empire, but it was not until the twentieth century that it was transcribed—first to written French and then to English. Recounted by a *griot*, who identifies himself in the opening passages, the epic immortalizes the adventures of Sundiata, the champion and founder of the Mali Empire. In the tradition of such Western heroes as Gilgamesh, Achilles, Alexander, and Roland, the "lion-child" Sundiata performs extraordinary deeds that bring honor and glory to himself and peace and prosperity to his people. The following excerpt includes the *griot's* intro-

Figure 18.4 Edo head of a queen mother, from Benin. Cast copper alloy and iron, height 16 3/4 in. The Metropolitan Museum of Art, New York (1977.187.36).

duction to the poem, the story of the battle of Tabon, and a brief description of the lively festival that celebrates Sundiata's triumphs. In the final passages of the poem, Mali is pictured as a place of peace and prosperity; it is eternal in the memory of those who know its history.

READING 3.14 From *Sundiata: An Epic of Old Mali*

I am a griot. It is I, Djeli Mamoudou Kouyaté, son of Bintou Kouyaté and Djeli Kedian Kouyaté, master in the art of eloquence. Since time immemorial the Kouyatés have been in the service of the Keita[1] princes of Mali; we are vessels of speech, we are the repositories which harbor secrets many centuries old. The art of eloquence has no secrets for us; without us the names of kings would vanish into oblivion, we are the memory of mankind; by the spoken word we bring to life the deeds and exploits of kings for younger generations.   10

I derive my knowledge from my father Djeli Kedian, who also got it from his father; history holds no mystery for us; we teach to the vulgar just as much as we want to teach them, for it is we who keep the keys to the twelve doors of Mali.[2]

I know the list of all the sovereigns who succeeded to the throne of Mali. I know how the black people divided into tribes, for my father bequeathed to me all his learning; I know why such and such is called Kamara, another Keita, and yet another Sibibé or Traoré; every name has a meaning, a secret import.   20

I teach kings the history of their ancestors so that the lives of the ancients might serve them as an example, for the world is old, but the future springs from the past.

My word is pure and free of all untruth; it is the word of my father; it is the word of my father's father. I will give you my father's words just as I received them; royal griots do not know what lying is. When a quarrel breaks out between tribes it is we who settle the difference, for we are the depositaries of oaths which the ancestors swore.   30

Listen to my word, you who want to know; by my mouth you will learn the history of Mali.

By my mouth you will get to know the story of the ancestor of great Mali, the story of him who, by his exploits, surpassed even Alexander the Great; he who, from the East, shed his rays upon all the countries of the West.

Listen to the story of the son of the Buffalo, the son of the Lion.[3] I am going to tell you of Maghan Sundiata, of Mari-Djata, of Sogolon Djata, of Naré Maghan Djata; the man of many names against whom sorcery could avail nothing.   40

· · · · · · · · · · ·

---

[1]The ruling Muslim family, the Mali emperors identified themselves as descendants of the prophet Muhammad.
[2]The twelve provinces of which Mali was originally composed.
[3]According to tradition, the buffalo was the totem of Sundiata's mother, Sogolon, while the lion was the totem of his father.

Kings have prescribed destinies just like men, and seers who probe the future know it. They have knowledge of the future, whereas we griots are depositaries of the knowledge of the past. But whoever knows the history of a country can read its future.

Other peoples use writing to record the past, but this invention has killed the faculty of memory among them.   50 They do not feel the past any more, for writing lacks the warmth of the human voice. With them everybody thinks he knows, whereas learning should be a secret. The prophets did not write and their words have been all the more vivid as a result. What paltry learning is that which is congealed in dumb books!

I, Djeli Mamoudou Kouyaté, am the result of a long tradition. For generations we have passed on the history of kings from father to son. The narrative was passed on to me without alteration and I deliver it without alteration, for I received it free from all untruth.

. . . .

Every man to his own land! If it is foretold that your destiny should be fulfilled in such and such a land, men can do nothing against it. Mansa Tounkara could not keep Sundiata back because the destiny of Sogolon's son was bound up with that of Mali. Neither the jealousy of a cruel stepmother, nor her wickedness, could alter for a moment the course of great destiny.

The snake, man's enemy, is not long-lived, yet the serpent that lives hidden will surely die old. Djata[4] was strong enough now to face his enemies. At the age of eighteen, he had the stateliness of the lion and the strength of the buffalo. His voice carried authority, his eyes were live coals, his arm was iron, he was the husband of power.

Moussa Tounkara, king of Mema, gave Sundiata half of his army. The most valiant came forward of their own free will to follow Sundiata in the great adventure. The cavalry of Mema, which he had fashioned himself, formed his iron squadron. Sundiata, dressed in the Muslim fashion of Mema, left the town at the head of his small but redoubtable army. The whole population sent their best wishes with him. He was surrounded by five messengers from Mali and Manding Bory rode proudly at the side of his brother. The horsemen of Mema formed behind Djata a bristling iron squadron. The troops took the direction of Wagadou, for Djata did not have enough troops to confront Soumaoro directly, and so the king of Mema advised him to go to Wagadou and take half of the men of the king, Soumaba Cissé. A swift messenger had been sent there and so the king of Wagadou came out in person to meet Sundiata and his troops. He gave Sundiata half of his cavalry and blessed the weapons. Then Manding Bory said to his brother, "Djata, do you think yourself able to face Soumaoro now?"

"No matter how small a forest may be, you can always find there sufficient fibers to tie up a man. Numbers mean nothing; it is worth that counts. With my cavalry I shall clear myself a path to Mali."

Djata gave out his orders. They would head south, skirting Soumaoro's kingdom. The first objective to be reached was Tabon, the iron-gated town in the midst of the mountains, for Sundiata had promised Fran Kamara that he would pass by Tabon before returning to Mali. He hoped to find that his childhood companion had become king. It was a forced march and during the halts the divines, Singbin Mara Cissé and Mandjan Bérété, related to Sundiata the history of Alexander the Great[5] and

several other heroes, but of all of them Sundiata preferred Alexander, the king of gold and silver, who crossed the world from west to east. He wanted to outdo his prototype both in the extent of his territory and the wealth of his treasury. . . .

In the evening, after a long day's march, Sundiata arrived at the head of the great valley which led to Tabon. The valley was quite black with men, for Sosso Balla had deployed his men everywhere in the valley, and some were positioned on the heights which dominated the way through. When Djata saw the layout of Sosso Balla's men he turned to his generals laughing.

"Why are you laughing, brother, you can see that the road is blocked."

"Yes, but no mere infantrymen can halt my course towards Mali," replied Sundiata.

The troops stopped. All the war chiefs were of the opinion that they should wait until the next day to give battle because, they said, the men were tired.

"The battle will not last long," said Sundiata, "and the men will have time to rest. We must not allow Soumaoro the time to attack Tabon."

Sundiata was immovable, so the orders were given and the war drums began to beat. On his proud horse Sundiata turned to right and left in front of his troops. He entrusted the rearguard, composed of a part of the Wagadou cavalry, to his younger brother, Manding Bory. Having drawn his sword, Sundiata led the charge, shouting his war cry.

The Sossos were surprised by this sudden attack for they all thought that the battle would be joined the next day. The lightning that flashes across the sky is slower, the thunderbolts less frightening and floodwaters less surprising than Sundiata swooping down on Sosso Balla and his smiths.[6] In a trice, Sundiata was in the middle of the Sossos like a lion in the sheepfold. The Sossos, trampled under the hooves of his fiery charger, cried out. When he turned to the right the smiths of Soumaoro fell in their tens, and when he turned to the left his sword made heads fall as when someone shakes a tree of ripe fruit. The horsemen of Mema wrought a frightful slaughter and their long lances pierced flesh like a knife sunk into a paw-paw.[7] Charging ever forwards, Sundiata looked for Sosso Balla; he caught sight of him and like a lion bounded towards the son of Soumaoro, his sword held aloft. His arm came sweeping down but at that moment a Sosso warrior came between Djata and Sosso Balla and was sliced like a calabash.[8] Sosso Balla did not wait and disappeared from amidst his smiths. Seeing their chief in flight, the Sossos gave way and fell into a terrible rout. Before the sun disappeared behind the mountains there were only Djata and his men left in the valley.

. . . .

---

[4]Sundiata.
[5]In Mali tradition, it is said that Alexander was the second great conqueror and Sundiata the seventh and last.

[6]Metalsmiths, within the clan, a powerful caste of men who were noted as makers of weapons and sorcerers or soothsayers.
[7]Papaya.
[8]The common bottle gourd.

The festival began. The musicians of all the countries were there. Each people in turn came forward to the dais under Sundiata's impassive gaze. Then the war dances began. The sofas[9] of all the countries had lined themselves up in six ranks amid a great clatter of bows and spears knocking together. The war chiefs were on horseback. The warriors faced the enormous dais and at a signal from Balla Fasséké, the musicians, massed on the right of the dais, struck up. The heavy war drums thundered, the bolons[10] gave off muted notes while the griot's voice gave the throng the pitch for the "Hymn to the Bow."[11] The spearmen, advancing like hyenas in the night held their spears above their heads; the archers of Wagadou and Tabon,[12] walking with a noiseless tread, seemed to be lying in ambush behind bushes. They rose suddenly to their feet and let fly their arrows at imaginary enemies. In front of the great dais the Kéké-Tigui, or war chiefs, made their horses perform dance steps under the eyes of the Mansa.[13] The horses whinnied and reared, then, overmastered by the spurs, knelt, got up and cut little capers, or else scraped the ground with their hooves.

The rapturous people shouted the "Hymn to the Bow" and clapped their hands. The sweating bodies of the warriors glistened in the sun while the exhausting rhythm of the tam-tams[14] wrenched from them shrill cries. But presently they made way for the cavalry, beloved by Djata. The horsemen of Mema threw their swords in the air and caught them in flight, uttering mighty shouts. A smile of contentment took shape on Sundiata's lips, for he was happy to see his cavalry manoeuvre with so much skill. . . .

· · · · · · · · · · · ·

After a year Sundiata held a new assembly at Niani, but this one was the assembly of dignitaries and kings of the empire. The kings and notables of all the tribes came to Niani. The kings spoke of their administration and the dignitaries talked of their kings. Fakoli, the nephew of Soumaoro, having proved himself too independent, had to flee to evade the Mansa's anger. His lands were confiscated and the taxes of Sosso were paid directly into the granaries of Niani. In this way, every year, Sundiata gathered about him all the kings and notables; so justice prevailed everywhere, for the kings were afraid of being denounced at Niani.

Djata's justice spared nobody. He followed the very word of God. He protected the weak against the strong and people would make journeys lasting several days to come and demand justice of him. Under his sun the upright man was rewarded and the wicked one punished.

In their new-found peace the villages knew prosperity again, for with Sundiata happiness had come into everyone's home. Vast fields of millet, rice, cotton,

indigo and fonio[15] surrounded the villages. Whoever worked always had something to live on. Each year long caravans carried the taxes in kind[16] to Niani. You could go from village to village without fearing brigands. A thief would have his right hand chopped off and if he stole again he would be put to the sword.

New villages and new towns sprang up in Mali and elsewhere. "Dyulas," or traders, became numerous and during the reign of Sundiata the world knew happiness.

There are some kings who are powerful through their military strength. Everybody trembles before them, but when they die nothing but ill is spoken of them. Others do neither good nor ill and when they die they are forgotten. Others are feared because they have power, but they know how to use it and they are loved because they love justice. Sundiata belonged to this group. He was feared, but loved as well. He was the father of Mali and gave the world peace. After him the world has not seen a greater conqueror, for he was the seventh and last conqueror. He had made the capital of an empire out of his father's village, and Niani became the navel of the earth. In the most distant lands Niani was talked of and foreigners said, "Travelers from Mali can tell lies with impunity," for Mali was a remote country for many peoples.

The griots, fine talkers that they were, used to boast of Niani and Mali saying: "If you want salt, go to Niani, for Niani is the camping place of the Sahel[17] caravans. If you want gold, go to Niani, for Bouré, Bambougou and Wagadou work for Niani. If you want fine cloth, go to Niani, for the Mecca road passes by Niani. If you want fish, go to Niani, for it is there that the fishermen of Maouti and Djenné come to sell their catches. If you want meat, go to Niani, the country of the great hunters, and the land of the ox and the sheep. If you want to see an army, go to Niani, for it is there that the united forces of Mali are to be found. If you want to see a great king, go to Niani, for it is there that the son of Sogolon lives, the man with two names."

This is what the masters of the spoken word used to sing. . . .

How many piled-up ruins, how much buried splendour! But all the deeds I have spoken of took place long ago and they all had Mali as their background. Kings have succeeded kings, but Mali has always remained the same.

Mali keeps its secrets jealously. There are things which the uninitiated will never know, for the griots, their depositaries, will never betray them. Maghan Sundiata, the last conqueror on earth, lies not far from Niani-Niani at Balandougou, the weir town.

After him many kings and many Mansas reigned over Mali and other towns sprang up and disappeared. Hajji Mansa Moussa, of illustrious memory, beloved of God, built houses at Mecca for pilgrims coming from Mali, but the towns which he founded have all disappeared,

---

[9]Sudanese infantrymen or soldiers.
[10]Large harps with three or four strings.
[11]A traditional song among the people of Mali.
[12]Kingdoms near Mali.
[13]Emperor.
[14]Large, circular gongs.

[15]A crabgrass with seeds that are used as a cereal.
[16]In produce or goods instead of money.
[17]A region of the Sudan bordering on the Sahara.

Karanina, Bouroun-Kouna—nothing more remains of these towns. Other kings carried Mali far beyond Djata's frontiers, for example Mansa Samanka and Fadima Moussa, but none of them came near Djata. **270**

Maghan Sundiata was unique. In his own time no one equalled him and after him no one had the ambition to surpass him. He left his mark on Mali for all time and his taboos still guide men in their conduct.

Mali is eternal. To convince yourself of what I have said go to Mali.

. . . .

Men of today, how small you are beside your ancestors, and small in mind too, for you have trouble in grasping the meaning of my words. Sundiata rests near Niani- **280** Niani, but his spirit lives on and today the Keitas still come and bow before the stone under which lies the father of Mali.

To acquire my knowledge I have journeyed all round Mali. At Kita I saw the mountain where the lake of holy water sleeps; at Segou, I learnt the history of the kings of Do and Kri; at Fadama, in Hamana, I heard the Kondé griots relate how the Keitas, Kondés and Kamaras conquered Wouroula. At Keyla, the village of the great **290** masters, I learnt the origins of Mali and the art of speaking. Everywhere I was able to see and understand what my masters were teaching me, but between their hands I took an oath to teach only what is to be taught and to conceal what is to be kept concealed.

Q How does Sundiata compare with other epic heroes: Gilgamesh, Achilles, and Roland?

Q What does the griot mean by the statement, "the future springs from the past?"

As lines 161–191 of this excerpt suggest, in African ritual celebration, the arts of music, dance, poetry, and decorative display formed a synthesis that mirrored shared spiritual and communal values (Figure **18.6**). Similarly, within the African community, the telling of stories was a group enterprise and an expression of social unity. Seated around the communal fire, the members of the tribe recited tales serially and from memory. Traditionally, such tales were told only after sundown, because, as favored entertainments, they might otherwise distract the group from daily labor.

Among the many genres of African literature was the mythical tale that accounted for the origins of the universe, of the natural forces, and of the community. African creation myths—like those of the Hebrews, Egyptians, and Mesopotamians—explained the beginnings of the world, the creation of human beings, and the workings of nature, while still other myths dealt with the origin of death. The following brief examples, which come from three different parts of Africa, represent only a sampling of the many African tales that explain how death came into the world.

READING 3.15 Three African Myths on the Origin of Death

1

In the beginning, Nzambi slid down to earth on a rainbow, and there created the animals and the trees. After this he also created a man and a woman, and he told them to marry and have children. Nzambi imposed only one prohibition upon men, that they should not sleep when the moon was up. If they disobeyed this command, they would be punished with death. When the first man had become old and had poor eyesight, it once happened that the moon was veiled behind the clouds, so that he could not see it shine. He went to sleep and died in his sleep. Since then all men have died, because they are unable to keep awake when the moon is up.

(Lunda)

2

One day God asked the first human couple who then lived in heaven what kind of death they wanted, that of the moon or that of the banana. Because the couple wondered in dismay about the implications of the two modes of death, God explained to them: the banana puts forth shoots which take its place, and the moon itself comes back to life. The couple considered for a long time before they made their choice. If they elected to be childless they would avoid death, but they would also be very lonely, would themselves be forced to carry out all the work, and would not have anybody to work and strive for. Therefore they prayed to God for children, well aware of the consequences of their choice. And their prayer was granted. Since that time man's sojourn is short on this earth.

(Madagascar)

3

Formerly men had no fire but ate all their food raw. At that time they did not need to die for when they became old God made them young again. One day they decided to beg God for fire. They sent a messenger to God to convey their request. God replied to the messenger that he would give him fire if he was prepared to die. The man took the fire from God, but ever since then all men must die.

(Darasa, Gada)

Q What aspects of ancient African culture do these myths reflect?

Q What do these myths have in common with those in Reading 1.2?

These myths offer valuable insights into ancient African culture. The directness with which the characters in these tales address the gods suggests the basic intimacy between Africans and the spirit world. Moreover, the tales stress

Figure 18.6 Bambara ritual *chi wara* dance, Mali. Photographic Archives, National Museum of African Art, Smithsonian Institution, Washington, D.C. (neg. no. VIII–58, 4A). Photo: Eliot Elisofon.

human fallibility (as in the disastrous blunder of the nearly blind "first man"), rather than (as in most Christian literature) human sinfulness. They describe a gentle and casual, rather than a forbidding and patriarchal, relationship between divine and human realms. Finally, as the second myth suggests, Africans placed great value on their children; as was the case in most agricultural societies, children were prized as helpers and as perpetuators of tradition. One African proverb reads, "There is no wealth where there are no children." Another asserts, "Children are the wisdom of the nation."

Africans invented a huge and colorful literature of tales, proverbs, and riddles. The animal tale explains why certain creatures look and act as they do. In the trickster tale, a small animal, such as a hare or spider, outwits a larger one, such as a hyena or elephant. Explanatory tales treat such themes as "Why some people are good-looking" and "Why one never tells a woman the truth." African tales, proverbs, and riddles—often playfully swapped—functioned as sources of instruction and entertainment. Like most forms of African expression, they were characterized by animism: consider, for instance, the riddle "who goes down the street and passes the king's house without greeting the king?" The answer is "rainwater." Many proverbs

call attention to the immutability of nature's laws. One states, "When it rains, the roof always drips in the same way." Africans used their riddles and proverbs to help teach moral values and even to litigate tribal disputes.

African Poetry

In ancient Africa, religious rituals and rites of passage featured various kinds of chant. Performed by shamans and priests, but also by nonprofessionals, and often integrated with mime and dance, the chant created a unified texture not unlike that of modern rap and Afro-pop music. Poets addressed the fragility of human life, celebrated the transition from one stage of growth to another, honored the links between the living and the dead, praised heroes and rulers, and recounted the experiences of everyday life. African poetry does not share the satiric thrust of Roman verse, the erotic mood of Indian poetry, the intimate tone of the Petrarchan or Shakespearean sonnet, or the reclusive spirit of Chinese verse; it is, rather, a frank and intensely personal form of vocal music.

African poetry is characterized by strong percussive qualities, by **anaphora** (the repetition of a word or words at the beginning of two or more lines), and by tonal patterns that—much like Chinese poetry—are based on voice inflections. Repetition of key phrases and call-and-response "conversations" between narrator and listeners add texture to oral performance. The rhythmic energy and raw vitality of African poetry set it apart from most other kinds of world poetry, including Chinese, which seems controlled and intellectualized by comparison. The poem of praise for the *oba* of Benin, reproduced in Reading 3.16, throbs with rhythms that invite accompanying drumbeats or hand-clapping of the kind familiar to us in gospel singing and contemporary rock music. African poetry is also notable for its inventive similes and metaphors. In the Yoruba poem "The God of War," warfare is likened to a needle "that pricks at both ends," a vivid image of the perils of combat—compare the plainspoken ode "On Civil War" by the Roman poet Horace (see chapter 6). And in the "Song for the Sun," the Hottentot poet invents the memorable image of God collecting the stars and piling them into a basket "like a woman who collects lizards and piles them in her pot."

READING 3.16 Selections from African Poetry

Song for the Sun that Disappeared behind the Rainclouds

The fire darkens, the wood turns black.   1
The flame extinguishes, misfortune upon us.
God sets out in search of the sun.
The rainbow sparkles in his hand,
the bow of the divine hunter.   5
He has heard the lamentations of his children.
He walks along the milky way, he collects the stars.
With quick arms he piles them into a basket
piles them up with quick arms
like a woman who collects lizards   10
and piles them into her pot, piles them up
until the basket overflows with light.

(Hottentot)

Longing for Death

I have been singing, singing I have cried bitterly   1
I'm on my way.
How large this world!
Let the ferryman bring his boat
on the day of my death.   5
I'll wave with my left hand,
I'm on my way.
I'm on my way,
the boat of death is rocking near,
I'm on my way,   10
I who have sung you many songs.

(Ewe)

The Oba of Benin

He who knows not the Oba   1
let me show him.
He has mounted the throne,
he has piled a throne upon a throne.

Plentiful as grains of sand on the earth   5
are those in front of him.
Plentiful as grains of sand on the earth
are those behind him.
There are two thousand people
to fan him.   10
He who owns you
is among you here.
He who owns you
has piled a throne upon a throne.
He has lived to do it this year;   15
even so he will live to do it again.

(Bini)

The God of War

He kills on the right and destroys on the left.   1
He kills on the left and destroys on the right.
He kills suddenly in the house and suddenly in the field.
He kills the child with the iron with which it plays.
He kills in silence.   5
He kills the thief and the owner of the stolen goods.
He kills the owner of the slave—and the slave runs away.
He kills the owner of the house—and paints the hearth
  with his blood.
He is the needle that pricks at both ends.
He has water but he washes with blood.   10

(Yoruba)

The Poor Man

The poor man knows not how to eat with the rich man.   1
When they eat fish, he eats the head.

Invite a poor man and he rushes in
licking his lips and upsetting the plates.

The poor man has no manners, he comes along   5
with the blood of lice under his nails.

The face of the poor man is lined
from the hunger and thirst in his belly.
Poverty is no state for any mortal man.
It makes him a beast to be fed on grass.   10

Poverty is unjust. If it befalls a man,
though he is nobly born, he has no power with God.

(Swahili)

A Baby is a European

A baby is a European   1
he does not eat our food:
he drinks from his own water pot.

A baby is a European
he does not speak our tongue: 5
he is cross when the mother understands him not.

A baby is a European
he cares very little for others;
he forces his will upon his parents.

| A baby is a European | 10 |

he is always very sensitive:
the slightest scratch on his skin results in an ulcer.

(Ewe)

The Moon

| The moon lights the earth | 1 |

it lights the earth but still
the night must remain the night.
The night cannot be like the day.

| The moon cannot dry our washing. | 5 |

Just like a woman cannot be a man
just like black can never be white.

(Soussou)

Q Based on these poems, how might one describe the African's response to nature? To the community? To European culture?

African Music and Dance

African music shares the vigorous rhythms of poetry and dance. In texture, it consists of a single line of melody without harmony. As with most African dialects, where pitch is important in conveying meaning, variations of musical effect derive from tonal inflection and timbre. The essentially communal spirit of African culture is reflected in the use of responsorial chants involving call-and-answer patterns similar to those of African poetry. The most distinctive characteristic of African music, however, is its polyrhythmic structure. A single piece of music may simultaneously engage five to ten different rhythms, many of which are repeated over and over. African dance, also communally performed, shares the distinctively dense polyrhythmic qualities of African music. The practice of playing "against" or "off" the main beat provided by the instruments is typical of much West African music and is preserved in the "off-beat" patterns of early modern jazz (see chapter 36).

A wide variety of percussion instruments, including various types of drums and rattles, is used in the performance of African ritual (see Fig. 18.6). Also popular are the *balafo* (a type of xylophone), the *bolon* or *kora* (a large harp), and the *sansa* (an instrument consisting of a number of metal tongues attached to a small

_____
♪ See Music Listening Selections at end of chapter.

wooden soundboard). The latter two of these instruments, used to accompany storytelling, were believed to contain such potent supernatural power that they were considered dangerous and were outlawed among some African tribes, except for use by *griots*. Africa was the place of origin for the banjo, which may have been the only musical instrument permitted on the slave ships that traveled across the Atlantic in the sixteenth century (bells, drums, and other instruments were forbidden). African culture is notably musical, and the dynamic convergence of chant, dance, music, and bodily ornamentation generates a singularly dramatic experience that has a binding effect on the participants.

African Sculpture

Perhaps no other art prior to the twentieth century confronts the viewer as boldly as African art or speaks as directly to the subconscious. The twentieth-century Spanish master Pablo Picasso, who tried to capture in his own work the power of African art, referred to African sculptures as "magical objects" (see chapter 32). Picasso perceived that African sculpture was of a magico-religious character, and that, like so much ancient and medieval art, it was inseparable from sacred ritual. Most African sculpture has a fierce, forbidding intensity that is not found in any art produced in the European West or, for that matter, in any other culture. This phenomenon is explained by the fact that such sculpture is intended as a channel through which spiritual energy may pass. The power-holding object, or **fetish**, channels magical forces that ward off evil, heal the sick, or communicate with ancestral spirits. For that reason, it resembles nothing in the ordinary world. The Gabon-Bakota statue (Figure **18.7**), which once stood above a container holding the bones of an ancestor, is not a representation of the deceased; rather, it worked to guard and protect the deceased from evil. Its aesthetic force derives, for the most part, from a unique synthesis of expressive abstraction and dynamic distortion. Similarly, the Congo nail fetish (Figure **18.8**) is a power-object used by healer-priests to protect against evil spirits or to cure (or inflict) disease. The act of driving a nail or sharp wedge into the figure invoked or liberated the powers of the medicinal herbs inserted into the cavity ("stomach") of the figure. Both the reliquary and the nail fetish mediate between sacred and profane worlds in order to restore spiritual equilibrium.

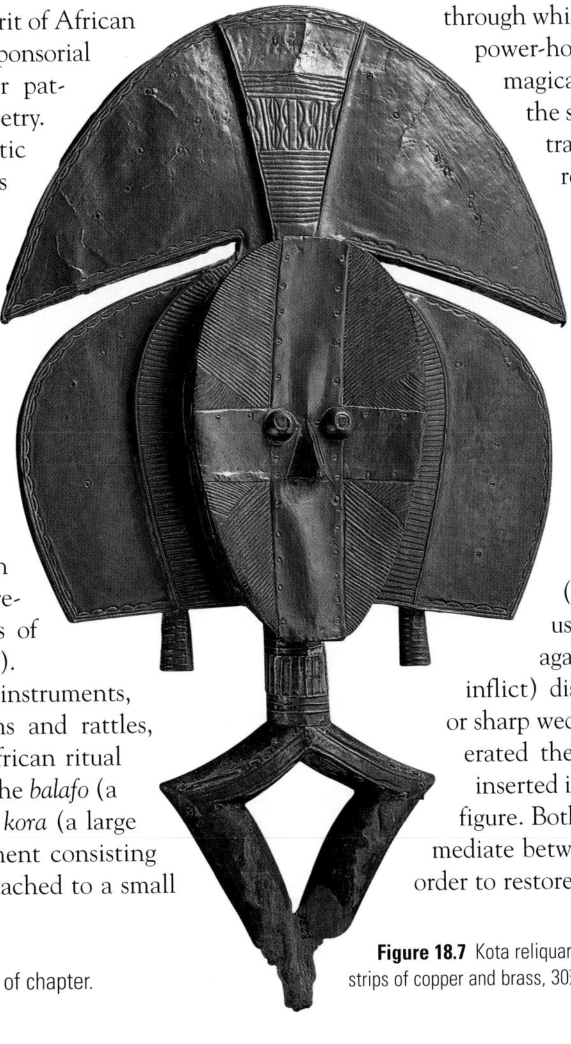

Figure 18.7 Kota reliquary figure, from Gabon. Wood covered with strips of copper and brass, 30¾ in. University Ethnographic Museum, Zürich.

African sculptures also serve in conjunction with rituals that marked rites of passage or honored a **totem** (the heraldic emblem of the tribe, family, or clan). The people of Mali have long regarded the antelope as their mythical ancestor, Chi Wara, who taught humankind how to cultivate the land. Chi Wara dance rituals incorporate movements that imitate those of the antelope (see Figure 18.6). The performers wear headdresses with huge crests that combine the features of the antelope, the anteater, and local birds (Figure **18.9**). In these magnificently carved fetishes, the triangular head of the antelope is repeated in the chevron patterns of the neck and the zigzags of the mane. The Chi Wara totem (which has become the logo for modern Mali's national airline) epitomizes the African taste for expressive simplification and geometric design.

Figure 18.9 Bambara antelope headpiece, from Mali, nineteenth century, based on earlier models. Wood, height 35¾ in., width 15¾ in. The Metropolitan Museum of Art, New York. The Michael C. Rockefeller Memorial Collection of Primitive Art. Gift of Nelson A. Rockefeller, 1964 (1978.412.435.436).

Figure 18.8 Congo nail fetish, 1875–1900. Wood with screws, nails, blades, cowrie shell, and other material, height 3 ft. 10 in. Photograph © 2000 The Detroit Institute of Arts. Founders Society Purchase, Eleanor Clay Ford Fund for African Art. 76.79.

African masks and headdresses, usually worn with elaborate cloth and fiber costumes, also appear in rituals of exorcism, initiation, purification, and burial. Masks function to disguise the wearer's identity; but they also channel the spirit of some animal, god, or ancestor, so that wearer becomes the agent of the supernatural. As a fetish, the mask has transformative powers. Throughout world history, religious rites and festivals of various cultures—from ancient Greek Dionysian ceremonies to the Catholic Mardi Gras carnival—have featured the act of masking, usually as part of a larger performance involving music and dance. Among the black Mardi Gras "Indians" of New Orleans, such traditions prevail to this day.

Over the course of centuries, African sculptors have mastered a wide variety of media and styles. The techniques of terracotta modeling, ivory carving, and casting in bronze, copper, and iron were known to Africans well before the end of the first millennium B.C.E. In Benin and other political centers along the Niger, royal portraits commanded the talents of sophisticated metalworkers (see Figures 18.4 and 18.5). But works in such enduring materials seem to have been produced mainly in the western and southern portions of Africa. The greater part of African sculptural productivity was in the medium of wood or, as in the case of Figure 18.7, wood covered with strips of metal. Using axes, knives, and chisels, professional sculptors carved their images from green or semidry timber. Rarely monumental in size, these objects still bear the rugged imprint of the artists' tools. Like the trunks of the trees from which they were hewn, they are often rigid, tubular,

and symmetrical (Figure **18.10**). African artists respected and patronized the life force that resided within the medium. Wooden caryatid stools like that shown in Figure 18.10, for instance, channeled the living spirit of the tree through the female form to the seated ruler. Feathers, shells, teeth, beads, raffia, hair, and other materials might be added to a fetish to increase textural contrast and enhance its vital powers (see Figure 18.8). And the surfaces of the fetish might be embellished with symbolic colors: red to represent danger, blood, and power; black to symbolize chaos and evil; and white to mean death.

On a Songe mask, whose neck holes indicate that it was attached to some type of costume, expressive linear patterns recreate the effects of scarification (Figure **18.11**). The artist has distorted and exaggerated human features so as to compress emotion and energy, and render the face dynamic and forbidding. A comparison of this mask with the head of an *oba* pictured in Figure 18.5 reminds us that African artists practiced a variety of styles ranging from idealized portraiture to stylized abstraction. The Benin bronzes fulfilled the community's political and commemorative needs, while the Songe mask probably served in ritual ceremonies that addressed the spirit world. Though many bronze, terracotta, gold, and ivory sculptures have outlasted the oldest African cultures, few examples in wood survive from before the nineteenth century. Eleventh-century Arab chronicles confirm, however, that the rich tradition of wood sculpture evidenced in the artworks illustrated here reaches far back into earlier African history.

African Architecture

As with the sculpture of ancient Africa, little survives of its early architecture, and that which does suggests a wide diversity of structural forms. A survey of traditional African house forms lists almost three dozen different types of structure. Construction materials consist of mud, stones, and brushwood, or adobe brick—a sun-dried mixture of clay and straw. Africans seem to have had little need for monumental religious or administrative buildings. But at the ancient trade center of Zimbabwe (the name means "House of Stone"), in South Central Africa, where a powerful kingdom developed before the year 1000, the remains of huge stone walls and towers indicate the presence of a royal residence or palace complex— the largest structures in Africa after the pyramids.

Figure 18.10 Front and back of Kuba stool with caryatid, from Zaire. Wood and glass beads, height 23¼ in. © Lee Boltin Picture Library, Crotin-on-Hudson, New York.

If rural Africans confirmed their sense of community in ways other than the construction of monumental architecture, urban Africans in Muslim-dominated cities built some of the most visually striking structures in the history of world architecture. The adobe mosques of Mali, for instance, with their bulging, organic contours, bulbous towers, and egglike finials (native symbols of fertility) resemble fantastic sand castles (see Figure 18.3). They have proved to be almost as impermanent: some have been rebuilt (and replastered) continuously since the twelfth century, hence their walls and towers bristle with sticks or wooden beams that provide a permanent scaffolding for restoration. African mosques are testimonials to the fusion of Muslim, Asian, and local ancestral traditions. Their domical shapes, like the temple shrines and burial mounds of early cultures, recall the primordial mountain and the womb—sites of spiritual renewal. Indeed, Africa's vernacular architecture calls to mind the sacred link between Mother Earth and the human community. Even the wooden pickets that serve as scaffolding have symbolic significance: used at Bambara initiation ceremonies and often buried with the dead, such tree branches are symbols of rebirth and regeneration.

Figure 18.11 Songe mask, from Zaire, nineteenth century, based on earlier models. Wood and paint, height 17 in. The Metropolitan Museum of Art, New York. The Michael C. Rockefeller Memorial Collection of Primitive Art. Bequest of Nelson A. Rockefeller, 1979 (1979.206.83).

Cross-Cultural Encounter

Ibn Battuta in West Africa

Islam was present in West Africa from at least the eighth century, and the religion increased in influence as Muslims came to dominate trans-Saharan trade. Occasional efforts to spread Islam by force were generally unsuccessful, yet the Islamization of the Sudan ultimately succeeded as the result of the peaceful and prosperous activities of Muslim merchants, administrators, and scholars. Mali's most famous ruler, Mansa ("King") Musa (1312–1337), came to symbolize the largesse of the African Muslim elite when, during his *hajj* of 1324, he and his retinue scattered large amounts of gold from Mali to Mecca. West African rulers like Musa patronized the arts, commissioned the construction of mosques, and encouraged conversion to Islam.

Nowhere in the literature of the age are the realities of cross-cultural encounter so well expressed as in the journal of the fourteenth-century Muslim traveler–scholar, Ibn Battuta (1304–1369). Born into an upper-class Muslim family in the North African city of Tangier, Battuta was educated in law and Arabic literature before he made the first of his seven pilgrimages in 1325. Over the course of his lifetime, this inveterate tourist journeyed on foot or by camel caravan some 75,000 miles, visiting parts of China, Indonesia, Persia, India, Burma, Spain, Arabia, Russia, Asia Minor, Egypt, and East and West Africa. Although his initial motives for travel were religious, he shared with other itinerant Muslim scholars an interest in Islamic law and a curiosity concerning the customs of Muslim communities throughout the world. In 1354, Battuta narrated the history of his travels, including his two-year trip from Morocco to Mali—his last recorded journey—to a professional scribe who recorded it in a *ribla* ("book of travels"). That portion of the *ribla* that recounts Battuta's visit to Mali is the only existing eyewitness account of the kingdom at the height of its power. It documents Battuta's keen powers of observation and reveals his efforts to evaluate social and cultural practices that differed sharply from his own.

READING 3.17 From Ibn Battuta's *Book of Travels* (1354)

We reached the city of Īwālātan[1] at the beginning   1
of the month of Rabi'I[2] after a journey of two full months
from Sijilmāsa. It is the first district of the country of the
Blacks....

When we arrived the merchants deposited their goods
in an open space and the Blacks took responsibility for
them. The merchants went to the Farbā who was sitting
on a rug under a shelter; his officials were in front of him
with spears and bows in their hands. The Massūfa[3]
notables were behind him. The merchants stood in front   10

---

[1]Near Timbuktu in Mali.
[2]April 1352.
[3]A Berber people of the Western Sahara.

of him and he spoke to them through an interpreter as a sign of his contempt for them, although they were close to him. At this I was sorry I had come to their country, because of their bad manners and contempt for white people. I made for the house of the Ibn Baddā', a kind man of Salā to whom I had written asking him to let[4] a house to me, which he did. . . .

. . . I stayed in Īwālātan about fifty days. Its people treated me with respect and gave me hospitality. Among them were the qāḍī[5] of the town Muḥ·ammad b. 'Abdallāh b. Yanūmar, and his brother the jurist and professor Yahyā. The town of Īwālātan is extremely hot. There are a few small palms and they sow melons in their shade. Water comes from underground sources. Mutton is plentiful. Their clothes are of fine quality and Egyptian origin. Most of the inhabitants belong to the Massūfa. The women are of outstanding beauty and are more highly regarded than the men.

Conditions among these people are remarkable and their life style is strange. The men have no jealousy. No one takes his name from his father, but from his maternal uncle. Sons do not inherit, only sister's sons![6] This is something I have seen nowhere in the world except among the infidel Indians of al-Mulāibar. Nevertheless these people are Muslims. They are strict in observing the prayers, studying the religious law, and memorizing the Qur'ān. Their women have no shame before men and do not veil themselves, yet they are punctilious about their prayers. Anyone who wants to take a wife among them does so, but they do not travel with their husbands, and even if one of them wished to, her family would prevent her. Women there have friends and companions among men outside the prohibited degrees for marriage, and in the same way men have women friends in the same category. A man goes into his house, finds his wife with her man friend, and does not disapprove.

One day I called upon the qāḍī at Īwālātan after he had given permission for me to enter. I found him with a young and exceptionally beautiful woman. When I saw her I hesitated and was going to go back, but she laughed at me and showed no embarrassment. The qāḍī said to me: "Why are you turning back? She is my friend." I was astonished at them, for he was a jurist and a Ḥājj.[7] I learnt that he had asked the Sultan's permission to go on pilgrimage that year with his female companion. I do not know whether this was the one or not, but permission was not given.

One day I called on Abū Muḥ·ammad Yandakān al-Massūfi, in whose company we had arrived, and found him sitting on a rug. In the middle of the room was a canopied couch and upon it was a woman with a man sitting and talking together. I said to him: "Who is this woman?" He said: "She is my wife." I said: "What about the man who is with her?" He said: "He is her friend." I

said: "Are you happy about this, you who have lived in our country and know the content of the religious law?" He said: "The companionship of women and men among us is a good thing and an agreeable practice, which causes no suspicion; they are not like the women of your country." I was astonished at his silliness. I left him and did not visit him again. Afterwards he invited me a number of times but I did not accept. . . .

The Blacks are the most respectful of people to their king and abase themselves most before him. . . . If he summons one of them at his session in the cupola we have mentioned, the man summoned removes his robe and puts on a shabby one, takes off his turban, puts on a dirty skull-cap and goes in with his robe and his trousers lifted half way to his knees. He comes forward humbly and abjectly, and strikes the ground hard with his elbows. He stands as if he were prostrating himself in prayer, and hears what the Sultan says like this. If one of them speaks to the Sultan and he answers him, he takes his robe off his back, and throws dust on his head and back like someone making his ablutions with water. I was astonished that they did not blind themselves.

When the Sultan makes a speech in his audience those present take off their turbans from their heads and listen in silence. Sometimes one of them stands before him, recounts what he has done for his service, and says: "On such and such a day I did such and such, and I killed so and so on such and such a day." Those who know vouch for the truth of that and he does it in this way. One of them draws the string of his bow, then lets it go as he would do if he were shooting. If the Sultan says to him: "You are right" or thanks him, he takes off his robe and pours dust on himself. That is good manners among them. . . .

Among their good practices are their avoidance of injustice; there is no people more averse to it, and their Sultan does not allow anyone to practice it in any measure; the universal security in their country, for neither the traveller nor the resident there has to fear thieves or bandits; they do not interfere with the property of white men who die in their country, even if it amounts to vast sums; they just leave it in the hands of a trustworthy white man until whoever is entitled to it takes possession of it; their punctiliousness in praying, their perseverance in joining the congregation, and in compelling their children to do so; if a man does not come early to the mosque he will not find a place to pray because of the dense crowd; it is customary for each man to send his servant with his prayer-mat to spread it out in a place reserved for him until he goes to the mosque himself; their prayer-mats are made of the leaves of a tree like the date-palm, but which has no fruit. They dress in clean white clothes on Fridays; if one of them has only a threadbare shirt he washes it and cleans it and wears it for prayer on Friday. They pay great attention to memorizing the Holy Qur'ān. If their children appear to be backward in learning it they put shackles on them and do not remove them till they learn it. I called on the qāḍī on the Feast Day. His children were in

[4]Rent.
[5]Muslim judges.
[6]In the matrilineal sub-Saharan tribes, the mother's brother is considered the most important male.
[7]One who has made the pilgrimage to Mecca.

shackles. I said to him: "Are you not going to free them?" He said: "Not till they learn the Qur'ān by heart." One day I passed by a handsome youth, who was very well dressed, with a heavy shackle on his foot. I said to the person with me: "What has he done? Has he killed someone?" The youth understood what I said and laughed. I was told: "He has been shackled to make him memorize the Qur'ān." 130

Among their bad practices are that the women servants, slave-girls and young daughters appear naked before people, exposing their genitals. I used to see many like this in Ramaḍān,[8] for it is customary for the farārīs[9] to break the fast in the Sultan's palace, where their food is brought to them by twenty or more slave-girls, who are naked. Women who come before the Sultan are naked and unveiled, and so are his daughters. On the night of the twenty-seventh of Ramaḍān I have 140 seen about a hundred naked slave-girls come out of his palace with food; with them were two daughters of the Sultan with full breasts and they too had no veil. They put dust and ashes on their heads as a matter of good manners. There is the clowning we have described when poets recite their works. Many of them eat carrion, dogs and donkeys.[10]

Q What aspects of African life did Ibn Battuta find congenial? Which did he find most unusual?

The Europeans in Africa

European commercial activity in Africa was the product of the quest for new sea routes to the East, and for control of the markets in gold, salt, and slaves that had long made Africa a source of wealth for Muslim merchants. During the sixteenth century, Portugal intruded upon the well-established Muslim-dominated trans-Saharan commercial slave trade. The Portuguese slave trade in West Africa, the Congo, and elsewhere developed according to the pattern that had already been established by Muslim traders: that is, in agreement with local African leaders who reaped profits from the sale of victims of war or raids on neighboring territories. By the year 1500, the Portuguese controlled the flow of both gold and slaves to Europe. Transatlantic slave trade commenced in 1551, when the Portuguese began to ship thousands of slaves from Africa to work in the sugar plantations of Brazil, a "New World" territory claimed by

[8]The Muslim month of fasting; the daily fast ends at sunset.
[9]Chiefs.
[10]The Quran forbids the eating of unclean meat.

Portugal. European forms of slavery were more brutal and exploitative than any previously practiced in Africa: slaves shipped overseas were branded, shackled in chains like beasts, underfed, and—if they survived the ravages of dysentery and disease—conscripted into oppressive kinds of physical labor (see chapter 25).

In their relations with the African states, especially those in coastal areas, the Europeans were equally brutal. They often ignored the bonds of family and tribe, the local laws and religious customs; they pressured Africans to adopt European language and dress and fostered economic rivalry. While in a spirit of missionary zeal and altruism they introduced Christianity and Western forms of education, they also brought ruin to some tribal kingdoms, and, in parts of Africa, they almost completely destroyed native black cultural life. These activities were but a prelude to

Figure 18.12 Benin plaque showing a Portuguese warrior surrounded by *manillas* (horseshoe-shaped metal objects used as a medium of exchange), from Nigeria, sixteenth century. Bronze. Museum für Volkerkunde, Vienna.

Figure 18.13 Mask, sixteenth century, Court of Benin, Nigeria. Ivory, height 9¾ in. Metropolitan Museum of Art, New York. The Michael C. Rockefeller Memorial Collection of Primitive Art. Gift of Nelson A. Rockefeller.

nally inlaid with iron. This commanding object, like the Edo head of the Queen Mother (see Figure 18.4) remained in Benin until British soldiers took it to London in 1897.

The Americas

Native American Cultures

Native cultures in the territories of North, Central, and South America began to develop at least twenty thousand years ago, following nomadic migrations across a land bridge that once linked Siberia and Alaska at the Bering Strait. The latest evidence suggests that it was mainly Asians who crossed the land bridge into Alaska in a single migration; however, many different ethnic groups from a variety of places peopled the Americas over a lengthy period of time. The earliest populations of the Americas formed a mosaic of migrant peoples and cultures. During the second millennium B.C.E., these migrant groups established communities throughout the Americas (Map 18.3). Like the ancient Africans, the Native Americans were culturally and linguistically diverse; and, much like the African populations, they shared a strong sense of communion with nature and deeply felt tribal loyalties.

In the five centuries prior to the first European contacts with the Americas, some one thousand individual tribal societies flourished. Many produced illustrious histories, and several achieved the status of empire. In Middle (or Meso-) America (present-day Mexico and Central America) and on the western coast of South America, villages grew into states that conquered or absorbed their rivals. Settlers of essentially tropical areas, these were agricultural peoples who traded only regionally and made frequent war on each other. Although after the ninth century copper came into use in Meso-America, iron was unknown until the arrival of the Spaniards in the fifteenth century. Most Native Americans fashioned their tools and weapons out of wood, stone, bone, and pieces of volcanic glass. They had no draft animals and no wheeled vehicles. These facts make all the more remarkable the material achievements of the Maya, Inka, and Aztec civilizations, all three of which developed into empires of considerable authority in the pre-Columbian era.

The Arts of Native North America

A holistic and animistic world view—one that perceives the world as infused with natural spirits—characterized early Native American culture. Indeed, the fact that there is no word for "art" in any Native American language reminds us that the aesthetically compelling objects of these (and many other) people were simply objects of daily use. Among Native Americans (as among Africans) ritual images took on special power and authority: they shared the magical powers of the fetish. The Hopi people of Arizona still produce small wooden *kachinas* ("spirit beings") for the purpose of channeling supernatural

the more disastrous forms of exploitation that prevailed during the seventeenth and eighteenth centuries, when the transatlantic slave trade, now dominated by the Dutch, the French, and the English, reached massive proportions. Between the years 1600 and 1700, the number of Africans taken captive may have reached over one million.

Considering the repeated intrusion of outsiders over the centuries, it is remarkable that local traditions in the arts of Africa have continued to flourish. Indeed, although the Portuguese and other Europeans to a great extent determined the course of African history (Figure 18.12), neither Western European styles nor Western forms of artistic expression would eclipse the unique characteristics of native African art, literature, and music. Perhaps the best evidence of this phenomenon is in the art of sixteenth-century Benin, where age-old African techniques of ivory carving and bronze casting were employed to depict the presence of the Portuguese in Africa. In one subtly carved ivory mask (used ceremonially as a belt or hip ornament), a row of bearded European heads, alternating with mudfishes (the emblem of Benin royalty), crowns the head, while a similar design forms a collar beneath the chin (Figure 18.13). The pupils of the eyes and the scarification patterns on the forehead were origi-

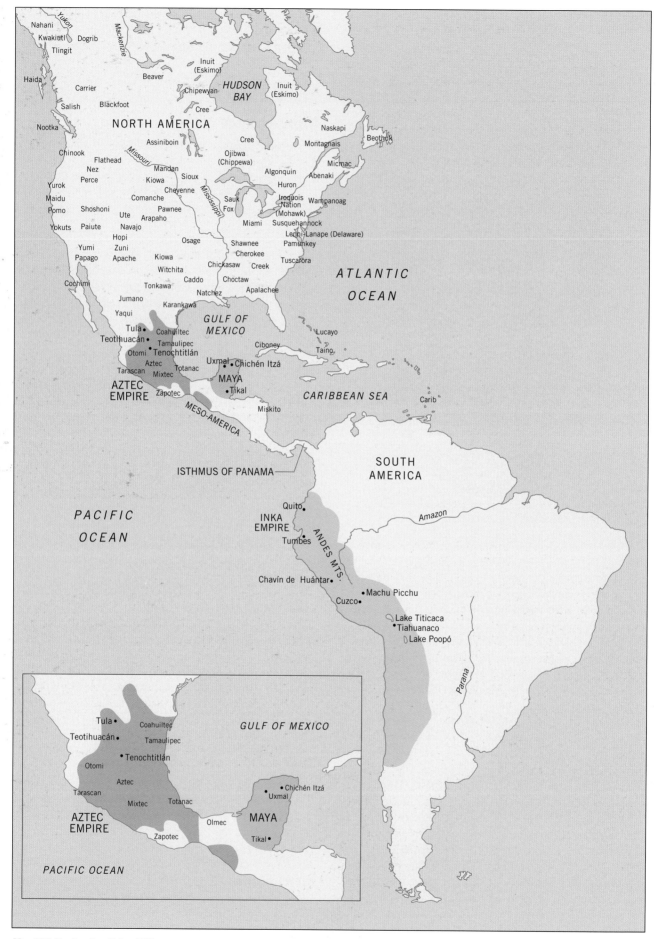

Map 18.3 The Americas Before 1500.

Figure 18.14 Butterfly maiden, Hopi Kachina. Carved wood, pigment and feathers, height 13 in. Courtesy Museum of Northern Arizona, photo archives.

powers (Figure **18.14**). These "dolls" are also given to children in order to familiarize them with the tribal gods. Masks, bowls, rattles, and charms depict gods and mythological heroes whose powers are sought in healing ceremonies and other sacred rites. Weaving, beadwork, pottery, and jewelry-making remain among the most technical and highly prized of Native American crafts. The Haida folk of the Queen Charlotte Islands, located near British Columbia, have revived the ancient practice of raising wooden poles carved and painted with *totems*— that is, heraldic family symbols that served as powerful expressions of social status, spiritual authority, and ancestral pride. The peoples of the Northwest Coast make portrait masks of spirits and ancestors whose powers help their shamans to cure the sick and predict events. Dance masks and clan helmets—which, like African masks, draw on the natural elements of wood, human hair and teeth, animal fur, seashell, and feathers—channel the metamorphic vitality of Northwest Coast creatures such as the raven (see Reading 3.19). Masks with hidden strings connected to moving parts that "become" different creatures or spirits are themselves vehicles of transformation (Figure **18.15**.)

Figure 18.15 Transformation mask, Kwakiutl, British Columbia. Carved wood, pigment and feathers, 24 x 18 in. American Museum of Natural History, New York. Neg/Transparency No: 4811, courtesy the Library, American Museum of Natural History

In various parts of the American Southwest, Native Americans raised communal villages, called "pueblos" by the Spanish. These communities consisted of flat-roofed structures built of stone or adobe arranged in terraces to accommodate a number of families. Among the most notable of the pueblo communities was that of the Anasazi (a Navajo word meaning "ancient ones"). Their settlements at Mesa Verde and Chaco Canyon in southwestern Colorado, which flourished between the eleventh and fourteenth centuries, consisted of elaborate multistoried living spaces with numerous rooms, storage areas, and circular underground ceremonial centers, known as *kivas*. Large enough to hold all of the male members of the community (women were not generally invited to attend sacred ceremonies), *kivas* served as cosmic symbols of the underworld and as theaters for rites designed to maintain harmony with nature. The Cliff Palace at Mesa Verde, Colorado, positioned under an overhanging cliff canyon wall, whose horizontal configuration it echoes, is one of the largest cliff dwellings in America (Figure **18.16**). Its inhabitants—an estimated 250 people—engineered the tasks of quarrying sandstone, cutting logs (for beams and posts), and hauling water, sand, and clay (for the adobe core structure) entirely without the aid of wheeled vehicles, draft animals, or metal tools.

The pueblo tribes of the American Southwest produced some of the most elegant ceramic wares in the history of North American art. Lacking the potter's wheel, women handbuilt vessels for domestic and ceremonial uses. They embellished jars and bowls with designs that vary from a stark, geometric abstraction to stylized human, animal, and plant forms. One Mimbres bowl shows a rabbit-man carrying a basket on his back (Figure **18.17**): the shape of the creature, which subtly blends human and animal features,

Figure 18.17 Classic Mimbres bowl showing rabbit-man with burden basket, from Cameron Creek village, New Mexico, 1000–1150. Black-on-white pottery, height 4⅜ in., diameter 10¾ in. Museum of Indian Arts and Culture/Laboratory of Anthropology, Santa Fe, New Mexico. Cat. 20420/11. Photo: Blair Clark.

works harmoniously with the curves of the bowl and animates the negative space that surrounds the image. Mimbres pottery—usually pierced or ritually "killed" before being placed with its owner in the grave—testifies to the rich imagination and sophisticated artistry of pueblo culture.

Native American religious rituals, like those of all ancient societies, blended poetry, music, and dance. The sun dance was a principal part of the annual ceremony that celebrated seasonal renewal. In the Navajo tribal community of the American Southwest, the shaman still conducts the healing ceremony known as the Night Chant. Beginning at sunset and ending some nine days later at sunrise, the Night Chant calls for a series of meticulously executed sand paintings and the recitation of song cycles designed to remove evil and restore good. Characterized by monophonic melody and hypnotic repetition, the Night Chant is performed to the accompaniment of whistles and percussive instruments such as gourd rattles, drums, and rasps. Its compelling rhythms are evident in both the Music Listening Selection and in the "Prayer of the Night Chant" reproduced below. Rituals like the Night Chant are not mere curiosities but, rather, living practices that remain sacred to the Navajo people.

READING 3.18 "A Prayer of the Night Chant" (Navajo)

Tségihi.	1
House made of dawn.	
House made of evening light.	
House made of the dark cloud.	
House made of male rain.	5
House made of dark mist.	
House made of female rain.	
House made of pollen.	
House made of grasshoppers.	
Dark cloud is at the door.	10
The trail out of it is dark cloud.	
The zigzag lightning stands high upon it.	
Male deity!	
Your offering I make.	
I have prepared a smoke for you.	15
Restore my feet for me.	
Restore my legs for me.	
Restore my body for me.	
Restore my mind for me.	
This very day take out your spell for me.	20
Your spell remove for me.	
You have taken it away for me.	
Far off it has gone.	
Happily I recover.	
Happily my interior becomes cool.	25
Happily I go forth.	
My interior feeling cool, may I walk.	
No longer sore, may I walk.	
Impervious to pain, may I walk.	

♩ See Music Listening Selections at end of chapter.

With lively feelings may I walk.   30
As it used to be long ago, may I walk.
Happily may I walk.
Happily, with abundant dark clouds, may I walk.
Happily, with abundant showers, may I walk.
Happily, with abundant plants, may I walk.   35
Happily, on a trail of pollen, may I walk.
Happily may I walk.
Being as it used to be long ago, may I walk.
May it be beautiful before me.
May it be beautiful behind me.   40
May it be beautiful below me.
May it be beautiful above me.
May it be beautiful all around me.
In beauty it is finished.

Q What is the purpose of repetition in the Night Chant?

Q What similarities do you detect between this chant (Music Listening Selection I-23), Gregorian Chant (MLS I-2), and Buddhist Chant (MLS I-3)?

Myths and folktales, transmitted orally for generations (and only recorded since the seventeenth century), feature themes that call to mind those of Africa. Creation myths, myths of destruction (or death), and myths that describe the way things are served to provide explanations of the workings of nature. Usually told by men who passed them down to boys, myths and tales often traveled vast distances, and, thus, may appear in many variant versions. As with African folklore, Native American myths feature heroes or heroines who work to transform nature; the heroes/tricksters may themselves be humans who are transformed into ravens, spiders, coyotes, wolves, or rabbits (see Figure 18.17). As with the African trickster tale, which usually points to a moral, the Native American trickster story means to teach or explain; nonetheless, heroes whose strategies involve deceit and cunning are often held in high regard.

READING 3.19 Two Native American Tales

How the Sun Came

There was no light anywhere, and the animal people   1
stumbled around in the darkness. Whenever one bumped
into another, he would say, "What we need in the world
is light." And the other would reply, "Yes, indeed, light is
what we badly need."

At last, the animals called a meeting, and gathered
together as well as they could in the dark. The red-
headed woodpecker said, "I have heard that over on the
other side of the world there are people who have light."

"Good, good!" said everyone.   10

"Perhaps if we go over there, they will give us some
light," the woodpecker suggested.

"If they have all the light there is," the fox said, "they
must be greedy people, who would not want to give any
of it up. Maybe we should just go there and take the
light from them."

"Who shall go?" cried everyone, and the animals all
began talking at once, arguing about who was strongest
and ran fastest, who was best able to go and get the light.

Finally, the 'possum said, "I can try. I have a fine big   20
bushy tail, and I can hide the light inside my fur."

"Good! Good!" said all the others, and the 'possum set
out.

As he traveled eastward, the light began to grow and
grow, until it dazzled his eyes, and the 'possum screwed
his eyes up to keep out the bright light. Even today, if you
notice, you will see that the 'possum's eyes are almost
shut, and that he comes out of his house only at night.

All the same, the 'possum kept going, clear to the
other side of the world, and there he found the sun. He   30
snatched a little piece of it and hid it in the fur of his
fine, bushy tail, but the sun was so hot it burned off all
the fur, and by the time the 'possum got home his tail
was as bare as it is today.

"Oh, dear!" everyone said. "Our brother has lost his
fine, bushy tail, and still we have no light."

"I'll go," said the buzzard. "I have better sense than to
put the sun on my tail. I'll put it on my head."

So the buzzard traveled eastward till he came to the
place where the sun was. And because the buzzard flies   40
so high, the sun-keeping people did not see him,
although now they were watching out for thieves. The
buzzard dived straight down out of the sky, the way he
does today, and caught a piece of the sun in his claws.
He set the sun on his head and started for home, but the
sun was so hot that it burned off all his head feathers,
and that is why the buzzard's head is bald today.

Now the people were in despair. "What shall we do?
What shall we do?" they cried. "Our brothers have tried
hard; they have done their best, everything a man can   50
do. What else shall we do so we can have light?"

"They have done the best a man can do," said a little
voice from the grass, "but perhaps this is something a
woman can do better than a man."

"Who are you?" everyone asked. "Who is that speaking
in a tiny voice and hidden in the grass?"

"I am your Grandmother Spider," she replied.
"Perhaps I was put in the world to bring you light. Who
knows? At least I can try, and if I am burned up it will
still not be as if you had lost one of your great warriors."   60

Then Grandmother Spider felt around her in the
darkness until she found some damp clay. She rolled it
in her hands, and molded a little clay bowl. She started
eastward, carrying her bowl, and spinning a thread
behind her so she could find her way back.

When Grandmother Spider came to the place of the
sun people, she was so little and so quiet no one noticed
her. She reached out gently, gently, and took a tiny bit of
the sun, and placed it in her clay bowl. Then she went
back along the thread that she had spun, with the sun's   70
light growing and spreading before her, as she moved

CHAPTER 18 Africa, the Americas, and Cross-Cultural Encounter from east to west. And if you will notice, even today a spider's web is shaped like the sun's disk and its rays, and the spider will always spin her web in the morning, very early, before the sun is fully up.

"Thank you, Grandmother," the people said when she returned. "We will always honor you and we will always remember you."

And from then on pottery making became woman's work, and all pottery must be dried slowly in the shade 80 before it is put in the heat of the firing oven, just as Grandmother Spider's bowl dried in her hand, slowly, in the darkness, as she traveled toward the land of the sun.

(Cheyenne)

Raven and the Moon

One day Raven learnt that an old fisherman, living alone 1 with his daughter on an island far to the north, had a box containing a bright light called the moon. He felt that he must get hold of this wonderful thing, so he changed himself into a leaf growing on a bush near to the old fisherman's home. When the fisherman's daughter came to pick berries from the wild fruit patch, she pulled at the twig on which the leaf stood and it fell down and entered into her body. In time a child was born, a dark-complexioned boy with a long, hooked nose, almost like 10 a bird's bill. As soon as the child could crawl, he began to cry for the moon. He would knock at the box and keep calling, "Moon, moon, shining moon."

At first nobody paid any attention, but as the child became more vocal and knocked harder at the box, the old fisherman said to his daughter, "Well, perhaps we should give the boy the ball of light to play with." The girl opened the box and took out another box, and then another, from inside that. All the boxes were beautifully painted and carved, and inside the tenth there was a net 20 of nettle thread. She loosened this and opened the lid of the innermost box. Suddenly light filled the lodge, and they saw the moon inside the box; bright, round like a ball, shining white. The mother threw it towards her baby son and he caught and held it so firmly they thought he was content. But after a few days he began to fuss and cry again. His grandfather felt sorry for him and asked the mother to explain what the child was trying to say. So his mother listened very carefully and explained that he wanted to look out at the sky and see the stars in the 30 dark sky, but that the roof board over the smoke hole prevented him from doing so. So the old man said, "Open the smoke hole." No sooner had she opened the hole than the child changed himself back into the Raven. With the moon in his bill he flew off. After a moment he landed on a mountain top and then threw the moon into the sky where it remains, still circling in the heavens where Raven threw it.

(Northwest Coast)

Q What creatures assume importance in these tales?

The Arts of Meso- and South America

The largest and most advanced of Native American societies were those of Meso-America. The earliest was the Olmec ("rubber people"), a name derived from the trees that flourished in their region. On the coast of the Gulf of Mexico near the modern Mexican city of Veracruz (see Map 18.3), the Olmecs established the first complex society of the Americas around 1200 B.C.E. Priestly rulers governed on behalf of the gods and rule was hereditary. From ceremonial centers, this elite cadre of priests oversaw the life of the community—a population consisting of farmers and artisans at the lower end of the class structure and an influential nobility at the upper end. The Olmecs honored their theocratic rulers by carving colossal stone heads weighing some twenty tons (Figure 18.18). Like the monumental temples that dominated their communities, these sculptures required the labor of thousands. Olmec culture survived until ca. 400 B.C.E., but Olmec political, religious, and artistic traditions survived for centuries throughout Meso- and South America, especially in this area's three great civilizations: the Maya, the Inka, and the Aztec.

During the two-thousand-year history of Meso- and South America, the techniques of metalwork, and

Figure 18.18 Collosal Olmec head, from San Lorenzo, Veracruz, Mexico, ca. 1000 B.C.E. Basalt, height 5 ft. 10⅛ in. Regional Museum of Veracruz, Jalapa, Mexico. Werner Forman Archive, London.

especially gold-working, passed from generation to generation and attained remarkable levels of proficiency. Gold was associated with the sun, whose radiance gave life to the crops, and with the gods, whose blood (in the form of rain) was considered procreative and thus essential to community survival. The choice medium for the glorification of gods and their earthly representatives, gold was used to produce extraordinary artworks ranging from small items of jewelry to masks and weapons, especially those associated with rituals of blood sacrifice (Figure **18.19**).

Figure 18.19 Ceremonial knife, from the Lambayeque valley, Peru, ninth to eleventh centuries. Hammered gold with turquoise inlay, 13 × 5⅛ in. The Metropolitan Museum of Art, New York. The Jan Mitchell Treasury for Precolumbian works of art in gold (1991.419.58).

In the sacrificial rites and royal ceremonies of pre-Columbian communities, human blood was shed to feed and repay the gods and save the world from destruction. The idea that human blood nourished the gods is a vivid example of the powerful sense of interdependence between earthly and spiritual realms. Nowhere is this more clearly illustrated than in the civilization of the Maya.

The Maya

The Maya were the most inventive heirs of the Olmec. Maya civilization reached its classic phase between 250 and 900 C.E. and survived with considerable political and economic vigor until roughly 1600. At sites in southern Mexico, Honduras, Guatemala, and the Yucatán Peninsula, the Maya constructed fortified cities consisting of elaborate palace complexes that are hauntingly reminiscent of those from ancient Mesopotamia (Figure **18.20**). The complex might include reclining stone figures known as "chacmools," which functioned as altars or bearers of sacrificial offerings. Like the Mesopotamian ziggurat (see chapter 2), the Maya temple was a terraced pyramid with a staircase ascending to a platform capped by a multi-roomed superstructure (Figure **18.21**).

A shrine and sanctuary that also served as a burial place for priests or rulers, the Maya temple was the physical link between earth and the heavens. On the limestone façades of temples and palaces, the Maya carved and painted scenes of religious ceremonies and war, as well as images of their gods: Tlaloc, the long-snouted rain deity (see Figure 18.21, far left), and Quetzalcoatl, the feathered serpent and legendary hero-god of Meso-America (Figure **18.22**).

The Maya were the only known Stone Age culture to produce a written language. This ancient script, comprised of hieroglyphs, was decoded during the second half of the twentieth century. Indeed, only since 1995 have the glyphs been recognized as a system of phonetic signs that operate like spoken syllables—a discovery made, in part, by studying the living language of modern-day descendants of the Maya who inhabit the Guatemalan highlands and the Yucatán. Despite the survival of some codices and many stone inscriptions, nearly all of the literary evidence of this people was destroyed during the sixteenth century by Spanish missionaries and colonial settlers. Perhaps the most important source of Meso-American mythology, however, survives in the form of an oral narrative believed to date from the Maya classic period, transcribed into the Quiche language around 1500. This narrative, known as the *Popol Vuh* (see Introduction), recounts the creation of the world. According to the Maya, the gods fashioned human beings out of maize—the principal Native American crop—but chose deliberately to deprive them of perfect understanding. As if to challenge the gods, the Maya became accomplished mathematicians and astronomers. Carefully observing the earth's movements around the sun, they devised a calendar that was more accurate than any used in medieval Europe before the twelfth century. Having developed a mathe-

Figure 18.20 Reconstruction drawing of post-classic Maya fortress city of Chutixtiox, Quiche, Guatemala, ca. 1000, from Richard Adams, *Prehistoric Mesoamerica*. Boston: Little Brown, 1977.

matical system that recognized "zero," they computed planetary and celestial cycles with some accuracy, tracked the paths of Venus, Jupiter, and Saturn, and successfully predicted eclipses of the sun and moon. They recorded their findings in stone, on the limestone-covered bark pages of codices and on the façades of temples, some of which may have functioned as planetary observatories. At

the principal pyramid at Chichén Itzá in the Yucatán (see Figure 18.21), the ninety-one steps on each of four sides, plus the platform on which the temple stands, correspond to the 365 days in the solar calendar. According to the Maya, the planets (and segments of time itself) were ruled by the gods, usually represented in Maya art as men and women carrying burdens on their shoulders. The Maya

Figure 18.21 Castillo, with Chacmool in the foreground, Chichén Itzá, Yucatán, Mexico. Maya, ninth to thirteenth centuries. © Lee Boltin Picture Library, Crotin-on-Hudson, New York.

and the various Meso-American peoples who followed them believed in the cyclical creation and destruction of the world, and they prudently entrusted the sacred mission of timekeeping to their priests.

A key feature of almost all Meso-American sacred precincts was the ballpark. It was used for the performance of ceremonial games played by two teams of nine to eleven men each. The object of the game was to propel a 5-pound rubber ball through the stone rings at either side of a high-walled court. Members of the losing team lost more than glory: they were sacrificed to the sun god, their hearts torn from their bodies on ritual altars adjacent to the court.

Blood sacrifice and bloodletting were also practiced by the Maya nobility. A low relief lintel from Yaxchilan in Chiapas, Mexico, shows a royal bloodletting ceremony that, according to hieroglyphs carved on the upper and left edges of the stone, took place in 709 C.E. (Figure **18.23**). It identifies King Shield Jaguar (the jaguar was a favorite symbol of military strength) and his queen, Lady Xoc. The king, holding a staff and wearing a feathered headdress adorned with the shrunken head of a sacrificial victim, witnesses the ritual by which the queen pulls a thorn-lined rope through her tongue. The blood-soaked rope falls into a basket filled with slips of paper that

Figure 18.23 Lintel relief, Yaxchilan, Chiapas, Mexico, late classic period, 725 C.E. Limestone. Reproduced by courtesy of the Trustees of the British Museum, London.

absorb the royal blood. These would have been burned in large sacrificial vessels, so that its smoke might lure the gods. The massive losses of blood may have produced hallucinogenic visions that enabled Maya rulers to communicate with the deities. Such ceremonies were performed on the accession of a new king, prior to waging war, and at ceremonies celebrating victory in battle. They served to appease the gods and confirm the political legitimacy of the ruler. A sophisticated blend of realistic detail and abstract design, the Yaxchilan lintel reveals the Maya genius for uniting representational and symbolic modes of expression.

Figure 18.22 Façade of the late classic Maya temple called "the Nunnery," Uxmal, Yucatán, Mexico, 600–1000 C.E. Photo: Ancient Art and Architecture Collection, Middlesex, U.K.

Science and Technology

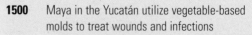

1500	Maya in the Yucatán utilize vegetable-based molds to treat wounds and infections
1568	Gerhard Kremen (Flemish) produces the first Mercator projection map
1596	Korean naval architects launch the first ironclad warship

The Empires of the Inkas and the Aztecs

In 1000 C.E., the Inkas were only one of many warring peoples but, by the fifteenth century, they had become the mightiest power in South America. Indeed, at its height in the late fifteenth century, the Inka settlement consisted of an astounding sixteen million individuals. Located amidst the mountains of the Andes in Peru, the Inka flourished in the rich soils of earlier Peruvian cultures noted for their fine pottery, richly woven textiles (Figure **18.24**), and sophisticated metalwork (see Figure 18.19). Like the ancient Romans, the Inka built thousands of miles of roads and bridges to expedite trade and communication within their empire, which, at its height extended almost three thousand miles from present-day Ecuador to Chile. Lacking writing, they kept records on a system of knotted and colored cords known as *quipu*. The cult of the sun dominated religious festivals at which sacrifices—primarily llamas or guinea pigs—were offered to the gods. Ceremonial objects were hammered from sheets of gold and silver, metals reserved for royal and religious use. With bronze tools and without mortar, they created temples and fortresses that are astonishing for their size and superb

Figure 18.24 Tapestry weave Inka tunic, from the south coast of Peru, 1440–1540. Camelid fiber and cotton, 35⅞ × 30 in. Dumbarton Oaks Research Library and Collections, Washington, D.C.

masonry. At Machu Picchu (see Map 18.3), they left an elaborately constructed three-square-mile city that straddles two mountain peaks some 9,000 feet above sea level.

Small by comparison with the Inka civilization, that of the Aztecs—the last of the three great Meso-American empires—is estimated to have numbered between three and five million people. In their earliest history, the Aztecs (who called themselves *Mexica*) were an insignificant tribe of warriors who migrated to central Mexico in 1325. Driven by a will to conquer matched perhaps only by the ancient Romans, they created in less than a century an empire that encompassed all of central Mexico and Meso-America as far south as Guatemala. Their capital at Tenochtitlán ("Place of the Gods"), a city of some 250,000 people, was constructed on an island in the middle of Lake Texcoco. It was connected to the Mexican mainland by three great causeways and watered by artificial lakes and dams. Like the Romans, the Aztecs were masterful engineers, whose roads, canals, and aqueducts astounded the Spaniards who arrived in Mexico in 1519. Upon encountering Tenochtitlán, with its huge temples and palaces connected by avenues and ceremonial plazas, Spanish soldiers reported that it rivaled Venice and Constantinople—cities that were neither so orderly nor so clean.

Both the Aztec and the Inka civilizations absorbed the cultural traditions of earlier Meso-Americans, including the Maya. They honored the pantheon of nature deities centering on the sun and extended the practice of blood sacrifice to the staggering numbers of victims captured in their incessant wars. They preserved the native Meso-American traditions of temple construction, ceramics, weaving, metalwork, and stone-carving. During

Figure 18.25 *Coatlique, Mother of the Gods*, Aztec, 1487–1520. Andesite, height 8 ft. 3¼ in. National Anthropological Museum, Mexico. Dagli Orti, Paris/Art Archive, London

Figure 18.26 Sun disk, known as the "Calendar Stone," Aztec, fifteenth century. Diameter 13 ft., weight 24½ tons. National Anthropological Museum, Mexico.

the fifteenth century, the Aztecs raised to new heights the art of monumental stone sculpture, carving great basalt statues that ranged from austere, realistic portraits to fantastic and terrifying icons of gods and goddesses such as Coatlique, Lady of the Skirt of Serpents and ancient earth mother of the gods (Figure **18.25**). Combining feline and human features, the over-life-sized "she-of-the-serpent-skirt" bears a head consisting of two snakes, clawed hands and feet, and a necklace of excised hearts and severed hands. Renaissance Europeans, whose idea of female divinity was shaped by Raphael's gentle madonnas, found these blood-drenched "idols" outrageous; they destroyed as many as they could find.

The Aztecs carried on the traditions of timekeeping begun by the Maya. Like the Maya, they devised a solar calendar of 365 days and anticipated the cyclical destruction of the world every fifty-two years. They produced the "Calendar Stone," a huge votive object that functioned not as an actual calendar, but as a symbol of the Aztec cosmos (Figure **18.26**). The four square panels

that surround the face of the sun god represent the four previous creations of the world. Arranged around these panels are the twenty signs of the days of the month in the eighteen-month Aztec year, and embracing the entire cosmic configuration are two giant serpents that bear the sun on its daily journey. The stone is the pictographic counterpart of Aztec legends that bind human beings to the gods and to the irreversible wheel of time.

Some of the most interesting records of Aztec culture are preserved in the form of codices, that is manuscripts—usually made of deer hide—with pictographic representations that recount tribal genealogy, history, and mythology. The most complex surviving Meso-American codex, which is housed today at the Vatican Library in Rome, illustrates the history of Quetzalcoatl in the underworld. A page showing the dual aspects of the universe—life and death—in the form of a pair of fantastically arrayed deities includes an inverted skull or earth monster (below) and twenty pictographic day signs on either side (Figure **18.27**).

Figure 18.27 Aztec peoples, *Mictlantecuhtli and Quetzalcoatl*. Manuscript illumination. Vatican Library, Rome. Codex Borgia, f.56.

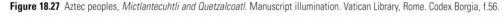

Cross-Cultural Encounter

The Spanish in the Americas

Columbus made his initial landfall on one of the islands now called the Bahamas, and on successive voyages he explored the Caribbean Islands and the coast of Central America. At every turn, he encountered people native to the area—people he called "Indians" in the mistaken belief that he had reached the "Indies," the territories of India and China. Other explorers soon followed and rectified Columbus' misconception. Spanish adventurers, called *conquistadores*, sought wealth and fortune in the New World. Although vastly outnumbered, the force of six hundred soldiers under the command of Hernán Cortés (1485–1547), equipped with fewer than twenty horses and the superior technology of gunpowder and muskets, overcame the Aztec armies in 1521. Following a seventy-five-day siege, the Spanish completely demolished the island city of Tenochtitlán, from whose ruins Mexico City would eventually rise. While the technology of gunpowder and muskets had much to do with the Spanish victory, other factors contributed, such as religious prophecy (that Quetzalcoatl would return as a bearded white man), support from rebellious Aztec subjects, and an outbreak of smallpox among the Aztecs.

The Spanish destruction of Tenochtitlán and the melting down of most of the Aztec goldwork left little tangible evidence of the city's former glory. Consequently, the description that is the subject of Cortés' second letter to Spain is doubly important: not only does it offer a detailed picture of Aztec cultural achievement, but it serves as a touchstone by which to assess the conflicted reactions of Renaissance Europeans to their initial encounters with the inhabitants of strange and remote lands.

READING 3.20 From Cortés' Letters from Mexico (1520)

This great city of Temixtitan[1] is built on the salt lake, and no matter by what road you travel there are two leagues from the main body of the city to the mainland. There are four artificial causeways leading to it, and each is as wide as two cavalry lances. The city itself is as big as Seville or Córdoba. The main streets are very wide and very straight; some of these are on the land, but the rest and all the smaller ones are half on land, half canals where they paddle their canoes. All the streets have openings in places so that the water may pass from one canal to another. Over all these openings, and some of them are very wide, there are bridges made of long and wide beams joined together very firmly and so well made that on some of them ten horsemen may ride abreast. [10]

Seeing that if the inhabitants of this city wished to betray us they were very well equipped for it by the design of the city, for once the bridges had been removed they could starve us to death without our being able to reach the mainland, as soon as I entered the city I made great haste to build four brigantines, and completed them in a very short time. They were such as could carry three hundred men to the land and transport the horses whenever we might need them. [20]

This city has many squares where trading is done and markets are held continuously. There is also one square twice as big as that of Salamanca,[2] with arcades all around, where more than sixty thousand people come each day to buy and sell, and where every kind of merchandise produced in these lands is found; provisions as well as ornaments of gold and silver, lead, [30] brass, copper, tin, stones, shells, bones, and feathers. They also sell lime, hewn and unhewn stone, adobe bricks, tiles, and cut and uncut woods of various kinds. There is a street where they sell game and birds of every species found in this land: chickens, partridges and quails, wild ducks, flycatchers, widgeons, turtledoves, pigeons, cane birds, parrots, eagles and eagle owls, falcons, sparrow hawks and kestrels, and they sell the skins of some of these birds of prey with their feathers, heads and claws. They sell rabbits and hares, and stags [40] and small gelded dogs which they breed for eating.

There are streets of herbalists where all the medicinal herbs and roots found in the land are sold. There are shops like apothecaries', where they sell ready-made medicines as well as liquid ointments and plasters. There are shops like barbers' where they have their hair washed and shaved, and shops where they sell food and drink. There are also men like porters to carry loads. There is much firewood and charcoal, earthenware braziers and mats of various kinds like mattresses for [50] beds, and other, finer ones, for seats and for covering rooms and hallways. There is every sort of vegetable, especially onions, leeks, garlic, common cress and watercress, borage, sorrel, teasels and artichokes; and there are many sorts of fruit, among which are cherries and plums like those in Spain.

They sell honey, wax, and a syrup made from maize canes, which is as sweet and syrupy as that made from the sugar cane. They also make syrup from a plant which in the islands is called *maguey*,[3] which is much better than [60] most syrups, and from this plant they also make sugar and wine, which they likewise sell. There are many sorts of spun cotton, in hanks of every color, and it seems like the silk market at Granada, except here there is a much greater quantity. They sell as many colors for painters as may be found in Spain and all of excellent hues. They sell deerskins, with and without the hair, and some are dyed white or in various colors. They sell much earthenware, which for the most part is very good; there are both large and small pitchers, jugs, pots, tiles, and many other sorts [70] of vessel, all of good clay and most of them glazed and painted. They sell maize both as grain and as bread and it is better both in appearance and in taste than any

---

[1]Tenochtitlán.

[2]A Spanish university town.

[3]Fermented aloe or *pulque*, a powerful liquor still popular today in Mexico.

found in the islands or on the mainland. They sell chicken and fish pies, and much fresh and salted fish, as well as raw and cooked fish. They sell hen and goose eggs, and eggs of all the other birds I have mentioned, in great number, and they sell *tortillas* made from eggs.

Finally, besides those things which I have already mentioned, they sell in the market everything else to be found in this land, but they are so many and so varied that because of their great number and because I cannot remember many of them nor do I know what they are called I shall not mention them. Each kind of merchandise is sold in its own street without any mixture whatever; they are very particular in this. Everything is sold by number and size, and until now I have seen nothing sold by weight. There is in this great square a very large building like a courthouse, where ten or twelve persons sit as judges. They preside over all that happens in the markets, and sentence criminals. There are in this square other persons who walk among the people to see what they are selling and the measures they are using; and they have been seen to break some that were false.

There are, in all districts of this great city, many temples or houses for their idols. They are all very beautiful buildings, and in the important ones there are priests of their sect who live there permanently; and, in addition to the houses for the idols, they also have very good lodgings. All these priests dress in black and never comb their hair from the time they enter the priesthood until they leave; and all the sons of the persons of high rank, both the lords and honored citizens also, enter the priesthood and wear the habit from the age of seven or eight years until they are taken away to be married; this occurs more among the first-born sons, who are to inherit, than among the others. They abstain from eating things, and more at some times of the year than at others; and no woman is granted entry nor permitted inside these places of worship.

Amongst these temples there is one, the principal one, whose great size and magnificence no human tongue could describe, for it is so large that within the precincts, which are surrounded by a very high wall, a town of some five hundred inhabitants could easily be built. All round inside this wall there are very elegant quarters with very large rooms and corridors where their priests live. There are as many as forty towers, all of which are so high that in the case of the largest there are fifty steps leading up to the main part of it; and the most important of these towers is higher than that of the cathedral of Seville. They are so well constructed in both their stone and woodwork that there can be none better in any place, for all the stonework inside the chapels where they keep their idols is in high relief, with figures and little houses, and the woodwork is likewise of relief and painted with monsters and other figures and designs. All these towers are burial places of chiefs, and the chapels therein are each dedicated to the idol which he venerated.

There are three rooms within this great temple for the principal idols, which are of remarkable size and stature and decorated with many designs and sculptures, both in stone and in wood. Within these rooms are other chapels, and the doors to them are very small. Inside there is no light whatsoever; there only some of the priests may enter, for inside are the sculptured figures of the idols, although, as I have said, there are also many outside.

The most important of these idols, and the ones in whom they have most faith, I had taken from their places and thrown down the steps; and I had those chapels where they were cleaned, for they were full of the blood of sacrifices; and I had images of Our Lady and of other saints put there, which caused Mutezuma[4] and the other natives some sorrow. First they asked me not to do it, for when the communities learnt of it they would rise against me, for they believed that those idols gave them all their worldly goods, and that if they were allowed to be ill treated, they would become angry and give them nothing and take the fruit from the earth leaving the people to die of hunger. I made them understand through the interpreters how deceived they were in placing their trust in those idols which they had made with their hands from unclean things. They must know that there was only one God, Lord of all things, who had created heaven and earth and all else and who made all of us; and He was without beginning or end, and they must adore and worship only Him, not any other creature or thing. And I told them all I knew about this to dissuade them from their idolatry and bring them to the knowledge of God our Saviour. All of them, especially Mutezuma, replied that they had already told me how they were not natives of this land, and that as it was many years since their forefathers had come here, they well knew that they might have erred somewhat in what they believed, for they had left their native land so long ago; and as I had only recently arrived from there, I would better know the things they should believe, and should explain to them and make them understand, for they would do as I said was best. Mutezuma and many of the chieftains of the city were with me until the idols were removed, the chapel cleaned and the images set up and I urged them not to sacrifice living creatures to the idols, as they were accustomed,[5] for, as well as being most abhorrent to God, Your Sacred Majesty's laws forbade it and ordered that he who kills shall be killed. And from then on they ceased to do it, and in all the time I stayed in that city I did not see a living creature killed or sacrificed.

The figures of the idols in which these people believe are very much larger than the body of a big man. They are made of dough from all the seeds and vegetables which they eat, ground and mixed together, and bound with the blood of human hearts which those priests tear out while still beating. And also after they are made they offer them more hearts and anoint their faces with the blood. Everything has an idol dedicated to it, in the same manner as the pagans who in antiquity honored their gods. So they have an idol whose favor they ask in war and another for

---

[4]Moctezuma II, the last Aztec monarch, who ruled from 1502 to 1520.
[5]In 1488, at the dedication of the Great Pyramid at Tenochtitlán, Aztec priests sacrificed more than twenty thousand war captives.

agriculture; and likewise for each thing they wish to be done well they have an idol which they honor and serve.

There are in the city many large and beautiful houses, and the reason for this is that all the chiefs of the land, who are Mutezuma's vassals, have houses in the city and live there for part of the year;[6] and in addition there are many rich citizens who likewise have very good houses. All these houses have very large and very good rooms and also very pleasant gardens of various sorts of flowers both on the upper and lower floors.

Along one of the causeways to this great city run two aqueducts made of mortar. Each one is two paces wide and some six feet deep, and along one of them a stream of very good fresh water, as wide as a man's body, flows into the heart of the city and from this they all drink. The other, which is empty, is used when they wish to clean the first channel. Where the aqueducts cross the bridges, the water passes along some channels which are as wide as an ox; and so they serve the whole city.

Canoes paddle through all the streets selling the water; they take it from the aqueduct by placing the canoes beneath the bridges where those channels are, and on top there are men who fill the canoes and are paid for their work. At all the gateways to the city and at the places where these canoes are unloaded, which is where the greater part of the provisions enter the city, there are guards in huts who receive a [percentage] of all that enters. I have not yet discovered whether this goes to the chief or to the city, but I think to the chief, because in other markets in other parts I have seen this tax paid to the ruler of the place. Every day, in all the markets and public places there are many workmen and craftsmen of every sort, waiting to be employed by the day. The people of this city are dressed with more elegance and are more courtly in their bearing than those of the other cities and provinces, and because Mutezuma and all those chieftains, his vassals, are always coming to the city, the people have more manners and politeness in all matters. Yet so as not to tire Your Highness with the description of the things of this city (although I would not complete it so briefly), I will say only that these people live almost like those in Spain, and in as much harmony and order as there, and considering that they are barbarous and so far from the knowledge of God and cut off from all civilized nations, it is truly remarkable to see what they have achieved in all things.

Q What aspects of Aztec life and culture favorably impressed Cortés? Of what was he critical?

---

[6]Provincial lords were required to spend part of each year at the capital.

The Aftermath of Conquest

Mexican gold and (after the conquest of the Inkas) Peruvian silver were not the only sources of wealth for the conquerors; the Spanish soon turned to the ruthless exploitation of the native populations, enslaving them for use as miners and field laborers. During the sixteenth century, entire populations of Native Americans were destroyed as a result of the combined effects of such European diseases as smallpox and measles and decades of inhumane treatment. When Cortés arrived, for example, Mexico's population was approximately 25 million; in 1600, it had declined to one million. Disease traveled from America to Europe as well: European soldiers carried syphilis from the "New World" to the "Old." Guns and other weaponry came into the Americas, even as Christian missionaries brought a pacifistic Catholicism to the native populations. The impact of colonialism is described in the following eyewitness account from a *History of the New World* (1565) by the Italian Girolamo Benzoni (1519–1570), who spent fifteen years in the Americas:

> After the death of Columbus, other governors were sent to Hispaniola;* both clerical and secular, till the natives, finding themselves intolerably oppressed and overworked, with no chance of regaining their liberty, with sighs and tears longed for death. Many went into the woods and having killed their children, hanged themselves, saying it was far better to die than to live so miserably serving such ferocious tyrants and villainous thieves. The women terminated their pregnancies with the juice of a certain herb in order not to produce children, and then following the example of their husbands, hanged themselves. Some threw themselves from high cliffs down precipices; others jumped into the sea and rivers; others starved themselves to death. Sometimes they killed themselves with their flint knives; others pierced their bosoms or sides with pointed stakes. Finally, out of two million inhabitants, through suicides and other deaths occasioned by the excessive labour and cruelties imposed by the Spaniards, there are not a hundred and fifty now to be found.

Such reports of Spanish imperialism in the Americas, brought to life by the illustrations of the Flemish engraver Theodore de Bry (1528–1598; Figure **18.28**), fueled the so-called "Black Legend" of Spanish cruelty toward the "Indians" and fed the heated debate that questioned the humanity of so-called "savage" populations. In this debate, the Spanish missionary-priest, Bartolomé de Las Casas (1474–1566), author of the infamous *Very Brief Account of the Destruction of the Indies* (1552), roundly denounced Spanish treatment of the "Indians." His humanitarian position prompted Pope Paul III to declare officially in

---

*The name Columbus gave to the island in the West Indies that now comprises Haiti and the Dominican Republic.

Figure 18.28 THEODORE DE BRY, *Spanish Cruelties Cause the Indians to Despair*, from *Grands Voyages*. Frankfurt, 1594. Woodcut. The John Carter Brown Library, Providence, Rhode Island. Photo: AKG, London.

1537 that "the said Indians and all other people who may later be discovered by Christians, are by no means to be deprived of their liberty or . . . property." (The papal edict, it is worth noting, failed to extend such protection to Africans.) Las Casas, known as the "Apostle to the Indians," pleaded, ". . . all the peoples of the world are men, and the definition of all men collectively and severally, is one: that they are rational beings. All possess understanding and volition, being formed in the image and likeness of God. . . ."

Unlike the civilizations of India, China, and Africa, which have each enjoyed a continuous history from ancient times until the present, none of the empires that once flourished in ancient America has survived into modern times. The European invasion of the Americas severely arrested the cultural evolution of native tribal populations. Remnants of these populations, however, remain today among such groups as the Hopi and the Pueblo of the Southwestern United States, the Maya of the Yucatán, and the Inuit of the Pacific Northwest. Among these and other tribes, the ancient crafts of pottery, weaving, beadwork, and silverwork still reach a high degree of beauty and technical sophistication.

The Columbian Exchange

While the immediate effect of European expansion and cross-cultural encounter was a dramatic clash of traditions and values, the long-range effects were more positive, especially in the realms of commerce and culture. The so-called "Columbian Exchange" describes the interchange of hundreds of goods and products between Western Europe and the Americas. The Europeans introduced into the Americas horses, cattle, pigs, sheep, chickens, wheat, barley, oats, onions, lettuce, sugar cane, and various fruits, including peaches, pears, and citrus. From America, Western Europe came to enjoy corn, potatoes, tomatoes, peppers, chocolate, vanilla, tobacco, avocados, peanuts, pineapples, pumpkins, and a variety of beans. The most important aspect of the Columbian Exchange, however, may be said to lie in the creation of vibrant new cultures and new peoples. The biological mix of Europeans, Native Americans, and Africans would alter the populations of the world to introduce the *mestizo* (a person of mixed European and Native American ancestry) and the various *creole* ("mixed") inhabitants of the Americas. Consequently, the Columbian Exchange generated new developments in all aspects of life, ranging from technology and industry to language, diet, and dance. On the threshold of modernity, the Euro-African and Euro-American exchanges opened the door to centuries of contact and diffusion that shaped the future of a brave new world.

SUMMARY

The civilizations of Africa and the Americas offer some startling features that set them apart from the culture of the West. Tribal organization and an animistic view of nature were primary characteristics of the diverse peoples who flourished in both of these vast regions. The literature, music, and art of the first kingdoms of West Africa reflect the communal and deeply spiritual nature of African society. The great body of African literature, from *Sundiata* to the tales, proverbs, and poems of various African tribes, emerges out of an oral tradition that, like African music and art, is characterized by strong rhythmic patterns. African music, dance, poetry, and the visual arts are traditionally integrated in ceremonial performance. African sculpture takes the form of masks, ancestor figures, and reliquaries, many of which function as fetishes. While some regions in Africa have produced art marked by great realism, others have shown a preference for expressive abstraction.

By comparison with Africa, the rich traditions of Native American cultures have almost disappeared. However, extant ceramics, textiles, baskets, metalwork, and sculpture, as well as the remains of pueblo architecture, testify to the vitality and originality of tribal people throughout the Americas. Among these, only the Maya left a system of writing, though the oral traditions of other early Native American cultures are known to us thanks to records of more recent vintage. The genius of the Maya, the Aztecs, and the Inkas—the three most notable of the Meso- and South American cultures—is still visible in the ruins of their great palaces, temples, and ballparks. The legacy of these imperial civilizations, their nature deities,

and their religious rituals takes the form of technically sophisticated goldwork, polychrome ceramics, and vividly carved stone sculptures.

Although they lived in different parts of the world and under different circumstances, ancient African and early Native American people shared similar world-views: they held that the universe and all natural objects were infused with spiritual power and that the community of the living was shared by the dead. They viewed time as cyclical rather than as moving toward a specific end or goal. Essentially, they sought the roots of their social order in nature and in the communion of human beings with nature. Such attitudes, closer in spirit to those of ancient India and China than to those of Renaissance Europe, would struggle to survive the aggressive momentum of European expansion and the critical scrutiny of the Christian world.

MUSIC LISTENING SELECTIONS

CD One Selection 21 Music of Africa, Senegal, "Greetings from Podor".

CD One Selection 22 Music of Africa, Angola, "Cangele Song".

CD One Selection 23 Music of Native America, "Navajo Night Chant," male chorus with gourd rattles.

GLOSSARY

anaphora the repetition of a word or words at the beginning of two or more lines of verse

animism the belief that the forces of nature are inhabited by spirits

fetish an object believed to have magical power

griot a class of poet-historians who preserved the legends and lore of Africa by chanting or singing them from memory

kiva the underground ceremonial center of the Southwest Indian pueblo community

scarification the act or process of incising the flesh as a form of identification and rank, and/or for aesthetic purposes

totem an animal or other creature that serves as a heraldic emblem of a tribe, family, or clan

CHAPTER 19

Protest and Reform: The Waning of the Old Order

"Now what else is the whole life of mortals but a sort of comedy, in which the various actors, disguised by various costumes and masks, walk on and play each one his part, until the manager waves them off the stage?"
Erasmus

The Temper of Reform

The Impact of Technology

In the transition from medieval to early modern times, technology played a crucial role. Gunpowder, the light cannon, and other military devices made warfare more impersonal and ultimately more deadly. At the same time, Western advances in navigation, shipbuilding, and maritime instrumentation brought Europe into a dominant position in world exploration and colonization. By the end of the sixteenth century, European expansion would change the map of the world.

Another kind of technology, the printing press, revolutionized the future of learning and communication. Block printing originated in China in the ninth century and movable type in the eleventh, but print technology did not reach Western Europe until the fifteenth century. By 1450, in the city of Mainz, the German goldsmith Johannez Gutenberg (ca. 1400–ca. 1468) had perfected a printing press that made it possible to fabricate books more cheaply, more rapidly, and in greater numbers than ever before (Figure **19.1**). As information became a commodity for mass production, vast areas of knowledge—heretofore the exclusive domain of the monastery, the Church, and the university—became available to the public. The printing press facilitated the rise of popular education and

encouraged individuals to form their own opinions by reading for themselves. Print technology proved to be the single most important factor in the success of the Protestant Reformation, as it brought the complaints of Church reformers to the attention of all literate folk. And, in the wake of such writers as Dante, Chaucer, Petrarch, and Boccaccio, the printing press nourished the growing interest in vernacular literature, which in turn enhanced national and individual self-consciousness.

Christian Humanism and the Northern Renaissance

The new print technology broadcast an old message of religious protest and reform. For two centuries, critics had attacked the wealth, worldliness, and unchecked corruption of the Church of Rome. During the early fifteenth century, the rekindled sparks of lay piety and anticlericalism spread throughout the Netherlands, where religious leaders launched the movement known as the *devotio moderna* ("modern devotion"). Lay Brothers and Sisters of the Common Life, as they were called, organized houses in which they studied and taught Scripture. Living in the manner of Christian monks and nuns, but taking no monastic vows, these lay Christians cultivated a devotional lifestyle that fulfilled the ideals of the apostles and the church fathers. They followed the mandate of Thomas a Kempis (1380–1471), himself a Brother of the Common Life and author of the *Imitatio Christi* (*Imitation of Christ*), to put the message of Jesus into daily practice. After the Bible, the *Imitatio Christi* was the most frequently published book in the Christian West well into modern times.

The *devotio moderna* spread quickly throughout Northern Europe, harnessing the dominant strains of anticlericalism, lay piety, and mysticism, even as it coincided with the revival of classical studies in the newly established universities of Germany. Although Northern humanists, like their Italian Renaissance counterparts, encouraged learning in Greek and Latin, they were more concerned with the study and translation of early Christian manuscripts than with the classical and largely

Science and Technology

1320	paper adopted for use in Europe (having long been in use in China)
1450	the Dutch devise the first firearm small enough to be carried by a single person
1451	Nicolas of Cusa (German) uses concave lenses to amend nearsightedness
1454	Johannes Gutenberg (German) prints the Bible with movable metal type

secular texts that preoccupied the Italian humanists. This critical reappraisal of religious texts is known as Christian humanism. Christian humanists studied the Bible and the writings of the church fathers with the same intellectual fervor that the Italian humanists had brought to their examination of Plato and Cicero. The efforts of these Northern scholars gave rise to a rebirth (or renaissance) that focused on the late classical world and, specifically, on the revival of Church life and doctrine as gleaned from early Christian literature. The Northern Renaissance put Christian humanism at the service of evangelical Christianity.

The leading Christian humanist of the sixteenth century—often called "the Prince of Humanists"—was Desiderius Erasmus of Rotterdam (1466–1536; Figure **19.2**). Schooled among the Brothers of the Common Life and learned in Latin, Greek, and Hebrew, Erasmus was a superb scholar and a prolific writer (see Reading 3.22). The first humanist to make extensive use of the printing press, he once dared a famous publisher to print his words as fast as he could write them. Erasmus was a fervent neoclassicist—he argued that almost everything worth knowing was set forth in Greek and Latin. He was also a devout Christian who advocated a return to the basic teachings of Christ. He criticized the Church and all Christians whose faith had been jaded by slavish adherence to dogma and ritual. Using four different Greek manuscripts of the Gospels, he produced a critical edition of the New Testament that corrected Jerome's mistranslations of key passages (see chapter 9). Erasmus' New Testament became the source of most sixteenth-century German and English vernacular translations of this central text of Christian humanism.

Luther and the Protestant Reformation

During the sixteenth century, papal extravagance and immorality reached new heights, and Church reform became an urgent public issue. In the territories of Germany, loosely united under the leadership of the Holy Roman Emperor Charles V (1500–1558), the voices of protest were more strident than anywhere else in Europe. Across Germany, the sale of indulgences (see chapter 15) for the benefit of the Church of Rome—specifically for the rebuilding of Saint Peter's Cathedral—provoked harsh criticism, especially by those who saw the luxuries of the papacy as a betrayal of apostolic ideals. As with most movements of religious reform, it fell to one individual to galvanize popular sentiment. In 1505, Martin Luther (1483–1546), the son of a rural coal miner, abandoned his legal studies to become an Augustinian monk (Figure **19.3**). Thereafter, as a doctor of theology at the University of Wittenberg, he spoke out against the Church. His inflammatory sermons and essays offered radical remedies to what he called "the misery and wretchedness of Christendom."

Luther was convinced of the inherent sinfulness of humankind, but he took issue with the traditional medieval view—as promulgated, for instance, in *Everyman*—that salvation was earned through the performance of good works and grace mediated by the Church and its priesthood. Inspired by the words of Saint Paul, "the just shall live by faith" (Romans 1:17), Luther maintained that salvation could be gained only by faith in the validity of Christ's sacrifice: human beings were saved by the unearned gift of God's grace, not by their good works on earth. The purchase of indulgences, the veneration of relics, making pilgrimages, and seeking the intercession of the saints were useless, because only the grace of God could save the Christian soul. Justified by faith alone, Christians should assume full responsibility for their own actions and intentions.

In 1517, in pointed criticism of Church abuses, Luther posted on the door of the collegiate church at Wittenberg a list of ninety-five issues he intended for dispute with the leaders of the Church of Rome. The *Ninety-Five Theses*, which took the confrontational tone of the sample below, were put to press and circulated throughout Europe:

27 They are wrong who say that the soul flies out of Purgatory as soon as the money thrown into the chest rattles.

32 Those who believe that, through letters of pardon [indulgences], they are made sure of their

Figure 19.2 ALBRECHT DÜRER, *Erasmus of Rotterdam*, 1526. Engraving, 9¾ × 7½ in. Reproduced by courtesy of the Trustees of the British Museum, London.

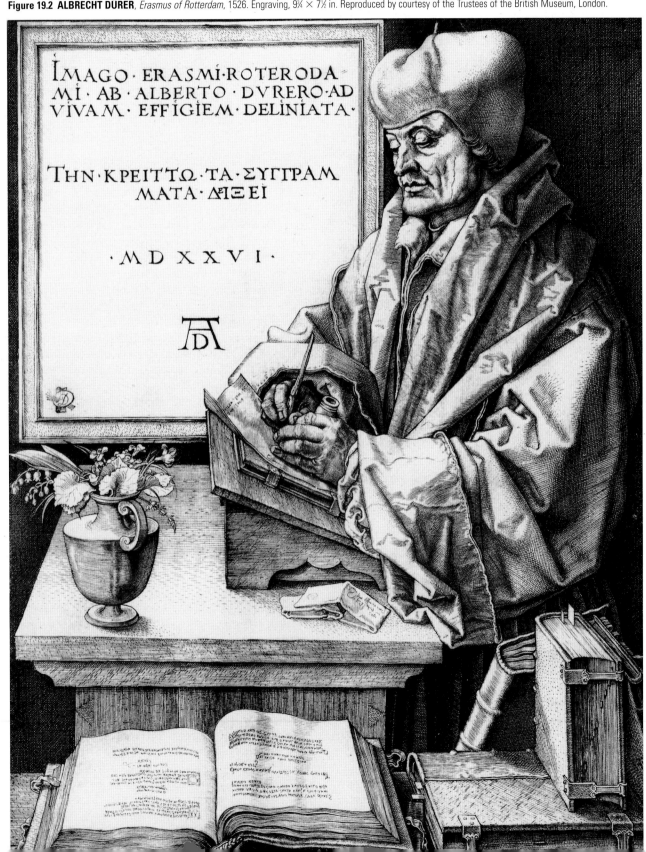

Figure 19.3 LUCAS CRANACH THE ELDER, *Portrait of Martin Luther*. 1533, panel, 8 × 5¾ in. City of Bristol Museum and Art Gallery.

own salvation will be eternally damned along with their teachers.

37 Every true Christian, whether living or dead, has a share in all the benefits of Christ and of the Church, given by God, even without letters of pardon.

43 Christians should be taught that he who gives to a poor man, or lends to a needy man, does better than if he bought pardons.

44 Because by works of charity, charity increases, and the man becomes better; while by means of pardons, he does not become better, but only freer from punishment.

45 Christians should be taught that he who sees any one in need, and, passing him by, gives money for pardons, is not purchasing for himself the indulgences of the Pope but the anger of God.

49 Christians should be taught that the Pope's pardons are useful if they do not put their trust in them, but most hurtful if through them they lose the fear of God.

50 Christians should be taught that if the Pope were acquainted with the exactions of the Preachers of pardons, he would prefer that the Basilica of St. Peter should be burnt to ashes rather than that it should be built up with the skin, flesh, and bones of his sheep.

54 Wrong is done to the Word of God when, in the same sermon, an equal or longer time is spent on pardons than on it.

62 The true treasure of the Church is the Holy Gospel of the glory and grace of God.

66 The treasures of indulgences are nets, wherewith they now fish for the riches of men.

67 Those indulgences which the preachers loudly proclaim to be the greatest graces, are seen to be truly such as regards the promotion of gain.

68 Yet they are in reality most insignificant when compared to the grace of God and the piety of the cross.

86 . . . why does not the Pope, whose riches are at this day more ample than those of the wealthiest of the wealthy, build the single Basilica of St. Peter with his own money rather than with that of poor believers? . . .*

Luther did not wish to destroy Catholicism, but rather, to reform it. Gradually he extended his criticism of Church abuses to criticism of Church doctrine. For instance, because he found justification in Scripture for only two of the sacraments dispensed by the Catholic Church—Baptism and Holy Communion—he rejected the other five. He attacked monasticism and clerical celibacy. (Luther himself married and and fathered six children.) Luther's boldest challenge to the old medieval order, however, was his unwillingness to accept the pope as the ultimate source of religious authority. He denied that the pope was the spiritual heir to Saint Peter and claimed that the head of the Church, like any other human being, was subject to error and correction. Christians, argued Luther, were collectively a priesthood of believers; they were "consecrated as priests by baptism." The ultimate source of authority in matters of faith and doctrine, held Luther, was Scripture, as interpreted by the individual Christian. To encourage the reading of the Bible among his followers, Luther translated the Old and New Testaments into German.

Luther's assertions were revolutionary because they defied both Church dogma and the authority of the Church of Rome. In 1520, Pope Leo X issued an edict excommunicating the outspoken reformer. Luther promptly burned the edict in the presence of his students at the University of Wittenberg. The following year, he was summoned to the city of Worms in order to appear before the Diet—the German parliamentary council. Charged with heresy, Luther stubbornly refused to back down, concluding, "I cannot and will not recant anything, for to act against our conscience is neither safe for us, nor open to us. On this I take my stand. I can do no other. God help me. Amen." Luther's confrontational temperament and down-to-earth style are captured in this excerpt from his *Address to the German Nobility*, a call for religious reform written shortly before the Diet of Worms and circulated widely in a printed edition.

*J. H. Robinson, ed., *Translations and Reprints from the Original Sources of European History*, II. No. 6. Philadelphia: University of Pennsylvania Press, 1894.

It has been devised that the Pope, bishops, priests, and **1**
monks are called the *spiritual estate*; princes, lords,
artificers, and peasants are the *temporal estate*. This is
an artful lie and hypocritical device, but let no one be
made afraid by it, and that for this reason: that all
Christians are truly of the spiritual estate, and there is no
difference among them, save of office alone. As St. Paul
says (1 Cor.: 12), we are all one body, though each
member does its own work, to serve the others. This is
because we have one baptism, one Gospel, one faith, and **10**
are all Christians alike; for baptism, Gospel, and faith,
these alone make spiritual and Christian people.

As for the unction by a pope or a bishop, tonsure,
ordination, consecration, and clothes differing from those
of laymen—all this may make a hypocrite or an anointed
puppet, but never a Christian or a spiritual man. Thus we
are all consecrated as priests by baptism. . . .

And to put the matter even more plainly, if a little
company of pious Christian laymen were taken prisoners
and carried away to a desert, and had not among them a **20**
priest consecrated by a bishop, and were there to agree to
elect one of them, born in wedlock or not, and were to
order him to baptise, to celebrate the mass, to absolve,
and to preach, this man would as truly be a priest, as if
all the bishops and all the popes had consecrated him.
That is why in cases of necessity every man can baptise
and absolve, which would not be possible if we were not
all priests. . . .

[Members of the Church of Rome] alone pretend to be
considered masters of the Scriptures; although they learn **30**
nothing of them all their life. They assume authority, and
juggle before us with impudent words, saying that the
Pope cannot err in matters of faith, whether he be evil or
good, albeit they cannot prove it by a single letter. That is
why the canon law contains so many heretical and
unchristian, nay unnatural, laws. . . .

And though they say that this authority was given
to St. Peter when the keys were given to him, it is plain
enough that the keys were not given to St. Peter alone,
but to the whole community. Besides, the keys were not **40**
ordained for doctrine or authority, but for sin, to bind or
loose; and what they claim besides this from the keys is
mere invention. . . .

Only consider the matter. They must needs
acknowledge that there are pious Christians among us
that have the true faith, spirit, understanding, word, and
mind of Christ: why then should we reject their word and
understanding, and follow a pope who has neither
understanding nor spirit? Surely this were to deny our
whole faith and the Christian Church. . . . **50**

Therefore when need requires, and the Pope is a cause
of offence to Christendom, in these cases whoever can best
do so, as a faithful member of the whole body, must do
what he can to procure a true free council. This no one can
do so well as the temporal authorities, especially since

they are fellow-Christians, fellow-priests, sharing one
spirit and one power in all things, . . . Would it not be most
unnatural, if a fire were to break out in a city, and every
one were to keep still and let it burn on and on, whatever
might be burnt, simply because they had not the mayor's **60**
authority, or because the fire perchance broke out at the
mayor's house? Is not every citizen bound in this case to
rouse and call in the rest? How much more should this be
done in the spiritual city of Christ, if a fire of offence breaks
out, either at the Pope's government or wherever it may!
The like happens if an enemy attacks a town. The first to
rouse up the rest earns glory and thanks. Why then should
not he earn glory that decries the coming of our enemies
from hell and rouses and summons all Christians?

But as for their boasts of their authority, that no one **70**
must oppose it, this is idle talk. No one in Christendom
has any authority to do harm, or to forbid others to
prevent harm being done. There is no authority in the
Church but for reformation. Therefore if the Pope wished
to use his power to prevent the calling of a free council,
so as to prevent the reformation of the Church, we must
not respect him or his power; and if he should begin to
excommunicate and fulminate, we must despise this as
the doings of a madman, and, trusting in God,
excommunicate and repel him as best we may. **80**

Q Which of Luther's assertions would the
Church of Rome have found heretical?
Why?

Q Which aspects of this selection might
be called anti-authoritarian? Which
might be called democratic?

The Spread of Protestantism

Luther's criticism constituted an open revolt against the
institution that for centuries had governed the lives of
Western Christians. With the aid of the printing press,
his "protestant" sermons and letters circulated throughout
Europe. Luther's defense of Christian conscience as
opposed to episcopal authority worked to justify protest
against all forms of dominion. In 1524, under the banner
of Christian liberty, German commoners instigated a series
of violent uprisings against the oppressive landholding
aristocracy. The result was full-scale war, the so-called
"Peasant Revolts," that resulted in the bloody defeat of
thousands of peasants. Although Luther condemned the
violence and brutality of the Peasant Revolts, social unrest
and ideological warfare had only just begun. His denunciation of the lower-class rebels brought many of the
German princes to his side; and some used their new religious allegiance as an excuse to seize and usurp Church
properties and revenues within their own domains. As the
floodgates of dissent opened wide, civil wars broke out
between German princes who were faithful to Rome and
those who called themselves Lutheran. The wars lasted for
some twenty-five years, until, under the terms of the Peace
of Augsburg in 1555, it was agreed that each German

prince should have the right to choose the religion to be practiced within his own domain. But religious wars resumed in the late sixteenth century and devastated German lands for almost a century.

All of Europe was affected by Luther's break with the Church. The Lutheran insistence that enlightened Christians could arrive at truth by way of Scripture led reformers everywhere to interpret the Bible for themselves. The result was the birth of many new Protestant sects, each based on its own interpretation of Scripture. In the independent city of Geneva, Switzerland, the French theologian John Calvin (1509–1564) set up a government in which elected officials, using the Bible as the supreme law, ruled the community. Calvin held that Christians were predestined from birth for either salvation or damnation, a circumstance that made good works irrelevant. The "Doctrine of Predestination" encouraged Calvinists to glorify God by living an upright life, one that required abstention from dancing, gambling, swearing, drunkenness, and from all forms of public display. For, although one's status was known only by God, Christians might manifest that they were among the "elect" by a show of moral rectitude. Finally, since Calvin taught that wealth was a sign of God's favor, Calvinists extolled the "work ethic" as consistent with the divine will.

In nearby Zürich, a radical wing of Protestantism emerged: the Anabaptists (given this name by those who opposed their practice of "rebaptizing" adult Christians) rejected all seven of the sacraments (including infant baptism) as sources of God's grace. Placing total emphasis on Christian conscience and the voluntary acceptance of Christ, the Anabaptists called for the abolition of the Mass and the complete separation of Church and state: holding individual responsibility and personal liberty as fundamental ideals, they were among the first Westerners to offer religious sanction for political disobedience. Many Anabaptist reformers met death at the hands of local governments—the men were burned at the stake and the women were usually drowned. English offshoots of the Anabaptists—the Baptists and the Quakers—would come to follow Anabaptist precepts, including the rejection of religious ritual (and imagery) and a fundamentalist approach to Scripture.

In England, the Tudor monarch Henry VIII (1491–1547) broke with the Roman Catholic Church and established a church under his own leadership. Political expediency colored the king's motives: Henry was determined to leave England with a male heir, but when eighteen years of marriage to Catherine of Aragon produced only one heir (a daughter), he attempted to annul the marriage and take a new wife. The pope refused, prompting the king—formerly a staunch supporter of the Catholic Church—to break with Rome. In 1526, Henry VIII declared himself head of the Church in England. His actions led to years of dispute and hostility between Roman Catholics and Anglicans (members of the new English Church). By the mid-sixteenth century, the consequences of Luther's protests were evident: the religious unity of Western Christendom was shattered

forever. Social and political upheaval had become the order of the day.

Music and the Reformation

Since the Reformation clearly dominated the religious and social history of the sixteenth century, it also touched, directly or indirectly, all forms of artistic endeavor, including music. Luther himself was a student of music, an active performer, and an admirer of Josquin des Prez (see chapter 17). Emphasizing music as a source of religious instruction, he encouraged the writing of hymnals and reorganized the German Mass to include both congregational and professional singing. Luther held that all religious texts should be sung in German, so that the faithful might understand their message. The text, according to Luther, should be both comprehensible and appealing.

Luther's favorite music was the **chorale**, a congregational hymn that served to enhance the spirit of Protestant worship. Chorales, written in German, drew on Latin hymns and German folk tunes. They were characterized by monophonic clarity and simplicity, features that encouraged performance by untrained congregations. The most famous Lutheran chorale (the melody of which may not have originated with Luther) is "Ein' feste Burg ist unser Gott" ("A Mighty Fortress Is Our God")—a hymn that has been called "the anthem of the Reformation." Luther's chorales had a major influence on religious music for centuries. And although in the hands of later composers the chorale became a complex polyphonic vehicle for voices and instruments, at its inception it was performed with all voices singing the same words at the same time. It was thus an ideal medium for the communal expression of Protestant piety.

Other Protestant sects, such as the Anabaptists and the Calvinists, regarded music as a potentially dangerous distraction to the faithful. In many sixteenth-century churches, the organ was dismantled and sung portions of the service edited or deleted. Calvin, however, who encouraged devotional recitation of psalms in the home, revised church services to include the congregational singing of psalms in the vernacular.

Northern Renaissance Art

The austerity of the Protestant reform cast its long shadow upon Church art. Protestants abandoned the traditional images of medieval piety, rejecting relics and sacred images as sources of superstition and idolatry. In Northern Europe, Protestant **iconoclasts** stripped the stained glass from Catholic churches, shattered statues, whitewashed church frescoes, and destroyed altarpieces. At the same time, however, Protestant reformers encouraged the proliferation of private devotional imagery—biblical subjects in particular.

♩ This Lutheran chorale inspired Johann Sebastian Bach's Cantata No. 80, an excerpt from which may be heard on CD Two, as Music Listening Selection Number 4.

Secular subject matter provided abundant inspiration for Northern artists. Portraiture, a favorite genre of the pre-Reformation master Jan van Eyck (see Figures 17.12, 17.13), remained popular among such sixteenth-century artists as Albrecht Dürer of Nuremberg (1471–1528), Lucas Cranach the Elder (1472–1553), and Hans Holbein the Younger (1497–1543), three of the greatest draftsmen of the Renaissance (see Figures 19.2, 19.3, 19.15). The natural world also intrigued artists: Dürer introduced landscape painting into Western art. His panoramic landscapes, often rendered in watercolors, were to be enjoyed for themselves (Figure **19.4**), rather than as settings for sacred or secular subjects (compare Figures 17.14, 17.28, 17.42). To these landscapes, as well as to his detailed studies of animals, birds, and plants, Dürer brought the eye of a scientific naturalist. Finally, the Flemish painter Pieter Brueghel the Elder (1525–1569) carried the tradition of the cosmic landscape to its peak in large panel paintings that describe the everyday labors of European peasants.

Dürer and Printmaking

Paralleling the invention of movable type, there developed in fifteenth-century Northern Europe a technology for reproducing images more cheaply and in greater numbers than ever before. The two new printmaking processes were **woodcut**, the technique of cutting away all parts of a design on a wood surface except those that will be inked and transferred to paper (Figure **19.5**), and **engraving** (Figure **19.6**), the process by which lines are incised on a

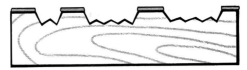

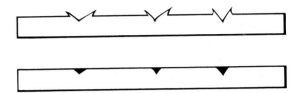

Figure 19.5 Woodcut. A relief printing process created by lines cut into the plank surface of wood. The raised portions of the block are inked and transferred by pressure to the paper by hand or with a printing press.

Figure 19.6 Engraving. An intaglio method of printing. The cutting tool, a *burin* or *graver*, is used to cut lines in the surface of metal plates. (a) A cross-section of an engraved plate showing burrs (ridges) produced by scratching a burin into the surface of a metal plate; (b) the burrs are removed and ink is wiped over the surface and forced into the scratches. The plate is then wiped clean, leaving ink deposits in the scratches; the ink is forced from the plate onto paper under pressure in a special press.

metal (usually copper) plate that is inked and run through a printing press. These relatively inexpensive techniques of mass-producing images made possible the proliferation of book illustrations and individual prints for private devotional use. Books with printed illustrations became cheap alternatives to the hand-illuminated manuscripts that were prohibitively expensive to all but wealthy patrons.

Figure 19.4 ALBRECHT DÜRER, *Wire Drawing Mill*, undated. Watercolor, 11¼ × 16¾in. State Museums, Berlin. Photo: B. P. K.

Figure 19.7 ALBRECHT DÜRER, *The Four Horsemen of the Apocalypse*, ca. 1496. Woodcut, 15½ × 11 in. Museum of Fine Arts, Boston.

The unassailed leader in Northern Renaissance print-making and one of the finest graphic artists of all time was Albrecht Dürer. Dürer earned international fame for his woodcuts and metal engravings. His mastery of the laws of linear perspective and human anatomy and his investigations into classical principles of proportions (enhanced by two trips to Italy) equaled those of the best Italian Renaissance artist–scientists. In the genre of portraiture, Dürer was the match of Raphael but, unlike Raphael, he recorded the features of his sitters with little idealization. His portrait engraving of Erasmus (see Figure 19.2) captures the concentrated intelligence of the Prince of Humanists. Dürer included a Latin inscription confirming that the portrait was executed from life, but added modestly in Greek, "The better image is [found] in his writings."

Dürer brought to the art of his day a profoundly religious view of the world and a desire to embody the spiritual message of Scripture in art. The series of woodcuts he produced to illustrate the last book of the New Testament, The Revelation According to Saint John (also called the "Apocalypse"), reveals the extent to which Dürer achieved his purpose. Executed two decades before Luther's revolt, The Four Horsemen of the Apocalypse—one of fifteen woodcuts in the series—brings to life the terrifying prophecies described in Revelation 6.1–8 (Figure 19.7). Amidst billowing clouds, Death (in the foreground),

Figure 19.8 ALBRECHT DÜRER, *Knight, Death, and the Devil*, 1513. Engraving, 9⅜ × 7½ in. The Metropolitan Museum of Art, New York. Harris Brisbane Dick Fund, 1943.

Famine (carrying a pair of scales), War (brandishing a sword), and Pestilence (drawing his bow) sweep down upon humankind; their victims fall beneath the horses' hooves, or, as with the bishop in the lower left, are devoured by infernal monsters. Dürer's image seems a grim prophecy of the coming age, in which 5 million people would die in religious wars.

Dürer was a humanist in his own right and a great admirer of both the moderate Erasmus and the zealous Luther. In one of his most memorable engravings, *Knight, Death, and the Devil*, he depicted the Christian soul in the allegorical guise of a medieval knight (Figure 19.8), a figure made famous in a treatise by Erasmus entitled *Handbook for the Militant Christian* (1504). The knight, the medieval symbol of fortitude and courage, advances against a dark and brooding landscape. Accompanied by his loyal dog, he marches forward, ignoring his fearsome companions: Death, who rides a pale horse and carries an hourglass, and the devil, a shaggy, cross-eyed, and horned demon. Here is the visual counterpart for Erasmus' message that the Christian must hold to the path of virtue, and in spite of "all of those spooks and phantoms" that come upon him, he must "look not behind." The knight's dignified bearing (probably inspired by heroic equestrian statues Dürer had seen in Italy) contrasts sharply with the bestial and cankerous features of his forbidding escorts. Dürer's engraving is remarkable for its wealth of microscopic detail. In the tradition of Jan van Eyck, but with a precision facilitated by the medium of metal engraving, Dürer records with scientific precision every leaf and pebble, hair and wrinkle; and yet the final effect is not a mere piling up of minutiae but, like nature itself, an astonishing amalgam of organically related substances.

The Paintings of Grünewald, Bosch, and Brueghel

Whether Catholic or Protestant, sixteenth-century Northern artists brought to religious subject matter spiritual intensity and emotional subjectivity that were unique. With the exception of Dürer, whose monumental paintings betray his admiration for classically proportioned figures and the Italianate unity of design, Northern Renaissance artists shared few of the aesthetic ideals of the Italian Renaissance masters. In the paintings of the German artist Matthias Gothardt Neithardt, better known as "Grünewald" (1460–1528), the gentle harmonies and idealized figures of Italian art are rejected in favor of brutal distortion and naturalistic detail. Grünewald's landmark work, the Isenheim Altarpiece, was designed to provide solace to the victims of disease and especially plague at the Hospital of Saint Anthony in Isenheim, near Colmar, France (Figure 19.9). Like the *Imitatio Christi*, which taught Christians to seek identification with Jesus, this multipaneled altarpiece reminded its beholders of their kinship with the suffering Jesus, depicted in the central panel. Following the tradition of the devotional German *Pietà* (see Figure 15.9), Grünewald made use of expressive exaggeration and painfully precise detail: the agonized body of Jesus is lengthened to emphasize its weight as it hangs from the bowed cross, the flesh putrefies

Figure 19.9 MATTHIAS GRÜNEWALD, Isenheim Altarpiece, ca. 1510–1515. Oil on panel, central panel 8 ft. × 10 ft. 1 in. Musée d'Unterlinden, Colmar, France. Photo: O. Zimmerman.

with clotted blood and angry thorns, the fingers convulse and curl, while the feet—broken and bruised—contort in a spasm of pain. Grünewald reinforces the mood of lamentation by placing the scene in a darkened landscape. He exaggerates the gestures of the attending figures, including that of John the Baptist, whose oversized finger points to the prophetic Latin inscription that explains his mystical presence: "He must increase and I must decrease" (John 3:30). A comparison of this painting with, for instance, Masaccio's *Trinity* (see Figure 17.17) provides a study in contrasts between German and Italian sensibilities in the age of the Renaissance.

More difficult to interpret are the works of the extraordinary Flemish artist Hieronymus Bosch (1460–1516). Like Grünewald, Bosch was preoccupied with matters of sin and salvation. Bosch's *Death and the Miser* (Figure **19.10**), for instance, belongs to the tradition of the *memento mori* (discussed in chapter 12), which works to warn the beholder of the inevitability of death. The painting also shows the influence of popular fifteenth-century handbooks on the art of dying (the *ars moriendi*), designed to remind Christians that they must choose between sinful pleasures and the way of Christ. As Death looms on his threshold, the miser, unable to resist worldly temptations even in his last minutes of life, reaches for the bag of

gold offered to him by a demon. In the foreground, Bosch depicts the miser storing gold in his money chest while clutching his rosary. Symbols of worldly power—a helmet, sword, and shield—allude to earthly follies. The depiction of such still-life objects to symbolize earthly vanity, transience, or decay would become a genre in itself among seventeenth-century Flemish artists.

Bosch's most famous work, *The Garden of Earthly Delights*—executed around 1510, the very time that Raphael was painting *The School of Athens*—underscores the enormous contrast between Renaissance art in Italy and in Northern Europe. Whereas Raphael celebrates the nobility and dignity of the human being, Bosch contemplates the inconstancy and degeneracy of humankind. In Bosch's **triptych** (a three-paneled painting), the Creation of Eve (left) and the Tortures of Hell (right) flank a central panel of extraordinary complexity (Figure **19.11**). Here, in an imaginary landscape, youthful nudes cavort in erotic and playful pastimes. They dally affectionately with each other amidst bizarre, oversized flora, fantastic birds and animals, egg-shaped vessels, and transparent tubes. This veritable "Garden of Earthly Delights" may be an exposition on the lustful behavior of the descendants of Adam and Eve, but its distance from conventional religious iconography (it was commissioned not by the

Church but by a private patron) has made it the subject of endless scholarly interpretation. The Roman Catholic Bosch derived his imagery from many sources, including the marginal grotesques of illuminated manuscripts, popular prints, Netherlandish proverbs, and the imagery of pilgrimage badges. He also drew on astrology and alchemy, both pseudosciences of some repute in his time. Astrology, the study of the influence of heavenly bodies on human affairs, and alchemy, the art of distillation (employed by apothecaries as well as by quacks who sought to transmute base metals into gold), attracted new attention when Islamic writings on both were introduced into late medieval Europe. Both, moreover, became subjects of serious study during the sixteenth century. Symbolic of the Renaissance quest to understand the operations of the material world, astrology (the ancestor of astronomy) and alchemy (precursor to chemistry) figured frequently in the works of sixteenth-century artists and writers.

In *The Garden of Earthly Delights*, alchemical devices reflect Bosch's familiarity with both the equipment and the distillation process that were used in experimental transmutation. Bosch seems to have embraced alchemy—and especially the cyclical theory of creation and destruction central to that pseudoscience—as a metaphor for the Christian myth of the Creation and Fall. The creatures of this garden participate in the mysteries of procreation, indulging their physical impulses with little regard for the inevitable consequences of their actions: the devastating punishments of Hell depicted in the right panel.

The fantastic demons in Bosch's Hell are products of an age that found the supernatural in natural and ordinary guises. Indeed, the witch-hunts that infested Europe (and especially Germany) during the sixteenth century were fueled by the popular belief that the devil was actively involved in human affairs. Belief in witches dates back to humankind's earliest societies; however, the practice of persecuting witches did not begin until the late fourteenth century. The first massive persecutions occurred at the end of the fifteenth century and reached their peak approximately one hundred years later. In 1484, two theologians published the *Malleus Maleficarum* (*Witches' Hammer*), an encyclopedia that described the nature of witches, their collusion with the devil, and the ways by which they were to be recognized and punished. Since women were traditionally regarded as inherently susceptible to the devil's temptations, they became the primary victims of this mass hysteria. Women—especially single, old, and eccentric women—constituted four-fifths of the witches executed between the fifteenth and early seventeenth centuries. A study published in 2004 suggests that witches were scapegoats blamed for the sharp drops in temperature that devastated sixteenth-century crops and left many Europeans starving.

The German artist Hans Baldung, called "Grien" (ca. 1484–1545), was one of a number of Northern

Figure 19.10 HIERONYMUS BOSCH, *Death and the Miser*, ca. 1485–1490. Oil on oak, 3 ft. ⅝in. × 12⅛ in. © 2000 Board of Trustees, National Gallery of Art, Washington, D.C. Samuel H. Kress Collection.

Figure 19.11 HIERONYMUS BOSCH, *The Creation of Eve: The Garden of Earthly Delights: Hell* (triptych), ca. 1510–1515. Oil on wood, 7 ft. 2⅝ in. × 6 ft. 4¾ in. (center panel), 7 ft. 2⅝ in. × 3 ft. 2¼ in. (each side panel). © Museo del Prado, Madrid.

Figure 19.12 HANS BALDUNG ("Grien"), *Witches*, 1510. *Chiaroscuro* woodcut, 15⅞ × 10¼ in. Louvre, Paris. Collection Rothschild. Photo: © R.M.N., Paris.

Renaissance artists who portrayed the activities of witches in painting and prints (Figure **19.12**). The witchcraft craze of this period dramatizes the prevailing gap between Christian humanism and rationalism on the one hand and barbarism and superstition on the other. Whether viewed as an instrument of post-Reformation political oppression, as an intensification of antifemale sentiment, or as an expression of the darker side of religious fanaticism, the witch-hunts of the early modern era force us to question the very notion of human progress.

The realities of violence, prejudice, and immorality did not go uncriticized among sixteenth-century Northern European artists. Bosch's contemporary, Pieter Brueghel the Elder, produced numerous paintings and prints that were cloaked condemnations of human folly, immorality, and war. Brueghel's *Triumph of Death* (Figure **19.13**), for instance, may be read as an indictment of the brutal wars that plagued sixteenth-century Europe: in a panoramic landscape that resembles the setting for a Last Judgment or a Bosch hell scene, Brueghel depicts armies of skeletons relentlessly slaughtering the living at work and at play. Some are crushed beneath the wheels of a death cart,

Figure 19.13 PIETER BRUEGHEL THE ELDER, *Triumph of Death*, ca. 1562–1564. Oil on panel, 3 ft. 10 in. × 5 ft. 3¾ in. © Museo del Prado, Madrid.

Figure 19.14 PIETER BRUEGHEL THE ELDER, *The Wedding Dance*, 1566. Oil on panel, 3 ft. 11 in. × 5 ft 2 in. Photo: © 2000 The Detroit Institute of Arts. City of Detroit Purchase. 30.374.

while others are subjected to torture and execution. Not divine judgment but human destiny rules here. Indeed, in Brueghel's hands, the late medieval Dance of Death (see chapter 15) has become a universal holocaust.

The last of the great sixteenth-century Flemish painters, Brueghel had traveled widely in Renaissance Italy; however, his paintings reflect only a passing interest in classical themes. His preoccupation with the details of rustic life, which earned him the title "Peasant Brueghel," continued the tradition of such medieval illuminators as the Limbourg brothers (see Figure 15.12). However, Brueghel's **genre paintings** (representations of the everyday life of ordinary folk) were not small-scale illustrations, but monumental (and sometimes allegorical) transcriptions of rural activities. *The Wedding Dance* (Figure **19.14**) depicts peasant revelry in a country setting whose earthiness is reinforced by rich tones of russet, tan, and muddy green. At the very top of the panel the bride and groom sit before an improvised dais, while the villagers cavort to the music of the bagpipe (right foreground). Although Brueghel's figures are clumsy and often ill proportioned, they share an ennobling vitality. In Brueghel's art, as in that of many other Northern Renaissance painters, we discover an unvarnished perception of human beings in mundane and unheroic circumstances—a sharp contrast to the idealized image of humankind found in the art of Renaissance Italy.

Sixteenth-Century Literature

Erasmus: *The Praise of Folly*

European literature of the sixteenth century was marked by heightened individualism and a progressive inclination to clear away the last remnants of medieval orthodoxy. It was, in many ways, a literature of protest and reform, and one whose dominant themes reflect the tension between medieval and modern ideas. European writers were especially concerned with the discrepancies between the noble ideals of classical humanism and the ignoble realities of human behavior. Religious rivalries and the horrors of war, witch-hunts, and religious persecution all seemed to contradict the optimistic view that the Renaissance

Science and Technology

1540	the Swiss physician Paracelsus (Philippus van Hohenheim) pioneers the use of chemistry for medical purposes
1543	Copernicus (Polish) publishes *On the Revolution of the Heavenly Spheres*, announcing his heliocentric theory
1553	Michael Servetus (Spanish) describes the pulmonary circulation of the blood

had inaugurated a more enlightened phase of human self-consciousness. Satire, a literary genre that conveys the contradictions between real and ideal situations, was especially popular during the sixteenth century. By means of satiric irony, Northern Renaissance writers held up prevailing abuses to ridicule, thus implying the need for reform.

The learned treatises and letters of Erasmus won him the respect of scholars throughout Europe; but his single most popular work was *The Praise of Folly*, a satiric oration attacking a wide variety of human foibles, including greed, intellectual pomposity, and pride. *The Praise of Folly* went through more than two dozen editions in Erasmus' lifetime, and influenced other humanists, including his lifelong friend and colleague Thomas More, to whom it was dedicated (in Latin, *moria* means "folly"). A short excerpt from *The Praise of Folly* offers some idea of Erasmus' keen wit as applied to a typical Northern Renaissance theme: the vast gulf between human fallibility and human perfectibility. The excerpt opens with the image of the world as a stage, a favorite metaphor of sixteenth-century painters and poets—not the least of whom was William Shakespeare. Dame Folly, the allegorical figure who is the speaker in the piece, compares life to a comedy in which the players assume various roles: in the course of the drama (she observes), one may come to play the parts of both servant and king. The lecturer then describes each of a number of roles (or disciplines), such as medicine, law, and so on, in terms of its affinity with folly. Erasmus' most searing words were reserved for theologians and church dignitaries, but his insights expose more generally (and timelessly) the frailties of all human beings.

READING 3.22 From Erasmus' *The Praise of Folly* (1511)

Now what else is the whole life of mortals but a sort of   1
comedy, in which the various actors, disguised by various
costumes and masks, walk on and play each one his
part, until the manager waves them off the stage?
Moreover, this manager frequently bids the same actor
go back in a different costume, so that he who has but
lately played the king in scarlet now acts the flunkey in
patched clothes. Thus all things are presented by
shadows; yet this play is put on in no other way. . . .

[The disciplines] that approach nearest to common   10
sense, that is, to folly, are held in highest esteem.
Theologians are starved, naturalists find cold comfort,
astrologers are mocked, and logicians are slighted. . . .
Within the profession of medicine, furthermore, so far as
any member is eminently unlearned, impudent, or
careless, he is valued the more, even in the chambers of
belted earls. For medicine, especially as now practiced
by many, is but a subdivision of the art of flattery, no
less truly than is rhetoric. Lawyers have the next place
after doctors, and I do not know but that they should   20
have first place; with great unanimity the philosophers—
not that I would say such a thing myself—are wont to

ridicule the law as an ass. Yet great matters and little
matters alike are settled by the arbitrament of these
asses. They gather goodly freeholds with broad acres,
while the theologian, after poring over chestfuls of the
great corpus of divinity, gnaws on bitter beans, at the
same time manfully waging war against lice and fleas. As
those arts are more successful which have the greatest
affinity with folly, so those people are by far the happiest   30
who enjoy the privilege of avoiding all contact with the
learned disciplines, and who follow nature as their only
guide, since she is in no respect wanting, except as a
mortal wishes to transgress the limits set for his status.
Nature hates counterfeits; and that which is innocent of
art gets along far the more prosperously.

What need we say about practitioners in the arts? Self-
love is the hallmark of them all. You will find that they
would sooner give up their paternal acres than any piece
of their poor talents. Take particularly actors, singers,   40
orators, and poets; the more unskilled one of them is,
the more insolent he will be in his self-satisfaction, the
more he will blow himself up. . . . Thus the worst art
pleases the most people, for the simple reason that the
larger part of mankind, as I said before, is subject to
folly. If, therefore, the less skilled man is more pleasing
both in his own eyes and in the wondering gaze of the
many, what reason is there that he should prefer sound
discipline and true skill? In the first place, these will
cost him a great outlay; in the second place, they will   50
make him more affected and meticulous; and finally,
they will please far fewer of his audience. . . .

And now I see that it is not only in individual men that
nature has implanted self-love. She implants a kind of it as
a common possession in the various races, and even
cities. By this token the English claim, besides a few other
things, good looks, music, and the best eating as their
special properties. The Scots flatter themselves on the
score of high birth and royal blood, not to mention their
dialectical skill. Frenchmen have taken all politeness for   60
their province; though the Parisians, brushing all others
aside, also award themselves the prize for knowledge of
theology. The Italians usurp *belles lettres* and eloquence;
and they all flatter themselves upon the fact that they
alone, of all mortal men, are not barbarians. In this
particular point of happiness the Romans stand highest,
still dreaming pleasantly of ancient Rome. The Venetians
are blessed with a belief in their own nobility. The Greeks,
as well as being the founders of the learned disciplines,
vaunt themselves upon their titles to the famous heroes of   70
old. The Turks, and that whole rabble of the truly
barbarous, claim praise for their religion, laughing at
Christians as superstitious. . . .

[Next come] the scientists, reverenced for their beards
and the fur on their gowns, who teach that they alone are
wise while the rest of mortal men flit about as shadows.
How pleasantly they dote, indeed, while they construct
their numberless worlds, and measure the sun, moon,
stars, and spheres as with thumb and line. They assign
causes for lightning, winds, eclipses, and other   80

inexplicable things, never hesitating a whit, as if they were privy to the secrets of nature, artificer of things, or as if they visited us fresh from the council of the gods. Yet all the while nature is laughing grandly at them and their conjectures. For to prove that they have good intelligence of nothing, this is a sufficient argument: they can never explain why they disagree with each other on every subject. Thus knowing nothing in general, they profess to know all things in particular; though they are ignorant even of themselves, and on occasion do not see the ditch or the stone lying across their path, because many of them are blear-eyed or absent-minded; yet they proclaim that they perceive ideas, universals, forms without matter. . . .

Perhaps it were better to pass over the theologians in silence, [for] they may attack me with six hundred arguments, in squadrons, and drive me to make a recantation; which if I refuse, they will straightway proclaim me an heretic. By this thunderbolt they are wont to terrify any toward whom they are ill-disposed.

They are happy in their self-love, and as if they already inhabited the third heaven they look down from a height on all other mortal men as on creatures that crawl on the ground, and they come near to pitying them. They are protected by a wall of scholastic definitions, arguments, corollaries, implicit and explicit propositions; . . . they explain as pleases them the most arcane matters, such as by what method the world was founded and set in order, through what conduits original sin has been passed down along the generations, by what means, in what measure, and how long the perfect Christ was in the Virgin's womb, and how accidents subsist in the Eucharist without their subject.

But those are hackneyed. Here are questions worthy of the great and (as some call them) illuminated theologians, questions to make them prick up their ears—if ever they chance upon them. Whether divine generation took place at a particular time? Whether there are several sonships in Christ? Whether this is a possible proposition: God the Father hates the Son? Whether God could have taken upon Himself the likeness of a woman? Or of a devil? Of an ass? Of a gourd? Of a piece of flint? Then how would that gourd have preached, performed miracles, or been crucified?. . . .

Coming nearest to these in felicity are the men who generally call themselves "the religious" and "monks"— utterly false names both, since most of them keep as far away as they can from religion and no people are more in evidence in every sort of place. . . . For one thing, they reckon it the highest degree of piety to have no contact with literature, and hence they see to it that they do not know how to read. For another, when with asinine voices they bray out in church those psalms they have learned, by rote rather than by heart, they are convinced that they are anointing God's ears with the blandest of oil. Some of them make a good profit from their dirtiness and mendicancy, collecting their food from door to door with importunate bellowing; nay, there is not an inn, public

90

100

110

120

130

conveyance, or ship where they do not intrude, to the great disadvantage of the other common beggars. Yet according to their account, by their very dirtiness, ignorance, these delightful fellows are representing to us the lives of the apostles.

140

Q What disciplines does Dame Folly single out as having "the greatest affinity with folly"?

Q How does Erasmus attack the religious community of his day?

More's *Utopia*

In England Erasmus' friend, the scholar and statesman Sir Thomas More (1478–1535), served as chancellor to King Henry VIII at the time of Henry's break with the Catholic Church (Figure **19.15**). Like Erasmus, More was a Christian humanist and a man of conscience. He denounced the modern evils of acquisitive capitalism and religious fanaticism and championed religious tolerance and Christian charity. Unwilling to compromise his position as a Roman Catholic, he opposed the actions of the king and was executed for treason in 1535.

In 1516, More completed his classic political satire on European statecraft and society, a work entitled *Utopia* (the Greek word meaning both "no place" and "a good place"). More's *Utopia*, the first literary description of an

Figure 19.15 HANS HOLBEIN THE YOUNGER, *Sir Thomas More*, ca. 1530. Oil on panel, 29½ × 23¼ in. © The Frick Collection, New York. Holbein's superb portrait reveals a visionary and a man of conscience ("a man for all seasons"), who died at the hands of Henry VIII rather than compromise his religious convictions.

ideal state since Plato's *Republic*, was inspired, in part, by accounts of wondrous lands reported by sailors returning from the "New World" across the Atlantic (see chapter 18). More's fictional island ("discovered" by a fictional explorer–narrator) is a socialistic state in which goods and property are shared, war and personal vanities are held in contempt, learning is available to all citizens (except slaves), and freedom of religion is absolute. In this ideal commonwealth, natural reason, benevolence, and scorn for material wealth ensure social harmony. More's ideal society differs from Plato's in that More gives to each individual, rather than to society's guardians, full responsibility for the establishment of social justice. Like Alberti (and Calvin), More regarded work—limited in Utopia to six hours a day—as essential to moral and communal well-being. Fundamental to *Utopia* as satire is the implicit contrast More draws between his own corrupt Christian society and that of his ideal community; although More's Utopians are not Christians, they are guided by Christian principles of morality and charity. They have little use, for instance, for precious metals, jewels, and the "trifles" that drive men to war.

READING 3.23 From More's *Utopia* (1516)

[As] to their manner of living in society, the oldest man **1** of every family . . . is its governor. Wives serve their husbands, and children their parents, and always the younger serves the elder. Every city is divided into four equal parts, and in the middle of each there is a marketplace: what is brought thither, and manufactured by the several families, is carried from thence to houses appointed for that purpose, in which all things of a sort are laid by themselves; and there every father goes and takes whatsoever he or his family stand in need of, **10** without either paying for it or leaving anything in exchange. There is no reason for giving a denial to any person, since there is such plenty of everything among them; and there is no danger of a man's asking for more than he needs; they have no inducements to do this, since they are sure that they shall always be supplied. It is the fear of want that makes any of the whole race of animals either greedy or ravenous; but besides fear, there is in man a pride that makes him fancy it a particular glory to excel others in pomp and excess. But by the **20** laws of the Utopians, there is no room for this. . . .

[Since the Utopians] have no use for money among themselves, but keep it as a provision against events which seldom happen, and between which there are generally long intervening intervals, they value it no farther than it deserves, that is, in proportion to its use. So that it is plain they must prefer iron either to gold or silver; for men can no more live without iron than without fire or water, but nature has marked out no use for the other metals so essential and not easily to be **30** dispensed with. The folly of men has enhanced the value of gold and silver, because of their scarcity. Whereas, on the contrary, it is their opinion that nature, as an

indulgent parent, has freely given us all the best things in great abundance, such as water and earth, but has laid up and hid from us the things that are vain and useless. . . .

. . . They eat and drink out of vessels of earth, or glass, which make an agreeable appearance though formed of brittle materials: while they make their chamber-pots **40** and close-stools[1] of gold and silver, and that not only in their public halls, but in their private houses: of the same metals they likewise make chains and fetters for their slaves; to some [slaves], as a badge of infamy, they hang an ear-ring of gold, and [they] make others wear a chain or coronet of the same metal; and thus they take care, by all possible means, to render gold and silver of no esteem. And from hence it is that while other nations part with their gold and silver as unwillingly as if one tore out their bowels, those of Utopia would look on **50** their giving in all they possess of those [metals] but as the parting with a trifle, or as we would esteem the loss of a penny. They find pearls on their coast, and diamonds and carbuncles on their rocks; they do not look after them, but, if they find them by chance, they polish them, and with them they adorn their children, who are delighted with them, and glory in them during their childhood; but when they grow to years, and see that none but children use such baubles, they of their own accord, without being bid by their parents, lay **60** them aside; and would be as much ashamed to use them afterward as children among us, when they come to years, are of their puppets and other toys. . . .

They detest war as a very brutal thing; and which, to the reproach of human nature, is more practiced by men than by any sort of beasts. They, in opposition to the sentiments of almost all other nations, think that there is nothing more inglorious than that glory that is gained by war. And therefore though they accustom themselves daily to military exercises and the discipline of war—in which not **70** only their men but their women likewise are trained up, that in cases of necessity they may not be quite useless— yet they do not rashly engage in war, unless it be either to defend themselves, or their friends, from any unjust aggressors; or out of good-nature or in compassion assist an oppressed nation in shaking off the yoke of tyranny. They indeed help their friends, not only in defensive, but also in offensive wars; but they never do that unless they had been consulted before the breach was made, and being satisfied with the grounds on which **80** they went, they had found that all demands of reparation were rejected, so that a war was unavoidable. . . .

If they agree to a truce, they observe it so religiously that no provocations will make them break it. They never lay their enemies' country waste nor burn their corn, and even in their marches they take all possible care that neither horse nor foot may tread it down, for they do not know but that they may have for it themselves. They hurt no man whom they find disarmed, unless he is a spy. When a town

---

[1] A covered chamber pot set in a stool.

is surrendered to them, they take it into their protection; and when they carry a place by storm, they never plunder it, but put those only to the sword that opposed the rendering of it up, and make the rest of the garrison slaves, but for the other inhabitants, they do them no hurt; and if any of them had advised a surrender, they give them good rewards out of the estates of those that they condemn, and distribute the rest among their auxiliary troops, but they themselves take no share of the spoil.

Q What sort of social organization does More set forth in his Utopia?

Q How would you describe More's views on precious metals and on war?

The Wit of Cervantes

While Erasmus and More wrote primarily in Latin—*Utopia* was not translated into English until 1551—other European writers favored the vernacular. The satiric novel and the **essay**, two new literary genres, were written in the language of everyday speech that sent defiant messages of social criticism. In Spain, Miguel de Cervantes (1547–1616) wrote *Don Quijote*, a novel that satirizes the outworn values of the Middle Ages as personified in a legendary Spanish hero. *Don Quijote* was not the first novel in world literature—the Chinese and Japanese had been writing novels since the eleventh century (see chapter 14)—but it was among the earliest Western examples of prose fiction in which a series of episodes converged on a fundamental theme. A chivalrous knight in an age of statecraft, the fifty-year-old Alonso Quixado, who assumes the title of Don Quijote de la Mancha, sets out to defend the ideals glorified in medieval books of chivalry and romance. (Such ideals may have been valued by Cervantes himself, who had fought in the last Crusade against the Muslim Turks.) Seeking to right all wrongs, and misperceiving the ordinary for the sublime, the Don pursues a long series of misadventures, including an armed attack on windmills which he thinks are giants—the episode inspired the expression "to tilt at windmills." After his illusions of grandeur are exposed, the hero laments that the world is "nothing but schemes and plots." Cervantes' Spain was itself the scene of dramatic transformation: its culture had been powerfully influenced by large populations of Jews and Muslims, both of whom were expelled from Spain, the former in 1492, and the latter between 1609 and 1614.

READING 3.24 From Cervantes' *Don Quijote* (1613)

The great success won by our brave Don Quijote in his dreadful, unimaginable encounter with two windmills, plus other honorable events well worth remembering

Just then, they came upon thirty or forty windmills, which (as it happens) stand in the fields of Montiel, and as soon as Don Quijote saw them he said to his squire: 1

"Destiny guides our fortunes more favorably than we could have expected. Look there, Sancho Panza, my friend, and see those thirty or so wild giants, with whom I intend to do battle and to kill each and all of them, so with their stolen booty we can begin to enrich ourselves. This is noble, righteous warfare, for it is wonderfully useful to God to have such an evil race wiped from the face of the earth." 10

"What giants?" asked Sancho Panza.

"The ones you can see over there," answered his master, "with the huge arms, some of which are very nearly two leagues long."

"Now look, your grace," said Sancho, "what you see over there aren't giants, but windmills, and what seem to be arms are just their sails, that go around in the wind and turn the millstone."

"Obviously," replied Don Quijote, "you don't know much about adventures. Those are giants—and if you're frightened, take yourself away from here and say your prayers, while I go charging into savage and unequal combat with them." 20

Saying which, he spurred his horse, Rocinante, paying no attention to the shouts of Sancho Panza, his squire, warning him that without any question it was windmills and not giants he was going to attack. So utterly convinced was he they were giants, indeed, that he neither heard Sancho's cries nor noticed, close as he was, what they really were, but charged on, crying: 30

"Flee not, oh cowards and dastardly creatures, for he who attacks you is a knight alone and unaccompanied."

Just then the wind blew up a bit, and the great sails began to stir, which Don Quijote saw and cried out:

"Even should you shake more arms than the giant Briareus himself, you'll still have to deal with me."

As he said this, he entrusted himself with all his heart to his lady Dulcinea, imploring her to help and sustain him at such a critical moment, and then, with his shield held high and his spear braced in its socket, and Rocinante at a full gallop, he charged directly at the first windmill he came to, just as a sudden swift gust of wind sent its sail swinging hard around, smashing the spear to bits and sweeping up the knight and his horse, tumbling them all battered and bruised to the ground. Sancho Panza came rushing to his aid, as fast as his donkey could run, but when he got to his master found him unable to move, such a blow had he been given by the falling horse. 40 50

"God help me!" said Sancho. "Didn't I tell your grace to be careful what you did, that these were just windmills, and anyone who could ignore that had to have windmills in his head?"

"Silence, Sancho, my friend," answered Don Quijote. "Even more than other things, war is subject to perpetual change. What's more, I think the truth is that the same Frestón the magician, who stole away my room and my books, transformed these giants into windmills, in order to deprive me of the glory of vanquishing them, so bitter is his hatred of me. But in the end, his evil tricks will have little power against my good sword." 60

"God's will be done," answered Sancho Panza.

Then, helping his master to his feet, he got him back up on Rocinante, whose shoulder was half dislocated. After which, discussing the adventure they'd just experienced, they followed the road toward Lápice Pass, for there, said Don Quijote, they couldn't fail to find adventures of all kinds, it being a well-traveled highway. But having lost his lance, he went along very sorrowfully, as he admitted to his squire, saying: **70**

"I remember having read that a certain Spanish knight named Diego Pérez de Vargas, having lost his sword while fighting in a lost cause, pulled a thick bough, or a stem, off an oak tree, and did such things with it, that day, clubbing down so many Moors that ever afterwards they nicknamed him Machuca [Clubber], and indeed from that day on he and all his descendants bore the name Vargas y Machuca. I tell you this because, the first oak tree I come to, I plan to pull off a branch like that, **80** one every bit as good as the huge stick I can see in my mind, and I propose to perform such deeds with it that you'll be thinking yourself blessed, having the opportunity to witness them, and being a living witness to events that might otherwise be unbelievable."

"It's in God's hands," said Sancho. "I believe everything is exactly the way your grace says it is. But maybe you could sit a little straighter, because you seem to be leaning to one side, which must be because of the great fall you took." **90**

"True," answered Don Quijote, "and if I don't say anything about the pain it's because knights errant are never supposed to complain about a wound, even if their guts are leaking through it."

"If that's how it's supposed to be," replied Sancho, "I've got nothing to say. But Lord knows I'd rather your grace told me, any time something hurts you. Me, I've got to groan, even if it's the smallest little pain, unless that rule about knights errant not complaining includes squires, too." **100**

Don Quijote couldn't help laughing at his squire's simplicity, and cheerfully assured him he could certainly complain any time he felt like it, voluntarily or involuntarily, since in all his reading about knighthood and chivalry he'd never once come across anything to the contrary. Sancho said he thought it was dinner-time. His master replied that, for the moment, he himself had no need of food, but Sancho should eat whenever he wanted to. Granted this permission, Sancho made himself as comfortable as he could while jogging along on his **110** donkey and, taking out of his saddlebags what he had put in them, began eating as he rode, falling back a good bit behind his master, and from time to time tilting up his wineskin with a pleasure so intense that the fanciest barman in Málaga might have envied him. And as he rode along like this, gulping quietly away, none of the promises his master had made were on his mind, nor did he feel in the least troubled or afflicted—in fact, he was thoroughly relaxed about this adventure-hunting business, no matter how dangerous it was supposed **120** to be.

In the end, they spent that night sleeping in a wood, and Don Quijote pulled a dry branch from one of the trees, to serve him, more or less, as a lance, fitting onto it the spearhead he'd taken off the broken one. Nor did Don Quijote sleep, that whole night long, meditating on his lady Dulcinea—in order to fulfill what he'd read in his books, namely, that knights always spent long nights out in the woods and other uninhabited places, not sleeping, but happily mulling over memories of their **130** ladies. Which wasn't the case for Sancho Panza: with his stomach full, and not just with chicory water, his dreams swept him away, nor would he have bothered waking up, for all the sunlight shining full on his face, or the birds singing—brightly, loudly greeting the coming of the new day—if his master hadn't called to him. He got up and, patting his wineskin, found it a lot flatter than it had been the night before, which grieved his heart, since it didn't look as if they'd be making up the shortage any time soon. Don Quijote had no interest in breakfast, **140** since, as we have said, he had been sustaining himself with delightful memories. They returned to the road leading to Lápice Pass, which they could see by about three that afternoon.

"Here," said Don Quijote as soon as he saw it, "here, brother Sancho Panza, we can get our hands up to the elbows in adventures. But let me warn you: even if you see me experiencing the greatest dangers in the world, never draw your sword to defend me, unless of course you see that those who insult me are mere rabble, people **150** of low birth, in which case you may be permitted to help me. But if they're knights, the laws of knighthood make it absolutely illegal, without exception, for you to help me, unless you yourself have been ordained a knight."

"Don't worry, your grace," answered Sancho Panza. "You'll find me completely obedient about this, especially since I'm a very peaceful man—I don't like getting myself into quarrels and fights. On the other hand, when it comes to someone laying a hand on me, I won't pay much attention to those laws, because whether **160** they're divine or human they permit any man to defend himself when anyone hurts him."

"To be sure," answered Don Quijote. "But when it comes to helping me against other knights, you must restrain your natural vigor."

"And that's what I'll do," replied Sancho. "I'll observe this rule just as carefully as I keep the Sabbath."

Q What does the phrase "tilting at windmills" imply?

Q What rules of chivalry forbid Sancho's assisting his master in battle, and with what exception?

Rabelais and Montaigne

In the earthier spirit of the prose burlesque, the French humanist François Rabelais (1495–1553) mocked the obsolete values of European society. Rabelais drew upon his experiences as a monk, a student of law, a physician, and a specialist in human affairs to produce *Gargantua and Pantagruel*, an irreverent satire filled with biting allusions to contemporary institutions and customs. The world of the two imaginary giants, Gargantua and Pantagruel, is one of fraud and folly drawn to fantastic dimensions. It is blighted by the absurdities of war, the evils of law and medicine, and the failure of scholastic education. To remedy the last, Rabelais advocates education based on experience and action, rather than rote memorization. In the imaginary Abbey of Thélème, the modern version of a medieval monastery, he pictures a coeducational commune in which well-bred men and women are encouraged to live as they please. *Gargantua and Pantagruel* proclaims Rabelais' faith in the ability of educated individuals to follow their best instincts for establishing a society free from religious prejudice, petty abuse, and selfish desire.

The French humanist Michel de Montaigne (1533–1592) was neither a satirist nor a reformer, but an educated aristocrat who believed in the paramount importance of cultivating good judgment. Trained in Latin, Montaigne was one of the leading proponents of classical learning in Renaissance France. He earned universal acclaim as the "father" of the personal **essay**, a short piece of expository prose that examines a single subject or idea. The essay—the word comes from the French *essayer* ("to try")—is a vehicle for probing or "trying out" ideas. Indeed Montaigne regarded his ninety-four vernacular French essays as studies in autobiographical reflection—in them, he confessed, he portrayed himself. Addressing such subjects as virtue, friendship, old age, education, and idleness, he pursues certain fundamentally humanistic ideas: that contradiction is a characteristically human trait, that self-examination is the essence of true education, that education should enable us to live more harmoniously, and that skepticism and open-mindedness are sound alternatives to dogmatic opinion. Like Rabelais, Montaigne defends a kind of teaching that poses questions rather than providing answers. In his essay on the education of children, he criticizes teachers who pour information into students' ears "as though they were pouring water into a funnel" and then demand that students repeat the information instead of exercising original thought.

Reflecting on the European response to overseas expansion (see chapter 18), Montaigne examined the ways in which behavior and belief vary from culture to culture.

Science and Technology

1556	Georg Agricola (German) publishes *On the Principles of Mining*
1571	Ambroise Paré (French) publishes five treatises on surgery
1587	Conrad Gesner (Swiss) completes his *Historiae Animalum*, the first zoological encyclopedia
1596	Sir John Harington (English) invents the "water closet," providing indoor toilet facilities

In his essay *On Cannibals*, a portion of which appears below, he weighted the reports of "New World" barbarism and savagery against the morals and manners of "cultured" Europeans. War, which he calls the "human disease," he finds less vile among "savages" than among Europeans, whose warfare is motivated by colonial expansion. Balancing his own views with those of classical Latin writers, whom he quotes freely throughout his essays, Montaigne questions the superiority of any one culture over another. Montaigne's essays, an expression of reasoned inquiry into human values, constitute the literary high-water mark of the French Renaissance.

READING 3.25 From Montaigne's *On Cannibals* (1580)

I had with me for a long time a man who had lived for   1
ten or twelve years in that other world which has been
discovered in our century, in the place where Villegaignon
landed, and which he called Antarctic France.[1] This
discovery of a boundless country seems worthy of
consideration. I don't know if I can guarantee that some
other such discovery will not be made in the future, so
many personages greater than ourselves having been
mistaken about this one. I am afraid we have eyes bigger
than our stomachs, and more curiosity than capacity. We   10
embrace everything, but we clasp only wind. . . .

This man I had was a simple, crude fellow—a character
fit to bear true witness; for clever people observe more
things and more curiously, but they interpret them; and to
lend weight and conviction to their interpretation, they
cannot help altering history a little. They never show you
things as they are, but bend and disguise them according to
the way they have seen them; and to give credence to their
judgment and attract you to it, they are prone to add
something to their matter, to stretch it out and amplify it.   20
We need a man either very honest, or so simple that he
has not the stuff to build up false inventions and give them
plausibility; and wedded to no theory. Such was my man;
and besides this, he at various times brought sailors and
merchants, whom he had known on that trip, to see me.
So I content myself with his information, without inquiring
what the cosmographers say about it.

We ought to have topographers who would give us an
exact account of the places where they have been. But
because they have over us the advantage of having seen   30
Palestine, they want to enjoy the privilege of telling us
news about all the rest of the world. I would like everyone
to write what he knows, and as much as he knows, not
only in this, but in all other subjects; for a man may have
some special knowledge and experience of the nature of a
river or a fountain, who in other matters knows only what
everybody knows. However, to circulate this little scrap of

___

[1] *La France antartique* was the French term for South America. In 1555, Nicolaus Durard de Villegaignon founded a colony on an island in the Bay of Rio de Janeiro, Brazil. The colony collapsed some years later, and many of those who had lived there returned to France.

knowledge, he will undertake to write the whole of physics. From this vice spring many great abuses.

Now to return to my subject, I think there is nothing barbarous and savage in that nation, from what I have been told, except that each man calls barbarism whatever is not his own practice; for indeed it seems we have no other test of truth and reason than the example and pattern of the opinions and customs of the country we live in. *There* is always the perfect religion, perfect government, the perfect and accomplished manners in all things. Those people are wild, just as we call wild the fruits that Nature has produced by herself and in her normal course; whereas really it is those that we have changed artificially and led astray from the common order, that we should rather call wild. The former retain alive and vigorous their genuine, their most useful and natural, virtues and properties, which we have debased in the latter in adapting them to gratify our corrupted taste. And yet for all that, the savor and delicacy of some uncultivated fruits of those countries is quite as excellent, even to our taste, as that of our own. It is not reasonable that art should win the place of honor over our great and powerful mother Nature. We have so overloaded the beauty and richness of her works by our inventions that we have quite smothered her. Yet wherever her purity shines forth, she wonderfully puts to shame our vain and frivolous attempts

> Ivy comes readier without our care;
> In lonely caves the arbutus grows more fair;
> No art with artless bird song can compare.
> Propertius

All our efforts cannot even succeed in reproducing the nest of the tiniest little bird, its contexture, its beauty and convenience; or even the web of the puny spider. All things, say Plato, are produced by nature, by fortune, or by art; the greatest and most beautiful by one or the other of the first two, the least and most imperfect by the last.

These nations, then, seem to me barbarous in this sense, that they have been fashioned very little by the human mind, and are still very close to their original naturalness. The laws of nature still rule them, very little corrupted by ours, and they are in such a state of purity that I am sometimes vexed that they were unknown earlier, in the days when there were men able to judge them better than we. I am sorry that Lycurgus[2] and Plato did not know of them; for it seems to me that what we actually see in these nations surpasses not only all the pictures in which poets have idealized the golden age and all their inventions in imagining a happy state of man, but also the conceptions and the very desire of philosophy. They could not imagine a naturalness so pure and simple as we see by experience; nor could they believe that our society could be maintained with so little artifice and human solder. This is a nation, I should say to Plato, in which there is no sort of traffic, no knowledge of letters, no science of numbers, no name for a magistrate or for political superiority, no custom of servitude, no riches or poverty, no contracts, no

successions, no partitions, no occupations but leisure ones, no care for any but common kinship, no clothes, no agriculture, no metal, no use of wine or wheat. The very words that signify lying, treachery, dissimulation, avarice, envy, belittling, pardon—unheard of. How far from this perfection would he find the republic that he imagined:

> *Men fresh sprung from the gods*
> Seneca

. . . .

They have their wars with the nations beyond the mountains, further inland, to which they go quite naked, with no other arms than bows or wooden swords ending in a sharp point, in the manner of the tongues of our boar spears. It is astonishing what firmness they show in their combats, which never end but in slaughter and bloodshed; for as to routs and terror, they know nothing of either.

Each man brings back as his trophy the head of the enemy he has killed, and sets it up at the entrance to his dwelling. After they have treated their prisoners well for a long time with all the hospitality they can think of, each man who has a prisoner calls a great assembly of his acquaintances. He ties a rope to one of the prisoner's arms, by the end of which he holds him, a few steps away, for fear of being hurt, and gives his dearest friend the other arm to hold in the same way; and these two, in the presence of the whole assembly, kill him with their swords. This done, they roast him and eat him in common and send some pieces to the absent friends. This is not, as people think, for nourishment, as of old the Scythians used to do; it is to betoken an extreme revenge.[3] And the proof of this came when they saw the Portuguese, who had joined forces with their adversaries, inflict a different kind of death on them when they took them prisoner, which was to bury them up to the waist, shoot the rest of their body full of arrows, and afterward hang them. They thought that these people from the other world, being men who had sown the knowledge of many vices among their neighbors and were much greater masters than themselves in every sort of wickedness, did not adopt this sort of vengeance without some reason, and that it must be more painful than their own; so they began to give up their old method and to follow this one.

I am not sorry that we notice the barbarous horror of such acts, but I am heartily sorry that, judging their faults rightly, we should be so blind as to our own. I think there is more barbarity in eating a man alive than in eating him dead; and in tearing by tortures and the rack a body still full of feeling, in roasting a man bit by bit, in having him bitten and mangled by dogs and swine (as we have not only read but seen within fresh memory, not among ancient enemies, but among neighbors and fellow citizens, and what is worse, on the pretext of piety and religion), than in roasting and eating him after he is dead.

Indeed, Chrysippus and Zeno, heads of the Stoic sect, thought there was nothing wrong in using our carcasses for

---

[2]The legendary lawgiver of ancient Sparta.

[3]Montaigne overlooks the fact that ritual cannibalism might also involve the will to consume the power of the opponent, especially if he were a formidable opponent.

any purpose in case of need, and getting nourishment from them; just as our ancestors, when besieged by Caesar in the city of Alésia, resolved to relieve their famine by eating old men, women, and other people useless for fighting.   150

> *The Gascons once, 'tis said, their life renewed*
> *By eating of such food.*
>
>   Juvenal

And physicians do not fear to use human flesh in all sorts of ways for our health, applying it either inwardly or outwardly. But there never was any opinion so disordered as to excuse treachery, disloyalty, tyranny, and cruelty, which are our ordinary vices.

So we may well call these people barbarians, in respect of the rules of reason, but not in respect of ourselves, who   160 surpass them in every kind of barbarity.

Their warfare is wholly noble and generous, and as excusable and beautiful as this human disease can be; its only basis among them is their rivalry in valor. They are not fighting for the conquest of new lands, for they still enjoy that natural abundance that provides them without toil and trouble with all necessary things in such profusion that they have no wish to enlarge their boundaries. They are still in that happy state of desiring only as much as their natural needs demand; any thing beyond that is superfluous to them.   170

 Q "Each man calls barbarian whatever is not of his own practice," writes Montaigne. What illustrations does he offer? Does this claim hold true in our own day and age?

The Genius of Shakespeare

No assessment of the early modern era would be complete without some consideration of the literary giant of the age: William Shakespeare (1564–1616; Figure **19.16**). A poet of unparalleled genius, Shakespeare emerged during the golden age of England under the rule of Elizabeth I (1533–1603). He produced thirty-seven plays—comedies, tragedies, romances, and histories—as well as 154 sonnets and other poems. These works, generally considered to be the greatest examples of English literature, have exercised an enormous influence on the evolution of the English language and the development of the Western literary tradition.*

Little is known about Shakespeare's early life and formal education. He grew up in Stratford-upon-Avon in the English Midlands, married Anne Hathaway (eight years his senior), with whom he had three children, and moved to London sometime before 1585. In London he formed an acting company, the Lord Chamberlain's Company (also called "the King's Men"), in which he was shareholder, actor, and playwright. Like fifteenth-century Florence, sixteenth-century London (and especially the Queen's court) supported a galaxy of artists, musicians, and writers who enjoyed a mutually stimulating interchange of ideas. Shakespeare's theater company performed at the court of Elizabeth I and that of her successor James I (1566–1625). But its main activities took place in the Globe Playhouse, one of a handful built just outside London's city limits—along with brothels and taverns, theaters were generally relegated to the suburbs.

---

*The complete works of Shakespeare are available at the following website: http://www-tech.mit.edu/shakespeare/works.html

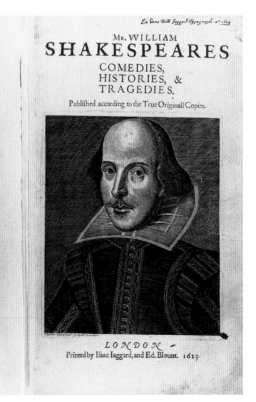

To the Reader.

This Figure, that thou here seest put,
    It was for gentle Shakespeare cut;
Wherein the Grauer had a strife
    with Nature, to out-doo the life :
O, could he but haue drawne his wit
    As well in brasse, as he hath hit
His face ; the Print would then surpasse
    All, that was euer writ in brasse.
But, since he cannot, Reader, looke
    Not on his Picture, but his Booke.
                    B. I.

Mr. WILLIAM
SHAKESPEARES
COMEDIES,
HISTORIES, &
TRAGEDIES.
Published according to the True Originall Copies.

LONDON
Printed by Isaac Iaggard, and Ed. Blount. 1623.

Figure 19.16 DROESHOUT, first Folio edition portrait of William Shakespeare, 1623. By permission of the Folger Shakespeare Library, Washington, D.C.

While Shakespeare is best known for his plays, he also wrote some of the most beautiful sonnets ever produced in the English language. Indebted to Petrarch, Shakespeare nevertheless devised most of his own sonnets in a form that would come to be called "the English sonnet": **quatrains** (four-line stanzas) with alternate rhymes, followed by a concluding **couplet**. Shakespeare's sonnets employ—and occasionally mock—such traditional Petrarchan themes as the blind devotion of the unfortunate lover, the value of friendship, and love's enslaving power. Some, like Sonnet 18, reflect the typically Renaissance (and classical) concern for immortality achieved through art and love. In Sonnet 18, Shakespeare contrives an extended metaphor: like the summer day, his beloved will fade and die. But, exclaims the poet, she will remain eternal in and through the sonnet; for, so long as the poem survives, so will the object of its inspiration remain alive. Stripped of sentiment, Sonnet 116 states the unchanging nature of love; Shakespeare exalts the "marriage of true minds" that most Renaissance humanists perceived as only possible among men. Sonnet 130, on the other hand, pokes fun at the literary conventions of the Petrarchan love sonnet. Satirizing the fair-haired, red-lipped heroine as object of desire, Shakespeare celebrates the real—though somewhat ordinary—features of his beloved.

READING 3.26 From Shakespeare's Sonnets (1609)

Sonnet 18

Shall I compare thee to a summer's day?   1
Thou art more lovely and more temperate.
Rough winds do shake the darling buds of May,
And summer's lease[1] hath all too short a date.
Sometime too hot the eye[2] of heaven shines,   5
And often is his gold complexion dimm'd;
And every fair from fair sometime declines,[3]
By chance or nature's changing course untrimm'd;[4]
But thy eternal summer shall not fade
Nor lose possession of that fair thou ow'st,   10
Nor shall Death brag thou wand'rest in his shade,
When in eternal lines to time thou grow'st.[5]
    So long as men can breathe or eyes can see,
    So long lives this[6] and this gives life to thee.

Sonnet 116

Let me not to the marriage of true minds   1
Admit impediments. Love is not love
Which alters when it alteration finds,
Nor bends with the remover to remove.[7]

O, no, it is an ever-fixed mark,[8]   5
That looks on tempests and is never shaken;
It is the star to every wand'ring bark,
Whose worth's unknown, although his height be taken.[9]
Love's not Time's fool, though rose lips and cheeks
Within his bending sickle's compass come;   10
Love alters not with his brief hours and weeks,
But bears it out even to the edge of doom.[10]
    If this be error, and upon me proved,
    I never writ, nor no man ever loved.

Sonnet 130

My mistress' eyes are nothing like the sun;   1
Coral is far more red than her lips' red:
If snow be white, why then her breasts are dun;
If hairs be wires, black wires grow on her head.
I have seen roses damasked, red and white,   5
But no such roses see I in her cheeks;
And in some perfumes is there more delight
Than in the breath that from my mistress reeks.
I love to hear her speak, yet well I know
That music hath a far more pleasing sound: 10
I grant I never saw a goddess go,—
My mistress, when she walks, treads on the ground:
    And yet, by heaven, I think my love as rare
    As any she belied with false compare.

Q What does each of these sonnets convey about love?

The Shakespearean Stage

Secular drama, Renaissance England's most original contribution to the humanistic tradition, was born in an era of high confidence: in 1588, the English navy defeated a Spanish fleet of 130 ships known as the "Invincible Armada." This event, a victory as well for the forces of Protestantism over Catholicism, encouraged a sense of national pride and a renewed confidence in the ambitious policies of the "Protestant Queen" Elizabeth I (Figure **19.17**). In its wake followed a period of high prosperity and commercial expansion. The rebirth of secular drama, stirred by the revival of interest in English history, is a major part of the Elizabethan legacy.

In the centuries following the fall of Rome, the Church condemned all forms of pagan display, including the performance of comedies and tragedies. Tragedy, in the sense that it was defined by Aristotle ("the imitation of an action" involving "some great error" made by an extraordinary man), was philosophically incompatible with the medieval worldview, which held that all events were predetermined by God. If redemption was the goal of Christian life, there was no place for literary tragedy in the

---

[1]Allotted time.
[2]The sun.
[3]Beautiful thing from beauty.
[4]Stripped of beauty.
[5]Your fame will grow as time elapses.
[6]The sonnet itself.
[7]Changes as the beloved changes.

[8]Sea mark, an aid to navigation.
[9]Whose value is beyond estimation.
[10]Endures to the very Day of Judgment.

Figure 19.17 GEORGE GOWER, *"Armada" Portrait of Elizabeth I*, ca. 1588. Oil on panel, 3 ft. 6 in. × 4 ft. 5 in. Woburn Abbey Collection, by kind permission of the Marquess of Tavistock and the Trustees of the Bedford Estates.

Christian cosmos. (Hence Dante's famous journey, though far from humorous, was called a "comedy" in acknowledgment of its "happy" ending in Paradise.) Elizabethan poets adapted classical and medieval literary traditions and texts to the writing of contemporary plays: while the context and the characters might be Christian, the plot and the dramatic action were secular in focus and in spirit. (The same might be said for the culture of the Renaissance in general.) Elizabethan London played host to groups of traveling actors (or "strolling players") who performed in public spaces or for generous patrons. In the late sixteenth century, a number of playhouses were built along the Thames River across from the city of London. Begun in 1599, the Globe, which held between 2,000 and 3,000 spectators, offered all levels of society access to professional theater (Figure **19.18**). The open-air structure consisted of three tiers of galleries and standing room for commoners (known as "groundlings") at the cost of only a penny—one-sixth of the price for a seat in the covered gallery. The projecting, rectangular stage, some 40 feet wide, included balconies (for musicians and special scenes such as required in *Romeo and Juliet*), exits to dressing

areas, and a trapdoor (used for rising spirits and for burial scenes, such as required in *Hamlet*). Stage props were basic, but costumes were favored, and essential for the male actors who played the female roles—women were not permitted on the public stage. Performances were held in the afternoon and advertised by flying a flag above the theater roof. A globe, the signature logo, embellished the theater, along with a sign that read "*Totus mundus agit histrionem*" (loosely, "All the World's a Stage"). The bustling crowd that attended the theater—some of whom stood through two or more hours of performance—often ate and drank as they enjoyed the most cosmopolitan entertainment of their time. A reconstruction of the Globe Playhouse, located on the south bank of the Thames River, opened in 1997 (Figure **19.19**).

Shakespeare's Plays

In Shakespeare's time, theater did not rank as high as poetry as a literary genre. As popular entertainment, however, Shakespeare's plays earned high acclaim in London's theatrical community. Thanks to the availability of printed editions, the Bard of Stratford was familiar with

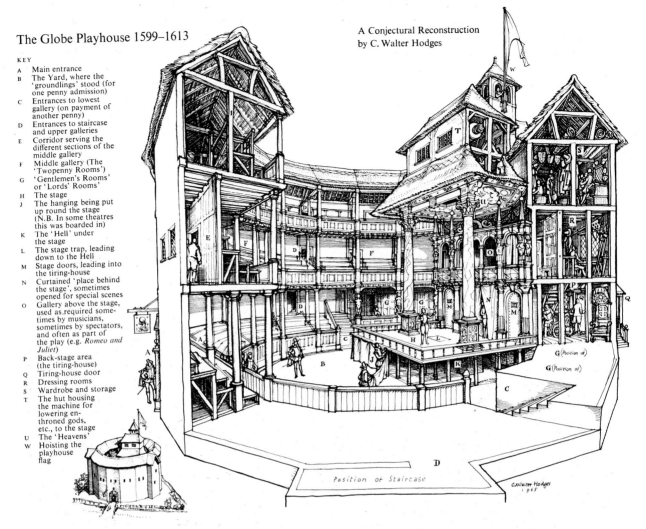

The Globe Playhouse 1599–1613

A Conjectural Reconstruction
by C. Walter Hodges

KEY
A Main entrance
B The Yard, where the 'groundlings' stood (for one penny admission)
C Entrances to lowest gallery (on payment of another penny)
D Entrances to staircase and upper galleries
E Corridor serving the different sections of the middle gallery
F Middle gallery (The 'Twopenny Rooms')
G 'Gentlemen's Rooms' or 'Lords' Rooms'
H The stage
J The hanging being put up round the stage (N.B. In some theatres this was boarded in)
K The 'Hell' under the stage
L The stage trap, leading down to the Hell
M Stage doors, leading into the tiring-house
N Curtained 'place behind the stage', sometimes opened for special scenes
O Gallery above the stage, used as required sometimes by musicians, sometimes by spectators, and often as part of the play (e.g. *Romeo and Juliet*)
P Back-stage area (the tiring-house)
Q Tiring-house door
R Dressing rooms
S Wardrobe and storage
T The hut housing the machine for lowering enthroned gods, etc., to the stage
U The 'Heavens'
W Hoisting the playhouse flag

Position of Staircase

G (Position of)
G (Position of)

Figure 19.18 Globe Playhouse, London, 1599–1613. Architectural reconstruction by **C. WALTER HODGES**, 1948. From *Introducing Shakespeare*, by G.B. Harrison, 3/e © G.B. Harrison, 1939, 1945, 1966.

the tragedies of Seneca and the comedies of Plautus and Terence. He knew the popular medieval morality plays that addressed the contest between good and evil, as well as the popular improvisational form of Italian comic theater known as the *commedia dell'arte*, which made use of stock or stereotypical characters. All of these resources came to shape the texture of his plays. For his plots, Shakespeare drew largely on classical history, medieval chronicles, and contemporary romances.

Like Machiavelli, Shakespeare was an avid reader of ancient and medieval history, as well as a keen observer of his own complex age; but the stories his sources provided became mere springboards for the exploration of human nature. His history plays, such as *Henry V* and *Richard III*, celebrate England's medieval past and its rise to power under the Tudors. The concerns of these plays, however, are not exclusively historical; rather, they explore the ways in which rulers behave under pressure: the weight of kingly responsibilities on mere humans and the difficulties of reconciling royal obligations and human aspirations.

Shakespeare's comedies, which constitute about one half of his plays, deal with such popular themes as the battle of the sexes, rivalry among lovers, and mistaken

identities. But here too, in such plays as *Much Ado About Nothing, All's Well That Ends Well,* and *The Taming of the Shrew,* it is Shakespeare's characters—their motivations exposed, their weaknesses and strengths laid bare—that command our attention.

It is in the tragedies, and especially the tragedies of his mature career—*Hamlet, Macbeth, Othello,* and *King Lear*—that Shakespeare achieved the concentration of thought and language that have made him the greatest English playwright of all time. Jealousy, greed, ambition, insecurity, and self-deception are among the many human experiences that Shakespeare examined in his plays, but in these last tragedies, they become definitive: they drive the action of the play. Indeed, these plays are the most significant evidence of the Renaissance effort to probe the psychological forces that motivate human action.

No discussion of Shakespeare's plays can substitute for the experience of live performance. Yet, in focusing on two of the late tragedies, *Hamlet* and *Othello,* it is possible to isolate Shakespeare's principal contributions to the humanistic tradition. These lie in the areas of character development and in the brilliance of the language with which characters are brought to life. Despite occasional passages in prose and rhymed verse, Shakespeare's plays were written in the current Renaissance verse form known as **blank verse**. This was popular among Renaissance humanists because, like classical poetry, it was unrhymed, and it closely approximated the rhythms of vernacular speech. In Shakespeare's hands, the English language took on a breadth of expression and a majesty of eloquence that has rarely been matched to this day. Shakespeare often used songs to create a special effect or develop the mood of a character. In the chilling scene just prior to her murder by Othello (see Reading 3.28), Desdemona sings a gentle ballad that serves to characterize her sense of frailty and futility as she anticipates her tragic fate at the hand of her husband, Othello.

Hamlet, the world's most quoted play, belongs to the popular Renaissance genre of revenge tragedy; the story itself came to Shakespeare from the history of medieval Denmark. Hamlet, the young heir to the throne of Denmark, learns that his uncle has murdered his father and married his mother in order to assume the throne; the burden of avenging his father falls squarely on Hamlet's shoulders. The arc of the play follows his inability to take action—his melancholic lack of resolve that, in the long run, results in the deaths of his mother (Gertrude), his betrothed (Ophelia), her father (Polonius), the king (Claudius), and, finally, Hamlet himself.

Shakespeare's protagonist differs from the heroes of ancient and medieval times: Hamlet lacks the sense of

Figure 19.19 Globe Theater, London, reconstructed 1997. © Yann Arthus-Bertrand/CORBIS.

obligation to country and community, the passionate religious loyalties, and the clearly defined spiritual values that drive such heroes as Gilgamesh, Achilles, and Roland. Yet Hamlet represents a new, more modern personality, one whose self-questioning disposition and brooding skepticism more closely resemble a modern existential antihero (see chapter 35). Though sunk in melancholy, he shares Pico della Mirandola's view (see Reading 3.8) that human nature is freely self-formed by human beings themselves. Hamlet marvels, "What a piece of work is a man! How noble in reason! How infinite in faculty! In form and moving how express and admirable! In action how like an angel! In apprehension how like a god! The beauty of the world! The paragon of animals." Nevertheless he concludes on a note of utter skepticism, "And yet, to me, what is this quintessence of dust?" (Act II, ii, ll. 303–309). It is in the oral examination of his innermost thoughts—the *soliloquy*—that Hamlet most fully reveals himself. In a painful process of self-examination, he questions the motives for meaningful action and the impulses that prevent him from action, but at the same time, he contemplates the futility of all human action.

READING 3.27 From Shakespeare's *Hamlet* (1602)

Hamlet, Act III, Scene 1

Enter King, Queen, Polonius, Ophelia, Rosencrantz, Guildenstern, lords.

King: And can you by no drift of conference   1
  Get from him why he puts on this confusion,
  Grating so harshly all his days of quiet
  With turbulent and dangerous lunacy?

Rosencrantz: He does confess he feels himself distracted,
  But from what cause 'a will by no means speak.

Guildenstern: Nor do we find him forward to be sounded,
  But with a crafty madness keeps aloof
  When we would bring him on to some confession
  Of his true state.

Queen: Did he receive you well?   10

Rosencrantz: Most like a gentleman.

Guildenstern: But with much forcing of his disposition.

Rosencrantz: Niggard of question, but of our demands
  Most free in his reply.

Queen: Did you assay him
  To any pastime?

Rosencrantz: Madam, it so fell out that certain players
  We o'erraught on the way. Of these we told him,
  And there did seem in him a kind of joy
  To hear of it. They are here about the court,
  And, as I think, they have already order   20
  This night to play before him.

Polonius: 'Tis most true,

And he beseeched me to entreat Your Majesties
  To hear and see the matter.

King: With all my heart, and it doth much content me
  To hear him so inclined.
  Good gentlemen, give him a further edge
  And drive his purpose into these delights.

Rosencrantz: We shall, my lord.

      Exeunt Rosencrantz and Guildenstern.

King: Sweet Gertrude, leave us too,
  For we have closely sent for Hamlet hither,
  That he, as 'twere by accident, may here   30
  Affront Ophelia.
  Her father and myself, lawful espials,
  Will so bestow ourselves that seeing, unseen,
  We may of their encounter frankly judge,
  And gather by him, as he is behaved,
  If 't be th' affliction of his love or no
  That thus he suffers for.

Queen: I shall obey you.
  And for your part, Ophelia, I do wish
  That your good beauties be the happy cause
  Of Hamlet's wildness. So shall I hope your virtues   40
  Will bring him to his wonted way again,
  To both your honors.

Ophelia: Madam, I wish it may.

                [*Exit Queen.*]

Polonius: Ophelia, walk you here.—Gracious, so please you,
  We will bestow ourselves. [*To Ophelia.*] Read on this
  book,   [*giving her a book*]
  That show of such an exercise may color
  Your loneliness. We are oft to blame in this—
  'Tis too much proved—that with devotion's visage
  And pious action we do sugar o'er
  The devil himself.

King [*aside*]:   O, 'tis too true!   50
  How smart a lash that speech doth give my conscience!
  The harlot's cheek, beautied with plastering art,
  Is not more ugly to the thing that helps it
  Than is my deed to my most painted word.
  O heavy burden!

Polonius: I hear him coming. Let's withdraw, my lord.

        [*The King and Polonius withdraw.*]

      Enter Hamlet. [*Ophelia pretends to read a book.*]

Hamlet: To be, or not to be, that is the question:
  Whether 'tis nobler in the mind to suffer
  The slings and arrows of outrageous fortune,
  Or to take arms against a sea of troubles   60
  And by opposing end them. To die, to sleep—

3.1. Location: The castle.
1 drift of conference directing of conversation **7 forward** willing **Sounded** questioned **12 disposition** inclination **13 Niggard** stingy **question** conversation **14 assay** try to win **17 o'erraught** overtook

---

3.1. Location: The castle.
26 edge incitement **29 closely** privately **31 Affront** confront, meet **32 espials** spies **41 wonted** accustomed **43 Gracious** Your Grace (i.e., the King) **44 bestow** conceal **45 exercise** religious exercise (The book she reads is one of devotion) **color** give a plausible appearance to **46 loneliness** being alone **47 too much proved** too often shown to be true, too often practiced **53 to** compared to **the thing** i.e., the cosmetic **56 s.d. withdraw** (The King and Polonius may retire behind an arras. The stage directions specify that they "enter" again near the end of the scene.) **59 slings** missiles

No more—and by a sleep to say we end
The heartache and the thousand natural shocks
That flesh is heir to. 'Tis a consummation
Devoutly to be wished. To die, to sleep;
To sleep, perchance to dream. Ay, there's the rub,
For in that sleep of death what dreams may come,
When we have shuffled off this mortal coil,
Must give us pause. There's the respect
That makes calamity of so long life.   70
For who would bear the whips and scorns of time,
Th' oppressor's wrong, the proud man's contumely,
The pangs of disprized love, the law's delay,
The insolence of office, and the spurns
That patient merit of th' unworthy takes,
When he himself might his quietus make
With a bare bodkin? Who would fardels bear,
To grunt and sweat under a weary life,
But that the dread of something after death,
The undiscovered country from whose bourn   80
No traveler returns, puzzles the will,
And makes us rather bear those ills we have
Than fly to others that we know not of?
Thus conscience does make cowards of us all;
And thus the native hue of resolution
Is sicklied o'er with the pale cast of thought,
And enterprises of great pitch and moment
With this regard their currents turn awry
And lose the name of action.—Soft you now,
The fair Ophelia. Nymph, in thy orisons   90
Be all my sins remembered.

Ophelia: Good my lord,
How does your honor for this many a day?

Hamlet: I humbly thank you; well, well, well.

Ophelia: My lord, I have remembrances of yours,
That I have longèd long to redeliver.
I pray you, now receive them.   [*She offers tokens.*]

Hamlet: No, not I, I never gave you aught.

Ophelia: My honored lord, you know right well you did,
And with them words of so sweet breath composed
As made the things more rich. Their perfume lost,   100
Take these again, for to the noble mind
Rich gifts wax poor when givers prove unkind.

There, my lord.   [*She gives tokens.*]

Hamlet: Ha, ha! Are you honest?

Ophelia: My lord?

Hamlet: Are you fair?

Ophelia: What means your lordship?

Hamlet: That if you be honest and fair, your honesty
should admit no discourse to your beauty.

Ophelia: Could beauty, my lord, have better commerce   110
than with honesty?

Hamlet: Ay, truly, for the power of beauty will sooner
transform honesty from what it is to a bawd than the
force of honesty can translate beauty into his likeness.
This was sometime a paradox, but now the time gives
if proof. I did love you once.

Ophelia: Indeed, my lord, you made me believe so.

Hamlet: You should not have believed me, for virtue
cannot so inoculate our old stock but we shall relish of
it. I loved you not.   120

Ophelia: I was the more deceived.

Hamlet: Get thee to a nunnery. Why wouldst thou be a
breeder of sinners? I am myself indifferent honest, but
yet I could accuse me of such things that it were better
my mother had not borne me: I am very proud,
revengeful, ambitious, with more offenses at my beck
than I have thoughts to put them in, imagination to
give them shape, or time to act them in. What should
such fellows as I do crawling between earth and
heaven? We are arrant knaves all; believe none of us.   130
Go thy ways to a nunnery. Where's your father?

Ophelia: At home, my lord.

Hamlet: Let the doors be shut upon him, that he may
play the fool nowhere but in 's own house. Farewell.

Ophelia: O, help him, you sweet heavens!

Hamlet: If thou dost marry, I'll give thee this plague for
thy dowry: be thou as chaste as ice, as pure as snow,
thou shalt not escape calumny. Get thee to a nunnery,
farewell. Or, if thou wilt needs marry, marry a fool, for
wise men know well enough what monsters you   140
make of them. To a nunnery, go, and quickly too.
Farewell.

Ophelia: Heavenly powers, restore him!

Hamlet: I have heard of your paintings too, well
enough. God hath given you one face, and you make
yourselves another. You jig, you amble, and you
lisp, you nickname God's creatures, and make your
wantonness your ignorance. Go to, I'll no more on 't;
it hath made me mad. I say we will have no more
marriage. Those that are married already—all but   150
one—shall live. The rest shall keep as they are. To a

---

66 rub (Literally, an obstacle in the game of bowls)   **68 shuffled**
sloughed, cast   **Coil** turmoil   **69 respect** consideration   **70 of . . . life**
so long-lived, something we willingly endure for so long (also
suggesting that long life is itself a calamity)   **72 contumely** insolent
abuse   **73 disprized** unvalued   **74 office** officialdom   **spurns**
insults   **75 of . . . takes** receives from unworthy persons   **76 quietus**
acquittance; here, death   **77 a bare bodkin** a mere dagger,
unsheathed   **fardels** burdens   **80 bourn** frontier, boundary   **85
native hue** natural color, complexion   **86 cast** tinge, shade of color
87 pitch height (as of a falcon's flight)   **moment** importance   **88
regard** respect, consideration   **currents** courses   **89 Soft you** i.e.,
wait a minute, gently   **90 orisons** prayers   **104 honest** (1) truthful (2)
chaste   **106 fair** (1) beautiful (2) just, honorable   **108 your honesty**
your chastity   **109 discourse to** familiar dealings with   **110–111
commerce** dealings, intercourse   **114 his** its   **115 sometime**
formerly   **a paradox** a view opposite to commonly held opinion
the time the present age   **119 inoculate** graft, be engrafted to

---

119–120 but . . . it that we do not still have about us a taste of the old
stock, i.e., retain our sinfulness   **122 nunnery** convent (with possibly
an awareness that the word was also used derisively to denote a
brothel)   **123 indifferent honest** reasonably virtuous   **126 beck**
command   **140 monsters** (An illusion to the horns of a cuckold)   **you**
i.e., you women   **146 jig** dance   **amble** move coyly   **147 you**
nickname . . . creatures i.e., you give trendy names to things in place
of their God-given names   **147–148 make . . . ignorance** i.e., excuse
your affectation on the grounds of pretended ignorance   **148 on 't** of it

nunnery, go.   *Exit.*

Ophelia: O, what a noble mind is here o'erthrown!
  The courtier's, soldier's, scholar's, eye, tongue,
    sword,
  Th' expectancy and rose of the fair state,
  The glass of fashion and the mold of form,
  Th' observed of all observers, quite, quite down!
  And I, of ladies most deject and wretched,
  That sucked the honey of his music vows,
  Now see that noble and most sovereign reason   160
  Like sweet bells jangled out of tune and harsh,
  That unmatched form and feature of blown youth
  Blasted with ecstasy. O, woe is me,
  T' have seen what I have seen, see what I see!
                 Enter King and Polonius.

King: Love? His affections do not that way tend;
  Nor what he spake, though it lacked form a little,
  Was not like madness. There's something in his soul
  O'er which his melancholy sits on brood,
  And I do doubt the hatch and the disclose
  Will be some danger; which for to prevent,   170
  I have in quick determination
  Thus set it down: he shall with speed to England
  For the demand of our neglected tribute.
  Haply the seas and countries different
  With variable objects shall expel
  This something-settled matter in his heart,
  Whereon his brains still beating puts him thus
  From fashion of himself. What think you on 't?

Polonius: It shall do well. But yet do I believe
  The origin and commencement of his grief   180
  Sprung from neglected love.—How now, Ophelia?
  You need not tell us what Lord Hamlet said;
  We heard it all.—My lord, do as you please,
  But, if you hold it fit, after the play
  Let his queen-mother all alone entreat him
  To show his grief. Let her be round with him;
  And I'll be placed, so please you, in the ear
  Of all their conference. If she find him not,
  To England send him, or confine him where
  Your wisdom best shall think.

King: It shall be so.   190
  Madness in great ones must not unwatched go. *Exeunt.*

---

155 **expectancy** hope   **rose** ornament   156 **The glass . . . form** the mirror of true self-fashioning and the pattern of courtly behavior   157 **Th' observed . . . observers** i.e., the center of attention and honor in the court   159 **music** musical, sweetly uttered   162 **blown** blooming   163 **Blasted** withered   **ecstasy** madness   165 **affections** emotions, feelings   168 **sits on brood** sits like a bird on a nest, about to *hatch* mischief (line 169)   169 **doubt** fear   **disclose** disclosure, hatching   172 **set it down** resolved   173 **For . . . of** to demand   175 **variable objects** various sights and surroundings to divert him   176 **This something . . . heart** the strange matter settled in his heart   177 **still** continually   178 **From . . . himself** out of his natural manner   185 **queen-mother** queen and mother   186 **round** blunt   188 **find him not** fails to discover what is troubling him

Q What profound question does Hamlet address in his soliloquy?

Q What conclusion does Ophelia reach at the end of her conversation with Hamlet?

The Tragedy of Othello, the Moor of Venice was based on a story from a collection of tales published in Italy in the sixteenth century. The life of the handsome and distinguished Othello, an African soldier whose leadership in the Venetian wars against the Turks has brought him heroic esteem, takes a tragic turn when his ensign Iago beguiles him into thinking that his beautiful wife Desdemona has betrayed him with another man. Enraged with jealousy, Othello destroys the person he loves most in the world, his wife; and, in the unbearable grief of his error, he takes his own life as well. No brief synopsis can capture the dramatic impact of this, one of Shakespeare's most sensational plays. While Othello's jealousy is the flaw that brings about his doom, it is Iago whose unmitigated evil drives the action of the plot. Conniving Iago is the Machiavellian villain, "a demi-devil," as he is called in the play. In contrast, Desdemona is the paragon of virtue and beauty. Such characters hark back to the allegorical figures in medieval morality plays, but Shakespeare transforms these figures into complex personalities, allowing them full freedom to falter and fail through their own actions.

That Shakespeare made a black man the hero of one of his tragedies is significant, since his treatment of the character seems to have challenged Elizabethan stereotypes. Medieval and Renaissance literature described blacks as vengeful, hot-blooded, and evil, black being the color traditionally associated with the devil. But in Shakespeare's play, the Moor (the Elizabethan name for any African) is unwitting, ingenuous, and pure, while Iago, the white man who confounds him, is the personification of evil. Perhaps more significant than this irony is Shakespeare's implication that underlying the most untainted acts of heroism and the purest emotions of love is the dark possibility of misguided action that leads to self-defeat. Shakespeare's plays generally preach no explicit moral; rather, they suggest that, in a universe in which order and disorder coexist, human choices play a vital and potentially destructive part. The nihilism that darkens *The Tragedy of Othello*, *Macbeth*, and *Hamlet* was unthinkable before the modern era.

READING 3.28 From Shakespeare's *Othello*

(1604)

Othello, Act IV, Scene III
Enter Othello, Lodovico, Desdemona, Emilia, and Attendants.

Lodovico: I do beseech you, sir, trouble yourself no further.   1
Othello: O, pardon me; 'twill do me good to walk.
Lodovico: Madam, good night. I humbly thank your
  ladyship.
Desdemona: Your honor is most welcome.

Othello: Will you walk, sir?
    O, Desdemona!

Desdemona: My lord?

Othello: Get you to bed on th' instant; I will be return'd
    forthwith. Dismiss your attendant there. Look 't be done.

Desdemona: I will, my lord.

                  Exit [Othello, with Lodovico and Attendants].

Emilia: How goes it now? He looks gentler than he did.   **10**

Desdemona: He says he will return incontinent,
    And hath commanded me to go to bed,
    And bade me to dismiss you.

Emilia: Dismiss me?

Desdemona: It was his bidding; therefore, good Emilia,
    Give me my nightly wearing, and adieu.
    We must not now displease him.

Emilia: I would you had never seen him!

Desdemona: So would not I. My love doth so approve him,
    That even his stubbornness, his checks, his frowns—
    Prithee unpin me—have grace and favor in them.   **20**

              [Emilia prepares Desdemona for bed.]

Emilia: I have laid those sheets you bade me on the bed.

Desdemona: All's one. Good faith, how foolish are our
    minds!
    If I do die before thee, prithee shroud me
    In one of those same sheets.

Emilia: Come, come, you talk.

Desdemona: My mother had a maid call'd Barbary.
    She was in love, and he she lov'd prov'd mad
    And did forsake her. She had a song of "Willow,"
    An old thing 'twas, but it express'd her fortune,
    And she died singing it. That song tonight
    Will not go from my mind; I have much to do   **30**
    But to go hang my head all at one side
    And sing it like poor Barbary. Prithee, dispatch.

Emilia: Shall I go fetch your nightgown?

Desdemona: No, unpin me here.
    This Lodovico is a proper man.

Emilia: A very handsome man.

Desdemona: He speaks well.

Emilia: I know a lady in Venice would have walk'd barefoot
    to Palestine for a touch of his nether lip.

Desdemona [*Singing*]:
    "The poor soul sat sighing by a sycamore tree,
      Sing all a green willow;   **40**
    Her hand on her bosom, her head on her knee,
      Sing willow, willow, willow.
    The fresh streams ran by her, and murmur'd her moans;
      Sing willow, willow, willow;
    Her salt tears fell from her, and soft'ned the stones"—
    Lay by these.

[*Singing*]: "Sing willow, willow, willow"—
    Prithee, hie thee; he'll come anon.

[*Singing*] "Sing all a green willow must be my garland.
      Let nobody blame him; his scorn I approve"—   **50**

Nay, that's not next.—Hark! Who is 't that knocks?

Emilia: It's the wind.

Desdemona [*Singing*]
    "I call'd my love false love; but what said he then?
      Sing willow, willow, willow;
    If I court moe women, you'll couch with moe men"—
    So, get thee gone; good night. Mine eyes do itch;
    Doth that bode weeping?

Emilia: 'Tis neither here nor there.

Desdemona: I have heard it said so. O, these men, these
    men!
    Dost thou in conscience think—tell me, Emilia—
    That there be women do abuse their husbands   **60**
    In such gross kind?

Emilia: There be some such, no question.

Desdemona: Wouldst thou do such a deed for all the world?

Emilia: Why, would not you?

Desdemona: No, by this heavenly light!

Emilia: Nor I neither by this heavenly light; I might do
    't as well i' th' dark.

Desdemona: Wouldst thou do such a deed for all the
    world?

Emilia: The world's a huge thing. It is a great price
    For a small vice.

Desdemona: Good troth, I think thou wouldst not.

Emilia: By my troth, I think I should; and undo 't when I
    had done. Marry, I would not do such a thing for a joint-   **70**
    ring, nor for measures of lawn, nor for gowns, petticoats,
    nor caps, nor any petty exhibition; but, for all the whole
    world—'ud's pity, who would not make her husband a
    cuckold to make him a monarch? I should venture
    purgatory for 't.

Desdemona: Beshrew me if I would do such a wrong for the
    whole world.

Emilia: Why, the wrong is but a wrong i' th' world; and
    having the world for your labor, 'tis a wrong in your own
    world, and you might quickly make it right.   **80**

Desdemona: I do not think there is any such woman.

Emilia: Yes, a dozen; and as many to th' vantage as
    would store the world they play'd for.
    But I do think it is their husbands' faults
    If wives do fall. Say that they slack their duties,
    And pour our treasures into foreign laps,
    Or else break out in peevish jealousies,
    Throwing restraint upon us? Or say they strike us,
    Or scant our former having in despite?
    Why, we have galls, and though we have some grace,
    Yet have we some revenge. Let husbands know   **90**
    Their wives have sense like them. They see, and smell,

---

48 hie thee hurry   **70–71 joint-ring** a ring made in separate halves
71 lawn fine linen   **72 exhibition** gift   **73 'ud's** i.e., God's   **82 to
th' vantage** in addition, to boot **store** populate   **85 pour . . . laps** i.e.,
are unfaithful, give what is rightfully ours (semen) to other women   **88
scant . . . despite** reduce our allowance to spite us   **89 have galls**
i.e., are capable of resenting injury and insult   **91 sense** physical
sense   **101 uses** habit, practice   **102 Not . . . mend** i.e., not to learn
bad conduct from others' badness (as Emilia has suggested women
learn from men), but to mend my ways by perceiving what badness is,
making spiritual benefit out of evil and adversity

IV.iii Location: The citadel.
11 incontinent immediately   **19 stubbornness** roughness **checks**
rebukes   **26 mad** wild, i.e., faithless   **30–31 I . . . hang** I can scarcely
keep myself from hanging

And have their palates both for sweet and sour,
As husbands have. What is it that they do
When they change us for others? Is it sport?
I think it is. And doth affection breed it?
I think it doth. Is 't frailty that thus errs?
It is so too. And have not we affections,
Desires for sport, and frailty, as men have?
Then let them use us well; else let them know,
The ills we do, their ills instruct us so. **100**

Desdemona: Good night, good night. God me such uses
send,
Not to pick bad from bad, but by bad mend!   *Exeunt.*

 Q How do Emilia's views on women as
wives compare with those of
Desdemona?

SUMMARY

The sixteenth century was a time of rapid change marked by growing secularism, advancing technology, and European geographic expansion. It was also an age of profound religious and social upheaval. Northern European humanists, led by Erasmus of Rotterdam, made critical studies of early Christian literature and urged a return to the teachings of Jesus and the early church fathers. Demands for Church reform went hand in hand with the revival of early Christian writings to culminate in the Protestant Reformation.

Aided by Gutenberg's printing press, Martin Luther contested the authority of the Church of Rome. He held that Scripture was the sole basis for religious interpretation and emphasized the idea of salvation through faith in God's grace rather than through good works. As Lutheranism and other Protestant sects proliferated throughout Europe, the unity of medieval Christendom was shattered.

The music and art of the Northern Renaissance reflect the mood of religious reform. In music, the Lutheran chorale became the vehicle of Protestant piety. In art, the increasing demand for illustrated devotional literature and private devotional art stimulated the production of woodcuts and metal engravings. The works of Dürer and Grünewald exhibit the Northern Renaissance passion for realistic detail and graphic expression, while the fantastic imagery of Hieronymus Bosch suggests a pessimistic and typically Northern concern with sin and death. Bosch's preoccupation with the palpable forces of evil found its counterpart in the witch-hunts of the sixteenth century. In painting, portraiture, landscapes, and scenes of everyday life mirrored the tastes of a growing middle-class audience for an unidealized record of the material world.

Northern Renaissance writers took a generally skeptical and pessimistic view of human nature. Erasmus, More, and Rabelais lampooned individual and societal failings and described the ruling influence of folly in all aspects of human conduct. In France, Montaigne devised the essay as an intimate form of rational reflection. In Spain, Cervantes' novel, *Don Quijote*, wittily attacked feudal values and outmoded ideals. The most powerful form of literary expression to evolve in the late sixteenth century, however, was secular drama. In the hands of William Shakespeare, Elizabethan drama became the ideal vehicle for exposing the psychological forces that motivate human behavior.

By the end of the sixteenth century, national loyalties, religious fanaticism, and commercial rivalries had splintered the European community, rendering ever more complex the society of the West. And yet, on the threshold of modernity, the challenges to the human condition—economic survival, communality, self-knowledge, and the inevitability of death—were no less pressing than they had been two thousand years earlier. If the technology of the sixteenth century offered greater control over nature than ever before, it also provided more devastating weapons of war and mass destruction. In the centuries to come, the humanistic tradition would be shaped and reshaped by changing historical circumstances and the creative imagination of indomitable humankind.

GLOSSARY

blank verse unrhymed lines of iambic pentameter, that is, lines consisting of ten syllables each with accents on every second syllable

chorale a congregational hymn, first sung in the Lutheran church

couplet two successive lines of verse with similar end-rhymes

engraving the process by which lines are incised on a metal plate, then inked and printed; see Figure 19.5

essay a short piece of expository prose that examines a single subject

genre painting art depicting scenes from everyday life; not to be confused with "genre," a term used to designate a particular category in literature or art, such as the essay (in literature) and portraiture (in painting)

iconoclast one who opposes the use of images in religious worship

quatrain a four-line stanza

triptych a picture or altarpiece with a central panel and two flanking panels; see also "diptych" in Glossary, chapter 9

woodcut a relief printing process by which all parts of a design are cut away except those that will be inked and printed; see Figure 19.7

Suggestions for Reading

INTRODUCTION

Chauvet, Jean-Marie and others. *The Dawn of Art: The Chauvet Cave*. New York: Abrams, 1996.

Clottes, Jean and D. Lewis-Williams. *The Shamans of Prehistory: Trance and Magic in the Painted Caves*. New York: Abrams, 1998.

Ehrenberg, Margaret. *Women in Prehistory*. London: British Museum Press, 1992.

Hadingham, E. *Lines to the Mountain Gods: Nazca and the Mysteries of Peru*. New York: Random House, 1987.

Hawkins, G. S. *Stonehenge Decoded*. New York: Dell, 1965.

James, E. O. *The Cult of the Mother Goddess*. New York: Barnes & Noble, 1994.

Johanson, Donald, and Blake Edgar. *From Lucy to Language*. New York: Simon & Schuster, 1996.

Jolly, Alison. *Lucy's Legend: Sex and Intelligence in Human Evolution*. Cambridge, Mass.: Harvard University Press, 1999.

Leakey, Richard. *Origins Reconsidered: In Search of What Makes Us Human*. New York: Doubleday, 1992.

Ruspoli, Mario. *The Cave of Lascaux*. London: Thames and Hudson, 1987.

Sandars, N. K. *Prehistoric Art in Europe*, 2nd ed. Baltimore: Penguin, 1985.

Schmandt-Besserat, Denise. *Before Writing: From Counting to Cuneiform*. Austin, Tex.: University of Texas Press, 1992.

Schwartz, Jeffrey. *What the Bones Tell Us*. New York: Henry Holt, 1993.

CHAPTER 1

Frankfort, Henri, et al. *Before Philosophy*. Baltimore: Penguin, 1961.

Hodges, Peter. *How the Pyramids Were Built*. Lonmead: Element Books, 1989.

Johnson, Paul. *The Civilization of Ancient Egypt*. New York: HarperCollins, 1999.

Lehrer, Mark. *The Complete Pyramids*. London: Thames and Hudson, 1998.

Malek, Jerome. *Egyptian Art*. New York: Phaidon Press, 2002.

Quirke, Stephen. *Ancient Egyptian Religion*. London: British Museum Press, 1992.

Robins, Gay. *Women in Ancient Egypt*. London: British Museum Press, 1993.

Taylor, John N. *Egypt and Nubia*. Cambridge, Mass.: Harvard University Press, 1991.

Tiradritti, Francesco, ed. *Egyptian Treasures from the Egyptian Museum in Cairo*. New York: Abrams, 1998.

Watterson, Barbara. *Women in Ancient Egypt*. New York: St. Martin's Press, 1992.

CHAPTER 2

Anderson, Bernhard. *Understanding the Old Testament*, 4th ed. Englewood Cliffs, N.J.: Prentice-Hall, 1986.

Aruz, Joan, ed. *Art of the First Cities: The Third Millennium BC from the Mediterranean to the Indus*. New Haven, Conn.: Yale University Press, 2003.

Collon, Dominique. *Ancient Near Eastern Art*. Berkeley: University of California Press, 1993.

Gabel, John B., and C. B. Wheeler. *The Bible as Literature: An Introduction*, 2nd ed. New York: Oxford University Press, 1990.

Gorden, Cyrus H. And Gary Rendsburg. *The Bible and the Ancient Near East.*, 4th edition. New York: Norton, 1997.

Holbrook, Clyde A. *The Iconoclastic Deity: Biblical Images of God*. Lewisburg, Pa.: Bucknell University Press, 1984.

Kramer, S. N. *History Begins at Sumer*, 3rd ed. Philadelphia: University of Pennsylvania Press, 1981.

Saggs, H. W. F. *The Babylonians*. Norman: University of Oklahoma, 1995.

——— *The Might That Was Assyria*. Salem, N.H.: Merrimack, 1984.

Snell, Daniel C. *Life in the Ancient Near East*. New Haven, Conn.: Yale University Press, 1997.

CHAPTER 3

Basham, A. L. *The Wonder That Was India: A Survey of the Culture of the Indian Subcontinent before the Coming of the Muslims*. 3rd edition. London: Sidgwick and Jackson, 1985.

Debaine-Frankfort, Corinne. *The Search for Ancient China*. New York: Abrams, 1999.

Jian, Li, ed. *External China: Splendors from the First Dynasties*. Dayton, Ohio: The Dayton Art Institute, 1998.

Loewe, Michael. *Everyday Life in Early Imperial China*. New York: Dorset Press, 1988.

Miller, James. *Daoism: A Short Introduction*. Oxford: Oneworld Publications, 2004.

Schwartz, Benjamin J. *The World of Thought in Ancient China*. Cambridge, Mass.: Harvard University Press, 1985.

Sommer, Deborah. *Chinese Religion: An Anthology of Sources*. New York: Oxford University Press, 1995.

Yang, Xiaoneng, ed. *The Golden Age of Chinese Archeology: Celebrated Discoveries from the People's Republic of China*. New Haven, Conn.: Yale University Press, 1999.

Zimmer, Heinrich. *Myths and Symbols in Indian Art and Civilization*. Reprint. Princeton: Princeton/Bollington, 1992.

CHAPTER 4

Blundell, Sue. *Women in Ancient Greece*. Cambridge, Mass.: Harvard University Press, 1995.

Cahill, Thomas. *Sailing the Wine-Dark Sea: Why the Greeks Matter*. New York: Talese/Doubleday, 2002.

Cartledge, Paul. *The Greeks: A Portrait of Self and Others*. New York: Oxford University Press, 1993.

Finley, M. I., ed. *The Legacy of Greece: A New Appraisal*. Oxford: Oxford University Press, 1981.

Green, Richard and Eric Handley. *Images of the Greek Theater*. Austin: University of Texas Press, 1995.

Hadot, Pierre. *What is Ancient Philosophy?* Trans. Michael Chase. Cambridge, Mass.: Belknap Press, 2002.

Lear, Jonathan. *Aristotle: The Desire to Understand.* New York: Oxford University Press, 1993.

Lefkowitz, Mary. *Greek Gods, Human Lives: What We Can Learn From Myths.* New Haven, Conn.: Yale University Press, 2003.

Martin, Thomas R. *Ancient Greece: From Prehistoric to Hellenistic Times.* New Haven, Conn.: Yale University Press, 1996.

Miller, Dean A. *The Epic Hero.* Baltimore, Md.: Johns Hopkins Press, 2000.

Reeder, Ellen D., ed. *Pandora: Women in Classical Greece.* Princeton: Princeton University Press, 1996.

Spivey, Nigel. *The Ancient Olympics.* New York: Oxford University Press, 2004.

Stone, I. F. *The Trial of Socrates.* New York: Doubleday, 1989.

Vlastos, Gregory. *Socrates, Ironist and Moral Philosopher.* Ithaca, N.Y.: Cornell University Press, 1991.

CHAPTER 5

Boardman, John. *Greek Art.* New York: Thames and Hudson, 2003.

—— and David Finn. *The Parthenon and its Sculptures.* Austin, Tex.: University of Texas Press, 1985.

Carpenter, Rhys. *The Architecture of the Parthenon.* Baltimore: Penguin, 1972.

Fildes, Alan and Joann Fletcher. *Alexander the Great: Son of the Gods.* Los Angeles, CA.: The J. Paul Getty Museum, 2002.

Francis, E. D. *Image and Idea in Fifth Century Greece: Art and Literature after the Persian Wars.* New York: Routledge, 1990.

Fullerton, Mark D. *Greek Art.* New York: Cambridge University Press, 2000.

Pedley, John G. *Greek Art and Archeology.* Englewood Cliffs, N.J.: Prentice-Hall, 1993.

Small, Jocelyn Penny. *The Parallel Worlds of Classical Art and Text.* New York: Cambridge University Press, 2003.

Spivey, Nigel. *Greek Art.* New York: Phaidon Press, 2003.

Walbank, F. W. *The Hellenistic World,* rev. ed. Cambridge, Mass.: Harvard University Press, 1993.

CHAPTER 6

Boatwright, Mary T. and others. *The Romans: From Village to Empire.* New York: Oxford University Press, 2004.

Bradley, K. R. *Slaves and Masters in the Roman Empire.* Berkeley, Calif.: University of California Press, 1987.

Christ, Karl. *The Romans: An Introduction to Their History and Civilization.* Berkeley, Calif.: University of California Press, 1984.

D'Ambra, Eve. *Roman Painting.* New York: Cambridge University Press, 1999.

Fantham, Elaine. *Roman Literary Culture: From Cicero to Apuleius.* Baltimore, Md.: Johns Hopkins University Press, 1999.

Galinsky, Karl. *Augustan Culture: An Interpretive Introduction.* Princeton: Princeton University Press, 1996.

Jones, P. V. and K. Sidwell, eds. *The World of Rome: An Introduction to Roman Culture.* New York: Cambridge University Press, 1997.

Kebric, Robert B. *Roman People.* Mountain View, Calif.: Mayfield, 1997.

Kleiner, Diana E. E. *Roman Sculpture.* New Haven, Conn.: Yale University Press, 1992.

Klingaman, William K. *The First Century: Emperors, Gods, and Everyman.* New York: Harper, 1986.

Stierlin, Henri. *The Roman Empire: From the Etruscans to the Decline of the Roman Empire.* Köln: Taschen, 2004.

Strong, Donald. *Roman Art: The Yale University Press Pelican History of Art,* 3rd edition. New Haven, Conn.: Yale University Press, 1992.

Zanker, Paul. *The Power of Images in the Age of Augustus.* Ann Arbor: University of Michigan Press, 1988.

CHAPTER 7

Bodde, Derk. *Chinese Thought, Society, and Science: The Intellectual and Social Background of Science and Technology in Pre-Modern China.* Honolulu: University of Hawaii Press, 1991.

Chang, Kwang-chin. *Art, Myth, and Ritual: The Path to Political Authority in Ancient China.* Cambridge, Mass.: Harvard University Press, 1983.

Fingarette, Herbert. *Confucius: The Secular as Sacred.* New York: Harper & Row, 1972.

Loewe, M. *Everyday Life in Early Imperial China.* New York: Dorset Press, 1988.

Miller, Barbara Stoler, ed. *Masterworks of Asian Literature in Comparative Perspective.* Armonk, N.Y.: M.E. Sharpe, 1994.

Needham, Joseph and Robert K. G. Temple. *The Genius of China: 3,000 Years of Science, Discovery, and Invention.* New York: Prion, 1986.

Rawson, Jessica, ed. *The British Museum Book of Chinese Art.* London: Thames and Hudson, 1993.

Schirokauer, Conrad. *A Brief History of Chinese Civilization.* New York: Harcourt, 1991.

Wang, Zhongshu. *Han Civilization,* trans., K. C. Chang. New Haven, Conn.: Yale University Press, 1982.

Watt, James C. V., ed. *China: Dawn of a Golden Age 200–750 A.D.* New York: Metropolitan Museum of Art, 2004.

CHAPTER 8

Brown, Peter. *The World of Late Antiquity, A.D. 150–750.* New York: Norton, 1989.

Chidester, David. *Christianity: A Global Perspective.* New York: Harper, 2002.

Crosson, John Dominic. *Jesus: A Revolutionary Biography.* New York: Harper, 1993.

Davies, Philp R. and others, eds. *The Complete World of the Dead Sea Scrolls.* New York: Thames and Hudson, 2002.

Ferguson, Everett. *Backgrounds of Early Christianity.* Grand Rapids, Mich.: Eerdmans, 1987.

Markus, R.A. *The End of Ancient Christianity.* Cambridge, UK: Cambridge University Press, 1998.

Nelson, Walter H. *Buddha: His Life and Teachings.* New York: Putnam, 2000.

Ross, Nancy W. *Three Ways of Asian Wisdom.* New York: Simon and Schuster, 1966.

Singh, Iqbal. *Gautama Buddha*. New York: Oxford University Press, 1997.

Strong, John S. *The Experience of Buddhism: Sources and Interpretations*. Belmont, Calif.: Wadsworth, 1995.

Walsh, Michael. *The Triumph of the Meek: Why Christianity Succeeded*. New York: Harper, 1986.

Wilson, A. N. *Jesus*. New York: Norton, 1992

CHAPTER 9

Beckwith, John. *Early Christian and Byzantine Art*. 2nd edition. New Haven, Conn.: Yale University Press, 1992.

Chadwick, Henry. *Augustine*. New York: Oxford University Press, 1986.

Durand, Jannic. *Byzantine Art*. New York: Terrail, 1999.

Fisher, Robert E. *Buddhist Art and Architecture*. New York: Thames and Hudson, 1993.

Jensen, Robin Margaret. *Understanding Early Christian Art*. New York: Routledge, 2000.

Lowden, John. *Early Christian and Byzantine Art*. New York: Phaidon, 1997.

Magoulias, H. J. *Byzantine Christianity: Emperor, Church and the West*. Detroit: Wayne State University Press, 1982.

Maguire, Henry. *Art and Eloquence in Byzantium*. Princeton, N.J.: Princeton University Press, 1995.

Menzies, Jackie, ed. *Buddha: Radiant Awakening*. New Haven, Conn: Yale University Press, 2003.

Milburn, Robert. *Early Christian Art and Architecture*. Berkeley, Calif.: University of California Press, 1988.

Zwalf, W., ed. *Buddhism: Art and Faith*. London: British Museum Press, 1985.

CHAPTER 10

Abu-Lughod, Janet L. *Before European Hegemony: The World System A.D. 1250–1350*. New York: Oxford University Press, 1989.

Armstrong, Karen. *Islam: A Short History*. New York: The Modern Library, 2002.

Bloom, Jonathan M., and Sheila S. Blair. *Islam: A Thousand Years of Faith and Power*. New Haven, Conn.: Yale University Press, 2002.

Brend, Barbara. *Islamic Art*. Cambridge, Mass.: Harvard University Press, 1980.

Hattstein, Markus and Peter Delius. *Islam: Art and Architecture*. Köln: Konemann, 2004.

Hillerbrand, Robert. *Islamic Art and Architecture*. London: Thames and Hudson, 1999.

Hiskett, Mervyn. *The Course of Islam in Africa*. New York: Columbia University Press, 1994.

Hodgson, Marshall. *The Venture of Islam*. 3 vols. Chicago: University of Chicago Press, 1974.

Lewis, Bernard, ed. *Islam from the Prophet Muhammad to the Capture of Constantinople*. New York: Oxford University Press, 1987.

Martin, Richard. *Islam: A Cultural Perspective*. New York: Prentice-Hall, 1982.

Otto-Dorn, Katharina. *The Art and Architecture of the Islamic World*. Berkeley, Calif. University of California Press, 1991.

Peters, F. E. *Muhammad and the Origins of Islam*. Ithaca, N.Y.: State University of New York, 1994.

Stanton, Charles M. *Higher Learning in Islam: The Classical Period, 700 A.D. to 1300 A.D.* Langham, Md.: Rowman and Littlefield, 1990.

Turner, Howard R. *Science in Medieval Islam: An Illustrated Introduction*. Austin: University of Texas Press, 1998.

CHAPTER 11

Bury, J. B. *Invasions of Europe by the Barbarians*. New York: Norton, 2000.

Diebold, William J. *Word and Image: An Introduction to Early Medieval Art*. New York: Harpercollins, 2000.

Dodwell, C. R. *The Pictorial Arts of the West 800–1200*. New Haven: Yale University Press, 1992.

Duby, George. *Love and Marriage in the Middle Ages*, translated by Jane Dunnett. Chicago: University of Chicago Press, 1994.

Erickson, Carolly. *Life in a Medieval City*. New York: Harper, 1981.

Evans, Angela Cane. *The Sutton Hoo Ship Burial*. London: British Museum Press, 1995.

Gies, Frances, and J. Gies. *Life in a Medieval Village*. New York: Harper, 1991.

Herlihy, David. *Opera Muliera: Women and Work in Medieval Europe*. New York: McGraw-Hill, 1990.

Labarge, Margaret Wade. *A Small Sound of the Trumpet: Women in Medieval Life*. Boston: Beacon Press, 1986.

Lewis, Archibald R. *Knights and Samurai: Feudalism in Northern France and Japan*. London: Temple Smith, 1974.

Maalouf, Amin. *The Crusades Through Arab Eyes*. New York: Schocken, 1984.

Maddon, Thomas F. *Crusades: The Illustrated History*. Ann Arbor: University of Michigan Press, 2004.

Stephenson, Carl. *Medieval Feudalism*. Ithaca, N.Y.: Cornell University Press, 1973.

CHAPTER 12

Adams, Henry. *Mont-Saint-Michel and Chartres*. New York: Penguin, 1986.

Cook, William R. and R. B. Herzman, *The Medieval World View: An Introduction*. New York: Oxford University Press, 2003.

De Ridder-Symoens, Hilde. *A History of the University in Europe: Universities in the Middle Ages*. Cambridge, UK: Cambridge University Press, 1991.

Duby, George. *The Age of the Cathedrals: Art and Society: 980–1420*, translated by E. Levieux and B. Thompson. Chicago: University of Chicago Press, 1981.

Gallagher, Joseph and John Freccero, *A Modern Reader's Guide to Dante's The Divine Comedy*. Liguori Publications, Liguori, Missouri, 2000.

LeGoff, Jacques. *The Medieval Imagination*, translated by A. Goldhammer. Chicago: University of Chicago Press, 1992.

Mazzotta, Giuseppe. *Dante's Vision and the Circle of Knowledge*. Princeton, N.J.: Princeton University Press, 1994.

Oakley, Francis. *The Medieval Experience: Foundations of Western Cultural Singularity*. Toronto: University of Toronto Press, 1988.

Rowling, Marjorie. *Everyday Life in Medieval Times*. New York: Hippocrene Books, 1987.

Shapiro, Marianne. *Dante and the Knot of Body and Soul.* New York: St. Martin's Press, 1998.

Vittorini, Domenico. *The Age of Dante.* New York: Greenwood Press, 1975.

CHAPTER 13

Calkins, Robert. *Monuments of Medieval Art.* Ithaca, N.Y.: Cornell University Press, 1989.

Dodwell, C. R. *The Pictorial Arts of the West 800–1200.* New Haven: Yale University Press, 1993.

Gies, Francis and Joseph. *Cathedral, Forge, and Waterwheel: Technology and Invention in the Middle Ages.* New York: Harperperennial, 1995.

Gimpel, Jean. *The Cathedral Builders*, translated by D. King. New York: HarperCollins, 1992.

Macauley, David. *Cathedral: The Story of its Construction.* Boston: Houghton Mifflin, 1981.

Martindale, Andrew. *Gothic Art from the Twelfth to the Fifteenth Century.* London: Thames and Hudson, 1985.

Seay, Albert. *Music in the Medieval World.* 2nd ed. Englewood Cliffs, N.J.: Prentice-Hall, 1991.

Sekules, Veronica. *Medieval Art.* New York: Oxford University Press, 2001.

Stokstad, Marilyn. *Medieval Art.* New York: Westview Press, 2004.

Toman, Rolf, ed. *Gothic Architecture, Sculpture, Painting.* Köln: Konemann, 2004.

Yudkin, Jeremy. *Music in the Middle Ages.* Upper Saddle River, N.J.: Prentice-Hall, 1989.

CHAPTER 14

Benn, Charles D. *China's Golden Age: Everyday Life in the Tang Dynasty.* New York: Oxford University Press, 2004.

Clunas, Craig. *Art in China.* New York: Oxford University Press, 1997.

Coomaraswamy, Ananda. *The Dance of Shiva.* Reprint edition. New York: South Asian Books, 1997.

Ellgood, Heather. *Hinduism and the Religious Arts.* London: Cassell, 1999.

Fisher, Robert E. *Buddhist Art and Architecture.* London: Thames and Hudson, 1993.

Massey, Reginald. *The Music of India.* New York: South Asian Books, 1998.

Morris, Ivan. *The World of the Shining Prince: Court Life in Ancient Japan.* New York: Kodansha International, 1994.

Murck, Alfreda, and Wen Fong. *Words and Images: Chinese Poetry, Calligraphy, and Painting.* Princeton, N.J.: Princeton University Press, 1991.

Rawson, Jessica, ed. *The British Museum Book of Chinese Art.* New York: Thames and Hudson, 1992.

Schirokauer, Conrad. *A Brief History of Chinese and Japanese Civilizations.* San Diego: Harcourt, 1991.

Stanley-Baker, Joan. *Japanese Art.* London: Thames & Hudson, 2000.

Varley, H. Paul. *Japanese Culture.* Honolulu: University of Hawaii Press, 2000.

Venkataramna, Leela and others. *Indian Classical Dance: Tradition in Transition.* Roli Books, Delhi, 2004.

CHAPTER 15

Cole, Bruce. *Giotto: The Scrovegni Chapel, Padua.* New York: Braziller, 1993.

Condren, Edward. I. *Chaucer and the Energy of Creation: The Design and Organization of the Canterbury Tales.* Gainesville, Fl.: University of Florida Press, 1999.

Goodrich, Michael E. *Violence and Miracle in the Fourteenth Century: Private Grief and Public Salvation.* Chicago: University of Chicago Press, 1995.

Gordon, Mary. *Joan of Arc.* New York: Viking Press, 2000.

Herlihy, David and S. K. Cohn. *The Black Death and the Transformation of the West.* Cambridge, Mass.: Harvard University Press, 1997.

Kelly, John. *The Great Mortality: An Intimate History of the Black Death, the Most Devastating Plague of all Time.* New York: HarperCollins Publishers, 2005.

Lerner, Robert E. *The Age of Adversity: The Fourteenth Century.* Ithaca, N.Y.: Cornell University Press, 1968.

Stejskal, Karel. *European Art in the Fourteenth Century*, translated by T. Gottheinerová. London: Octopus Books, 1978.

Tuchman, Barbara. *A Distant Mirror: The Calamitous 14th Century.* New York: Ballantine, 1987.

Warner, Marina. *Joan of Arc: The Image of Female Heroism.* New York: Knopf, 1981.

CHAPTER 16

Bertelli, Sergio. *The Courts of the Italian Renaissance.* New York: Oxford University Press, 1986.

Brown, Alison, ed. *Language and Images of Renaissance Italy.* New York: Oxford University Press, 1995.

Brucker, G. A. *Renaissance Florence*, rev. ed. Berkeley, Calif.: University of California Press, 1983.

Burke, Peter. *The Italian Renaissance: Culture and Society in Italy.* Princeton, N.J.: Princeton University Press, 1986.

Hale, J. R. *The Civilization of Europe in the Renaissance.* New York: Atheneum, 1994.

Holmes, George, ed. *Art and Politics in Renaissance Italy.* New York: Oxford University Press, 1994.

Johnson, Paul. *The Renaissance: A Short History.* New York: Modern Library, 2002.

Kekewich, Lucille, ed. *The Impact of Humanism (The Renaissance in Europe: A Cultural Inquiry).* New Haven, CT: Yale University Press, 2000.

King, Margaret and Catherine R. Stimpson. *Women of the Renaissance.* Chicago: University of Chicago Press, 1991.

Stephens, John. *The Italian Renaissance: The Origins of Intellectual and Artistic Change Before the Reformation.* New York: Longman, 1990.

CHAPTER 17

Acidini, Cristina and others. *The Medici, Michelangelo, and the Art of Late Renaissance Florence.* New Haven, Conn.: Yale University Press, 2002.

Adams, Laurie Schneider. *Italian Renaissance Art.* Boulder, Co.: Westview Press (Icon Books), 2001.

Baxandall, Michael. *Painting and Experience in Fifteenth Century Italy*. 2nd ed. New York: Oxford University Press, 1988.

Clark, Kenneth. *Leonardo da Vinci: An Account of His Development as an Artist*. Rev. ed. Baltimore, Md.: Penguin, 1993.

Cole, Bruce. *The Renaissance Artist at Work: From Pisano to Titian*. New York: Harper, 1993.

Kempers, Bram. *Painting, Power and Patronage: The Rise of the Professional Artist in Renaissance Italy*. Translated by Beverley Jackson. New York: Penguin, 1987.

Nicholl, Charles, *Leonardo da Vinci: Flights of the Mind*. New York: Viking, 2004.

Palisca, Claude V. *Humanism in Italian Renaissance Musical Thought*. New Haven: Yale University Press, 1985.

Perkins, Leeman L. *Music in the Age of the Renaissance*. New York: Norton & Company, 1999.

Smith, Christine. *Architecture in the Culture of Early Humanism: Ethics, Aesthetics, and Eloquence 1400–1470*. New York: Oxford University Press, 1992.

Turner, A. Richard. *Renaissance Florence: The Invention of a New Art*. Upper Saddle River, N.J.: Prentice Hall, 2003.

CHAPTER 18

Bacquart, Jean-Baptiste. *The Tribal Arts of Africa*. New York: Thames & Hudson, 2000.

Bierhorst, John. *The Mythology of Mexico and Central America*. New York: William Morrow, 1990.

Brody, J. J., et al. *Mimbres Pottery: Ancient Art of the American Southwest*. New York: Hudson Hills Press, 1983.

Coe, Michael, *Breaking the Maya Code*. London: Thames and Hudson, 1995.

Coquet. Michèle. *African Royal Court Art*. Translated by J. M. Todd. Chicago: University of Chicago Press, 1998.

Feder, Norman. *American Indian Art*. New York: Abradale Books, 1995.

Levathes, Louise. *When China Ruled the Seas: The Treasure Fleet of the Dragon Throne, 1405–1433*. New York: Oxford University Press, 1996.

Levenson, Jay A., ed. *Circa 1492: Art in the Age of Exploration*. New Haven: Yale University Press, 1991.

Mbiti, John S. *African Religions and Philosophy*. New York: Heinemann, 1992.

Penney, David, and George Longfish. *Native American Art*. New York: Scribners, 1994.

Prussin, Labelle. *African Nomadic Architecture: Space, Place, and Gender*. Washington, D.C.: Smithsonian Institution Press, 1995.

Schele, Linda, and Mary Ellen Miller. *The Blood of Kings: Dynasty and Ritual in Maya Art*. New York: Braziller, 1986.

Smita, Michael E. *The Aztecs*. London: Blackwell, 2002.

Stannard, David E. *American Holocaust: The Conquest of the New World*. New York: Oxford University Press, 1993.

Willett, Frank. *African Art: An Introduction*. Rev. Ed. New York: Thames and Hudson, 1993.

CHAPTER 19

Bloom, Harold. *Shakespeare: The Invention of the Human*. New York: Riverhead Books, 1998.

Eisenstein, Elizabeth L. *The Printing Press as an Instrument of Change*. Cambridge, U.K. Cambridge University Press, 1979.

Farrell, Kirby. *Play, Death, and Heroism in Shakespeare*. Chapel Hill. N.C.: University of North Carolina Press, 1989.

Harbison, Craig. *The Mirror of the Artist: Northern Renaissance Art in its Historical Context*. New York: Abrams, 1995.

Holden, Anthony. *William Shakespeare: The Man Behind the Genius*. Boston: Little, Brown and Company, 2000.

Holl, Karl. *The Cultural Significance of the Reformation*, translated by K. and B. Herz and J. H. Lichtblau. Cleveland, Ohio: Meridian, 1962.

Kermode, Frank. *The Age of Shakespeare*. New York: The Modern Library, 2004.

Pettegree, Andrew. *The Reformation World*. New York: Routledge, 2000.

Schoeck, Richard. *Erasmus of Europe: Prince of the Humanists 1501–1536*. New York: Columbia University Press, 1995.

Smith, Jeffrey Chips. *The Northern Renaissance*. New York: Phaidon Press, 2004.

Strong, Roy. *The Cult of Elizabeth: Elizabethan Portraiture and Pageantry*. London: Pimlico, 1999.

Tillyard, E. M. W. *The Elizabethan World Picture*. New York: Random House, 1964.

Credits

The author and publishers wish to thank the following for permission to use copyright material. Every effort has been made to trace or contact copyright holders, but if notified of any omissions, Laurence King Publishing would be pleased to insert the appropriate acknowledgement in any subsequent edition of this publication.

CHAPTER 1

READING 1.1 (p. 4): From Leo Frobenius and Douglas C. Fox, *Prehistoric Rock Pictures in Europe and Africa* (1937). Reprinted by permission of The Museum of Modern Art, New York.

READING 1.2 (p. 16): "The Song of Creation" (translated from the *Rig Veda*) in *The Wonder That Was India* by A. L. Basham (Macmillan, 1954). Reprinted by permission of the publisher; "How Man Was Created" (Mohawk Tale) from *American Indian Legends*, edited by Allan MacFarlan (The Heritage Press, 1968).

READING 1.3 (p. 21): From "The Hymn to the Aten" in *The Literature of Ancient Egypt*, edited by William Kelly (Yale University Press, 1973), © 1973 Yale University Press. Reprinted by permission of the publisher.

READING 1.4 (p. 35); "I will lie down within…", "My sister has come to me" and "The Voice of the goose sounds forth…" from *Love Lyrics of Ancient Egypt*, translated by Barbara Hughes Fowler (University of North Carolina Press).

CHAPTER 2

READING 1.5 (p. 39): From *Poems of Heaven and Hell from Ancient Mesopotamia*, translated by N. K. Sandars (Penguin Classics, 1971), © N. K. Sandars, 1971. Reprinted by permission of the publisher.

READING 1.6 (p. 41): From *The Epic of Gilgamesh*, translated by N. K. Sandars (Penguin Classics, 1960; Second revised edition, 1972), © N. K. Sandars, 1960, 1964, 1972. Reprinted by permission of the publisher.

READING 1.7 (p. 46): From "The Code of Hammurabi" in *The Hammurabi Code and the Sinaitic Legislation*, translated by Chilperic Edwards (Kennikat Press, 1971).

READING 1.8a (p. 50), 1.8b (p. 50), 1.8c (p. 52): From *The Jerusalem Bible*, edited by Alexander Jones (Darton, Longman & Todd Ltd./Doubleday, 1966), © 1966 by Darton, Longman & Todd Ltd. and Doubleday, a division of Bantam Doubleday Dell Publishing group Inc. Reprinted by permission of Doubleday.

CHAPTER 3

READING 1.9 (p. 62): From *The Bhagavad-Gita* in *The Song of God: The Bhagavad-Gita*, translated by Swami Prabhavanda to Christopher Isherwood (1951). Reprinted by permission of Vedanta Press, California.

READING 1.10 (p. 67): Lao Tzu, "Thirty spokes will converge…" from *The Way of Life*, translated by Raymond B. Blakney (New American Library, 1955), © 1955 by Raymond B. Blakney, renewed (c) 1983 by Charles Philip Blakney. Reprinted by permission of Dutton Signet, a division of Penguin Putnam Inc.

CHAPTER 4

READING 1.11 (p. 75): From *The Iliad of Homer*, translated by R. Lattimore (University of Chicago Press, 1965), © 1965 The University of Chicago Press. Reprinted by permission of the publisher.

READING 1.12 (p. 82): Pericles' "Funeral Speech" from Thucydides, *History of the Peloponnesian War*, translated by Benjamin Jowett, in *The Greek Historian*, edited by F. R. B. Godolphin (Random House, 1942).

READING 1.13 (p. 85): From Sophocles, *Antigone*, translated by Shaemas O'Sheel, in *Ten Greek Plays in Contemporary Translations*, edited by L. R. Lind (1957), © the Estate of Shaemas O'Sheel.

READING 1.14 (p. 95): From Aristotle, *Poetics*, translated by Ingram Bywater, in *The Works of Aristotle*, Vol. 11, edited by W. D. Ross (Oxford University Press, 1925). Reprinted by permission of the publisher.

READING 1.15 (p. 99): From Plato, *Crito*, in *Authyphro, Apology, Crito*, translated by F. J. Church (Macmillan Library of the Liberal Arts, 1956), © 1955. Reprinted by permission of Prentice-Hall Inc., Upper Saddle River, NJ.

READING 1.16 (p. 101): Plato, "Allegory of the Cave" in *The Republic of Plato*, translated by F. M. Cornford (Oxford University Press, 1941). Reprinted by permission of the publisher.

READING 1.17 (p. 105): From Aristotle, *Ethics*, in *The Nicomachean Ethics of Aristotle*, translated by J. E. C. Welldon (Macmillan, 1927). Reprinted by permission of the publisher.

CHAPTER 5

READING 1.18 (p. 110): From Vitruvius, *Principles of Symmetry*, in *Ten Books on Architecture*, translated by Morris Hicky Morgan (Dover Publications, 1960). Reprinted by permission of the publisher.

READING 1.19 (p. 122): From Mary Barnard, *Sappho: A New Translation* (University of California Press, 1958), © 1958 The Regents of the University of California; © renewed 1984 Mary Barnard. Reprinted by permission of the publisher.

READING 1.20 (p. 123): From Pindar, *Nemean Ode VI*, translated by C. M. Bowra (Oxford University Press, 1964). Reprinted by permission of the publisher; from Pindar, *Pythian Ode VIII*, translated by Roy Arthur Swans, in *Pindar's Odes* (Bobbs-Merrill Company).

CHAPTER 6

READING 1.21 (p. 133): From Josephus, *The Jewish War*, Vol. II, translated by S. St. J. Thackeray (Harvard University Press, 1927). Reprinted by permission of the publisher and the Loeb Classical Library.

READING 1.22 (p. 137): From Seneca, *On Tranquility of Mind*, in *The Stoic Philosophy of Seneca*, translated by Moses Hadas (Doubleday, 1958), © 1958 by Moses Hadas. Reprinted by permission of Doubleday, a division of Bantam Doubleday Dell Publishing Group Inc.

READING 1.23 (p. 138): From Cicero, *On Duty*, in *Cicero: De Officiis*, Vol. XXI, translated by Walter Miller (Harvard University Press, 1961). Reprinted by permission of the publisher and the Loeb Classical Library.

READING 1.24 (p. 139): From Tacitus, *Dialogue on Oratory*, in *Tacitus: Dialogus*, translated by W. Peterson (Harvard University Press, 1958). Reprinted by permission of the publisher and the Loeb Classical Library.

READING 1.25 (p. 140): From Virgil, *Aeneid*, in *The Aeneid of Virgil*, translated by Rolfe Humphries (Scribner, 1951), © 1951 by Charles Scribner's Sons. Reprinted by permission of Scribner, a division of Simon & Schuster.

READING 1.26 (p. 141): Poems #5, 16, 51, 92 from *The Poems of Catullus*, translated by Horace Gregory (Grove Press, 1956).

READING 1.27 (p. 142): "Civil War", "To be Quite Frank" and "Carpe Diem" from *Selected Poems of Horace*, introduction by George F. Whicher (Van Nostrand Reinhold, 1947), copyright 1947 Van Nostrand Reinhold; copyright renewed 1975 Susan W. Whicher, Stephen F. Whicher and Nancy Whicher Greene.

READING 1.28a (p. 143), 1.28b (p. 144): From Juvenal, "Against the City of Rome" and "Against Women" in *The Satires of Juvenal*, translated by Rolfe Humphries (Indiana University Press, 1958), © 1958 by Indiana University Press. Reprinted by permission of the publisher.

CHAPTER 7

READING 1.29 (p. 161): From *The Analects of Confucius*, translated by Simon Leys (W. W. Norton, 1997).

[Extracts (p. 162): From Mencius and Han Fei, in *Sources of Chinese Tradition*, compiled by William Theodore de Bary and others (Columbia University Press, 1960).

READING 1.30 (p. 167): From Sima Qian, *Records of the Grand Historian*, in *Wisdom of China and India* by Lin Yutang (Random House, 1942), © 1942 and renewed 1970 by Random House Inc. Reprinted by permission of the publisher.

READING 1.31 (p. 169): Han poems, in *The Columbia Book of Chinese Poetry*, translated by Burton Watson (Columbia University Press, 1984), © 1984 by Columbia University Press. Reprinted by permission of the publisher.

CHAPTER 8

READING 2.1 (p. 179): From Apuleius, *Metamorphoses* in *Apuleius: Volume II.* Loeb Classical Library Volume L453, translated by Arthur Hanson (Cambridge, Mass.: Harvard University Press, 1989). The Loeb Classical Library is a registered trademark of the President and Fellows of Harvard College. Reprinted by permission of the publisher and the Trustees of the Loeb Classical Library.

READING 2.2 (p. 181), 2.3 (p. 185): From "Sermon on the Mount" and "Paul's Epistle to the Church in Rome" in *The Jerusalem Bible* (Doubleday/Darton, Longman & Todd, 1966), © 1966 by Darton, Longman & Todd Ltd and Doubleday, a division of Bantam Doubleday Dell Publishing Group Inc. Reprinted by permission of Bantam Doubleday Dell Publishing Group.

READING 2.4A AND 2.4B (pp. 187 & 188): From Buddha's "Sermon at Benares" and "Sermon on Abuse" in *The Wisdom of China and India* by Lin Yutang (Random House, 1970), copyright 1942 and renewed 1970 by Random House Inc. Reprinted by permission of the publisher.

CHAPTER 9

READING 2.5 (p. 192): From "The Nicene Creed" in *Documents of the Christian Church*, edited by Henry Bettenson (Oxford University Press, 1963), selection © Oxford University Press, 1963. Reprinted by permission of the publisher.

READING 2.7 (p. 194): From St. Augustine, *Confessions of St. Augustine*, translated by Rex Warner (E. P. Dutton, 1991), © 1963 by Rex Warner, renewed © 1991 by F. C. Warner. Reprinted by permission of Dutton Signet, a division of Penguin Putnam Inc.

READING 2.8 (p. 195): From St. Augustine, *City of God Against the Pagans* in *St. Augustine: Volume IV.* Loeb Classical Library Volume L414, translated by Phil Levine (Cambridge, Mass.: Harvard University Press, 1966). The Loeb Classical Library is a registered trademark of the President and Fellows of Harvard College. Reprinted by permission of the publisher and the Trustees of the Loeb Classical Library.

CHAPTER 10

READING 2.9 (p. 222): From the *Qur'an*, translated by M.A.S. Haleem (Oxford University Press, 2004). Reprinted by permission of the publisher.

READING 2.10 (p. 228): Ibn Zaydun, 'Two Fragments' and Ibn Abra, 'The Beauty-Spot' from *Anthology of Islamic Literature from the Rise of Islam to the Modern World*, edited by James Kritzeck (Henry Holt, 1964), © 1964 by James Kritzeck. Reprinted by permission of the publisher.

READING 2.11 (p. 230): Rumi, 'The Man of God', 'Empty the Glass of Your Desire' and "The One True Light" from *Love is a Stranger*, translated by Rabir Edmund Helminski (Threshold Books, 1993). Reprinted by permission of the publisher.

READING 2.12 (p. 232): From *Arabian Nights*, translated by Jack Zipes (Dutton Signet, 1991), © 1991 by Jack Zipes. Reprinted by permission of Dutton Signet, a division of Penguin Putnam Inc.

CHAPTER 11

READING 2.13 (p. 245): From *Beowulf*, translated by Burton Raffel (New American Library, 1963), © 1963 by Burton Raffel. Reprinted by permission of Dutton Signet, a division of Penguin Putnam Inc.

READING 2.14 (p. 252): From *The Song of Roland*, translated by Patricia Terry (Prentice-Hall, 1965), © 1965. Reprinted by permission of Prentice-Hall Inc., Upper Saddle River, NJ.

READING 2.15 (p. 260): From Chrétien de Troyes, *Lancelot*, translated by W. W. Comfort (Everyman, 1970). Reprinted by permission of the publisher.

CHAPTER 12

READING 2.20 (p. 280): From Dante Alighieri, *The Divine Comedy*, translated by John Ciardi (Norton, 1970), copyright 1954, 1957, 1959, 1960, 1961, 1965, 1967, 1970 by the Ciardi Family Publishing Trust. Reprinted by permission of the publisher.

READING 2.21 (p. 285): Saint Francis, 'The Canticle of Brother Sun' from *Francis and Clare: The Complete Works*, translated by Regis J. Armstrong and I. C. Brady (Paulist Press, 1982). Reprinted by permission of the publisher.

READING 2.22 (p. 288): From Thomas Aquinas, *Summa Theologica* in *Aquinas, Basic Writings: Volume 1*, edited by Anton C. Pegis (Hackett Publishing Co., 1997). Reprinted by permission of the publisher.

Index

Numbers in **bold** refer to figure numbers.
Text excerpts are indicated by (quoted).